Hornbook Series and Basic Legal Texts
Nutshell Series

and

Black Letter Series

of

WEST PUBLISHING COMPANY
P.O. Box 64526
St. Paul, Minnesota 55164–0526

Accounting
FARIS' ACCOUNTING AND LAW IN A NUTSHELL, 377 pages, 1984. Softcover. (Text)

Administrative Law
GELLHORN AND LEVIN'S ADMINISTRATIVE LAW AND PROCESS IN A NUTSHELL, Third Edition, 479 pages, 1990. Softcover. (Text)

Admiralty
MARAIST'S ADMIRALTY IN A NUTSHELL, Second Edition, 379 pages, 1988. Softcover. (Text)

SCHOENBAUM'S HORNBOOK ON ADMIRALTY AND MARITIME LAW, Student Edition, 692 pages, 1987 with 1989 pocket part. (Text)

Agency—Partnership
REUSCHLEIN AND GREGORY'S HORNBOOK ON THE LAW OF AGENCY AND PARTNERSHIP, Second Edition, 683 pages, 1990. (Text)

STEFFEN'S AGENCY-PARTNERSHIP IN A NUTSHELL, 364 pages, 1977. Softcover. (Text)

American Indian Law
CANBY'S AMERICAN INDIAN LAW IN A NUTSHELL, Second Edition, 336 pages, 1988. Softcover. (Text)

Antitrust—see also Regulated Industries, Trade Regulation
GELLHORN'S ANTITRUST LAW AND ECONOMICS IN A NUTSHELL, Third Edition, 472 pages, 1986. Softcover. (Text)

HOVENKAMP'S BLACK LETTER ON ANTITRUST, 323 pages, 1986. Softcover. (Review)

HOVENKAMP'S HORNBOOK ON ECONOMICS AND FEDERAL ANTITRUST LAW, Student Edition, 414 pages, 1985. (Text)

SULLIVAN'S HORNBOOK OF THE LAW OF ANTITRUST, 886 pages, 1977. (Text)

Appellate Advocacy—see Trial and Appellate Advocacy

Art Law
DUBOFF'S ART LAW IN A NUTSHELL, 335 pages, 1984. Softcover. (Text)

Banking Law
LOVETT'S BANKING AND FINANCIAL INSTITUTIONS LAW IN A NUTSHELL, Second Edition, 464 pages, 1988. Softcover. (Text)

Civil Procedure—see also Federal Jurisdiction and Procedure
CLERMONT'S BLACK LETTER ON CIVIL PROCEDURE, Second Edition, 332 pages, 1988. Softcover. (Review)

FRIEDENTHAL, KANE AND MILLER'S HORNBOOK ON CIVIL PROCEDURE, 876

Civil Procedure—Cont'd

pages, 1985. (Text)

KANE'S CIVIL PROCEDURE IN A NUTSHELL, Third Edition, 303 pages, 1991. Softcover. (Text)

KOFFLER AND REPPY'S HORNBOOK ON COMMON LAW PLEADING, 663 pages, 1969. (Text)

SIEGEL'S HORNBOOK ON NEW YORK PRACTICE, Second Edition, Student Edition, 1068 pages, 1991. Softcover. (Text)

Commercial Law

BAILEY AND HAGEDORN'S SECURED TRANSACTIONS IN A NUTSHELL, Third Edition, 390 pages, 1988. Softcover. (Text)

HENSON'S HORNBOOK ON SECURED TRANSACTIONS UNDER THE U.C.C., Second Edition, 504 pages, 1979, with 1979 pocket part. (Text)

NICKLES' BLACK LETTER ON COMMERCIAL PAPER, 450 pages, 1988. Softcover. (Review)

SPEIDEL'S BLACK LETTER ON SALES AND SALES FINANCING, 363 pages, 1984. Softcover. (Review)

STOCKTON'S SALES IN A NUTSHELL, Second Edition, 370 pages, 1981. Softcover. (Text)

STONE'S UNIFORM COMMERCIAL CODE IN A NUTSHELL, Third Edition, 580 pages, 1989. Softcover. (Text)

WEBER AND SPEIDEL'S COMMERCIAL PAPER IN A NUTSHELL, Third Edition, 404 pages, 1982. Softcover. (Text)

WHITE AND SUMMERS' HORNBOOK ON THE UNIFORM COMMERCIAL CODE, Third Edition, Student Edition, 1386 pages, 1988. (Text)

Community Property

MENNELL AND BOYKOFF'S COMMUNITY PROPERTY IN A NUTSHELL, Second Edition, 432 pages, 1988. Softcover. (Text)

Comparative Law

GLENDON, GORDON AND OSAKWE'S COMPARATIVE LEGAL TRADITIONS IN A NUTSHELL. 402 pages, 1982. Softcover. (Text)

Conflict of Laws

HAY'S BLACK LETTER ON CONFLICT OF LAWS, 330 pages, 1989. Softcover. (Review)

SCOLES AND HAY'S HORNBOOK ON CONFLICT OF LAWS, Student Edition, approximately 1025 pages, 1992. (Text)

SIEGEL'S CONFLICTS IN A NUTSHELL, 470 pages, 1982. Softcover. (Text)

Constitutional Law—Civil Rights

BARRON AND DIENES' BLACK LETTER ON CONSTITUTIONAL LAW, Third Edition, 440 pages, 1991. Softcover. (Review)

BARRON AND DIENES' CONSTITUTIONAL LAW IN A NUTSHELL, Second Edition, 483 pages, 1991. Softcover. (Text)

ENGDAHL'S CONSTITUTIONAL FEDERALISM IN A NUTSHELL, Second Edition, 411 pages, 1987. Softcover. (Text)

MARKS AND COOPER'S STATE CONSTITUTIONAL LAW IN A NUTSHELL, 329 pages, 1988. Softcover. (Text)

NOWAK AND ROTUNDA'S HORNBOOK ON CONSTITUTIONAL LAW, Fourth Edition, 1357 pages, 1991. (Text)

VIEIRA'S CONSTITUTIONAL CIVIL RIGHTS IN A NUTSHELL, Second Edition, 322 pages, 1990. Softcover. (Text)

WILLIAMS' CONSTITUTIONAL ANALYSIS IN A NUTSHELL, 388 pages, 1979. Softcover. (Text)

Consumer Law—see also Commercial Law

EPSTEIN AND NICKLES' CONSUMER LAW IN A NUTSHELL, Second Edition, 418 pages, 1981. Softcover. (Text)

Contracts

CALAMARI AND PERILLO'S BLACK LETTER ON CONTRACTS, Second Edition, 462 pages, 1990. Softcover. (Review)

CALAMARI AND PERILLO'S HORNBOOK ON

Contracts—Cont'd

CONTRACTS, Third Edition, 1049 pages, 1987. (Text)

CORBIN'S TEXT ON CONTRACTS, One Volume Student Edition, 1224 pages, 1952. (Text)

FRIEDMAN'S CONTRACT REMEDIES IN A NUTSHELL, 323 pages, 1981. Softcover. (Text)

KEYES' GOVERNMENT CONTRACTS IN A NUTSHELL, Second Edition, 557 pages, 1990. Softcover. (Text)

SCHABER AND ROHWER'S CONTRACTS IN A NUTSHELL, Third Edition, 457 pages, 1990. Softcover. (Text)

Copyright—see Patent and Copyright Law

Corporations

HAMILTON'S BLACK LETTER ON CORPORATIONS, Second Edition, 513 pages, 1986. Softcover. (Review)

HAMILTON'S THE LAW OF CORPORATIONS IN A NUTSHELL, Third Edition, 518 pages, 1991. Softcover. (Text)

HENN AND ALEXANDER'S HORNBOOK ON LAWS OF CORPORATIONS, Third Edition, Student Edition, 1371 pages, 1983, with 1986 pocket part. (Text)

Corrections

KRANTZ' THE LAW OF CORRECTIONS AND PRISONERS' RIGHTS IN A NUTSHELL, Third Edition, 407 pages, 1988. Softcover. (Text)

Creditors' Rights

EPSTEIN'S DEBTOR-CREDITOR LAW IN A NUTSHELL, Fourth Edition, 401 pages, 1991. Softcover. (Text)

NICKLES AND EPSTEIN'S BLACK LETTER ON CREDITORS' RIGHTS AND BANKRUPTCY, 576 pages, 1989. (Review)

Criminal Law and Criminal Procedure— see also Corrections, Juvenile Justice

ISRAEL AND LaFAVE'S CRIMINAL PROCEDURE—CONSTITUTIONAL LIMITATIONS IN A NUTSHELL, Fourth Edition, 461

pages, 1988. Softcover. (Text)

LaFAVE AND ISRAEL'S HORNBOOK ON CRIMINAL PROCEDURE, Second Edition, approximately 1350 pages, 1992. (Text)

LaFAVE AND SCOTT'S HORNBOOK ON CRIMINAL LAW, Second Edition, 918 pages, 1986. (Text)

LOEWY'S CRIMINAL LAW IN A NUTSHELL, Second Edition, 321 pages, 1987. Softcover. (Text)

LOW'S BLACK LETTER ON CRIMINAL LAW, Revised First Edition, 443 pages, 1990. Softcover. (Review)

Domestic Relations

CLARK'S HORNBOOK ON DOMESTIC RELATIONS, Second Edition, Student Edition, 1050 pages, 1988. (Text)

KRAUSE'S BLACK LETTER ON FAMILY LAW, 314 pages, 1988. Softcover. (Review)

KRAUSE'S FAMILY LAW IN A NUTSHELL, Second Edition, 444 pages, 1986. Softcover. (Text)

MALLOY'S LAW AND ECONOMICS: A COMPARATIVE APPROACH TO THEORY AND PRACTICE, 166 pages, 1990. Softcover. (Text)

Education Law

ALEXANDER AND ALEXANDER'S THE LAW OF SCHOOLS, STUDENTS AND TEACHERS IN A NUTSHELL, 409 pages, 1984. Softcover. (Text)

Employment Discrimination—see also Gender Discrimination

PLAYER'S FEDERAL LAW OF EMPLOYMENT DISCRIMINATION IN A NUTSHELL, Third Edition, approximately 270 pages, 1992. Softcover. (Text)

PLAYER'S HORNBOOK ON EMPLOYMENT DISCRIMINATION LAW, Student Edition, 708 pages, 1988. (Text)

Energy and Natural Resources Law— see also Oil and Gas

LAITOS AND TOMAIN'S ENERGY AND NATURAL RESOURCES LAW IN A NUTSHELL,

Energy and Natural Resources Law—Cont'd

Approximately 525 pages, 1992. Softcover. (Text)

Environmental Law—see also Energy and Natural Resources Law; Sea, Law of

FINDLEY AND FARBER'S ENVIRONMENTAL LAW IN A NUTSHELL, Third Edition, approximately 375 pages, February, 1992 Pub. Softcover. (Text)

RODGERS' HORNBOOK ON ENVIRONMENTAL LAW, 956 pages, 1977, with 1984 pocket part. (Text)

Equity—see Remedies

Estate Planning—see also Trusts and Estates; Taxation—Estate and Gift

LYNN'S AN INTRODUCTION TO ESTATE PLANNING IN A NUTSHELL, Third Edition, 370 pages, 1983. Softcover. (Text)

Evidence

BROUN AND BLAKEY'S BLACK LETTER ON EVIDENCE, 269 pages, 1984. Softcover. (Review)

GRAHAM'S FEDERAL RULES OF EVIDENCE IN A NUTSHELL, Third Edition, approximately 475 pages, 1992. Softcover. (Text)

LILLY'S AN INTRODUCTION TO THE LAW OF EVIDENCE, Second Edition, 585 pages, 1987. (Text)

MCCORMICK'S HORNBOOK ON EVIDENCE, Fourth Edition, Student Edition, approximately 1150 pages, March, 1992 Pub. (Text)

ROTHSTEIN'S EVIDENCE IN A NUTSHELL: STATE AND FEDERAL RULES, Second Edition, 514 pages, 1981. Softcover. (Text)

Federal Jurisdiction and Procedure

CURRIE'S FEDERAL JURISDICTION IN A NUTSHELL, Third Edition, 242 pages, 1990. Softcover. (Text)

REDISH'S BLACK LETTER ON FEDERAL JURISDICTION, Second Edition, 234 pages, 1991. Softcover. (Review)

WRIGHT'S HORNBOOK ON FEDERAL COURTS, Fourth Edition, Student Edition, 870 pages, 1983. (Text)

First Amendment

Future Interests—see Trusts and Estates

Gender Discrimination—see also Employment Discrimination

THOMAS' SEX DISCRIMINATION IN A NUTSHELL, Second Edition, 395 pages, 1991. Softcover. (Text)

Health Law—see Medicine, Law and

Human Rights—see International Law

Immigration Law

WEISSBRODT'S IMMIGRATION LAW AND PROCEDURE IN A NUTSHELL, Second Edition, 438 pages, 1989, Softcover. (Text)

Indian Law—see American Indian Law

Insurance Law

DOBBYN'S INSURANCE LAW IN A NUTSHELL, Second Edition, 316 pages, 1989. Softcover. (Text)

KEETON AND WIDISS' INSURANCE LAW, Student Edition, 1359 pages, 1988. (Text)

International Law—see also Sea, Law of

BUERGENTHAL'S INTERNATIONAL HUMAN RIGHTS IN A NUTSHELL, 283 pages, 1988. Softcover. (Text)

BUERGENTHAL AND MAIER'S PUBLIC INTERNATIONAL LAW IN A NUTSHELL, Second Edition, 275 pages, 1990. Softcover. (Text)

FOLSOM'S EUROPEAN COMMUNITY LAW IN A NUTSHELL, Approximately 425 pages, 1992. Softcover. (Text)

FOLSOM, GORDON AND SPANOGLE'S INTERNATIONAL BUSINESS TRANSACTIONS IN A NUTSHELL, Third Edition, 509 pages, 1988. Softcover. (Text)

Interviewing and Counseling

SHAFFER AND ELKINS' LEGAL INTERVIEWING AND COUNSELING IN A NUTSHELL, Second Edition, 487 pages, 1987. Softcover. (Text)

Introduction to Law—see Legal Method and Legal System

Introduction to Law Study

HEGLAND'S INTRODUCTION TO THE STUDY AND PRACTICE OF LAW IN A NUTSHELL, 418 pages, 1983. Softcover. (Text)

KINYON'S INTRODUCTION TO LAW STUDY AND LAW EXAMINATIONS IN A NUTSHELL, 389 pages, 1971. Softcover. (Text)

Judicial Process—see Legal Method and Legal System

Juvenile Justice

FOX'S JUVENILE COURTS IN A NUTSHELL, Third Edition, 291 pages, 1984. Softcover. (Text)

Labor and Employment Law—see also Employment Discrimination, Workers' Compensation

LESLIE'S LABOR LAW IN A NUTSHELL, Third Edition, approximately 400 pages, 1992. Softcover. (Text)

NOLAN'S LABOR ARBITRATION LAW AND PRACTICE IN A NUTSHELL, 358 pages, 1979. Softcover. (Text)

Land Finance—Property Security—see Real Estate Transactions

Land Use

HAGMAN AND JUERGENSMEYER'S HORNBOOK ON URBAN PLANNING AND LAND DEVELOPMENT CONTROL LAW, Second Edition, Student Edition, 680 pages, 1986. (Text)

WRIGHT AND WRIGHT'S LAND USE IN A NUTSHELL, Second Edition, 356 pages, 1985. Softcover. (Text)

Legal Method and Legal System—see also Legal Research, Legal Writing

KEMPIN'S HISTORICAL INTRODUCTION TO ANGLO-AMERICAN LAW IN A NUTSHELL,

Third Edition, 323 pages, 1990. Softcover. (Text)

REYNOLDS' JUDICIAL PROCESS IN A NUTSHELL, Second Edition, 308 pages, 1991. Softcover. (Text)

Legal Research

COHEN'S LEGAL RESEARCH IN A NUTSHELL, Fourth Edition, 452 pages, 1985. Softcover. (Text)

COHEN, BERRING AND OLSON'S HOW TO FIND THE LAW, Ninth Edition, 716 pages, 1989. (Text)

Legal Writing and Drafting

MELLINKOFF'S DICTIONARY OF AMERICAN LEGAL USAGE, Approximately 900 pages, March, 1992 Pub. (Text)

SQUIRES AND ROMBAUER'S LEGAL WRITING IN A NUTSHELL, 294 pages, 1982. Softcover. (Text)

Legislation—see also Legal Writing and Drafting

DAVIES' LEGISLATIVE LAW AND PROCESS IN A NUTSHELL, Second Edition, 346 pages, 1986. Softcover. (Text)

Local Government

MCCARTHY'S LOCAL GOVERNMENT LAW IN A NUTSHELL, Third Edition, 435 pages, 1990. Softcover. (Text)

REYNOLDS' HORNBOOK ON LOCAL GOVERNMENT LAW, 860 pages, 1982, with 1990 pocket part. (Text)

Mass Communication Law

ZUCKMAN, GAYNES, CARTER AND DEE'S MASS COMMUNICATIONS LAW IN A NUTSHELL, Third Edition, 538 pages, 1988. Softcover. (Text)

Medicine, Law and

HALL AND ELLMAN'S HEALTH CARE LAW AND ETHICS IN A NUTSHELL, 401 pages, 1990. Softcover (Text)

JARVIS, CLOSEN, HERMANN AND LEONARD'S AIDS LAW IN A NUTSHELL, 349 pages, 1991. Softcover. (Text)

KING'S THE LAW OF MEDICAL MALPRACTICE IN A NUTSHELL, Second Edition,

Medicine, Law and—Cont'd

342 pages, 1986. Softcover. (Text)

Military Law

SHANOR AND TERRELL'S MILITARY LAW IN A NUTSHELL, 378 pages, 1980. Softcover. (Text)

Mortgages—see Real Estate Transactions

Natural Resources Law—see Energy and Natural Resources Law, Environmental Law

TEPLY'S LEGAL NEGOTIATION IN A NUTSHELL, Approximately 250 pages, 1992. Softcover. (Text)

Office Practice—see also Computers and Law, Interviewing and Counseling, Negotiation

HEGLAND'S TRIAL AND PRACTICE SKILLS IN A NUTSHELL, 346 pages, 1978. Softcover (Text)

Oil and Gas—see also Energy and Natural Resources Law

HEMINGWAY'S HORNBOOK ON THE LAW OF OIL AND GAS, Third Edition, Student Edition, approximately 700 pages, 1992. (Text)

LOWE'S OIL AND GAS LAW IN A NUTSHELL, Second Edition, 465 pages, 1988. Softcover. (Text)

Partnership—see Agency—Partnership

Patent and Copyright Law

MILLER AND DAVIS' INTELLECTUAL PROPERTY—PATENTS, TRADEMARKS AND COPYRIGHT IN A NUTSHELL, Second Edition, 437 pages, 1990. Softcover. (Text)

Products Liability

PHILLIPS' PRODUCTS LIABILITY IN A NUTSHELL, Third Edition, 307 pages, 1988. Softcover. (Text)

Professional Responsibility

ARONSON AND WECKSTEIN'S PROFESSIONAL RESPONSIBILITY IN A NUTSHELL, Second Edition, 514 pages, 1991. Soft-

cover. (Text)

ROTUNDA'S BLACK LETTER ON PROFESSIONAL RESPONSIBILITY, Third Edition, approximately 400 pages, 1992. Softcover. (Review)

WOLFRAM'S HORNBOOK ON MODERN LEGAL ETHICS, Student Edition, 1120 pages, 1986. (Text)

Property—see also Real Estate Transactions, Land Use, Trusts and Estates

BERNHARDT'S BLACK LETTER ON PROPERTY, Second Edition, 388 pages, 1991. Softcover. (Review)

BERNHARDT'S REAL PROPERTY IN A NUTSHELL, Second Edition, 448 pages, 1981. Softcover. (Text)

BOYER, HOVENKAMP AND KURTZ' THE LAW OF PROPERTY, AN INTRODUCTORY SURVEY, Fourth Edition, 696 pages, 1991. (Text)

BURKE'S PERSONAL PROPERTY IN A NUTSHELL, 322 pages, 1983. Softcover. (Text)

CUNNINGHAM, STOEBUCK AND WHITMAN'S HORNBOOK ON THE LAW OF PROPERTY, Student Edition, 916 pages, 1984, with 1987 pocket part. (Text)

HILL'S LANDLORD AND TENANT LAW IN A NUTSHELL, Second Edition, 311 pages, 1986. Softcover. (Text)

Real Estate Transactions

BRUCE'S REAL ESTATE FINANCE IN A NUTSHELL, Third Edition, 287 pages, 1991. Softcover. (Text)

NELSON AND WHITMAN'S BLACK LETTER ON LAND TRANSACTIONS AND FINANCE, Second Edition, 466 pages, 1988. Softcover. (Review)

NELSON AND WHITMAN'S HORNBOOK ON REAL ESTATE FINANCE LAW, Second Edition, 941 pages, 1985 with 1989 pocket part. (Text)

Regulated Industries—see also Mass Communication Law, Banking Law

GELLHORN AND PIERCE'S REGULATED INDUSTRIES IN A NUTSHELL, Second Edi-

Regulated Industries—Cont'd

tion, 389 pages, 1987. Softcover. (Text)

Remedies

DOBBS' HORNBOOK ON REMEDIES, 1067 pages, 1973. (Text)

DOBBYN'S INJUNCTIONS IN A NUTSHELL, 264 pages, 1974. Softcover. (Text)

FRIEDMAN'S CONTRACT REMEDIES IN A NUTSHELL, 323 pages, 1981. Softcover. (Text)

O'CONNELL'S REMEDIES IN A NUTSHELL, Second Edition, 320 pages, 1985. Softcover. (Text)

Sea, Law of

SOHN AND GUSTAFSON'S THE LAW OF THE SEA IN A NUTSHELL, 264 pages, 1984. Softcover. (Text)

Securities Regulation

HAZEN'S HORNBOOK ON THE LAW OF SECURITIES REGULATION, Second Edition, Student Edition, 1082 pages, 1990. (Text)

RATNER'S SECURITIES REGULATION IN A NUTSHELL, Third Edition, 316 pages, 1988. Softcover. (Text)

Sports Law

SCHUBERT, SMITH AND TRENTADUE'S SPORTS LAW, 395 pages, 1986. (Text)

Tax Practice and Procedure

MORGAN'S TAX PROCEDURE AND TAX FRAUD IN A NUTSHELL, 400 pages, 1990. Softcover. (Text)

Taxation—Corporate

SCHWARZ AND LATHROPE'S BLACK LETTER ON CORPORATE AND PARTNERSHIP TAXATION, 537 pages, 1991. Softcover. (Review)

WEIDENBRUCH AND BURKE'S FEDERAL INCOME TAXATION OF CORPORATIONS AND STOCKHOLDERS IN A NUTSHELL, Third Edition, 309 pages, 1989. Softcover. (Text)

Taxation—Estate & Gift—see also Estate Planning, Trusts and Estates

MCNULTY'S FEDERAL ESTATE AND GIFT TAXATION IN A NUTSHELL, Fourth Edition, 496 pages, 1989. Softcover. (Text)

PEAT AND WILLBANKS' FEDERAL ESTATE AND GIFT TAXATION: AN ANALYSIS AND CRITIQUE, 265 pages, 1991. Softcover. (Text)

Taxation—Individual

DODGE'S THE LOGIC OF TAX, 343 pages, 1989. Softcover. (Text)

HUDSON AND LIND'S BLACK LETTER ON FEDERAL INCOME TAXATION, Third Edition, 406 pages, 1990. Softcover. (Review)

MCNULTY'S FEDERAL INCOME TAXATION OF INDIVIDUALS IN A NUTSHELL, Fourth Edition, 503 pages, 1988. Softcover. (Text)

POSIN'S HORNBOOK ON FEDERAL INCOME TAXATION, Student Edition, 491 pages, 1983, with 1989 pocket part. (Text)

ROSE AND CHOMMIE'S HORNBOOK ON FEDERAL INCOME TAXATION, Third Edition, 923 pages, 1988, with 1991 pocket part. (Text)

Taxation—International

DOERNBERG'S INTERNATIONAL TAXATION IN A NUTSHELL, 325 pages, 1989. Softcover. (Text)

BISHOP AND BROOKS' FEDERAL PARTNERSHIP TAXATION: A GUIDE TO THE LEADING CASES, STATUTES, AND REGULATIONS, 545 pages, 1990. Softcover. (Text)

BURKE'S FEDERAL INCOME TAXATION OF PARTNERSHIPS IN A NUTSHELL, Approximately 400 pages, February, 1992 Pub. Softcover. (Text)

SCHWARZ AND LATHROPE'S BLACK LETTER ON CORPORATE AND PARTNERSHIP TAXATION, 537 pages, 1991. Softcover. (Review)

Taxation—State & Local

GELFAND AND SALSICH'S STATE AND LOCAL TAXATION AND FINANCE IN A NUT-

Taxation—State & Local—Cont'd
SHELL, 309 pages, 1986. Softcover. (Text)

Torts—see also Products Liability
KIONKA'S BLACK LETTER ON TORTS, 339 pages, 1988. Softcover. (Review)

KIONKA'S TORTS IN A NUTSHELL, Second Edition, approximately 500 pages, March, 1992 Pub. Softcover. (Text)

MALONE'S TORTS IN A NUTSHELL: INJURIES TO FAMILY, SOCIAL AND TRADE RELATIONS, 358 pages, 1979. Softcover. (Text)

PROSSER AND KEETON'S HORNBOOK ON TORTS, Fifth Edition, Student Edition, 1286 pages, 1984 with 1988 pocket part. (Text)

Trade Regulation—see also Antitrust, Regulated Industries
McMANIS' UNFAIR TRADE PRACTICES IN A NUTSHELL, Second Edition, 464 pages, 1988. Softcover. (Text)

SCHECHTER'S BLACK LETTER ON UNFAIR TRADE PRACTICES, 272 pages, 1986. Softcover. (Review)

Trial and Appellate Advocacy—see also Civil Procedure
BERGMAN'S TRIAL ADVOCACY IN A NUTSHELL, Second Edition, 354 pages, 1989. Softcover. (Text)

GOLDBERG'S THE FIRST TRIAL (WHERE DO I SIT? WHAT DO I SAY?) IN A NUTSHELL, 396 pages, 1982. Softcover. (Text)

HEGLAND'S TRIAL AND PRACTICE SKILLS IN A NUTSHELL, 346 pages, 1978. Softcover. (Text)

HORNSTEIN'S APPELLATE ADVOCACY IN A NUTSHELL, 325 pages, 1984. Softcover. (Text)

JEANS' HANDBOOK ON TRIAL ADVOCACY, Student Edition, 473 pages, 1975. Softcover. (Text)

Trusts and Estates
ATKINSON'S HORNBOOK ON WILLS, Second Edition, 975 pages, 1953. (Text)

AVERILL'S UNIFORM PROBATE CODE IN A NUTSHELL, Second Edition, 454 pages, 1987. Softcover. (Text)

BOGERT'S HORNBOOK ON TRUSTS, Sixth Edition, Student Edition, 794 pages, 1987. (Text)

McGOVERN, KURTZ AND REIN'S HORNBOOK ON WILLS, TRUSTS AND ESTATES–INCLUDING TAXATION AND FUTURE INTERESTS, 996 pages, 1988. (Text)

MENNELL'S WILLS AND TRUSTS IN A NUTSHELL, 392 pages, 1979. Softcover. (Text)

SIMES' HORNBOOK ON FUTURE INTERESTS, Second Edition, 355 pages, 1966. (Text)

TURANO AND RADIGAN'S HORNBOOK ON NEW YORK ESTATE ADMINISTRATION, 676 pages, 1986 with 1991 pocket part. (Text)

WAGGONER'S FUTURE INTERESTS IN A NUTSHELL, 361 pages, 1981. Softcover. (Text)

Water Law—see also Environmental Law
GETCHES' WATER LAW IN A NUTSHELL, Second Edition, 459 pages, 1990. Softcover. (Text)

Wills—see Trusts and Estates

Workers' Compensation
HOOD, HARDY AND LEWIS' WORKERS' COMPENSATION AND EMPLOYEE PROTECTION LAWS IN A NUTSHELL, Second Edition, 361 pages, 1990. Softcover. (Text)

THE LAW OF
CONTRACTS

By

John D. Calamari
Wilkinson Professor of Law, Fordham University

and

Joseph M. Perillo
Alpin J. Cameron Professor of Law, Fordham University

THIRD EDITION

HORNBOOK SERIES

WEST PUBLISHING CO.
ST. PAUL, MINN., 1987

Hornbook Series, WESTLAW, the West Publishing Co. Logo, the key number appearing on the front cover and the WESTLAW Computer/Book design are registered trademarks of West Publishing Co. Registered in U.S. Patent and Trademark Office.

Library of Congress Cataloging-in-Publication Data

Calamari, John D.
  The law of contracts.

  (Hornbook series)
  Includes index.
  1. Contracts—United States. I. Perillo, Joseph M.
II. Title. III. Series.
KF801.C26 1987   346.73'02   87–2077
               347.3062
  ISBN 0–314–34698–8

  Calamari & Perillo, Contracts, 3rd Ed. HB
  3rd Reprint—1992

Preface to Third Edition

Our primary purpose in offering the second edition was "to offer coverage of subject matters not included in the first edition." The purpose of the third edition is not only to update and refine but to substantially improve the prior editions.

Our students have often complained that in the earlier editions many important matters are contained in footnotes. This problem has been alleviated. In addition, use of this book has revealed a few trouble spots. These have been remedied. Our main purpose in this edition is to make the text as clear as possible. However, clarity is not gained at the expense of oversimplification.

We express our gratitude to the many students who have helped in the preparation of this manuscript. These include Paul G. Calamari, Mark Dietrich, Michael J. Getzler, Vincent J. Handal, Jr., Tony Harwood, Amy Heirman, Gretta Heaney, Caryn Hemsworth, Mladen Kresic, Frederick Z. Lodge, Joseph Mazzarulli, Georgianne Mezzone, Marilyn Palone, Eric S. Reff, and Andrea Schacht. Our special thanks to Andrew M. Calamari, Patrick S. Dunleavy, Patrick Fogarty, Joseph Ramognoli, Neils Schaumann, and John Wolak. We also express our appreciation to Marilyn Alexander, Mary Dowdell, Helen Herman, Ann Maloney, Barbara McFadden, Beverly O'Meally, Lourdes Ramirez, Mary Whelan, secretaries, who worked above and beyond the call of duties in preparing this manuscript.

Finally we express our thanks to Dean John D. Feerick for his encouragement and his help.

JOHN D. CALAMARI
JOSEPH M. PERILLO

Fordham University School of Law
January, 1987

*

Preface to Second Edition

The first edition of this book has received a gratifying response from students and teachers of the law as well as from the courts and practitioners. The primary purpose in offering a second edition is to offer coverage of subject matters not included in the first edition. In particular specific performance, avoidance and reformation for mistake or misconduct and consumer protection are new topics discussed in this edition. In addition, each of the chapters has been updated and refined.

We were aided in our task by thoughtful reviewers of the first edition, comments received from students and professors throughout the country, but primarily from first year students at Fordham Law School whose challenging questions and comments have added to our continuing legal education. Comments on this second edition will indeed be welcome.

We are grateful to Professors Earl Phillips and Thomas Quinn who reviewed portions of the manuscript. We are indebted to many students who assisted in the checking of citations. These include Vincent N. Amato, Danny Chin, John J. Gallagher, George O. Guldi, Helen Hadjiyannakis, Thomas M. Herlihy, Francis Hertz, Joanne Keenan, Mark Koslowe, Michael Landron, Edward W. Larkin, Thomas C. Meriam, Glen Niemy, Jeffrey G. Steinberg, William Troy and particularly Joseph B. Valentine who carried a great part of the load. This book would not have been possible without the aid of the typists who skillfully prepared various parts of the manuscript. Therefore, special appreciation is expressed for the work of Janice Armstrong, Estelle Fabian, Ann Maloney, Ann Sullivan, Sandy Tchou and Barbara Valentine.

JOHN D. CALAMARI
JOSEPH M. PERILLO

Fordham University School of Law
June, 1977

*

Preface to First Edition

Contract law is rapidly changing. In particular, the enactment of the Uniform Commercial Code by forty-nine states has caused a major change of approach in some of the fundamental doctrines. It is believed that the time is ripe for a new introductory text which emphasizes new developments, without, however, neglecting traditional rules and doctrines. This volume is offered as such a text.

An attempt to introduce so vast a subject matter in a one volume text has obvious dangers. Over-simplifications are inevitable. Generalizations are always more dogmatic than the law in action. Nonetheless, the practitioner is aware and the student soon becomes aware of the uses and limitations of introductory texts. A text of this kind seeks to provide an introduction to the doctrines, concepts and fundamental rules of the subject. Its citations are designed to provide a guide to deeper knowledge of the subject.

We wish to express our indebtedness to the two giants in the field, Professors Arthur L. Corbin and Samuel Williston, whose treatises are cited liberally throughout the text, as well as to innumerable scholars and students who have contributed to the literature in legal periodicals and texts. We are indebted to Professors Paul S. Graziano and Joseph M. McLaughlin and Dean Malachy T. Mahon for their valued comments on portions of the manuscript. We particularly express our gratitude to George W. Bacon, Professor Emeritus, for making available to his successors the insights gained from his many years as a teacher and scholar.

We express our appreciation to Dean William Hughes Mulligan of the Fordham University School of Law who in many ways facilitated our task. We are grateful to Miss Anne McKim who ably prepared each draft of the manuscript and to Sandra Behrle, Manuel Bernardo, Andrew Bongiorno, Benjamin Goldman, Frederic Ingraham and James Maloney, each of whom gave us invaluable help in the checking of citations.

Last, but most important, we express our thanks to our wives for their patience and understanding.

JOHN D. CALAMARI
JOSEPH M. PERILLO

March, 1970

*

WESTLAW Introduction

Calamari and Perillo's *Contracts, Third Edition* offers a detailed and comprehensive treatment of basic rules, principles, and issues in contracts. However, readers occasionally need to find additional authority. In an effort to assist with comprehensive research of the law of contracts, preformulated WESTLAW references are included after most sections of the text in this edition. The WESTLAW references are designed for use with the WESTLAW computer-assisted legal research service. By joining this publication with the extensive WESTLAW databases in this way, the reader is able to move straight from the hornbook into WESTLAW with great speed and convenience.

Some readers may desire to use only the information supplied within the printed pages of this hornbook. Others, however, will encounter issues in contracts that require further information. Accordingly, those who opt for additional material can rapidly and easily gain access to WESTLAW, an electronic law library that possesses extraordinary currency and magnitude.

The preformulated WESTLAW references in this text provide illustrative searches for readers who wish to do additional research on WESTLAW. The WESTLAW references are approximately as general as the material in the text to which they correspond. Readers should be cautioned against placing undue emphasis upon these references as final solutions to all possible issues treated in the text. In most instances, it is necessary to make refinements to the search references, such as the addition of other search terms or the substitution of different proximity connectors, to adequately fit the particular needs of an individual reader's research problem. The freedom, and also the responsibility, remains with the reader to "fine tune" the WESTLAW references in accordance with his or her own research requirements. The primary usefulness of the preformulated references is in providing a basic framework upon which further query construction can be built. The Appendix gives concise, step-by-step instruction on how to coordinate WESTLAW research with this book.

THE PUBLISHER

*

Copyright Acknowledgments

The authors are indebted for the generous permission of various publishers to reprint published materials. A particular debt is owed to the American Law Institute for extensive quotes from the Restatements and to the American Law Institute and the National Conference of Commissioners on Uniform State Laws for permission to reproduce Official Comments on the Uniform Commercial Code. In addition various quotations from Duesenberg & King, Sales and Bulk Transfers and Williston on Contracts are reproduced with the permission of Matthew Bender & Co. and Baker Voorhis & Co., Inc., respectively. The consent of the Brooklyn Law Review for a quotation from Vol. 30, p. 185, is gratefully acknowledged as is the consent of the Fordham Law Review for adaptation of articles in Vol. 27, p. 332, and Vol. 43, p. 341, and the Indiana Law Journal for adaptation of an article in Vol. 42, p. 333.

*

Summary of Contents

*

Table of Contents

CHAPTER 3. PAROL EVIDENCE AND INTERPRETATION

A. INTRODUCTION

B. THE PAROL EVIDENCE RULE

CHAPTER 5. INFORMAL CONTRACTS WITHOUT CONSIDERATION OR DETRIMENTAL RELIANCE

A. PAST CONSIDERATION AND MORAL OBLIGATION AS CONSIDERATION

CHAPTER 7. CONTRACTS UNDER SEAL

CHAPTER 8. CAPACITY OF PARTIES

A. INFANTS

B. THE MENTALLY INFIRM

C. SELF–DEALING

CHAPTER 9. AVOIDANCE OR REFORMATION FOR MISCONDUCT OR MISTAKE

A. INTRODUCTION

CHAPTER 11. CONDITIONS

A. INTRODUCTION

CHAPTER 14. DAMAGES

A. INTRODUCTION

B. NON–COMPENSATORY DAMAGES

C. COMPENSATORY DAMAGES

D. FORESEEABILITY

E. CERTAINTY

F. THE CONCEPT OF VALUE

G. AVOIDABLE CONSEQUENCES

H. DAMAGES IN PARTICULAR ACTIONS

CHAPTER 18.   ASSIGNMENT AND DELEGATION

A.   INTRODUCTION

B.   ASSIGNMENTS—GENERAL BACKGROUND

C.   DEVIANTS FROM THE NORM

D.   ARE THERE RIGHTS WHICH ARE NOT ASSIGNABLE?

E.   DEFENSES OF THE OBLIGOR

CHAPTER 20. JOINT AND SEVERAL CONTRACTS

II. DISCHARGES BY OPERATION OF LAW

J. ALTERATION

K. BANKRUPTCY

L. PERFORMANCE

CHAPTER 22. ILLEGAL BARGAINS

*

THE LAW OF
CONTRACTS

THIRD EDITION

*

Chapter 1

INTRODUCTION

Table of Sections

§ 1–1. What Is a Contract?

No entirely satisfactory definition of the term "contract" has ever been devised. The difficulty of definition arises from the diversity of the expressions of assent which may properly be denominated "contracts" and from the various perspectives from which their formation and consequences may be viewed.

Every contract involves at least one promise which has legal consequences. The usual, but not the inevitable, legal consequence is that performance of the promise may be enforced in court by a decree for specific performance or a money judgment. The promissory element present in every contract is stressed in a widely quoted definition: "A contract is a promise, or set of promises, for breach of which the law gives a remedy, or the performance of which the law in some way

1

recognizes as a duty."[1] This, like similar definitions, is somewhat misleading. While it is true that a promise is a necessary element in almost every contract, frequently the promise is coupled with other elements such as physical acts, recitals of fact, and the immediate transfer of property interests. In ordinary usage the contract is not the promise alone, but the entire complex of these elements. The definition also fails to point out that a contract usually requires the assent of more than one person. An additional criticism is that there are "voidable" and "unenforceable" contracts containing promises which at times may be dishonored with impunity. While promises contained in such contracts may have legal consequences, to say that the law recognizes them as duties is to stretch the concept of duty beyond its usual limitations.[2]

Another common definition of a contract is that it is a legally enforceable agreement. While this definition has the advantage of emphasizing that "agreement"[3] is at the core of the law of contracts, the troublesome fact is that there are certain kinds of contracts that may be formed without an agreement.[4] Also, like other definitions of the term "contract," it is unenlightening, and of little help in determining whether a given complex of words and acts are legally enforceable. In sum, knowledge of much of the law of contracts is a prerequisite to an understanding of what a contract is.

A recent definition of contract is "the relations among parties to the process of projecting exchange into the future."[5] One of the merits of this definition is that it stresses that a contract establishes an interrelationship among the contracting parties that is broader than their promises and agreement. The agreement is fleshed out by its social matrix which includes such matters as custom, cognizance of the social and economic roles of the parties, general notions of decent behavior, basic assumptions shared but unspoken by the parties, and other factors in the particular and general context in which the parties find themselves. This definition also underscores that the economic core of contract is an exchange between at least two parties and that contract is an instrument for planning future action. As helpful as this defini-

1. 1 Williston, Contracts § 1 (3d ed. 1957) [hereinafter Williston]; Restatement, Contracts § 1 (1932) [hereinafter Restatement, Contracts]. The definition is carried over into Restatement, Second, Contracts § (1981) [hereinafter Restatement, Second, Contracts]. Compare, 1 Corbin, Contracts § 3 (1963) [hereinafter Corbin] (" * * * a contract is a promise enforceable at law directly or indirectly.")

2. "A duty is a legal relation that exists whenever certain action or forbearance is expected of an individual, and in default of it the representatives of organized society will act in some predetermined manner injurious to the defaulting individual." 1A Corbin § 182. While the aggrieved party

to an unenforceable or voidable contract sometimes has a remedy against the defaulting promisor, quite often there is none. Where there is no remedy for non-performance it seems inappropriate to speak of a "duty" of performance.

3. The term "agreement" may also be defined in various ways. The definition adopted by Restatement, Second, Contracts § 3 is: "An agreement is a manifestation of mutual assent on the part of two or more persons." Compare, 1 Corbin § 9; 1 Williston § 2.

4. See ch. 5 infra.

5. Macneil, The New Social Contract 4 (1980).

tion may be, it often takes a great deal of imagination to see how the implications of this relational view of contract are worked out in the details of contract law.

Apart from the difficulty, even when there is little or no substantive disagreement, of defining a legal term so as to achieve universal acceptance, it should be stressed that technical terms share an affliction in common with non-technical language. Words, carefully defined in one context, have the frequently disagreeable habit of appearing in different contexts with widely divergent meanings. To illustrate, Article I, Section 10, of the United States Constitution, provides that "No State shall * * * pass any * * * Law impairing the Obligation of Contracts." The United States Supreme Court has held that this clause prohibits the Legislature of New Hampshire from modifying a charter granted by King George III to Dartmouth College.[6] A study of the treatises on the law of contracts would indicate clearly that this charter is not a contract as that term is used in the law of contracts. Nonetheless, by considering the purpose of the constitutional clause, and the presumed intention of the framers of the Constitution, the court held that the charter was a contract within the meaning of the Constitution. The re-defining of a term based on the purpose for which the term was used in its particular context is one of the subtle techniques of the legal art.[7]

Sometimes a legislative act will define terms used in the act in a manner different from standard definitions. The Uniform Commercial Code in essence defines a contract as the total legal obligation created by a bargain.[8] Thus by act of the legislature, the term "contract" for purposes of the Uniform Commercial Code, has a somewhat different meaning than it has in transactions not governed by the Code, since the term "bargain" as used in legal parlance includes transactions in which no promise is made, such as the immediate sale of property without warranty in exchange for cash.[9]

The term "contract" is also used by laymen and lawyers alike to refer to a document in which the terms of a contract are written. Use of the word in this sense is by no means improper so long as it is clearly understood that rules of law utilizing the concept "contract" rarely refer to the writing itself. Usually, the reference is to the agreement; the writing being merely a memorial of the agreement.

6. Trustees of Dartmouth College v. Woodward, 17 U.S. (4 Wheat.) 518, 4 L.Ed. 629 (1819).

7. "The tendency to assume that a word which appears in two or more legal rules, and so in connection with more than one purpose, has and should have precisely the same scope in all of them, runs all through legal discussions. It has all the tenacity of original sin and must constantly be guarded against." Cook, Substance and Procedure in the Conflict of Laws, 42 Yale L.J. 333, 337 (1933).

8. See U.C.C. § 1–201(11), read with § 1–201(3). The Uniform Commercial Code is discussed in § 1–7 infra.

9. See Reporter's Note, Restatement, Second, Contracts § 3. In addition, for purposes of Article 2 of the U.C.C. § 2–106(1) specifically includes sales of goods within the term "contracts."

WESTLAW REFERENCES
"legal consequence" /s contract

di contract

contract /s "specific performance" /s "money judgment"

contract /s performance /s promise /s duty

contract /s "physical act"

contract /s "legally enforceable agreement"

contract /s remedy /s nonperformance

di agreement

contract /s tacit! /s agree!

"obligation of contract" /p dartmouth +s woodward

writing written /s memorial /s agreement /s contract

§ 1–2. Contracts Distinguished From Executed Agreements

The law gives effect to certain agreements other than contracts. These include barters, gifts, sales of goods, conveyances of interests in real property, and the creation of bailments.[10] The distinction is that a contract is executory in nature. It contains a promise or promises that must be executed, that is, performed. For example, an agreement to sell a parcel of land is a contract; the sale of a parcel of land is not.

The distinction, like many legal distinctions, is helpful for the purpose of analysis, but is not rigid and is often artificial.[11] Looked at from a transactional perspective, probably most sales, conveyances and bailments are mixed transactions, involving both an executed transfer of property interests or possession and promises such as warranties or promises to surrender possession.

Even from a purely analytic point of view, the distinction between executed agreements and contracts is not firm. As noted in the preceding section, the Uniform Commercial Code includes sales of goods within its definition of contract. This was not an arbitrary legislative decision. One of the basic purposes of Article 2 of the Code is to bring the rules governing sales of goods closer to the rules governing contracts to sell goods than had been true under the Uniform Sales Act which the Code has replaced in most jurisdictions.[12]

 WESTLAW REFERENCES
perform! /s contract /s executory /s agreement

---

10. See 1 Corbin § 4. A bailment is not necessarily formed by agreement. For example, a finder of personal property is a bailee. Brown, Personal Property § 3.1 (3d ed. 1975).

11. See Wagstaff v. Peters, 203 Kan. 108, 453 P.2d 120 (1969).

12. See U.C.C. § 2–106, Comment 1 ("* * * the rights of the parties do not vary according to whether the transaction is a present sale or a contract to sell unless the Article expressly so provides.") Contrast, Uniform Sales Act § 1.

§ 1–3. Freedom of Contract

The law of contracts permeates every aspect of our society. Every day it reaches into the life of the individual, governing to some extent his employment, his purchase and sale of land and goods, the insuring of his possessions and the financing of these transactions. On a vaster scale it enters into practically every aspect of domestic and international trade.

It was not always thus. In medieval England contract law was rudimentary.[13] The protection of expectations engendered by promissory agreements was generally not regarded as important enough for the state to concern itself with. True, a remedy might be had in local courts, the proceedings of which we have few records.[14] The ecclesiastical courts took jurisdiction over some contract cases [15] and merchants and craftsmen often utilized their own courts and arbitrators.[16] However, the central parts of the legal system—the courts of common law and the chancery—tended to regard the non-performance of promises as unworthy of the King's justice unless the promise was made pursuant to certain solemn forms.[17] The feudal society of the time assigned each man a niche, a status, which rather rigidly delineated the conduct expected of him and which he might expect from others. Enforcement of a voluntary assumption of duties of the kind we now call contractual tended to disrupt this status oriented society.

No attempt will be made here to trace the step by step evolution of the law of contracts. The crux is that as England changed from a relatively primitive backwater to a commercial center with a capitalistic ethic, the law changed with it. As freedom became a rallying cry for political reforms, freedom of contract was the ideological principle for development of the law of contract. In Maine's classic phrase, it was widely believed that "the movement of the progressive societies has hitherto been a movement from *Status to Contract.*" [18] Williston adds: "Economic writers adopted the same line of thought. Adam Smith, Ricardo, Bentham and John Stuart Mill successively insisted on freedom of bargaining as the fundamental and indispensable requisite of

---

13. See Simpson, A History of the Common Law of Contract (1975); Farnsworth, The Past of Promise: An Historical Introduction to Contract, 69 Colum.L.Rev. 576 (1969); McGovern, Contract in Medieval England: The Necessity for Quid Pro Quo and a Sum Certain, 13 Am.J.Leg.Hist. 173 (1969); McGovern, The Enforcement of Oral Covenants Prior to Assumpsit, 65 Nw. U.L.Rev. 576 (1970); Pollock, Contracts in Early English Law, 6 Harv.L.Rev. 389 (1893), Selected Readings on the Law of Contracts 10 (1931) [hereinafter Selected Readings.]

14. See Fifoot, History and Sources of the Common Law: Tort and Contract 293–298 (1949).

15. Woodcock, Medieval Ecclesiastical Courts in the Diocese of Canterbury 89–102 (1952); Select Pleas from the Bishop of Ely's Court of Littleport, in Maitland and Baildon, The Court Baron 115–18, 125–26, 139, 144 (Volume 4 of the Selden Society Series 1891).

16. Gross, Selected Cases Concerning the Law Merchant, A.D. 1270–1638, Vol I (Volume 23 of the Selden Society Series 1908).

17. See Hazelitine, The Formal Contract of Early English Law, 10 Colum.L. Rev. 608 (1910), Selected Readings 1.

18. Maine, Ancient Law 165 (3rd American ed. 1873).

progress; and imposed their theories on the educated thought of their times with a thoroughness not common in economic speculation." [19]

In the twentieth century the tide has turned away from the nineteenth century tendency toward unrestricted freedom of contract. While the parties' power to contract as they please for lawful purposes remains a basic principle of our legal system, it is hemmed in by increasing legislative restrictions. Two areas of the law serve to illustrate this. Contracts of employment are controlled by a wide range of Federal and State laws concerning minimum wages, hours, working conditions and required social insurance programs. Contracts of insurance, perhaps to a greater extent than labor contracts, are controlled by law. Often terms of the policy are dictated by statute.

Apart from legislative restrictions on freedom of contract it seems likely that in the future there will be greater restrictions imposed by courts in the exercise of their function of developing the common law. There has been increasing recognition in legal literature that the bargaining process has become more limited in modern society. In purchasing a new automobile, for example, the individual may be able to dicker over price, model, color and certain other factors, but, if he wishes to consummate the contract to purchase, he usually must sign the standard form prepared by the manufacturer (although he is contracting with an independent dealer). He has no real choice. He must take that form or leave it. Such contracts, called contracts of "adhesion," [20] constitute a serious challenge to much of contract theory.

Most of contract law is premised upon a model consisting of two alert individuals, mindful of their self-interest, hammering out an agreement by a process of hard bargaining. The process of entering into a contract of adhesion, however " * * * is not one of haggle or cooperative process but rather of a fly and flypaper." [21] Courts, legislators and scholars have become increasingly aware of this divergence between the theory and practice of contract formation, and new techniques are evolving for coping with the challenges stemming from this divergence.[22]

 WESTLAW REFERENCES
"status to contract" /s society
"freedom of bargaining"
restrict! /s "power to contract"
law /s employment /1 contract
contract /2 insurance /s statut!
"freedom of contract"
"contract of adhesion"

---

19. Williston, Freedom of Contract, 6 Cornell L.Q. 365, 366 (1921), Selected Readings 100, 101–102.

20. See Kessler, Contracts of Adhesion—Some Thoughts About Freedom of Contract, 43 Colum.L.Rev. 629 (1943).

21. Leff, Contract as Thing, 19 Am.U.L. Rev. 131, 143 (1970).

22. See §§ 9–37 to 9–46 infra.

§ 1–4. The Philosophical Foundations of Contract Law

For centuries philosophers of the law have attempted to explain why the legal system recognizes and enforces private agreements.[23] As is so frequently the case in philosophical discourse no consensus has been reached, but the range of disagreement, although significant, is surprisingly small. The exponents of different schools of thought have tended to focus variously on five factors: (a) the human will either as a source of sovereignty or (b) as a source of moral compulsion, (c) private autonomy, (d) reliance, and (e) the needs of trade.

(a) The Sovereignty of the Human Will and (b) the Sanctity of Promise

In the heyday of the Enlightenment era there was widespread belief in, and great stress was placed upon, the existence of inalienable rights which existed prior to, and independent of, government. Indeed, government itself was believed to be based upon a social contract that derived its binding force from the sovereignty of the individual wills of the contracting parties. The social contract theory was pithily put by an English lawyer in the mid 1600's. "[B]oth judge and prisoner have consented to a law that if either of them steal they shall be hanged." And again, "to know what obedience is due to the prince you must look into the contract betwixt him and the people; as if you would know what rent is due from the tenant to the landlord you must look into the lease." [24] An American exponent of this viewpoint, Chief Justice John Marshall, had this to say about the law of contract: [25]

> "If, on tracing the right to contract, and the obligations created by contract, to their source, we find them to exist anterior to, and

23. For further discussion of the topics discussed in this section, see Atiyah, Promises, Morals and Law (1981); Atiyah, The Rise and Fall of Freedom of Contract (1979); Barnett, A Consent Theory of Contract, 86 Colum.L.Rev. 269 (1986); Bentham, Theory of Legislation 192–194 (Odgen ed. 1931); Cohen, The Basis of Contract, 46 Harv.L.Rev. 553, 558–85 (1933); Cohen, Jewish and Roman Law, 78–79 (1966); Ehrlich, Fundamental Principles of the Sociology of Law 111 (Moll. trans. 1962); Farnsworth, The Past of Promise, 69 Colum.L.Rev. 576 (1969); Fried, Contract as Promise (1981); Fuller, Consideration and Form, 41 Colum.L.Rev. 799, 806–14 (1941); Grotius, The Rights of War and Peace, book II, chs. 11, 12 (Whewell trans. 1853); Kant, The Philosophy of Law 134–144 (Albrecht trans. 1921); Kronman & Posner, The Economics of Contract Law (1979); Lorenzen, Causa and Consideration in the Law of Contracts, 28 Yale L.J. 621–44 (1919); Macneil, Efficient Breach of Contract: Circles in the Sky, 68 Va.L.Rev. 947 (1982); Pound, The Role of the Will in Law, 68 Harv.L.Rev. 1 (1954); Pufendorf, The Two Books on the Duty of Man and Citizen According to the Natural Law, book I, ch. 9 § 3 (Moore trans. 1927); Radin, Contract Obligation and the Human Will 43 Colum.L.Rev. 575 (1943); St. Thomas Acquinas, The Summa Theologica, Part II, Q. 88, Arts. 1, 2, 3, Q. 89, Art. 7 (Dominican trans. 1922); Sharp, Pacta Sunt Servanda, 41 Colum.L.Rev. 783–85 (1941); Vinogradoff, Reason and Conscience in Sixteenth Century Jurisprudence, 24 L.Q.Rev. 373 (1908); Willis, Rationale of the Law of Contracts, 11 Ind.L.J. 227 (1936). The flavor of contemporary debate is most easily approached by reading book reviews of the works of Atiyah and Fried supra.

24. Selden, Table-Talk (headings Equity and War).

25. Ogden v. Saunders, 25 U.S. (12 Wheat.) 213, 345, 6 L.Ed. 606 (1827). See generally Isaacs, John Marshall on Contracts: A Study in Early American Juristic Theory, 7 Va.L.Rev. 413 (1921).

independent of society, we may reasonably conclude that those original and pre-existing principles are, like many other natural rights brought with man into society; and, *although they may be controlled, are not given by human legislation.*"

Although, this natural law viewpoint could be logically consistent with other possible views, historically it was interwined with the idea that, "I am bound because I intend to be bound." Intention is regarded as the keystone of contract law.

Although the Enlightenment concept of natural law was the natural law concept that had the most direct impact upon Anglo-American courts, it was preceded by canon law and rabbinical thinking about the sanctity of promise. According to the canon lawyers and rabbinical scholars of the late middle ages and the Renaissance, promises were binding in natural law as well as in morality because failure to perform a promise made by a free act of the will was an offense against the Deity. Inasmuch as some training in theology was part of the education of every literate person during the formative era of the Anglo-American law of contracts it is inferable that this doctrine had an impact upon the thinking of lawyers and judges as well as upon the teaching of philosophers. Indeed, it was often utilized by Enlightenment philosophers as an additional argument to support the notion of the sovereignty of the individual will. The difference was a shift in emphasis from a theological to an humanistic basis. This does not imply that the religious basis was abandoned. English college students in the 18th and 19th century were exposed to it in the many editions of Paley's Principles of Moral and Political Philosophy.[26] American college students received the same message from Paley or his principle American successor, Wayland.[27]

(c) Private Autonomy

A less radical analysis of the efficacy of the human will is made by the exponents of the theory of private autonomy. Simply put, the theory sees the foundation of contract law as a sort of delegation of power by the State to its inhabitants. Recognizing the desirability of allowing individuals to regulate, to a large extent, their own affairs, the State has conferred upon them the power to bind themselves by expression of their intention to be bound, provided, always, that they operate within the limits of their delegated powers.

> * * * [I]nsofar as the law of contract places the coercions of the legal order behind the terms of a contract settled by private parties, the legal order may and indeed should set socially approved limits to the support which it gives to the terms which one party is in a position to impose on the other.[28]

26. Book II, chs. I–III, Book III, chs. V–IX.

27. The Elements of Moral Science 260–64 (1963).

28. Stone, Social Dimensions of Law and Justice 253 (1966).

This power, it is argued, stems from the law of the State rather than the law of nature.

(d) Reliance

Proponents of the reliance theory of contracts profess to see the foundation of contract law not in the will of the promisor to be bound but in the expectations engendered by, and the promisee's consequent reliance upon, the promise. Although this idea is not in opposition to some aspects of the theories discussed under (a), (b) and (c) above, it is in opposition to a finding that the efficacy of a contract is based upon the power of the will of the promisor. It is significant that the earliest cases in which the courts of common law gave relief to a promise were those in which damage had been incurred in reliance upon a promise. On the other hand, it is clear that under modern law a contract once made is binding and an action for breach may be instituted although the contract is repudiated before it induces any action or inaction in reliance upon it.[29] We will see, however, that in many areas of contract law reliance by the promisee is often crucial.

(e) Needs of Trade

Some students of the law urge that contract law is based upon the needs of trade, sometimes stated in terms of the mutual advantage of the contracting parties, but more often of late in terms of a tool of the economic and social order. Such students find discussions of the efficacy of the will, private autonomy, and reliance to be irrelevant, or at least subordinate to what they perceive to be its main utilitarian economic pillar. Consequently, proponents of this basis of the law of contracts do not necessarily exclude some validity to any of the theories discussed above. In stressing the role of the state, however, proponents undercut emphasis on the intention of the parties.

(f) Synthesis

It cannot be said that any of the five competing philosophic premises discussed above is officially enshrined in our law of contract. Each of them, however, together with the pervasive desire of the law to prevent unjust enrichment, coexists as part of our frequently utilized stock of legally acceptable arguments. The contradictions among them are rarely noticed. The premises were neatly synthesized by Sir Frederick Pollock.[30]

"The law of Contract may be described as the endeavor of the State, a more or less imperfect one by the nature of the case, to establish a positive sanction for the expectation of good faith which has grown up in the mutual dealings of men of average rightmindedness. * * * He who has given the promise is bound to him who accepts it, not merely because he had or expressed a

---

29. Hochster v. De La Tour, 118 Eng. Rep. 922 (1853).

30. Pollock, Principles of Contract 9 (Preface to 4th ed. 1888).

certain intention, but because he so expressed himself as to entitle the other party to rely on his acting in a certain way."

Such a synthesis, while serving well for the generality of cases, breaks down when many difficult choices must be made. Illustrative of the questions which receive different answers depending upon which premise is accepted, are the following:

(1) If a person who intentionally causes another to rely upon his word, at the same time disclaims any intention to be bound, should the law protect the interests of the person so relying? The will premise and the reliance premise have produced conflicting decisions.[31]

(2) Should a contract-breaker who deliberately goes back upon his pledged word be treated differently from one who is merely negligent or unfortunate? Proponents of the moral basis of contract enforcement may answer the question differently from those who adopt the view that contract law is designed to meet the needs of trade.[32]

Questions such as the above permeate our law of contracts and receive no consistent or easily predictable reply. Different premises have been more strongly stressed and more dogmatically asserted in given historical eras than in others.[33] Readers of judicial opinions will note that rarely is a conscious choice made between competing theories, and perhaps this is to the good. Each of the five theories are based upon values and interests which our legal system holds in high regard. We can, at the risk of oversimplification, draw the following equations:

Theory		Underlying Social Value
(1) Sovereignty of the Individual Will	=	Individual Responsibility of Promisors
(2) Sanctity of Promise	=	The Law Upholds Moral Values

31. See § 2–4 infra.

32. For example, on the question of whether a party who has intentionally breached his contract may recover for the value of the benefits he has conferred upon the other party, compare the statements of New York's Chief Judge Cardozo with those of California's Chief Justice Traynor. Cardozo: "The willful transgressor must accept the penalty of his transgression * * *. The transgressor whose default is unintentional and trivial may hope for mercy if he will offer atonement for his wrong." Jacob & Youngs v. Kent, 230 N.Y. 239, 244, 129 N.E. 889, 891 (1921). Traynor: "* * * to deny the remedy of restitution because a breach is wilful would create an anomalous situation * * *." Freedman v. Rector, Wardens & Vestrymen of St. Mathias Parish, 37 Cal.2d

16, 22, 230 P.2d 629, 632, 31 A.L.R.2d 1, 7 (1951). See § 11–22 infra. Compare further, the language of economic analysis: "The opportunity cost of completion to the breaching party is the profit that he would make from a breach, and if it is greater than his profit from completion, then completion will involve a loss to him. If that loss is greater than the gain to the other party from completion, breach would be value maximizing and should be encouraged." Posner, Economic Analysis of Law 90 (2d ed. 1977). For another example of a split of authority turning on whether or not a contract breaker ought to be characterized as a "bad man," see Perillo, Restitution in a Contractual Context, 73 Colum.L.Rev. 1208, 1224 n. 104 (1973).

33. See generally Pound, Liberty of Contract, 18 Yale L.J. 454 (1909).

Theory		Underlying Social Value
(3) Private Autonomy	=	Freedom of the Private Sector With Controls Against Excesses
(4) Reliance	=	Fairness to Promisees
(5) Needs of Trade	=	Economic Efficiency

It seems unrealistic to expect our legal system to select one of these social values as the sole and exclusive basis of the law of contract. Realism aside, it is doubtful whether it would be desirable in each and every case to subordinate four of these values to any one of the five. It should also be reiterated that in many cases there is no irreconcilable clash among them.

§ 1–5. Scope, Relevance and Adequacy of the Law of Contracts

Contract Law interlocks with and overlaps all other legal disciplines. In particular, labor, sales, commercial financing, agency, suretyship, quasi contracts, damages, personal property—to name but a few—are contract permeated subjects about which specialized treatises have been written.

Of late, it has been suggested that there is no law of contracts, or that if there is, it ought to be done away with. The thrust of the argument is that the variety of contractual contexts is so extensive and that the social and economic needs of each kind of transaction is so different that a disservice is done if one attempts to resolve transactional disputes by the application of supposed general principles of contract law.[34] Critics of contract law find additional support in the fact that when disputes arise in business and non-business transactions the parties involved usually resolve the dispute without reference to rules of law.[35] The latter argument is rather simple to dispose of. If neighboring children walk through one's yard as a short-cut to school one has the choice of greeting them with a welcome or with a snarl, and if one wishes, one may resort to a variety of legal remedies to punish or stop them from trespassing. The fact that in this context legal remedies are rarely resorted to hardly means that the law of property is irrelevant. Rather it is the weapon of last resort when other methods of attaining one's goals fail. Similarly the reluctance of many to resort to law to resolve contract disputes may indicate a healthy social system rather than the irrelevance of contract law.

The first argument is much more serious however. Can general principles be formulated to regulate adequately such diverse transac-

34. See Atiyah, Contracts, Promises and the Law of Obligations, 94 L.Q.Rev. 193, 199–201 (1978); Mueller, Contract Remedies: Business Fact and Legal Fantasy, 1967 Wis.L.Rev. 833; see also Gilmore, The Death of Contract (1974). For a good analysis of this thesis, see Speidel, An Essay on the Reported Death and Continued Vitality of Contract, 27 Stanford L.Rev. 1161 (1975).

35. Friedman and Macaulay, Contract Law and Contract Teaching: Past, Present and Future, 1967 Wis.L.Rev. 805.

tions as military enlistments,[36] credit card purchases,[37] collective bargaining agreements,[38] government construction contracts, maritime charters, house purchases, and the wide variety of other consensual transactions? The answer is, and for centuries has been, a broad mixture of yes and no. There are legal questions common to all of these transactions, particularly those involving the nature of consent, capacity of parties, methods of interpretation, necessary formalities, the relationship between the parties' performances, rights of third parties, the discharge of obligations, as well as others. There are also questions unique to each kind of transaction; the business context of maritime charters requires that special rules should apply that do not apply to a contract for sale of a house.

Moreover, legislators and regulators have staked out various kinds of transactions for the enactment of special rules for the protection of the consumer, for economic regulation, or for other purposes. The coexistence of general rules common to all transactions and special rules for particular transactions was recognized in one of the earliest discussions of contracts available to us in English, by Hugo Grotius,[39] and continues to be recognized in most of the current American literature. Possibly surprising to some, the same general problems addressed by Grotius are addressed in much the same way in the recent recodification of contract law in Russia.[40] It is believed that the persistency of approaching general problems of contract, along with special rules for particular contracts throughout the centuries and in countries with diverse economic systems, stems not from academic conservatism but from the persistency of similar problems that run through all consensual transactions. To study one kind of transaction in isolation from others would be to ignore the persistency of human behavior and the utility of generalizations.[41] Those who rebel at generalizations might well be reminded of the tale of the empire whose

36. Dilloff, A Contractual Analysis of the Military Enlistment, 8 U. Richmond L.Rev. 121 (1974).

37. Macaulay, Private Legislation and the Duty to Read—Business Run By IBM Machine, the Law of Contracts and Credit Cards, 19 Vand.L.Rev. 1051 (1966).

38. Summers, Collective Agreements and the Law of Contracts, 78 Yale L.J. 525 (1969).

39. Grotius, The Rights of War and Peace, book II, chs. 11, 12 (Whewell trans. 1853).

40. Civil Code of the R.S.F.S.R., part III (Gray and Stults trans. 1965).

41. "[I]n any intellectual enterprise * * * there must always be a certain difference between theory and practice or experience. A theory must certainly be simpler than the factual complexity or cha-

os that faces us when we lack the guidance which a general chart of the field affords us. A chart or map would be altogether useless if it did not simplify the actual contours and topography which it describes. * * * No science offers us an absolutely complete account of its subject matter. It is sufficient if it indicates some general pattern to which the phenomena approximate more or less. For practical purposes any degree of approximation will do if it will lead to a greater control over nature than we should have without our ideal pattern. But for theoretic purposes we need the postulate that all divergences between the ideal and the actual will be progressively minimized by the discovery of subsidiary principles deduced from, or at least consistent with, the principles of our science." Cohen, Reason and Law 63–64 (Free Press ed. 1950).

exacting map makers produced a map so accurate that it coincided with the empire point by point.[42] Its uselessness was, of course, total.

Serious criticism has been levelled of late against the adequacy of contract law. The criticism is of two kinds. First, that contract law has not forged adequate tools for coping with contracts of adhesion. This is discussed elsewhere in this book.[43] The second criticism is made by Professor Ian Macneil in several challenging articles.[44] The thrust of the criticism is that traditional contract doctrine takes as its model the discrete transaction: the contract to sell a horse, a house, a plot of land, or short term services. In today's world such transactions continue but are overshadowed by long-term relational contracts: franchises, collective bargains, long-term supply contracts and the like. The need in the future is to recast much of contract doctrine to consider more adequately the needs of on-going relational contracts. In this he is surely right.

§ 1–6. Sources of Contract Law

Except in a few American jurisdictions the basic law of contracts is not codified. Contract law is thus primarily common law, embodied in court decisions. Many legislative enactments do, however, bear on the subject. Generally, only a few statutes purport to modify a principle running throughout contract law. For the most part legislatures have concentrated on regulating particular types of contracts such as insurance policies and employment contracts. Of particular relevance in recent legislation is Article 2 of the Uniform Commercial Code.[45]

For the guidance of the bench and bar, the American Law Institute in 1932 published a code-like document called the Restatement of Contracts. The Restatement, having been issued by a private organization, does not have the force of law. Nevertheless, it is highly persuasive authority. Leaders of the profession analyzed the often conflicting maze of judicial decisions, attempted to cull the sound from the less sound and to state the sounder views in systematic form.[46] The principal draftsman of the Restatement of Contracts was Samuel Williston.

After a passage of some thirty years, it was felt that there had been sufficient developments in the law for a new Restatement to be issued. In 1964 the first tentative draft of the initial portion of a second edition was circulated. The chief draftsman of Chapters 1–9 of the second Restatement has been Professor Robert Braucher, who resigned to serve as a Justice of the Supreme Judicial Court of Massachusetts. Subsequent chapters have been drafted primarily by Professor E. Allan

---

42. Borges, A Universal History of Infamy 141 (di Giovanni trans., E. P. Dutton & Co. 1972).

43. See § 9–44 infra.

44. Macneil, The Many Futures of Contract, 47 So.Calif.L.Rev. 691 (1974); Mac-

neil, Restatement (Second) of Contracts and Presentation, 60 Va.L.Rev. 589. (1974); Symposium, 1985 Wis.L.Rev. 483.

45. See § 1–7 infra.

46. For a fuller discussion, see Preface, Restatement of Contracts (1932).

Farnsworth. The final draft was approved in 1979 and published in 1981. It is fair to say that just as the first Restatement largely reflected the views of Professor Williston, the Second Restatement has drawn heavily on the views of Professor Arthur L. Corbin.[47]

The law of contracts is the subject of two of the best treatises in Anglo-American legal literature. The first edition of Professor Williston's treatise was published in 1920 and has had enormous impact on the law. Professor Corbin's, first published in 1950, promises to be equally influential. Research into any contract problem necessarily requires consultation of both of these authors' views as well as the cases and statutes. Both treatises are masterful analyses. To capsulate the basic difference in approach of the two authors, requires an introduction to two schools of jurisprudence: the so-called positivist and realist schools.

Stated in its extreme form the positivist idea is this:

> "Justice is an irrational idea. * * * that only one of two orders is 'just' cannot be established by rational cognition. Such cognition can grasp only a positive order * * *. This order is positive law * * *. It presents the law as it is, without defending it by calling it just, or condemning it to call it unjust." [48]

The positivist usually believes that the legal system may be analyzed into component rules, principles and concepts and that any fact situation may be solved by the careful pigeonholing of the facts into the appropriate legal concepts, principles and rules. In other words, once the facts are determined, a carefully programmed computer would produce the correct decision. This approach has been criticized as "mechanical jurisprudence." [49]

The realist is skeptical whether decisions are in fact so arrived at and furthermore questions the propriety of such an approach. Again stated in extreme form, the realist believes:

> "[T]he law, with respect to any particular set of facts, is a decision of a court with respect to those facts so far as that decision affects that particular person. Until a court has passed on those facts no law on that subject is yet in existence." [50]

The realist is skeptical of the formulation of generalizations and definitions. He believes that courts in reaching a decision do in fact and should take into account the moral, ethical, economic and social situation in reaching a decision. This approach is subject to criticism in that it tends toward the creation of a legal system based on non-law and

---

47. See Braucher, Freedom of Contract and the Second Restatement, 78 Yale L.J. 598, 616 (1969).

48. Kelsen, General Theory of Law and State 13 (1961). Kelsen is the leading modern exponent of the positivist approach.

49. Pound, Mechanical Jurisprudence, 8 Colum.L.Rev. 605 (1908).

50. Frank, Law and the Modern Mind 46 (1930). See generally Fuller, American Legal Realism, 82 U.Pa.L.Rev. 429 (1934); Savarese, American Legal Realism, 3 Houston L.Rev. 180 (1965).

to defeat society's expectations of order and certainty in legal relationships.

Neither Professor Williston nor Professor Corbin adopts either of the extreme positions just discussed. However, the reader might find his comprehension of their treatises enhanced if he realizes at the outset that the former tends towards the positivist position and the latter towards the realist school.

The neophyte should also be apprised that although courts usually articulate their decisions in positivist terms, it is only the unsophisticated attorney who will phrase his argument purely in those terms without reference to social, economic and ethical considerations.

§ 1–7. The Uniform Commercial Code and the United Nations Convention

The Uniform Commercial Code is the product of a Permanent Editorial Board under the joint auspices of the American Law Institute and the National Conference of Commissioners on Uniform State Laws.[51] A draft was approved by these bodies in 1952. In 1953, it was enacted by Pennsylvania as the law of that Commonwealth. No other state followed. In 1956 the New York Law Revision Commission recommended against enactment unless extensive amendments were made. Reacting to the New York report, the Permanent Editorial Board made extensive revisions. As so revised it was enacted by all the states except Louisiana between 1957 and 1967. The enactments were not wholly uniform, as many of the states have varied from the uniform text at some points. In addition, the Code contained several optional provisions. These variations are noted in the "Uniform Laws Annotated" edition of the Code. Editions published in local state collections of statutes will usually indicate instances in which the local enactment varies from the uniform text.

The Uniform Commercial Code contains nine articles.[52] Article 1 contains general provisions applicable to all transactions governed by the Code. Article 2 governs the sale of goods; Article 3, commercial paper; Article 4, bank deposits and collections; Article 5, letters of credit; Article 6, bulk transfers; Article 7, warehouse receipts, bills of lading and other documents of title; Article 8, investment securities; Article 9, secured transactions, sales of accounts and chattel paper.

Most of the provisions of the Code do not affect basic contract law; those that do are mostly contained in Article 2, which deals with the sale of goods[53] and in Article 9 which deals, among other things, with the assignment (transfer) of some contract rights. As the most recent

---

51. See Schnader, A Short History of the Preparation and Enactment of the Uniform Commercial Code, 22 U. Miami L.Rev. 1 (1967); White and Summers, Uniform Commercial Code 1–21 (2d ed. 1980).

52. The citation "U.C.C. § 2–238" indicates that the provision is in Article 2.

The citation "U.C.C. § 3–211" indicates the provision is in Article 3.

53. The term "goods" is defined in § 2–105, with a cross reference to § 2–107. This definition is discussed in § 19–16 infra.

legislative statement of certain contract principles and rules, Article 2 of the Code has increasingly been looked to by courts for guidance in transactions other than the sale of goods.[54]

The Code was published with official comments prepared by the Permanent Editorial Board. The "General Comment" introduction to the Code indicates that the purpose of the comments is to promote uniformity and "to aid in viewing the Act as an integrated whole, and to safeguard against misconstruction." The Act itself is law in the 49 states that have adopted the Code, but the comments are not since they have not been enacted by the legislatures.[55] The comments have proved valuable. The courts have repeatedly turned to them in resolving issues. Of course, if the Code and a comment are in conflict, the Code must prevail.

The contract provisions of Article 2 of the Code make many changes in traditional contract law with the result that very often there is a different rule for "contracts for sale" than for other contracts such as for labor, services and the sale of land.[56] The Code does not change all the traditional rules; where it is silent, the traditional rules prevail even as to contracts for sale.[57] As indicated above,[58] there is a marked tendency to employ the Code by analogy, to transactions outside its coverage. In addition, the Restatement Second has recast many of the provisions of the Restatement First to harmonize them with the Code. The foreseeable result is that in future decades the principles underlying the contract provisions of Article 2 will be the law of the land even for contracts not governed by the Code.

Article 2 of the Uniform Commercial Code governs contracts for the sale of goods, whether the seller is a merchant or a casual seller. However, some of its provisions treat merchants differently. The Code defines a merchant, as paraphrased in a leading case,[59] as follows:

> [A] person is a "merchant" if he (1) deals in goods of the kind, or (2) by his occupation holds himself out as having knowledge or skill peculiar to the *practices* involved in the transaction, or (3) by his occupation holds himself out as having knowledge or skill peculiar to the *goods* involved in the transaction, or (4) employs an intermediary who by his occupation holds himself out as having such knowledge or skill, and that knowledge or skill may be attributed to the person whose status is in question.

54. See U.C.C. § 1–102(1); Murray, Under the Spreading Analogy of Article 2 of the Uniform Commercial Code, 39 Fordham L.Rev. 447 (1971); Note, 65 Colum.L. Rev. 880 (1965).

55. See Miller v. Preitz, 442 Pa. 383, 221 A.2d 320 (1966).

56. The result of having two sets of contract rules has been criticized. Williston, The Law of Sales in the Proposed Uniform Commercial Code, 63 Harv.L.Rev. 561, 576 (1950); but see Corbin, The Uniform Commercial Code—Sales; Should it be enacted? 59 Yale L.J. 821 (1950).

57. U.C.C. § 1–103.

58. See note 54 supra.

59. Nelson v. Union Equity Co-op Exch., 548 S.W.2d 352, 355, 95 A.L.R.3d 471 (Tex.1977).

Despite the clarity of this definition there are many borderline situations. For example, the courts are divided on the question of whether a farmer who sells his crop once a year is a merchant or a "casual seller." [60]

On October 9, 1986, the United States Senate, at the request of the President, consented to his ratification of the United Nations Convention on Contracts for the International Sale of Goods. This convention, governing certain international sales contracts, is not considered in this treatise.

§ 1–8. Classification of Contracts

Contracts have been classified and distinguished in various ways for different purposes. Some of these classifications will be discussed briefly in the following sections.

§ 1–9. Formal and Informal Contracts

The distinction between formal and informal contracts is based on the method of the formation of the contract. Under the early common law a promise was not binding unless accompanied by certain formalities.[61] Three kinds of formal contracts are still important: (1) the contract under seal; [62] (2) the recognizance; [63] and (3) negotiable instruments and letters of credit.[64]

All other kinds of contracts are considered to be informal and are enforceable not because of the form of the transactions but because of their substance. Such contracts have also been called "simple" or "parol" contracts.

 WESTLAW REFERENCES

"formal contract"

"informal contract"

formation /2 contract

"contract under seal"

recognizance /s contract

"negotiable instrument" /s "letter of credit" /s contract

§ 1–10. Unilateral and Bilateral Contracts

Every contract involves at least two contracting parties. In some contracts, however, only one party has made a promise and therefore

60. See Wallach, The Law of Sales Under the U.C.C. § 1.06[1][b] (1981); Dolan, The Merchant Class of Article 2: Farmers, Doctors and Others, 1977 Wash.U.L.Q. 1; Annot., 95 A.L.R.3d 484 (1979).

61. See Hazeltine, The Formal Contract of Early English Law, 10 Colum.L.Rev. 608 (1910), Selected Readings 1 (1931).

62. The seal has lost all or some of its effect in many jurisdictions. See ch. 7 infra.

63. A recognizance is a acknowledgment in court by the recognizor that he is bound to make a certain payment unless a specified condition is performed. Restatement, Second, Contracts § 6, Comment c. Recognizances are discussed in 76 C.J.S. 73–104 (1952).

64. Negotiable instruments and letters of credit are treated in specialized works. These are governed by Articles 3 and 5 of the Uniform Commercial Code.

only he is subject to a legal obligation. Such a contract is said to be unilateral. If both parties have made promises, the contract is bilateral. Of course this assumes that there are only two parties to the contract. If there are more than two, the contract is deemed bilateral if one party is both a promisor and a promisee.[65]

If A says to B, "If you walk across Brooklyn Bridge, I promise to pay you ten dollars," A has made a promise but he has not asked B for a return promise. He has requested B to perform an act, not a commitment to do the act. A has thus made an offer to a unilateral contract which arises when and if B performs the act called for. If A has said to B, "If you promise to walk across Brooklyn Bridge, I promise to pay you ten dollars," his offer requests B to make a commitment to walk the bridge. A bilateral contract arises when the requisite return promise is made by B.

A number of recent authorities, including the Second Restatement and the Uniform Commercial Code avoid the terms "bilateral" and "unilateral." Their abandonment of this terminology is part of an effort to soften the rigor of some of the rigid consequences thought to flow from the mechanical application of this dichotomy.[66]

 WESTLAW REFERENCES

"unilateral contract"

"bilateral contract"

"unilateral contract" /s define*

§ 1–11. Enforceable, Void, Voidable and Unenforceable Contracts

When a promisee is entitled to either a money judgment,[67] an injunction or specific performance [68] because of a breach, the contract is said to be enforceable.

A contract is void, a contradiction in terms, when it produces no legal obligation upon the part of a promisor. For example, an exchange of promises which lacks consideration is frequently said to be a void contract.[69] It would be more exact to say that no contract has been created.

A contract is voidable if one or more of the parties has the power to elect to avoid the legal relations created by the contract or by ratification to extinguish the power of avoidance. This power to avoid or ratify is sometimes given to an infant contracting party and to persons who have been induced to enter contracts by fraud, mistake or duress.[70]

---

65. Restatement, Contracts § 12.

66. See Reporter's Note to § 12 in Restatement, Second, Contracts (Tent.Draft No. 1, 1964). For fuller discussion see §§ 2–10, 2–26 infra.

67. A money judgment may be based on either the remedy of damages or of restitution, or both. See chs. 14, 15 infra.

68. See ch. 16 infra.

69. See ch. 4 infra.

70. See ch. 9 infra.

Unenforceable contracts are those which have some legal consequences but which may not be enforced in an action for damages or specific performance in the face of certain defenses such as the Statute of Frauds and the statute of limitations. Certain contracts which are tainted by illegality but are neither wholly void nor voidable may also be classified as unenforceable,[71] as can be contracts with those governmental units which still retain a doctrine of sovereign immunity.[72] Unenforceable contracts share many of the features of voidable contracts, the main difference being that unenforceable contracts have a variety of legal consequences that voidable contracts do not share, including various methods of indirect enforcement.[73]

WESTLAW REFERENCES

"enforceable contract" /s enjoin! injunction

"legal! obligat!" /s "enforceable contract"

to(95) /p "enforceable contract"

void! /s contract /s "legal! obligat!"

void! /s contract /s lack! want! fail! +2 consideration

"voidable contract" /s definition define* defining

"voidable contract" /s fraud! mistake!

"unenforceable contract"

to(95) /p "statute of frauds"

to(95) /p "statute of limitations"

taint! /s contract /s illegal!

"sovereign immunity" /s contract /s enforce! unenforce!

§ 1–12. Express and Implied Contracts—Quasi Contracts

When the parties manifest their agreement by words the contract is said to be express. When it is manifested by conduct it is said to be implied in fact.[74] If A telephones a plumber to come to A's house to fix a broken pipe, it may be inferred that A has agreed to pay the plumber a reasonable fee for his services although nothing is said of this. The contract is partly express and partly implied in fact. There are cases of contracts wholly implied in fact.[75] The distinction between this kind of contract and a contract expressed in words is unimportant: both are true contracts formed by a mutual manifestation of assent.[76]

A contract implied in law is not a contract at all but an obligation imposed by law to do justice even though it is clear that no promise was ever made or intended.[77] To illustrate, if a physician gives a child

---

71. Restatement, Second, Contracts § 8, Comment b.

72. Restatement, Second, Contracts § 8, Comment c.

73. Restatement, Second, Contracts § 8, ills. 2, 3, 4, 5; Corbin, Offer and Acceptance, and Some of the Resulting Legal Relations, 26 Yale L.J. 169, 179–181 (1917), Selected Readings 170, 178–77.

74. Erickson v. Goodell Oil Co., 384 Mich. 207, 180 N.W.2d 798 (1970).

75. E.g., Day v. Caton, 119 Mass. 513 (1876).

76. Elias v. Elias, 428 Pa. 159, 237 A.2d 215 (1968); Bailey v. West, 105 R.I. 61, 249 A.2d 414 (1969).

77. Bradkin v. Leverton, 26 N.Y.2d 192, 309 N.Y.S.2d 192, 257 N.E.2d 643 (1970).

necessary medical care in the face of parental neglect, the physician may recover from the parents, in quasi contract, the value of his services.[78] There is nothing contractual about this at all. The quasi-contractual label arose from a procedural quirk. Since in the earlier law there was no writ for an obligation of this kind, courts permitted the use of the contractual writ of assumpsit and allowed the plaintiff's attorney to plead a fictitious promise. The crux is that a quasi contract is not a peculiar brand of contract. It is a non-contractual obligation that used to be treated procedurally as if it were a contract. The principal function of quasi contract is generally said to be that of prevention of unjust enrichment.[79]

Very often, however, quasi-contractual remedies are employed in contractual contexts. When the parties negotiate an agreement which fails because the subject matter is too indefinite, or because the agent for one of the parties had no power to bind his principal, or the parties each had a different reasonable understanding of the agreement, or because the agreement is illegal, it is the law of quasi contracts that is looked to for a determination of to what extent any performance rendered under the agreement, or other acts in reliance on the agreement, are to be compensated. Similarly, when a contract is made and avoided for incapacity, mistake, fraud, or duress or is unenforceable for non-conformity with form requirements, or discharged for impossibility or frustration, quasi contract is the body of law to which we look for the reallocation of gains and losses between the parties. It should be noticed that in the illustration given in the preceding paragraph, the law of quasi contract is the exclusive source of the plaintiff's rights and remedies. In the illustrations given in this paragraph any recovery is based on the interplay of rules of contract and quasi contract. When there is no agreement between the parties the basis of the plaintiff's recovery is the fact of the unjust enrichment of the defendant and the amount of recovery is measured on that basis. When there is an agreement which has failed from the start or because of subsequent avoidance or discharge, unjust enrichment, unjust impoverishment, relative fault, the allocation of risks in the failed agreement, and fairness of alternative risk allocations are all factors that go into the measure of recovery.[80]

WESTLAW REFERENCES

to(95) /p ''express contract'' /p agree!

95k3

95k4

95k27

''implied in fact'' /s contract

to(95) /p ''implied in law''

''quasi contract!'' /s ''implied in law''

---

78. Greenspan v. Slate, 12 N.J. 426, 97 A.2d 390 (1953), noted in 39 Cornell L.Q. 337 (1954).

79. Restatement, Restitution § 1 (1937).

80. See Perillo, Restitution in a Contractual Context, 73 Colum.L.Rev. 1208 (1973).

```
assumpsit  /s  ''implied in law''
95k5
205hk2
42k1
42k4
to(95)  /p  ''quasi contract!''  /p  ''unjust! enrich!''
''quasi contract''  /s  ''subject matter''
''quasi contract!''  /s  illegal!
''quasi contract!''  /s  perform!
''quasi contract!''  /s  mistake! fraud! duress
''quasi contract''  /s  impossib! frustrat!
''quasi contract''  /s  remedy
```

Chapter 2

OFFER AND ACCEPTANCE

Table of Sections

Table of Sections

A. INTENT TO CONTRACT

A.   INTENT TO CONTRACT

Table of Sections

§ 2–1.   Mutual Assent

Usually an essential prerequisite to the formation of a contract is an agreement: a mutual manifestation of assent to the same terms.[1] This mutual assent ordinarily is established by a process of offer and acceptance.[2] But it is possible to have mutual assent even though it is impossible to identify the offer and the acceptance.[3] Thus if A and B are together and C suggests the terms of an agreement for them, there would be a contract without any process of offer and acceptance if they simultaneously agreed to these terms.[4] Frequently, especially in transactions of considerable magnitude, the parties negotiate the terms of a proposed contract until a final draft is typed or printed. The contract may be formed when the copies of the writing are signed and exchanged.[5] Again neither an offer nor an acceptance can be identified in this circumstance.

But, as indicated above, mutual assent usually arises through a process of offer acceptance and, even in cases where the offer and acceptance cannot be identified, the conceptual model of offer and acceptance may be a helpful analytical tool.[6] We shall explore the framework of offer and acceptance after establishing some important ground rules.[7]

 WESTLAW REFERENCES
prerequisite /s formation /s contract /s agree!

1. Russell v. Union Oil Co., 7 Cal.App. 3d 110, 86 Cal.Rptr. 424 (1970); Quality Sheet Metal Co. v. Woods, 2 Hawaii App. 160, 627 P.2d 1128 (1981); Brown v. Considine, 108 Mich.App. 504, 310 N.W.2d 441 (1981); Christenson v. Billings Livestock Comm'n Co., 201 Mont. 207, 653 P.2d 492 (1982); Cessna Fin. Corp. v. Mesilla Valley Flying Serv., 81 N.M. 10, 462 P.2d 144 (1969), certiorari denied 397 U.S. 1076, 90 S.Ct. 1521, 25 L.Ed.2d 811 (1970).

2. Dura-Wood Treating v. Century Forest Indus., 675 F.2d 745 (5th Cir.1982), certiorari denied 459 U.S. 865, 103 S.Ct. 144, 74 L.Ed.2d 122 (1982); Hahnemann Medical College & Hosp. v. Hubbard, 267 Pa.

Super. 436, 406 A.2d 1120 (1979); Eisenberg v. Continental Casualty Co., 48 Wis.2d 637, 180 N.W.2d 726 (1970).

3. Restatement, Second, Contracts § 22, Comment a.

4. 1 Corbin § 12.

5. Formation of Contracts: A Study of the Common Core of Legal Systems, 1584–86 (R. Schlesinger ed. 1968). Contract obligations may, however, attach at an earlier stage. See § 2–7 infra.

6. See, for example, the problem of identical cross offers in § 2–12 infra.

7. See §§ 2–2 to 2–4 infra.

"mutual manifestation of assent"
"offer and acceptance" /s contract

§ 2–2. Objective and Subjective Assent and Intent

In the previous section it is stated that mutual assent is a prerequisite to the formation of the contract. However, over the years a debate has raged as to whether the assent of the parties should be actual mental assent so that there is a "meeting of the minds" [8] or whether assent should be determined solely from objective manifestations of intent—namely what a party says and does rather than what he subjectively intends or believes or assumes.[9] Thus under the objective theory the mental assent and intent of the parties is irrelevant.[10] However, even under the objective theory the acts manifesting assent must be done either intentionally or negligently.[11] For at least a century the objective theory of contracts has been dominant.[12]

Another portion of the credo of the objectivists is that objective manifestations of intent of the party should be viewed from the vantage point of a reasonable man in the position of the other party.[13] The phrase "in the position of the other party" means that the other party is charged not only with the knowledge of a reasonable man but also with what he knows or should know because of his superior knowledge.[14] This will become clearer in the section that follows.

There are other versions of the objective approach and even some more modern subjective approaches. These will be discussed in Chap-

8. Williston, Mutual Assent In the Formation of Contracts, in Selected Readings On the Law of Contracts 119 (1931). However even under this theory, there would be no contract unless there were also external acts indicating assent. Restatement of Contracts § 20 (1932). The same is true in France where the subjective theory dominates thinking about contract. See 2 Formation of Contracts, supra note 5, at 1316–19; Chloros, Comparative Aspects of the Intention to Create Legal Relations in Contract, 33 Tul.L.Rev. 607, 613–17 (1959).

9. See Williston, Freedom of Contract, 6 Cornell L.Q. 365 (1921), Selected Readings 100 (1931). The objective theory was borrowed by American law from the writings of Paley, the moral philosopher, and is referred to in nineteenth century cases as "Dr. Paley's Law." See Palmer, The Effect of Misunderstanding on Contract Formation and Reformation under the Restatement of Contracts Second, 65 Mich.L.Rev. 33, 44–47 (1966). See also Ricketts v. Pennsylvania R.R., 153 F.2d 757, 761 n. 2 (2d Cir.1946); 2 Parsons on Contracts *498 n. (p) (9th ed. 1904).

10. Fairway Center Corp. v. U.I.P. Corp., 502 F.2d 1135 (8th Cir.1974);

Blackhawk Heating & Plumbing Co. v. Data Lease Fin. Corp., 302 So.2d 404 (Fla. 1974).

11. Whittier, The Restatement of Contracts and Mutual Assent, 17 Calif.L.Rev. 441, 447–48 (1929). To act intentionally means to act with the intent to do the acts and not necessarily to desire the consequences.

12. A great judge has stated the objective approach as follows, "A contract has, strictly speaking, nothing to do with the personal, or individual, intent of the parties. A contract is an obligation attached by mere force of law to certain acts of the parties, usually words, which ordinarily accompany and represent a known intent." Hotchkiss v. National City Bank, 200 Fed. 287, 293 (S.D.N.Y.1911) (L. Hand J.).

13. Ricketts v. Pennsylvania R. Co., 153 F.2d 757, 760–61 (2d Cir.1946) (FRANK, J., concurring opinion).

14. Sands v. Sands, 252 Md. 137, 249 A.2d 187 (1969); Embry v. Hargadine-McKittrick Dry Goods Co., 127 Mo.App. 383, 105 S.W. 777 (1907).

ter 3. In the meantime the approach outlined above will be employed as an acceptable tentative test. In other words, a party's intention will be held to be what a reasonable man in the position of the other party would conclude his manifestation to mean.

 WESTLAW REFERENCES

"actual mental assent"

di("meeting of the mind" /p contract)

"objective theory" /s contract

"objective! manifest! of intent!"

"objective theory" /p "intent of the party" "mental assent"

"objective theory" /p reasonable +l man person

"position of the party" /s contract /s know!

contract /s "superior knowledge"

§ 2–3. Must the Parties Be Serious?

If A and B enter into what otherwise appears to be a contract and, at the trial B asserts as a defense that he was joking, assuming that B is believed, would there be an enforceable contract? Under the subjective approach discussed in the preceding section, the answer would be in the negative. Under the tentative test proposed in the preceding section, the issue would be whether a reasonable man in the position of A would conclude from B's manifestations that B was serious. This, as we shall see, is ordinarily a question of fact.[15]

Under this test, if it is determined that B did not appear serious, there is no contract because B has in fact manifested an intention not to be bound by the apparent agreement.[16] If a reasonable man would conclude that B was serious, there is a contract unless A knows or should know B is not serious.[17] For example, if B appears to be serious to a by-stander who could be considered to be a reasonable man, there could still be no contract if A and B had joked about the matter under discussion many times before.[18] In that case A would be charged with superior knowledge of B's intent not to contract.[19]

The same rules would apply if a party were to claim that he was not serious because he was angry or excited,[20] or because the entire matter was intended as a "frolic and banter".[21] Very often, as indicat-

---

15. See § 2–8 infra.

16. Davis v. Davis, 119 Conn. 194, 175 A. 574 (1934); McClurg v. Terry, 21 N.J.Eq. 225 (1870).

17. Lucy v. Zehmer, 196 Va. 493, 84 S.E.2d 516 (1954); Plate v. Durst, 42 W.Va. 63, 24 S.E. 580 (1896); 1 Williston § 21. If a purely objective theory were followed, B should not be permitted to testify that he was not serious but could only point to words and conduct which showed that he was not serious. Since the test is partially subjective, B should be permitted to testify that he was not serious because, as stated,

if A knew or should have known that he was joking there would be no contract. See also 1 Corbin § 34.

18. Smith v. Richardson, 31 Ky.L.R. 1082, 104 S.W. 705 (1907).

19. See § 2–2 supra.

20. Higgins v. Lessig, 49 Ill.App. 459 (1893).

21. Keller v. Holderman, 11 Mich. 248 (1863). See also Graves v. Northern N.Y. Publishing Co., 260 App.Div. 900, 22 N.Y.S.2d 537 (4th Dep't 1940), appeal dismissed 285 N.Y. 547, 32 N.E.2d 832 (1941)

ed above, these issues are questions of fact rather than questions of law.[22]

WESTLAW REFERENCES

contract　/s　joke joked joking jest

lucy　+s　zehmer

95k14　/p　joke joked joking jest anger angry excit!

graves　+3　northern

§ 2–4. Must the Parties Intend to Be Bound or Intend Legal Consequences?

As asked, the question in the caption must be answered in the negative because it is well settled that the parties need not manifest an intent to be bound or consciously advert to legal consequence that might arise upon breach.[23]　In other words, if A and B go through a process of offer and acceptance, they need not in addition manifest an intent to be bound or to invoke legal sanctions in order to have mutual assent.　This is a sound rule because parties at the time of contracting hardly think about these matters much less discuss them.　Professor Corbin gives an illustration of this situation when he states that if two ignorant persons agreed to exchange a horse for a cow there would be a mutual assent, under the objective theory, even if the parties were unaware that society offers remedies for the breach of such an agreement.[24]　This rule is consistent with the rule that mistake as to a rule of law does not necessarily deprive an agreement of parties of legal effect.[25]　The same result can be reached by employing the reasonable man test because "a normally constituted person" would know, however dimly, that legal sanctions exist.[26]

However, if, from the statements or conduct of the parties or the surrounding circumstances, it appears that the parties do not intend to be bound or do not intend legal consequences, then under the great majority of the cases there will be no contract.[27]　Two types of cases arise in this area.　In one, the parties expressly agree that they do not

(offer published in newspaper's "joke column" to pay $1,000 to anyone who would provide defendant with telephone number of Western Union).

22.　Theiss v. Weiss, 166 Pa. 9, 31 A. 63 (1895); Chiles v. Good, 41 S.W.2d 738 (Tex. Civ.App.1931), reversed on other grounds 57 S.W.2d 1100 (Tex.Comm.App.1933). On the distinction between questions of law and questions of fact, see § 2–8 infra.

23.　1 Corbin § 34; 1 Williston § 21; Restatement, Second, Contracts § 21.

24.　1 Corbin § 34.

25.　Restatement, Second, Contracts § 21, Comment a.

26.　New York Trust Co. v. Island Oil & Transport Corp., 34 F.2d 655 (2d Cir.1929).

27.　United States v. Aetna Casualty & Surety Co., 480 F.2d 1095 (8th Cir.1973); Nice Ball Bearing Co. v. Bearing Jobbers, 205 F.2d 841 (7th Cir.1953), certiorari denied 346 U.S. 911, 74 S.Ct. 242, 98 L.Ed. 408 (1953); New York Trust Co. v. Island Oil Transport Corp., 34 F.2d 655 (2d Cir. 1929); contra 9 J. Wigmore, Evidence § 2406 (3d ed.1940).　There have been cases where the sham arrangement has been enforced against a promisor by a third party upon a theory of promissory estoppel or on public policy grounds. Bersani v. General Acc. Fire & Life Ass'n Corp., 36 N.Y.2d 457, 369 N.Y.S.2d 108, 330 N.E.2d 68 (1975); Mt. Vernon Trust Co. v. Bergoff, 272 N.Y. 192, 5 N.E.2d 196 (1936). See chapters 6 & 22 infra.

intend to be bound. In the other, the parties do not expressly so agree but the conclusion is reached from the surrounding circumstances.

Under the majority rule, when the parties expressly state that they do not intend to be bound by their agreement or do not intend legal consequences—the so-called gentlemen's agreement—the courts conclude that a contract does not arise.[28] The type of case envisaged is one where the parties enter into agreements regulating commercial relations but further agree that the agreement is to create no legal obligation. In such a case, as stated above, the general rule is that the agreement is not binding. There is, however, a strong minority current which holds that, when the parties have acted under the agreement and it is unfair not to enforce the agreement, if should be enforced.[29] Such cases have been explained as instances where "the principle of reimbursing reliance is regarded as overriding the principle of private autonomy."[30] Failure by one party to perform may also result in his unjust enrichment, presenting an additional ground for enforcement in contract or quasi contract.[31] Many of the minority cases have involved pension plans upon which employers could reasonably expect employees to rely and which in fact did induce reliance. In addition, the minority view has been used in bonus and employee death benefit cases.[32] Under the majority rule no protection is available to an employee where the agreement explicitly stated that it was non-contractual. This is one of the abuses the Pension Reform Act of 1974 was designed to curtail.[33]

As indicated above, the intent not to be bound or to intend legal consequences need not be stated in so many words; it may be inferred from the circumstances of the case. Thus, if A invites B to dinner and

28. Smith v. MacDonald, 37 Cal.App. 503, 174 P. 80 (1918); Osgood v. Skinner, 211 Ill. 229, 71 N.E. 869 (1904); McKevin v. Solvay Process Co., 32 A.D. 610, 53 N.Y.S. 98 (1898), affirmed 167 N.Y. 530, 60 N.E. 1115 (1901); Hirschkorn v. Severson, 319 N.W.2d 475 (N.D.1982); Rose & Frank Co. v. J. R. Crompton, [1923] 2 K.B. 261 (C.A.); Annot., 42 A.L.R.2d 461 (1955); Annot., 96 A.L.R. 1093 (1935). The exclusion of legal consequences is common in English collective bargaining agreements. See Kahn-Freund, Pacta Sunt Servanda—A Principle and Its Limits: Some Thoughts Prompted By Comparative Labor Law, 48 Tul.L.Rev. 894 (1974).

29. Greene v. Howard Univ., 412 F.2d 1128 (D.C.Cir.1969); Tilbert v. Eagle Lock Co., 116 Conn. 357, 165 A. 205 (1933); Mabley & Carew Co. v. Borden, 129 Ohio St. 375, 195 N.E. 697 (1935). See § 6–5 infra.

30. Fuller, Consideration and Form, 41 Colum.L.Rev. 799, 811 n. 16 (1941). Most of the cases, however, do not articulate their rationale in these terms, but use the fact of reliance as a predicate for often

strained interpretation. In addition to the cases cited in the prior note, see Novack v. Bilnor Corp., 26 A.D.2d 572, 271 N.Y.S.2d 117 (1966). See also Fridman, Freedom of Contract, 2 Ottawa L.Rev. 1, 5–6 (1967) ("the parties are free to 'agree' without contracting, but only to the extent to which the courts permit them to do so. The courts could decide that their language or intentions did not have the effect of rendering the law of contract inapplicable").

31. Cf. Schott v. Westinghouse Elec. Corp., 436 Pa. 279, 259 A.2d 443 (1969), noted in 74 Dick.L.Rev. 798 (1970) and 31 U.Pitt.L.Rev. 742 (1970). In addition, other doctrines may come into play. Restatement, Second, Contracts § 21, Comment b.

32. See Annot., 28 A.L.R.3d (1969); Annot., 42 A.L.R.2d 461 (1955). See also § 6–5 infra.

33. Employee Retirement Income Security Act of 1974, § 2(c), 88 Stat. 829, 29 U.S.C.A. § 1101 et seq.

B accepts the invitation and arrives at A's house at the appointed time and A is not there, B would not have a cause of action because it is a reasonable factual presumption that the parties intended that only a social obligation should result.[34] In other words, the conclusion is that the parties did not intend legal consequence with the result that there is no contract. The result would be different if the parties manifest an intent to be bound.

The same presumption that the parties do not intend to be bound exists when a husband and wife live together amicably and make an agreement with respect to a housekeeping allowance.[35] In this case, even if the parties expressly state that they intend legal consequences, there are still questions of public policy to be considered. About one-half of the courts have refused to enforce such an agreement because they fear that the courts would be flooded by such actions or that the suits would interfere with family harmony or that the agreements are unfair because changed circumstances may require a greater or lesser allowance.[36]

Other kinds of cases might be discussed under this heading. If A promises B a gift, A's promise, absent further facts, is not binding. Courts in England tend to consider such cases to be based on the absence of contractual intent, while American cases have generally analyzed such cases in terms of the absence of consideration.

The discussions in §§ 2–3 and 2–4 to some extent overlap. In § 2–3 a party is claiming that there is no mutual assent because he manifested an intent not to be bound by manifesting an intent not to be serious. In § 2–4 the issue is again intent to be bound but here the question of intent to be bound arises by virtue of the parties manifesting a serious intent not to be bound either expressly or impliedly.

34. Mitzel v. Hauck, 78 S.D. 543, 105 N.W.2d 378 (1960). Absence of contractual intention will also be assumed when a candidate for public office makes preelection promises to the electorate. O'Reilly v. Mitchel, 85 Misc. 176, 148 N.Y.S. 88 (1914) (candidate for mayor promised not to change Civil Service Law). If contractual intention existed in such a case, however, the agreement so formed would doubtless be void on grounds of public policy. The ceremonious Jewish marriage agreement known as the Ketubah creates no legal obligations because it is understood by modern participants to be a symbolic ritual rather than a contract. In re White's Estate, 78 Misc.2d 157, 356 N.Y.S.2d 208 (Sur. Ct.1974).

35. Balfour v. Balfour [1919] 2 K.B. 571 (C.A.); see Fridman, supra note 30, at 4–7; see also Havighurst, Services in the Home—A Study of Contract Concepts in Domestic Relations, 41 Yale L.J. 386 (1932); McDowell, Contracts in the Family, 45 B.U.L.Rev. 43 (1965). Separation agreements (where the parties are not living in amity) are ordinarily enforceable. Lacks v. Lacks, 12 N.Y.2d 268, 238 N.Y.S.2d 949, 189 N.E.2d 487 (1963).

36. See generally H. Clark, Domestic Relations 522 n. 4 (1968) and McKinney's N.Y. Gen'l Obl. Law § 5–311, as interpreted in Lacks v. Lacks, 12 N.Y.2d 268, 238 N.Y.S.2d 949, 189 N.E.2d 487 (1963), prior to its revision.

WESTLAW REFERENCES

95k14 /p bind bound binding enforc!

di(intend! intent /p bound bind binding /p statement conduct circumstan!)

"gentlem*n agreement"

rely! relied reliance /s contract /s bind binding bound /s agree!

contract /s pension /s employ**** /s reliance rely! relied

29 +4 1101

contract /s "social! obligat!"

contract /s "changed circumstance"

contract /s gift /s consideration

contract /s gift /s bind bound binding

B. OFFER

Table of Sections

§ 2–5. What Is an Offer?—Its Legal Effect

An offer, with minor exceptions discussed below, is essentially a promise to do or refrain from doing some specified thing in the future. A promise has been defined as "a manifestation of intent to act or refrain from acting in a specified way, so made as to justify a promisee in understanding that a commitment has been made." [37] It also has been defined as an assurance that a thing will or will not be done.[38]

While the First Restatement included the word "promise" in its definition of offer, the Second Restatement does not. It defines an offer

---

37. Restatement, Second, Contracts § 2, accord Day v. Amax, Inc., 701 F.2d 1258 (8th Cir.1983).

38. Bowman v. Hill, 45 N.C.App. 116, 262 S.E.2d 376 (1980).

as "a manifestation of willingness to enter into a bargain so made as to justify another person in understanding that his assent to that bargain is invited and will conclude it." [39]   Apparently the reason why the word "promise" is not used in the Restatement Second's definition of "offer" is that it intends to include in the word "offer" an executed sale or barter where no promise is made by the offeror or the offeree.[40]   For example, assume that A says to B, "my car which is in your possession is yours if you pay me $1000."   If B pays the $1000 there is an acceptance of the offer and a complete exchange without any promise being made.   This situation should be compared with what is described below as a "reverse unilateral contract" another situation where the offeror does not make a promise.   However, the offeree does promise.[41]

One analyst, although not noting the omission of the word "promise" in the Second Restatement concludes that the omission of the word in the Uniform Commercial Code is of great significance.[42]   He emphasizes that the Code instead stresses the word "agreement" and defines it as "the bargain of the parties in fact as found in their language or by implication from other circumstances including course of dealing or usage of trade or course of performance as provided in this Act * * *."[43]   It is difficult to see how this definition undermines the importance of promise in determining the existence of an offer.[44]

Once it is decided that a party has made an offer it follows that the offer invites an acceptance.   In other words, an offer empowers the offeree to create a contract by his acceptance.[45]   Despite the extended discussion above the typical offer is promissory in character.   The acceptance of a promissory offer transforms the offeror's promise into a contract [46] unless there is some other impediment to the existence of a contract.[47]

 WESTLAW REFERENCES
di offer

39. Restatement, Second, Contracts § 24.

40. Restatement, Second, Contracts § 24, Comment a.

41. See § 2–10 infra.

42. Mooney, Old Kontract Principles and Karl's New Kode: An Essay on the Jurisprudence of Our New Commercial Law, 11 Vill.L.Rev. 213 (1966).

43. U.C.C. § 1–201(3). The Code defines a contract as "the total obligation which results from the parties' agreement as affected by this Act and any other applicable rules of law." (U.C.C. § 1–201(11). In other words the court, by applying rules of law, decides whether an agreement is a contract and the legal effect of the contract.

44. See also Barndt, The Possible Words of Promise, 45 Tex.L.Rev. 44 (1966) (there cannot be a contract unless there is

a promise). See also Sharp, Promissory Liability, 7 U.Chi.L.Rev. 1 (1939).

45. League Gen. Ins. Co. v. Tvedt, 317 N.W.2d 40 (Minn.1982).

46. Philadelphia Newspapers, Inc. v. Commonwealth Unemployment Compensation Bd. of Review, 57 Pa.Cmwlth. 639, 426 A.2d 1289 (1981). Corbin, Offer and Acceptance and Some of the Resulting Legal Relations, 26 Yale L.J. 169 (1917), revised in Selected Readings 170 (1931).

47. It is often stated that the requisites of a contract in addition to mutual assent are 1) a promise by a party having legal capacity to act, 2) two or more contracting parties, 3) consideration, 4) the agreement must not be void. 1 Williston § 18. All of these matters are discussed elsewhere in this volume as is the question of the genuineness of mutual assent.

```
offer  /s  "legal effect"
offer  /s  refrain!  /s  act action
di promise
promise  /s  manifest!  /s  intent!
manifest!  /s  willing!  /s  bargain
"uniform commercial code"  /s  bargain  /s  "course of dealing"
offer  /s  power empower!  /s  offeree  /s  accept!
contract  /s  "legal capacity to act"
```

§ 2–6. Offers Distinguished From Statements That Are Not Offers

(a) Introduction

There are a number of kinds of expressions that border on, but are not, promises. To facilitate the drawing of distinctions between these expressions and promises, the discussion will be subdivided into several somewhat arbitrary categories.

(b) Offer Distinguished From an Expression of Opinion and Predictions

Since an expression of an opinion is not a promise it follows that it is not an offer. This distinction is often crucial, particularly in the doctor-patient relationship. It is generally held that a doctor is not liable in contract for breach of an implied promise to possess "skill commensurate to that possessed by his collegues in similar localities".[48] For a breach of such an implied promise or failure to live up to that standard it has generally been held that the patient is limited to a malpractice (negligence) action.[49]

It is, however, also generally recognized that a physician is free to enter into an express contract.[50] Thus, courts have held a physician liable for breach of a promise to cure,[51] or obtain a specified result,[52] or administer a prescribed treatment.[53] There is a minority view that such actions are contrary to public policy because they encourage the practice of defensive medicine and discourage a physician from reassuring his patient.[54] There are also a few cases requiring that as a

48. Note, Contractual Liability in Medical Malpractice—Sullivan v. O'Connor, 24 De Paul L.Rev. 212, 214 (1974).

49. Note, Physicians and Surgeons—Sullivan v. O'Connor: A Liberal View of the Contractual Liability of Physicians and Surgeons, 54 N.C.L.Rev. 885, 887 (1976).

50. Note, Express Contracts to Cure: The Nature of Contractual Malpractice, 50 Ind.L.J. 361 (1975).

51. Hawkins v. McGee, 84 N.H. 114, 146 A. 641 (1929) (defendant guaranteed to make the hand one hundred percent perfect). But in the same case a statement that the patient would go back to work in a few days with a good hand was deemed to be an opinion.

52. Sullivan v. O'Connor, 363 Mass. 579, 296 N.E.2d 183 (1973) (defendant promised to make plaintiff more beautiful).

53. Stewart v. Rudner, 349 Mich. 459, 84 N.W.2d 816 (1957) (defendant promised to perform a Caesarian section).

54. See Annot., 43 A.L.R.3d 1221 (1972).

condition to such an action, defendant's promise be supported by a consideration other than payment for services rendered.[55]

Under the majority view the issue in most cases is whether the doctor has made a promise or merely stated his opinion or given a therapeutic assurance. The cases are in confusion [56] and one commentator has referred to the problem as a "legal thicket".[57] For the most part the courts have held that the question is one of fact.[58] This means the reasonable man test should be employed.[59]

In determining the question of fact it is important to take into account not only what was said, but also the surrounding circumstances. For example, when the doctor is presented with an emergency situation it is less likely that his words should be taken as a promise.[60] One case has tried to balance the competing views by saying that the action is a "little suspect" and that therefore "clear proof" should be required. It also suggests that the jury should be instructed that it is unlikely that a physician will make such a promise and that an optimistic statement of encouragement should not be taken as a promise when it is intended only as a therapeutic reassurance.[61] At least one state has made such a promise subject to the writing requirements of the Statute of Frauds.[62]

The same problem arose in a different context in the well-known case of Anderson v. Backlund.[63] In that case B, a tenant farmer, was behind in his rent. He told A, his landlord, about his problems, and A suggested that he should get more cattle. B replied, "If I stock up too heavy in the pasture and there be a short spell I will be up against it and that is the reason I am waiting for you." A then told B, "Never mind the water, John, I will see there will be plenty of water because it never failed in Minnesota yet." On the strength of A's statement B purchased 107 cattle and lost money when the water supplied failed. The court held as matter of law that A's statement was not a promise; it was nothing more than an opinion or a prediction.[64] If A had said, "I will make good any loss you suffer due to a water shortage," the result could well have been different even though the rainfall was not within the control of the promisor.[65] Lack of control over the event is an important factor to consider but it is not determinative.

Some important considerations are: (1) that in each of these cases the question is whether the defendant made an offer or merely expressed an opinion; (2) that under the tentative standard adopted, this

55. See, e.g., Gault v. Sideman, 42 Ill. App.2d 96, 191 N.E.2d 436 (1963).

56. Note, supra note 48, at 214–16.

57. Note, supra note 49, at 888.

58. Note, supra note 49.

59. See §§ 2–2 supra and 2–8 infra.

60. Note, supra note 50, at 75–84.

61. Sullivan v. O'Connor, 363 Mass. 579, 296 N.E.2d 183 (1973).

62. See Gilmore v. O'Sullivan, 106 Mich.App. 35, 307 N.W.2d 695 (1981).

63. 159 Minn. 423, 199 N.W. 90 (1924).

64. Accord, Sears Boston Employees Fed. Credit Union v. Cummings, 322 Mass. 81, 76 N.E.2d 150 (1947); cf. Kail v. Department of Pub. Welfare, 62 Misc.2d 302, 306 N.Y.S.2d 563 (Jus.Ct.1969).

65. Restatement, Second, Contracts § 2, Comment d.

is determined by inquiring whether a reasonable man in the position of the plaintiff would conclude that the defendant made a promise or merely stated his opinion; and (3) that sometimes this is a question of law and at other times this is a question of fact.[66]

(c) Statements of Intention, Hopes and Desires and Estimates

If A says to B, "I'm going to sell my car for $500.00," and B replies, "All right here is $500.00 I will take it," there is no contract because a reasonable man would conclude that A was stating his intention and was not making a promise.[67] So also an announcement that an auction will be held is deemed to be a statement of intention,[68] despite the fact that "will" is a word commonly used as a promise. For example, if A says to B, "If you paint my house I will pay $1000," it is clear that in context the words "I will pay" mean "I promise to pay."

Businessmen frequently exchange what they term "letters of intent." These are usually understood to be noncommittal statements preliminary to a contract. There is, however, no magic attached to the phrase "letter of intent" and a commitment may be found to have been made.[69] Also, in a modern business context, statements of intention to act in a given manner may often be regarded as statements of policy rather than promises.[70]

It is well settled that statements of wishes, hopes, or desires are not considered to be promises or offers.[71] So also an estimate is not considered to be an offer. This is upon the theory that a reasonable man would conclude that the party who is giving an estimate is not promising that he will do the job for the price named but that he thinks that he can do the job for a sum in that neighborhood.[72] It should be

66. See § 2–8 infra.

67. Cutler-Hammer, Inc. v. United States, 441 F.2d 1179 (Ct.Cl.1971); Pappas v. Bever, 219 N.W.2d 720 (Iowa 1974); Forbes v. Wells Beach Casino, Inc., 307 A.2d 210 (Me.1973); Pacific Cascade Corp. v. Nimmer, 25 Wn.App. 552, 608 P.2d 266 (1980); Randall v. Morgan, 33 Eng.Rep. 26 (Ch. 1805); 1 Williston § 26.

68. Kinmon v. J. P. King Auction Co., 290 Ala. 323, 276 So.2d 569 (1973); Benjamin v. First Citizens Bank & Trust Co., 248 A.D. 610, 287 N.Y.S. 947 (1936) (plaintiff's assignor came from South Africa to attend an auction announced to be without reserve which was cancelled; no recovery); cf. Peters v. Bower, 63 So.2d 629 (Fla.1953) (affidavit of intent to grade streets in a subdivision held not enforceable).

69. See California Food Service Corp. v. Great Am. Ins., 128 Cal.App.3d 28, 182 Cal. Rptr. 67 (1982); compare Dunhill Sec. Corp. v. Microthermal Applications, 308 F.Supp. 195 (S.D.N.Y.1969) and Garner v. Boyd, 330 F.Supp. 22 (N.D.Tex.1970), judg-

ment affirmed 447 F.2d (5th Cir.1970) with Arthur Anderson v. Source Equities, 43 A.D.2d 921, 353 N.Y.S.2d 1 (1974).

70. Estate of Bogley v. United States, 514 F.2d 1027 (Ct.Cl.1975); Beverage Distrib., Inc. v. Olympia Brewing Co., 440 F.2d 21, 29 (9th Cir.1971), certiorari denied 403 U.S. 906, 91 S.Ct. 2209, 29 L.Ed.2d 682 (1971) ("it is our intention that, if they show the ability and application required to make the business successful under reasonable direction of our organization, they shall have a reasonable amount of the new common stock, which will be issued exclusively to members of our organization.") (No promise here.)

71. Bowman v. Hill, 45 N.C.App. 116, 262 S.E.2d 376 (1980); 1 Corbin § 15.

72. Denniston & Partridge Co. v. Mingus, 179 N.W.2d 748 (Iowa 1970); Malmin v. Grabner, 282 Minn. 82, 163 N.W.2d 39 (1968); Clark Sanitation, Inc. v. Sun Valley Disposal Co., 87 Nev. 338, 487 P.2d 337 (1971).

clear, however, that the word "estimate" itself is not conclusive because "estimate" in context may be used in the sense of "offer." For example, if the party in response to an invitation to bid says "I estimate" such an amount, this may be deemed to be an offer.[73]

An estimate was held to be binding upon a theory of equitable estoppel in United States v. Briggs Mfg. Co.[74] The key finding in the case was "that as an inducement for Toombs to purchase the housing involved, Briggs quoted prices on freight, terminal, longshoring and lightering charges. And while these quotations were estimated both parties anticipated they would be reasonably accurate and Toombs was entitled to rely on the estimate." [75] Equitable estoppel traditionally requires misrepresentation, reliance and injury.[76] The reliance and injury are clear. Apparently the estimate is treated as a misrepresentation because Briggs was an expert.[77] But how would the case apply to an auto mechanic who was giving an estimate with respect to hidden damage?

(d) Inquiry or Invitation to Make an Offer

If A writes to B saying, "Will you sell me your property on Rockledge Drive for $50,000?", this is not an offer but an inquiry. A question is not an offer because it seeks information and does not amount to a commitment. In the same illustration, if B replied, "make me an offer" this is a statement inviting A to make an offer.

The same process is illustrated in the case of Owen v. Tunison.[78] In that case plaintiff wrote to defendant, "Will you sell me your store property * * * for the sum of $6,000.00?" This was an inquiry. Defendant answered, "it would not be possible for me to sell it unless I was to receive $16,000 cash." The court held that defendant had not made an offer. The defendant had not promised to sell for $16,000; he was really saying, "I will not entertain an offer of less than $16,000." Consequently defendant's statement amounts to an invitation to make an offer.[79]

(e) Is the Ordinary Advertisement, Catalog or Circular Letter, etc., an Offer?

If a clothing store advertised a well-known brand of suits in the following terms, "nationally advertised at $220, today only at $150," and A came to the store in response to the advertisement, selected a suit and tendered $150, would there be a contract? The answer is in

---

73. See Parker v. Meneley, 106 Cal. App.2d 391, 235 P.2d 101 (1951); 1 Corbin § 23; 1 Williston § 27; cf. United States v. Briggs Mfg. Co., 460 F.2d 1195 (9th Cir. 1972).

74. 460 F.2d 1195 (9th Cir.1972); cf. K. M. Young Ltd. v. Cosgrove [1963] N.Z.L.R. 967, noted in 4 Vict. U.W.L.Rev. 98 (1965).

75. 460 F.2d at 1196.

76. See § 11–29 infra.

77. See § 9–17 infra.

78. 131 Me. 42, 15 A. 926 (1932).

79. Accord Blakeslee v. Nelson, 212 A.D. 219, 207 N.Y.S. 676 (1925), affirmed 240 N.Y. 697, 148 N.E. 763 (1925).

the negative.[80] Since the store has not stated any quantity and there is no language of commitment, the cases hold that an advertisement of this kind is only a statement of intention to sell or a preliminary proposal inviting offers. Would the reasonable man so conclude? While it would be onerous to hold that the advertiser has committed himself to have an unlimited supply of the article, it could be argued that he was impliedly promising to sell one to a customer or a reasonable number to a customer on a first come, first served basis so long as the supply lasts. The reasonable man test tends to be used by the courts to resolve cases of first impression which then serve as precedents in later cases. By this process certain hardened categories emerge. The newspaper advertisement case relating to the sale of goods illustrate this process. Rightly or wrongly, at an early date it was decided and the law is now settled that there is no offer in cases like the hypothetical illustration just discussed. Consumer protection legislation may not have changed this contract rule.[81]

It does not follow that an advertisement for the sale of goods never constitutes an offer. In a leading case,[82] the following advertisement

---

80. See Georgian Co. v. Bloom, 27 Ga. App. 468, 108 S.E. 813 (1921); Steinberg v. Chicago Medical School, 69 Ill.2d 320, 13 Ill.Dec. 699, 371 N.E.2d 634 (1977); O'Keefe v. Lee Calan Imports, Inc., 128 Ill. App.2d 410, 262 N.E.2d 758 (1970); Rhen Marshall, Inc. v. Purolator Filter Div., 211 Neb. 306, 318 N.W.2d 284 (1982); Craft v. Elder & Johnston Co., 38 N.E.2d 416 (Ohio App.1941); Restatement, Second, Contracts § 26; Annot., 43 A.L.R.3d 1102 (1972). In some cases it has been held that no offer has been made because the goods are insufficiently described. Lovett v. Frederick Loeser & Co., 124 Misc. 81, 207 N.Y.S. 753 (Mun.Ct.1924). This involves the question of indefiniteness. See § 2–9 infra.

81. The result reached on the facts now under discussion would not appear to be changed by any of the following:

(1) Section 52(b) of the Federal Trade Commission Act, 15 U.S.C.A. §§ 41 et seq. (1970), which gives power to the Commission to proceed against "unfair or deceptive" practices.

(2) A Printer's Ink Statute, which has been adopted by most states, making false or misleading advertising a misdemeanor. See, e.g., Ohio Rev.Code § 2911.42 (1953); McKinney's N.Y. Penal Law § 190.20, which was revised in 1973 to make a cross reference to the Truth in Lending Act, 15 U.S.C.A. §§ 1601 et seq. (1970).

(3) Statutes which permit the Attorney General to obtain an injunction against deceptive practices or which permit him to receive for the state five-

hundred dollars for each violation. See, e.g., McKinney's N.Y. Gen.Bus.Law §§ 349, 350–c and McKinney's N.Y. Exec. Law § 63.

(4) A statute such as the New York City Consumer Protection Law ch. 64, § 2203d–4.0 (1969) which permits an action to be brought by a public official for the benefit of the public.

(5) A statute which makes it a misdemeanor to "offer" goods or services for sale with "an intent not to sell." See Note, State Control of Bait Advertising, 69 Yale L.J. 830 (1960).

Is it changed by the Uniform Deceptive Trade Practices Act § 2(9), (10) (1966) and the New York City Consumer Protection Law ch. 64, § 2203d–2.0 (1969) which condemn, inter alia, advertising "goods or services with intent not to sell them as advertised" and "advertising goods or services with intent not to supply reasonably expectable public demand, unless the advertisement discloses a limitation of quantity" The Uniform Act permits any injured person to obtain an injunction and provides that costs and attorney's fees may be awarded. In addition it provides that common law remedies are continued. See Dole, Merchant and Consumer Protection: The Uniform Deceptive Trade Practices Act, 76 Yale L.J. 485 (1967). See also § 3 of the Uniform Consumer Sales Practices Act.

82. Lefkowitz v. Great Minneapolis Surplus Store, Inc., 251 Minn. 188, 86 N.W.2d 689 (1957).

appeared in the newspaper: "1 Black Lapin Stole, Beautiful, Worth $139.50 * * * $1.00 FIRST COME FIRST SERVED." The plaintiff was the first to present himself and tendered a dollar. The court held that there was an offer. The Restatement Second indicates that the basis of the decision is that the words "FIRST COME FIRST SERVED" are promissory, an element which is ordinarily lacking in advertisements for the sale of goods.[83] In addition there is a statement of quantity (one) which is ordinarily lacking in advertisements. One is not only a quantity but also a quantity per person. The existence of all of these factors appears to be important. In the same case, if the ad had related to ten lapin stoles and listed a price per stole, would there be an offer if the advertisement did not state the quantity allocated per person? There does not appear to be a ready answer to this question.

So also if an advertiser announces that, "We will pay $100.00 for each share of the common stock of the XYZ Company mailed to us before July 1," an offer has been made.[84] Here again it should be observed that there is a quantity, "each share" (every share), and also language of promise ("We will pay"). If an advertiser promises to pay a fixed sum to anyone who contracts influenza after using his patent medicine, an offer has been made.[85] The problem here is quite different because there is language of promise and no problem with respect to quantity as in the case of the advertisement for the sale of goods. Even though an advertisement is not an offer it is possible that its terms may be tacitly included in a contract which is subsequently entered into by the parties.[86]

In the same category as advertisements for the sale of goods are catalogs,[87] circular letters,[88] price lists[89] and articles displayed in a window with a price tag.[90] As a result of some recent cases, the law with respect to a display on a shelf, as for example in a supermarket, has become more complicated. Under the traditional rule such a display is held not to be an offer presumably because there is no language of promise or because no quantity is stated or at least no

---

83. Restatement, Second, Contracts § 26, ill. 1.

84. R.E. Crummer & Co. v. Nuveen, 147 F.2d 3 (7th Cir.1945); Seymour v. Armstrong, 62 Kan. 720, 64 P. 612 (1901).

85. Carlill v. Carbolic Smoke Ball Co., [1893] 1 Q.B. 256 (C.A.1892); accord, Minton v. F.G. Smith Piano Co., 36 App.D.C. 137 (1911); Whitehead v. Burgess, 61 N.J. Law 75, 38 A. 802 (1897). Cf. Crowe v. Hertz Corp., 382 F.2d 681 (5th Cir.1967), (on a theory of misrepresentation), further proceedings sub nom. Hertz Corp. v. Cox, 430 F.2d 1365 (5th Cir.1970), rehearing denied 436 F.2d 1376 (5th Cir.1971), appeal after remand 472 F.2d 552 (5th Cir.1973), certiorari denied 414 U.S. 825, 94 S.Ct. 129, 38 L.Ed.2d 59 (1973).

86. Willis v. Allied Insulation Co., 174 So.2d 858 (La.App.1965); Johnson v. Capital City Ford Co., 85 So.2d 75 (La.App. 1955); Turner v. Central Hardware Co., 353 Mo. 1182, 186 S.W.2d 603 (1945); Rinkmasters v. Utica, 75 Misc.2d 941, 348 N.Y.S.2d 940 (Civ.Ct.1973) (applying U.C.C.).

87. Schenectady Stove Co. v. Holbrook, 101 N.Y. 45, 4 N.E. 4 (1885).

88. Montgomery Ward & Co. v. Johnson, 209 Mass. 89, 95 N.E. 290 (1911); Moulton v. Kershaw, 59 Wis. 316, 18 N.W. 172 (1884).

89. 1 Corbin § 28.

90. Fisher v. Bell, [1960] 3 All E.R. 731.

quantity per person.[91] There is a recent trend holding that the display of goods in a supermarket constitutes an offer.[92] These cases can only be defended on theory that placing the goods on the shelf with a unit price amounts to implied language of promise and that the quantity offered is the quantity on the shelf. But again, the question of how many to customer must be answered. It is interesting to note that French law concludes that there is an offer in this situation.[93]

Although not relevant here, it is interesting to examine how these cases handled the question of acceptance. They have stated that the acceptance occurs when the customer places the goods in his cart, subject to the customer's power to terminate the contract before going through the check-out counter. This is strained reasoning because ordinarily an acceptance gives rise to a contract and a contract may not be terminated. This reasoning appears to be designed to allow plaintiffs to recover under a warranty theory in a products liability type case as where a soft drink bottle explodes, causing injury to the customer.[94]

(f) Auction Sales—Who Makes the Offer?

If the auctioneer says, "What am I bid?", it seems clear that he is not making an offer to sell, but is inviting offers to purchase which he is free to accept or reject. The law so decided at an early date.[95] Even if the auctioneer announces that he will sell to the highest bidder the cases generally hold that such a statement does not constitute an offer,[96] presumably because a reasonable man would not believe that the seller has manifested a willingness to risk a sale of property at a price far below its value. However, as discussed below, the situation is different if the auction is announced to be "without reserve."

The rules governing auction sales, at least as to the sale of goods,[97] are now incorporated in § 2–328 of the Uniform Commercial Code. Subdivision 3 of that section continues the important common law

---

91. Lasky v. Economy Grocery Stores, 319 Mass. 224, 65 N.E.2d 305 (1946); Day v. Grand Union Co., 280 App.Div. 253, 113 N.Y.S.2d 436 (1952), affirmed 304 N.Y. 821, 109 N.E.2d 609 (1952); Pharmaceutical Soc'y of Great Brittain v. Boots Cash Chemists Ltd. [1953] 1 Q.B. 401.

92. Giant Food, Inc. v. Washington Co-ca-Cola Bottling Co., 273 Md. 592, 332 A.2d 1 (1975); Gillispie v. Great Atlantic & Pac. Tea Co., 14 N.C.App. 1, 187 S.E.2d 441 (1972).

93. 1 Formation of Contracts, supra note 5, at 364–65. The advertisement is deemed to be a conditional offer which may be accepted by any member of the public subject to the offeror's power to reject an unreasonable acceptance.

94. See U.C.C. §§ 2–314 and 2–106(1).

95. Payne v. Cave, 100 Eng.Rep. 502 (K.B.1789). On the question of what is an

auction, see Hawaii Jewelers Ass'n v. Fine Arts Gallery, Inc., 51 Hawaii 502, 463 P.2d 914 (1970).

96. Anderson v. Wisconsin Cent. R. Co., 107 Minn. 296, 120 N.W. 39 (1909); Drew v. John Deere Co. of Syracuse, Inc., 19 A.D.2d 308, 241 N.Y.S.2d 267 (1963); Spencer v. Harding, L.R. 5 C.P. 561 (1870); 1 Corbin § 108. Cf. Restatement, Second, Contracts § 27, ill. 3.

97. There is a tendency to apply these rules in auction sales of real property. See Freeman v. Poole, 37 R.I. 489, 93 A. 786 (1915); Hoffman v. Horton, 212 Va. 565, 186 S.E.2d 79 (1972); see generally U.C.C. § 1–102, Comment 1; Murray, Under the Spreading Analogy of Article 2 of the Uniform Commercial Code, 39 Fordham L.Rev. 47 (1971); Note, The Uniform Commercial Code as a Premise for Judicial Reasoning, 65 Colum.L.Rev. 880 (1965).

distinction between auctions "with reserve" and auctions "without reserve." In an auction "with reserve" the common law rule is retained. The bidder is the offeror and contract is complete when the auctioneer so announces, usually by the fall of the hammer.[98] The bidder may withdraw his bid before that time. A bid terminates all prior bids but a bidder's retraction does not revive any prior bids.[99]

An anomaly exists in the rules governing auctions announced to be "without reserve." The Code retains the common law rule that the auctioneer may not withdraw the article from sale after he calls for a bid on an article (provided that a bid is received within a reasonable time),[1] but it permits the bidder to withdraw until the article is knocked down to him.[2] This rule diverges substantially from standard contract principles. It is difficult to identify the offeror. If the auctioneer is deemed the offeror then it must be said that the bid is a conditional acceptance, subject to no higher bid being made and subject to the bidder's right to withdraw. If the bidder is said to be the offeror, an unusual situation exists since the offeree is not free to reject the offer. Since the rule is statutory, identification of the offeror is of purely intellectual interest.

The auction is deemed to be "with reserve" unless otherwise indicated.[3] Even if the auction is advertised as being without reserve, this may be changed, as indicated above, before the goods are "put up" for sale and a bid has been obtained within a reasonable time.

Subdivision 4 of § 2–328 is quite puzzling. It reads:

> If the auctioneer knowingly receives a bid on the seller's behalf or the seller makes or procures such a bid, and notice has not been given that liberty for such bidding is reserved, the buyer may at his option avoid the sale or take the goods at the price of the last good faith bid prior to the completion of the sale. This subsection shall not apply to any bid at a forced sale.[4]

It would have been better if the word "reserved" in this subdivision had been changed to "retained". Then there could have been no confusion with phrases "with reserve" and "without reserve" used in subdivision 3. Clearly subdivision 4 was not designed to change subdivision 3.[5] It governs the rights of the parties where the auctioneer receives a bid from his agent or the agent of the seller when he has not retained ("reserved") right to have such bids made—sometimes called puffing.[6]

---

98. In a judicial sale, the bid remains open until the auctioneer's acceptance is confirmed by the court. Well v. Schoeneweis, 101 Ill.App.3d 254, 56 Ill.Dec. 797, 427 N.E.2d 1343 (1981).

99. U.C.C. § 2–328(2), (3); Note, 12 B.U.L.Rev. 240 (1932).

1. Zuhak v. Rose, 264 Wis. 286, 58 N.W.2d 693 (1953); 1 Williston § 30.

2. U.C.C. § 2–328(3).

3. Holston v. Pennington, 225 Va. 551, 304 S.E.2d 287 (1983).

4. Berg v. Hogan, 322 N.W.2d 448 (N.D. 1982).

5. U.C.C. § 2–328, Comment 2.

6. The history of this ancient, if dishonorable, practice is colorfully traced in McMillan v. Harris, 110 Ga. 72, 35 S.E. 334 (1900).

When this has occurred "*the buyer* may at his option avoid the sale or take the goods at the price of the last good faith bid prior to the completion of the sale." This provision raises some difficult problems. Note first that it is only a "buyer" who may use this subdivision. Therefore, if the auction is "with reserve" the seller has the privilege of removing the goods from the auction block and, even if he accomplishes this removal through the subterfuge of having his agent make the high bid, the next highest bidder may not complain by virtue of this provision because he is not a buyer.[7] If the auction, however, is "without reserve" the highest legitimate bidder would be a "buyer" and have the option set forth in subdivision 4.

The next question then is the meaning of the phrase "at the price of the last good faith bid prior to the completion of the sale." Suppose only B and A, an agent, bid. B makes the first bid of $40 and each party alternatively raised the price by bidding $10 more until the price of $100 was bid by B and at that point the goods are knocked down to B. Note first that B is the buyer even if the auction is "with reserve". At what price may B claim the goods? Since the Code provision was designed to protect B against puffing, it has been suggested that B should have the goods at $40 despite the fact that all of his bids were literally in good faith, including the last. But suppose that C, a legitimate bidder, had made the $90 bid? Although there has been puffing, a third person bid $90. It has been suggested that, in order to protect C's interests, B, if he elects to buy, must pay $90.[8] It is difficult to see, however, what legally protected interest C has or should have at the stage of the transaction because the contest is now between B and the seller. Nevertheless, the suggestion that B should pay $90 for the goods may have some merit in that a third person in good faith valued the goods to be worth this sum and B himself valued them at a higher price.

The statute specifically states that this subdivision does not apply to a "forced sale". The Code does not define "forced sale". But undoubtedly a forced sale is one which takes place because the debtor has defaulted and the property must or may be sold to terminate the interest of the debtor therein and/or to satisfy the debt.[9] Under this statute it appears that both the secured party (execution creditor) and the party whose interest is being foreclosed may bid.[10]

Subdivision 4 creates one additional problem. Up until now we have assumed that the existence of the agent has not been disclosed.

7. Drew v. John Deere Co., 19 A.D.2d 308, 241 N.Y.S.2d 267 (1963); Freeman v. Poole, 37 R.I. 489, 93 A. 786 (1915). This does not mean that the auctioneer may not encounter licensing difficulties or even criminal charges. See, e.g., McKinney's N.Y.Gen.Bus.Law § 24.

8. See 1 W. Hawkland, A Transactional Guide to the Uniform Commercial Code 40 (1964) [hereinafter cited as Hawkland].

9. See U.C.C. §§ 9–504, 9–505; State v. Lacey, 8 Wn.App. 542, 507 P.2d 1206 (1973), judgment affirmed 84 Wn.2d 33, 524 P.2d 1351 (1974).

10. See, e.g., U.C.C. § 9–504(3). Whether other statutes or decisions limit this right is beyond the scope of this text.

But what if it is disclosed, for example, in the case of an auction "without reserve" where the agent becomes the high bidder. It is clear that subdivision 3 says that the goods may not be withdrawn and this should be equally true if the withdrawal is through the medium of an agent. Yet subdivision 4 might be taken to say at least inferentially that the goods may be withdrawn from sale by knocking them down to an agent whose identity has been disclosed. The same type of problem can also arise in the case of a forced sale. It would appear that the problem should be resolved in favor of the provisions of subdivision 3.

The problems raised by the Statute of Frauds in the case of an auction sale are discussed below.[11]

(g) Invitation to Bid—Bid

In the construction industry it is common for someone who wishes to build a large complex to send out invitations to bid to people in the industry. The invitation to bid will ordinarily specify in detail the work to be done and in effect or in so many words asks the recipient to state his lowest price for the work. It should be obvious that the situation is analogous to an auction "with reserve". The request to bid is not the offer; the bid itself is the offer.[12] Occasionally there have been invitations to bid that have been held to be offers because of the unusual language contained therein.[13] Then the bid is the acceptance. In such a case the analogy would be to an auction "without reserve."

The situation is more complicated when the invitation to bid is prepared by municipalities, counties, states, and other governmental units. The situation then may be covered by a statute stating that a contract shall be awarded to the lowest responsible bidder. If such a statute is read into the invitation to bid, it could be argued that the invitation to bid is the offer and the bid is the acceptance, but this result has not generally been reached. The bid is looked upon as the offer and a contract is not formed until the lowest responsible bid is accepted.[14] It is clear that it need not be accepted.

If for no adequate reason the contract is awarded to another, has the disappointed low bidder legal cause to complain? Under the traditional rule he could not bring an action because he had not standing to sue[15] or because the statute is solely for the benefit of the public.[16] This traditional rule has been relaxed by a growing number of decisions permitting the

---

11. See § 19–32 infra.

12. Carriger v. Ballenger, ___ Mont. ___, 628 P.2d 1106 (1981); 1 Corbin § 46.

13. Short v. Sun Newspapers, Inc., 300 N.W.2d 781 (Minn.1980); Gulf Oil v. Clark City, 94 Nev. 116, 575 P.2d 1332 (1978); Jenkins Towel Serv., Inc. v. Fidelity—Philadelphia Trust Co., 400 Pa. 98, 161 A.2d 334 (1960).

14. 1 Williston § 31. "In the case of public contracts, the requirements of certain formalities by law or by the request for bids, such as a written contract, or the furnishing of the bond, often indicates that even after acceptance of the bid no contract is formed until the requisite formality has been complied with." Id. See § 2–7 infra.

15. Cf. Perkins v. Lukens Steel Co., 310 U.S. 113, 60 S.Ct. 869, 84 L.Ed. 1108 (1940).

16. M.A. Stephen Constr. Co. v. Borough of Rumson, 125 N.J.Super. 67, 308 A.2d 380 (1973), certification denied 64 N.J. 315, 315 A.2d 404 (1973).

disappointed bidder to recover the costs of preparing his bid and/or to obtain an injunction preventing the contract from being awarded to another.[17] In this event new bids may be requested.[18]

(h) Price Quotations—Personal and Real Property

(1) Personal Property

A price quotation is usually a statement of intention to sell at a given unit price.[19] When the quotation is addressed to many people and this is disclosed, it is similar to an advertisement, circular letter and catalog.[20] Even if the word "quote" is used in a communication addressed to an individual, it is commonly understood to mean that an offer is invited.[21] This, however, is far from a hard and fast rule because the word "quote" in context may mean "offer". It is the communication as a whole rather than the label the party puts upon it that must be interpreted.[22]

In a well-known case [23] the plaintiff asked for the defendant's price on 1000 gross of Mason green jars. The defendant answered, stating detailed terms including price, and using the word "quote", but also stating that the price was "for immediate acceptance". The court decided that defendant's communication was an offer despite the use of the word "quote." There were three factors which led the court to the conclusion that the word "quote" in context meant "offer". First, it came in response to an inquiry that obviously sought an offer. Second, the defendant's communication contained detailed terms and included by implication the quantity of 1000 gross inquired about by the plaintiff. Finally there was the use of the words "for immediate acceptance."

What would the result have been if one of these factors were missing? There is no easy answer to this question. As in other cases, the two key issues are whether there is language of commitment and

17. Merriam v. Kunzig, 476 F.2d 1233 (3d Cir.1972), certiorari denied 414 U.S. 911, 94 S.Ct. 233, 38 L.Ed.2d 149 (1973); Scanwell Laboratories, Inc. v. Shaffer, 424 F.2d 859 (D.C.Cir.1970); Lombard Corp. v. Resor, 321 F.Supp. 687 (D.D.C.1970); Datatrol Inc. v. State Purchasing Agent, 379 Mass. 679, 400 N.E.2d 1218 (1980); Zurenda v. Commonwealth, 46 Pa.Cmwlth. 67, 405 A.2d 1124 (1979); for a detailed discussion of this entire problem see Pierson, 12 B.C.Indus., & Com.L.Rev. 1 (1970). See also Lent, Standing to Sue Leaves the Army Standing Where?, Grossbaum, Procedural Fairness in Public Contracts: 53 Mil. L.Rev. 73 (1971); The Procurement Regulations, 57 Va.L.Rev. 171, 227–54 (1971); Annots., 30 A.L.R.Fed. 355 (1976); 23 A.L.R. Fed. 301 (1975).

18. 1 Williston § 31; see Clemens v. United States, 295 F.Supp. 1339 (D.Or.

1968), judgment affirmed 439 F.2d 705 (9th Cir.1971).

19. Restatement, Second, Contracts § 26, Comment c.

20. See § 2–6(e) supra.

21. Interstate Indus. v. Barclay Indus., 540 F.2d 868 (7th Cir.1976); Thos. Sheehan Co. v. Crane Co., 418 F.2d 642 (8th Cir. 1969); Restatement, Second, Contracts § 26, Comment c.

22. Cannavino & Shea, Inc. v. Water Works Supply Corp., 361 Mass. 363, 280 N.E.2d 147 (1972); Nickel v. Theresa Farmers Co-op. Ass'n, 247 Wis. 412, 20 N.W.2d 117 (1945).

23. Fairmount Glass Works v. Grunden-Martin Woodenware Co., 106 Ky. 659, 51 S.W. 196 (1899); accord, Gibson v. De La Salle Institute, 66 Cal.App.2d 609, 152 P.2d 774 (1944).

whether the terms, including quantity, are sufficiently definite.[24]   In another case S wrote to B, "We quote Hungarian [flour] $5.40 [per barrel] car lots only and subject to sight draft with bill of lading. We would suggest your using wire to order as prices are rapidly advancing that they may be beyond reach before a letter would reach us." The court held that there was not an offer because S's communication did not specify any quantity.[25] In this case if the word "offer" had been substituted for the word "quote" the result would still be the same because of the failure to specify quantity.[26]

Suppose S sent a letter to B saying, "We quote you two cars Hungarian flour at $5.40 per barrel." Is this an offer? Williston indicates that it is when he says, "where the property to be sold is accurately defined and an amount stated as the price in the communication made, not by general advertisement, but to one person individually, no reasonable interpretation seems possible except that the writer offers to sell the property described for the price mentioned." [27] This statement does not appear to place sufficient emphasis on the question of promise or commitment.[28] Nor does it give sufficient importance to the question of whether the communication is an initial communication as opposed to an answer to an inquiry.[29]

The Restatement Second is more restrained. Nonetheless, it seems to indicate that there would be an offer in the Mason green jar case even without the words "for immediate acceptance." It stresses the importance of detailed terms, and the fact that the communication was in response to an inquiry.[30] When are terms detailed? In the hypothetical cases above are the terms detailed? Obviously there are no easy answers to any of these questions.

(2) Real Property

Although the problems in the real property cases are somewhat different, there are analogous cases. A discussion of two cases will suffice.

In Mellen v. Johnson [31] the defendant wrote the plaintiff that his price for certain property was $7500 and that he was writing to several other interested persons. The plaintiff wired, stating that he accepted. The case is similar to the price quotation cases discussed above where the communication is addressed to many persons. The additional fact to be considered is that defendant made it clear that he had only one piece of real property to sell. This is not normally true in the case of personal property.

24. See, for example, § 2–6(e) supra.

25. Johnston Bros. v. Rogers Bros., 30 Ont. 150 (1899).

26. Earl M. Jorgensen Co. v. Mark Constr. Inc., 56 Hawaii 466, 540 P.2d 978 (1975); Moulton v. Kershaw, 59 Wis. 316, 18 N.W. 172 (1884).

27. 1 Williston § 27.

28. See, e.g., Nebraska Seed Co. v. Harsh, 98 Neb. 89, 152 N.W. 310 (1915).

29. See, e.g., Cox v. Denton, 104 Kan. 516, 180 P. 261 (1919).

30. Restatement, Second, Contracts § 26, Comment c, ill. 3.

31. 322 Mass. 236, 76 N.E.2d 658 (1948).

The court held that a reasonable man should have concluded that the defendant was not making an offer, especially since it would be unreasonable to assume that the defendant was willing to subject himself to the possibility of being bound by more than one contract. This is not to say that a person may not be held to have made offers to sell the same property to more than one offeree. If he is so unwise, each of the offerees who has accepted will have a remedy against the offeror.[32] When a person is interested in disposing of real property, however, he is likely to negotiate with more than one potential buyer. If in some way he indicates that proposals to sell have been addressed to others, in the absence of a clear promise to sell at given terms, his proposal is not reasonably construed as an offer. Rather, in this case it should be looked upon as an invitation to make an offer or a mere price quotation.

In Harvey v. Facey [33] the plaintiff sent a telegram to the defendant saying, "Will you sell us Bumper Hall Pen? Telegraph lowest cash price. The defendant answered, "Lowest price for Bumper Hall Pen £ 900." Plaintiff sent a letter of acceptance. The court held that defendant had not made an offer. It reasoned that, since the plaintiff's first question had not been answered, defendant's communication did not contain a promise to sell. But couldn't defendant's communication be reasonably understood to say, "Yes, I will sell you Bumper Hall Pen for £ 900?".[34] It is interesting to compare this case with the Mason green jar case above. In each case the plaintiff made an inquiry with respect to price and the defendant gave the price. The question in each case is whether the defendant promised to sell at that price. In the green jar case the word used in defendant's communication was "quote" but he also said "for immediate acceptance." But, according to the Restatement Second, these words are not essential to the decision. Are the cases contradictory? The answer is not necessarily for two reasons to be discussed below.

There are additional facts in the case of Harvey v. Facey that are important even though the court does not explicitly rely upon them. The plaintiffs, who were solicitors in Kingston, dispatched their initial telegram the day after the City Council had publicly discussed an offer by the defendant to sell the premises to the City. Although the opinion does not state that the plaintiffs were aware of the Council meeting, the inference is clear that they were. This makes the case analogous to Mellen v. Johnson (discussed above) because plaintiff is aware that the defendant is negotiating with others with respect to the same subject matter. Under the circumstances the failure to reply to the first question could well indicate that defendant did not intend to commit himself.

32. See Tymon v. Linoki, 16 N.Y.2d 293, 266 N.Y.S.2d 357, 213 N.E.2d 661 (1965).

33. 1893 A.C. 552 (P.C.) (Jamaica). See also Courteen Seed Co. v. Abraham, 129 Or. 427, 275 P. 684 (1929), criticized in 9 Ore.L.Rev. 72 (1929).

34. 1 Corbin § 26 n. 20.

Another possible explanation is that courts are quite properly reluctant to construe a communication as an offer unless it quite clear that a promise has been made. Once a contract is made, courts tend to interpret language freely and, if justice seems to require, without finicky regard for grammatical nicety. However, they will not lightly determine that a person has taken the significant step of creating a power of acceptance unless he quite clearly made a commitment.[35] But again there is no such hard and fast rule and as a matter of fact both Restatements take the position that the same rules of interpretation that apply to contracts also apply to offers.[36] If there is any validity to the opening sentence of this paragraph, it is probably more true in cases involving real property.

If you have concluded that there are no precise answers to many problems, you have achieved the beginning of wisdom. This theme is continued immediately below.

(i) Offer vs. Preliminary Negotiations—Some Factors to Be Considered

Preliminary negotiations can be defined to include any communication prior to the acceptance [37] or any communication prior to the operative [38] offer in the case.[39] Since we are here discussing offers, for our purposes the second definition is preferable. Under this definition, many of the types of communications already discussed often are made in preliminary negotiations. These include statements of opinion, statements of intention, hopes and desires, estimates, inquiries, invitations to make offers, advertisements, catalogs, circular letters, invitations to make bids, and price quotations.[40]

But as we have seen, there is not always a clear answer to the question of whether a particular communication is preliminary to the offer or whether it is an offer. The essential difficulty is that, under the objective theory of contracts, the test is whether a reasonable man in the position of the plaintiff would conclude that the defendant had made a commitment. Under such a test, it is not surprising to find that there are often differences of opinion as to the correct result in a concrete case.[41] The problem is further complicated by the distinction

---

35. United States v. Braunstein, 75 F.Supp. 137, 139 (S.D.N.Y.1947), appeal dismissed 168 F.2d 749 (2d Cir.1948). ("It is true that there is much room for interpretation once the parties are inside the framework of a contract, but it seems that there is less in the field of offer and acceptance. Greater precision of expression may be required, and less help from the court given, when the parties are merely at the threshold of a contract."); accord Henry Simons Lumber Co. v. Simons, 232 Minn. 187, 44 N.W.2d 726 (1950).

36. See chapter 3 infra.

37. 1 Corbin § 22.

38. The word "operative" is added to take into account the rule that a counter-offer normally terminates an offer. In such a case the initial offer could be classified as a preliminary negotiation.

39. Restatement, Second, Contracts § 26.

40. All of these topics have been covered in this section.

41. 1 Corbin § 23; J. Murray, Contracts: A Revision of Grismore on Contracts § 24 (1974) [hereinafter cited as Murray]. Since the question is essentially one of the intent of the parties as gleaned from the facts of a particular case, it is not

between questions of fact and questions of law—a topic to be discussed below.[42]

In determining whether a communication is an offer or not, some of the important factors to be considered are:

1) Whether the communication alleged to be an offer is an initial communication as opposed to an answer to an inquiry. An answer to an inquiry is more likely to be an offer. In such a case the language of the inquiry is important. Does the inquiry ask for an offer as in Fairmount? Compare Harvey v. Facey.

2) The language used. Is it language generally associated with promise or noncommittal language?

3) Are there detailed terms or are only relatively few terms covered? Are the quantity and quality terms covered?

4) Is it clear that the party who sends the communication is dealing with other people with respect to the same subject matter?

5) Does the case involve real or personal property?

6) What is the relationship of the parties: husband and wife, physician and patient?

7) Surrounding circumstances; for example, in the case of a doctor, whether he is treating a patient under emergency conditions or not.

8) Usages of the trade, prior practices of the parties ("course of dealing") to be discussed later.[43]

 WESTLAW REFERENCES

(b) *Offer Distinguished from an Expression of Opinion and Predictions*

"skill commensurate" /s doctor medical! physician

contract /s doctor physician medical! /s malpractice

physician doctor medical! /s "express contract"

"promise to cure"

doctor physician medical! /p sullivan +s o'connor

find 199 nw 90

reasonable +1 man person /s conclud! conclusion /s promise

(c) *Statements of Intention, Hopes and Desires and Estimates*

statement /s intent! /s offer! /s contract

"letter of intent" /s preliminary /s contract

hope wish /s promise offer /s statement /s contract

"letter of intent" /s commit committed committing noncommit!

estimat! /s offer /s contract

invit! /s bid bidding /s contract

estimat! /s "equitabl! estop!"

surprising that the cases do not always appear to be in harmony. See Alpen v. Chapman, 179 N.W.2d 585 (Iowa 1970).

42. See § 2–8 infra.

43. See § 3–17 infra.

"equitabl! estop!" /s misrepresent! /s rely! relied reliance /s
  injur!

156k87

(d) *Inquiry or Invitation to Make an Offer*

owen +s tunison

invit! /s make making /s offer!

(e) *Is the Ordinary Advertisement, Catalog or Circular Letter, etc.*
  an Offer?

advertis! /s offer /s contract /s enforc!

"intention to sell" /s contract

advertis! /s invit! /s offer!

"preliminary proposal" /s contract bind binding bound

advertis! /s contract /s consumer /s protect!

ci(15 +4 41)

"printers ink" /s statut! law legislat!

"attorney general" /s "deceptive practice"

"consumer protection law"

contract /s "intent not to sell"

"uniform deceptive trade practices act"

"language of promise"

to(92) /p "consumer protection"

(f) *Auction Sales—Who Makes the Offer?*

di auction

auction /s offer! /s contract

"auction without reserve"

"uniform commercial code" /s 2–328

bidder /s offeror

auction! /s bid /s withdr*w!

bid bidding bidder /s puff puffing

bid bidder bidding /s "forced sale"

(g) *Invitation to Bid—Bid*

offer! accept! /s invit! /s bid bidding /s construction

statut! law legislat! /s contract /s "lowest responsible bidder"

bid bidding /s offer! /s "lowest responsible bidder"

requir! /s bid bidding /s "public contract"

316ak8

standing /s perkins +s lukens

"disappointed bidder" /s enjoin! injunction

(h) *Price Quotations—Personal and Real Property*

  (1) *Personal Property*

quot! /s invit! /s offer!

cannavino +s water

contract /s "immediate acceptance" /s offer!

"detailed term" /s contract

343k22(1)

  (2) *Real Property*

find 76 ne2d 658

"real property" /s offer! /s contract

real +1 estate property /s propos! /s negotiat! /s offer!
  contract

"communication as an offer" /s contract

"power of acceptance" /s contract

(i) *Offer vs. Preliminary Negotiations—Some Factors to Be Considered*

offer! accept! /s "preliminary negotiat!"

"preliminary negotiat!" /s operative

di("preliminary negotiat!")

"preliminary negotiat!" /s commit!

contract /s "initial communication" "answer to an inquiry"

contract /s "relationship of the party"

contract /s "surrounding circumstance"

C. OTHER MATTERS RELATING TO MUTUAL ASSENT

Table of Sections

§ 2–7. Intention That Agreement Be Memorialized—Effect of Signing Duplicate Originals

During the process of negotiation parties often manifest an intention that when an agreement is reached it should be formalized. In such a situation, does a contract arise when the parties reach an otherwise binding agreement or is there no contract unless the formal document is adopted by both parties?

The problem is another aspect of the question of intending legal consequences.[44] If the parties make it clear that they do not intend that there should be legal consequences unless and until a formal writing is executed, there is no contract until that time.[45] Conversely, if they make it clear that the prospective writing is merely to be a

---

44. See § 2–4 supra.

45. Warrior Constructors, Inc. v. International Union of Operating Engineers, Local 926, 383 F.2d 700 (5th Cir.1967);

Apablasa v. Merritt & Co., 176 Cal.App.2d 719, 1 Cal.Rptr. 500 (1959); Smissaert v. Chiode, 163 Cal.App.2d 827, 330 P.2d 98 (1958).

convenient memorial of the agreement previously reached, the agreement is binding when reached even though a memorial is never adopted.[46] In this case a party's refusal to execute the memorial constitutes a breach of contract.[47]

The difficult case is where the parties have not expressly manifested their intent other than by the fact that they intended that there should be a writing. In this situation some of the cases have held that the parties are not bound until the writing is executed.[48] Other cases, however, have concluded that the contract becomes binding when the agreement is reached.[49]

This does not mean that there is a conflict in the cases even though at times they are difficult to reconcile.[50] What is being decided is a question of the intention of the parties[51] and frequently this is a question of fact.[52] Some of the cases talk in terms of a presumption that the writing is intended merely as a convenient memorial, while others indicate that the burden of proof is upon the party who says that a formal document was required to complete the contract.[53] There is not a great deal of difference in these two formulations. There is, however, a third and contrary formulation to the effect that an understanding that the agreement will be reduced to writing raises a presumption that the parties did not intend the negotiation to amount to an agreement and therefore prevents a contract from arising until the writing is executed.[54]

However, it has been concluded, and apparently properly so, that it does not seem fruitful to analyze the problem in these terms.[55] It would seem to be more fruitful to identify some of the important factors which influence the decisions of the courts.[56] The Restatement Second

46. Mesa Petroleum Co. v. Coniglio, 629 F.2d 1022 (5th Cir.1980); 1 Corbin § 30; 1 Williston §§ 28, 28A.

47. Restatement, Second, Contracts § 27.

48. Wharton v. Stoutenburg, 35 N.J.Eq. 266 (1882); Scheck v. Francis, 26 N.Y.2d 466, 311 N.Y.S.2d 841, 260 N.E.2d 493 (1970); Schwartz v. Greenberg, 304 N.Y. 250, 107 N.E.2d 65 (1952).

49. Barton v. Chemical Bank, 577 F.2d 1329 (5th Cir.1978); H.B. Zachry Co. v. O'Brien, 378 F.2d 423 (10th Cir.1967); Miles v. Wichita, 175 Kan. 723, 267 P.2d 943 (1954); Dohrman v. Sullivan, 310 Ky. 463, 220 S.W.2d 973 (1949); Peoples Drug Stores, Inc. v. Fenton Realty Corp., 191 Md. 489, 62 A.2d 273 (1948); Sanders v. Pottlitzer Bros. Fruit Co., 144 N.Y. 209, 39 N.E. 75 (1894); see V'Soske v. Barwick, 404 F.2d 495 (2d Cir.1968), certiorari denied 394 U.S. 921, 89 S.Ct. 1197, 22 L.Ed.2d 454 (1969); cf. Sands v. Arruda, 359 Mass. 591, 270 N.E.2d 826 (1971).

50. 1 Corbin § 30.

51. Smith v. Onyx Oil & Chem. Co., 218 F.2d 104 (3d Cir.1955); Mitchell v. Siqueiros, 99 Idaho 396, 582 P.2d 1074 (1978).

52. Babdo Sales, Inc. v. Miller-Wohl Co., 440 F.2d 962 (2d Cir.1971); Patrolmen's Benevolent Ass'n v. New York, 27 N.Y.2d 410, 318 N.Y.S.2d 477, 267 N.E.2d 259 (1971); Scott v. Ingle Bros. Pac., Inc., 489 S.W.2d 554 (Tex.1972), noted in 26 Baylor L.Rev. 132 (1974); see Short v. Sunflower Plastic Pipe, Inc., 210 Kan. 68, 500 P.2d 39 (1972); 1 Corbin § 30.

53. Sanders v. Pottlitzer Bros. Fruit Co., 144 N.Y. 209, 39 N.E. 75 (1894); 1 Williston § 28.

54. Valjar, Inc. v. Maritime Terminals, Inc., 220 Va. 1015, 265 S.E.2d 734 (1980); 1 Williston § 28A.

55. 2 Formation of Contracts, supra § 2–1, note 5, at 1625.

56. Mississippi & Dominion S.S. Co. v. Swift, 86 Me. 248, 29 A. 1063 (1894); Michigan Broadcasting Co. v. Shawd, 352 Mich. 453, 90 N.W.2d 451 (1958).

lists the following factors: "the extent to which express agreement has been reached on all terms to be included, whether the contract is a type usually put in writing, whether it needs a formal writing for its full expression, whether it has few or many details, whether the amount involved is large or small, whether it is a common or unusual contract, whether a standard form of contract is widely used in similar transactions, and whether either party takes any action in preparation for performance during the negotiations".[57] In addition, if the agreement is reached by correspondence, it is likely that the parties intend to be bound when they reach agreement.[58]

In the previous discussion it has been assumed that the parties have manifested the same intent or have not manifested any intention. Obviously, where there is litigation, one party claims that he did not intend to be bound until there was a formal writing. This issue is to be determined by the tentative test previously suggested. If a reasonable man in the position of the other party either knew or should have known that the other party did not intend to be bound in the absence of a formal agreement, there is no contract until formal agreement is executed.[59]

When the parties do not intend to be bound before a formal document is duly executed, the question sometimes arises whether the contract is formed when both parties sign duplicate originals or only when the signed writings are exchanged. The cases appear to be in hopeless conflict.[60] This is because a question of intention is being decided. This has been specifically recognized in the case of Aspen Acres Association v. Seven Associates, Inc.[61] As stated there: "[T]he mere affixing of the signatures to the document did not conclusively prove that there was a binding contract. In addition, there must be a delivery, not in the traditional sense of a manual transfer, but in the sense that it was the intent of the parties to have the document become

---

57. Restatement, Second, Contracts § 28, Comment c. See also 2 Formation of Contracts, supra § 2–1, note 5, at 1627–1632, where additional factors are identified.

58. Sanders v. Pottlitzer Bros. Fruit Co., 144 N.Y. 209, 39 N.E. 75 (1894).

59. Restatement, Second, Contracts § 27, Comment b. "In New York, as elsewhere it is quite plain that if either of the parties manifests an intention not to be bound until a written contract is executed then the parties are not bound until that event occurs." Lizza & Sons, Inc. v. D'Onfro, 186 F.Supp. 428, 432 (D.Mass. 1959), judgment affirmed 282 F.2d 175 (1st Cir.1960); accord, Merritt-Chapman & Scott Corp. v. Public Utility Dist. No. 2, 237 F.Supp. 985 (S.D.N.Y.1965). At times the rule is stated as if the parties are bound upon agreement "in the absence of a positive agreement that it should not be

binding until so reduced to writing and formally executed." Disken v. Herter, 73 App.Div. 453, 455, 77 N.Y.S. 300, 302 (1902), affirmed 175 N.Y. 480, 67 N.E. 1081 (1903); accord, 12 Am.Jr., Contracts §§ 23, 25 (1938). This statement is incorrect since it implies that the manifest intent of one of the parties may be ignored by the other. See also Municipal Consultants v. Ramapo, 47 N.Y.2d 144, 417 N.Y.S.2d 218, 390 N.E.2d 1143 (1979).

60. Compare Schwartz v. Greenberg, 304 N.Y. 250, 107 N.E.2d 65 (1952) with Generes v. Justice Court, 106 Cal.App.3d 678, 165 Cal.Rptr. 222 (1980) and Whitley v. Patrick, 226 Ga. 87, 172 S.E.2d 692 (1970) and Besser v. K.L.T. Associates, 42 A.D.2d 725, 345 N.Y.S.2d 659 (1973), affirmed 34 N.Y.2d 687, 356 N.Y.S.2d 295, 312 N.E.2d 478 (1974).

61. 29 Utah 2d 303, 508 P.2d 1179 (1973).

legally operative at some definite point in time, however, such intent might be indicated." [62]

 WESTLAW REFERENCES

intend! intent! /s agree /s formal!

contract /s "formal! document"

contract /s intend! intent! /s "legal consequence"

contract /s agree! /3 memorial!

"question of fact" (factual +l question matter) /s write writing
   written /s contract /s "intent of the party"

valjar +s maritime

manifest! /s intend! intent /s bind binding bound /s write
   writing written

manifest! /s intend! intent! /s bind binding bound /s formal +l
   agreement document

§ 2–8. Questions of Law and Fact

The distinction between questions of law and fact is analyzed in detail in treatises on procedure. Here it is sufficient to note that at the trial level questions of fact are determined by the triers of fact, often a jury, and questions of law are determined by the trial judge. Appellate courts as a general rule, subject to some exceptions, review only questions of law.[63]

To illustrate: Whether and to what extent subjective intention is relevant in making a particular determination is a question of law. Whether a person said "50" or "100" on a particular occasion is a question of fact. Whether a reasonable man in the position of the plaintiff would conclude that the defendant had made a commitment is a question of fact unless the court rules that reasonable men could reach only one reasonable conclusion.[64] Even where reasonable men could reach different conclusions the question is often held to be one of law when it involves the interpretation of a writing.[65] As Corbin points out "since two cases are never identical * * * the decision made in one of them can never be regarded as a conclusive precedent for the other." [66] It must also be remembered that the printed report never gives all of the facts and may well omit one of the decisive factors that led to the decision. There is also a tendency to rule as a matter of law

62. Id. at 310–11, 508 P.2d at 1184; see also Cortlandt v. E.F. Hutton, Inc., 491 F.Supp. 1 (S.D.N.Y.1979); cf. 2 Formation of Contracts, supra § 2–1, note 5, at 1584–86.

63. United States ex rel. Howard Steel Co. v. United Pac. Ins. Co., 427 F.2d 366 (7th Cir.1970).

64. Construction Aggregates Corp. v. Hewitt-Robins, Inc., 404 F.2d 505 (7th Cir. 1968), certiorari denied 395 U.S. 921, 89 S.Ct. 1174, 23 L.Ed.2d 238 (1969).

65. General Dynamics Corp. v. Miami Aviation Corp., 421 F.2d 416 (5th Cir.1970). Although the general rule is that the interpretation of a writing is a question of law, in reality the court is deciding a question of the intention of the parties which but for this rule would ordinarily be a question of fact. This point is discussed in greater detail at § 3–14 infra.

66. 1 Corbin § 23.

in certain recurring situations, as in the advertising situation,[67] where the law has hardened as to the proper decision.

WESTLAW REFERENCES

distinct! distinguish! /s "question of law or fact"

judge /s "question of law"

di(jury /s "question of fact")

appeal! appellate /s "question of law"

"question of law" /s interpret! /s write written writing wrote

di("question of law")

§ 2–9. Indefiniteness

We have already seen that indefiniteness in a communication would be some evidence of an intent not to contract.[68] The more terms that are omitted the more likely it is that the parties do not intend to contract.[69] But, even if the parties intend to contract, if the content of their agreement is unduly uncertain no contract is formed.[70] This rule must be understood as a necessary limitation upon freedom of contract because an agreement must be sufficiently definite before a court can enforce it.[71] The traditional rule is that if the agreement is not *reasonably* certain [72] as to its *material* terms there is a fatal indefiniteness with the result that the agreement is void.[73] The rule does not supply a precise standard. Vagueness and indefiniteness are matters of degree.[74]

It is the contract which must be definite and not the offer. For example, if A makes an offer to B to sell from 1 to 10 copies of a specified book at a certain price and adds "state the number in your acceptance" and B replies "I'll take 5," there is a contract, although considered alone the offer might seem indefinite as to quantity.

What are material terms? Material terms include subject matter, price, payment terms, quantity, quality, duration, the work to be done. Given the infinite variety of contracts, it is obvious that no precise

67. See § 2–6(e) supra.

68. Owen v. Owen, 427 A.2d 933 (D.C. App.1981); Hill v. McGregor Mfg. Corp., 23 Mich.App. 342, 178 N.W.2d 553 (1970). See § 2–6 supra.

69. Soar v. National Football League Player's Ass'n, 550 F.2d 1287, 1290 (1st Cir. 1977) ("while an enforceable contract might be found in some circumstances if one or more of such questions were left unanswered, the accumulation in the instant case of so many unanswered questions is convincing evidence that there never was a consensus ad idem between the parties").

70. Parks v. Atlanta News Agency, Inc., 115 Ga.App. 842, 156 S.E.2d 137 (1967); Restatement, Second, Contracts § 33(1); 1 Corbin § 95; 1 Williston § 37.

71. Snug Harbor Property Owners Ass'n v. Curran, 55 N.C.App. 199, 284 S.E.2d 752 (1981), review denied 305 N.C. 302, 291 S.E.2d 151 (1982).

72. Coastland Corp. v. Third Nat'l Mortgage Co., 611 F.2d 969 (4th Cir.1979).

73. Riis v. Day, 188 Mont. 253, 613 P.2d 696 (1980); Restatement, Second, Contracts § 32. See § 1–11 supra.

74. Palmer v. Albert, 310 N.W.2d 169 (Iowa 1981).

listing can be made or definition stated.[75]   It is clear that indefiniteness as to an immaterial term is not fatal.[76]

It is even more difficult to determine when a material term is reasonably certain.[77]   If the agreement is reasonably certain, it is enforced even though all of the terms are not set forth with "optimal specificity." [78]   It is enough that the agreement is sufficiently explicit so that the court can perceive what are the respective obligations of the parties.[79]   In other words, the requirements of definiteness cannot be pushed to extreme limits.[80]   As has been stated, "what is reasonable in any case must depend upon the subject matter of the agreement, the purpose for which it was entered into, the situation and relation of the parties and the circumstances under which it was made." [81]

Indefiniteness problems arise primarily in three types of cases: 1) Where the parties have purported to agree upon a material term but left it indefinite (not reasonably certain).   2) Where the parties are silent as to a material term.   3) Where the parties have agreed to agree later as to a material term.   Since at common law the problems in each category are treated somewhat differently each will be discussed separately.

(a) The Common Law

(1) Where the Parties Have Purported to Agree Upon a Material Term but Have Left It Indefinite

If A says to B, "If you work for me for one year as the foreman of my plant I promise to pay you a fair share of the profits," it has been held that the promise it too vague and indefinite to be enforced.[82]   If, however, B performs under the agreement, he may obtain a quasi-contractual recovery measured by the reasonable value of services

---

75. See 1 Corbin §§ 95–100; 1 Williston §§ 38–48.

76. Purvis v. United States, 344 F.2d 867 (9th Cir.1965) (leaving open a $9,300 item in a construction contract involving $1,000,000 held immaterial); Yellow Run Coal Co. v. Alma-Elley-Yv Mines, 285 Pa. Super. 84, 426 A.2d 1152 (1981); Touche Ross & Co. v. Dasd Corp., 162 Ga.App. 438, 292 S.E.2d 84 (1982); Restatement, Second, Contracts § 332, ill. 11.

77. 1 Corbin § 95.

78. Soar v. National Football League Player's Ass'n, 550 F.2d 1287, 1290 n. 6 (1st Cir.1977).

79. Id., Lambert Corp. v. Evans, 575 F.2d 132 (7th Cir.1978); Barry M. Dechtman v. Sidpaul Corp., 89 N.J. 547, 446 A.2d 518 (1982); Berg Agency v. Sleepworld-Willingboro, 136 N.J.Super. 369, 346 A.2d 419 (App.Div.1975).

80. V'Soske v. Barwick, 404 F.2d 495 (2d Cir.1968), certiorari denied 394 U.S.

921, 89 S.Ct. 1197, 22 L.Ed.2d 454 (1969); Jack Richards Aircraft Sales, Inc. v. Vaughn, 203 Kan. 967, 457 P.2d 691 (1969); Davco Realty Co. v. Picnic Foods, Inc., 198 Neb. 193, 252 N.W.2d 142 (1977).

81. Marcor Housing Sys. v. First Am. Title Co., 41 Colo.App. 90, 92–93, 584 P.2d 86, 88 (1978), judgment affirmed in part, reversed in part 197 Colo. 530, 595 P.2d 679 (1979).

82. T'Ai Corp. v. Kalso Systemet, Inc., 568 F.2d 145 (10th Cir.1977); Gray v. Aiken, 205 Ga. 649, 54 S.E.2d 587 (1949); Varney v. Ditmars, 217 N.Y. 223, 111 N.E. 822 (1916). Additional cases are collected in 1 Williston § 41. A number of more liberal cases have enforced promises of this nature. See Noble v. Joseph Burnett Co., 208 Mass. 75, 94 N.E. 289 (1911); Allan v. Hargadine-McKittrick Dry Goods Co., 315 Mo. 254, 286 S.W. 16 (1926). A promise of reasonable recognition for future inventions was upheld in Corthell v. Summit Thread Co., 132 Me. 94, 167 A. 79 (1933).

rather than by a share of the profits.[83] A promise to make a tailor-made suit for fifty dollars, where the material is not specified, also suffers from indefiniteness.[84] Indefiniteness of this kind can be cured by the subsequent conduct of the parties.[85] If the tailor commences making the suit with cotton cloth and the customer acquiesces in this, the indefiniteness is cured by the conduct of the parties.[86] Indefiniteness can also be cured by agreement rather than by conduct. A good illustration is the case of Perreault v. Hall [87] where the defendant promised to pay the plaintiff "well and enough." Upon retirement the defendant promised to give plaintiff a pension of $20.00 per week, an offer which plaintiff apparently accepted. Here the indefiniteness was cured by the new agreement.[88] In the "fair share of the profits" case the indefiniteness was never cured and so plaintiff was limited to a quasi-contractual recovery; in the other two cases (tailor-made suit, pay "well and enough") the indefiniteness was cured and therefore a contractual recovery was in order.[89]

That the entire question of reasonable certainty is relative may be shown by a comparison of two fact patterns. In one assume that there was an agreement that the plaintiff, contractor, would build "a first class ranch house" for the defendant for a stated price. Before there was any performance defendant refused to perform. There are cases indicating that the agreement is too vague and indefinite to be enforced.[90]

In a well known case plaintiff agreed to sell and did sell his real property to defendant for a fixed sum that was paid. In addition defendant promised to build a "first class theatre" on the site sold. Plaintiff, as the defendant knew, desired the theatre to enhance the value of his other properties in the area. After defendant became the owner he sold the property to a third party without having built the theatre. Plaintiff sued for damages for breach of contract and defendant argued fatal indefiniteness. The court reached a contrary conclusion.[91]

---

83. Kearns v. Andree, 107 Conn. 181, 139 A. 695 (1928); Varney v. Ditmars, 217 N.Y. 223, 111 N.E. 822 (1916); 1 Corbin § 102; 1 Williston § 49.

84. Factor v. Peabody Tailoring Sys., 177 Wis. 238, 187 N.W. 984 (1922). There are many cases which have held an agreement to be too indefinite because of the indefiniteness of the subject matter of the contract. E.g., Greater Serv. Homebuilders Inv. Ass'n v. Albright, 88 Colo. 146, 293 P. 345 (1930); see 1 Corbin § 100.

85. Morris v. Ballard, 16 F.2d 175 (D.C. Cir.1926); Barto v. Hicks, 124 Ga.App. 472, 184 S.E.2d 188 (1971); Dreazy v. North Shore Pub. Co., 53 Wis.2d 38, 191 N.W.2d 720 (1971); 1 Corbin § 101.

86. See 1 Corbin § 101; 1 Williston § 49; City of Bremerton v. Kitsap County Sewer Dist., 71 Wn.2d 689, 430 P.2d 956 (1967). The related question of forging a good unilateral contract out of bad bilateral contract is discussed at § 4–12(a)(7) infra.

87. 94 N.H. 191, 49 A.2d 812 (1946).

88. 1 Williston § 49. This agreement might be looked upon as some species of accord and satisfaction. See § 4–11 infra and 1 Corbin § 143.

89. 1 Williston § 49.

90. See, for example, Hart v. Georgia Ry., 101 Ga. 188, 28 S.E. 637 (1897).

91. Bettancourt v. Gilroy Theatre Co., 120 Cal.App.2d 364, 261 P.2d 351 (1953).

The cases are not necessarily in conflict. The second court begins with a statement made by a number of courts that "the law leans against the destruction of contracts because of uncertainty."[92] This is especially true, where, as here, there has been full performance by the plaintiff.[93] Perhaps the most significant factor in the case is that evidence of subjective understanding, and other evidence aliunde the writing was admitted and was of help in explaining what the words "a first class theatre" meant. This type of evidence should be admissible in any case where the expression is ambiguous and the evidence can help resolve the problem.[94]

In addition it may be perceived that the purpose of the plaintiff was different in the two cases. In the hypothetical case how "first class" the ranch house was, was of great importance to the defendant because his purpose was to use and or sell it. Since the plaintiff's purpose in the second case was to enhance the value of his other properties, his purpose could be served by the erection of any theatre that fit the definition of a first class theatre.

Finally, the court stated another well-recognized rule to the effect that less certainty is required where the action is for damages than in an action for specific performance.[95] The reason for requiring greater certainty before specific performance is granted is discussed elsewhere.[96]

(2) Where the Parties Are Silent as to a Material Term

As stated above, under the traditional rule where the parties have purported to agree upon a material term and left it indefinite, the agreement is considered to be too vague and indefinite. But if the parties are silent as to material term or discuss the term but do not purport to agree upon it and do not condition their agreement upon an agreement as to this term, there is a strong possibility that a term may be implied from surrounding circumstances or supplied by a court using a gap-filler.[97] Thus, in these situations the missing term may be supplied by external sources, including standard terms, usages by which the parties are bound, and a course of dealing between the

92. Id. at 367, 261 P.2d at 353; accord In re Wonderfair Stores, Inc., 511 F.2d 1206 (9th Cir.1975); In re Sing Chong Co., 1 Hawaii App. 236, 617 P.2d 578 (1980); Gift v. Ehrichs, 284 N.W.2d 435 (N.D.1979); Mag Constr. Co. v. McLean County, 181 N.W.2d 718 (N.D.1970).

93. Butler v. Westgate State Bank, 3 Kan.App.2d 403, 596 P.2d 156 (1979), judgment reversed on other grounds 226 Kan. 581, 602 P.2d 1276 (1979). The case states that even partial performance can be important.

94. Kleinheider v. Phillips Pipe Line Co., 528 F.2d 837 (8th Cir.1975); 3 Corbin § 583. See ch. 3 infra.

95. Caisson Corp. v. Ingersoll-Rand Co., 622 F.2d 672 (3d Cir.1980); Rego v. Decker, 482 P.2d 834 (Alaska 1971); Davis v. Davis, 261 Iowa 992, 156 N.W.2d 870 (1968).

96. See § 16–8 infra.

97. Southwest Eng'r Co. v. Martin Tractor Co., 205 Kan. 684, 473 P.2d 18 (1970); Flemming v. Ranson Corp., 107 N.J.Super. 311, 258 A.2d 153 (1969), affirmed 114 N.J. Super. 221, 275 A.2d 759 (1971); 1 Williston, Contracts § 40.

parties prior to the agreement and a course of performance after it.[98] Here the term becomes part of the contract by implying that the parties contracted on the basis of these sources.

A gap-filler, on the other hand, is a term supplied by the courts either because the court feels that the parties would have agreed upon the term if it had been brought to their attention or because it is "a term which comports with community standards of fairness and policy." [99] The important point to remember, as elaborated below, is that it is difficult to know, without research, when the courts will or will not supply a gap-filler.

In the language of one court, "[t]erms are implied not because they are just or reasonable, but rather for the reason that the parties must have intended them and have only failed to express them * * * or because they are necessary to give business efficacy to the contract as written, or to give the contract the effect which parties, as fair and reasonable men, presumably would have agreed if, having in mind the possibility of the situation which had arisen, they contracted expressly in reference thereto." [1] This topic is related to the topic of supplying "omitted terms" which is discussed at various places in this volume.

If A and B agree that A will perform a service for B and no mention is made of the price to be paid, it will be concluded that the parties intended that a reasonable price should be paid and received.[2] It has also been held that, where one hires a contractor and no price is set, the term supplied is that the contractor is to be paid his usual charges for work.[3] In the case of a sale of goods where no price is stated, it will be assumed that the parties contracted in terms of a reasonable price and this rule has been continued by the Uniform Commercial Code.[4] The same rule has been applied even in the case of

---

98. Metro-Goldwyn-Mayer, Inc. v. Scheider, 40 N.Y.2d 1069, 392 N.Y.S.2d 252, 360 N.E.2d 930 (1976); § 3–17 infra.

99. Restatement, Second, Contracts § 204 comment d. There is authority that the Restatement's provision is sound from a sociological point of view. See E. Durkheim, The Division of Labor in Society 213–14 (Free Press ed. 1964).

1. Barco Urban Renewal Corp. v. Housing Auth., 674 F.2d 1001, 1007 (3d Cir. 1982).

2. Charlotte Aircraft Corp. v. Braniff Airways, Inc., 497 F.2d 1016 (5th Cir.1974); A.M. Webb & Co. v. Robert P. Miller Co., 157 F.2d 865 (3d Cir.1946); S.F. Bowser & Co. v. F.K. Marks & Co., 96 Ark. 113, 131 S.W. 334 (1910); Olberding Const. Co. v. Ruden, 243 N.W.2d 872 (Iowa 1976); Sitzler v. Peck, 162 N.W.2d 449 (Iowa 1968); Konitzky v. Meyer, 49 N.Y. 571 (1872); Dixon v. Kittle, 109 Ohio App. 257, 164 N.E.2d 806 (1959); but see Campbell v. Wabc Towing Corp., 78 Misc.2d 671, 356

N.Y.S.2d 455 (1974) (consumer protection legislation requires price to be revealed at outset of automobile repair contract; no recovery).

3. La Velle v. De Luca, 48 Wis.2d 464, 180 N.W.2d 710 (1970). But see Hemenover v. Depatis, 86 Ill.App.3d 586, 42 Ill. Dec. 9, 408 N.E.2d 387 (1980) wherein it is held that the contractor is entitled to the reasonable value of goods used and the customary price for labor.

4. The Uniform Commercial Code provides detailed rules applicable to agreements in which the price has not been decided upon. U.C.C. § 2–305 provides:

"(1) The parties if they so intend can conclude a contract for sale even though the price is not settled. In such a case the price is a reasonable price at the time for delivery if

(a) nothing is said as to price; or

(b) the price is left to be agreed by the parties and they fail to agree; or

a sale of real property.[5] A reasonable price may be measured by the market price [6] and where there is no market price the reasonable price may be determined by actual cost plus a reasonable profit [7] or other means of valuation.[8] If no time is stated for the delivery of goods [9] or for the completion of a building contract,[10] a reasonable time is assumed. This is also true in other cases as for example in a case involving a transfer of real property.[11]

However, a gap-filler is not supplied to cover every material term with respect to which the parties have been silent. Thus, where the parties have omitted from their agreement the kind or quantity of goods [12] or the specifications of a building contract,[13] the courts have refused to fill the gap because no objective standard can ordinarily be found in such cases.[14] Unfortunately, despite the business necessity for such contracts, courts have sometimes included within this category agreements to deliver one's entire output to, or to take all of one's

(c) the price is to be fixed in terms of some agreed market or other standard as set or recorded by a third person or agency and it is not so set or recorded.

(2) A price to be fixed by the seller or by the buyer means a price for him to fix in good faith.

(3) When a price left to be fixed otherwise than by agreement of the parties fails to be fixed through fault of one party, the other may at his option treat the contract as cancelled or himself fix a reasonable price.

(4) Where, however, the parties intend not to be bound unless the price be fixed or agreed and it is not fixed or agreed, there is no contract. In such a case the buyer must return any goods already received or if unable so to do must pay their reasonable value at the time of delivery and the seller must return any portion of the price paid on account."

For an analysis, see Note, U.C.C. § 2–305(1)(c): Open Price Terms and the Intention of the Parties in Sales Contracts, 1 Val.U.L.Rev. 381 (1967); see Schmieder v. Standard Oil Co. of Indiana, 69 Wis.2d 419, 230 N.W.2d 732, 91 A.L.R.3d 1231 (1975).

5. Shayeb v. Holland, 321 Mass. 429, 73 N.E.2d 731 (1947).

6. Credit Serv. Co. v. Country Realty Co., 46 Or.App. 867, 612 P.2d 773 (1980).

7. Kuss Mach. Tool & Die Co. v. El-tronics, Inc., 393 Pa. 353, 143 A.2d 38 (1958) (a case decided under § 2–305 of the U.C.C.); cf. Restatement, Second, Contracts § 33, ill. 7.

8. Economic and legal methods of valuation are considered in C. McCormick, Damages ch. 6 (1935).

9. U.C.C. § 2–309(1). Comment 5 requires that reasonable notice be given before a contract may be treated as breached on the ground that delivery or demand for performance has not been made within a reasonable time. If the parties allow the reasonable time for delivery or demand to pass in silence, the reasonable time may be extended. At some point, if the parties do not act, the contract may be considered tacitly rescinded. See § 21–2 infra.

10. American Concrete Steel Co. v. Hart, 285 Fed. 322 (2d Cir.1922) (reasonableness of time sometimes a question of fact, sometimes of law). So also every contract of employment in the absence of a contrary agreement "includes an obligation ∗ ∗ ∗ to perform in a diligent and reasonably skillful ∗ ∗ ∗ manner." Nash v. Sears, Roebuck & Co., 383 Mich. 136, 142, 174 N.W.2d 818, 821 (1970). Where a person contracts to perform work or render service, in the absence of a contrary agreement, he promises to perform "in a workmanlike manner and to exercise reasonable care." Gilley v. Farmer, 207 Kan. 536, 542, 485 P.2d 1284, 1289 (1971).

11. Rodin v. Merritt, 48 N.C.App. 64, 268 S.E.2d 539 (1980), review denied 301 N.C. 402, 274 S.E.2d 226 (1980).

12. Burke v. Campbell, 258 Mass. 153, 154 N.E. 759 (1927); Guthing v. Lynn, 109 Eng.Rep. 1130 (K.B.1831).

13. Bissenger v. Prince, 117 Ala. 480, 23 So. 67 (1898); Peoples Drug Stores v. Fenton Realty Corp., 191 Md. 489, 62 A.2d 273 (1948).

14. E.g., Wright v. Mark C. Smith & Sons, 283 So.2d 85 (La.1973); Klimek v. Perisich, 231 Or. 71, 371 P.2d 956 (1962); 1 Corbin § 100; 1 Williston § 42.

requirements of a product from, the other contracting party.[15] The Uniform Commercial Code explicitly validates such agreements.[16]

There are also situations where the courts are in disagreement as to whether a gap should be filled. For example, in employment contracts, if no duration term is provided either expressly or by implication, a majority of the courts have refused to fill the gap and have held that the hiring is at will (either party may terminate at will) even if the parties have set the compensation at a specified sum per month, day or year.[17] However, an appropriate evidentiary showing of surrounding circumstances may change the result.[18] In addition, some courts have held that an agreement for a specified sum per day, month or year gives rise to a contract for such period in the absence of evidence to the contrary.[19] Under either view it is of course possible for the parties by use of appropriate language to bind themselves to an employment contract for a definite number of days, months or years.[20] Under either view, if a hiring for a specified term is found, performance after the term expires usually gives rise to an inference that the parties have renewed their agreement for the same duration.[21] There is a similar division in cases involving the duration of a franchise agreement that is silent on the point of duration. This facet of the problem will be

---

15. See § 4–13 infra; 1 Corbin § 100.

16. U.C.C. § 2–306(1); see § 4–13 infra.

17. Boatright v. Steinite Radio Corp., 46 F.2d 385 (10th Cir.1931); Elliott v. Delta Air Lines, Inc., 116 Ga.App. 36, 156 S.E.2d 656 (1967); Feola v. Valmont Industries, 208 Neb. 527, 304 N.W.2d 377 (1981); Parker v. Borock, 5 N.Y.2d 156, 182 N.Y.S. 2d 577, 156 N.E.2d 297 (1959); Watson v. Gugino, 204 N.Y. 535, 98 N.E. 18 (1912); Bihlmaier v. Carson, 603 P.2d 790 (Utah 1979); Plaskitt v. Black Diamond Trailer Co., 209 Va. 460, 164 S.E.2d 645 (1968); but see Elizaga v. Kaiser Foundation Hosp., Inc., 259 Or. 542, 487 P.2d 870 (1971) (recovery on misrepresentation theory). "[A] contract which is terminable upon the occurrence of an event is not terminable at will." Consolidated Laboratories, Inc. v. Shandon Scientific Co., 413 F.2d 208 (7th Cir.1969). Although a contract is terminable at will, an employee who is discharged without fault on his part has been held entitled to a proportionate share of a promised bonus according to time spent. Sinnett v. Hie Food Prod., Inc., 185 Neb. 221, 174 N.W.2d 720 (1970). In many countries of the world, except for strictly seasonal labor, employees are entitled to job security. Unless they are dismissed for cause, they are entitled to a statutory period of notice and severance pay. See, e.g., 2 H.

Blake, Business Regulation in the Common Market Nations 437 (1969).

18. In re Estate of Miller, 90 N.J. 210, 447 A.2d 549 (1982); Weiner v. McGraw-Hill, Inc., 57 N.Y.2d 458, 457 N.Y.S.2d 193, 443 N.E.2d 441 (1982); Providence v. Board of Regents for Education, 112 R.I. 288, 308 A.2d 788 (1973); but see Wexler v. Newsweek, Inc., 109 A.D.2d 714, 487 N.Y.S.2d 330 (1st Dep't 1985).

19. Dennis v. Thermoid Co., 128 N.J.L. 303, 25 A.2d 886 (1942); accord Restatement, Second, Contracts § 32, ill. 6.

20. Eales v. Tanana Valley Medical-Surgical, 663 P.2d 958 (Alaska 1983).

21. Steed v. Busby, 268 Ark. 1, 593 S.W.2d 34 (1980); Steranko v. Inforex, Inc., 5 Mass.App.Ct. 253, 362 N.E.2d 222 (1977), appeal after remand 8 Mass.App.Ct. 523, 395 N.E.2d 1303 (1979); Cinefot Int'l Corp. v. Hudson Photographic Indus., 13 N.Y.2d 249, 246 N.Y.S.2d 395, 196 N.E.2d 54 (1963); Restatement, Second, Contracts § 33 ill. 6. There are statutes, however, which do not permit the inference of a continued contractual relationship even in the face of an automatic renewal provision unless notice is given by the dominant party to the subservient party. See, e.g., McKinney's N.Y. Gen'l Obl.Law § 5–903.

discussed below.[22] In other situations where the agreement is silent as to duration most courts will decide that a reasonable time is intended.[23]

Although it is not strictly relevant to the topic under discussion, a few words should be said about some other problems that arise in employment contracts. One of the problems arises when the parties agree that employment shall be "permanent." In the case of an agreement for "permanent employment" the majority of courts have held that, in the absence on contrary indication, a hiring at will results.[24] Most courts have felt that by use of this term all that is meant is that the employment is foreseen as steady rather than seasonal or for a particular project. According to the minority view the employee is entitled to work so long as he is able to do the work properly and the employer continues in the business in which the employee was hired.[25] If this is the express or implied agreement of the parties, there is no problem.[26]

Even under the majority view, if a consideration over and above the consideration supplied by the employee's services or promises of services is exchanged for the promise of permanent employment, some courts have indicated that the hiring will not then be considered to be at will.[27] This approach gropes toward a fair result but confuses the questions of indefiniteness and consideration. It is possible to reach just results without confusing issues so diverse. Terms such as "permanent employment" have no immutable meaning. When used in different concrete situations by different individuals different meanings may fairly be attached to the term. If the employee has paid in money or in some other way for the promise of "permanent employment", it is likely that both parties understood that employment was to endure as long as the employee is able to perform the work for which he is hired or at least until retirement age. The payment of a consideration is an evidentiary factor bearing on the proper interpretation of the parties'

---

22. See § 4–12(4) infra.

23. Compare Smith v. Smith, 375 So.2d 1138 (Fla.App.1979) with Schultz v. Atkins, 97 Idaho 770, 554 P.2d 948 (1976) and Haines v. New York, 41 N.Y.2d 769, 396 N.Y.S.2d 155, 364 N.E.2d 820 (1977) and East Coast Corp. v. Alderman-250 Corp., 30 N.C.App. 598, 228 S.E.2d 72 (1976). There are still cases concluding that an agreement that is silent as to duration is at will even in non-employment cases. 1 Corbin § 96.

24. Benson Co–op Creamery Ass'n v. First Dist. Ass'n, 276 Minn. 520, 151 N.W.2d 422, 35 A.L.R. 1417 (1967); Skagerberg v. Blandin Paper Co., 197 Minn. 291, 266 N.W. 872 (1936); Mau v. Omaha Nat'l Bank, 207 Neb. 308, 299 N.W.2d 147 (1980); Arentz v. Morse Dry Dock & Repair Co., 249 N.Y. 439, 164 N.E. 342 (1928); Roberts v. Wake Forest Univ., 55 N.C.App. 430, 286 S.E.2d 120 (1982),

review denied 305 N.C. 586, 292 S.E.2d 571 (1982).

25. 1 Williston § 39.

26. Stauter v. Walnut Grove Prods., 188 N.W.2d 305 (Iowa 1971); Toussaint v. Blue Cross & Blue Shield, 408 Mich. 579, 292 N.W.2d 880 (1980); Parker v. United Airlines, Inc., 32 Wn.App. 722, 649 P.2d 181 (1982); but see Fleming v. Mack Trucks, Inc., 508 F.Supp. 917 (E.D.Pa.1981).

27. Bixby v. Wilson & Co., 196 F.Supp. 889 (D.Iowa 1961); United Sec. Life Ins. Co. v. Gregory, 281 Ala. 264, 201 So.2d 853 (1967); Collins v. Parsons College, 203 N.W.2d 594, Annot., 60 A.L.R.3d 218 (Iowa 1973); Burkhimer v. Gealy, 39 N.C.App. 450, 250 S.E.2d 678 (1979), certiorari denied 297 N.C. 298, 254 S.E.2d 918 (1979); Humphrey v. Hill, 55 N.C.App. 359, 285 S.E.2d 293 (1982); see 1 Corbin § 96; 1A Corbin § 152; 3A Corbin § 684.

intention. It follows that other evidentiary factors can perform the same function. In each case all of the circumstances are to be considered. It may be shown that the parties meant or did not mean something definite. The presence or absence of an additional consideration should not be conclusive on this score. Unfortunately, however, the courts have tended to deal with the question mechanically, as if a *stare decisis* could provide the method by which the intention of the parties could be determined.

The same dichotomy exists in the case of a promise of lifetime employment. Some cases hold that such a promise amounts to a hiring at will unless there are other factors such as an additional consideration being given.[28] But others take the position that the term should be accepted as written.[29] Despite the reluctance of the courts to take the terms "permanent" or "lifetime" literally, there are cases where a perpetual obligation to pay money has been upheld.[30] In the absence of an express agreement, however, the courts are reluctant to find that an obligation in perpetuity exists.[31]

Another point to be made concerning employment contracts relates to the rule that such agreement are ordinarily terminable at will. The orthodox rule as to agreements terminable at will (or even upon reasonable notice) has been that the agreement may be terminated "for good cause, for no cause or even for a cause morally wrong." [32] The traditional reason given for this harsh rule is that it would not be good policy to keep the parties locked in the close relationship of employer-

---

28. Page v. Carolina Coach Co., 667 F.2d 1156 (4th Cir.1982); McDole v. Duquesne Brewing Co., 281 Pa.Super. 78, 421 A.2d 1155 (1980); Smith v. Beloit Corp., 40 Wis.2d 550, 162 N.W.2d 585 (1968); Forrer v. Sears, Roebuck & Co., 36 Wis.2d 388, 153 N.W.2d 587 (1967).

29. Roberts v. Southern Wood Piedmont Co., 571 F.2d 276 (5th Cir.1978); Arentz v. Morse Dry Dock & Repair Co., 249 N.Y. 439, 164 N.E. 342 (1928).

30. Payroll Express Corp. v. Aetna Casualty and Sur. Co., 659 F.2d 285 (2d Cir. 1981); Warner-Lambert Pharmaceutical Co. v. John J. Reynolds, Inc., 178 F.Supp. 655 (S.D.N.Y.1959), affirmed 280 F.2d 197 (2d Cir.1960); Holmgren v. Utah-Idaho Sugar Co., 582 P.2d 856 (Utah 1978).

31. Haines v. New York, 41 N.Y.2d 769, 396 N.Y.S.2d 155, 364 N.E.2d 820 (1977); 1 Williston § 38; Barton v. State, 104 Idaho 338, 659 P.2d 92 (1983). See also Baum Assocs. v. Society Brand Hat Co., 477 F.2d 255 (8th Cir.1973); Martocci v. Greater New York Brewery, Inc., 301 N.Y. 57, 92 N.E.2d 887 (1950), motion denied 301 N.Y. 662, 93 N.E.2d 926 (1950); City of Gastonia v. Duke Power Co., 19 N.C.App. 315, 199 S.E.2d 27 (1973), certiorari denied 284 N.C. 252, 200 S.E.2d 652 (1973). Compare

Southern Bell Tel. & Tel. Co. v. Florida East Coast Ry., 399 F.2d 854 (5th Cir.1968) (an agreement in 1917 for free passage of telephone lines over railroad property was held not perpetual but terminable on reasonable notice) with City of Gainesville v. Board of Control, 81 So.2d 514 (Fla.1955) (an agreement by the City to provide free water to the University of Florida was held non-terminable so long as the University remained in Gainesville on the ground that the promise of free water had induced the University to locate in Gainesville).

32. Payne v. Western & A.R. Co., 81 Tenn. 507, 519–20 (1884), overruled on other grounds Hutton v. Watters, 132 Tenn. 527, 179 S.W. 134 (1915); Kilbride v. Dushkin Publishing Group, Inc., 186 Conn. 718, 443 A.2d 922 (1982); accord Brockmeyer v. Dun & Bradstreet, 113 Wis.2d 561, 335 N.W.2d 834 (1983). See De Giuseppe, The Effect of the Employment-At-Will Rule on Employee's Rights to Job Security and Fringe Benefits, 10 Fordham Urban L.J. 1 (1981); Comment, Employment at Will and The Law of Contracts, 23 Buffalo L.Rev. 211 (1973); Comment, Implied Contract Rights to Job Security, 26 Stan.L.Rev. 335 (1974).

employee when one of the parties wishes to terminate it,[33] but this rule is being overturned in many jurisdictions in cases where the discharge is viewed as contrary to public policy.[34]

Federal legislation prohibits dismissal of employees because of union activity,[35] on grounds of racial discrimination,[36] or because of age.[37] Recently it has been held that a worker whose hiring is at will cannot be discharged in retaliation for his filing of a worker's compensation claim.[38] It has also been held that the manager of a consumer credit department whose employment was at will could not be discharged because he wished to adhere to the dictates of consumer protection legislation.[39] So, also, it has been held that a tenancy at will cannot be terminated in retaliation for the tenant's exercise of his rights to complain to the authorities about building violations.[40] The same rule applies if an employee is discharged solely to avoid paying pension benefits under ERISA.[41]

A New Hampshire [42] case has radically pushed the doctrine of these cases a giant step forward, holding that the firing of a female worker because she resisted the sexual advances of her foreman was wrongful, stating:

> "We hold that a termination by the employer of a contract of employment at will which is motivated by bad faith or malice or based on retaliation is not in the best interest of the economic

33. Blades, Employment at Will v. Individual Freedom; On Limiting the Abusive Exercise of Employer Power, 67 Colum.L. Rev. 1404 (1967); Summers, Individual Protection Against Unjust Dismissal, Time for a Statute, 62 Va.L.Rev. 481 (1976); Note, Individual Rights for Organized and Unorganized Employees under the National Labor Relations Act, 58 Tex.L.Rev. 991, 994 (1980).

34. Perks v. Firestone Tire & Rubber Co., 611 F.2d 1363 (3d Cir.1979); Palmateer v. International Harvester Co., 85 Ill.2d 124, 52 Ill.Dec. 13, 421 N.E.2d 876 (1981), appeal after remand 140 Ill.App.3d 857, 95 Ill.Dec. 253, 489 N.E.2d 474 (1986); Pierce v. Ortho Pharmaceutical Corp., 84 N.J. 58, 417 A.2d 505 (1980). To the effect that such a significant change should be made by the legislature, see Murphy v. American Home Products, 58 N.Y.2d 293, 461 N.Y.S.2d 232, 448 N.E.2d 86 (1983).

35. 29 U.S.C.A. § 158(a)(3).

36. 42 U.S.C.A. § 2000(e)–(e)(2).

37. 29 U.S.C.A. §§ 621–34.

38. Frampton v. Central Indiana Gas Co., 260 Ind. 249, 297 N.E.2d 425, Annot. 63 A.L.R.3d 973 (1973); Shanholtz v. Monongahela Power Co., 165 W.Va. 305, 270 S.E.2d 178 (1980); accord, Petermann v. Teamsters Local 396, 174 Cal.App.2d 184,

344 P.2d 25 (1959) (employee fired because he refused to commit perjury). Contra, Christy v. Petrus, 365 Mo. 1187, 295 S.W.2d 122 (1956); cf. Martinez v. Behring's Bearings Serv., 501 F.2d 104 (5th Cir.1974).

39. Harless v. First Nat'l Bank in Fairmont, 162 W.Va. 116, 246 S.E.2d 270 (1978). See De Guiseppe, The Effect of the Employment-at-Will Rule on Employee Rights to Job Security and Fringe Benefits, 10 Fordham Urban L.J. 1 (1981).

40. Robinson v. Diamond Housing Corp., 463 F.2d 853 (D.C.Cir.1972), noted in 18 Vill.L.R. 1119 (1973); Note, The Use of the Federal Remedy to Bar Retaliatory Eviction, 39 U.Cin.L.Rev. 712 (1970).

41. Moore v. Home Ins. Co., 601 F.2d 1072 (9th Cir.1979). New Jersey has a retaliatory discrimination statute in favor of employees. N.J.Stat.Ann. 34–15–39.1.

42. Monge v. Beebe Rubber Co., 114 N.H. 130, 316 A.2d 549, 551, Annot., 62 A.L.R.3d 264, 268 (1974), noted in 43 Fordham L.Rev. 300 (1974) and 8 Ga.L.Rev. 996 (1974); accord Siles v. Travenol Laboratories, 13 Mass.App.Ct. 354, 433 N.E.2d 103 (1982), review denied 386 Mass. 1103, 440 N.E.2d 1176 (1982); see Blades, supra note 33.

system or the public good and constitutes a breach of the employment contract ∗ ∗ ∗. Such a rule affords the employee a certain stability of employment and does not interfere with the employer's normal exercise of his right to discharge, which is necessary to permit him to operate his business efficiently and profitably."

There are a number of cases in accord with these new approaches,[43] but others have declined to follow this new lead.[44]

(3) Where the Parties Agree to Agree

The traditional rule is that an agreement to agree as to a material term does not result in a binding contract.[45] Two reasons are given. First, such an agreement leaves a material term too vague and indefinite to be enforced.[46] It also may show a lack of present agreement.[47] Thus, an agreement to agree is equated for indefinite purposes with a case where the parties purport to agree upon a term and leave it indefinite. But an agreement to agree must be distinguished from a situation where the parties agree to use reasonable efforts to reach agreement for in such a case there is a duty to negotiate in good faith and failure to do so results in a breach.[48] In such a case there may still be a question of what, if any, remedy is available.[49]

Some of the more modern cases (even without relying on the Uniform Commercial Code and the Restatement Second to be discussed below) have recognized that agreements to agree serve a valuable commercial purpose and that the traditional rule may operate unfairly

---

43. Jackson v. Minidoka Irrigation District, 98 Idaho 330, 563 P.2d 54 (1977). The cases are collected in Daniel v. Magma Copper Co., 127 Ariz. 320, 620 P.2d 699 (App.1980).

44. Green v. Amerada-Hess Corp., 612 F.2d 212 (5th Cir.1980), rehearing denied 614 F.2d 1298 (1980); Loucks v. Star City Glass Co., 551 F.2d 745 (7th Cir.1977); Hinrichs v. Tranquilaire Hospital, 352 So. 2d 1130 (Ala.1977); Amaan v. Eureka, 615 S.W.2d 414 (Mo.1981), certiorari denied 454 U.S. 1084, 102 S.Ct. 642, 70 L.Ed.2d 619 (1981); Bottijliso v. Hutchison Fruit Co., 96 N.M. 789, 635 P.2d 992 (App.1981). It has also been held that the doctrine of prima facie tort should not be applied in this type of case. Cartwright v. Golub Corp., 51 A.D.2d 407, 381 N.Y.S.2d 901 (1976); but see Ivy v. Army Times Publishing Co., 428 A.2d 831 (D.C.App.1981); Parnar v. Americana Hotels, Inc., 65 Hawaii 370, 652 P.2d 625 (1982).

45. Joseph Martin, Jr., Delicatessen v. Schumacher, 52 N.Y.2d 105, 436 N.Y.S.2d 247, 417 N.E.2d 541 (1981); Gregory v. Perdue, Inc., 47 N.C.App. 655, 267 S.E.2d 584 (1980). This rule is criticized in Macneil, Contracts: Adjustment of Long-Term

Economic Relations Under Classical, Neoclassical, and Relational Contract Law, 72 Nw.U.L.Rev. 854 (1978).

46. Willowood Condominium Ass'n, Inc. v. HNC Realty Co., 531 F.2d 1249 (5th Cir. 1976); Transamerica Equip. Leasing Corp. v. Union Bank, 426 F.2d 273 (9th Cir.1970); Western Airlines, Inc. v. Lathrop Co., 499 P.2d 1013 (Alaska 1972); Burgess v. Rodom, 121 Cal.App.2d 71, 262 P.2d 335 (1953); Weil & Associates v. Urban Renewal Agency, 206 Kan. 684, 479 P.2d 875 (1971); Willmott v. Giarraputo, 5 N.Y.2d 250, 184 N.Y.S.2d 97, 157 N.E.2d 282 (1959); Sun Printing & Publishing Ass'n v. Remington Paper & Power Co., 235 N.Y. 338, 139 N.E. 470 (1923); Deadwood Lodge No. 508 v. Albert, 319 N.W.2d 823 (S.D.1982). Annot., 68 A.L.R.2d 1221 (1959).

47. Restatement, Contracts § 33, Comment C.

48. Itek Corp. v. Chicago Aerial Indus., 248 A.2d 625 (Del.1968), on remand 257 A.2d 232 (Del.Super.1969). See Knapp, Enforcing the Contract to Bargain, 44 N.Y. U.L.Rev. 673 (1969).

49. See the discussion below.

where a party uses the rule to defeat an agreement that the parties intended to be binding.[50]

A good illustration of the modern cases is an option in an existing lease that permits the tenant to extend the lease at a rental fee to be agreed upon at the time of the exercise of the option. Some cases still follow the older view that the agreement to agree prevents the exercise of the option.[51] But, as a recent case stated, "The better view, however, would hold that such a clause intends renewal at a 'reasonable' rent and would find that market conditions are ascertainable with sufficient certainty to make the clause specifically enforceable."[52] The case argues that the result coincides with the true intention of the parties and with fairness because the lessee has already paid for the option and so should not be denied the benefit of his bargain on a technicality.

The case discussed above might be regarded as only a small departure from the traditional rule. If so, let us examine a case that takes a giant step away from the traditional rule.[53] Plaintiff entered into an arrangement with defendant whereby he obtained an option to buy a piece of real property for the sum of $23,500 "on payments and terms to be negotiated provided the same is exercised by June 1, 1968." On May 15, plaintiff sought to exercise the option. He offered to pay $5300 in cash and to assume two mortgages in the combined amount of $18,200. The court found as a fact that defendant refused to negotiate because he changed his mind about selling. The court stated that plaintiff was free to suggest a method of payment, that the parties were obliged to negotiate in good faith, and that defendant breached this duty. The court concluded that plaintiff's proposal would satisfy a reasonable man (in any event he also offered to pay the entire $23,500 in cash) and therefore a Court of Equity could do what equity and good conscience requires, decree specific performance based upon the offer of the plaintiff. It is obvious that here the court constructs a duty requiring the parties to negotiate in good faith even though there is no such provision in the contract.[54]

The Restatement Second[55] and the Uniform Commercial Code[56] are in accord with the modern view on this question of agreements to agree. The Uniform Commercial Code expresses the modern philosophy as follows: "This article rejects * * * the formula that an

50. Opdyke Inv. Co. v. Norris Grain Co., 413 Mich. 354, 320 N.W.2d 836 (1982); Vigano v. Wylain, Inc., 633 F.2d 522 (8th Cir.1980) (citing text); see also 1 Corbin § 29 and Macneil, A Primer of Contract Planning, 48 S.Cal.L.Rev. 627, 662 (1975).

51. Walker v. Keith, 382 S.W.2d 198 (Ky.1964).

52. Moolenaar v. Co-Build Co., 354 F.Supp. 980, 982 (D.V.I.1973); accord Joseph Martin, Jr., Delicatessen, Inc. v. Schumacher, 70 A.D.2d 1, 419 N.Y.S.2d 558 (1979), order reversed 52 N.Y.2d 105, 436 N.Y.S.2d 247, 417 N.E.2d 541 (1981); Playmate Club, Inc., v. Country Clubs, Inc., 62 Tenn.App. 383, 462 S.W.2d 890, Annot., 58 A.L.R.3d 494 (1970).

53. Kier v. Condrack, 25 Utah 2d 139, 478 P.2d 327 (1970).

54. See note 48 supra. See also Yackey v. Pacifica Development Co., 99 Cal.App.3d 776, 160 Cal.Rptr. 430 (1979).

55. Restatement, Second, Contracts § 33, ill. 8.

56. U.C.C. §§ 2–305(1)(b), 2–204(3).

agreement to agree is unenforceable * * * and rejects also defeating such agreements on the ground of 'indefiniteness'." Instead this article recognizes the dominant intention of the parties to have the deal continue to be binding upon both.[57]

(b) The Uniform Commercial Code

The provisions of the Uniform Commercial Code relating to indefiniteness are of two types. There are provisions relating to specific problems. Some of these have already been discussed, for example the provision relating to open price terms.[58] There is also an important general provision that has not been mentioned as yet. Before covering this general provision, however, let us discuss another specific provision.

The problem governed by this specific provision is illustrated by the facts in Wilhelm Lubrication Co. v. Brattrud.[59] The seller agreed to sell and the buyer agreed to buy five thousand gallons of "Worthmore Motor Oil SAE 10–70." The term "SAE 10–70" designates seven weights of oil. In this agreement the price for each weight was definite. Three weeks after the agreement was made and before any specifications were submitted, the buyer repudiated the agreement. The court held that the agreement was too vague and indefinite to be enforceable because the contract was indefinite as to the assortment. There were many cases in accord which had held that, unless the assortment is specified, the agreement was too vague and indefinite to be enforceable and perhaps an equal number of cases which had held that agreement was sufficiently definite.[60] The latter cases ordinarily assessed damages upon the alternative least onerous to the defendant.[61]

Subsection 1 of Section 2–311 of the Code resolves this problem by providing that, "despite the fact that the agreement leaves particulars of performance to be specified by one of the parties," there is a contract. Under subsection 3 the contract would be breached if the buyer fails to specify the assortment or if the seller refuses to permit him to specify the assortment. Although subsection 2 says that the specifications relating to the assortment of goods are at the buyer's option, it does not mean that the buyer is free to specify or not specify as he chooses, but rather he has both the right and obligation.[62] The problem of indefiniteness is solved by requiring the specification to be made in "good faith and within limits set by commercial reasonableness." [63]

The general provision of the Uniform Commercial Code is most important because it is designed to prevent, where it is at all possible, a

57. U.C.C. § 2–305, Comment 1.

58. U.C.C. § 2–305 discussed above.

59. 197 Minn. 626, 268 N.W. 634 (1936) noted in 37 Colum.L.Rev. 309 (1937).

60. The cases are collected in Annots., 106 A.L.R. 1284 (1937), 105 A.L.R. 1100 (1936) and are commented upon in 11 Temp.L.Q. 250 (1936).

61. Restatement, Contracts § 344; 5 Williston § 1407. The Code sections relating to remedies and damages as they apply to this type of case are discussed in 23 U.Chi.L.Rev. 499 (1956).

62. See U.C.C. § 2–322, Comments 1, 2.

63. Id. § 2–311(1).

contracting party who is dissatisfied with his bargain from taking refuge in the doctrine to renounce his agreement.[64] Section 2–204(3) of the Code states the guiding principle to be:

> "Even though one or more terms are left open a contract for sale does not fail for indefiniteness if the parties have intended to make a contract and there is a reasonably certain basis for giving an appropriate remedy."

Before the section is satisfied the parties must intend to contract and indefiniteness as to material terms does not prevent this intent from existing.[65] However, in the language of a recent case, "when a dispute over material terms manifests a lack of intention to contract, no contract results." [66]

But even if there is an intent to contract there may still be a question of indefiniteness. The section changes the traditional common law rules in all three types of cases discussed above. Under the Code, contrary to common law, a gap-filler is available even though the parties agreed to agree or purported to agree upon a term that was left indefinite. But the section goes beyond gap-fillers and permits a court to use any reasonably certain basis for giving an appropriate remedy. When such a basis exists must be decided on a case-by-case approach. In this respect Comment 3 points out:

> "The test is not certainty as to what the parties were to do nor as to the exact amount of damages due the plaintiff. Nor is the fact that one or more terms are left to be agreed upon enough of itself to defeat an otherwise adequate agreement. Rather, commercial standards on the point of 'indefiniteness' are intended to be applied, this act making provision elsewhere for missing terms needed for performance, open price, remedies and the like."

What is clear is that the omission of an important term or terms does not necessarily prevent a contract from arising.[67] What is not clear is when a court will find that "there is a reasonably certain basis for giving an appropriate remedy." The type of approach envisaged is

---

64. Restatement, Second, Contracts § 33 Comment b. See, e.g., Kearns v. Andree, 107 Conn. 181, 139 A. 695, Annot., 59 A.L.R. 599 (1928); Fairmount Glass Works v. Grunden–Martin Woodenware Co., 106 Ky. 659, 51 S.W. 196 (1899); Scammel v. Ouston, [1941] 1 All E.R. 14 (1940); Foley v. Classique Coaches, Ltd. [1934] 2 K.B. 2 (C.A.).

65. Pennsylvania Co. v. Wilmington Trust Co., 39 Del.Ch. 453, 166 A.2d 726 (1960). U.C.C. § 2–204, Comment 3 on this point states: "The more terms the parties leave open, the less likely it is that they have intended to conclude a binding agreement, but their actions may be frequently conclusive on the matter despite omissions."

66. Kleinschmidt Div. of SCM Corp. v. Futuronics Corp., 41 N.Y.2d 972, 975, 395 N.Y.S.2d 151, 152, 363 N.E.2d 701, 702 (1977).

67. It is interesting to note that Professor Williston wished to limit the section to "minor" omissions. Williston, The Law of Sales in The Proposed Uniform Commercial Code, 63 Harv.L.Rev. 561 (1950). His recommendation was rejected. See Pennsylvania Co. v. Wilmington Trust Co., 39 Del.Ch. 453, 166 A.2d 726 (1960).

the type employed in the Kier and Itek cases mentioned above.[68]　It will take many years before it becomes clear how this provision will be implemented, but it certainly offers an artful court wide scope in employing its ingenuity.　The question of whether there is a reasonably certain basis for giving an appropriate remedy is one of law while the question of whether the parties intended to contract will ordinarily be one of fact.

The Restatement Second is in accord with the Code.[69]　The Restatement Second also considers questions of detrimental reliance in this context but we will defer this topic for later consideration.[70]　The Restatement Second does not discuss the question of severability that may arise because of indefiniteness.　In other words, if part of an agreement is indefinite and part of it is not, should the part that is indefinite be disregarded and the remainder enforced?　The test seems to be whether the parties would have entered into the agreement without the offending clauses.[71]

WESTLAW REFERENCES

di(indefiniteness /s contract)

to(95) /p indefiniteness

contract /s term /s agreement /s uncertain

contract /s indefiniteness /s term

vague! /s agreement /s enforc!

"material term" /s "reasonably certain"

agreement /s indefiniteness /s void!

contract /s indefinite! /s quantity

contract /s "material term" /s price "material term"

"reasonabl! certain!" /s "material term"

"obligation of the party" /s contract agreement

silent silence /s "material term"

(a) *The Common Law*

　　(1) *Where the Parties Have Purported to Agree Upon a Material Term But Have Left it Indefinite*

"material term" /s indefinite!

(quasi +1 contractual contract) "material term" indefinite! /s "subsequent conduct"

indefiniteness /s agree! /s cure* curing

indefiniteness /s "reasonabl! certain!"

agreement contract /s "fatal! indefinite!"

evidence /s agreement contract /s ambigu! /s writing wr*te written

---

68. These two cases are cited in note 48 and note 53 supra.

69. Restatement, Second, Contracts §§ 33, 34; Firstul Mortgage Co. v. Osko, 604 P.2d 150 (Okl.App.1979).

70. Restatement, Second, Contracts § 34, Comment d.　See ch. 6 infra.

71. See, e.g., Eckles v. Sharman, 548 F.2d 905 (10th Cir.1977); Wilhelm Lubrication Co. v. Brattrud, 197 Minn. 626, 268 N.W. 634, Annot., 106 A.L.R. 1279 (1936).

evidence /s agreement contract /s ambigu! /s term

agreement contract /s certain! /s ''specific performance''

(2) *Where the Parties are Silent as to a Material Term*

implication implied! imply! /s ''surrounding circumstance'' /s term

term /s imply! implied! implication /s course +2 dealing
   performance

''gap filler'' /s term

term /s imply! implied! implication /s intend! intent! /s party

''reasonable price'' /s contract agree!

contractor /s ''reasonable value''

real +1 property estate /s ''reasonable price''

deliver! /s ''reasonable time''

''reasonable price'' /s market

''output contract'' /s quantity

''customary price'' /s labor

employ**** /s cause fault /s ''terminable at will''

''employment contract'' /s duration

255k20

discharg! /s entitl! /s ''terminable at will''

employ**** /s duration /s ''reasonable time''

expir! /s employ**** /s ''specified term''

duration /s silen! /s ''reasonable time''

''hiring at will'' ''reasonable time'' /s ''permanent employment''

''permanent employment'' /s perform! compensat!

obligat! /2 perpetu!

contract agreement /s indefinite! /s duration /s intend! intent!

''employment contract'' /s ''terminable at will''

''agreement terminable at will''

''reasonable notice'' /s termina! /s perpetu!

union compensation /s retaliat! /s employ**** /s discharg!

employ**** /s racial! race /s dismiss! discharg! /s discriminat!

ci(29 +4 158)

employ**** /s perjur! /s dismiss! discharg! fire fired

employ**** /s retaliat! /s discriminat!

breach! /s employ**** /s ''bad faith'' malic! /s terminat!
   discharg! dismiss!

(3) *Where the Parties Agree to Agree*

''joseph martin'' +s schumacher

''material term'' /s vague!

lack! void! /s ''present agreement''

walker +s keith

future /s lease /s exten! /s option /s agree!

''reasonable rent'' /s renew!

find 478 p2d 327

2–305

(b) *The Uniform Commercial Code*

''uniform commercial code'' /s indefinite!

wilhelm +s brattrud

"uniform commercial code" /s open /s term

"uniform commercial code" /s intend! intent! +4 contract

"commercial standard" /s indefinite!

"uniform commercial code" /s "reasonably certain basis"

contract /s indefinite! /s sever severed severing severable

---

§ 2–10. Unilateral, Bilateral and Reverse Unilateral Contracts and Some of Their Implications

If A says to B, "If you walk across the Brooklyn Bridge I will pay you $10," A has made an offer looking to a unilateral contract.[72] B cannot accept this offer by promising to walk the bridge.[73] He must accept, if at all, by performing the act.[74] Since no promise is requested of him, at no point is he bound to perform.[75] If he performs there is a contract involving two parties, but the contract is classified as unilateral because only one party is ever under an obligation.

If A says to B, "If you promise to walk across the Brooklyn Bridge I will pay you $10," he makes an offer looking to a bilateral contract.[76] If B makes the promise both parties are bound, which is to say that there is a contract.[77] A contract would also arise if B made an implied promise. B's promise could be inferred if he started to walk the bridge in A's presence. If B started to walk the bridge but not in A's presence, there would be no implied promise because the requisite communication would be lacking.[78] Thus the rule is that in the case of an offer looking to a bilateral contract there can be no contract unless B makes the requested promise either expressly or by implication. All of these conclusions are premised on the notion that the offeror is "the master of his offer" and is thus free to indicate in what manner he wants the offeree to assent.[79] There is perhaps one exception to this last statement. If the offeree actually performs the act he was requested to promise to perform, there is some authority to the effect that a contract is formed if the performance is completed while the offer is still open [80]

---

72. See § 1–10 supra.

73. Suhre v. Busch, 343 Mo. 170, 120 S.W.2d 47 (1938); Restatement, Second, Contracts § 59, ill. 2; Simpson, Contracts 46 (2d ed. 1965) [hereinafter cited as Simpson].

74. Becker v. Missouri Dep't of Social Services, 689 F.2d 763 (8th Cir.1982); United Steel Works v. United States Steel Corp., 492 F.Supp. 1 (N.D.Ohio 1980).

75. This matter is discussed in greater detail in § 2–22 infra.

76. Bleecher v. Conte, 29 Cal.3d 345, 173 Cal.Rptr. 278, 626 P.2d 1051 (1981). See § 1–10 supra.

77. Judd Realty, Inc. v. Tedesco, ___ R.I. ___, 400 A.2d 952 (1979).

78. Note, Contracts: Unilateral or Bilateral: Notice, 10 Cornell L.Q. 220 (1924); see Allied Steel & Conveyors, Inc. v. Ford Motor Co., 277 F.2d 907 (6th Cir.1960); United States ex rel. Worthington Pump & Mach. Co. v. John A. Johnson Contracting Corp., 139 F.2d 274 (3d Cir.1943), certiorari denied 321 U.S. 797, 64 S.Ct. 937, 88 L.Ed. 1085 (1944); Vermillion v. Marvel Merchandising Co., 314 Ky. 196, 234 S.W.2d 673 (1950).

79. Wormser, The True Conception of Unilateral Contracts, 26 Yale L.J. 136 (1916).

80. Restatement, Contracts § 63; 1 Williston § 78A.

and the requisite notice of performance is given.[81] However, this rule violates the theory that the offeror is master of his offer.[82]

At times it is easy to decide whether an offer looks to a unilateral or a bilateral contract, but at other times the manifestations are ambiguous. In such a case the original Restatement espoused the traditional common law rule that it would be presumed that the offer looked to a bilateral contract.[83] The reason for this presumption is that an offeror wants the security of promise that binds the offeree. At times an offer may be phrased so as expressly to permit an acceptance either by the making of a promise or by the doing of an act.[84]

In a reverse unilateral contract, the promise is made by the offeree. In the usual unilateral contract the promise is made by the offeror.[85] However, this is not always true. If A, a house owner, pays $500 to an insurance company asking for company's promise to pay A $100,000 if A's house is destroyed by fire, A is the offeror but he has made no promise. Rather he has requested a promise from B, the offeree. Thus, when B makes the promise there is a reverse unilateral contract.[86]

Another preliminary question of some importance is the question of what is the act called for in a unilateral contract. For example, in the case involving the insurance company above, if the facts were changed so that the insurance company is the offeror, the act called for would be the payment of the premium. That is, the payment of the premium would create the unilateral contract, but the owner could not recover unless there was a fire. The occurrence of the fire is a condition precedent to the insurance company's obligation to pay. This distinction between an act necessary to the formation of a contract and an act or event that must occur before the performance of a contractual duty

---

81. On the question of notice see § 2–15 infra. This exception, based on the thought that performance is as desirable as a promise, has been eliminated in the Second Restatement. But under the new approach of the Second Restatement, the need for this exception has been eliminated. Reporter's Note to Restatement, Second, Contracts § 63. This matter is discussed in § 2–15 infra. See also Braucher, Offer and Acceptance in the Second Restatement, 74 Yale L.J. 302, 307 (1964); Goble, Is Performance Always as Desirable as a Promise to Perform?, 22 Ill.L.Rev. 789 (1928); Williston, Reply, 22 Ill.L.Rev. 791 (1928); cf. Crook v. Cowan, 64 N.C. 743 (1870).

82. Note, Acceptance by Performance When the Offeror Demands a Promise, 52 S.Cal.L.Rev. 1917 (1979).

83. Restatement, Contracts § 31; see Craddock v. Greenhut Constr. Co., 423 F.2d

111 (5th Cir.1970); Davis v. Jacoby, 1 Cal. 2d 370, 34 P.2d 1026 (1934); Motel Services, Inc. v. Central Maine Power Co., 394 A.2d 786 (Me.1978).

84. Ever-Tite Roofing Corp. v. Green, 83 So.2d 449 (La.App.1955); Koppers Co. v. Kaiser Aluminum & Chem. Corp., 9 N.C. App. 118, 175 S.E.2d 761 (1970); 49 Iowa L.Rev. 960 (1964); cf. Lazarus v. American Motors Corp., 21 Wis.2d 76, 123 N.W.2d 548 (1963).

85. See § 2–5 supra.

86. Restatement, Second, Contracts § 55, ill. 1; 1 Corbin § 71; 1 Williston § 24A; see also Goble, The Non-Promissory Offer, 48 Nw.U.L.Rev. 590 (1953); Goble, Is an Offer a Promise?, 22 Ill.L.Rev. 567 (1928); Green, Is an Offer Always a Promise?, 23 Ill.L.Rev. 301 (1928); Stoljar, The Ambiguity of Promise, 47 Nw.U.L.Rev. 1 (1952).

is due will be of importance in a number of matters to be discussed hereafter.[87]

The importance of the distinction between an offer looking to a unilateral and a bilateral contract has been diminished by the Uniform Commercial [88] Code and the Restatement Second.[89] This will be discussed below.[90]

WESTLAW REFERENCES

unilateral /s obligat! /s agree! contract

"bilateral contract"

to(95) /p unilateral

to(95) /p bilateral

bilateral /s "implied promise"

"bilateral contract" /s bind binding bound /s promis!

"bilateral contract" /s communicat!

"bilateral contract" /s infer!

"master of his offer"

contract agree! /s unilateral /s communicat!

bilateral /s accept! /s perform! /s promis!

unilateral /s bilateral /s offer!

"reverse unilateral"

"unilateral contract" /s act

D. ACCEPTANCE

Table of Sections

87. See § 2–15 infra.

88. U.C.C. § 2–206.

89. Restatement, Second, Contracts § 32.

90. See § 2–26 infra.

§ 2–11.   Introduction

We have seen that an offer creates a power of acceptance in the offeree. This power of acceptance permits the offeree to transform the offer into a contractual obligation.[91] Thus, an acceptance has been defined as "a voluntary act of the offeree whereby he exercises the power conferred upon him by the offer and thereby creates the set of legal relations called a contract."[92] The acceptance of the offer terminates the power of revocation that the offeror ordinarily has.[93]

 WESTLAW REFERENCES
di accept!

define* definition defining +2   accept! /s   contract agree!

terminat! /s   accept! /s   revok! revoc!

offeree /s   reasonable +1   person man

§ 2–12.   Must the Offeree Know of the Offer and, if so, When?

As a general proposition no contract can be formed unless the offeree knew of the offer at the time of the alleged acceptance.[94] Anglo-American law generally requires that before a person can recover on a promise he must exchange his own performance or promise for the promise he seeks to enforce.[95] In the case of a bilateral contract, however, the general rule may come into conflict with the objective theory of contracts and, if so, the objective theory prevails. Thus, in the case of a bilateral contract it is possible that an offeree may be bound by an acceptance even if he does not know of the offer. A far-fetched illustration will make the point. A sends an offer to B by mail looking to a bilateral contract. When B receives the letter, without opening it and without suspecting that it is an offer, he decides to confuse A by sending a letter which states "I accept." Here, because A as a reasonable man would conclude that B accepted, under the objec-

91. See § 2–5 supra.

92. Corbin, Offer and Acceptance, and Some of the Resulting Legal Relations, 26 Yale L.J. 169, 199–200 (1917), reprinted and revised in Selected Readings 170, 193 (1931) (footnote omitted); accord Cinciarelli v. Carter, 662 F.2d 73 (D.C.Cir.1981).

93. See § 2–20 infra.

94. 1 Corbin § 59; 1 Williston § 33.

95. For further development of the importance of the exchange requirement, see ch. 4 infra.

tive theory of contracts, there is an acceptance (and therefore a contract) although B did not know of the offer.[96]

The situation is quite different if the offer looks to a unilateral contract. In the case above, if the offer were to a unilateral contract and B performed the act called for, he could not recover from A because he did not know of the offer and this result would follow even if he did the act called for in the presence of A. Although B's performance in the presence of A may be considered to be a promise, under the traditional rule relating to unilateral contracts, the promise is a nullity because no promise was requested.[97] There is not even a possibility of justifiable reliance on the part of A because he could not justifiably rely upon a promise that was neither requested nor expected and that was a nullity. Thus, in this case B may not recover. The same result obtains where an offer of reward has been made to the public. In such a case a person who has performed the act called for has no contractual claim[98] against the offeror unless he knows of the offer.[99]

The principle that an offeree must know of the offer also gives rise to the rule that identical cross-offers do not create a contract. For example, if A sends an offer through the mail to B offering to sell a certain item at a certain price and in ignorance of this offer B mails an offer to buy the same item at the same price, it has been held that no contract results.[1] The Restatement Second attempts a partial fictionalized subversion of this rule when it asserts that the two offerors could assent in advance to cross-offers and suggests that such assent may be inferred when both parties think a contract has been made.[2] It would be better to say that identical cross-offers constitute a contract despite the objective theory because there is subjective assent to the same deal and objective evidence of that subjective intent.[3] The Restatement Second takes precisely that approach in the case of a similar problem discussed in the same section that discusses cross-offers.[4]

96. Restatement, Second, Contracts § 23, Comment b. See § 2–2 supra.

97. See § 2–10 supra.

98. In some states an offer for a reward made by a public agency is deemed to create a non-contractual liability toward a person performing the desired act. Sullivan v. Phillips, 178 Ind. 164, 98 N.E. 868 (1912); Smith v. State, 38 Nev. 477, 151 P. 512 (1915); Choice v. Dallas, 210 S.W. 753 (Tex.Civ.App.1919). In these jurisdictions knowledge of the offer is not a prerequisite to recovery.

99. Glover v. Jewish War Veterans, 68 A.2d 233 (D.C.1949); Fitch v. Snedaker, 38 N.Y. 248, 97 Am.Dec. 791 (1868); Broadnax v. Ledbetter, 100 Tex. 375, 99 S.W. 1111 (1907). Contra Russell v. Stewart, 44 Vt. 170 (1872). See Annot., 86 A.L.R.3d 1142 (1978).

1. Tinn v. Hoffman & Co., 29 L.T.R. (n.s.) 271 (Ex.1873).

2. Restatement, Second, Contracts § 23, Comment d., ill. 5; cf. Morris Asinof & Sons, Inc. v. Freudenthal, 195 A.D. 79, 186 N.Y.S. 383 (1921), affirmed 233 N.Y. 564, 135 N.E. 919 (1922); Perillo, Book Review, 37 Fordham L.Rev. 144, 148–49 (1968).

3. See Litvinoff, Offer and Acceptance in Louisiana Law: A Comparative Analysis: Part II Acceptance, 28 La.L.Rev. 153, 201 (1968).

4. See Restatement, Second, Contracts § 23, Comment d, ill. 6. The illustration is based upon the case of Mactier's Adm'rs v. Frith, 6 Wend. (N.Y.) 102, 21 Am.Dec. 262 (1830). This problem is discussed in § 2–23, infra.

At what point in time must the offeree know of the offer? Suppose, for example, that A offers a reward of $100 to anyone who finds and returns his lost watch and B finds the watch, learns of the reward and returns it to A, is B entitled to the money? A number of authorities have concluded that B may not recover because B did not know of the offer when he started to perform.[5] This is obviously based upon the notion that to satisfy the rule relating to knowledge of the offer the knowledge must occur before the performance begins. As stated by the First Restatement, "the whole consideration requested by an offer must be given after the offeree knows of the offer."[6] The more modern view is that it is sufficient that he completes performance with knowledge of the offer.[7] The theory of the second view is that it should be enough that the offer induces the completion of performance because this is the "common understanding" of the parties.[8]

The discussion immediately above relates to unilateral contracts. As stated above, an acceptance of an offer looking to a bilateral contract can be effective under the objective theory of contracts even if the offeree did not know of the offer. In such a case the promise of the offeree creates the contract and thus when the offeree starts to perform is not usually relevant on the issue of acceptance.[9]

WESTLAW REFERENCES

95k18

accept! /s offeree /s know! knew

promis! /s exchang! /s perform! /s recover!

"cross offer!" /s contract agree!

340k1/2

§ 2–13. Must the Offeree Intend to Accept? When?

In order to accept the offeree must not only know of the offer but he must also intend to accept.[10] Again, as above, it is quite clear that a bilateral contract is formed when the offeree makes the requested promissory acceptance even if the offeree did not intend to accept, because under the prevailing objective theory the offeree will be held to what appeared from his expression to be his intention unless the offeror knows or has reason to know that the offeree did not intend to accept.[11]

When the offer looks to a unilateral contract, the question is more complicated. If A says to B, "I will pay you $10 if you walk across the Brooklyn Bridge" and B walks, is there necessarily an intent to accept? It is readily apparent that B may have walked in order to collect the

---

5. Restatement, Contracts § 53; Fitch v. Snedaker, 38 N.Y. 248, 97 Am.Dec. 791 (1868).

6. Restatement, Contracts § 53.

7. Restatement, Second, Contracts § 51.

8. Restatement, Second, Contracts § 51, Comment b; accord 1 Corbin § 60. See also Annot., 86 A.L.R.3d 1142 (1978).

9. Restatement, Second, Contracts § 51, Comment a; see also Restatement, Contracts § 53, Comment a.

10. 1 Williston §§ 66, 67.

11. Nationwide Resources Corp. v. Massabni, 134 Ariz. 557, 658 P.2d 210 (1982); see §§ 2–2, 2–12 supra.

$10, or to gain exercise or from a combination of these two motives or even for other reasons. Thus, in the case of unilateral contract, the performance of the requested act is an ambiguous manifestation on the issue of intent to accept. Consequently, the traditional view is that evidence of the offeree's subjective intention to accept or not to accept is relevant and admissible.[12] Thus, if he testifies that he intended to accept and is believed, he will prevail. If the offeree proves that he performed for many reasons, one of which was to receive the $10., again he will prevail.[13] It is enough that the offer was some part of the reason for the offeree's performance.[14] Some cases have indicated the contrary.[15] A realistic reading of these cases, mostly involving offers of rewards, may indicate that they diverge from the normal view because courts seem in reward cases, more than in others, to emphasize the ethical position of the particular claimant and the public policy considerations involved in the reward situations. In many of these cases it was concluded that the act of acceptance was not voluntarily performed.[16]

A more modern view is that the offeree may not testify to his subjective intention. The Restatement Second, instead of allowing the offeree to testify to his subjective intention, takes the position that intent to accept is presumed in the absence of words or conduct indicating the contrary. The theory is that inquiry into the motives of the offeree is ordinarily unnecessary.[17] Since the intent to accept is only assumed, if the offeree manifests an intent not to accept before the offeror performs his promise, the disclaimer is effective and renders the promise of the offeror inoperative from the beginning.[18]

Presumably the question of when the necessary intent must be formulated will follow the same lines as indicated in the previous section.

 WESTLAW REFERENCES

    offeree /s intend! intent! +3 accept!

    reynolds +s "eagle pencil"

    motiv! /s offer! /s reward

    340k7

    motiv! /s offeree

---

12. The relevance of subjective intention in this situation is based on the traditional view that subjective intention is relevant when a manifestation is ambiguous. See § 3–10 infra.

13. 1 Corbin § 58.

14. Simmons v. United States, 308 F.2d 160 (4th Cir.1962); Industrial America, Inc. v. Fulton Indus., 285 A.2d 412 (Del.Supr. 1971); Restatement, Contracts § 55, Comment b.

15. Reynolds v. Eagle Pencil Co., 285 N.Y. 448, 35 N.E.2d 35 (1941), reversing 260 A.D. 482, 23 N.Y.S.2d 101 (1940); Vitty

v. Eley, 51 A.D. 44, 64 N.Y.S. 397 (1900); The Crown v. Clarke, 40 C.L.R. 227 (Austl. 1927), 1 Austl.L.J. 287 (1928).

16. Sheldon v. George, 132 App.Div. 470, 116 N.Y.S. 969 (1909).

17. Restatement, Second, Contracts § 53, Comment c. Industrial America, Inc. v. Fulton Indus., 285 A.2d 412 (Del.Supr. 1971); see also Braucher, Offer and Acceptance in Second Restatement, 74 Yale L.J. 302, 308 (1964).

18. Restatement, Second, Contracts § 53(3) & Comment c.

§ 2–14. Who May Accept the Offer?

Because the offeror is master of his offer he controls the person or persons in whom a power of acceptance is created.[19] In other words, an offer may be accepted only by the offeree or the offerees to whom it is made.[20] Since the power of acceptance is personal to the offeree it follows that the offeree may not transfer his *power* of acceptance to another.[21] If the offeree accepts the offer so that a contract is created he may thereafter have a right to transfer his rights under the contract. This question is discussed below.[22] The point made here is that, if A makes an offer to B, C may not accept. So, also, if A makes an offer jointly to B and C, B or C alone may not accept.[23]

Ordinarily the identity of the offerees will be determined by the reasonable man test.[24] Thus, it has been determined that a reward offer may ordinarily be accepted by anyone who knows of the offer, but once the offer has been accepted no one else may accept.[25] On the other hand, an offer to pay a sum of money to anyone who uses a certain medicine and contracts influenza may be accepted by any who knows of the offer and by any number of persons.[26] Although in both cases the offer is made to the public, a reasonable man would reach different conclusions as to how many times it can be accepted.

None of the cases discussed above are particularly difficult but there are more complicated situations. For example, if A individually is doing business under the trade name of "Acme Supply Co." and B sends in an order (offer) to "Acme Supply Co." and C, who buys out A including the name, fills the order, is there a contract? The question to be answered is whether C as a reasonable man would conclude that B manifested an intention to make the offer to "Acme Supply Co." irrespective of the ownership of the establishment or that B manifested an intention to make the offer to "Acme" only so long as A was the proprietor. This could be a difficult question and in making the determination all admissible evidence should be considered. The question may be one of fact.[27] If it is concluded that the offer was not made to C, the question of a quasi-contractual recovery would have to be addressed.[28] Even if the offer was not made to C but he delivered the

19. 1 Corbin § 56.

20. Boulton v. Jones, 157 Eng.Rep. 232 (Ex.1857); see Daru v. Martin, 89 Ariz. 373, 363 P.2d 61 (1961); Apostolic Revival Tabernacle v. Charles J. Febel, Inc., 131 Ill. App. 579, 266 N.E.2d 545 (1970); Trimount Bituminous Products Co. v. Chittenden Trust Co., 117 N.H. 946, 379 A.2d 1266 (1977); Wagner, How and by Whom May an Offer Be Accepted?, 11 Vill.L.Rev. 95, 95–96 (1965).

21. Restatement, Second, Contracts § 52.

22. See ch. 18 infra.

23. Meister v. Arden–Mayfair, Inc., 276 Or. 517, 555 P.2d 923 (1976).

24. Restatement, Second, Contracts § 29.

25. 1 Williston §§ 32, 33A. It has been argued that if no one person performs the requested act but a number of persons do, the reward should be divided among them even though they were not acting in concert. 1 Corbin § 64; 34 Mich.L.Rev. 854 (1936).

26. Carlill v. Carbolic Smoke Ball Co., [1893] 1 Q.B. 256 (C.A.1892).

27. See ch. 3 infra. The fact pattern is based in part upon the case of Boulton v. Jones, 157 Eng.Rep. 232 (Ex.1857).

28. See Michigan Cent. R.R. Co. v. State, 85 Ind.App. 557, 155 N.E. 50 (1927);

goods and disclosed that he was the new owner there would be a contract if B accepted the goods. This would be so because C made an offer which B accepted.[29]

In most cases the offeree is also the promisee. But this is not necessarily so. Thus, if A makes a promise to pay B $10 if C walks across Brooklyn Bridge, B is the promisee but C is the offeree and, for B to obtain the money, C, and C alone, must walk the bridge.[30]

 WESTLAW REFERENCES
offeree /s "power of acceptance"
carlill +s "carbolic smoke"

§ 2–15. Must the Offeree Give Notice of Acceptance of an Offer to a Unilateral Contract?

When an offer to a unilateral contract is made the offeror has requested not words, but deeds. Consequently it is well settled that the offeree need not give notice that he is going to perform,[31] but another question is whether the offeree must give notice that he has performed.[32] A reason why notice should be required is so that the offeror will know that the act requested is done and thus not enter into a contract with another with respect to the same matter. On the other hand, if the offeror is in a position to learn of performance, it can be argued that notice should not be required. The two Restatements, in an effort to balance these two propositions, take the position that a contract arises at least upon performance, but if the offeree has reason to know that the offeror has no adequate means of learning of the performance with reasonable promptness and certitude, the duty of the offeror is discharged unless the offeree exercises reasonable diligence to notify the offeror or the offeror otherwise learns of performance within a reasonable time or the offer expressly or by implication indicates that notification is not necessary.[33] There is a second view that is the same as above except that, if notice is required, no contract is consummated unless and until notice of performance has been communicated.[34]

An illustration will help explain the difference between the two views. A makes an offer looking to a unilateral contract on November 1, the act of acceptance occurs on November 2, a revocation takes place

Parker v. Dantzler Foundry & Mach. Works, 118 Miss. 126, 79 So. 82 (1918). There are also related questions of agency, Kelly Asphalt Block Co. v. Barber Asphalt Paving Co., 211 N.Y. 68, 105 N.E. 88 (1914), and possible questions of mistake. See 3 Corbin § 601.

29. Orcutt v. Nelson, 67 Mass. (1 Gray) 536 (1854).

30. Restatement, Second, Contracts § 52, Comment b & ill. 3.

31. Carlill v. Carbolic Smoke Ball Co., [1893] 1 Q.B. 256 (C.A.1892).

32. See generally 1 Williston §§ 69–69AA; Calhoun, Acceptance of Offer for Unilateral Contract—Necessity of Notice to Offeror, 4 U.Cin.L.Rev. 57 (1930); Campbell, The Notice Due to a Guarantor, 35 Mich.L.Rev. 529 (1936); Dole, Notice Requirements of Guaranty Contracts, 62 Mich.L.Rev. 57 (1963).

33. Restatement, Contracts § 56; Restatement, Second, Contracts § 54.

34. Kresge Dep't Stores, Inc. v. Young, 37 A.2d 448 (D.C.Mun.App.1944).

on November 3, and the notice of performance is sent on November 4. According to the second view there would be no contract because the revocation occurred prior to the act of acceptance.[35] According to the two Restatements the revocation would not be effective because the acceptance had already occurred and so there would be a contract. However, the contract would be discharged if notice is necessary and not given unless otherwise received or dispensed with. Thus notice, if necessary, is a condition precedent to the obligation of the defendant to perform.

Under both views one is faced with the question of under what circumstances does the offeree have "reason to know that the offeror has no adequate means of learning of performance with reasonable promptness and certitude." The Restatement indicates that it is an exceptional case in which the offeror does not have means of ascertaining what has occurred.[36] The cases have carried this a step beyond by saying that the offeror has a duty of inquiry unless inquiry is not reasonably feasible and places the burden of proof on the offeror to show that inquiry is not reasonably feasible.[37] But the Restatement does give an illustration of a case where it believes that the offeror sustains this burden. It is a case where the offeror is a guarantor and a friend in another country makes the requested loan to the guarantor's brother.[38] The fact that the situation involves a guaranty appears to be important.[39]

There is also a third view on this question of whether notice of performance must be given that at least has the merit of simplicity. Under this view notice is not required unless requested by the offeror.[40]

 WESTLAW REFERENCES

unilateral /s contract /s aris! /s perform!

"condition precedent" /s notice notif! /s perform! /s obligat!

bishop +s eaton /p offer! guarant!

---

§ 2–16. Acceptance of an Offer Looking to a Series of Contracts

The preceding discussion has been confined to offers looking to a single unilateral or bilateral contract. An offer may instead look to the formation of a series of contracts, unilateral or bilateral. For example, A on Jan. 1 writes to B: "In consideration of your advancing moneys

35. As the illustration is worded the possibility of the offer becoming irrevocable by virtue of the beginning of performance does not arise. See § 2–24 infra.

36. Restatement, Contracts § 56, Comment a.

37. Ross v. Leberman, 298 Pa. 574, 148 A. 858 (1930).

38. Restatement, Second, Contracts § 54, ill. 5. The illustration is based on

the case of Bishop v. Eaton, 161 Mass. 496, 37 N.E. 665 (1894).

39. Restatement, Second, Contracts § 54, Comment d.

40. Midland Nat'l Bank v. Security Elevator Co., 161 Minn. 30, 200 N.W. 851 (1924); City Nat'l Bank of Poughkeepsie v. Phelps, 86 N.Y. 484 (1881). This is described as the minority view in Dole, supra note 32 at 64.

from time to time over the next twelve calendar months, up to a total of $5,000, to X, at X's request, at your option, I hereby undertake to make good any losses you may sustain in consequence." [41] In reliance upon the letter, B lends $1,000 to X on February 1, another $1,000 on March 1. A revokes the offer on March 15 and B makes an additional loan of $1,000 on April 1. A has made an offer looking to a series of unilateral contracts. The advance made on Feb. 1 gave rise to one unilateral contract and the advance on March 1 gave rise to a second unilateral contract.[42] The offer continues into the future but is effectively revoked and thus the alleged third acceptance is ineffective because of the earlier effective revocation. In other words, the offer continued prospectively but, as in the case of offers generally, could be revoked prior to the next acceptance.[43]

Not only are there offers looking to a series of unilateral contracts, there are also offers looking to a series of bilateral contracts. If A offers B stated quantities of certain goods as B may order from time to time during the next year at a fixed price, A has made an offer looking to a series of bilateral contracts. The series is bilateral because each time B places an order he impliedly promises to pay.[44] As above, each time an order is placed one bilateral contract arises but as to the future the offer remains revocable.

Care must be taken to distinguish an offer looking to a series of contracts from an offer that looks to one acceptance with a number of performances.[45] If A offers to sell B between 4000 to 6000 tons of a specified type of coal, deliveries to be made in equal monthly installments during the months of May, June, July and August, the acceptance to specify the quantity the offer looks to one bilateral contract which will arise when B accepts and specifies the quantity. However, there will be four performances under the contract.[46]

Whether an offer looks to one contract or a series of contracts is a question of interpretation to be decided in the same manner as any question of interpretation—that is to say under the reasonable man test as modified below.[47] For example, A, a newspaper, requests B to discontinue publication of a rival newspaper and promises to pay B $1000.00 per week as long as B abstains from such publication so long as A remains in the publishing business. It is conceivable that this

41. The illustration is based upon the facts of Offord v. Davies, 142 Eng.Rep. 1336 (C.P.1862).

42. Restatement, Contracts § 30; Restatement, Second, Contracts § 31 Comments a, b. Offers to guarantee the credit of another are usually held to look to a series of contracts are at times are referred to as "continuing guaranties." Walter E. Heller & Co. v. Aetna Bus. Credit, Inc., 158 Ga.App. 249, 280 S.E.2d 144 (1981).

43. Restatement, Contracts § 44; Restatement, Second, Contracts § 47.

44. Great Northern Ry. v. Withan, L.R., 9 C.P. 16 (1873); Strang v. Witkowski, 138 Conn. 94, 82 A.2d 624 (1951); 1 Corbin § 65.

45. Hollidge v. Gussow, Kahn & Co., 67 F.2d 459 (1st Cir.1933).

46. Chicago and Great E. Ry. v. Dane, 43 N.Y. 240 (1870); Restatement, Second, Contracts § 31, ill. 2.

47. See § 2–2 supra and chapter 3 infra.

offer could be looked upon as an offer looking to a series of unilateral contracts. However, the court held that what was involved was an offer looking to one unilateral contract with a series of performances under that one unilateral contract.[48] In other words, the contract arose with the discontinuance of publication but B would not become entitled to $1000 until he had not published for a week. Thus not publishing for a week is a condition precedent to A's obligation to pay. Thus far it would seem that there is little practical difference between an offer looking to a series of unilateral contracts and an offer looking to one unilateral contract with a number of performances under it. But it would make a great difference if A wished to revoke his offer prospectively. He could do so if the offer looked to a series of unilateral contracts but not where there was only one unilateral contract with a series of performances.

Where there is an offer looking to series of unilateral contracts and it is assumed that notice of performance is required under one or more of the rules stated above,[49] there is authority that one notification may be sufficient even though there are multiple acceptances.[50]

WESTLAW REFERENCES

series /s "unilateral contract"

revoc! revok! /s accept! /s "continuing guarant!"

series /s "bilateral contract"

series /s contract /s perform! /s installment

§ 2–17. The Necessity of Communicating Acceptance of an Offer to a Bilateral Contract

Under the common law a unilateral contract arises upon performance.[51] But in the case of a bilateral contract, the general rule is that the offeree's promise must be communicated to the offeror or to his agent.[52] Clearly the offeree, as a reasonable man, should understand that the offeror expects to know that the offeree has made the requested return promise so that he may guide his conduct accordingly.[53] Whether it is actually necessary for the communication to come to the offeror's attention is a matter to be discussed below.[54]

Since the offeror is the master of his offer he may dispense with communication if he so desires. In a recurring situation A, an agent for B Corporation, presents C with a document that states the terms of a bilateral arrangement but adds that a contract will arise when approved by an executive officer of B Corporation. C signs the docu-

48. American Publishing & Engraving Co. v. Walker, 87 Mo.App. 503 (1901); Restatement, Second, Contracts § 31, ill. 3, § 47, ill. 3, § 54, ill. 3.

49. See § 2–15 supra.

50. Restatement, Second, Contracts § 31, Comment b, § 54, Comment d.

51. See § 2–10 supra.

52. Zamore v. Whitten, 395 A.2d 435 (Me.1978); Ardente v. Horan, 117 R.I. 254, 366 A.2d 162 (1976).

53. 1 Corbin § 67; 1 Williston § 70; see A & J Trounstine & Co. v. Sellers, 35 Kan. 447, 11 P. 441 (1886).

54. See § 2–23 infra.

ment setting forth the deal at the place indicated. How should the problem be analyzed? B Corporation has not made an offer because it has not committed itself to anything since it states that approval by an executive offer will be its commitment. Although B Corp. has not made an offer, C does when he signs the document. C's offer includes the term relating to approval by an executive officer. Thus we have an offer by C looking to a bilateral contract. Some cases have held that this offer is accepted by B corporation when it indicates its assent even though the assent is not communicated.[55] The theory is that the language used (a contract will arise when approved by an executive officer of B Company) dispenses with the necessity for communication.[56]

Even if this reasoning is accepted it would appear reasonable to imply that notice of acceptance should be required by analogy to the rules established by the Restatement for giving notice of performance in the case of a unilateral contract.[57] Such notice would not be necessary for the formation of the contract but the failure to give notice would discharge the obligation of the offeror and could amount to a breach of the contract.[58]

In the fact pattern discussed above it is interesting to analyze some of the advantages and disadvantages to the corporation in doing business in such a fashion. One advantage is that such a form prevents an agent from exceeding his authority.[59] A disadvantage is that the customer is free to withdraw the offer at any time until there is an acceptance by an executive officer.[60]

In other cases involving the same basic pattern, except that communication of the acceptance was necessary, the Corporation wrote back stating that you may be assured of our very best attention to your order or similar language. The question is whether such language in context amounts to language of acceptance. The cases appear to be in conflict.[61]

 WESTLAW REFERENCES

offeree /s reasonable +1 man person
95k22(3)
requir! necess! /s communicat! /s accept! /s contract
offer! /s promis! /s communicat! /s contract
bilateral /s communicat! /s contract

55. Meekins-Bamman Prestress, Inc. v. Better Constr., Inc., 408 So.2d 1071 (Fla. App.1982); Pacific Photocopy, Inc. v. Canon U.S.A., Inc., 57 Or.App. 752, 646 P.2d 647 (1982), review denied 293 Or. 635, 652 P.2d 810 (1982).

56. International Filter Co. v. Conroe Gin, Ice & Light Co., 277 S.W. 631 (Tex. Com.App.1925).

57. See § 2–15 supra.

58. See Restatement, Second, Contracts § 56, ill. 1; compare Neal-Cooper Grain Co. v. Texas Gulf Sulphur Co., 508 F.2d 283

(7th Cir.1974) with Venters v. Stewart, 261 S.W.2d 444 (Ky.1953).

59. See Carl Wagner and Sons v. Appendagez, Inc., 485 F.Supp. 762 (S.D.N.Y. 1980).

60. West Penn Power Co. v. Bethlehem Steel Corp., 236 Pa.Super. 413, 348 A.2d 144 (1975).

61. Compare Hill's, Inc. v. William B. Kessler, Inc., 41 Wn.2d 42, 246 P.2d 1099 (1952) with Courtney Shoe Co. v. E.W. Curd & Son, 142 Ky. 219, 134 S.W. 146 (1911).

343k23(3) /p communicat!

assent! /s communicat! /s contract

"language of acceptance"

contract /s notice notif! /s perform /s discharg! /s obligat!

---

§ 2–18. Acceptance by Silence—Implied in Fact Contracts

The question here is whether silence may amount to a promise. Although it is conceivable that an offer may be made by silence most of the cases have involved the question of acceptance by silence. Silence ordinarily does not give rise to an acceptance of an offer or a counter offer.[62] But there are cases where this general rule has not been applied. The issue to be resolved is whether the relationship of the parties and the fact pattern justify the offeror's expectation of a reply.[63] When such expectation is justified the offeror may reasonably conclude that silence is acceptance.[64] The same notion is expressed in a different way when it is stated that there is a duty to speak when silence "would be deceptive and beguiling."[65] Thus, the question of acceptance by silence comes down to an issue of whether the offeree has a duty to speak.[66] It is obvious that a text of this size cannot explore all or even many of the cases that may arise.[67] But we shall continue with a discussion of the cases that commonly occur.

If A makes an unsolicited offer to B by mail and states, "If I do not hear from you by next Tuesday, I shall assume you accept", every one agrees that B need not reply because it would be unfair to impose such a duty. Thus, it has been said that "a party cannot by the wording of his offer turn the absence of a communication into an acceptance and compel the recipient of his offer to remain silent at his peril"[68] But

---

62. Restatement, Second, Contracts § 69, Comment a; accord Beech Aircraft Corp. v. Flexible Tubing Corp., 270 F.Supp. 548 (D.Conn.1967); Thomson v. United States, 357 F.2d 683 (Ct.Cl.1966); Cincinnati Equip. Co. v. Big Muddy River Consol. Coal Co., 158 Ky. 247, 164 S.W. 794 (1914); Bowen v. McCarthy, 85 Mich. 26, 48 N.W. 155 (1891); Albrecht Chem. Co. v. Anderson Trading Corp., 298 N.Y. 437, 84 N.E.2d 625 (1949); More v. New York Bowery Fire Ins. Co., 130 N.Y. 537, 29 N.E. 757 (1892); Royal Ins. Co. v. Beatty, 119 Pa. 6, 12 A. 607 (1888); J.C. Durick Ins. v. Andrus, 139 Vt. 150, 424 A.2d 249 (1980). However, as indicated below, silence is acceptance when there is a duty to speak. Brooks Towers Corp. v. Hunkin-Conkey Constr. Co., 454 F.2d 1203 (10th Cir.1972); see Helen Whiting, Inc. v. Trojan Textile Co., 307 N.Y. 360, 121 N.E.2d 367 (1954). See generally Comment, When Silence Gives Consent, 29 Yale L.J. 441 (1920); Laufer, Acceptance by Silence: A Critique, 7 Duke B.A.J. 87 (1939).

63. R.A. Berjian, D.O., Inc. v. Ohio Bell Tel. Co., 54 Ohio St.2d 147, 375 N.E.2d 410 (1978); Anderson Chevrolet/Olds, Inc. v. Higgins, 57 N.C.App. 650, 292 S.E.2d 159 (1982).

64. John J. Brennan Constr. Co. v. Shelton, 187 Conn. 695, 448 A.2d 180 (1982).

65. Brennan v. National Equitable Inv. Co., 247 N.Y. 486, 490, 160 N.E. 924, 925 (1928); accord Brooks Towers Corp. v. Hunkin-Conkey Constr. Co., 454 F.2d 1203 (10th Cir.1972).

66. Garcia v. Middle Rio Grande Conservancy Dist., 99 N.M. 802, 664 P.2d 1000 (App.1983); Chorba v. Davlisa Enterprises, Inc., 303 Pa.Super. 497, 450 A.2d 36 (1982).

67. See Comment, When Silence Gives Consent, 29 Yale L.J. 441 (1920); Laufer, Acceptance by Silence: A Critique, 7 Duke B.A.J. 87 (1939).

68. Clark, Contracts §§ 31, 32; accord William F. Klingensmith, Inc. v. District of Columbia, 370 A.2d 1341 (D.C.1977); J.C.

from the fact that B has no duty to reply it does not follow that B may not accept. Certainly he may accept by communication of an acceptance and there are cases holding that this is the only way in which he may accept.[69] This limitation is clearly incorrect because the offeror has authorized the offeree to accept by remaining silent.[70] The Restatement rejects this limitation and takes the position that since the offeree's silence is ambiguous (his silence may indicate an intent to accept or the contrary) his subjective intent in remaining silent is relevant and admissible and a contract exists if he intended to accept.[71] The case is analogous to the problem of intent to accept in the case of an offer looking to a unilateral contract. In that situation the First Restatement permitted the offeree to testify as to subjective intent.[72] Since the offeror is responsible for the existence of the ambiguity created by silence he may not complain that he did not conclude that the silence constituted acceptance.[73]

To be distinguished are cases where the parties have mutually agreed that silence will manifest assent. For example, A says to B, "I offer to sell you my black horse for $200. B replies, "If you do not hear from me by next Tuesday you may assume I accept." A agrees. Here by the agreement of both parties B has a duty to speak and if he does not he is bound in accordance with his agreement.[74]

A duty to speak may also arise by virtue of a prior course of dealing.[75] If A (offeror) on a number of occasions has without request sent goods to B who has always kept the goods and paid for them without protest and A makes an additional shipment of similar goods and B retains the goods for a long period of time without complaint, has B accepted A's offer by his retention of the goods in light of the prior course of dealing?[76] B's silence is concededly ambiguous. The question to be decided is whether B should be permitted to testify as to his subjective intent or whether the case should be decided under the tentative objective test stated earlier. The Restatement Second explicitly takes the position that B may not testify as to his subjective intention[77] and thus the issue to be decided is whether A as a reasona-

---

Durick Ins. v. Andrus, 139 Vt. 150, 424 A.2d 249 (1980). The same is true if the offeror says, "I shall conclude you accept if you watch the Giant game on television this Sunday."

69. Prescott v. Jones, 69 N.H. 305, 41 A. 352 (1898); Felthouse v. Bindley, 142 Eng. Rep. 1037 (C.P.1862).

70. Restatement, Contracts § 72(1)(b).

71. Restatement, Contracts § 72(1)(b); Restatement, Second, Contracts § 69(1)(b).

72. See § 2–13 supra.

73. Cavanaugh v. D.W. Ranlet Co., 229 Mass. 366, 118 N.E. 650 (1918).

74. Attorney Grievance Comm'n v. McIntire, 286 Md. 87, 405 A.2d 273 (1979); Freinuth v. Glen Falls Ins. Co., 50 Wn.2d

621, 314 P.2d 468 (1957). "The offeree may authorize the offeror to regard silence as an acceptance of his offer." 1 Williston § 91C.

75. William F. Klingensmith, Inc. v. District of Columbia, 370 A.2d 1341 (D.C.1977); 1 Corbin § 75.

76. These are the facts of Hobbs v. Massasoit Whip Co., 158 Mass. 194, 33 N.E. 495 (1893). The same principle is involved in Krauss Bros. Lumber Co. v. Bossert, 62 F.2d 1004 (2d Cir.1933); Ballard v. Tingue Mill, Inc., 128 F.Supp. 683 (D.Conn.1954); Holt v. Swenson, 252 Minn. 510, 90 N.W.2d 724 (1958).

77. Restatement, Second, Contracts § 69(1)(c), Comment d. The original Restatement appears to be in accord.

ble man would conclude that B's silence under the circumstances amounted to an acceptance.[78] This is undoubtedly a jury question.[79] It is important to note that the ambiguity here is the fault of B, the offeree, and so he is not permitted to testify to his subjective intent. Whereas in the case that introduced this section the ambiguity was the fault of the offeror and thus the offeree was permitted to testify as to his subjective intent.

A similar problem arises when A, through a salesman, has frequently solicited orders from B, the contract to arise when approved by A at A's home office. As we have seen in this situation B is the offeror and A the offeree.[80] A has always shipped the goods to B without prior notification and has billed them after shipment. A's salesman solicits and receives another order from B and A remains silent for a period of time.[81] As above, and for the same reasons, A is not permitted to testify to his subjective intention and so again, as above, the tentative objective test would be applied on the issue of whether the offeror (B) would conclude that A's silence indicated assent. Again the issue is basically one of fact.[82]

Under the explanation of the Restatement in the case above there is true assent and so there is a contract even if B does not change his position in reliance on A's silence, for example, by refraining from buying elsewhere. Some cases have indicated that B should recover only if there was reliance followed by a change of position—a theory of estoppel.[83] There are occasional cases which seem to place the entire doctrine of acceptance by silence upon an estoppel theory.[84] But even these cases are talking about silence as being misleading rather than the necessity for reliance and change of position.[85]

Similar problems arise in connection with solicitation by insurance agents. As one court has stated: "It is the general rule that mere delay in passing upon an application for insurance is not sufficient in and of itself to amount to acceptance even though the premium is retained. * * * But an acceptance may be implied from retention of

---

78. The original Restatement made this question turn upon the subjective understanding of the offeror. Restatement, Contracts § 72(1)(c).

79. See, e.g., William F. Klingensmith, Inc. v. District of Columbia, 370 A.2d 1341 (D.C.1977); Terminal Grain Corp. v. Rozell, 272 N.W.2d 800 (S.D.1978).

80. See § 2–17 supra.

81. This is a recurring fact pattern. See, e.g., Ammons v. Wilson & Co., 176 Miss. 645, 170 So. 227 (1936); Ercanbrach v. Crandall-Walker Motor Co., 550 P.2d 723 (Utah 1976); Hendrickson v. International Harvester Co., 100 Vt. 161, 135 A. 702 (1927).

82. Again, the first Restatement made this question turn upon the subjective understanding of the offeror. See note 78 and accompanying text supra.

83. See, e.g., Cole-McIntyre-Norfleet Co. v. Holloway, 141 Tenn. 679, 214 S.W. 817 (1919); Hills, Inc. v. William B. Kessler, Inc., 41 Wn.2d 42, 246 P.2d 1099 (1952).

84. See, e.g., Tanenbaum Textile Co. v. Schlanger, 287 N.Y. 400, 404, 40 N.E.2d 225, 227 (1942) (dictum).

85. Comment, When Silence Gives Consent, 29 Yale L.J. 441 (1920); Laufer, Acceptance by Silence: A Critique, 7 Duke B.A.J. 87 (1939). The same can be true when the insured silently retains renewal policies. Bohn Mfg. Co. v. Sawyer, 169 Mass. 477, 48 N.E. 620 (1897).

the premium and failure to reject within a reasonable time * * *. Having accepted and retained the premium paid upon an application solicited by its agent, the company was bound to act with reasonable promptitude." [86] It is significant to observe that the acceptance here is not predicated upon a course of dealing.

Another, and more common, instance of acceptance by silence arises where the offeree takes offered services with reasonable opportunity to reject them and with reason to believe that they are offered with expectation of compensation.[87] The words "opportunity to reject" imply that there is a duty to speak. The duty arises because it is impossible to return services that have been accepted. That duty does not arise, however, unless the offeree knows of the services and has "reason to believe that they are offered with expectation of compensation." The cases relate primarily to the question of "expectation of compensation" and as usual, everything depends on the totality of the facts. In other words, if a reasonable man would conclude that the services are rendered gratuitously there can be no recovery.[88]

A very important factor is whether the services are rendered within the family relationship. Where the services are rendered within the family relationship the offeree ordinarily has no reason to conclude that compensation is expected. A family relationship can arise through consanguinity (blood) or affinity (marriage). It may also arise by living as a family.[89] A family for this purpose has been defined "as a collective body of persons who form one household, under one head and one domestic government." [90] At times the two elements of relationship and living together will co-exist and both factors will be considered in making the decision. There are many complicated cases on this question of family relationship.[91] If services are rendered within the family relationship there is a presumption that they were rendered without expectation of compensation.[92] On the other hand if

---

86. American Life Ins. Co. v. Hutcheson, 109 F.2d 424, 427–28 (6th Cir.1940), certiorari denied 310 U.S. 625, 60 S.Ct. 898, 84 L.Ed. 1397 (1940); see Joseph Schultz & Co. v. Camden Fire Ins. Ass'n, 304 N.Y. 143, 106 N.E.2d 273 (1952); U.C.C. § 2–208; 12 Appleman, Insurance, Law & Practice § 7226 (1943); Annot., 32 A.L.R.2d 487 (1953).

87. Old Jordan Mining Co. v. Societe Anonyme de Mines, 164 U.S. 261, 17 S.Ct. 113, 41 L.Ed. 427 (1896); James v. P.B. Price Constr. Co., 240 Ark. 628, 401 S.W.2d 206 (1966); Porter v. General Boiler Casing Co., 284 Md. 402, 396 A.2d 1090 (1979); Spencer v. Spencer, 181 Mass. 471, 63 N.E. 947 (1902); Day v. Caton, 119 Mass. 513, 20 Am.R. 347 (1876); Stout v. Smith, 4 N.C. App. 81, 165 S.E.2d 789 (1969); Restatement, Contracts § 72(1)(a); see Minerals & Chem. Philipp Corp. v. Milwhite Co., 414 F.2d 428 (5th Cir.1969).

88. Lirtzman v. Fuqua Industries, Inc., 677 F.2d 548 (7th Cir.1982). In such a case there is not even an offer.

89. When an unmarried couple lives together, it has been held that services rendered by the parties are gratuitous because of the intimate nature of the relationship. Morone v. Morone, 50 N.Y.2d 481, 429 N.Y.S.2d 592, 413 N.E.2d 1154 (1980). But see Marvin v. Marvin, 18 Cal.3d 660, 134 Cal.Rptr. 815, 557 P.2d 106 (1976) where it was held that a nonmarital partner may recover reasonable value for household services if it can be shown that such services were offered with expectation of monetary reward.

90. Annot., 7 A.L.R.2d 36 (1949).

91. Annot., 7 A.L.R.2d 8 (1949).

92. Worley v. Worley, 388 So.2d 502 (Ala.1980); In re Barnet's Estate, 320 Pa. 408, 182 A. 699 (1936); Matter of Estate of

there is not a family relationship the presumption is that compensation is expected.[93] In either case the presumption may be rebutted.[94] Since we are discussing cases where the parties have not explicitly agreed with respect to the services rendered we are talking about the possibility of an implied in fact contract arising from the conduct of the offeror and an acceptance by the offeree in silently allowing the services to be performed despite the existence of a duty to speak. Whether an implied in fact contract exists is ordinarily a question of fact.[95] The ultimate question is whether a reasonable man would conclude that the services were rendered gratuitously.[96]

A recent case has stated that, in order to demonstrate the existence of an implied-in-fact contract for services, "the party seeking payment must show that services were carried out under such circumstances as to give the recipient reason to understand that the services were rendered for the recipient and not for some other person * * * demonstrate the existence of such circumstances as to put the recipient on notice that the services were not rendered gratuitously and prove that the services were beneficial to the recipient.[97]

The first and last factors mentioned seem to be important in cases where medical services are rendered to a patient at the request of a third party. In such a case it has been stated as a general rule that "the mere request to a medical practitioner or hospital to attend a third person to whom the person making such request is under no legal obligation to furnish such services has been held not to raise an implied promise to pay therefor in the absence of an express undertaking to do so, or special circumstances justifying a proper inference of an intention to incur such liability." [98]

In a case where a party renders services to another not in a family relationship is it necessary that the offeror subjectively intend to be paid? This requirement has been posited in a number of the cases.[99] For example, if A's car is disabled and B, the owner of a tow truck begins to move the vehicle and the owner stands by and does or says nothing, under the rules previously stated it seems clear that there would be an implied in fact contract. But what if the truck owner acted carelessly? Could B avoid contractual liability by showing that B subjectively intended to offer the services gratuitously? Since on the facts presented any ambiguity resulted from the failure of the tow

Steffes, 95 Wis.2d 490, 290 N.W.2d 697 (1980); McDowell, Contracts in the Family, 45 B.U.L.Rev. 43 (1965); Annot., 7 A.L.R.2d 8 (1949).

93. McKeon v. Van Slyck, 233 N.Y. 392, 119 N.E. 851 (1918).

94. Wilhoite v. Beck, 141 Ind.App. 543, 230 N.E.2d 616 (1967).

95. Shapira v. United Medical Serv., Inc., 15 N.Y.2d 200, 257 N.Y.S.2d 150, 205 N.E.2d 293 (1965); see Sheldon v. Thornburg, 153 Iowa 622, 133 N.W. 1076 (1912).

96. Sturgeon v. Estate of Wideman, 608 S.W.2d 140 (Mo.App.1980), appeal after remand 631 S.W.2d 55 (1981).

97. H.G. Smithy Co. v. Washington Medical Center, 374 A.2d 891, 893 (D.C.1977).

98. Annot., 34 A.L.R.3d 176, 183 (1970).

99. See Wilhoite v. Beck, 141 Ind.App. 543, 230 N.E.2d 616 (1967); Bourisk v. Amalfitano, 379 A.2d 149 (Me.1977); Day v. Caton, 119 Mass. 513, 20 Am.R. 347 (1876).

truck operator to mention his subjective intent it would seem that subjective intent should not be considered.[1] If the case is one where the operator seeks to be paid but he will testify that he was acting gratuitously should that evidence be excluded? There do not appear to be any clear answers to these problems.[2]

Another case where it is difficult to tell whether one should conclude that services were rendered gratuitously arises when a person renders services prior to the formation of an express contract. The question is whether it is reasonable to conclude that he rendered these services gratuitously in hopes of obtaining the contract or whether he expects to be paid for the preliminary services irrespective of obtaining the ultimate contract.[3]

 WESTLAW REFERENCES

silen! /s promis! /s offer! accept!

"implied in fact contract"

silen! /s accept! /s contract agreement

to(95) /p "implied in fact"

95k27

silen! /s accept! /s offer!

"relationship of the party" /s silen! /s accept!

silen! /s offer! /s expect! /s reply! replied answer!

95k15 /p silen!

offeree /s "duty to speak"

silen! /s conclud! conclus! /s accept! /s offer!

silen! /s authoriz! /s accept!

"course of dealing" /s silen! /s accept!

silence! /s accept! /s circumstance

"joseph schultz" +s camden

156k95

95k4

217k130(3)

"reasonable opportunity" /s service /s expect! /s compensat!

"reasonable opportunity" /s service /s reject!

"expectation of compensation" /s service perform!

family familial consanguin! sanguin! /s "expectation of compensation"

affinity family familial sanguin! consanguin! /s service /s expect! /s compensat!

"implied in fact" /s "question of fact"

95k4

"implied in fact" /s service

service /s "beneficial to the recipient"

service /s "implied promise to pay"

---

1. See Prince v. McRae, 84 N.C. 674 (1889).

2. See ch. 3.

3. Compare Arden v. Freydberg, 9 N.Y.2d 393, 214 N.Y.S.2d 400, 174 N.E.2d 495 (1961) and Vitale v. Russell, 332 Mass. 523, 126 N.E.2d 122 (1955) and Cronin v. National Shawmut Bank, 306 Mass. 202, 27 N.E.2d 717 (1940) with Hill v. Waxberg, 237 F.2d 936 (9th Cir.1956).

"express contract" /s gratuit! /s service
205hk91

§ 2–19. Acceptance by Conduct or an Act of Dominion

In the prior section we discussed acceptance arising as a result of silence and inaction. It is, of course, possible for acceptance to arise by affirmative conduct. Thus if A, on passing a market picks up an apple from a box marked "10 cents each" and holds it up so that the clerk sees it and nods assent, A has made an offer by conduct and B has accepted in the same way.[4] This is so because a reasonable man would conclude that there has been an offer and an acceptance. Thus, U.C.C. § 2–204(1) provides, "a contract for the sale of goods may be made in any manner sufficient to show agreement, including conduct by both parties which recognizes the existence of such a contract." Comment 1 makes it clear that this is also the rule at common law. As one court has stated, "a contract implied in fact arises under circumstances which, according to the ordinary course of dealing and common understanding of men, show a mutual intention to contract * * *. A contract is implied in fact where the intention is not manifested by direct or explicit words between the parties, but is to be gathered by implication or proper deduction from the conduct of the parties, language used or things done by them, or other pertinent circumstances attending the transaction."[5]

Whether a promise will be implied under particular circumstances is ordinarily a question of fact.[6] This matter is discussed in more detail below.[7]

An act of dominion is conduct but it is a particular type of conduct because an act of dominion relates to the tort of conversion.[8] Before an act of dominion becomes a conversion it must be wrongful.[9] It is not our purpose here to study the tort of conversion. Rather emphasis should be on a number of cases that have held that the exercise of dominion constitutes a contractual acceptance.[10] This occurs when the offeree's act of dominion is referrable to the power of acceptance granted by the offeror—a difficult question.[11] Once it is decided that

4. Restatement, Second, Contracts § 4, ill. 2.

5. Miller v. Stevens, 224 Mich. 626, 195 N.W. 481 (1923); quoted in Schwartz v. Michigan Sugar Co., 106 Mich.App. 471, 308 N.W.2d 459 (1981); Bell v. Hegewald, 95 Wn.2d 686, 628 P.2d 1305 (1981).

6. Kane v. New Hampshire State Liquor Comm'n, 118 N.H. 706, 393 A.2d 555 (1978).

7. See § 4–12(c) infra.

8. W. Prosser and W. Keeton, Torts § 15 (5th ed. 1984).

9. Restatement, Second, Contracts § 69, Comment e; U.C.C. § 2–606(1)(c) (1977).

10. Raible v. Puerto Rico Indus. Dev. Co., 392 F.2d 424 (1st Cir.1968); Louisville Tin & Stove Co. v. Lay, 251 Ky. 584, 65 S.W.2d 1002 (1933); Austin v. Burge, 156 Mo.App. 286, 137 S.W. 618 (1911); Indiana Mfg. Co. v. Hayes, 155 Pa. 160, 26 A.6 (1893); Ferrous Prods. Co. v. Gulf States Trading Co., 160 Tex. 399, 332 S.W.2d 310 (1960). The cases do not seem to concern themselves with the necessity for communication in this situation. See § 2–17 supra.

11. Restatement, Second, Contracts § 69, Comment e. But according to this section, the offeree is not bound by the offered terms where these are manifestly

there is a contractual acceptance it follows that there is no conversion. Where the act of dominion is not referrable to the power of acceptance granted by the offer it is wrongful and therefore there is a conversion.[12] According to both Restatements in such a case the party who is not a converter has the option of proceeding either upon a contract or a tort theory.[13]

Section 2–606(1)(c) of the Uniform Commercial Code which relates to "What Constitutes Acceptance of Goods" provides that there is an acceptance of goods when the buyer "does any act inconsistent with the seller's ownership; but if the act is wrongful as against the seller it is an acceptance only if ratified by him." Comment 4 states in part, "the second clause of paragraph (c) modifies some of the prior case law and makes it clear that "acceptance" in law based on the wrongful act of the accepter is acceptance only as against the wrongdoer and then only at the option of the wronged party."

Although the meaning and purpose of the provisions quoted are somewhat obscure,[14] they seem to be in accord with the rules stated above. Illustrative of the section is the case of F.W. Lang Co. v. Fleet.[15] In that case the plaintiff (seller) sent a freezer unit on approval to defendant (buyer) and the buyer used the compressor of the freezer unit to operate an air-conditioner. The court held that the use made of the compressor amounted to a wrongful act of dominion and so the plaintiff had the option of suing in tort or contract.[16]

In order to discourage the unsolicited sending of goods to unwary customers, several states have enacted legislation making it unlawful to offer merchandise for sale by the unsolicited sending of goods and also providing that a person who receives such goods has a complete defense to an action for the price or for the return of the goods.[17] The Postal Reorganization Act of 1970[18] provides that one who receives "unordered merchandise"[19] by mail may treat the transaction as a gift.[20]

unreasonable. See Wright v. Sonoma Country, 156 Cal. 475, 105 P. 409 (1909); Whittier, The Restatement of Contracts and Mutual Assent, 17 Calif.L.Rev. 441, 452 (1929). In such a case the offeror would be limited to a recovery based upon a quasi-contractual theory.

12. Restatement, Second, Contracts § 69, Comment e and ill. 7.

13. Restatement, Contracts § 72, ill. 8; Restatement, Second, Contracts 69, ill. 9.

14. See Annot., 67 A.L.R.3d 363 (1975).

15. 193 Pa.Super. 365, 165 A.2d 258 (1960).

16. See also Columbia Rolling-Mill Co. v. Beckett Foundry & Machine Co., 55 N.J. Law 391, 26 A. 888 (1893).

17. See, e.g., McKinney's N.Y.Gen.Obl. Law § 5–332; cf. Neb.Rev.Stat. § 63–101 (1936) (limited to newspapers and other publications).

18. 39 U.S.C.A. § 3009 (1976).

19. The statute defines the words "unordered merchandise" as "merchandise mailed without the prior expressed request or consent of the recipient." 39 U.S.C.A. § 3009 (1976).

20. For a discussion of this type of statute, see Note, Unsolicited Merchandise: State and Federal Remedies for a Consumer Problem, 1970 Duke L.J. 991. At common law the recipient is an involuntary bailee and is required to keep the goods for a reasonable time before discarding them.

WESTLAW REFERENCES

"affirmative conduct" /s contract

2–204 /p conduct contract

"implied in fact" /s conduct /s contract /s party

"implied in fact" /s "conduct of the party"

"act of dominion" /s tort

"act of dominion" /s contract

389k8

389k1

"act of dominion" /s wrong!

"act of dominion" /s accept!

conversion /s contract /s accept!

conversion /s contract /s tort

conversion /s "act of dominion"

"uniform commercial code" /s 2–606

find 165 a2d 258

"postal reorganization act" /p "unordered merchandise"

"unordered merchandise"

§ 2–20. Termination of the Power of Acceptance Created by Revocable Offers

The power of acceptance created by a revocable offer may be terminated in a variety of ways prior to its exercise.[21]

(a) Lapse of Time

Lapse of time relates to the duration of an offer. The cases are of two kinds. One where the duration of the offer is specified, the other when it is not. Both types of cases will be discussed.

On Jan. 29 A sends a letter to B dated Jan. 29 which states "Will give you eight days to accept or reject." B receives the offer on Feb. 2 and on Feb. 8 sends a letter of acceptance which is received by A on Feb. 9. It is clear that the offer lapses in eight days but should the eight days be measured from Jan. 29 or from February 2? Both Professor Williston and Corbin seem to suggest that since the offeree should realize that the offer is ambiguous and that the limitation is imposed for the benefit of the offeror that the eight days should be reckoned from Jan. 29 rather than Feb. 2.[22] However, the case upon which the illustration is based took the position that in the absence of countervailing indications the eight days should be measured from the day the offer is received[23] and this view appears to have been adopted by the Restatement Second.[24] Another question is how are the eight

21. Restatement, Contracts § 36. The rules relating to termination of irrevocable offers are discussed in § 2–25 infra.

22. 1 Corbin § 35; 1 Williston § 53A.

23. Caldwell v. Cline, 109 W.Va. 553, 156 S.E. 55 (1930). In this case if the offer

had read, "You have eight days from the date hereof," there would have been such a countervailing indication.

24. Restatement, Second, Contracts § 41, Comment e.

days calculated. What date is eight days from February 2? The normal rule is that in measuring eight days the day from which the time is reckoned should be excluded.[25] Thus eight days from Feb. 2 is Feb. 10. The same rule would apply if an act was to be done *within* 90 days. But in another case an employee became eligible for a benefit *on* the date that he completed 90 days of service. The court held that first day of service is to be included in calculating the 90 days.[26] This topic ultimately becomes quite confusing and is better left to other courses.[27]

Under the assumption that the eight days are to be measured from Feb. 2 the matter can be further complicated by assuming that there is a delay in the transmission of the offer. In such a case, should the eight days be measured from the date that the offer was received or from the date when it would have been received. The answer appears to be that if the offeree knows or has reason to know of the delay, the eight days should be measured from the date it would have been received.[28] According to Corbin, "In most cases the offeree will have some indication of the delay from the date of the letter, the postmarks, the condition of the envelope, or statements of the messenger. All such indications must be considered." [29]

If the duration of the power of acceptance is not stated, it is deemed to be open for a reasonable time [30] and what is a reasonable time is ordinarily a question of fact depending upon the circumstances [31] of the case. Factors considered are whether the transaction is speculative or not,[32] the manifest purpose of the offeror,[33] and according to the new Restatement, whether or not the offeree is in good faith.[34]

The offeror may stipulate in his offer that the power of acceptance shall terminate upon the happening of a certain event. If the event occurs before the acceptance, the power of acceptance lapses even though the offeree is not informed that the event has occurred.[35]

25. Clements v. Pasadena Fin. Co., 376 F.2d 1005 (9th Cir.1967); Housing Auth. of Lake Arthur v. T. Miller & Sons, 239 La. 966, 120 So.2d 494 (1960); Barnet v. Cannizzaro, 3 A.D.2d 745, 160 N.Y.S.2d 329 (2d Dep't 1957); West's Ann. California Civ. Code § 10; McKinney's N.Y.Gen.Constr. Law § 20.

26. Polan v. Travelers Ins. Co., 156 W.Va. 250, 192 S.E.2d 481 (1972).

27. See, for example, Livesey v. Copps Corp., 90 Wis.2d 577, 280 N.W.2d 339 (1979). This matter is discussed in Procedure courses.

28. Restatement, Contracts § 51.

29. 1 Corbin § 37.

30. Caldwell v. E.F. Spears & Sons, 186 Ky. 64, 216 S.W. 83 (1919); Restatement, Contracts § 41.

31. Kaplan v. Reid Bros., Inc., 104 Cal. App. 268, 285 P. 868 (1930); Starkweather v. Gleason, 221 Mass. 552, 109 N.E. 635

(1915); Orlowski v. Moore, 198 Pa.Super. 360, 181 A.2d 692 (1962).

32. Minnesota Linseed Oil Co. v. Collier White Lead Co., 17 F.Cas. 447 (C.C.D.Minn. 1876) (No. 9635); Brewer v. Lepman, 127 Mo.App. 693, 106 S.W. 1107 (1908); Restatement, Second, Contracts § 41, Comment f and ills. 7, 8. Comment of states that absence of actual fluctuation is a factor to be considered in determining the reasonable time for acceptance.

33. In re Kelly, 39 Conn. 159 (1872); Mitchell v. Abbott, 86 Me. 338, 29 A. 1118 (1894); Loring v. Boston, 48 Mass. (7 Metc.) 409 (1844); Restatement, Second, Contracts § 41; cf. Carr v. Mahaska County Bankers Ass'n, 222 Iowa 411, 269 N.W. 494 (1936).

34. Restatement, Second, Contracts § 41, Comment f.

35. Oliphant, The Duration and Termination of an Offer, 18 Mich.L.Rev. 201 (1920).

Where an offer is made in a face to face or telephone conversation or in any situation where there are direct negotiations, the offer is deemed, in the absence of a manifestation of a contrary intention, to be open only while the parties are conversing.[36]

(b) Effect of a Late Acceptance

If an offer lapses before an acceptance becomes effective it would seem to follow that the late acceptance is an offer which in turn can be accepted only by a communicated acceptance. This is only one of three views.[37] A second but untenable view is that the offeror may at his option treat the late acceptance as an acceptance by waiving the lateness without communicating this fact to the offeree at any particular time or "perhaps without any limitation of time."[38] This approach violates "a vital principle of the law of contract" namely the necessity for communication of the acceptance.[39] Under an intermediate view if the acceptance is late but sent in what could plausibly be argued to be a reasonable time the original offeror has a duty to reply within a reasonable time. If he fails to do so there is a contract. The theory is that, as in the first view, the late acceptance is an offer but here the original offeror accepts by remaining silent when he has a duty to speak. Since it is not clear that the original acceptance was late there is a duty to speak.[40]

Although the Restatement Second rejects the second view set forth above[41] it is not clear if it accepts the third view in a case where it could be plausibly argued that the late acceptance was timely. In Comment b, in discussing late acceptances and in particular the type of case under discussion, it states that "the failure of the original offeror to object to an acceptance and his subsequent preparation for performance may be evidence that the acceptance was made within a reasonable time."[42] This is not an adoption of the third view because it assumes that the acceptance was timely. Elsewhere the Restatement Second comes closer to the third view when its says, "But the original offeror may have a duty to speak, for example, if the purported acceptance embodies a plausible but erroneous reading of the original offer."[43] This statement embodies the theory of the third view but does not specifically relate it to a late acceptance because it speaks of an "erroneous reading" and the illustration used is discussed in terms of "ambiguity". But if an offer is open for a reasonable time, can't the offeree "misread" the time available and isn't a reasonable time to some extent indefinite?

36. Akers v. J.B. Sedberry, Inc., 39 Tenn.App. 633, 286 S.W.2d 617 (1955).

37. Houston Dairy v. John Hancock Mut. Life Ins. Co., 643 F.2d 1185 (5th Cir. 1981); Maclay v. Harvey, 90 Ill. 525 (1878); Ferrier v. Storer, 63 Iowa 484, 19 N.W. 288 (1844); Cain v. Noel, 268 S.C. 583, 235 S.E.2d 292 (1977); Wax v. Northwest Seed Co., 189 Wn. 212, 64 P.2d 513 (1937).

38. The cases are collected in 1 Williston § 92.

39. 1 Williston § 92.

40. Phillips v. Moor, 71 Me. 78 (1880).

41. Restatement, Second, Contracts § 70, Comment a.

42. Id., Comment b.

43. Id., Comment a.

A well known case has raised a difficult problem in this area of late acceptance. A made an offer to B, stating no time limitation on acceptance. Consequently the power of acceptance was open for a reasonable time. B sent a letter of acceptance after a reasonable time had expired. The acceptance, however, crossed a letter from A indicating that the offer was still open. B sent no other acceptance. Had B accepted after receiving A's second letter it would be easy to conclude that although the offer has lapsed it had been revived by the second communication and so was effectively accepted.[44]

The court decided that there was a contract and that it was the original offer that was accepted despite the fact that the acceptance came too late. The court does not appear to apply any of the three views stated above. What the court is really saying is that objective evidence not known to the offeree was sufficient to show an agreement. The result appears to be just. However, the decision is not in accord with the objective theory of contracts because under that approach one should take into account only what the offeree knew or should have known about the intent of the offeror at the time of acceptance.[45] The Restatement Second approves the result upon the theory that the second offer may be used in interpreting the duration of the first offer.[46] This does not explain how or if the decision accords with the objective theory. Ultimately the question is not whether the case accords with objective theory of contracts but whether it accords with any of the more modern subjective theories of contracts.[47] This case is related to and has already been mentioned in connection with our prior discussion of identical cross-offers.[48]

(c) Death or Lack of Capacity of the Offeror and Offeree

It is well settled in most jurisdictions that a power of acceptance is terminated when the offeror dies.[49] It must be carefully kept in mind that the rule has reference to death which occurs between the making of the offer and the acceptance. To illustrate, if A makes an offer to B looking to a bilateral contract and A dies before B accepts, the offer is terminated. This is true under the majority view even if B was unaware of A's death at the time of acceptance.[50] The rule is logical when B is aware of A's death because knowledge of death would be tantamount to a revocation. If B is not aware of A's death there does not seem any good reason to say that the offer is terminated. This is

44. Santa Monica Unified School Dist. v. Persh, 5 Cal.App.3d 945, 85 Cal.Rptr. 463 (1970); Livingston v. Evans, [1925] 4 D.L.R. 769 (Alberta).

45. See § 2–2 supra. The case is Mactier's Adm'rs v. Frith, 6 Wend. 102, 21 Am.Dec. 262 (N.Y.1830).

46. Restatement, Second, Contracts § 23, Comment d and ill. 6.

47. See ch. 3.

48. See § 2–12 supra.

49. New Headley Tobacco Warehouse Co. v. Gentry's Ex'r, 307 Ky. 857, 212 S.W.2d 325 (1948); Jordan v. Dobbins, 122 Mass. 168 (1877); Jones v. Union Cent. Life Ins. Co., 265 App.Div. 388, 40 N.Y.S.2d 74 (4th Dep't, 1943), affirmed 290 N.Y. 883, 50 N.E.2d 293 (1943); Restatement, Contracts § 48.

50. Pearl v. Merchants Warren Nat'l Bank, 9 Mass.App.Ct. 853, 400 N.E.2d 1314 (1980); Restatement, Second, Contracts § 48, Comment a.

the basis of the minority view.[51] The majority view is a frequently criticized relic of the subjective theory. It does not conform to the objective theory because the offeree should be charged only with what he knows or should know of the offeror's situation.[52] Despite the criticism of the rule, however, it is still the majority rule.[53] If B accepts before A dies there is a contract and the only question presented would be whether A's estate would have the defense of impossibility of performance, a matter to be discussed later.[54]

The same rules apply to a unilateral contract except in that situation there is the additional problem of determining up to what point the offer may be revoked. This matter is discussed below.[55] But if the offer becomes irrevocable or a contract arises by virtue of any of these rules death no longer terminates the offer.[56]

The problem with respect to incapacity of the offeror terminating the offer is more complicated and more limited. Here as in the case of death we are talking about an incapacity that arises between the making of the offer and the acceptance. Most of the cases in this area arise where there is an adjudication of mental illness or defect and as a result the property of the mental defective is placed under guardianship. In such a case the supervening insanity terminates the offer whether or not the offeree is aware of the adjudication.[57] But, as in the case of death, there is a minority view to the effect that the offer is not terminated unless the offeree knows of the adjudication.[58] If there is no adjudication of insanity the rule is that supervening mental incapacity in fact terminates an offer if the offeree is aware of the incapacity.[59]

What constitutes incapacity is discussed in chapter 8 below. There are, in addition, a whole host of other problems discussed in that chapter. It is important to remember that the only topic being discussed here is incapacity that is adjudicated or arises between the making of the offer and the acceptance—a most unusual situation.

The supervening death or incapacity of the offeree will prevent his representative from accepting the offer because presumably the offer is

51. Grey v. Ward, 67 Conn. 147, 34 A. 1025 (1895); 1 Corbin § 54.

52. See § 2–2 supra. See also Oliphant, Duration and Termination of an Offer, 18 Mich.L.Rev. 201, 209–211 (1920).

53. Restatement, Second, Contracts § 48, Comment a. The Comment states that some inroads have been made upon the rule by statute and decisions in certain specific areas.

54. See § 13–7 infra.

55. See § 2–22 infra.

56. See § 2–25 infra.

57. Beach v. First Methodist Episcopal Church, 96 Ill. 177 (1880); Restatement, Second, Contracts § 48, Comment b. The same rule was applied where a guardian was appointed because of physical incapacity in the case of Union Trust & Sav. Bank v. State Bank, 188 N.W.2d 300 (Iowa 1971). It is the appointment of the guardian that terminates the offer. Restatement, Second, Contracts § 118.

58. Swift & Co. v. Smigel, 115 N.J. Super. 391, 279 A.2d 895 (1971) affirmed mem. 60 N.J. 348, 289 A.2d 793 (1972). The case involved an offer looking to a series of unilateral contracts and the court adverts to "the diminished business utility of continuing guarantees" under the majority rule. The case also states that the adjudication is only prima facie evidence of incapacity. This is also a minority view.

59. 1 Williston § 62A.

made only to the offeree. The situation would be different if the representative were made an additional offeree.[60]

(d) Revocation

The most obvious way of terminating the power of acceptance created by a revocable offer is by revocation[61]—a manifestation of intent not to enter into the proposed contract.[62] A revocable offer may be revoked at any time prior to effective acceptance by the offeree.[63] The question of whether the particular language used is language of revocation is a question of interpretation.[64]

The general rule is that a revocation is effective when received.[65] Some states have the rule that a revocation is effective when sent.[66] According to the Restatement a written communication is received "when the writing comes into the possession of the person addressed, or of some person authorized by him to receive it for him, or when it is deposited is some place which he has authorized as the place for this or similar communications to be deposited for him."[67] The Restatement permits the offeror to reserve the right to revoke the offer without notice either in the original offer or in a later communication. Of course even in this situation the revocation will not be effective if it occurs after an acceptance.[68]

When an offer is made to a number of persons whose identity is unknown to the offeror as, for example, in a newspaper advertisement, it is clear that it is impossible to revoke in the usual manner that is to say by sending a letter of revocation. In such a case the power of acceptance may be terminated by giving equal publicity to the revocation.[69] Normally this is accomplished by using the same medium for the revocation as was used for the offer.[70] Even then it would appear necessary that the publication of the revocation continue for as long as the offer did in as prominent a location, and in at least the same size

60. See § 2–14 supra; see also Restatement, Second, Contracts § 48, Comment c, and ill. 3.

61. 1 Corbin § 38; see Boston & M.R. v. Bartlett, 57 Mass. (3 Cush.) 224 (1849).

62. Restatement, Contracts § 42.

63. Calvin v. Rupp, 471 F.2d 1346 (8th Cir.1973); K.L. House Constr. Co. v. Watson, 84 N.M. 783, 508 P.2d 592 (1973); Leigh v. New York, 33 N.Y.2d 774, 350 N.Y.S.2d 414, 305 N.E.2d 493 (1973); R.J. Taggart, Inc. v. Douglas County, 31 Or. App. 1137, 572 P.2d 1050 (1977); Merritt Land Corp. v. Marcello, 110 R.I. 166, 291 A.2d 263 (1972); see generally, Wagner, Some Problems of Revocation and Termination of Offers, 38 N.D.L.Rev. 138 (1963).

64. See, e.g., Hoover Motor Express Co. v. Clements Paper Co., 193 Tenn. 6, 241 S.W.2d 851 (1951); Restatement, Second, Contracts § 42, Comment d.

65. Patrick v. Bowman, 149 U.S. 411, 13 S.Ct. 811, 37 L.Ed. 790 (1893); Wertheimer, Inc. v. Wehle-Hartford Co., 126 Conn. 30, 9 A.2d 279 (1939); Wheat v. Cross, 31 Md. 99 (1869).

66. See, e.g., West's Ann.Cal.Civ. Code § 1587.

67. Restatement, Contracts § 69; accord, Howard v. Daly, 61 N.Y. 362, 19 Am. R. 285 (1875); U.C.C. § 1–201 (26) (1977).

68. Restatement, Second, Contracts § 42, Comment b.

69. Shuey v. United States, 92 U.S. (2 Otto) 73, 23 L.Ed. 697 (1875); Restatement, Contracts § 43.

70. Restatement, Second, Contracts § 42, Comment b.

ad.[71] However, if the same medium is not available the doctrine requires only the best means of notice available under the circumstances of the case.[72] Should the offeror know the identity of a person who is taking action upon the offer the offeror must, to have an effective revocation, communicate the revocation to him.[73] If the attempted revocation actually comes to the attention of any offeree that, in and of itself, will amount to a revocation from the moment he is aware of it.[74]

An offer may also be terminated by indirect revocation. In Dickinson v. Dodds [75] the defendant was the owner of real property. He first made an offer to sell the property to the plaintiff and later while the first offer was still open made an offer with respect to the same property to one Allan. Allan accepted the offer. Later the plaintiff accepted but at the time he accepted he was aware that Allan had accepted. The court held that the offer to the plaintiff was revoked when the plaintiff received reliable information that Allan had accepted. The point is that at this juncture the plaintiff as a reasonable man should have concluded that the defendant no longer wished his offer to be operative.

The case raises three problems. Should the doctrine of indirect revocation be limited to cases involving the sale of land and chattels? The original Restatement so stated.[76] The Restatement Second is to the contrary.[77] Under the rule of the Restatement Second the removal of this limitation will make it more difficult to decide in a given case whether a reasonable man should conclude that the defendant no longer wished his offer to be operative. The second problem is, what information is reliable. The cases hold that the information must be both objectively and subjectively reliable.[78] Objectively reliable means that the information heard must in fact be true. For example, in Dickenson v. Dodds if Allan had not in fact accepted the offer there would not have been indirect revocation. Subjectively reliable means that the information must come from a reliable source. If the source is not reliable it may be ignored but if it is reliable, reasonable inquiry should be made to ascertain its validity.

The most difficult question is what information should lead a reasonable man to conclude that the offeror wishes to terminate his offer? In Dickinson v. Dodds the information was that Allan had

---

71. See 1 Corbin § 41.

72. Williston § 59A.

73. Long v. Chronicle Publishing Co., 68 Cal.App. 171, 228 P. 873 (1924); Restatement, Second, Contracts § 46, ill. 1. Presumably the rule is one of reason.

74. If the offer has become irrevocable by conduct, then obviously the offer may not be revoked. See § 2–25 infra.

75. 2 Ch. D. 463 (1876); see Bancroft v. Martin, 144 Miss. 384, 109 So. 859 (1926). On the issue of indirect acceptance, see

Southern Nat'l Bank v. Tri Financial Corp., 317 F.Supp. 1173 (S.D.Tex.1970), judgment affirmed in part, vacated in part 458 F.2d 688 (5th Cir.1972).

76. Restatement, Contracts § 43.

77. Restatement, Second, Contracts § 43, ill. 2; see also 1 Corbin § 40.

78. Coleman v. Applegarth, 68 Md. 21, 11 A. 284 (1887); Watters v. Lincoln, 29 S.D. 98, 135 N.W. 712 (1912); Frank v. Stratford-Handcock, 13 Wyo. 37, 77 P. 134 (1904).

accepted the offer made to him. When plaintiff heard this reliable information as a reasonable man he should have concluded that the offeror would not want his offer to continue since he would not want to run the risk of contracting to sell the same property twice when he could fulfill only one of two contracts. The same would be true if he heard that the property had actually been sold.[79]

What if the first offeree (the plaintiff in Dickinson v. Dodds) heard only that an offer had been made to Allan, should that give rise to an indirect revocation? A reasonable man might conclude that the offeror would not want to make two offers because of the potential liability discussed above or he may decide that since the offeror has not bothered to communicate a revocation he is willing to run the risk of making two offers. In general the second conclusion seems preferable.[80] If the second offeree learned of the first offer he could without a doubt reasonably believe that the offer to him still existed since it was made to him while the first offer was in existence thus indicating that the offeror was willing to run the risk of having two outstanding offers.

(e) Rejection—Counter-Offer

It is clear that an offeree's power of acceptance is terminated by rejection.[81] The same rule is applied in the case of a counter-offer.[82] According to the Restatement this result merely carries out the usual understanding that a new proposal supercedes an earlier proposal.[83] But neither a rejection nor a counter-offer will operate to terminate an offer if the offeror or offeree manifest such an intention.[84] Thus if the offeree makes a counter-offer but says that he is "keeping the offer under advisement" the original offer is not terminated.[85]

It is necessary to distinguish a counter-offer and a rejection from a counter-inquiry, a comment upon the terms, a request for a modification of the offer, a request for a modification of a contract, an acceptance plus a separate offer,[86] or even what has been referred to as a "grumbling assent."[87]

---

79. 1 Corbin § 40.

80. 1 Corbin § 40; 1 Murray § 32; Restatement, Contracts § 40.

81. Collins v. Thompson, 679 F.2d 168 (9th Cir.1982). But see Pepsi-Cola Bottling Co. v. N.L.R.B., 659 F.2d 87 (8th Cir.1981) (applying a contrary rule in the case of collective bargaining).

82. Nodland v. Chirpick, 307 Minn. 360, 240 N.W.2d 513 (1976); Corr v. Braasch, 97 N.M. 279, 639 P.2d 566 (1981); Financial Indem. Co. v. Bevans, 38 Or.App. 369, 590 P.2d 276 (1979); 1 Williston § 51. A counter-offer has been described as a reply to an offer that adds qualifications or requires performance of conditions. In such a case even if the reply purports to accept the offer, as a common law proposition, it is a counter-offer. Gleeson v. Frahm, 211

Neb. 677, 320 N.W.2d 95 (1982). This common law rule and recent changes therein are discussed in § 2–21 infra. It should be noted that a counter-offer not only terminates the original offer but is itself an offer that can be accepted. Steele v. Harrison, 220 Kan. 422, 552 P.2d 957 (1976).

83. Restatement, Second, Contracts § 39, Comment a.

84. Restatement, Second, Contracts § 39.

85. Radford & Guise v. Practical Premium Co., 125 Ark. 199, 188 S.W. 562 (1916); Restatement, Second, Contracts § 39, ill. 3.

86. Restatement, Second, Contracts § 39, Comment b.

87. Johnson v. Federal Union Sur. Co., 187 Mich. 454, 153 N.W. 788, 792 (1915);

For example, if A makes an offer to B to sell an object for $5000, the offer to remain open for thirty days, and B says "I'll pay $4800", this would be a counter-offer but if he said "will you take $4800?", this would be a counter-inquiry.[88] If B said "your price is too high" this could be considered to be a comment on the terms.[89] If he said "send lowest cash price", this would be a request for a modification of the offer and not a rejection.[90] If B said "I accept but I would appreciate it if you gave me the benefit of a 5% discount," this would be an acceptance which requests or suggests a modification of the contract.[91] If B said, "I accept your offer and I hereby order a second object", there is a contract and B has made a separate offer and not a counter-offer.[92] A "grumbling assent" has been described as an acceptance that expresses dissatisfaction at some terms "but stops short of dissent".[93] If an acceptance contains a term that is not expressly stated in the offer but is implied therein there is an acceptance and not a counter-offer.[94]

A counter-offer must also be distinguished from what could be termed a future acceptance.[95] For example, a general contractor who is about to make a bid may in turn receive a bid (offer) from a subcontractor and accept that offer upon the condition that he is awarded the contract, a condition that the subcontractor either expressly or impliedly agrees to.[96] The parties are not presently bound and so either party is entitled to withdraw until the future event occurs. Once that event occurs the parties are bound without the necessity for any further manifestation of intent. When the future event occurs fairness may

see also Podany v. Erickson, 235 Minn. 36, 49 N.W.2d 193 (1951).

88. Restatement, Contracts § 39, ills. 1 and 2.

89. Restatement, Second, Contracts § 39, Comment b.

90. Home Gas Co. v. Magnolia Petroleum Co., 143 Okl. 112, 287 P. 1033 (1930); Stevenson, Jaques & Co. v. McLean, 5 Q.B.D. 346 (1880).

91. Kodiak Island Borough v. Large, 622 P.2d 440 (Alaska 1981); Culton v. Gilchrist, 92 Iowa 718, 61 N.W. 384 (1894); Collin v. Wetzel, 163 Md. 194, 161 A. 18 (1932); Butler v. Foley, 211 Mich. 668, 179 N.W. 34 (1920); Valashinas v. Koniuto, 308 N.Y. 233, 124 N.E.2d 300 (1954); Rucker v. Sanders, 182 N.C. 607, 109 S.E. 857 (1921); Restatement, Second, Contracts § 61.

The case of Martindell v. Fiduciary Counsel, Inc., 131 N.J.Eq. 523, 26 A.2d 171 (1942), affirmed 133 N.J.Eq. 408, 30 A.2d 281 (1943) is illustrative. In that case A gave B an option to purchase 27 shares of certain stock. Within the time specified in the option, the optionee wrote as follows: "I hereby exercise my option. I have deposited the purchase price with the Colorado National Bank to be delivered to you upon transfer of the stock. If you do not accept such procedure, I demand that you designate the time and place for same." The court held that there was an acceptance and that the language relating to how the purchase price would be paid did not give rise to a counter-offer because it merely suggested a way to perform the contract and the acceptance was otherwise unconditional.

92. 1 Corbin § 84.

93. Johnson v. Federal Union Sur. Co., 187 Mich. 454, 153 N.W. 788 (1915); 1 Corbin § 84.

94. Pickett v. Miller, 76 N.M. 105, 412 P.2d 400 (1966); Burkhead v. Farlow, 266 N.C. 595, 146 S.E.2d 802 (1966); Restatement, Second, Contracts § 59, ill. 3. Contra, Phoenix Iron & Steel Co. v. Wilkoff Co., 253 Fed. 165 (6th Cir.1918).

95. Reed Bros. v. Bluff City Motor Co., 139 Miss. 441, 104 So. 161 (1925), noted in 24 Mich.L.Rev. 302 (1926); Orr v. Doubleday, Page & Co., 223 N.Y. 334, 119 N.E. 552 (1918); see 1 Williston § 77A, where this type of acceptance is called "an acceptance in escrow."

96. Frederick Raff Co. v. Murphy, 110 Conn. 234, 147 A. 709 (1929).

require that the offeree give the offeror notice that the event has occurred.[97]

A rejection or a counter-offer does not terminate an offer until it is received.[98] The definition of a counter-offer is found in the first sentence of the next section and in note 82 supra.

(f) Supervening Death or Destruction

The power of acceptance created by an offer is terminated by the death or destruction, prior to acceptance, of a person or thing essential to performance of the contract.[99]

(g) Supervening Illegality

The power of acceptance is terminated by illegality supervening between the making of an offer and its acceptance.[1]

 WESTLAW REFERENCES

(a) *Lapse of Time*

offer /s reviv! /s accept!

95k20

time! /s accept! /s offer /s limit!

time /s laps! /s offer

terminat! /s laps! /s offer

laps! /s offer /s duration

delay! /s transmit! transmission /s offer

offer /s laps! /s "reasonable time"

receiv! receipt /s offer /s laps!

"power of acceptance" /s time laps! duration period

"power of acceptance" /s terminat!

offer /s conver! /s laps!

(b) *Effect of a Late Acceptance*

offer /s "late acceptance"

contract /s late /s accept! /s waiv!

400k187

(wax +s "northwest seed") ("houston dairy" +s "john hancock")

"duty to reply" /s accept!

(c) *Death or Lack of Capacity of the Offeror or Offeree*

"revocable offer" /s accept!

"power of acceptance" /s death die deceas!

death /s offeror

---

97. See Craddock v. Greenhut Constr. Co., 423 F.2d 111 (5th Cir.1970); Premier Elec. Constr. Co. v. Miller-Davis Co., 422 F.2d 1132 (7th Cir.1970); Los Angeles Rams Football Club v. Cannon, 185 F.Supp. 717 (S.D.Cal.1960); see also Note, 24 Mich. L.Rev. 302 (1926).

98. Glacier Park Foundation v. Watt, 663 F.2d 882 (9th Cir.1981); Harris v. Scott, 67 N.H. 437, 32 A. 770 (1893); Restatement, Second, Contracts § 40. Contra, Hunt v. Higman, 70 Iowa 406, 30 N.W. 769 (1886).

99. Restatement, Contracts § 49.

1. Restatement, Contracts § 50.

die deceas! death /s contract /s unilateral

terminat! /s offer /s irrevoc!

insan! incapacit! /s contract /s offer!

"revocable offer" /s offeree

(d) *Revocation*

"power of acceptance" /s . revok! revoc!

di(revoc! revok! /p offer /p contract)

"language of revocation"

revoc! revok! /s effect! /s send sending sent

95k19

reserv! /s notice notif! /s revocation

"indirect! revo!"

revo! /s accept! offer! /s reasonable +1 man person

terminat! /s offer! /s revo!

communicat! /s offer! /s revo!

(e) *Rejection—Counter—Offer*

"power of acceptance" /s reject!

reject! /s "counter offer!"

"counter offer!" /s reply! replied

"counter offer!" /s terminat!

"counter offer!" /s accept!

"counter inquir!"

"counter offer!" counteroffer! /s term

"counter offer!" counteroffer! /s modif!

"grumbling assent"

"counter offer!" counteroffer! /s future /s contract agreement
    accept!

reject! counteroffer! "counter offer" /s receipt receiv! /s terminat!

(f) *Supervening Death or Destruction*

"subject matter" /s destroy! destruct! /s contract

(g) *Supervening Illegality*

contract /s superven! /s illegal! unlawful!

---

§ 2–21. Acceptance Varying From Offer—The Common Law and Modern Rule

(a) The Common Law Rule

As has been indicated the common law rule is that a purported acceptance which adds qualifications or conditions operates as a counter-offer and thereby a rejection of the offer.[2] This is so even if the

---

2. See § 2–20 supra. In re Pago Pago Aircrash of January 30, 1974, 637 F.2d 704 (9th Cir.1981).

qualification or condition relates to a trivial matter.[3] The rule, sometimes called the "ribbon matching" or "mirror-image" rule, has been enforced with a rigor worthy of a better cause.[4] In the words of one court "acceptance [of an offer] must be 'positive, unconditional, unequivocal and unambiguous, and must not change, add to, or qualify the terms the offer.' "[5] Rigid application of the rule has proved detrimental to commerce, particularly since business today is largely done through the mails on printed forms and the buyer's and seller's forms frequently clash as to ancillary terms of the transaction.[6]

(b) U.C.C. § 2–207

This common law rule has been changed by § 2–207 of the Uniform Commercial Code [7] which reads as follows:

> (1) A definite and seasonable expression of acceptance or a written confirmation which is sent within a reasonable time operates as an acceptance even though it states terms additional to or different from those offered or agreed upon, unless acceptance is expressly made conditional on assent to the additional or different terms.

> (2) The additional terms are to be construed as proposals for addition to the contract. Between merchants such terms become part of the contract unless:

> (a) the offer expressly limits acceptance to the terms of the offer;

> (b) they materially alter it; or

> (c) notification of objection to them has already been given or is given within a reasonable time after notice of them is received.

> (3) Conduct by both parties which recognizes the existence of a contract is sufficient to establish a contract for sale although the writings of the parties do not otherwise establish a contract. In such cases the terms of the particular contract consist of those terms on which the writings of the parties agree, together with

---

3. Restatement, Contracts § 60; accord, Craddock v. Greenhut Constr. Co., 423 F.2d 111 (5th Cir.1970); Dickey v. Hurd, 33 F.2d 415 (1st Cir.1929), certiorari denied 280 U.S. 601, 50 S.Ct. 82, 74 L.Ed. 646 (1929); Rounsaville v. Van Zandt Realtors, Inc., 247 Ark. 749, 447 S.W.2d 655 (1969); Polhamus v. Roberts, 50 N.M. 236, 175 P.2d 196 (1946); Poel v. Brunswick-Balke-Collender Co., 216 N.Y. 310, 110 N.E. 619 (1915); see Llewellyn, On Our Case-Law of Contract: Offer and Acceptance I, 48 Yale L.J. 1, 30 (1938).

4. Dorton v. Collins & Aikman Corp., 453 F.2d 1161 (6th Cir.1972).

5. Gyurkey v. Babler, 103 Idaho 663, 651 P.2d 928 (1982); Wagner v. Rainier Mfg. Co., 230 Or. 531, 371 P.2d 74 (1962).

6. Macauley, Non-Contractual Relations in Business: A Preliminary Study, 28 Am.Soc.Rev. 55 (1963).

7. Hohenberg Bros. Co. v. Killebrew, 505 F.2d 643 (5th Cir.1974), rehearing denied 507 F.2d 1280 (5th Cir.1975); Dorton v. Collins & Aikman Corp., 453 F.2d 1161 (6th Cir.1972).

supplementary terms incorporated under any other provisions of this Act.

(1) Basic Design of Statute

a) Subdivision 1.   Subdivision 1 speaks of "a definite and seasonable expression of acceptance" but also speaks of a "confirmation which is sent within a reasonable time." These are two separate and distinct issues. The "confirmation" problem will be discussed at the end of this section. Subdivision 1 raises two important questions on the issue of acceptance, that is to say on the issue of mutual assent. The section appears to assume that there is an offer looking to a bilateral contract. The two critical issues are: 1) was there a definite and seasonable expression of acceptance? 2) Is the acceptance *expressly conditional on assent* to the additional or different terms?

We do not attempt to explore the meaning of these words at this point. Suffice it to say here if the first question is answered in the affirmative and the second in the negative we know that there is an acceptance (and hence mutual assent) by virtue of the negotiations (communications) of the parties. In other words under the statute where there is a "definite and seasonable expression of acceptance" there is an acceptance unless the acceptance is expressly made conditional on assent to the additional or different terms in which event there is a rejection and in most cases a counter-offer.

b) Subdivision 2—Additional Terms.   Once it is determined that there is an acceptance under subdivision 1 then subdivision 2 becomes relevant not to learn if there is a contract, that has already been decided under subdivision 1, but to ascertain what the terms of the contract are. This depends in part upon whether the parties are merchants and may also depend upon whether the term introduced by the offeree is an additional or a different term. It should be noted that subdivision 2 does not mention different terms and so we will reserve that topic for later discussion.

When either party is not a merchant [8] the first part of subdivision 2 applies. It says that "additional terms are to be construed as proposals for addition to the contract". In other words in the language of the common law the additional term is a request for the modification of an existing contract and so becomes part of the contract only if assented to by the offeror. The silence of the offeror will not normally be considered assent.[9] As between merchants the additional terms become part of the contract unless: (a) the offer expressly limits acceptance to the

---

8.   Merchant is defined in § 2–104 as "a person who deals in goods of the kind or otherwise by his occupation holds himself out as having knowledge or skill peculiar to the practices or goods involved in the transaction or to when such knowledge or skill may be attributed by his employment of an agent or broker or other intermediary who by his occupation holds himself out as having such knowledge or skill." See § 1–7 supra.

9.   Although Comment 6 talks in terms of acceptance by silence, it relates to a situation involving two merchants, and more specifically to the last part of 2(c). Dorton v. Collins & Aikman Corp., 453 F.2d 1161 (6th Cir.1972); cf. Hohenberg v. Killebrew, 505 F.2d 643 (5th Cir.1974), re-

terms of the offer,[10] (b) they materially alter it, or (c) notification of objection to them has already been given or is given within a reasonable time after notice of them is received.

c) Subdivision 3. If it is decided that there was no contract under subdivision 1 then one goes to subdivision 3 to see if there was mutual assent by virtue of the conduct of the parties. If so subdivision 3 gives the rule for determining the terms of the agreement.[11] This subdivision will receive further mention below.

d) Different Terms. There are two problems relating to different terms. The first is what is a different term? If a term is *expressly* contradictory of an express term in the offer the term is a "different term". But what if a term of the acceptance contradicts an implied term of the offer should it be deemed to be "different"? There is authority to that effect.[12]

The text of the Code does not state a rule relating to what happens to different terms and thus it would appear that different terms do not become part of contract unless the different terms are accepted by the offeror.[13] However, Comment 3 to section 2–207 provides that the rule that is applied to additional terms should be applied to different terms.[14] Under this approach if one of the parties is a non-merchant a different term will become part of the contract only if in turn accepted by the offeror. As to merchants the different term would become part of the contract unless it is ejected under the provisions of subdivision (2).[15] Under Professor Summer's approach stated in note 15 the different term does not become part of the contract unless the offeror expressly agrees to the different term as for example by signing and returning an expression of acceptance.[16]

Professor White [17] following the lead of the Bosway [18] case argues that different terms cancel each other out but that any provision of the Code may be used as a gap-filler for the term that has been eliminated.

hearing denied 507 F.2d 1280 (5th Cir. 1975).

10. See, e.g., CBS, Inc. v. Auburn Plastics, Inc., 67 A.D.2d 811, 413 N.Y.S.2d 50 (4th Dep't 1979).

11. Duesenberg & King, Sales & Bulk Transfers, § 3.04(1) (2d ed. 1966) [hereinafter cited as Duesenberg & King]. Although subdivision (3) of the statute uses the word "writings", it would seem clear that oral communications should also be taken into account.

12. Steiner v. Mobil Oil Corp., 20 Cal.3d 90, 141 Cal.Rptr. 157, 569 P.2d 751 (1977). But there is also contrary authority. See Roto-Lith, Ltd. v. F.P. Bartlett, & Co., 297 F.2d 497 (1st Cir.1962).

13. Duesenberg & King, § 3.03(1) at 3–33 to 3–38.

14. Boese-Hilburn Co. v. Dean Machinery Co., 616 S.W.2d 520 (Mo.App.1981).

15. American Parts Co. v. American Arbitration Ass'n, 8 Mich.App. 156, 154 N.W.2d 5 (1967); Air Products & Chem., Inc. v. Fairbanks Morse, Inc., 58 Wis.2d 193, 206 N.W.2d 414 (1973). Prof. Summers suggests that this ejection would occur in every case by virtue of § 2–207(2)(c). Is there truly notification of objection? J. White and J. Summers, § 1–2.

16. N. & D. Fashions, Inc. v. DHJ Indus., Inc., 548 F.2d 722 (8th Cir.1976); see Construction Aggregates Corp. v. Hewitt-Robins, Inc., 404 F.2d 505 (7th Cir.1968), certiorari denied 395 U.S. 921, 89 S.Ct. 1774, 23 L.Ed.2d 238 (1969).

17. White & Summers, § 1–2. This notion was followed in Owens-Corning Fiberglas v. Sonic Dev. Corp., 546 F.Supp. 533 (D.C.Kan.1982). For a criticism of this approach, see Duesenberg, Contract Creation:

18. See note 18 on page 105.

However, as his co-author correctly states, the Bosway case is not on point because it relates to confirmations.

(2) The Roto-Lith Case

The operation of this section and some of the problems created by it can best be demonstrated by examining a concrete case. We shall examine the case of Roto-Lith, Ltd. v. F.P. Bartlett & Co.,[19] an early decision under this section, which for reasons of its own did not follow the language of the statute. However, it is still an excellent case to illustrate the problems created by this section.

a) The Facts. The plaintiff, a merchant, made an offer to buy a drum of emulsion from the defendant who was also a merchant. The offer did not refer to warranties but did state the particular purpose for which the goods were to be used. The defendant sent an acknowledgment and an invoice, both of which provided: "all goods sold without warranties express or implied and subject to the terms on the reverse side." One of these terms on the reverse side stated: "Seller's liability hereunder shall be limited to the replacement of any goods that materially differ from the Seller's sample order on the basis of which the order for such goods was made. If these terms are not acceptable, Buyer must so notify the Seller at once." Plaintiff did not object to these terms, accepted the goods when delivered and paid for them. Plaintiff's action is for breach of implied warranty.

b) Is There a Definite and Seasonable Expression of Acceptance? The only facts stated that bear on this question are that the defendant sent an acknowledgement and an invoice. We are not told what these forms stated other than the provisions relating to warranties quoted above. Thus, whether these forms amounted to a definite and seasonable expression of acceptance "cannot be learned from the report of the decision."[20] The court, without discussing the point assumed that there was a definite and seasonable expression of acceptance and so shall we. We shall return to the general topic of definite and seasonable expression of acceptance below.

c) Is the Acceptance Expressly Conditional on Assent to the Additional or Different Terms? The key words here are "expressly conditional on assent". The question is whether the quoted language relating to warranties makes the acceptance "expressly conditional on *assent* to the additional or different terms." The court does not take these words literally for it states, "If plaintiff's contention is correct that a reply to an offer stating additional conditions unilaterally burdensome upon the offeror is a binding acceptance of the original

The Continuing Struggle with Additional and Different Terms Under Uniform Commercial Code Section 2–207, 34 Bus.L.Rev. 1477 (1979).

18. Bosway Tube & Steel v. McKay Mach. Co., 65 Mich.App. 426, 237 N.W.2d 488 (1975).

19. 297 F.2d 497 (1st Cir.1962).

20. Duesenberg & King § 3.04(1); see also Murray, Intention Over Terms: An Explanation of U.C.C. § 2–207 and New Section 60, Restatement of Contracts, 37 Fordham L.Rev. 317 (1969).

offer plus simply a proposal for additional conditions, the statute would lead to an absurdity. Obviously no offeror will subsequently assent to such conditions." The court recognized that the statute, taken literally, requires the offeree to say in so many words, "I will not accept your offer unless you assent to the following." The court argues that businessmen "cannot be expected to act by rubric" and concludes that the statute requires "a practical construction" so that the acceptance was expressly conditional on assent.[21] Under this approach there was no agreement by virtue of the communications of the parties.

Since this case it has been widely recognized that the statute was intended to be and should be taken literally.[22] In the language of one case this provision is intended to apply "only to an acceptance which clearly reveals that the offeree is unwilling to proceed with the transaction unless he is assured of the offeror's assent to the additional or different terms."[23] A number of later cases have held that language similar to that used in Roto-Lith case did not make acceptance expressly conditional on assent.[24] A conclusion that the language should be taken literally does not solve all problems because it is still difficult to apply the language of the statute to a particular set of facts.[25]

As we have seen the court above decided that there was no contract by virtue of the communications of the parties but later cases reached a different conclusion. It will be helpful to an understanding of the statute to analyze the result under either approach.

It should be recalled that we have already assumed that there was a definite and seasonable expression of acceptance and thus if the acceptance is not expressly conditional on assent there is mutual assent.

d) Assumption That There Was an Agreement by Virtue of the Communications of the Parties. Under this assumption we go to subdivision 2 to ascertain what the terms of the agreement are. As we have seen this depends in part upon whether we are dealing with two merchants or not and whether the term sought to be included in the agreement (here no warranty) is additional or different. On the facts it is clear that we are dealing with two merchants. In any event it would be prudent in explaining the statute to analyze all of the possibilities.

---

21. Roto-Lith, Ltd. v. F.P. Bartlett & Co., 297 F.2d 497, 500 (1st Cir.1962).

22. Idaho Power Co. v. Westinghouse Elec. Corp., 596 F.2d 924 (9th Cir.1979); C. Itoh & Co. (American) Inc. v. Jordan Int'l Co., 552 F.2d 1228 (7th Cir.1977); Hohenberg Bros. Co. v. Killebrew, 505 F.2d 643 (5th Cir.1974), rehearing denied 507 F.2d 1280 (5th Cir.1975); Dorton v. Collins & Aikman, 453 F.2d 1161 (6th Cir.1972); Ebasco Serv., Inc. v. Pennsylvania P & L Co., 460 F.Supp. 163 (E.D.Pa.1978); Steiner v. Mobil Oil Corp., 20 Cal.3d 90, 141 Cal. Rptr. 157, 569 P.2d 751 (1977).

23. Dorton v. Collins & Aikman, 453 F.2d 1161 (6th Cir.1972); see Annot., 22 A.L.R.4th 939 (1983).

24. Idaho Power Co. v. Westinghouse Elec. Corp., 596 F.2d 924 (9th Cir.1977); Dorton v. Collins & Aikman, 453 F.2d 1161 (6th Cir.1972); Leonard Pevar Co. v. Evans Prod. Co., 524 F.Supp. 546 (D.D.C.1981).

25. For example, in Kleinschmidt v. Futuronics Corp., 41 N.Y.2d 972, 395 N.Y.S.2d 151, 363 N.E.2d 701 (1977), it was held that the language used, "We request that the following conditions be made a part of the order," was expressly conditional on the assent of the offeror.

e) Additional Terms. If we assume that one of the parties is a non-merchant and the term sought to be included (no warranty) is an additional term the result is that the term will not be included unless it is in turn assented to by the offeror.

If we assume that the two parties are merchants then "additional terms become part of the contract unless (a) the offer expressly limits acceptance to the terms of the offer (b) they materially alter it, or (c) notification of objection to them has already been given or is given or is given within a reasonable time after notice of them is received."

Since subdivisions 2(a) and (c) do not apply to the fact pattern the question becomes whether a no warranty clause in the acceptance amounts to a material alteration of the contract. The court indicated that it does and so the no warranty term would not be included. The question of material alteration will be discussed below as not to interfere with the flow of the analysis of the Roto-Lith case.

f) Different Terms. The court in the Roto-Lith case looked at the no warranty term as being additional presumably because the offer said nothing about warranties. Under this reasoning the no-warranty clause in the acceptance is not a different term. It certainly could be argued that the offer by implication carried with it at least an implied warranty of fitness for the purpose. Thus a clause in the acceptance saying no implied warranties would appear to contradict an implied term of the offeror. If so the term is a different term.[26]

Assuming that this is a different term the question is what becomes of the different term in this case. As we have seen in section (d) above there are three views. One view is that a different term should be treated as an additional term. That analysis has already been made. A second view is that the different terms cancel out but the provisions of the Code may be used as gap-fillers. Under this approach the warranties would form part of the contract. A third view is that different terms do not become part of the contract unless the different terms are accepted by the offeror.

g) Assumptions That There Was No Agreement by Virtue of the Communications of the Parties. In the Roto-Lith case the court concluded that there was no agreement by virtue of the communications of the parties. It then reasoned that the communication of the offeree with the no warranty term was a counter-offer that in turn was accepted when the offeror received, retained and paid for the goods that were delivered subsequent to the counter-offer. This result was correct under the "last-shot" principle of the common-law.[27] But the Roto-Lith court should have looked to subdivision 3 of § 2–207 for the answer to this problem. Under subdivision 3 it seems clear that there was an agreement by conduct. What are the terms of the agreement? Subdivision 3 says, "The terms of the particular contract consist of those

26. Air Prod. & Chem., Inc. v. Fairbanks Morse, Inc., 58 Wis.2d 193, 206 N.W.2d 414 (1973). See note 12 supra.

27. Indiana Mfg. Co. v. Hayes, 155 Pa. 160, 26 A. 6 (1893).

terms on which the writings of the parties agree, (including terms on which confirmations agree) [28] together with any supplementary terms incorporated under any other provisions of this act."

The act referred to is the entire U.C.C. except that subdivision 2 is not relevant because there was no mutual assent under subdivision 1 hence the use of the word "other". On the facts the question becomes is there a provision in the Code relating to warranties? The answer is in the affirmative. Hence the warranty provisions of the Code would become part of the contract and the contract would include at least a warranty of merchantability and possibly a warranty of fitness for the purpose.[29]

(3) The Pretermitted Topics

Three topics mentioned above were postponed for later discussion. They will be considered briefly at this point.

a) Definite and Seasonable Expression of Acceptance. The Code is not clear on the meaning of this phrase. For example, if the offeree's form indicates acceptance but shows a change in the quantity can there be a definite and seasonable expression of acceptance? A recent case has held that there is not.[30] This is in accord with some authorities that take the position that there is not a definite and seasonable expression if the alleged acceptance "diverges significantly as to a dickered term". Dickered terms should certainly include the description of the goods, price quantity and delivery terms.[31] Other courts reach the same result but stress U.C.C. § 2–204(3) to the effect that the parties must "have intended to make a contract". The notion undoubtedly is that if the parties fail to agree as to a dickered term the parties do not intend to make a contract, and the parties do not have the necessary commercial understanding that a deal has been closed.[32]

There are contrary cases. For example, there is a case where the seller's acceptance called for a 30% increase in price. The court held that there was a definite and seasonable expression of acceptance and then under subdivision 2 held that the price increase amounted to a material alteration and so the seller's price term (whether additional or different) did not become part of the contract and the offeror's term

---

28. Jones & McKnight Corp. v. Birdsboro Corp., 320 F.Supp. 39 (N.D.Ill.1970).

29. Bosway Tube & Steel v. McKay Mach. Co., 65 Mich.App. 426, 237 N.W.2d 488 (1975); see U.C.C. §§ 2–314 and 2–315.

30. Duval & Co. v. Malcom, 233 Ga. 784, 214 S.E.2d 356 (1975).

31. United States Indus. v. Semco Mfg., 562 F.2d 1061 (8th Cir.1977), certiorari denied 434 U.S. 986, 98 S.Ct. 613, 54 L.Ed.2d 480 (1977); [Duesenberg & King § 3.04(1)]; White & Summers § 1–2.

32. Dorton v. Collins & Aikman Corp., 453 F.2d 1161 (6th Cir.1972); Steiner v. Mobil Oil Corp., 20 Cal.3d 90, 141 Cal.Rtpr. 157, 569 P.2d 751 (1977); Kleinschmidt v. Futuronics Corp., 41 N.Y.2d 972, 395 N.Y.S.2d 151, 363 N.E.2d 701 (1977); U.C.C. § 2–207, Comment 2. Professor Murray argues that subdivision 1 should not be read mechanically and the issue should be whether the parties should reasonably conclude that there was a deal or that a counter offer was made. 39 Pitt.L. Rev. 597 (1978).

prevailed.[33] Another relevant case is the Bosway Case.[34] In that case the offer contained one delivery date and the acceptance a different delivery date. The court looked upon the problem as one of different terms. However, under one view stated above it could have been decided that there was no definite and seasonable expression of acceptance. An acceptance that negates an express warranty is still deemed to be a definite expression of acceptance because this is considered not to be a dickered term.[35]

b) Material Alteration. What is a material as opposed to an immaterial alteration is not made clear. Comments 4 and 5 to U.C.C. § 2–207 give some illustrations of each. "Generally a material alteration is an addition or change to the contract which would result in surprise or hardship if incorporated without the express awareness by the other party."[36] Many of the cases have arisen when the offeree merchant includes an arbitration clause in his acceptance. The facts assumed are that two merchants have reached agreement by virtue of their communications and offeree seeks to include in the contract an arbitration clause contained in his acceptance when arbitration was not mentioned by the offeror. The issue becomes whether the arbitration clause is a material alteration. The majority of the cases have responded in the affirmative.[37] Others have held that the materiality of the arbitration clause must be proved and not assumed.[38]

If there is a usage of the trade with respect to arbitration but the offeror's form does not include it and the offeree's acceptance does, does the arbitration clause become part of the contract by virtue of the custom or a course of performance or a course of dealing even though it would otherwise be deemed to be a material alteration?[39] If a material alteration is assented to by the offeror it becomes part of the contract.[40]

33. CBS, Inc. v. Auburn Plastics, Inc., 67 A.D.2d 811, 413 N.Y.S.2d 50 (1979). See generally Stewart-Decatur Sec. Systems v. Von Weise Gear Co., 517 F.2d 1136 (8th Cir.1975); 31 Bus.Law. 1543–44 (1976); 37 Fordham L.Rev. 317, 322 (1969).

34. Bosway Tube & Steel v. McKay Mach. Co., 65 Mich.App. 426, 237 N.W.2d 488 (1975).

35. General Time Corp. v. Eye Encounter, Inc., 50 N.C.App. 467, 274 S.E.2d 391 (1981).

36. McMahan v. Koppers Co., 654 F.2d 380 (5th Cir.1981); U.C.C. § 2–207, Comment 4.

37. Windsor Mills, Inc. v. Collins & Aikman Corp., 25 Cal.App.3d 987, 101 Cal. Rptr. 347 (2d Dist.1972); Andy Associates, Inc. v. Bankers Trust Co., 49 N.Y.2d 13, 424 N.Y.2d 139, 399 N.E.2d 1160 (1979); Matter of Marlene Indus. Corp., 45 N.Y.2d 327, 408 N.Y.S.2d 410, 380 N.E.2d 239

(1978); Frances Hosiery Mills, Inc. v. Burlington Indus., Inc., 285 N.C. 344, 204 S.E.2d 834 (1974). See generally Furnish, Commercial Arbitration Agreements and the Uniform Commercial Code, 67 Calif.L. Rev. 317 (1979).

38. Dorton v. Collins & Aikman Corp., 453 F.2d 1161 (6th Cir.1972).

39. The cases are in conflict. See Baumgold Bros. v. Alan M. Fox Co., East, 375 F.Supp. 807 (N.D.Ohio 1973); Application of Gaynor-Stafford Indus., Inc./Mafco Textured Fibers, 52 A.D.2d 481, 384 N.Y.S.2d 788 (1st Dep't 1976); White & Summers § 1–2; see also Shubtex, Inc. v. Snyder, 49 N.Y.2d 1, 424 N.Y.S.2d 133, 399 N.E.2d 1154 (1979), reargument denied 49 N.Y.2d 801, 426 N.Y.S.2d 1029, 403 N.E.2d 466 (1980).

40. See Coastal Indus. v. Automatic Steam Products, 654 F.2d 375 (5th Cir. 1981).

c) Confirmations. At the very beginning of this section it was noted that subdivision 1 talks about "a definite and seasonable expression of acceptance". This has already been covered. It also mentions "a written confirmation which is sent within a reasonable time." On this point subdivision 1 reads, "a written confirmation which is sent within a reasonable time operates as an acceptance even though it states terms additional to or different from those * * * agreed upon, * * *" It appears strange to say that "a written confirmation" operates as an acceptance because a confirmation presumably would be a confirmation of a contract already formed. However, this part of the section seems to be limited primarily to two situations: (1) "where an agreement has been reached either orally or by informal correspondence between the parties and is followed by one or both parties sending formal acknowledgements or memoranda embodying the terms so far agreed upon and adding terms not discussed."[41] The assumption here is that the terms are additional and that there is no conflict between the additional terms in the two memoranda or acknowledgements. In this type of case it is easy to understand that the rules previously stated with respect to "additional" terms should apply. (2) Where there are "additional" terms in the memoranda sent and they conflict with each other, each party is deemed to object to the other party's terms "and the conflicting terms to do not become part of the contract." The contract then consists of the terms originally expressly agreed to, terms on which the confirmations agree and terms supplied by the Act including subsection 2. The reference to subsection 2 here seems to relate to terms brought into the contract under rule (1) above and additional or different terms that became part of the original agreement.[42]

If a written confirmation omits a term that was actually agreed upon, it would appear that the actual term agreed upon may be proved and will govern the transaction.[43] However, this situation also presents a problem to be discussed under the parol evidence rule.[44]

(c) Conclusion

It is clear that U.C.C. § 2–207 was designed to change the mirror-image rule and to do away with the battle of the forms—drawing forms designed to give advantage to the drafter.[45] To some extent the Code

41. U.C.C. § 2–207, Comment 1.

42. U.C.C. § 2–207, Comment 6. The "unless" clause of subdivision 1 does not apply to written confirmations. Dorton v. Collins & Aikman Corp., 453 F.2d 1161 (6th Cir.1972); American Parts Co. v. American Arbitration Ass'n, 8 Mich.App. 156, 154 N.W.2d 5 (1967).

43. Album Graphics, Inc. v. Beatrice Foods, 87 Ill.App.3d 338, 42 Ill.Dec. 332, 408 N.E.2d 1041 (1980).

44. I.S. Joseph Co., Inc. v. Citrus Feed Co., Inc., 490 F.2d 185 (5th Cir.1974), rehearing denied 492 F.2d 1242 (5th Cir. 1974); U.C.C. § 2–201(2), Comment 3; see ch. 3 infra.

45. See Apsey, The Battle of the Forms, 34 Notre Dame Law. 556 (1959); Lipman, On Winning the Battle of the Forms: An Analysis of Section 2–207 of the Uniform Commercial Code, 24 Bus.Law. 789 (1969); Macauley, Non-Contractual Relations in Business: A Preliminary Study, 28 Am.

has succeeded because it has structured a statute that is designed to favor the offeror, who apparently is the "have not" in most transactions. The statute has been properly described as a "murky bit of prose," [46] "not too happily drafted" [47] and as "not altogether satisfactory." [48] The initial advantage that it may confer upon the offeror will disappear after the attorneys for the large corporations learn to move within the crevices of the statute.[49] For example it has been suggested that the offeree may avoid the statute altogether by rejecting the offer and explicitly making a counter-offer.[50]

 WESTLAW REFERENCES

(a) *The Common Law Rule*

95k24 /p "common law"

accept! /s "common law" /s contract /s condition! vary! varied

counter offer! "counter offer!" /s "common law"

"mirror image" /s "common law"

343k22(4)

"mirror image rule"

(b) *U.C.C. § 2–207*

"uniform commercial code" /s 2–207

   (1) *Basic Design of Statute*

      (b) *Subdivision 2—Additional Terms*

"additional terms" /s merchant

      (d) *Different Terms*

"different term" /s offer! /s contract

"different term" /s contract /s express!

"different term" /s offeror /s accept!

"different term" /s "additional term"

"different term" /s merchant

   (2) *The Roto-Lith Case*

"roto lith" +s bartlett

   (3) *The Pretermitted Topics*

      (a) *Definite and Seasonable Expression of Acceptance*

"definite and seasonable expression of acceptance"

"dickered term"

accept! /s negat! /s "express warranty"

Soc.Rev. 55, 59–60 (1963); Comment, Section 2–207 of the Uniform Commercial Code—New Rules for the Battle of Forms, 32 Pitt.L.Rev. 209 (1970); Comment, Nonconforming Acceptances under Section 2–207 of the Uniform Commercial Code: An End to the Battle of the Forms, 30 U.Chi.L. Rev. 540 (1963).

46. Southwest Engineering Co. v. Martin Tractor Co., 205 Kan. 684, 694, 473 P.2d 18, 25 (1970).

47. Roto-Lith, Ltd. v. F.P. Bartlett & Co., 297 F.2d 497, 500 (1st Cir.1962).

48. Duesenberg & King § 3.03; see also Barron and Dunfee, Two Decades of 2–207: Review, Reflection and Revision, 24 Clev. St.L.Rev. 171 (1975).

49. Weintraub, Disclaimer of Warranties and Limitation of Damages for Breach of Warranty Under the U.C.C., 53 Tex.L. Rev. 60, 70–74 (1974).

50. E. Farnsworth, Contracts, § 3.21.

       (b) *Material Alteration*

"material alteration" /s immaterial

"material alteration" /s contract

"immaterial alteration"

"material alteration" /s "arbitration clause"

"material alteration" /s assent!

       (c) *Confirmations*

di("written confirmation" /p "reasonable time")

"written confirmation" /s acceptance

"written confirmation" /s "oral agreement"

di("written confirmation" /p additional)

di("written confirmation" /p differ!)

95k24 /p differ!

343k23 /p confirm!

(c) *Conclusion*

"uniform commercial code" 2–207 /s "mirror image"

battle +2 form "last shot"

---

§ 2–22.   Up to What Point of Time May an Offeror Revoke a Revocable Offer Looking to a Unilateral Contract?

May an offer to a unilateral contract be revoked (terminated) or changed after the offeree has partially performed?[51] The common law has three views on the question. The oldest view is that the offer may be revoked at any time until the act constituting performance is completed.[52] The theory is that since the offeree is free not to complete performance the offeror should be free not to perform. In addition the argument goes that it is logical to assume that the offeror is asking for a completed act.[53]

But even if this is so, logic is not justice. Clearly once the offeree has relied upon the offer by starting to perform he deserves some protection from an arbitrary revocation. To provide such protection a second view concludes that a bilateral contract arises when the offeree starts to perform.[54] This view is illogical because the offeror did not ask for a promise and because the beginning of performance may not indicate that the offeree intended to pursue his performance to completion.[55]

51. A change in terms is tantamount to a revocation of the offer and the substitution of a new one. Sylvestre v. State, 298 Minn. 142, 214 N.W.2d 658 (1973).

52. Bartlett v. Keith, 325 Mass. 265, 90 N.E.2d 308 (1950); Petterson v. Pattberg, 248 N.Y. 86, 161 N.E. 428 (1928); Hummer v. Engeman, 206 Va. 102, 141 S.E.2d 716 (1965).

53. Wormser, The True Conception of Unilateral Contracts, 26 Yale L.J. 136

(1916), Selected Readings 307. But see Wormser, Book Review, 3 J.Legal.Educ. 145 (1950); see also Stoljar, The False Distinction Between Bilateral and Unilateral Contracts, 64 Yale L.J. 515 (1954).

54. Los Angeles Traction Co. v. Wilshire, 135 Cal. 654, 67 P. 1086 (1902).

55. See Ashley, Offers Calling for Consideration Other than a Counter Promise, 23 Harv.L.Rev. 159 (1910).

The third view stakes out a middle ground between the two other competing views. This view states that once the offeree begins to perform the offer becomes irrevocable.[56] The term irrevocable offer is often used interchangeably with the expression used in the Restatement Second that there is an option contract.[57] Under this view the offeree does not become bound to complete performance. Even though there is an option contract the offeree will not be entitled to a contractual recovery unless he completes performance within the time allowable. But this will not be true if the offeror repudiates his promise after the offeree has commenced performance. In such a case the offeree has a contractual cause of action because his failure to complete performance is excused.[58] But he must show that he would have been ready, willing and able to perform but for the repudiation.[59] What his measure of damages is need not be discussed here but the situation in this respect is analogous to a bilateral contract.[60] Also, as in the case of a bilateral contract, he must mitigate damages.[61] Usually, this rule requires that he cease performance.[62]

There are two additional problems that must be considered under this approach. One is that the offer becomes irrevocable only if the offeree has actually started to perform. Mere preparation is not enough.[63] This is a somewhat tenuous distinction.[64] The other rule is that if performance requires the cooperation of the offeror and cooperation is withheld, tender of part performance is the equivalent of part performance.[65]

The two problems may be exemplified in one illustration. A makes an offer stating that he will pay B $1,000.00 if B paints (assume unilateral) A's living room. B arrives at the front door ready, willing and able to perform and tenders his services. A sends him away. The first question is whether what B did prior to being sent away could be

56. Marchiondo v. Scheck, 79 N.M. 440, 432 P.2d 405 (1967); Jenkins v. Vaughn, 197 Tenn. 578, 276 S.W.2d 732 (1955); Hutchinson v. Dobson–Bainbridge Realty Co., 31 Tenn.App. 490, 217 S.W.2d 6 (1946); Harding v. Rock, 60 Wn.2d 292, 373 P.2d 784 (1962); Restatement, Second, Contracts § 45.

57. See the discussion on this point in § 2–24 infra.

58. Restatement, Second, Contracts § 45, Comment 3, wherein it is stated that performance is excused "for example if the offeror prevents performance, waives it or repudiates." See also Motel Services, Inc. v. Central Maine Power Co., 394 A.2d 786 (Me.1978).

59. Restatement, Second, Contracts § 45; Restatement, Contracts § 315.

60. See § 11–31 infra.

61. Simpson § 199.

62. See § 14–15 infra.

63. See Bretz v. Union Cent. Life Ins. Co., 134 Ohio St. 171, 16 N.E.2d 272 (1938); Peizer v. Bergeon, 111 Ohio App. 205, 164 N.E.2d 790 (1960); see also Doll & Smith v. A. & S. Sanitary Dairy Co., 202 Iowa 786, 211 N.W. 230 (1926); Restatement, Second, Contracts § 45, Comment f; Comment, Unilateral Contracts: An Examination of Traditional Concepts and the Proposed Solution of the ALI Restatement of Contracts, Second (Tent. Draft No. 1), 5 Duq.L. Rev. 175 (1966).

64. See Restatement, Second, Contracts § 45, Comment f, to the effect that many factors must be considered in applying this distinction to a set of facts.

65. Restatement, Contracts § 45, Comment d. It seems that the word "tendered" here is used in its technical significance as it apparently was used by the majority of the Court of Appeals in Petterson v. Pattberg, 248 N.Y. 86, 161 N.E. 428 (1928); see also Restatement, Contracts § 263, Comment b.

considered to be the beginning of performance or only preparation. If it is decided that it is only preparation then the second rule comes into play. The act of painting on these facts requires the cooperation of the offeror because the offeree is a trespasser if he does not have the permission of the offeror to enter upon the premises. Thus even though it is assumed that the offeree has not entered upon performance the tender of performance (or even part performance) prior to revocation makes the offer irrevocable.

The Uniform Commercial Code has not resolved this conflict because cases involving this issue are essentially placed on a different basis. The same is true of the Restatement Second.[66]

WESTLAW REFERENCES

"unilateral contract" /s revo!

"unilateral contract" /s chang!

"unilateral contract" /s part partial! partly /2 perform! /s revo! chang! terminat!

revoc! revok! chang! terminat! /s "unilateral contract" /s offer! /s perform!

bilateral /s unilateral /s contract /s offeree /s perform!

offeree /s perform! /s irrevo!

"option contract" /s "irrevocable offer"

"option contract" /s bind binding bound /s perform!

perform! /s "wrongful! revo!"

perform! /s excus! /s offer! /s waiv! repudiat! prevent!

perform! /s repudiat! /s "ready, willing and able"

§ 2–23.   Up to What Point in Time May a Revocable Offer Looking to a Bilateral Contract Be Revoked?

(a) Parties at a Distance

A revocable offer to a bilateral contract may be revoked at any time prior to its acceptance. Thus, stated differently the question in the caption is, when is an attempted acceptance effective? In a general way the answer is that it is effective when it is communicated.[67] But when is it communicated? As we have seen a revocation and a rejection are effective when received.[68] This is generally true of other communications in the absence of unusual circumstances.[69]

However, as a result of an historical accident some early cases held that an acceptance is effectively communicated when it is put out of the possession of the offeree as for example into a public mail box. This rule is sometimes referred to as the "mailbox rule" or the rule of

66. See the discussion in § 2–26 infra.

67. See § 2–17 supra.

68. Lynch v. Webb City School Dist., 418 S.W.2d 608 (Mo.App.1967); Restatement, Contracts § 68. See § 2–20 supra.

69. See Hoch v. Hitchens, 122 Mich. App. 142, 332 N.W.2d 440 (1982); Sy Jack

Realty Co. v. Pergament Syosset Corp., 27 N.Y.2d 449, 318 N.Y.S.2d 720, 267 N.E.2d 462 (1971); § 11–35 infra. But see Birznieks v. Cooper, 405 Mich. 319, 275 N.W.2d 221 (1979).

Adams v. Lindsell.[70] This rule has been defended on the ground that at this point the offeree has done all he can do and so he should be protected against an intervening revocation.[71] The rule applies even if the communication is delayed or lost in transit.[72] The rule of Adams v. Lindsell prevails generally throughout the United States with the qualification that the acceptance to be effective when sent must be dispatched in an authorized manner.[73] The First Restatement states that, in the absence of contrary indications, the offer authorizes the means of communication used in transmitting the offer and any other manner customary at the time and place received.[74] The test is very general and has resulted in conflicting decisions. Thus, it is often held that a telegram is an authorized method of accepting an offer sent by post.[75] There are contrary decisions.[76] So also it has been held that an acceptance of a telegraphed offer by post has been held to be authorized.[77] Again there are contrary decisions.[78]

70. Adams v. Lindsell, 106 Eng.Rep. 250 (K.B.1818). The decision seems to have been rendered to protect offerees from an application of the subjective theory as previously announced in the case of Cooke v. Oxley, 100 Eng.Rep. 785 (K.B.1790). The rule that acceptance takes effect upon dispatch was reaffirmed in Dunlop v. Higgins, 9 Eng.Rep. 805 (Ch. 1848). For critiques of the decisions, see Macneil, Time of Acceptance: Too Many Problems for a Single Rule, 112 U.Pa.L. Rev. 947 (1964); Sharp, Reflections on Contract, 33 U.Chi.L.Rev. 211, 213–15 (1965).

71. Restatement, Second, Contracts § 63, Comment a.

72. Household Fire & Carriage Acc. Ins. Co. v. Grant, 4 Ex.D. 216 (C.A.1879); Restatement, Second, Contracts § 63, Comment b. But see Macneil, Time of Acceptance: Too Many Problems for a Single Rule, 112 U.Pa.L.Rev. 947 (1964). See also Llewellyn, Our Case Law of Contract: Offer and Acceptance (Pt. 2), 48 Yale L.J. 779, 795 n. 23 (1939).

73. Morrison v. Thoelke, 155 So.2d 889 (Fla.App.1963); Reserve Ins. Co. v. Duckett, 249 Md. 108, 238 A.2d 536 (1968); Pribil v. Ruther, 200 Neb. 161, 262 N.W.2d 460 (1978); Scottish American Mortgage Co. v. Davis, 96 Tex. 504, 74 S.W. 17 (1903); Henthorn v. Fraser, [1892] 2 Ch. 27. Contra, Rhode Island Tool Co. v. United States, 128 F.Supp. 417 (Ct.Cl.1955) (relying on the privilege, under postal regulation to withdraw letter from the mails, but this position has not gained any substantial recognition); 38 Tul.L.Rev. 566 (1964). Even if the letter is actually withdrawn, it still amounts to an acceptance. Restatement, Second, Contracts § 63, Comment c.

74. Restatement, Contracts § 65. It is also generally held that a letter which is properly addressed, stamped and mailed is presumed to have been delivered in due course of the post. Legille v. Dann, 544 F.2d 1 (D.C.Cir.1976). The presumption is rebuttable. Charlson Realty Co. v. United States, 384 F.2d 434 (Ct.Cl.1967); News Syndicate Co. v. Gatti Paper Stock Corp., 256 N.Y. 211, 176 N.E. 169 (1931). For a more detailed statement of this rule, see Public Finance Co. v. Van Blaricome, 324 N.W.2d 716 (Iowa 1982); see Wagner Tractor, Inc. v. Shields, 381 F.2d 441 (9th Cir. 1967); Annot., 24 A.L.R.3d 1434 (1967) (applying the same presumption to a telegram). However, proof of office practice is not sufficient to give rise to the presumption. Pribil v. Ruther, 200 Neb. 161, 262 N.W.2d 460 (1978); Caprino v. Nationwide Mut. Ins. Co., 34 A.D.2d 522, 308 N.Y.S.2d 624 (1st Dep't 1970). But see Cushing v. Thomson, 118 N.H. 292, 386 A.2d 805 (1978).

75. Stephen M. Weld & Co. v. Victory Mfg. Co., 205 Fed. 770 (E.D.N.C.1913).

76. Dickey v. Hurd, 33 F.2d 415 (1st Cir. 1929); Tucas v. Western Tel. Co., 131 Iowa 669, 109 N.W. 191 (1906). But cf. Elkhorn-Hazard Coal Co. v. Kentucky River Coal Co., 20 F.2d 67 (6th Cir.1927) (use of mail for acceptance not authorized where written offer delivered in person).

77. Farmers' Produce Co. v. McAlester Storage & Comm'n Co., 48 Okl. 488, 150 P. 483 (1915).

78. Richard v. Credit Suisse, 124 Misc. 3, 206 N.Y.S. 150 (1924), affirmed 214 App. Div. 705, 209 N.Y.S. 909 (1st Dep't 1925), affirmed 242 N.Y. 346, 152 N.E. 110 (1926).

The Uniform Commercial Code and the Restatement Second have changed the concept from authorized to reasonable. If an offer is accepted by "any medium reasonable in the circumstances" it is effective when it is put out of the possession of the offeree.[79] The Restatement Second and the Code make it clear that the concept of reasonability is intended to be flexible and may be enlarged. They indicate that acceptance by mail is ordinarily reasonable where the parties are negotiating at a distance unless there is a reason for speed and that it may be reasonable where the offer is transmitted by telegraph. Telegraphic acceptance of an offer made by mail is ordinarily reasonable.[80]

If the offeree uses an unauthorized or an unreasonable medium of acceptance under the traditional rule, the acceptance is effective when received rather than when sent.[81] The Restatement Second, however, takes the position that even if an unreasonable method of acceptance is utilized, it is, nevertheless, effective when sent provided that it is seasonably dispatched and provided that it is received within the time a seasonably dispatched acceptance sent in a reasonable manner would normally have arrived.[82] Even if an authorized (reasonable) means of communications is utilized, failure to address it properly or to take other reasonable precautions to insure safe transmission has traditionally been believed to result in the loss of the benefit of the rule that the acceptance takes effect when dispatched. That is to say that the acceptance in such a case is effective when received provided it is timely.[83] The Second Restatement has also changed this rule. It states that the acceptance is effective when sent provided that it is seasonably dispatched and provided that it is received within the time a seasonably dispatched properly stamped and addressed acceptance would normally have arrived.[84]

79. Fujimoto v. Rio Grande Pickle Co., 414 F.2d 648 (5th Cir.1969); Albemarle Educ. Foundation, Inc. v. Basnight, 4 N.C. App. 652, 167 S.E.2d 486 (1969); Restatement, Contracts (2d) § 63; U.C.C. § 2–206(1)(a).

80. Restatement, Second, Contracts § 65, Comments b, c and d; see U.C.C. § 2–206, Comment 1.

81. Restatement, Contracts § 67. Of course the acceptance must be received before the power of acceptance has lapsed or has been revoked. Williston § 87. There are some difficult problems. For example, if A in Los Angeles sends an offer to B by mail in New York, and a reasonable time within which to reply by mail would be two days after receipt of the letter, and B accepts on the third day by telegram (assume unauthorized) and the telegram is received by the offeror "within the time within which an acceptance sent in authorized manner would probably have been received by him," (Restatement, Con-

tracts § 67) there would be a contract. But would the result be the same if the offer was stated to be open for 2 days from the time it was received?

82. Restatement, Second, Contracts § 67, Comment a indicates that the offeree should not be allowed to use the extra time to speculate at the expense of the offeror.

83. Restatement, Contracts § 67.

84. Restatement, Second, Contracts § 67. In discussing the two problems raised by this paragraph, the Restatement Second makes a cross-reference to U.C.C. § 1–201(38). The Reporter's Note states, "the provision that timely receipt has the effect of proper sending is also new; it conforms to Uniform Commercial Code § 1–201(38) * * *." This section reads, " 'Send' in connection with any writing or notice means to deposit in the mail or deliver for transmission by any other usual means of communication with postage or cost of transmission provided for and prop-

In the logical order before one considers whether the medium used by the offeree is reasonable (authorized) it is necessary to decide whether the offeror prescribes a medium of communication. When the offeror prescribes the place, time or medium of acceptance the offer controls [85] with the result that no contract is formed unless the terms of the offer are followed.[86] If for example, the offeror states, "you must accept, if at all by telegram" a contract will be formed when the telegram is duly deposited with the telegraph company. The prescribed method has been followed and so the acceptance is effective when it is put out of the possession of the offeree.[87] If the offeree uses another method of acceptance no contract is formed but the offeree has made a counter-offer.[88]

Courts are reluctant to interpret language as calling for a prescribed medium of acceptance. Thus, even though a medium of acceptance is stated in the offer the tendency of the courts is to hold that the offeror has merely suggested, rather than required, this form of acceptance.[89] If the suggested form of acceptance is not used the question remains whether the medium actually used could be considered reasonable or authorized under the circumstances of the case.[90]

The offeror, it must be remembered, is master of his offer and so he has power to negate the mailbox rule. He can do this by framing his

erly addressed * * *. The receipt of any writing or notice within the time at which it would have arrived if properly sent has the effect of a proper sending." It seems clear that the provision does not relate to an unauthorized method of acceptance. However, it does appear to apply to a misdirected acceptance. But the rule is slightly different than the one announced in the Restatement. The Restatement talks about when a seasonably dispatched acceptance would be received, whereas the U.C.C. takes into account when this particular communication was actually sent in determining whether it arrives within the time at which it would have arrived if properly sent.

85. Eliason v. Henshaw, 17 U.S. (4 Wheat.) 225, 4 L.Ed. 556 (1819); Glenway Indus., Inc. v. Wheelabrator-Frye, Inc., 686 F.2d 415 (6th Cir.1982); Golden Dipt Co. v. Systems Eng'r & Mfg. Co., 465 F.2d 215 (7th Cir.1972); Goode v. Universal Plastics, Inc., 247 Ark. 442, 445 S.W.2d 893 (1969); Brophy v. Joliet, 14 Ill.App.2d 443, 144 N.E.2d 816 (1957); Spratt v. Paramount Pictures, Inc., 178 Misc. 682, 35 N.Y.S.2d 815 (1942); Cochran v. Connell, 53 Or.App. 933, 632 P.2d 1385 (1981), review denied 292 Or. 109, 642 P.2d 311 (1981); Restatement, Contracts § 60. Where the method of acceptance is prescribed on the offeree's form, the offeree may waive compliance. Neal-Cooper Grain Co. v. Texas Gulf

Sulphur Co., 508 F.2d 283 (7th Cir.1974) ("Contract shall not be binding * * * until duly accepted at its New York Office").

86. Lexington Housing Auth. v. Continental Cas. Co., 210 F.Supp. 732 (W.D. Tenn.1962); Town of Lindsay v. Cooke County Elec. Coop. Ass'n, 502 S.W.2d 117 (Tex.1973), certiorari denied 416 U.S. 970, 94 S.Ct. 1993, 40 L.Ed.2d 559 (1974); see Brach v. Matteson, 298 Ill. 387, 131 N.E. 804 (1921).

87. Restatement, Second, Contracts § 60, ill. 3.

88. Avila Group, Inc. v. Norma J., 426 F.Supp. 537 (S.D.N.Y.1977); Executive Leasing Ass'n, Inc. v. Rowland, 30 N.C. App. 590, 227 S.E.2d 642 (1976); Vaulx v. Cumis Ins. Society, 407 A.2d 262 (D.C. 1979); Zinni v. Royal Lincoln-Mercury, Inc., 84 Ill.App.3d 1093, 40 Ill.Dec. 511, 406 N.E.2d 212 (1980).

89. Fujimoto v. Rio Grande Pickle Co., 414 F.2d 648 (5th Cir.1969); Allied Steel & Conveyors, Inc. v. Ford Motor Co., 277 F.2d 907 (6th Cir.1960); Mid–Continent Petroleum Corp. v. Russel, 173 F.2d 620 (10th Cir. 1949); Zimmerman Bros. & Co. v. First Nat'l Bank, 219 Wis. 427, 263 N.W. 361 (1935); see also Restatement, Second, Contracts § 60, ill. 5.

90. Cf. In re Klauenberg, 32 Cal.App.3d 1067, 108 Cal.Rptr. 669 (1973).

offer so as to require actual receipt of an acceptance as a precondition to the formation of the contract.[91] However, such a requirement must be clearly expressed.[92] The Second Restatement states that such a condition is normally implied "where the receipt of the notice is essential to enable the offeror to perform."[93]

The rule that an acceptance is effective when sent is troublesome when the offeree sends both an acceptance and a rejection. The rejection, as we have seen is effective when received.[94] Consider the following sequences (a) rejection sent, acceptance sent, rejection received, acceptance received; (b) rejection sent, acceptance sent, acceptance received, rejection received. The Restatement rule with respect to these two situations is that an acceptance dispatched after a rejection has been sent is not effective until received and only if received prior to the rejection.[95] Under this rule there is a contract in sequence (b)[96] but not in (a). Under this approach in each case the expectation of the offeror is protected. In case (a) the acceptance is regarded as a counter-offer.[97]

A more troublesome sequence arises in sequence (c), acceptance sent, rejection sent, rejection received, acceptance received. If the expectations of the offeror were followed, there would be no contract and some courts have so held.[98] However, there is significant authority, including the Restatement, that a contract is formed.[99] Otherwise the offeree could speculate at the offeror's expense by seeing how the market went. If it moved in the offeree's favor he would allow the acceptance to stand. If it moved in the offeror's favor, the offeree could use an earlier-arriving communication to undo the acceptance.[1] This would be unfair because if the offeror is bound by the offeree's communication this should also be true of the offeree. This view is sometimes qualified by saying that if the offeror relies on the rejection before receiving the acceptance the offeree will be estopped from enforcing the contract.[2] Under the Restatement view the over-taking rejection may

91. Union Interchange, Inc. v. Sierota, 355 P.2d 1089 (Colo.1960); Holland v. Riverside Park Estates, 214 Ga. 244, 104 S.E.2d 83 (1958); Lewis v. Browning, 130 Mass. 173 (1881); Vassar v. Camp, 11 N.Y. (1 Kern.) 441 (1854); Western Union Tel. Co. v. Gardner, 278 S.W. 278 (Tex.Civ.App. 1925); 1 Williston § 88. Restatement, Second, Contracts § 63, Comment b.

92. Vassar v. Camp, 11 N.Y. (1 Kern.) 441 (1854); 1 Williston § 88.

93. Restatement, Second, Contracts § 63, Comment b.

94. Restatement, Second, Contracts § 68.

95. Restatement, Second, Contracts § 40.

96. But under this rule in sequence (b) a revocation that became effective prior to the receipt of the acceptance would terminate the offer.

97. Restatement, Second, Contracts § 40.

98. Dick v. United States, 82 F.Supp. 326 (Ct.Cl.1949); 1 Corbin § 94.

99. Morrison v. Thoelke, 155 So.2d 889 (Fla.App.1963); Restatement, Second, Contracts § 63, Comment c and ill. 7.

1. Restatement, Second, Contracts § 63, Comment c.

2. E. Frederics, Inc. v. Felton Beauty Supply, 58 Ga.App. 320, 198 S.E. 324 (1938); Restatement, Second, Contracts § 63, Comment c.

be looked upon as an offer to rescind the contract or a repudiation.[3] In case (c) if the acceptance arrived before the rejection there would also be a contract.

(b) Parties in the Presence of One Another

When the parties are in the presence of each other an acceptance is inoperative unless the offeror hears it or is at fault in not hearing.[4] It would be an unusual case in which the offeror is at fault in not hearing.[5] Even if the offeror is at fault in not hearing, there still would be no contract if the offeree knew or had reason to know that the offeror had not heard.[6] It is clear this rule is not in accord with "mailbox" rule discussed above.

Should a conversation conducted by telephone or similar media be governed by the rules developed for face to face conversation? The text writers all but unanimously agree that these means of communication should be governed by the *in praesentes* rules.[7] The majority of the cases appear to be to the contrary, holding that the acceptance takes place when spoken by the offeree rather than when heard by the offeror, but it should be noted that they have arisen in the context of conflict of laws and concern the question of where the contract was formed rather than whether there was a contract.[8]

These cases do no involve a break in the connection. In such a case the Restatement argues that even if a court wished to apply the "at a distance" rule the issue of fault would have to be confronted. If the parties are equally blameless or equally at fault there would be no contract.[9]

 WESTLAW REFERENCES

(a) *Parties at a Distance*

"bilateral contract" /s revo!

accept! /s communicat! /s effective

revo! reject! /s receiv! receipt /s effective

"mail box" mailbox +1 rule

adams +s lindsell

accept! /s effect! /s dispatch!

mail*** post*** /s telegram! /s accept! /s offer!

"medium reasonable"

"medium of acceptance"

offeror /s precondition! prerequisite /s contract agreement

3. Restatement, Second, Contracts § 63, Comment c; see also U.C.C. § 2–608 (1977).

4. 1 Williston § 82.

5. 1 Corbin § 104.

6. 1 Corbin § 79.

7. Id., 1 Williston § 82A; Restatement, Contracts § 64.

8. Perrin v. Pearlstein, 314 F.2d 863 (2d Cir.1963). Contra, Entores Ltd. v. Miles Far East Corp., [1955] 2 Q.B. 327.

9. Restatement, Second, Contracts § 64, Comment b.

(lewis +2 browning) ("union interchange" +s sierota)
offeror /s expectation

(b) *Parties in the Presence of One Another*
perrin +s pearlstein

§ 2–24. Risk of Mistake in Transmission by an Intermediary

If A intends to sell his horse to B for $110, but inadvertently says "I offer to sell you my horse for $100," it is settled that if B does not know or have reason to know of A's mistake and accepts the offer, a contract for the sale of the horse at $100 is formed.[10] The same would be true if A's agent made a similar mistake. But what if the mistake is made in transmission by an intermediary and not an agent? This problem arose in a number of cases that involve a mistake in transmission by a telegraph company. A majority of the cases have held in such a case that there is a contract based upon the $100 figure.[11]

Three reasons are assigned by the majority for this result. One reason is that the telegraph company is the agent of A.[12] But this is simply not true because the telegraph company is an independent contractor.[13] A second reason advanced for the rule is that it results in better business convenience. This argument may have some validity but it is at least a debatable proposition.

The third rationale is that the first party to utilize the telegraph company should bear the risk of loss because his choice of the telegraph company makes him more responsible for the error.[14] But this reason is not consistent with a complete statement of the majority rule. The true majority view is that the message as transmitted is operative unless the other party knows or has reason to know of the mistake.[15] Thus the offeree, who is the second to use the telegraph, would be bound if he had accepted an offer that had been raised as a result of an error in transmission. So also if the offeree had indicated an intent not to accept an offer but the telegraph company by a mistake in transmission sent an affirmative message, there would be a contract.

The minority view is based upon the notion, mentioned above, that the telegraph company is an independent contractor. The general rule is that a person who hires an independent contractor is not liable for the negligence of the contractor. This means that no contract will

---

10. Wender Presses, Inc. v. United States, 343 F.2d 961 (Ct.Cl.1965); Restatement, Contracts § 71(c). The possibility of avoiding a contract on the grounds of unilateral mistake is considered at § 9–27 infra.

11. 1 Corbin § 105; 1 Williston § 94.

12. Des Arc Oil Mill v. Western Union Tel. Co., 132 Ark. 335, 201 S.W. 273 (1918).

13. Butler v. Foley, 211 Mich. 668, 179 N.W. 34 (1920).

14. Ayer v. Western Union Tel. Co., 79 Me. 493, 10 A. 495 (1887).

15. 1 Corbin § 105. If it is apparent from the face of the message, or otherwise, that an error has been made, no contract results since the addressee is not justified in relying upon its contents. Germain Fruit Co. v. Western Union Tel. Co., 137 Cal. 598, 70 P. 658 (1902).

arise in the case of a mistake in transmission.[16] It might be argued that the majority view is more consistent with the objective theory of contracts because the recipient of the erroneous telegram would normally take it at face value. But, as we have seen, for the objective theory to apply the acts manifesting assent must be done either intentionally or negligently.[17] Here there is no wrongful intentional or negligent conduct on the part of the sender of the message because he is not responsible for the misconduct of the telegraph company. This section does not apply to a misdirected acceptance. It applies to a message that has not been faithfully transmitted.

Once it is determined which of the two innocent parties should suffer a loss as a result of a mistake in transmission it should be clear that said party has an action against the telegraph company upon a negligence theory and perhaps also for breach of contract.[18] However the remedy may prove to be unsatisfactory because telegraph companies by contract usually limit their liability. These limitations of liability have been upheld and this question is now governed by federal regulations.[19]

 WESTLAW REFERENCES
contract /s mistak! /s transmi! /s telegram! telegraph!

§ 2-25. Option Contracts—Irrevocable Offers

(a) Introduction

We have previously mentioned the topic of option contracts and that these words are often used interchangeably with the words irrevocable offer.[20] In this section we will discuss what makes an offer irrevocable, the nature of an option contract, the termination of irrevocable offers and when the acceptance of an irrevocable offer is effective. Incidentally we shall point out that the two sets of words are not precisely interchangeable but that the distinction does not carry any important implications.

(b) What Makes an Offer Irrevocable?

Most offers are revocable offers. One of the classic ways of rendering an offer irrevocable is by the acceptance of a consideration by the offeror in exchange for this promise to keep the offer open.[21] As we have seen, if A makes an offer to sell specific real property to B for a specified price and states that the offer is open for ten days, the offer is revocable. The same would be true if A stated that the offer was

---

16. Western Union Tel. Co. v. Cowin & Co., 20 F.2d 103 (8th Cir.1927); see Restatement, Second, Contracts § 64, Comment b.

17. See § 2-2 supra.

18. Webbe v. Western Union Tel. Co., 169 Ill. 610, 48 N.E. 670 (1897).

19. Western Union Tel. Co. v. Priester, 276 U.S. 252, 48 S.Ct. 234, 72 L.Ed. 555 (1928); Annots., 20 A.L.R.2d 761 (1951); 94 A.L.R. 1056 (1935).

20. See § 2-22 supra; Beall v. Beall, 291 Md. 224, 434 A.2d 1015 (1981).

21. Restatement, Contracts § 46, accord Crockett v. Lowther, 549 P.2d 303 (Wyo. 1976).

irrevocable for ten days.[22] But if, for example, A bargained for and received $10 in exchange for A's promise to keep the offer open for ten days there would be an irrevocable offer because A's promise is supported by consideration.[23]

Certain statutes permit the creation of irrevocable offers without consideration. For example, a New York statute set out in full in the note,[24] provides, in essence that if the offeror in a signed writing states that the offer is irrevocable it is irrevocable despite the absence of consideration. There is a similar provision in the Uniform Commercial Code.[25] The two statutory formulations are compared in the notes.[26] A third way in which an offer can become irrevocable without consideration is in the case of an offer looking to a unilateral contract. According to § 45 of the Restatement—old and new—an option contract arises when the offeree begins to perform the act requested in the offer.[27] An offer may also be made irrevocable without consideration under the doctrine of promissory estoppel.[28] In some jurisdictions an offer may be made irrevocable by the use of a seal.[29]

22. Hummer v. Engeman, 206 Va. 102, 141 S.E.2d 716 (1965); 7 Wm. & Mary L.Rev. 186 (1966). See § 2–20 supra. This common law rule is criticized in Eisenberg, The Principles of Consideration, 67 Cornell L.Rev. 640, 653 (1982).

23. If A gives B an "option" to buy property but there is no consideration to support the "option", the "option" is nothing more or less than a revocable offer. Beall v. Beall, 45 Md.App. 489, 413 A.2d 1365 (1980), judgment reversed 291 Md. 224, 434 A.2d 1015 (1981); Troutman v. Erlandson, 44 Or.App. 239, 605 P.2d 1200 (1980).

24. McKinney's N.Y.Gen.Obl.Law § 5–1109 provides:

"Except as otherwise provided in section 2–205 of the uniform commercial code with respect to an offer by a merchant to buy or sell goods, when an offer to enter into a contract is made in a writing signed by the offeror, or by his agent, which states that the offer is irrevocable during a period set forth or until a time fixed, the offer shall not be revocable during such period or until such time because of the absence of consideration for the assurance of irrevocability. When such a writing states that the offer is irrevocable but does not state any period or time of irrevocability, it shall be construed to state that the offer is irrevocable for a reasonable time."

25. U.C.C. § 2–205 provides:

"An offer by a merchant to buy or sell goods in a signed writing which by its terms gives assurance that it will be held open is not revocable, for lack of consideration, during the time stated or if no time is stated for a reasonable time, but in no event may such period of irrevocability exceed three months; but any such term of assurance on a form supplied by the offeree must be separately signed by the offeror." On the meaning of "signed", see U.C.C. § 2–205, Comment 2, and § 1–210(39).

26. See notes 24–25 supra. At least four differences are rapidly perceptible. The Code section is (1) limited to offers by merchants and (2) is limited to offers to buy and sell goods. Under the Code, (3) the period of irrevocability may not exceed three months. The option may be renewed. U.C.C. § 2–205, Comment 3. Finally, the Code provides that (4) where the term of assurance is contained on a form supplied by the offeree, it must be separately signed by the offeror. For a critical comment on the necessity for such statutes see Schultz, The Firm Offer Puzzle: A Study of Business Practice in the Construction Industry, 19 U.Chi.L.Rev. 237 (1952); see Note, Another Look at Construction Bidding and Contracts at Formation, 53 Va.L.Rev. 1720 (1967).

27. See § 2–22 supra.

28. See § 6–5(a).

29. See ch. 7 infra.

(c) Nature of an Option Contract

An option contract is hybrid in nature. The first question that must be considered is did the option contract arise. This has already been discussed above. Once it arises so that there is an irrevocable offer then one is dealing essentially with an offer and acceptance situation and thus the rules of acceptance discussed above apply.[30] In the illustration given above B (the optionee) would have the option of accepting or not accepting the offer relating to the real property in question.[31] This is similar to any other offer and acceptance situation except, as discussed below, the offer is less easily terminated.[32]

The option contract itself may be either unilateral or a bilateral.[33] For example, in the case discussed above A asked for $10 and this was paid. Thus the option contract itself was unilateral.[34] If A had asked for and received a promise to pay $10 there would be a bilateral option contract. Of course the money must be paid at the time stated in the agreement otherwise the option could not be exercised.[35] In either case, B has an option if he does what is required and there is no difference in the two situations. So also the underlying offer (in the illustration the offer looking to the sale of the real property) may look to a unilateral or a bilateral contract and the ordinary rules of acceptance should be applied.[36]

But it is possible to conceive of a situation in which there is only one contract—the option contract—and therefore only one acceptance. For example A says to B "If you pay me $100 today I promise to sell Blackacre to you for $10,000 on condition that you tender $10,000 within thirty days." The payment of $100 gives rise to a unilateral contract. The payment of $10,000 is then only a condition precedent to A's obligation to give a deed.[37] This might be described as a true option contract. On the other hand if the underlying contract requires a promise by B to purchase there are two potential contracts—the option contract and the underlying bilateral contract. Here the payment of $10 is more properly described as creating an irrevocable offer. It has been suggested in the second case that A has no right to revoke but that he has the power to revoke. Consequently, if A revoked, B would be entitled to damages for breach of the irrevocable offer (sometimes

30. Plantation Key Developers v. Colonial Mortgage, Co., 589 F.2d 164 (5th Cir. 1979); Graham v. Anderson, 397 So.2d 71 (Miss.1981); Northwestern Bell Tel. Co. v. Cowger, 303 N.W.2d 791 (N.D.1981).

31. Central Bank & Trust Co. v. Kincaid, 617 S.W.2d 32 (Ky.1981).

32. Civic Plaza Nat'l Bank v. First Nat'l Bank, 401 F.2d 193 (8th Cir.1968); Katz v. Pratt St. Realty Co., 257 Md. 103, 262 A.2d 540 (1970); Westinghouse Broadcasting Co. v. New England Patriots, 10 Mass.App.Ct. 70, 406 N.E.2d 399 (1980); Schacht v. First Wyoming Bank N.A. Rawlins, 620 P.2d 561 (Wyo.1980).

33. 1A Corbin § 260.

34. Dixon v. Kinser, 54 N.C.App. 94, 282 S.E.2d 529 (1981), review denied 304 N.C. 725, 288 S.E.2d 805 (1982).

35. 1A Corbin § 260. But see 1 Williston § 61B wherein it is stated that "an option is necessarily a unilateral contract. * * *"

36. See Herring v. Prestwood, 414 So.2d 52 (Ala.1982); Blakeslee v. Davoudi, 54 Or. App. 9, 633 P.2d 857 (1981), review denied 292 Or. 108, 642 P.2d 310 (1981).

37. Diggs v. Siomporas, 248 Md. 677, 237 A.2d 725 (1968).

called the collateral contract) but not to specific performance of the main (underlying) contract.[38] This view is rejected by the modern text writers [39] and most of the decided cases.[40] In either case the result should be the same.[41] Thus, we are still free to say as we did at the beginning that the words option contract and irrevocable offer are used interchangeably.

(d) Termination of Irrevocable Offers

(1) Introduction

Since an irrevocable offer is still an offer the question of termination of the offer prior to acceptance must be considered. (We have already covered the topic of termination of revocable offers).[42] According to the Restatement Second an irrevocable offer is terminated by lapse of time, death or destruction of a person or thing essential for the performance of the contract and supervening legal prohibition of the proposed contract. However an irrevocable offer is not terminated by rejection, revocation or supervening death or incapacity of the offeror, nor does the death or supervening incapacity of the offeree terminate the offer.[43] A few words on each of these topic is appropriate.

(2) Specific Headings

a) *Lapse of Time.* As stated above an irrevocable offer is terminated by lapse of time. Thus it is frequently stated that time is of the essence in the exercise of an irrevocable offer.[44] One reason given is that the offer is usually made irrevocable in exchange for a small consideration. But there are cases that have not followed this approach where a forfeiture would have resulted.[45]

b) *Death or Destruction etc. and Supervening Legal Prohibition.* Since death or destruction of a person or thing essential for the performance of the contract discharges a contract upon a theory of impossibility of performance it follows that the same impossibility terminates an irrevocable offer. Since supervening legal prohibition also involves a question of impossibility of performance the same rule

---

38. Langdell, Summary of the Law of Contracts § 178 (1880). Since damages for breach of the collateral contract would be the same as for breach of the underlying proposed contract, the distinction between the right and the power to revoke can be raised only if specific performance is sought. McGovney, Irrevocable Offers, 27 Harv.L.Rev. 644 (1914), reprinted in Selected Readings 220.

39. 1 Corbin §§ 42–44; 1 Williston §§ 61–61D.

40. Simpson & Harper v. Sanders & Jenkins, 130 Ga. 265, 60 S.E. 541 (1908); Solomon Mier Co. v. Hadden, 148 Mich. 488, 111 N.W. 1040 (1907); Crocker v. Page, 210 App.Div. 735, 206 N.Y.S. 481 (3d Dep't 1924), affirmed 240 N.Y. 638, 148 N.E. 738 (1925). Time is generally consid-

ered to be of the essence in an option contract. Wesley v. United States, 384 F.2d 100 (9th Cir.1967). See also § 11–35 infra.

41. See 1A Corbin § 262. See generally Hauser, Some Aspects of the Law of Option Contracts, 23 Brooklyn L.Rev. 69 (1957).

42. See § 2–20 supra.

43. Restatement, Second, Contracts §§ 35A, 48, Comment d.

44. Western Sav. Fund, Etc. v. Southeastern, Etc., 285 Pa.Super. 187, 427 A.2d 175 (1981).

45. Loitherstein v. I.B.M. Corp., 11 Mass.App.Ct. 91, 413 N.E.2d 1146 (1980), review denied 441 N.E.2d 1042 (1981); 1A Corbin § 273; 1 Williston § 61D. See § 11–35 infra.

applies.[46] In general the rules relating to discharge of contracts apply to option contracts.[47]

c) Revocation and Rejection. It is obvious that revocation should not and does not terminate an irrevocable offer.[48] The authorities are somewhat divided on the question of rejection. The earlier view was that rejection terminated an irrevocable offer.[49] But the more modern view is that rejection should not terminate an irrevocable offer because the offeree has paid a consideration for irrevocability.[50] If the offeror relies on the rejection to his injury the offeree should be estopped from accepting it later.[51] A counter-offer does not normally operate as a rejection where the offer is irrevocable.[52]

d) Supervening Death or Incapacity of the Offeror. Although supervening death and incapacity of the offeror or offeree do not terminate an irrevocable offer, death or incapacity creates a variety of other problems. These are discussed under the headings of Prospective Inability to Perform,[53] Impossibility of Performance[54] and the Assignability of Option Contracts.[55]

(e) When Acceptance of an Irrevocable Offer Is Effective

We have already seen that in the case of a revocable offer the acceptance may be effective under the "mailbox" rule when sent.[56] But in the case of an irrevocable offer the weight of authority is that the acceptance is operative when received by the offeror rather than when dispatched.[57] The result would be different if the option agreement otherwise provided.[58] The rule that an acceptance is effective when sent is designed to protect an offeree against revocation.[59] Since here we are dealing with an irrevocable offer the offeree does not require the protection of the rule of Adams v. Lindsell. A right of first refusal supported by consideration is not strictly speaking an option because it creates in the holder only a right to purchase on the same terms offered by other parties.[60] The same is true of a first option to buy.[61]

46. See Restatement, Second, Contracts § 37, Comment b. See also 13–5 and 13–7 infra.

47. Restatement, Second, Contracts § 37.

48. Smith v. Banham, 156 Cal. 359, 104 P. 689 (1909); O'Brien v. Boland, 166 Mass. 481, 44 N.E. 602 (1896).

49. Restatement, Contracts § 44.

50. Restatement, Second, Contracts § 37. McCormick v. Stephany, 61 N.J.Eq. 208, 48 A. 25 (1900); Silverstein v. United Cerebral Palsy Ass'n, 17 A.D.2d 160, 232 N.Y.S.2d 968 (1st Dep't 1962); Humble Oil & Ref. Co. v. Westside Inv. Corp., 428 S.W.2d 92 (Tex.1968).

51. Restatment, Second, Contracts § 36, Ill. 2.

52. 1 Corbin § 91.

53. See ch. 11 infra.

54. See ch. 13 infra.

55. See § 18–32 infra.

56. See § 2–23 supra.

57. Restatement, Second, Contracts § 63, Comment f; 1 Corbin § 264. For a recent contrary case see Worms v. Burgess, 620 P.2d 455 (Okl.App.1980).

58. Jameson v. Foster, 646 P.2d 955 (Colo.App.1982).

59. McAfee v. Brewer, 214 Va. 579, 203 S.E.2d 129 (1974). But see Duesenberg & King § 4.02(1).

60. Gyurkey v. Babler, 103 Idaho 663, 651 P.2d 928 (1982); Smith v. Mitchell, 301 N.C. 58, 269 S.E.2d 608 (1980).

61. Dimaria v. Michaels, 90 A.D.2d 676, 455 N.Y.S.2d 875 (4th Dep't 1982).

WESTLAW REFERENCES

(b) *What Makes an Offer Irrevocable?*

offer /s consideration /s revo! irrevocable

crockett +s lowther

irrevocable revo! /s option /s consideration

5–1109

2–205 /p merchant

"unilateral contract" /s consideration

offer! /s "option contract" /s perform!

"unilateral contract" /s "option contract"

"promissory estoppel" /s offer /s consideration

"firm offer" /s revo! irrevocable /s consideration

seal /s offer /s irrevocable revo!

(c) *Nature of an Option Contract*

"option contract" /s define* definition

"option contract" /s bilateral

"option contract" /s revo! irrevocable

(d) *Termination of Irrevocable Offers*

  (1) *Introduction*

"irrevocable offer" /s terminat!

  (2) *Specific Headings*

    (a) *Lapse of Time*

95k20

time +4 essence /s irrevocable

time +4 essence /s "option contract"

time +4 essence /s laps!

    (b) *Death or Destruction etc. and Supervening Legal Prohibi-
tion*

"impossibility of performance" /s destruction

95k309(2)

"essential for the performance" /s contract agreement

"impossibility of performance" /s illegal!

"option contract" /s discharg!

irrevocable /s terminat! /s offer

    (c) *Revocation and Rejection*

silverstein +s "united cerebral"

"option contract" /s reject!

"option contract" /s terminat!

"counter offer!" counteroffer! /s "option contract" irrevocable

    (e) *When Acceptance of an Irrevocable Offer is Effective*

accept! /s effective /s irrevocable /s offer

"option contract" (irrevocable /s offer) /s accept! /s receiv!
receipt

"right of first refusal"　/s　"right to purchase"　/s　option
"right of first refusal"　/s　consideration　/s　option

§ 2–26.　U.C.C. § 2–206 and Related Provisions in Restatement Second

Extensive changes in the common law in the area of offer and acceptance have been made by the Uniform Commercial § 2–206. Despite variations in the language the Restatement Second adopts the same basic approach. We shall first discuss the U.C.C. section and later point out some of the substantive differences in the Restatement Second. This U.C.C. Section reads as follows:

(a) U.C.C. § 2–206

"(1) Unless otherwise unambiguously indicated by the language or circumstances

(a) an offer to make a contract shall be construed as inviting acceptance in any manner and by any medium reasonable in the circumstances;

(b) an order or other offer to buy goods for prompt or current shipment shall be construed as inviting acceptance either by a prompt promise to ship or by the prompt or current shipment of conforming or non-conforming goods, but such a shipment of nonconforming goods does not constitute an acceptance if the seller seasonably notifies the buyer that the shipment is offered only as an accommodation to the buyer.

(2) Where the beginning of a requested performance is a reasonable mode of acceptance an offeror who is not notified of acceptance within a reasonable time may treat the offer as having lapsed before acceptance."

(1) Subdivision (1)(a)

The word "manner" in subdivision (a) relates to the common law distinction between a unilateral and bilateral contract. At common law, except in unusual cases, an offer looked either to a bilateral or a unilateral contract. The conclusion reached (unilateral or bilateral) determined the manner of acceptance.[62] If the offer was ambiguous on this point it was presumed that the offer invited a promise.[63] This section has substituted for this presumption the notion that in the vast majority of cases the offeror is indifferent as to the manner of acceptance. Thus in most cases the offeree is free to proceed by act or promise.[64]

However the introductory language ("unless otherwise unambiguously" etc.) specifically permits the offeror to insist upon a particular

62. See § 2–10 supra.

63. See § 2–10 supra.

64. Murray, Contracts: A New Design for the Agreement Process, 53 Corn.L.Rev. 785 (1968).

manner of acceptance.[65]   In other words the offeror is free, despite the new approach of the Uniform Commercial Code, "to prescribe as many conditions, terms or the like as he may wish, including but not limited to, the time, place and method of acceptance."[66]   In a word he is master of his offer.

Essentially, then, the question is when does an offeror "unambiguously indicate" that he is insisting on a particular manner of acceptance. The Code does not offer much help in illuminating this thought.

The Restatement Second furnishes some helpful illustrations that show that it will be an unusual case where the offer is not indifferent.[67] The use in the offer of unilateral words such as "deliver" is not enough to prevent an acceptance by promise.[68] Conversely the use of the word promise does not prevent an acceptance by performance.[69] However in a recent case under the U.C.C. the buyer's order stated that "seller shall mail to purchaser a signed duplicate copy hereof" it was held that the offer unambiguously indicated that a promise by writing was the only manner of acceptance.[70]

The phrase "by any medium reasonable in the circumstances" in subdivision (1)(a) relates to the "mailbox" rule. In other words when an acceptance is made by promise and that is a reasonable manner of acceptance it will be effective when sent provided it is sent "by any medium reasonable in the circumstance". As we have already seen, the concept of "reasonableness" is intended to be more flexible than the previously prevailing concept of an "authorized" means of transmission.[71]

(2) Section (1)(b)

Subsection (1)(b) appears to be designed to accomplish two results. First if one reads up to the comma and ignores the word "nonconforming" it seems reasonably clear that the section "exemplifies" the more general provision of subsection 2–106(1)(a) quoted above that is to say, it shows that an "indifferent" offer "to buy goods for prompt or current shipment" invites an acceptance either by performance or promise.[72] Parenthetically it should be noted that if the offeree per-

---

65. Empire Machinery Co. v. Litton Business Tel. Sys., 115 Ariz. 568, 566 P.2d 1044 (1977).

66. Kroeze v. Chloride Group Ltd., 572 F.2d 1099, 1105 (5th Cir.1978); Southwestern Stationery & Bank Supply Co. v. Harris Corp., 624 F.2d 168 (10th Cir.1980).

67. Restatement, Second, Contracts § 32.

68. Restatement, Second, Contracts § 32, Comment a. An offer of reward would not be considered to be indifferent. Restatement, Second, Contracts § 31, ill. 3.

69. Restatement, Second, Contracts § 32, ills. 2 and 5; see also U.C.C. § 2–206, Comment 2.

70. Southwestern Stationery & Bank Supply Co. v. Harris, 624 F.2d 168 (10th Cir.1980). The common law cases were split on the question of whether similar language prescribed the method of acceptance. Compare, for example, Fujimoto v. Rio Grande Pickle Co., 414 F.2d 648 (5th Cir.1969) and Allied Steel & Conveyors, Inc. v. Ford Motor Co., 277 F.2d 907 (6th Cir.1960) with Markoff v. New York Life Ins. Co., 92 Nev. 268, 549 P.2d 330 (1976).

71. See § 2–23 supra.

72. Hawkland § 1.1303.

forms U.C.C. § 2–504(c) requires prompt notification of shipment.[73] Under that provision failure to give notice is a ground for rejection only if there is a material delay in shipment or if loss ensues. The Restatement Second takes the position that notice is unnecessary.[74] This is unfortunate because the Uniform Commercial Code will in any event prevail since the situation relates to a sale of goods.

This section was also designed to prevent the offeree from utilizing what Hawkland calls the "unilateral contract trick." The word that accomplishes this is "non-conforming".[75] What is said is that even if the seller sends non-conforming goods there is a contract. At common law a shipment of non-conforming goods amounted only to a counter-offer. But under the Code there is a contract and simultaneously a breach.[76] However there is no contract if "the seller seasonably notifies the buyer that the shipment is offered only as an accommodation to the buyer". In that event the shipment would be treated as a counter-offer.[77]

It is important to stress that under this subdivision shipment is performance and not merely the beginning of performance. As comment 2 says shipment is not the beginning of performance it is performance. Loading goods on the seller's own truck is not shipment but it may be the beginning of performance.[78] It is subdivision 2 that applies to the beginning of performance.

(3) Subdivision (2)

As stated above subdivision 2 relates to the effect of beginning performance. To understand this subdivision the background of the common law must be recalled. If the offer looked to a unilateral contract there were three views on the effect of beginning performance. One view is that the beginning of performance creates a bilateral contract. A second view is that beginning performance does not bind the offeree to continue but makes the offer irrevocable. Under the third view the beginning of performance has no effect.[79] In the case of an offer looking to a bilateral contract the beginning of performance was of no effect unless done in the presence of the offeror.[80] Subdivi-

---

73. Notice here, apparently means that reasonable and prompt efforts to notify the offeror should be taken.

74. Restatement, Second, Contracts § 62, Comment b. See also U.C.C. § 1–201(26) (1977).

75. Goods are conforming "when they are in accordance with the obligations under the contracts." See U.C.C. § 2–106(2).

76. Gilbride, The Uniform Commercial Code: Impact on the Law of Contracts, 30 Brooklyn L.Rev. 177, 185 (1964). The offeror is not hurt by such a provision because he undoubtedly has the right to rescind the agreement. In a proper case the

offeree would have a right to cure the defect. See § 11–20 infra.

77. Weintraub, Disclaimer of Warranties and Limitation of Damages for Breach of Warranty under the U.C.C., 53 Texas L.Rev. 60 (1974).

78. U.C.C. § 2–206, Comment 2.

79. See § 2–22 supra.

80. This is perhaps an overstatement. Although an offer to a bilateral contract is usually accepted by an express or implied promise, as we have seen, there is some authority to the effect that a contract is formed if the performance is completed while the offer is still open and the requi-

sion 2 of the Uniform Commercial Code has made radical changes in the common law.

The subdivision starts out with the phrase, "where the beginning of performance is a reasonable mode of acceptance." It seems clear that if the beginning of performance is not a reasonable mode of acceptance (as for example where it is unambiguously clear that a promise is sought) then we are returned to the common law for solutions.

If the beginning of performance is a reasonable mode of acceptance the offeree is bound when he starts to perform if "the beginning of performance unambiguously expresses the offeree's intent to engage himself." [81] The theory appears to be that in such a case the offeree has made an implied promise to complete the performance already begun.[82] The net result is that bilateral arrangements are favored over unilateral arrangements. Even if the offeree is bound when he starts to perform the offeror is not bound to perform his promise unless notice of beginning performance is given within a reasonable time. During the time between the beginning of performance and the reasonable time for giving notice to the offeror he would not be free to revoke in a jurisdiction that followed two of common law rule stated above.[83] If timely notice is not given the offeror, despite the fact that he is not bound to perform may at his option proceed as if there is a contract.[84] In other words the basic notion is that offeror is not bound unless he is given notice but the offeree is bound when he begins performance.

(b) Restatement Second

The Restatement Second states a somewhat different position on the effect of beginning performance. The Restatement Second agrees that if it is clear that acceptance can be only by promise beginning performance will be without effect. If beginning performance is a reasonable mode of acceptance then beginning performance constitutes acceptance unless the offeror knows or should know that the offeree does not intend to be bound.[85] The Restatement adds that in such a case notice of the beginning of performance will ordinarily be re-

site notice of performance is given. See § 2–10 supra. The rule relates to completed performance rather than the beginning of performance. It might be argued, however, that the beginning of performance would make the offer irrevocable under the second view stated above. In any event, the Restatement Second asserts that this rule, which is a departure "from the basic principle that the offeror is master of his offer," is rendered unnecessary by the new approach being discussed. Restatement, Second, Contracts § 62 (Reporter's Note).

81. U.C.C. § 2–206, Comment 3. What this means in the concrete is far from clear. But in the abstract it means that if the offeror as a reasonable man should know that the offeree in starting to per-

form does not intend to be bound, the offeree is not bound. This would certainly be true if the offeree actually notifies the offeror within a reasonable time that he is not accepting. Murray, Contracts: A New Design for the Agreement Process, 53 Cornell L.Rev. 785 (1968).

82. Murray, Contracts: A New Design for the Agreement Process, 53 Cornell L.Rev. 785 (1968).

83. See U.C.C. § 2–206, Comment 3 and § 2–22 supra.

84. U.C.C. § 2–206, Comment 3.

85. Murray, Contracts: A New Design for the Agreement Process, 53 Cornell L.Rev. 785 (1968).

quired.[86] If notice is not given, the offeror is discharged but presumably the offeror at his option may still sue the offeree because a contract has already arisen.

The major difference between the Restatement and the U.C.C. on this point is that under the Restatement Second the beginning of performance creates the contract whereas under the Uniform Commercial Code it is the notice that creates the contract. Professor Murray argues that this is not necessarily so because the basis for the difference is in a comment to the Code that should be ignored because it is in conflict with the statute itself.[87]

 WESTLAW REFERENCES
(a) *U.C.C. § 2–206*

> (1) *Subdivision (1)(a)*
> "uniform commercial code" u.c.c. /s 2–206
> kroeze +s chloride

---

86. Restatement, Second, Contracts § 54, comment b. But notice would not be required, for example, if the offer or a prior course of dealing indicates that notice is not required. Restatement, Second, Contracts § 56, ill. 1.

87. Murray, Contracts: A New Design for the Agreement Process, 53 Cornell L.Rev. 785 (1968).

Chapter 3

PAROL EVIDENCE AND INTERPRETATION [1]

Table of Sections

Table of Sections

A. INTRODUCTION

Sec.
3–1. The Difficulty of the Subject Matter.

B. THE PAROL EVIDENCE RULE

3–2. Introduction.
    (a) To What Type of Evidence Does the Parol Evidence Rule Relate—Prior—Contemporaneous, and Subsequent Agreements.
    (b) Policy and Analytical Rationales Involved.
    (c) The Role of the Judge and Jury.
    (d) Is the Rule One of Substantive Law or Procedure?
3–3. Is the Writing Integrated?
3–4. Is the Writing a Total Integration?
    (a) The "Four-Corners" Rule.
    (b) The "Collateral Contract" Concept.
    (c) Williston's Rules.
    (d) Corbin's Rule.
    (e) The U.C.C. Rule.
        (1) Clause (b).
        (2) Clause (a).
    (f) The Restatement Second.

---

1. An earlier version of this chapter appeared in Calamari and Perillo, A Plea for a Uniform Parol Evidence Rule and Principles of Contract Interpretation, 42 Ind.L.J. 333 (1967).

A. INTRODUCTION

Table of Sections

§ 3–1. The Difficulty of the Subject Matter

Professor Thayer, speaking of the parol evidence rule, aptly observed, "Few things are darker than this, or fuller of subtle difficulties." [2] Much of the fog and mystery surrounding these subjects stems from the fact that there are basic disagreements as to the application of the parol evidence rule and as to the best method of ascertaining the intention of the parties—the process of contractual interpretation.[3] The cases and treatises of the contract giants tend to conceal this conflict. While frequently masking disagreement by using the same terminology, Professors Williston and Corbin are often poles apart in the meaning they attach to the same terms. Often starting from what superficially appear to be the same premises, they frequently advocate different results in similar fact situations. The polarity of their views reflects conflicting value judgments as to policy issues that are as old as our legal system and that are likely to continue as long as courts of law exist. Although many writers and courts have expressed their views on the subject and have made major contributions to it, concentration on the analyses of Professors Williston and Corbin will point up the fundamental bases upon which the conflicting cases and views rest.[4]

 WESTLAW REFERENCES

"parol* evidence rule" /s apply! applied application /s "subject matter"

"parol* evidence rule" /s determin! ascertain! /s intend! intent!

B. THE PAROL EVIDENCE RULE

Table of Sections

2. J. Thayer, A Preliminary Treatise on Evidence at Common Law 390 (1898).

3. According to some authorities the parol evidence rule also applies to exclude some or all types of extrinsic evidence offered in aid of interpretation. See § 3–15 infra.

4. For some recent articles see Childres & Spitz, Status in the Law of Contracts, 47 N.Y.U.L.Rev. 1 (1971); Corbin, The Interpretation of Words and the Parol Evidence Rule, 50 Cornell L.Q. 161 (1965); Farnsworth, "Meaning" in the Law of Contracts, 76 Yale L.J. 939 (1967); Havighurst, Principles of Construction and the Parol Evidence Rule as Applied to Releases, 60 Nw. U.L.Rev. 599 (1965); Murray, The Parol Evidence Rule; A Clarification, 4 Dug.L. Rev. 337 (1966); Murray, The Parol Evidence Process and Standardized Agreements Under the Restatement (Second) of Contracts, 123 U.Pa.L.Rev. 1342 (1975); Patterson, The Interpretation and Construction of Contracts, 64 Colum.L.Rev. 833 (1964); Sweet, Contract Making and Parol Evidence: Diagnosis and Treatment of a Sick Rule, 53 Cornell L.Q. 1036 (1968); Young, Equivocation in the Making of Agreements, 64 Colum.L.Rev. 619 (1964); Note, The Parol Evidence Rule: Is It Necessary? 44 N.Y.U.L.Rev. 972 (1969); Note, Chief Judge Traynor and The Parol Evidence Rule, 22 Stan.L.Rev. 547 (1970). See also note 20 infra.

§ 3–2.   Introduction

There is a rule of substantive law which states that whenever contractual intent is sought to be ascertained from among several expressions of agreement by the parties, an earlier tentative agreement will be rejected in favor of a later expression that is final.[5] More simply stated, the final agreement made by the parties supersedes tentative terms discussed in earlier negotiations. Consequently, in determining the content of the contract, earlier tentative agreements and negotiations are inoperative.[6]

The parol evidence rule comes into play only where the last expression is in writing[7] and is a binding contract.[8] The parol evidence rule has been stated in many ways but the basic notion is that a writing intended by the parties to be a final embodiment of their agreement

5. 3 Corbin § 573; McCormick, Evidence § 213 (1954) [hereinafter cited as McCormick]. The new edition of McCormick does not deal with the parol evidence rule.

6. As to interpretation, see note 3 supra. In the meantime the emphasis here is on what terms outside of the writing may be considered to be part of the contract.

7. Restatement, Second, Contracts § 213, Comment d and subd. (3); Restate-

ment, Contracts § 228, Comment b, which suggests that the words of an oral agreement may be chosen with such precision that there is an equivalent of an integration. It adds that such a case is so unusual as not to require separate discussion. See 3 Corbin § 573 n. 11; Restatement, Second, Contracts § 215.

8. See § 3–7 infra.

may not be contradicted by certain kinds of evidence.[9]   A writing that is final is at least a partial integration.[10]   If the writing is final and also complete, it is a total integration and may not only not be contradicted by the type of evidence in question but may not even be supplemented by consistent (non-contradictory) additional terms.[11]   If it is final and incomplete it may be supplemented by consistent additional terms.   It is obvious that the important questions to be addressed are whether a particular writing is deemed to be an integrated writing and if so whether it is a total or only a partial integration.   However, before taking up these questions it would probably be helpful to consider a number of preliminary questions that will help increase understanding

(a) To What Type of Evidence Does the Parol Evidence Rule Relate—Prior—Contemporaneous, and Subsequent Agreements

The parol evidence rule applies to terms [12] agreed upon prior to the integration regardless of whether the term agreed upon is written or oral.[13]   It does not apply to subsequent agreements.[14]   Whether it applies to contemporaneous agreements is in some confusion.   Williston and the first Restatement take the position that contemporaneous terms should be treated in the same way as prior agreements except that a contemporaneous writing should be deemed to be a part of the integration.[15]   Corbin appears to argue that the terms are either prior or subsequent and that therefore the word "contemporaneous" merely clouds the issue.[16]   This matter will again be mentioned at various places in the ensuing discussion.[17]   It is sufficient to note here that Williston's rule is generally accepted.[18]

9.   See Farmers Co–op Ass'n v. Garrison, 248 Ark. 948, 454 S.W.2d 644 (1970); Ely Constr. Co. v. S & S Corp., 184 Neb. 59, 165 N.W.2d 562 (1964); Corbin § 574.

10.   J. Murray, Contracts § 104, at 225 (2d revised ed. 1974). 4 Williston § 636. While Corbin is in agreement with the statement in the text, he advocates abandonment of the term "partial integration" and argues that parties rarely intend that an incomplete writing be considered final. 3 Corbin § 581; see Leyse v. Leyse, 251 Cal.App.2d 629, 59 Cal.Rptr. 680 (1967).

11.   Restatement, Second, Contracts § 210(1) and Comment a (1981); J. Murray, Contracts § 104, at 226.

12.   § 1–201(42) of the U.C.C. defines "term" as "that portion of an agreement which relates to a particular matter."

13.   3 Corbin § 576.

14.   Connell v. Diamond T. Truck Co., 88 N.H. 316, 188 A. 463 (1936).   There are statutes, however, which prevent any subsequent modification or rescission if such an intent is expressed in the writing. These statutes are discussed in § 5–14 infra.

15.   Restatement, Contracts § 237, Comment a; 4 Williston § 628; Jenkins v. Watson-Wilson Transp. System, 183 Neb. 634, 163 N.W.2d 123 (1968); Sonfield v. Eversole, 416 S.W.2d 458 (Tex.Civ.App.1967); Hathaway v. Ray's Motor Sales, Inc., 127 Vt. 279, 247 A.2d 512 (1968).   This position has been adopted by the Uniform Commercial Code.   The parol evidence provision applies to "evidence of any [oral or written] prior agreement or of a contemporaneous oral agreement."   U.C.C. § 2–202 (1970). A covering letter may be considered to be part of the integration.   Sawyer v. Arum, 690 F.2d 590 (6th Cir.1982); Brown v. Financial Service Corp., 489 F.2d 144 (5th Cir.1974).

16.   3 Corbin § 577.   Corbin's position appears to be adopted in Restatement, Second, Contracts § 213 Comment a.   But in § 241 the reference is to "prior or contemporaneous agreements or negotiations." See also 48 ALI Proceedings 449 (1971).

17.   See § 3–4 infra.

18.   See 4 Williston § 628; Restatement, Contracts § 237; Jenkins v. Watson-Wilson Transp. Sys., Inc., 183 Neb. 634, 163 N.W.2d 123 (1968); Sonfield v. Eversole,

Thus in a typical case one of the parties offers into evidence a term that is not found in the writing but which he alleges was orally agreed to prior to or contemporaneously with the writing. The question is whether the parol evidence rule excludes this evidence. For example, assume that landlord and tenant sign a two year lease. Under the terms of the writing the tenant agrees not to sell tobacco in any form but is permitted to sell soft drinks. At the trial the tenant seeks to introduce into evidence an oral agreement made prior to or contemporaneously with the writing that, in consideration of his promise not to sell tobacco, the landlord gave him an *exclusive* right to sell soft drinks on the premises and that the landlord breached this promise. The question is whether the exclusivity term may be received into evidence even though it does not appear in the writing.[19]

(b) Policy and Analytical Rationales Involved

The policy behind the rule is to give the writing a preferred status so as to render it immune to perjured testimony and the risk of "uncertain testimony of slippery memory." [20] The rule also proceeds at least in part upon the analytical rationale that the offered term is excluded because it has been superseded by the writing—that is to say it was not intended to survive the writing—a theory of merger.[21] This theory relates to prior agreements.

The rule is also designed to require parties to put their complete agreement (including oral contemporaneous agreements) in writing at the risk of losing the benefit of any term agreed upon that is not in writing.[22] The desired object is to secure business stability.[23] Critics answer that the rule has never had the effect of forcing people to reduce their entire agreement to writing and that commerce has nevertheless managed to survive.[24] The other major criticism is that it results in injustice because the rule in practice may exclude as much truthful evidence as it excludes perjurious testimony.[25] Another criti-

---

416 S.W.2d 458 (Tex.Civ.App.1967); Hathaway v. Ray's Motor Sales, Inc., 127 Vt. 279, 247 A.2d 512 (1968); see also U.C.C. § 2–202 (1977) (rule applies to "evidence of any prior agreement or of a contemporaneous oral agreement").

19. The facts are based upon the case of Gianni v. R. Russell & Co., 281 Pa. 320, 126 A. 791 (1924).

20. McCormick, The Parol Evidence Rule as a Procedural Device for Control of the Jury, 41 Yale L.J. 365, 366–67 & n. 3 (1932); Wallach, The Declining "Sanctity" of Written Contracts—Impact of the Uniform Commercial Code on the Parol Evidence Rule, 44 Mo.L.Rev. 651, 653 (1979); Binks Mfg. Co. v. National Presto Industries, Inc., 709 F.2d 1109 (7th Cir.1983).

21. 3 A Corbin § 585.

22. 3 Corbin § 575; 4 Williston § 633; Note, The Parol Evidence Rule: Is It Really Necessary? 44 N.Y.U.L.Rev. 972, 982 & n. 54 (1969) [hereinafter cited as Note, The Parol Evidence Rule].

23. See Cargill Comm'n Co. v. Swartwood, 159 Minn. 1, 7, 198 N.W. 536, 538 (1924); S.W. Bridges & Co. v. Candland, 88 Utah 373, 380, 54 P.2d 842, 845 (1936).

24. E.g., Sweet, Contract Making and Parol Evidence: Diagnosis and Treatment of a Sick Rule, 53 Cornell L.Q. 1036 (1968) [hereinafter cited as Sweet I]; Note, The Parol Evidence Rule, supra note 22, at 983.

25. See 3 Corbin § 575, at 381; Note, The Parol Evidence Rule, supra note 22, at 974–75.

cism is that the rule is simply too complicated and that it has not been applied consistently.[26]

The issue to be resolved is whether the public is better served by giving effect to the parties' entire agreement (written and oral) even at the risk of injustice caused by the possibility of perjury and the possibility that superseded agreements will be treated as operative, or does the security of transactions require that, despite occasional injustices, persons adopting a formal writing be required, on the penalty of voidness of their side agreements, to put their entire agreement in the writing.[27]

The conflict is an old one. Rules excluding evidence on the ground that it is likely to be false are not strangers to the law. Formerly, parties and interested third parties were incompetent to testify on the ground that their testimony would be unworthy of belief.[28] The Statute of Frauds and the Statute of Wills embody similar considerations.[29] The authors believe, however, that the possibility of perjury is an insufficient ground for interfering with freedom of contract by refusing to effectuate the parties' entire agreement.

The whole thrust of our law for over a century has been directed to the eradication of exclusionary rules of evidence in civil cases. Thus the parties may now testify, their interest in the outcome affecting only the weight and not the admissibility of evidence. Dissatisfaction with rigid application of the parol evidence rule has resulted in the strained insertion of fact situations into categories where the parol evidence rule is inapplicable. Thus to circumvent the rule fraud has been found[30] and reformation granted[31] in situations where those concepts are not normally deemed applicable. Moreover, whole categories of exceptions have been carved out, for example, a deed absolute may be shown to be a mortgage.[32] Thus it is often stated that parol evidence is admissible

---

26. Professor Sweet describes the rule as a "maze of conflicting tests * * * and exceptions adversely affecting both the counseling of clients and the litigation process." Sweet I, supra note 24, at 1036. Note, The Parol Evidence Rule, supra note 22, at 973–74.

27. For the policy considerations involved, see 3 Corbin § 575; 4 Williston § 633; McCormick §§ 210–16. The same conflict is found in cases involving the question whether the parol evidence rule may be invoked by and against a person who is not a party to the agreement. "However, a number of courts have hesitated or refused to routinely apply Williston's strict formulation of the parol evidence rule to certain third parties." Comment, The Parol Evidence Rule and Third Parties, 41 Fordham L.Rev. 945, 959 (1973); see also Annot., 13 A.L.R.3d 313 (1967) and § 3–8 infra.

28. See McCormick § 65.

29. See 3 Corbin § 575.

30. E.g., Bareham & McFarland, Inc. v. Kane, 228 A.D. 396, 240 N.Y.S. 123 (4th Dep't 1930) (language sounding in warranty of performance held to be factual representation); see Sweet, Promissory Fraud and the Parol Evidence Rule, 49 Calif.L. Rev. 877, 896 (1961) ("It does not take much manipulation to classify a promise as either a warranty or a fact.").

31. E.g., Winslett v. Rice, 272 Ala. 25, 128 So.2d 94 (1960) (breach of oral collateral agreement constituted "fraud" justifying reformation).

32. 3 Corbin § 587; 9 Wigmore § 2437; 4 Williston § 635. See Fogelman, The Deed Absolute as a Mortgage in New York, 32 Fordham L.Rev. 299 (1963). In addition parol evidence is admissible to show that a mortgage absolute on its face was in fact intended to secure future advances. Gos-

to show the true nature of the transaction between the parties.[33] Professor Thayer's observation concerning the parol evidence rule problem warrants repetition: "Few things are darker than this, or fuller of subtle difficulties."[34] When any rule of law is riddled through with exceptions and applications difficult to reconcile,[35] it is believed that litigation is stimulated rather than reduced.[36] If the policy of the parol evidence rule is to reduce the possibility of judgments predicated upon perjured testimony and superseded negotiations, it may be effectuated to a large extent by continuing to leave control over determining the question of intent to integrate in the hands of the trial judge.[37]

(c) The Role of the Judge and Jury

As indicated above, the parol evidence rule is generally stated in terms of the intent of the parties. Did the parties intend an integration and did they intend it to be total? Questions of intent are ordinarily questions of fact and would normally be submitted to a jury.[38] However, under the parol evidence rule the question of intent, whether actual

selin v. Better Homes Inc., 256 A.2d 629 (Me.1969).

33. Mahoney v. May, 207 Neb. 187, 297 N.W.2d 157 (1981).

34. J. Thayer, supra note 2, at 390.

35. The Supreme Court of California has acknowledged that its decisions have not been consistent. It disapproved of the restrictive approach previously adopted in many cases. Masterson v. Sine, 68 Cal.2d 222, 65 Cal.Rptr. 545, 436 P.2d 561 (1968). Inconsistencies in the Virginia decisions are discussed in Note, 7 Wm. & Mary L.Rev. 189 (1966). Pennsylvania inconsistencies are discussed in 3 Corbin § 577 n. 34 (Supp.1971).

It is interesting that an occasional jurisdiction appears to reach consistent results although on the most varied reasoning. For example, in Connecticut the leading cases appear to be State Finance Corp. v. Ballestrini, 111 Conn. 544, 150 A. 700 (1930) in which Williston's test is articulated but a result more consistent with Corbin's approach was reached; Harris v. Clinton, 142 Conn. 204, 112 A.2d 885 (1955), in which although he is not cited, the reasoning seems to be pure Corbin; Greenwich Plumbing & Heating Co. v. A. Barbaresi & Son, Inc., 147 Conn. 580, 164 A.2d 405 (1960), in which parol evidence of a collateral agreement was admitted because the writing was ambiguous. The analysis, but not the result of this last decision is criticized in 3 Corbin § 582 n. 84 (Supp.1964).

A degree of consistency is shown in some jurisdictions which adopt a Willistonian approach. McDonough, The Parol Evi-

dence Rule in South Dakota and the Effect of Section 2–202 of the Uniform Commercial Code, 10 S.D.L.Rev. 60 (1965); Comment, The Parol Evidence Rule in Missouri, 27 Mo.L.Rev. 269, 279–82 (1962). New York is one such jurisdiction. Oxford Commercial Corp. v. Landau, 12 N.Y.2d 362, 239 N.Y.S.2d 865, 190 N.E.2d 230 (1963), 49 Cornell L.Q. 311 (1964); Mitchill v. Lath, 247 N.Y. 377, 160 N.E. 646 (1928); Meadow Brook Nat'l Bank v. Bzura, 20 A.D.2d 287, 246 N.Y.S.2d 787 (4th Dep't 1964). This apparent consistency is often achieved by strained characterization of the facts to bring the case within one of the exceptions to the parol evidence rule. See e.g., Peo v. Kennedy, 16 A.D.2d 306, 227 N.Y.S.2d 971 (4th Dep't 1962) (condition precedent to the formation of a contract); Bareham & McFarland, Inc. v. Kane, 228 A.D. 396, 240 N.Y.S. 123 (4th Dep't 1930) (fraud). For Washington, see Comment, Parol Evidence Rule—In Need of Change, 8 Gonzaga L.Rev. 88 (1972).

36. See 3 Corbin § 575; see also Fisch, New York Evidence § 64, at 42 (1959): "Because the decisions are ineffective as guides to determine in advance whether or not the facts of a given transaction will come within one of the exceptions to the rule, the assumption, frequently enunciated in judicial opinions, that the rule is indispensable to business stability is specious * * *. The decisions as to these matters are valueless, contrary holdings being reached on almost identical facts."

37. See subdivision (c) of this section.

38. See § 2–8 supra.

or presumed,[39] is ordinarily decided by the trial judge as a question of law.[40]

The policy of leaving this question to the trial judge is based on the belief that unsophisticated jurors would be easily beguiled by an artful presentation and would not give the writing the protection it deserved.[41] As stated by one commentator it gives the trial judge a polite means of keeping suspect oral evidence from the jury.[42] Making the question one of law strengthens the hand of an appellate court because ordinarily appellate courts do not handle questions of fact.[43] Critics are quick to point out that jurors routinely handle more complicated and sophisticated questions.[44] Recent never ending anti-trust cases provide a good illustration.[45] It has also been observed that distrust of jurors is hardly a reason for excluding a prior written agreement[46] and that there are other ways in which juries can be controlled.[47]

If the judge decides that the parol evidence rule applies he excludes the offered term not because it was not agreed upon but because under the rule it is legally immaterial. Conversely, if he decides that the parol evidence rule does not apply he admits the term agreed upon into evidence but then leaves to the jury the issue of fact as to whether such a term was actually agreed upon.[48]

(d) Is the Rule One of Substantive Law or Procedure?

Although the earlier decisions considered the parol evidence rule as a rule of evidence Professor Thayer railed against this notion and argued (apparently convincingly because almost all of the modern cases seem to agree)[49] that it is a rule of substantive law. A rule of evidence, he maintained, excludes relevant evidence and does not define obliga-

39. See § 3–4(g) infra.

40. Restatement, Second, Contracts § 210(3); McCormick, supra note 20, at 380–82. Corbin generally agrees, but sees no harm in the judge's obtaining the aid of the jury on the issue. 3 Corbin § 595; accord, McCormick, supra note 20, at 378–79. The cases are in conflict. See Sullivan v. Massachusetts Mut. Life Ins. Co., 611 F.2d 261 (9th Cir.1979) (discussing the conflict).

41. J. Murray, supra note 10 at, § 105, at 228; J. White & R. Summers, Handbook of the Law Under the Uniform Commercial Code § 2–9, at 75 (2d ed. 1980); McCormick; supra note 20, at 367.

42. Wallach, supra note 20, at 654.

43. See § 2–8 supra.

44. Sweet I, supra note 24, at 1055 & n. 86.

45. See, In re United States Financial Securities Litigation, 609 F.2d 411 (9th Cir. 1979), certiorari denied sub nom. Gant v. Union Bank, 446 U.S. 929, 100 S.Ct. 1866, 64 L.Ed.2d 281 (1980).

46. Murray, The Parol Evidence Rule: A Clarification, 4 Dug.L.Rev. 337, 342 (1965–1966) [hereinafter cited as Murray I].

47. Other methods of jury control include the trial judge's comments on the evidence, the power of cross-examination, the judge's charge to the jury, and where the judge is convinced the jury reached an erroneous result, the granting of a motion for a new trial. Sweet I, supra note 24, at 1056.

48. 9 J. Wigmore, Anglo-American System of Evidence in Trials at Common Law § 2430, at 99 (3d ed. 1940).

49. E.g., Prophet v. Builders, Inc., 204 Kan. 268, 462 P.2d 122 (1969); Fogelson v. Rackfay Constr. Co., 300 N.Y. 334, 90 N.E.2d 881 (1950), reargument denied 301 N.Y. 552, 93 N.E.2d 349 (1950); O'Brien v. O'Brien, 362 Pa. 66, 66 A.2d 309 (1949); Adams v. Marchbanks, 253 S.C. 280, 170 S.E.2d 214 (1969); In re Spring Valley Meats, Inc., 94 Wis.2d 600, 288 N.W.2d 852 (1980); see 3 Corbin § 573.

tions.[50]　Rather, he stated that the rule is simply a statement of the substantive law principle that if the parties so intend their final expression will prevail over any antecedent expression of agreement.[51] This is true whether the final expression is oral or written.[52]　However, as Professor McCormick points out, making the question of intent to integrate a question of law gives the parol evidence rule a procedural function since the rule has as a basis distrust of the jury.

In reality the question is one that may be answered either way depending on how it is phrased.　When one says that an integrated writing supersedes prior or collateral agreements, a rule of substantive law is stated.[53]　When it is said that a particular writing is conclusively presumed to contain the entire agreement and other evidence is thus inadmissible, the principle being announced is evidentiary.[54]

The main consequence of this determination relates to whether the parol evidence question can be raised for the first time on appeal.　In the case of a rule of evidence, ordinarily a failure to object waives any error in the admission of improper evidence.　However, in the area of parol evidence there are cases (probably a majority) that say that the question may be raised for the first time on appeal despite the failure to object.[55]

 WESTLAW REFERENCES

"final agreement" /s supersed!

di("parol* evidence rule" /p contradict! /p evidence)

157k445(1) /p "parol* evidence rule"

"parol* evidence rule" /s "binding contract"

final /s "partial! integrat!"

"final embodiment" /s evidence

complete! /s "total! integrat!"

157k397(2) /p "parol* evidence rule"

integrat! /s supplement! /s term

agreement contract /s final! /s incomplete! /s term

157k429 /p "parol* evidence rule"

(a) *To What Type of Evidence Does the Parol Evidence Rule Relate—Prior Contemporaneous, and Subsequent Agreements*

"prior or contemporaneous agreements or negotiations"

157k448 /p "parol* evidence rule"

"parol* evidence rule" /s prior /s term /s integrat!

"parol* evidence rule" /s "subsequent agreement"

50. J. Thayer, supra note 2, at 405–10.

51. Id.

52. J. Murray, supra note 10, at § 105, at 227.

53. Id.

54. See Note, The Parol Evidence Rule, supra note 22, at 972 n. 2.

55. E.g., Tahoe Nat'l Bank v. Phillips, 4 Cal.3d 11, 92 Cal.Rptr. 704, 480 P.2d 320 (1971); Ruscito v. F–Dyne Elec. Co., 177 Conn. 149, 411 A.2d 1371 (1979); Snow v. Winn, 607 P.2d 678 (Okl.1980); Bulis v. Wells, 565 P.2d 487 (Wyo.1977); see also Annot., 81 A.L.R.3d 249 (1977) (collecting cases; Restatement, Second, Contracts § 213, Comment a.　But see Higgs v. De Maziroff, 263 N.Y. 473, 189 N.E. 555 (1934) (parol evidence rule is both a rule of substantive law and a rule of evidence).

di("parol* evidence rule" /p contemporaneous! /p agreement)

williston restatement corbin /p "parol* evidence rule" /p
    contemporaneous! /p agreement

restatement /p contemporaneous! /s term writing

corbin /p prior subsequent! contemporaneous! /s term writing

(b) *Policy and Analytical Rationales Involved*

"parol* evidence rule" /s perjur!

"uncertain testimony of slippery memory"

writing written /s merg! /s term /s supersed!

"prior agreement /s merge!

"parol* evidence rule" /s "public policy"

"parol* evidence rule" /s reform!

"parol* evidence rule" /s fraud! /s except!

157k433(1) /p "parol* evidence rule"

"parol* evidence rule" /s mortgag!

"parol* evidence rule" /s "third party"

157k384 /p "parol* evidence rule"

(c) *The Role of the Judge and Jury*

"parol* evidence rule" /s fact*** /2 question

integrat! contract agreement /s law legal /2 question /s intent!
    intend! /s party

to (95) /p intent! intend /p party /p question /2 law legal

"parol* evidence rule" /s question /2 law legal

"parol* evidence rule" /s judge

(d) *Is the Rule of Substantive Law or Procedure?*

157k384 /p "parol* evidence rule" /p substantive

"parol* evidence rule" /s "substantive law"

integrat! /s write writing written /s substantive!

write written writing /s eviden! /s conclusive! /s presum! /s
    integrat! agreement contract

"parol* evidence rule" /s fail! /s object!

"parol* evidence rule" /s appeal! appellate /s rais***

30k204(3)

---

§ 3–3. Is the Writing Integrated?

We have already seen that the first issue in a parol evidence problem is whether the parties intended the writing to be a final embodiment of their agreement. If so, there is at least a partial integration and the writing may not be contradicted by the type of evidence discussed above.[56] A writing that evidences a contract is not necessarily a final embodiment of the contract.[57] For example, a note or a memorandum prepared by one party, but not shown to the other, is not an integration because not only is it not final it is not even assented

56. See § 3–2(a) supra.

57. Cornwell Quality Tools Co. v. C.T.S. Co., 446 F.2d 825 (9th Cir.1971), certiorari

denied 404 U.S. 1049, 92 S.Ct. 715, 30 L.Ed. 2d 740 (1972).

to by the other party.[58] The writing is merely evidence of the agreement. So also, the parties may have intended their writings to be tentative and preliminary to a final draft.[59] In these cases, the parol evidence rule does not apply.[60] Unlike a note or memorandum placed in one's own files, a letter of confirmation is sent to the other party. At common law it is often held that such a letter acts as a total integration if the other party makes no response to it prior to performance.[61] However, it is possible that a letter of confirmation may act only as a partial integration particularly where it is clear that the memorandum is incomplete.[62]

It is agreed that any relevant evidence is admissible to show that the writing was not intended to be final.[63] Although the question of finality is ordinarily characterized as one of law in order to remove it from the province of unsophisticated jurors, it is actually a question of fact—one of intention—which the trial judge determines.[64] To be considered final the writing need not be in any particular form and need not be signed. The crucial requirement is that the parties have regarded the writing as the final embodiment of their agreement.[65] Undoubtedly the completeness of the agreement does have some bearing on the question of finality (integration); that is to say, the more complete and formal the instrument is, the more likely it that it is intended as an integration.[66]

58. That is to say, ordinarily there is no evidence of assent to the note by both parties much less evidence that it is assented to by both parties as a final expression. See Donald Friedman & Co. v. Newman, 255 N.Y. 340, 174 N.E. 703 (1931); Hoots v. Calaway, 282 N.C. 477, 193 S.E.2d 709 (1973).

59. Restatement, Second, Contracts § 209, ill. 1.

60. Atwater v. Cardwell, 21 Ky.L.Rev. 1297, 54 S.W. 868 (1900); Hechinger v. Ulacia, 194 A.D. 330, 185 N.Y.S. 323 (1st Dep't 1920).

61. Tow v. Miners Memorial Hosp. Ass'n, 305 F.2d 73 (4th Cir.1962); Newburger v. American Surety Co., 242 N.Y. 134, 151 N.E. 155 (1926); Restatement, Contracts § 228, ill. 2; Restatement, Second, Contracts § 209, ill. 2. The U.C.C. rule on this point is discussed in § 3–4(e) infra.

62. Reconstruction Finance Corp. v. Commercial Union of America Corp., 123 F.Supp. 748 (S.D.N.Y.1954); Flavorland Industries v. Schnoll Packing Corporation, 167 N.J. 376, 400 A.2d 883 (1979); Hoots v. Calaway, 282 N.C. 477, 193 S.E.2d 709 (1973); Levy v. Leaseway Systems, Inc., 190 Pa.Super. 482, 154 A.2d 314 (1959).

63. In re William Rakestraw Co., 450 F.2d 6 (9th Cir.1971); National Cash Register Co. v. I.M.C., Inc., 260 Or. 504, 491 P.2d

211 (1971); Bullfrog Marina, Inc. v. Lentz, 28 Utah 2d 261, 501 P.2d 266 (1972); 3 Corbin § 588; 4 Williston § 633 n. 13; Restatement, Contracts § 228, Comment a; Restatement, Second, Contracts § 209(2) and Comments b and c; id. § 214(a).

64. McCormick §§ 214–15. Corbin would allow greater participation by the jury. See 3 Corbin § 595; Restatement, Second, Contracts § 209, Comment c.

65. Kitchen v. Stockman Nat'l Life Ins. Co., 192 N.W.2d 796 (Iowa 1971); J. Murray, supra 10, § 104; J. Wigmore, Anglo-American System of Evidence at Common Law § 2408 (2d ed. 1923). Thus even an offer may amount to an integration, if the parties both assent to it as an integration. Restatement, Second, Contracts § 209, Comment b.

66. Antonellis v. Northgate Const. Corp., 362 Mass. 847, 291 N.E.2d 626 (1973); Di Menna v. Cooper & Evans Co., 220 N.Y. 391, 397–98, 115 N.E. 993, 995 (1917); 3 Corbin § 581; Restatement, Second, Contracts § 210, Comment c. "Where the parties reduce an agreement to a writing which in view of its completeness and specificity reasonably appears to be a complete agreement it is taken to be an integrated agreement unless it is established by other evidence that the writing did not constitute a final expression." Restate-

WESTLAW REFERENCES

note memorandum /s party /s integrat! /s assent! agree! contract

relevan! /s eviden! /s write written writing /s final!

"consistent additional term" /s integrat!

integrat! /s contract agreement /s question /2 legal law fact intend! intent!

(a) The "Four Corners" Rule

"four corners" /s integrat!

anchor +s "bird island"

(b) The "Collateral Contract" Concept

collateral +1 agreement contract /s integrat!

collateral +1 agreement contract /s "parol evidence"

collateral +1 agreement contract /s inconsisten! contradict!

collateral +1 agreement contract /s independen!

collateral +1 agreement contract /s introduc!

collateral ancillary +1 agreement contract /s admit! admissible

ancillary collateral +1 agreement contract /s separat!

silen! /s collateral ancillary +1 agreement contract

seitz +s refrigerating

(c) Williston's Rules

williston /s merg! integrat!

mitchell +s lath

consisten! /s addition! /s term /s incomplete!

reasonable +1 man person /s integrat!

(d) Corbin's Rule

corbin /s intend! intent! /s Party /s complete! incomplete! integrat! merg!

corbin /p ("dix steel" +s miles) (black +s "evergreen land")

corbin /s integrat!

(e) The U.C.C. Rule

"uniform commercial code" u.c.c. /s 2–202

(1) Clause (b)

"uniform commercial code" u.c.c. /s 2–202 /p integrat!

"hunt foods" +s doliner

find 380 a2d 618

(2) Clause (a)

"uniform commercial code" u.c.c. /s 2–202 /p consisten! /s term

"uniform commercial code" u.c.c. /s 2–202 /p confirmatory memoranda

"uniform commercial code" u.c.c. /s 2–202 /p "express! warrant!"

ment, Second, Contracts § 209(3). Illustration 3 of this section makes it clear that even if such a writing is not a total integration it ordinarily would be a partial integration. However this does not accord with Williston's rules discussed below as to what constitutes a total integration.

(f) *The Restatement Second*

restatement /s second 2d /p intend! intent! /s integrat!

restatement /s second 2d /p consisten! /s term

(g) *Is the Existence of a Total Integration Determined by the Intention of the Parties?*

"intention of the party" /s integrat! /s contract transaction agreement

bussard +s thomas /p integrat!

§ 3–4.   Is the Writing a Total Integration?

Once it is decided that the writing is an integration the next issue is whether the writing is a total integration. When it is concluded that there is an integration this decides only that the writing was a final statement of part of the agreement of the parties—that is to say, that there is a partial integration. If the writing is final and complete then there is a total integration with the result that it may not be contradicted or supplemented. However, while a partial integration may not be contradicted it may be supplemented by consistent additional terms.[67]

Whether the integration is total or partial is very often the key issue in parol evidence disputes. This issue is also ordinarily treated as a question of law even though so very often it is suggested that this is a question of the intention of the parties.[68] There are many approaches used to determine whether the integration is total and in many of them the intention of the parties is not the basis of the determination.[69] The leading tests used to determine the existence of a total integration will now be briefly discussed.

(a) The "Four Corners" Rule

The earliest view is the so-called "four corners" rule. Under that view if the instrument is complete on its face—a determination to be made by the trial judge by looking solely at the writing—the instrument is conclusively presumed to be a total integration.[70] This approach is in decline.[71]

(b) The "Collateral Contract" Concept

The "four corners" rule is not only illogical but can produce harsh results since it is impossible to determine whether an agreement is

67. See § 3–2 supra.

68. Restatement, Second, Contracts § 210(3); McCormick, Evidence § 215; Hanslin v. Keith, 120 N.H. 361, 415 A.2d 329 (1980).

69. A recent article indicates that the courts are more likely to find the existence of a total integration in the case of a formal contract negotiated by attorneys or

sophisticated parties. Childres & Spitz, Status In The Law of Contracts, 47 N.Y. U.L.Rev. 1, 7 (1972).

70. Anchor Cas. Co. v. Bird Island Produce, Inc., 249 Minn. 137, 82 N.W.2d 48 (1957).

71. J. Murray, supra note 10, at § 106; J. White & R. Summers, supra n. 41, § 2–10, at 79–80.

complete on its face simply by looking at the writing.[72] In an attempt to obtain fairer results some of the courts looked for another approach and the "collateral contract" concept was born.[73] Under this rule the existence of a total integration did not prevent "collateral agreements"—those that are independent of the writing in question—from being introduced so long as the main agreement was not contradicted.[74]

The problem became that courts applied the concept to situations that were logically distinct. For example if S and B in a signed writing agreed to sell and buy a specific automobile for $1,000.00 and they contemporaneously orally agreed that B may keep the automobile in A's garage for one year in return for B's promise to pay $15.00 per month for the year for garaging the car, the second agreement may be looked upon as being in a sense independent of the first agreement because there is consideration on both sides in the agreement relating to the storage of the car. In this situation under the collateral contract concept and all of the views to be discussed, it is held that the ancillary agreement is admissible unless it contradicts the main agreement.[75] Here it does not and thus the agreement relating to the garage is admissible even in the face of a merger clause.[76] At times it may be difficult to determine which is the main and which is the ancillary agreement but as indicated above this is important only when the two agreements are contradictory.[77]

If we take the illustration relating to the garage and change the facts so that B seeks to prove that S promised to allow him to use the garage but testifies to no consideration for this collateral promise other than the consideration stated in the writing, the situation is quite different. Yet under the "collateral contract" concept there were "many cases where parol evidence was admitted to prove the existence of a separate oral agreement as to any matter on which the document is silent and which is not inconsistent with its terms—even though the instrument appeared to state a complete agreement." [78] Wigmore seems to approve of this test.[79]

72. But see Note, The Parol Evidence Rule, supra note 22, at 975–6. There are still cases in which it is said that a writing is presumed to embody the final and entire agreement of the parties. See Piercy v. Citibank N.A., 101 Misc.2d 302, 424 N.Y.S.2d 76 (1978).

73. Wallach supra note 20 at 657.

74. Wallach, supra note 20, at 658; see Markoff v. Kreiner, 180 Md. 150, 154, 23 A.2d 19, 23 (1941); Buyken v. Ertner, 33 Wn.2d 334, 339–42, 205 P.2d 628, 633–36 (1949).

75. E. Farnsworth, Contracts § 7.3, at 458.

76. Gem Corrugated Box Corp. v. National Kraft Container Corp., 427 F.2d 499

(2d Cir.1970); Restatement, Second, Contracts § 216(2)(a) and Comment c. Merger clauses are discussed below in § 3–6 infra.

77. See Gem Corrugated Box Corp. v. National Kraft Container Corp., 427 F.2d 499 (2d Cir.1970); E. Farnsworth, Contracts § 7–3 at 458.

78. Masterson v. Sine, 68 Cal.2d 222, 65 Cal.Rptr. 545, 436 P.2d 561 (1968); Lee v. Kimura, 2 Hawaii App. 538, 634 P.2d 1043 (1981); Crow-Spieker # 23 v. Robinson, 97 Nev. 302, 629 P.2d 1198 (1981).

79. 9 J. Wigmore, supra note 48, § 2430, 98; Lanning Constr., Inc. v. Rozell, 320 N.W.2d 522 (S.D.1982).

Under this approach it seems clear that no writing could be considered more than a partial integration. However, many courts stated the "collateral contract" concept much more narrowly. For example, the Supreme Court of the United States in a leading case stated:

> "Undoubtedly the existence of a separate oral agreement as to any matter on which the written contract is silent, and which is not inconsistent with its term, may be proven by parol, if under the circumstances of the particular case it may properly be inferred that the parties did not intend the written paper to be a complete and final statement of the whole of the transaction between them. But such an agreement must not only be collateral, but must also relate to a subject distinct from that to which the written contract applies; that is, it must not be so closely connected with the principal transaction as to form part and parcel of it." [80]

The narrower view makes a distinction between promises which "are inherently and substantially collateral to the main purpose of the contract" and those "which directly relate to the main object." This distinction is unworkable.[81] Williston therefore suggested a new "reasonable man" test which is discussed below. Since that time the "collateral contract" rule has been declining in popularity, although at times Williston rules and the "collateral contract rule" are employed in the same case.[82] Despite its decline, the "collateral contract rule" is still alive.[83]

(c) Williston's Rules

Professor Williston's rules can be summarized as follows: (1) If the writing expressly declares that it contains the entire agreement of the parties in what is usually referred to as a merger clause,[84] this declaration conclusively establishes that the integration is total unless the document is obviously incomplete or the merger clause was included as a result of fraud or mistake or any reason exists that is sufficient to set aside a contract.[85] As previously indicated, even a merger clause does not prevent enforcement of a separate agreement supported by a

---

80. Seitz v. Brewers' Refrigerating Mach. Co., 141 U.S. 510, 12 S.Ct. 46, 35 L.Ed. 837 (1891).

81. See 4 Williston, § 638. Professor McCormick points out that the net result was that the courts could and did select the version of the rule that suited them in a particular case. McCormick, supra note 20, at 372; see also Murray, The Parol Evidence Process and Standardized Agreements Under the Restatement (Second) of Contracts, 123 U.Pa.L.Rev. 1342, 1349 (1975) [hereinafter cited as Murray II].

82. See, e.g., Mitchill v. Lath, 247 N.Y. 377, 160 N.E. 646 (1928) and more recently, Lee v. Joseph E. Seagram & Sons, 552 F.2d 447 (2d Cir.1977).

83. FMA Financial Corp. v. Hansen Dairy, Inc., 617 P.2d 327 (Utah 1980).

84. See § 3–6 infra.

85. 4 Williston § 633; cf. 3 Corbin § 578. See also Hartsfield, The Merger Clause and the Parol Evidence Rule, 27 Tex.L.Rev. 361 (1949); Note in Uniform Commercial Code—Effect of Entire Agreement Clause on Admission of Parol Evidence, 19 Ala.L.Rev. 556 (1967). The Restatement Second suggests that a merger clause should not have any effect unless the merger clause was actually agreed to. Restatement, Second, Contracts § 216, Comment e.

separate consideration.[86] (2) In the absence of a merger clause, the determination is made by looking to the writing.[87] Consistent additional terms may be proved if the writing is obviously incomplete on its face [88] or if it is apparently complete but, as in the case of deed, bonds, bills and notes, expresses the undertaking of only one party.[89] (3) Where the writing appears to be a complete instrument expressing the rights and obligations of both parties, it is deemed a total integration unless the alleged additional terms were such as might naturally be made as a separate agreement by parties situated as were the parties to the written agreement,[90] in which event it is a partial integration.[91]

The second rule makes clear that if the writing is obviously incomplete it cannot amount to more than a partial integration. This is a logical and generally accepted approach.[92] The second part of this rule is really a corollary of the third rule because it would be natural not to include all of terms agreed upon in the type of instruments discussed.[93]

It is the third rule that has had great influence in the area of parol evidence. As indicated above, Professor Williston found the "four corners" and the "collateral contract" rules unworkable. He therefore selected the "reasonable man" approach embodied in the third rule as the basis of determining whether there was a total integration when the other two rules did not apply. Thus when Williston talks about intent in this area, he is not talking about the actual intent of the parties but a presumed or fictitious intent.[94] More fully expressed Williston's third rule states that when a term not found in the writing is offered into evidence by one of the parties and the court concludes that it would have been natural for the parties situated as they were to have included that term in the writing, there is a total integration with respect to that term and the term may not be admitted into evidence even if it does not contradict the writing. If a second term were

---

86. See discussion in 3–4(b).

87. 4 Williston § 633.

88. "The test of the completeness of the writing proposed as a contract is the writing itself. If this bears evidence of careful preparation, of a deliberate regard for the many questions which would naturally arise out of the subject-matter of the contract, and if it is reasonable to conclude from it that the parties have therein expressed their final intentions in regard to the matters within the scope of the writing, then it will be deemed a complete and unalterable exposition of such intentions. If, on the other hand, the writing shows its informality on its face, there will be no presumption that it contains all the terms of the contract. In every case, therefore, the writing must be critically examined in the light of its surrounding circumstances, with a view of determining whether it is a memorial of the transaction." Brady v.

Central Excavators, Inc., 316 Mich. 594, 606, 25 N.W.2d 630, 635 (1947).

89. 4 Williston §§ 633, 636; see Restatement, Second, Contracts § 216 Comment c.

90. 4 Williston § 645; 3 Corbin § 587; Restatement, Second, Contracts § 216, Comment d.

91. 4 Williston §§ 638–39; see Ratta v. Harkins, 268 Md. 122, 299 A.2d 777 (1973); Restatement, Second, Contracts § 216(2)(b) and Comment d.

92. Chertkof v. Spector Baltimore Terminal, Inc. 263 Md. 550, 284 A.2d 215 (1971); Land Reclamation, Inc. v. Riverside Corp., 261 Or. 180, 492 P.2d 263 (1972); Restatement Contracts § 240.

93. Wallach, supra note 20, at 659.

94. See Murray II, supra note 81, at 1369–70; see also 3A Corbin § 587; 4 Williston § 645.

offered, it would be admitted if it would have been natural not to include that particular term in the writing. The question is not in fact what the parties did but what parties similarly situated would normally do with respect to the particular term offered.[95] It is obvious that there can be great difficulty in applying this test to a particular set of facts.[96]

In time, Williston's rule was adopted by the First Restatement [97] and it probably became and probably still is the majority rule in the country. But, in time, Williston was challenged by Professor Corbin's bold new approach to the problem.

(d) Corbin's Rule

Earlier we discussed the question of whether the parol evidence rule applied to a contemporaneous agreement. We noted that Williston's view on this point is the majority view. His view is that a contemporaneous writing becomes part of the integration but that a contemporaneous oral agreement is subject to the rule.[98] Corbin concludes that terms are either prior or subsequent to the writing and that the word "contemporaneous" merely clouds the issue.[99] If "contemporaneous" agreements do not exist, then obviously the rule does not apply to them.

However, Corbin agrees that the rule applies to prior agreements, whether written or oral. He rejects Williston's "reasonable man" approach and is determined to search out the actual intention of the parties. The issue for him is whether the parties actually agreed or intended that the writing was a total and complete statement of their agreement.[1] Stated differently the trial judge determines whether the parties intended that the prior agreement should be merged.[2] According to Corbin all relevant evidence should be included on this issue of intent including evidence of prior negotiations.[3] In other words the very evidence whose admissibility is challenged is admissible on the issue of total integration.[4] It is clear that Corbin's approach undercuts the traditional parol evidence rule.[5] The trend is now in the direction

95. J. Murray, supra n. 10, § 106; 4 Williston § 633.

96. Compare Gianni v. Russell & Co., 281 Pa. 320, 126 A. 791 (1924) with Masterson v. Sine, 68 Cal.2d 222, 65 Cal.Rptr. 545, 436 P.2d 561 (1968).

97. Wallach, supra note 20, at 658 & n. 21; see Restatement, Contracts § 240.

98. See 3–2(a) supra.

99. See 3–2(a) supra.

1. 3A Corbin § 577.

2. Wallach, supra note 20, at 664; 3A Corbin § 585; Sherman v. Mutual Benefit Life Ins. Co., 633 F.2d 782, 784 (9th Cir. 1980); Bunbury v. Krauss, 41 Wis.2d 522, 164 N.W.2d 473, 476 (1969).

3. 3A Corbin § 582; J. Murray, supra note 10, § 106, at 231; Silver Syndicate, Inc. v. Sunshine Mining Co., 101 Idaho 226, 611 P.2d 1011 (1979).

4. 3A Corbin § 582; Restatement, Second, Contracts § 209(2); In re Eickman Estate, 291 N.W.2d 308 (Iowa 1980); Alexander v. Snell, 12 Mass.App.Ct. 323, 424 N.E.2d 262 (1981).

5. 3A Corbin § 582; J. Wigmore, supra note 49, § 2403(2); Connell v. Aetna Life & Tax Co., 436 A.2d 408 (Me.1981); Rainbow Constr. Co., Inc. v. Olsen, 64 Or.App. 699, 669 P.2d 814 (1983); In re Spring Valley Meats, 94 Wis.2d 600, 288 N.W.2d 852 (1980).

of Corbin [6] and will be accelerated by the Restatement Second which, as we shall see, has staked out a position similar to that of Corbin.[7]

(e) The U.C.C. Rule

Uniform Commercial Code section 2–202 contains the Code's Parol Evidence Rule, It provides:

Final Written Expression: Parol or Extrinsic Evidence

Terms with respect to which the confirmatory memoranda of the parties agree or which are otherwise set forth in a writing intended by the parties as a final expressions of their agreement with respect to such terms as are included therein may not be contradicted by evidence of any prior agreement or of a contemporaneous oral agreement but may be explained or supplemented:

(a) by course of dealing or usage of trade (Section 1–205) or by course of performance (Section 2–208); and

(b) by evidence of consistent additional terms unless the court finds the writing to have been intended also as a complete and exclusive statement of the terms of the agreement.

(1) Clause (b)

Clause (b) states the traditional rule that a total integration may not be contradicted or supplemented. However, the section does not determine the existence of a total integration according to any of the rules previously discussed. Rather the presumption appears to be that the writing does not include all of the terms; that is to say, that it is only a partial integration.[8] As stated in the statute this presumption may be overcome if the parties actually intend the writing to be a total integration *or,* as stated in Comment 3, if it is *certain* that parties similarly situated would have included the offered term in the writing. In making these determinations the courts appear willing to receive all relevant extrinsic evidence.[9] There appears to be some conflict as to what evidence is relevant based upon whether an objective or a subjective approach should be taken.[10]

It is clear that the statute embraces Corbin's rule that the actual intention of the parties should be sought. It also contains a variation

---

6. Ample authority for this proposition can be found in the cases relying upon Professor Corbin's analysis and cited by him in 3 Corbin §§ 573–95. See, more recently, Aboussie v. Aboussie, 441 F.2d 150 (5th Cir.1971); United States v. Clementon Sewerage Authority, 365 F.2d 609 (3d Cir.1966) (New Jersey law); Masterson v. Sine, 68 Cal.2d 222, 65 Cal.Rptr. 545, 436 P.2d 561, (1968); 17 Cath.U.L.Rev. 489 (1968). Corbin's approach was adopted for admiralty law in Battery Steamship Corp. v. Refineria Panama, S.A., 513 F.2d 735 (2d Cir.1975).

7. See § 3–4(f) infra.

8. U.C.C. § 2–202, Comment 3; J. White & R. Summers, supra note 41 at 69; Wallach, supra note 20, at 666; cf. Restatement, Second, Contracts § 209(3).

9. Cosmopolitan Fin. Corp. v. Runnels, 2 Hawaii App. 33, 625 P.2d 390 (1981).

10. Wallach, supra note 20, at 674. Compare Hunt Foods & Indus., Inc. v. Doliner, 26 A.D.2d 41, 270 N.Y.S.2d 937 (1966) and Whirlpool Corp. v. Regis Leasing Corp., 29 A.D.2d 395, 288 N.Y.S.2d 337 (1968).

of Williston's reasonable man test in its certainty test. It is equally clear that a total integration can result from either the intention test or the certainty test. Under this alternative rule it is apparent that under the U.C.C. there will be fewer determinations that there is a total integration than under Williston's rule [11] not to mention the four corners rule and the collateral contract rule. The effect of a merger clause will be discussed below.[12] Finally it should be noted that the Code follows Williston's rules with respect to contemporaneous agreements and that the integration question is treated as one of law.[13]

(2) Clause (a)

Under this clause a course of dealing usage of the trade or a course of performance may be used to supply a consistent additional term even though the writing is deemed to be a total integration under the rule stated in clause (b) above.[14] Thus under this rule there is at most a partial integration and the only question to be decided is whether the course of dealing etc. offered contradicts the integration. This sounds as if it would make an important change in the prior common law decisions that followed Williston's rules. However, under Williston's rule it would be natural for parties similarly situated not to include a course of dealing or the like in the writing. Thus under Williston's rule the integration would be partial and the question would be whether the term offered is contradictory. This section would change the result under the "four corners rule." [15] The topic of course of dealing, usage of the trade and course of performance will be discussed in more detail below.[16]

The final problem presented by this section arises as a result of its use of the words "confirmatory memoranda." We have previously seen that at common law a confirmation often acts as a total integration if the other party makes no response to it prior to performance.[17] Under the Code even if there are "confirmatory memoranda" it does not follow that the result is a total integration. This will be so only if the parties intend a total integration or the term offered would certainly have been included.[18] This represents a change in the common law rule.

Another interesting question is whether it is possible under the Code to have a total integration based upon a single confirmatory memorandum. It has been argued that this result may no longer obtain because of the use of the words "confirmatory memoranda." [19]

---

11. Bersner v. Bolles, 20 Cal.App.3d 635, 97 Cal.Rptr. 846 (1971); Snyder v. Hubert Greenbaum & Associates, Inc., 38 Md.App. 144, 380 A.2d 618 (1977); Hunt Foods & Indus. v. Doliner, supra note 10.

12. See § 3–6 infra.

13. U.C.C. § 2–202 (1977), Comment 3.

14. J. White & R. Summers, supra n. 41, § 2–10, at 85.

15. As a matter of fact the Code appears to completely reject "the four cor-

ners rule." J. White & R. Summers, supra n. 41, § 2–10, at 79; see also U.C.C. § 2–202, Comment 1(a) (1977).

16. See § 3–17 infra.

17. See § 3–3 supra.

18. Paymaster Oil Mill Co. v. Mitchell, 319 So.2d 652 (Miss.1975).

19. Album Graphics, Inc. v. Beatrice Foods Co., 87 Ill.App.3d 338, 42 Ill.Dec. 332, 408 N.E.2d 1041 (1980).

Professor Murray [20] disagrees and argues that a single confirmatory memorandum may still operate as total integration under the Code and Professor Farnsworth agrees with him.[21]

(f) The Restatement Second

The most recent formulation of the parol evidence rule has been pronounced by the Second Restatement. Unfortunately the Restatement has failed to make its position clear and has only perpetuated and added to the confusion.[22] There is some dispute as to whether the Restatement Second adopted Corbin's approach or that of the Uniform Commercial Code.[23] In our opinion the Restatement Second appears to be more in accord with Corbin.[24] Its major premise is that Corbin's rule of ascertaining actual intent should be used in determining whether there is a total or partial integration. It goes on to say that, even if this test leads to a determination of a total integration, consistent additional terms are still admissible a) if the alleged agreement is made for a separate consideration *or* b) if the offered agreement is not within the scope of the integrated writing.[25] (This seems to be a throwback to the more liberal cases under the collateral contract theory) or c) if the offered terms might naturally be omitted from the writing.[26] In fact the Restatement Second appears to say that it is impossible to have more than a partial integration.[27] Thus the Restatement Second appears to have buried the parol evidence rule in a shallow grave of verbiage without even tendering the accoutrements of a decent burial.

Finally, it should be noted that the Restatement Second does not take a clear position on the issue of contemporaneous agreements. Corbin's position appears to be adopted in Restatement, Contracts 2d

---

20. J. Murray, supra n. 10, at 225 & n. 9.

21. E. Farnsworth, supra note 75, § 7–3 at 453 n. 9. § 2–202 has a cross-reference to § 2–316(1). The question is whether an express warranty not contained in the writing may be introduced into evidence in the face of an integration. The answer generally given is in the negative. S.M. Wilson & Company v. Smith Intern., Inc., 587 F.2d 1363 (9th Cir.1978). Prof. Broude, however, argues that printed form disclaimers do not become part of the agreement, and in any event Comment 2 of § 2–316 clearly indicates that the section protects only against a "false" allegation of oral warranties. Therefore, an oral warranty which, in fact, has been made is admissible. Broude, The Consumer and the Parol Evidence Rule: Section 2–202 of the Uniform Commercial Code 1970 Duke L.J. 881. See also C. Birnbaum, L.A. Stahl, M.P. West, Standardized Agreements and the Parol Evidence Rule: Defining and Explaining the Expectations Principle, 26 Arizona L.Rev. 793 (1984).

22. J. Murray, supra n. 10, § 107.

23. As we have seen, the rule of the Uniform Commercial Code actually adopts a part of Williston's approach and a part of Corbin's rule. See (e) supra.

24. Fortune Furniture Mfg., Inc. v. Pate's Elec. Co., 356 So.2d 1176 (Miss.1978); FDIC v. First Mortgage Investors, 76 Wis. 2d 151, 250 N.W.2d 362 (1976). The U.C.C. agrees on this point. U.C.C. § 2–202 Comment 3 (1977).

25. Professor Murray has sought to demonstrate that this notion is nebulous and probably unnecessary. See Murray II, supra note 81, at 1364–66.

26. J. Murray, Contracts § 107. For a detailed treatment of the position of the Restatement (Second) of Contracts, see Murray II, supra note 81.

27. See Restatement, Second, Contracts § 213, Comment a; see also Lane v. Pfeifer, 264 Ark. 162, 568 S.W.2d 212 (1978).

§ 239, Comment a. However, in section 241 the reference is to prior or contemporaneous agreements or negotiations.[28] The Restatement Second takes the position that integration is a question for the court, but with a nod toward Corbin's position that this is only ordinarily true.[29]

(g) *Is the Existence of a Total Integration Determined by the Intention of the Parties?*

It is obvious that the "four corners rule" and the "collateral contract" concept do not determine the existence of a total integration on the basis of the intention of the parties. Both Williston and Corbin assert that the existence of a total integration depends upon the intention of the parties. Williston does so primarily in a section entitled. "Integration Depends Upon Intent.[30] Corbin's emphasis on intent runs throughout his entire discussion of the rule.[31] It appears, however, that in this context they use the term "intent" in ways that are remarkably dissimilar. A typical fact pattern will illustrate this. A agrees to sell and B agrees to purchase Blackacre for $10,000. The contract is in writing and in all respects appears complete on its face. Prior to the signing of the contract A, in order to induce B's assent, orally promises him in the presence of a number of reputable witnesses that if B will sign the contract, A will remove an unsightly shack on A's land across the road from Blackacre. May this promise be received into evidence and made part of the contract?[32] This depends upon whether the writing is a total integration. Williston argues that if the intention to have a total integration were to be determined by the ordinary process of determining intention the parol evidence rule would be emasculated because the very existence of the collateral agreement would conclusively indicate that the parties intended only a partial integration.[33] In other words the only questions that would be presented is whether the alleged prior or contemporaneous agreement was made.

Williston makes it clear that in determining the issue of total integration the fact of agreement is irrelevant and thus he excludes the evidence of prior and oral contemporaneous agreements in making this determination.[34] In addition his rules for determining the existence of a total integration, as we have seen, do not seek out the actual intention of the parties in determining whether the writing was a complete integration.[35]

As we have seen Corbin's notion is to ascertain the actual intention of the parties and he is even willing to receive evidence of the prior

28. See 48 ALI Proceedings 226 (1971); Murray II, supra note 81, at 1362.

29. See Restatement, Second, Contracts § 209.

30. 5 Williston § 633.

31. 3 Corbin §§ 573–596.

32. These facts are suggested by Mitchill v. Lath, 247 N.Y. 377, 160 N.E. 646 (1928).

33. 4 Williston § 633.

34. 4 Williston § 633.

35. See § 3–4(c) supra.

negotiations.[36] As we have also seen the U.C.C. and the Restatement Second are substantially in accord with Corbin's approach.[37]

§ 3–5. Is the Offered Term Consistent or Contradictory?

Several times we have adverted to the rule that a partial integration may not be contradicted but may be supplemented by consistent additional terms. Is there a clear distinction between a contradictory and a consistent term? For example, if a written real estate contract lists a number of obligations of the seller and the buyer offers proof that the seller orally assumed an additional obligation, would the term offered impliedly contradict the writing? There are some cases that have held the offered term is inconsistent because it contradicts an inference that all of the seller's obligations were listed in the contract.[38]

An additional and more difficult problem is presented when the term offered contradicts an implied in fact or an implied in law term. For example, if a writing is silent as to the time of performance, it is implied as a fact that performance within a reasonable time was intended by the parties. Under some of the cases, if a party offered evidence of an agreement that performance would take place at a particular time, the evidence would be excluded because it contradicts an implied in fact term that is part of the integration.[39] There are fewer cases that exclude the term offered when it contradicts an implied in law term.[40]

This problem is illustrated by the case of Masterson v. Sine.[41] In that case D.M. and his wife conveyed a ranch to D.M.'s sister and her husband. The deed contained an option to repurchase. In time D.M. was adjudicated a bankrupt. His trustee in bankruptcy and his wife seek to exercise the option to purchase. The grantees assert that there was a prior oral agreement that the option to purchase was personal to D.M. and his wife. If this agreement in fact occurred and was admissible in evidence, it is clear that the option could not be exercised by the trustee in bankruptcy and D.M.'s wife. The admissibility of this evidence was decided under Williston's rule. The majority opinion decided that it would have been natural not to include this term in the writing (a deed) because of the close relationship of the parties and because it would be natural not to include all of the terms agreed upon in this type of instrument.[42] Thus the majority held that there was only a partial integration. It then went on to hold that the term offered was a consistent additional term even though it contradicted an

---

36. See § 3–4(d) supra.

37. See § 3–4(e) and (f) supra.

38. See, e.g., Mitchill v. Lath, 247 N.Y. 377, 160 N.E. 646 (1928); see also 4 Williston § 642.

39. See 4 Williston § 640. Some courts, however, admit such evidence on the issue of what is a reasonable time. Sweet I, supra note 24, at 1039.

40. See 4 Williston Contracts § 640 (collecting cases).

41. 68 Cal.2d 222, 65 Cal.Rptr. 545, 436 P.2d 561 (1968). For an excellent discussion of this entire area see Hadjiyannakis, The Parol Evidence Rule and Implied Terms: The Sounds of Silence, 54 Fordham L.Rev. 35 (1986).

42. See § 3–4(c) supra.

implied in law term of the writing—namely free assignability of the option.

There is no clear distinction between implications of fact that in theory become part of the agreement by consent and rules of law that are read into the agreement by the court in order to fill its gaps.[43] Both Williston and Corbin appear to favor the rule that an implied in law term may be contradicted.[44] The cases under the Code also appear to be taking the position that to be inconsistent a term must contradict an express term of the integration.[45]

All of the cases discussed above relate to whether an implied term or inference may be contradicted. It is equally difficult to tell whether an offered term contradicts an express term of the agreement. For example is a demand note contradicted by evidence that it was to be paid only out of the proceeds of a sale? There are contradictory cases.[46] Is an agreement that calls for the sale of a specific quantity of goods contradicted by evidence of a custom to the effect that quantity terms in such contracts "are mere projection to be adjusted according to market, forces?" The court in Columbia Nitrogen Corp. v. Royster Co.,[47] held that there was no contradiction.

All that can be said is that there is little or no consistency in the cases on the question of what is contradictory and what is consistent. A recent U.C.C. case has defined "inconsistency" as "the absence of reasonable harmony in terms of the language and respective obligations of the parties."[48]

 WESTLAW REFERENCES

imply! implied! implicat! /2 law /s term /s contradict!

offered /s term /s contradict! /s express!

43. "There is no clear line between implications of fact and rules of law filling gaps; although fairly clear examples of each can be given other cases will involve almost imperceptable shadings." Restatement (Second) of Contracts § 216, Comment b. See note 40 supra. See also id.; § 204, Comment e; id. § 214, Comment c; Hayden v. Hoadley, 94 Vt. 345, 111 A. 343 (1920); 4 Williston § 640.

44. 3 Corbin § 593; 4 Williston § 640.

45. Anderson & Nafziger v. G.T. Newcomb, Inc., 100 Idaho 175, 595 P.2d 709 (1979); Snyder v. Greenbaum & Assoc., Inc., 38 Md.App. 144, 380 A.2d 618 (1977); Hunt Foods & Industries, Inc. v. Doliner, 26 A.D.2d 41, 270 N.Y.S.2d 937 (1st Dep't 1966). See generally J. White & R. Summers, Uniform Commercial Code (2d ed. 1980) § 2–9, at 82–84; Wallach, supra § 3–

2 note 20, at 674–76. For an extended discussion of this point as it relates to the U.C.C., see Broude, The Consumer and the Parol Evidence Rule: Section 2–202 of the Uniform Commercial Code, 1970 Duke L.J. 881, 886–88.

46. Compare Mozingo v. North Carolina Nat. Bank, 31 N.C.App. 157, 229 S.E.2d 57 (1976), review denied 291 N.C. 711, 232 S.E.2d 204 (1977) with London & Lancashire Indem. Co. v. Allen, 272 Wis. 75, 74 N.W.2d 793 (1956).

47. 451 F.2d 3 (4th Cir.1971).

48. Luria Bros. & Co., Inc., v. Pielet Bros., Scrap Iron & Metal, Inc., 600 F.2d 103, 111 (9th Cir.1979); see also Anderson & Nafziger v. G.T. Newcomb, Inc., 100 Idaho 175, 595 P.2d 709 (1979).

"columbia nitrogen"   +s   royster

"uniform commercial code" u.c.c.   /p   "absence of reasonable
   harmony"

§ 3–6. Merger Clauses

A merger clause is a clause in the instrument that states that the writing is a final expression of all the terms agreed upon and is a complete and exclusive statement of those terms.[49] Williston's first rule states that a merger clause will ordinarily resolve the issue of total integration.[50] The only two exceptions listed are where the instrument is obviously incomplete on its face and where the merger clause was included in the instrument as a result of fraud or mistake or for any reason that is sufficient to set aside a contract.[51] Note that we are here talking about the merger clause being voidable whereas in the next section we are talking about the entire contract being voidable.[52]

Williston's position reflects the traditional rule and the vast majority of courts still follow it.[53] However there is some motion in the other direction. There is now some authority that a merger clause is only one of the factors to be considered in determining whether there is a total integration.[54] A suggestion gaining currency is that the merger clause should not have any effect unless the merger clause was actually agreed upon.[55] This approach is based upon notions ordinarily discussed under the headings of Duty to Read, Unconscionability and Contracts of Adhesion.[56] This is a sensible approach since it is logical to make a distinction between a "dickered" merger clause and one that is merely "boiler plate."[57]

The Columbia Nitrogen[58] case concerns the effect of a merger clause upon a usage of the trade and a course of dealing. It indicates that a merger clause should not rule out this type of evidence unless specific reference is made to this type of evidence. How specific must the clause be? For example, must the clause negate the custom being offered or only customs in general? It would seem to be sufficient if it

---

49. J. White & R. Summers, supra n. 45, § 2–12, 89.

50. See § 3–4(c) supra.

51. See § 3–4(c) supra.

52. The distinction between voidability of the merger clause and voidability of the contract is not always observed; see for example, J. White & R. Summers, supra n. 45, § 2–12, at 78–81.

53. Id. § 2–12; Wallach, § 3–2 supra note 20, at 677–78.

54. See Corbin § 578; J. Murray, Contracts § 106; see also Betz Laboratories, Inc. v. Hines, 647 F.2d 402 (3d Cir.1981); Luther Williams, Jr., Inc. v. Johnson, 229 A.2d 163 (D.C.1967); Zwierzycki v. Owens, 499 P.2d 996 (Wyo.1972).

55. See Broude, supra note 45, at 897–99. Interestingly, Comment 3 to U.C.C. § 2–202 originally contained language referring to the effect of a merger clause "specifically agreed to by both parties". This language, however, was deleted between 1950 and 1952. See id. at 889 & n. 36.

56. Seibel v. Layne & Bowler, Inc. 56 Or.App. 387, 641 P.2d 668 (1982), review denied 293 Or. 190, 648 P.2d 852 (1982), see ch. 9 infra.

57. Restatement, Second, Contracts § 216, Comment e; see O'Keeffe v. Hicks, 74 A.D.2d 919, 426 N.Y.S.2d 315 (1980).

58. 451 F.2d 3 (4th Cir.1971).

excluded customs in general because it is difficult to anticipate what custom a party will claim exists.

 WESTLAW REFERENCES

di merger clause
williston /s "merger clause"
"merger clause" /s final!
"merger clause" /s voidable
"merger clause" /s integrat!
"merger clause" /s fraud! mistak!
"merger clause" /s agreed
"merger clause" /s effect!
"merger clause" /s boilerplate "boiler plate" dicker!

§ 3–7. The Parol Evidence Rule Does Not Apply Until It Is Decided That There Is a Contract

There is a general agreement that parol evidence is admissible to show that a contract was never formed.[59] This general rule may be restated by saying that despite the existence of a merger clause parol evidence is admissible to show that the agreement is void or voidable or to show grounds for granting or denying rescission, reformation, specific performance or other remedy.[60] A good example of what is being discussed is duress. A party may show that he was forced into executing what is or appears to be an integrated writing.[61] All "defect in formation" cases are not equally simple and some require extended discussion.

(a) Writing Was Not Intended to Be Operative

A party may testify that what appears to be a total integration was never intended to be operative—in other words that it was a sham agreement[62] or that the writing was never intended to be binding.[63] This rule, although logical, because a sham agreement is not a contract,[64] really is at war with the notion that the parol evidence rule is designed to prevent perjury. A party who has decided to commit

59. Murray I, supra § 3–2 note 46, at 343–44; Wallach, supra § 3–2 note 20 at 654; see Creamer v. Helferstay, 47 Md. App. 243, 422 A.2d 395 (1980), vacated 294 Md. 107, 448 A.2d 332 (1982), appeal after remand 58 Md.App. 263, 473 A.2d 47 (1984), certiorari denied 300 Md. 794, 481 A.2d 239 (1984).

60. Branstetter v. Cox, 209 Kan. 332, 496 P.2d 1345 (1972); Broome Constr. Co. v. Beaver Lake Recreation Center, Inc., 229 So.2d 545 (Miss.1970); Mitchell v. Kimbrough, 491 P.2d 289 (Okl.1971); National Bank of Commerce v. Thomsen, 80 Wn.2d 406, 495 P.2d 332 (1972); Restatement, Second, Contracts § 214(d), (e) & Comment c.

61. 4 Williston § 634.

62. Drink, Inc. v. Martinez, 89 N.M. 662, 556 P.2d 348 (1976). There are, however, contrary cases that relate to negotiable instruments. See Houck v. Martin, 82 Ill.App.3d 205, 37 Ill.Dec. 531, 402 N.E.2d 421 (1980).

63. Johnston v. Holiday Inns, Inc., 565 F.2d 790 (1st Cir.1977); Arnold Palmer Golf Co. v. Fuqua Indus., Inc., 541 F.2d 584 (6th Cir.1976).

64. See § 2–3 supra.

perjury instead of offering an additional or contradictory term may simply testify that the agreement was sham. If he is believed he will have succeeded in piercing the protective shield of the parol evidence rule. Here there is a clash between the policy basis of the rule and the analytic rationale and, the analytic rationale displaces the policy basis. The same observation applies equally well to the sub-divisions that follow.

(b) Contract Was Intended to Be Effective Only on the Happening of an Express Condition

When the parties agree that a condition precedent must occur before the contract is effective it is generally agreed that the failure of the condition to occur may be shown despite a total integration.[65] The same is true of conditional manual transfer of a formal instrument with an oral condition attached to delivery.[66] This is true even if there is a merger clause.[67] The theory is that the agreement is not to take effect until the condition occurs and thus there is no contract to be added to or contradicted until that time.[68] This rule presents a conceptual difficulty that is not encountered in the case of a defense such as duress. This is so because the condition precedent offered is a term of the agreement and therefore arguably could be made subject to the parol evidence rule.[69] Some courts have made what appears to be a compromise. They adopt the rule stated above but do not apply it where the condition precedent to the formation of the contract offered contradicts a specific term of the writing.[70] If conditions precedent to the formation of a contract are expressed in the writing some courts refuse to permit evidence of other oral conditions precedent upon the theory of an implied contradiction.[71]

Under some authorities the condition may not only be a condition precedent to the formation of a contract but may also be "a condition precedent to the activation of a duty under an existing contract"—that is to say a condition precedent to the performance of a contract.[72] A good illustration of this situation is the well-known case of Pym v. Campbell.[73] In that case the parties entered into an agreement to buy

---

65. 3 Corbin, 589; Nord v. Herreid, 305 N.W.2d 337 (Minn.1981); Restatement, Second, Contracts § 217 (1981); Restatement Contracts, § 241 (1932).

66. Paine v. Paine, 458 A.2d 420 (Mc. 1983); Marquess v. Geuy, 47 Or.App. 351, 614 P.2d 142 (1980); Sweet I, supra § 3–2 note 24, at 1039–40.

67. Luther Williams, Jr., Inc. v. Johnson, 229 A.2d 163 (D.C.App.1967); see also 1 N.Y. State Law Revision Comm'n, 1955 Report 683 (1955). Some cases disagree. See Broude note 45, 897–98.

68. Cumnock-Reed Co. v. Gilvin, 278 Ky. 496, 128 S.W.2d 926 (1939).

69. Wallach, supra note 20, at 654.

70. Bank of Suffolk County v. Kite, 49 N.Y.2d 827, 427 N.Y.2d 782, 404 N.E.2d 1323 (1980).

71. E.g., Stafford v. Russell, 117 Cal. App.2d 326, 255 P.2d 814 (1953); Whirlpool Corp. v. Regis Leasing Corp., 29 A.D.2d 395, 288 N.Y.S.2d 337 (1st Dep't 1968); see Antonellis v. Northgate Constr. Corp., 362 Mass. 847, 291 N.E.2d 626 (1973); Hamon v. Akers, 159 W.Va. 396, 222 S.E.2d 822 (1976).

72. J. Murray, Contracts 237 & n. 5. See also § 11–5 infra.

73. 6 El. & Bl. 340 (Q.B.1856).

and sell a certain patent. The sale however, was orally conditioned upon the approval of the patent by a named third party. The court held that the oral condition was admissible because until the condition occurred no binding contract existed. As Corbin points out there was a binding contract when the parties mutually agreed and thus the condition was actually a condition precedent to the performance of the contract and thus the case should have been decided under the rules stated in section 3–4.[74]

(c) Fraud

The general rule is that a proof of fraud in the inducement may be shown to avoid the written agreement even in the face of a merger clause.[75] This is also generally held to be true even if the evidence offered specifically contradicts the writing or a merger clause.[76] There are, however, cases saying if the written contract includes a "specific disclaimer of the very representation later alleged to be foundation for rescission" the parol evidence rule will exclude the allegation of fraud.[77]

A problem in this area is also created under the doctrine of promissory fraud. The majority of jurisdictions now hold that the making of a promise with intent not to perform is a misrepresentation of fact that can give rise to fraud.[78] The question remains whether such a promise may be shown in the face of a total integration. The

74. 3 Corbin § 589. But would there be a binding contract if neither party had the duty to seek the approval of the third party? Corbin also provides an illustration of a condition precedent to the formation of the contract: A makes a written offer to B and B is to accept by signing. A, however, orally tells B that the offer is to be operative only if a certain event happens. Here, the condition is clearly a condition precedent to the existence of the contract. Id. § 589, at 536–37.

75. See, e.g., Ott v. Midland-Ross Corp., 600 F.2d 24 (6th Cir.1979); Parker v. Mc-Gaha, 294 Ala. 702, 321 So.2d 182 (1975); 3 Corbin § 580. Nor does the parol evidence rule prevent an action for reformation. See § 9–34 infra.

76. Ott v. Midland-Ross Corp., 600 F.2d 24 (6th Cir.1979); Barash v. Pennsylvania Terminal Real Estate Corp., 26 N.Y.2d 77, 308 N.Y.S.2d 649, 256 N.E.2d 707 (1970); Marshall v. Keaveny, 38 N.C.App. 644, 248 S.E.2d 750 (1978); 3 Corbin § 580. There are some cases to the contrary. See, for example, 80th Division Veteran's Ass'n v. Johnson, 100 Pa.Super. 447, 159 A. 467 (1931).

77. E.g., Centronics Fin. Corp. v. El Conquistador Hotel Corporation, 573 F.2d 779 (2d Cir.1978); Bank of America v. Pendergrass, 4 Cal.2d 258, 48 P.2d 659 (1935); Danann Realty Corp. v. Harris, 5 N.Y.2d 317, 184 N.Y.S.2d 599, 157 N.E.2d 597 (1959). See also LeDonne v. Kessler, 256 Pa.Super. 280, 389 A.2d 1123 (1978).

78. E.g., United States v. 1,557.28 Acres of Land, 486 F.2d 445 (10th Cir.1973); Entron, Inc. v. General Cablevision of Palatka, 435 F.2d 995 (5th Cir.1970); Walker v. Woodall, 288 Ala. 510, 262 So.2d 756 (1972); Abbott v. Abbott, 188 Neb. 61, 195 N.W.2d 204 (1972); Anderson v. Tri-State Home Improvement Co., 268 Wis. 455, 67 N.W.2d 853 (1955), rehearing denied 268 Wis. 455, 68 N.W.2d 705 (1955). See generally Restatement (Second) of Contract § 171(2); W. Prosser, Handbook of the Law of Torts 728–30 (4th Ed.1971); 12 Williston § 1496; Keeton, Fraud: Statements of Intention, 15 Tex.L.Rev. 185 (1937); Note, The Legal Effect of Promises Made with Intent Not to Perform, 38 Colum.L.Rev. 1461 (1938).

cases are in utter confusion.[79] Ultimately the question is how strong a public policy the parol evidence rule represents.[80]

If a party cannot prevail on a claim of fraud in the inducement it is possible that he may be able to establish a claim of fraud in the execution. Fraud in the inducement relates to false statements of fact, warranties, and promises that lead a party into contracting. It does not concern the contents of the writing. Fraud in the execution relates to deception about the contents of the instrument. This may occur when one party tells the other that a provision to which they have orally agreed is in the writing when it is not or when one party inserts a provision knowing that it was not part of the agreement.[81] The assumption, of course, is that the writing is an integration and the question is whether fraud in the execution may be shown in the face of the integration. There are two views. One is that the failure to read the instrument precludes this evidence from being offered.[82] The other reaches the opposite conclusion on the theory that fraud is a greater evil than the failure to read.[83]

(d) Mistake

If there is a mistake recognized in law an agreement is ordinarily voidable [84] and the parol evidence rule does not prevent a party from showing that a contract was not formed.[85] In addition a party may claim that a writing which is integrated, does not reflect the true agreement of the parties. It is clear that in such case that the writing may be reformed to reflect the true agreement if certain conditions are met.[86] The point made here is that compliance with the parol evidence rule is not one of these conditions.[87] In other words the parol evidence

79. Professor Sweet has presented an outstanding analysis of the problem. Sweet, Promissory Fraud and the Parol Evidence Rule, 41 Cal.L.Rev. 877 (1961) [hereinafter cited as Sweet II]. According to Professor Sweet, the majority of courts allow the evidence despite the parol evidence rule; a minority opts instead for excluding the evidence and strengthening the rule as a matter of public policy. Id. at 888–90. He also points out that admissibility may depend upon whether the promise is consistent with the writing, and upon what relief is sought. For example, on the basis of promissory fraud, rescission is more likely to be granted than reformation. Id. at 890–93.

80. Sweet II, supra note 79, at 888.

81. Whether this kind of fraud makes the agreement void or voidable is discussed in § 9–22 infra. This is not important here.

82. E.g., Mitchell v. Excelsior Sales & Imports, Inc., 243 Ga. 813, 256 S.E.2d 785 (1979); Knight & Bostwick v. Moore, 203 Wis. 540, 234 N.W. 902 (1931).

83. Belew v. Griffis, 249 Ark. 589, 460 S.W.2d 80 (1970); Estes v. Republic Nat'l Bank of Dallas, 462 S.W.2d 273 (Tex.1970).

84. For the rules relating to voidability for mistake, see §§ 9–25 to 9–30 infra.

85. E.g., F.R. Hoar & Sons, Inc. v. McElroy Plumbing & Heating Co., 680 F.2d 1115 (5th Cir.1982); Garot v. Hopkins, 266 Ark. 243, 583 S.W.2d 54 (1979); General Equip. Mfrs. v. Bible Press, Inc., 10 Mich.App. 676, 160 N.W.2d 370 (1968); see Wallach, supra n. 20 at 654.

86. See §§ 9–31 to 9–36 infra.

87. Sweet I, supra note 24, at 1042. Central Transp., Inc. v. Board of Assessment Appeals of Cambria County, 490 Pa. 486, 417 A.2d 144 (1980).

rule does not bar the process of reformation even though this results in the enforcement of the alleged oral agreement.[88]

(e) Illegality and Unconscionability

Illegality may make a contract either void or voidable.[89] In either case the parol evidence is admissible to prove the illegality and this is so even though there is a contradiction of the integration.[90] For example an agreement that contains a "liquidated damages" clause may be shown to be a "penalty." Thus the clause is excised because it is contrary to public policy and the parol evidence rule does not prevent the process.[91] The same is true under modern notions of unconscionability and duty to read.[92] Under these doctrines, for example, a clause or clauses may be excised from an agreement because there was not "true assent" to a given term. In such a case, obviously, the parol evidence rule will not deter a court from receiving parol evidence to show the lack of true assent.[93]

(f) Consideration

It is frequently said that the parol evidence rule does not preclude a showing of absence of consideration.[94] The problem arises in radically different fact patterns. A majority of the cases have held that a recital of consideration in the writing may be contradicted upon the theory that the rule does not relate to recitals of fact.[95] There is a minority view that reaches an opposite conclusion upon the theory that the parties are estopped from contradicting the writing or that the recital gives rise to an implied promise to pay.[96] The minority view is applied primarily to option and guaranty cases.[97]

However, the situation is somewhat different when there is an attempt to show that the only promise made by one party in what appears to be a binding total integration was not in fact made. A few cases have held that the writing may not be contradicted.[98] The

---

88. See § 9–34 infra; see also Neeley v. Kelsch, 600 P.2d 979 (Utah 1979).

89. § 22–2 infra.

90. 3 Corbin § 580; see Bunn v. Weyerhaeuser Co., 268 Ark. 445, 598 S.W.2d 54 (1980).

91. 3 Corbin § 580.

92. Mellon Bank, N.A. v. Aetna Business Credit, 619 F.2d 1001 (3d Cir.1980).

93. Murray II, supra note 81, at 1343.

94. Sweet I, supra note 24, at 1040. Weintraub v. Cobb Bank & Trust Co., 249 Ga. 148, 288 S.E.2d 553 (1982). Discussed here is lack of consideration, rather than failure of consideration. Failure of consideration relates to performance of the contract rather than its formation and is thus unrelated to the parol evidence rule. Id. at 1041 & n. 35; see § 11–25 infra.

95. 3 Corbin § 586.

96. See Smith v. Wheeler, 233 Ga. 166, 210 S.E.2d 702 (1974); Jones v. Smith, 206 Ga. 162, 56 S.E.2d 462 (1949); Real Estate Co. of Pittsburgh v. Rudolph, 301 Pa. 502, 153 A. 438 (1930). The Second Restatement takes the position that promises to keep an offer firm or guarantying credit are binding if they are in writing and contain a "recital of purported consideration" whether or not it has been paid. Restatement, Second, Contracts §§ 87, 88. See § 4–6 infra.

97. See note 96 supra.

98. See W.P. Fuller & Co. v. McClure, 48 Cal.App. 185, 191 P. 1027 (1920); Schneider v. Turner, 130 Ill. 28, 22 N.E. 497 (1889); In re Emery's Estate, 362 Pa. 142, 66 A.2d 262 (1949); Lakeway Co. v. Leon Howard, Inc., 585 S.W.2d 660 (Tex.

majority view is to the effect that it may be contradicted because of the rule that the parol evidence rule does not apply until it is decided that there is a contract.[99]

The problem is reversed where a writing fails to show consideration on one or both sides of a writing. Here the rule is that it may in fact be shown that consideration exists even if the consideration takes the form of a promise. This does not create any serious theoretical problem because a look at the writing would indicate that it is not complete and thus it is not a total integration and at most it is a partial integration. The term being offered is obviously not contradictory.[1]

(g) The Rule of Non-formation of Contract Under the U.C.C.

Section 2–202 of the U.C.C. makes no reference to the general rule that a party may show that there was no contract despite the existence of an integration. However, U.C.C. Section 1–103 provides that where the Code is silent the common law should be applied. This section has already been applied in a case permitting evidence of fraud in the inducement even though fraud is not mentioned in section 2–202.[2] There have also been U.C.C. cases in the area of "conditions precedent" discussed above.[3] The cases assumed that the doctrine was applicable even though § 2–202 does not mention it. These cases, however, have served only to further complicate an already confused topic.[4] It may safely be assumed that the courts will apply all aspects of the non-formation rule to U.C.C. cases.[5]

 WESTLAW REFERENCES

    "parol* evidence" /s admit! admissib! /s form** formation
       nonform! /s contract

    "parol* evidence" /s admit! admissib! /s void avoid! voidab! /s
       contract

    "parol* evidence" /s "merger clause"

    "parol* evidence" /s "specific! perform!"

    "parol* evidence" /s rescind! rescission

    parol* extrinsic +1 evidence /s reform!

    parol* extrinsic +1 evidence /s duress

    parol* extrinsic +1 evidence /p defect! /2 form** formation

(a) When Writing was Not Intended to be Operative

"sham agreement"

1979); see also 4 Williston, § 642, at 1071 n. 15; Annot., 100 A.L.R. 17 (1936) (collecting cases).

99. 3 Corbin §§ 577, 586; see § 3–2 supra; cf. Restatement, Second, Contracts § 218.

1. Restatement, Second, Contracts § 218; Restatement, Contracts § 214.

2. Associated Hardware Supply Co. v. Big Wheel Distrib. Co., 355 F.2d 114 (3d Cir.1965); George Robberecht Seafood, Inc.

v. Maitland Bros., Co., Inc., 220 Va. 109, 255 S.E.2d 682 (1979).

3. See § 3–7(b) supra.

4. Whirlpool Corp. v. Regis Leasing Corp., 29 A.D.2d 395, 288 N.Y.S.2d 337 (1968); Hunt Foods & Indus., Inc. v. Doliner 26 A.D.2d 41, 270 N.Y.S.2d 937 (1966); see Broude, supra note 21, at 890–99.

5. J. White & R. Summers, Uniform Commercial Code § 2–11 (2d ed. 1980).

contract agreement /s bind binding bound /s operative /s
   integrat!

contract agreement /s sham /s parol

write writing wrote written /s contract agreement /s intend! intent!
   /s operative

(b) *Contract was Intended to be Effective Only on the Happening of*
an Express Condition

intend! intent! /s contract agreement /s effect! /s happen!
   occur! /s condition

''condition precedent'' /s contract agreement /s effect!

''condition precedent'' /s contract agreement /s fail! /s parol

''express condition'' /s contract agreement /s effect!

''condition precedent'' /s term /s contradict! /s agreement
   contract

''condition precedent'' /s agreement contract /s duty /s
   perform!

pym +s campbell

''express! condition!'' /s duty /s perform!

''parol* evidence rule'' /s event /s occur! happen!

(c) *Fraud*

''fraud in the inducement'' /s parol

''fraud in the inducement'' /s merg!

avoid! /s ''fraud in the inducement''

di(''fraud in the inducement'' /p write writing written wrote /p
   agreement contract)

di(''fraud in the inducement'' /p oral)

''fraud in the inducement'' /s contradict!

''fraud in the inducement'' /s disclaim!

''fraud in the inducement'' /s ''parol* evidence rule''

fraud! /s exclud! exclusion /s ''parol* evidence rule'' /s alleg!

''promissory fraud'' /s ''parol* evidence rule''

''promissory fraud'' /s misrepresent!

''promissory fraud'' /s integrat!

''promissory fraud'' /s perform!

''fraud in the execution'' /s ''parol* evidence rule''

''fraud in the inducement'' /s fals! /s state* stating statement

''fraud in the inducement'' /s warrant!

''fraud in the execution'' /s content

''fraud in the execution'' /s integrat!

''promissory fraud'' /p rescission rescind! reform!

(d) *Mistake*

agreement contract /s mistak! /s voidable

95k93(5) /p voidable

''parol* evidence rule'' /s mistak! /s reform! /s contract
   agreement

''parol* evidence rule'' /s true +1 intent agreement /s mistak!

328k19(1) /p oral! parol*

328k44 /p oral! parol* /p mistak! error erroneous!

(e) *Illegality and Unconscionability*

illegality /s contract agreement /s void voidable /s parol oral!

parol* oral! /s illegal! /s integrat!

contradict! /s illegal! /s oral! parol*

unconscionab! /s agreement contract /s parol* oral!

(f) *Consideration*

"parol* evidence rule" /s consideration /s absen! lack***

"parol* evidence rule" /s consideration /s fail!

157k432 /p parol* oral!

consideration /s wr*te written writing /s parol* oral! /s
    contradict!

party /s estop! /s consideration /s contradict!

contradict! /s recit! /s consideration /s parol* oral!

guarant! firm /s recit! /s parol* oral! /s consideration

parol* oral! /s integrat! /s consideration

bind binding bound /s parol* /s consideration

parol* /s consideration /s fail! /s write writing written wrote

§ 3–8. Application of the Rule in the Case of Third Persons

The question presented here is who is bound by the parol evidence rule? It is clear that the parties to the contract are bound by it, but the question is whether others are bound by it. The answer should be in the affirmative because the policy of the rule should be the same whether a party or a third party seeks to defeat the integration.[6] There are many cases to the contrary.[7] These cases usually take the position that the parol evidence rule applies only to the parties to the contract and their privies and that it cannot be invoked for or against other persons sometimes referred to as strangers.[8] The courts are less likely to apply the parol evidence rule in non-contractual actions.[9]

 WESTLAW REFERENCES

third +1 party person /s "parol* evidence rule" /s binding
    bind bound

party /s contract agreement /s bind bound binding /s "parol*
    evidence rule"

157k424

---

6. Atlantic Northern Airlines v. Schwimmer, 12 N.J. 293, 96 A.2d 652 (1953); 3 Corbin § 596.

7. 3 Corbin § 596; 4 Williston § 647; see also Brakenbrough v. MacCloskey, 42 Or.App. 231, 600 P.2d 481 (1979). See note 27 supra.

8. 3 Corbin § 596; 4 Williston § 647. For a more detailed discussion of this topic

see Comment, The Parol Evidence Rule and Third Parties, 41 Fordham L.Rev. 945 (1973); see Annot., 13 A.L.R.3d 313 (1967).

9. Comment, The Statute of Frauds As a Bar To An Action In Tort For Fraud, 53 Fordham L.Rev. 1231 (1985).

C. INTERPRETATION

Table of Sections

§ 3–9. Introduction

The Restatement says "Interpretation of words and of other manifestations of intent forming an agreement [or having reference to the formation of an agreement] is the ascertainment of the meaning to be given to such words and manifestations." [10] At times a distinction is drawn between interpretation and construction. Interpretation relates to ascertaining the meaning of the parties. Construction relates to the legal effect of the words used. The construction placed upon an agreement will not necessarily coincide with the meaning of the parties.[11] The distinction is, for the most part, not dwelled upon by the courts, with the result that it is difficult to tell which process is being employed. It is even difficult to tell whether the Restatement definition of interpretation refers to interpretation or construction or both.[12] For these reasons this distinction will not be pursued here.

In deciding what a communication means there are two fundamental questions. First, whose meaning is to be given to a communication—in technical language what standard of interpretation is to be used? [13] The second question is what evidence may be taken into account in applying the standard of interpretation selected. The sec-

10. Restatement, Contracts § 226.

11. Fashion Fabrics of Iowa, Inc. v. Retail Investors Corp., 266 N.W.2d 22 (Iowa 1978); 3 Corbin § 534; 4 Williston § 602; Restatement, Contracts 2d § 200, Comment C. Construction is a question of law. Farm Bureau Mut. Ins. Co. v. Sandbulte, 302 N.W.2d 104 (Iowa 1981); Park View Manor, Inc. v. Housing Authority of County of Stutsman, 300 N.W.2d 218 (N.D.1980).

12. See generally Friedman, Law Rules and Interpretation of Written Documents, 59 Nw.U.L.Rev. 751 (1965); Patterson, The Interpretation and Construction of Contracts, 64 Colum.L.Rev. 833 (1964).

13. The Restatement, Contracts § 227 lists six possible standards of interpretation, that is, six vantage points which might be used in the interpretation process. These standards are:

"1. The standard of general usage;

"2. A standard of limited usage, which would attach the meaning given to language in a particular locality, or by a sect or those engaged in a particular occupation, or by an alien population or those using a local dialect (the distinction between 1 and 2 is a difference in degree, since generality of usage does not necessarily imply universality);

ond phase relates to the parol evidence rule. Here, however, the issue relates to the admissibility of *extrinsic* evidence on the question of *meaning.* By way of contrast in the preceding sections the discussion of the parol evidence rule related to the admissibility of prior and contemporaneous agreements. Extrinsic evidence is a very broad term. It includes not only prior and contemporaneous agreements but also surrounding circumstances (e.g. market conditions), evidence of subjective intention, what the parties said to each other with respect to meaning and customs, course of dealing and course of performance.

As in the case of the other portion of the parol evidence rule (section B) there is a wide variety of views and consistency in result is seldom achieved. It has been observed that there is no "lawyer's Paradise [where] all words have a fixed, precisely ascertained meaning, * * * and where, if the writer has been careful, a lawyer, having a document referred to him may sit in his chair, inspect the text, and answer all questions without raising his eyes." [14] Despite this observation there is one school of thought that has taken an opposite approach. This approach goes under the name of the Plain Meaning Rule.

 WESTLAW REFERENCES

di interpret!

"legal effect" /s contract agreement /s constru!

di(question /2 law legal /p constru! /p agreement contract)

"standard of interpretation" /s contract agreement

"standard of interpretation" /s extrinsic parol*

"standard of interpretation" /p (mutual individual +1 standard)
    (standard +2 reasonable +1 expectation understanding)
    (general limited +1 usage)

"extrinsic evidence" /s "surrounding circumstance" /s includ!
    inclus!

§ 3–10.   The Plain Meaning Rule and Its Opposite—Ambiguity

The Plain Meaning Rule states that if a writing, or the term in question, appears to be plain and unambiguous on its face, its meaning

"3. A mutual standard, which would allow only such meaning as conforms to an intention common to both or all parties, and would attach this meaning although it violates the usage of all other persons;

"4. An individual standard, which would attach to words or other manifestations of intention whatever meaning the person employing them intend them to express, or that the person receiving the communication understood from it;

"5. A standard of reasonable expectation, which would attach to words or

other manifestations of intention the meaning which the party employing them should reasonably have apprehended that they would convey to other party;

"6. A standard of reasonable understanding, which would attach to words or other manifestations of intention the meaning which the person to whom the manifestations are addressed might reasonably give to them."

14. J. Thayer, A Preliminary Treatise on the Law of Evidence 428–429 (1898).

must be determined from the four corners of the instrument without resort to extrinsic evidence of any nature.[15] The rule has been properly condemned because the meaning of words varies with the "verbal context and surrounding circumstances and purposes in view of the linguistic education and experience of their users and their hearers or readers (not excluding judges)."[16] In other words meaning may not be ascertained simply by reading a document.[17] Although the Plain Meaning Rule has been condemned by the writers,[18] the Uniform Commercial Code,[19] the Restatement Second[20] and an increasing number of courts,[21] it is undoubtedly still employed frequently or on occasion by the great majority of the jurisdictions in this country.[22]

If the term in question does not have a plain meaning it follows that the term is ambiguous.[23] It is for the court to say whether there is a "plain meaning" or an ambiguity exists.[24] As one author has stated it is difficult to reconcile the cases where the plain meaning rule has been applied with those in which it has been found that there is an ambiguity.[25]

Once it is found that an ambiguity exists the question becomes what extrinsic evidence may be admitted to clarify the ambiguity. In the earlier cases it was held that extrinsic evidence could be received in the case of a latent ambiguity but not if there was a patent ambiguity.[26]

15. J.B. Service Court v. Wharton, 632 P.2d 943 (Wyo.1981). There have been cases professing to apply the Plain Meaning Rule that have on occasion permitted some types of extrinsic evidence. See Craig v. Jo B. Gardner, Inc., 586 S.W.2d 316 (Mo.1979); 9 Wigmore §§ 2462, 2463(2); Patterson, The Interpretation and Construction of Contracts, 64 Colum.L.Rev. 833, 838 et seq. (1964).

16. 3 Corbin § 579, at 225 n. 74 (1964 supp).

17. Corbin, The Interpretation of Words and the Parol Evidence Rule, 50 Cornell L.Q. 161, 187 (1965). See generally Levie, The Interpretation of Contracts in New York Under the Uniform Commercial Code, 10 N.Y.L.F. 350 (1964).

18. 3 Corbin § 542; 9 Wigmore §§ 2461–62; 4 Williston § 629.

19. U.C.C. § 2–202, Comment 2.

20. Restatement, Second, Contracts §§ 200–204.

21. E.g. Pacific Gas Elec. Co. v. G.W. Thomas Drayage & Rigging Co., 69 Cal.2d 33, 69 Cal.Rptr. 561, 442 P.2d 641 (1968); Delta Dynamics, Inc. v. Arioto, 69 Cal.2d 525, 446 P.2d 785 (1968); Hamilton v. Wosepka, 261 Iowa 299, 154 N.W.2d 164 (1967).

22. The number of cases decided under the Plain Meaning Rule is simply stagger-

ing. Therefore no list of cases will be supplied.

23. St. Paul Mercury Ins. Co. v. Price, 359 F.2d 74 (5th Cir.1966).

24. Id.

25. Patterson, The Interpretation and Construction of Contracts; 64 Colum.L. Rev. 833, 839 (1964).

26. Mass Appraisal Services, Inc. v. Carmichael, 404 So.2d 666 (Ala.1981); McBaine, The Rule Against Disturbing Plain Meaning, 31 Calif.L.Rev. 145, 147 (1942). In theory a patent ambiguity is one that is apparent on the face of the document, a latent ambiguity exists when the term in question appears clear but extrinsic evidence makes it ambiguous. St. Joseph Data Serv., Inc., v. Thomas Jefferson Life Insurance Company of America, 73 Ill.App.3d 935, 30 Ill.Dec. 575, 393 N.E.2d 611 (1979); Hokama v. Relinc Corp., 57 Hawaii 470, 559 P.2d 279 (1977). The best known illustration of a latent ambiguity is Raffles v. Wickelhaus, 159 Eng.Rep. 375 (Ex.1864) (The case of the two ships Peerless discussed in section 3–11). In actuality as Professor Thayer states, "The old distinction between a patent and latent ambiguity was never more than 'an unprofitable subtlety.' " Thayer, Preliminary Treatise on Evidence 424 (1896–98). Whether an ambiguity is patent or latent is also a question of law. Ross Bros. Const.

In the case of patent ambiguities these earlier cases chose to resolve the problem by deciding what the term meant without the aid of extrinsic evidence.[27] The more modern cases, however, hold that all types of extrinsic evidence are admissible in both types of ambiguities.[28] Williston's more enlightened approach, discussed next, undoubtedly had something to do with this change in attitude.

 WESTLAW REFERENCES

"plain meaning" /p "four corners"

"plain meaning" /s extrinsic parol* +1 evidence

157k448 /p "plain meaning"

"plain meaning rule" /s contract agreement

di("plain meaning" /p ambigu! /p court)

ambigu! /s admit! admissible /s extrinsic /s agreement contract

latent patent +1 ambiguity /s extrinsic parol* /s evidence /s contract agreement

latent patent +1 ambiguity /s question /2 law legal

§ 3–11. Williston's Rule

Except in the case of a non-integration that is ambiguous,[29] Williston employs an objective standard of interpretation. In addition, but for the exception made above, he does not permit all types of extrinsic evidence. He also has different rules for an integration and non-integration.

As to integrated writings Williston's standard of interpretation is the meaning that would be attached to the integration by a reasonably intelligent person acquainted with all operative usages [30] and knowing all of the circumstances prior to and contemporaneous with the making of the integration.[31] However, he excludes what the parties said to each other about meaning (e.g. "buy" was to mean "sell") and what the parties subjectively believed the writing meant at the time of agreement.[32]

Where there is no integration and no ambiguity the standard is the meaning that the party making the manifestation should reasonably expect the other party to give it—the standard of reasonable expectation, a test based primarily upon the objective theory of contracts.[33]

Co., Inc. v. State By and Through Its Transportation Commission, Highway Division, 59 Or.App. 374, 650 P.2d 1080 (1982).

27. McBaine, supra note 26, at 147. The type of rules used are discussed in section 3–13 infra.

28. Christopher v. Safeway Stores, Inc., 644 F.2d 467 (5th Cir.1981); Wiginton v. Hill Soberg Co., Inc., 396 So.2d 97 (Ala. 1981); Cody v. Remington Elec. Shavers, 179 Conn. 494, 427 A.2d 810 (1980); Hokama v. Relinc Corp., 57 Hawaii 470, 559 P.2d 279 (1977).

29. This is covered in the last part of this section.

30. An operative usage is one that becomes part of the contract under the rules stated in § 3–17 infra.

31. Restatement, Contracts § 230.

32. Restatement, Contracts §§ 230, 231; First Nat'l Bank in Dallas v. Rozelle, 493 F.2d 1196 (10th Cir.1974). There are a few limited exceptions to this statement that are also stated in these two sections.

33. 4 Williston § 605.

This should bring to mind the tentative working test set up in § 2–2, where it is stated, "a party's intention will be held to be what a reasonable man in the position of the other party would conclude the manifestation to mean." In other words if A says something to B, what A means depends upon what a reasonable man in the position of B would conclude that he meant. The words "in the position of B" make it clear that what B knows or should know about A's intention should be taken into account. The tentative working test employs a standard or reasonable understanding (standard 6 note 13, § 3–9, supra).

However, Williston has chosen a slightly different standard for a non-integration—the standard of reasonable expectation the meaning that the party making the manifestation should reasonably expect the other party to give it. In the illustration given above, what A as a reasonable man should conclude that B would take it to mean. In reaching that conclusion the reasonable man should take into account what A knows or should know about B's knowledge.[34]

In the case of a non-integration where there is no ambiguity, all extrinsic evidence is admissible except evidence of subjective intention.[35] If there is an ambiguity in the case of a non-integration, evidence of subjective intention is also admissible. When such evidence is introduced and it shows that the parties had conflicting understandings as to the meaning of a material term, there is contract based on the meaning of the party who is unaware of the ambiguity if the other party knows or has reason to know of the ambiguity. If the understandings conflict as to a material term and each party is guilty or blameless on the issue of knowledge or reason to know of the ambiguity, there is no contract. If the parties place the same meaning on the term, there is a contract based on the meaning.[36]

A good illustration of this problem is presented by the case of Raffles v. Wichelhaus.[37] The seller agreed to sell cotton to the buyer. Shipment was to be made from Bombay on the ship Peerless. It happened that there were two ships Peerless.[38] One was to sail from Bombay in October and the other in December. The evidence was to the effect that the buyer meant the ship Peerless that sailed in October and the seller meant the ship Peerless that sailed in December. Under the rules stated, the question is whether one party knew or should have known of the ambiguity and the other did not. For example, if the seller knew or should have known of the ambiguity and the buyer did

---

34. Sometimes the test is stated in terms of what a reasonable person in the position of the parties would have concluded. James v. Goldberg, 256 Md. 520, 261 A.2d 753 (1970).

35. 4 Williston § 605; Restatement, Contracts § 235(d).

36. Jet Forwarding, Inc. v. United States, 437 F.2d 987 (Ct.Cl.1971); 4 Williston § 605; Restatement, Contracts §§ 71 and 233. Williston does not employ the

standard of reasonable expectation "where the law gives to certain words an established meaning" because "this meaning is less readily controlled by the standard of interpretation * * * than is the meaning of other words." 4 Williston §§ 641, 615; see Restatement, Contracts § 234.

37. 159 Eng.Rep. 375 (Ex. 1864).

38. This case is a good illustration of a latent ambiguity. See § 3–10 supra.

not, there would be a contract based upon the buyer's meaning—the ship Peerless that sailed in October. If neither party knew or had reason to know or if both parties knew or had reason to know, there would be no contract. If both parties meant the same ship Peerless there would be a contract. What the parties know or should have known is ordinarily a question of fact.

In all cases except that of a non-integration in which there is ambiguity Williston employs an objective approach. This means that his standards of interpretation may result in an interpretation that does not conform to the intention of either party.[39] For him the contract acquires a life and meaning of its own, separate and apart from the meaning the parties attach to their agreement.[40] "It is not primarily the intention of the parties which the court is seeking, but the meaning of the words at the time and place when they were used.[41] He is explicit in stating why this should be so. "A facility and certainty of interpretation is obtained, which, though not ideal, is so much greater than is obtainable" by use of a less rigid standard.[42] The certainty so obtained is "more than adequate compensation for the slight restriction put upon the power to grant and contract." [43]

 WESTLAW REFERENCES

williston /s integrat! /s wr*te writing written contract agreement

williston /s reasonabl! /s intelligen! expect! /s contract agreement

williston /s "objective theory"

williston /s subjective!

williston /s parol* extrinsic /s evidence

williston /s contract agreement /s ambigu!

williston /p "material term"

39. 4 Williston §§ 607–07A; Restatement, Contracts § 230, ill. 1.

40. This is the very heart of the divergence between the positions of Corbin and Williston. Corbin's position, as forcefully restated by Professor Murray, is that: "Any written expression of the agreement—whether it is not final, final, or final and complete—is nothing more than the manifestation of the agreement. It is not the agreement." Murray, The Parol Evidence Process and Standardized Agreements under the Restatement (Second) of Contracts, 123 U.Pa.L.Rev. 1342, 1353 (1975). Williston's view has support in legal history where the distinction has been drawn between " 'carta' (a document which is the contract) and 'memoratorium' (a document which evidences a contract outside itself)." Lucke, Contracts in Writing, 40 Austl. L.J. 265, 266 (1966). The basic issue is whether the historical distinction rests on any sound basis in the modern world, or ought to be silently ignored, as it has been by Corbin and his supporters. That Williston's approach is very much alive, see Rodolitz v. Neptune Paper Products, Inc., 22 N.Y.2d 383, 292 N.Y.S.2d 878, 239 N.E.2d 628, 630 (1968) ("While the Appellate Division's conclusion as to the real intent of the parties may be correct, the rule is well settled that a court may not, under the guise of interpretation, make a new contract for the parties or change the words of a written contract so as to make it express the real intentions of the parties if to do would contradict the clearly expressed language of the contract * * * ").

41. 4 Williston § 613, at 583.

42. Id. § 612, at 577.

43. Id.

```
raffles  +s  wichelhaus
williston  /s  intend! intent!  /s  conform!
```

§ 3–12. Corbin's Rules—Restatement Second—U.C.C.

Under Corbin's rules all relevant extrinsic evidence is admissible on the issue of meaning including evidence of subjective intention and what the parties said to each other with respect to meaning.[44] This is true even if there is an integration and there is no ambiguity.[45]

This is a subjective approach because in most cases evidence of what the parties intended the language to mean will be introduced. When such evidence is introduced the problem is similar to the Peerless case discussed in the preceding section. Corbin is in agreement with Williston's conclusion that if the parties meant the same ship Peerless there is a contract based on that meaning. If the meanings do not coincide as to a material term there is no contract unless one of the parties is more guilty than the other for the difference in meaning attached. In that case the meaning attached is the meaning of the party who is less at fault. Again, as under Williston's rules, it is important to ascertain what a party knew or should have known about the existence of two ships Peerless, for that will help determine who is more at fault. It should be observed that Corbin's rule is not exactly the same as Williston's. Under Williston's rule if both parties know or should know of the ambiguity there is no contract. Under Corbin's view if one knows and the other should know there is an agreement based upon the meaning of the party who should know—the party who is less at fault. In other words Corbin is willing to weigh fault and Williston is not.[46]

If evidence of subjective intention at the time of contracting is not introduced into evidence the parties may still assert the meaning that they now attach to the language in question. In this situation Corbin uses a standard based on the balance between the standard of reasonable expectations and the standard of reasonable understanding.[47] A contract exists in accord with the meaning the promisee could rely upon, provided the promisor had reason to foresee that the promisee had reason to attach this meaning. Actually this means that the issue is who is more responsible for the difference in meaning attached to the language in question. This properly takes into account that speech is

---

44. 3 Corbin § 542; Mississippi State Highway Commission v. Dixie Contractors, Inc., 375 So.2d 1202 (Miss.1979), appeal after remand 402 So.2d 811 (1981); Security Credit Corp. v. Jesse, 46 Or.App. 399, 611 P.2d 702 (1980).

45. 3 Corbin § 542; Corbin, The Interpretation of Words and the Parol Evidence Rule, 50 Cornell L.Q. 161, 189 (1965). Under Corbin's rule the parties may testify that they agreed that "buy means sell" and there is no special rule for words with an established meaning. Restatement, Second, Contracts § 201, Comment c, and § 212, Comment b. The Uniform Commercial Code is in accord. U.C.C. § 2–202, Comment 1(a). Peterson v. Wirum, 625 P.2d 866 (Alaska 1981); Mississippi State Highway Commission v. Dixie Contractors, Inc., 375 So.2d 1202 (Miss.1979), appeal after remand 402 So.2d 811 (1981).

46. Corbin §§ 538, 539.

47. 3 Corbin § 538.

not only and not primarily the expression of thought, but is used "in order to influence the conduct of others." [48]

Professor Corbin tempers his more liberal rules by stating that the trial judge must initially decide whether the asserted meaning is one to which the language, taken in context, is reasonably susceptible in the light of all of the evidence.[49] If it is not, then that asserted meaning may not be attached to the language in question.

The Restatement Second is generally in accord with Corbin.[50] Since the U.C.C. rules relating to interpretation relate primarily to usage of the trade, course of performance, and course of dealing we will delay that discussion until these topics are discussed below.[51]

 WESTLAW REFERENCES

corbin /s meaning /s evidence
corbin /s subjective!
corbin /s reasonabl! /s expect! understand!

§ 3–13. Rules in Aid of Interpretation and Their Relationship to Standards of Interpretation

Rules in aid of interpretation are used primarily in cases where extrinsic evidence is not permitted or not introduced. This occurs most frequently when a court refuses to admit extrinsic evidence in cases where there is a patent ambiguity.[52] At times these rules are used to bolster decisions already reached under the rules stated in the preceding section. Sometimes these rules are in conflict and a court chooses the one that suits the conclusion it wishes to reach.

Williston distinguishes between primary and secondary rules of interpretation. The primary rules as stated in section 235 of the Restatement are set forth in the footnote.[53] The primary rules apply to both integrated and non-integrated transactions and "serve merely as

48. Gardiner, The Theory of Speech and Language 19 (1932).

49. 3 Corbin § 579; Brobeck, Phleger & Harrison v. The Telex Corp., 602 F.2d 866 (9th Cir.1979), certiorari denied 444 U.S. 981, 100 S.Ct. 483, 62 L.Ed.2d 407 (1979); International Broth. of Painters and Allied Trades v. Hartford Acc. & Indem. Co., 388 A.2d 36 (D.C.1978); Harrigan v. Mason & Winograd, Inc., 121 R.I. 209, 397 A.2d 514 (1979).

50. Restatement, Second, Contracts §§ 210, 212, 215, Comment b.

51. See § 3–17 infra.

52. Payne v. Commercial National Bank, 177 Cal. 68, 169 P. 1007 (1917); Carson v. Palmer, 139 Fla. 570, 190 So. 720 (1939); Hunt v. First National Bank of Tampa, 381 So.2d 1194 (Fla.App.1980).

53. The following rules aid the application of the standards stated in Restatement §§ 230, 233.

(a) The ordinary meaning of language throughout the country is given to words unless circumstances show that a different meaning is applicable.

(b) Technical terms and words of art are given their technical meaning unless the context or a usage which is applicable indicates a different meaning.

(c) A writing is interpreted as a whole and all writings forming part of the same transaction are interpreted together.

(d) All circumstances accompanying the transaction may be taken into consideration, subject in case of integrations to the qualifications stated in § 230.

guides to achieving a final result, namely, the correct application of the proper standard.[54] The secondary rules set forth in the footnote [55] are also applicable to both integrated and non-integrated transactions, but should not be used except where the meaning of the words or other manifestations of intent remain doubtful after application of the appropriate standard of interpretation, aided by primary rules of interpretation.[56]

The Restatement Second also has two sections on the topic discussed herein. One is entitled Rules in Aid of Interpretation [57] and the other Standards of Preference in Interpretation.[58] The matters discussed in those two sections are generally consistent with Williston's rules although they do not coincide precisely. The Restatement Second seems to agree with Corbin's notions that the rules of interpretation can be applied whether or not there is an ambiguity and that these rules "are to be taken as suggestive working rules only." [59]

The Restatement Second has given new importance to two of the rules in aid of interpretation by putting them in individual sections. They are that a contract should be interpreted against the draftsman [60]

(e) If the conduct of the parties subsequent to a manifestation of intention indicates that all the parties placed a particular interpretation upon it, that meaning is adopted if a reasonable person could attach it to the manifestation.

54. Restatement, Contracts § 235, Comment a.

55. Restatement, Contracts § 236 reads as follows: Where the meaning to be given to an agreement or to acts relating to the formation of an agreement remains uncertain after the application of the standards of interpretation stated in §§ 230, 233, with the aid of the rules stated in § 235, the following rules are applicable:

(a) An interpretation which gives a reasonable, lawful and effective meaning to all manifestations of intention is preferred to an interpretation which leaves a part of such manifestations unreasonable, unlawful or of no effect.

(b) The principal apparent purpose of the parties is given great weight in determining the meaning to be given to manifestations of intention or to any part thereof.

(c) Where there is an inconsistency between general provisions and specific provisions, the specific provisions ordinarily qualify the meaning of the general provisions.

(d) Where words or other manifestations of intention bear more than one reasonable meaning an interpretation is preferred which operates more strongly

against the party from whom they proceed, unless their use by him is prescribed by law.

(e) Where written provisions are inconsistent with printed provisions, an interpretation is preferred which gives effect to the written provisions.

(f) Where a public interest is affected an interpretation is preferred which favors the public.

Corbin's statement of these rules generally corresponds to Williston's. See 3 Corbin §§ 545–50. Corbin adds some additional rules in § 552.

56. Restatement, Contracts § 236, Comment a. In his text Williston makes it clear that in the case of an integration these secondary rules come into play "only where after the primary rules or principles have been applied, the local meaning of the writing is still uncertain or ambiguous." He adds "the same rules are applicable to informal parol agreements, but, as has been seen, the standard there sought to be applied is slightly different." 4 Williston § 617, at 703–04.

57. Restatement, Second, Contracts § 202.

58. Restatement, Second, Contracts § 203.

59. Restatement, Second, Contracts § 202; 3 Corbin §§ 535, 542.

60. Restatement, Second, Contracts § 206.

and should be construed in favor of the public.[61]   The Restatement Second has included in its interpretation chapter matters not ordinarily considered to relate to interpretation.   Section 231 relates to "Duty of Good Faith and Fair Dealing" and Section 234 to "Unconscionable Contract or Term."   These matters are discussed elsewhere in this volume.[62]   Also included in the material on interpretation is a section entitled "Supplying An Omitted Essential Term."[63]   This topic is discussed below.[64]

 WESTLAW REFERENCES

"rule in aid of interpretation"

"standard of preference in interpretation"

restatement /2 contract +s second 2d +5 206 207

§ 3–14.   Are Questions of Interpretation Questions of Fact or Questions of Law?

Although the meaning of language is essentially a question of fact, it has been determined that this question should often be treated as a question of law.   The general rule is that the interpretation of a writing is for the court.[65]   This approach again reflects the unwillingness of the judicial system to trust unsophisticated jurors and the desire of judges to increase the judicial scope of review.

Where, however, extrinsic evidence [66] is introduced,[67] in aid of its interpretation, the question of its meaning should be left to the jury [68] except where, after taking the extrinsic evidence into account, the meaning is so clear that reasonable men could reach only one reasonable conclusion, in which event, as pointed out above, the question is treated as one of law.[69]   Where extrinsic evidence is not introduced, as indicated above, the question is one of law.[70]   Even where the contract is oral, if the exact words used by the parties are not in dispute the

61. Restatement, Second, Contracts § 207.

62. See § 11–38 and Ch. 9G infra.

63. Restatement, Second, Contracts § 204.

64. See § 3–18 infra.

65. Langer v. Iowa Beef Packers, Inc., 420 F.2d 365 (8th Cir.1970); Parsons v. Bristol Development Co., 62 Cal.2d 861, 44 Cal.Rptr. 767, 402 P.2d 839 (1965); Carroll v. Littleford, 225 Ga. 636, 170 S.E.2d 402 (1969); Hartford Accident & Indem. Co. v. Wesolowski, 33 N.Y.2d 169, 350 N.Y.2d 895, 305 N.E.2d 907 (1973); Restatement, Second, Contracts 212, Comment d; 4 Williston § 616; 3 Corbin § 554.

66. "Extrinsic Evidence" includes all evidence outside of the writing.   See § 3–9 supra.

67. Under the Plain Meaning Rule no extrinsic evidence is received.   See § 3–10 supra.

68. Restatement, Second, Contracts § 212, Comment e; Hoover, Inc. v. McCullough Indus., Inc., 380 F.2d 798 (5th Cir. 1967), appeal after remand 456 F.2d 170 (5th Cir.1971); Transport Indem. Co. v. Dahlen Transport, Inc., 281 Minn. 253, 161 N.W.2d 546 (1968); Marso v. Mankato Clinic Ltd., 278 Minn. 104, 153 N.W.2d 281 (1967); Root v. Allstate Ins. Co., 272 N.C. 580, 158 S.E.2d 829 (1968); see Worland School Dist. v. Bowman, 445 P.2d 364 (Wyo.1968), appeal after remand 531 P.2d 889 (1975).

69. See § 2–8 supra.

70. See § 2–8 supra.

court will deal with the matter in the same way as if the contract were written.[71]

 WESTLAW REFERENCES

wr*te written writing /s contract agreement /s interpret! /s
   question /2 law legal

contract agreement /s interpret! /s question /2 law legal /s
   court

95k176(2) /p question

question /s interpret! /s contract agreement /s extrinsic parol*
   +1 evidence /s meaning

reasonable +1 man person /s interpret! /s contract agreement
   /s question meaning /s law legal

§ 3–15.   Parol Evidence Rule and Interpretation

It has already been mentioned that the parol evidence rule has two components.[72] In part B of this chapter we dealt with the question of whether a term agreed upon prior to or contemporaneously with the writing should be received in evidence when there is an integrated writing.

The second phase of the parol evidence rule (at least this is what it is called by many courts) relates to what, if any, extrinsic evidence is admissible in interpreting a writing. The two phases are related because a basic notion of the traditional parol evidence rule (see B above) is that an integrated writing may not be varied or contradicted.[73] A contradiction, however, may take place not only by offering into evidence a term which contradicts the writing, but also by offering evidence as to meaning of the language of the agreement which contradicts the apparent meaning of the language.[74]

To what extent this can be done depends upon the various views discussed immediately above. For example, under the Plain Meaning Rule, if it is determined that language has a plain meaning, no contradiction is permitted because extrinsic evidence of all types is excluded.[75] Williston obviously foresaw the possibility of undermining the parol evidence rule (see B above) under the guise of interpretation and, as we have seen, structured a rule for an integration that does not permit an integration to be contradicted by what the parties said to one another about the meaning of language in the written contract, or evidence of subjective intent.[76]

71. See § 2–8 supra.

72. See § 3–1 supra.

73. The Restatement (Second) suggests that the proper word is "contradict" because the word "vary" might include cases "where more than one meaning is reasonably possible." Restatement, Second, Contracts § 215 (Reporter's Note).

74. McBaine, The Rule Against Disturbing Plain Meaning of Writings, 31 Calif.L.Rev. 145 (1942).

75. See § 3–10 supra.

76. See § 3–11 supra.

Corbin's basic position is contrary as is the Restatement Second. They take the position that the parol evidence rule should have no effect on the question of interpretation—the meaning of language.[77] Corbin states that before the parol evidence rule may be invoked to exclude extrinsic evidence, the meaning of the writing must be ascertained, since one may not determine whether a writing is being contradicted or even supplemented until one knows what the writing means.[78] This means that all types of extrinsic evidence are admissible on the issue of meaning.[79] The only limitation is that "the asserted meaning must be one to which the language of the writing read in context, is reasonably susceptible in the light of all of the evidence introduced." [80] The U.C.C. rule is discussed below.[81]

The discussion above has proceeded upon the assumption that there is a clear cut distinction between offering evidence of a consistent additional term and offering evidence on the issue of meaning. Nothing could be further from the truth. For example, a written integrated contract between buyer and seller calls for the purchase and sale of "all cotton planted on 400 acres." If one party claims that the agreement meant 400 acres planted "solid" and the other said it meant 400 acres "however planted" it sounds as if there is an interpretation problem.[82] If the seller says that the parties in fact agreed on the "however planted" term and offers it in evidence, this would be looked upon as an additional term just as the exclusive right to sell soft drinks in the Gianni case was looked upon as an additional term.[83] Generally speaking, and certainly under the rule of the Restatement Second and Corbin, it would appear to be to the advantage of the party offering the evidence to couch his offer of proof in terms of interpretation.

 WESTLAW REFERENCES

```
"parol* evidence"  /s  admit! admissible  /s  interpret!  /s  writing
157k448  /p  interpret!  /p  writing
157k428
di("extrinsic evidence"  /p  interpret!  /p  writing  /p  ambigu!
    intend! intent!)
parol* extrinsic  +1  evidence  /s  varied  /s  integrat!
di(parol extrinsic  +1  evidence  /p  inconsisten! contradict!  /p
    integrat!  /p  writing)
```

77. 3 Corbin, Contracts § 543. The question of the meaning of language should be resolved according to the rules of interpretation. Restatement, Second, Contracts § 214, Comment a, b.

78. 3 Corbin, Contracts § 543; Kitchen v. Stockman Nat'l Life Ins. Co., 192 N.W.2d 796 (Iowa 1971); Restatement, Second, Contracts § 214, Comment b.

79. 3 Corbin §§ 542, 542A, 543, 579; Restatement, Second, Contracts § 212, Comment a, c.

80. Restatement, Second, Contracts § 215, Comment b.

81. The U.C.C. rules of interpretation are for the most part limited to a course of dealing, cause of performance and usage. See § 3–17 infra.

82. The facts are based upon the case of Loeb & Co., Inc. v. Martin, 295 Ala. 262, 327 So.2d 711 (1976), appeal after remand 349 So.2d 11 (1977).

83. See note 19, supra and accompanying text at § 3–2.

vary! varied inconsisten! contradict!   /s   meaning   /s   language   /s
     writing   /s   parol* extrinsic

157k384   /p   interpret!

corbin "restatement contract"   /s   "parol* evidence"   /s   interpret!

corbin "restatement contract"   /s   parol* extrinsic   /s   meaning

§ 3–16.   Some Practical Observation About Parol Evidence and Interpretation

It is obvious from the foregoing that there is no unanimity as to the content of the parol evidence rule or the process called interpretation, and that the rules are complex, technical and difficult to apply. It would, however, be a mistake to suppose that the courts follow any of these rules blindly, literally or consistently.[84] As often as not they choose the standard or the rule that they think will give rise to a just result in the particular case.[85] We have also seen that often under a guise of interpretation a court will actually enforce its notions of "public policy" which is "nothing more than an attempt to do justice." [86]

 WESTLAW REFERENCES

"course of dealing"   /s   define* definition defining   /s   "uniform
     commercial code" u.c.c.

1–205(1)

"usage of trade" "course of performance"   /s   definition define*
     defining   /s   "uniform commercial code" u.c.c.

2–208(1)

1–205(2)

course   +2   dealing performance   /s   party plaintiff defendant   /s
     testimon! testif!

expert   /s   testif! testimon!   /s   use usage   /3   trade

84. The Restatement Second states that the chapter on interpretation sets forth separate rules "with respect to various aspects of the process. Such separate statements may convey an erroneous impression of the psychological reality of the judicial process in which many elements are typically combined in a single ruling." Restatement, Contracts (2d) § 200, Introductory Comment. It has been suggested that we are in a time of transition. In earlier days, courts were almost the only agency concerned with the flow of commerce. Objective criteria were utilized by courts as devices for creating order and stability in business practices. As other governmental agencies now have the primary function of regulating business practices, courts receive only a variety of specialized, nonrecurrent issues for determination. Consequently standardized interpretation is not seen as necessary for business stability. See Friedman, Law, Rules and the Interpretation of Written Documents, 59 Nw.U.L.Rev. 751, 774–80 (1965).

85. See, e.g., Crow v. Monsell, 200 So.2d 700 (La.App.1967), certiorari denied 251 La. 226, 203 So.2d 558 (1967).

86. See Brezina Constr. Co. v. United States, 449 F.2d 372, 375 (Ct.Cl.1971) ("it is in cases such as this one, where the contract is ambiguous and where there are no extraneous aids to interpretation, that the courts are forced to resort to guidelines based on what is thought to be sound policy rather than on the intent of the contracting parties"); Restatement, Contracts § 230, Comment d. There is, for example, a tendency to interpret insurance policies against the insurance company. Century Bank v. St. Paul Fire & Marine Ins. Co., 4 Cal.3d 319, 93 Cal.Rptr. 569, 482 P.2d 193 (1971).

purpose /s use usage /3 trade /s meaning term

1–205(4)

"parol* evidence" /s "course of performance"

"course of performance" /s term /s modif! waiv!

"course of performance" of /s term /s interpret! meaning

"express term /s "course of performance"

D. COURSE OF DEALING, COURSE OF PERFORMANCE AND USAGE

Table of Sections

Sec.

3–17. Course of Dealing, Course of Performance and Usage.

§ 3–17. Course of Dealing, Course of Performance and Usage

We have already mentioned course of dealing, usage of the trade and course of performance in connection with our discussion of the parol evidence rule and interpretation. Here our main purpose is to define these terms and to determine when a trade usage exists, and assuming it exists, when the parties are bound by it. In addition we shall discuss the effect of an established course of dealing, custom of the trade, or course of performance. This latter discussion may to some extent overlap our prior discussion of the parol evidence rule and interpretation.

The Uniform Commercial Code has attempted to draw a careful distinction between a "course of dealing," a "course of performance" and a "trade usage" whereas the common law decisions often inartistically meshed the three together under the usual classification of custom.[87]

A course of dealing is defined in the Code as "a sequence of previous conduct between the parties to a particular transaction which is fairly to be regarded as establishing a common basis of understanding for interpreting their expressions and other conduct." [88] A course of dealing relates to the conduct prior to the agreement in question.[89] A course of performance relates to conduct after the agreement in question, according to the Code, as "where the contract for sale involves repeated occasions for performance by either party with knowledge of the nature of the performance and opportunity for objection to it by the

---

87. Duesenberg & King, Sales and Bulk Transfers § 4.08(3)[b]; Carroll, "Harpooning Whales, of which Karl N. LLewellyn is the Hero of the Piece; or Searching for More Expansion Joints in Karl's Crumblin Cathedral," 12 B.C.Ind. & Com.L.Rev. 139 (1970); Note, Custom and Trade Usage: Its Application to Commercial Dealings and the Common Law, 55 Colum.L.Rev. 1192 (1955).

88. U.C.C. § 1–205(1); accord, Sinkwich v. E. F. Drew & Co., 9 A.D.2d 42, 189 N.Y.S.2d 630 (3rd Dep't 1959).

89. U.C.C. § 1–205, Comment 2.

other, any course of performance accepted or acquiesced in without objection shall be relevant to determine the meaning of the agreement." [90] These concepts are not limited to cases involving sales of goods. [91] The Code defines a usage of the trade as "any practice or method of dealing having such regularity of observance in a place, vocation or trade as to justify an expectation that it will be observed with respect to the transaction in question." [92] Under this definition a trade usage may be limited to a particular area or to a particular activity or both. [93] It is obvious that a course of performance or a course of dealing can be established by the testimony of the parties. A trade usage is usually established by expert testimony. At early common law in order to establish a usage, [94] including a trade usage, it had to be "(1) legal (2) notorious, (3) ancient or immemorial and continuous, (4) reasonable (5) certain, (6) universal and obligatory." [95] These requisites, however, even as a common law proposition have been watered down. [96]

Under the Code the trade usage need not be ancient or immemorial [97] or universal. [98] The requirement of certainty is also eliminated. [99]

90. U.C.C. § 2–208(1). Under the Restatement of Contracts a course of performance is treated as a primary rule of interpretation: "If the conduct of the parties subsequent to a manifestation of intent indicates that all the parties placed a particular interpretation upon it, that meaning is adopted if a reasonable person could attach it to the manifestation." Restatement, Contracts § 235. See § 3–13. Sometimes it has been stated that this type of evidence "is entitled to the greatest weight" or is referred to as "convincing evidence." R.F.C. v. Sherwood Distilling Co., 200 F.2d 672 (4th Cir.1952); Department of Revenue v. Jennison–Wright Corp., 393 Ill. 401, 66 N.E.2d 395 (1946); Martinson v. Brooks Equipment Leasing, Inc., 36 Wis.2d 209, 152 N.W.2d 849 (1967), rehearing denied 36 Wis.2d 209, 154 N.W.2d 353 (1967). Some courts have held that the parties would be bound by a course of performance even though it did not conform to the contract. H.B. Deal Constr. Co. v. Labor Discount Center, Inc., 418 S.W.2d 940 (Mo.1967).

91. Restatement, Contracts § 245.

92. U.C.C. § 1–205(2).

93. U.C.C. § 1–205(2); Restatement, Second, Contracts § 219, Comment a.

94. Although the Uniform Commercial Code limits its discussion to trade usages, there are usages other than trade usages. A usage is an habitual or customary practice. Restatement, Second, Contracts § 219. As in the case of trade usages these usages may be used in interpretation or to add terms or under more modern authori-

ties to qualify an agreement even though it is integrated. Restatement, Contracts § 246; Restatement, Second, Contracts §§ 220, 221. A usage is employed for these purposes (i) if both parties manifest assent that the usage shall be operative, or (ii) if one of the parties intends the usage to apply and the other knows or has reason to know of this intent or (iii) if each party knows or has reason to know of the usage but neither party manifests an intent with respect to it, unless one party knows or has reason to know that the other has an intent inconsistent with usage. Compare Restatement, Contracts § 247 with Restatement, Second, Contracts §§ 220, 221. Thus, the rules as to trade usages set forth infra are a particular application of the rules stated herein. Restatement, Second, Contracts § 222, Comment a. The relationship between trade usages and the parol evidence rule is discussed infra.

95. Levie, Trade Usage and Custom Under the Common Law and the Uniform Code, 40 N.Y.U.L.Rev. 1101 (1965).

96. Restatement, Second, Contracts § 222, Comment b.

97. U.C.C. § 1–205, Comment 5.

98. U.C.C. § 1–205(2). It is enough that it be "currently observed by the great majority of decent dealers." U.C.C. § 1–205, Comment 5.

99. § 1–205, Comment 9 states: "In cases of a well established line of usage varying from the general rules of this act where the precise amount of variation has not been worked out into a single standard,

Reasonableness is also abolished and substituted in its place is the requirement against "unconscionable contracts and clauses."[1] The notion that the custom be notorious is carried forward in the definition of usage in § 1–205(2) which requires "regularity of observance * * * as to justify an expectation that it will be observed with respect to the transaction in question."

Assuming that a usage of the trade has been established, the question remains whether the parties are bound by the usage. The general notion is that a person is bound by a usage of the trade if he is aware of it or should be aware of it. Under the Code, if a party is engaged in a particular trade he is bound by the usages of that trade even if he does not know of them, on the theory that he should know of them.[2] Of course the parties by agreement may negate the usage.

Once it is shown that there is a usage of the trade and that the parties are bound by it, the remaining question is for what purposes the usage of the trade may be used. The answer is that the usage of the trade may be used on the issue of meaning and also to add a term to the agreement.[3] At common law a usage of the trade (and a course of dealing) may be added as an additional term to a writing "if the term is not inconsistent" with the agreement.[4] U.C.C. § 2–202 which contains this phase of the parol evidence rule states the same rule.[5]

However, as stated above, another phase of the parol evidence rule relates to interpretation. Under the modern common law rule a usage of the trade (or a course of dealing) may be shown to contradict the plain meaning of the language (e.g. a contract to sell 10,000 shingles, custom shown that 2 packs equals 10,000 even though they contain less than 10,000).[6] Under the Code there are conflicting provisions as to

the party relying on the usage is entitled, in any event, to the minimum variation demonstrated. The whole is not to be disregarded because no particular line of detail has been established. In case a dominant pattern has been fairly evidenced, the party relying on the usage is entitled under this section to go to the trier of the fact on the question of whether such dominant pattern has been incorporated into the agreement."

1. U.C.C. § 1–205, Comment 6. "The policy of this Act controlling explicit unconscionable contracts and clauses (Sections 1–203, 2–302) applies to implicit clauses which restrain usage of the trade and carries forward the policy underlying the ancient requirement that a custom or usage must be reasonable. However, the emphasis is shifted. The very fact of commercial acceptance makes out a prima facie case that the usage is reasonable, and the burden is no longer on the usage to establish itself as being reasonable. But the anciently established policing of usage by the courts is continued to the extent

necessary to cope with situation arising if an unconscionable or dishonest practice should become standard."

2. U.C.C. § 1–205(3). See Valentine v. Ormsbee Exploration Corp., 665 P.2d 452 (Wyo.1983); Warren, Trade Usage and Parties in the Trade: An Economic Rationale for an Inflexible Rule, 42 U.Pitt.L.Rev. 515 (1981).

3. Restatement, Contracts § 246.

4. Restatement, Contracts § 246; Reynolds Bros. Lumber Co. v. W. S. Newell Constr. Co., 284 Ala. 352, 224 So.2d 899 (1969); Maskel Constr. Co. v. Glastonbury, 158 Conn. 592, 264 A.2d 557 (1969); Valente v. Two Guys From Harrison, N.Y., Inc., 35 A.D.2d 862, 315 N.Y.S.2d 220 (3d Dep't 1970); contra, Hurst v. W. J. Lake & Co., 141 Or. 306, 16 P.2d 627 (1932); Restatement, Second, Contracts § 220, Comments c, d.

5. See § 3–4(e) supra.

6. Eie v. St. Benedict's Hospital, 638 P.2d 1190 (Utah 1981).

whether this can still be done. Comment 2 to § 2–202 indicates that it continues this rule when it states, "such writings are to be read on the assumption that the course of prior dealings between the parties and the usages of the trade were taken for granted when the document was phrased. Unless carefully negated they become an element of the meaning of the word used."[7] However, subdivision 4 of U.C.C. 1–205(4) seems to indicate the opposite when it says, "the express terms of an agreement and an applicable course of dealing or usage of the trade shall be construed wherever reasonable as consistent with each other; but when such construction is unreasonable express terms control both course of dealing and usage of the trade and course of dealing controls usage of the trade."[8]

A course of performance is different in some respects from a course of dealing. Since a course of performance is subsequent to the writing in question the part of the parol evidence rule that deals with additional terms does not apply to it. Thus, if a course of performance is used to add a term to the writing the issue is modification or waiver.[9] A course of performance may add a term to the agreement or subtract one.

A course of performance may also be relevant on the issue of meaning. At common law it could be used in aid of interpretation "if a reasonable man could attach it [that meaning] to the manifestation."[10] Under U.C.C. section 2–208(1) "any course of performance accepted or acquiesced in without objection shall be relevant to determine the meaning of the agreement" and a comment states that "a course of performance is always relevant to determine the meaning of the agreement."[11] This rule appears to be contradicted by subdivision 2 which states, "The express terms of the agreement and any such course of performance, as well as any course of dealing and usage of the trade, shall be construed whenever reasonable as consistent with each other; but when such construction is unreasonable, express terms shall control course of performance and course of performance shall control both course of dealing and usage of the trade."[12]

7. Federal Express Corp. v. Pan American World Airways, Inc., 623 F.2d 1297 (1980); see also Nanakuli Paving & Rock Co. v. Shell Oil Co., Inc., 664 F.2d 772 (9th Cir.1981).

8. Professor Krist in an excellent article demonstrates that the intent of the Code was that a usage of the trade must be examined in its commercial setting to ascertain if the parties wished the usage of the trade to take priority over the writing. His position then is in accord with the Comment to § 2–202 rather than the literal language to § 1–205(4). Professor Krist's formulation would mean that ordinarily there is a question of fact. See Krist, Usage of Trade and Course of Deal-

ing: Subversion of the UCC Theory, 1977 Ill.L.F. 811.

9. U.C.C. § 2–208, Comment 3; see Comment, Evaluating the Conduct of Successors in the Interpretation of Contract Terms: Practical Construction and the Judicial Method, 57 Iowa L.Rev. 215 (1971). Waiver is discussed in chapter 11.

10. Restatement, Contracts § 235(e).

11. See Comment 2.

12. U.C.C. § 2–208(1). These conflicting provisions create a problem similar to the one discussed immediately above relating to a course of dealing and a usage of the trade.

E. DECIDING OMITTED CASES

Table of Sections

§ 3–18. Deciding Omitted Cases

This section relates to a situation where the parties have not agreed upon a term that relates to the dispute in question. It is clear that the rules of interpretation, discussed above, have no relevancy to this situation because the assumption is that there is no term that applies to the situation. This situation arises primarily where the parties fail to foresee the contingency that arises or if they do foresee it for one reason or another they fail to make any provision with respect to it.[13]

One illustration will suffice. An Advertising Co. (A) entered into an agreement with a Transit Co. (T) by the terms of which A was to obtain advertisers, collect from them for "advertising displays" and pay to T a specified percentage of the "gross receipts." Many years after the agreement was made, advertising displays containing "take one" pads—pads of individually removable tickets that can be pulled off and kept by interested passengers—came into existence. The evidence made it clear that the parties had never considered how this type of advertising should be handled, because it was different from other ads because of the additional work required to install and maintain advertising displays containing "take one" pads. The parties had never considered this contingency. Assume further that there was no tacit assumption or agreement as to this contingency and a term could not be supplied by logical assumption. This is an omitted term.[14]

Once it is decided that one is dealing with an "omitted case," the court should supply a term "which comports with community standards of fairness and policy rather than analyze a hypothetical model of the bargaining process." [15] Under this rule courts have supplied terms such as "good faith," "best" or "reasonable efforts" and "reasonable notice." [16] Although additional promises or agreements between the parties as to the omitted term may be barred by the parol evidence

---

13. Farnsworth, Disputes over Omission in Contracts, 68 Colum.L.Rev. 860 (1968).

14. Restatement, Second, Contracts § 204, Comment b.

15. Restatement, Second, Contracts § 204, Comment d.

16. Farnsworth, Contracts § 7–17. Other cases base the result upon the intention of the parties. See, for example, Barco Urban Renewal Corp. v. Housing Auth. of City of Atlantic City, 674 F.2d 1001 (3d

Cir.1982) wherein it is stated: "Terms are implied not because they are just or reasonable, but rather for the reason that the parties must have intended them and have only failed to express them * * * or because they are necessary to give business efficacy to the contract as written, or to give the contract the effect which the parties, as fair and reasonable men, presumably would have agreed on if, having in mind the possibility of the situation which has arisen, they contracted expressly in reference thereto."

rule, the term may be shown, "if relevant" on the question of what is reasonable in the circumstances.[17]

The problem of omitted cases (terms) arises in many areas of contract law, most notably in the areas of constructive conditions of exchange and under the doctrines of impractibility and frustration.[18]

WESTLAW REFERENCES

contract agreement /s contingen! /s fail! /s foresee!

"omission in contract"

omitted +1 case term /s agreement contract

omitted +1 case term /s intent! intend! /s party

"barco urban" +s housing

---

17. Restatement, Contracts § 230, Comment e.

18. See chapters 11 and 13 infra. See also § 2–9 supra and § 4–12(7) supra.

Chapter 4

CONSIDERATION

Table of Contents

184

---

§ 4–1.   Introduction

Consideration relates to what types of promises the law will enforce.[1] Apparently no legal system has ever enforced all promises. Fundamentally, the idea is that the coercive power of the State will not be employed to impose sanctions on the defaulting promisor unless the promisor has made a commitment which the law deems socially useful.[2] In the words of one court, "consideration is the glue that binds the parties to a contract together."[3]

Under the doctrine of consideration gratuitous promises are not enforced.[4] As we shall see, this conclusion is tempered by other doctrines. Thus, historically, a formal gratuitous promise—that is one made pursuant to a recognized form—has been enforceable.[5] Remnants of this notion are preserved in those common law jurisdictions which still give effect to the seal.[6] So also a gratuitous promise relied upon by the promisee may be enforced under the doctrine of promissory estoppel.[7] Under certain circumstances a promise to make restitution for material benefits received in the past will be enforced.[8]

1.   1A Corbin, Contracts § 210.

2.   Cohen, The Basis of Contract, 46 Harv.L.Rev. 553, 571–574 (1933). Many European, Latin American, African and Asiatic countries which have derived their legal systems from Roman law require either that contracts be made in solemn form or contain the elements of causa. See Von Mehren, Civil Analogues to Consideration: An Exercise in Comparative Analysis, 72 Harv.L.Rev. 1009 (1959); Lorenzen, Causa and Consideration in the Law of Contracts, 28 Yale L.J. 621 (1919). On formal contracts in civil law systems derived from Roman Law, see Schlesinger, The Notary and the Formal Contract in Civil Law, 1941 Report of the New York Law Revision Commission 403. A modern formulation of the causa requirement is that a promise is enforceable if it is directed to the realization of interests worthy of protection in accordance with the principles of the legal system. Ital.C.Civ. art. 1322 (paraphrase).

3.   In Matter of Deed of Trust of Owen, 62 N.C.App. 506, 303 S.E.2d 351 (1983).

4.   See § 4–5.

5.   See Hazeltine, The Formal Contract of Early English Law, 10 Colum.L.Rev. 608 (1910), Selected Readings 1; Maine, Ancient Law Ch. IX (5th ed. 1873); Perillo, The Statute of Frauds in the Light of the Functions and Dysfunctions of Form, 43 Fordham L.Rev. 39, 43–48 (1974).

6.   See ch. 7 infra.

7.   See ch. 6 infra. See also chapter 5 relating to the question of Moral Obligation.

8.   See ch. 5 infra.

The end result is that an informal unrelied-upon gratuitous promise generally will not be enforced.[9] Professor Eisenberg argues that this is a tenable position.[10] He advances both substantive and administrative reasons to support the conclusion. In addition to difficulties of proof he points out that the injury in this type of case is relatively slight; there are not significant costs on the part of the promisee and no enrichment on the part of the promisor at the expense of the promisee.[11] There is in addition an ideological concept that economic activity and commercial activity in particular are to be encouraged and that this is best done by encouraging, and giving legal protection to, trade; that is, exchanges, and not to gratuitous unrelied upon promises.[12] Furthermore a gratuitous promise may be made without sufficient deliberation and, even if not, there might be reason not to enforce it if it was made improvidently or if the promisee showed ingratitude.[13]

Whatever the reasons, it is clear that the common law usually requires that informal promises be made for a consideration if they are to be binding. Despite the apparently sound theoretical basis for the doctrine of consideration, at least as it relates to informal, not relied upon, donative promises, it must nevertheless be confessed that the doctrine of consideration is an historical phenomenon and therefore in some of its aspects affected by fortuitous circumstances.[14] Despite the fact that the history of this requirement of consideration is tortuous, confused and wrapped in controversy,[15] a brief overview of this history seems appropriate.

The history relates to the writ system and more particularly to the writs of covenant, debt and assumpsit. The writ of covenant was used to enforce contracts made under seal.[16] Under this writ a gratuitous promise under seal could be enforced because the form would encourage deliberateness and because the writing was deemed trustworthy evidence of the terms of the contract.[17] The second writ was debt. This

---

9. See Eisenberg, Donative Promises, 47 U.Chi.L.Rev. 1, 6 (1979). But see Wright, Ought the Doctrine of Consideration to be Abolished from the Common Law?, 49 Harv.L.Rev. 1225, 1251–53 (1936) and 1 Corbin § 111.

10. Eisenberg, note 9, pp. 2–8.

11. Id. pp. 2–6.

12. C. Bufnoir, Propiete et Contract 487 (1900).

13. Eisenberg, note 9, pp. 5–6.

14. See the eloquent discussion in 1 Corbin § 109; Sharp, Pacta Sunt Servanda, 41 Colum.L.Rev. 783 (1941). "Learned Americans are still engaged from time to time in valiant efforts to reduce the common-law rules of contract, and the doctrine of consideration in particular, to strict logical consistency. Legal rules exist not for their own sake, but to further justice and convenience in the business of

human life; dialectic is the servant of their purpose, not their master." Pollock, Principles of Contract, x–xi (9th ed. 1921). See also G. Gilmore, The Death of Contract (1974) and Speidel, An Essay on the Reported Death and Continued Vitality of Contract, 27 Stanford L.Rev. 1161 (1975).

15. See Ames, The History of Assumpsit, 2 Harv.L.Rev. 1, 53 (1888), Selected Readings 33; Farnsworth, The Past of Promise: An Historical Introduction to Contract, 69 Colum.L.Rev. 576 (1969); City of Highland Park v. Grant–MacKenzie Co., 366 Mich. 430, 115 N.W.2d 270 (1962); Quattlebaum v. Gray, 252 Ark. 610, 480 S.W.2d 339 (1972).

16. See the text relating to note 6 supra and ch. 7 infra.

17. Fuller, Consideration and Form, 41 Colum.L.Rev. 799 (1941).

writ could be used to sue for a definite sum owing as a result of performance by the promisee. The theory was that the promisor should pay because he had received a benefit.

The third writ, assumpsit, grew out of cases where a promisor had undertaken (assumpsit) to do something and had done it carelessly (misfeasance) to the detriment of the promisee. At the outset assumpsit did not lie where the promisor simply did not perform (nonfeasance). Later the common law courts began to honor the writ of assumpsit in cases of non-performance but they postulated a requirement of detrimental reliance on the promise—as for example by a change of position in reliance on the promise. In time an action in assumpsit was allowed for breach of a promise even though there was no change of position.

Eventually the writ of assumpsit supplanted the writ of debt. Before this occurred the word consideration had already come into existence. Several elements were included in the concept. It included the notion of the writ of debt that there must be a benefit to the promisor. It also included the notion of the writ of assumpsit that there must be detriment on the part of the promisee.[18]

 WESTLAW REFERENCES

consideration /s enforc! /s law legal! /s promise

"doctrine of consideration"

form formal! /s "doctrine of consideration"

"promissory estoppel" /s reliance /s gratuit! /s promise

"gratuitous promise" /s enforc! /s consideration

"writ of covenant"

"writ of debt"

"writ of assumpsit"

§ 4–2. What Is Consideration?

Having examined in the previous section some justification for the doctrine of consideration and its historical background, it is time to attempt to define or describe it even though an encompassing definition is perhaps impossible. A learned judge has identified the three elements which concur before a promise is supported by consideration.[19]

(a) The promisee must suffer legal detriment; that is, do or promise to do what he is not legally obligated to do; or refrain from doing or promise to refrain from doing what he is legally privileged to do.

---

18. For a detailed treatment of the history see Holdsworth, Debt, Assumpsit and Consideration, 11 Mich.L.Rev. 347 (1913); Farnsworth, The Past of Promise: An Historical Introduction to Contract, 69 Colum. L.Rev. 576 (1969); A. W. B. Simpson, A History of the Common Law of Contract (1975). See also Holt v. Feigenbaum, 52 N.Y.2d 291, 437 N.Y.S.2d 654, 419 N.E.2d 332 (1981).

19. Cardozo, C. J., in Allegheny College v. National Chautauqua County Bank of Jamestown, 246 N.Y. 369, 159 N.E. 173 (1927). This formulation was not new. See, e.g., Wisconsin & Michigan R. Co. v. Powers, 191 U.S. 379, 24 S.Ct. 107, 48 L.Ed. 229 (1903).

(b) The detriment must induce the promise. In other words the promisor must have made the promise because he wishes to exchange it at least in part for the detriment to be suffered by the promisee.

(c) The promise must induce the detriment. This means in effect, as we have already seen, that the promisee must know of the offer and intend to accept.

(a) The Promisee Must Suffer Legal Detriment

There are two additional points to be made in relation to this portion of the rule. First, although the rule stated above is in terms of legal detriment suffered by the promisee it is often stated in terms of "either legal detriment to the promisee or legal benefit to the promisor." [20] This phrasing relates back to our historical discussion where it is pointed out that the concept of consideration carried with it elements of the writ of debt (benefit to the promisor) and of the writ of assumpsit (detriment to the promisee).[21] Since we are talking about *legal* benefit and *legal* detriment the result is invaribly the same no matter which of the two approaches is taken.[22] If the promisee suffers legal detriment the promisor obtains a legal benefit.[23] In the balance of the chapter the approach will be primarily in terms of detriment to be suffered by the promisee.

The other point to be made is that the quoted rule speaks of "legal detriment to the promisee." Although this is the usual case the statement of the rule is inaccurate. It is well settled in the United States that the detriment may be given by a person other than the promisee and run to a person other than the promisor.[24] As the Restatement Second states it does not matter from whom or to whom

20. Rickett v. Doze, 184 Mont. 456, 603 P.2d 679 (1979); Arledge v. Gulf Oil Corp., 578 F.2d 130 (5th Cir.1978); Currie v. Misa, L.R. 10 Ex. 153, 162 (1875); Stonestreet v. Southern Oil Co., 226 N.C. 261, 37 S.E.2d 676 (1946); Wells v. Hartford Accident & Indem. Co., 459 S.W.2d 253 (Mo.1970); Hyde v. Shapiro, 216 Neb. 785, 346 N.W.2d 241 (1984); First Wisconsin Nat'l Bank of Milwaukee v. Oby, 52 Wis.2d 1, 188 N.W.2d 454 (1971); Albemarle Educational Foundation, Inc. v. Basnight, 4 N.C.App. 652, 167 S.E.2d 486 (1969); Doggett v. Heritage Concepts, Inc., 298 N.W.2d 310 (Iowa 1980); Omaha Nat'l Bank v. Goddard Realty, Inc., 210 Neb. 604, 316 N.W.2d 306 (1982). It has on occasion been suggested that neither legal benefit or legal detriment is necessary under the doctrine of consideration. In fact both Restatements may have embraced this approach. See particularly Restatement, Second, Contracts §§ 71 and 79 and Martin v. Federal Life Ins. Co., 109 Ill.App.3d 596, 65 Ill.Dec. 143, 440 N.E.2d

998 (1982). However, there are very few cases that have applied this notion. See E. Farnsworth, Contracts § 2–2 (1980). This approach will be ignored in our discussion of this chapter.

21. See § 4–1 supra.

22. 1 Williston § 102. For a possible exception see § 4–9 infra.

23. 1 Williston § 102A.

24. Restatement, Contracts § 75(2); Cechettini v. Consumer Associates, Limited, 260 Cal.App.2d 295, 67 Cal.Rptr. 15 (1968); McClellan v. McClellan, 52 Md. App. 525, 451 A.2d 334 (1982), certiorari denied 462 U.S. 1135, 103 S.Ct. 3119, 77 L.Ed.2d 1372 (1983); City of Highland Park v. Grant–MacKenzie Co., 366 Mich. 430, 115 N.W.2d 270 (1962); Quattlebaum v. Gray, 252 Ark. 610, 480 S.W.2d 339 (1972); Quazzo v. Quazzo, 136 Vt. 107, 386 A.2d 638 (1978). Contra, Dunlap Pneumatic Tyre Co. v. Selfridge & Co., [1915] A.C. 847.

the consideration moves so long as it is bargained for and given in exchange for the promise of the promisor.[25]

The promisor may raise the defense of lack of consideration where the promisee seeks to enforce an executory agreement but it is not grounds for avoiding a contract that has been fully performed.[26] In other words the promisor is not entitled to restitution once he has performed. At that point he has made an effective gift of money, property or services.

(b) Detriment Must Induce Promise

This means that the promisor makes his promise to induce the conduct of the offeree. Another way of stating the same thought is that the promisor has manifested an offering state of mind looking to an acceptance rather than a gift-making state of mind. The point is that a gratuitous promise is not an offer and in terms of consideration there is no consideration because the promise being gratuitous was not made with an offering (exchanging) state of mind and thus any detriment that ensues did not induce the promise.[27]

(c) The Promise Must Induce the Detriment

As stated above, this means that the offeree must know of the offer and intend to accept. In other words the offeree is induced to act by virtue of and because of the offer.[28]

The essence of consideration, then, is legal detriment,[29] that has been bargained for by the promisor and exchanged by the promisee in return for the promise of the promisor.[30]

A simple illustration will help clarify the concept of consideration. A says to B, "If you paint my house according to my specifications I promise to pay you $2,000." B performs. A is the promisor and B the promisee. (a) The promisee (B) has suffered legal detriment. He has performed an act (painting) that he was not legally obligated to perform. (b) On the facts as stated it is reasonable conclusion that the promisor (A) was exchanging his promise for the act of painting. (c) It

---

25. Restatement, Second, Contract § 71, Comment e.

26. Ope Shipping, Ltd. v. Allstate Ins. Co., Inc., 687 F.2d 639 (2d Cir.1982), certiorari denied 460 U.S. 1069, 103 S.Ct. 1523, 75 L.Ed.2d 946 (1983); Zubik v. Zubik, 384 F.2d 267 (3d Cir.1967), certiorari denied 390 U.S. 988, 88 S.Ct. 1183, 19 L.Ed.2d 1291 (1968). But see § 4–10 infra.

27. This question is discussed in greater detail in § 4–5 infra.

28. See §§ 2–12, 2–13 supra. As pointed out in those section, at times this requirement is eliminated in a bilateral contract in order to protect the expectations of the offeror.

29. The use of the term detriment in this context is criticised in 1 Corbin §§ 122–23. Its use has been avoided in the Restatement, Second, Contracts. See § 79, Comment b. The criticism of this traditional term by these authorities is based upon the thought that it is unrealistic to speak of detriment in cases involving no economic loss. This criticism has merit, but similar criticism may be directed at legal terms such as "consideration" which frequently differ in meaning from use of the same words by non-lawyers.

30. Key Pontiac, Inc. v. Blue Grass Savings Bank, 265 N.W.2d 906 (Iowa 1978); Baehr v. Penn-O-Tex Oil Corp., 258 Minn. 533, 104 N.W.2d 661 (1960).

also is a reasonable conclusion that the offeree (B) painted knowing of the offer and intending to accept.

It should be observed that the questions listed at the beginning of this section and the illustration above are set up in terms of a unilateral arrangement in which there is only one promisor. Of course in a bilateral contract there are two promisors. This gives rise to some complicated problems to be discussed below.[31]

This text does not distinguish between "consideration" and "sufficient consideration" as did the original Restatement. According to that terminology there is "sufficient consideration" if all three elements listed above are present. If elements (b) and (c) are present but not (a) then there was "consideration" (exchange) but not "sufficient consideration."[32] The Second Restatement has wisely dropped this distinction.[33] Accordingly when we say that there is consideration it means that all three elements discussed above are present.

WESTLAW REFERENCES

di consideration

consideration /2 define*

(a) *The Promise Must Suffer Legal Detriment*

promisee /s "legal detriment"

promisor /s "legal benefit"

"highland park" +s "grant mackenzie"

lack*** absen! /s consideration /s executory /s agreement

(b) *Detriment Must Induce Promise*

detriment /s induc*** /s promise

di(promisor /p induc*** /p promisee /p action)

(c) *The Promise Must Induce the Detriment*

consideration /s "legal detriment" /s bargain! /s promis!

"sufficient consideration" /s exchang! /s promis!

"sufficient consideration" /s bargain!

"sufficient consideration" /s restatement

---

§ 4–3. Motive and Past Consideration Are Not Consideration; Necessity of an Exchange

If the promisor says to one of his sons, "In consideration of the fact that you are not as wealthy as your brothers, I promise to pay you $500 thirty days from today." This promise is not enforceable because the promisor has neither requested nor induced any detriment in exchange.[34] The promisor merely has stated the motive for his gratuitous promise and this is not consideration.[35] This is not to say that motive

---

31. See § 4–12 infra.

32. Restatement, Contracts § 80.

33. Restatement, Second, Contracts § 71, Reporter's Note.

34. Fink v. Cox, 18 Johns. 145 (N.Y. 1820).

35. Lesnik v. Estate of Lesnik, 82 Ill. App.3d 1102, 38 Ill.Dec. 452, 403 N.E.2d 683 (1980); Rose v. Lurvey, 40 Mich.App. 230, 198 N.W.2d 839 (1972).

is irrelevant to the question of consideration. In the illustration given there was no detriment and thus there could be no consideration. Once there is detriment the motive of the promisor in entering into the transaction may be important on the issue of consideration for his motive often is to induce action on the part of the promisee and conversely the motive of the promisee is to gain what is offered by the promisor. Thus, motive does relate to the issue of whether an exchange is intended.[36] The relationship between motive and consideration will be explored at greater length below.[37]

If the promisor had stated to his son, "In consideration of the fact that you have named your child after me I promise to pay $500 thirty days from today", the promise is equally unenforceable because the detriment (naming the child after the promisor) could not induce the promise since the child had already been named.[38] Nor did the promise induce the detriment because there was no knowledge of any offer or any intent to accept when the act was done.[39] Thus, it is frequently stated that past consideration is not consideration.[40]

As a matter of fact the term "past consideration" is itself a contradiction in terms. As we have seen consideration is essentially an exchange and parties do not bargain or exchange for something that has already occurred.[41] In the illustration above, however, if the transaction had been prospective—that is if the promisor bargained for the naming of child before the child was named and thereby induced the parents to name the child after the promisor, consideration would exist.[42]

The idea of "exchange" is central to the law of contracts, as it is to any advanced economic system.[43] Should it, however, set the boundaries of the law of contracts? One may question the adequacy of a legal system which refuses to enforce a promise such as this: "In consideration of your forty years of faithful service, you will be paid a pension of $200.00 per month."[44] It is not surprising that some legislatures[45] have turned their attention to promises of this kind which, if seriously made, deserve to be enforced. The requirement of an "exchange" may

---

36. 1 Corbin § 118.

37. See § 4–7 infra.

38. Hayes v. Plantations Steel Co., ___ R.I. ___, 438 A.2d 1091 (1982).

39. Lanfier v. Lanfier, 227 Iowa 258, 288 N.W. 104 (1939); 1 Williston § 142.

40. 1 Williston § 142; Pershall v. Elliott, 249 N.Y. 183, 163 N.E. 554 (1928). There are exceptions to this rule. They are studied under the heading of Moral Obligation in Chapter 5. See also Brody, Performance of a Pre-Existing Contractual Duty as Consideration: The Actual Criteria for the Efficacy of an Agreement Altering Contractual Obligations, 52 Denver L.J. 433 (1975).

41. 1 Williston § 142.

42. Schumm by Whyner v. Berg, 37 Cal. 2d 174, 231 P.2d 39, 21 A.L.R.2d 1051 (1951).

43. This concept of exchange is discussed in more detail in §§ 4–4, 4–5 infra.

44. Cf. Bogley's Estate v. United States, 206 Ct.Cl. 695, 514 F.2d 1027 (1975); Perreault v. Hall, 94 N.H. 191, 49 A.2d 812 (1946); and see 1 Williston § 1308; Somers and Schwartz, Pension and Welfare Plans: Gratuities or Compensation?, 4 Ind. & Lab. Rel.Rev. 77 (1950); Notes, 23 Cornell L.Q. 310 (1938), 44 Geo.L.J. 145 (1955).

45. See §§ 5–12 to 5–18 infra.

have seemed indispensable (with few exceptions)[46] to eighteenth and nineteenth century lawyers whose understanding of the proper role of contract law was conditioned by the pervasive influence of Adam Smith's theory of economics. Twentieth century lawyers seem less inclined to ideological dogmatism of any school and more inclined to ask whether the community conscience would deem a particular promise worthy of enforcement. Although the exchange requirement still remains central to the law of contracts, lawyer influenced legislation and the development of the doctrine of promissory estoppel[47] dispense with the exchange requirement in a number of instances. These instances will doubtless increase in the future.

WESTLAW REFERENCES

motive! /s gratuit! /s contract agreement

fink +3 cox

gratuit! /s promis! /s detriment

consideration /s "gratuit! promis!"

"past consideration" /s enforc!

"past consideration" /s promis!

"past consideration" /s detriment

"past consideration" /s support!

"past consideration" /s rule axiom maxim

95k79

"past consideration" /s contract agreement

§ 4–4. Adequacy of Detriment

As a general rule it is settled that any detriment no matter how economically inadequate will support a promise.[48] But this does not necessarily mean that there is consideration to support the promise because economic inadequacy of the detriment is one of the factors to be considered in determining whether the promisor exchanged his promise in return for this small detriment.[49] Courts, however, have believed that it would be an unwarranted interference with freedom of contract if they were to relieve an adult party from a bad exchange.[50] This

---

46. See ch. 5 infra.

47. See ch. 6 infra.

48. In re American Coils Co., 187 F.2d 384 (3d Cir.1951); Western Fed. Sav. & Loan Ass'n of Denver v. National Homes Corp., 167 Colo. 93, 445 P.2d 892 (1968); Hotze v. Schlanser, 410 Ill. 265, 102 N.E.2d 131 (1951); Earle v. Angell, 157 Mass. 294, 32 N.E. 164 (1892); Spaulding v. Benenati, 57 N.Y.2d 418, 456 N.Y.S.2d 733, 442 N.E.2d 1244 (1982). See generally Braucher, Freedom of Contract and the Second Restatement, 78 Yale L.J. 598 (1969).

49. See § 4–5 infra.

50. Black Indus., Inc. v. Bush, 110 F.Supp. 801, 805 (D.N.J.1953) (Even if it were proved that the plaintiff was to have received a far greater profit than the defendants for a much smaller contribution, the defendant would nevertheless be bound by his agreement by the familiar rule that relative values of the consideration in a contract between business men dealing at arm's length without fraud will not affect the validity of the contract."); Guaranteed Foods of Neb., Inc. v. Rison, 207 Neb. 400, 299 N.W.2d 507 (1980); Trans-Fuel, Inc. v. Saylor, 440 Pa. 51, 269 A.2d 718 (1970); Reliable Pharmacy v. Hall, 54 Wis.2d 191, 194 N.W.2d 596 (1972); Tsiolis v. Hatter-

reluctance to interfere with economic freedom has been carried to its logical conclusion.

A good illustration is the case of Haigh v. Brooks.[51] Defendant for a consideration had executed a guaranty of payment of a debt of 10000£ owed by a third party to the plaintiffs. The guaranty was legally ineffective at its inception because, among other reasons, it was unstamped and therefore worthless under then existing English law. Defendant subsequently promised that if the plaintiffs would return the document he would pay the plaintiffs the sum stated. Plaintiffs performed. When sued on his promise defendant argued that the surrender of the document—a worthless piece of paper—did not constitute detriment. Therefore, he argued, his promise was not enforceable. The court followed the traditional rule indicating that it was not the court's function to concern itself with the adequacy or the inadequacy of the detriment. The court also considered the question of what defendant bargained for and concluded on the facts that he did bargain for the paper.[52]

This landmark case should be compared with another well-known case, Newman & Snell's State Bank v. Hunter,[53] in which a widow had promised plaintiff to pay the debt of her deceased husband's insolvent estate. In exchange, the bank returned the husband's note to the widow. The court, ruling in her favor, indicated that surrender of a worthless note did not constitute consideration. If the court meant that the surrender of the note was not legal detriment, the case is in radical opposition to the weight of authority.[54] Since the court apparently decided the case on this basis, it was unnecessary for the court to determine what in fact was bargained for.[55] In any event, the case may be made consistent with basic concepts of contract law if it is based on the ground that economic inadequacy may constitute some circumstantial evidence of fraud, duress, over-reaching, undue influence or mistake.[56]

scheidt, 85 S.D. 568, 187 N.W.2d 104 (1971); Patterson, An Apology for Consideration, 58 Colum.L.Rev. 929 (1958). The classic philosophical discussion supporting this point of view and which had enormous impact on nineteenth century law is in Bentham, Defence of Usury: Showing the Impolicy of the Present Legal Restraints on the Terms of Pecuniary Bargains (Phila. 1796). Cf. "The Norwegian Price Act provides as follows: 'Charging, demanding or contracting unreasonable prices shall be prohibited.'" Danish Committee on Comparative Law, Danish and Norwegian Law 82 (1963).

51. 113 Eng.Rep. 119 (K.B. 1839); Mullen v. Hawkins, 141 Ind. 363, 40 N.E. 797 (1895) (quitclaim deed from grantor who had no interest in the premises). See also Brooks v. Ball, 18 Johns. 337 (N.Y.1820). Compare, however, the situation where a recording act requires "valuable consideration." Hood v. Webster, 271 N.Y. 57, 2 N.E.2d 43, 107 A.L.R. 497 (1936).

52. The question of what is bargained for in this type of a case is discussed in § 4-8 infra.

53. 243 Mich. 331, 220 N.W. 665, 59 A.L.R. 311 (1928).

54. See criticism of the case in 1 Corbin § 127 n. 83.

55. On this issue, see § 4-8 infra.

56. Bowl-Opp, Inc. v. Bayer, 255 Or. 318, 458 P.2d 435 (1969); Restatement, Second, Contracts § 79, Comment e. Gross inadequacy of consideration is also an important factor to be taken into account on the issue of whether specific performance will be granted. Restatement, Contracts § 367, Comment b.

There is one kind of transaction in which the court will evaluate the economic adequacy of consideration. This involves a promise to exchange a specific amount of money or fungible goods for a lesser amount of money or goods at the same time and place.[57] The reasoning behind this exception is that in such a case the court takes judicial notice of the value of the things exchanged and cannot indulge in the supposed normal presumption of equivalence between the detriment and the promise.[58] This exception would not apply to an exchange of different currencies or an exchange for a rare coin since these are generally dealt with in the market place as commodities.[59]

Williston extends the rule to a promise to exchange a specific sum of money or fungible goods for the same amount of money or goods at the same time and place.[60] He gives as an illustration "a bargain stated to be 'in consideration of one dollar by each to the other paid'" where the one dollar was actually paid by each party.[61] This illustration does not fit within the reasoning of the preceding paragraph since in this case a court need not presume equivalence because there is actual equivalence. However, the result would likely be the same because it would be ludicrous to assume that each party bargained for the dollar in question.[62] In any event the Second Restatement of Contracts omits this exception on the ground that an agreement of this kind is highly unlikely to be made.[63]

The cases discussed above are to be distinguished from case in which a sum is exchanged for a promise to return a larger sum if a contingent event occurs. In one case a party released from a mental institution solicited $50 from a friend for the purpose of travelling to Alaska to recover a gold mine. He promised that if he were successful he would repay $10,000. It was held that since the loan was repayable only on the happening of a contingency there was sufficient consideration for this promise to pay two hundred times the amount received.[64]

Economic inadequacy, then, except in one unusual situation, does not prevent any bargained for detriment from constituting consideration. On the other hand, economic inadequacy may constitute some circumstantial evidence of fraud,[65] duress, over-reaching, undue influence, mistake,[66] or that the detriment was not in fact bargained for.[67]

57. 1 Corbin § 129; Schnell v. Nell, 17 Ind. 29, 79 Am.Dec. 453 (1861).

58. American University v. Todd, 39 Del. (9 W.W. Harr.) 449, 1 A.2d 595 (Del. Super.1938); see 1 Corbin § 129; 1 Williston § 115. On the supposed equivalence between the detriment and the promise, see Verplanck, An Essay on the Doctrine of Contracts 86–97 (1825).

59. 1 Corbin § 129.

60. 1 Williston § 115.

61. 1 Williston § 115, p. 460.

62. 1 Corbin § 129.

63. Restatement, Second, Contracts § 72, Reporter's Note, citing Whittier, The Restatement of Contracts and Consideration, 18 Calif.L.Rev. 611, 623 (1930). But see Robertson v. Garvan, 270 Fed. 643 (S.D. N.Y.1920).

64. Embola v. Tuppela, 127 Wash. 285, 220 P. 789 (1923). See § 4–12(5) infra.

65. Dreyer v. Dreyer, 48 Or.App. 801, 617 P.2d 955 (1980).

66. See n. 56 supra; West Gate Bank of Lincoln v. Eberhardt, 202 Neb. 762, 277 N.W.2d 104 (1979).

Relief from this harshly individualistic principle under the doctrine of unconscionability will be considered elsewhere in this volume.[68]

It should also be noted that the distinction between "sufficiency" of consideration and "adequacy" of consideration employed in the original Restatement is not used in this text or in the Second Restatement.[69]

 WESTLAW REFERENCES

adequa! /4 detriment

inadequa! /2 consideration /s support! /s promis!

"freedom of contract" /p adequa! inadequa! /s consideration

adequa! inadequa! /s consideration /s unreasonable
   unconscionabl!

haigh +s brooks

"sufficient consideration" /s support! /s agreement contract

"sufficient consideration" /s agreement contract /s duress fraud!
   "undue infuence" mistake

"sufficient consideration" /s "specific! perform!"

§ 4-5. Conditions to Gift Distinguished From Bargained for Detriment

If A gratuitously says to B, "If it rains tomorrow I promise to pay you $10," B may not enforce the promise even if it rains. A has merely made an unenforceable conditional promise to make a gift.[70]

In a well known case the defendant wrote to "Dear Sister Antillico", his sister-in-law, promising her a place to raise her family "If you will come down and see me." [71] In response to the promise she moved to the defendant's land incurring certain losses and expenses. The court held that the defendant's promise was a promise to make a gift and that her expenses arising from the move were merely necessary conditions to acceptance of the gift.[72] The defendant did not appear to be bargaining for the plaintiff's presence on his plantation; rather it appeared he wished to help her out of a difficult situation. In other

67. See § 4–5 infra and 1 Williston § 112.

68. See §§ 9–37 to 9–40; In Matter of Last Will and Testament of Johnson, 351 So.2d 1339 (Miss.1977).

69. Restatement, Second, Contracts § 71, Reporter's Note.

70. A gift ordinarily is ineffective until there has been delivery of the subject matter. See Brown, Personal Property 76–112 (3d ed. 1975). In Hoffmann v. Wausau Concrete Co., 58 Wis.2d 472, 207 N.W.2d 80 (1973) the four elements of a gift were listed as: intent to give, actual or constructive delivery, termination of the donor's dominion and dominion in the donee.

71. Kirksey v. Kirksey, 8 Ala. 131 (1845). Compare Matter of Baer's Estate,

196 Misc. 979, 92 N.Y.S.2d 359 (Sur.Ct. 1949) (in accord with Kirksey, supra) with Maughs v. Porter, 157 Va. 415, 161 S.E. 242 (1931) (prize offered to anyone who would attend auction; attendance is sufficient detriment and was bargained for). See City Stores Co. v. Ammerman, 266 F.Supp. 766 (D.D.C. 1967), affirmed 394 F.2d 950 (D.C.Cir.1968); Bredemann v. Vaughan Mfg. Co., 40 Ill.App.2d 232, 188 N.E.2d 746 (1963), noted in 13 De Paul L.Rev. 158 (1964); Coder v. Smith, 156 Kan. 512, 134 P.2d 408 (1943).

72. For a discussion of the doctrine of promissory estoppel and its application to cases of this kind, see ch. 6 infra.

words the promisor made a gratuitous promise rather than an offer.[73] Two observations should be made with respect to this case. First, although, as we have seen, adequacy of detriment is not important in itself, it is relevant in determining whether the promisor manifests a gift making state of mind or a contract making state of mind since it is less likely that a promisor will bargain for a small detriment. In other words the smallness of the detriment is one of the factors to be considered in determining whether the promisor has bargained for the named detriment or whether the detriment is merely a condition of a gift.[74]

Another factor to be considered in making this determination is whether the happening of the contingency would be a benefit to the promisor.[75] For example, if in the case under discussion the defendant had wanted his sister-in-law to come to his house as a housekeeper the result doubtlessly would have been different.[76] In other words, selfish benefit to the promisor is an indication of a contract making state of mind, whereas if the benefit is merely the pleasure of altruism a gift making state of mind may be present. The distinction is obviously not a clear one and the test is not conclusive—merely one of the factors to be considered.

In another well known case a promise was made by an uncle to his nephew to pay $5,000 if the nephew refrained from "drinking, using tobacco, etc., until he was twenty-one." The nephew fulfilled his uncle's requirements and the court held that there was sufficient evidence to sustain the lower court's finding that there was a contract.[77] Although it could be argued that the uncle was motivated by altruism this factor obviously did not turn the case. Ultimately this question is nothing more nor less than a question of interpretation. The rules relating to subjective and objective intention and the dividing line between questions of law and fact again become relevant.[78]

It is interesting and instructive to compare the case above involving "Dear Sister Antillico" with a case such a Bard v. Kent.[79] In the latter case the lessor offered to extend the lease of the lessee for an additional four years if the lessee promised to make improvements that would cost approximately $10,000. Before the "option" was given the lessor suggested that the promisee retain an architect to check figures on the proposed improvements of the promises. This was done after the offer ("Option") was given. One question in the case was whether the offer was irrevocable.

---

73. See § 4–2 supra.

74. 1 Williston § 112.

75. 1 Williston § 112.

76. Davis v. Jacoby, 1 Cal.2d 370, 34 P.2d 1026 (1934); Brackenbury v. Hodgkin, 116 Me. 399, 102 A. 106 (1917).

77. Hamer v. Sidway, 124 N.Y. 538, 27 N.E. 256 (1891); see also Schumn by Whyner v. Berg, 37 Cal.2d 174, 231 P.2d

39, 21 A.L.R.2d 1051 (1951) (naming a child after actor Wallace Berry).

78. 1 Williston § 112; 1 Corbin § 151. See ch. 3 and §§ 2–2 and 2–8 supra.

79. 19 Cal.2d 449, 122 P.2d 8 (1942). See Fisher v. Jackson, 142 Conn. 734, 118 A.2d 316 (1955); Stelmack v. Glen Alden Coal Co., 339 Pa. 410, 14 A.2d 127 (1940).

Although a revocable offer is gratuitous, it involves a contract making state of mind, because it looks to an exchange.[80] As stated, one question in the case is whether the offer was made irrevocable (assuming that the offer manifested an intent to make the offer irrevocable) by engaging the architect. This is important on the facts because the offeror died prior to an acceptance and thus the offer was terminated unless there was consideration to make it irrevocable.[81] The court sustained the finding of fact made by the trial court that the hiring of the architect was not consideration because it was merely suggested and not bargained for. Thus the offer was revocable and death terminated the offer. This would not have been true if the offer were irrevocable.[82]

 WESTLAW REFERENCES

sy(gift /s deliver! /s "subject matter")

intend! intent! +2 give /s deliver! /s dominion /s gift

to(191) /p detriment

to(191) /p bargain!

to(191) /p gratuit!

unenforc! /s gift

benefit! /s gift /s promisor offeror

motiv! /s gift

revoc! /s gift

revoc! /s gratuit! /s offer!

di gift

§ 4–6. Of Sham and Nominal Consideration

The basic question discussed here is whether a pretense of consideration will suffice as consideration. In the case of Bard v. Kent discussed immediately above, the instrument in question recited that the option in question was given in "consideration of ten dollars and other valuable consideration."[83] The facts showed that the $10.00 had not been paid. The question is whether this false (sham) recital[84] of

80. See § 4–2 supra.

81. See §§ 2–20 and 2–25 supra.

82. See § 2–25 supra.

83. The words "for value received" raise a rebuttable presumption that consideration has been given. Matter of Estate of Mingesz, 70 Wis.2d 734, 235 N.W.2d 296 (1975). Some courts say that these or similar words are prima facie evidence of consideration. Farrar v. Young, 158 W.Va. 977, 216 S.E.2d 575 (1975).

84. The word "recital" here is not used in its technical sense. In its technical sense a recital in a contract is usually prefixed by the word "Whereas". It is not usually drafted as a promise or condition. It appears to be generally agreed that a recital of fact is prima facie evidence of

that fact, subject, however, to refutation. Eastern Plank Road Co. v. Vaughan, 14 N.Y. 546 (1856). Oregon has a statute which makes the truth of recitals in a written instrument conclusive presumptions between the parties thereto. See High v. Davis, 283 Or. 315, 584 P.2d 725 (1978). As to the relationship of recitals to the body of the instrument, the rule usually followed is the one stated by Lord Esher in Ex Parte Dawes, 17 Q.B.D. 275, 286 (1886) wherein he stated: "If the recitals are clear and the operative part is ambiguous, the recitals govern the construction. If the recitals are ambiguous, and the operative part is clear, the operative part must prevail. If both the recitals and the operative part are clear, but they are inconsistent with each other, the operative part is

consideration constitutes consideration as to make the offer irrevocable. There are a number of views.

The vast majority of cases have held that it may be shown that the consideration has not been paid and that no other consideration has been given.[85] This result does not contravene the parol evidence rule since this rule does not prohibit the contradiction of a recital of fact.[86] There is a minority view—mostly involving options and guarantees— that reaches the opposite result either upon the theory that the parties are estopped from contradicting the writing [87] or upon the theory that the recital gives rise to an implied promise to pay.[88] Under the minority view it is assumed that there is an exchange.[89] For this reason the Restatement Second says that in many cases the minority view is fictitious and as a result takes a different approach,[90] singling out option contracts and credit guarantees for special treatment.

Section 87 provides, "an offer is binding as an option contract if it is in writing and signed by the offeror, recites a purported consideration for the making of the offer, and proposes an exchange on fair terms within a reasonable time; ＊ ＊ ＊. There is a similar provision with respect to a guaranty. It reads, "A promise to be a surety for the performance of a contractual obligation made to the obligee is binding if the promise is in writing and signed by the promisor and recites a purported consideration." [91]

It should be observed that these sections are placed in topic 2 of Chapter 4 entitled "Contracts Without Consideration." Thus the Restatement explicitly recognizes that these are enforceable transactions in which there is no exchange. The reason for giving special treatment to options and guaranties is their economic utility.[92] The form used also insures that there is sufficient reflection.[93] These sections would

to be preferred." See Note, 41 Cornell L.Q. 126 (1955); Note, 35 Colum.L.Rev. 565 (1935); United Virginia Bank Nat. v. Best, 223 Va. 112, 286 S.E.2d 221 (1982), certiorari denied 459 U.S. 879, 103 S.Ct. 175, 74 L.Ed.2d 144 (1982).

85. Bard v. Kent, 19 Cal.2d 449, 122 P.2d 8 (1942); Neils v. Deist, 180 Mont. 542, 591 P.2d 652 (1979); Komp v. Raymond, 175 N.Y. 102, 67 N.E. 113 (1903). See Ehrlich v. American Moninger Greenhouse Mfg. Corp., 26 N.Y.2d 255, 309 N.Y.S.2d 341, 257 N.E.2d 890 (1970); Lewis v. Fletcher, 101 Idaho 530, 617 P.2d 834 (1980) (citing text).

86. 1 Williston § 115B. We have already discussed one aspect of the parol evidence rule as it relates to consideration in § 3–4 supra.

87. Real Estate Co. of Pittsburgh v. Rudolph, 301 Pa. 502, 153 A. 438 (1930); Hubbard v. Schumaker, 82 Ill.App.3d 476, 37 Ill.Dec. 855, 402 N.E.2d 857 (1980).

88. Baumer v. United States, 580 F.2d 863 (5th Cir.1978), rehearing denied 585 F.2d 520 (5th Cir.1978); Smith v. Wheeler, 233 Ga. 166, 210 S.E.2d 702 (1974); Jones v. Smith, 206 Ga. 162, 56 S.E.2d 462 (1949). The problem under discussion arises only if there is a recital of fact and so it cannot arise if there is a promise rather than a recital of fact.

89. Lawrence v. McCalmont, 43 U.S. (2 How.) 426, 452, 11 L.Ed. 326 (1844).

90. Restatement, Second, Contracts § 87(1)(a), Comments b and c.

91. Restatement, Second, Contracts § 88(a).

92. Restatement, Second, Contracts § 88, Comment a.

93. Restatement, Second, Contracts § 87, Comments a and c.

appear to apply to a recital of "for value received"[94] but it is unclear whether they would apply to a recital of past consideration.

A related but slightly different problem arises where the parties, having learned that a gratuitous promise is unenforceable, attempt to make the promise of the promisor enforceable by cloaking the gratuitous promise with the form of a bargain. Thus, suppose that A wishes to make a binding contract to convey certain property worth $10,000 to his son B one year later. A intends a gift but, being aware of the doctrine of consideration, drafts an instrument in which he promises to convey in return for B's promise to pay $10. If B knows or should know that the $10 is merely a token should A's promise be enforced if B tenders the $10 in accordance with terms of the document? There are two views.

Since the exchange is only a charade used to circumvent the doctrine of consideration, one view is that the agreement should not be enforced because the exchange is a formality rather than a genuine intended bargain. The token payment was consideration in name only (nominal consideration) rather than true consideration.[95] The Restatement Second adopts this view.[96] The contrary view is supported by the original Restatement and some other authorities.[97]

The question is one of philosophical approach. According to the first view if a pretense is accepted as consideration then the doctrine of consideration is undermined. The other view argues that there ought to be a way to make a gratuitous promise binding especially since this can no longer be done in many jurisdictions through the mechanism of a seal.[98]

It is important to note in this situation that there is not an admixture of bargain and gift (the topic of the next section) but rather that there is only a gratuitous promise and a pretense of a bargained-for exchange rather than a bargain in fact.

 WESTLAW REFERENCES

"nominal consideration"

consideration /s agreement contract /s sham

"value received" /s presum! /s consideration

56k493(1)

recital /s sham fals! /s consideration /s revoc! revok! irrevoc!
   offer! agreement contract

recital /s "implied! promis! to pay"

---

94. See note 83 supra.

95. Axe v. Tolbert, 179 Mich. 556, 562, 146 N.W. 418, 420 (1914); Wallace v. Figone, 107 Mo.App. 362, 81 S.W. 492 (1904).

96. Restatement, Second, Contracts § 71, ill. 5. It should be recalled, however, that the Restatement Second has created a special rule for options and guarantees under which a recited consideration is allowed even though it is a pretense.

97. Restatement, Contracts § 84, ill. 1; Holmes, The Common Law 293–95 (1881).

98. Note, Restatement of Contracts (Second)—A Rejection of Nominal Consideration?, 1 Valparaiso U.L.Rev. 102 (1966); see generally Von Mehren, Civil Law Analogues to Consideration: An Exercise in Comparative Analysis, 72 Harv.L.Rev. 1009 (1959).

option guarant** /s binding /s consideration

195k17

195k16(2)

§ 4–7. Admixture of Gift and Bargain

We have already seen that motive and consideration are not synonomous terms but that motive is related to consideration because the promisor in making his promise is ordinarily motivated by his desire to obtain the detriment sought.[99] It must be recalled, however, that the detriment to be surrendered by the promisee need not be the sole or even the predominant inducement,[1] but it must be enough of an inducement so that it is in fact bargained for.[2]

Suppose A is moved by friendship to promise to sell his horse to B for $100 and the horse is worth $500. Should the promise be enforced? If there is an element of exchange the generally accepted answer appears to be in the affirmative even though A's primary motive in entering into the transaction is friendship.[3] Once the element of exchange is found there is a mixture of gift and bargain. The Restatement Second makes it clear that such an agreement should be enforced.[4] A law review article, however, has suggested that only the part as to which there is a bargain should be enforced. This suggestion would work, for example, in a case where the promisor has promised to pay $10 for a $5 book but not in the illustration above.[5]

Under the traditional rule, the ultimate question is how does one determine if there is an admixture of bargain and gift or whether any named consideration is not in fact bargained for. One answer is that this should be treated as a question of fact unless reasonable men on the facts could reach only one reasonable conclusion.[6] The Restatement Second, however, makes the following significant comment. "Even in the typical commercial bargain, the promisor may have more than one motive, and the person furnishing the consideration need not inquire into the promisor's motives. Unless both parties know that the purported consideration is a mere pretense, it is immaterial that the promisor's desire for consideration is incidental to other objectives and even that the other party knows this to be so."[7] But elsewhere the Restatement Second talks about the distinction between bargain and

---

99. See § 4–3 supra; 1 Williston § 111.

1. See § 4–2 supra; 1 Williston § 111.

2. 1 Corbin § 118.

3. Restatement, Second, Contracts § 71, Comment c, Thomas v. Thomas, 114 Eng. Rep. 330 (1842); Matter of Doran, 96 Misc. 2d 846, 410 N.Y.S.2d 44 (Surr.Ct.1978).

4. Restatement, Second, Contracts § 71, Comment c.

5. Note, Restatement of Contracts (Second)—A Rejection of Nominal Consideration?, 1 Valparaiso U.L.Rev. 102 (1966).

6. Fischer v. Union Trust Co., 138 Mich. 612, 101 N.W. 852 (1904) ("To say that one dollar was the real, or such valuable consideration as would of itself sustain a deed of land with several thousand dollars, is not in accord with reason or common sense.") See also § 4–5 supra.

7. Restatement, Second, Contracts § 81, Comment b.

gift being a fine line and dependent upon a number of factors.[8] Ultimately what the Restatement Second appears to say is that if the promisee does not know or does not have reason to know that the promisor is introducing detriment into the transaction as a pretense, then the promise should be enforced under the objective theory but if it clear from the facts that the consideration is merely pretense the promise will not be enforced.[9]

 WESTLAW REFERENCES
motiv! /s friendship /s gift
motiv! /s transaction /s gift
motiv! /s enforc! /s gift
191k15
gift /s "question of fact"

---

§ 4–8.   Surrender of or Forbearance to Assert an Invalid Claim as Detriment

A promise to surrender a valid claim constitutes a detriment and, if bargained for, constitutes consideration.[10] There is no unanimity, however, with respect to the surrender of an invalid claim. Everyone has a duty not to assert a claim known to be unfounded and a contract entered into under threat of such a claim may well be set aside on the ground of duress and restitution awarded to the aggrieved party.[11] If a party believes that he has a valid claim, however, should his surrender of an invalid claim still be considered non-detrimental? There are a number of views.

The earliest view, still preserved in some jurisdictions, is that the surrender of an invalid claim cannot constitute detriment because a person has no right to assert an unfounded claim.[12] This rule runs contrary to the policy of the law to favor settlements.[13] A more modern view, therefore, is that the surrender of an invalid claim serves as detriment if the claimant has asserted it in good faith and a reasonable man could believe that the claim is well founded.[14] Still other courts have held that the only requirement is good faith,[15] but some of these courts qualify the good faith requirement by insisting that the invalidi-

---

8. Restatement, Second, Contracts § 71, Comment c.

9. Restatement, Second, Contracts § 79, Comment d, and illustrations 5 and 6.

10. Mustang Equipment, Inc. v. Welch, 115 Ariz. 206, 564 P.2d 895 (1977).

11. § 9–8 infra.

12. Renney v. Kimberly, 211 Ga. 396, 86 S.E.2d 217 (1955); Gunning v. Royal, 59 Miss. 45, 42 Am.Rep. 350 (1881); Hooff v. Paine, 172 Va. 481, 2 S.E.2d 313 (1939).

13. Stanspec Corp. v. Jelco, Inc., 464 F.2d 1184 (10th Cir.1972). Restatement, Second, Contracts § 74, Comment a.

14. In re Windle, 653 F.2d 328 (8th Cir. 1981); Dick v. Dick, 167 Conn. 210, 355 A.2d 110 (1974); Dom J. Moreau & Son, Inc. v. Federal Pac. Elec. Co., 378 A.2d 151 (Me.1977); Fiege v. Boehm, 210 Md. 352, 123 A.2d 316 (1956); Melotte v. Tucci, 319 Mass. 490, 66 N.E.2d 357 (1946); Restatement, Contracts § 76(b); 1 Williston § 135B.

15. Ralston v. Mathew, 173 Kan. 550, 250 P.2d 841 (1952); Carter v. Provo, 87 N.H. 369, 180 A. 258 (1935); Byrne v. Padden, 248 N.Y. 243, 162 N.E. 20 (1928); Sanders v. Roselawn Memorial Gardens, Inc., 152 W.Va. 91, 159 S.E.2d 784 (1968); see cases cited in 1 Corbin § 140 n. 79.

ty of the claim not be obvious; i.e. "unless the claim is so obviously unfounded that the assertion of good faith would affront the intelligence of the ordinary reasonable layman." [16] In other words even if there is good faith there is no detriment if "the plaintiff has not the shadow of a right as the basis of his claim." [17] When this qualification is added this view is very similar to the view set forth immediately above.[18] The new Restatement takes the position that either good faith or objective uncertainty as to the validity of the claim is sufficient.[19]

The same rules that apply to surrender of the invalid claim also apply to forbearance to assert an invalid claim.[20] Some of the earlier decisions had erroneously held that while a promise to forbear could constitute consideration, forbearance without a promise could not.[21] Where the forbearance is intended to be temporary so that a claim may be asserted later there may be a question whether the forbearance is bargained for.[22]

Having stated the rules with respect to invalid claims it is important to determine when they apply. For example, we have previously discussed the case of Haigh v. Brooks where the defendant had guaranteed in writing an obligation of a third party to the plaintiff and promised to pay the amount stated in the writing if the plaintiff returned the written document. The court not only held that the return of the document constituted detriment but also that what was bargained for was the return of the paper. It so held even though the document was invalid under the existing English law.[23] The court obviously decided that what was bargained for was the piece of paper.[24] It could just as easily have decided that what was bargained for was the surrender of the claim embodied in the document and in that event the rules stated above relating to invalid claims would apply. A clearer illustration of a case where a piece of paper is bargained for is a case where A, an owner of property, who has lost a previous quit claim deed from B promises B to pay him $50 for a second quit-claim deed in order to facilitate his obtaining a mortgage.[25]

---

16. Hall v. Fuller, 352 S.W.2d 559, 562 (Ky.1961), 51 Ky.L.J. 174 (1962).

17. Sharp, Pacta Sunt Servanda, 41 Colum.L.Rev. 783, 787 (1941).

18. 1 Corbin § 140.

19. Restatement, Second, Contracts § 74. The requirement of the first Restatement that a dispute be honest and reasonable was dropped in favor of the alternative test set forth for reasons suggested in Whittier, The Restatement of Contracts and Consideration, 13 Calif.L. Rev. 611, 618–23 (1930). See Restatement, Second, Contracts, Reporter's Note to § 73.

20. In re All Star Feature Corp., 232 Fed. 1004 (S.D.N.Y.1916); Palmer v. Dehn, 29 Tenn.App. 597, 198 S.W.2d 827 (Tenn. App.1946); Veilleux v. Merrill Lynch Relo-

cation Management, Inc., 226 Va. 440, 309 S.E.2d 595 (1983); Restatement, Second, Contracts § 74, Comment d.

21. Shaw v. Philbrick, 129 Me. 259, 151 A. 423 (1930); Reid-Strutt, Inc. v. Wagner, 65 Or.App. 475, 671 P.2d 724 (1983) (implied promise to forbear).

22. Restatement, Second, Contracts § 74, Comment d.

23. A claim is invalid if there is a defense to it as for example in many cases where the contract that gives rise to a claim is void, voidable or unenforceable. See, for example, 1 Corbin § 132.

24. See § 4–4 supra.

25. See Restatement, Second, Contracts § 74, Comment e and illustration 10.

A word might also be said about the case of Newman & Snell's State Bank v. Hunter discussed above. In that case the husband died insolvent and was liable to the plaintiff bank on a note. The bank agreed to return the note in exchange for the widow's promise to pay her husband's obligation. The court improperly held that the surrender of the note was not detriment,[26] but assuming the existence of detriment a number of problems are presented. First the bank had a valid claim against the husband and therefore the topic of invalid claim can be relevant only if the claim can be treated as invalid simply because it is a worthless (uncollectible) claim. Assuming the invalid claim approach is not available the question is what, if anything, did she bargain for—a worthless piece of paper, her husband's honor, or some other intangible benefits? The Restatement Second in discussing this case suggests as a possible explanation that plaintiff failed to sustain its burden of proof that the desire to secure the note motivated the promisor.[27] In other words it was not established that the widow bargained for the note.

Both Corbin and the Restatement Second agree that in the cases being discussed it is important to ascertain what is being bargained for. For example, they indicate that cases involving "worthless pieces of paper" and "invalid claims" should be kept distinct on the grounds that in one case the promisor is bargaining for the discharge of a duty.[28] In an attempt to explain how the distinction should be applied to a set of facts Professor Corbin states that "as a matter of fact a promisor bargains for the acts he describes rather than for a change in the legal relations they may produce."[29] This means that if the promisor asks for possession of the paper he is bargaining for the paper, but if he asks for the surrender of the claim, he is bargaining for the surrender of the claim. As we have seen, all cases do not neatly fit this pattern and it could be argued that all these cases should be decided under the tests of good faith and reasonableness.

Of course if the promisor makes clear precisely what he is bargaining for there is no problem. For example, if he bargains for the surrender of the claim but only on the express condition that it is valid or that a certain condition exists, then, unless the condition or conditions exist or come to pass the party surrendering the claim will not prevail.

 WESTLAW REFERENCES

"invalid claim" /s detriment

"invalid claim" /s consideration

invalid unfounded +1 claim /s forbear!

26. See § 4–4 supra.

27. Restatement, Second, Contracts § 79, ill. 6.

28. 1 Corbin § 127 n. 76 discussing Neikirk v. Williams, 81 W.Va. 558, 94 S.E. 947 (1918); Restatement, Second, Contracts § 79, ill. 2.

29. 1 Corbin § 132.

§ 4–9. The Pre-existing Duty Rule

(a) Introduction

The pre-existing duty rule states that where a party does or promises to do what he is legally obligated to do or promises to refrain from doing or refrains for doing what he is not legally privileged to do he has not incurred detriment.[30] It is clear that if a party does only what he is legally obligated to do or less he is not suffering legal detriment because he is not surrendering a legal right.[31]

The pre-existing duty rule has been the subject of debate. Although the rule is a logical consequence of the doctrine of consideration and its requirement for detriment, it can be and has been argued that the rule can defeat the justifiable expectations of the parties. This is particularly true in the area of a modification of an existing contract where under the modified agreement one party is only doing what he is legally obligated to do.[32] Dissatisfaction with the rule has led to a number of exceptions, some of which are illogical or tenuous at best. These matters are discussed below as is the relationship between this rule and the topic of duress.[33]

(b) The Pre-existing Duty Rule: Duties Imposed by Law

The pre-existing duty rule applies not only to a modification of an existing contract but to a duty that is not contractual in nature—that is to say a duty imposed by law.[34] Thus, for example, if one promises to pay his or her spouse $1,000 at the end of the year if the spouse carries out the obligations of the marriage, the spouse would not be entitled to the money because the spouse would merely have performed a pre-existing legal duty.[35] Where a guest was by statute entitled to use the hotel safe to store valuables a promise by the guest to limit the liability

30. Agristor Credit Corp. v. Unruh, 571 P.2d 1220 (Okl.1977).

31. See § 4–3 supra; Hyatt v. Hyatt, 273 Pa.Super. 435, 417 A.2d 726 (1979); Hoffa v. Fitzsimmons, 673 F.2d 1345 (D.C. Cir.1982).

32. Rye v. Phillips, 203 Minn. 567, 282 N.W. 459 (1938) in which the court indicated in dictum that the rule would be discarded. This dictum was followed in Winter Wolff & Co. v. Co–Op. Lead & Chem. Co., 261 Minn. 199, 111 N.W.2d 461 (1961); Angel v. Murray, 113 R.I. 482, 322 A.2d 630 (1974); 1A Corbin § 171. See also Patterson, An Apology for Consideration, 58 Colum.L.Rev. 929, 936 (1958); Recter,

Courts, Consideration and Common Sense, 27 Toronto L.J. 439 (1977).

33. The topic of duress as it relates to a modification is discussed in Chapters 5 and 9.

34. 1 Williston, Contracts § 132; Keith v. Miles, 39 Miss. 442 (1860).

35. Salmeron v. United States, 724 F.2d 1357 (9th Cir.1983); Lee v. Savannah Guano Co., 99 Ga. 572, 27 S.E. 159 (1869); Young v. Cockman, 182 Md. 246, 34 A.2d 428 (1943); Ritchie v. White, 225 N.C. 450, 35 S.E.2d 414 (1945); Blaechinska v. Howard Mission & Home for Little Wanderers, 130 N.Y. 497, 29 N.E. 755 (1892).

of the hotel in exchange for using the safe is not supported by consideration because of the pre-existing duty rule.[36]

(c) The Pre-existing Duty Rule: Modification in a Two Party Case

If in August B hires A at $90 per week for one year the term to commence in November and in October the parties agree to modify the agreement so that the salary is to be $100 per week, B's promise to pay the additional $10 weekly is not enforceable because A has not suffered detriment. He is merely doing what he is legally obligated to do.[37] This involves a purported modification without consideration.[38] If, however, A assumed even a slight additional duty that was bargained for, there would be a binding modification with consideration.[39]

Again, if the parties had rescinded their original contract by mutual agreement and subsequently entered into a new employment agreement at a salary of $100 per week, the promise would be enforceable since A would have been under no obligation to B at the time the new agreement was entered into.[40] Note carefully that in this situation there are three separate and distinct agreements, each of which is supported by consideration. There is the initial agreement, the agreement of rescission in which each party gives up something, and finally the subsequent agreement. At the time of the subsequent agreement there is no pre-existing duty on the part of either party because their duties were discharged by the agreement of rescission.

Although the pre-existing duty rule is generally followed,[41] as indicated above, there are many decisions in which ingenuity has been

36. Goncalves v. Regent Intern. Hotels, Ltd., 58 N.Y.2d 206, 460 N.Y.S.2d 750, 447 N.E.2d 693 (1983), reargument denied 59 N.Y.2d 761, 463 N.Y.S.2d 1030, 450 N.E.2d 254 (1983).

37. Ruffin v. Mercury Record Productions, Inc., 513 F.2d 222 (6th Cir.1975), certiorari denied 423 U.S. 914, 96 S.Ct. 219, 46 L.Ed.2d 142 (1975); Alaska Packers' Ass'n v. Domenico, 54 C.C.A. 485, 117 Fed. 99 (1902); Continental Cas. Co. v. Wilson-Avery, Inc., 115 Ga.App. 793, 156 S.E.2d 152 (1967); Dunn v. Utica Mut. Ins. Co., 108 Ga.App. 368, 133 S.E.2d 60 (1963), 15 Mercer L.Rev. 506 (1964); Insurance Agents, Inc. v. Abel, 338 N.W.2d 531 (Iowa App. 1983); Healy v. Brewster, 59 Cal.2d 455, 30 Cal.Rptr. 129, 380 P.2d 817 (1963); Rudio v. Yellowstone Merchandising Corp., 200 Mont. 537, 652 P.2d 1163 (1982). See Corbin, Does a Pre-existing Duty Defeat Consideration, 27 Yale L.J. 362 (1918); Havighurst, Consideration, Ethics and Administration, 42 Colum.L.Rev. 1 (1942); Hillman, Contract Modification in Iowa— Recker v. Gustafson and the Resurrection of the Preexisting Duty Doctrine, 65 Iowa L.Rev. 343 (1980). Before the considera-tion question is reached, it is of course necessary to see if there was an agreement. It is often stated that a modification agreement must be demonstrated by clear and/ or satisfactory evidence. Grizzly Bar, Inc. v. Hartman, 169 Colo. 178, 454 P.2d 788 (1969); St. Louis Fire & Marine Ins. Co. v. Lewis, 230 So.2d 580 (Miss.1970).

38. W.L. Thaxton Constr. Co. v. O.K. Constr. Co., ___ W.Va. ___, 295 S.E.2d 822 (1982). See U.C.C. § 2–209(1) which permits a modification without consideration in cases involving the sale of goods discussed in § 5–14 infra.

39. West India Industries, Inc. v. Tradex, Tradex Petroleum Services, 664 F.2d 946 (5th Cir.1981); Blakeslee v. Board of Water Comm'rs, 106 Conn. 642, 139 A. 106 (1927).

40. Leonard v. Downing, 246 Ark. 397, 438 S.W.2d 327 (1969); Jura v. Sunshine Biscuits, 118 Cal.App.2d 442, 258 P.2d 90 (1953); Restatement, Contracts § 406, ill. 1.

41. Heckman & Shell v. Wilson, 158 Mont. 47, 487 P.2d 1141 (1971).

employed, in circumventing the rule, often on tenuous grounds. These decisions show that the courts are not impressed with the fairness of the rule.[42]

A number of cases have held the pre-existing duty rule does not apply where an existing agreement is subsequently rescinded by mutual agreement and the rescission and the new agreement are entered into simultaneously.[43] The rescission, however, must be express and not implied from the new agreement.[44] This is similar to the last case discussed above except there the rescission and the new agreement were not simultaneous but separated by an interval of time. Where the rescission and the subsequent agreement are simultaneous, the pre-existing duty rule is violated because the parties clearly intend the rescission to be contingent on the new contract, which, in turn, is contingent on the rescission.[45] The Restatement Second rejects these cases as employing fictions.[46]

Another exception to the pre-existing duty rule recognized by some jurisdictions is that a modification will be upheld even if it is without consideration if the modification was made after unforeseen difficulties had arisen in the performance of the prior agreement.[47] These decisions violate the pre-existing rule unless the difficulties encountered amount to impossibility or impracticability of performance, in which event the excuse given by the law for non-performance would erase the pre-existing duty problem.[48] Suppose A agrees to do excavation work for B for a stated price. When solid rock is unexpectedly encountered A notifies B and they agree that A will complete the job and that B will pay double the contract price, which is reasonable in relation to the work to be done. Under the pre-existing duty rule B's promise to pay double the price is not enforceable because the unforeseen difficulty did not amount to impossibility of performance and therefore did not excuse B from performing. In jurisdictions recognizing the exception the promise would be binding.

The Restatement Second has adopted the spirit of the exception. Its rule has also been strongly influenced by U.C.C. § 2–209(1), dis-

42. Angel v. Murray, 113 R.I. 482, 322 A.2d 630 (1974).

43. Martiniello v. Bamel, 255 Mass. 25, 150 N.E. 838 (1926); Schwartzreich v. Bauman-Basch, Inc., 231 N.Y. 196, 131 N.E. 887 (1921); cf. Frommeyer v. L. & R. Constr. Co., 261 F.2d 879 (3d Cir.1958).

44. Armour & Co. v. Celic, 294 F.2d 432 (2d Cir.1961). See Patterson, An Apology for Consideration, 58 Colum.L.Rev. 929 (1958).

45. 1 Williston § 130A; 1 Corbin § 186.

46. Restatement, Second, Contracts § 89, Comment b. But it reaches the same conclusion under § 89(a). See ill. 3.

47. Pittsburgh Testing Laboratory v. Farnsworth & Chambers Co., 251 F.2d 77 (10th Cir.1958); Lange v. United States, 120 F.2d 886 (4th Cir.1941); King v. Duluth M. & N. R. Co., 61 Minn. 482, 63 N.W. 1105 (1895); Watkins & Son v. Carrig, 91 N.H. 459, 21 A.2d 591, 138 A.L.R. 131 (1941).

48. Restatement, Contracts § 76, ill. 8; Burton v. Kenyon, 46 N.C.App. 309, 264 S.E.2d 808 (1980); McGovern v. New York, 234 N.Y. 377, 138 N.E. 26 (1923). Restatement, Second, Contracts § 89, Comment c, indicates that a decision such as the one in McGovern might in some states be based upon "statutes or constitutional provisions [which] flatly forbid the payment of extra compensation to Government contractors." See generally 1A Corbin § 184.

cussed below.[49]   It looks upon the exception as being fair and useful because a modification is "ancillary" to the original exchange.[50]   It states that a promise to modify "under a contract not fully performed on either side is binding if the modification is fair and equitable[51] in view of circumstances not anticipated when the contract was made." * * *[52]   An event that is foreseen as a remote possibility may, according to the Restatement Second, "be unanticipated for this purpose if it was not adequately covered in the agreement."[53]   Whether the modification is fair and equitable depends upon many factors.[54] Professor Eisenberg suggests that the doctrine of unconscionability does what this section was intended to achieve and does it better.[55]

There are a number of other theories adopted to defeat the pre-existing duty rule. The best known of these is based on the idea that a party suffers legal detriment in giving up his legal right to breach his contract.[56]   This is clearly unsound. Although a contracting party often can refuse to perform his agreement and respond in damages, his ability to breach his contract is neither a right nor a lawful exercise of power.[57]   The law has generally regarded a breach of contract to be as much a wrong as the commission of a tort,[58] although some economic

49. See § 5–14 infra.

50. Restatement, Second, Contracts § 89, Comment a.

51. Guilford Yacht Club Ass'n, Inc. v. Northeast Dredging, Inc., 438 A.2d 478 (Me.1981). See generally, Horowitz, The Historical Foundations of Modern Contract Law, 87 Harv.L.Rev. 917 (1974). The reference to "fair and equitable" seems to relate to the issue of duress. Comment b states in part, "The limitation to a modification which is 'fair and equitable' goes beyond the absence of coercion and requires an objectively demonstrable reason for seeking a modification." This language is found in Comment 2 to U.C.C. § 2–209, a comment which clearly deals with the issue of duress. See § 5–14 infra.

52. Restatement, Second, Contracts § 89(a); it is interesting to note that the position of the Second Restatement had been widespread in the nineteenth century. In Meech v. Buffalo, 29 N.Y. 198, 218 (1864), the following language appears. "The contractor, finding that the contract price must prove wholly inadequate on account of this hidden and wholly unforeseen obstacle, quitted the work and declined to proceed further without additional compensation. It was under these circumstances that the new agreement, providing for the additional compensation, was made; and the law will uphold it." One judge went further, saying, "It is conceded that the parties might have cancelled the agreement, and, if they could do this, they could certainly modify it." 29 N.Y. at 213–14.

53. Restatement, Second, Contracts § 89, Comment b.

54. Restatement, Second, Contracts § 89, ills. 4 and 5.

55. See Eisenberg, The Principles of Consideration, 67 Corn.L.Rev. 640, 644–649 (1982).

56. Swartz v. Lieberman, 323 Mass. 109, 80 N.E.2d 5 (1948). In Lattimore v. Harsen, 14 Johns. 330 (N.Y.1817), the court construed a contract containing a penalty clause as giving the defendant an option to perform or pay the penalty. The decision is clearly obsolete. Wirth & Hamid Fair Booking v. Wirth, 265 N.Y. 214, 192 N.E. 297 (1934); Bradshaw v. Millikin, 173 N.C. 432, 92 S.E. 161 (1917); Restatement, Contracts § 378; 11 Williston § 1444. And see Armstrong v. Stiffler, 189 Md. 630, 56 A.2d 808 (1948) ("Forfeiture and damage clauses are means to insure performance, not optional alternatives for performance.") 56 A.2d at 810.

57. Barbour, The "Right" to Breach a Contract, 16 Mich.L.Rev. 106 (1917), Selected Readings 500; Note, 55 L.Q.Rev. 1 (1939). It should also be noted that the mere fact that the business convenience of the promisor is served does not mean that the promisee has suffered a detriment or that the promisor has received legal benefit.

58. See 1A Corbin § 182.

analysts, who applaud "efficient breaches," regard this attitude as wrong.[59] In addition, a modifying promise that is not supported by consideration has been enforced under the Wisconsin rule which employs the fiction that the original consideration is imported into the new agreement.[60] A few jurisdictions have held that no consideration is required for a modifying agreement.[61] Still others have looked upon the modification as an attempt to mitigate damages.[62] A scattering of cases have held modification to be binding upon the theory of promissory estoppel.[63]

At the beginning of this section the pre-existing duty rule was criticized upon the ground that it is not reasonable for the law to prevent adult contracting parties from modifying their legal obligations even if there is no consideration. In conflict with the reasonableness of this last proposition is the realization that modifications are frequently agreed to under conditions that approach duress. In a typical situation, the building contractor threatens to terminate operations if the price is not increased. The landowner succumbs rather than face the pitfalls of litigation and the difficulty of procuring a substitute contractor with dispatch. Although the courts have generally followed the pre-existing duty rule there is a trend in the direction of making a modification without consideration binding.[64] At the same time the rules of duress are being changed in the case of modifications to make it easier to set aside a modification on grounds of duress. These matters are discussed elsewhere.[65]

(d) The Pre-existing Duty Rule: The Three Party Case

As we have just seen, if A, a jockey, enters into a bilateral contract with B, the owner of a horse, to ride in a race for $1,000 and the contract is modified by the parties to provide for compensation of $1,500, under the majority view the promise to pay more is not supported by consideration because A will only be doing what he is legally obligated to do. But if C, an outsider, who does not have a right to performance under the contract, but owns the dam of B's horse and would receive a prize if B's horse wins, promises to pay a bonus of $500

---

59. See Posner, Economic Analysis of Law 57 (1972).

60. Jacobs v. J.C. Penney Co., 170 F.2d 501 (7th Cir.1948); Everlite Mfg. Co. v. Grand Valley Machines & Tool Co., 44 Wis. 2d 404, 171 N.W.2d 188 (1969); Holly v. First Nat'l Bank of Kenosha, 218 Wis. 259, 260 N.W. 429 (1935); Mid-Century, Ltd. of American v. United Cigar-Whelan Stores Corp., 109 F.Supp. 433 (D.D.C.1953). Minnesota and New Hampshire seem to be in accord. See Kramas v. Beattie, 107 N.H. 321, 221 A.2d 236 (1966) and Rye v. Phillips, 203 Minn. 567, 282 N.W. 459 (1938). See also § 4–10.

61. Industrial Development Bd. of Town of Section, Alabama v. Fuqua Indus-

tries, Inc., 523 F.2d 1226 (5th Cir.1975) (Alabama law); see Shattuck, Contracts in Washington, 1937–1957, 34 Wash.L.Rev. 24, 58–59 (1959) (Washington contract law prior to 1937).

62. Scanlon v. Northwood, 147 Mich. 139, 110 N.W. 493 (1907); Evans v. Oregon & Washington R.R. Co., 58 Wash. 429, 108 P. 1095 (1910).

63. Canada v. Allstate Ins. Co., 411 F.2d 517 (5th Cir.1969); this matter is discussed in more detail in § 6–5 infra.

64. See § 5–13 infra. Note that section 89 of the Restatement Second mentioned above is part of the trend mentioned.

65. See § 5–15 infra.

to A if A rides, there are conflicting views as to whether C's promise is supported by consideration.[66]

The majority of courts have taken the traditional and rigorously logical view that since the jockey is merely promising to perform his legal obligation the agreement is a nullity.[67] The result is different even under this view if the third party bargains for and causes the original contracting parties to refrain from rescinding their previous agreement because in that event A and B have suffered a legal detriment because together they have a legal right to rescind; [68] so also if A merely gives up his right to make such a proposal to B.[69] But in either case the question is whether this is what C bargained for.

A second and untenable view would enforce the promise of C if the contract between the jockey and C is bilateral and not unilateral.[70] The fallacy in this is that it does not make any difference if the agreement is bilateral or unilateral because A's promise can be consideration only if the performance which is promised would be consideration and it is not.[71]

A third view is that C's promise is enforceable whether or not his arrangement with A is unilateral or bilateral. This view is ordinarily justified on one of two grounds. One approach is that C's promise should be enforced because A's pre-existing duty was owed to B and not to C.[72] As a result A confers a benefit upon C and some courts have held that a benefit conferred upon the promisor is sufficient even if there is no detriment.[73]

The second reason given is that there is less likelihood of duress or unfair pressure in the three party cases than in the two party cases.[74] This is the approach of the two Restatements.[75] Thus the Restatements say that there is consideration for C's promise but the Restatement Second adds that B may be the party who is entitled to the additional payment on the theory that A may be acting as the agent of B.[76] The Restatement Second, however, refuses to apply its rule if the pre-

---

66. See generally, Bronaugh, A Secret Paradox of the Common Law, 2 Law and Philosophy 193 (1983).

67. McDevitt v. Stokes, 174 Ky. 515, 192 S.W. 681 (1917); Arend v. Smith, 151 N.Y. 502, 45 N.E. 872 (1897).

68. De Cicco v. Schweizer, 221 N.Y. 431, 117 N.E. 807 (1917).

69. Restatement, Second, Contracts § 73, Comment d.

70. Beale, Notes on Consideration, 17 Harv.L.Rev. 71 (1903); Pollock, Afterthoughts on Consideration, 17 L.Q.R. 4 (1901).

71. See § 4–12 infra; 1 Williston § 131A.

72. Restatement, Second, Contracts § 73, Comment d.

73. Briskin v. Packard Motor Car Co., 269 Mass. 394, 169 N.E. 148 (1929); Neal v. Hagedorn Constr. Co., 192 N.C. 816, 135 S.E. 120 (1926). See § 4–2 supra. See also Morgan, Benefit to the Promisor as Consideration for a Second Promise for the Same Act, 1 Minn.L.Rev. 383 (1915), Selected Readings on Contracts 491 (1931).

74. Morrison Flying Serv. v. Deming Nat'l Bank, 404 F.2d 856 (10th Cir.1968), certiorari denied 393 U.S. 1020, 89 S.Ct. 628, 21 L.Ed.2d 565 (1969); Restatement, Second, Contracts § 73, Comment d.

75. Restatement, Contracts § 84(d); Restatement, Second, Contracts § 73, Comment d.

76. Restatement, Second, Contracts § 73, ill. 12.

existing duty is owed to the promisor as a member of the public.[77] For example the public duty of a police officer would prevent him from recovering a reward for performing an act within the scope of his employment.[78]

If the arrangement between the jockey and the owner was an offer to a unilateral contract, because the jockey would not be under a duty to perform, there could be no question of the pre-existing duty rule applying.

WESTLAW REFERENCES

(a) *Introduction*

"legally bound" /s consideration

"pre-existing duty rule"

"pre-existing duty" /s consideration

"pre-existing duty" /s support! (legal! +1 right obligat!) modif!

"pre-existing duty" /s promis! sufficien! insufficien!

(b) *The Pre-Existing Duty Rule: Duties Imposed by Law*

"pre-existing duty" /s law legal!

"pre-existing duty" /s requir! impos!

"pre-existing duty" /s statut!

lee +s "savannah guano"

"existing legal obligation" /s promis! consideration detriment

(c) *The Pre-Existing Duty Rule: Modification in a Two Party Case*

modif! /s consideration /s "pre existing duty" (legal! +1 obligat! bound)

"modification agreement" (contract*** /3 modif!) /s "pre existing duty" (legal! +1 bound obligat!)

modif! consideration /s exception /s "pre existing duty" (legal! +1 bound obligat!)

pittsburgh +s farnsworth

"pre-existing duty" (legal** +1 bound obligat!) /s foresee! unforesee! impossib! impractica! unexpected! /s perform! modif!

modif! /s promise /s "fair and equitable" /s perform!

"efficient breach"

forfeiture damage penalty +1 clause /s perform! /s breach!

modif! /s "promissory estoppel"

(d) *The Pre-Existing Duty Rule: The Three Party Cases*

briskin +s packard

---

77. Restatement, Second, Contracts § 73, Comment b.

78. Restatement, Second, Contracts § 73, ills. 1 and 2; Denney v. Reppert, 432

S.W.2d 647 (Ky.1968). This problem also presents overtones of illegality.

§ 4–10.   The Pre-existing Duty Rule: Agreements to Accept Part Payment as Satisfaction of a Debt: Pinnel's Case and Foakes v. Beer

In Pinnel's Case, Lord Coke in dictum stated "that payment of a lesser sum on the [due] day in satisfaction of a greater, cannot be any satisfaction of the whole, because it appears to the judges that by no possibility, a lesser sum can be a satisfaction of to the plaintiff for a greater sum." [79] What this means is that part payment by a debtor of an amount here and now undisputedly due is not detriment to support a promise by the creditor to discharge the entire amount due.[80] The same would be true if there was a purported present discharge as for example if the creditor delivered a release to the debtor.[81] Clearly this rule is a particular application of the pre-existing duty rule since the debtor in making part payment of an amount here and now undisputedly due is only doing what he is legally obligated to do. Since, consideration primarily relates to the enforcement of executory promises, the question of a present discharge of duties, as an original proposition could have been distinguished and exempted from the requirement of consideration.[82] Lord Coke's dictum was not put to the test in an authoritative fashion until the case of Foakes v. Beer [83] arose in 1884. The plaintiff had obtained a judgment of some £ 2000 against the defendant. The parties agreed that the plaintiff would accept in full satisfaction of the judgment, £ 500 in cash and the balance in installments. There was no promise to pay interest. The defendant fully complied with the agreement and the amount of the judgment was fully paid. Plaintiff subsequently brought suit for interest on the judgment. The defendant argued that pursuant to the agreement of the parties he was fully discharged. The House of Lords ruled that payment, even if bargained for in satisfaction of an obligation, could not discharge the obligation to pay interest which attached as a matter of law because defendant had only done what he was legally obligated to do.[84]

Despite its overwhelming acceptance, the rule of Foakes v. Beer has been persistently criticized. In Frye v. Hubbell,[85] the rule was

79. 77 Eng.Rep. 237 (1602).

80. Voight & McMakin Air Conditioning, Inc. v. Property Redevelopment Corp., 276 A.2d 239 (D.C.App.1971); In re Cunningham's Estate, 311 Ill. 311, 142 N.E. 740 (1924); Warren v. Hodge, 121 Mass. 106 (1876); Bunge v. Koop, 48 N.Y. 225 (1872); 1 Williston § 120.

81. See § 21–10 infra.

82. Schiffman v. Atlas Mill Supply, Inc., 193 Cal.App.2d 847, 14 Cal.Rptr. 708 (1961); 15 Williston § 1851; see § 4–2 supra.

83. 9 App.Cas. 605 (1884).

84. See generally, Ames, Two Theories of Consideration, 12 Harv.L.Rev. 515, 521–

531 (1899); Ferson, The Rule of Foakes v. Beer, 31 Yale L.J. 15 (1921); Hemingway, The Rule in Pennel's Case, 13 Va.L.Rev. 380 (1927); Gold, The Present Status of the Rule in Pinnel's Case, 30 Ky.L.J. 72, 187 (1942); Comment, 11 Ariz.L.Rev. 344 (1969).

85. 74 N.H. 358, 68 A. 325 (1907), further explained in Watkins & Son v. Carrig, 91 N.H. 459, 21 A.2d 591 (1941). This view was advanced in Rye v. Phillips, 203 Minn. 567, 282 N.W. 459 (1938) (dictum); cf. Winter Wolff & Co. v. Co–Op. Lead & Chemical Co., 261 Minn. 199, 111 N.W.2d 461 (1961).

rejected and it was held that part payment of a debt accepted in full payment discharged liability for the balance. A small number of other cases have followed this minority view.[86] Other cases have held that where unforseen hardships make full payment more onerous than anticipated acceptance of part payment will discharge the balance. This would occur, for example, if there was an economic depression and an impecunious debtor has made a part payment in satisfaction of the whole.[87] The Restatement Second seems to have adopted this rule.[88]

Even in jurisdictions that follow the rule of Foakes v. Beer, dissatisfaction with the rule have made the courts eager to ferret out some kind of detriment in the fact pattern. Lord Coke's dictum in Pinnel's Case indicated that delivery of a "horse, hawk or robe" in addition to or in place of part payment of the pre-existing debt would provide the necessary detriment to support the discharge of the debt. Of course the question of whether the detriment mentioned was bargained for must be examined and a pretense may not be enough.[89] Consideration has been found where the part payment was prior to the due date,[90] or was made at a place other than that stated in the agreement,[91] or if the debtor gives security in addition to the part payment,[92] or if the part payment is by a third person.[93] On the other hand it is generally held that the debtor's execution of his own promissory note or check is not sufficient consideration.[94] This holding is probably correct in most cases: the execution of a note or check, although a detriment, is rarely bargained for as such. If the creditor in fact bargained for the note or check to obtain evidence or secure facility of collection, consideration is present.[95]

More complicated problems have been presented where the debtor is insolvent. In making a part payment it is clear that the insolvent is only doing what he is legally obligated to do and therefore most courts have held that he is obligated to pay the balance.[96] But the situation is different if the debtor refrains from bankruptcy or insolvency proceedings at the request of the creditor[97] or if there is a composition agreement among creditors.[98]

---

86. See cases cited in note 85.

87. Liebreich v. Tyler State Bank & Trust Co., 100 S.W.2d 152 (Tex.Civ.App. 1936) (economic depression). As we have seen some courts have adopted the same rule with respect to a modification of an executory contract. See § 4–8 supra; Restatement, Second, Contracts § 89.

88. Restatement, Second, Contracts § 73, Comment c.

89. Restatement, Second, Contracts § 71, Comment b.

90. Codner v. Siegel, 246 Ga. 368, 271 S.E.2d 465 (1980); Princeton Coal Co. v. Dorth, 191 Ind. 615, 133 N.E. 386 (1921); see 1 Williston § 121 n. 7.

91. 1 Williston § 121 n. 9.

92. Jaffray v. Davis, 124 N.Y. 164, 26 N.E. 351 (1891).

93. Welsh v. Loomis, 5 Wn.2d 377, 105 P.2d 500 (1940).

94. Shanley v. Koehler, 80 App.Div. 566, 80 N.Y.S. 679 (1st Dep't 1903); cf. U.C.C. § 3–408.

95. Id.

96. 1 Williston § 120.

97. Melroy v. Kemmerer, 218 Pa. 381, 67 A. 699 (1907); Brown Shoe Co. v. Beall, 107 S.W.2d 456 (Tex.Civ.App.1937); Restatement, Second, Contracts § 73, ill. 6.

98. Although composition agreements are invariably sustained, there has been a certain amount of difficulty in ascertaining the consideration which sustains

There are decisions, even in states which adopt the rule of Foakes v. Beer, which are difficult to reconcile with the rule. It is generally held that if a creditor agrees, in consideration of part payment, to discharge a retiring partner, the promise is binding.[99] There are occasional decisions holding that when a promisee is entitled to money payable in installments, as for example, under a lease or separation agreement, acceptance of a lesser sum in full payment discharges the debtor as to that installment despite the absence of detriment.[1] This would not be true as to any unpaid future installment. These cases should be carefully compared with a case such as McKenzie v. Harrison.[2] A lease called for payment of $1250 per quarter. The lessor subsequently agreed to accept and accepted $875 per quarter. Upon each payment he gave the tenant a receipt marked "payment in full." On these facts alone, under the rule of Foakes v. Beer, the lessor would have the right to demand payment of the difference between the amount called for in the lease and the amount he received. The court, however, found that the lessor had a donative intent and the receipts constituted sufficient delivery of the gift.[3] As to future installments, the promise to accept reduced rental payments was not binding since gratuitous promises are unforceable.

them. As stated in Restatement, Contracts § 84, Comment d: "The consideration for which each assenting creditor bargains may be any or all of the following: (1) part payment of the sum due him; (2) the promise of each other creditor to forgo a portion of his claim; (3) forbearance (or promise thereof) by the debtor to pay the assenting creditors more than equal proportions; (4) the action of the debtor in securing the assent of the other creditors; (5) the part payment made to other creditors. Of these, number 1 is not a sufficient consideration; but each of the other four is sufficient. Numbers 4 and 5 are seldom bargained for in fact; but numbers 2 and 3 are practically always bargained for, by reasonable implication if not in express terms. Still other considerations may be agreed upon in any case." See Massey v. Del-Valley Corp., 46 N.J.Super. 400, 134 A.2d 802 (1957); White v. Kuntz, 107 N.Y. 518, 14 N.E. 423 (1887); A. & H. Lithoprint, Inc. v. Bernard Dunn Advertising Co., 82 Ill.App.2d 409, 226 N.E. 2d 483 (1967).

99. Ludington v. Bell, 77 N.Y. 138, 23 Am.R. 601 (1879); 1 Williston § 123 (pointing out the possibility of detriment in the event of subsequent insolvency); see also J. Crane and A. Bromberg, Law of Partnership 450 (1968) who state that "Changing a joint obligation as partners into a separate obligation, thereby giving the creditor a parity with other creditors of the separate estate, will operate as consideration." Query, is this the bargained for consideration?

1. Julian v. Gold, 214 Cal. 74, 3 P.2d 1009 (1931); Russo v. De Bella, 220 N.Y.S.2d 587 (1961); see Annot., 30 A.L.R.3d 1259 (1970); contra, Levine v. Blumenthal, 117 N.J.L. 23, 186 A. 457 (1936), affirmed 117 N.J.L. 426, 189 A. 54 (1937); Pape v. Rudolph Bros., 257 App. Div. 1032, 13 N.Y.S.2d 781 (4th Dep't 1939), affirmed 282 N.Y. 692, 26 N.E.2d 817 (1940). This type of case is discussed in more detail in the chapter on Discharge, ch. 21 infra. Cf. Restatement, Contracts § 416.

2. 120 N.Y. 260, 24 N.E. 458 (1890); see also Gray v. Barton, 55 N.Y. 68 (1873).

3. In McKenzie v. Harrison the court found a completed gift because in its judgment there was evidence of donative intent and sufficient delivery. But see Brown, Personal Property § 8.5 (3d ed. 1975). In the cases listed in note 1, there could not possibly be sufficient delivery so that the finding of a gift is precluded. But see Restatement, Second, Contracts § 275, Comment a, ill. 2 and § 21–12 infra.

Injurious reliance on the creditor's promise to accept part payment in full satisfaction of an obligation could result in enforceability of the promise [4] under the doctrine of promissory estoppel discussed below.[5]

Statutory changes in the rule of Foakes v. Beer, discussed below, have been made in a number of jurisdictions and by the Uniform Commercial Code.[6]

WESTLAW REFERENCES

"part***   payment"   /s   (legal!   +1   bound obligat!)   "pre existing duty"

"pre-existing duty" (legal!   +1   bound obligat!)   /s   satisf!   /s debt indebtedness

consideration   /s   "part***   payment"   /s   discharg! satisf!   /s debt indebtedness

foakes   +s   beer

"pinnel's case"

"part***   payment"   /s   consideration   /s   insolven! "composition agreement" bankrupt!

§ 4–11. The Doctrine of Accord and Satisfaction—Of Liquidated and Unliquidated Claims

(a) Introduction

Earlier, in section 4–8, the settlement of claims was discussed. The focus was on the surrender of, or forbearance from pursuing an invalid claim as consideration for a promise made to the claimant. In this section we shall discuss the other side of the transaction. The claimant is asserting that his agreement to discharge a claim or his purported discharge of the claim is not supported by consideration.

(b) Discussion

The rule of Foakes v. Beer (discussed in § 4–10) applies only to liquidated claims: that is, claims that are undisputed as to their existence and where the amount due has been agreed upon or can be precisely determined. On the other hand if there is a dispute as to liability or the amount due or even as to some other question, for example the method of payment, the claim is generally said to be unliquidated even if a party's assertion is incorrect provided that the assertion is made in good faith and, according to some jurisdiction, if it is reasonably asserted.[7]

An accord is an offer to give or to accept a stipulated performance in the future in satisfaction or discharge of the obligor's existing duty

4. Central London Property Trust, Ltd. v. High Trees House, Ltd. [1947] 1 K.B. 130.

5. See ch. 6 infra. In re Stein's Estate, 50 Misc.2d 627, 271 N.Y.S.2d 449 (1966).

6. See § 5–16 infra.

7. Tanner v. Merrill, 108 Mich. 58, 65 N.W. 664 (1895); Fuller v. Kemp, 138 N.Y.

231, 33 N.E. 1034 (1893); Restatement, Second, Contracts § 74, Comments b and c. See also Eames Vacuum Brake Co. v. Prosser, 157 N.Y. 289, 51 N.E. 986 (1898); Restatement, Contracts § 420; 1 Williston § 128; 1A Corbin § 188.

plus an acceptance of that offer.[8] The performance of this stipulated performance is the satisfaction.[9] If the agreement is not performed then the special rules relating to breach of an accord apply. These rules are discussed below.[10] Also discussed at the same point is a more detailed discussion of how the rules of accord and satisfaction apply in a situation that does not involve the rule of Foakes v. Beer.

When a question of accord and satisfaction is presented the analysis should be divided into three parts. 1) Have the parties gone through a process of offer and acceptance (accord)? 2) Has the accord reached been carried out (satisfaction)? Once it is determined that there is an offer and acceptance and that the agreement has been performed, the third question is whether the offer and acceptance is supported by consideration.[11] If so there is a binding accord and satisfaction; if not one could say that there is no accord and satisfaction or that any accord and satisfaction reached is not binding. The wording of the conclusion is not important since the result is the same.

The rule relating to an offer of accord is that the offer must make it clear that the offeror seeks a total discharge. If this is not done any payment made and accepted will be treated as part payment.[12] An acceptance of such an offer may take place by verbal assent or by conduct including under most authorities the cashing of a check sent "in full payment" or according to some authorities by the retention of such check. All of these matters and others will be explored in greater detail below and clarified by a discussion of the following six fact patterns.

(c) Cases

Case 1. The debtor, D, owes C, the creditor $100 here and now undisruptedly due, the claim is liquidated. D sends a check for $50 marked "payment in full" and C cashes the check. What is the result?

We have already seen that the offer of accord must make it clear that the offeror is seeking a complete discharge. Do the quoted words achieve this result? According to the vast majority of the cases they do.[13] But there is a growing number of recent cases to the effect that this language is only one of the factors to be considered in determining

---

8. Electric Ad Sign Co., Inc. v. Cedar Rapids Truck Center, 316 N.W.2d 876 (Iowa 1982); Christensen v. Abbott, 595 P.2d 900 (Utah 1979), appeal after remand 671 P.2d 121 (1983).

9. Id.

10. See §§ 21–4 to 21–7 inclusive infra.

11. Geisco, Inc., v. Honeywell, Inc., 682 F.2d 54 (2d Cir.1982).

12. See Calamari, The New York "Check Cashing" Rule, 1 N.Y.C.L.E. No. 2, p. 113 (1963); Scantlin v. Superior Homes, Inc., 6 Kan.App.2d 144, 627 P.2d 825 (1981); Pincus-Litman Co., Inc. v. Canon U.S.A., Inc., 98 A.D.2d 681, 469 N.Y.S.2d 756 (1st Dep't 1983); Hall GMC, Inc. v. Crane Carrier Co., 332 N.W.2d 54 (N.D.1983). The burden of proof on this issue is on the party who asserts the existence of the accord and satisfaction. Bryson v. Kenney, 430 A.2d 1102 (Me. 1981). But see Sam Finley, Inc. v. Barnes, 147 Ga.App. 432, 249 S.E.2d 147 (1978), appeal after remand 156 Ga.App. 802, 275 S.E.2d 380 (1980).

13. Calamari, The New York "Check Cashing" rule, 1 N.Y.C.L.E. No. 2, p. 113 (1963).

whether an offer of accord has been made.[14] Of course, the precise words "payment in full" are not necessary, it is enough that the intent to obtain a total discharge is manifested.[15] At times, on particular language and under particular circumstances, courts have had difficulty in making this determination.[16]

Assuming the existence of an offer of accord, the second question would be one of acceptance. Most cases hold that the cashing of the check would amount to an acceptance.[17] Beyond that, many cases have held that the retention of the check for an unreasonable period is the same as cashing it and therefore operates as an acceptance.[18] A second view is that the retention of the check does not amount to an acceptance.[19] Still other cases have held that the retention of the check creates a question of fact on this issue of acceptance.[20]

Assuming an offer and acceptance the next issue is performance. As explained in more detail later the cashing of the check may operate not only as the necessary acceptance but also as the completion of performance.

On the facts, the alleged accord and satisfaction is not supported by consideration because the claim is here and now undisputedly due. Thus, under the rule of Foakes v. Beer there is no consideration to support C's promise to take or his actual taking of a lesser amount in full satisfaction.[21] In other words D is only doing what he was legally obligated to do. The rule stated here would not apply to the satisfaction of a judgment where the satisfaction is entered on the record.[22]

Case 2. If we assume the same facts as in Case 1 but further assume that there was a good faith dispute between the parties, what would be the result? For example, assume C tells D that he is entitled to $100 and D replies that C is only entitled to $50, D then sends a check for $75 marked "payment in full" and C cashes it. Is there a binding accord and satisfaction? The issues of offer, acceptance and

14. Ensley v. Fitzwater, 59 Or.App. 411, 651 P.2d 734 (1982); Kibler v. Garrett & Sons, Inc., 73 Wn.2d 523, 439 P.2d 416 (1968).

15. Hastings v. Top Cut Feedlots, Inc., 285 Or. 261, 590 P.2d 1210 (1979).

16. See, for example, Kibler v. Garrett & Sons, Inc., 73 Wn.2d 523, 439 P.2d 416 (1968).

17. Mobil Oil Corp. v. Prive, 137 Vt. 370, 406 A.2d 400 (1979); Malarchick v. Pierce, 264 N.W.2d 478 (N.D.1978). Some contrary cases are discussed in 15 Williston § 1854.

18. Morris v. Aetna Life Ins. Co., 160 Ga.App. 484, 287 S.E.2d 388 (1981); FCX, Inc. v. Ocean Oil Co., 46 N.C.App. 755, 266 S.E.2d 388 (1980); Malarchick v. Pierce, 264 N.W.2d 478 (N.D.1978). Furgat Tractor & Equipment, Inc. v. Lynn, 135 Vt. 329, 376 A.2d 760 (1977). So also if the check is

cashed and not honored. Curran v. Bray Wood Heel Co., 116 Vt. 21, 68 A.2d 712, 717 (1949) or if a check is deposited and withdrawn, Peckham Industries, Inc. v. A.F. Lehmann, 49 A.D.2d 172, 374 N.Y.S. 2d 144 (3d Dep't 1975).

19. Cole Associates, Inc. v. Holsman, 181 Ind.App. 431, 391 N.E.2d 1196 (1979).

20. American Oil Co. v. Studstill, 230 Ga. 305, 196 S.E.2d 847 (1973); Hoffman v. Ralston Purina Co., 86 Wis.2d 445, 273 N.W.2d 214 (1979).

21. See § 4–10 supra; Air Power, Inc. v. Omega Equipment Corp., 54 Md.App. 534, 459 A.2d 1120 (1983); Adams v. B.P.C., Inc., 143 Vt. 308, 466 A.2d 1170 (1983).

22. Hazelwood Lumber Co., Inc. v. Smallhoover, 500 Pa. 180, 455 A.2d 108 (1982).

performance are the same as Case 1. Here it is clear that there is consideration to support the accord and satisfaction because of the existence of the good faith dispute and a compromise which involved the surrender of detriment by both parties.[23]

What is the key difference between the two cases? In the first case it is stated as a fact that the sum of $100 was "here and now undisputedly due" whereas the second case talks in terms of a "good faith dispute." [24] When the first case says that the $100 was here and now undisputedly due, it assumes that there was no good faith dispute and no basis for any dispute. But don't the words "payment in full" without more indicate the possibility of a good faith dispute? One answer appears to be that if there is no dispute this phrase does not create one but if there is a basis for a dispute the words are sufficient to indicate a dispute even though the other party does not know the basis of the dispute.[25] However, other cases have said that an accord and satisfaction will not arise unless the other party is aware of the basis of the dispute.[26]

Case 3. Assume the same facts as in Case 2 except that while D admits that he owes $50 he sends a check in that amount and C cashes the check. As above, according to the majority view there is offer, acceptance and performance.[27] This fact pattern, however, produces a division of authority on the issue of consideration. The majority of the courts have held that claim is unliquidated and from this premise have concluded that there is consideration to support the accord and satisfaction.[28] This is a non sequitur. Even though the claim is unliquidated it does not follow that D is doing any more than he is legally obligated to do. A minority of courts have adopted the position that he is only doing what he is legally obligated to do.[29] Professor Corbin agrees with the logic of the minority view but sides with the majority for policy reasons involving the notion that the law favors resolution of disputes.[30]

23. In re Lloyd, Carr and Co., 617 F.2d 882 (1st Cir.1980); Flowers v. Diamond Shamrock Corp., 693 F.2d 1146 (5th Cir. 1982); Amino Bros. Co. v. Twin Caney Watershed (Joint) Dist. No. 34 of Chautauqua, 206 Kan. 68, 476 P.2d 228 (1970); Lafferty v. Cole, 339 Mich. 223, 63 N.W.2d 432 (1954); Farmland Service Coop., Inc. v. Jack, 196 Neb. 263, 242 N.W.2d 624 (1976); cf. Gottlieb v. Charles Scribner's Sons, 232 Ala. 33, 166 So. 685 (1936) (dispute related to the method rather than the amount of payment).

24. Grettenberger Pharmacy, Inc. v. Blue Cross–Blue Shield of Michigan, 98 Mich.App. 1, 296 N.W.2d 589 (1980).

25. Corbin § 187; Gottlieb v. Charles Scribner's Sons, 232 Ala. 33, 166 So. 685 (1936).

26. Holm v. Hansen, 248 N.W.2d 503 (Iowa 1976); Matter of Leckie's Estate, 54 A.D.2d 205, 388 N.Y.S.2d 858 (4th Dep't 1976); Hagerty Oil Company v. Chester County Security Fund, Inc., 248 Pa.Super. 456, 375 A.2d 186 (1977); Cannon v. Stevens School of Business, Inc., 560 P.2d 1383 (Utah 1977).

27. See discussion in Cases 1 and 2.

28. Air Van Lines, Inc. v. Buster, 673 P.2d 774 (Alaska 1983); Van Riper v. Baker, 61 Or.App. 540, 658 P.2d 537 (1983), review denied 295 Or. 122, 666 P.2d 1344 (1983); Chicago & North Western Transportation Co. v. Thoreson Food Products, Inc., 71 Wis.2d 143, 238 N.W.2d 69 (1976).

29. Medd v. Medd, 291 N.W.2d 29 (Iowa 1980).

30. 6 Corbin § 1289.

The Restatement Second in discussing this case concludes that there is consideration to support the accord and satisfaction if D is not contractually bound by his admission.[31] The original Restatement took the position that D was not bound by his admission and that there would be an accord and satisfaction.[32] The Restatement Second adds, "But payment of less than is admittedly due may in some circumstances tend to show that a partial defense or offset was not asserted in good faith."[33] The original Restatement seems to indicate the contrary.[34]

The majority view in Case 3 unfairly places the creditor on the horns of a dilemma for he must either return the check even though it is in an amount concededly due or cash it and forgo the balance of his claim. Creditors have sought to evade this harsh result by striking out the words "payment in full" written on the check or by notifying the debtor that he is cashing the check in part payment, but to no avail.[35] For in cashing the check in violation of the conditions upon which it was tendered, the creditor is held to assent to its terms much as in the cases where an offeree exercises dominion over unordered personal property sent him.[36] In the words of Chief Judge Cardozo, "protest will be unavailing if the money is retained. What is said is overridden by what is done, and assent imputed as an inference of law."[37] Thus in this type of case assent is imputed rather than actual.[38] Just as the offeree of a contract for the sale of goods can be estopped from claiming he took and used the goods as a converter,[39] one who cashes a check is estopped from alleging that he acted in violation of the conditions on which it was tendered. According to some authorities, however, cash-

31. Restatement, Second, Contracts § 74, Comment c. It does not answer the question of whether D is bound by his admission.

32. Restatement, Contracts § 420, ill. 2.

33. Restatement, Second, Contracts § 74, Comment c.

34. Restatement, Contracts § 420, ill. 2. See also, American Food Purveyors, Inc. v. Lindsay Meats, Inc., 153 Ga.App. 383, 265 S.E.2d 325 (1980).

35. Chrietzberg v. Kristopher Woods, Ltd., 162 Ga.App. 517, 292 S.E.2d 100 (1982); Hannah v. James A. Ryder Corp., 380 So.2d 507 (Fla.App.1980); Goes v. Feldman, 8 Mass.App.Ct. 84, 391 N.E.2d 943 (1979); Olson v. Wilson & Co., 244 Iowa 895, 58 N.W.2d 381 (1953); Nassoiy v. Tomlinson, 148 N.Y. 326, 42 N.E. 715 (1896). But see 6 Corbin § 1279.

36. See § 2–19 supra and 15 Williston § 1854.

37. RTL Corp. v. Manufacturer's Enterprises, Inc., 429 So.2d 855 (La.1983), on remand 444 So.2d 144 (1983); T.B.M.

Properties v. Arcon Corp., 346 N.W.2d 202 (Minn.App.1984); Hudson v. Yonkers Fruit Co., 258 N.Y. 168, 171, 179 N.E. 373, 374 (1932); Welbourne & Purdy, Inc. v. Mahon, 54 A.D.2d 1046, 388 N.Y.S.2d 369 (3d Dep't 1976). If the check is inadvertently cashed, the cases are split on the question of whether the effect of the cashing may be set aside for mistake. Relief on the grounds of mistake was granted in Dalrymple Gravel & Contracting Co. v. State, 23 A.D.2d 418, 261 N.Y.S.2d 566 (3d Dep't 1965), affirmed 19 N.Y.2d 644, 278 N.Y.S. 2d 616, 225 N.E.2d 210 (1967); cf. Hotz v. Equitable Life Assur. Soc. of United States, 224 Iowa 552, 276 N.W. 413 (1937); see also Teledyne Mid-America Corp. v. HOH Corp., 486 F.2d 987 (9th Cir.1973); Kirk Williams Co., Inc. v. Six Industries, Inc., 11 Ohio App.3d 152, 463 N.E.2d 1266 (1983) (bookkeeper who made deposit lacked authority to contract); see McKinney's N.Y. State Finance Law § 145.

38. Most of what is said in this paragraph applies also to Case 2.

39. See § 2–9 supra.

ing the check under protest may reserve the rights of the creditor if the transaction is governed by the U.C.C.[40]

Case 4. Plaintiff (P) and defendant (D) entered into an agreement that specified the work to be done by P and that D would pay $6,000 when the work was completed. On completion D complained that there were certain defects in performance. The parties discussed the matter and settled the claim for $5,500 and D later sent P a check for $5,500 and P cashed it. On these facts it is clear that there is an accord and satisfaction. Here there is an express agreement of accord and satisfaction but unlike Cases 1, 2, and 3 the offer and acceptance took place prior to the sending and cashing of the check and thus the sending and cashing do not involve offer and acceptance (for that has already occurred) but relate only to the performance of the agreement. In the first three cases discussed above the cashing of the check amounts both to the acceptance and the performance of the accord.[41]

Case 5. P owned a quantity of apples and requested D to obtain a purchaser, which D did, collecting the price. P claimed the service was to be gratuitous; D that there was an agreement to pay him a 10% commission. P cashed the check but immediately protested to D that the deduction was erroneous and P subsequently brought suit for the amount of the deduction. The jury found for P thus accepting P's version that the service was gratuitous. The New York Appellate Division reversed on the ground that P's cashing of the check created a binding accord and satisfaction.[42] This is in accord with the majority view discussed in Case 3 above. However, the New York Court of Appeals reversed not because it did not agree with the majority rule in Case 3 above, but because it found that there is an important distinction in the two cases. In Case 3 the relationship between D and C was debtor-creditor. In this case the relationship between the plaintiff and defendant was principal and agent—a fiduciary relationship. The court states the importance of the distinction in two ways. First that a debtor paying his own money may attach the condition that the check is sent in full payment but that where, as here, the agent-defendant was accounting for money belonging to this principal even though the agent may have had a claim against his principal he may not lawfully impose such a condition. Second that to allow a fiduciary to proceed in this way is "a flagrant abuse of the opportunities and powers of a fiduciary position."[43]

An interesting question is what would be the result in Case 2 (where there is a compromise) if it is also assumed that there was a fiduciary relationship. The court expressly left this question open. The court also makes it clear that the assent in the actual case was imputed. Would the result be different if the assent were not imputed?

40. See the discussion at the end of this section.

41. Sherwin–Williams Co. v. Sarrett, 419 So.2d 1332 (Miss.1982).

42. Hudson v. Yonkers Fruit Co., 233 App.Div. 884, 250 N.Y.S. 991 (3d Dep't 1931).

43. Hudson v. Yonkers Fruit Co., 258 N.Y. 168, 171, 179 N.E. 373, 374 (1932).

Presumably not, because the public policy should protect the principal even though he does not protest.[44] There are contrary cases.[45] Again what is it that makes the assent imputed? Apparently there is imputed assent when there is prompt protest.[46]

Case 6. Defendant (D) in exchange for plaintiff's (P) promise to do certain work promised P, among other things that P would receive ⅓ of the receipts from the product of D's dairy. This contract was entered into on October 7, 1904. Prior to this arrangement P had been working for D on a daily (per diem) basis and as of March 1, 1905, there was concededly due to P on this per diem arrangement the sum of $17.15. Soon after March 1, 1905, P received $17.15 from D and signed and delivered a receipt stating the $17.15 was received in "full of all accounts and demands to date." P's action relates to an amount allegedly due to him on the second contract for the period between October 7, 1904 and March 1, 1905. The trial court found that there was an accord and satisfaction and there is some logic to this conclusion because the case is similar to Case 3.

The New York Court of Appeals reversed.[47] The court could have said that there was no accord and satisfaction because D did not make it sufficiently clear that the offer related to both arrangements.[48] However, the court states a much broader proposition when it says, "The payment of an admitted liability is not a payment of or a consideration for an alleged accord and satisfaction of another and independent alleged liability." [49]

The important factor is not that there is an admitted liability because that is the situation in Case 3 where under the majority view there is a binding accord and satisfaction supported by consideration. Thus, there is no consideration because payment of a liquidated obligation is not consideration to support the surrender of a second claim that is wholly distinct.[50] If the disputed claim is closely related to the undisputed claim, payment of the amount admittedly due on one claim may be consideration for the surrender of the two claims in the absence of unfair pressure or economic coercion.[51] Whether the claims are separate or not is a most obscure question,[52] and actually the obscurity of the question serves as a safety-valve that a court can use to insure that justice is done in a particular case.

The common law rules discussed above may have been changed by the U.C.C. Section 1–207 of the Code which provides:

44. The assent of the creditor, whether expressed or inputed, should be immaterial when there is an abuse of the powers of a fiduciary.

45. 15 Williston § 1854.

46. 15 Williston § 1854.

47. Manse v. Hossington, 205 N.Y. 33, 98 N.E. 203 (1912).

48. Mademoiselle Fashions, Inc. v. Buccaneer Sportswear, Inc., 11 Ark.App. 158, 668 S.W.2d 45 (1984); Messick v. PHD Trucking Service, Inc., 615 P.2d 1276 (Utah 1980), appeal after remand 678 P.2d 791 (1984).

49. Manse v. Hossington, 205 N.Y. 33, 98 N.E. 203 (1912).

50. 1A Corbin § 188.

51. Restatement, Second, Contracts § 74, Comment c.

52. 1A Corbin § 188.

"A party who with explicit reservation of rights performs or promises performance or assents to performance in a manner demanded or offered by the other party does not thereby prejudice the rights reserved. Such words as 'without prejudice', 'under protest' or the like are sufficient."

Commentaries to the U.C.C. in five states,[53] indicated that a check tendered in full payment could be cashed under protest so as to reserve the creditor's claim to the balance allegedly due. While most textbooks ignored the relationship between 1–207 and the rules governing accord and satisfaction, at least three treatises took the position that a reservation of rights written on a full payment check was made possible by this provision.[54] The first three cases to discuss this relationship were in accord,[55] although law review commentary was mostly to the contrary.[56] In 1978 Dean Rosenthal published a thought-provoking article [57] questioning whether § 1–207 is applicable to the formation of an accord and satisfaction in the check cashing context. While also making textual and historical arguments, the main thrust of his article is that the common law rules as applied to check cashing cases are sensible and provide a simple means for resolving disputes. A later article by Professor Caraballo focuses on the phrase "explicit reservation of rights," pointing out that a reservation of rights marked on a check and then cashed explicates nothing to the debtor prior to its cashing and therefore, he argues, fails to meet the statutory test.[58] Since publication of the 1978 article a majority of jurisdiction that have ruled on the issue have held that Section 1–207 is inapplicable to the rules of accord and satisfaction in the check cashing context and governs primarily waivers and modifications.[59]

However, the New York Court of Appeals, in a recent well reasoned opinion, refused to adopt the view that U.C.C. § 1–207 does not

---

53. Delaware, Florida, Massachusetts, New Hampshire, New York. See Rosenthal, Discord and Dissatisfaction: Section 1–207 of the Uniform Commercial Code, 78 Colum.L.Rev. 48, 61–63 (1978).

54. 1 Anderson, Uniform Commercial Code 186 (2d ed. 1970); Calamari & Perillo, Contracts 168 (1970), p. 197 (2d ed. 1977); White & Summers, Uniform Commercial Code 453 (1972) pp. 545–47 (2d ed. 1980). Is there a clear cut distinction between a discharge by way of an accord and satisfaction and a modification? See Anderson, The Part Payment Check under the Code, 9 Am.Bus.L.J. 103 (1971). A modification under the Code does not require consideration. See § 5–14 infra.

55. Hanna v. Perkins, 2 U.C.C.Rep. Serv. 1044 (Co.Ct.N.Y.1965) (Dictum); Baillie Lumber Co. v. Kincaid Carolina Corp., 4 N.C.App. 342, 167 S.E.2d 85 (1969) (alternative holding); Scholl v. Tallman, 247 N.W.2d 490 (S.D.1976).

56. Hawkland, The Effect of U.C.C. § 1–207 on the Doctrine of Accord and Satisfaction by Conditional Check, 74 Comm.L.J. 329 (1969); Comment, 18 Buffalo L.J. 539 (1969); Comment, 11 Creighton L.Rev. 515 (1969); but see Anderson, The Part Payment Check under the Code, 9 Am.Bus.L.J. 103, 131 (1971); Comment, 1 Mem.St.U.L.Rev. 425 (1971).

57. Rosenthal supra note 53.

58. Caraballo, The Tender Trap: U.C.C. § 1–207 and Its Applicability to an Attempted Accord and Satisfaction by Tendering a Check in a Dispute Arising from a Sale of Goods, 11 Seton Hall L.Rev. 445 (1981); see also McDonnell, Purposive Interpretation of the Uniform Commercial Code: Some Implications for Jurisprudence, 126 Pa.L.Rev. 795, 824–28 (1978).

59. See Les Schwab Tire Centers of Oregon, Inc. v. Ivory Ranch, Inc., 63 Or.App. 364, 664 P.2d 419 (1983) (collecting cases).

apply to an accord and satisfaction in a check cashing case.[60] The decision, after taking note of the split of authority, and after delineating the arguments and considerations on both sides of the issue states its reasons for concluding that section 1–207 does apply in the case of a full payment check.

These include: (1) the rule of U.C.C. § 1–207 is a fairer rule than the traditional common law rule; (2) the language of section 1–207, taken literally, makes it clear that the section was designed to cover the accord and satisfaction problem; (3) a literal reading of the section promotes "the underlying policies and purposes of the Code." In other words one of the purposes of the Code is "to modernize" the law governing commercial transactions.[61]

The case also deals with another important problem under U.C.C. § 1–207. Assuming that the section relates to an accord and satisfaction will it apply only where the underlying transaction is a Code-covered transaction? In the case under discussion the underlying transaction was an action for work, labor and services. This is not a Code-covered transaction. However, the case involves check cashing, and a check is a negotiable instrument covered by Article 3 of the Code. The question is whether the use of a check brings the case within § 1–207 even though the underlying transaction is not a Code-covered transaction. The Court concludes that the transaction is covered by U.C.C. § 1–207.[62]

This case goes contrary to what is the majority view on the question of whether § 1–207 relates to an accord and satisfaction in a check cashing context. It shows that this question is far from settled and that this question eventually will be adjudicated by the highest court of each jurisdiction. In any state where this has not yet occurred it would be wise for the debtor, when issuing a full payment check, to add language restricting the creditor's right to reserve his rights.[63]

A New York statute (McKinney's N.Y.Gen'l Obl.Law § 5–1103) also raises an interesting question in the area of accord and satisfaction. We have previously seen that where D owes C a liquidated debt and he sends a check for a lesser amount the debt is not discharged even if D

---

60. Horn Waterproofing Corp. v. Bushwick Iron & Steel Co., Inc., 66 N.Y.2d 321, 497 N.Y.S.2d 310, 488 N.E.2d 56 (1985). For a recent contrary opinion, see Marton Remodeling v. Jensen, 706 P.2d 607 (Utah 1985). See also Annot., 37 A.L.R. 4th 773 (1985).

61. "Still, where the creditor is presented with partial payment as satisfaction in full, but nevertheless, wishes to preserve his claim to the balance left unpaid, it cannot be gainsaid that conflicting considerations of policy and fairness are implicated. This is particularly so in the case of a full payment check. On the one hand, the debtor, as master of his offer, has reason to

expect that his offer will either be accepted or his check returned. At the same time, however, the creditor has good cause to believe that he is fully entitled to retain the partial payment that is rightfully his and presently in his possession without having to forfeit entitlement to whatever else is his due." (id. at 325, 497 N.Y.S.2d at 312.)

62. Rosenthal, supra note at 53. But see Comment, 1 Mem.St.U.L.Rev. 425 (1971).

63. For suggested language see Hawkland, note 53, supra at 342.

sends a check marked "payment in full" and C cashes it. D is only doing what he is legally obligated to do and there is therefore no consideration and the alleged accord and satisfaction is therefore invalid.[64] What is the result under the New York Statute in such a case? It could be argued that the phrase "payment in full" is a writing and that the creditor's endorsement of the check is a signing within the meaning of the statute and that therefore there is an accord and satisfaction since, because of the statutory provision, consideration is not necessary to support it. However, this argument appears to have been rejected by the New York cases.[65] The apparent rationale is that such endorsement does not show the kind of circumspection and deliberateness that the writing requirement was intended to ensure.[66]

WESTLAW REFERENCES

(b) Discussion

unliquidated /s claim debt indebtedness liab! /s "good faith"
   "reasonabl! asser!"

unliquidated /s disput /s faith assert!

di accord

accord /s discharg! /s duty

"existing duty" /s discharg!

"existing duty" /s accord

di satisfaction

satisfaction /s "existing duty"

accord /s satisfaction /s perform! /s duty

accord /4 breach!

"burden of proof" /s accord /s satisfaction

8k26(1)

"part*** payment" /s offer /s accord

accord /s accept! /s "part*** payment"

accord /s accept! /s paid payment /2 full*

(c) Cases

  Case 1

retain! retention /s check /s accord

accord /s satisfaction /s accept! /s cash*** /s check

accord /s satisf! /s consideration /s due

accord /s satisf! /s legal! +l obligat! bound

  Case 2

accord /s satisf! /s compromis!

accord /s satisf! /s "good faith"

accord /s satisf! /s detriment

64. See Case 1 supra. The statute would seem to apply where a creditor states in a signed writing that he will take a lesser amount in discharge of a liquidated debt and the lesser amount is paid by the debtor.

65. King Metal Products, Inc. v. Workman's Compensation Bd., 20 A.D.2d 565, 245 N.Y.S.2d 882 (2d Dep't 1963); Glen Navigation Corp. v. Trodden, 97 N.Y.S.2d 228 (N.Y.City Ct.1950); Horan v. John F. Trommer, Inc., 15 Misc.2d 347, 137 N.Y.S.2d 26 (1954).

66. On the various functions of writing requirements see, Perillo, The Statute of Frauds in the Light of Functions and Dysfunctions of Form, 43 Fordham L.Rev. 39, 43–69 (1974).

Case 3

accord   /s   satisf!   /s   assent!   /s   imply! implied! imput!

accord   /s   satisf!   /s   protest

8k11(3)

accord   /s   satisf!   /s   mistak! inadverten!

Case 4

accord   /s   satisf!   /s   perform!   /s   defect

Case 5

principal   /s   agent   /s   accord   /s   satisf!

Case 6

"admit! liab!"   /s   accord   /s   satisf!

independen! distinct prior   /s   liab!   /s   accord   /s   satisf!

"explicit reservation of right"

accord   /s   satisf!   /s   check   /s   condition!

1–207   /p   modif! waiv!

1–207   /p   check

1–207   /p   "accord and satisfaction"

§ 4–12. Problems Arising in Bilateral Contracts

(a) Introduction

When the topic of consideration was introduced it was observed that there are some peculiar problems in the case of bilateral contracts that would be deferred to this point.[67] There are two topics to be discussed. The first is whether the exchange of promises constitutes consideration in a bilateral contract or whether it is the promised performances which are the considerations. The second and more difficult problem is treated under the heading of mutuality of obligation.

(b) Consideration in Bilateral Contracts

It has sometimes been asserted that in a bilateral contract each party's promise is consideration for the promise of the other since each party in making a promise is doing something he is not legally bound to do.[68] Closer analysis of decided cases, however, shows that the uttering of the promise does not supply the consideration; rather it is the content of the promise which must be scrutinized to determine its sufficiency as consideration.[69] The cases hold that a promise in a bilateral agreement is consideration for the counter-promise only if the performance which is promised would be consideration.[70] For example,

---

67. See § 4–2 supra.

68. Knack v. Industrial Commission, 108 Ariz. 545, 503 P.2d 373 (1972). See Ames, Two Theories of Consideration, 12 Harv.L.Rev. 515 (1898), 13 Harv.L.Rev. 29 (1899), Selected Readings 320.

69. See Williston § 103. See also Langdell, Mutual Promises as a Consideration

for Each Other, 14 Harv.L.Rev. 496 (1900); Williston, Consideration in Bilateral Contracts, 27 Harv.L.Rev. 503 (1914).

70. Coca-Cola Bottling Corp. v. Kosydar, 43 Ohio St.2d 186, 331 N.E.2d 440 (1975).

B says to A, "If you pay me the $50 you owe me, I promise to give you a hat worth $10." B's promise is not enforceable because A, if he performs, would merely be doing what he was legally obligated to do.[71] The result would be the same if B had asked for and received A's counter-promise to pay the amount admittedly due. Therefore, it is clear that the mere utterance of words of promise does not constitute legal detriment in a bilateral contract.

It is possible to hypothesize a case in which one party bargains for the making of a promise rather than for its ultimate performance. For example, a nephew may, for past grievances, refuse to speak to his uncle. The uncle makes the following promise, "I will give you $1,000 if you say 'I promise to accept'". If the nephew speaks the works of promise he has incurred detriment in speaking them but this is because the offer looks to a unilateral contract—the uttering of the words requested.

(c) Mutuality of Obligation

(1) Introduction

The meaning of the phrase "mutuality of obligation" as here used is best indicated by an illustration.[72] B here and now owes A a liquidated debt of $1,000. They agree that A will not seek to collect the debt for six months and B will pay the debt without interest at the end of this period.[73] If each side of the arrangement were approached as a unilateral arrangement it is clear that A's promise is not supported by detriment because B is only doing what he is legally obligated to do. Conversely B's promise should be enforceable because A, in forbearing suit, is suffering a detriment and this is so even though B is only promising to do what he is legally obligated to do. But the doctrine of mutuality of obligation concludes that since A is free not to perform because there is no detriment to support his promise, B, as a matter of fairness, should be equally free not to perform.[74] Without mutuality of consideration there is a void bilateral contract.[75]

---

71. See § 4–9 supra.

72. The illustration is based upon the case of Hay v. Fortier, 116 Me. 455, 102 A. 294 (1917). Another aspect of this case is discussed in § 4–12 infra.

73. If under the agreement D was to pay interest under the majority view, his promise would be detrimental since he is surrendering the privilege of discharging the debt and thereby terminating the running of interest. Hackin v. First Nat'l Bank of Arizona, 101 Ariz. 350, 419 P.2d 529 (1966); Adamson v. Bosick, 82 Colo. 309, 259 P. 513 (1927); Benson v. Phipps, 87 Tex. 578, 29 S.W. 1061 (1895); Restatement, Second, Contracts § 73, ill. 8; cf. Rogers v. First Nat'l Bank of Birmingham, 282 Ala. 379, 211 So.2d 796 (1968). A minority of jurisdictions has incorrectly concluded that since interest accrues by operation of law on overdue debts, the debtor in promising to pay interest is merely promising to perform a pre-existing legal duty. Harburg v. Kumpf, 151 Mo. 16, 52 S.W. 19 (1899); Olmstead v. Latimer, 158 N.Y. 313, 53 N.E. 5 (1899). This reasoning overlooks that the debtor has surrendered his right to tender payment thereby stopping the further accumulation of interest. 1 Williston § 121. There may be a question as to whether this was bargained for.

74. 1A Corbin § 152.

75. See Marcrum v. Embry, 291 Ala. 400, 282 So.2d 49 (1973). Cf., Restatement, Second, Contracts § 1, comment b which appears to do away even with the doctrine

The doctrine of mutuality of obligation is commonly expressed in the phrase that in a bilateral contract "both parties must be bound or neither is bound." [76] But this phrase is over-generalization because the doctrine is not one of mutuality of obligation but rather one of mutuality of consideration.[77] Phrasing the rule in terms of mutuality of obligation rather than in terms of consideration has lead to so-called exceptions and judicial circumventions to be discussed below. It has been suggested that the term "mutuality of obligation" should be abandoned and we must agree in the light of the confusion that this term has engendered.[78]

(2) Unilateral Contracts and the Mutuality Doctrine

Under the traditional view of a unilateral contract it is clear that there is no mutuality of obligation. At no time has the offeree been requested to bind himself to do anything and even if he starts to perform he is not bound to complete the performance.[79] Even if he should promise to do the act called for his unsolicited promise would be a nullity.[80] In a unilateral arrangement only the promisor may become bound to perform and thus there is no possibility of mutuality of obligation. In most cases if the offeree performs the act called for there will be the necessary consideration. More specifically if the act called for is detrimental and the offeror bargains for it the offeree's performance is the bargained for detriment and despite the absence of mutuality of obligation it has long been recognized that a contract exists.[81]

It would not make any difference if the promisor was only doing what he was legally obligated to do because the doctrine of mutuality of consideration[82] applies only to a bilateral contract. For example, assume A owed B $100.00 and A promised to pay B the $100.00 he owed if B walked the Brooklyn Bridge. B performed. B would be in a position in which he could sue on the original claim or on the unilateral contract but there could be only one recovery.[83]

---

of mutuality of consideration. See § 4–12(6) infra.

76. See Sala & Ruthe Realty, Inc. v. Campbell, 89 Nev. 483, 515 P.2d 394 (1973); 1 Williston § 105A.

77. R.S. Mikesell Assoc. v. Grand River Dam Authority, 627 F.2d 211 (10th Cir. 1980); Consolidated Laboratories, Inc. v. Shandon Scientific Co., 413 F.2d 208 (7th Cir.1969); Marcrum v. Embry, 291 Ala. 400, 282 So.2d 49 (1973); S.J. Groves & Sons Co. v. State, 93 Ill.2d 397, 67 Ill.Dec. 92, 444 N.E.2d 131 (1982), appeal dismissed 462 U.S. 1126, 103 S.Ct. 3103, 77 L.Ed.2d 1359 (1983); ACME Cigarette Services, Inc. v. Gallegos, 91 N.M. 577, 577 P.2d 885 (App.1978); Jackson Hole Builders v. Piros, 654 P.2d 120 (Wyo.1982).

78. Smith v. Atlas Off-Shore Boat Service, Inc., 653 F.2d 1057 (5th Cir.1981), on remand 552 F.Supp. 128 (S.D.Miss.1982);

1A Corbin § 152; Murray § 90; Oliphant, Mutuality of Obligation in Bilateral Contracts at Law, 25 Colum.L.Rev. 705 (1925), 28 Colum.L.Rev. 907 (1928); Jackson Hole Builders v. Piros, 654 P.2d 120 (Wyo.1982).

79. See § 2–10. This traditional doctrine has been changed by the Restatement Second and the Uniform Commercial Code. See § 2–10.

80. See § 2–10.

81. See 1A Corbin §§ 152–154; Jackson Hole Builders v. Piros, 654 P.2d 120 (Wyo. 1982) (citing text).

82. Chrisman v. Southern Cal. Edison Co., 83 Cal.App. 249, 256 P. 618 (1927).

83. Ward v. Goodrich, 34 Colo. 369, 372, 82 P. 701 (1905) where it is said, "While it is settled that promising to do, or the doing of, that which the promisor is already legally bound to do, does not, as a rule,

(3) Voidable and Unenforceable Promises and the Doctrine of Mutuality

If the doctrine of mutuality of obligation were to be accepted at face value (both parties must be bound or neither is bound) it would follow that a voidable or unenforceable promise on one or both sides of a bilateral contract would create a mutuality problem with the result that the agreement would be void.[84] But, as we have seen, the issue in a bilateral contract is mutuality of consideration. It is well settled that a voidable or unenforceable promise is consideration for a counter-promise and thus there is mutuality of consideration even though one or both of the parties make a voidable or unenforceable promise.[85]

What is stated above solves the mutuality problem but it does not answer why a voidable or unenforceable promise should be treated as consideration. Why, for example, despite the infant's power to avoid his agreement, does his promise serve as consideration to support the adult's promise though the adult has no such right?

A number of explanations have been advanced. One is that an infant incurs legal detriment in making a promise which he must act affirmatively to avoid. Alternatively, it may be said that the infant's promise creates an expectation which the other party bargains for and, generally, for consideration to exist the possibility of detriment rather than the absolute certainty of detriment is sufficient.[86] But in either case is the detriment argued for in these explanations really bargained for by the adult party?[87]

The real explanation for the rule is grounded in public policy. The policy is that it is desirable that the infant should be able to enforce the promise of the adult even though the infant has the power of avoidance. To achieve this result the law must say the promise of the infant is consideration. If his promise were not deemed to be consideration there would not be mutuality of consideration and the agreement would be void and the policy of the law in classifying certain promises as being voidable or unenforceable would be subverted.

---

constitute consideration for a reciprocal promise, or support a reciprocal undertaking given by the promisee, it by no means follows that such promise may not be enforced against such promisor by the promisee, although its enforcement compels the performance of that which was already a legal obligation."

84. See text at note 76 supra.

85. Restatement, Second, Contracts § 80; see 1 Williston 105. The essence of a voidable contract is that the law gives to a party (for example an infant) the option of avoiding the contract or of ratifying it and performing. A contract may also be voidable for lack of capacity, fraud, duress, mistake, etc. (See Chapters 7 and 9 and § 1–11 supra). An unenforceable contract may also be avoided, but it may not be ratified.

Even though it may not be ratified, it may still produce some legal consequences. A contract may be unenforceable because of the Statute of Frauds or the Statute of Limitations (see § 1–11 supra and § 19–35 infra). In theory a void contract of itself produces no legal obligations (see § 1–11 infra but see also § 4–12(7)). An agreement is void when there is not mutuality of consideration. By way of illustration, this occurs in the case of an illusory promise or indefiniteness. In addition, illegality may create a void contract. (See Ch. 22).

86. Holt v. Ward Clarencieux, 93 Eng. Rep. 954 (K.B.1732); Atwell v. Jenkins, 163 Mass. 362, 40 N.E. 178 (1895).

87. Compare Restatement, Second, Contracts § 78, Comment a with 1 Williston § 105.

(4) Illusory and Alternative Promises

As seen above, a bilateral contract is void if there is no mutuality of consideration. This will occur if the promise made by one or both parties is illusory or indefinite.[88] An illusory promise is an expression cloaked in promissory terms, but which, upon closer examination, reveals that the promisor has committed himself not at all. For example, the promise of a creditor made to a guarantor to forbear "until such time as I want my money" is an illusory promise and renders the bilateral contract void under the doctrine of mutuality of consideration.[89]

As a Texas court has stated, "the modern decisional tendency is against lending the aid the courts to defeat contracts on technical grounds of want of mutuality."[90] These courts have recognized that countless bargains, freely entered into and openly arrived at, have been struck down because of zealous judicial concern that one party's promise appeared illusory. It mattered not that the party who made the illusory promise was prepared to carry out the bargain and that it was the other party who reneged because under the doctrine of mutuality the other party is allowed free access to this escape hatch.

One of the methods of circumventing the illusory promise problem is interpolating into an agreement that otherwise seems illusory the requirement of good faith or reasonableness.[91] A good illustration of this approach is found in the case of Furrer v. International Health Assurance Co.[92] where a promise "to spend such time as he personally sees fit in developing" a business was held not to be illusory under the modern approach. There are now many cases that have employed this technique. In the Furrer case it should be noted that the law is implying good faith or the like against the express declaration of the promisor. Some cases—usually older ones—do not go this far.[93]

The new approaches being taken to the illusory promise problem may also be illustrated by cases relating to the question of alternative promises involving a right to terminate the agreement by virtue of a provision contained therein. In the case of alternative promises the rule is that each alternative must be detrimental.[94] Let us proceed by

---

88. Corbin, The Effect of Options on Consideration, 34 Yale L.J. 571 (1925). The question of indefiniteness in this context is discussed in § 4–12(7) infra.

89. Strong v. Sheffield, 144 N.Y. 392, 39 N.E. 330 (1895). Since a negotiable instrument was involved in this case under modern law, past consideration is sufficient to support the promise. U.C.C. § 3–408, see Hardy v. Brookhart, 259 Md. 317, 270 A.2d 119 (1970); see also § 5–18 infra.

90. Texas Gas Utilities Co. v. Barrett, 460 S.W.2d 409 (Tex.1970).

91. See, for example, Richard Bruce & Co. v. J. Simpson & Co., 40 Misc.2d 501, 243 N.Y.S.2d 503 (1963). But see Automat-ic Sprinkler Corp. of America v. Anderson, 243 Ga. 867, 257 S.E.2d 283 (1979); De Los Santos v. Great Western Sugar Co., 217 Neb. 282, 348 N.W.2d 842 (1984).

92. 256 Or. 429, 474 P.2d 759 (1970).

93. Flemming v. Ronson Corp., 107 N.J. Super. 311, 258 A.2d 153 (1969), judgment affirmed 114 N.J.Super. 221, 275 A.2d 759 (1971).

94. See, for example, Osborn v. Boeing Airplane Co., 309 F.2d 99 (9th Cir.1962); Blish v. Thompson Automatic Arms Corp., 30 Del.Ch. 538, 64 A.2d 581 (1948); Stopford v. Boonton Molding Co., 56 N.J. 169, 265 A.2d 657 (1970).

way of background to examine the traditional views in four fact patterns in the area under discussion and then discuss the more modern approach.

(1) If A and B enter into a bilateral agreement whereby A agrees to provide services for a year at a certain wage that B promises to pay and in addition B retains the power to terminate the agreement upon giving thirty days notice, there is no doubt that there is an agreement supported by consideration. B has agreed either to pay the wages for one year or for 30 days. Since either alternative constitutes consideration the rule stated above with respect to alternative promises is satisfied.[95]

(2) In the same case if B reserved the right to terminate the agreement at any time without notice the cases almost unanimously agree that the promise is illusory.[96]

(3) Where a party reserves the right of termination simply by giving notice at any time the older cases have held that the alternative promise of giving notice is not detrimental and therefore the alternative promises do not constitute detriment.[97] But Corbin and the later decisions take the position that the requirement for notice, even though it may be given at any time, constitutes detriment.[98] Thus each alternative is detrimental. The question that would remain is whether notice is bargained for but this question seems to have been ignored in an effort to make the agreement enforceable.

(4) Many cases have arisen in this type of situation where the language is that the "contract may be terminated at any time". The agreement leaves unanswered the question of whether notice is required or not. Once that issue is decided it is clear that the case will fall either into case (2) or (3). This issue is one of interpretation and the cases have gone both ways.[99]

Even where the language of the agreement seems to reserve the right to terminate at any time without notice (Case 2) some cases have sustained the agreement by ignoring the words "without notice." For example, in a well known case, Sylvan Crest Sand & Gravel Co. v. United States,[1] the United States promised to purchase trap rock from the plaintiff. The agreement read, "cancellation by the Procurement Division may be effected at any time." The court, could have read the quoted words as stating that the cancellation could be affected at any

95. Daughtry v. Capital Gas Co., 285 Ala. 89, 229 So.2d 480 (1969); Ventanas Del Caribe, S.A. v. Stanley Works, 158 Conn. 131, 256 A.2d 228 (1969); Long v. Foster & Associates, Inc., 242 La. 295, 136 So.2d 48 (1961), 22 La.L.Rev. 872 (1962); Klug v. Flambeau Plastics Corp., 62 Wis.2d 141, 214 N.W.2d 281 (1974); 1A Corbin § 164, 1 Williston § 105.

96. See note 95 immediately above.

97. 1A Corbin § 163; 1 Williston § 104; see Patterson, Illusory Promises and Promisors' Options, 6 Iowa L.Bull. 129 (1920).

98. 1A Corbin § 163.

99. Compare Miami Coca-Cola Bottling Co. v. Orange Crush Co., 296 Fed. 693 (5th Cir.1924) with A.S. Rampell, Inc. v. Hyster, 3 N.Y.2d 369, 165 N.Y.S.2d 475, 144 N.E.2d 371 (1957).

1. 150 F.2d 642 (2d Cir.1945). See Gurfein v. Werbelovsky, 97 Conn. 703, 118 A. 32 (1922).

time without notice. Instead the court concluded that the government had promised to purchase trap rock, or alternatively to give notice of termination within a reasonable time after the time of acceptance. Under either alternative there is detriment. As the court interprets the facts, the case seems to be closer to Case (1) than to Case (3). Again the court does not consider the question of whether the notice was bargained for. The decision is explained in part by the court's emphasis on the fact that the parties intended their agreement to be a contract and not a nullity.[2] The court is saying that if the parties intended to make a contract that intent should not be frustrated by overly technical rules of law. The decision also undoubtedly accords with business convenience in that it fulfills the expectations of the parties. However not all modern cases have followed this approach.[3]

Dispensing with the fiction, the Sylvan Crest case supports this proposition. "A promise is not rendered insufficient as consideration by reason of a power of termination reserved to the promisor." The statement of the rule in these terms has the advantage of bringing the law governing a promisor's right to terminate into symmetry with the law governing contingent contracts generally and in particular with the rule governing unenforceable and voidable contracts.

U.C.C. Section 2–309(2) and (3) also relate to this topic. Subdivision (2) states that a contract which provides for successive performances but is indefinite in duration "is valid for a reasonable time but unless otherwise agreed[4] may be terminated at any time by either party." Subdivision (3) states, "Termination of a contract by one party except on the happening of an agreed event requires that reasonable notification be received by the other party and an agreement dispensing with notification is invalid if its operation would be unconscionable."

The section is far from clear but it seems to stand for these propositions. 1) Even though an agreement is silent as to duration it is valid but it terminates after a reasonable time or in addition it may be terminated by giving reasonable notice. One of the comments talks in terms of recognizing "that the application of principles of good faith and sound commercial practice normally call for such notification of the termination of a going contract relationship as will give the other party reasonable time to seek a substitute arrangement."[5] 2) If the agreement provides that it may be terminated "at any time" (Case 4 above) reasonable notice would still be required. A fortiori the same result would apply in Case 3 above. 3) If the agreement specifically states that it may be terminated at "any time without notice" the issue is unconscionability. If it is decided that the arrangement is not unconscionable a court may nevertheless take into account the consid-

2. This is a recurrent theme in the modern cases. See e.g., Sonnenblick-Goldman Corp. v. Murphy, 420 F.2d 1169 (7th Cir.1970). See also U.C.C. § 2–204(3) discussed in § 2–9 supra.

3. See, for example, Zeyher v. S.S. & S. Mfg. Co., 319 F.2d 606 (7th Cir.1963); Baber v. Lay, 305 S.W.2d 912 (Ky.1957).

4. Besco, Inc. v. Alpha Portland Cement Co., 619 F.2d 447 (5th Cir.1980).

5. U.C.C. § 2–309, Comment 8.

eration problem. If it is unconscionable the term should be stricken and a reasonable time substituted. 4) If the time for giving notice is specified (e.g. 30 days as in Case 1, above) although there is no consideration problem, there may still be an issue of unconscionability.[6]

This section applies to franchises for the resale of goods and should go a long way toward eliminating the unjust result previously reached in a majority of franchise cases.[7] These cases had held that if the franchise agreement is silent as to duration it may be terminated at will; they also held that a notice provision will be enforced as written.[8] There are contrary and sounder decisions. Some are based upon the theory that the arrangement may be terminated only for good cause [9] and others saying that the franchise is entitled to a reasonable time to recoup his investment and presumably to wind up his affairs and make other arrangements.[10] This last view is akin to U.C.C. § 2–309 discussed above.

Another legislative technique aimed at curtailing termination of contracts in an unfair manner is found in the Automobile Dealers' Day in Court Act [11] which requires an automobile manufacturer "to act in good faith * * * in terminating, cancelling or not renewing" a dealership.[12] This Congressional legislation was enacted in response to numerous cases in which automobile manufacturers have terminated dealerships in an allegedly arbitrary fashion pursuant to one-sided adhesion agreements drafted by the manufacturers. The requirement of good faith imposed as a condition to termination has the additional effect of removing any question of whether the typical dealership contract is illusory.[13]

6. See U.C.C. § 2–309, Comment 8.

7. Note, 28 Miami L.Rev. 710 (1974). On what constitutes a franchise arrangement, see A & M Fix-It, Inc. v. Schwinn Bicycle Co., 494 F.Supp. 175 (D.Utah 1980).

8. 19 A.L.R.3d 196; Comment, Article Two of the Uniform Commercial Code and Franchise Distribution Agreements, 1969 Duke Law Journal 959.

9. Shell Oil Co. v. Marinello, 63 N.J. 402, 307 A.2d 598 (1973), certiorari denied 415 U.S. 920, 94 S.Ct. 1421, 39 L.Ed.2d 475 (1974), noted in 28 U.Miami L.Rev. 710 (1974) and 45 Miss.L.J. 252 (1974). Contra, Division of Triple T Serv., Inc. v. Mobil Oil Corp., 60 Misc.2d 720, 304 N.Y.S.2d 191 (1969), affirmed 34 A.D.2d 618, 311 N.Y.S.2d 961 (2d Dep't 1970); cf. McKinney's Gen.Bus.L.Art. 11–13. In some states this rule has been adopted by statute. See, for example, Conn.Gen.Stat.Ann. § 42–133f; Fornaris v. Ridge Tool Co., 423 F.2d 563 (1st Cir.1970), reversed on other grounds 400 U.S. 41, 91 S.Ct. 156, 27 L.Ed. 2d 174 (1970); Wisconsin Fair Dealership Law W.S.A. 135.01; Boatland, Inc. v. Brunswick Corp., 558 F.2d 818 (6th Cir.

1977); Witmer v. Exxon Corp., 260 Pa. Super. 537, 394 A.2d 1276 (1978), affirmed 495 Pa. 540, 434 A.2d 1222 (1981).

10. McGinnis Piano & Organ Co. v. Yamaha Intern. Corp., 480 F.2d 474 (8th Cir.1973); Bak-A-Lum Corp. of America v. Alcoa Bldg. Products, Inc., 69 N.J. 123, 351 A.2d 349 (1976). In general see The Federal Trade Commission Disclosure Requirements and Prohibitions Concerning Franchising and Business Opportunity Ventures, effective Oct. 21, 1979. There are also similar state statutes, for example, in New York and Illinois.

11. 15 U.S.C.A. § 1222. This statute is similar to the statutes discussed above in connection with the franchise cases.

12. See Annot. 50 A.L.R.Fed. 245; 54 A.L.R.Fed. 314.

13. Similar statutes exist in some states in other industries. See, for example, the Petroleum Market Practices Act adopted in some jurisdictions (e.g., Conn., Mich.). Federal regulation includes the Petroleum Marketing Practices Act, 15 U.S.C.A. §§ 2801–2841.

Although there is a strong trend toward limiting the concept of illusory promise by adopting a judicial or legislative construction or interpretation of the agreement which will sustain it,[14] the draftsman would do well to take note of the many cases which have failed to sustain an inartful agreement despite the parties intention to be bound.[15]

(5) Are Conditional and Aleatory Promises Illusory?

A promise to pay $500 is not illusory; but a promise to pay $500 "if I feel like it", is.[16] There is no doubt that if the happening of the condition is outside the control of the party who makes the promise, the promise is not illusory and does not fail for lack of consideration.[17] This is also true if the condition relates to an event that is outside of the promisor's unfettered discretion, such as the promisee's non-performance, or the happening of some event such as a strike, war, decline in business, etc.[18]

At times an illusory promise problem is avoided by treating the express language of condition attached to the promise as implied language of promise. Typically the question is posed in connection with sales of real estate contingent upon the purchaser's ability to obtain a specified mortgage loan. Although the promise by the buyer to pay the purchase price is clearly not illusory the condition would render the promise illusory if the buyer was not under any obligation to try to obtain a mortgage loan, the cases have held that the buyer has impliedly promised to use his best efforts to bring about the condition. His conditional promise is thus by no means illusory.[19] The same type of problem arises in sales of businesses contingent upon the purchaser being able to obtain an extended lease from the landlord and in agreements to lease contingent upon the lessee obtaining a license for the kind of business he intends to engage in on the premises.[20]

14. Jackson Hole Builders v. Piros, 654 P.2d 120 (Wyo.1982) (citing text).

15. 1A Corbin § 158.

16. Call v. Alcan Pacific Co., 251 Cal. App.2d 442, 59 Cal.Rptr. 763 (1967); Endres v. Warriner, 307 N.W.2d 146 (S.D.1981) (citing text). 1A Corbin § 166; 1 Williston § 105.

17. Tuggle v. Wilson, 158 Ga.App. 411, 280 S.E.2d 628 (1981), judgment reversed 248 Ga. 335, 282 S.E.2d 110 (1981), on remand 161 Ga.App. 347, 289 S.E.2d 824 (1982); Omni Group, Inc. v. Seattle-First Nat'l Bank, 32 Wn.App. 22, 645 P.2d 727 (1982).

18. 1A Corbin § 166; 1 Williston § 105.

19. Brack v. Brownlee, 246 Ga. 818, 273 S.E.2d 390 (1980) (citing text); Lach v. Cahill, 138 Conn. 418, 85 A.2d 481 (1951);

Carlton v. Smith, 285 Ill.App. 380, 2 N.E.2d 116 (1936); Eggan v. Simonds, 34 Ill.App. 2d 316, 181 N.E.2d 354 (1962); but see Paul v. Rosen, 3 Ill.App.2d 423, 122 N.E.2d 603 (1954). For a more complete discussion of this problem, see § 11–10 infra. It is important that the terms of the contemplated mortgage financing be agreed upon. Otherwise the agreement may fail for indefiniteness. Burgess v. Rodom, 121 Cal.App. 2d 71, 262 P.2d 335 (1953); Willmott v. Giarraputo, 5 N.Y.2d 250, 184 N.Y.S.2d 97, 157 N.E.2d 282 (1959); Gerruth Realty Co. v. Pire, 17 Wis.2d 89, 115 N.W.2d 557 (1962); Note, Contingency Financing Clauses in Real Estate Contracts in Georgia, 8 Ga.L.Rev. 186, 186–93 (1973).

20. Raner v. Goldberg, 244 N.Y. 438, 155 N.E. 733 (1927).

Agreements of this kind serve a vital purpose. They are entered into with the understanding that both parties are firmly committed to the performance of the agreement provided that cooperation is forthcoming from a financial institution, landlord or licensing authority. The purchaser or lessee has wisely protected himself, with the other party's consent, against the possibility that he will be unable to obtain the financing, lease or license. His promise, as explained above, is not rendered illusory by the condition attached.

In Dibenedetto v. Dirocco,[21] the Supreme Court of Pennsylvania went further than have the courts in the cases just discussed. The agreement provided, "In the event that the buyer cannot make the settlement, he may cancel this agreement." The buyer's obligation was held not to be made illusory by virtue of the condition. The Court reasoned that the word "cannot" meant objective inability, rather than subjective unwillingness (will not). Therefore, the performance of the promise made was not left to the whim and caprice of the buyer. In other words the buyer was obliged to make a good faith effort to perform the agreement. To be disapproved are numerous cases contrary in spirit to this well reasoned decision. Parties must be permitted to contract with flexibility to meet the complexities of modern life. Typical of the cases in which such flexibility serves a valuable economic need are requirements and output contract to be discussed below.

An aleatory promise is conditional on the happening of a fortuitous event, or an event supposed by the parties to be fortuitous.[22] Thus an insurance company's promise to pay a sum of money in the event of fire or other casualty supplies consideration for the insured's payment of a premium even if no casualty occurs. So also a valid contract exists if in consideration of a payment of $50, a promise is made to repay $10,000 "if I recover my gold mine." [23] In each of these cases the promise is aleatory because it is conditional on a fortuitous event.

An illustration of a promise conditioned on "an event supposed by the parties to be fortuitous" is in order for, by definition, this is also an aleatory promise. Suppose a man with two sons has made a will and one son makes the following proposition to the other: "you know how eccentric our father is. Let us agree now that no matter what his will contains, we will divide whatever he leaves to either of us equally." If the second son agrees, there is consideration, although it turns out that the testator bequeathed all of his assets to the second son. The first son incurred no actual detriment but he may enforce the promise of the second son because the second son bargained against the possibility that the first son would be favored. This result would obtain even if the will

21. 372 Pa. 302, 93 A.2d 474 (1953).

22. Restatement, Contracts § 291. See § 11–26 infra.

23. Embola v. Tuppela, 127 Wash. 285, 220 P. 789 (1923).

in favor of the second son had already been drawn. The point is that the parties believed that the event was fortuitous.[24]

Neither type of aleatory contract is illusory because the condition is based upon an event outside of the control of the promisors.

(6) Consideration Supplied by Implied Promises

In subdivision 4 of this section we discussed cases where an illusory promise problem was resolved by implying a promise from language of condition. Here we will discuss the resolving of an illusory promise problem not by implying a promise from language of condition,[25] but rather by inferring a promise from the entire fact pattern.[26]

The leading case is Wood v. Lucy, Lady Duff-Gordon.[27] In an elaborate written instrument defendant promised to give the plaintiff an exclusive agency and plaintiff promised to pay one-half of the profits resulting from the agency. It is obvious that plaintiff's promise was illusory if he was not required to do anything that would bring about profits.

The Court pointed out, however, that the plaintiff had an organization adapted to, and a financial self-interest in, carrying out the exclusive agency. It inferred a promise on plaintiff's part to use reasonable efforts to bring about profits. In the language of the Court, "It is true that he does not promise in so many words that he will use reasonable efforts to place the defendant's endorsements and market her designs. We think, however, such a promise is fairly to be implied. The law has outgrown its primitive stage of a formalism when the precise word was the sovereign talisman, and every slip was fatal. It takes a broader view today. A promise may be lacking, and yet the whole writing, may be instinct with an obligation imperfectly expressed * * *. If that is so there is a contract." [28]

The method of the case is to find a promise by inferences drawn from the facts. Under some circumstances the promise inferred is called an implied promise and in others it is referred to as a constructive promise. But whichever conclusion is reached, the result is the same. In other words an implied promise and a constructive promise are not treated differently. The theoretical difference between the two is that a promise implied from the conduct of the parties arises by

---

24. Minehan v. Hill, 144 App.Div. 854, 129 N.Y.S. 873 (1911); see Beckley v. Newman, 24 Eng.Rep. 691 (Ch. 1723).

25. See also 11–10 infra.

26. Hammond v. C.I.T. Financial Corp., 203 F.2d 705 (2d Cir.1953); United Press Int'l, Inc. v. Sentinel Publishing Co., 166 Colo. 47, 441 P.2d 316 (1968); cf. Celeste v. Owen, 279 App.Div. 1117, 112 N.Y.S.2d 290 (3d Dep't 1952).

27. 222 N.Y. 88, 118 N.E. 214 (1917). The implication may vary from "reasonable" efforts to "good faith" efforts, to "best

results." Whatever the adjective, heroic efforts are not implied. Compare Joyce Beverages of N.Y. v. Royal Crown Cola Co., 555 F.Supp. 271 (S.D.N.Y.1983), with Zilg v. Prentice-Hall, Inc., 717 F.2d 671 (2d Cir. 1983), certiorari denied 466 U.S. 938, 104 S.Ct. 1911, 80 L.Ed.2d 460 (1984).

28. Wood v. Lucy, Lady Duff-Gordon, 222 N.Y. 88 at 90–91, 118 N.E. 214 at 214 (1917); accord Bailey v. Chattem, Inc., 684 F.2d 386 (6th Cir.1982); Licocci v. Cardinal Associates, Inc., 445 N.E.2d 556 (Ind.1983), appeal after remand 492 N.E.2d 48 (1986).

construction of law, only when justice requires it under the circumstances. A promise is implied in fact when the conduct of the parties reasonably indicates that a promise has been made.[29] The distinction between the two is obviously not precise, but it would appear that the promise in the Lucy case was implied rather than constructive.[30] Constructive promises will be discussed later in a more appropriate context.[31]

The Uniform Commercial Code adopts and goes beyond the reasoning of Wood v. Lucy, Lady Duff-Gordon. It provides in § 2–306(2):

> "A lawful agreement by either the seller or the buyer for exclusive dealing in the kind of goods concerned imposes unless otherwise agreed an obligation by the seller to use best efforts to supply the goods and by the buyer to use best efforts to promote their sale."

Of course the Code provision has reference only to exclusive dealings in "goods" as defined by the Code.[32] It thus would probably not be applicable to an agreement such as was involved in the Wood case, but it adopts and extends its rationale by imposing the obligation of best efforts as a matter of legislative fiat rather than as a matter of construction. This approach had already been taken in a number of cases.[33]

(7) A Void Contract is Not Necessarily a Nullity

We have seen that if there is no consideration on one side of a bilateral contract the entire contract is void.[34] We have also seen that a void contract produces no legal obligations.[35] This is not necessarily true where there has been performance under the void bilateral contract.

For example, in Hay v. Fortier[36] the defendant was under an undisputed obligation to pay the plaintiff a liquidated debt. The parties entered into an agreement whereby the plaintiff agreed to forbear from suing on the obligation for six months and defendant promised to pay the debt at the end of six months without interest. Under the pre-existing duty rule the plaintiff's promise was unsupported by consideration and not binding on the defendant.[37] Under the doctrine of mutuality of consideration, plaintiff could not enforce defendant's promise and the court so stated.[38] However the plaintiff did forbear for six months and then brought action not on the debt but

29. A recent case has listed five requirements for finding an implied promise. Brown v. Safeway Stores, Inc., 94 Wn.2d 359, 617 P.2d 704 (1980).

30. Farnsworth, Disputes over Omissions in Contracts, 68 Colum.L.Rev. 860, 865 (1968); see also 3A Corbin, Contracts §§ 632 and 653.

31. See § 11–13 infra.

32. U.C.C. § 2–105.

33. See Mandel v. Liebman, 303 N.Y. 88, 100 N.E.2d 149 (1951).

34. See § 4–12 supra.

35. See § 4–12 supra.

36. 116 Me. 455, 102 A. 294 (1917). See the discussion of this case at note 72 supra.

37. See § 4–9 supra.

38. See § 4–12 supra.

upon the defendant's promise to pay the debt. The court found for the plaintiff, despite the voidness of the bilateral contract stating as follows: "If a contract, although not originally binding for want of mutuality, is nevertheless executed by the party not originally bound, so that the party asserting the invalidity of the contract has actually received the benefit contracted for, the latter will be estopped from refusing performance on his part on the ground that the contract was not originally binding on the other, who has performed." [39]

Although the court speaks in terms of estoppel,[40] a better analysis is that if there is performance under a void bilateral contract, the situation should be treated as if an offer looking to unilateral contract had been made to the party who performed.[41] Under that assumption, plaintiff's act was detrimental and the fact that defendant promised to do only what he was already bound to do is immaterial.[42] On the facts, plaintiff could sue either on the original claim or on the subsequent promise but would be entitled to only one recovery.[43] This process has been described as forging a good unilateral contract out of a bad bilateral contract.[44] A law review article has identified at least two requirements that are essential before this forging can take place.[45] 1) All of the requisites of the law of offer and acceptance must be fulfilled including the requirement that the promise requested must have been given. Otherwise there would be no bilateral contract rather than a void bilateral contract.[46] 2) The act performed by the party seeking to enforce the contract must be detrimental. If this were not so there would be no consideration to support the unilateral contract being forged.

This process of forging a good unilateral contract out of a bad bilateral is relevant in the case of any void bilateral contract. Thus, for example, it applies to a bilateral arrangement that is too vague and indefinite to be enforced. If the side of the agreement which was too vague and indefinite becomes definite by performance, the other side of the agreement, although not originally enforceable, can become en-

---

39. 102 A. at 295 (quoting from 6 R.C.L.) 690 (Perm.Supp.ed W. McKinney 1929); First Wis. Nat'l Bank of Milwaukee v. Oby, 52 Wis.2d 1, 188 N.W.2d 454 (1971); contra, Commonwealth Department of Transportation v. First Pennsylvania Bank, 77 Pa.Cmwlth. 551, 466 A.2d 753 (1983).

40. The relationship between this problem and promissory estoppel is discussed in chapter 6.

41. See Eisenberg, The Principles of Consideration 640, 649 (1982); Wright & Seaton, Inc. v. Prescott, 420 So.2d 623 (Fla. App.1982).

42. See § 4–12 supra.

43. On the facts it would appear that it would have been wise to sue on the origi-

nal debt, but, because of the number of obligors on the debt, there may have been procedural impediments to such an action. See § 20–1 to 20–5 infra.

44. See Calamari, Forging a Good Unilateral or a Series of Good Contracts or a Series of Good Contracts out of a Bad Bilateral Contract, 1961 Wash.U.L.Q. 367; Finn, The Forging of Good Unilaterals out of Bad Bilaterals, 3 Brooklyn L.Rev. 6 (1933).

45. See Calamari, supra n. 44.

46. Obviously nothing said here would apply to an offer that from the beginning looks to a unilateral or a series of unilateral contracts. The problem under discussion arises because there is a bad bilateral contract.

forceable under the doctrine of forging a good unilateral contract out of a bad bilateral contract.[47]

For example, in a case involving the sale of goods, if the parties fail to agree on the quality of the goods but the seller sends a particular quality which buyer accepts it can be said that there is a contract based upon a theory of acquiescence [48] or under the notion of forging a good unilateral contract out of a bad bilateral contract.[49]

Closely related to the doctrine of forging a good unilateral contract out of a bad bilateral contract is the doctrine of forging a series of good contracts out of a bad bilateral contract.[50] We have previously discussed the concept of an offer looking to a series of contracts.[51] The doctrine of forging a series of contracts is analogous. The point is that in a proper case a void bilateral contract is looked upon as creating an offer looking to a series of contracts.

One illustration will suffice. In Rubin v. Dairymen's League Co-Op. Association,[52] the defendant agreed to appoint the plaintiff as his exclusive agent within a certain territory in exchange for plaintiff's promise to develop a market for defendant's products. Plaintiff was to be paid a commission on each sale he made. No time was stated for the duration of the contract and the court held that the contract was terminable at will.[53] The court also held that although the contract was void because of indefiniteness, nevertheless the plaintiff was entitled to be paid under the agreement his commission for any sale he made—thus forging a series of good unilateral contracts out of a bad bilateral contract.[54]

Above it is stated that at a minimum there are two requirements for the process of forging. If these two elements are not present there can be no forging. If they are present it does not follow that forging will take place. Three illustrations will suffice. 1) In the case of indefiniteness, if only the promise which was originally definite is performed, even though the two requirements stated are met, the indefinite promise is still indefinite and therefore there is only the possibility of quasi-contractual recovery.[55] 2) In a case such as Strong v. Sheffield [56] where the plaintiff promised in effect to forbear for as long as he felt like and did forbear for two years, assuming that the two requisites are met, there is still a question of whether any period of performance is sufficient because no time for performance is stated in

---

47. Swafford v. Sealtest Foods Div. of Nat'l Dairy Products Corp., 252 Ark. 1182, 483 S.W.2d 202 (1972); 1 Williston § 49, 104. See § 4-12(7) supra.

48. See § 2-9 supra.

49. Continental Bank & Trust Co. v. American Bonding Co., 605 F.2d 1049 (8th Cir.1979), appeal after remand 630 F.2d 606 (8th Cir.1980); Swafford v. Sealtest Foods Div. of Nat'l Dairy Products Corp., 252 Ark. 1182, 483 S.W.2d 202 (1972).

50. See Calamari Note 44 supra.

51. See § 2-16 supra.

52. 284 N.Y. 32, 29 N.E.2d 458 (1940), reargument denied 284 N.Y. 816, 31 N.E.2d 927 (1940).

53. See § 2-9 supra. But see § 4-12(4) wherein U.C.C. § 2-309(2), (3) are discussed.

54. See § 4-12(7) supra.

55. 1 Williston § 49. See § 2-9 supra.

56. 144 N.Y. 392, 39 N.E. 330 (1895). This case was discussed in § 4-12(4) supra.

the agreement. Of course, it could be argued that forbearance for a reasonable time is sufficient.[57] 3) Finally, suppose the party who seeks to use the doctrine has made the requisite promise, starts to perform and the other party revokes. Presumably the result would depend on the three views stated in § 2–22.

As previously indicated the Restatement Second appears to have done away with the doctrine of mutuality of consideration even in bilateral contracts.[58] Illustration 4 to section 75 sets up a case in which A promises to forbear suit against B in exchange for B's promise to pay a liquidated debt to A. Under the rule of mutuality of consideration even though A's promise was detrimental he could not enforce B's promise. The conclusion of the Restatement Second is that A's promise is nevertheless consideration for B's promise but that "B's promise is conditional on A's forbearance and can be enforced only if the condition is met." The net result is that the Restatement Second is employing the theory of forging a good unilateral contract out of a bad bilateral contract.

 WESTLAW REFERENCES

(b) Consideration in Bilateral Contracts
promis! /s consideration /s bilateral /s contract agreement
bilateral /s contract agreement /s promis! /s detriment
consideration /s "word of promise"

(c) Mutuality of Obligation
"doctrine of mutuality of obligation"
"mutuality of consideration"
mutuality +2 obligation consideration /s bilateral
mutuality +2 obligation consideration /s void! avoid!
"both parties must be bound or neither is bound"

 (2) Unilateral Contracts and the Mutuality Doctrine
mutuality +2 obligation consideration /s unilateral!
unilateral /s promisor /s bind binding bound
promisor /s consideration /s legal! +1 bound obligat!

 (3) Voidable and Unenforceable Promises and the Doctrine of Mutuality
mutuality +2 obligation consideration /s unenforceable void! avoid!
bilateral /s void! unenforceable /s promis!
counter-promis! /s unenforceable void!
void! avoid! /s unenforceable /s ratif!

 (4) Illusory and Alternative Promises
"illusory promise" /s consideration
illusory indefinite! /s mutuality
illusory indefinite! /s promis! /s void!

57. The court avoided the problem by suggesting that there is no such process as forging a good unilateral contract out of a bad bilateral contract. "The consideration is to be tested by the agreement, and not by what was done under it." 144 N.Y. at 396, 39 N.E. at 331.

58. Restatement, Second, Contracts § 79, Comment f.

illusory indefinite! /s promis! /s ''good faith'' reasonabl!

''alternative promise'' /s detriment!

''alternative promise'' % ''statute of frauds''

terminat! /s notice notif! /s illusory

''contract may be terminated at any time''

''sylvan crest'' +s ''united states''

2–309(2) 2–309(3)

franchise /s agreement contract /s silen! /s terminat! duration

ci(15 +4 1222)

''automobile dealers' day in court act''

ci(15 +4 280*)

(5) *Are Conditional and Aleatory Promises Illusory?*

condition! /s promis! /s illusory

control! /s promis! /s illusory

wartime strike war /s illusory /s promis!

express +1 language condition /s promis! /s imply! implication
     implied

illusory /s contingen! /s promis!

illusory /s perform! /s ''good faith''

''good faith'' /s promis! /s illusory

aleatory /s promis!

aleatory /s condition! contingen! event occur! change luck fortuit!

(6) *Consideration Supplied by Implied Promises*

consideration /s ''implied! promis!''

consideration /s infer! /s promis!

imply! implied! implication /s consideration /s supply! supplied
     /s promis!

infer! imply! implied! implication /s ''reasonable effort'' ''best result''
     /s promise* promising

wood +s ''lady duff''

law /s imply! implied! implication /s promise /s conduct /s
     party

promise /s ''implied in fact''

2–306(2)

(7) *A Void Contract is Not Necessarily a Nullity*

''void! contract'' /s null!

''forging a good unilateral''

''theory of acquiescence''

rubin +s ''dairymen's league''

vague! indefinite! /s quasi +1 contract contractual

---

§ 4–13. Requirements and Output Contracts

(a) Introduction

In a typical requirements contract the buyer expressly agrees to buy all of his requirements of a stated item from the seller who agrees to sell that amount to the buyer. But this may be implied if that is the apparent intention of the parties.[59] In a typical output contract the seller agrees to sell all of his output of a certain item to the buyer and the buyer agrees to buy that output from the seller. In other words in these situations the quantity term is measured by the requirements of the buyer (requirements contract) or by the output of the seller (output contract). If the buyer agrees to buy all of his requirements up to a specified amount from the seller the contract is deemed by some courts to be a requirement contract,[60] but there are contrary cases.[61] The same problem can arise in the case of an output contract. Since the rules relating to output and requirements contracts are basically the same, as a matter of convenience emphasis will be on the topic of requirements contracts.

(b) Validity of Requirements Contracts

At one time requirements contracts were not enforced.[62] They were deemed illusory because the buyer might refrain from having requirements.[63] In time a majority of the courts upheld requirements contracts on the theory that consideration could be found in the surrender of the buyer's privilege of purchasing elsewhere.[64] Nevertheless, a minority of courts refused to enforce the agreement when the buyer was entering into a new business or was a middleman.[65] In these cases, the stated thinking was the lack of any basis for prediction of the amount of goods to be purchased rendered the agreement illusory or indefinite and thus void. Perhaps the real reason for striking down the agreement was the one-sidedness of the arrangement. The business value of such agreements has been recognized by the Uniform Commercial Code and other authorities.

Output and requirements contracts involving the sale of goods are now governed by § 2–306 of the Uniform Commercial Code, which provides:

59. Brem-Rock, Inc. v. Warnack, 28 Wn. App. 483, 624 P.2d 220 (1981).

60. City of Louisville v. Rockwell Manufacturing Company, 482 F.2d 159, 164 (6th Cir.1973). See also U.C.C. § 2–306, Comment 3 which refers to "any maximum or minimum stated by the agreement."

61. 96 A.L.R.3d 1275, 1282 (1980).

62. Swindell & Co. v. First Nat'l Bank, 121 Ga. 714, 49 S.E. 673 (1905) (agreement to supply required loan funds up to $30,000); Crane v. C. Crane & Co., 45 C.C.A. 96, 105 Fed. 869 (1901); Miami Butterine Co. v. Frankel, 190 Ga. 88, 8 S.E.2d 398 (1940); G. Loewus & Co. v. Vischia, 2 N.J. 54, 65 A.2d 604 (1949). See generally, Havighurst & Berman, Requirement and Output Contracts, 27 Ill.L.Rev. 1 (1932); Note, Requirements Contracts: Problems of Drafting & Construction, 78 Harv.L.Rev. 1212 (1965). For treatment of such cases in the British Commonwealth, see Howard,

The Requirements and the Output Contracts, 2 U.Tasmania L.Rev. 446 (1967).

63. Lima Locomotive & Mach. Co. v. National Steel Castings Co., 83 C.C.A. 593, 155 Fed. 77 (1907); Simon Bros. Co., Inc. v. Miller Brewing Co., 83 Wis.2d 701, 266 N.W.2d 369 (1978).

64. G. Loewus & Co. v. Vischia, 2 N.J. 54, 65 A.2d 604 (1949); Nassau Supply Co. v. Ice Service Co., 252 N.Y. 277, 169 N.E. 383 (1929), 43 Harv.L.Rev. 828 (1930) (a reading of the opinion may indicate that the court felt the transaction fraudulent); cf. McMichael v. Price, 177 Okl. 186, 58 P.2d 549 (1936).

65. Oscar Schlegel Mfg. Co. v. Peter Cooper's Glue Factory, 231 N.Y. 459, 132 N.E. 148 (1921). The case may be read less broadly, since the middleman did not expressly promise not to purchase glue elsewhere.

"A term which measures the quantity by the output of the seller or the requirements of the buyer means such actual output or requirements as may occur in good faith, except that no quantity unreasonably disproportionate to any stated estimate or in the absence of a stated estimate to any normal or otherwise comparable prior to output or requirements may be tendered or demanded."

This provision assumes the general validity of requirements contracts.[66] The Code makes clear that the "good faith" provision is designed to eliminate any lingering questions of indefiniteness and mutuality and is intended to include in the case of merchants the notion of "commercial standards of fair dealing." [67]

(c) How Much Is Requirements Buyer Entitled to Demand?

At common law there were two views on this question. Under one view the buyer was entitled to his normal requirements; under the other to his actual good faith requirements. At common law an estimate by the buyer had no effect except if made in bad faith in which event it operated as a maximum to the seller's liability.[68]

The basic notion of the Code is that the buyer is entitled to his good faith requirements. Insisting on unneeded goods is not good faith.[69] However, two limitations are placed on the rule of good faith. 1) If there is a stated estimate the buyer is not entitled to any quantity unreasonably disproportionate to the estimate. Comment 3 states, "any maximum or minimum set by the agreement shows a clear limit on the intended elasticity." In similar fashion it is stated, "the agreed estimate is to be regarded as a center around which the parties intend the variation to occur." [70] While at common law in the absence of bad faith, an estimate was for the convenience of the parties and of little operative significance, under the Code the estimate limits the risk of the seller even though the buyer is making his demand in good faith.[71] 2) If there is no estimate or maximum or minimum stated in the contract, the buyer may demand only "any normal or otherwise comparable prior requirements." [72] What this means is an amount reasonably foreseeable at the time of contracting.[73] If the requirements are measured by a particular plant a normal as opposed to a sudden expansion undertaken in good faith would ordinarily be proper. On the

---

66. U.C.C. §§ 2–306, Comment 2, 2–708 Comment 2 (final sentence); Teigen Constr., Inc. v. Pavement Specialists, Inc., 267 N.W.2d 574 (S.D.1978); Dusenberg & King § 4.05(1); Note, Requirements Contracts under Uniform Commercial Code, 102 U.Pa.L.Rev. 654 (1954); 96 A.L.R.3d 1275.

67. U.C.C. § 2–306, Comment 2. But see Farnsworth, Contracts § 2–15, p. 82. See § 11–38 infra.

68. See generally, Havighurst & Berman, supra note 62.

69. Homestake Mining Co. v. Washington Pub. Power Supply Sys., 476 F.Supp.

1162 (N.D.Cal.1979), affirmed per curiam 652 F.2d 28 (9th Cir.1981).

70. Orange & Rockland Utilities, Inc. v. Amerada Hess Corp., 59 A.D.2d 110, 397 N.Y.S.2d 814 (2d Dep't 1977).

71. McLouth Steel Corp. v. Jewell Coal & Coke Co., 570 F.2d 594 (6th Cir.1978), certiorari dismissed 439 U.S. 801, 99 S.Ct. 43, 58 L.Ed.2d 94 (1978).

72. See Note, Requirements Contracts under the Uniform Commercial Code, 102 U.Pa.L.Rev. 654 (1954).

73. See U.C.C. § 2–306, Comment 2.

question of good faith one should always take into account whether the market price had increased greatly in the case of a requirements contract containing a fixed price.[74]

(d) May a Requirements Buyer Diminish or Terminate His Requirements?

Essentially the question here is whether a requirements buyer may go out of business so that he has no requirements or change his way of doing business so that he has less or no requirements. At common law there were three views. 1) The buyer was free to go out of business with impunity and free to change his method of business at will.[75] It was this view that lead some courts to believe that the buyer's promise was illusory. 2) The buyer is liable if he goes out of business or changes his method of doing business in bad faith.[76] Perhaps this test is best expressed in terms of whether the purchaser has used commercial judgment as opposed to an attempt to defeat the particular obligation.[77] 3) If the buyer goes out of business or changes his way of doing business so as to lessen his requirement, he must respond in damages.[78]

Under the Uniform Commercial Code he may go out of business or change his method of doing business if he acts in good faith. This is so even if the reductions are highly disproportionate to normal prior requirements or stated estimates.[79] Thus the issue is good faith. Putting in more modern equipment so that the buyer has fewer requirements is not considered bad faith.[80]

On this issue of good faith Comment 2 states: "A shut down by a requirements buyer for lack of orders may be permissible when a shut down merely to curtail losses would not." But the case of Feld v. Henry S. Levy & Sons, Inc.[81] appears to disagree when it states that an output seller may curtail losses if he acts in good faith and the losses

74. U.C.C. § 2–306, Comment 2.

75. In re United Cigar Stores Co. of America, 8 F.Supp. 243 (S.D.N.Y.1934), affirmed 72 F.2d 673 (2d Cir.1934); cf. Dickey v. Philadelphia Minit-Man Corp., 377 Pa. 549, 105 A.2d 580 (1954).

76. Fort Wayne Corrugated Paper Co. v. Anchor Hocking Glass Corp., 130 F.2d 471 (3d Cir.1942); Royal Paper Box Co. v. E.R. Apt Shoe Co., 290 Mass. 207, 195 N.E. 96 (1935); New York Central Ironworks Co. v. United States Radiator Co., 174 N.Y. 331, 66 N.E. 967 (1903).

77. Cf. McKeever v. Canonsburg Iron Co., 138 Pa. 184, 16 A. 97 (1888). (Defendant agreed to buy requirements of coal. Upon discovery of natural gas on its own land, defendant converted to gas. Held: Defendant was privileged to convert.)

78. Texas Industries v. Brown, 218 F.2d 510 (5th Cir.1955); Wigand v. Bachman-Bechtel Brewing Co., 222 N.Y. 272, 118 N.E. 618 (1918); Wells v. Alexandre, 130

N.Y. 642, 29 N.E. 142 (1891); Humble Oil & Refining Co. v. Cox, 207 Va. 197, 148 S.E.2d 756 (1966); cf. 407 East 61st Garage, Inc. v. Savoy Fifth Avenue Corp., 23 N.Y.2d 275, 296 N.Y.S.2d 338, 244 N.E.2d 37 (1968).

79. R.A. Weaver & Assoc., Inc. v. Asphalt Const., Inc., 587 F.2d 1315 (D.C. Cir.1978); Angelica Uniform Group, Inc. v. Ponderosa Systems, Inc., 636 F.2d 232 (8th Cir.1980); Wilsonville Concrete Products v. Todd Building Co., 281 Or. 345, 574 P.2d 1112 (1978). See Weistart, Requirements and Output Contracts. Quantity Variations under the U.C.C., 1973 Duke L.J. 599; Note, Requirements Contracts: Problems of Drafting & Construction, 78 Harv.L.Rev. 1212, 1220 n. 34; 1A Corbin § 158, n. 49.

80. Southwest Natural Gas Co. v. Oklahoma Portland Cement Co., 102 F.2d 630 (10th Cir.1939).

81. 37 N.Y.2d 466, 373 N.Y.S.2d 102, 335 N.E.2d 320 (1975).

are more than trivial. In that case these questions were held to be questions of fact.

It is obvious that a requirements contract is ordinarily an exclusive dealing contract. Thus § 2–306(2) would appear to apply and to impose upon the buyer an obligation "to use best efforts to promote" the sale of the goods in question. It would seem obvious that if a requirements buyer does not purchase the goods for resale (e.g. a houseowner who agrees to buy his requirements of oil), no such implication can be made. But if he does purchase for resale Comment 5 must be taken into account. That comment talks in terms of an "exclusive agent" who has an "exclusive territory." In such a case it is logical to imply such a promise.[82] But whether a promise should be implied when the buyer does not have an exclusive territory is more debatable. The same type of questions may also arise in connection with an output contract.[83]

It is important to distinguish requirements and output contracts from continuing offers. A promise by X to bottle all milk produced by Y, is merely an offer looking to a series of contracts and therefore revocable at will,[84] unless made irrevocable by payment of consideration or by compliance with statutory formalities. If however, a return promise by Y to supply his output of milk is expressed or can be implied, a bilateral contract exists at least if it is assumed that a return promise was requested.[85]

WESTLAW REFERENCES

"requirement contract" /s buy*** /s sell***

infer! imply! implied! implication /s "requirement contract"

"requirement contract" /s quantity

"output contract" /s quantity

(b) *Validity of Requirement Contracts*

requirement output +1 contract /s unenforc! illusory

requirement output +1 contract /s consideration mutual!

requirement output +1 contract /s enforc!

requirement output +1 contract /s void! vague! indefinite!

requirement output +1 contract /s exclusiv!

2–306

(c) *How Much is Requirements Buyer Entitled to Demand?*

requirement output +1 contract /s "good faith" normal!

requirement output +1 contract /s estimat! minimum maximum

requirement output +1 contract /s vary! varied variance limit!
 disproportion!

---

82. See § 4–12(6) supra.

83. Feld v. Henry S. Levy & Sons, Inc., 37 N.Y.2d 466, 373 N.Y.S.2d 102, 335 N.E.2d 320 (1975).

84. Balsam Farm, Inc. v. Evergreen Dairies, Inc., 6 A.D.2d 720, 175 N.Y.S.2d 517 (2d Dep't 1958), reargument and appeal denied 6 A.D.2d 829, 176 N.Y.S.2d 931

(1958); see also Halloway v. Mountain Grove Creamery Co., 286 Mo. 489, 228 S.W. 451 (1920). See § 2–16 supra.

85. McNussen v. Graybeal, 146 Mont. 173, 405 P.2d 447 (1965); Western Sign, Inc. v. State, 180 Mont. 278, 590 P.2d 141 (1979).

```
requirement output  +1  contract  /s  prior decreas! increas!
    foresee!

requirement output  +1  contract  /s  number amount

requirement output  +1  contract  /s  reasonabl!

requirement output  +1  contract  /s  fix*** price market

requirement output  +1  contract  /s  "bad faith"
```

(d) *May a Requirements Buyer Diminish or Terminate His Requirements?*

```
requirement output  +1  contract  /s  terminat! diminish!

requirement output  +1  contract  /s  demand!

requirement output  +1  contract  /s  reduc! chang! fluctuat!

feld  /s  henry  /s  levy

"continuing offer"
```

§ 4–14. Must All of the Considerations Be Valid? Alternative and Conjunctive Promises Compared

We have already seen that in the case of alternative promises the rule is that each alternative must be detrimental.[86] Thus if A promises to paint for B and in exchange B promises to do masonry work for A *or* to pay A the liquidated debt of $500 that B owes A, B has made alternative promises. Because one of the alternative promises is not detrimental, B's promises are not consideration for A's promise and thus there is a void bilateral contract under the mutuality doctrine. The Restatement Second qualifies this rule by stating that alternative promises are detrimental provided there is or appears to the parties to be a substantial possibility that events may eliminate the alternative which is not detrimental before the promisor exercises his choice.[87]

The rule relating to conjunctive promises is quite different. Here the rule is that if one of the conjunctive promises is consideration that is sufficient to support a counter-promise.[88] For example, if A says to B, "I promise to give you my black horse if you promise to pay me the liquidated debt of $50 you owe me *and* to paint my fence," although in paying his debt, B is only doing what he is legally obligated to do, in painting the fence, he is suffering detriment and thus B is supplying consideration for A's counter-promise.[89] A separate and distinct question that has no connection with the topic of consideration is what must B do to enforce A's promise. The answer is that he must paint and pay the debt. Even though the payment is not consideration it is a condition that must be performed if B is to recover on A's promise.[90]

86. See § 4–12 supra; Restatement, Second, Contracts § 77(a) and Comment b.

87. Restatement, Second, Contracts § 77(b).

88. Restatement, Second, Contracts § 80(2), 1 Corbin § 126, 1 Williston § 134.

89. Spaulding v. Benenati, 86 A.D.2d 707, 446 N.Y.S.2d 543 (3d Dep't 1982), appeal dismissed 56 N.Y.2d 803, 452 N.Y.S.2d 402, 437 N.E.2d 1159 (1982), order reversed 57 N.Y.2d 418, 456 N.Y.S.2d 733, 442 N.E.2d 1244 (1982) which also states that there may be an exception in the case of a divisible contract.

90. 1 Williston § 134. There is a related question in the area of illegality which is discussed in § 22–6 infra.

A promise by uncle to his nephew, "In consideration of your past good conduct and in consideration of your promise to refrain from smoking for a year, I will pay you $500, would be supported by the consideration if the counter-promise were given and performed. In this illustration we have neither alternative nor conjunctive promises. The rule that applies is that all of the considerations need not be valid.[91] The fact that part of the consideration is invalid (past consideration) does not prevent the valid part (refraining from smoking) from operating as consideration. In this respect the situation is similar to conjunctive promises.

In discussing alternative promises, it was assumed that the choice of alternatives resided in the promisor. If the choice of alternative is in the promisee, however, the alternative promises supply consideration for a counter-promisee if any of the alternative performances is detrimental.[92] Thus in the illustration above where A promised to paint and B promised to do masonry work or to pay a liquidated debt, B's alternative promise is detrimental because A is free to choose to have B perform the masonry work.

§ 4-15. One Consideration Will Support Many Promises

In many cases there is only one promise on the part of each party to a bilateral contract. But in some cases the number of promises made by the two promisors may not be equal. For example, in consideration of an employee's promised services, the employer may promise a salary, a year-end bonus and other fringe benefits. All three promises of the employer are supported by the one promise of the employee. The rule is that one consideration will support many promises.[93] This rule is qualified by the rules relating to alternative promises discussed above.[94]

Similarly, one consideration will support the promises of more than one promisor. Thus a lease executed by a lessor will support not only the tenant's promise to pay rent, but also the promise of a guarantor guaranteeing that the rent will be paid.[95]

 WESTLAW REFERENCES
files +s schaible

---

91. 1 Corbin § 126; 1 Williston § 134.

92. Restatement, Second, Contracts § 77 Comment c.

93. Restatement, Second, Contracts § 80(1); 1 Corbin § 125; 1 Williston § 137A; Files v. Schaible, 445 So.2d 257 (Ala.1984); Krasselt v. Koester, 99 Idaho 124, 578 P.2d 240 (1978); Koehler & Hinrichs Mercantile Co. v. Illinois Glass Co., 143 Minn. 344, 173 N.W. 703 (1919);

Keane v. Aetna Life Ins. Co. of Hartford, Conn., 22 N.J.Super. 296, 91 A.2d 875 (1952).

94. See § 4-14 supra.

95. John Mohr & Sons v. Apex Terminal Warehouses, Inc., 422 F.2d 638 (7th Cir.1970); Citizens Bank of Oregon v. Pioneer Investment Co., 271 Or. 60, 530 P.2d 841 (1975).

Chapter 5

INFORMAL CONTRACTS WITHOUT CONSIDERATION OR DETRIMENTAL RELIANCE

Table of Sections

Table of Sections

A. PAST CONSIDERATION AND MORAL OBLIGATION AS CONSIDERATION

B. CONSIDERATION NOT REQUIRED IN CERTAIN COMMERCIAL AND WRITTEN CONTRACTS

C.　STIPULATIONS

A.　PAST CONSIDERATION AND MORAL OBLIGATION AS CONSIDERATION

Table of Sections

§ 5–1.　Introduction

Not all contracts require consideration. The formal contract under seal survives in some jurisdictions,[1] as do recognizances and other kinds of specialties. In addition there are cases in which informal contracts are exempt from the requirement of consideration. Promises which are enforceable because they have induced unbargained for reliance are the subject of the next chapter. This chapter is concerned with informal promises enforceable without detrimental reliance or consideration. One group of promises of this kind, promises to perform a duty despite failure of a condition, will be discussed in chapter 11, where the context will make the discussion clearer.

---

1. See ch. 7 infra.

Lord Mansfield, perhaps the greatest judge in the history of Anglo-American law,[2] introduced revolutionary changes into the doctrine of consideration. This revolution proved abortive, but had certain residual effects on court decisions and the ideas he espoused have in part been revived by legislation. In the case of Pillans and Rose v. Van Mierop[3] he laid down two radical propositions. First, no consideration is required if a promise is expressed in a writing. Second, no consideration is required in a commercial transaction. Both of these propositions were quickly overruled[4] but, as indicated in part B of this chapter, have found limited acceptance in Twentieth Century legislation.

In Lee v. Muggeridge,[5] Chief Justice Mansfield (no relation to Lord Mansfield), took up certain *dicta* of his more famous namesake and squarely ruled that a promise made in fulfillment of an antecedent moral obligation to pay for a benefit that had been conferred by the promisee was sufficiently supported by moral consideration. This ruling was reasonably well grounded in the older law.[6] It is important to note that the moral obligation that served as consideration was not the moral obligation created by the promise itself, but rather the consideration was found in the antecedent moral obligation that induced the promise.[7] This broad proposition was also overruled[8] but not entirely and not in every common law jurisdiction. The first part of this chapter will discuss the moral obligation problem. This will be followed by a discussion of statutes that eliminate the necessity for consideration under certain circumstances. The chapter will close with a brief discussion of stipulations, a category unto itself.

 WESTLAW REFERENCES

"formal contract" /s seal

recognizance /s agreement contract

informal +1 agreement contract /s exempt! consideration

"moral! obligat!" /s antecedent /s promis! consideration

"moral consideration" /s promise agreement contract

95k76

95k79

---

2. His major achievement was the incorporation of the law merchant into the common law. In contracts, he is responsible for the doctrine of constructive conditions and substantial performance. He also introduced the Roman law idea of quasi contracts into the common law.

3. 3 Burr. 1663, 97 Eng.Rep. 1035 (K.B. 1765). A concurring judge remarked: "many of the old cases are strange and absurd; so also are some of the modern ones * * *" 3 Burr. at 1671, 97 Eng.Rep. at 1039.

4. Rann v. Hughes, 7 T.R. 350, 101 Eng. Rep. 1014 n. (Ex.1778).

5. 2 Taunt. 36, 128 Eng.Rep. 599 (C.P. 1813).

6. E.g., Lampleigh v. Brathwait, Hobart 106, 80 Eng.Rep. 255 (C.P.1615). Occasion-

ally a more modern case has stated the rule almost as broadly. In re Schoenkerman's Estate, 236 Wis. 311, 294 N.W. 810 (1940). Wisconsin is the jurisdiction most frequently cited as following a broad version of the moral obligation concept. See § 5–4 infra.

7. 1A Corbin §§ 230, 231, 232. Although commonly moral and legal obligations are distinguished, it would be a mistake to regard moral obligations as devoid of legal consequences. For a list of fifteen legal consequences attaching to the existence of an unenforceable moral obligation, see Dias, The Unenforceable Duty, 33 Tulane L.Rev. 473, 483–88 (1959).

8. Eastwood v. Kenyon, 11 Ad. 8c E. 438, 113 Eng.Rep. 482 (Q.B.1840).

"moral! obligat!"   /s   induc!

moral!   +1   duty obligat! consideration   /s   statut!

promis!   /s   recogni!   /s   "moral! obligat!"

§ 5–2. The Relationship Between Past Consideration and Moral Obligation

We have already seen the general rule that past consideration is not consideration.[9] We have also seen immediately above that at early common law there was authority to the effect that a promise made in recognition of a moral obligation arising out of a benefit previously received is enforceable. This notion is now generally rejected or, where accepted, it is accepted with a great deal of circumspection and qualification. Where it is accepted, cases generally divide themselves into five categories: (1) Where the promise relates to a prior contractual or quasi-contractual debt that still exists as an enforceable obligation (§ 5–3); (2) where material benefits were previously received by the promisor (§ 5–4); (3) where there was a prior legal obligation that was discharged by operation of law (§§ 5–5, 5–6, 5–7); (4) where there is a promise not to avoid an avoidable duty (§ 5–8); (5) where there is a promise based upon a previous unenforceable obligation under the Statute of Frauds (§ 5–9). Section 5–10 discusses certain other promises not included in the categories listed above.

WESTLAW REFERENCES

past /4 consideration /s moral! +1 obligat! duty consideration

§ 5–3. Promises to Pay Pre-existing Debts

At early common law it was well settled that a pre-existing debt was consideration for a promise to pay the debt. Under this early common law rule, if C loaned D $1,000 which was to be repaid by D on January 2, 1600, and D failed to repay the debt when due, D's promise made on March 1, 1600, to repay the debt would be deemed to be supported by consideration. Under modern definitions of consideration, the promise is unsupported by consideration, since the past debt was not incurred in exchange for the subsequent promise. The rule that the pre-existing debt constitutes consideration had significant practical impact at that time. In an action on the promise to pay the pre-existing indebtedness the writ of assumpsit was available under which the plaintiff was entitled to trial by jury. If the writ of debt was employed, defendant was entitled to trial by wager of law.[10]

There is some question whether the rule continues in effect. Some authorities take the position that if the past debt is still existing and enforceable a promise to pay the debt is enforceable provided that the promise is co-extensive with the pre-existing debt.[11] Other authorities

---

9. See § 4–2 supra.

10. Ames, The History of Assumpsit, 2 Harv.L.Rev. 53 (1888), Selected Readings 33.

11. 1A Corbin § 211. If the debtor promised to pay less, the promise is still enforceable. 1A Corbin § 212.

indicate that the promise is unenforceable.[12] The question is almost purely of academic interest since the creditor may sue on the original obligation.[13] The primary context in which the new promise may become important is that of the running of the statute of limitations. Promises in this context, however, have a particular set of rules, discussed below.[14] The Uniform Commercial Code makes it clear in § 3–408 that if the promise is made in an instrument, such as a note or a check governed by Article 3 of the Code, for a pre-existing indebtedness no new consideration is required for the enforceability of the instrument.

 WESTLAW REFERENCES

"common law" /s consideration /s indebtedness debt /s
  promis!

promis! /s pay paid paying payment /s debt indebtedness /s
  "pre-exist!" /s consideration

"original! obligat!" /s creditor

"original! obligat!" /s "statute of limitation"

"statute of limitation" /s "new promise"

241k197(3)

3–408

§ 5–4. Promises to Pay for Benefits Received

At early common law if A requested B to perform a certain act without making an express promise in return, unlike the cases discussed in the preceding section, an action for debt would not lie because the obligation was unliquidated. Assumpsit would not lie because A made no express promise.[15] For example, if A requested B to paint A's house but made no express promise to pay for the services A would not be liable to B either under the writ of debt or under the writ of assumpsit. To help overcome this unjust result it was held that a subsequent express promise to pay for the acts performed was enforceable.[16] In time it was held that this was true even if the services had been performed as a favor rather than in expectation of payment.[17] Under modern law, however, this last point is controversial.

Under the modern law it is clear that if A requests B to perform services, A would be liable on his implied promise to pay the reasonable value of the services, unless the services were rendered gratuitously.[18] A subsequent promise defining the amount which A is willing to pay for the services, assented to by B, is, of course, supported by considera-

---

12. 1 Williston § 143.

13. An account stated (§ 21–9 infra) is enforceable without consideration and gives the claimant certain advantages of pleading and proof. This is perhaps a result of the rule here discussed.

14. See § 5–7 infra.

15. Ames, The History of Assumpsit, 2 Harv.L.Rev. 1 (1888).

16. Bosden v. Thinne, 80 Eng.Rep. 29 (K.B.1603).

17. Lampleigh v. Brathwait, 80 Eng. Rep. 255 (C.P.1615); contra, Moore v. Elmer, 180 Mass. 15, 61 N.E. 259 (1901) (per Holmes, J.).

18. See 1A Corbin § 233 n. 72; 1 Williston §§ 144–147.

tion.[19] If a promise to pay a fixed amount is made by A, and withdrawn prior to B's acceptance, no mutual assent and no consideration is present. In a number of cases it has been held that there is no reason to enforce such a promise. Under this view A's promise is at best a rebuttable evidentiary admission of the value of the services.[20]

It is, nonetheless, much more commonly held that a new promise to pay a fixed sum in discharge of a pre-existing obligation arising from services or other material benefit rendered at request is enforceable without new consideration and without mutual assent. The rule, of course, does not apply where the promise is made in an offer that requires a return promise or performance by the promisee.[21] Professor Corbin [22] and a number of cases [23] take the view that the promise will be enforced only to the extent that it is not disproportionate to the value of the services. Under this view the new promise is of little value except to the extent that it may be prima facie proof of the value of the prior acts. According to Professor Williston's analysis, "the weight of authority supports the validity of a subsequent promise defining the extent of the promisor's undertaking," even if the promise is disproportionate to the value of the prior acts.[24] That is, the new promise will be enforced according to its terms. Many of the cases are analytically unsatisfactory in one respect. In many, if not most, of the cases in which the court relied on the majority rule as stated by Professor Williston, the facts show that the new promise was assented to by the promisee; the promise could equally have been treated as one side of an accord and satisfaction.[25] The new Restatement appears to avoid the question.[26]

An important problem is whether a promise to pay for services rendered at request, but as a favor, without expectation of payment, is enforceable. In a majority of jurisdictions, such a promise is unenforceable.[27] As discussed earlier,[28] the majority of cases have held that past consideration is ordinarily not sufficient to support a promise. Yet, Mansfield's ruling that the past consideration creates a moral obligation which supports a subsequent promise lingers on. In some jurisdictions, it continues to be held to constitute the law, although frequently the decisions are sustainable on other grounds.[29]

19. Each party is suffering detriment in arriving at the compromise. However, the agreement may instead be an executory accord. See §§ 21–4 and 21–5 infra.

20. See 1 Williston §§ 144–145.

21. Restatement, Second, Contracts ch. 4, topic 2, introductory note.

22. 1A Corbin § 233.

23. In re Estate of Gerke, 271 Wis. 297, 73 N.W.2d 506 (1955).

24. 1 Williston § 146.

25. E.g., In re Bradbury, 105 A.D. 250, 93 N.Y.S. 418, (3d Dep't 1905); see n. 19 supra.

26. Compare Restatement, Second, Contracts § 82(1) with § 86(2)(b).

27. Moore v. Lawrence, 252 Ark. 759, 480 S.W.2d 941 (1972); Allen v. Bryson, 67 Iowa 591, 25 N.W. 820 (1885); Moore v. Elmer, 180 Mass. 15, 61 N.E. 259 (1901); Pershall v. Elliott, 249 N.Y. 183, 163 N.E. 554 (1928).

28. See § 4–2 supra.

29. Old American Life Ins. Co. v. Biggers, 172 F.2d 495, 8 A.L.R.2d 781 (10th Cir.1949); Medberry v. Olcovich, 15 Cal. App.2d 263, 59 P.2d 551 (1936), appeal denied on other grounds 15 Cal.App.2d 263, 60 P.2d 281 (1936); Sargent v. Crandall,

Under the rules of quasi contracts, in limited circumstances, there is a right of action to recover the value of benefits conferred upon another without his request.[30] When such a right exists a promise to pay for benefits so received is governed by the same rules as govern a promise to pay for acts previously performed at request. In the ordinary case, however, receipt of unrequested benefits creates no legal obligation.[31] If a subsequent promise is made to pay for these benefits, the majority of cases hold that the promise is unenforceable.[32] A minority of cases, accepting the moral obligation concept, are to the contrary,[33] and accept a doctrine of "promissory restitution."[34]

The Restatement Second has accepted the minority view that a receipt of a material benefit with or without a prior request, followed by the receiver's promise to pay for the benefit is enforceable without consideration "to the extent necessary to prevent injustice."[35] Despite the absence of a bargained for exchange, the Restatement rightly takes the position that an expressed intention to be bound founded upon receipt of a material benefit ought to be enforced. The Restatement judiciously qualifies the right to recovery by refusing enforcement if

143 Colo. 199, 352 P.2d 676 (1960); In re Hatten's Estate, 233 Wis. 199, 288 N.W. 278 (1940) (the decision, however, is supported by the majority view since payment for the services was promised prior to their complete rendition).

30. Chase v. Corcoran, 106 Mass. 286 (1871) (rescue and repair of a boat); Cotnam v. Wisdom, 83 Ark. 601, 104 S.W. 164 (1937) (medical services to an unconscious person); see Restatement, Second, Contracts § 86, Comments b, c, d, e and f; Wade, Restitution for Benefits Conferred Without Request, 19 Vand.L.Rev. 1183 (1966).

31. Restatement, Restitution § 112; see Dawson, The Self-Serving Intermeddler, 87 Harv.L.Rev. 1409 (1974).

32. In re Greene, 45 F.2d 428 (S.D.N.Y. 1930) ("the doctrine that past moral obligation is consideration is now generally exploded"); Mills v. Wyman, 20 Mass. (3 Pick.) 207 (1825) (father promised to pay for services rendered to ailing son; court suggests that the enforcement of such promise be left to the Tribunal of Conscience); Estate of Voight, 95 N.M. 625, 624 P.2d 1022 (1981); Harrington v. Taylor, 225 N.C. 690, 36 S.E.2d 227 (1945) (plaintiff injured in saving defendant's life; promise to pay damages).

33. Webb v. McGowin, 232 Ala. 374, 168 So. 199 (1936) (plaintiff injured in saving defendant's life; promise to pay an annuity); Desny v. Wilder, 46 Cal.2d 715, 299 P.2d 257 (1956) (defendant promised to pay for plaintiff's idea which he was free to utilize without compensation); Worner

Agency, Inc. v. Doyle, 133 Ill.App.3d 850, 88 Ill.Dec. 855, 479 N.E.2d 468 (1985) (subsequent promise to pay for services as a finder); Holland v. Martinson, 119 Kan. 43, 237 P. 902 (1925), noted in 11 Cornell L.Q. 357 (1926); Brickell v. Hendricks, 121 Miss. 356, 83 So. 609 (1920), noted in 5 Cornell L.Q. 450 (1920); Edson v. Poppe, 24 S.D. 466, 124 N.W. 441 (1910) (tenant orders well dug; landlord promised to pay well digger). The moral obligation doctrine was applied in the United States prior to its demolition (§ 5–1 supra) in England. E.g. Beach v. Lee, 2 Dall. 257 (Pa. 1796).

At times the same result is reached by covert manipulation of consideration concepts. See, e.g., Griffin v. Louisville Trust Co., 312 Ky. 145, 226 S.W.2d 786 (1950) (conventional consideration found by a series of inferences); Yarwood v. Trusts & Guarantee Co., Ltd., 94 A.D. 47, 87 N.Y.S. 947 (4th Dep't 1904) (wealthy vagabond is taken in from the bitter cold; subsequently promises $5,000 for this apparently charitable act); Matter of Todd, 47 Misc. 35, 95 N.Y.S. 211 (Surr.Ct.1905) (same vagabond promises $5,000 for similar kindnesses).

34. The term "promissory restitution" appears to have been coined by Henderson, Promises Grounded in the Past: The Idea of Unjust Enrichment and the Law of Contract, 57 Va.L.Rev. 1115, 1118 n. 4 (1971). An economic justification for this doctrine appears in Kronman & Posner, The Economics of Contract Law 51–52 (1979).

35. Restatement, Second, Contracts § 86.

"the promisee conferred the benefit as a gift or for other reasons the promisor has not been unjustly enriched." [36] It also provides that the promise will not be enforced "to the extent that its value is disproportionate to the benefit." [37] As the Restatement reporter for this section grants, the section "fairly bristles with unspecific concepts," [38] such as "gift," "unjust enrichment" and "injustice." The primary thrust of the section is to provide for recovery on promises made to compensate for benefits received which are on the outer fringes of the law of quasi contract. The section comments and illustrations focus upon promises made because of benefits received in emergencies,[39] or in a business setting,[40] and promises made to rectify mistakes.[41]

Professor Corbin's treatise is generally in accord and suggests that the moral consideration concept is part of the legal resources of all jurisdictions to be utilized "as an escape from more hardened and definitely worded rules of law." [42] In New York, by statute, past consideration will support a written promise if certain formalities are complied with.[43] The statute is broader in scope than the Restatement rule. The Restatement indicates that a promise to pay an additional sum for benefits conferred under a contract would not be enforceable because no element of unjust enrichment would be present.[44] Under the New York Statute such a promise would seem to be enforceable if the required formalities are complied with.

 WESTLAW REFERENCES

request! /s perform! /s service /s "implied! promis!" /s pay payment paying paid

205hk35

gratuit! /s "reasonable value" /s "implied! promis!"

service /s "implied! promis!" /s "reasonable value"

"subsequent! promis!" /s pay payment paying paid

service /s benefit! /s receiv! receipt /s promis! /s pay payment paying paid

36. Id. § 86(2)(a).

37. Id. § 86(2)(b).

38. Braucher, Freedom of Contract and the Second Restatement, 78 Yale L.J. 598, 605 (1969). He also states that: "The new section seeks to draw a distinction between the cases involving moral obligations based on gratitude or sentiment and those cases which are on the borderline of quasi-contract or unjust enrichment, where the subsequent promise removes an objection which might otherwise bar quasi-contractual relief." Ibid.

39. Restatement, Second, Contracts § 86, ills. 6, 7.

40. Id., ills. 8, 9, 10, 11.

41. Id., ills. 4, 5.

42. 1A Corbin § 230; see also Fuller, Consideration and Form, 41 Colum.L.Rev.

799, 821–22 (1941); Grosse, Moral Obligation as consideration in Contracts, 17 Vill. L.Rev. 1 (1971); Havighurst, Consideration, Ethics and Administration, 42 Colum.L. Rev. 1, 18–20 (1942); Henderson supra note 34; Kronman & Posner, The Economics of Contract Law 51–53 (1979); cf. Von Mehren, Civil-Law Analogues to Consideration: An Exercise in Comparative Analysis, 72 Harv.L.Rev. 1009, 1033–47 (1959).

43. See § 5–18 infra. Statutory formulations in California, Georgia and other Civil Code states are discussed in Henderson, supra, note 34, at 1129–35.

44. Restatement, Second, Contracts § 86, Comment f; see 1A Corbin § 235; but see cases such as Griffin v. Louisville Trust Co., 312 Ky. 145, 226 S.W.2d 786 (1950), discussed in note 33 supra.

"pre-exist!" /s "new promise"

"new promise" /s enforc! /s term

favor /s service /s expect! /s pay paid paying payment /s
   service enforc! unenforc!

"quasi contract***" /s benefit! /s confer! /s expect! request!

"material benefit" /s promis!

"material benefit" /s consideration

---

§ 5–5.   Promises to Pay Debts Discharged by Operation of Law: Rationale

Until recently it has been held that a promise to pay a debt discharged in bankruptcy, barred by the statute of limitations, or otherwise rendered unenforceable by operation of law [45] is enforceable without consideration. The rule with respect to bankruptcy has been drastically changed. (§ 5–6). The cases frequently articulate the rationale in terms that the debt coupled with the moral obligation to pay is sufficient consideration to support the new promise to pay.[46] Other cases speak in terms of the promise reviving a debt barred by operation of law.[47] Others adopt the rationale that the promise operates as a waiver of the debtor's defense; the right is said to have continued to exist, only the remedy having been barred.[48] In truth, the rule is a particular application of the older view that an antecedent debt is sufficient consideration for a subsequent promise to pay it. When this doctrine was abandoned by most courts, these courts generally agreed that promises to pay a debt discharged by operation of law should be enforced and carved out an exception for this type of case.[49] That the reason for the rule is historical rather than purely logical is shown by the cases holding that a promise to pay a tort claim which is barred by the statute of limitations [50] is unenforceable despite the fact that the elements of waiver and moral obligation are equally as strong in such a case. The survival of the moral obligation rule has been justified on the ground that the promisor "is only promising to do what he should have done without a promise." [51] An economic theorist finds economic utility in the rule because of the enhancement of the *promisor's* credit worthiness.[52]

45. Other illustrations of this doctrine may be found in § 5–10 infra.

46. Stanek v. White, 172 Minn. 390, 215 N.W. 784 (1927); Herrington v. Davitt, 220 N.Y. 162, 115 N.E. 476 (1917); Kopp v. Fink, 204 Okl. 570, 232 P.2d 161 (1951).

47. See 1 Williston § 202.

48. Way v. Sperry, 60 Mass. (6 Cush.) 238 (1851).

49. See § 5–3 supra; 1 Williston §§ 201, 203; Stanek v. White, 172 Minn. 390, 215 N.W. 784 (1927); Carshore v. Huyck, 6 Barb. (N.Y.) 583 (1849); Restatement, Second, Contracts §§ 82–83.

50. Marchetti v. Atchison T. & S.F. Ry. Co., 123 Kan. 728, 255 P. 682 (1927) (negli-

gence); Hollenbeck v. Guardian Nat. Life Ins. Co., 144 Neb. 684, 14 N.W.2d 330 (1944) (fraud); Armstrong v. Levan, 109 Pa. 177, 1 A. 204 (1885) (but a promise made before the statute has run may be enforceable by estoppel); contra, Opitz v. Hayden, 17 Wn.2d 347, 135 P.2d 819 (1943) (promise made after expiration of statute of limitations to compensate for seduction held enforceable). Even under the majority rule, the promise may be enforced under the doctrine of estoppel if the promisee relied upon the promise. See note 79 infra.

51. Fuller, supra note 42, at 821.

52. Kronman & Posner, supra note 42, at 51.

§ 5–6. Promises to Pay Debts Discharged in Bankruptcy

A bankruptcy court can discharge a debtor's obligations by decree. Not infrequently, after discharge, the bankrupt promises one or more of his creditors that he will pay them despite the discharge. Until enactment of the Bankruptcy Reform Act of 1978, such promises were binding and formed perhaps the bulk of the past consideration cases. Because of perceived abuses by financing institutions, this Statute bars enforcement of such promises except those made in the bankruptcy proceeding itself.[53]

 WESTLAW REFERENCES
51k434

bankrupt! /s discharg! /s decree

bankrupt! /s bind binding bound /s promis!

§ 5–7. Promises to Pay Debts—Effect on Statute of Limitations

A promise to pay a contractual or quasi-contractual debt has the effect of starting the statute of limitations running anew.[54] This occurs whether the promise is made after the debt has been barred by the passage of the statutory period or whether it is not yet barred.[55] A promise not to plead the statute of limitations generally has the same effect as a promise to pay the debt,[56] but, in most jurisdictions if the promise is made in the original contract or before maturity of the debt, it is void as contrary to public policy.[57] Most cases invalidate attempts to provide for a longer period of limitations than provided for by statute,[58] as does the U.C.C.[59]

53. 11 U.S.C.A. § 524(c).

54. United States v. Upper Valley Clinic Hospital, Inc., 615 F.2d 302 (5th Cir. 1980) (quasi-contractual action for medicare reimbursement); Restatement, Second, Contracts § 82. See generally Kocourek, A Comment on Moral Consideration and the Statute of Limitations, 18 Ill. L.Rev. 538 (1924).

55. Harper v. Fairley, 53 N.Y. 442 (1873); 1A Corbin § 214; 1 Williston § 160. For example, assume a six year period of limitation. If A lends B $1,000 on January 2, 1986, the money to be repaid on January 2, 1987, the statute of limitations begins to run in January of 1987. If B on January 2, 1987, made a new promise to pay, the six year period would commence to run again from this date so that the debt would be barred in 1993. If instead, after the statute had run, B in 1994 promised to pay, the statute would start to run again so that it will expire in 2000.

56. Restatement, Second, Contracts § 82, Comment f; United States v. Curtiss Aeroplane Co., 147 F.2d 639 (2d Cir.1945); 1 Williston §§ 183–184. But if the debtor makes the promise indicating he reserves the right to raise other defenses, there is no implied promise to pay the debt. The promise may, however, be enforced if supported by consideration or if the claimant relies on the promise to his detriment. 1 Williston § 184.

57. 1 Williston § 183; Restatement, Contracts § 558; see McKinney's N.Y. C.P. L.R. 201.

58. E.L. Burns Co., Inc. v. Cashio, 302 So.2d 297, 84 A.L.R.3d 1162 (La.1974); Kassner v. New York, 46 N.Y.2d 544, 415 N.Y.S.2d 785, 389 N.E.2d 99 (1979).

59. U.C.C. § 2–725(1).

An acknowledgment of the existence of the debt is treated as an implied promise to pay,[60] unless there is an indication of a contrary intention. For example, a statement that "I know I owe the money * * * and I will never pay it," although an acknowledgment of the debt, rebuts any implication of a promise to pay.[61]

Statutes in most of our states require the promise or the acknowledgment to be in a signed writing.[62] Part payment of principal or interest or the giving of collateral may have the same effect as an acknowledgment and be treated as the equivalent of a writing.[63] To have this effect the part payment must be voluntary.[64]

The creditor's claim is based on the new promise and therefore is limited by the terms of the new promise.[65] Thus, the promise may be to pay in part or in installments [66] or on specified conditions.[67] Whether the promise or acknowledgment must specify the amount of the debt is a matter on which the courts are divided.[68] A promise by one joint obligor does not bind the others if there is no agency relationship.[69]

Originally, the rule enforcing new promises to pay debts barred by the statute of limitations was limited to antecedent obligations enforceable pursuant to the writ known as indebitatus assumpsit or general assumpsit.[70] Generally, this writ was available to enforce claims for liquidated amounts or for the reasonable value of an executed perform-

---

60. Curtiss–Wright Corp. v. Intercontinent Corp., 277 App.Div. 13, 97 N.Y.S.2d 678 (1st Dep't 1950). Some courts are reluctant to infer a promise. See Wipf v. Blake, 72 S.D. 10, 28 N.W.2d 881 (1947) ("I am planning to make a settlement" insufficient); Dolby v. Fisher, 1 Wn.2d 181, 95 P.2d 369 (1939); see generally, 1A Corbin § 216; 1 Williston §§ 166–173. Some courts require that the communication contain directly or impliedly an expression by the debtor of the justness of the debt. Freeman v. Wilson, 107 Ariz. 271, 485 P.2d 1161 (1971); Restatement, Second, Contracts § 82, Comment d.

61. A'Court v. Cross, 3 Bing. 329, 130 Eng.Rep. 540 (C.P.1825).

62. 1 Williston § 164; Restatement, Second, Contracts § 82, Comment a; e.g., McKinney's N.Y. General Obligations Law § 17–101; Manwill v. Oyler, 11 Utah 2d 433, 361 P.2d 177 (1961).

63. Restatement, Second, Contracts § 82, Comment e. The word "may" is used in the text because the question is whether the part payment is to be interpreted as an implied promise to pay the balance. Lew Morris Demolition Co., Inc. v. Board of Education, 40 N.Y.2d 516, 355 N.E.2d 369, 10 A.L.R. 4th 925 (1976). This is often a question of fact. Jones v. Jones, 242

F.Supp. 979 (S.D.N.Y.1965); see also 1A Corbin § 217; 1 Williston § 174.

64. Security Bank v. Finkelstein, 160 App.Div. 315, 145 N.Y.S. 5 (1st Dep't 1913), affirmed 217 N.Y. 707, 112 N.E. 1076 (1916); Restatement, Second, Contracts § 82, Comment e; 1 Williston § 175.

65. Tebo v. Robinson, 100 N.Y. 27, 2 N.E. 383 (1885).

66. Gillingham v. Brown, 178 Mass. 417, 60 N.E. 122 (1901); Cross v. Stackhouse, 212 S.C. 100, 46 S.E.2d 668 (1948); 1 Williston § 181.

67. E.g., Big Diamond Milling Co. v. Chicago, M. & St. P. Ry., 142 Minn. 181, 171 N.W. 799 (1919); Barker v. Heath, 74 N.H. 270, 67 A. 222 (1907). As the Restatement Second states: "The claim is based on the new promise and is limited by the terms of the new promise" and the statute of limitations is governed by the terms of the new promise. Restatement, Second, Contracts § 82, Comment c; see 1 Williston §§ 179, 182.

68. See Annot, 21 A.L.R. 4th 1121 (1983).

69. Roth v. Michelson, 55 N.Y.2d 278, 449 N.Y.S.2d 159, 434 N.E.2d 228 (1982).

70. Restatement, Second, Contract § 82, Comment b.

ance.[71] New promises to pay obligations enforceable in special assumpsit or covenant were apparently not enforced; the former writ was applicable to a breach of an executory contract and the latter was applicable to the enforcement of a sealed instrument or a judgment. Consequently, the first Restatement stated the rule that a promise to pay all or part of any antecedent contractual or quasi-contractual obligation for the payment of money whether liquidated or not, commences the running of the statute of limitations anew.[72]

This means by way of illustration that if A, a painter, painted B's house at B's request and B subsequently promised to pay for the services, B's subsequent promise would start the statute of limitations running anew even though the obligation was unliquidated.[73] However, if A and B entered into a bilateral contract with respect to the painting and B breached the contract before A performed, a subsequent promise by B to pay the damages caused by his breach would have no effect upon the statute of limitations.[74]

With the abolition of the writ system a number of cases began to hold that the subsequent promise would have the effect of starting the obligation running anew even though the promise was to pay an obligation under seal or to pay a judgment.[75] The original Restatement took the position that the antecedent duty may be under seal but that "an antecedent duty under a judgment is not, however, included." [76] The Restatement Second takes no position with regard to sealed instruments or judgments.[77] It makes specific what appears to have been generally recognized: a promise to pay a tort claim has no effect upon the statute of limitations unless the tort claim involves unjust enrichment.[78] Such a promise may, however, be effective on a theory of estoppel where the promise lulls the promisee into a false feeling of security.[79]

 WESTLAW REFERENCES
     promis! /s pay payment paid paying /s "statute of limitation" /s
     debt indebtedness

71. See Shipman, Common Law Pleading 254–55 (1923).

72. Restatement, Second, Contracts § 82.

73. Restatement, Second, Contracts § 82(1), Comment b. But some cases have held that the indebtedness must be defined by the new promise. Bell v. Morrison, 26 U.S. (1 Pet.) 351, 7 L.Ed. 174 (1828).

74. 1 Williston § 188; Restatement, Second, Contracts § 82, Comment b.

75. Spilde v. Johnson, 132 Iowa 484, 109 N.W. 1023 (1906); Trustees of St. Mark's Evang. Lutheran Church v. Miller, 99 Md. 23, 57 A. 644 (1904).

76. Restatement, Contracts § 86(1), Comment b; accord, Mutual Trust & Deposit Co. v. Boone, 267 S.W.2d 751, 45 A.L.R.2d 962 (Ky.1954). Williston asserts that there is no logical basis for this distinction (1 Williston § 187), and Corbin takes the position that a promise to pay a specialty debt or a barred judgment should be enforceable. 1A Corbin § 220.

77. Restatement, Second, Contracts § 82, Comment b.

78. Restatement, Second, Contracts § 82, Comment b; 1 Williston § 186.

79. State Farm Mutual Ins. Co. v. Budd, 185 Neb. 343, 175 N.W.2d 621, 44 A.L.R.3d 476 (1970); see also Annot., 43 A.L.R.3d 756 (1972).

commenc! start! run running /s pomis! /s "statute of limitations"
/s debt indebtedness

promis! /s debt indebtedness /s bar barring barred /s "statute
of limitations"

acknowledg! /s debt indebtedness /s promis! /s "statute of
limitation"

moral! "pre-exist!" +1 duty obligat! consideration /s "statute of
limitation" /s debt indebtedness

"statute of limitation" /s debt indebtedness /s writing wr*te
written

"new promise" /s "statute of limitation"

241k145(5)

241k141

241k148(1)

"statute of limitation" /s unliquidated

§ 5–8. Promises to Perform Voidable Duties

If A is induced by fraud to promise to pay B $100 in return for
property worth much less, his promise is voidable. If, upon discovering
the fraud, he again promises to pay $100, or some lesser sum, the new
promise is enforceable without consideration,[80] provided of course, that
the new promise is not itself voidable because it is induced by fraud or
suffers from some other infirmity. If the second promise is made
without knowledge of the fraud, it is not enforceable.[81]

The same analysis is applicable to contracts voidable on other
grounds, such as duress, mistake and infancy. However it has not been
generally applied to void contracts[82] although there is an occasional
case to the contrary.[83]

The rule of law discussed here may also be explained on grounds
other than the presence or absence of consideration. A voidable
promise gives the promisor the right to elect to avoid or to affirm the
promise. In promising to make payment he has given notice of his
election not to exercise his power of avoidance.[84]

 WESTLAW REFERENCES

fraud! /s induc /s voidable /s promis!

duress mistak! infant infancy /s promis! /s voidable

---

80. Restatement, Second, Contracts § 85.

81. Restatement, Second, Contracts § 93. The promisor need only know the essential facts. According to the Restatement, it is not necessary that he know that the facts give him a legal power of avoidance or other remedy. But see § 8–5 infra as to infants; and see also 3 Black, Rescission of Contracts and Cancellation of Written Instruments § 591 (2d ed.1929).

82. Restatement, Second, Contracts § 85.

83. Hansen v. Kootenai County Bd. of County Com'rs, 93 Idaho 655, 471 P.2d 42 (1970); Sheldon v. Haxtun, 91 N.Y. 124 (1883) (usury).

84. 1 Williston § 204.

§ 5–9.　New Promise Based Upon a Previous Promise Within the Statute of Frauds

If A and B enter into a contract which is unenforceable under the Statute of Frauds,[85] should a subsequent oral promise based upon the previous agreement within the Statute of Frauds be enforceable? Assuming first that the arrangement within the Statute of Frauds is still executory, it might seem that the case is analogous to the voidable promises discussed above and that therefore the subsequent oral promise should be enforceable despite the absence of consideration.[86] However, an important difference is that enforcement of the subsequent oral promise would violate the policy of the Statute of Frauds which is to curtail perjured claims.[87] Consequently, the subsequent oral promise is not enforced.

A different problem is presented if the subsequent promise is in writing. Under the Statute of Frauds it is well settled that a memorandum subsequent to the agreement that sufficiently outlines the details of the transaction satisfies the Statute of Frauds and it is immaterial that there is no consideration for the memorandum.[88] Thus, if the subsequent promise is contained in a sufficient memorandum it will be enforceable. But there is some authority for the proposition that where the writing definitely states the terms of the promise, as in a promissory note to pay a sum certain, it should be enforceable even though it does not serve as a sufficient memorandum.[89]

The situation is also different where the agreement that is unenforceable under the Statute of Frauds has been performed by one of the parties. Under these circumstances it is generally accepted that the party who has performed is entitled to a quasi-contractual recovery.[90] A subsequent promise to pay what is owing under this quasi-contractual obligation raises the problems discussed in section 5–4 above. Occasionally a statute is drawn in such a way as to prevent a quasi-contractual recovery. In such a case the subsequent promise should be enforced unless the subsequent promise is included in the prohibition.[91]

A major conservative force in this area has been the over-generalized but influential note made by the reporters to the case of Wennall v. Adney.[92] This asserted that a new promise to pay a debt that had been barred by operation of law is enforceable while a new promise to pay a debt unenforceable at its inception is not enforceable. This over-

85. See ch. 19 infra.

86. See § 5–8 supra.

87. Hill v. Dodge, 80 N.H. 381, 117 A. 728 (1922).

88. See § 19–30 infra.

89. 1 Williston § 199; 1A Corbin § 238. The Restatement, Second, Contracts § 86, Comment g, states that "the new promise is binding if the policy of the statute is satisfied." See, e.g., Muir v. Kane, 55 Wash. 131, 104 P. 153 (1909); Fellom v. Adams, 274 Cal.App.2d 855, 79 Cal.Rptr. 633 (1969); Bagaeff v. Prokopik, 212 Mich. 265, 180 N.W. 427, 17 A.L.R. 1292 (1920).

90. See § 19–40 infra.

91. 1A Corbin § 238.

92. 127 Eng.Rep. 137 (K.B.1802).

generalization frequently has been criticized in the cases [93] and the treatises,[94] and should be discarded.

WESTLAW REFERENCES
"statute of fraud" /s subsequent! /s enforc! unenforc!
di(wr*te writing written /p subsequent! /s "statute of fraud")
"subsequent! promis!" /s "statute of fraud"
"statute of fraud" /s unenforc! /s perform!
"statute of fraud" /s "quasi contract***"

§ 5–10. Miscellaneous Promises Supported by Antecedent Events

On moral obligation and related grounds a number of cases which have not been previously discussed have enforced promises based on antecedent events. These include promises by sureties or indorsers who have been discharged on technical grounds,[95] promises to repay sums collected by force of an erroneous but valid judgment [96] and promises to pay for benefits received under an illegal bargain when the illegality does not involve moral turpitude,[97] as well as others.[98] The cases in this category are closely allied in reasoning and rationale with the cases involving prior legal obligations discharged by the statute of limitations. Therefore they should be authoritative even in jurisdictions that do not accept a broad view of moral obligation as an equivalent of consideration.

WESTLAW REFERENCES
surety endors! /s promis! /s discharg!

§ 5–11. To Whom the Promise Must Be Made

A new promise to pay an antecedent obligation, to be enforceable, must be made to an obligee of the antecedent duty or his representative.[99] A promise made to a stranger to the transaction has no operative effect unless it can be anticipated that this person will communicate the promise to the obligee.[1] In a few jurisdictions, where a mere admission of the indebtedness is sufficient to revive the debt, an admission or promise made to a third person is sufficient.[2]

93. Bagaeff v. Prokopik, 212 Mich. 265, 180 N.W. 427 (1920); Goulding v. Davidson, 26 N.Y. 604 (1863) (contract usurious in its inception); Muir v. Kane, 55 Wash. 131, 104 P. 153 (1909); but see Stout v. Humphrey, 69 N.J.L. 436, 55 A. 281 (1903).

94. 1A Corbin § 239; 1 Williston § 202.

95. 1A Corbin § 224.

96. Bentley v. Morse, 14 Johns. 468 (N.Y.1817); 1A Corbin § 225.

97. 1A Corbin § 236.

98. 1A Corbin §§ 210–239.

99. City of Fort Scott v. Hickman, 112 U.S. 150, 5 S.Ct. 56, 28 L.Ed. 636 (1884); Restatement, Second, Contracts § 92; 1 Williston §§ 154, 185, esp. 189. Beneficiaries, sureties, assignees, and distributees are included in the term obligee. Restatement, Second, Contracts § 92, Comments b and c.

1. Miller v. Teeter, 53 N.J.Eq. 262, 31 A. 394 (1895).

2. In re Stratman's Estate, 231 Iowa 480, 1 N.W.2d 636 (1942).

WESTLAW REFERENCES

"new promise" /s obligee representative represent***

"new promise" /s assignee distributee surety

B. CONSIDERATION NOT REQUIRED IN CERTAIN COMMERCIAL AND WRITTEN CONTRACTS

Table of Sections

§ 5–12. Scope of the Discussion

At common law, persons wishing to enter into a contract without consideration were empowered to resort to a sealed instrument.[3] In recent decades, by legislation and judicial decision, the legal effect of the seal has been abolished or substantially curtailed in a majority of jurisdictions.[4] Partly in an attempt to fill the gap thus created, legislatures have reacted with a number of statutes which provide that specified kinds of promises are enforceable without consideration. The abolition of the seal was not the only motive for these statutes. Ever since Lord Mansfield's day[5] there has been a lingering feeling that written agreements show sufficient deliberation and that the requirement of consideration, as applied to them, tends, without sufficient justification, to defeat the expectations of the parties.[6] Similarly, the doctrine has sometimes seemed to have defeated commercial expectations without any countervailing benefit to the state's interest in regulating private contracts.

This text does not purport to attempt complete coverage of local variations. Only the most significant types of statutes will be considered.

---

3. See ch. 7 infra.

4. Id.

5. See § 5–1 supra.

6. For a contrary point of view, see Hays, Formal Contracts and Consideration: A Legislative Program, 41 Colum.L.Rev.

849, 852 (1941) ("deliberation, seriousness of purpose, intent to be legally bound, even if they were actually indicated by the formal device, are not, in themselves and apart from other factors, proper grounds for enforcing promises.")

§ 5–13. The Model Written Obligations Act

Pennsylvania is the only state which presently has on its books [7] the Model (formerly Uniform) Written Obligations Act.[8] This provides:

> "A written release or promise, hereafter made and signed by the person releasing or promising, shall not be invalid or unenforceable for lack of consideration, if the writing also contains an additional express statement, in any form of language, that the signer intends to be legally bound."

Under this statute, a written promise is not sufficient; there must be "an additional express statement" indicating the promisor's intent to be bound.[9] It has been held that the following language is insufficient to meet the statutory requirements: [10]

> "We, Pauline and Mike, release you from all obligations under the Lease, for the balance thereof, and will not hold you responsible whatsoever under the Lease if you sell to Mr. Brown."

Subsequent cases appear more ready to infer an intent to be bound from the use of legalistic language.[11]

§ 5–14. Modification of Contracts

(a) Consideration Not Required

As previously discussed, according to the majority of cases, under the pre-existing duty rule an enforceable agreement to modify a contract requires consideration on both sides.[12] This rule has been mitigated in a number of states when unforeseen difficulties arise in the performance of the contract,[13] and eliminated by judicial decision in a distinct minority of jurisdictions.[14] There are also some statutes less sweeping than the Model Written Obligations Act that relate specifically to modifications.

The Sales Article of the Uniform Commercial Code provides in § 2–209(1):

> "An agreement modifying a contract within this Article needs no consideration to be binding." [15]

The Code does not require the modifying agreement to be written except in two important instances. First, a writing is required if the

7. 33 Purdon's Statutes Ann. §§ 6–8.

8. 9C U.L.A. 378 (adopted 1925); see Note, 29 Colum.L.Rev. 206 (1929). The Act is criticized in Hays, supra note 6, at 850–52.

9. Gershman v. Metropolitan Life Ins. Co., 405 Pa. 585, 176 A.2d 435 (1962) (words, "Approved by" followed by a signature are insufficient to meet the statutory requirement).

10. Fedun v. Mike's Cafe, Inc., 204 Pa. Super. 356, 204 A.2d 776 (1964), affirmed 419 Pa. 607, 213 A.2d 638 (1965).

11. Paul Revere Protective Life Ins. Co. v. Weis, 535 F.Supp. 379 (E.D.Pa.1981), affirmed 707 F.2d 1403 (3d Cir.1982); Fasco, A.G. v. Modernage, Inc., 311 F.Supp. 161 (W.D.Pa.1970).

12. See § 4–8 supra.

13. See § 4–8 supra.

14. See § 4–8 supra.

15. See also Restatement, Second, Contracts § 89, discussed in § 4–9 supra.

contract as modified is within the Statute of Frauds provision of the Code.[16] Also, a writing is required if the original contract by its terms excludes modification or rescission by mutual consent except by a signed writing.[17]

This section which dispenses with the necessity for consideration and which does not generally require a writing raises the question of whether there can be a modification without an express agreement and without a course of performance. In Gateway Co. v. Charlotte Theatres[18] the parties had reduced their agreement to writing. In a covering letter the buyer specified a completion date although none had been set in the original agreement. The seller ignored this and started performance but did not complete within the time specified by the buyer. The court held that the seller had accepted the proposed modification by its conduct.[19]

An illustrative case under § 2–209 involving an express modification is Skinner v. Tober Foreign Motors, Inc.[20] The defendant sold and delivered an airplane to the plaintiff who agreed to pay the purchase price at the rate of $200 per month. Soon after delivery, it was discovered that the engine was faulty. Apparently, the airplane was not warranted. Since the plaintiff would have to incur considerable expense in repairing the engine, defendant orally agreed that for one year plaintiff would have to pay only $100 per month toward the price. Several months later, defendant demanded that the payments be increased to $200. Plaintiff refused and defendant repossessed the aircraft. It was held that the modification was binding without consideration and that defendant was liable for substantial damages.[21]

Outside of the Uniform Commercial Code, other statutory provisions relating to modification without consideration exist. For example, there is a New York statute that is substantially the same as § 2–209 of the Uniform Commercial Code, except that a writing is required in every case of a modification without consideration.[22] In the New York scheme the writing serves more than merely an evidentiary

16. U.C.C. § 2–209(3). See § 19–37 infra.

17. U.C.C. § 2–209(2). See text at notes 25–31 infra.

18. 297 F.2d 483 (1st Cir.1961).

19. Could the case be explained on the basis of U.C.C. § 2–207? See § 2–21 supra.

20. 345 Mass. 429, 187 N.E.2d 669 (1963), noted in 65 W.Va.L.Rev. 330 (1963).

21. Since the defendant did not plead the defense of Statute of Frauds, the court did not reach the question whether a writing was required by § 2–201 of the Code.

Not only is a modification involved here but also a discharge. In fact there may be no distinction between these terms because accepting $100.00 per month in place of

$200.00 could be considered a modification even if there were no prior agreement. Anderson, The Part Payment Check under the Code, 9 Am.Bus.L.J. 103, 121 (1971).

22. McKinney's N.Y. General Obligations Law § 5–1103, effective in 1936, Mich.Comp.L.Annot. § 566.1 is substantially to the same effect. Compare such statutes as Mass.G.L.A. c. 4 § 9A, providing that an instrument reciting that it is a sealed instrument will be treated as a sealed instrument. Compare also such statutes as Miss.Code 1972, § 75–19–1 which appear to give the effect of a sealed instrument to all writings. The effect of the statutes such as these depends on the effect seals have heretofore had in the particular jurisdiction. See § 7–9 infra.

purpose. The writing requirement is designed also to assure that the modification was a deliberate act of the will.[23] Consequently, unlike the writing requirements of the Statute of Frauds, the modification itself must be in writing; a written memorandum of the modification is not sufficient.[24]

(b) Effect of No-Oral-Modification Clause

Apart from statute, the common law rule is that "even where the contract specifically states that no non-written [modification] will be recognized, the parties may yet alter their agreement by parol." [25] This rule stems from the notion that contracting parties cannot today restrict their power to contract with each other tomorrow.[26] The Uniform Commercial Code, however, gives effect, within limits, to clauses prohibiting oral modifications or rescissions, recognizing that parties seek protection against false allegations of oral modifications.[27] If the contract is between a merchant [28] and a non-merchant, a term on the merchant's form requiring that modification or rescission be in a signed writing must be separately signed by the non-merchant.[29]

The Code in Section 2–209 directly confronts the situation where an oral modification or rescission is made in violation of a clause forbidding such oral agreements. Subdivision 4 provides that the attempted modification can operate as a waiver. A waiver is effective, but retractable by giving reasonable notification "unless the retraction would be unjust in view of a material change of position in reliance on the waiver." [30]

The Code's provisions with respect to no-oral-modification clauses were patterned on a prior New York Statute.[31] The New York Statute is unclear on the question of the effect of part performance of an oral

23. Second Annual Report of the [N.Y.] Law Revision Commission 67, 172 (1936). ("Without undertaking to enforce all promises and agreements, the common law might conceivably establish a more comprehensive basis or theory for the enforcement of deliberate promises intentionally made when they are of a character ordinarily relied upon by men in their economic or business dealings. The necessary deliberation, certainty and security could be insured by evidentiary and formal requirements.")

24. Cf. Dfi Communications, Inc. v. Greenberg, 41 N.Y.2d 602, 394 N.Y.S.2d 586, 363 N.E.2d 312 (1977), motion denied 41 N.Y.2d 1017, 395 N.Y.S.2d 639, 363 N.E.2d 1384 (1977) (decided under McKinney's N.Y. General Obligations Law § 15–301).

25. Wagner v. Graziano Constr. Co., 390 Pa. 445, 136 A.2d 82, 84 (1957). Universal Builders, Inc. v. Moon Motor Lodge, Inc., 430 Pa. 550, 244 A.2d 10 (1968) rejects the suggestion made in C.I.T. Corp. v. Jonnet,

419 Pa. 435, 214 A.2d 620 (1965) that to have a waiver the requirement for a writing must be explicitly waived. In accord with Wagner are First Nat'l Bank v. Acra, 462 N.E.2d 1345 (Ind.App.1984); University Nat'l Bank v. Wolfe, 279 Md. 512, 369 A.2d 570 (1977); Son-Shine Grading, Inc. v. Adc Construction Co., 68 N.C.App. 417, 315 S.E.2d 346 (1984), review denied 312 N.C. 85, 321 S.E.2d 900 (1984); but see Mathis v. Daines, 196 Mont. 252, 639 P.2d 503 (1982).

26. Restatement, Second, Contracts § 283, Comment b.

27. U.C.C. § 2–209, Comment 3.

28. See § 1–7 supra.

29. U.C.C. § 2–209(2).

30. U.C.C. § 2–209(5); see Note, The Scope and Meaning of Waiver in § 2–209 of The Uniform Commercial Code, 5 Ga.L. Rev. 783 (1971).

31. McKinney's N.Y. General Obligations Law § 15–301.

modification that violates a clause barring such modifications. The courts have interpreted the statute to conform to the U.C.C. in most respects,[32] although points of difference may remain.[33] This is a sound interpretation inasmuch as conduct that makes the oral agreement unretractable is (1) highly probative of the oral modifying agreement and (2) good grounds for estopping a party from shielding himself against liability.

 WESTLAW REFERENCES

A. Consideration Not Required

2–209(1)

gateway +s "charlotte theatre"

accept! /s modif! /s contract agreement /s conduct

"express! modif!" /s consideration

95k236 /p consideration

McKinney's +s 5–1103

343k89 /p consideration

B. Effect of No-Oral-Modification Clause

wagner +s graziano

"oral modification clause"

oral! parol* /s modif! /s "non merchant" merchant

343k89 /p wr*te writing written

95k238(2) /p prohibit!

mckinney's +s 15–301

C. Modifications Under Compulsion

contract agreement /s alter*****modif! /s compulsion

lingenfelder +s wainwright

u.c.c. "uniform commercial code" /s 2–614 2–615

"presupposed condition"

modif! alter***** /s duress /s consideration

"business compulsion" /s duress

D. Release and Accord and Satisfaction

effect! ineffect! /s "accord and satisfaction" /s releas! /s
    consideration

u.c.c. "uniform commercial code" /s 1–107

331k37 /p consideration

di release

releas! /s duty /s consideration

"common law" /s release! /s seal

renounc! renunciation /s releas! /s intend! intent!

---

32. Nassau Trust Co. v. Montrose Concrete Prods. Corp., 56 N.Y.2d 175, 451 N.Y.S.2d 663, 436 N.E.2d 1265 (1982), reargument denied 57 N.Y.2d 674, 454 N.Y.S.2d 1032, 439 N.E.2d 1247 (1982); Rose v. Spa Realty Assocs., 42 N.Y.2d 338, 397 N.Y.S.2d 922, 366 N.E.2d 1279 (1977).

33. E.g., the distinction between waiver and modification is stressed in Nassau Trust Co. v. Montrose Concrete Prods., cited in the prior note where the court suggests that an estoppel will more readily be found in the case of an oral waiver than in the case of an oral modification.

§ 5–15. Modifications Under Compulsion

The pre-existing duty rule, in addition to the conceptual ground sustaining it, has had an important policy rationale. In an early decision, a sailor who had signed for a voyage at a stipulated wage sued to recover for additional wages promised him during the voyage. Lord Kenyon, in rendering his decision, was little concerned about concepts of consideration. Rather, he urged:

> "If this action was to be supported, it would materially affect the navigation of this kingdom * * * [I]f sailors were * * * in times of danger entitled to insist on an extra charge on such a promise as this, they would in many cases suffer a ship to sink, unless the captain would pay any extravagant demand they might think proper to make." [34]

In repeated instances, courts have defended the pre-existing duty rule as a salutary method of preventing the coerced modification of contracts.[35] Now that the Uniform Commercial Code and other legislation permit a contractual modification without consideration it seems clear that other techniques need to be developed to avoid coerced modifications.

The Code must be read as an integrated document. As the comments to § 2–209 make clear the good faith standard of § 2–103 ("the observance of reasonable commercial standards of fair dealing in the trade") [36] is applicable to a request for modification. It will, of course, require a good deal of creative interpretation of the Code before standards are developed for distinguishing between reasonable and unreasonable demands for modification. Clearly, if unforeseen difficulties arise that are sufficient to excuse performance for failure of presupposed conditions,[37] a modification is permissible because detriment would exist in the surrender of the privilege not to perform. If unforeseen difficulties of a less significant kind arise, such as had led a minority of states, prior to enactment of the Code, to permit a modification without new detriment,[38] it is equally clear that a modification would be enforced under the Code. Indeed, the language permits a far broader permissibility of modifications unilaterally favorable to one party.

As to modifications entered into under other statutory dispensations from the requirement of consideration, the common law doctrine of duress is relevant. The doctrine, in most jurisdictions has been rather narrow in scope. Generally, it has been held that a threat to break a contract does not constitute duress.[39] Of late, however, courts

34. Harris v. Watson, 170 Eng.Rep. at 94 (K.B.1791); see also Stilk v. Myrick, 170 Eng.Rep. 1168 (C.P.1809); Bartlett v. Wyman, 14 Johns. (N.Y.) 260 (1817) (similar facts; cases decided on grounds of lack of consideration); see § 4–9 supra.

35. See, e.g., Lingenfelder v. Wainwright Brewery Co., 103 Mo. 578, 15 S.W. 844 (1891).

36. On "good faith" see 11–38 infra.

37. U.C.C. §§ 2–614, 2–615. See § 13–22 infra.

38. See § 4–9 supra.

39. Hartsville Oil Mill v. United States, 271 U.S. 43, 46 S.Ct. 389, 70 L.Ed. 822 (1926); Austin Instruments, Inc. v. Loral Corp., 29 N.Y.2d 124, 324 N.Y.S.2d 22, 272

have begun to hold that various kinds of "business compulsion" constitute duress.[40]   Only recently has this concept been expanded, to the point where a bad faith demand for modification, if coupled with other factors, will be treated as duress.[41]   In this way the various statutory provisions permitting contractual modifications without consideration will be brought into harmony with the Code.

§ 5–16.   Release and Accord and Satisfaction

The pre-existing duty concept led to the rule that a release of a duty, except in an instrument under seal, is ordinarily ineffectual without consideration.[42]   Section 1–107 of the U.C.C. provides, however, that: "any claim of right arising out of alleged breach can be discharged in whole or in part by a written waiver or renunciation signed and delivered by the aggrieved party."   The section appears to relate to a discharge by way of release since the word renunciation is the word of art used in connection with an oral release.[43]

The section is comparable to § 15–303 of the New York General Obligations Law which provides: "A written instrument which purports to be a total or partial release of any particular claim * * * shall not be invalid because of the absence of consideration or of a seal." [44]   It should be noted that the Code section applies only to a claim or right arising out of an "alleged breach" whereas the New York statute covers the release of any claim or obligation even if there has been no breach.   Both statutes merely dispense with the requirements of consideration.   They do not make a release invulnerable to attack because of duress or other invalidating cause.[45]   These statutes were designed to fill the vacuum left by the demise of the common law release under seal.[46]   To be effective as a release the writing must contain an expression of present intention to renounce a claim.[47]

We have previously considered the recurring fact pattern where D, who owes C a liquidated debt, sends C a check for less than the debt and clearly marks it as "payment in full."   When C cashes the check no accord and satisfaction or release occurs because, under the pre-existing duty rule, D has furnished no consideration.[48]   Would the statutes discussed in this section change the outcome?   C, by endorsing the check, has signed a writing containing language of present discharge. Nevertheless, the New York Courts have consistently ruled that no discharge results.   The apparent rationale is that an indorsement does not show the kind of circumspection and deliberateness that the writing

N.E.2d 533 (1971), reargument denied 29 N.Y.2d 749, 326 N.Y.S.2d 1027, 276 N.E.2d 238 (1971).

40. See § 9–6 infra.

41. See § 9–6 infra.

42. See § 4–9 supra.

43. See §§ 21–10, 21–12 infra.

44. Statutes similar to the New York statute are cited in 1 Williston § 120 n. 9.

45. New Again Constr. Co. v. New York, 76 Misc.2d 943, 351 N.Y.S.2d 895 (1974).

46. See Second Annual Report of the [N.Y.] Law Revision Commission 67 (1936).

47. Carpenter v. Machold, 86 A.D.2d 727, 447 N.Y.S.2d 46 (3d Dep't 1982) (N.Y. Statute).

48. See § 4–11 supra.

requirement was intended to insure.[49] No comparable cases appear to have arisen under U.C.C. § 1–107. It is doubtful whether return of the cashed check to D by D's bank would meet the delivery requirement of the Statute. The argument has been made that such a check cashing would constitute a valid modification without consideration under U.C.C. § 2–209,[50] but a discharge is not generally deemed to be a modification.

§ 5–17. Firm Offers

As previously discussed, under the U.C.C. and under a number of other statutes, an offer may be made irrevocable without consideration, if the statutory formalities are met.[51]

§ 5–18. Past Consideration: Moral Obligation and Guarantees of Pre-existing Debts

As indicated,[52] past events do not constitute consideration, in the bargain sense, for a promise. For example, a promise by C to guarantee payment of an existing debt owed by B to A, requires new consideration,[53] and a promise made after an employee's retirement to pay him a pension, is unenforceable.[54] A provision of the New York General Obligations Law [55] states that:

> "A promise in writing and signed by the promisor or by his agent shall not be denied effect as a valid contractual obligation on the ground that consideration for the promise is past or executed, if the consideration is expressed in the writing and is proved to have been given or performed and would be valid consideration but for the time it was given or performed."

Similar results are obtainable under broader statutes, such as the Model Written Obligations Act.[56]

The New York Statute was designed primarily to permit recovery on a promise based on a prior moral obligation created by benefits conferred upon the promisor or a third person.[57] The writing require-

---

49. King Metal Products, Inc. v. Workman's Compensation Bd., 20 A.D.2d 565, 245 N.Y.S.2d 882 (2d Dep't 1963); Glen Navigation Corp. v. Trodden, 97 N.Y.S.2d 228 (N.Y.City Ct.1950); Horan v. John F. Trommer Inc., 15 Misc.2d 347, 137 N.Y.S.2d 26 (1954); Armour & Co. v. Schlacter, 159 N.Y.S.2d 135 (County Ct. 1957).

50. Anderson, The Part Payment Check Under the Code, 9 Am.Bus.L.J. 103 (1971).

51. See § 2–25 supra.

52. See § 4–3 supra.

53. Strong v. Sheffield, 144 N.Y. 392, 39 N.E. 330 (1895).

54. Perreault v. Hall, 94 N.H. 191, 49 A.2d 812 (1946).

55. § 5–1105 (enacted in 1941, as since amended).

56. See § 5–13 supra.

57. See 1941 Report of the [N.Y.] Law Revision Commission 345, 395–96. The legislature's failure to coordinate this section with other provisions relating to the effect on the statute of limitations of a new promise to pay a debt, and the effect of a new promise to pay a debt discharged by bankruptcy has caused confusion. See, as an expression that confusion, Persico Oil Co., Inc. v. Levy, 64 Misc.2d 1091, 316 N.Y.S.2d 924 (1970).

ment is expected to assure that the promise is made with deliberation.[58] The statute has been the subject of strong criticism [59] and has been but little applied.

It was foreseen, and experience has borne out, that a principal application of the New York past consideration statute would be in cases where a promisor guarantees payment of a pre-existing debt of another.[60] The Uniform Commercial Code has largely preempted this function of the statute, making it clear that no consideration is necessary to validate commercial paper governed by article 3 of the Code if the instrument is given for an antecedent indebtedness.[61] Similarly no consideration is required to validate an indorsement made to guaranty payment of a pre-existing debt of another.[62]

The term "past consideration" is not defined by the statute. From the Law Revision Commission report it seems rather clear that it includes past bargained for detriment, even by a third person and past material benefit received by the promisor even without request. It is not clear whether past unbargained for detriment would constitute past consideration. Suppose an uncle promises his nephew $5,000 in a signed writing "in consideration of the fact that you have refrained from using tobacco and alcohol for five years." It is doubted whether such a promise would be enforceable. If it were to be, any gift promise could be made enforceable by searching out past unbargained for detriment and reciting it in a signed writing. This would stretch the statute beyond its legislative purpose. The courts have been insistent that the writing contain an "unequivocal" promise.[63] In view of the gratuitous nature of the promise, this construction of the Statute seems sound.[64]

 WESTLAW REFERENCES

"past consideration" /s statut!

u.c.c. "uniform commercial code" /s 3–408

"unequivocal! promis!" /s consideration

---

58. See 1941 Report of the [N.Y.] Law Revision Commission 345, 395–96.

59. Braucher, Freedom of Contract and the Second Restatement, 78 Yale L.J. 598, 605 ("This provision is too broad is scope and too restrictive in formal requirements; it does not seem to have had any significant effect."); 1A Corbin § 210 n. 1 ("This is not a useful statute: indeed it is likely to do positive harm."). For criticism from the opposite direction, to the effect that this and other New York provisions do not go far enough, see Lloyd, Consideration and the Seal in New York—An Unsatisfactory Legislative Program, 46 Colum.L.Rev. 1 (1946) (gift promises ought to be enforceable). Another overall look at the New York statutory scheme is Comment, 46 Mich.L.Rev. 58 (1947).

60. 1941 Report of the [N.Y.] Law Revision Commission 345, 395–96; Hays, supra note 6, at 859. See Weyerhaeuser Co. v. Gershman, 324 F.2d 163 (2d Cir.1963); Central State Bank v. Botwin, 66 Misc.2d 1085, 323 N.Y.S.2d 74 (Civ.Ct.1971) reversed on other grounds 71 Misc.2d 1012, 337 N.Y.S.2d 856 (App.Term 1972).

61. U.C.C. § 3–408.

62. U.C.C. § 3–408, Comment 2.

63. Umschied v. Simnacher, 106 A.D.2d 380, 482 N.Y.S.2d 295 (2d Dep't 1984).

64. Perillo, The Statute of Frauds in the Light of the Functions and Dysfunctions of Form, 43 Fordham L.Rev. 39, 55–56, 79 (1974).

C. STIPULATIONS

Table of Sections

§ 5–19. Stipulation Defined

A stipulation is a promise or agreement with reference to a pending judicial proceeding, made by a party to the proceeding or his attorney.[65] Stipulations are favored by the courts. They tend to relieve court congestion and place the settlement of litigation or details of litigation on the litigants where it primarily belongs.

 WESTLAW REFERENCES
di stipulation
stipulat! /s "judicial proceeding"

§ 5–20. Consideration and Formality in Stipulations

Generally, statutes or rules of court provide that a stipulation should be in writing or made in open court.[66] Stipulations are enforced without regard to consideration [67] but as in the case of any other kind of contract, fraud or other vitiating circumstances can be shown to avoid its legal effect.[68] Indeed, a court has power to relieve a party from a stipulation if there is no prejudice to the other party, for reasons such as inadvertence, improvidence or excusable neglect.[69]

An oral stipulation made out of court is not a nullity. It is dishonorable for an attorney to avoid performance of an oral agreement and a court will enforce an oral stipulation upon which a party relies to his detriment.[70]

 WESTLAW REFERENCES
"oral! stipulat!" /s enforc!
363k6
stipulat! /s detriment! /s rely! reli****

---

65. See Restatement, Second, Contracts § 94; 1 Williston § 204A.

66. Id. It has been held that "open court" does not include judge's chambers. Matter of Dolgin Eldert Corp., 31 N.Y.2d 1, 334 N.Y.S.2d 833, 286 N.E.2d 228 (1972).

67. Crunden-Martin Mfg. Co. v. Christy, 188 P. 875 (1920); Connors v. United Metal Products Co., 209 Minn. 300, 296 N.W. 21 (1941); Restatement, Second, Contracts § 94.

68. 1 Williston § 204A.

69. Hester v. New Amersterdam Cas. Co., 268 F.Supp. 623 (D.S.C.1967); Matter of Frutiger, 29 N.Y.2d 143, 324 N.Y.S.2d 36, 272 N.E.2d 543 (1971).

70. Mutual Life Ins. Co. v. O'Donnell, 146 N.Y. 275, 40 N.E. 787 (1895); Restatement, Second, Contracts § 94(c).

Chapter 6

PROMISSORY ESTOPPEL: DETRIMENTAL RELIANCE AS A SUBSTITUTE FOR CONSIDERATION

Table of Sections

§ 6–1. Introduction

We say in the chapter on consideration that a donative promise would not be enforced even though the promisee relied upon it to his injury.[1] It was felt that consideration was necessary to insure that the promise was made with sufficient deliberation.[2] Despite a general adherence to the law of consideration, a relied upon donative promise was enforced in certain categories even though reliance was not necessarily the stated basis for enforcement of the promise.[3] There can be little doubt that the reliance interest should be entitled to protection.[4]

1. See § 4–1 supra.

2. See the more extended discussion in 4–2 supra.

3. See Boyer, Promissory Estoppel: Principle from Precedents (pts. 1–2), 50 Mich.L.Rev. 639 (1952); see also Boyer, Promissory Estoppel: Requirements and Limitations of the Doctrine, 98 U.Pa.L.Rev. 459 (1950). See § 6–2 infra.

4. Fuller & Perdue, The Reliance Interest in Contract Damages (pts. 1–2), 46 Yale L.J. 52 (1936).

271

In 1932, Professor Williston, as chief architect of the First Restatement, gave birth to the doctrine of promissory estoppel—a doctrine that states reliance may in a proper case make a donative promise enforceable.[5] As a result this doctrine became a separate and specific doctrine recognized in American contract law.[6]

Section 90 stated the doctrine in the following terms: "A promise which the promisor should reasonably expect to induce action or forbearance of a definite and substantial character on the part of the promisee and which does induce such action or forbearance is binding if injustice can be avoided only by the enforcement of the promise."

It is obvious that a promise is necessary to create promissory estoppel.[7] Thus a statement of future intent is not sufficient.[8] The same is true of a precatory remark.[9] So also reliance on an estimate is not generally sufficient.[10]

Secondly the promise must be one which the promisor should reasonably anticipate will lead the promisee to act or to forbear.[11] This looks at the matter from the point of view of the promisor. In addition the promisee must reasonably rely upon the promise.[12]

Furthermore, the reliance of the promisee must be of a definite and substantial character. Substantiality is obviously a quantitative factor. The word "definite" creates a particular problem that can best be illustrated by an example used by Professor Williston. He says that a promise of $1,000.00 with which to buy an automobile is binding if it induces the purchase of a car whereas a promise of $1,000.00 for no specific purpose will not be binding if it induces similar action. In other words, the reliance which occurs must not only be reasonable but also must be foreseeable.[13] Corbin identifies the question as one of

5. Restatement, Contracts § 90 (1932).

6. Eisenberg, Donative Promises, 47 U.Chi.L.Rev. 1 (1979).

7. Burst v. Adolph Coors Co., 650 F.2d 930 (8th Cir.1981); United States Jaycees v. Bloomfield, 434 A.2d 1379 (D.C.App. 1981); Irwin Concrete Inc. v. Sun Coast Properties, 33 Wn.App. 190, 653 P.2d 1331 (1982).

8. School Dist. No. 69 of Maricopa County v. Altherr, 10 Ariz.App. 333, 458 P.2d 537 (1969); Pappas v. Bever, 219 N.W.2d 720 (Iowa 1974).

9. Woodmere Academy v. Steinberg, 41 N.Y.2d 746, 395 N.Y.S.2d 434, 363 N.E.2d 1169 (1977).

10. Robert Gordon, Inc. v. Ingersoll-Rand Co., 117 F.2d 654 (7th Cir.1941); cf. Leo F. Piazza Paving Co. v. Bebek & Brkich, 141 Cal.App.2d 226, 296 P.2d 368 (1956). But see United States v. Briggs Mfg. Co., 460 F.2d 1195 (9th Cir.1972).

11. Smith v. Boise Kenworth Sales, Inc., 102 Idaho 63, 625 P.2d 417 (1981); Dial v. Deskins, 221 Va. 701, 273 S.E.2d 546 (1981).

12. Landess v. Borden, Inc., 667 F.2d 628 (7th Cir.1981); Atlanta Nat'l Real Estate Trust v. Tally, 243 Ga. 247, 253 S.E.2d 692 (1979); Malaker Corp Stockholder's Protective Comm. v. First Jersey Nat'l Bank, 163 N.J.Super. 463, 395 A.2d 222 (1978), certification denied 79 N.J. 488, 401 A.2d 243 (1979).

13. 4 A.L.I. Proceeding at 92–93. RCM Supply Co. v. Hunter Douglas, Inc. 686 F.2d 1074 (4th Cir.1982); Levitt Homes v. Old Farm Homeowner's Ass'n, 111 Ill.App. 3d 300, 67 Ill.Dec. 155, 444 N.E.2d 194 (1982); Ripple's of Clearview, Inc. v. Le Havre Assoc., 88 A.D.2d 120, 452 N.Y.2d 447 (2d Dep't 1982), appeal denied 57 N.Y.2d 609, 456 N.Y.S.2d 1026, 442 N.E.2d 1277 (1982).

foreseeability but argues that the rules should be in accord with the standards of foreseeability followed in negligence law.[14]

Finally the promise will be enforced only if injustice can be avoided by the enforcement of the promise.[15] To some extent this relates to Williston's notion (not expressly stated in the First Restatement) that any recovery under the doctrine of promissory estoppel should be a full contractual recovery and not be limited to reliance damages. Under this approach, in deciding what is just one must consider this premise of full recovery and this is probably the reason for including in the section the provisions for definite and substantial reliance.[16] The question of avoidance of injustice is one of law; the other elements raise questions of fact.[17]

The authorities are not in accord on whether the promisee's reliance must be detrimental in the consideration sense or whether the reliance must be injurious to the promisee.[18] It would seem that injury is what is required because without injury there would be no injustice in not enforcing the promise.

Section 90 of the Restatement Second has made four very important changes in the formulation of the doctrine. (1) It has excised the words "of a definite, and substantial character" in text of the section.[19] (2) It added a new sentence permitting flexibility of remedy; that is to say a promise that is reasonably relied upon is enforceable to the extent of the reliance. As explained above this new provision contributed to the omission of the words "of a definite and substantial character".[20] (3) It has also provided for the contingency of reliance by a third party on a promise made to the promisee.[21] (4) It contains a provision that a

14. 1A Corbin § 200; see Sanders v. Arkansas-Mo. Power Co., 267 Ark. 1009, 593 S.W.2d 56 (App.1980).

15. Restatement, Second, Contracts § 90.

16. Eisenberg, supra note 6, at 23.

17. R.S. Bennett & Co., Inc. v. Economy Mech. Industries, Inc., 606 F.2d 182 (7th Cir.1979).

18. See Northern State Constr. Co. Robbins, 76 Wn.2d 357, 457 P.2d 187 (1969). But see Henderson, Promissory Estoppel and Traditional Contract Doctrine, 78 Yale L.J. 343 (1969).

19. However, Comment b to the Restatement Second § 90 makes it clear that the definite and substantial nature of the reliance is one of the factors to be considered. The comment goes on to list a number of other factors to be considered and concludes, "The force of particular factors varies in different types of cases: thus reliance need not be of a substantial character in charitable subscription cases, but must in cases of firm offers and guaranties." The Second Restatement thus provides not only for a flexible approach on remedies but also as to the substantive doctrine itself.

20. See Restatement, Second, Contracts § 90 Reporter's Note.

21. An illustration of a third party reliance is found in the case of Mount Vernon Trust Co. v. Bergoff, 272 N.Y. 192, 5 N.E.2d 196 (1936). At the request of B, a bank, D gave B a note in the sum of $35,000. At the same time B gave D a written statement to the effect that D would not be held liable on the note. The note, however, was treated on B's books as an asset of B and was shown to bank examiners. The bank became bankrupt. The court held that the bank's liquidators could enforce the note against D because of third party reliance. On the related question of enforcement by a third party beneficiary based upon reliance by the promisee, see Broxson v. Chicago Milwaukee, St. Paul & P.R. Co., 446 F.2d 628 (9th Cir.1971); Note, Should a Beneficiary Be Allowed to Invoke Promisee's Reliance to Enforce Promisor's Gratuitous Promise? 6 Val.U.L.Rev. 352 (1972);

charitable subscription or a marriage settlement is binding without proof that the promise induced action or forbearance.[22]

Ordinarily the key difference between a promise supported by consideration and a gratuitous promise supported by promissory estoppel is that in the former case the detriment is bargained for in exchange for the promise of the promisor; in the latter, there is no bargain. The injury is a consequence of the promise but does not induce the making of the promise.[23] Justice Holmes, in arguing for strict adherence to the concept of consideration, said, "[i]t is not enough that the promise induces the detriment or that the detriment induces the promise if the other half is wanting."[24] Elsewhere he lamented that the courts "have gone far" in losing sight of this fact.[25] The modern law has tended to hold firm to Holmes' view of consideration and to develop a separate doctrine of promissory estoppel from the cases which he had critized as stretching the doctrine of consideration beyond its conceptual boundaries.[26]

Perhaps at this point it would be wise to say just a word about the traditional distinction between promissory estoppel and equitable estoppel. Traditionally, estoppel *in pais* (equitable estoppel) has been limited to cases in which one party has represented a fact to the other who injuriously relies on the representation that is in fact false. In such cases the court bars the party who has made the representation from contradicting it.[27] Courts have traditionally held that an equitable estoppel could not be created by reliance on a promise.[28] Thus there was a need for the creation of this new doctrine of promissory estoppel.

 WESTLAW REFERENCES

williston /s "promissory estoppel" /s rely! reli****

gift donat! /s "promissory estoppel" /s rely! reli****

"future intent" /s promis! estop! rely! reli****

promis! /s estop! /s reasonabl! /s anticipat! act action forbear!

"promis! estop!" /s rely! reli**** /s reasonabl!

"promis! estop!" /s definite! substantial! /s rely! reli****

156k87

"promis! estop!" /s injusti! unjust! /s avoid!

see also Restatement, Second, Contracts § 90 Comment c.

22. See § 6–2(d) infra. For an extensive discussion of the Restatement Second, see Knapp, Reliance in the Revised Restatement: The Proliferation of Promissory Estoppel, 81 Colum.L.Rev. 52 (1981).

23. Youngman v. Nevada Irrigation Dist., 70 Cal.2d 240, 74 Cal.Rptr. 398, 449 P.2d 462 (1969).

24. Wisconsin & Mich. Ry. Co. v. Powers, 191 U.S. 379, 386, 24 S.Ct. 107, 108, 48 L.Ed. 229, 231 (1903).

25. O. Holmes, The Common Law, 292 (1881).

26. A legal system that does not impose a requirement of consideration has little need for a doctrine of promissory estoppel. See Comment, Promissory Estoppel and Louisiana, 31 La.L.Rev. 84 (1970).

27. See § 11–29 infra.

28. Henderson, supra note 18, p. 376; Commonwealth of Pennsylvania, Dep't of Pub. Welfare v. School Dist. of Philadelphia, 49 Pa.Cmwlth. 316, 410 A.2d 1311 (1980); see Restatement, Second, Contracts § 90, Comment a. A promise, at times, has been looked upon as a misrepresentation if the party who made it did not intend to carry it out when it was made. See § 9–19 infra.

"promis! estop!" /s rely! reli**** /s damage

"reliance damage"

"definite and substantial character" /s remedy!

"promis! estop!" /s "gratuitous promise"

di equitable estoppel

---

§ 6–2. The Roots of the Doctrine of Promissory Estoppel

As we have already seen, the doctrine of promissory estoppel as a separate and distinct doctrine is a twentieth century innovation. Nonetheless, it has ancient roots. It has been extracted as a general principle from a number of recurring decisions which were difficult, and sometimes impossible, to explain in terms of the doctrine of consideration.[29] In this section we will briefly consider these historical antecedents to the doctrine of promissory estoppel.

(a) Promises in the Family

In the case of Devecmon v. Shaw,[30] an uncle of the plaintiff promised him that, if plaintiff would take a trip to Europe, he would reimburse his expenses. The nephew made the trip but the uncle's executor[31] refused to make payment. The court concluded that the uncle's promise was supported by consideration. Surely there was detriment, but the court did not consider whether the detriment was bargained for in exchange for the promise.

The court came to grips with the conceptual problem in Ricketts v. Scothorn.[32] A grandfather had given his granddaughter a promissory note, indicating that it was for the purpose of freeing her from the necessity of working. It was clear that he was not demanding that she cease working in exchange for the note. The court recognized that there was no consideration for the note and held that the note would be enforced against the grandfather's estate on the grounds of estoppel *in pais*. Traditionally, as we have seen estoppel *in pais* has been limited to cases in which one party has represented a fact to the other who relies on the representation.[33] The court in Ricketts extended the doctrine of estoppel to promissory expressions.

Recognition of the doctrine of promissory estoppel as an independent ground for enforcing intrafamily promises can lead to a profitable reexamination of many similar cases decided on grounds of consideration.[34]

---

29. See § 6–1 supra.

30. 69 Md. 199, 14 A. 464 (1888).

31. How often it is in these cases that the promise is not repudiated by the promisor. Frequently, it is the executor, conscious of the possibility of being surcharged, who refused the payment. One cannot but conjecture the importance of this factor on the decisions.

32. 59 Neb. 51, 77 N.W. 365 (1898); see In re Estate of Bucci, 488 P.2d 216 (Colo. App.1971).

33. See note 27 supra.

34. E.g., Kirksey v. Kirshey, 8 Ala. 131 (1845); Hamer v. Sidway, 124 N.Y. 538, 27 N.E. 256 (1891). See § 4–5 supra for a discussion of these cases.

(b) Promise to Make a Gift of Land

Cases involving a promise to make a gift of land generally arise in a family context and are related to the cases discussed in the preceding section. If the promise is oral the case also involves non-compliance with Statute of Frauds [35] as well as the absence of consideration and has an historical background somewhat different from other kinds of intrafamily promises.

A promise to give land, standing alone, is unenforceable as a gift because of the lack of delivery of a conveyance to complete the gift. Not infrequently, however, acting in reliance on the gratuitous promise to convey land, the promisee, with the knowledge and assent of the promisor, takes possession of the land and makes improvements. Courts of equity in almost all states in such circumstances have granted the promisee specific performance [36] or other equitable remedies [37] even though the oral promise contravenes the Statutes of Frauds.[38] Traditionally, the expressed rationales of the decisions have been of two kinds. Sometimes, the court has relied on an analogy from the law of gifts, treating the entry upon the land and the making of improvements as the equivalent of physical delivery of a chattel.[39] Perhaps more frequently the courts have said that the taking of possession and the making of improvements constitute "good consideration in equity." [40] Under modern ideas of the relationship between law and equity it is indeed anomalous that a different definition of consideration should prevail in the equity and law sides of the court. It is now recognized that the decisions enforcing promises to give land are based on promissory estoppel.[41]

35. The Statute of Frauds generally requires that a contract to create or the creation of an interest in land be in writing. See §§ 19–14, 19–15 and 19–16 infra.

36. Seavey v. Drake, 62 N.H. 393 (1881); Freeman v. Freeman, 43 N.Y. 34 (1870); cf. Miller v. Lawlor, 245 Iowa 1144, 66 N.W.2d 267, 48 A.L.R.2d 1058 (1954). Some courts have distinguished between promises to make a gift in the future and promises to make a present gift stating that the former are not enforceable. Prior v. Newsom, 144 Ark. 593, 223 S.W. 21 (1920); Burris v. Landers, 114 Cal. 310, 46 P. 162 (1896); Hagerty v. Hagerty, 186 Iowa 1329, 172 N.W. 259 (1919).

37. King's Heirs v. Thompson, 34 U.S. (9 Pet.) 204, 9 L.Ed. 102 (1835) (equitable lien); see Frady v. Irvin, 245 Ga. 307, 264 S.E.2d 866 (1980). In addition, an action for restitution at law or equity is available. Carter v. Carter, 182 N.C. 186, 108 S.E. 765 (1921); see also Tozier v. Tozier, 437 A.2d 645 (Me.1981). Of course, an action in damages should also be available.

38. See Annot., 83 A.L.R.3d 1294 (1978).

39. Roberts–Horsfield v. Gedicks, 94 N.J.Eq. 82, 118 A. 275 (1922).

40. Young v. Overbaugh, 145 N.Y. 158, 163, 39 N.E. 712, 713 (1895); see Lindell v. Lindell, 135 Minn. 368, 371, 160 N.W. 1031, 1032 (1917) ("A parol promise by an owner to give land to another either by deed or will accompanied by actual delivery of possession, becomes an enforceable promise, when the promisee induced thereby has made substantial improvements upon the premises with knowledge of the promisor. The promise to give is no longer *nudum pactum*. It has become a promise upon a consideration.")

41. Greiner v. Greiner, 131 Kan. 760, 293 P. 759 (1930).

(c) Gratuitous Agencies and Bailments

The early case of Coggs v. Bernard [42] has been highly influential in this area. A carter agreed to transport a keg of brandy for the plaintiff free of charge. By reason of the carter's negligence, the freight was damaged. It was held that an action for assumpsit would lie for breach of the carter's implied promise to use requisite care. The court reasoned that the "bare being trusted with another man's goods, must be taken to be a sufficient consideration." [43] It is clear, however, that in such a case the gratuitous bailee does not bargain for the privilege of being trusted with the goods; consequently, the decision is not in accord with modern ideas of consideration. [44] In cases such as Coggs a distinction was drawn between nonfeasance and misfeasance. If the gratuitous promisor takes possession of the goods and fails to carry out his promise to use requisite care, liability has traditionally been found to exist. [45] If, however, he fails to take possession, traditionally there is no liability on the gratuitous promise to take the goods. [46]

A similar distinction between nonfeasance and misfeasance has been made in cases of gratuitous agencies. Here, the influential case has been Thorne v. Deas. [47] The parties were co-owners of a brig. On the day it was to sail the defendant promised to procure insurance for the voyage. Ten days later, the defendant told the plaintiff that no insurance had been procured. The plaintiff, upset at this revelation, said he would procure insurance himself. The defendant, however, told the plaintiff to "make himself easy" and that he would procure coverage that very day. Defendant failed to act and the brig was wrecked. It was held that the defendant was not liable since there was no consideration for the promise and no liability for mere nonfeasance pursuant to a gratuitous promise. If, however, the defendant has negligently procured insurance that was somehow defective, he would have been guilty of misfeasance and liable in contract. [48]

The gratuitous agency and bailment cases coalesced in the case of Siegel v. Spear & Co. [49] The defendant agreed to store plaintiff's furniture free of charge and also agreed to procure insurance at the plaintiff's expense, stating that he could obtain the insurance at a cheaper rate than could the plaintiff. The defendant failed to procure the insurance but did enter upon the bailment. The uninsured furniture was destroyed by fire. It was held that the defendant was liable on his promise. The court characterized the case as one of gratuitous

42. 92 Eng.Rep. 107 (K.B.1703).

43. Id. at 114.

44. See § 4–2 supra.

45. Siegel v. Spear & Co., 234 N.Y. 479, 138 N.E. 414 (1923); 1 Williston § 138.

46. Tomko v. Sharp, 87 N.J.L. 385, 94 A. 793 (Sup.Ct.1915).

47. 4 Johns. 84 (N.Y.1809), followed in Comfort et al. v. McCorkle, 149 Misc. 826, 268 N.Y.S. 192 (1933).

48. Barile v. Wright, 256 N.Y. 1, 175 N.E. 351 (1931); Elam v. Smithdeal Realty & Ins. Co., 182 N.C. 599, 109 S.E. 632 (1921).

49. 234 N.Y. 479, 138 N.E. 414 (1923), noted in 23 Colum.L.Rev. 573 (1923), 32 Yale L.J. 609 (1923); accord Schroeder v. Mauzy, 16 Cal.App. 443, 118 P. 459 (1911).

bailment, indicating that once possession of the goods was taken by the bailee, failure to carry out the promise to insure was misfeasance.

The distinction between misfeasance and nonfeasance in gratuitous agency cases has been abandoned by a large number of recent cases.[50] These courts are in actuality following the approach stated in the Restatements.[51] Under this approach, if a promisee relies upon a gratuitous agency promise to his injury, he may enforce the promise by virtue of the doctrine of promissory estoppel. These cases recognize that there is a potential for injurious reliance, not only in the misfeasance cases, but also in the nonfeasance cases. Some of these cases have related to a promise to procure insurance. The Restatement Second points out that this type of case should be approached with caution because the promisor is in effect treated as an insurer and so exposed to a large liability. It suggests that at times the promisee may not be justified in relying on the promise or that such reliance may be justified only for a short time.[52]

There does not seem to have any parallel development in the case of the nonfeasance of a gratuitous bailee and properly so. In such a case there can be no negligence with respect to the goods because there is no change of possession. In addition the potential for injurious reliance is remote. When the promisor refuses to undertake his promise of bailment, the other party may have the promised performance rendered by another. In actuality, the case involves the promise of a gratuitous agent to undertake a bailment. Such a promise will not ordinarily cause injurious justifiable reliance.

The distinction between misfeasance and nonfeasance is untenable and, as indicated above, the issue should be injurious reliance. To some extent the distinction appears to be traceable to the writ system in England. The rule of liability of a gratuitous bailee or agent for misfeasance "appears to have its origin in the writs allowing actions in case, granted pursuant to the Statute of Westminister Second."[53] The writ of assumpsit rose much later and grew out of cases similar to Coggs v. Bernard where the emphasis was on a physical injury to person or property as a result of negligently carrying out a consensual

50. Northern Commercial Co. v. United Airmotive, 101 F.Supp. 169 (D.Alaska 1951); Graddon v. Knight, 138 Cal.App.2d 577, 292 P.2d 632 (1956); Franklin Investment Co. v. Huffman et al., 393 A.2d 119 (D.C.App.1978); Brawn v. Lyford, 103 Me. 362, 69 A. 544 (1907); Lusk-Harbison-Jones, Inc. v. Universal Credit Co., 164 Miss. 693, 145 So. 623 (1933); Spiegel v. Metropolitan Life Ins. Co., 6 N.Y.2d 91, 188 N.Y.S.2d 486, 160 N.E.2d 40 (1959), reargument denied 7 N.Y.2d 805, 194 N.Y.S.2d 1025, 163 N.E.2d 677 (1959); East Providence Credit Union v. Geremia, 103 R.I. 597, 239 A.2d 725 (1968). The Restatement (Second) of Agency § 378 states a particular application of promissory estoppel in the field of agency. It provides: "One who, by a gratuitous promise or other conduct which he should realize will cause another reasonably to rely upon the performance of definite acts of service by him as the other's agent, causes the other to refrain from having such acts done by other available means is subject to a duty to use care to perform such service or, while other means are available, to give notice that he will not perform."

51. See § 6–1 supra.

52. Restatement, Second, Contracts § 90 Comment f.

53. Shattuck, Gratuitous Promises—A New Writ?, 35 Mich.L.Rev. 908, 917 (1937).

arrangement. These decisions initially did not go far enough to impose liability for nonfeasance.[54]

Despite the ultimate development of the writ of assumpsit to encompass generally any action for breach of promise, the distinction still plagues us in these cases—further proof that the writs still rule us from the grave.[55]

(d) Charitable Subscriptions and Marriage Settlements

With great frequency but not with complete uniformity, charitable subscriptions have been enforced in this country.[56] There are cases in which it has been held that the promise to give money to a charity is supported by consideration in the strict sense of the term. For example, the promisor may have bargained for and received a commitment from the charity that the "gift" be employed in a specified way or that a memorial be built bearing the promisor's name.[57]

In the usual case, however, there is no bargain in fact and the promisor manifests a gift-making state of mind.[58] Courts have, however, purported to find consideration on various tenuous theories. Some courts have found consideration on the theory that the donee impliedly promises to use the promised gifts for charitable purposes.[59] Undoubtedly this is not bargained for by the subscriber. In effect, the charity is a trustee with a duty to use the fund for charitable purposes. Obviously a gift promise to a trustee is no more enforceable under the doctrine or consideration than any other gift promise.[60] Other cases have found consideration in the purported exchange of promises between the subscribers.[61] If such an exchange actually is bargained for and actually occurs, consideration exists.[62] This is hardly what occurs in large fund-raising campaigns. A subscriber may be motivated by the

---

54. A. Simpson, A History of the Common Law of Contract (1975). See generally Holdsworth, Debt, Assumpsit and Consideration, 11 Mich.L.Rev. 347 (1913).

55. F. Maitland, The Forms of Action at Common Law 2 (1936).

56. See 1A Corbin § 198; 1 Williston §§ 116, 140; Billig, The Problem of Consideration in Charitable Subscriptions, 12 Cornell L.Q. 467 (1927). See generally Page, Consideration: Genuine and Synthetic, 1947 Wis.L.Rev. 483; Shattuck, Gratuitous Promises—A New Writ?, 35 Mich. L.Rev. 908 (1937). In England, charitable subscriptions generally are not enforced. In re Hudson, 54 L.J.Ch. 811 (1885).

57. Rogers v. Galloway Female College, 64 Ark. 627, 44 S.W. 554 (1898) (in consideration of locating a college in a particular town); American Legion, Christie E. Wilson Post No. 324, Rexford Kan. v. Thompson, 121 Kan. 124, 245 P. 744 (1926) (in consideration of building a particular building); Allegheny College v. National

Chautauqua County Bank of Jamestown, 246 N.Y. 369, 159 N.E. 173 (1927) (in consideration of perpetuating the name of the founder of a memorial).

58. Floyd v. Christian Church Widows & Orphans Home of Kentucky, 296 Ky. 196, 176 S.W.2d 125 (1943); In re Taylor's Estate, 251 N.Y. 257, 167 N.E. 434 (1929).

59. Nebraska Wesleyan Univ. v. Griswold's Estate, 113 Neb. 256, 202 N.W. 609 (1925).

60. See 1 Williston § 116.

61. First Presbyterian Church of Mt. Vernon v. Dennis, 178 Iowa 1352, 161 N.W. 183 (1917); Congregation B'nai Sholom v. Martin, 382 Mich. 659, 173 N.W.2d 504 (1969); In re Upper Peninsula Dev. Bureau, 364 Mich. 179, 110 N.W.2d 709 (1961).

62. Floyd v. Christian Church Widows & Orphans Home of Kentucky, 296 Ky. 196, 176 S.W.2d 125 (1943); 1A Corbin § 198; 1 Williston §§ 117, 118.

fact that others have given or will give but there is ordinarily no element of exchange among the various promisors. As we have seen motive and consideration are not necessarily equivalents.[63] Moreover, the prior subscriptions are past and therefore cannot constitute consideration.[64] A large number of cases have held that the subscription is an offer to a unilateral contract which is accepted by the charity's performance or starting to perform the terms of the subscription.[65] This is a rationalization because there is nothing to indicate a contract making state of mind upon the part of the promisor and therefor there is no offer.

This wide variation in reasoning indicates the difficulty of enforcing a charitable subscription on grounds of consideration. Yet, the courts have generally striven to find grounds for enforcement, indicating the depth of feeling in this country that private philanthropy serves a highly important function in our society.[66]

Of late, some courts have tended to abandon the attempt to utilize traditional contract doctrines to sustain subscriptions and have placed their decisions on the grounds of promissory estoppel.[67] Surprisingly, however, if promissory estoppel in its traditional form is the doctrine under which subscriptions are to be tested, fewer subscriptions are likely to be enforced than previously. This is because in the majority of the cases the charity would not be able to show substantial injurious reliance—that is that it did anything differently than it would have done in reliance on a particular promise.[68] This would appear to be true even in a case where the first subscriber has promised to pledge a large sum if others would pledge an equal amount.[69]

---

63. See § 4–3 supra.

64. See § 4–3 supra.

65. I. & I. Holding Corp. v. Gainsburg, 276 N.Y. 427, 12 N.E.2d 532 (1938), noted in 39 Colum.L.Rev. 283 (1939), 7 Fordham L.Rev. 264 (1938), 12 St. John's L.Rev. 339 (1938). See § 2–10 supra.

66. Danby v. Osteopathic Hosp. Ass'n, 34 Del.Ch. 427, 104 A.2d 903 (1954). For a recent case taking the position that the traditional doctrine of consideration should be applied to charitable subscriptions, see Maryland Nat'l Bank et al. v. United Jewish Appeal Federation of Greater Washington, Inc., 286 Md. 274, 407 A.2d 1130 (1979).

67. Danby v. Osteopathic Hosp. Ass'n, 34 Del.Ch. 427, 104 A.2d 903 (1954); Estate of Timko v. Oral Roberts Evangelistic Ass'n, 51 Mich.App. 662, 215 N.W.2d 750 (1974); Alleghany College v. National Chautauqua County Bank of Jamestown, 246 N.Y. 369, 159 N.E. 173 (1927) (dictum). But cf. I. & I. Holding Corp. v. Gainsburg, 276 N.Y. 427, 12 N.E.2d 532 (1938) (reverting to unilateral contract analysis and applying Restatement, Contracts § 45). Neither promissory estoppel nor a unilateral contract theory was held to support a charitable subscription, at least in the absence of demonstrable reliance, in the case of Jordan v. Mount Sinai Hosp. of Greater Miami, Inc., 276 So.2d 102 (Fla.Dist.App. 1973), affirmed 290 So.2d 484 (Fla.1974), noted in 26 Baylor L.Rev. 256 (1974); the doctrine was not applied in a case where the charity assured the subscriber that the pledge was not binding. Pappas v. Hauser, 197 N.W.2d 607 (Iowa 1972). For an early case using an estoppel rationale, see Miller v. Western College, 177 Ill. 280, 52 N.E. 432 (1898).

68. Salsbury v. Northwestern Bell Tel. Co., 221 N.W.2d 609 (Iowa 1974) (quoting a previous edition of this text).

69. At times in this fact pattern, the promise of the "bellwether" has been enforced on a consideration theory. Congregation B'nai Sholom v. Martin, 382 Mich. 659, 173 N.W.2d 504 (1969).

The Restatement Second appears to have reached a similar conclusion by providing that, "A charitable subscription * * * is binding * * * without proof that the promise induced action or forbearance." [70] It recognizes that the courts have favored charitable subscriptions and have found consideration where none existed and thus sets forth a rule stating that a charitable subscription is enforceable without consideration and without injurious reliance.[71] Recognition of such a rule would put an end to the flood of needless litigation created by the caution of executors and administrators who, for self-protection against surcharging, will not pay out on a subscription without a court decree. It would also insure the future accuracy of Professor Corbin's assertion that "promises of this kind are now almost universally enforced." [72]

Marriage settlements pose a problem quite similar to charitable subscriptions. There is a policy in favor of sustaining marriage settlements and this had led courts to conclude that there is consideration when none in fact existed.[73] A good illustration is the case of DeCicco v. Schweizer.[74] There Judge Cardozo concluded that there was a manifestation of a contract making state of mind, in other words, the father of the bride bargained for the marriage of his daughter and the count. However, in the Allegheny College case he confesses that there was a manifestation of gift making state of mind and that the promise was enforced under the doctrine of promissory estoppel. However, there was nothing in the facts to indicate that the engaged couple would not have married even if the father had not made his promise. Thus, there was no proof of injurious reliance as required under the promissory estoppel doctrine. For this reason and to carry out the public policy set forth above, the Restatement Second has classified marriage settlement contracts with charitable subscriptions. That is to say both are enforceable "without proof that the promise induced action or forbearance." [75]

(e) Other Roots of the Doctrine of Promissory Estoppel

It is clear that the doctrine of equitable estoppel is an historical antecedent of promissory estoppel. The relationship of the two doctrines will be discussed in more detail below.[76] Other roots of the doctrine include cases where a debtor has induced a creditor not to bring an action by a promise of payment or a promise not to plead the statute of limitations even though there was no consideration for the promise.[77]

70. Restatement, Second, Contracts § 90(2).

71. Restatement, Second, Contracts § 90 Comment c, ill. 7.

72. 1A Corbin § 198.

73. Phelan v. Brady, 186 N.Y. 178, 78 N.E. 943 (1906); Restatement, Second, Contracts § 90 Comment c, ill. 8.

74. 221 N.Y. 431, 117 N.E. 807 (1917).

75. Restatement, Second, Contracts § 90(2). See note 57 supra.

76. See § 11–29 infra.

77. 1 Williston § 140. If the promise is made with reference to certain contract claims, no reliance is needed. See § 5–7 supra. The rule here discussed is primarily applied in non-contract cases. State Farm Ins. Mut. Auto. Co. v. Budd, 185 Neb. 343, 175 N.W.2d 621, 44 A.L.R.3d 476

WESTLAW REFERENCES

(a) *Promises in the Family*

devecmon +s shaw

ricketts +s scothorn

consideration /s "estoppel in pais"

represent! /s "estoppel in pais"

(b) *Promise to Make a Gift of Land*

gift /s promis! /s land realty (real +1 estate property)

oral! /s promis! /s "statute of fraud" /s realty land (real +1 estate property)

promis! /s land realty (real +1 estate property) /s possess! /s improv!

"promis! estop!" /s realty land (real +1 estate property)

(c) *Gratuitous Agencies and Bailments*

gratuitous +1 agency bailment /s liab!

gratuitous +1 agency bailment /s possess!

to(50) /p gratuitous! /p negligen!

50k9 /p gratuitous!

coggs +s bernard

volunt! +1 bailment agency

thorne +s deas

"gratuitous! promis!" /s liab! /s consideration

"promis! estop!" /s gratuitous! volunt! +1 bailment agency promis!

volunt! gratuitous! +1 agency bailment promis! /s rely! relied reliance /s injur! detriment!

(d) *Charitable Subscriptions and Marriage Settlements*

"charitable subscripton" /s enforc! unenforc!

to(367) /p charitable

"charitable subscription" /s gift

"charitable subscription" /s charity

"charitable subscription" /s consideration

"charitable subscription" /s unilateral bilateral perform!

trustee /s gift /s promis! /s consideration enforc! unenforc!

"charitable subscription" /s "promis! estop!"

"charitable subscription" /s reli**** rely!

"marriage settlement" /s consideration

"marriage settlement" /s enforc! unenforc! sustain!

---

§ 6–3. Traditional Approach to the Promissory Estoppel Doctrine

Before looking to the doctrine of promissory estoppel the courts ordinarily look to see if conventional consideration is present.[78] If not

(1970). In New York the principle of estoppel in cases involving the statute of limitations has been codified. McKinney's N.Y. General Obligations Law § 17–103. As to the effect of a promise to pay a debt on the statute of limitations, see § 5–7 supra.

78. Walker v. KFC Corp., 515 F.Supp. 612 (S.D.Cal.1981), affirmed in part, reversed in part 728 F.2d 1215 (9th Cir.1984).

they determine whether the elements for a promissory estoppel are present. However, even if all of the elements for a promissory estoppel are present the plaintiff will lose unless a given jurisdiction accepts promissory estoppel as a substitute for consideration under the facts of a particular case. As a minimum most jurisdictions will accept the doctrine in the fact patterns discussed above. Thus, Section 90 of the Restatement has been applied to a promise to make a gift of land,[79] promises relating to gratuitous bailments and agencies,[80] charitable subscriptions,[81] and promises not to plead the statute of limitations in tort cases.[82]

§ 6–4. Present Approach to a Gift Promise

Although initially the courts used promissory estoppel as a substitute for consideration for the most part in the case of a gift promise made in the types of cases listed in § 6–2, with the impetus given to the doctrine by the two Restatements it is fair to say that the present tendency is to use promissory estoppel as a substitute for consideration in the case of a gift promise in just about any case where all of the elements for promissory estoppel are present.[83] A recent case has spoken "of the widespread acceptance of the doctrine as formulated by the two Restatements." [84]

Since the kinds of promises which are likely to induce reliance on a gift promise are as varied as human ingenuity no exhaustive listing of the cases will be attempted. The doctrine has recently been applied to a promise that prior service of an employee would be included for certain purposes; [85] to a promise by an insurance company that it would give the plaintiff a full and complete settlement,[86] to a promise by an insurance company to notify a bank of a premium default [87] to gratuitous advice given by an attorney,[88] to a gratuitous promise to pay an employee a pension [89] and to a gratuitous promise to guarantee a debt.[90]

79. Greiner v. Greiner, 131 Kan. 760, 293 P. 759 (1930).

80. Lusk-Harbison-Jones, Inc. v. Universal Credit Co., 164 Miss. 693, 145 So. 623 (1933).

81. Danby v. Osteopathic Hosp. Ass'n, 34 Del.Ch. 427, 104 A.2d 903 (1954).

82. Jackson v. Kemp, 211 Tenn. 438, 365 S.W.2d 437 (1963).

83. Landro v. Glendenning Motorways, Inc., 625 F.2d 1344 (8th Cir.1980); Wroten v. Mobil Oil Corp., 315 A.2d 728 (Del.Supr. 1973); Kirkpatrick v. Seneca Nat'l Bank, 213 Kan. 61, 515 P.2d 781 (1973); Fretz Constr. Co. v. Southern Nat. Bank of Houston, 626 S.W.2d 478 (Tex.1982).

84. Chapman v. Bomann, 381 A.2d 1123 (Me.1978); see also Knapp, Reliance in the Revised Restatement: The Proliferation of Promissory Estoppel, 81 Colum.L.Rev. 52 (1981).

85. Schmidt v. McKay, 555 F.2d 30 (2d Cir.1977); Alix v. Alix, —— R.I. ——, 497 A.2d 18 (1985).

86. Huhtala v. Travelers Ins. Co., 401 Mich. 118, 257 N.W.2d 640 (1977).

87. Northwestern Bank of Commerce v. Employers Life Ins. Co., of America, 281 N.W.2d 164 (Minn.1979).

88. Togstad et al. v. Vesely, Otto, Miller & Keefe, 291 N.W.2d 686, 693 (Minn.1980).

89. Hessler, Inc. v. Farrell, 226 A.2d 708 (Del.1967); Feinberg v. Pfeiffer Co., 322 S.W.2d 163 (Mo.App.1959).

90. W.B. Saunders Co. v. Galbraith, 40 Ohio App. 155, 178 N.E. 34 (1931); Restatement, Second, Contracts § 88. See also Baehr v. Penn-O-Tex Oil Corp., 258 Minn.

WESTLAW REFERENCES

"promis! estop!" /s substitut! /s gift consideration

§ 6–5. Doctrine Not Limited to Enforcing Gratuitous Promises

Although initially there was some authority to the effect that the doctrine of promissory estoppel should be limited to enforcing gratuitous promises and should not be applied in transactions contemplating a bargain,[91] the trend today is in the other direction.[92] This is made clear by consideration of the representative cases discussed below.

(a) Reliance on Offers

In a recurring fact pattern a general contractor receives a low bid from a subcontractor and uses that low bid in preparing his own bid on a project. The bid of the subcontractor is an offer.[93] Under the traditional common law rule the offer may be withdrawn prior to acceptance even though the general contractor has relied upon it in submitting his own bid.[94] Nor does the use of the bid by the general contractor amount to an acceptance even if the name of the subcontractor is used in the bid of the general contractor.[95] The majority of courts which have considered the problem have held that justifiable injurious reliance on the offer will render it irrevocable.[96] Thus the offer is rendered irrevocable under the doctrine of promissory estoppel. The Restatement Second had explicitly adopted this approach.[97] Of course

533, 104 N.W.2d 661 (1960); cf. Glitsos v. Kadish, 4 Ariz.App. 134, 418 P.2d 129 (1966); Fried v. Fisher, 328 Pa. 497, 196 A. 39 (1938).

91. See, e.g., James Baird Co. v. Gimbel Brothers, 64 F.2d 344 (2d Cir.1933). This case was specifically repudiated in Debron Corp. v. National Homes Constr. Corp., 493 F.2d 352 (8th Cir.1974); see also Fridman, Promissory Estoppel, 35 Can.B.Rev. 279 (1957); 28 Ill.L.Rev. 419 (1933); 22 Minn.L. Rev. 843 (1938); 20 Va.L.Rev. 214 (1933).

92. Universal Computer Sys., Inc. v. Medical Servs. Ass'n, 628 F.2d 820 (3d Cir. 1980).

93. See § 2–6(g) supra.

94. See § 2–6(g) supra.

95. Holman Erection Co. v. Orville E. Madsen & Sons, Inc., 330 N.W.2d 693 (Minn.1983). A number of commentators and some courts have disagreed with this view. See, e.g., Closen & Weiland, The Construction Industry Building Cases: Application of Traditional Contract, Promissory Estoppel, and Other Theories to the Relations Between General Contractors and Subcontractors, 13 John Marshall L.Rev. 565 (1980); Note, Another Look at Construction Bidding and Contracts at For-

mation, 53 Va.L.Rev. 1720 (1967). Under this approach the general contractor becomes bound when he uses the bid if his bid is adopted. This is so even if the subcontractor's name is not listed in the bid of the general contractor.

96. Montgomery Industries International Ins. v. Thomas Constr. Co., Inc., 620 F.2d 91 (5th Cir.1980); N. Litterio & Co. v. Glassman Constr. Co., 319 F.2d 736 (D.C. Cir.1963); Reynolds v. Texarkana Constr. Corp., 237 Ark. 583, 374 S.W.2d 818 (1964), noted in 18 Ark.L.Rev. 351 (1965); Drennan v. Star Paving Co., 51 Cal.2d 409, 333 P.2d 757 (1958); Harry Harris, Inc. v. Quality Constr. Co. of Benton, Ky., 593 S.W.2d 872 (Ky.1980); E.A. Coronis Associates v. M. Gordon Constr. Co., 90 N.J.Super. 69, 216 A.2d 246 (App.Div.1966); Northwestern Eng'r Co. v. Ellerman, 69 S.D. 397, 10 N.W.2d 879 (1943); Restatement, Second, Contracts § 87 and ill. 6; cf. Harris v. Lillis, 24 So.2d 689 (La.App.1946) (bid held to be irrevocable pursuant to local custom); see also Comment, The "Firm Offer" Problem in Construction Bids and the Need for Promissory Estoppel, 10 Wm. & Mary L.Rev. 212 (1968).

97. Restatement, Second, Contracts § 87. See also M.L. Closen & D.G. Wei-

there must be something upon which the contractor may justifiably rely. An estimate is not enough [98] and if the subcontractors bid is so palpably low as to indicate that it is based on a mistake, reliance is not justified.[99] One case has stated: "It bears noting that a general contractor is not free to delay acceptance after he has been awarded the general contract in the hope of getting a better price nor can he reopen bargaining with the subcontractor and at the same time claim a continuing right to accept the original offer." [1] In other words bid shopping and bid chiseling by the general contractor will terminate the option contract.[2] It may also be observed that in the cases which apply the doctrine of promissory estoppel, although the subcontractor is bound by his bid, the general contractor is not bound to accept the bid because the general contractor has not made any promise upon which the subcontractor reasonably relies.[3] The result is different under the Subletting and Subcontracting Fair Practices Act where the statute requires the listing of the subcontractor. Under that statute the contractor may not without the consent of the owner substitute another subcontractor for the one listed.[4]

The case under discussion relates to an offer looking to a bilateral contract. When an offer looks to a bilateral contract it will be an

land, The Construction Bidding Cases; Application of Traditional Contract, Promissory Estoppel, and Other Theories to the Relations Between General Contractors and Subcontractors, 13 John Marshall L.Rev. 565 (1980). This restatement provision receives strong criticism in Kniffen, Innovation or Aberration: Recovery for Reliance on an Offer as Permitted by the New Restatement, Second, Contracts, 62 U.Detroit L.Rev. 23 (1984).

98. Robert Gordon, Inc. v. Ingersoll-Rand Co., 117 F.2d 654 (7th Cir.1941); Leo F. Piazza Paving Co. v. Bebek & Brkich, 141 Cal.App.2d 226, 296 P.2d 368, 371 (1956).

99. Robert Gordon, Inc. v. Ingersoll-Rand Co. 117 F.2d 654 (7th Cir.1941).

1. Drennan v. Star Paving Co., 51 Cal. 2d 409, 333 P.2d 757, 760 (1958). This view is adopted by the Restatement, Second, Contracts § 87(2). Although the cases allow an expectancy measure of damages, the section talks of a recovery that would "avoid injustice."

2. Preload Technology, Inc. v. A.B. & J. Constr. Co., Inc., 696 F.2d 1080 (5th Cir. 1983), rehearing denied 703 F.2d 557 (5th Cir.1983).

3. Seacoast Elec. Co. v. Franchi Bros. Constr. Corp., 437 F.2d 1247 (1st Cir.1971); Cortland Asbestos Prods., Inc. v. J. & K. Plumbing & Heating Co., 33 A.D.2d 11, 304 N.Y.S.2d 694 (3d Dep't 1969); Southern California Acoustics Co. v. C.V. Holder, Inc., 71 Cal.2d 719, 79 Cal.Rptr. 319, 456 P.2d 975 (1969). "In contrast, the subcontractor does not rely on the general and suffers no detriment. A subcontractor submits bids to all or most of the general contractors that it knows are bidding on a project. The subcontractor receives invitations to bid from some generals and submits bids to others without invitation. The time and the expense involved in preparing a bid is not segregated to any particular general. The total cost is part of the overhead of doing business. The same bid is submitted to each general. Thus, whether or not a particular general wins the contract is of little or no concern to the subcontractor. The subcontractor engages in the same work and expense in preparing its bid regardless of who wins the general contract and whether the subcontractor wins the contract on which it bid. No further expense is incurred until a formal agreement is reached with the general and actual work commences. Clearly, the promissory estoppel concept is not applicable in this situation. With no detrimental reliance, there can be no estoppel claim. Ample justification exists for binding the subcontractor and not binding the general. The two situations are very different." Holman Erection Co. v. Orville E. Madsen & Sons, 330 N.W.2d 693 (Minn.1983).

4. West's Ann.Cal.Gov.Code § 4100 et seq.; cf. Air Technology Corp. v. General Elec. Co., 347 Mass. 613, 199 N.E.2d 538 (1964).

unusual situation where the offer becomes irrevocable under the doctrine of promissory estoppel because ordinarily the offeree is not justified in relying on the offer.[5] If he wishes to rely on the offer normally he need only accept it.[6] This is not true in the fact pattern discussed above.[7]

The situation is quite different in the case of an offer looking to a unilateral contract. We saw earlier that part performance in response to an offer for a unilateral contract has the effect of rendering the offer irrevocable under the Restatement Second.[8] However, this is not true if what is done was merely preparation.[9] Under the promissory estoppel doctrine reliance in the form of preparation may render the offer irrevocable.[10]

(b) Promissory Estoppel as a Result of a Defective Contract

A good illustration of this concept is presented by the case of Wheeler v. White.[11] In that case plaintiff owned a lot and desired to construct a commercial enterprise thereon. Plaintiff entered into an agreement with the defendant by the terms of which defendant was to obtain a loan in the sum of $70,000.00 in favor of plaintiff from a third party or provide it himself. Defendant in turn was to be paid $5,000.00 plus 5% of the rent of tenants procured by defendant. The loan was to be payable in monthly installments over fifteen years and bear interest at a rate of not more than 6% per annum. After the agreement was signed defendant assured plaintiff that the money would be available and urged plaintiff to demolish the buildings presently on the site. Plaintiff complied.

The majority of the court held that the loan arrangement was too vague and indefinite to be enforced because of the payment terms of the loan. In other words there was a void bilateral agreement.[12] The court did not consider the possibility of forging a good unilateral contract out of a bad bilateral and properly so because the court indicates that what the plaintiff did amounted to preparation rather than the beginning of performance.[13] Parenthically it might also be noted that a quasi-

---

5. Friedman v. Tappan Development Corp., 22 N.J. 523, 126 A.2d 646 (1956); Hill v. Corbett, 33 Wn.2d 219, 204 P.2d 845 (1949); cf. Grouse v. Group Health Plan, Inc., 306 N.W.2d 114 (Minn.1981).

6. Berryman v. Kmoch, 221 Kan. 304, 559 P.2d 790 (1977).

7. See generally Schultz, The Firm Offer Puzzle: A Study of Business Practice in the Construction Industry, 19 U.Chi.L.Rev. 237 (1952) (business practice indicates to the author that subcontractor's bids should not be treated as irrevocable); Sharp, Promises, Mistakes and Reciprocity, 19 U.Chi.L.Rev. 28 (1952); Note, Another Look at Construction Bidding and Contracts at Formation, 53 Va.L.Rev. 1720 (1967).

8. See § 2–22 supra.

9. See § 2–22 supra.

10. Abbott v. Stephany Poultry Co., 44 Del. 513, 62 A.2d 243 (Super.Ct.1948); Kucera v. Kavan, 165 Neb. 131, 84 N.W.2d 207 (1957); Spitzli v. Guth, 112 Misc. 630, 183 N.Y.S. 743 (1920); Restatement, Second, Contracts § 87, Comment e.

11. 398 S.W.2d 93 (Tex.1965), noted in 18 Baylor L.Rev. 546 (1966); see also Bixler v. First Nat'l Bank of Oregon, 49 Or.App. 195, 619 P.2d 895 (1980).

12. See § 2–9 supra.

13. See § 4–12(7) supra. The two doctrines may be applied in the case of void bilateral contracts. The main difference is that in forging, the act done must be detri-

contractual recovery would not be available because there was no unjust enrichment.[14] The court, however, applied the promissory estoppel doctrine and allowed a reliance measure of damages based upon the value of the improvements destroyed and the lost rental.[15]

Another illustration of this approach arises in a number of pension cases. With surprising frequency,[16] employers have offered pension plans, death benefits and other fringe benefits while retaining the power to withdraw or modify the offer at will. Such an offer is an illusory promise or could be looked at as a situation in which the parties do not intend legal consequences.[17] Yet a minority of courts by a process of interpretation have eliminated the clause in question so as to preclude withdrawal or modification after the employee has retired [18] or died.[19] Detrimental reliance on the promise doubtlessly is a primary factor in impelling the courts to so interpret the offer.

Once it is decided that a void bilateral contract may be the basis for applying the doctrine of promissory estoppel the possibilities are almost limitless. For example, the Restatement has a specific section covering each of two other fact patterns that fall within the ambit of the problem being discussed. The first is a modification without consideration,[20] and the other relates to the promise of a surety inducing detrimental reliance.[21]

In the first situation the Restatement provides that a modification is binding "to the extent that justice requires enforcement in view of a material change of position in reliance on the promise." [22] The reason for the special rule is the "presumptive utility" of a modification without consideration. Thus even though the promise is not binding when made, it may become binding by reliance but the terms of the original contract may be reinstated as to the future by reasonable

---

mental in the consideration sense while in the case of promissory estoppel, injurious reliance is necessary.

14. See § 15–2 infra.

15. But see Bickerstaff v. Gregston, 604 P.2d 382 (Okl.App.1979) wherein it is concluded that injurious reliance on a void agreement creates no rights under a theory of promissory estoppel because reliance on a void contract is considered unreasonable. This notion seems to be applied in employment cases. Bixby v. Wilson & Co., 196 F.Supp. 889 (N.D.Iowa 1961), 47 Iowa L.Rev. 725 (1962); Tatum v. Brown, 29 N.C.App. 504, 224 S.E.2d 698 (1976).

16. See Note, Consideration for the Employer's Promise of a Voluntary Pension Plan, 23 U.Chi.L.Rev. 96 (1955); Note, Contractual Aspects of Pension Plan Modification, 56 Colum.L.Rev. 251 (1956).

17. See § 4–12(4) and § 2–4.

18. West v. Hunt Foods, Inc., 101 Cal. App.2d 597, 225 P.2d 978 (1951); Kari v.

General Motors Corp., 79 Mich.App. 93, 261 N.W.2d 222 (1977), reversed 402 Mich. 726, 282 N.W.2d 925 (1978); Schofield v. Zion's Co–Op Mercantile Inst., 85 Utah 281, 39 P.2d 342 (1934) (pension).

19. Stopford v. Boonton Molding Co., 56 N.J. 169, 265 A.2d 657 (1970); Mabley & Carew Co. v. Borden, 129 Ohio St. 375, 195 N.E. 697 (1935) (death benefit); see Annot. 46 A.L.R.3d 464 (1972). For a recent case following the majority view, see Abelson v. Genesco, Inc., 58 A.D.2d 774, 396 N.Y.S.2d 394 (1977). See also, Note, Public Employee Benefits—A Promissory Estoppel Approach, 10 Wm. Mitchell L.Rev. 287 (1984).

20. Restatement, Second, Contracts § 89.

21. Restatement, Second, Contracts § 88.

22. Restatement, Second, Contracts § 89 Comment a.

notification unless this would be unfair because of a change of position.[23]

The Restatement gives the following illustration based upon the case of Central London Property Trust, Ltd. v. High Trees House, Ltd.[24] "A is the lessee of an apartment house under a 99 year lease from B at a rent of $10,000 per year. Because of war conditions many of the apartments became vacant, and in order to enable A to stay in business B agrees to reduce the rent to $5,000. The reduced rent is paid for five years. The war being over, the apartments are then fully rented, and B notifies A that the full rent called for by the lease must be paid. A is bound to pay the full rent only from a reasonable time after the receipt of the notification."

It is clear that under the traditional rule the modification is without consideration and the assumption is that the reliance, although not detrimental in the consideration sense, is injurious. A is allowed to reinstate the $10,000 term as to the future because there has been no change of position that would make reinstatement unfair.

As indicated above the Restatement Second takes a similar approach in the case of a guaranty. The provision is directed to a situation where the surety makes his promise after the creditor has already furnished the consideration so that there is no consideration for the surety's promise. If the creditor relies on the promise of the surety, as for example by refraining from bringing action against the principal at a time when the amount due could have been recovered, the promise may be enforced.[25]

In the cases discussed above in each case the agreement enforced under the doctrine of promissory estoppel was void. It is also possible to use promissory estoppel to enforce an unenforceable agreement, as for example a case involving the Statute of Frauds.[26] Presumably promissory estoppel could be used in cases involving voidable contracts but the rules employed in this area take into account the element of reliance together with the policy to be attained.[27]

(c) Promises Made During the Course of Preliminary Negotiations

In the cases discussed above the parties intended to contract, had reached agreement and believed that they had entered into a contract. Yet for some reason there was a legal defect in the formation of the

23. Restatement, Second, Contracts § 89 Comment d; see also U.C.C. § 2–209(4) and (5).

24. [1947] 1 K.G. 130; Restatement, Second, Contracts § 89, ill. 7. However, there is some doubt as to whether this case should be classified as a modification. The case could equally well be classified as involving an accord and satisfaction. See § 4–11 supra.

25. Restatement, Second, Contracts § 88 Comments a and d, and illustrations 2 and 3; see also U.C.C. § 3–404(2).

26. See § 19–48 infra. The promissory estoppel doctrine can be used to overcome the parol evidence rule. The Parol Evidence Rule: Promissory Estoppel's Next Conquest, 36 Vanderbilt L.Rev. 1383 (1983).

27. See generally ch. 9.

contract. The situation here is different. The assumption is that the parties were still negotiating, had not as yet reached agreement and did not expect to be bound until some later time.

Although there are a number of cases [28] that may appear to fit this mold, the clearest example is the well known case of Hoffman v. Red Owl Stores.[29] In that case, the plaintiff was assured that if he took certain steps and raised $18,000 worth of capital he would be granted a supermarket franchise. In compliance with the recommendation of the defendant, he sold his bakery, purchased a grocery store to gain experience, resold it, acquired an option on land for building a franchised outlet, and moved his residence near to where the franchise was to be. He raised the necessary capital by borrowing the major portion of it from his father-in-law. This arrangement was approved by the defendant's agent. Later, however, the defendant's more highly placed agents insisted that plaintiff's credit standing was impaired by his loan and demanded that the plaintiff procure from his father-in-law a statement that these funds were an outright gift. Plaintiff refused and sued. The court ruled for the plaintiff on the theory of promissory estoppel, limiting his recovery to the amounts he had lost and expended in reliance on the promise.[30]

As the court pointed out there was indefiniteness, because the parties had not agreed upon the "size, cost, design and layout of the store building; and the terms of the lease with respect to rent, maintenance, renewal, and purchase options." [31] In this respect the case is like Wheeler v. White discussed above. Not only was there indefiniteness, but the parties did not intend to be bound at the time the rupture occurred so that there was nothing more than preliminary negotiations.

The court specifically held that promissory estoppel can sustain a cause of action despite the absence of an intent to be bound. In the court's view promissory estoppel is more than an equivalent of or substitute for consideration. It is the basis of a cause of action that is not contract, tort, or quasi-contract.[32] The court's result is close in spirit to the doctrine of culpa in contrahendo recognized in a number of

---

28. See, e.g., Goodman v. Dicker, 169 F.2d 684, 83 U.S.App.D.C. 353 (1948); Chrysler Corporation v. Quimby, 51 Del. 264, 144 A.2d 123 (1958), rehearing denied 51 Del. 264, 144 A.2d 885 (1958). However, in these cases recovery could just as easily have been granted on the tort theory of misrepresentation. See Guilbert v. Phillips Petroleum Co., 503 F.2d 587 (6th Cir. 1974).

29. 26 Wis.2d 683, 133 N.W.2d 267 (1965), noted in 51 Com.L.Q. 351 (1966); 65 Mich.L.Rev. 351 (1966).

30. But see Smith v. Boise Kenworth Sales, Inc., 102 Idaho 63, 625 P.2d 417 (1981).

31. Hoffman v. Red Owl Stores, Inc., 26 Wis.2d 683, 617, 133 N.W.2d 267, 274 (1965).

32. The decision may be read as indicating that "Section 90 should serve as a distinct basis of liability without regard to theories of bargain, contract, or consideration. The criteria which justify and limit the application of promissory estoppel are to be determined exclusively by what Section 90 says about the effects of nonperformance of promises." Henderson, § 6–2 Note 18 supra, at 359. See also Debron Corp. v. National Homes Construction Corp., 40 Mo.L.Rev. 163 (1975); Metzger & Phillips, The Emergence of Promissory Estoppel as an Independent Theory of Recovery, 35 Rutgers L.J. 472 (1983).

European countries, under which, where justice demands, recovery is awarded for losses sustained as a result of unsuccessful negotiations.[33]

 WESTLAW REFERENCES

(a) *Reliance on Offers*

withdr*w! /s bid /s subcontractor /s offer!

"promis! estop!" /s bid /s subcontractor

"promis! estop!" /s bid /s irrevoc! revoc! revok!

bid bidding /s "general contractor" /s subcontractor /s bind binding bound

bid bidding /s mistak! /s subcontractor /s "general contractor"

bid +1 shopping chiseling

"promis! estop!" /s unilateral

(b) *Promissory Estoppel as a Result of a Defective Contract*

find 398 sw2d 93

void! /p agreement contract /s "promis! estop!"

pension retirement (death fringe +1 benefit) /s plan /s modif! /s employ**** /s power empower!

"promis! estop!" /s surety guaranty

"promis! estop!" /s "parol* evidence rule" "statute of frauds"

(c) *Promises Made During the Course of Preliminary Negotiations*

hoffman +s "red owl store"

"promis! estop!" /s "preliminary negotiation"

promise /s "preliminary negotiation"

rely! reli**** /s "preliminary negotiation"

"culpa in contrahendo"

"promis! estop!" /s bargain!

§ 6–6. Flexibility of Remedy

As we have seen, the unspoken premise of the First Restatement is that if the elements of a promissory estoppel are present a contract is formed and therefore ordinary remedies for breach of promise would be available.[34] As Professor Williston explained to the American Law Institute, either a contract was formed or it was not, "you have to take one leg or the other."[35] This overly conceptual approach has very likely hindered full judicial acceptance of the doctrine.

Some courts, however have broken the conceptual barrier and have decided that the remedy need not be as broad as that which would be available for breach of a contract founded in consideration.[36] For

---

33. See Kessler & Fine, Culpa in Contrahendo, Bargaining in Good Faith, and Freedom of Contract: A Comparative Study, 77 Harv.L.Rev. 401 (1964).

34. See § 6–1.

35. Williston, IV American Law Institute Proceedings, Appendix p. 103 (1926); 1A Corbin § 205.

36. Grouse v. Group Health Plan, Inc., 306 N.W.2d 114 (Minn.1981). See the thorough discussion in Comment, Once More into the Breach; Promissory Estoppel and Traditional Damage Doctrine, 37 U.Chi.L. Rev. 559 (1970); see also Seavey, Reliance on Gratuitous Promises or Other Conduct, 64 Harv.L.Rev. 913 (1951); Shattuck, Gratuitous Promises—A New Writ? 35 Mich.L.

example in Goodman v. Dicker,[37] the court, in enforcing a promise to grant the plaintiff a franchise under the promissory estoppel theory, limited the plaintiff's recovery for loss of profits. Reliance damages were also awarded in the cases of Wheeler v. White, London Property Trust Ltd. v. High Trees House and Hoffman v. Red Owl Stores discussed above.[38]

Such flexibility is to be encouraged.[39] If reliance on an extremely valuable promise is moderate courts should not be compelled to choose between full contractual recovery or none at all.[40]

The Restatement Second specifically states that the remedy for breach of a contract based upon promissory estoppel should be flexible.[41] Thus the Restatement Second makes it clear that it is proper in a given case to award reliance damages to protect the reliance interest but that "full-scale enforcement by normal remedies is often appropriate."[42] It is not a simple matter to determine in a given case which remedy is appropriate.[43] In addition Professor Eisenberg has pointed out that there may be many difficult problems in determining how reliance damages are "to be measured in the donative-promise context."[44]

WESTLAW REFERENCES
"promis! estop!" /s los* +2 profit
"promis! estop!" /s remedy
goodman +s dicker
"promis! estop!" /s damage /s rely! reli****

§ 6–7. The Future of Promissory Estoppel

Just as the original Restatement gave great impetus to promissory estoppel it may be expected that the Second Restatement with its liberalization of the doctrine will give added impetus to the utilization of the doctrine in the types of cases discussed above.[45] The ultimate and important point to be remembered is that promissory estoppel may

Rev. 908 (1936). But see Note, 13 Vand.L. Rev. 705 (1960).

37. 169 F.2d 684, 83 U.S.App.D.C. 353 (1948).

38. All of these cases are discussed in § 6–5. See also RCM Supply Co., Inc. v. Hunter Douglas, Inc., 686 F.2d 1074 (4th Cir.1982).

39. Associated Tabulating Services, Inc. v. Olympic Life Ins. Co., 414 F.2d 1306 (5th Cir.1969).

40. Fuller and Perdue, The Reliance Interest in Contract Damages, 46 Yale L.J. 373, 405 (1937).

41. See § 6–1 supra.

42. Restatement, Second, Contracts § 90, Comment d (Reporter's Note to Section 90).

43. See Restatement, Second, Contracts § 90, Comment d, ills. 8–11.

44. Eisenberg, op. cit. supra pp. 26–31. See also Seavey, Reliance upon Gratuitous Promises or Other Conduct, 64 Harv.L.Rev. 913 (1951); Comment, 37 U.Chi.L.Rev. 559 (1970).

45. Knapp, Reliance in the Revised Restatement: The Proliferation of Promissory Estoppel, 81 Colum.L.Rev. 52 (1981) which states in conclusion, "The revised Restatement provides a useful summary of the current status of the section 90 principle, but it is not likely to be the end of the story. Indeed, by the time its force is finally felt, section 90 may well have transformed the face of contract law in ways undreamt by its drafters—or its revisers."

be used in any context in order to do justice. As one court has stated the doctrine of promissory estoppel is "an attempt by the courts to keep remedies abreast of increased moral consciousness of honest and fair representations in all business dealing. * * *"[46]

46. People's Nat'l Bank of Little Rock v. Linebarger Constr. Co., 219 Ark. 11, 17, 240 S.W.2d 12, 16 (1951).

Chapter 7

CONTRACTS UNDER SEAL

---

§ 7–1. Introduction

For centuries before the doctrine of consideration was developed and long before informal contracts were enforced, contracts under seal were enforced.[1] As we have seen a contract under seal is one type of formal contract;[2] indeed, the outstanding kind of formal contract from the late middle ages down to recent times, at least in non-mercantile transactions.[3] The sealed instrument required no consideration,[4] although, at times, courts, losing sight of its historical origins, have said that the seal "imports a consideration."[5] The promise under seal is

---

1. 1A Corbin § 252; 1 Williston § 205. See generally, Backus, The Origin and Use of Private Seals under the Common Law, 51 Am.L.Rev. 369 (1917); Crane, The Magic of Private Seal, 15 Colum.L.Rev. 598 (1915), Selected Readings 598; Praeger, The Distinction between Sealed and Unsealed Instruments, 74 Cent.L.J. 172 (1912); Riddell, The Mystery of the Seal, 4 Can.B. Rev. 156 (1926); New York Law Revision Commission Reports: 1936 p. 287ff., 1940 p. 173ff.; Comment, the Seal in North Carolina and the Need for Reform, 15 Wake Forest L.Rev. 251 (1979).

2. See § 1–10 supra. The efficacy of the seal has not been limited to contracts. Traditionally, many executed transactions such as conveyances and releases have been under seal.

3. This is not to say that sealed instruments have not been used in mercantile transactions, but other forms of formal instruments are more important in commercial law; e.g., negotiable instruments and letters of credit.

4. Milde v. Harrison, 162 Ga.App. 809, 293 S.E.2d 56 (1982); Johnson v. Norton Housing Authority, 375 Mass. 192, 375 N.E.2d 1209 (1978).

5. See discussion of this terminology in Hartford-Connecticut Trust Co. v. Devine, 97 Conn. 193, 116 A. 239 (1922); Hensel v. United States Electronics Corp., 262 A.2d 648 (Del.1970); Twining v. National Mtg. Corp., 268 Md. 549, 302 A.2d 604 (1973); Minch v. Saymon, 96 N.J.Super. 464, 233 A.2d 385 (1967); Thomason v. Bescher, 176 N.C. 622, 97 S.E. 654, 2 A.L.R. 626 (1918).

enforced because of the form of the instrument. The required formalities are three: a sufficient writing, a seal, and delivery.[6]

Formalities serve important functions in many legal systems,[7] particularly in relatively primitive societies. Important among these is the evidentiary function. Compliance with formalities provides reliable evidence that a given transaction took place. A cautionary function is also served. The ceremony of melting sealing wax onto parchment followed by impressing the melted wax with a signet ring was imposing. Before performing the required ritual the promisor had ample opportunity to reflect and deliberate on the wisdom of his act. Therefore the document can be accepted by the legal system as a serious act of volition. A third function is an earmarking or channeling function. The populace is made aware that the use of a given device will attain a desired result. When the device is used, the judicial task of determining the parties' intentions is facilitated. A fourth function is clarification. When the parties reduce their transaction to writing (and a contract under seal must be in writing) they are more likely to work out details not contained in their oral agreement. In addition, form requirements can work to serve regulatory and fiscal ends, to educate the parties as to the full extent of their obligations, to provide public notice of the transaction, and also to help management efficiency in an organizational setting.

Toward the end of this brief chapter you will learn that legal effect of the seal has been abolished or downgraded in most jurisdictions. Despite the numerous advantages to formal requirements, in time the disadvantages of the rules regarding sealed instruments outweighed the advantages. Perhaps more importantly, the ceremony of sealing degenerated to such an extent that it lost its almost magical power to impress the parties with the seriousness of their conduct.[8] There are those, however, who lament the weakened condition of the seal.[9]

 WESTLAW REFERENCES

"contract under seal"

import! /s consideration /s seal

formality /s seal sealed /3 instrument contract agreement

seal sealed /s evidenc! evidentiary /s transaction

"private seal"

---

6. Restatement, Second, Contracts § 95. In addition, the promisor and promisee must have legal capacity and the contract must not be void as, for example, because of illegality. Also, if the promisee is to render some performance under the contract, such performance may be required as a condition precedent to enforcement of the promise under the same rules as are applicable to an informal contract. See ch. 11 infra; In re Conrad's Estate, 333 Pa. 561, 3 A.2d 697 (1939).

7. See, generally, Perillo, The Statute of Frauds in the Light of the Functions and Dysfunctions of Form, 43 Fordham L.Rev. 39, 43–69 (1974).

8. See Cardozo, The Paradoxes of Legal Science 70–72 (1928).

9. See A. Kronman & R. Posner, The Economics of Contract Law 53 (1979).

§ 7–2.   Sufficiency of the Writing

The sealed instrument "must be written on paper or parchment, but an instrument written or printed on any substance capable of receiving and retaining legible characters, would probably have equal validity." [10] Although today sealed instruments are invariably signed, a signature is not a requirement for the efficacy of the instrument.[11] The instrument must contain a promise which is sufficiently definite as to be capable of performance.[12] In addition, the promisor and the promisee must be named or sufficiently described in the instrument so as to be capable of identification.[13] Thus, for example, the rule of agency law that a principal may sue or be sued on a contract, although the contract by its term appears to be made with his agent, is inapplicable to sealed instruments.[14] Some courts, however, have circumvented this rule in part by holding that if the contract was such that no seal is required, it will be treated as an informal contract.[15]

Although there was an initial reluctance to permit a suit by a third party beneficiary upon a sealed contract, the prevailing view today is that there is no greater obstacle to such an action than in the case of informal contracts.[16]

WESTLAW REFERENCES
seal sealed   /s   "third party beneficiary"
seal sealed   +1   instrument   /s   requir!
seal sealed   +1   instrument   /s   sufficien! insufficien!

---

§ 7–3.   What Constitutes a Seal

For some period in history seals were required to consist of wax affixed to the parchment or paper on which the terms of the instrument were written. The wax was required to have an identifiable impression made upon it.[17] Usually this was made by a signet ring.

In time when ordinary people, who did not have signet rings, learned to read and write, it was to be expected that substitutes for the traditional seal would be accepted by the law. Thus, today it would be generally accurate to say that a seal may consist of wax, a gummed wafer, an impression on the paper, the word "seal," the letters "L.S." (locus sigilli) or even a pen scratch.[18]

---

10. 1 Williston § 206.

11. Restatement, Second, Contracts § 95, Comment c; Parks v. Hazlerigg, 7 Blackf. 536, 43 Am.Dec. 106 (Ind.1845).

12. On definiteness, see § 2–13 supra.

13. Restatement, Second, Contracts § 108.

14. Crowley v. Lewis, 239 N.Y. 264, 146 N.E. 374 (1925); 1 Williston § 215.

15. Harris v. McKay, 138 Va. 448, 122 S.E. 137, 32 A.L.R. 156 (1924); contra, New England Dredging Co. v. Rockport Granite Co., 149 Mass. 381, 21 N.E. 947 (1889).

16. Wilmington Housing Authority, for Use of Simeone v. Fidelity & Deposit Co., 43 Del. (4 Terry) 381, 47 A.2d 524, 170 A.L.R. 1288 (1946); Coster v. Mayor of Albany, 43 N.Y. 399 (1871); 1A Corbin § 255; Restatement, Second, Contracts § 303.

17. Coke, 3 Institutes 169 (1812 ed.). See 1A Corbin § 241; 1 Williston § 207.

18. Loraw v. Nissley, 156 Pa. 329, 27 A. 242 (1893); Restatement, Second, Contracts

To have a sealed instrument, in addition to the formalities mentioned above, it must appear that the party executing it intended it to be a sealed instrument.[19] The most common way in which this intent is shown is by a witnessing clause; that is, a clause which states "In Witness Whereof I have hereunto set my hand and seal" or words to that effect. Some cases have held that a recital is necessary at least where the seal is other than a wax impression.[20] Others, contrary to the formerly prevailing view that one must determine from the face of the instrument whether it is sealed, have admitted extrinsic evidence to show the necessary intention.[21] The Restatement of Contracts Second adopts the approach that a recital of sealing is neither required nor conclusive.[22] Generally, however, an objective test of sealing is incorporated in its definition of a seal as "a manifestation in tangible and conventional form of an intention that a document be sealed."[23] The Restatement recognizes, however, that extrinsic evidence should be freely admitted to determine whether or not there was a manifestation of intention to seal.[24]

WESTLAW REFERENCES

"locus sigilli"

seal sealed /s wax signet

seal sealed /s wax /s instrument

"witness whereof i have hereunto set my hand and seal"

seal sealed /s extrinsic /s intend! intent!

§ 7–4. The Adoption of a Seal Already on the Instrument

In the section above it was assumed that the seal was placed on the writing by the promisor before delivery. It is to be noted, however, that under modern practice very often the parties adopt a printed form purchased from a legal stationer upon which the word "seal," the letters "L.S." or some other form of seal has been printed or otherwise

§ 96; 1A Corbin § 241; 1 Williston § 207. This listing is not necessarily completely accurate for each jurisdiction. For example, a pen scrawl was held to be sufficient in Woodbury v. United States Cas. Co., 284 Ill. 227, 120 N.E. 8 (1918).

19. Empire Trust Co. v. Heinze, 242 N.Y. 475, 152 N.E. 266 (1926). However, there are cases indicating that the intent to seal is sufficient, as for example, where there is a clause which says "In Witness Whereof, I have hereunto set my hand and seal," not accompanied by a seal. Beach v. Beach, 141 Conn. 583, 107 A.2d 629 (1954).

20. Alropa Corp. v. Rossee, 86 F.2d 118 (5th Cir.1936); Dawsey v. Kirven, 203 Ala. 446, 83 So. 338, 7 A.L.R. 1658 (1919); Bradley Salt Co. v. Norfolk Importing and Exporting Co., 95 Va. 461, 28 S.E. 567 (1897).

21. Jackson v. Security Mut. Life Ins. Co., 135 Ill.App. 86 (1907), affirmed 233 Ill.

161, 84 N.E. 198 (1908); Matter of Pirie, 198 N.Y. 209, 91 N.E. 587 (1910), modified 199 N.Y. 524, 91 N.E. 1144 (1910).

22. Restatement, Second, Contracts § 100.

23. Restatement, Second, Contracts § 96(1); contra, Mobil Oil Corp. v. Wolfe, 297 N.C. 36, 252 S.E.2d 809 (1979) (recital conclusive).

24. Restatement, Second, Contracts § 100, Comment b: "A recital may give meaning to a manifestation of intention, indicating that a dash or scrawl after a signature is intended as a seal or that the promisor intends to adopt a seal affixed by another party. * * * [R]ecitals are often false and their falsity may be shown by any relevant evidence."

affixed, or they adopt a form prepared by the attorney for one of the parties. It is well settled that the promisor need not himself attach the seal [25] and that one seal may serve for several persons.[26] In other words a seal which is on the instrument may be adopted. Since the question of adoption is one of intent and the writing is seldom unambiguous, extrinsic evidence is ordinarily admissible to determine this issue of adoption.[27] It also seems to be generally agreed that if the instrument contains a recital of sealing and some form of seal, all who signed will be presumed to have adopted the seal.[28]

§ 7–5. Delivery of a Sealed Instrument

It is unanimously agreed that delivery of a sealed instrument is required for its validity.[29] The difficult question is what constitutes delivery. The earlier cases seemed to have assumed that when the obligor placed the instrument in the possession of the obligee or of some third person as agent of the obligee, delivery was effectuated.[30] It soon became recognized, however, that possession of the paper could be relinquished without an intent that the obligation should exist as, for example, when it is given merely for inspection. Consequently, it was held that, in addition to the surrendering of possession, an intent to deliver was required.[31] Under the more modern cases, the only requirement is an intent to deliver, that is to say, a manifestation of intent by the obligor that the document be immediately operative, even where the instrument has never left the possession of the obligor.[32] This view is not sufficiently widespread, however, to cause the Second Restatement to depart from the traditional rule that the promisor must part with possession.[33]

  WESTLAW REFERENCES

deliver! /s seal sealed /2 instrument

intend! intent! /s deliver! /s instrument /2   sealed seal

surrender! /s instrument /2   seal sealed

deliver! transfer! /s agent custodian (third +1 person party) /s
   seal sealed /2   instrument

---

25. Commonwealth v. Gutelius, 287 Pa. 441, 135 A. 214 (1926); Van Domelen v. Westinghouse Electric Corp., 382 F.2d 385 (9th Cir.1967).

26. Restatement, Second, Contracts § 99; McNulty v. Medical Science of D.C., Inc., 176 A.2d 783 (D.C.App.1962).

27. F.D.I.C. v. Barness, 484 F.Supp. 1134 (E.D.Pa.1980); Restatement, Second, Contracts § 98; 1 Williston § 208.

28. Cammack v. J.B. Slattery & Bro., 241 N.Y. 39, 148 N.E. 781 (1925); Branton v. Martin, 243 S.C. 90, 132 S.E.2d 285 (1963).

29. Restatement, Second, Contracts § 95(1)(b).

30. If the instrument is transferred to an agent or custodian of the obligor, there is no delivery by virtue of the transfer. 1A Corbin § 244.

31. Moore v. Trott, 162 Cal. 268, 122 P. 462 (1912). See generally, Gavitt, The Conditional Delivery of Deeds, 30 Colum.L.Rev. 1145 (1930); Corbin, Delivery of Written Contracts, 36 Yale L.J. 443 (1926); Patterson, The Delivery of a Life Insurance Policy, 33 Harv.L.Rev. 198 (1919).

32. Maciaszek v. Maciaszek, 21 Ill.2d 542, 173 N.E.2d 476 (1961); McMahon v. Dorsey, 353 Mich. 623, 91 N.W.2d 893 (1958).

33. Restatement, Second, Contracts § 102, Comment b.

§ 7–6. Is the Acceptance of the Obligee Necessary to Complete a Delivery?

There are cases which have stated that an expression of assent by the other party is necessary to complete a delivery.[34] However, this is not required where the instrument expresses an obligation only on the part of the obligor.[35] It has sometimes been said that the promisee's assent is presumed absent a disclaimer from him. A more direct statement is that the instrument is effective upon delivery without assent, but that it may be disclaimed by the obligee within a reasonable time after learning of the existence of the instrument.[36]

The situation is different if the instrument delivered by the obligor calls for a return promise. In such a case, in order for the promisee to be bound by a sealed promise, he must seal and deliver the instrument (or another instrument). If the promisee does not seal and deliver, but makes the required return promise, the parties are bound by a bilateral contract. The original promisor is bound by a promise under seal and the second promisor is bound by his informal promise.[37] It is sometimes held, however, that acceptance of the sealed instrument containing a return promise justifies a holding that the acceptor is liable on the instrument by adoption or estoppel.[38] Since such a transaction involves consideration, the effects of the distinction between action on a sealed promise and an informal promise are primarily two: (1) where common law pleading survives, the action of the sealed promise is in covenant rather than assumpsit; a (2) in many jurisdictions the statutory period of limitations is appreciably longer in the case of an action on a sealed instrument.

Under any view of the matter, if the sealed instrument calls for a return promise, the delivery is deemed conditional until the return promise is made as the promisor has no intent to deliver until there is an expression of assent by the other party.[39]

 WESTLAW REFERENCES

    seal sealed /2 instrument /s deliver! /s assent! effect!

    seal sealed /2 instrument /s deliver! obligee promis! /s accept!

    seal sealed /2 instrument document contract promise /s estop!

34. Bowen v. Prudential Ins., Co., 178 Mich. 63, 144 N.W. 543 (1913); 1 Williston § 213.

35. Restatement, Second, Contracts § 104.

36. Branton v. Martin, 243 S.C. 90, 132 S.E.2d 285 (1963); Restatement, Second, Contracts § 104(2); 1 Williston § 213; 1A Corbin § 245.

37. Restatement, Second, Contracts § 107; 1A Corbin § 256; 1 Williston § 214.

38. Atlantic Dock Co. v. Leavitt, 54 N.Y. 35 (1873); 1 Williston § 214. In Blass v. Terry, 156 N.Y. 122, 50 N.E. 953 (1898), the court has held that sufficient delivery of a deed so as to vest title in the grantee did not necessarily result in a sufficient manifestation of assent to a mortgage assumption clause in the deed. Under the facts the grantee was not given the opportunity to read the deed. Under ordinary circumstances the grantee who accepts a deed is chargeable with its contents whether he reads it or not. See § 9–42 infra.

39. Diebold Safe & Lock Co., v. Morse, 226 Mass. 342, 115 N.E. 431 (1917).

seal sealed /2 instrument contract document promise /s "statute
of limitation" (time /4 bar barred barring)
241k22(2)

§ 7–7. Delivery in Escrow—Conditional Delivery

We have already seen that delivery can be effectuated by the transfer of possession to a third party other than an agent of the promisor. The question here is the effect of such a delivery when instructions are given to the third party to deliver the instrument to the grantee or promisee only upon the occurrence of a condition not specified in the instrument itself. The function of the conditional delivery is to make the promisor bound upon the instrument in the sense that, unless the power of revocation is reserved, the instrument is irrevocable;[40] however, the obligor is not bound to perform until the condition takes place.[41] When the condition occurs he is bound even though the third party does not deliver the instrument.[42] The main legal problem presented by this fact pattern is with the parol evidence rule. However, the weight of authority is to the effect that the parol evidence rule is no bar to proof that the delivery was conditional.[43]

A similar problem arises where the instrument is delivered not to a third person but to the promisee and is delivered subject to the occurrence of a condition not stated in the instrument. Many of the older cases, particularly those involving conveyances, held that the condition not stated in the writing should be disregarded because of the parol evidence rule.[44] The weight of authority under the modern cases is to the contrary.[45]

Of course it is possible that the condition is one which prevents any delivery from taking place so that the instrument is not effective in any way. For example, if A hands B a sealed instrument which contains a promise in favor of B and says "hold this for me until tomorrow," there is no delivery and therefore the instrument is not effective.[46] At times it is difficult to determine whether the condition imposed prevents a delivery or whether it is merely a condition to performance. "Without doubt, interpretations have been variable and inconsistent."[47]

 WESTLAW REFERENCES
seal sealed /2 instrument document promise contract /s escrow!

40. Moore v. Downing, 289 Ill. 612, 124 N.E. 557 (1919); Restatement, Second, Contracts § 103.

41. Sunset Beach Amusement Corp. v. Belk, 31 N.J. 445, 158 A.2d 35 (1960); as to conditional delivery of conveyances, see Aigler, Is a Contract Necessary to Create an Effective Escrow, 16 Mich.L.Rev. 569 (1918).

42. Gardiner v. Gardiner, 36 Idaho 664, 214 P. 219 (1923).

43. Restatement, Second, Contracts § 103; Corbin, Conditional Delivery of Written Contracts, 36 Yale L.J. 443, 455 (1927); 1A Corbin § 249; 1 Williston § 212.

44. Hume v. Kirkwood, 216 Ala. 534, 113 So. 613 (1927).

45. 1A Corbin § 250; 1 Williston § 212; Notes, 18 Mich.L.Rev. 314 (1920), 5 Minn.L.Rev. 287 (1921).

46. See § 7–5 supra.

47. 1A Corbin § 251; see also, Puckett v. Hoover, 146 Tex. 1, 202 S.W.2d 209 (1947); 1 Williston § 212.

seal sealed /2 instrument document promise contract /s deliver!
    /s condition!

seal sealed /2 instrument document promise contract /s bind
    bound binding /s condition! perform!

seal sealed /2 instrument document promise contract /s "parol*
    evidence"

§ 7–8. Some Effects of the Seal

As we have seen, a sealed instrument is binding without consideration.[48] However, the absence of consideration can be taken into account by a court of equity in determining whether specific performance or other equitable remedies should be granted.[49]

At early common law it was held that the discharge or modification of a sealed contract could be accomplished only by another sealed instrument.[50] Later it was held that a sealed instrument could be discharged or modified by an accord and satisfaction but not by an unperformed executory bilateral contract.[51] The more modern view is that a sealed instrument may be modified or rescinded in the same manner as any other instrument.[52] Traditionally, an undisclosed principal cannot sue on a sealed instrument, but this rule is also changing.[53]

Under common law pleading, an action on a sealed instrument was required to be brought under the writ of covenant rather than assumpsit. While the distinction between writs is now largely a matter of history, it still remains the law in a good number of jurisdictions that a longer statutory period of limitations is applicable to an action on an instrument under seal.[54]

 WESTLAW REFERENCES
seal sealed /2 instrument document promise contract /s "specific!
perform!" equit!

48. Goulet v. Goulet, 105 N.H. 51, 192 A.2d 626 (1963); see also § 7–1 supra.

49. Capitol Investors Co. v. Estate of Morrison, 584 F.2d 652 (4th Cir.1978), certiorari denied 440 U.S. 981, 99 S.Ct. 1790, 60 L.Ed.2d 241 (1979); see Restatement, Contracts § 366; Restatement, Second, Contracts § 95, reporter's note. An option contract under seal will be enforced in equity despite the absence of consideration. The common law rule is that an offer under seal is irrevocable for the time stated within the offer, or for a reasonable time if no time is stated. O'Brien v. Boland, 166 Mass. 481, 44 N.E. 602 (1896); Clark on Contracts 43 (4th ed. 1931).

50. See 1A Corbin § 253.

51. Tussing v. Smith, 125 Fla. 578, 171 So. 238 (1936).

52. Koth v. Board of Education of Jasper County, 141 S.C. 448, 140 S.E. 99 (1927); Restatement, Contracts § 407. See generally, Costigan, Waiver, Alteration or Modification by Parol of Contracts under Seal, 6 Ill.L.Rev. 280 (1911). At early common law many other defenses that could be raised against simple contracts could not be raised against sealed instruments, necessitating the intervention of equity to stay the unconscionable exercise of the obligee's legal right to enforce the sealed instrument despite the defense of fraud, payment or the like. See Ames, Specialty Contracts and Equitable Defenses, 9 Harv. L.Rev. 49 (1895).

53. See § 7–9 infra.

54. See the statutory note preceding Restatement, Second, Contracts § 95 which compiles the relevant statutes.

seal sealed   /s   instrument document promise contract   /s   modif!
discharg!

seal sealed   /2   instrument document promise contract   /s   "accord
and satisfaction" rescind! rescission

§ 7–9. Statutory Changes Affecting the Seal

In its original conception, the sealing of an instrument was surrounded by impressive solemnity. Individuals who owned signet rings or similar devices guarded them as they would guard treasure. The community was aware of the consequences of the ceremony of sealing and delivery. As times changed and the ceremony was abandoned and supplanted by the mere presence on a printed form of the word "seal" or the initials "L.S." [55] on or near the signature line, the community lost its awareness of the distinction between sealed and unsealed instruments.

Taking cognizance of the change in community expectations, legislatures have enacted statutes affecting the seal.[56] Some statutes make private seals wholly inoperative.[57] The Uniform Commercial Code is in this class. It "makes clear that every effect of the seal which relates to 'sealed instruments' is wiped out insofar as contracts for sale are concerned." [58] In some states where the effectiveness of the seal has been abolished, and under the Uniform Commercial Code, as we have seen, it has been deemed necessary to enact statutory substitutes to perform one or more of its functions, particularly the function of sustaining a transaction without consideration.[59]

Another group of state statutes has abolished the distinction between sealed and unsealed instruments but provide that any written promise is rebuttably presumed to be supported by consideration.[60] A

55. The abandonment of the ceremony apparently occurred early in American history. See the remarks of Brackenridge, J. in Alexander v. Jameson, 5 Bin. 238, 244 (Pa.1812), quoted in the learned decision, Loraw v. Nissley, 156 Pa. 329, 27 A. 242 (1893).

56. The courts had previously taken cognizance of the deterioration of the ceremony of sealing. Their piecemeal attempts to deal with the problem, however, tended to place the law in confusion. See Crane, The Magic of the Private Seal, 15 Colum.L.Rev. 24 (1915), Selected Readings 598.

57. Arkansas, Illinois, Indiana, Minnesota, Nebraska, New York, Ohio, Utah, Wyoming. The presence or absence of a seal has always been irrelevant in Louisiana. See the statutory note preceding Restatement, Second, Contracts § 95. Another statutory classification appears in 1 Williston § 219A.

58. § 2–203, Comment 1. A seal, however, may have the effect of a signature. Id., Comment 2.

59. See ch. 5(B) supra.

60. Arizona, California, Idaho, Iowa, Kansas, Kentucky, Missouri, Montana, Nevada, North Dakota, Oklahoma, Tennessee, Texas. Two states, Mississippi and New Mexico, have statutes which appear to have elevated all written contracts to the level of sealed instruments. In each state, however, the court decisions must be consulted to determine the interpretation given to the local statute.

Citations to the statutes are compiled in the statutory note preceding Restatement, Second, Contracts § 95.

The rebuttable presumption of consideration conferred on all written promises can have a significant impact upon the decision of a concrete case. See Patterson v. Chapman, 179 Cal. 203, 176 P. 37, 2 A.L.R. 1467 (1918).

third group of state statutes provide that a seal is only presumptive evidence of consideration on executory instruments, generally leaving unchanged the effect of the seal on executed instruments such as releases.[61] There are, of course, variations within these groups and no lack of additional statutes of miscellaneous types.

Not all statutes of the same type have received similar interpretations. For example, the New Jersey legislature enacted legislation to the effect that the seal is merely presumptive evidence of consideration. This was held not to deprive a sealed gratuitous promise of its efficacy if no bargained for exchange was intended.[62] A subsequent statutory change was enacted to the effect that in an action on a sealed promise the defendant may prove the absence of consideration with the same effect as if the instrument were not sealed. In the face of this statute the court still adhered to its view that no consideration is necessary on a sealed instrument.[63]

It is apparent that the different kinds of statutes may give rise to different results. Thus, for example, if a jurisdiction has not overruled the common law principle that a sealed instrument may only be modified or rescinded by an instrument under seal,[64] a statute abolishing the effect of a seal would obliterate this rule, but a statute which modifies the effect of a seal by providing that it is presumptive evidence of consideration would have no direct effect on this rule.

The same analysis would apply in the case of the common law rule that an undisclosed principal may not sue or be sued upon a sealed instrument. Under a statute providing that the seal gives rise to a presumption of consideration, this common law rule would not be changed. Of course, the courts could change the common law rule as has been done by courts in other jurisdictions.[65] Indeed, the legislative policy to reduce the sanctity of a sealed instrument should be given effect even as to rules such as this. A similar analysis is applicable to the rules retained in some jurisdictions that a third party beneficiary may not sue on a sealed instrument [66] and that an agent's authority to execute a sealed instrument must be granted by a sealed instrument.[67]

---

61. Alabama, Connecticut, Florida, Michigan, New Jersey, Oregon, Washington, Wisconsin. See the Restatement's statutory note.

62. Aller v. Aller, 40 N.J.L. 446 (1878); see 1A Corbin § 254; 1 Williston § 219. Cf. Cochran v. Taylor, 273 N.Y. 172, 7 N.E. 2d 89 (1937), decided under the former New York statute that a seal created a presumption of consideration. It was held that the parties were estopped from contradicting a recital of $1.00 as consideration. An estoppel is not created in New York by

such a recital on an unsealed instrument. See § 4–6 supra.

63. Zirk v. Nohr, 127 N.J.L. 217, 21 A.2d 766 (1941).

64. See § 7–8 supra.

65. See Nalbandian v. Hanson Restaurant & Lounge, Inc., 369 Mass. 150, 338 N.E.2d 335 (1975).

66. See § 7–2 supra.

67. Restatement, Second, Agency § 28, Comment g (1958).

WESTLAW REFERENCES

seal sealed /2 instrument document promise contract /s statut!

u.c.c. ''uniform commercial code'' /s 2–203

statut! /s wr*te writing written /s instrument contract agreement
/s presum! /s consideration

Chapter 8

CAPACITY OF PARTIES

Table of Sections

Table of Sections

C. SELF–DEALING

§ 8–1. Introduction

There are certain classes of persons whose contractual capacity is limited. Their agreements are either void, or more often, voidable. These classes include infants and persons suffering from mental infirmity.[1] In addition, limitations upon one's ability to contract with oneself may be viewed as limitations upon contractual capacity.

A. INFANTS

Table of Sections

1. **Other classes exist.** Formerly, the agreements of married women were void. This disability has largely been eliminated by statutory enactments. The statutes are compiled in 2 Williston §§ 269–269A. Some disabilities of married women may continue to exist in various jurisdictions. See Restatement, Second, Contracts § 12, Comment d.

In a number of jurisdictions a spendthrift may be placed under guardianship and his contracts are voidable. See Lilienthal v. Kaufman, 239 Or. 1, 395 P.2d 543 (1964).

Convicts are under disabilities which vary from state to state. See 2 Williston § 272; Note, 14 Colum.L.Rev. 592 (1914); Note, 5 Cornell L.Q. 320 (1920).

The problem of capacity to contract arises as to corporations in connection with the doctrine of *ultra vires;* that is, in relation to agreements entered into outside the scope of the powers of the corporation. This doctrine is extensively discussed in works on corporation law. For summary treatment, see 2 Williston § 271.

A related problem exists in relation to the contracts of municipal corporations and other public agencies. Public contracts not awarded pursuant to the procedures provided by law are void or voidable.

There is much disagreement in the cases as to whether and under what circumstances the private party who has performed under such a contract may recover in quasi contract. Extensive discussion and citations will be found in American-LaFrance, Inc. v. Philadelphia, 183 Miss. 207, 184 So. 620 (1938); Hudson City Contracting Co. v. Jersey City Incinerator Authority, 17 N.J. 297, 111 A.2d 385 (1955); Federal Paving Corp. v. Wauwatosa, 231 Wis. 655, 286 N.W. 546 (1939). Some jurisdictions will in almost no case grant such relief. See Seif v. Long Beach, 286 N.Y. 382, 387–88, 36 N.E.2d 630, 632 (1941), motion denied 287 N.Y. 836, 41 N.E.2d 164 (1942); but see Gerzof v. Sweeney, 22 N.Y.2d 297, 292 N.Y.S.2d 640, 239 N.E.2d 521 (1968), reargument denied 22 N.Y.2d 884, 293 N.Y.S. 2d 1025, 239 N.E.2d 927 (1968). See also Haight, The Problem of the Defective Public Contract in New York State, 14 Syracuse L.Rev. 426 (1963). Others are quite liberal. See Campbell v. Tennessee Valley, 421 F.2d 293 (5th Cir.1969). See also Gitleman, Contractual and Quasi-Contractual Liability of Arkansas Local Government Units, 20 Ark.L.Rev. 292 (1967); Vaubel, Relief Under a Defective Municipal Contract in Ohio, 2 Akron L.Rev. 20 (1968); Note, 19 S.Dak.L.Rev. 485 (1974).

§ 8–2.   Introduction

The law often preserves archaic terminology. In everyday language we distinguish between adults and minors. Lawyers refer to the latter as "infants." If this label were changed volumes of digests, texts and encyclopedias would immediately become obsolete. At common law a person remained an infant until he reached the age of twenty-one.[2] By legislation enacted mostly in the 1970's, the age of majority is now eighteen in almost all jurisdictions.[3] In accordance with the maxim that the law often disregards fractions of a day, it is commonly held that one's infancy ends at the very first moment of the day preceding one's twenty-first (or eighteenth) birthday.[4] Emancipation of the infant by his parents does not enlarge his capacity to contract.[5]

Formerly, it was the rule that the contracts of infants were void.[6] Later it was held that they were voidable but that certain kinds of transactions entered into by an infant such as his appointment of an agent, his execution of a promissory note and his agreement to be surety were void. It is now almost everywhere agreed that even such

2. Gastonia Personnel Corp. v. Rogers, 276 N.C. 279, 172 S.E.2d 19, 41 A.L.R.3d 1062 (1971); Restatement, Second, Contracts § 14, Comment a.

3. The Legal Status of Adolescents 1980 (U.S.Dept. of Health and Human Services 1981) p. 41. Statutes changing the age of majority are not retroactive and do not generally affect preexisting rights. Stewart v. Stewart, 85 N.M. 637, 515 P.2d 641 (1973). See Note, 5 Fordham Urb.L.J. 365 (1977).

4. Turnbull v. Bonkowski, 419 F.2d 104 (9th Cir.1969); Nelson v. Sandkamp, 227 Minn. 177, 34 N.W.2d 640, 5 A.L.R.2d 1136 (1948). In several jurisdictions, an infant attains his majority at the first moment of his twenty-first (or eighteenth) birthday. See 2 Williston § 224.

5. Commonwealth v. Graham, 157 Mass. 73, 31 N.E. 706 (1892); Daubert v. Mosley, 487 P.2d 353, 56 A.L.R.3d 1328 (Okl.1971); Schoenung v. Gallet, 206 Wis. 52, 238 N.W. 852 (1931). Emancipation occurs upon the express or implied renun-

ciation by his parents of their common law right of control over the infant and particularly of the infant's obligation to provide his parent with his services and to turn over to them his earnings. See Katz, Schroeder & Sidman, Emancipating Our Children, 7 Family L.Q. 211 (1973). In most jurisdictions emancipation also occurs by operation of law upon marriage. See 2 Williston § 225. In some jurisdictions it is also held that contractual capacity is attained upon marriage, but this is a distinctly minority view. See Succession of Hecker, 191 La. 302, 185 So. 32 (1938).

Several jurisdictions permit judicial emancipation upon the petition of the minor and the decree may also remove in whole or in part the infant's lack of capacity. See 1938 Report of the New York Law Revision Commission 139, for discussion of such statutes.

6. For the historical development of this rule, see the learned opinion in Henry v. Root, 33 N.Y. 526 (1865); see also 2 Williston § 226.

transactions are voidable rather than void.[7] Not only a contract, but also an executed transaction, such as a sale, conveyance or release may be avoided.[8] The power of avoidance resides only in the infant[9] or in the event of his death, in his heirs, administrators or executors.[10] Occasional decisions permitting a parent or other guardian to disaffirm the infant's contract can, however, be found and would seem to be sound if the infant is not emancipated.[11] It is quite clear that an adult party to the transaction cannot avoid the contract on the ground of the other's infancy.[12]

Because of the one-sided power of avoidance held by the infant it might seem anomalous to speak in terms of the limited capacity of infants. To some observers it has seemed that the infant has capacity to contract coupled with an additional power of disaffirmance. It has been said that "the law confers a privilege rather than a disability."[13] This, however, represents but one side of the coin. Adult parties frequently will refuse to contract with or sell to infants because an infant is incapable of giving legal assurance that he will not disaffirm.[14] From this point of view the infant is under both a legal and practical disability.[15] Protection, as is so often the case, involves "limitations on the individual liberty of the protected person."[16] It has been strenuously argued of late, that the price of protection is too high and that the

---

7. See Casey v. Kastel, 237 N.Y. 305, 142 N.E. 671, 31 A.L.R. 995 (1924); 2 Williston § 226; Restatement, Second, Contracts § 14. In England certain infants' contracts are "wholly void." Infants Relief Act, 1874, § 1.

8. Even a sheriff's sale was held to be voidable in G.M.A.C. v. Stotsky, 60 Misc.2d 451, 303 N.Y.S.2d 463 (Sup.Ct.1969).

9. Quality Motors v. Hays, 216 Ark. 264, 225 S.W.2d 326 (1949) (father cannot disaffirm for son); Oliver v. Houdlet, 13 Mass. 237 (1816) (guardian may not disaffirm for ward); Dostal v. Magee, 272 Wis. 509, 76 N.W.2d 349 (1956) (father cannot ratify for son).

10. Gendreau v. North American Life & Cas. Co., 158 Minn. 259, 197 N.W. 257 (1924); Eagan v. Scully, 29 App.Div. 617, 51 N.Y.S. 680 (3d Dep't 1898), affirmed 173 N.Y. 581, 65 N.E. 1116 (1902); cf. Kline v. L'Amoureaux, 2 Paige's Ch. 419 (N.Y.1831).

11. Crockett Motor Co. v. Thompson, 177 Ark. 495, 6 S.W.2d 834 (1928); Hughes v. Murphy, 5 Ga.App. 328, 63 S.E. 231 (1908) (action brought by guardian to disaffirm sale permissible although infant objected); Boudreaux v. State Farm Mutual Automobile Insurance Co., 385 So.2d 480 (La.App.1980); Champa v. New York Central Mut. Relief Ass'n, 57 Ohio App. 522, 15 N.E.2d 172 (1936).

12. Holt v. Ward Clarencieux, 93 Eng. Rep. 954 (K.B.1732); Shaw v. Philbrick, 129 Me. 259, 151 A. 423 (1930). For the relationship between this rule and the doctrine of "mutuality of obligation," see § 4–12 supra.

A contract between two infants is voidable at the option of either. Hurwitz v. Barr, 193 A.2d 360 (D.C.App.1963) (sale of motor scooter).

13. Simpson, Contracts 216 (2d ed. 1965).

14. As a practical matter the adult party may refuse to contract with the infant unless the infant's parent or other responsible adult agrees to become jointly liable with the infant. In such a case, disaffirmance by the infant does not discharge his co-obligor. Campbell v. Fender, 218 Ark. 290, 235 S.W.2d 957 (1951); 2 Williston § 327; 10 Williston § 1214; but if the contract has been rescinded and the status quo restored, the co-obligor may be discharged. Allen v. Small, 129 Vt. 77, 271 A.2d 840, 44 A.L.R.3d 1412 (1970).

15. See Warner Bros. Pictures, Inc. v. Brodel, 31 Cal.2d 766, 192 P.2d 949, 3 A.L.R.2d 691 (1948), certiorari denied 335 U.S. 844, 69 S.Ct. 67, 93 L.Ed. 394 (1948), rehearing denied 335 U.S. 873, 69 S.Ct. 165, 93 L.Ed. 417 (1948).

16. Dicey, Law and Public Opinion in England 151 (2d ed. 1962).

interests of infants of any age would be best served by granting them full freedom of contract.[17] A comprehensive enactment in New South Wales goes very far in this direction although maintaining some protection for infants as to contracts which are not beneficial to them.[18]

After the infant has exercised his power to avoid the contract the transaction is treated for many purposes as if it were void from the beginning. Thus, by disaffirming his conveyance the infant may reclaim the real property from a subsequent purchaser who purchased in good faith and without notice of the fact that an infant had preceded his vendor in the chain of title.[19] So also an infant may disaffirm his liability on a negotiable instrument even as to a holder in due course.[20] As to sales of goods, however, the Uniform Sales Act provided that a subsequent bona fide purchaser for value obtained goods free from an infant's power of disaffirmance[21] and this rule has been continued by the Uniform Commercial Code.[22]

 WESTLAW REFERENCES

"twenty one" /s capacity /s contract***

"age of majority" /s eighteen

emancipat! /s infan! /s contract***

voidable /s infan! /s contract***

211k46

power +2 avoid! /s infan!

disaffirm! /s infan!

"legal! disab!" /s infan!

3-305 /p infan!

infan! /s "negotiable instrument"

infan! minor /s disaffirm! /s privileg!

---

§ 8–3.   Transactions Which the Infant Cannot Avoid

There are certain situations where the infant cannot avoid the contract.[23] No clear-cut test can be formulated except to state that the infant cannot disaffirm certain contracts because public policy so requires or because a statute so provides or because he has done or promised to do something which the law would compel him to do even

---

17. Holt, Escape from Childhood, 172, 236–37 (1974); see also, Navin, The Contracts of Minors Viewed from the Perspective of Fair Exchange, 50 N.Car.L.Rev. 517, 544–45 (1972) (suggesting age of majority of fourteen years); Mehler, Infant Contractual Responsibility: A Time for Reappraisal and Realistic Adjustment?, 11 U.Kan.L. Rev. 361, 373 (1963); Edge, Voidability of Minors' Contracts: A Feudal Doctrine in a Modern Economy, 1 Ga.L.Rev. 205 (1966).

18. See Harland, The Contractual Capacity of Minors—A New Approach, 7 Sydney L.Rev. 41 (1973); Pearce, Reform of the Law of Infancy, 44 Austl.L.J. 269 (1970).

19. Ware v. Mobley, 190 Ga. 249, 9 S.E.2d 67 (1940) (collecting cases).

20. U.C.C. § 3–305(2)(a). But he may not assert any claim against a holder in due course predicated upon his infancy. U.C.C. § 3–207.

21. Uniform Sales Act § 24; see Jones v. Caldwell, 216 Ark. 260, 225 S.W.2d 323, 16 A.L.R.2d 1416 (1949), 28 Chi.-Kent L.Rev. 253 (1950).

22. U.C.C. § 2–403.

23. Restatement, Second, Contracts § 14, Comment b.

in the absence of the contract.[24] Thus, if an infant contracts to support his illegitimate child his promise cannot be disaffirmed as infants are under an obligation to support their illegitimate children.[25] An infant employee's promise not to utilize secret customer lists will be enforced by injunction as his promise merely defines the scope of a legal duty existing apart from the express contractual provision.[26] An infant is generally held liable on his bail bonds on the ground that public policy would otherwise be offended.[27] A small number of cases hold an infant contractually liable if he has received benefits under the contract.[28]

Exceptions to the general rule of the voidable nature of infant's contract can be found in the statutes of most jurisdictions. Insurance legislation, banking laws, educational loan statutes, federal and state legislation regarding military enlistments,[29] and the like, must be consulted. Some statutes provide that a contract made by an infant may not be disaffirmed when it has been approved by a court.[30] It is nonetheless probably true everywhere that the great bulk of infants' transactions continue to be voidable.

To be distinguished from legislation permitting infants to contract are statutes in almost all jurisdictions permitting a guardian to sell the property of an infant under specified conditions. Usually a court order is required to effectuate such a sale, and when made pursuant to the statutory procedure, the sale is not disaffirmable.[31] To facilitate gifts of securities to minors almost all jurisdictions have enacted the Uniform Gifts to Minors Act which permits a custodian of the securities given to the minor pursuant to the terms of the Act to sell the infant's securities and to reinvest the proceeds with great freedom and without the possibility of disaffirmance.[32]

 WESTLAW REFERENCES

"public policy" statut! /s liab! /s infan! /s contract***

minor infan! /s liab! /s necess! /s contract***

24. 2 Williston § 228.

25. Gavin v. Burton, 8 Ind. 69 (1856); Township of Bordentown v. Wallace, 50 N.J.L. 13, 11 A. 267 (1887).

26. Mutual Milk & Cream Co. v. Prigge, 112 App.Div. 652, 98 N.Y.S. 458 (1st Dep't 1906) (decided on other grounds); Career Placement of White Plains, Inc. v. Vaus, 77 Misc.2d 788, 354 N.Y.S.2d 764 (Sup.Ct. 1974).

27. Commonwealth v. Harris, 11 Pa.D. & C. 2, noted in 77 U.Pa.L.Rev. 279 (1928).

28. See § 8–9 infra.

29. See United States v. Williams, 302 U.S. 46, 58 S.Ct. 81, 82 L.Ed. 39 (1937), rehearing denied 302 U.S. 779, 58 S.Ct. 361, 82 L.Ed. 602 (1937), noted in 12 St. John's L.Rev. 346 (1938).

30. West's Ann.Cal.Civ.Code § 36(2) (contracts of employment as an entertainer or athlete); West's Ann.Cal.Labor Code § 1700.37 (contracts with theatrical employment agencies and artists' managers); McKinney's N.Y. General Obligations Law § 3–105 (contracts with infant athletes or artists); McKinney's N.Y.C.P.L.R. 1207 (compromise of claims). In several states, a court may in whole or in part remove the disabilities of infants. See note 5, supra.

31. See 4 Tiffany, Real Property § 1244 (3d ed. 1939).

32. See generally, Newman, The Uniform Gifts to Minors Act in New York and Other Jurisdictions, 49 Cornell L.Q. 12 (1963); Newman, Tax and Substantive Aspects of Gifts to Minors, 50 Cornell L.Q. 446 (1965).

211k50

"uniform gifts to minors act"

§ 8–4. Avoidance and Ratification

As we have seen, the general rule is that an infant's contract is voidable by him. The exercise of this power of avoidance is often called disaffirmance. The effective surrender of this power is known as ratification.[33] An effective ratification obviously cannot take place prior to the attainment of majority; any purported ratification prior to that time suffers from the same infirmity as the contract itself.[34]

An infant may disaffirm his contract at any time prior to ratification. Except as to his conveyance of real property, it is clear that a disaffirmance may effectively be made during infancy and once made is irrevocable.[35] It seems to be the weight of authority, however, that a conveyance of real property executed by an infant may be disaffirmed only after his majority,[36] but sound modern authority permits disaffirmance during minority.[37] The older rule based on a desire to protect the infant's interests has a tendency to keep land unmarketable for an excessive period.

No particular form of language or conduct is required to effectuate a disaffirmance. It may be oral.[38] Any manifestation of unwillingness to be bound by the transaction is sufficient.[39] Often disaffirmance is manifested for the first time by a plea of infancy as a defense,[40] or by the commencement of an action to set aside the transaction.[41]

The entire contract must be avoided. The infant is not entitled to enforce portions that are favorable to him and at the same time disaffirm other portions that he finds burdensome.[42]

33. In England, by statute, any non-necessary debt contracted during infancy is incapable of being ratified even for a new consideration. Infants' Relief Act, 1874, § 2.

34. Elkhorn Coal Corp. v. Tackett, 261 Ky. 795, 88 S.W.2d 943 (1935); Morris v. Glaser, 106 N.J.Eq. 585, 151 A. 766 (1930), affirmed 110 N.J.Eq. 661, 160 A. 578 (1932).

35. Smith v. Wade, 169 Neb. 710, 100 N.W.2d 770 (1960); McNaughton v. Granite City Auto Sales, 108 Vt. 130, 183 A. 340 (1936). Michigan appears to stand alone in holding that no effective disaffirmance may occur until majority. Poli v. National Bank of Detroit, 355 Mich. 17, 93 N.W.2d 925 (1959).

36. 2 Williston § 235.

37. New Domain Oil & Gas Co. v. McKinney, 188 Ky. 183, 221 S.W. 245 (1920) (infant's action to set aside conveyance). Even in jurisdictions in which it is held that the infant may not disaffirm during his minority it has been held that the infant may enter onto the land to take profits or recover the income of the premises conveyed. Sims v. Bardoner, 86 Ind. 87 (1882); Bool v. Mix, 17 Wend. 119 (N.Y. 1836).

38. But see Ray v. ACME Finance Corp., 367 So.2d 186 (Miss.1979) (statutory writing requirement).

39. Tracey v. Brown, 265 Mass. 163, 163 N.E. 885 (1928); McNaughton v. Granite City Auto Sales, 108 Vt. 130, 183 A. 340 (1936).

40. Lesnick v. Pratt, 116 Vt. 477, 80 A.2d 663 (1951).

41. Del Santo v. Bristol County Stadium, Inc., 273 F.2d 605 (1st Cir.1960) (disaffirmance of release accomplished by bringing suit on underlying negligence claim); accord, Slaney v. Westwood Auto, Inc., 366 Mass. 688, 322 N.E.2d 768 (1975).

42. Dairyland County Mut. Ins. Co. v. Roman, 498 S.W.2d 154 (Tex.1973).

Ratification may take place in three ways: failure to make a timely disaffirmance, express ratification, and conduct manifesting an intent to ratify. No consideration is required to create an effective ratification.[43]

(a) Failure to Make a Timely Disaffirmance

Leaving aside for the moment special rules in connection with conveyances, an infant may disaffirm his contracts until a reasonable time after reaching majority.[44] What is a reasonable time is often a question of fact dependent upon such circumstances as whether or not there has been any performance by either or both parties, the nature of the transaction and the extent to which the other party has been prejudiced by any extensive delay in disaffirming.[45]

A good many cases speak in terms of a firm rule that executed contracts are binding if not disaffirmed within a reasonable time after majority, but executory contracts are not binding unless ratified by words or conduct after majority.[46] The rule is a carryover from the older view than an infant's executory contract is void rather than voidable.[47] It is apparent, however, that this "rule" as to executory contracts is not applied when the infant's failure to disaffirm within a reasonable time after attaining his majority works injustice.[48] Ordinarily, however, if the infant has obtained no benefits under the contract [49] as will usually be the case if the contract is wholly executory or executed only by the infant, there is no reason to bar the infant from disaffirming at any time up until the time the statute of limitations has run. Where it has been executed by the adult or by both parties, it will ordinarily be inequitable to permit the infant to retain the benefits of the contract for a long time and then disaffirm. However, for example, it has been pointed out that where pursuant to contract the infant received and paid for services during his minority, there is no reason not to permit the infant to disaffirm long after reaching his majority as the infant's inaction constituted neither benefit to him nor prejudice to

---

43. Restatement, Second, Contracts § 85; see § 5–8 supra.

44. In some jurisdictions this is the rule by statute and is applicable to executory and executed transactions. See Pottawatomie Airport & Flying Service v. Winger, 176 Kan. 445, 271 P.2d 754 (1954). Similar statutory provisions exist elsewhere. 1938 Report of the New York Law Revision Commission 132–137.

45. Harrod v. Kelly Adjustment Co., 179 A.2d 431 (D.C.App.1962); Adamowski v. Curtiss-Wright Flying Service, 300 Mass. 281, 15 N.E.2d 467 (1938); Johnson v. Storie, 32 Neb. 610, 49 N.W. 371 (1891); International Text Book Co. v. Connelly, 206 N.Y. 188, 99 N.E. 722 (1912); Merchants' Credit Bureau v. Kaoru Akiyama, 64 Utah 364, 230 P. 1017 (1924); and see Wooldridge v. Lavoie, 79 N.H. 21, 104 A.

346 (1918), where disaffirmance at trial was deemed reasonable.

46. Nichols & Shepard Co. v. Snyder, 78 Minn. 502, 81 N.W. 516 (1900); Warwick Municipal Employees Credit Union v. McAllister, 110 R.I. 399, 293 A.2d 516 (1972).

47. See Henry v. Root, 33 N.Y. 526 (1865), where the court traces the historical changes in the law of infants' contracts.

48. E.g., Jones v. Godwin, 187 S.C. 510, 198 S.E. 36 (1938) (in reliance upon a mortgage executed by infant, creditor advanced money to infant's father after infant attained majority).

49. Whether or not the infant had received any benefit was said to be the test in Cassella v. Tiberio, 150 Ohio St. 27, 80 N.E.2d 426, 5 A.L.R.2d 1 (1948).

the other.[50]   In summary, the true rule, reflecting what the courts have done in fact, has been expressed in a Texas case in terms of "the effect which mere nonaction by the minor has upon the respective rights or interest of the parties, rather than upon arbitrary test of whether the contract be regarded as executed or executory in whole or in part." [51]

In a good number of cases often cited as announcing a rule on the question, close reading of the opinion indicates that the court merely held that there were sufficient facts to sustain the verdict of the jury or findings of fact of the trial court,[52] and ordinarily the question is the factual one of whether, because of the passage of time after attaining full legal capacity, it is unreasonable to disaffirm.   However, if different inferences cannot reasonably be drawn from the facts it becomes a question of law.[53]

As to conveyances of real property, it is the general rule that these also are ratified if not disaffirmed within a reasonable time after reaching majority,[54] but many cases hold that in the absence of estoppel, the former infant has the right to avoid his conveyance until the statute of limitations has run.[55]

(b) Express Ratification

In the absence of statute an express ratification may be oral.[56]   It has been said frequently that "ratification depends upon intent" [57] and, as to contracts not yet performed by the former infant, many cases hold that a mere acknowledgment of the contract is not enough [58] and that

50. Adamowski v. Curtiss-Wright Flying Service, 300 Mass. 281, 15 N.E.2d 467 (1938).

51. Walker v. Stokes Bros. & Co., 262 S.W. 158 (Tex.Civ.App.1924); and see Terrace Co. v. Calhoun, 37 Ill.App.3d 757, 347 N.E.2d 315 (1976).

52. Adamowski v. Curtiss-Wright Flying Service, 300 Mass. 281, 15 N.E.2d 467 (1938); Johnson v. Storie, 32 Neb. 610, 49 N.W. 371 (1891); International Text Book Co. v. Connelly, 206 N.Y. 188, 99 N.E. 722 (1912).

53. Nationwide Mut. Ins. Co. v. Chantos, 25 N.C.App. 482, 214 S.E.2d 438 (1975), certiorari denied 287 N.C. 465, 215 S.E.2d 624 (1975).

54. Sims v. Everhardt, 102 U.S. (12 Otto) 300, 26 L.Ed. 87 (1880); Martin v. Elkhorn Coal Corp., 227 Ky. 623, 13 S.W.2d 780 (1929); Sprecher v. Sprecher, 206 Md. 108, 110 A.2d 509 (1955); Muncey v. Norfolk & Western Ry. Co., 106 W.Va. 348, 145 S.E. 581 (1928); cf. 2 Williston § 239.

55. Gibson v. Hall, 260 Ala. 539, 71 So. 2d 532 (1954); Walker v. Ellis, 212 Ark. 498, 207 S.W.2d 39 (1947); Mott v. Iossa, 119 N.J.Eq. 185, 181 A. 689 (1935).   Of course, many of the same factors which go

into a finding of whether there is an estoppel are the same as those which go into a determination under the majority rule of whether a reasonable time has elapsed. The equitable doctrine of laches may also be applicable and much the same factors as create an estoppel give rise to the application of that doctrine.   Curtis v. Curtis, 398 Ill. 442, 75 N.E.2d 881 (1947).   Very often it is unclear which rule the court is applying.   E.g., Green v. Green, 69 N.Y. 553 (1877).

56. Statutes requiring that a ratification be in writing were enacted in Arkansas, Kentucky, Maine, Mississippi, Missouri, New Jersey, South Carolina, Virginia and West Virginia.   See 1938 Report of the New York Law Revision Commission 139.

57. International Text Book Co. v. Connelly, 206 N.Y. 188, 99 N.E. 722 (1912).   If ratification occurs because of failure to make a timely disaffirmance, it is obvious that subjective intention is immaterial.

58. E.g., Lee v. Thompson, 124 Fla. 494, 168 So. 848 (1936).   See 2 Page, Contracts § 1372 (2d ed. 1920): "By the weight of authority the rule in ratification of an infant's contract * * * is that mere acknowledgement that the obligation has

nothing less than a promise will suffice.[59] Still, a jury may be entitled to find that a promise can reasonably be implied from the language and circumstances.[60] It has been pointed out in an able opinion that the requisite that there be a new promise is an erroneous carryover from the obsolete view that the contracts of infants are void,[61] and that therefore a ratification must, by analogy, meet the requisites of a new promise to pay a debt discharged by operation of law.[62]

The authorities agree that if the contract is fully executed, an acknowledgment or other words consistent with an intention to stand on the transaction is sufficient to constitute ratification.[63]

(c) Ratification by Conduct

Ratification by failure to make a timely disaffirmance, previously discussed, may be considered a kind of ratification by conduct; at least if inaction be deemed conduct. Retention and enjoyment of property received pursuant to contract for more than a reasonable time after attaining majority involves both kinds of conduct; that is, active use of the property coupled with a failure to disaffirm. Under such circumstances a ratification will often be found to have occurred.[64] Receipt of performance from the other party after attaining majority will also be normally considered to be a ratification.[65] On the other hand part payment or other performance by the infant, without more, will not ordinarily be deemed a ratification.[66] Frequently, the question is for the jury to determine.

 WESTLAW REFERENCES

infan! minor /s power empower! /s disaffirm!

minor infan! /s ratif! /s power empower!

majority /s infan! minor /s ratif!

infan! minor /s land (real +1 estate property) /s ratif! avoid! disaffirm!

infan! /s contract*** /s defens! defend!

"del santo" +s bristol

been incurred, or even a part payment thereon is not a ratification. Even payment of interest, part payment of principal, and a mere acknowledgment of the debt, or a statement, 'I owe a debt and you will get your pay' was held not to be a ratification." (Citations omitted).

59. Thus, it is generally held that part payment made by an infant after attaining his majority is not, without more, a ratification. International Accountants Soc'y v. Santana, 166 La. 671, 117 So. 768, 59 A.L.R. 276 (1928).

60. Camp v. Bank of Bentonville, 230 Ark. 414, 323 S.W.2d 556 (1959); Hook v. Harmon Nat'l Real Estate Corp., 250 App. Div. 689, 295 N.Y.S. 249, amended 251 App.Div. 722, 295 N.Y.S. 249 (2d Dep't 1937).

61. Henry v. Root, 33 N.Y. 526 (1865). Inconsistent language in subsequent New York opinions should be disapproved.

62. On these requisites, see § 5–6 supra.

63. E.g., Lee v. Thompson, 124 Fla. 494, 168 So. 848 (1936).

64. Jones v. Dressel, 623 P.2d 370 (Colo. 1981); Bobby Floars Toyota Inc. v. Smith, 48 N.C.App. 580, 269 S.E.2d 320 (1980); and see notes 48–51 supra.

65. Turner v. Little, 70 Ga.App. 567, 28 S.E.2d 871 (1944); Clark v. Kidd, 148 Ky. 479, 146 S.W. 1097 (1912).

66. See notes 58, 59 supra.

(a) *Failure to Make a Timely Disaffirmance*

infan! minor /s fail! /s time! /s disaffirm!

disaffirm! /s "question of fact"

infan! minor /s "reasonable time" /s disaffirm!

211k57(2)

disaffirm! /s minor infan! /s perform!

infan! minor /s executory +1 contract agreement

minor! infan! /s disaffirm! /s estop! laches "statute of limitation"

(b) *Express Ratification*

minor infan! /s "express! ratif!"

oral! acknowledg! intend! intent! /s ratif! /s minor infan!

imply! implied! implication /s ratif! /s infan! minor

"new promise" /s infan!

minor infan! /s "fully executed"

(c) *Ratification by Conduct*

ratif! /s minor infan! /s conduct (retain! retention enjoy! "active use" /s property)

find 269 se2d 320

§ 8–5. Effect Upon Ratification of Ignorance of Law or Fact

The former infant's ratification is ineffective unless he knows the facts upon which his liability depends,[67] but the cases are in conflict as to whether he must know that the law gives him the power to avoid the original contract. Perhaps the majority of cases have applied the maxim that everyone is presumed to know the law and have held that lack of knowledge of the law is immaterial.[68] A significant number of cases, however, have held that there can be no ratification without full knowledge of the legal consequences.[69]

 WESTLAW REFERENCES

ratif! /s infan! minor! /s consequence

§ 8–6. Obligations of Restitution Upon Disaffirmance

A variety of questions and a number of conflicting views exist as to the adjustment of the economic relations of the parties after an infant

67. Thus in a case in which an infant partner upon reaching majority was alleged to have ratified his partnership obligations by accepting benefits under the partnership, it was held that he did not ratify certain outstanding bad checks of which he was unaware. Tobey v. Wood, 123 Mass. 88 (1877).

68. Shepherd v. Shepherd, 408 Ill. 364, 97 N.E.2d 273 (1951); Campbell v. Sears, Roebuck & Co., 307 Pa. 365, 161 A. 310 (1932); see Annot., 5 A.L.R. 137 (1920).

69. Trader v. Lowe, 45 Md. 1 (1876); International Text Book Co. v. Connelly, 206 N.Y. 188, 99 N.E. 722 (1912). An intermediate position was taken in Ogborn v. Hoffman, 52 Ind. 439 (1876), where it was held that the presumption that everyone knows the law is rebuttable.

has disaffirmed. If either or both parties have rendered some performance questions of restitution may arise.[70]

(a) Infant as Defendant

If an infant has purchased an automobile on credit [71] and effectively disaffirms, in an action against him for the balance of the price his avoidance is an affirmative defense.[72] It would be an obvious injustice, however, if he were to be allowed to retain the automobile while escaping from his obligation to pay. Thus it is everywhere recognized that the infant is under an obligation to return any consideration which he has received and still possesses.[73] If he no longer has the consideration he need not return it. This is true even if he has squandered, wasted or negligently destroyed what he has received.[74] Thus the infant purchaser of the automobile on credit is not accountable for the automobile if he no longer has it.[75] This rule is subject to one exception. If the infant has exchanged or sold the property and still possesses the property received in the exchange or the investment, the infant will be liable as if he still had the original consideration or such portion of it as is represented by the exchange or investment.[76]

(b) Infant as Plaintiff

Suppose that instead of purchasing an automobile on credit, the infant purchases the automobile for $12,000, pays cash and proceeds to wreck it. If the infant then disaffirms and brings an action for restitution, application of the rule that an infant need account only for that part of the consideration which he retains would seem to dictate that the infant may have full recovery of the $12,000 upon restoration of the wreck. This is the traditional view.[77] Many courts have,

70. See Restatement, Second, Contracts § 14, Comment c; Restatement, Restitution §§ 61 to 62.

71. It is assumed here that the automobile is not a necessary. If it is a necessary other rules come into play. See § 8–8 infra.

72. Clark, Code Pleading 611, 621 (2d ed. 1947).

73. It is generally agreed that the infant need not tender restitution of the consideration as a condition precedent to a defensive plea of infancy. 2 Williston § 238.

"When property is bought by an infant on credit, and being sued for the price, he pleads infancy, the seller may recover at law the property, the title being revested in him by the result of the suit for the price * * *" Evans v. Morgan, 69 Miss. 328, 329, 12 So. 270, 270–71 (1891) (citations omitted).

74. Drude v. Curtis, 183 Mass. 317, 67 N.E. 317, 62 L.R.A. 755 (1903) (rule applied

where both parties were infants); Star Chevrolet Co. v. Green, 473 So.2d 157 (Miss.1985); Terrace Co. v. Calhoun, 37 Ill. App.3d 757, 347 N.E.2d 315 (1976) (because services cannot be returned, no duty of restitution); but see Wheeless v. Eudora Bank, 256 Ark. 644, 509 S.W.2d 532 (1974) (statute requiring full restitution by infant).

75. 2 Williston § 238.

76. Macgreal v. Taylor, 167 U.S. 688, 17 S.Ct. 961, 42 L.Ed. 326 (1897) (subrogation theory); Whitman v. Allen, 123 Me. 1, 121 A. 160, 36 A.L.R. 776 (1923) (infant had proceeds of sale); Evans v. Morgan, 69 Miss. 328, 12 So. 270 (1891) (infant businessmen purchased goods from plaintiffs on credit and goods were intermingled with other stock; plaintiffs could execute on entire stock).

77. Quality Motors v. Hays, 216 Ark. 264, 225 S.W.2d 326 (1949) (wrecked automobile); Weisbrook v. Clyde C. Netzley, Inc., 58 Ill.App.3d 862, 16 Ill.Dec. 327, 374

however, ruled that the infant's recovery will be offset by the value of the use to him of the automobile or the amount of depreciation in value of the vehicle.[78] Although the texts have not usually emphasized the distinction in result based upon whether the infant is the plaintiff or defendant in the action, it explains a good many cases which otherwise appear contradictory. The distinction has been recognized explicitly in some of the decisions.[79] A distinction in result based upon the procedural position of the parties may seem arbitrary, but to some extent it reflects the risks foreseeable to the parties. A seller on credit recognizes that he is assuming legal and practical risks of nonpayment. A seller for cash would usually be astounded if he were made to restore the price paid without receiving in return the goods delivered. There is rough justice in holding that an infant who takes a flight from New York to Los Angeles and pays cash may not demand his money back after taking the flight; [80] but that if he flies on the "pay later plan," the risk of nonpayment is taken by the extender of credit. What is involved is an attempt to protect an infant from improvident commitments; but not from improvident cash expenditures, at least where protection of the infant would work a harsh forfeiture against the other party. This approach, pioneered in New Hampshire,[81] has led to a complete breakthrough in the ordinary rules relating to infancy in that

N.E.2d 1102 (1978); Carpenter v. Grow, 247 Mass. 133, 141 N.E. 859 (1923); Rotondo v. Kay Jewelry Co., 84 R.I. 292, 123 A.2d 404 (1956) (burden of proof on adult party that infant still has the consideration); Hines v. Cheshire, 36 Wn.2d 467, 219 P.2d 100 (1950) (return of damaged automobile); Halbman v. Lemke, 99 Wis.2d 241, 298 N.W.2d 562 (1980); Annots., 16 A.L.R. 1475 (1922); 36 A.L.R. 782 (1925).

On the manner of evaluation of the consideration supplied by the infant when he supplies goods rather than money, see Robertson v. King, 225 Ark. 276, 280 S.W.2d 402, 52 A.L.R.2d 1108 (1955). The traditional view does not always hold if the infant misrepresents his age. See § 8–7 infra.

78. Myers v. Hurley Motor Co., 273 U.S. 18, 47 S.Ct. 277, 71 L.Ed. 515, 50 A.L.R. 1181 (1927) (depreciation caused by negligent use of automobile); Worman Motor Co. v. Hill, 54 Ariz. 227, 94 P.2d 865, 124 A.L.R. 1363 (1939); Creer v. Active Automobile Exchange, 99 Conn. 266, 121 A. 888 (1923) (value of depreciation deducted from infant's recovery but not value of use); Marceiliac v. Stevens, 206 Ky. 383, 267 S.W. 229 (1924) (rental value of house; alternate ground as house was also a necessary); Latrobe v. Dietrich, 114 Md. 8, 78 A. 983 (1910); Johnson v. Northwestern Mut. Life Ins. Co., 56 Minn. 365, 57 N.W. 934, affirmed 56 Minn. 365, 59 N.W. 992, 26 L.R.A. 187 (1894) (infant must account for

benefits received); Wooldridge v. Lavoie, 79 N.H. 21, 104 A. 346 (1918) (infant must account for benefit received from use but not depreciation caused by negligence); Rice v. Butler, 160 N.Y. 578, 55 N.E. 275, 47 L.R.A. 303 (1899); Pettit v. Liston, 97 Or. 464, 191 P. 660, 11 A.L.R. 487 (1920) (value of use of motorcycle); Barber v. Gross, 74 S.D. 254, 51 N.W.2d 696 (1952) (statutory result). See also Annot., 12 A.L.R.3d 1174 (1967).

79. The distinction is suggested in 2 Kent's Commentaries *240. Many of the cases making the distinction rely upon and cite these influential commentaries. E.g., Rice v. Butler, 160 N.Y. 578, 55 N.E. 275, 45 L.R.A. 303, and Pettit v. Liston, 97 Or. 464, 191 P. 660, 11 A.L.R. 487 (1920).

80. Vichnes v. Transcontinental & Western Air, Inc., 173 Misc. 631, 18 N.Y.S.2d 603 (App.Term 1940), noted in 15 St. John's L.Rev. 98 (1940); contra, Adamowski v. Curtiss-Wright Flying Service, 300 Mass. 281, 15 N.E.2d 467 (1938), criticized 27 Georgetown L.J. 233 (1938), 7 Fordham L.Rev. 445 (1938).

81. Hall v. Butterfield, 59 N.H. 354 (1879); Bartlett v. Bailey, 59 N.H. 408 (1879); Wooldridge v. Lavoie, 79 N.H. 21, 104 A. 346 (1918). See Notes, 12 S.Dak.L. Rev. 426 (1967); 43 N.Dak.L.Rev. 89 (1966); 19 Hastings L.J. 1199 (1968), approving this approach.

jurisdiction, discussed in § 8–9 infra. Another suggested approach is that each contract be judged by criteria of fairness, and that restitutionary principles, based on concepts of conscionability, be applied on a case by case basis.[82]

 WESTLAW REFERENCES
211k58(2)
infan! minor! /s disaffirm! /s restitution

(a) Infant as Defendant
infan! minor! /s disaffirm! /s consideration
infan! minor! /s disaffirm! /s car auto automobile
infan! minor! /s disaffirm! /s property
infan! minor! /s disaffirm! /s proceed
infan! minor! /s disaffirm! /s exchang! sale sold sell selling

(b) Infant as Plaintiff
minor! infan! /s disaffirm! /s recover!
minor! infan! /s disaffirm! /s valu! depreciat!
(weisbrook +s netzley) (rotondo +s "kay jewelry")

§ 8–7. Torts Connected With Contracts

Very often tort liability is intimately connected with a contractual relation. Although an infant is not generally liable on his contracts he is liable for his torts.[83] At least three kinds of problems arise from the interplay of tort and contract liability in cases involving infants.

(a) Infant's Torts Stemming From His Contracts

The other party to a contractual relation may not sue the infant for tort if the tort is in essence a breach of contractual duty. While it is possible in some jurisdictions to frame an action for negligence in respect to a bailment in terms of tort or in terms of breach of contract,[84] the almost universal holding is that the action cannot be brought against the infant no matter how it is couched.[85] It is believed that to allow such an action would in effect be enforcing the contract. The infant, however, would be liable if he converted the chattel since this kind of wrong is deemed to be independent of the contract, rather than a breach of an implied promise not to convert.[86] The same analysis is made as to breach of warranty, although such a breach may often give

82. Navin, supra note 17 (as to infants over age fourteen).

83. See Prosser, Torts § 134 (4th ed. 1971).

84. Although a bailment is not a contract, it is often formed by a contract, (see § 1–2 supra) and as a common law proposition, "assumpsit" could be brought for negligence in relation to a bailment.

85. Jones v. Milner, 53 Ga.App. 304, 185 S.E. 586 (1936); Eaton v. Hill, 50 N.H. 235 (1870); Brunhoelzl v. Brandes, 90 N.J.L. 31, 100 A. 163 (1917); contra, Daggy v. Miller, 180 Iowa 1146, 162 N.W. 854 (1917).

86. Williams v. Buckler, 264 S.W.2d 279 (Ky.1954); Young v. Muhling, 48 App.Div. 617, 63 N.Y.S. 181 (2d Dep't 1900); Vermont Acceptance Corp. v. Wiltshire, 103 Vt. 219, 153 A. 199 (1931).

rise to an action in tort, since it stems from a contract, it is not maintainable against an infant.[87]

(b) False Representations by the Infant

If the infant willfully misrepresents his age, the majority view is that he nevertheless may exercise his power of avoidance.[88] However, it often has been held that in equity the rule is different to the extent that if the infant wishes to disaffirm under these circumstances he must place the adult party in the status quo ante.[89]

Despite the general recognition of the rule that a misrepresentation of age does not inhibit the infant's power of avoidance, there is a marked split of authority on the question of whether an infant is liable in tort for a willful misrepresentation of his age. The division stems from the rule that a tort action will not lie against an infant if in essence it involves the enforcement of a contract. Some courts assert that ultimately the fraud action is based on the contract.[90] Others take the position that the tort is sufficiently independent of the contract and that the granting of tort relief does not involve indirect enforcement of the contract.[91] A case can be made for either point of view. The basic dispute is as to what extent the law's policy of protecting infants should apply to a fraudulent infant. The same kind of split of authority exists as to other kinds of fraudulent statements made by infants in connection with their contracts.[92]

87. Collins v. Gifford, 203 N.Y. 465, 96 N.E. 721, 38 L.R.A.,N.S. 202 (1911).

88. Myers v. Hurley Motor Co., 273 U.S. 18, 47 S.Ct. 277, 71 L.Ed. 515, 50 A.L.R. 1181 (1927); Del Santo v. Bristol County Stadium, Inc., 273 F.2d 605 (1st Cir.1960); Creer v. Active Automobile Exchange, 99 Conn. 266, 121 A. 888 (1923); Tracey v. Brown, 265 Mass. 163, 163 N.E. 885 (1928); Sternlieb v. Normandie Nat'l Sec. Corp., 263 N.Y. 245, 188 N.E. 726, 90 A.L.R. 1437 (1934); contra, Nichols v. English, 223 Ga. 227, 154 S.E.2d 239, 29 A.L.R.3d 1265 (1967); La Rosa v. Nichols, 92 N.J.L. 375, 105 A. 201, 6 A.L.R. 412 (1918); Haydocy Pontiac, Inc. v. Lee, 19 Ohio App.2d 217, 250 N.E.2d 898 (1969), noted in 31 Ohio St. L.J. 403 (1970). In some jurisdictions the estoppel is mandated by statute. Thosath v. Transport Motor Co., 136 Wash. 565, 240 P. 921 (1925). See generally, Miller, Fraudulent Misrepresentations of Age as Affecting the Infant's Contract—A Comparative Study, 15 U.Pitt.L.Rev. 73 (1953).

89. Lewis v. Van Cleve, 302 Ill. 413, 134 N.E. 804 (1922); Stallard v. Sutherland, 131 Va. 316, 108 S.E. 568 (1921); contra, Sims v. Everhardt, 102 U.S. (12 Otto) 300, 26 L.Ed. 87 (1880); Watson v. Billings, 38 Ark. 278 (1881). In line with the usual flexibility of equitable doctrine, however,

the decisions have varied with questions such as whether the infant is the plaintiff or defendant and whether the contract is executed or executory. See Note, 20 Iowa L.Rev. 785, 790–91 (1935).

90. Drennen Motor Car Co. v. Smith, 230 Ala. 275, 160 So. 761 (1935); Slayton v. Barry, 175 Mass. 513, 56 N.E. 574 (1900); Sternlieb v. Normandie Nat'l Sec. Corp., 263 N.Y. 245, 188 N.E. 726, 90 A.L.R. 1437 (1934); Greensboro Morris Plan Co. v. Palmer, 185 N.C. 109, 116 S.E. 261 (1923).

91. Keser v. Chagnon, 159 Colo. 209, 410 P.2d 637 (1966) (adult may counterclaim for fraud in infant's action for restitution); Byers v. LeMay Bank & Trust Co., 365 Mo. 341, 282 S.W.2d 512 (1955); Wisconsin Loan & Finance Corp. v. Goodnough, 201 Wis. 101, 228 N.W. 484, 67 A.L.R. 1259 (1930). See generally Miller, supra note 88.

92. Not liable: Collins v. Gifford, 203 N.Y. 465, 96 N.E. 721, 38 L.R.A.(NS) 202 (1911); Lesnick v. Pratt, 116 Vt. 477, 78 A.2d 487 (1951), reargument denied 116 Vt. 477, 80 A.2d 663 (1951). Liable: Wisconsin Loan & Finance Co. v. Goodnough, 201 Wis. 101, 228 N.W. 484, 67 A.L.R. 1259 (1930).

It is recognized that the infant's fraudulent misrepresentation as to his age or other material facts will permit the other party to avoid the contract on grounds of fraud.[93]

(c) Torts and Agency Relationships

Under the doctrine of respondeat superior a principal is liable for the torts of his agent committed within the scope of the agent's employment. An infant may appoint an agent but such an appointment is subject to disaffirmance. Accordingly the majority view is that infants may avoid their liabilities for the torts of their agents,[94] at least insofar as the tort liability stems from respondeat superior.[95]

 WESTLAW REFERENCES

infan! minor! /s disaffirm! /s tort

infan! /s liab! /s tort

(a) *Infant's Torts Stemming from His Contracts*

infan! /s breach! /s tort /s contract***

infan! minor /s conversion /s liab!

(b) *False Representations by the Infant*

211k62

infan! minor /s misrepresent! /s age

211k56

infan! minor /s age /s misrepresent! represent! /s tort

(c) *Torts and Agency Relationships*

infan! minor /s agen** /s disaffirm!

palmer +s miller /p liab!

§ 8–8. Liability of an Infant for Necessaries

It is well settled that an infant is liable for necessaries furnished him, and it is generally recognized that this liability is quasi-contractual rather than contractual. As a consequence of the quasi-contractual nature of the action, the infant may disaffirm an executory contract for necessaries.[96] Moreover, the infant is not liable for the contract price, but for the reasonable value of the necessaries furnished.[97]

93. Beardsley v. Clark, 229 Iowa 601, 294 N.W. 887 (1940), noted in 39 Mich.L. Rev. 1417 (1941); Neff v. Landis, 110 Pa. 204, 1 A. 177 (1885); Fredeking v. Grimmett, 140 W.Va. 745, 86 S.E.2d 554 (1955). See generally Miller, supra note 88 and appendix thereto.

94. Palmer v. Miller, 380 Ill. 256, 43 N.E.2d 973 (1942); Payette v. Fleischman, 329 Mich. 160, 45 N.W.2d 16 (1950); Hodge v. Feiner, 338 Mo. 268, 90 S.W.2d 90, 103 A.L.R. 483 (1936); Covault v. Nevitt, 157 Wis. 113, 146 N.W. 1115, 51 L.R.A.(NS) 1092 (1914) (infant businessman not liable for negligence of his janitor); contra, Scott v. Schisler, 107 N.J.L. 397, 153 A. 395,

noted in 44 Harv.L.Rev. 1292 (1931). See generally Gregory, Infant's Responsibility for His Agent's Torts, 5 Wis.L.Rev. 453 (1930).

95. Cf. Sikes v. Johnson, 16 Mass. 389 (1820) (infant procured another to commit a battery).

96. Gregory v. Lee, 64 Conn. 407, 30 A. 53, 25 L.R.A. 618 (1894); Wallin v. Highland Park Co., 127 Iowa 131, 102 N.W. 839 (1905).

97. Sceva v. True, 53 N.H. 627 (1873); see 2 Williston §§ 240–244; Woodward, Quasi Contracts § 202 (1913).

The concept of "necessaries" is relative to the infant's status in life.[98] It would seem clear that the range of what is necessary is considerably larger if the infant is emancipated, and larger yet if he is married,[99] as compared with what is necessary for an unemancipated infant. Thus it is a somewhat fruitless quest to analyze the cases to determine, for example, whether an automobile is a necessary.[1] When reasonable men would differ, the question is for the jury. It is obvious, however, that food,[2] shelter,[3] and clothing[4] are necessaries. But the kind of food,[5] shelter,[6] and clothing[7] is another question. Medical services can generally be considered as necessaries.[8] Legal services are necessaries in many instances, particularly for the enforcement or defense of tort claims and criminal prosecutions,[9] but are often not considered such if the attorney is retained to protect property rights. This result is reached on the ground that a guardian should be appointed to protect such rights and the attorney should contract with the guardian.[10]

Education is of course a necessary, but the kind of education which is necessary is dependent upon the circumstances of the infant. While a basic public school education is recognized as a necessary, it appears that generally a college education has not been deemed to be,[11] but

98. "The word 'necessaries' as used in the law is a relative term, except when applied to such things as are obviously requisite for the maintenance of existence, and depends on the social position and situation in life of the infant as well as upon his own fortune and that of his parents." International Text Book Co. v. Connelly, 206 N.Y. 188, 195, 99 N.E. 722, 725 (1912).

99. Ragan v. Williams, 220 Ala. 590, 127 So. 190, 68 A.L.R. 1182 (1930); Spaulding v. New England Furniture Co., 154 Me. 330, 147 A.2d 916 (1959).

1. Generally the cases have held that the automobile was not a necessary under the facts of the particular case. See Harris v. Raughton, 37 Ala.App. 648, 73 So.2d 921 (1954), noted in 6 Hastings L.J. 112 (1954) (an excellent note pointing out the changing place of the automobile in society); Star Chevrolet Co. v. Green, 473 So.2d 157 (Miss.1985). Contra, Rose v. Sheehan Buick, Inc., 204 So.2d 903 (Fla.App.1967); Ehrsam v. Borgen, 185 Kan. 776, 347 P.2d 260 (1959); Bancredit, Inc. v. Bethea, 65 N.J.Super. 538, 168 A.2d 250 (1961) (remanded for jury determination); Daubert v. Mosley, 487 P.2d 353, 56 A.L.R.3d 1328 (Okl.1971).

2. O'Donniley v. Kinley, 220 Mo.App. 284, 286 S.W. 140 (1926) (loan to purchase groceries).

3. Ragan v. Williams, 220 Ala. 590, 127 So. 190, 68 A.L.R. 1182 (1930) (house rental

for married infant); Gregory v. Lee, 64 Conn. 407, 30 A. 53, 25 L.R.A. 618 (1894) (lodging for Yale student); but see Moskow v. Marshall, 271 Mass. 302, 171 N.E. 477 (1930) (lodging for Harvard student).

4. Lynch v. Johnson, 109 Mich. 640, 67 N.W. 908 (1896).

5. Kline v. L'Amoureux, 2 Paige 419 (N.Y.1831); L'Amoureux v. Crosby, 2 Paige 422 (N.Y.1831) (liquor not a necessary).

6. The purchase of a house was held to be a necessary in Johnson v. Newberry, 267 S.W. 476 (Tex.Civ.App.1924), noted in 13 Georgetown L.J. 416 (1925), although this would not ordinarily be the case.

7. Lefils & Christian v. Sugg, 15 Ark. 137 (1854) (cologne, cravats, kid gloves, and walking canes not necessaries).

8. Scott Country School District I v. Asher, 263 Ind. 47, 324 N.E.2d 496 (1975); Cole v. Wagner, 197 N.C. 692, 150 S.E. 339 (1929).

9. Crafts v. Carr, 24 R.I. 397, 53 A. 275 (1902); Plummer v. Northern Pac. R. Co., 98 Wash. 67, 167 P. 73, 7 A.L.R. 104 (1917). See Annot., 13 A.L.R.3d 1251 (1967).

10. Grissom v. Beidleman, 35 Okl. 343, 129 P. 853 (1913); 2 Williston § 242.

11. Moskow v. Marshall, 271 Mass. 302, 171 N.E. 477 (1930); La Salle Extension University v. Campbell, 131 N.J.L. 343, 36 A.2d 397 (1944); Hawley v. Doucette, 43 A.D.2d 713, 349 N.Y.S.2d 801 (2d Dep't

education in a trade has been said to qualify as a necessary.[12]　The language of the decisions shows sufficient flexibility, however, to allow for changing community standards in this regard.[13]

Business and employment expenses have received variable treatment [14] but a North Carolina case has broken with the ordinary strictures as to what constitutes a necessary, holding a married infant liable for the reasonable value of an employment service fee, stating:

> "In our view, the concept of 'necessaries' should be enlarged to include such articles of property and such services as are reasonably necessary to enable the infant to earn the money required to provide the necessities of life for himself and those who are legally dependent upon him." [15]

If the infant borrows money for the purpose of purchasing necessaries and so uses it, the infant is liable to the lender as if the lender had supplied the necessaries.[16]　The same result should follow if a loan is in fact used for necessaries although there was no agreement with the lender as to the use to which the money is to be put.[17]　If the funds are advanced for the purpose of purchasing necessaries but are squandered for other purposes, the cases are divided as to the infant's liability.[18]

The liability of an infant for necessaries is relative not only to his status in life but also is dependent upon whether or not he has an

---

1973); Middlebury College v. Chandler, 16 Vt. 683 (1844).

12. Mauldin v. Southern Shorthand & Bus.Univ., 126 Ga. 681, 55 S.E. 922 (1906) (stenography may qualify, but not under the facts); Curtiss v. Roosevelt Aviation School, 5 Air L.Rev. 382 (Mun.Ct.N.Y.1934) (mechanical training course). In Siegel & Hodges v. Hodges, 20 Misc.2d 243, 191 N.Y.S.2d 984 (1959), affirmed 10 A.D.2d 646, 197 N.Y.S.2d 246 (2d Dep't 1960), affirmed 9 N.Y.2d 747, 214 N.Y.S.2d 452, 174 N.E.2d 533 (1961), it was held that voice training could constitute a necessary for a ten year old prodigy who made many television appearances, but that a parent could not recover from the child, as the primary duty of furnishing the necessaries is upon the parent. See also Siegel v. Hodges, 15 A.D.2d 571, 222 N.Y.S.2d 989 (2d Dep't 1961).

It was subsequently held that whether a third person could recover for managerial and coaching services as necessaries was a question of fact for the jury. Siegel v. Hodges, 24 A.D.2d 456, 260 N.Y.S.2d 405 (2d Dep't 1965).

13. See International Text Book Co. v. Connelly, 206 N.Y. 188, 195, 99 N.E. 722, 725 (1912). Cases in other contexts, e.g., family court support orders, petitions for invasion of trust funds, welfare program administration, etc., have indicated that a college education can be a necessary. 1961 Report of the New York Law Revision Commission 283–84.

14. Bancredit, Inc. v. Bethea, 65 N.J. Super. 538, 168 A.2d 250 (1961); Annot. 56 A.L.R.3d 1335 § 4 (1974). For a special situation, see Beane, The Role of an Infant as a Member of a Partnership, 87 Commercial L.J. 622 (1982).

15. Gastonia Personnel Corp. v. Rogers, 276 N.C. 279, 172 S.E.2d 19, 24, 41 A.L.R.3d 1062 (1970); but see Fisher v. Cattani, 53 Misc.2d 221, 278 N.Y.S.2d 420 (Dist.Ct.1966).

16. Norwood Nat'l Bank v. Allston, 152 S.C. 199, 149 S.E. 593, 65 A.L.R. 1334 (1929), noted in 43 Harv.L.Rev. 498 (1930). Sometimes this result is attained by the equitable doctrine of subrogation by which the lender is placed in the position of the party who supplied the necessaries. Price v. Sanders, 60 Ind. 310 (1878).

17. 2 Williston § 243 argues strongly for this position.

18. The infant was held to be liable in Norwood Nat'l Bank v. Allston, 152 S.C. 199, 149 S.E. 593, 65 A.L.R. 1334 (1929), noted in 43 Harv.L.Rev. 498 (1930). A strong contrary dictum appears in Randall v. Sweet, 1 Denio 460 (N.Y.1845).

existing supply of necessaries, or parents or guardians who are able and willing to supply him with the necessities of life.[19] The mere fact that the goods or services are in general considered necessaries does not make them necessary to the particular infant if he is already supplied with them.[20] Also an infant who has not been emancipated cannot be liable for necessaries unless his parent or guardian refuses to supply him with his needs and broad discretionary latitude is granted the parent or guardian in determining the manner in which he will meet the needs of his child or ward.[21] Moreover, even if all other tests of what is necessary are met it must appear that the goods or services were supplied on the credit of the infant and not of his parent, guardian or third person.[22] Therefore, the mere fact that the creditor has supplied necessaries to the family unit of which the infant is a part does not render the infant liable unless he contracted for the necessaries.[23] Thus, the liability, although quasi-contractual, requires that there be a contract with the infant. The basis of this liability is thus considerably different from the liability of a parent for necessaries furnished his children.[24]

 WESTLAW REFERENCES

infan! minor /s liab! /s necessary necessity /s "quasi contract***"

infan! minor /s liab! /s necessary necessity /s disaffirm!

211k50

infan! minor /s disaffirm! /s execut! /s necess!

infan! minor /s necess! /s food shelter cloth***

infan! minor /s necess! /s "reasonable value"

moskow +s marshall

infan! minor /s necessary necessity /s contract*** /s liab!

---

19. 2 Williston § 244.

20. Conboy v. Howe, 59 Conn. 112, 22 A. 35 (1890); Trainer v. Trumbull, 141 Mass. 527, 6 N.E. 761 (1886).

21. Mauldin v. Southern Shorthand & Bus. Univ., 126 Ga. 681, 55 S.E. 922 (1906); International Text Book Co. v. Connelly, 206 N.Y. 188, 99 N.E. 722 (1912).

"It would be subversive of parental authority and dominion if interested third persons could assume to judge for the parent, and subject him to liability for their unauthorized interference in supplying the supposed wants of the child." Lefils & Christian v. Sugg, 15 Ark. 137, 140 (1854).

"A third party has no right to usurp the rights and duties of the guardian." McKanna v. Merry, 61 Ill. 177, 180 (1871).

22. McManus v. Arnold Taxi Corp., 82 Cal.App. 215, 255 P. 755 (1927); Mackey v. Shreckengaust, 27 S.W.2d 752 (Mo.App. 1930); Foster v. Adcock, 161 Tenn. 217, 30 S.W.2d 239, 70 A.L.R. 569 (1930); but see Gardner v. Flowers, 529 S.W.2d 708 (Tenn. 1975); Scott County School District I v. Asher, 263 Ind. 47, 324 N.E.2d 496 (1975), allowing infant to recover necessary medical expenses against a tortfeasor on theory infant is bound to pay when his parents cannot.

23. Foster v. Adcock, 161 Tenn. 217, 30 S.W.2d 239, 70 A.L.R. 569 (1930).

24. See § 1–12 supra.

§ 8–9. Infant's Liability for Benefits Received: The New Hampshire View

It has been pointed out that many jurisdictions now require that an infant who seeks to disaffirm a contract and obtain restitution must return or account for the benefits he has received under the contract.[25] If, however, the infant is a defendant and sets up a defense of infancy the infant is liable only for necessaries [26] or for the value of tangible consideration he still retains.[27]

In New Hampshire, however, the courts have taken the position that it is immaterial whether the infant is the plaintiff or defendant. If the infant has received benefits, whether necessaries or not, he is liable in an action for restitution for the value of the benefits. Thus, it has been held that an infant dealer in milk is liable for the value of milk supplied to him in the course of his business,[28] and that an infant orphan is liable for the reasonable value of legal services received to contest the appointment of a particular guardian, the court deeming it irrelevant to determine whether or not the services were necessary.[29] The approach adopted by New Hampshire commends itself to good sense as it protects the infant from executory contracts, and transactions which are not beneficial to him.[30] At the same time it recognizes the legitimate interests of those who have dealt with the infant.

B. THE MENTALLY INFIRM

Table of Sections

25. See § 8–6 supra.

26. Id.

27. Id.

28. Bartlett v. Bailey, 59 N.H. 408 (1879).

29. Porter v. Wilson, 106 N.H. 270, 209 A.2d 730, 13 A.L.R.2d 1247 (1965); adopted in Valencia v. White, 134 Ariz. 139, 654 P.2d 287 (1982); accord, under a statute, Spencer v. Collins, 156 Cal. 298, 104 P. 320 (1909). Similar reasoning is found in Pankas v. Bell, 413 Pa. 494, 198 A.2d 312 (1964), noted in 42 U.Det.L.J. 218 (1964), in enjoining a former infant employee from violation of a covenant not to compete, and in Cidis v. White, 71 Misc.2d 481, 336 N.Y.S.2d 362 (Dist.Ct.1972) (infant required to pay for contact lenses). See also Frank v. Volkswagenwerk, A.G., 522 F.2d 321 (3d Cir.1975). A similar approach has been taken in New South Wales by statute. See § 8–2 supra; but see CBS, Inc. v. Tucker, 412 F.Supp. 1222, 1226 (S.D.N.Y.1976).

30. See Notes, 12 S.Dak.L.Rev. 426 (1967); 43 N.Dak.L.Rev. 89 (1966); 19 Hastings L.J. 1199 (1968). On the question of the effect of supervening mental disability on offers, see § 2–20 supra.

§ 8–10. Introduction

Although there is older authority to the effect that the contracts and executed transactions of the mentally infirm [31] are void,[32] the overwhelming weight of modern authority is to the effect that they are merely voidable,[33] except that if the person so afflicted has been adjudicated an incompetent and a guardian of his property has been appointed prior to entering into the transaction, in many jurisdictions they are deemed void.[34] Commitment to an asylum is not equivalent to the appointment of a guardian of property [35] nor is the appointment of a conservator.[36]

Although the problems we are now considering are ordinarily grouped under the heading of "Contracts of Insane Persons," [37] a significant number of the cases do not deal with insanity, but with other forms of mental infirmity, such as senility,[38] mental retardation,[39] temporary delirium deriving from physical injuries sustained in accidents,[40] intoxication,[41] and the side effects of medication.[42]

---

31. On mental infirmity, see generally Allen, Ferster & Weihofen, Mental Impairment and Legal Incompetency (1968); Cotton, Agreements of the Mentally Disabled: A Problem of New Jersey Law, 3 Rutgers-Camden L.Rev. 241 (1971); Comment, 57 Mich.L.Rev. 1020 (1959).

32. Hovey v. Hobson, 53 Me. 451 (1866).

33. Levine v. O'Malley, 33 A.D.2d 874, 307 N.Y.S.2d 919 (4th Dep't 1969); see 2 Williston §§ 249–252. As one consequence of this rule, as in the case of infancy, a bona fide purchaser of personal property takes free of the incompetent's interest in the property. See 2 Williston § 252.

As to real property, unlike in the case of infants, the majority rule protects the bona fide purchaser on the basis of the rule requiring restoration of the status quo, discussed in the next section. See Note, 47 Colum.L.Rev. 675 (1947).

34. Restatement, Second, Contracts § 13; Church v. Rosenstein, 85 Conn. 279, 82 A. 568 (1912); Dupont v. Dupont, 308 So.2d 512 (La.App.1975) (Mississippi law); Hughes v. Jones, 116 N.Y. 67, 22 N.E. 446, 5 L.R.A. 632 (1889); Fixico v. Fixico, 186 Okl. 656, 100 P.2d 260 (1940) (despite acquiescence of guardian); John P. Bleeg Co. v. Peterson, 51 S.D. 502, 215 N.W. 529 (1927), noted in 41 Harv.L.Rev. 536 (1928); but see, In re Estate of Cline, 250 Iowa 265, 93 N.W.2d 708 (1958) (voluntary guardianship). An adjudication without appointment of a guardian is merely evidence of incompetency. McCormick v. Littler, 85 Ill. 62 (1877). An appointment of a guardian is prima facie evidence that the person was incapable of contracting just prior to

the adjudication but is not conclusive. Hughes v. Jones, 116 N.Y. 67, 22 N.E. 446, 5 L.R.A. 632 (1889); cf. L'Amoureux v. Crosby, 2 Paige 422 (N.Y.1831) (judgment entered by confession void where judgment creditor knew incompetency proceedings were pending against judgment debtor).

It is often held that if the guardianship falls into disuse because the ward has regained sanity, the ward's contracts are enforceable. Fugate v. Walker, 204 Ky. 767, 265 S.W. 331 (1924); Schultz v. Oldenburg, 202 Minn. 237, 277 N.W. 918 (1938); Restatement, Second, Contracts § 13, Comment d.

See generally, Note, Contractual Capacity of a Ward, 1967 Wash.U.L.Q. 545.

35. Finch v. Goldstein, 245 N.Y. 300, 157 N.E. 146 (1927); Restatement, Second, Contracts § 13, ill. 2.

36. Board of Regents v. Davis, 14 Cal.3d 33, 120 Cal.Rptr. 407, 533 P.2d 1047 (1975), appeal after remand 74 Cal.App.3d 862, 141 Cal.Rptr. 670 (1977).

37. E.g., 2 Williston ch. 10.

38. E.g., Dupont v. Dupont, 308 So.2d 512 (La.App.1975); Krasner v. Berk, 366 Mass. 464, 319 N.E.2d 897 (1974).

39. E.g., Edmunds v. Chandler, 203 Va. 772, 127 S.E.2d 73 (1962).

40. E.g., Kilgore v. Cross, 1 Fed. 578 (E.D.Ark.1880).

41. See § 8–14 infra.

42. Cf. Sharpe, Medication as a Threat to Testamentary Capacity, 35 N.Car.L.Rev. 380 (1957).

It is generally said that insanity exists where a party does not understand the nature and consequences of his act at the time of the transaction.[43] This test, as well as subsidiary tests of whether the person was rational except for "insane delusions" as to the particular transaction in question, has been attacked as unscientific.[44] Some observers have pointed out, however, that the very fact that psychiatric tests are not employed has enabled the courts to work out just results.[45] In other words, if the contract is fair and beneficial to the alleged incompetent there will be a great tendency to find that he was sane; otherwise the tendency is to find him incompetent.[46] Of course, a tendency must not be confused with doctrine, and there must be some arguable basis for a determination of incompetency and this tendency merely reflects judicial treatment of borderline cases. It is clear, however, that incompetency may be proved by circumstantial evidence including disparity of value in the considerations exchanged.[47]

The more modern view espoused by the Second Restatement adopts in addition to the cognitive test "of ability to understand", the position that the contract is also voidable if the party "by reason of mental illness or defect * * * is unable to act in a reasonable manner in relation to the transaction and the other party has reason to know of this condition." [48] This approach permits disaffirmance of contracts

---

43. Cundick v. Broadbent, 383 F.2d 157 (10th Cir.1967), certiorari denied 390 U.S. 948, 88 S.Ct. 1037, 19 L.Ed.2d 1139 (1968); Hendricks v. Hendricks, 272 N.C. 340, 158 S.E.2d 496 (1968), vacated 273 N.C. 733, 161 S.E.2d 97 (1968); Kruse v. Coos Head Timber Co., 248 Or. 294, 432 P.2d 1009 (1967); Poole v. Hudson, 46 Del. (7 Terry) 339, 83 A.2d 703 (Del.Super.1951); Schneider v. Johnson, 357 Mo. 245, 207 S.W.2d 461 (1948). See Guttmacher and Weihofen, Mental Incompetency, 36 Minn.L.Rev. 179 (1952); Note, 32 Colum.L.Rev. 504 (1932).

44. See Comment, "Civil Insanity," 44 Cornell L.Q. 76, 88–93 (1958).

45. A series of articles by Green demonstrates that the legal fact of insanity or sanity tends to be determined by the finding which will better serve the interests of the alleged incompetent or his heirs. The courts are primarily concerned, he demonstrates, with the question of whether the transaction was abnormal, tending to determine the question of sanity by that criterion. Green, Fraud, Undue Influence, and Mental Incompetency, 43 Colum.L. Rev. 176 (1943); Green, Public Policies Underlying the Law of Mental Incompetency, 38 Mich.L.Rev. 1189 (1940); Green, Judicial Tests of Mental Incompetency, 6 Mo.L. Rev. 141 (1941); Green, The Operative Effect of Mental Incompetency on Agreements and Wills, 21 Tex.L.Rev. 554 (1943);

Green, Proof of Mental Incompetency and the Unexpressed Major Premise, 53 Yale L.J. 271 (1944).

See also Virtue, Restitution from the Mentally Infirm, 26 N.Y.U.L.Rev. 132 and 291 (1951).

46. E.g., in discussing the contests surrounding life support contracts frequently entered into by aged persons, one observer concludes "if it was a reasonable contract and the recipient was a worthy object of trust and faith, then that shows sufficient capacity to uphold the contract; but if support was not given, or if there was fraud, then the grantor was incapacitated because no one in his right mind would have made such a contract." Virtue, supra note 45, at 151. It is to be noted that in many of such cases, it is the heirs of the alleged incompetent who are attempting to set aside the contract or conveyance, thereby seeking to frustrate a bargain which was beneficial to the deceased.

47. Gindhart v. Skourtes, 271 Or. 115, 530 P.2d 827 (1975); Bach v. Hudson, 596 S.W.2d 673 (Tex.App.1980).

48. Restatement, Second, Contracts § 15; accord, Ortelere v. Teachers' Retirement Board of the City of New York, 25 N.Y.2d 196, 303 N.Y.S.2d 362, 250 N.E.2d 460 (1969), noted in 36 Brooklyn L.Rev. 145 (1969), 45 N.Y.U.L.Rev. 585 (1970), 16 Wayne L.Rev. 1188 (1970). For further

made by persons who understand what they are doing but cannot control their behavior in a rational manner.

Although there has been debate about the appropriate test to determine incompetency, the apparently unanimous assumption has been that incompetents, properly defined, require protection from their own actions. A forceful attack has been made against that assumption by a psychiatrist and a legal scholar.[49] Among the points made is that protection of the incompetent in effect masks protection of the relatives of the incompetent at the expense of his freedom of action. "The result of such solicitude can easily be that the contractor is protected into a straitjacket, both figuratively and literally." Further, it is argued that the setting aside of his transactions "is punishment for deviancy, not protection against helplessness."[50] Deprivation of contractual capacity also deprives a psychiatric patient of his power to withhold consent from lobotomy or electro-shock treatment or even therapy that consists of battering and bruising the patient.[51] This criticism of the protective policy of the law may be more severe than the existing state of the law merits, but, as in the case of infants' contracts, a comprehensive review of the policy bases and operative rules applicable to the contracts of the mentally infirm seems appropriate.[52]

 WESTLAW REFERENCES

"mental! infirm!" /s void!

"mental infirm! /s adjudicat! incompeten! /s agreement contract***

"set aside" /s mental! +1 disab! impair! infirm!

guardian! /s contract*** agreement /s mental! +1 infirm! disab! impair!

120k68(4)

257ak373

contract*** agreement /s void! /s senil! deliri! (mental! /s retard! incapacitat!)

di insanity

insan! /s contract*** agreement /s transact!

insan! /s "understand the nature and consequences of his act"

insan! /s "sufficient capacity"

di incompeten!

incompeten! /s capacity incapacit! /s contract***

---

facts and analysis of this leading case, see Danzig, The Capability Problem in Contract Law 148–204 (1978). The Restatement's and Ortelere's insistence that the incapacity be a product of "mental disease or defect" is criticised in Hardisty, Mental Illness: A Legal Fiction, 48 Wash.L.Rev. 735 (1973).

49. Alexander & Szasz, From Contract to Status Via Psychiatry, 13 Santa Clara L.Rev. 537 (1973).

50. Id. at 546.

51. Id. at 548–52.

52. See Id. at 557–59 for some suggestions in this regard.

§ 8–11. Requirement of Restitution

To some extent the rationale of the rules concerning the transactions of infants and incompetents coincide. The law desires to protect these classes of persons from their own presumed improvidence. As to incompetents an additional factor is present. Contracts are based on mutual assent. A person incapable of rational volition cannot give his intelligent assent. Under a purely subjective test his contracts would be void. But under a purely objective test the inquiry would be whether he appeared to a reasonable man in the position of the other to be capable of rational assent. This purely objective approach, however, conflicts with the policy of protecting the incompetent from his own improvidence.

Under the majority view a kind of compromise has evolved. Contracts which are executory,[53] or based upon grossly inadequate consideration [54] are voidable, but if the transaction is executed and the other party took no advantage of the incompetent and had no reason to know of his infirmity, it is not voidable unless the incompetent can place the other party in the status quo ante.[55] If the incompetency would be obvious to a reasonable man, there is no obligation upon the incompetent to make restitution if the consideration has been consumed or dissipated.[56] Under a minority view the appearance of sanity is immaterial and the incompetent need restore the consideration only if he still has it.[57]

WESTLAW REFERENCES

restitution /s contract*** agreement /s "mental! retard!" insan!
    incompeten!

contract*** agreement /s "mental! retard!" insan! incompeten! /s
    (consideration /s adequa! inadequa!) executory

257ak391

53. Cundell v. Haswell, 23 R.I. 508, 51 A. 426 (1902). The English rule is contrary. Where the other party did not take advantage of the incompetent and had no reason to know of his mental infirmity the executory contract is enforceable. York Glass Co., Ltd. v. Jubb, 134 L.T.R.(N.S.) 36 (C.A.1925). See Note, 25 Colum.L.Rev. 230 (1925).

54. Alexander v. Haskins, 68 Iowa 73, 25 N.W. 935 (1885) (land conveyed for about one third of its value).

55. Restatement, Second, Contracts § 15(2); Knighten v. Davis, 358 So.2d 1022 (Ala.1978); Sparrowhawk v. Erwin, 30 Ariz. 238, 246 P. 541, 46 A.L.R. 413 (1926); Coburn v. Raymond, 76 Conn. 484, 57 A. 116 (1904); Perper v. Edell, 160 Fla. 477, 35 So.2d 387, noted in 47 Mich.L.Rev. 269 (1948) (incompetent must pay real estate broker's commission); Atlanta Banking & Savings Co. v. Johnson, 179 Ga. 313, 175

S.E. 904, 95 A.L.R. 1436 (1934); cf. Georgia Power Co. v. Roper, 201 Ga. 760, 41 S.E.2d 226 (1947); Verstandig v. Schlaffer, 296 N.Y. 62, 70 N.E.2d 15 (1946), noted in 47 Colum.L.Rev. 675 (1947); Edmunds v. Chandler, 203 Va. 772, 127 S.E.2d 73 (1962). Restoration of the status quo ante often requires a complex evaluation of the equities and a complex accounting. See Virtue, supra note 45, esp. at 291–320.

That the modern tendency is to bring the rules regarding infants' contracts into harmony with those governing the contracts of mental incompetents. See § 8–6 supra as to infants' obligations to make restitution.

56. Spence v. Spence, 239 Ala. 480, 195 So. 717 (1940); Hardy v. Dyas, 203 Ill. 211, 67 N.E. 852 (1903); Restatement, Second, Contracts § 15, Comment e.

57. The leading case is Seaver v. Phelps, 28 Mass. (11 Pick.) 304 (1821).

"mental! retard!" insan! incompeten! infirm! /s restitution /s void!
    consideration

§ 8–12. Avoidance and Ratification

As in the case of infants' contracts there is no power of avoidance in the competent party.[58] The power of avoidance and ratification is reserved to the incompetent and his heirs or personal representative after death.[59] If a guardian is appointed, the power is vested in the guardian.[60] Once the incompetent recovers his capacity he may ratify the contract.[61] As in the case of infants' contracts, ratification can be effected by conduct or words, and once ratified the contract may not be avoided.[62] After ratification, the former incompetent or guardian may have an action for damages if exploitation of the incompetent amounted to actionable fraud.[63]

 WESTLAW REFERENCES
    ratif! /s "mental! retard!" insan! incompeten! infirm! /s contract***
        agreement % infirmary
    ratif! /s "mental! retard!" insan! incompeten! infirm! /s guardian!

§ 8–13. Liability for Necessaries

As in the case of an infant, a mental incompetent is liable in a quasi-contractual action for necessaries furnished him [64] or his dependents.[65] Roughly the same classes of goods and services considered necessaries for infants are necessaries for incompetents, including money advanced to procure necessaries.[66] Obviously, the incompetent's

---

58. Atwell v. Jenkins, 163 Mass. 362, 40 N.E. 178 (1895). If the contract is executory the competent party, upon discovery of the incompetency of the other, may refuse to perform until a guardian is appointed. Rattner v. Kleiman, 36 S.W.2d 249 (Tex. Civ.App.1931).

The competent party could obtain a declaration of nullity of a transaction entered into with an incompetent under guardianship as such a transaction is void rather than merely voidable.

59. Orr v. Equitable Mortgage Co., 107 Ga. 499, 33 S.E. 708 (1899); 2 Williston § 253. See also Reed v. Brown, 215 Ind. 417, 19 N.E.2d 1015 (1939) (administrator prevailed over adversary grantee-heir); Bullard v. Moor, 158 Mass. 418, 33 N.E. 928 (1893) (administrator's ratification binding on heirs).

Some jurisdictions permit creditors to attack transfers of his property. Chandler v. Welborn, 156 Tex. 312, 294 S.W.2d 801 (1956).

60. Finch v. Goldstein, 245 N.Y. 300, 157 N.E. 146 (1927) (ratification); Kline v.

L'Amoureaux, 2 Paige 419 (N.Y.1831) (avoidance); 2 Williston § 253; contra, Gingrich v. Rogers, 69 Neb. 527, 96 N.W. 156 (1903).

Strangers cannot generally avail themselves of the incompetency of a party to the transaction. Safe Deposit & Trust Co. v. Tait, 54 F.2d 383 (4th Cir.1931) (Commissioner of Internal Revenue).

61. Strodder v. Southern Granite Co., 99 Ga. 595, 27 S.E. 174 (1896).

62. First Nat. Bank v. Bunker, 494 F.2d 435 (8th Cir.1974); Bunn v. Postell, 107 Ga. 490, 33 S.E. 707 (1899).

63. Hunt v. Golden, 271 Or. 321, 532 P.2d 26 (1975).

64. Coffee v. Owens' Adm'r, 216 Ky. 142, 287 S.W. 540 (1926), noted in 15 Ky. L.J. 361 (1927).

65. Dalton v. Dalton, 172 Ky. 585, 189 S.W. 902 (1916); Linch v. Sanders, 114 W.Va. 726, 173 S.E. 788 (1934).

66. Bank of Rector v. Parrish, 131 Ark. 216, 198 S.W. 689 (1917); Henry v. Knight, 74 Ind.App. 562, 122 N.E. 675 (1919).

need for nursing and medical attention is salient among his necessaries.[67] Also legal services availed of to procure release from custody and guardianship, whether or not successful, are ordinarily compensable.[68]

 WESTLAW REFERENCES

"mental! retard!" insan! incompeten! infirm! /s "quasi contract***"

"mental! retard!" insan! incompeten! infirm! /p carter +s beckwith

"mental! retard!" insan! incompeten! infirm! /s liab! /s medical
legal /s service

§ 8–14. Intoxicated Persons

When a person is so far intoxicated or under the influence of narcotics that he does not understand the nature and consequences of the transaction in issue, the legal effect is much the same as in the case of any other kind of mental infirmity having the same effect.[69] Since the incompetency is self-induced, however, there is a different emphasis in the cases and particularly in the older cases, a good deal of moral indignation is often voiced at the intoxicated person [70] or the person plying him with liquor.[71] The contract of an intoxicated person is voidable by him but only under circumstances similar to those available to other classes of the mentally infirm. Cases permitting avoidance for intoxication alone are rare. This may be explainable on grounds that it would be unusual for the admittedly competent party to contract unknowingly with a person who is so intoxicated as not to understand the nature and consequences of his acts.[72] Under the rule laid down in the Restatement (Second), contracts made by an intoxicated party are voidable only if the other party has reason to know that the intoxicated party is unable to act in a reasonable manner in relation to the

67. In re Weber's Estate, 256 Mich. 61, 239 N.W. 260 (1931), noted in 17 Cornell L.Q. 502 (1932).

68. Kay v. Kay, 53 Ariz. 336, 89 P.2d 496, 121 A.L.R. 1496 (1939); Carr v. Anderson, 154 Minn. 162, 191 N.W. 407, 26 A.L.R. 557 (1923); Carter v. Beckwith, 128 N.Y. 312, 28 N.E. 582 (1891); In re Weightman's Estate, 126 Pa.Super. 221, 190 A. 552 (1937), noted in 85 U.Pa.L.Rev. 852 (1937).

69. Reiner v. Miller, 478 S.W.2d 283 (Mo.1972). See Poole v. Hudson, 46 Del. (7 Terry) 339, 83 A.2d 703 (Super.1951); Van Horn v. Persinger, 202 Mo.App. 236, 215 S.W. 930 (1919) (but need not return consideration which he no longer has); Seminara v. Grisman, 137 N.J.Eq. 307, 44 A.2d 492 (1945); Lucy v. Zehmer, 196 Va. 493, 84 S.E.2d 516 (1954).

See generally, McCoid, Intoxication and its Effect upon Civil Responsibility, 42 Io-wa L.Rev. 38 (1956); Annot. 36 A.L.R. 619 (1925); 2 Williston §§ 258–263.

Chronic alcoholism is grounds in many jurisdictions for an adjudication of incompetency and for the appointment of a guardian.

70. See Cook v. Bagnell Timber Co., 78 Ark. 47, 94 S.W. 695 (1906), expressing a minority view that intoxication per se is never a defense. If coupled with fraud by the other, the transaction is voidable on grounds of fraud. Accord, Burroughs v. Richman, 13 N.J.L. 233 (1832). See also Somers v. Ferris, 182 Mich. 392, 148 N.W. 782 (1914); Christensen v. Larson, 77 N.W.2d 441 (N.D.1956).

71. See L'Amoureux v. Crosby, 2 Paige 422 (N.Y.1831), where the Chancellor expressed regret that he did not possess the power of the English Chancellor to commit plaintiff innkeeper to Fleet Prison.

72. See 2 Williston § 259.

transaction or lacks understanding of it.[73]   This limitation is not generally found in the language of the cases.   Where the other party is aware of the intoxication the rules alluded to in the next section also come into play.

 WESTLAW REFERENCES
intoxicat! /s "understand the nature"
intoxicat! /s contract*** agreement /s voidable
95k92 /p intoxicat!

§ 8–15.   Exploitation of Alcoholics and Weak Minded Persons

Mental infirmity, feebleness of intellect or intoxication may exist to a lesser degree than required by law for the avoidance of a contract.   In such a case the person so afflicted is of course bound by his contract if no other grounds for avoidance exist.   The cases, however, frequently reveal exploitation of such persons.   The law offers a number of other doctrines for their protection.   It is obvious that where a feeble minded illiterate woman is made to execute a conveyance at pistol point the transaction is voidable.[74]   The woman's mental powers are barely relevant in such circumstances.   The factual patterns, however, usually involve more subtle forms of duress, fraud, undue influence or overreaching.   To ply an alcoholic with liquor and then induce him to enter into a contract for a grossly inadequate consideration has been deemed a species of fraud.[75]   Such cases are not decided on grounds of lack of capacity, but because the person's limited mental ability is coupled with unconscionable exploitation by the other.   This is further illustrated by cases holding that a hard bargain aggressively pressed upon a sober alcoholic by a party who knows of his consuming desire for cash to obtain liquor is voidable for overreaching.[76]

The situation in which persons who suffer from some infirmity, but who are not legally insane, and have been exploited are as varied as the expressions of human avarice.   Typical situations which recur involve deeds extracted from the aged bedridden,[77] and releases extracted from

73.   Restatement, Second, Contracts § 16.

74.   This illustration is suggested by Phillips v. Bowie, 127 S.W.2d 522 (Tex.Civ. App.1939).

75.   Thackrah v. Haas, 119 U.S. 499, 7 S.Ct. 311, 30 L.Ed. 486 (1886); Tubbs v. Hilliard, 104 Colo. 164, 89 P.2d 535 (1939); Ealy v. Tolbert, 209 Ga. 575, 74 S.E.2d 867 (1953); Matthis v. O'Brien, 137 Ky. 651, 126 S.W. 156 (1910).

76.   Kendall v. Ewert, 259 U.S. 139, 42 S.Ct. 444, 66 L.Ed. 862 (1922), noted in 3 Tenn.L.Rev. 84 (1925); Harlow v. Kingston, 169 Wis. 521, 173 N.W. 308, 6 A.L.R. 327 (1919); see § 9–9 to 9–12 infra.

77.   An analysis of 123 cases involving contracts and conveyances with aged persons attacked for want of capacity leads one observer to conclude that in addition to evidence of the extent of the infirmity and the fairness of the bargain the courts place emphasis on whether there is a fiduciary relationship, secrecy or unkindness.   Of the 62 transactions which were set aside, undue influence and fraud rather than want of capacity seems to have been the basis of most of the decisions.   The observer concludes: "These are perhaps the most difficult cases of all for the courts, which are virtually without doctrinal guidance, and must base their decisions solely on the individual equities, as disclosed by witness-

injured persons suffering great shock or pain.[78] In each case the court has the difficult task of sifting through the facts. Some degree of infirmity coupled with the unfairness of the bargain will often result in a finding of fraud, undue influence, overreaching or even mental incapacity.[79] The recent enlargement of the doctrine of unconscionability offers another and more forthright approach to cases of this kind.[80]

 WESTLAW REFERENCES

intoxicat! (feeble weak /s mind**) "mental infirm!" /s fraud!
    duress overreach! "undue influence" /s void!

intoxicat! (feeble weak /s mind**) "mental! infirm!" /s contract***
    agreement /s unconscionab! exploit!

thackrah +s haas

void! "set aside" /s "undue influence" fraud! /s old age* elderly
    /s deed agreement contract***

120k211(1)

120k211(3) /p old age* elderly (mental! +1 capacity incapacit!)

120k211(4) /p old age* elderly (mental! +1 incapacit! capacity

95k92 /p old age* elderly

120k196(3) /p old age* elderly

C. SELF–DEALING

Table of Sections

§ 8–16. Contracting With Oneself

If a person promises himself that if he abstains from smoking for one year he will spend $2,000 on a Caribbean vacation for himself, the promise, although accepted in accordance with its terms, creates no legal duty.[81] The same result would follow even if the promise were made in a formal document containing a recital of an intention that his promise be legally binding. Perhaps no better illustration than this exists to demonstrate that intention to be bound is not the exclusive basis of contract law. From illustrations such as this, large generalizations have been drawn. The First Restatement adamantly asserted: "It is not possible under existing law for a man to make a contract with

es who are usually deeply involved emotionally in some variant of the King Lear situation." Virtue, supra note 45, at 298–99.

78. Union Pacific R. Co. v. Harris, 158 U.S. 326, 15 S.Ct. 843, 39 L.Ed. 1003 (1895) (release signed while injured person was under the influence of morphine); Carr v. Sacramento Clay Products Co., 35 Cal.App. 439, 170 P. 446 (1918). For additional cases, see Virtue, supra note 45, at 296–97.

79. Williamson v. Matthews, 379 So.2d 1245 (Ala.1980); McPheters v. Hapke, 94 Idaho 744, 497 P.2d 1045 (1972); Patterson v. Ervin, 230 So.2d 563 (Miss.1970).

80. See §§ 9–37 to 9–40 infra.

81. 1 Corbin § 55; 1 Williston § 18; C.J.S. Contracts § 26; Restatement, Second, Contracts § 9.

himself." [82]   Such a transaction has been said to be void.[83]   This statement of the rule ought to be tempered by an awareness that the needs of concrete cases requires greater flexibility than such a rule suggests.[84]

On the ground that one cannot contract with himself it has been said that a dealer in mobile homes who purportedly contracted to sell a mobile home to himself on credit and who, as seller, purported to retain a security interest in the home, created no change in legal relations. Certainly if he were suing himself such an analysis would be appropriate. But to hold that a purchaser of the business who agreed to take an assignment of all the rights and to assume all the liabilities of the business would not be protected and limited by the terms of the "contract" of sale that the prior owner of the business made with himself would be palpably unfair.[85] Businessmen tend to conceive of their business assets as something other than their personal assets. When they deal with them on such a basis interested third parties have a right to hold them to this promise, even if originally the promise was made to the promisor himself.

At times a person has more than one legal capacity.[86] Can John Jones contract with the same John Jones in his capacity as executor of the estate of John Smith, or as president of XYZ Corporation, or both? Suppose Jones, as executor of Smith's estate has title to certain equipment and wishes to transfer the equipment on a credit sale to XYZ Corporation which he heads, and also agrees personally to guarantee payment of the price. This may be a sensible transaction for the benefit of all concerned. A lawyer would advise Jones to arrange the transaction through a strawman, transferring the equipment to Y, who would then transfer to XYZ. But if Jones is not guided by a lawyer, should the transaction be struck down merely because of the notion that one cannot contract with himself? Certainly not. A more important question is, shouldn't the transaction be struck down because of Jones' conflict of interest? As seller is he likely to get the best possible price for the equipment by bargaining with himself? The answer is that the transaction ought to be treated as voidable at the election of the beneficiaries of the estate. Indeed, it is unlikely that a transaction of the type here hypothesized would be entered into without the consent of the beneficiaries or the probate court.

The same problem is shown in a somewhat clearer light when we consider multi-divisional entities such as banks. May a bank acting as executor for an estate contract with its loan division to borrow money for estate purposes? There is authority to the effect that this may be

---

82. Restatement, Contracts § 15, Comment a.

83. Restatement, Contracts § 15, ill. 2; Schmaeling v. Schmaeling, 127 Misc.2d 763, 487 N.Y.S.2d 494 (Dist.Ct.1985).

84. See Restatement, Second, Contracts § 9, Comment a.

85. Cf. Forest Investment Corp. v. Chaplin, 55 Ill.App.2d 429, 205 N.E.2d 51 (1965).

86. Restatement, Second, Contracts § 9, Comment b.

done.[87] Statutes have been enacted explicitly to govern aspects of multi-department banking, permitting contracts between departments.[88]

In a significant case the United States appointed the defendant steamship company as its agent for the management of a government owned merchant ship. As agent, the company contracted with its stevedoring division to stevedore the ship. Despite the company's subsequent contention that it could not contract with itself, the court ruled that the contract was binding on the defendant upon ratification of the contract by the United States.[89] A contrary result based upon the supposed incapacity of a person to contract with himself would clearly have sacrificed a sound result from an overgeneralized rule. The case is in tune with the same realistic approach which permits one department of the executive branch of government to sue another department of the executive branch.[90]

 WESTLAW REFERENCES

contract*** /s "self dealing"

"conflict of interest" /s "self dealing" void! /s "self dealing"

find 89 f2d 324

§ 8–17. Contracting With Oneself and Another

Courts of equity have long enforced contracts between an individual and a group of individuals which includes himself. Thus a member of an unincorporated club may contract with the club [91] and a partner may contract with his partnership.[92] In each of these instances the member is both a promisor and a promisee in the contractual relation.[93]

87. Breedlove v. Freudentstein, 89 F.2d 324 (5th Cir.1937), certiorari denied 302 U.S. 701, 58 S.Ct. 20, 82 L.Ed. 541 noted in 51 Harv.L.Rev. 351 (1937).

88. See Bogert, Trusts & Trustees § 598, pp. 335–49 (2d ed. 1960).

89. United States v. Alaska Steamship Co., 491 F.2d 1147 (9th Cir.1974).

90. United States v. Nixon, 418 U.S. 683, 94 S.Ct. 3090, 41 L.Ed.2d 1039 (1974).

91. Anderson v. Amidon, 114 Minn. 202, 130 N.W. 1002, 34 L.R.A.,N.S., 647 (1911).

92. Forsyth v. Butler, 152 Cal. 396, 93 P. 90 (1907).

93. See Restatement, Second, Contracts § 11; 1 Williston § 18; 1 Corbin § 55.

Chapter 9

AVOIDANCE OR REFORMATION FOR MISCONDUCT OR MISTAKE

Table of Sections

Table of Sections

A. INTRODUCTION

Sec.
9–1. Scope of This Chapter.

B. DURESS

9–2. The History and Elements of Duress.
9–3. What Acts or Threats Are Wrongful—Abuse of Rights.
9–4. Threats of Imprisonment or Criminal Prosecution.
9–5. Duress of Property: Assertion of Liens.
9–6. Coerced Settlements or Contract Modifications.
9–7. Business Compulsion.
9–8. Remedies for Duress.

C. UNDUE INFLUENCE

9–9. Background of Undue Influence.
9–10. Elements of Undue Influence.
9–11. Undue Influence in the Absence of a Confidential Relationship.
9–12. Remedies for Undue Influence.

D.   MISREPRESENTATION AND NON–DISCLOSURE

E.   MISTAKE

F.   REFORMATION

G.   UNCONSCIONABILITY

A. INTRODUCTION

Table of Sections

§ 9–1. Scope of This Chapter

Even though the parties have gone through a process of offer and acceptance and their agreement or apparent agreement is supported by consideration or one of its equivalents and they have contractual capacity, the agreement may be void, voidable, or reformable because it is contaminated by duress, undue influence, misrepresentation, mistake or unconscionability. These topics will now receive brief consideration as well as the question of duty to read.

B. DURESS

Table of Sections

§ 9–2. The History and Elements of Duress

Few areas of the law of contracts have undergone such radical changes[1] in the nineteenth and twentieth centuries as has the law governing duress. In Blackstone's time relief from an agreement on grounds of duress was a possibility only if it was coerced by actual (not threatened) imprisonment or fear of loss of life or limb. "A fear of

---

1. So characterized in Tallmadge v. Robinson, 158 Ohio St. 333, 338–340, 109 N.E.2d 496, 499 (1952). For the history of duress, see 13 Williston §§ 1601–1602.

battery * * * is no duress; neither is the fear of having one's house burned, or one's goods taken away or destroyed;" he wrote, "because in these cases, should the threat be performed, a man may have satisfaction by recovering equivalent damages: but no suitable atonement can be made for the loss of life, or limb." [2]

Today the general rule is that any wrongful act or threat which overcomes the free will of a party constitutes duress.[3] This simple statement of the law conceals a number of questions, particularly as to the meaning of "free will" and "wrongful". Also, as in the case of all contractual rules which make reference to mental processes, we must ask whether the test is objective or subjective. This last is the easiest of the questions posed. The overwhelming weight of modern authority is to the effect that the issue is whether the will of the particular person has been overcome,[4] and not, as the earlier cases had held, whether a brave man would be put in fear or whether the will of a person of ordinary firmness would be overcome.[5] Evidence showing whether a reasonable person would be put in fear is relevant, however, as circumstantial evidence of whether the person's free will was overcome.[6] Where the coercion involves economic pressure rather than threat of physical injury, however, an objective element continues to be demanded by the court. In the face of a threat of "either * * * or," did the person threatened have some reasonable third alternative? For example, was there a judicial proceeding that could have produced prompt and adequate relief? If so, a case for duress would not be made out.[7]

2. 1 Blackstone's Commentaries * 131. The rule in England seems to have been relaxed but slightly. On the other hand, the doctrine of undue influence has been expanded to fill part of the void. See Cheshire, Fifoot & Furmston, The Law of Contract 280–84 (8th ed. 1972). Blackstone was not strictly correct, for the doctrine of duress of goods already had been originated when he wrote. See § 9–5 infra. In the United States the defense of duress to a criminal charge has remained close to the Blackstonian rule. See Newman & Weitzer, Duress, Free Will and the Criminal Law, 30 So.Cal.L.Rev. 313 (1957).

3. Kaplan v. Kaplan, 25 Ill.2d 181, 185, 182 N.E.2d 706, 709 (1962); Austin Instrument, Inc. v. Loral Corp., 29 N.Y.2d 124, 130, 324 N.Y.S.2d 22, 25, 272 N.E.2d 533, 535 (1971), reargument denied 29 N.Y.2d 749, 326 N.Y.S.2d 1027, 276 N.E.2d 238 (1971). See 2 Palmer on Restitution § 9.2 (1978).

4. Kaplan v. Kaplan, 25 Ill.2d 181, 186, 182 N.E.2d 706, 709 (1962); Silsbee v. Webber, 171 Mass. 378, 50 N.E. 555 (1898) (classic exposition by Holmes); Rubenstein v. Rubenstein, 20 N.J. 359, 120 A.2d 11 (1956); 13 Williston § 1605; but see Three

Rivers Motors Co. v. Ford Motor Co., 522 F.2d 885 (3d Cir.1975).

5. Young v. Hoagland, 212 Cal. 426, 298 P. 996, 75 A.L.R. 654 (1931). At times the "mind of a person of ordinary firmness" rule is routinely stated, but usually in a case where the precise test is not really in issue. See, e.g., Bata v. Central-Penn Nat'l Bank of Philadelphia, 423 Pa. 373, 224 A.2d 174 (1966), certiorari denied 386 U.S. 1007, 87 S.Ct. 1348, 18 L.Ed.2d 433 (1967) where the old rule is stated but in a context where "we find it inconceivable that appellant was subject to any degree of restraint or danger." 224 A.2d at 180.

6. Restatement, Contracts § 492, Comment b; Restatement, Second, Contracts § 175, Comment b.

7. Leeper v. Beltrami, 53 Cal.2d 195, 1 Cal.Rptr. 12, 347 P.2d 12, 77 A.L.R.2d 803 (1959); Austin Instrument, Inc. v. Loral Corp., 29 N.Y.2d 124, 324 N.Y.S.2d 22, 272 N.E.2d 533 (1971), reargument denied 29 N.Y.2d 749, 326 N.Y.S.2d 1027, 276 N.E.2d 238 (1971); see Dalzell, Duress by Economic Pressure II, 20 N.C.L.Rev. 341, 367–82 (1942).

The idea of "free will" requires some elaboration. This, of course, is not the place to deal with the millenia old concern of philosophers as to whether free will exists. It is quite obvious, however, that contract law is very much premised on its existence.[8] Older doctrine was often premised on the idea that an agreement made under duress lacks "real" consent and produces only apparent assent. However, as has been pointed out, when a parent pays a kidnapper because he wishes to save his daughter's life, his choice may be the "expression of the most genuine, heartfelt consent."[9] The consent is real enough, the vice of it is that it was coerced in a manner that society brands as wrongful and is therefore not deemed the product of free will. Consequently, in determining whether a transaction may be avoided for duress the main inquiry is to ascertain what acts or threats are branded as wrongful. It is, of course, important in every case to inquire not only whether the act or threat was wrongful but also whether the transaction was in fact induced by the wrong.[10] In addition, another factor, not generally articulated as a rationale in the cases or treatises, is often emphasized in the court's review of the facts; that is, the degree of economic imbalance in the transaction.[11] Duress will generally not be found to exist unless the party exercising the coercion has been unjustly enriched.[12] Remedies for duress are primarily aimed at the cancellation of unjust gain.[13] Of course, where the coercion is extreme the legal system's interest in the protection of individual freedom will prevail regardless of any inquiry into the unfairness of the transaction itself.[14]

8. See for an introduction, Macneil, The Many Futures of Contracts, 47 S.Cal.L.Rev. 691, 701–06 (1974).

9. Dalzell, Duress by Economic Pressure I, 20 N.C.L.Rev. 237, 237–238 (1942); see also 13 Williston § 1627A; Sharp, The Ethics of Breach of Contract, 45 Int'l J. of Ethics, 27, 30–31 (1934); Note, Restitution—Duress—The Law in Oregon, 38 Or. L.Rev. 246, 248 (1959); Note, The Nature and Effect of Duress, 26 Harv.L.Rev. 255 (1912). The classic statement of this analysis is by Justice Holmes in Union Pac. R.R. Co. v. Public Service Comm'n of Missouri, 248 U.S. 67, 39 S.Ct. 24, 63 L.Ed. 131 (1918). Similar analysis, in a broader discussion of the idea of liberty, is found in Hale, Bargaining, Duress and Economic Liberty, 43 Colum.L.Rev. 603 (1943).

10. United States v. Bethlehem Steel Corp., 315 U.S. 289, 62 S.Ct. 581, 86 L.Ed. 855 (1942); Hellenic Lines, Ltd. v. Louis Dreyfus Corp., 372 F.2d 753 (2d Cir.1967). The fear must induce the contract, but need not be the sole cause. Restatement, Contracts § 492, Comment f.

11. This is the primary thrust of the analysis in Dawson, Economic Duress—An Essay in Perspective, 45 Mich.L.Rev. 253 (1947); see also Dawson, Unconscionable

Coercion: The German Version, 89 Harv.L. Rev. 1041 (1976); Dawson, Duress through Civil Litigation I, II, 45 Mich.L.Rev. 571, 679 (1947); Dawson, Economic Duress and Fair Exchange in French and German Law, 11 Tul.L.Rev. 345 (1937). Another commentator argues that lack of balance is merely evidence of coercion and not a substantive basis for a finding of duress. Dalzell, Duress by Economic Pressure I, 20 N.C.L.Rev. 237, 263 (1942); compare Note, Unbalanced Transactions under Common and Civil Law, 43 Colum.L.Rev. 1066 (1943) (focusing on consideration doctrine).

12. First Data Resources, Inc. v. Omaha Steaks Int'l, Inc., 209 Neb. 327, 307 N.W.2d 790 (1981) (coercion must result in a contract that is illegal, unjust or unconscionable).

13. 2 Palmer on Restitution § 9.4 (1978); Dawson, Economic Duress—An Essay in Perspective, 45 Mich.L.Rev. 253, 283–285 (1947); Restatement, Second, Contracts § 176, see § 9–8 infra.

14. Dawson, supra note 13, at 284–285; Restatement, Second, Contracts § 176(1); cf. Pound, Interests of Personality, 28 Harv.L.Rev. 343, 357–359 (1915) (duress doctrine is designed to protect freedom of will).

One commentator, focusing on the means of coercion, rather than its result, has argued that the law of duress has developed to control the bargaining process. Inasmuch as the democratic state has allowed the exchange process to be handled through the mechanism of contracts, the state has an interest in regulating that mechanism of exchange.[15]

The two possible vantage points—(1) the end result of the coercion and (2) the means of coercion—help explain some of the confusion surrounding differing views concerning coerced modifications of contracts, discussed in § 9–6 below.

WESTLAW REFERENCES

duress /s actual /s imprison! (fear /s life limb)

agreement contract*** /s duress /s coerc! /s fear!

di duress

"doctrine of duress"

duress /s wrong! /s "free will"

to(95) /p duress /p "free will" coerc! fear!

duress /s "free will" /s overc*m!

"economic duress" /s "reasonable alternative"

duress /s consent! /s assent!

duress /s induc! /s wrong!

di(duress /p "unjust! enrich!")

duress /s subjectiv!

§ 9–3. What Acts or Threats Are Wrongful—Abuse of Rights

Violence and threats of violence are wrongful and, although not as rare as one would hope,[16] such threats no longer make up the bulk of duress cases. The law has evolved so as to permit relief for duress in a vast variety of situations. These roughly may be categorized into four principal classes:[17]

1. Violence or threats of violence.

2. Imprisonment or threats of imprisonment.

3. Wrongful seizing or withholding, or threats wrongfully to seize or withhold, goods or lands.

15. Carlston, Restitution—The Search for a Philosophy, 6 J.Leg.Ed. 330, 336–38 (1954). For a similar discussion to the effect that "moralistic" arguments "prevent serious analysis." By "serious analysis" is meant analysis in terms of the functioning of the market. Dobbs, Remedies 654–55 (1973). For such an analysis, see Eisenberg, The Bargain Principle and its Limits, 95 Harv.L.Rev. 741 (1982).

A release executed by a person under arrest in exchange for a prosecutor's agreement to dismiss charges has been held against public policy because of the inherently coercive nature of the bargaining context. Boyd v. Adams, 513 F.2d 83 (7th Cir.1975). See Annot., 86 A.L.R.3d 1230.

16. Williams v. Macchio, 69 Misc.2d 94, 329 N.Y.S.2d 405 (1972); Rubenstein v. Rubenstein, 20 N.J. 359, 120 A.2d 11 (1956).

17. See, e.g., Restatement of Contracts § 493 (Restatement categories (a) and (c) are merged in our category No. 1). Restatement, Second, Contracts § 176 contains a longer list of categories.

4. Other wrongful acts.

It will be helpful to the discussion if the miscellaneous category of "other wrongful acts" is discussed first. Within this category of course comes such criminal conduct as blackmail.[18] The evolving case law, however, has for the most part dealt with threats to exercise legal rights in oppressive or abusive ways. For example, a threat to bring a law suit is a legitimate form of coercion protected by law and the Constitution. However, where a husband threatens his wife with a suit demanding custody of their children on grounds of her adultery unless she assigns certain securities to him, it is at least a jury question whether the assignment is voidable for duress. In the words of the court:

> "The weight of modern authority supports the rule, which we here adopt, that the act done or threatened may be wrongful even though not unlawful, per se; and that the threat to instigate legal proceedings, criminal or civil, which might be justifiable, per se, becomes wrongful, within the meaning of this rule, if made with the corrupt intent to coerce a transaction grossly unfair to the victim and not related to the subject of such proceedings."[19]

Similarly, an employee under a hiring at will may be fired without cause. However, a threat to fire him unless he agrees to sell his shares of stock in the employing corporation back to the employer constitutes an abuse of the employer's rights and the employee who succumbs to the threat may recover his shares if the trier of fact finds that the employee had been coerced by the threat.[20] To summarize, in the context of duress, an act or threat is wrongful if it is "an abuse of the powers of the party making the threat; that is, any threat the purpose of which was not to achieve the end for which the right, power, or privilege was given."[21] Looked at from the point of view of the coerced party, he may ethically protect himself by making a contract he has no intent to keep in order to save himself from the abusive invasion or threatened invasion of his rights.[22]

18. This would include also lesser tortious threats such as a threat to use one's influence to cause a lender to refuse to consummate a loan agreement, Criterion Holding Co. v. Cerussi, 140 Misc. 855, 250 N.Y.S. 735 (1931), and a threat to induce a person's employer to fire him. Wise v. Midtown Motors, 231 Minn. 46, 42 N.W.2d 404, 20 A.L.R.2d 735 (1950).

19. Link v. Link, 278 N.C. 181, 194, 179 S.E.2d 697, 705 (1971).

20. Laemmar v. J. Walter Thompson Co., 435 F.2d 680 (7th Cir.1970); but see Vines v. General Outdoor Advertising Co., 171 F.2d 487 (2d Cir.1948); see also Mitchell v. C.C. Sanitation Co., 430 S.W.2d 933 (Tex.Civ.App.1968), error refused n.r.e. (re-

lease void for duress where employer threatens to fire employee unless he signed release); Annots., 20 A.L.R.2d 743 (1951); 30 A.L.R.4th 294 (1984).

What of the situation where, when threatened with being fired, the employee accedes to the employer's threats by agreeing to the employer's terms and is soon thereafter fired? See McCubbin v. Buss, 180 Neb. 624, 144 N.W.2d 175 (1966) (coerced agreement may be rescinded).

21. Dalzell, Duress by Economic Pressure II, 20 N.C.L.Rev. 341, 364 (1942); see also 13 Williston § 1607; Restatement, Contracts § 492, Comment g.

22. Sharp, supra note 9, at 34.

It should be noted, however, that where there is a good faith dispute, a refusal to pay under a contract until a dispute is settled or adjudicated, does not constitute duress.[23] A party's refusal to settle does not constitute a wrongful threat.[24] When an employee is offered the chance of being fired for cause or resigning, it will usually be held that the resignation cannot be avoided,[25] unless the threat to fire is made for bad faith reasons or is accompanied by threats to ruin the reputation of the employee.[26] In short, absent a *wrongful* threat, the driving of a hard bargain is not duress.[27] This is true even if one party benefits from the financial distress of the other.[28]

WESTLAW REFERENCES

duress /s "wrongful act"

duress /s blackmail

duress /s "legal right" /s claim suit

claim /s duress /s threat!

employ**** /s duress /s fire* firing hire* hiring

"good faith" /s duress

"wrong! threat!" /s duress

§ 9–4.   Threats of Imprisonment or Criminal Prosecution

Civil imprisonment or the threat of it, if caused or threatened in good faith and allowed by law, cannot normally justify a finding of duress.[29] Coercive it may be, but it is not wrongful. On the other hand if the imprisonment is not allowed by law or is oppressively exercised or threatened so as to constitute an abuse of rights there is sufficient foundation for a finding of duress.[30] Similarly, a threat of a legitimate civil suit coupled with threats to ruin the other party by enmeshing him in difficulties with licensing and regulatory authorities may be the basis for a finding of duress.[31]

23. Selmer Co. v. Blakeslee-Midwest Co., 704 F.2d 924 (7th Cir.1983); Labeach v. Beatrice Foods Co., 461 F.Supp. 152 (S.D. N.Y.1978); Landers v. State, 56 A.D.2d 105, 391 N.Y.S.2d 723 (3d Dep't 1977), affirmed 43 N.Y.2d 784, 402 N.Y.S.2d 386, 373 N.E.2d 281 (1977).

24. Wiesen v. Short, 43 Colo.App. 374, 604 P.2d 1191 (1979). Otherwise, if the claim is in bad faith. Adams v. Crater Well Drilling, Inc., 276 Or. 789, 556 P.2d 679 (1976); see also International Underwater Contractors, Inc. v. New England Telephone and Telegraph Co., 8 Mass.App. Ct. 340, 393 N.E.2d 968 (1979).

25. City of Miami v. Kory, 394 So.2d 494 (Fla.App.1981), review denied 407 So. 2d 1104 (1981).

26. Humana, Inc. v. Fairchild, 603 S.W.2d 918 (Ky.App.1980).

27. Selmer Co. v. Blakeslee-Midwest Co., supra note 23; Grand Motors, Inc. v. Ford Motor Co., 564 F.Supp. 34 (W.D.Mo. 1982).

28. Chouinard v. Chouinard, 568 F.2d 430 (5th Cir.1978); First Texas Sav. Ass'n of Dallas v. Dicker Center, Inc., 631 S.W.2d 179 (Tex.Civ.App.1982).

29. Restatement, Contracts § 493, Comment b. Cases are collected and discussed in Dawson, Duress through Civil Litigation 1, 45 Mich.L.Rev. 571, 586–91 (1947); 13 Williston §§ 1609–1610.

30. See all authorities cited in the prior note.

31. Jamestown Farmers Elevator, Inc. v. General Mills, Inc., 552 F.2d 1285 (8th Cir.1977).

When a transaction is induced by a threat of arrest, criminal prosecution, or criminal imprisonment, the most varied results and reasonings are found.[32] Few generalizations can be made. The reason for the confusing disparity of results can perhaps be understood by examining a typical fact pattern. A fiduciary is charged by his principal with embezzlement. The fiduciary is threatened with being turned over to the authorities unless he makes restitution. Induced by the threat, he produces part of the demand in cash and he and a concerned relative sign a promissory note for the balance. The following propositions can be stated, some of which tug in a different direction than others. The first two propositions point to a finding of duress. (1) The principal has a legal right to report his suspicions to the authorities. The threat to exercise this right solely for private gain is, however, an abuse of this right. (2) The threat is coercive and capable of inducing a settlement against the free will of the fiduciary and his relative.[33] Whether it did in fact induce the settlement is a question of fact. A third proposition points, however, to an opposite result. If the fiduciary was in fact guilty, the principal is not unjustly enriched by the fiduciary's doing and promising what he has a legal obligation to do.[34]

A fourth proposition must be injected into the equation, if, as so frequently occurs, the principal agrees not to prosecute a criminal proceeding against the fiduciary. Such an agreement is emphatically illegal.[35] As to illegal agreements the general proposition is that the court will leave the parties where it finds them.[36] If this proposition stood alone the court would neither enforce the promissory note nor would it compel restitution of the amount paid. This result, however,

32. See generally 2 Palmer on Restitution § 9.11; 13 Williston §§ 1609–1615; Woodward, Quasi Contracts §§ 141–142, 214–215; Dawson, Economic Duress—An Essay in Perspective, 45 Mich.L.Rev. 253, 285–287 (1947). As to a release of claims of false arrest exchanged for a prosecutor's dismissal of charges see note 15 supra. A threat to turn one's claim over to one's attorney for prosecution does not justify an inference of a threat of criminal prosecution. Rivervalley Co. v. Deposit Guaranty Nat'l Bank, 331 F.Supp. 698 (N.D.Miss. 1971).

33. Some courts distinguish between the accused and his relative, expressing a greater willingness to consider a claim of duress where the party coerced is a relative. Kronmeyer v. Buck, 258 Ill. 586, 101 N.E. 935 (1913). Others do not accept the distinction. Union Exchange Nat'l Bank of New York v. Joseph, 231 N.Y. 250, 131 N.E. 905, 17 A.L.R. 323 (1921).

There must be a threat. A statement to the accused that he could be subject to a penitentiary offense has been held not to be a threat. Buhrman v. International

Harvester Co., 181 Neb. 633, 150 N.W.2d 220 (1967).

34. If a finding of duress is made and there is no complicating factor of illegality, the recovery is frequently limited to the excess of the amount paid over the amount of the indebtedness. Merrel v. Research & Data, Inc., 3 Kan.App.2d 48, 589 P.2d 120 (1979); see also cases cited by Dawson, Economic Duress—An Essay in Perspective, 45 Mich.L.Rev. 253, 285–87 (1947). For similar reasons, courts which are unwilling to allow duress to be raised as a defense or as a basis for an action for restitution where the settlement is fair, are willing to allow the claim of duress to be proved where the settlement is out of proportion to the legal obligation. Kronmeyer v. Buck, 258 Ill. 586, 101 N.E. 935 (1913).

35. If there is no such agreement and the withholding of prosecution is merely an unbargained for result of the settlement, the transaction is not illegal. Restatement, Contracts § 548, ill. 1; Blair Milling Co. v. Fruitager, 113 Kan. 432, 215 P. 286, 32 A.L.R. 416 (1923).

36. See § 22–1 infra.

is placed in doubt by a fifth proposition. A party who is pressured into an illegal bargain by duress is deemed not to be equally guilty with the party exercising the pressure and generally will be awarded restitution.[37]

In view of the tensions among these propositions it is not surprising that courts have reached differing results. At times the decisions show a sophisticated awareness of the nature of the choice to be made.[38] Frequently, however, the competing factors are submerged beneath dubious reasoning.[39]

WESTLAW REFERENCES

duress /s imprison! /s threat!
prosecut! /s duress /s criminal!
"question of fact" /s duress
illegal! /s bargain! agreement contract*** /s duress

---

§ 9–5. Duress of Property: Assertion of Liens

A wrongful threat to detain or the detention of the property of another amounts to duress if it coerces the assent of the other to a transaction and the party coerced had no reasonable alternative but to assent.[40] There is often a legal right to assert a retaining lien on property of another, to obtain an attachment of goods, to foreclose a mortgage, etc. The exercise of such rights is inherently coercive even if scrupulously employed. If a right is employed in a particularly oppressive manner or to force a settlement disproportionate to what is owed, the exercise of the right constitutes duress unless the coerced party could have obtained judicial or other relief that would have been reasonably prompt and efficacious under the circumstances.[41] The

---

37. See § 22–7 infra.

38. See Union Exchange Nat'l Bank of New York v. Joseph, 231 N.Y. 250, 131 N.E. 905, 17 A.L.R. 323 (1921) (no enforcement of note against accused's brother-in-law and no restitution; restitution perhaps available if criminal charge is asserted in bad faith) ("there is to be no traffic in the privilege of invoking the public justice of the state."); contra, and equally cognizant of competing state interests, Gorringe v. Reed, 23 Utah 120, 63 P. 902, 90 Am.St. Rep. 692 (1901) ("as civilization has advanced the law has tended much more strongly than it formerly did to overthrow everything which is built on violence and fraud.") Restatement, Second, Contracts § 176, Comment c, takes the position that duress renders executory transactions of the kind considered here voidable. It takes no position on the question of restitution of money paid pursuant to a threat.

39. See, e.g., Harrell v. Allen, 439 F.2d 1005 (5th Cir.1971) (as a matter of law a threat of arrest cannot overcome free will).

40. The doctrine of duress of goods originated with the case of Astley v. Reynolds, 2 Strange 915, 93 Eng.Rep. 939 (K.B.1732) where a pledgee refused to surrender pledged property to the pledgor except upon payment of an unjustified bonus. The pledgor made the payment and recovered the excess payment, the court stating the owner "might have such an immediate want of his goods, that an action of trover would not do his business." For a modern application, see S.P. Dunham & Co. v. Kudra, 44 N.J.Super. 565, 131 A.2d 306 (1957), 32 Tulane L.Rev. 512 (1958).

41. See generally, 13 Williston §§ 1616–1619; Dalzell, Duress by Economic Pressure I, II, 20 N.C.L.Rev. 237, 341 (1942); Dawson, Duress Through Civil Litigation I, II, 45 Mich.L.Rev. 571, 679 (1947).

classic case is that of Chandler v. Sanger,[42] where a creditor whose claim had been discharged in bankruptcy procured a writ of attachment and attached the plaintiff's ice wagon in the pre-dawn hours after they had been loaded with ice. To dissolve the attachment the plaintiff paid the creditor's claim. His alternative was to move in court that the attachment be dissolved and a bond posted by him be substituted therefor. He was advised, however, that three days would be required to obtain such relief, by which time the ice would have melted and, perhaps, his ice business crippled. Note that the property chosen for attachment was deliberately selected to deprive the plaintiff of freedom of choice and that the claim was known to be unfounded. Where these elements co-exist in the same fact pattern duress can easily be found. Where the oppression is no greater than that which is inherent in the typical attachment or assertion of a lien and the claim is made in bad faith, again a finding of duress is generally indicated if the evidence shows that the pressured party was indeed coerced by the lien and had no reasonable alternative but to agree to the offered terms.[43] Where the claim is made in good faith but is factually unfounded or the claim although in good faith is in excess of what is in fact owed, a claim of duress is extremely difficult to sustain.[44] There are strong judicial policies favoring the settlement of disputes and encouraging use of the courts where settlement can not satisfactorily be attained. On the other hand, there is increasing willingness to realize that liens asserted, even in good faith, have the power to coerce unjustified settlements resulting in unjust enrichment. In what is perhaps the leading modern case, plaintiff acceded to the defendant's demands for payment of repairs to his motor boat in order to secure release of the boat.[45] The court allowed recovery of the overcharges without making reference to the presence or absence of the defendant's good faith. In addition, the court made no reference to whether the plaintiff had any reasonable alternative (e.g., posting a bond pending litigation) to acceding to defendant's demands. Some courts would distinguish, however, between a judicial attachment and a common law possessory lien, allowing redress in the latter, but not in the former case.

 WESTLAW REFERENCES
duress /s wrong! /s threat! /s property
duress /s lien!

42. 114 Mass. 364, 19 Am.Rep. 367 (1874); accord, Fenwick Shipping Co. v. Clarke Bros., 133 Ga. 43, 65 S.E. 140 (1909) (attachment of baggage of a traveller when he has abundant other attachable assets within the jurisdiction); Restatement, Second, Contracts § 176, ill. 7; compare the tort doctrine of abuse of process. Prosser & Keeton, Torts § 121 (5th ed. 1984).

43. First Nat'l Bank of Cincinnati v. Pepper, 454 F.2d 626 (2d Cir.1972) (attorney's retaining lien), second appeal 547 F.2d 708 (2d Cir.1976); Leeper v. Beltrami,

53 Cal.2d 195, 1 Cal.Rptr. 12, 347 P.2d 12, 77 A.L.R.2d 803 (1959) (threatened mortgage foreclosure); Kilpatrick v. Germania Life Ins. Co., 183 N.Y. 163, 75 N.E. 1124 (1905) (refusal of mortgagee to discharge a mortgage on tender by mortgagor).

44. See Annot., 18 A.L.R. 1233 (1922).

45. Murphy v. Brilliant Co., 323 Mass. 526, 83 N.E.2d 166 (1948); compare Hensel v. Cahill, 179 Pa.Super. 114, 116 A.2d 99 (1955). See Joannin v. Ogilvie, 49 Minn. 564, 52 N.W. 217, 16 L.R.A. 376 (1892).

"duress of goods"
duress /s attach! (foreclos! /s mortgag!)
duress /s "abuse of process"

---

§ 9–6.   Coerced Settlements or Contract Modifications

The doctrine of duress has tended to be compartmentalized into various categories: rules governing threats of imprisonment, duress of property, etc., often being treated as separate doctrines rather than separate manifestations of common legal principles. Threats to breach contracts have been deemed one such category and traditionally the general rule has been that a threat to breach a contract does not constitute duress,[46] except in coercive situations in which the threat is made by the government, a common carrier or a public utility.[47] Hackley v. Headley[48] has been regarded as a leading case. The defendant admittedly owed the plaintiff $4,260, and knowing that the plaintiff was in great need of money and could be financially ruined if he were not quickly paid, offered the plaintiff his note for $4,000 on a take it or sue me basis. The plaintiff took the note and signed a release demanded by the defendant. The court held that the release was not avoidable for duress. The courts are open to compel payment of debts, argued the court, and the fact that plaintiff was in dire financial straits and needed relief more quickly than could be supplied by the courts was not pressure supplied by the defendant.[49] Consequently, the inadequacy of the judicial remedy was due to subjective factors personal to the plaintiff.[50]

46. 2 Palmer on Restitution § 9.12; Dalzell, Duress by Economic Pressure I, 20 N.C.L.Rev. 237, 255–276 (1942).

47. Id. at 254–55. The government contract exception was based on the inadequacy of remedy against the government. Now that in most jurisdictions sovereign immunity no longer presents a significant barrier to actions against the government, a plea of duress is nonetheless available. The federal standards are restated in Loral Corp. v. United States, 193 Ct.Cl. 473, 434 F.2d 1328, 1332–1333 (1970); and Urban Plumbing & Heating Co. v. United States, 187 Ct.Cl. 15, 408 F.2d 382 (1969), certiorari denied 398 U.S. 958, 90 S.Ct. 2164, 26 L.Ed.2d 542 (1970); compare state standards stated in Pearlman v. State, 18 Misc. 2d 494, 191 N.Y.S.2d 422 (1959). The carrier and utility cases are based on the monopolistic position of the public service company. See Woodward, Quasi Contracts §§ 220–21 (1913).

48. 45 Mich. 569, 8 N.W. 511 (1881).

49. If the plaintiff had urgent need for cash, why did he accept the note? Presumably the note would be used as collateral security for a loan or, as was customary in the nineteenth century, discounted at a bank, or used as a medium of exchange. Promissory notes served many of the functions of money. See Lincoln Nat'l Bank of Lincoln, Ill. v. Perry, 14 C.C.A. 273, 66 F. 887, 894 (8th Cir.1895) ("as notes and bills are designed to circulate freely, and to take the place of money in commercial transaction."); see also Bakken, Contract Law in the Rockies, 1850–1912, 18 Am.J.Leg.Hist. 33, 41 (1974).

50. Compare Selmer Co. v. Blakeslee-Midwest Co., 704 F.2d 924 (7th Cir.1983) with Totem Marine Tug & Barge, Inc. v. Alyeska Pipeline Service Co., 584 P.2d 15, 9 A.L.R.4th 928 (Alaska 1978). See also Rich & Whillock, Inc. v. Ashton Development, Inc., 157 Cal.App.3d 1154, 204 Cal. Rptr. 86 (1984).

Two things should be noted. First, that the case is inconsistent with the subjective approach to duress which dominates the law today [51] and is squarely inconsistent with at least one recent persuasive case in which duress was deemed well pleaded where it was alleged that a liquidated obligation of $157,000 was released for $5,000 where money was immediately required to prevent foreclosure of a mortgage on the coerced party's house and repossession of his personal property.[52] Second, in both of the cases just described relief was available to the parties coerced under the doctrine of consideration.[53] The persistence of the pre-existing duty rule has relieved the pressure for expansion of the doctrine of duress to cases of threatened contractual breach. With, however, the decline of the doctrine of consideration under the U.C.C. and certain other statutes, and its deemphasis in the Restatement Second,[54] an additional impetus for the expansion of the duress doctrine into the threatened breach area has been given.[55] Thus, recent cases [56] have held that a threat to breach a contract constitutes duress if the threatened breach would, if carried out, result in irreparable injury

51. See § 9–2 supra. On the question of the pressure of circumstances taken advantage of by one party, see 13 Williston § 1608. If the wrongful pressure is exerted by a third party unbeknownst to the party benefiting from the pressure, duress will not generally be a defense. The party benefiting will normally be in the position of a bona fide purchaser for value. See 13 Williston § 1622A. Contra, Barry v. Equitable Life Assur. Soc., 59 N.Y. 587 (1875). See Restatement, Second, Contracts § 175(2).

52. Capps v. Georgia Pacific Corp., 253 Or. 248, 453 P.2d 935 (1969). On releases by employees, see Annot., 30 A.L.R.4th 294 (1984).

53. In subsequent litigation the release in Headley v. Hackley was held void for want of consideration. Headley v. Hackley, 50 Mich. 43, 14 N.W. 693 (1883). In Capps v. Georgia Pacific Corp., Justice Denecke, concurring specially, was of the opinion that the doctrine of duress was inapplicable but the release would be void for want of consideration if the facts were as alleged.

See generally, Note, Unbalanced Transactions under Common and Civil Law, 43 Colum.L.Rev. 1066 (1943) (focusing on consideration doctrine).

54. See § 4–9 supra.

55. See § 5–15 supra.

56. Thompson Crane & Trucking Co. v. Eyman, 123 Cal.App.2d 904, 267 P.2d 1043

(1954), 28 So.Cal.L.Rev. 317 (1955); Ross Systems v. Linden Dari-Delite, Inc., 35 N.J. 329, 173 A.2d 258 (1961) (refusal to pay overcharges would result in loss of source of supply); Austin Instrument, Inc. v. Loral Corp., 29 N.Y.2d 124, 324 N.Y.S.2d 22, 272 N.E.2d 533 (1971), reargument denied 29 N.Y.2d 749, 326 N.Y.S.2d 1027, 276 N.E.2d 238 (1971) (overcharges by sub-contractor where substitute components were unavailable on the market); compare New Again Construction Co. v. New York, 76 Misc.2d 943, 351 N.Y.S.2d 895 (1974) (purported release of claims without consideration under statute denied effect because of City's "bad faith"); Equity Funding Corp. v. Carol Management Corp., 66 Misc.2d 1020, 322 N.Y.S.2d 965 (1971), affirmed 37 A.D.2d 1047, 326 N.Y.S.2d 384 (1st Dep't 1971) (coerced increase in rent). The above cases, although classified as "threatened" breaches could be viewed as actual breaches by anticipatory repudiation (See ch. 12 infra). In Pecos Constr. Co. v. Mortgage Investment Co. of El Paso, 80 N.M. 680, 459 P.2d 842 (1969), plaintiff was awarded restitution for amounts paid because of duress plus damages for breach caused by delay between the time of defendant's unjustified demand and the time of the coerced settlement. See also, Gilbert Kobatake, Inc. v. Kaiser Hawaii-Kai Dev. Co., 56 Hawaii 39, 526 P.2d 1205 (1974); Wurtz v. Fleischman, 97 Wis.2d 100, 293 N.W.2d 155, 12 A.L.R.4th 1254 (1980).

because of the absence of an adequate legal or equitable remedy [57] or other reasonable alternative.[58]

Not every threatened breach, however, will justify a finding of duress even if these criteria are met. According to the Restatement of Contracts Second, § 176(1)(d), the threatened breach must be a "breach of the duty of good faith and fair dealing." The Restatement Second follows the U.C.C. in this respect. Although the U.C.C. permits modifications and releases without consideration, it requires that a request for a modification or release be made in good faith. The Restatement Second gives this illustration,[59] which conceals as many problems as it clarifies:

> *A* contracts to excavate a cellar for *B* at a stated price. *A* unexpectedly encounters solid rock and threatens not to finish the excavation unless *B* modifies the contract to state a new price that is reasonable but is nine times the original price. *B*, having no reasonable alternative, is induced by *A*'s threat to make the modification by a signed writing that is enforceable by statute without consideration. *A*'s threat is not a breach of his duty of good faith and fair dealing, and the modification is not voidable by *B*. See Illustration 1 to § 89.

If we assume that nine times the original price meets only *A*'s costs and a reasonable profit, we might conclude that *A* is not unjustly enriched. We are, however, told nothing about *B*'s situation. Suppose *B* is a general contractor working under a fixed price contract with *C*. The illustration makes it clear that the modification is induced by coercion. Unless *C* is willing to modify the contract price upward with *B*, the coercion has resulted in *B*'s unjust impoverishment. If he cannot get relief under the doctrine of duress, can he not get protection under the doctrine of unconscionability? As indicated earlier, there have been two different vantage points from which the doctrine of duress has been analyzed: (1) unjust enrichment and (2) policing the bargaining process.[60] The Restatement Second has concentrated on the first,[61] while some commentators focus on the second,[62] as does a leading

---

57. On what constitutes an adequate remedy in this context, see Dalzell, Duress by Economic Pressure II, 20 N.C.L.Rev. 341, 367–382 (1942).

58. For example, retaining another contractor. Tri-State Roofing Co. of Uniontown v. Simon, 187 Pa.Super. 17, 142 A.2d 333 (1958).

59. Restatement, Second, Contracts § 176, ill. 8.

60. See § 9–2 supra.

61. As has its reporter. See Farnsworth, Coercion in Contract Law, 5 U.Ark. Little Rock L.J. 329 (1982).

62. Brody, Performance of a Pre-Existing Contractual Duty as Consideration, 52 Denv.L.J. 433 (1975); Hillman, Contract Modification Under the Restatement (Second) of Contracts, 67 Cornell L.Rev. 680 (1982); Hillman, A Study of Uniform Commercial Code Methodology: Contract Modification Under Article Two, 59 N.C.L.Rev. 335 (1981); Hillman, Policing Contract Modifications Under the U.C.C.: Good Faith and the Doctrine of Economic Duress, 64 Iowa L.Rev. 849 (1979); Mather, Contract Modification Under Duress, 33 S.Car.L.Rev. 615 (1982); Compare Robison, Enforcing Extorted Contract Modifications, 68 Iowa L.Rev. 699 (1983).

case under the U.C.C. which holds that coercive conduct itself is bad faith, unless it is justified by the contract.[63]

Under the U.C.C. the party who is subjected to coercion has an additional vehicle for setting aside a coerced modification or settlement. He may agree, at the same time indicating that his agreement is under protest. If he does this, he has preserved his rights.[64] It is obvious, however, that there will be occasions when the coercing party will insist that the protest be withdrawn. Under such circumstances a withdrawn protest should act as a protest. Outside of the Code, protest is merely some evidence of duress.[65]

There are conflicting policies at work in this area. Modifications and settlements are encouraged. Such transactions will be discouraged, however, if they are easily upset. At the same time coercion, unjust enrichment and unjust impoverishment are not favorites of the law. Neither the U.C.C. nor the Restatement Second offer much guidance on how to reconcile these policies. The courts are likely to continue to balance the competing concerns in arriving at decisions in concrete cases.

 WESTLAW REFERENCES

duress /s "public utility"

"doctrine of duress"

threat! /s breach! /s agreement contract*** /s duress

95k95(3) /p duress

duress /s "irreparabl! injur!"

duress /s "economic pressure"

duress /s inadequa! /s remedy

agreement contract*** /s duress /s settl! /s coerc!

agreement contract*** /s coerc! duress /s modif!

"economic duress" /s "good faith" modif!

u.c.c. "uniform commercial code" /s 1–207

331k18

§ 9–7. Business Compulsion

There has been a tendency to categorize cases involving threatened contract breaches and other forms of economic pressure as something other than duress; to restrict duress to its nineteenth century categories of duress to person and property and to group the more modern problems under a separate heading of "business compulsion."[66] There is little justification for this tendency and it has not been accepted by the two in-depth scholarly analyses of this area.[67] Rather, cases recog-

---

63. Roth Steel Products v. Sharon Steel Corp., 705 F.2d 134 (6th Cir.1983).

64. U.C.C. § 1–207.

65. 2 Palmer on Restitution § 9.17.

66. E.g., Ramp Buildings Corp. v. Northwest Building Co., 164 Wash. 603, 4 P.2d 507, 79 A.L.R. 651 (1931).

67. Dalzell, Duress by Economic Pressure I, II, 20 N.C.L.Rev. 237, 341 (1942); Dawson, Economic Duress—An Essay in Perspective, 45 Mich.L.Rev. 253 (1947); see also 25 Am.Jur.2d, Duress & Undue Influence § 6 (1966).

nizing business compulsion as grounds for setting aside a transaction have adapted the principles of duress and have modernized them but have created no separate doctrine.

 WESTLAW REFERENCES

di("business compulsion")

"economic pressure" /s breach!

"set aside" /s "business compulsion" (economic +1 duress pressure)

§ 9–8. Remedies for Duress

Normally, duress renders a transaction voidable at the election of the coerced party.[68] In highly unusual situations it would render the transaction void. These situations involve the absence of consent rather than coerced consent, as where a party is made to sign an instrument at gun point without knowledge of its contents.[69] In the usual case where the duress produces coerced consent, the coerced party is deemed to ratify the voidable transaction if after the coercion is removed he recognizes its validity by acting upon it, accepting benefits under it or merely fails to act to avoid it with reasonable promptness.[70] Where, however, the initial coercion continues for a period of time, it has been held that the wrong is a continuing one and the statute of limitations does not commence to run until the coercion ceases.[71]

Normally, the remedy for duress is in the nature of a quasi-contractual action for money had and received. Because the principal economic function of duress has been to redress unjust enrichment, the normal recovery is the amount paid to the party to the extent the payment exceeds what was fairly owed.[72] However, in a good number of cases the plaintiff has not parted with money but with property or services. In such cases he may recover the market value of the property or services with an offset for any money received.[73] Alternatively, he may be able to invoke the equity arm of the court to assert a constructive trust or equitable lien on the property handed over or an equitable lien upon the property his services have benefited.[74] Indeed,

68. Restatement, Contracts § 496; 13 Williston §§ 1624, 1627; cf. Lanham, Duress and Void Contracts, 29 Modern L.Rev. 615 (1966). On the availability of reformation as a remedy for duress, see § 9–35 infra.

69. Restatement, Contracts § 495; Restatement, Second, Contracts § 174; 13 Williston § 1624.

70. Gallon v. Lloyd-Thomas Co., 264 F.2d 821, 77 A.L.R.2d 417 (8th Cir.1959); see Williston § 1627. Also, where the transaction is merely voidable, the party who obtains property by duress can transfer good title to a bona fide purchaser for value. See note 51 supra.

71. Pierce v. Haverlah's Estate, 428 S.W.2d 422 (Tex.Civ.App.1968), rehearing denied. On the question of which statute of limitations is applicable, see Annot., 77 A.L.R.2d 821 (1961).

72. First National Bank of Cincinnati v. Pepper, supra note 43; Jamestown Farmers Elevator, Inc. v. General Mills, Inc., supra note 31; Dawson, supra note 67, at 283–285 (1947); Restatement, Restitution § 150.

73. Restatement, Restitution §§ 151–152.

74. Restatement, Restitution § 51, Comment g; § 152, Comment a.

the aid of equity may be essential to cancel a deed of record or other instrument.[75]

Professor Woodward has made a persuasive argument that, as in the case of fraud, the plaintiff who has a restitutionary action based on duress ought to be able to elect instead to bring a tort action.[76] In particular cases this could be highly advantageous.[77] Yet, the tort of duress has been recognized only in "odd cases,"[78] and cases in which counsel argued for such a doctrine also appear to be very rare.[79] To be distinguished of course are cases where the coercion itself involves a battery, false imprisonment or other traditional tort. In such cases, a tort action, in addition to an action to recover back what one has parted with, lies.[80]

Duress may be raised by way of an affirmative defense to an action on the executory portion of the agreement.[81] If the action brought is for specific performance, less coercion and oppression is required to sustain a defense than in a case seeking relief at law.[82] This stems from the discretionary nature of the remedy of specific performance.[83] If the instrument executed under duress is a release or its equivalent, duress may be raised by way of reply in a case where the coerced party brings an action on the underlying claim and the release is raised by defense.[84]

75. See 1 Pomeroy, Equity Jurisprudence §§ 110, 171 (1918); 2 id. § 950.

76. Woodward, The Law of Quasi Contracts § 211 (1913); see also Note, Economic Duress After the Demise of Free Will Theory: A Proposed Tort Analysis, 53 Iowa L.Rev. 892 (1968).

77. Outlined in Note, Duress as a Tort, 39 Harv.L.Rev. 108 (1925).

78. Prosser & Keeton, Torts 121 (5th ed. 1984); see also Dawson, Economic Duress—An Essay in Perspective, 45 Mich.L. Rev. 253, 285 n. 80; Note, Economic Duress After the Demise of Free Will Theory: A Proposed Tort Analysis, 53 Iowa L.Rev. 892, 901 n. 57; Note, Restitution—Duress—The Law in Oregon, 38 Or.L.Rev. 246, 257–258 (1959). In addition to the cases cited by these sources, the tortious nature of duress may be induced from those cases holding that in addition to restitution the plaintiff may recover punitive damages. Edquest v. Tripp & Dragstedt Co., 93 Mont. 446, 19 P.2d 637 (1933); Adams v. Crater Well Drilling, Inc., supra note 24; Southwestern Gas & Elec. Co. v. Stanley, 123 Tex. 157, 70 S.W.2d 413 (1934).

79. The argument was made unsuccessfully in Davis v. Hargett, 244 N.C. 157, 92 S.E.2d 782, 58 A.L.R.2d 494 (1956).

80. Prosser & Keeton, Torts 121 (5th ed. 1984).

81. Austin Instrument, Inc. v. Loral Corp., 29 N.Y.2d 124, 324 N.Y.S.2d 22, 272 N.E.2d 533 (1971), reargument denied 29 N.Y.2d 749, 326 N.Y.S.2d 1027, 276 N.E.2d 328 (1971); Great American Indem. Co. v. Berryessa, 122 Utah 243, 248 P.2d 367 (1952) (burden of proof of this affirmative defense on the defendant.)

82. Scheinberg v. Scheinberg, 249 N.Y. 277, 164 N.E. 98 (1928), motion granted, 250 N.Y. 538, 166 N.E. 315 (1929), reargument denied 250 N.Y. 540, 166 N.E. 316 (1929).

83. See § 16–7 infra.

84. Wise v. Midtown Motors, 231 Minn. 46, 42 N.W.2d 404, 20 A.L.R.2d 735 (1950); Fleming v. Ponziani, 24 N.Y.2d 105, 299 N.Y.S.2d 134, 247 N.E.2d 114 (1969) (useful discussion of burden of proof in such a case). Similarly, duress may be raised by way of estopping the defendant from asserting other affirmative defenses. Bayshore Industries, Inc. v. Ziats, 232 Md. 167, 192 A.2d 487 (1963) (employee failed to file timely workmen's compensation claims because of employer's threats).

WESTLAW REFERENCES

duress /s elect*** /s void!

duress /s agreement contract*** /s void!

duress /s contract*** agreement /s ratif!

95k97(2) /p duress coerc!

duress coerc! /s "statute of limitation" /s continu!

duress coerc! /s "quasi contract***"

agreement contract*** /s duress coerc! /s recover! /s money "market value"

duress coerc! /s "measure of recovery"

390k91 /p duress coerc!

duress coerc! /s "equitable lien"

duress coerc! /s cancel! /s deed instrument

120k71

duress /s tort

duress /s affirmative! +1 defens! defend! /s execut! agreement contract***

C. UNDUE INFLUENCE

Table of Sections

§ 9–9. Background of Undue Influence

Undue influence is a concept originated by courts of equity as a ground for setting aside transactions that have been imposed by a dominant party upon a subservient party.[85] In the nineteenth century the concept was expanded to allow relief on grounds akin to duress but which failed to come within the rigid Blackstonian concept of duress as employed in courts of common law. As stated in one case: "Undue influence * * * is 'any improper or wrongful constraint, machination, or urgency of persuasion, whereby the will of a person is overpowered, and he is induced to do or forbear an act which he would not do, or would do if left to act freely'." [86]

When at the turn of the twentieth century, the common law doctrine of duress was expanded to provide relief for coercion irrespective of the means of coercion,[87] much of the work of undue influence

---

85. Early cases are cited by Dawson, supra note 67, at 262 (1947).

86. Smith v. Henline, 174 Ill. 184, 203, 51 N.E. 227, 233 (1898). 2 Pomeroy, A Treatise on Equity Jurisprudence § 951 (4th ed. 1918); see also 1 Story, Commenta-

ries on Equity Jurisprudence § 239 (13th ed. 1886).

87. The turning point appears to have been Holmes' opinion in Silsbee v. Webber, 171 Mass. 378, 50 N.E. 555 (1898).

became unnecessary. The doctrine has a much more specialized role today, although often enough the precedents decided when the more general doctrine prevailed are cited and quoted to the general confusion of the profession.[88] Today the gist of the doctrine is unfair persuasion rather than coercion. Euphoria rather than fear is often, but certainly not always, the state of mind of the party unduly influenced.[89]

 WESTLAW REFERENCES
di undue influence

"undue influence" /s "court of equity" "equitable relief"

"undue influence" /s dominan! /s subservien!

"undue influence" /s "unfair! persua!"

§ 9–10. Elements of Undue Influence

There are two broad classes of undue influence cases. In the first, one party uses his dominant psychologic position in an unfair manner to induce the subservient party to consent to an agreement to which he would not otherwise have consented.[90] The doctrine requires neither threats nor deception although often enough one or the other is present. In the second, one uses his position of trust and confidence, rather than dominance, to unfairly persuade the other into a transaction.[91] Very often the line between these two categories is blurred, as when the dominant party dominates by virtue of the trust and confidence, rather than the subservience, he has engendered. The rules are elusive. The primary problem is to attempt to describe what is meant by "unfair" persuasion. Most statements of the problem focus on the means of persuasion, but Professor Dawson has indicated that the key is perhaps not the means, but the results.[92] The foremost indicator of undue influence is an unnatural transaction resulting in the enrichment of one of the parties at the expense of the other.

By far the majority of undue influence cases arise after the death of the person alleged to have been unduly importuned. Typically, disappointed relatives seek to set aside a will or inter vivos transfer. Since unfair persuasion normally takes place in privacy, its proof must normally be made by circumstantial evidence. Evidence of four elements are sufficient to make out a prima facie circumstantial case of

---

88. See note, 22 Baylor L.Rev. 572 (1970).

89. For a psychological study of undue influence, see Shaffer, Undue Influence, Confidential Relationship, and the Psychology of Transference, 45 Notre Dame Law. 197 (1970).

90. Restatement, Contracts § 497; see e.g., In re Kaufmann's Will, 20 A.D.2d 464, 247 N.Y.S.2d 664 (1964), affirmed 15 N.Y.2d 825, 257 N.Y.S.2d 941, 205 N.E.2d 864 (1965).

91. Restatement, Contracts § 497; Restatement, Second, Contracts § 177, Comment a; see e.g., Schroeder v. Ely, 161 Neb. 252, 73 N.W.2d 165 (1955) (unfairness in not revealing facts to friend who trusted implicitly). Cases such as this are often treated under fraudulent non-disclosure rather than undue influence. See § 9–20 infra.

92. Dawson, supra note 67, at 264; compare the discussion with respect to the mentally infirm § 8–15 supra.

undue influence.[93] First, facts showing the susceptibility of the party influenced. Mental and physical weakness and psychological dependency go to show susceptibility. Second, there must be evidence of the opportunity to exercise undue influence. The existence of a confidential relationship such as husband-wife, parent-child, trustee-beneficiary, guardian-ward, attorney-client, administrator-legatee, physician-patient, pastor-parishioner, or fiance-fiancee is strong evidence of such an opportunity.[94] Third, there must be evidence of a disposition to exercise undue influence. Such a disposition may be shown by evidence that the alleged influencer took the initiative in the transaction. An additional factual element stressed in many of the cases is whether the influenced party had reasonable access to independent advice.[95] Fourth, evidence of the unnatural nature of the transaction may take the form of evidence of inadequacy of consideration or neglect of the natural objects of the transferor's or testator's bounty.

A prima facie case of undue influence can be rebutted by evidence of the fairness of the transaction.[96]

Many cases ease the proof requirements even further. Upon proof of the existence of a confidential relationship and of a transaction benefiting the person in whom trust and confidence is reposed, the burden of proof is placed upon the party benefited to show that the transaction was not procured by undue influence.[97] The decision is preeminently one of fact and rarely is the finding of the trial court reversed.[98]

WESTLAW REFERENCES
"undue influence" /s psycholog!
"undue influence" /s induc! /s party
"undue influence" /s consent!

93. For extensive discussion, see Note, Undue Influence in Intervivos Transactions, 41 Colum.L.Rev. 707, 717–23 (1941); Note, Undue Influence—Judicial Implementation of Social Policy, 1968 Wis.L.Rev. 569, 571–585; Contra, Blackmer v. Blackmer, 165 Mont. 69, 525 P.2d 559 (1974), 37 Mont.L.Rev. 250 (1976).

94. These relationships are itemized, with citations, in Note, 49 Notre Dame Law. 631, 632 (1974).

95. 13 Williston § 1625; 2 Black, Rescission of Contracts and Cancellation of Written Instruments § 244 (2d ed. 1929) [hereinafter Black].

96. Kase v. French, 325 N.W.2d 678 (S.D.1982); Simmons v. Foster, 622 S.W.2d 838 (Tenn.App.1981).

97. Francois v. Francois, 599 F.2d 1286 (3d Cir.1979), certiorari denied 444 U.S. 1021, 100 S.Ct. 679, 62 L.Ed.2d 653 (1980); McCollough v. Rogers, 431 So.2d 1246 (Ala. 1983); Lipson v. Lipson, 183 So.2d 900

(Miss.1966), 38 Miss.L.J. 156 (1966); Ruggieri v. West Forum Corp., 444 Pa. 175, 282 A.2d 304 (1971). Frequently it is unclear whether the court is laying down a rule concerning the burden of proof in the sense of burden of persuasion or the burden of going forward with the evidence. Dobbs, Remedies 676–77 (1973). For a sophisticated discussion, see In re Wood's Estate, 374 Mich. 278, 132 N.W.2d 35, 5 A.L.R.3d 1 (1965); see also, Note, 41 Colum.L.Rev. 707, 711–16 (1941); Note, The Presumption of Undue Influence, 17 U.N. Brunswick L.J. 46 (1967). Under the rule shifting the burden of proof, it is not surprising that frequently the main trial battle concerns whether there is a confidential relation. See, e.g., Clyde v. Hodge, 460 F.2d 532 (3d Cir.1972); Woodbury v. Pfliiger, 309 N.W.2d 104 (N.D.1981).

98. E.g., Robert O. v. Ecmel A., 460 A.2d 1321 (Del.1983); Kase v. French, supra note 96; For a statistical sampling in one state, see Note, 1968 Wis.L.Rev. 569.

```
95k96
"undue influence"    /s   fiduciary   /s   transact!
"undue influence"    /s   "trust and confidence"
"undue influence"    /s   unfair!
"undue influence"    /s   "prima facie"
"undue influence"    /s   "set aside"   /s   will transfer!
120k211(4)
"undue influence"    /s   weak! susceptib! dependen!   /s   party
di "undue influence"   /p   "confidential relationship")
"undue influence"    /s   "independent advice"
"undue influence"    /s   "burden of proof"
"undue influence"    /s   "question of fact"
```

§ 9–11.   Undue Influence in the Absence of a Confidential Relationship

Although there has been no stated requirement that there be a confidential relationship between the parties, the overwhelming bulk of twentieth century cases on the subject in which a finding of undue influence was made and upheld [99] have involved such relationships. In a significant California case undue influence was found where no such relationship existed.[1] The transaction in question was the resignation of a school teacher who had been arrested on charges, later dismissed, of homosexual activity. After forty hours without sleep and soon after his release on bail he was visited by school officials who persuaded him that it was in his best interests to resign. The resignation was set aside by the court with the statement: "The difference between legitimate persuasion and excessive pressure, like the difference between seduction and rape, rests to a considerable extent in the manner in which the parties go about their business."[2] The court in the following language lays down criteria for determining the distinction:

"However, overpersuasion is generally accomplished by certain characteristics which tend to create a pattern. The pattern usually involves several of the following elements: (1) discussion of the transaction at an unusual or inappropriate time, (2) consummation of the transaction in an unusual place, (3) insistent demand that the business be finished at once, (4) extreme emphasis on untoward consequences of delay, (5) the use of multiple persuaders by the dominant side against a single servient party, (6) absence of third-party advisers to the servient party, (7) statements that there is no time to consult financial advisers or attorneys. If a number of these elements are simultaneously present, the persuasion may be characterized as excessive."[3]

99. See 49 Notre Dame Law. 631, 632–33.

1. Odorizzi v. Bloomfield School District, 246 Cal.App.2d 123, 54 Cal.Rptr. 533 (1966).

2. Id. at 134, 54 Cal.Rptr. at 542.

3. Id. at 133, 54 Cal.Rptr. at 541. Further application of these criteria is the subject of the Note, 49 Notre Dame Law. 631 (1974). See also Methodist Mission

§ 9–12. Remedies for Undue Influence

We know of no case in which undue influence has been deemed to constitute a tort. The doctrine originated in equity and the remedy given was cancellation of any instrument contaminated by undue influence, avoidance of the transaction and restoration of the status quo ante.[4] In a jurisdiction where law and equity have been merged and all that is sought is a money judgment, a quasi-contractual action may be brought at law.[5]

Undue influence may be raised as an affirmative defense if the transaction sought to be enforced was the alleged product of unfair persuasion. If the relief sought is specific performance, the defense of undue influence can be successful even if the unfair persuasion would not have been sufficient to set aside an executed transaction.[6] As is the case with voidable transactions generally, the party having the power to avoid the transaction may be deemed to have elected to affirm the transaction unless he disaffirms it within a reasonable time after he is free from the wrongful persuader and has knowledge of the essential facts.[7]

D. MISREPRESENTATION AND NON–DISCLOSURE

Table of Sections

Home of Tex. v. N___ A___ B___, 451 S.W.2d 539 (Tex.Civ.App.1970).

4. This may be done through the device of a constructive trust, an equitable lien or an accounting. See Dobbs, Remedies 673 (1973); see also 2 Black § 239. Punitive damages were awarded in Kennedy v. Thomsen, 320 N.W.2d 657 (Iowa App.1982).

5. Woodbury v. Woodbury, 141 Mass. 329, 5 N.E. 275 (1886); Eldridge v. May, 129 Me. 112, 150 A. 378 (1930).

6. This stems from the discretionary nature of the remedy of specific performance. Scheinberg v. Scheinberg, 249 N.Y. 277, 164 N.E. 98 (1928). See § 16–7 infra.

7. 3 Black §§ 610–615; Restatement, Restitution § 70, Comment a.

§ 9–13. Elements of Misrepresentation

Whenever a party has fraudulently induced another to enter into a transaction under circumstances giving the latter the right to bring a tort action for deceit, the deceived party may instead elect to avoid the transaction and claim restitution.[8] The converse, however, is not true. There are many instances when a transaction may be avoided for misrepresentation or non-disclosure despite the fact that a tort action for fraud would not lie. Tortious fraud—the action of deceit—involves five elements, each of them, although tersely stated, is quite complex: (1) representation, (2) falsity, (3) scienter, (4) deception, and (5) injury.[9] It is not the province of this book to examine the tort law of fraud [10] but reference will be made to these elements as they relate to the remedy of restitution. Inasmuch as this remedy is designed merely to restore the situation that existed prior to the transaction, it is not surprising that the requisites necessary to make out a case are far less demanding than those necessary to make out a tort action.[11]

 WESTLAW REFERENCES
95k96
"undue influence" /s fiduciary /s transact!

§ 9–14. Knowledge of Falsity and Materiality of the Misrepresentation

Where the representation is made with the knowledge of its falsity, with an intent to deceive and that it shall be acted upon in a certain

---

8. Pursuant to certain statutes no election is necessary and both remedies may be pursued. See § 9–23 infra. On some occasions the remedy of reformation is available. See § 9–25 infra. On rare occasions the transaction is void and avoidance is not needed. See § 9–22 infra.

9. Reno v. Bull, 226 N.Y. 546, 124 N.E. 144 (1919); see Prosser & Keeton, Torts 727–29 (5th ed. 1984).

10. In addition to Prosser & Keeton supra note 9, see generally James & Gray, Misrepresentation, Part I, 37 Md.L.Rev.

286 (1977) and id. Part II, 37 Md.L.Rev. 488 (1978).

11. A number of jurisdictions use the out of pocket rule to measure damages for deceit. That rule is an essentially restitutionary measure of damages designed to restore the status quo ante rather than to compensate for loss of bargain. See ch. 14 infra. Even in such jurisdictions however, consequential damages are frequently awarded. Such damages are generally not available in an action for restitution.

way, the scienter element of tort liability is made out. Less rigorous tests are employed in some contexts and tort liability for negligent and even innocent misrepresentation is not unknown. In tort law the question is quite complex,[12] but it has long been the rule in equity that avoidance and restitution are available for a negligent and even an innocent misrepresentation [13] and the same rule now prevails in quasi-contractual actions for restitution at law.[14] There is perhaps one qualification in some jurisdictions. A few scattered cases have followed the English view that avoidance for nonfraudulent misrepresentation will not be available if the contract is fully performed on both sides.[15] In England, this view has been overturned by statute.[16]

There is one distinction frequently made between intentional and unintentional misrepresentation. The distinction relates to materiality. For avoidance to be available for an unintentional misrepresentation it is usually held that the fact misrepresented must be material.[17] Materiality exists whenever the misrepresentation would be likely to affect the conduct of a reasonable man or if "the maker of the representation knows that the recipient is likely to regard the fact as important although a reasonable man would not." [18] This objective requisite is to be contrasted with the subjective test employed in cases of duress.[19] Where the misrepresentation is intentional, however, a subjective test is employed and avoidance is available even if the fact represented is immaterial,[20] because in this last case the wrongdoer has accomplished his intended purpose, whereas one who innocently mis-

12. See Prosser & Keeton, supra note 9, at 748–49; Keeton, Fraud: The Necessity for an Intent to Deceive, 5 UCLA L.Rev. 583 (1958). Prosser's analysis of innocent misrepresentation as a tort is severely criticized in Hill, Breach of Contract as a Tort, 74 Colum.L.Rev. 40 (1974).

13. Smith v. Richards, 38 U.S. (13 Pet.) 26, 10 L.Ed. 42 (1839); 1 Story, Commentaries on Equity Jurisprudence § 193 (13th ed. 1866); 1 Black §§ 102, 106; 2 Parsons, The Law of Contracts * 786 (6th ed. 1873).

14. Seneca Wire & Mfg. Co. v. A.B. Leach & Co., 247 N.Y. 1, 159 N.E. 700 (1928); Restatement, Second, Contracts § 164, Comment b; see 12 Williston § 1500. The rule is criticized as unduly harmful to the security of transactions in Keeton, Actionable Misrepresentation: Legal Fault as a Requirement, II. Rescission, 2 Okla.L.Rev. 56 (1949); but see Prosser & Keeton, supra note 9, at 729–33; 1 Palmer on Restitution § 3.19.

15. E.g., Thompson v. Jackson, 24 Va. (3 Rand.) 504, 15 Am.Dec. 721 (1825). Such decisions stem from the general idea that equity will deny specific performance more readily than it will award restitution.

16. Misrepresentation Act of 1967 § 7(b); see Cheshire, Fifoot & Furmston, The Law of Contract 267–68 (1972).

17. Restatement, Second, Contracts § 164(2) and Comment b; Restatement, Restitution § 9(2). Materiality is also required for a tort action. Restatement, Torts § 538(1) and Comment g.

18. Restatement, Torts § 538(2)(b). Accord, Restatement, Second, Contracts § 162(2).

19. See § 9–2 supra. A subjective test is stated in 2 Parsons on Contracts *769–70 (6th ed. 1873) ("if the fraud be such, that, had it not been practiced, the contract would not have been made, or the transaction completed, then it is material to it.") Parsons makes no distinction for this purpose between intentional and unintentional misrepresentations. This test has been quoted or paraphrased in many cases.

20. Restatement, Second, Contracts § 162(1); Restatement, Restitution § 9, Comment b; 12 Williston § 1490. On what constitutes an intentional misrepresentation, see Restatement, Second, Contracts § 162 and Comment b.

states an unimportant fact has no reason to know that his statement will cause action.[21]

WESTLAW REFERENCES
misrepresent! /s ''knowledge of its falsity''
tort /s scienter
di(avoid! /p misrepresentation /s agreement contract***)
restitution /s misrepresentation
unintentional! /s avoid! /s misrepresent!
intentional! /s avoid! /s misrepresent!

§ 9–15. Deception and Reliance

Before relief for misrepresentation may be awarded, causation must be shown. It must be proved that the party was in fact deceived by the misrepresentation and relied upon it in entering into the transaction.[22] Obviously, if the party to whom a falsehood is addressed, does not believe it, he cannot later use the falsehood as a ground for avoidance.[23] There has been no deception. A rebuttable presumption of deception and reliance arises if the misrepresentation is material.[24]

There are two main problems in the area of reliance: (1) Did the person deceived have a right to rely? (2) Did he in fact rely? On the question of one's right to rely upon the representation of another, in the absence of a confidential relationship, the nineteenth and earlier twentieth century cases were quite strict. Many cases took the position that it was the duty of every person to take notice of obvious facts and to investigate the truth of representations.[25] The credulous were deemed to have invited their own misfortunes. Although there were many qualifications of the rule [26] there were frequent harsh applications. But the tide turned. The Vermont Court proclaimed that "the law will afford relief even to the simple and credulous who have been duped by art and falsehood." [27] The same court stated, "no rogue should enjoy his ill-gotten plunder for the simple reason that his victim is by chance a fool." [28]

As Vermont went, so has gone the nation. It is the exceptional case today where, especially in the face of an intentional misrepresentation,[29] relief will be denied on the ground of the undue credulity or

21. Restatement, Second, Contracts § 162, Comment c.

22. Restatement, Second, Contracts § 167; 12 Williston §§ 1515–1515C; 1 Black, §§ 109–111.

23. Woodtek, Inc. v. Musulin, 263 Or. 644, 503 P.2d 677 (1972) (some officers of plaintiff were aware of misstatements); Lundy v. Palmetto State Life Ins. Co., 256 S.C. 506, 183 S.E.2d 335 (1971); Pennybacker v. Laidley, 33 W.Va. 624, 11 S.E. 39 (1890).

24. Restatement, Contracts § 479; cf. Restatement, Second, Contracts § 107, Comment b.

25. 1 Black § 113.

26. Id. §§ 118–120, 122–125.

27. Kendall v. Wilson, 41 Vt. 567, 571 (1869).

28. Chamberlin v. Fuller, 59 Vt. 247, 9 A. 832, 836 (1887).

29. Investors Equity Exchange, Inc. v. Whiteley, 269 Or. 309, 524 P.2d 1211 (1974); Black § 124; Restatement, Second,

negligence of the defrauded party.[30]   It has been suggested that the nineteenth century attitude is particularly relaxed where the relief sought is restitution rather than tort damages.[31]   On the other hand, the old approach is often reasserted,[32] but seemingly with little consistency.[33]   One frequently receives the impression that when the old rule is applied, the court is covertly acting upon its conviction that the trier of fact erred in its finding of reliance.[34]

On the issue of whether the party did in fact rely upon representation, it would appear that the question is preeminently a question of fact.   Normally it is so treated.   But where the party receiving the representation in fact made his own investigation, many courts have ruled that, as a matter of law, there is no reliance.[35]

WESTLAW REFERENCES

di(misrepresent! /p cause /p rely! reliance relied)

fraud! /s "right to rely"

di(fraud! /p duty /p investigat!)

schupp +s "davey tree"

fraud! misrepresent! /s dup***

§ 9–16. Injury

A necessary element of the tort of deceit is pecuniary injury.   In the nineteenth century leading text writers appear to have uncritically cited tort cases for the proposition that injury was an element of the power to avoid a contract for fraud.[36]   The courts followed, and in the late nineteenth and early twentieth centuries a large number of courts stated their agreement.[37]   Yet, the statement of the rule was often so

Contracts § 164, Comment b, § 169(c), § 172.

30. See 12 Williston § 1515B; Schupp v. Davey Tree Expert Co., 235 Mich. 268, 209 N.W. 85 (1926).

31. Dobbs, Remedies 620 (1973).

32. Danann Realty Corp. v. Harris, 5 N.Y.2d 317, 184 N.Y.S.2d 599, 157 N.E.2d 597 (1959); Gladstone Hotel, Inc. v. Smith, 487 P.2d 329 (Wyo.1971).

33. Compare with the prior note, Weaver Organization, Inc. v. Manette, 41 A.D.2d 138, 341 N.Y.S.2d 631 (1st Dep't 1973), order modified 34 N.Y.2d 923, 359 N.Y.S.2d 552; 316 N.E.2d 869 (1974). "The older rule that the buyer is generally required to make an independent inspection or investigation wherever possible and is put upon notice of and bound by any knowledge that a reasonable inspection or investigation would have revealed * * * has been cast aside in favor of a more elastic requirement of inspection and investigation which has been altered, reshaped, and somewhat distorted from year to year and case to

case." (footnotes omitted). Comment, 3 Willamette L.J. 183, 184 (1965). For an attempt to rationalize the cases in terms of "the implied rules of the business game" and "community-wide assumptions in connection with business practices," see Harper & McNeely, A Synthesis of the Law of Misrepresentation, 32 Minn.L.Rev. 939, 1006–07 (1938). The Restatement, Second, Contracts § 172 makes the inquiry turn upon whether the person duped failed "to act in good faith and in accordance with reasonable standards of fair dealing".

34. For additional comments, see § 9–24 infra.

35. McCormick & Co. v. Childers, 468 F.2d 757 (4th Cir.1972); but see Fisher v. Mr. Harold's Hair Lab, Inc., 215 Kan. 515, 527 P.2d 1026 (1974); but see Restatement, Second, Contracts § 167, ill. 1.

36. McCleary, Damage as Requisite to Rescission for Misrepresentation, 36 Mich. L.Rev. 1, 20–23 (1937).

37. Id. at 17.

qualified as almost to eradicate the requirement. A frequently cited case stated that whenever misrepresentation is material, damage will be presumed.[38] Such holdings, which in essence cancel out the requirement, lead to the Restatement rule that it is not relevant whether damage was caused.[39] The Restatement undoubtedly goes a little further than the cases. An in depth analysis has shown that the cases can readily be divided into three categories: [40] (1) the defrauded party obtains what he bargains for but because of the misrepresentation it is worth less than he had reason to expect; (2) the defrauded party obtains something substantially different from what he was led to expect; (3) the defrauded party obtains what he expected and it is as valuable as he was led to expect. In the first two classes the defrauded party has been deprived of his reasonable expectations and this is sufficient harm upon which to base an avoidance.[41] In the last case, the court may find that the social interest in the security of transactions outweighs any social interest in redress for the trick played upon the defrauded party.[42] Another court may balance the scales differently.[43] Certain recurring situations have frequently been passed upon. Where a person knowing that another will not deal with him, misrepresents his identity or acts through an undisclosed agent, most courts have been willing to set aside the transaction even if a fair exchange has been agreed upon.[44] On the other hand, where the misrepresentation causes the other to perform a legal duty, or to sign a promissory note for a preexisting debt, the equities are weighed differently and the transaction cannot be avoided.[45]

 WESTLAW REFERENCES

"pecuniary injury" /s fraud! misrepresent! deceit

184k25

38. Stewart v. Lester, 49 Hun. 58, 1 N.Y.S. 699 (1888).

39. Restatement, Contracts § 476, Comment c; Restatement, Second, Contracts § 164, Comment c; § 165. Gross v. State Cooperage Export Crating & Shipping Co., 32 A.D.2d 540, 299 N.Y.S.2d 773 (2d Dep't 1969).

40. McCleary, Damage as Requisite to Rescission for Misrepresentation II, 36 Mich.L.Rev. 227 (1937).

41. Id. at 258; Kelsey v. Nagy, 410 N.E. 2d 1333 (Ind.App.1980).

42. See the curious case of Mott v. Tri-Continental Financial Corp., 330 F.2d 468 (2d Cir.1964) (avoidance would be futile where defrauded party has sold at no loss what he has received). This case may also illustrate a proposition that rescission will be denied where the remedy would be of no practical value. McCleary, Damages as Requisite to Rescission for Misrepresentation II, 36 Mich.L.Rev. 227, 251–53 (1937).

43. See Earl v. Saks & Co., 36 Cal.2d 602, 226 P.2d 340 (1951) (avoidance allowed where plaintiff got what in economic terms was worth more than he bargained for); but see, Reed v. King, 145 Cal.App.3d 261, 193 Cal.Rptr. 130 (1983) (pecuniary loss required for avoidance based on nondisclosure).

44. McCleary, Damages as Requisite to Rescission for Misrepresentation II, 36 Mich.L.Rev. 227, 245–248 (1937). McCleary includes in this category cases where a purchaser misrepresents the purpose for which he is purchasing land, but the cases generally do not support this proposition unless the defrauded party owns other land that will be adversely affected by the purchaser's use. See Finley v. Dalton, 251 S.C. 586, 164 S.E.2d 763, 35 A.L.R.3d 1364 (1968).

45. McCleary, Damage as Requisite to Rescission for Misrepresentation II, 36 Mich.L.Rev. 227, 251–52 (1937).

injur! damag!   /s   fraud! misrepresent! deceit   /s   power empower!
      /s   void! avoid!

harm harmed harming damag! injur***   /s   fraud deceit misrepresent!
      /s   "reasonabl! expect"   %   "statute of frauds"

§ 9–17. The Representation: Fact Versus Opinion

Relief is granted for misrepresentations of fact, and not for erroneous statements of opinion.[46] The distinction between fact and opinion is extremely tenuous. Statements such as, "it is hot today" contain both a factual element—a statement about the temperature and the speaker's characterization of the temperature; a characterization which may well differ from that of the reasonable man. The distinction between fact and opinion has long been regarded by keen analysts as a logical absurdity.[47] The opinion rule doubtless arose as a means of denying relief to persons who unjustifiably (by community standards) relied upon sellers' "puff" or "trade talk." Descriptions of what one puts on the market as "best buys," "finest quality," etc. have been deemed by the courts not the kind of statements which, if false, ought to be redressed by the legal system.[48] There have been three ways of analyzing such language so as to deny relief. Trade talk could be deemed "immaterial"; second, it could be said that one has "no right to rely" upon such puffery; third, it could be deemed a statement of opinion.[49] Yet, if the court's sympathies are sufficiently with the party who relies upon a used car salesman's statement that a car is in "A–1 shape" and "mechanically perfect," the court may find that the opinion line has crossed into the area of fact.[50] And, although statements of value are usually deemed to be opinions,[51] where a farmer is induced by a confidence man to exchange his homestead for a store with a represented inventory value of $9,000 to $11,000, he may avoid the contract when the inventory value is found to be $2,500.[52] On the other hand, other litigants have not been so fortunate. One observer notes:

> "And then there is always the friendly doctrine of sellers' puff to shield the advertiser from liability. If such statements as, 'these second hand tires are as good as new,' 'this suit of clothes will wear

46. See generally, Keeton, Fraud: Misrepresentations of Opinion, 21 Minn.L.Rev. 643 (1937); 12 Williston §§ 1491–1494; Restatement, Contracts § 474; Black §§ 76–88.

47. See 7 Wigmore, Evidence § 1919 (3d ed.1940); Keeton, Fraud: Misrepresentation of Opinion, 21 Minn.L.Rev. 643, 656–57 (1937).

48. For a jurisprudential analysis to the effect that the legal standards must be less stringent than the demands of morality, see 2 Parsons, The Law of Contracts *768–69 (6th ed.1873). A contrary view is expounded by Verplanck, An Essay on the Doctrine of Contracts: Being an Inquiry How Contracts Are Affected in Law and Morals by Concealment, Error, or Inadequate Price 170 (1825).

49. See Keeton, Fraud: Misrepresentations of Opinion, 21 Minn.L.Rev. 643, 667–68 (1937).

50. Wat Henry Pontiac Co. v. Bradley, 202 Okl. 82, 210 P.2d 348 (1949). "A–1" was deemed to be language of opinion in Deming v. Darling, 148 Mass. 504, 20 N.E. 107 (1889).

51. Fifty Associates v. Prudential Ins. Co. of America, 450 F.2d 1007 (9th Cir. 1971).

52. Foote v. Wilson, 104 Kan. 191, 178 P. 430 (1919).

like iron,' 'these bicycles are unsurpassable, having been subjected to severe and practical tests; we are in a position to guarantee them to be all that is claimed for them, perfect of their kind,' or 'this article will give first class satisfaction, it is the best upon the market, it will sell like hot cakes and will be the best drawing card ever handled,' are regarded as puffs, then all the copy writer has to do is to give free rein to his fancy and avoid any useful information about the article. The facts besides being dull do not sell the article and may involve liability. (Citations omitted)."[53]

Some opinions are in the nature of predictions as to future events. A statement to a potential shareholder that shares priced at $8.00 will be worth $25.00 in a year has been held to be a statement of opinion, not "susceptible of knowledge."[54] The same court, however, held that representations that a chicken raising franchise would "return to the careful broiler raiser an income roughly equal to half as much as is obtained from an average size farm in the Midwest—and it will do so for about 6 hours of one person's attention daily," together with related "highly colored" and "overly optimistic" statements were actionable.[55] Wherein lies the distinction? In an early and philosophical American discussion of fraud, the author lamented, "whilst I had little difficulty in deciding on the morality of a single given case, I found it much less easy to lay down any general rules or definitions, at once comprehending all that strict integrity enjoined, and not requiring too much."[56] Sharing his embarrassment, we can point not to rules, but to factors which justify the differing results in the two cases. Among the factors are that in the second case the representations were printed in a glossy brochure rather than made orally; the business experience of the representee was far less in the second case than in the first; the representations in the second case were part of a regional selling campaign which gave the representor an aura of expertise and no such appearance of expertise was found in the first case.[57]

Some of the factors relevant to a decision of opinion cases are sometimes stated as rules of law; that is, as exceptions to the general rule of no relief for reliance upon an opinion. These include: (1) where there is a relation of trust and confidence between the parties;[58] (2)

53. Handler, False and Misleading Advertising, 39 Yale L.J. 22, 25–26 (1929) (footnotes omitted); see also Prosser & Keeton, Torts § 109 (5th ed.1984); Nordstrom, Sales § 70 (1970).

54. Kennedy v. Flo-Tronics, Inc., 274 Minn. 327, 143 N.W.2d 827 (1966).

55. Hollerman v. F.H. Peavey & Co., 269 Minn. 221, 130 N.W.2d 534 (1964). Compare Clements Auto Co. v. Service Bureau Corp., 298 F.Supp. 115 (D.Minn.1969), affirmed 444 F.2d 169 (8th Cir.1971).

56. Verplanck, supra note 48, at 101.

57. Another case in which avoidance of a transaction was permitted when representations of value were made pursuant to a sophisticated and well organized "hard sell" is Vertes v. G a C Properties, Inc., 337 F.Supp. 256 (S.D.Fla.1972). The Restatement, Second, Contracts § 168 places emphasis on whether the statement purports to be based on knowledge rather than judgment. If it purports to be based on knowledge it is more than a statement of opinion.

58. Restatement, Second, Contracts § 169; Keeton, Fraud: Misrepresentations of Opinion, 21 Minn.L.Rev. 643, 645–47 (1937).

where the representor is or claims to be an expert; [59] (3) where the representor has superior access to knowledge of facts making the opinion false; [60] (4) where the opinion is stated by a third person posing as a disinterested person; [61] (5) where the opinion intentionally varies so far from reality that no reasonable man in the representor's position could have such an opinion.[62] It is obvious that consistent application of these "exceptions" would signal the death knell of the opinion rule as a significant barrier to relief. Furthermore, in doubtful cases whether or not a statement is a representation of fact or opinion can be a question of fact,[63] further weakening the general rule.

To the extent that the fact-opinion dichotomy of prior law is still viable, it is continued by the Uniform Commercial Code.[64]

WESTLAW REFERENCES

relief /s "misrepresentation of fact"

misrepresentation /s distinguish! distinction /s fact /s opinion

misrepresentation /s "statement of opinion"

misrepresent! /s puff! "trade talk"

puff! /s rely! reliance relied

"statement of valu!" /s misrepresent!

misrepresent! puff! /s advertis! /s fact opinion

misrepresent! puff! /s predict! /s future

misrepresent! puff! /s expertise "business experience"

misrepresent! puff! /s "trust and confidence"

misrepresent! puff! /s superior /s access know!

sophisticat! unsophisticat! /s misrepresent! puff!

§ 9–18. The Representation: Fact Versus Law

(1) Everyone is presumed to know the law.[65] (2) A statement of the law governing a given set of facts is merely the expression of an opinion: no lawyer or layman ought to rely upon such an opinion

---

59. Id. at 647–48; Vokes v. Arthur Murray, Inc., 212 So.2d 906 (Fla.App.1968); Restatement, Contracts § 474(a); Restatement, Second, Contracts § 169(b). Where both parties are experts, there is generally no reason why the party to whom a representation of value is addressed should be entitled to rely upon it. Fifty Associates v. Prudential Ins. Co. of America, 450 F.2d 1007 (9th Cir.1971).

60. Ryan v. Glenn, 489 F.2d 110 (5th Cir.1974); Keeton, Fraud: Misrepresentations of Opinion, 21 Minn.L.Rev. 643, 648–54 (1937).

61. Keeton, Fraud: Misrepresentations of Opinion, 21 Minn.L.Rev. 643, 654–56 (1937); cf. Farnsworth v. Feller, 256 Or. 56, 471 P.2d 792 (1970) (forged appraiser's report).

62. Restatement, Contracts § 474(b).

63. Condas v. Adams, 15 Utah 2d 132, 388 P.2d 803 (1964).

64. U.C.C. § 2–313(2) provides " * * * an affirmation merely of the value of the goods or a statement purporting to be merely of the value of the goods or a statement purporting to be merely the seller's opinion or commendation of the goods does not create a warranty." If the word "merely," repeated thrice in this provision, is stressed, the opinion rule is further weakened. On the relationship between representations and warranties, see §§ 9–20, 9–23 infra.

65. "The maxim 'a man is presumed to know the law,' is a trite, sententious saying, 'by no means universally true.' " Municipal Metallic Bed Mfg. Corp. v. Dobbs, 253 N.Y. 313, 317, 171 N.E. 75, 76, 68 A.L.R. 1376, 1378 (1930); but see, Platt v. Scott, 6 Blackf. 389, 390 (Ind.1843) ("It is

without further research. Based upon either or both of these mutually contradictory rationales, the rule has been stated that: "One cannot rescind a contract or withdraw from an obligation into which he was induced to enter by representations made to him by the other party, however false and fraudulent, when such representations related to a matter of law, as distinguished from a matter of fact." [66] In so far as this rule has its foundation in the opinion rule, it shares the same logical absurdity. Does a representation that a given college has the legal authority to award the degree of D.M.D. represent fact or law? [67] It also shares with the opinion rule common exceptions,[68] the most important of which is the expertise exception. If the representor is a lawyer expressing an opinion about the law of his state, the representee may normally rely upon that opinion,[69] even if the representee is an adversary rather than a client.[70] Other situations of trust and confidence or supposed superior knowledge of the representor will be treated on the same basis.[71] Some jurisdictions may have abolished the law-fact distinction.[72]

An additional exception, over and above the exceptions generally involved in the opinion category, exists in the misrepresentation of law category. A misrepresentation of the law of another state or country is treated as a misrepresentation of fact.[73] This originates from the rule, now changed in many jurisdictions, that for purposes of pleading and proof the law of another jurisdiction is a fact.[74] There was little logic in importing the rule into the context of misrepresentation. Yet, any relief from the broad generalization that misrepresentation of law is not grounds for avoidance is to be welcomed.

 WESTLAW REFERENCES
"misrepresentation of law"

---

considered that every person is acquainted with the law, both civil and criminal, and no one can, therefore, complain of the mis-representations of another respecting it.").
Platt v. Scott is the ancestor of hundreds of decisions on point.

66. Black § 71; see generally 12 Williston § 1495; Restatement, Second, Contracts § 170; Prosser & Keeton, Torts 758–60 (5th ed.1984); Keeton, Fraud—Misrepresentations of Law, 15 Tex.L.Rev. 409 (1937); Note, Misrepresentation of Law, 32 Colum.L.Rev. 1018 (1932).

67. Kerr v. Shurtleff, 218 Mass. 167, 105 N.E. 871 (1914) (fact); see Note, Misrepresentation of Law, 32 Colum.L.Rev. 1018, 1021–23 (1932).

68. Restatement, Second, Contracts § 170, Comment b. See § 9–17 supra.

69. See the authorities cited in note 60 supra.

70. Sainsbury v. Pennsylvania Greyhound Lines, 183 F.2d 548, 21 A.L.R.2d 266 (4th Cir.1950).

71. Note, Misrepresentations of Law, 32 Colum.L.Rev. 1018, 1023–25 (1932); cf. Farnsworth v. Feller, 256 Or. 56, 471 P.2d 792 (1970) (seller concealed his knowledge of zoning ordinances).

72. Peterson v. First Nat'l Bank of Ceylon, 162 Minn. 369, 375, 203 N.W. 53, 55 (1925) ("useless duffle of an older and more arbitrary day"); National Conversion Corp. v. Cedar Building Corp., 23 N.Y.2d 621, 627–28, 298 N.Y.S.2d 499, 504, 246 N.E.2d 351, 355 (1969) ("the law has outgrown the oversimple dichotomy between law and fact in the resolution of issues of deceit.")

73. Bernhan Chemical & Metal Corp. v. Ship-A-Hoy, 200 App.Div. 399, 193 N.Y.S. 372 (1st Dep't 1922), 22 Colum.L.Rev. 591 (1922); 12 Williston § 1495; 1 Black § 72.

74. Cf. 30 Mich.L.Rev. 301 (1931).

§ 9–19. The Representation: Fact Versus Intention and Promise

If an issuer of debentures misrepresents the purpose to which he intends to put the proceeds, has he misrepresented a fact? In such a case the court gave the classic answer: "The state of a man's mind is as much a fact as the state of his digestion." [75] It should be borne in mind, however, that frequently a representation of purpose is of no great importance to the representee and would be deemed immaterial.[76]

Since a promise is a statement of intention coupled with a commitment to act in accordance with that statement,[77] it should follow that the making of a promise with an intent not to perform it is a misrepresentation of fact. The majority of jurisdictions now so hold.[78] The rationale is that: "Every promise involves an implied representation that the promisor intends to carry out the promise at the time it is made." [79]

Special problems exist when the promise would be void or unenforceable on the grounds of lack of consideration, the parol evidence rule, the Statute of Frauds, illegality, etc. The courts are far from unanimous on the resolution of these problems.[80] Some take the position that such contractual doctrines applicable in an action to enforce a promise have no relevance in an action for restitution or deceit.[81] Other courts are of the opinion that to allow a restitutionary

75. Edgington v. Fitzmaurice, L.R., 29 Ch.D. 459, 483 (1885); cf. "In an ancient case, Y.B. 17 Edw. IV, 2, Brian, C.J., remarked, perhaps erroneously, that 'the devil himself knoweth not the thought of man.'" 3 Corbin § 597 n. 5.

76. See generally, Keeton, Fraud: Statements of Intention, 15 Tex.L.Rev. 185 (1937); Note, The Legal Effect of Promises Made With Intent Not to Perform, 38 Colum.L.Rev. 1461 (1938); 12 Williston § 1496; Prosser, Torts 728–30 (4th ed. 1971); 1 Black §§ 89–91; Restatement, Second, Contracts § 171.

77. See § 2–6 supra.

78. See the authorities cited in note 76 supra. See also Dirose v. PK Management Corp., 691 F.2d 628 (2d Cir.1982), certiorari denied 461 U.S. 915, 103 S.Ct. 1896, 77 L.Ed.2d 285 (1983); United States v. 1,557.28 Acres of Land in Osage County, Kansas, 486 F.2d 445 (10th Cir.1973) (promise by federal agent); Entron, Inc. v. General Cablevision of Palatka, 435 F.2d 995 (5th Cir.1970) (reason to know of inability to carry out the promise is sufficient); Walker v. Woodall, 288 Ala. 510, 262 So.2d 756 (1972); Abbott v. Abbott, 188 Neb. 61, 195 N.W.2d 204 (1972); Anderson v. Tri-State Home Improvement Co., 268 Wis. 455, 67 N.W.2d 853 (1955), rehearing denied 268 Wis. 455, 68 N.W.2d 705 (1955);

Sabo v. Delman, 3 N.Y.2d 155, 164 N.Y.S.2d 714, 143 N.E.2d 906 (1957) (parol evidence rule no defense). Adhering to the view that a promise is not a representation, but carving out exceptions, is Fayette v. Ford Motor Credit Co., 129 Vt. 505, 282 A.2d 840 (1971).

79. Keeton, Fraud: Statements of Intention, 15 Tex.L.Rev. 185, 195 (1937).

80. See Prosser & Keeton, Torts 763–64 (5th ed. 1984). Keeton, Fraud: Statements of Intention, 15 Tex.L.Rev. 185, 200–16 (1937); Sweet, Promissory Fraud and the Parol Evidence Rule, 49 Cal.L.Rev. 877 (1961); Note, Action for Misrepresentation When Statute of Frauds Denies Recovery on the Contract, 7 Buffalo L.Rev. 332 (1958); Note, The Legal Effect of Promises Made with Intent Not to Perform, 38 Colum.L.Rev. 1461, 1465–72 (1938); Note, The Statute of Frauds as a Bar to an Action in Tort for Fraud, 53 Fordham L.Rev. 1231 (1985).

81. In a parol evidence rule case the court said: "Objectivity and certainty in the law of contracts are desirable, but at times they are too weak to protect legitimate expectations of fair dealing." Abbott v. Abbott, 188 Neb. 61, 66, 195 N.W.2d 204, 208 (1972). See also § 9–21 infra on disclaimer clauses.

or tort action would open the gate to circumvention of these contract doctrines by artful recasting of the facts in pleadings and testimony, or, if the question is lack of consideration, circumvention of the old rule that one has no right to rely upon a promise made without consideration, a rule which is now pretty well exploded by acceptance of the doctrine of promissory estoppel.[82]

 WESTLAW REFERENCES

misrepresent! /s "state of mind" "mental state"

"misrepresentation of fact" /s intend! intent!

"statement of intent!" /s fraud! deceit! misrepresent!

"promissory fraud"

§ 9–20. The Representation: Non-Disclosure, Implied Warranty

Information is valuable. Possession of it frequently permits an individual to enter into a transaction that is profitable precisely because he is acting on the information possessed by him but not by the other party. To what extent must a contracting party share information with the other party when that information bears on the relative exchange of values? Poker players do not share information concerning the content of their hands. Is this an apt analogy to a bargaining transaction? The answer is complex. The kinds of information that affect values are many. Means of gathering information are multiple. The circumstances surrounding the negotiation of contracts vary greatly, and the relationships between negotiating parties are diverse.

Every schoolboy knows that the Battle of New Orleans took place after a treaty of peace had been signed in Ghent ending the War of 1812. Every lawyer ought to be familiar with a case which had its genesis soon thereafter.[83] The British blockade had drastically curtailed the export of tobacco, depressing the price. Plaintiff, through special circumstances, learned of the treaty of peace before news of it had reached the general public in New Orleans. He called upon the defendant soon after sunrise at his New Orleans trading company, and purchased a large quantity of tobacco. Within hours the news of the treaty became public, the market price rose substantially and the seller sought to avoid the sale. The dictum was delivered by Chief Justice Marshall that:

> The question in this case is, whether the intelligence of extrinsic circumstances, which might influence the price of the commodity, and which was exclusively within the knowledge of the vendee, ought to have been communicated by him to the vendor? The court is of the opinion, that he was not bound to communicate it.

A Statute of Frauds case in accord is Burgdorfer v. Thielemann, 153 Or. 354, 55 P.2d 1122 (1936); contra, Caplan v. Roberts, 506 F.2d 1039 (9th Cir.1974).

82. See ch. 6 supra.

83. Laidlaw v. Organ, 15 U.S. (2 Wheat.) 178, 4 L.Ed. 214 (1817).

It would be difficult to circumscribe the contrary doctrine within proper limits * * *.[84]

In short, the bargaining process was treated as if it were a poker game. On the question of whether the decision conforms to community expectations of good faith and fair dealing, one observer has noted: "If those facts were given to the normal person, as an abstract question, he would probably say that the buyer's conduct was unethical; on the other hand, if the same individual were given the opportunity the buyer had * * * he would do precisely the same thing." [85] This case is very likely good law on its facts [86] and can be cited for the general rule that in a bargaining transaction there is generally no duty to disclose information to the other party.[87] This rule contains numerous exceptions. The first exception or group of exceptions is where a statute or regulation requires disclosure. The number of such statutes perhaps attests to the inadequacy of common law disclosure rules. The Securities Act,[88] Truth-in-Lending,[89] The Interstate Land Sales Full Disclosure Act,[90] The Truth-in-Negotiation Act,[91] are some of the more prominent legislation in this field displacing the common law. These all involve transactions where one party is in possession of information which can be obtained by the other, if at all, only by extremely expensive means *and* where abuses of the information monopoly frequently took the form of false or misleading statements.

A second exception or qualification of the general rule is the distinction made between non-disclosure and concealment. Positive action designed to hide the truth or to stymie the other party's investigation is deemed to constitute misfeasance that can result in liability for misrepresentation.[92]

A third exception is that where partial disclosure is made, lack of full disclosure (a half truth) may constitute misrepresentation.[93] Thus

84. Id. at 194.

85. Keeton, Fraud—Concealment and Non-disclosure, 15 Tex.L.Rev. 1, 32 (1936). For a contemporary criticism of the decision, see Verplanck, supra note 48, passim, and his suggested contrary rule at 125–26, 227.

86. But see Palmer, Mistake and Unjust Enrichment 83–4 (1962) ("Today, I believe many courts would reach the opposite conclusion.")

87. See generally, Keeton, note 85 supra; 12 Williston §§ 1497–99; Prosser & Keeton, Torts 737–40 (5th ed.1984); 1 Black § 41; Berger & Hirsch, Pennsylvania Tort Liability for Concealment & Nondisclosure in Business Transactions, 21 Temple L.Q. 368 (1948); Goldfarb, Fraud and Nondisclosure in the Vendor-Purchaser Relation, 8 West.Res.L.Rev. 5 (1956); Note, Is the Duty to Disclose a Question of Fair Conduct?, 2 Idaho L.Rev. 112 (1965).

88. See generally, Loss, Securities Regulation (2d ed.1961).

89. See generally, Clontz, Truth-In-Lending Manual (5th ed.1982).

90. See on this act: 27 Ark.L.Rev. 65 (1973); 47 Notre Dame Law. 267 (1971); 51 Or.L.Rev. 381 (1972); 24 S.Car.L.Rev. 331 (1972); 25 Stan.L.Rev. 605 (1973). Related state legislation is discussed in 60 Ill. B.J. 16 (1971); 9 Ga.St.B.J. 369 (1973).

91. This Act, applicable to United States government contracts, is discussed at 2 Pub.Cont.L.J. 88 (1968).

92. Keeton, Note 85 supra at 2–6; 1 Black § 43. E.g., covering over a defect in a machine with paint. Kuelling v. Roderick Lean Mfg. Co., 183 N.Y. 78, 75 N.E. 1098, 2 L.R.A. (NS) 303 (1905). See also Restatement, Second, Contracts § 160.

93. Norton v. Poplos, 443 A.2d 1 (Del. 1982); Russ v. Brown, 96 Idaho 369, 529 P.2d 765 (1974); Kannavos v. Annino, 356

where one party reads a suggested contract to another, leaving out portions, he has run afoul of this exception.[94] Where a resident of the Philippines was offered a job in Oregon, without disclosure that the existence of the job slot is under review, non-disclosure was deemed fraudulent and damages were awarded when the slot was cancelled as of the date of the promised employment.[95]

A fourth exception is where a party has made a statement in good faith, but supervening events make it no longer true, or he discovers new information demonstrating to him that it was not true when made. If he knows that the other is relying upon it, he is under a duty to disclose the truth.[96] Similarly, if one party becomes aware that the other is operating under a mistake as to a basic assumption upon which he is contracting,[97] he has a duty to correct the mistake even if he did not cause it.[98] Under this heading come the numerous cases holding that the seller of goods, lands or securities is under an obligation to disclose latent defects. This is very old doctrine, certainly prevalent in the early nineteenth century. "A sound price warrants a sound commodity" was the maxim.[99] But later in that century the phrase *caveat emptor* had thoroughly eradicated the earlier maxim.[1] Although the dust has not settled, it may safely be said that the older law once again prevails as to latent defects[2] although some citadels of *caveat emptor* remain. Thus, in Massachusetts a seller of a house need not disclose that the house is infested with termites,[3] although he must disclose conditions dangerous to health and safety.[4]

Mass. 42, 247 N.E.2d 708 (1969); Krause v. Eugene Dodge, Inc., 265 Or. 486, 509 P.2d 1199 (1973) ("new car" had 5,000 miles of use); 12 Williston § 1497 n. 4.

94. Ten-Cate v. First Nat'l Bank of Decatur, 52 S.W.2d 323 (Tex.Civ.App.1932). Additional "half-truth" cases in Prosser & Keeton, Torts 736–40 (5th ed. 1984); 1 Black § 67; see also Coral Gables v. Mayer, 241 App.Div. 340, 271 N.Y.S. 662 (1st Dep't 1934), second appeal 246 App.Div. 518, 282 N.Y.S. 596 (1st Dep't 1935), affirmed 270 N.Y. 670, 1 N.E.2d 991 (1936).

95. Elizaga v. Kaiser Foundation Hospitals, Inc., 259 Or. 542, 487 P.2d 870 (1971). See also Restatement, Second, Contracts § 159, Comment b.

96. Restatement, Contracts § 472 (similarly where he knowingly tells an untruth not expecting the other to rely and discovers that he is relying); Keeton, note 85 supra, at 6; 12 Williston §§ 1497, 1499. See also Restatement, Second, Contracts § 161(a).

97. Restatement, Second, Contracts § 161(b).

98. Davis v. Reisinger, 120 App.Div. 766, 105 N.Y.S. 603 (1st Dep't 1907); Re-

statement, Contracts § 472(b); 12 Williston §§ 1497, 1499.

99. See Horwitz, The Historical Foundations of Modern Contract Law, 87 Harv. L.Rev. 917, 926 (1974), and authorities there cited. In addition, see Cowen, A Treatise on the Civil Jurisdiction of a Justice of the Peace in the State of New York 146–147 (1821).

1. By 1873 a leading text could state that the maxim "a sound price implies a sound article" is peculiar to South Carolina. 2 Parsons, The Law of Contracts, *775 n. j (6th ed.1873).

2. Neuman v. Corn Exchange Nat'l Bank & Trust Co., 356 Pa. 442, 51 A.2d 759 (1947), reargument refused 356 Pa. 442, 52 A.2d 177 (1947); 12 Williston § 1498; 3 Williston, Sales § 631 (1948); Prosser & Keeton, Torts 736–40 (5th ed.1984); Goldfarb, supra note 87, at 5, 19.

3. Swinton v. Whitinsville Sav. Bank, 311 Mass. 677, 42 N.E.2d 808 (1942); contra, Obde v. Schlemeyer, 56 Wn.2d 449, 353 P.2d 672 (1960); Williams v. Benson, 3 Mich.App. 9, 141 N.W.2d 650 (1966), re-

4. See note 4 on page 369.

Where the transaction involves the sale of goods, in most cases the question of non-disclosure is of no relevance, inasmuch as the Uniform Commercial Code supplies an array of implied warranties granting the purchaser relief for defects in the goods whether or not these are known to the seller.[5] Thus the question of whether non-disclosure constitutes a misrepresentation becomes significant primarily in those cases where warranties have been effectively disclaimed,[6] where the non-disclosure is by a buyer rather than by a seller,[7] and perhaps on the question of consequential damages for breach of warranty.[8] Although at common law there were no warranties attaching to a sale of real property other than those recited in the deed, there is a modern trend recognizing an implied warranty of habitability in the sale of new housing.[9] There is also an increasing trend toward recognition of such a warranty in the leasing of new or old housing.[10]

A fifth exception centers on the nature of the transaction. Contracts of suretyship[11] and insurance[12] are transactions in which, by long established precedent, broad duties of disclosure are required.[13]

A sixth exception focuses upon the relationship of the parties. If there is a fiduciary or confidential relation between the parties, there is a duty of disclosure of material facts.[14] Indeed, the duty extends somewhat beyond such relationships. Whenever one party to a trans-

versed 378 Mich. 721 (1966); see also Weintraub v. Krobatsch, 64 N.J. 445, 317 A.2d 68 (1974) (roaches); Greenberg v. Glickman, 50 N.Y.S.2d 489 (1944), modified 268 App.Div. 882, 51 N.Y.S.2d 96 (2d Dep't 1944), second appeal denied 268 App.Div. 987, 51 N.Y.S.2d 861 (2d Dep't 1944) (duty to disclose sub-surface water conditions); De Meo v. Horn, 70 Misc.2d 339, 334 N.Y.S.2d 22 (1972); Lawson v. Citizens & Southern Nat'l Bank of South Carolina, 259 S.C. 477, 193 S.E.2d 124 (1972) (filled earth); Ollerman v. O'Rourke Co., Inc., 94 Wis.2d 17, 288 N.W.2d 95 (1980).

4. Cutter v. Hamlen, 147 Mass. 471, 18 N.E. 397 (1888) (child of prior tenant died of diphtheria because of defective drains); accord, Cesar v. Karutz, 60 N.Y. 229 (1875) (prior tenant died of smallpox).

5. U.C.C. §§ 2–312 to 2–318.

6. U.C.C. § 2–316.

7. It is only rarely that a buyer is held to be under a duty to disclose. See generally, Goldfarb, supra note 87, at 26–31; Keeton, supra note 85, at 22–27. If he fails to disclose material facts known to him, however, specific performance will be denied him. See note 18 infra.

8. Undisclosed knowledge of a defect will give the seller reason to know of consequential damages and will inhibit the purchaser from minimizing injury. On consequential damages, see § 14–4 infra.

9. Tassan v. United Development Co., 88 Ill.App.3d 581, 43 Ill.Dec. 769, 410 N.E.2d 902 (1980); Yepsen v. Burgess, 269 Or. 635, 525 P.2d 1019 (1974); see 12 Williston § 1506A; Demko, Caveat Aedificator—Home Builders Beware!, 71 Ill.B.J. 724 (1983); Moskowitz, Implied Warranty of Habitability: A New Doctrine Raising New Issues, 62 Cal.L.Rev. 1444 (1974); Note, 23 U.Fla.L.Rev. 626 (1971).

10. Green v. Superior Court, 10 Cal.3d 616, 111 Cal.Rptr. 704, 517 P.2d 1168 (1974); Berzito v. Gambino, 63 N.J. 460, 308 A.2d 17 (1973); Love, Landlord's Liability for Defective Premises: Caveat Lessee, Negligence or Strict Liability?, 1975 Wis.L.Rev. 19; Notes, 2 Fordham Urb.L.J. 433 (1974); 28 Stan.L.Rev. 729 (1976).

11. Simpson, Suretyship 86–93 (1950).

12. Keeton, Basic Text on Insurance Law 326–28 (1971); Patterson, Essentials of Insurance Law, ch. 10 (1957); Vance, Insurance 368–86 (3d ed.1951).

13. Long ago, an observer sought to demonstrate that a distinction between insurance and other transactions rested on no logical basis and that the insurance rule ought to be broadened to encompass all business dealings. Verplanck, supra note 48, ch. 7.

14. Restatement, Second, Contracts § 161(d); Keeton, supra note 85, at 11–14; 12 Williston § 1499; 1 Black §§ 48–58.

action justifiably believes the other is looking out for his interests, a duty of disclosure arises.[15]

In the law of medical malpractice, a rule of "informed consent" to therapy has evolved in recent years. One statement of the doctrine is that "true consent to what happens to one's self is the informed exercise of a choice, and that entails an opportunity to evaluate knowledgeably the options available and the risks attendant upon each."[16] Disclosure of the risks by the physician is a necessary precondition to the patient's ability to evaluate knowledgeably whether to accept the proposed therapy. It would indeed be salutary if the doctrine of "informed consent" were adapted to the general law of contracts so as to require disclosure of all facts which "if known, would so affect the value of the thing sold or done, in the general estimation of those whose use or estimation fixes the market price of similar things, as to make the price of the actual subject of the contract vary materially from that of other things of the same nature or use."[17] The adoption of such a principle would bring the law with respect to avoidance into harmony with the rule governing the remedy of specific performance, where the governing principle is that "equity only compels the specific performance of a contract which is fair and open, and in regard to which all material matters known to each have been communicated to the other."[18] The United States Court of Claims appears to have gone far toward adoption of such a principle. A government agency is required to disclose information possessed by it "which it knew that bidders did not have and would need in order to make an intelligent appraisal of the problems and costs that would be involved in the performance of the proposed contract."[19]

This rule is closely tied to and overlaps the doctrine of undue influence. See § 9–10 supra. See e.g., Village of Burnsville v. Westwood Co., 290 Minn. 159, 189 N.W.2d 392 (1971); Jackson v. Seymour, 193 Va. 735, 71 S.E.2d 181 (1952) (constructive fraud; could have been based on innocent misrepresentation).

15. Restatement, Contracts § 472(c); 1 Black § 49; Goldfarb, supra note 87, at 32–34; contra, requiring a confidential relationship, Grow v. Indiana Retired Teachers Community, 149 Ind.App. 109, 271 N.E.2d 140 (1971).

16. Karp v. Cooley, 493 F.2d 408, 419 (5th Cir.1974), rehearing denied 496 F.2d 878 (5th Cir.1974).

17. Verplanck, supra note 48, at 228; see also Holmes, A Contextual Study of Commercial Good Faith: Good Faith Disclosure in Contract Formation, 39 U.Pitt.L. Rev. 381 (1978). Such a rule is approximated in some jurisdictions.

"It is now settled in California that where the seller knows of facts materially affecting the value or desirability of the property which are known or accessible only to him and also knows that such facts are not known to, or within the reach of the diligent attention and observation of the buyer, the seller is under a duty to disclose them to the buyer."

Lingsch v. Savage, 213 Cal.App.2d 729, 29 Cal.Rptr. 201, 204, 8 A.L.R.3d 537, 543 (1963); accord, Ollerman v. O'Rourke Co., Inc., 94 Wis.2d 17, 288 N.W.2d 95 (1980); see also Kaas v. Privette, 12 Wn.App. 142, 529 P.2d 23, 80 A.L.R.3d 1 (1974). Compare Sharp, The Ethics of Breach of Contract, 45 Int'l Journal of Ethics 27, 45 (1934).

18. Rothmiller v. Stein, 143 N.Y. 581, 592, 38 N.E. 718, 721 (1894); cf. Amend v. Hurley, 293 N.Y. 587, 59 N.E.2d 416 (1944); McClintock, Equity § 73 (2d ed.1948).

19. T.F. Scholes, Inc. v. United States, 174 Ct.Cl. 1215, 357 F.2d 963, 970 (1966), followed in J.A. Jones Constr. Co. v. United States, 182 Ct.Cl. 615, 390 F.2d 886 (1968).

Despite the desirability of a broad rule of disclosure an exception must, however, be made for collateral information deliberately acquired at some cost in time or money such as by scientific market research or careful investment analysis. The nondisclosure of such information is no breach of the obligation of good faith and fair dealing.[20]

 WESTLAW REFERENCES

duty +2 disclos! /s transact!

184k17

"securities act" /s disclos! nondisclos!

nondisclos! "non disclos!" /s conceal!

misfeasance /s misrepresent!

"half truth" "partial! disclos!" /s misrepresent!

nondisclos! disclos! /s "latent defect"

"caveat emptor" /s disclos! nondisclos! defect!

"implied warranty of habitability"

"nature of the transaction" /s duty

"informed consent" /s duty /s disclos! nondisclos!

§ 9–21. Disclaimers of Representations; Merger Clauses; "As Is"

Written contracts frequently contain merger clauses stating that the writing contains the entire contract and that no representations other than those contained in the writing have been made. Despite the existence of a merger clause, parol evidence is admissible for purposes of demonstrating that the agreement is void or voidable or for proving an action for deceit.[21] *Fraus omnia corrumpit:* fraud vitiates everything it touches.

A peculiar distinction is, however, made in New York. A general merger clause is not deemed to bar parol evidence of misrepresentations, but a specific merger clause disclaiming specific representations is deemed to bar such evidence.[22] The distinction is more subtle than practical and has produced the proverbial flood of litigation. At the root of it there is a tension between the seemingly reasonable proposition that parties by agreement ought to be able to provide that a purchaser is relying solely upon his own inspection and the also reasonable proposition that a party ought not by the use of magic words insulate himself from fraud. The distinction doubtless will cause

20. See Kronman & Posner, The Economics of Contract Law 116–121 (1979); L & N Grove, Inc. v. Chapman, 291 So.2d 217 (Fla.Dist.Ct.App.1974), certiorari dismissed 298 So.2d 412 (1974).

21. Norton v. Poplos, supra note 93 (even innocent misrepresentations); 3 Corbin § 580; 1 Palmer on Restitution § 3.20; 5 Williston § 811; accord, under the U.C.C., Associated Hardware Supply Co. v. Big Wheel Distribr. Co., 355 F.2d 114 (3d Cir.1965); see also Sweet, Promissory Fraud and the Parol Evidence Rule, 49 Cal. L.Rev. 877 (1961); Comment, The "Merger Clause" and the Parol Evidence Rule, 27 Tex.L.Rev. 361 (1949).

22. Danann Realty v. Harris, 5 N.Y.2d 317, 184 N.Y.S.2d 599, 157 N.E.2d 597 (1959) noted in many law reviews with unanimous disapproval. See 47 Cornell L.Q. 655 n. 7 (1962) for citations.

draftsmen of standard forms to draft lengthier, more verbose merger clauses. A sounder distinction, if, indeed, any is needed, would be between a negotiated clause and a standard form clause.[23]

Even under the majority rule, a merger clause may not be entirely ineffective. If the clause states that no representations have been made and that the purchaser relies on nothing but his own inspection, the clause, although not conclusive, is at least an evidentiary admission against him.[24] If the clause states that the company's agents have no authority to make representations, it places the other party on notice of the agent's lack of authority. There are holdings applying this concept rather rigidly.[25] Under the Restatement view, a compromise has been put forward, permitting a party who has relied on unauthorized representations of an agent to rescind and have restitution but not to recover damages.[26]

Expressions such as "as is" are commonly understood to exclude all implied warranties,[27] but do not bar an action for deceit or restitution.[28]

WESTLAW REFERENCES

"merger clause" /s fraud! deceit misrepresent!

"specific merger clause"

2–316 /s "uniform commercial code" u.c.c.

§ 9–22. Fraud in the Factum (or Execution) Versus Fraud in the Inducement

In the great majority of cases actionable misrepresentation renders a transaction voidable rather than void. There is some loose language in the cases on this score, for seldom is the distinction of importance. It becomes of crucial importance if property has been transferred by virtue of the misrepresentation. If the property has been subsequently transferred to a bona fide purchaser for value, the defrauded party may recover the property only if the initial transaction is void.[29] The void-voidable dichotomy also has an effect on the burden of proof. While

23. The disclaimer in the Danann case was a typewritten rider to a printed form. Brief for Defendant p. 10. The distinction suggested in the text is considered in Citibank, N.A. v. Plapinger, 66 N.Y.2d 90, 495 N.Y.S.2d 309, 485 N.E.2d 974 (1985), reargument denied 67 N.Y.2d 647, 490 N.E.2d 558 (1986).

24. Omar Oil & Gas Co. v. MacKenzie Oil Co., 33 Del. 259, 289, 138 A. 392, 398 (1926); Abbott v. Abbott, 188 Neb. 61, 195 N.W.2d 204 (1972).

25. E.g., Holland Furnace Co. v. Williams, 179 Kan. 321, 295 P.2d 672 (1956) (furnace salesman untruthfully told customer his present furnace emitted carbon monoxide into his house).

26. Restatement, Second, Agency § 260 (1958); Herzog v. Capital Co., 27 Cal.2d

349, 164 P.2d 8 (1945); cf. Anderson v. Tri-State Home Improvement Co., 268 Wis. 455, 67 N.W.2d 853 (1955), rehearing denied 268 Wis. 455, 68 N.W.2d 705 (1955) (damages for deceit allowed where representor was the corporate president).

27. U.C.C. § 2–316(3)(a); Chamberlain v. Bob Matick Chevrolet, Inc., 4 Conn.Cir. 685, 239 A.2d 42, 24 A.L.R.3d 456 (1967).

28. Lingsch v. Savage, 213 Cal.App.2d 729, 29 Cal.Rptr. 201, 8 A.L.R.3d 537 (1963) (non-disclosure); New England Foundation Co. v. Elliott & Watrous, Inc., 306 Mass. 177, 27 N.E.2d 756 (1940); Packard-Dallas, Inc. v. Carle, 163 S.W.2d 735 (Tex.App. 1942).

29. 1 Palmer on Restitution § 3.2; Restatement, Second, Contracts § 163, Comment c.

the defendant has the burden of proof on matters of avoidance, the plaintiff has the burden of establishing the existence of the contract.[30]

On the question of what kind of misrepresentation renders a transaction void, the House of Lords in 1970 [31] laid down a twofold criteria. First, the plaintiff must have signed an instrument that is radically different from that which the plaintiff is led to believe that he is signing.[32] Second, the plaintiff must have acted without negligence in the sense that a reasonable person would have signed it under the circumstances of the case. When these two factors coexist, plaintiff can claim *non est factum:* it is not my deed.

A similar test is laid down in Article 3 of the Uniform Commercial Code. Commercial paper is void even against a holder in due course if the paper is vitiated by "such misrepresentation as has induced the party to sign the instrument with neither knowledge nor reasonable opportunity to obtain knowledge of its character or its essential terms." [33]

WESTLAW REFERENCES

"bona fide" bonafide /s fraud +3 factum execution

fraud +3 factum execution /s burden +2 proof proving

fraud! misrepresent! /s 3–305 /s u.c.c. "uniform commercial code"

"fraud in the inducement" /s burden +2 proof proving

---

§ 9–23. Remedies for Misrepresentation: Election, Express Warranty, Restitution, Measure of Restitution

If the fraud constitutes the tort of deceit, the defrauded party may elect to stand on the transaction, keep what was received, and sue for damages.[34] Instead, he may choose to avoid the transaction and claim restitution.[35] In many cases restitutionary recovery has included reliance damages.[36] Under statutes in some states,[37] and under the sales

---

30. Boxberger v. New York, N.H. & H.R. Co., 237 N.Y. 75, 142 N.E. 357 (1923).

31. Gallie v. Lee, [1969] 1 All E.R. 1062 (C.A.); Saunders v. Anglia Building Soc., [1970] 3 All E.R. 961 (H.L.), aff'g sub nom. In this case the court deals with, and overthrows, a good number of precedents. See Note 87 L.Q.Rev. 145 (1971); Cheshire, Fifoot & Furmston, The Law of Contract 237–40 (8th ed.1972).

32. Accord, Restatement, Second, Contracts § 163; Operating Engineers Pension Trust v. Gilliam, 737 F.2d 1501 (9th Cir. 1984); Curtis v. Curtis, 56 N.M. 695, 248 P.2d 683 (1952) (wife signed separation agreement on representation it was a property division for income tax purposes).

33. U.C.C. § 3–305(2)(c).

34. The measure of damages is discussed at § 14–21 infra.

35. A third remedy, reformation, is considered at §§ 9–31 to 9–36 infra. A number of authorities permit a restitution action to be brought against all participants in the fraud even as to those who are not contracting parties. Metge v. Baehler, 762 F.2d 621 (8th Cir. 1985), cert. denied ___ U.S. ___ 106 S.Ct. 798, 88 L.Ed.2d 774 (1986); Gordon v. Burr, 506 F.2d 1080 (2d Cir.1974).

36. Hammac v. Skinner, 265 Ala. 9, 89 So.2d 70 (1956); Jennings v. Lee, 105 Ariz. 167, 461 P.2d 161 (1969); Mock v. Duke, 20 Mich.App. 453, 174 N.W.2d 161 (1969); see 1 Palmer on Restitution § 3.9.

37. E.g., McKinney's N.Y.C.P.L.R. 3002(e).

article of the Uniform Commercial Code,[38] no election is necessary. The defrauded party may pursue and obtain both remedies so long as items of recovery are not duplicated. For example, where plaintiff was induced to purchase a horse by a representation that it was a stallion, he was permitted to return the horse, recover the price plus expenses for food, maintenance and veterinary care, when it was discovered that the horse was a gelding.[39] This case also illustrates another rule of the Uniform Commercial Code. The factual representation that the horse is a stallion is deemed an express warranty;[40] an absolute undertaking that the representation is true. When pursuing a remedy for breach of warranty, questions such as the seller's knowledge of the falsity of the representation disappear.[41] The only requisite is that the representation be "part of the basis of the bargain," which appears to mean that reliance in some broad, vague sense is required, although some courts have held no reliance is required.[42]

Where an election is still required by common law, there is a great diversity of views about what constitutes an election and when it must be made.[43] The older view demanded a prompt and irrevocable election.[44] This is still the present tendency if the remedy sought is restitution and the other party would be prejudiced by delay.[45] Otherwise, the time at which the election must be made varies with local practice, but the modern tendency is to allow an election even after the pleading stage of a lawsuit.[46]

38. U.C.C. § 2–721.

39. Grandi v. LeSage, 74 N.M. 799, 399 P.2d 285 (1965).

40. U.C.C. § 2–313(1)(a), (b); see also Steadman v. Turner, 84 N.M. 738, 507 P.2d 799 (1973) (warranty as to real property).

41. A number of jurisdictions allow an action against a manufacturer based on breach of warranty even where there is no privity of contract and no personal injuries. Restitution against such a manufacturer is not, however, permitted. Voytovich v. Bangor Punta Operations, Inc., 494 F.2d 1208 (6th Cir.1974); see Restatement, Second, Torts § 402B.

42. See generally, Nordstrom, Sales 199–228 (1970); White & Summers, Uniform Commercial Code § 9–4 (2d ed.1980).

43. See generally, 1 Palmer on Restitution § 3.10.

44. 3 Black §§ 561–564; 12 Williston §§ 1526–1528A.

45. Johns Hopkins Univ. v. Hutton, 488 F.2d 912 (4th Cir.1973), certiorari denied 416 U.S. 916, 94 S.Ct. 1622, 40 L.Ed.2d 118 (1974); Moore v. Farm & Ranch Life Ins. Co., 211 Kan. 10, 505 P.2d 666 (1973). If after discovery of the fraud, some modification of the contract is agreed upon, it is likely that this will be deemed to release any claims for tort damage as well as the power to rescind. United Forest Products Co. v. Baxter, 452 F.2d 11 (8th Cir.1971). If after discovery of the fraud, the defrauded party merely continues to accept the other's performance, he may be deemed to have released the fraud claim unless it would be economically unreasonable to terminate the relationship, or there has been substantial performance. Clements Auto Co. v. Service Bureau Corp., 444 F.2d 169 (8th Cir.1971).

46. Moore, Federal Practice §§ 8.31[2] (1984). It is sometimes suggested that the election between restitution and deceit is a substantive law election, rather than a procedural election and thereby governed by different principles. Id. § 405; see also, Jackson, The History of Quasi-Contract in English Law 81–84 (1936). This is cogently answered in Ebner v. Haverty Furn. Co., 138 S.C. 74, 136 S.E. 19 (1926) and in Comment, Election of Remedies: The California Basis, 19 Hastings L.J. 1233 (1968). Cf. Restatement, Second, Contracts § 378.

Avoidance and restitution on grounds of misrepresentation was originally an equitable remedy.[47] The common law courts, however, also opened the courts of law to claimants for restitution by development of the law of quasi contracts; restitution being based upon the fictional promise to refund that which had been obtained by fraud. Today in many jurisdictions, equity has ceded its power except in cases where equitable relief is required to provide relief other than a money judgment as where the cancellation of a written instrument is required for complete relief.[48] In an equitable action it is not essential for the plaintiff to tender restoration of that which he has received as a precondition of relief. The flexibility of the equity decree is such that relief can be conditioned upon restoration, or the value of what has been received may be offset from the relief granted.[49]

Where restitution is sought at law, the general rule is that as a precondition to relief the defrauded party must offer to return that which he has received under the contract.[50] Strictly applied it has been held that failure to tender restoration prior to commencement of an action is grounds for dismissal of the action.[51] It is certainly arguable that the equity rule should, in all states where law and equity are merged, be applied at law.[52] In New York, this is made explicit by statute.[53] In other jurisdictions a tendency towards adoption of the equity rule can be discerned, primarily by the proliferation of exceptions to the well eroded general rule requiring an offer to restore.[54] Some of the stated exceptions are where the defrauded party is a governmental unit,[55] where what has been received was wholly worthless, has become worthless because of the fault of the other party or because of the absence of represented qualities,[56] where what has been received consists of money which can be credited to the plaintiff's claim,[57] etc.[58] In essence, these and other exceptions state that an offer to restore is unnecessary where it would be useless or unfair to insist upon it. Nonetheless it is everywhere the rule that, if upon discovering the truth the aggrieved party fails to act with reasonable promptness to

---

47. 2 Pomeroy, Equity Jurisprudence §§ 910–915 (4th ed.1918).

48. Herrick v. Robinson, 267 Ark. 576, 595 S.W.2d 637 (1980); Schank v. Schuchman, 212 N.Y. 352, 106 N.E. 127 (1914), or where specific restitution of lands or goods is appropriate. Restatement, Contracts § 489; § 15–5 infra. See generally, 1 Palmer on Restitution § 3.7.

49. Knaebel v. Heiner, 663 P.2d 551 (Alaska 1983); Jennings v. Lee, 105 Ariz. 167, 461 P.2d 161 (1969); Limoli v. Accettullo, 358 Mass. 381, 265 N.E.2d 92 (1970); Restatement, Contracts § 481; 3 Black § 625.

50. See 3 Black §§ 616–637; 12 Williston §§ 1529–1530; see also Professor Patterson's studies in N.Y. Law Rev. Comm'n Rep. 31–78 (1946); 339–54 (1952).

51. 3 Black § 625.

52. 12 Williston § 1529 n. 3.

53. McKinney's N.Y.C.P.L.R. 3004.

54. See generally, 1 Palmer on Restitution § 3.11–3.12.

55. Restatement, Contracts § 480(1).

56. Restatement, Contracts § 384(2)(a); Restatement, Restitution § 65(d).

57. Restatement, Contracts § 480(2)(c); Restatement, Restitution § 65(f).

58. Restatement, Contracts § 480(2)(d), (e); Restatement, Second, Contracts § 384; Restatement, Restitution § 65(a), (b), (e); § 66(3), (4), (5).

avoid the contract, he will be deemed to have ratified the contract, thus destroying his power of avoidance and relegating him to his tort action, if any.[59]

The offer to restore need only be conditional; that is conditioned upon the return of what he parted with.[60] If the offer is rejected, the plaintiff must retain what he has received as bailee.[61]

"Restitution" is an ambiguous term, sometimes referring to the disgorging of something which has been taken and at times referring to compensation for injury done.[62] Often, the result under either meaning of the term would be the same. If the plaintiff has been defrauded into paying $1,000 to the defendant, his loss and the defendant's gain coincide. Where they do not coincide, as where the plaintiff is out of pocket more than the defendant has gained and the defendant's conduct is tortious, the plaintiff will recover his loss in a quasi-contractual or equitable action for restitution.[63] Unjust impoverishment as well as unjust enrichment is a ground for restitution.[64] If the defendant is guilty of a non-tortious misrepresentation, the measure of recovery is not rigid[65] but, as in other cases of restitution, such factors as relative fault, the agreed upon risks, and the fairness of alternative risk allocations not agreed upon and not attributable to the fault of either party need to be weighed.[66]

Where what the fraudulent party has received increases in value, the most appropriate remedy is the imposition, by a court of equity, of a constructive trust on what he has received or its proceeds, thus permitting the defrauded party to recover the enhanced value.[67]

A misrepresentation may also give rise to an estoppel, preventing the party who made the representation from denying the truth of the assertion. Contrary to a widely quoted statement that estoppel is merely the basis of a defense and not of a cause of action,[68] estoppel may be raised affirmatively. For example, prior to any legislation on the point, a good number of jurisdictions had ruled that a carrier or warehouseman was estopped from denying the accuracy of a receipt for

59. Gannett Co., Inc. v. The Register Pub. Co., 428 F.Supp. 818 (D.Conn.1977); Herrick v. Robinson, supra note 48; Restatement, Second, Contracts §§ 380–381.

60. Restatement, Contracts § 480(3); Restatement, Second, Contracts § 384.

61. Restatement, Restitution § 67.

62. See Perillo, Restitution in a Contractual Context, 73 Colum.L.Rev. 1208, 1219–22 (1973).

63. See Restatement, Restitution pp. 595–96 (topic note) and §§ 151–153; Jennings v. Lee, 105 Ariz. 167, 461 P.2d 161 (1969).

64. Restatement, Restitution § 154, ill. 1; see also note 36 supra.

65. No opinion on the question is expressed by the Restatement, Restitution § 155, Caveat to Subsection 1.

66. Perillo, supra note 62, at 1224–25.

67. Janigan v. Taylor, 344 F.2d 781 (1st Cir.1965) (constructive trust measure applied at law), certiorari denied 382 U.S. 879, 86 S.Ct. 163, 15 L.Ed.2d 120 (1965); Sher v. Sandler, 325 Mass. 348, 90 N.E.2d 536 (1949), 63 Harv.L.Rev. 1463 (1950); Falk v. Hoffman, 233 N.Y. 199, 135 N.E. 243 (1922).

68. "Estoppel is only a rule of evidence; you cannot found an action upon estoppel." Low v. Bouverie, [1891] 3 Ch. 82, 105 (Bowen, L.J.).

goods as against a bona fide purchase for value.[69]   Estoppel is a doctrine, though never exclusively equitable, which has acquired a good deal of its sustenance from equitable principles.   It is quite clear, therefore, that even an innocent misrepresentation can provide the basis of an estoppel.[70]

Fraud may also be used as an affirmative defense to an action to enforce the contract.   If the remedy sought is specific performance, the court may deny relief although the fraud would not constitute grounds for avoidance.[71]   This rule stems from the discretionary nature of the remedy of specific performance.[72]

As is the case with any kind of voidable transaction, the aggrieved party may affirm the contract thereby ratifying it.   The ratification may be express or it may occur by actions inconsistent with disaffirmance after acquisition of facts putting him on notice that a misrepresentation has been made.[73]

    WESTLAW REFERENCES

fraud! /s deceit /s elect*** /s recover!

fraud! deceit /s void! avoid! /s restitution

fraud! deceit /s "express warranty" /s recover! /s damage

143k3(1) /p fraud! deceit

warrant! /s breach! /s basis +3 bargain

remedy /s misrepresentation /s restitution

restitution /s tender! /s good property

misrepresent! fraud! deceit /s ratif! /s deem!

misrepresent! fraud! deceit /s offer! +2 restor! restitution

di restitution

restitution /s quasi-contract*** /s equit!

misrepresent! fraud! deceit /s remedy /s "constructive trust" %
    "statute of limitation"

honest! innocen! /s misrepresent! /s estop!

§ 9–24. Adequacy of the Case Law of Fraud

The rules governing fraud are quite elastic.   Seemingly erratic approaches towards the issues of materiality, reliance, non-disclosure and the fact-opinion distinction often mask appellate judges' covert imposition of control over the findings of fact of the court below.   In addition, there is ideological tension between rules forged in the nineteenth century in an era where risk taking and self-reliance were

69. See Ewart, Principles of Estoppel 235–36 (1900); Williston, Liability for Honest Misrepresentation, 24 Harv.L.Rev. 415, 423–27 (1911).

70. Ewart, supra note 69, at 85–97; Williston, supra note 69, at 424; see generally, Atiyah, Misrepresentation, Warranty and Estoppel, 9 Alberta L.Rev. 347 (1971).

71. Clayburg v. Whitt, 171 N.W.2d 623 (Iowa 1969) (equity rule applied to law action for the price).

72. See § 16–7 infra.

73. Restatement, Second, Contracts §§ 380, 381; 1 Palmer on Restitution § 3.10.

extolled and judicially applied in the maxim of *caveat emptor*,[74] and twentieth century recognition that individuals and even companies often have no real alternative but to rely upon statements made by sellers in today's mass, impersonal, nation-wide market.

The elasticity and lack of definiteness of the law of fraud has had its defenders on the ground that fraud is too multifarious to be reduced to firm rules.[75] This may be true but it makes the business of advising clients difficult. Perhaps the main difficulty with the law of fraud in modern society is that much fraud is aimed at the public generally and aggrieved members of the public are unable to investigate the representations made, and when injured, it is often by a lesser sum than it would cost in legal expenses to obtain redress. In addition, unsophisticated members of the public are often unable to comprehend aspects of the transaction—such as true interest rates—when cloaked in obfuscating language. It is to problems such as these that the doctrine of unconscionability (§§ 9–37 to 9–40) and consumer protection legislation (Ch. 10) address themselves.

E. MISTAKE

Table of Sections

§ 9–25. Subject of This Discussion

Certain kinds of error may prevent the formation of contracts. These include misunderstandings and mistake in transmission, topics dealt with elsewhere in this treatise.[76] Primarily we are concerned

---

74. "It is one of that tribe of anonymous Latin maxims that infest our law ＊ ＊ ＊ they fill the ear and sound like sense, and to the eye look like learning; while their main use is to supply the place of either or both." Verplanck, An Essay on the Doctrine of Contracts: Being an Inquiry How Contracts Are Affected in Law and Morals by Concealment, Error, or Inadequate Price 218 (1825). On the history (by no means ancient) of the maxim as a rule of law, see Hamilton, The Ancient Maxim Caveat Emptor, 40 Yale L.J. 1133 (1931).

75. 2 Parsons, The Law of Contracts ＊769 (6th ed. 1873).

76. For misunderstanding, see §§ 3–11, 3–10 supra; for mistake in transmission, see § 2–24 supra.

here with mistake as a ground for avoiding a transaction.[77] Nowhere in the law of contracts do objective elements supporting the certainty and stability of transactions and subjective elements supporting fairness and the autonomy of the will clash as frequently as in the subject matter of mistake.[78]

 WESTLAW REFERENCES
mistak! /s ground /s void! avoid! /s contract*** bargain agreement

§ 9–26. Mutual Mistake

Not long ago it was a common statement of the law that while relief is available for certain kinds of mutual mistake, it is unavailable for unilateral mistake unless the other party knew or had reason to know of the mistake.[79] This statement is no longer entirely accurate and it has been strongly argued that the distinction between mutual and unilateral mistake should be dropped.[80] This argument may be accepted in the long run, but for the present the distinction is so embedded in the cases it cannot be ignored.[81]

Where both parties share a common assumption about a vital existing fact upon which they based their bargain and that assumption is false, the transaction may be avoided if, because of the mistake, a quite different exchange of values occurs from the exchange of values the parties contemplated, unless the risk is otherwise allocated by agreement, custom or law.[82] The same rule holds if the parties are operating under differing mistakes about the same vital fact.[83] It is immaterial whether the mistake relates to factors traditionally stressed as most likely to be vital such as to the identity of the subject matter. The important thing is that it be a basic assumption upon which both parties acted.[84] Normally, for example, tax considerations are important factors entering into the calculations of each party to a bargain. That the parties are mistaken in their belief of these tax consequences will be grounds for setting the bargain aside if a mutual error as to tax

---

77. The remedy of reformation is discussed at §§ 9–31 to 9–36 infra.

78. For discussions of mistake in the framework of objective and subjective theories of contracts, see McKeag, Mistake in Contract 127–132 (1905); Patterson, Equitable Relief for Unilateral Mistake, 28 Colum.L.Rev. 859, 861–67 (1928); Sabbath, Effect of Mistake in Contracts: A Study in Comparative Law, 13 Int. & Comp.L.Q. 798 (1964).

79. Foulke, Mistake in Formation and Performance of a Contract, 11 Colum.L. Rev. 197, 224 (1911); Restatement, Contracts § 503; Restatement, Restitution § 12.

80. See Rabin, A Proposed Black-Letter Rule Concerning Mistaken Assumptions in Bargain Transactions, 45 Tex.L.Rev. 1273, 1277–79 (1967).

81. See 3 Corbin § 608.

82. Restatement, Second, Contracts § 152; see Palmer, Mistake and Unjust Enrichment 38–40, 47 (1962).

83. Restatement, Contracts § 503; cf. Restatement, Second, Contracts § 152, Comment h. Where the parties are mistaken about different facts, it is a case of two unilateral mistakes. Alden Auto Parts Warehouse, Inc. v. Dolphin Equipment Leasing Corp., 682 F.2d 330 (2d Cir. 1982).

84. Restatement, Second, Contracts § 152, Comment a.

liability was a basic assumption upon which they proceeded.[85] With the understanding that the following categories represent typical fact patterns rather than legally distinct compartments, we shall examine several classes of cases.

(a) Existence, Ownership, or Identity of the Subject Matter

Absent a contrary assumption of the risk, if at the time of contracting for the sale of specific goods, unbeknownst to the parties, the goods never existed or are no longer in existence, no contract is made.[86] Where the seller is negligent in his mistaken belief, however, liability may be found on an implied warranty of existence or a negligence theory.[87]

If the question involves ownership of goods, the question is resolved by an implied warranty of title which the seller makes to the buyer under the Uniform Commercial Code.[88] Where the transfer carries no implied warranty, as may be the case with a transfer of a patent, the problem may be dealt with under mistake. Absent an assumption of the risk by the transferee, it may be held that if the patent is found to be invalid, the transferee may have rescission and restitution.[89] Where a life insurance policy is surrendered after the insured is dead, but before his death is known to the parties, the surrender can be retracted because of the mistaken assumption upon which the parties acted.[90]

Where the parties are mistaken as to the identity of the subject matter the contract may be avoided. For example, if both A and B

85. Future Plastics, Inc. v. Ware Shoals Plastics, Inc., 407 F.2d 1042 (4th Cir.1969) (stipulation); West Los Angeles Inst. for Cancer Research v. Mayer, 366 F.2d 220 (9th Cir.1966), certiorari denied 385 U.S. 1010, 87 S.Ct. 718, 17 L.Ed.2d 548 (1967) (decided under related doctrine of frustration), noted 42 Notre Dame Law. 557 (1967); Stone v. Stone, 319 Mich. 194, 29 N.W.2d 271 (1947); accord, Dover Pool & Racquet Club, Inc. v. Brooking, 366 Mass. 629, 322 N.E.2d 168 (1975) (mistake as to zoning); cf. Walton v. Bank of California, Nat. Assoc., 218 Cal.App.2d 527, 32 Cal. Rptr. 856 (1963) (mistake not inducing cause of transaction).

86. Restatement, Second, Contracts § 266; 3 Corbin § 600; 13 Williston §§ 1561–62. If the goods are in existence at the time of contracting and are destroyed subsequently, the question is one of risk of loss and impossibility of performance. See §§ 13–3, 13–26 infra.

87. McRae v. Commonwealth Disposals Comm'n, 84 Commw.L.R. 377 (Austl.1951); In re Zellmer's Estate, 1 Wis.2d 46, 82 N.W.2d 891 (1957); see Krasnowiecki, Sale of Non-Existent Goods: A Problem in the Theory of Contracts, 34 Notre Dame Law. 358 (1959); Nicholas, Rules and Terms—Civil Law and Common Law, 48 Tul.L.Rev. 946, 966–72 (1974).

88. U.C.C. § 2–312; cf. Restatement, Second, Contracts § 152, Comment g ("A buyer usually finds it more advantageous to rely on the law of warranty than on the law of mistake").

89. Herzog v. Heyman, 151 N.Y. 587, 45 N.E. 1127 (1897); cf. 1 Black §§ 87, 157. Where an owner of securities owned American Israeli Paper Mills, Ltd., Ordinary B shares, but thought he owned American Israeli Paper Mills, Ltd., American shares (listed on a stock exchange) and ordered them sold, it was held the mistake was unilateral and no rescission was permitted. A sounder ground was that the defendant broker would not have been restored to the status quo ante. Morris Speizman Co. v. Williamson, 12 N.C.App. 297, 183 S.E.2d 248 (1971), certiorari denied 279 N.C. 619, 184 S.E.2d 113 (1971); cf. Ohio Co. v. Rosemeier, 32 Ohio App.2d 116, 288 N.E.2d 326, 61 O.O.2d 105 (1972).

90. Riegel v. American Life Ins. Co., 153 Pa. 134, 25 A. 1070 (1893); accord, Duncan v. New York Mut. Ins. Co., 138 N.Y. 88, 33 N.E. 730 (1893) (policy surrendered after insured ship had been lost).

believe that a cask contains lime and enter into an agreement on that basis, and the cask contains sand, the agreement would be avoidable for mistake.[91] Under the U.C.C. if the seller describes the cask as containing lime, he has made an express warranty to that effect.[92] Although the Code thus throws the risk upon the seller that his description is accurate, it does not foreclose the possibility that the warranty itself can be avoided for mistake.[93] The extent to which this will be allowed is not at all clear. It is assumed that barring very exceptional circumstances it will be deemed that the seller has assumed the risk that his description is accurate.

(b) Qualities of the Subject Matter and Conscious Uncertainty

Two famous cases illuminate the law with respect to mistaken qualities. In Sherwood v. Walker [94] a cow of good breeding stock, Rose 2d of Aberlone, was believed to be sterile and the owner contracted to sell her at a price far under that which she would have brought if fertile. Before she was delivered it was discovered that she was with calf and thereby worth about ten times the sales price. The court ruled that the transaction was voidable, saying, "Yet the mistake was not of the mere quality of the animal, but went to the very nature of the thing. A barren cow is substantially a different creature than a breeding one. There is as much difference between them * * * as there is between an ox and a cow * * *." [95] One explanation for the decision is that in any contract parties take certain risks, but do not take risks of the existence of facts materially affecting their bargain which both shared as a common pre-supposition.[96] In deciding which facts are vital and basic to their bargain one must search the facts for unexpected, unbargained for gain on the one hand and unexpected, unbargained for loss on the other. A perceptive analyst of the case states, "Here the buyer sought to retain a gain that was produced, not by a subsequent change in circumstances, nor by the favorable resolution of known uncertainties when the contract was made, but by the presence of facts quite different from those on which the parties based their bargain." [97]

In Wood v. Boynton [98] the plaintiff found a small pretty stone and sold it for one dollar to the defendant after two conversations in which

---

91. Cf. Conner v. Henderson, 15 Mass. 319 (1818).

92. U.C.C. § 2–313.

93. U.C.C. § 1–103; see Nordstrom, Sales 173 (1970); Kavanagh, Mistake and Related Matters: Impact of the Sales Article of the Uniform Commercial Code, 1 Ottawa L.Rev. 113 (1966); Restatement, Second, Contracts § 152, Comment g.

94. 66 Mich. 568, 33 N.W. 919 (1887), reexamined and questioned in Lenawee County Board of Health v. Messerly, 417 Mich. 17, 331 N.W.2d 203 (1982).

95. 66 Mich. at 577, 33 N.W. at 923. See Smith v. Zimbalist, 2 Cal.App.2d 324, 38 P.2d 170 (1934) (violin was assumed to be a Stradivarius); Beachcomber Coins, Inc. v. Boskett, 166 N.J.Super. 442, 400 A.2d 78 (App.Div.1979) (counterfeit coin).

96. 3 Corbin § 605. For an economic analysis of risk assumption in this context, see Kronman, Mistake, Disclosure, Information and the Law of Contracts, 7 J.Leg. Stud. 1, 2–9 (1978).

97. Palmer, supra note 82, at 16–17.

98. 64 Wis. 265, 25 N.W. 42 (1885).

the parties expressed their ignorance of the nature of the stone and guessed it to be a topaz. It turned out to be an uncut diamond worth from $700 to $1,000, but the court refused to allow a rescission. The court made three points. First, the action was at law and not in equity, expressing no opinion on the question of whether the more liberal equity approach to mistake would produce a contrary decision.[99] Second, that the subject matter of the sale was a particular stone and there was no mistake as to which stone was sold. Third, and most fundamental, there was no mistake about the nature of the stone; there was conscious uncertainty. Therefore, each party took the risk that it was something more or less valuable than the agreed price.

Where there is conscious uncertainty there is an assumption of the risk that the resolution of the uncertainty may be unfavorable.[1] This principle is particularly noticeable in cases involving settlements by insurers. Where both the insured and insurer act under a mistaken belief that a given death or casualty loss has occurred, the settlement of the policy can be avoided.[2] Where, however, there is conscious doubt whether the death or casualty loss has occurred the settlement stands.[3]

The application of the leading precedents on the question of the basic nature of particular assumptions is most difficult. It may be quite obvious that a fire insurance binder issued when neither party knows that the insured premises are afire is rescindable because of mistake.[4] That a fire was in progress is not a risk assumed by the insurer. Put another way, a house ablaze is as different in kind from a house not ablaze as a barren cow is from a pregnant cow. On the other hand, consider the case of a settlement of a paternity suit. It is quite clear that paternity is one of the risks assumed by the male party to such a settlement and, if scientific evidence becomes available that he is not the father of the child, the settlement nonetheless stands.[5] It is not clear, however, whether the settlement involves the assumption of the risk that the pregnancy is a false one.[6]

99. See 13 Williston § 1579 as to the continued viability of the law-equity dichotomy as to mistake.

1. Restatement, Second, Contracts § 154(b); Backus v. Maclaury, 278 App. Div. 504, 106 N.Y.S.2d 401 (4th Dep't 1951), appeal denied 278 App.Div. 1043, 107 N.Y.S.2d 568 (1951) (conscious uncertainty as to potency of a bull). Where there is conscious ignorance and an opportunity to investigate the facts, *a fortiori* avoidance is not permitted. Southern Nat. Bank v. Crateo, Inc., 458 F.2d 688 (5th Cir.1972). The distinction between ignorance and mistake is discussed in Culbreath v. Culbreath, 7 Ga. 64, 70 (1849); see Restatement, Second, Contracts § 154, Comment c.

2. Continental Cas. Co. v. Van Deventer, 277 App.Div. 553, 101 N.Y.S.2d 342 (1st Dep't 1950).

3. New York Life Ins. Co. v. Chittenden & Eastmen, 134 Iowa 613, 112 N.W. 96 (1907); Sears v. Grand Lodge, AOUW, 163 N.Y. 374, 57 N.E. 618, 50 L.R.A. 204 (1900); contra, Phoenix Indem. Co. v. Steiden Stores, 267 S.W.2d 733 (Ky.1954), 40 Cornell L.Q. 618 (1955).

4. Powderly v. Aetna Cas. & Sur. Co., 72 Misc.2d 251, 338 N.Y.S.2d 555 (1972); accord, Richardson Lumber Co. v. Hoey, 219 Mich. 643, 189 N.W. 923 (1922) (sale of lumber which neither party knew was in imminent danger of fire).

5. Fiege v. Boehm, 210 Md. 352, 123 A.2d 316 (1956).

6. Rheel v. Hicks, 25 N.Y. 289 (1862) (mistake a good defense; pregnancy a vital fact not in issue); cf. Heaps v. Dunham, 95 Ill. 583, 590 (1880); Thompson v. Nelson, 28 Ind. 431 (1867). Of course, if the claim

A similarly difficult case was decided by the House of Lords.[7] Defendants were the chairman of the board and a director of a subsidiary of Lever Brothers. When the subsidiary was merged with another corporation, defendants agreed to release their rights under their employment contracts in return for a payment of £ 50,000. Soon thereafter, Lever Brothers became aware that defendants had committed breaches of trust and could have been fired without compensation.[8] Lever Brothers sought restitution on grounds of mistake. The court ruled for the defendants, saying, in effect, a contract to rescind a breached contract is not different in kind from a contract to rescind a contract not breached.

The difference "in kind" test employed by the cases if taken literally is subject to criticism, as being overly metaphysical.[9] But it is more generally employed in a metaphorical than metaphysical sense. When the court rules that there must be a difference in kind between the state of facts and the facts the parties had assumed to be true, it is employing an analogy to the early cases allowing rescission for a mistake in identity of the subject matter, and suggesting that the mistake must be about as vital as in those early cases. Metaphors, however, are dangerous for there are those who will take them literally. It would be beneficial if the rule were stated to be that for relief to be granted for mistake as to quality, the mistake must relate to a vital fact upon which the parties based their bargain.[10]

(c) Mistake in Acreage—Realty Contracts

A fact pattern which recurs with remarkable frequency involves a contract to convey or a conveyance of land under a mistake as to the number of acres in the parcel. If the acreage is materially at variance with what was believed, the aggrieved party may avoid the contract.[11] Where relief other than avoidance is sought a broad distinction is drawn between sales in gross and per acre sales. If the sale is on a per

---

is asserted in bad faith, there is no consideration. See § 4–8 supra.

7. Bell v. Lever Bros. Ltd., [1932] A.C. 161; criticized, Palmer, supra note 82, at 92–94.

8. Cf. Hadden v. Consolidated Edison Co. of New York, Inc., 34 N.Y.2d 88, 356 N.Y.S.2d 249, 312 N.E.2d 445 (1974), second appeal 45 N.Y.2d 466, 410 N.Y.S.2d 274, 382 N.E.2d 1136 (1978) (plaintiff was under suspicion of wrongful conduct when he retired with pension).

9. Palmer, supra note 82, at 46. The author favors a test of whether the mistake is "objectively basic." Id. at 47, 92. The court abandoned the "difference in kind" test in Lenawee County Board of Health v. Messerly, supra note 94.

10. For such an approach, see Davey v. Brownson, 3 Wn.App. 820, 478 P.2d 258, 50

A.L.R.3d 1182 (1970) (neither party knew motel contracted to be sold contained termites); Faria v. Southwick, 81 Idaho 68, 337 P.2d 374 (1959) (parties wrongly assumed productivity of leasehold); Hinson v. Jefferson, 24 N.C.App. 231, 210 S.E.2d 498 (1974), modified 287 N.C. 422, 215 S.E.2d 102 (1975); Vermette v. Andersen, 16 Wn.App. 466, 558 P.2d 258 (1976).

11. McGeorge v. White, 295 Ky. 367, 174 S.W.2d 532, 153 A.L.R. 1 (1943); D'Antoni v. Goff, 52 A.D.2d 973, 383 N.Y.S.2d 117 (3d Dep't 1976); Enequist v. Bemis, 115 Vt. 209, 55 A.2d 617, 1 A.L.R.2d 1 (1947), reargument denied 115 Vt. 209, 56 A.2d 5 (1947); see also 13 Williston § 1571; Comment, Real Estate: Purchaser's Remedies for Deficiency of Quantity, 49 Marquette L.Rev. 767 (1966).

acre basis, the purchaser may have pro rata restitution of the purchase price for any missing acres [12] and the seller has an action for additional payment for any excess acres.[13] If the sale is in gross, generally no relief other than avoidance of the entire transaction for a material variance is available.[14] It is often difficult to determine whether the sale is on an in gross or per acre basis. Among the factors to consider is whether the purchase price is an equimultiple of the acreage, whether the property is described by a name, as the XYZ ranch, or by acreage, whether the acreage had a uniform value, and whether personal property has been included in the sale price.[15]

(d) Releases—Mistake as to Injuries

A release of a personal injury claim is not a commercial transaction.[16] Social policies favoring the assumption of entrepreneurial risks as a means of improving market efficiency are not present. Instead, a policy of adequate compensation for injury tortiously done is strong. Boilerplate release forms releasing all injuries, known and unknown, present and future are not automatically honored.[17] The main tool for dishonoring them is a doctrine of mistake somewhat more flexible than is employed in commercial transactions.[18] Most of the cases involve mistake as to existence, nature or gravity of personal injuries.[19] There appear to be at least four views on the problem. The most strict view refuses to distinguish between personal injury and commercial releases.[20] Next in the spectrum is a view which distinguishes between unknown injuries and unknown consequences of known injuries; relief for mistake being available in the former but not in the latter case.[21] Application of this test has proved erratic. Where an injured party's symptom was a bruise on a foot, a settlement for $275 was allowed to

12. Paine v. Upton, 87 N.Y. 327, 41 Am. Rep. 371 (1882); Restatement, Second, Contracts § 158, ill. 1.

13. Cases of this type are very few. A relatively recent one is Lyons v. Keith, 316 S.W.2d 785 (Tex.App.1958), ref. n.r.e.

A good discussion is in Lawrence v. Staigg, 8 R.I. 256 (1866); see Restatement, Second, Contracts § 158, ill. 2. Contra, Ford v. Delph, 203 Mo.App. 659, 220 S.W. 719 (1920).

14. As to what constitutes a material variance, see Branton v. Jones, 222 Va. 305, 281 S.E.2d 799, 801 (1981). Granting an abatement in price contrary to the general rule is Glover v. Bullard, 170 Ark. 58, 278 S.W. 645 (1926).

15. Speedway Enterprises v. Hartsell, 75 Ariz. 36, 251 P.2d 641 (1952).

16. See Ricketts v. Pennsylvania R. Co., 153 F.2d 757, 767–68 (2d Cir.1946) (Frank, J., concurring).

17. See generally Dobbs, Conclusiveness of Personal Injury Settlements: Basic

Problems, 41 N.Car.L.Rev. 665 (1963); Havighurst, Problems Concerning Settlement Agreements, 53 Nw.U.L.Rev. 283 (1958); Keefe, Validity of Releases Executed Under Mistake of Fact, 14 Fordham L.Rev. 135 (1945); Annots., 71 A.L.R.2d 82, 13 A.L.R. 4th 686; 9 Wigmore, Evidence § 2416; Restatement, Second, Contracts § 154, Comment f.

18. Of course releases are frequently also attacked on grounds of duress, misrepresentation and mistake of law.

19. Other cases involve (a) mistake as to the nature of the instrument executed or (b) mistake as to the contents of the instrument. Keefe, supra note 17, at 136–40.

20. Bernstein v. Kapneck, 290 Md. 452, 430 A.2d 602 (1981).

21. Mangini v. McClurg, 24 N.Y.2d 556, 301 N.Y.S.2d 508, 249 N.E.2d 386 (1969); Reynolds v. Merrill, 23 Utah 2d 155, 460 P.2d 323 (1969).

stand despite the fact that the injury subsequently required amputation of the leg. The amputation was deemed the consequence of a known injury.[22] On the other hand, knowledge of superficial injury to the knee was held not knowledge of serious bone injury.[23]

A third view, often indistinguishable from the second; but somewhat more relaxed, distinguishes between mistake as to the nature and *extent* of an injury for which relief is available and mistaken belief as to its future course [24] for which no relief is available. Diagnosis is distinguished from prognosis.

A fourth approach is difficult to synthesize. It is clearly the approach most favorable to the injured party. It operates from the general principle allowing relief for vital mistake rather than from any particular formulation. Thus a vital mistake as to prognosis is grounds for setting aside the release.[25]

A special rule governs as to seamen, who, as wards of admiralty receive paternalistic treatment. A release will not be sustained unless it is fair, just and reasonable.[26] "The tender consideration of admiralty for those 'favorites' of the court who are 'a class of persons remarkable for their rashness, thoughtlessness and improvidence' " [27] is the asserted basis for this rule.

(e) Mistaken Predictions

The doctrine of mistake concerns itself with mistaken understandings of existing facts.[28] If the mistake relates to future events, relief is available, if at all, only under the doctrines of impracticability or frustration.[29]

 WESTLAW REFERENCES

"unilateral mistake" /s relief

contract! bargain agreement /s void! avoid! /s "mutual mistake"

22. Mack v. Albee Press, 263 App.Div. 275, 32 N.Y.S.2d 231 (1st Dep't), affirmed 288 N.Y. 623, 42 N.E.2d 617 (1942), motion denied 288 N.Y. 734, 43 N.E.2d 354 (1942).

23. Lockrow v. Church of the Holy Family, 5 A.D.2d 959, 171 N.Y.S.2d 622 (4th Dep't 1958), affirmed 5 N.Y.2d 1024, 185 N.Y.S.2d 549, 158 N.E.2d 249 (1959).

24. Newborn v. Hood, 86 Ill.App.3d 784, 42 Ill.Dec. 96, 408 N.E.2d 474, 13 A.L.R. 4th 681 (1980); Poti v. New England Road Mach. Co., 83 N.H. 232, 140 A. 587 (1928).

25. Witt v. Watkins, 579 P.2d 1065 (Alaska 1978); Reed v. Harvey, 253 Iowa 10, 110 N.W.2d 442 (1961); Sloan v. Standard Oil Co., 177 Ohio St. 149, 203 N.E.2d 237, 29 O.O.2d 355 (1964), 16 West Res.L. Rev. 1004 (1965).

26. See the opinion of Mr. Justice Story in Harden v. Gordon, 11 Fed.Cas. 480 (No. 6,047) (C.C.Me.1823); and Garrett v.

Moore-McCormack Co., 317 U.S. 239, 63 S.Ct. 246, 87 L.Ed. 239 (1942).

27. Bonici v. Standard Oil Co. of New Jersey, 103 F.2d 437, 438 (2d Cir.1939), quoting from Mr. Justice Story in Brown v. Lull, 4 Fed.Cas. 407, 409 (No. 2018) (C.C. Mass.1836).

28. Backer Management Corp. v. Acme Quilting Co., 46 N.Y.2d 211, 413 N.Y.S.2d 135, 385 N.E.2d 1062 (1978); Leasco Corp. v. Taussig, 473 F.2d 777 (2d Cir.1972).

29. Metropolitan Life Ins. Co. v. Kase, 718 F.2d 306 (9th Cir.1983), on rehearing 720 F.2d 1081 (9th Cir.1983); but see Aluminum Co. of America v. Essex Group, Inc., 499 F.Supp. 53, 71 (W.D.Pa.1980), criticised in Wabash, Inc. v. Avnet, Inc., 516 F.Supp. 995 (N.D.Ill.1981), distinguished in Louisiana Power & Light Co. v. Allegheny Ludlum Indus., 517 F.Supp. 1319 (E.D.La.1981).

"mutual mistake" /s contemplat! /s party

95k93(5)

"subject matter" /s mistak! /s seller vendor % jurisdiction

(a) Existence, Ownership, or Identity of Subject Matter

di("mutual mistake" /s "subject matter" % jurisdiction)

own*** ownership /s "implied warranty of title"

mistak! /s identity /s "subject matter"

(b) Qualities of the Subject Matter and Conscious Uncertainty

mistak! +3 quality

sherwood +2 walker

mistak /s fact /s material! /s affect! /s contract***

assum! +2 risk /s uncertain! /s contract*** agreement

mistak! /s "vital fact" "basic assumption"

(c) Mistake in Acreage—Realty Contracts

contract*** agreement /s mistak! /s number /s acre***

mistak! /s acre*** /s gross

mistak! /s quantity /s acre***

mistak! /s acre*** /s description describ!

(d) Releases—Mistake as to Injuries

"personal injury" /s releas! /s mistak!

mistak! /s injur! /s "settlement agreement"

mistak! /s exist! serious! nature gravity /s "personal injury"

releas! /s "personal injury" /s commercial

injur! /s unknown /s consequence /s mistak!

settlement releas! /s injur! /s future /s mistak!

releas! /s injur! /s mistak! /s prognosis

331k16 /p injur!

seaman /s releas! /s injur!

(e) Mistaken Predictions

§ 9–27. Unilateral Mistake

Until recently the common generalization has been that avoidance is not available for unilateral mistake except where the other party knows or has reason to know the mistake,[30] but, as Professor Corbin has pointed out, "the decisions that are inconsistent with it are too numerous and too appealing to the sense of justice to be disregarded.[31] Since those words were written, an increasing number of cases have permitted avoidance where only one party was mistaken. Today avoidance is

---

30. Foulke, Mistake in the Formation and Performance of a Contract, 11 Colum. L.Rev. 197, 299 (1911); Restatement, Contracts § 503; Restatement, Restitution § 12. Such statements continue to be found in many cases. E.g., Cohen v. Merrill, 95 Idaho 99, 503 P.2d 299, 304 (1972). But frequently in one jurisdiction one finds the generalization repeated, but specific cases to the contrary. See, e.g., Rescission of Contracts—Unilateral Mistake in Florida, 18 U.Miami L.Rev. 954 (1964).

31. 3 Corbin § 608, at 675. The existence of such cases had been noted by some earlier authorities but dismissed as aberrations. One saying, "the doctrine is opposed by the great preponderance of the authorities." 1 Black § 128, at 397; cf. 1 Page, The Law of Contracts § 256 (2d ed. 1920).

generally allowed if two conditions concur: 1) enforcement of the contract against the mistaken party would be oppressive, or, at least, result in an unconscionably unequal exchange of values and 2) rescission would impose no substantial hardship on the other.[32]

The most frequent fact pattern in which relief for unilateral mistake is sought involves a mistaken bid by a construction contractor, usually caused by computational error or misconstruction of the invitation to bid. Several decades ago relief generally was not allowed unless the error was "palpable;" that is, known or obvious to the party receiving the bid.[33] Recent cases are, however, to the contrary, permitting relief even for impalpable mistake.[34] It is quite apparent that if liberally applied, such a rule would erode, if not totally deluge, the prevailing objective theory of contracts.[35] It is therefore not surprising that there are strict limitations upon the right to avoid a contract for unilateral impalpable mistake.[36] First, relief is not available unless the agreement is entirely executory or the other party can be placed in the status quo ante.[37] Second, the mistake must be vital. If the mistake is large enough that it should be obvious, then the mistake is classified as palpable and relief is easily given.[38] If, on the opposite end, the mistake is not substantial, relief is not given.[39] Therefore, if the

32. Restatement, Second, Contracts § 153(a) and Comment d; Maryland Casualty Co. v. Krasnek, 174 So.2d 541, 577 (Fla.1965); Gethsemane Lutheran Church v. Zacho, 258 Minn. 438, 104 N.W.2d 645 (1960); Da Silva v. Musso, 53 N.Y.2d 543, 428 N.E.2d 382 (1981); cf. Beatty v. Depue, 78 S.D. 395, 103 N.W.2d 187, 1 A.L.R.3d 531 (1960) (less restrictive approach); 13 Williston §§ 1577–1578.

33. See Lubell, Unilateral Palpable and Impalpable Mistake in Construction Contracts, 16 Minn.L.Rev. 137 (1932); cf. Centex Constr. Co. v. James, 374 F.2d 921 (8th Cir.1967) (ambiguous specifications); Patterson, Equitable Relief for Unilateral Mistake, 28 Colum.L.Rev. 859, 884–94 (1928). In our text, as in the Restatement, the question of mistake of one party known to the other is dealt with under the heading of misrepresentation and non-disclosure. See § 9–20 supra.

34. White v. Berenda Mesa Water Dist., 7 Cal.App.3d 894, 87 Cal.Rptr. 338 (1970); Boise Junior College Dist. v. Mattefs Constr. Co., 92 Idaho 757, 450 P.2d 604 (1969); see Fields, Relief from Mistake in Bids, 32 Ins.Couns.J. 259 (1965); Hume, Mistakes in Bids and Bid Bond Liability, 35 Ins.Couns. J. 36 (1968); Owens, A Primer of Procurement by Formal Advertising and Relief for Mistakes in Bids, 42 N.Y.St.B.J. 428 (1970).

35. See 13 Williston § 1579. As to gifts given under mistake there is no such danger in granting relief for mistake and such

relief is granted with great liberality. Deskovick v. Porzio, 78 N.J.Super. 82, 187 A.2d 610 (App.Div.1963); In re Agnew's Will, 132 Misc. 466, 230 N.Y.S. 519 (1928); Comment, 58 Mich.L.Rev. 90 (1959).

36. That satisfactory techniques for dealing with this problem have not been worked out, see Palmer, Mistake and Unjust Enrichment 96–98 (1962). For a proposed statute, see 1967 Report, Recommendations and Studies of the N.Y.Law Revision Commission 377.

37. Monarch Marking System Co. v. Reed's Photo Mart, Inc., 485 S.W.2d 905 (Texas 1972); contra, Crenshaw County Hosp. Bd. v. St. Paul Fire & Marine Ins. Co., 411 F.2d 213 (5th Cir.1969) (other party's expectations are to be compensated).

38. City of Syracuse v. Sarkisian Bros., Inc., 87 A.D.2d 984, 451 N.Y.S.2d 945 (4th Dep't 1982), affirmed 57 N.Y.2d 618, 454 N.Y.S.2d 71, 439 N.E.2d 880 (1982). If the bidder notifies the other party before the bid is accepted, even if a statute makes the bid irrevocable, the mistake becomes palpable and rescission is allowed. Ruggiero v. United States, 190 Ct.Cl. 327, 420 F.2d 709 (1970); M.F. Kemper Constr. Co. v. Los Angeles, 37 Cal.2d 696, 235 P.2d 7 (1951). Such cases actually support relief for unilateral mistake, since the mistake is used as a basis for relief from the irrevocable offer which is itself a contract.

39. Fields, supra note 34, at 260.

mistake involved is impalpable, it must be substantial, but not astronomical. The test of substantiality is probably met in the bidding cases if the mistake swallows up the allocation made in the bid for profit.[40] A third restriction is that the mistake must be of a clerical or computational error or a misconstruction of the specifications or something of that sort. Rescission is not allowed for a mistake of judgment.[41] Many of the cases routinely state that the error should not have been negligent. But, of course, the essence of the holdings is that there must have been negligence of a particular sort. When this is realized, courts have floundered with "culpable" versus ordinary negligence, "bad faith" versus "good faith" negligence and other such nonsense.[42] Unilateral mistake is grounds for rescission by the mistaken party at his election. It cannot be invoked by the other party.[43]

The remedy of specific performance is a discretionary one and unilateral mistake may be raised as a defense under circumstances in which an action for restitution would not be permitted.[44] It has been urged that the rule applicable to specific performance be applied to restitution.[45] Not surprisingly, proponents of extension of relief for unilateral mistake are much attached to the will theory of contracts [46] and opponents tend to regard the will theory as an outlandish transplant into American law.[47]

WESTLAW REFERENCES

"unilateral mistake" /s void! avoid! /s unconscionab!

unilateral /s mistak! /s palpable

"unilateral mistake" /s bid bidding /s construction

"unilateral mistake" /s executory

"unilateral mistake" /s comput! clerical

"unilateral mistake" /s negligen!

"unilateral mistake" /s recission rescind!

"unilateral mistake" /s "specific! perform!"

358k52 /p unilateral

§ 9–28. Mistake of Law

In 1802 Lord Ellenborough committed a mistake of law when he ruled that, because ignorance of the law is no excuse, money paid under

40. Boise Junior College Dist. v. Mattefs Constr. Co., 92 Idaho 757, 450 P.2d 604 (1969).

41. President and Council of Mt. St. Mary's College v. Aetna Cas. & Sur. Co., 233 F.Supp. 787 (D.Md.1964), affirmed 344 F.2d 331 (4th Cir.1965).

42. See Fields, supra note 260–61; Annot. 52 A.L.R.2d 792 (1957).

43. United States v. Systron-Donner Corp., 486 F.2d 249 (9th Cir.1973).

44. 4500 Suitland Rd. Corp. v. Ciccarello, 269 Md. 444, 306 A.2d 512 (1973); Panco

v. Rogers, 19 N.J.Super. 12, 87 A.2d 770 (Ch.1952) (rescission and specific performance denied).

45. Newman, Relief for Mistake in Contracting, 54 Cornell L.Rev. 232, 237–48 (1969).

46. For good concise treatment, see Sharp, Williston on Contracts, 4 U.Chi.L. Rev. 30, 31–39 (1936).

47. Patterson, Equitable Relief for Unilateral Mistake, 28 Colum.L.Rev. 859 (1928).

a mistake of law that a debt was owed need not be repaid.[48] On the broad principle that relief is not available for mistake of law, he was confuted by a number of earlier cases.[49] Nonetheless, the plausibility of the principle, imported from the criminal law, was such that it was soon adopted by almost all of the United States; Connecticut[50] and Kentucky,[51] apparently, being the only exceptions. Others have since joined them,[52] some by statute.[53] On the whole, however, the rule denying relief has been eroded by so many qualifications and exceptions,[54] varying from jurisdiction to jurisdiction, that it has little, if any, vitality. It is common to find cases where the issue is not even raised.[55] The Restatement of Contracts Second expressly treats the old rule as non-existent and the Restatement of Restitution regards the rule as surviving only as to payments made pursuant to an honest demand under a mistaken belief of law that payment was owed.[56] The most common fact pattern to which this rule is applicable is distinctly non-contractual. It involves the payment of taxes or fees to a public agency which are subsequently determined to be unconstitutional or otherwise illegal. Mistake of law is not grounds for relief in such cases[57] although, on occasion, duress may be, as where one would be forced to discontinue doing business if a license fee is not paid.[58]

48. Bilbie v. Lumley, 2 East 469, 102 E.R. 448 (K.B.1802); see generally 3 Corbin §§ 616–620; 13 Williston §§ 1581–1592; 1 Black §§ 147–153; Woodward, The Law of Quasi Contracts §§ 35–44 (1913); Comment, 19 Hastings L.J. 1225 (1968).

49. See Ireton, Mistake of Law, 67 U.S.L.Rev. 405 (1933); Comment, Relief for Mistake of Law, 4 Fordham L.Rev. 466 (1935).

50. Park Bros. & Co. v. Blodgett & Clapp Co., 64 Conn. 28, 29 A. 133 (1894); Northrop's Ex'rs v. Graves, 19 Conn. 548 (1849).

51. McMurtry v. Kentucky Cent. R. Co., 84 Ky. 462, 1 S.W. 815 (1886); Ray v. Bank of Ky., 42 Ky. (3 Monroe) 510, 39 Am.Dec. 479 (Ky.1843).

52. Gartner v. Eikill, 319 N.W.2d 397 (Minn.1982); McFarland v. Stillwater County, 109 Mont. 544, 98 P.2d 321 (1940); contra, Marriott Fin. Services v. Capitol Funds, Inc., 23 N.C.App. 377, 209 S.E.2d 423 (1974).

53. E.g., McKinney's N.Y.C.P.L.R. 3005 (" * * * relief shall not be denied merely because the mistake is one of law rather than one of fact.") Other state statutes are considered in Act, Recommendation and Study Relating to Restitution of Money Paid Under Mistake of Law, Report of the [N.Y.] Law Rev.Comm. 27 (1942).

54. 13 Williston §§ 1581–1592; Smith, Correcting Mistakes of Law in Texas, 9 Tex.L.Rev. 309 (1931); Comment, Relief for

Mistake of Law, 4 Fordham L.Rev. 466, 471–75 (1935); Note, 30 Mich.L.Rev. 301 (1931). Compare the discussion relating to misrepresentation of law, § 9–18 supra.

55. 4500 Suitland Rd. Corp. v. Ciccarello, 269 Md. 444, 306 A.2d 512 (1973) (zoning ordinance).

56. Restatement, Second, Contracts § 151, Comment b; Restatement, Restitution, Introductory Note to Ch. 2, Topic 3, p. 179. A defense of the rule of no recovery for mistake of law may be found in Sutton, Kelly v. Solari: The Justification for the Ignorantia Juris Rule, 2 N.Z.U.L.Rev. 173 (1966); Note, Mistake of Law: A Suggested Rationale, 45 Harv.L.Rev. 336 (1931). It is followed in Commonwealth Department of General Services v. Collingdale Millwork Co., 71 Pa.Cmwlth. 286, 454 A.2d 1176 (1983); Webb v. Webb, ___ W.Va. ___, 301 S.E.2d 570 (1983).

57. Paramount Film Distributing Corp. v. State, 30 N.Y.2d 415, 334 N.Y.S.2d 388, 285 N.E.2d 695 (1972) (despite statute quoted note 53, supra). Canadian taxpayers appear to be more fortunate. See Crawford, Restitution: Mistake of Law and Practical Compulsion, 17 U. Toronto L.J. 344 (1967).

58. Manufacturer's Cas. Ins. Co. v. Kansas City, 330 S.W.2d 263, 80 A.L.R.2d 1035 (Mo.App.1959); Five Boro Elec. Contrs. Ass'n Inc. v. New York, 12 N.Y.2d 146, 237 N.Y.S.2d 315, 187 N.E.2d 774 (1962). If the payment is stated to be "under protest,"

WESTLAW REFERENCES
"mistake of law" /s restitution

§ 9–29. Mistake in Performance

When a valid and enforceable contract exists between the parties and one of the parties pays money to the other in the mistaken belief that the payment is required by the contract, he may recover the payment.[59] The same rule holds true if excess payment is made.[60] If something other than money has been transferred to the other, generally the same rule holds.[61] The transferor may recover the value of what has been transferred,[62] and, under proper circumstances, have specific restitution. Relief for mistake in performance is given far more readily than in cases of mistake in formation of a contract. It matters not that the mistake is merely unilateral and that it is negligent.[63] Inasmuch as the contract itself defines the rights of the parties, mistaken overpayment or the equivalent clearly involves the unjust enrichment of the payee and unjust impoverishment of the payor.

Exceptions to the mistake in performance rule exist. If the person who pays or transfers something is under a moral obligation to do so, he may not have restitution.[64] Thus if the obligation is unenforceable or discharged by bankruptcy or the statute of limitations or is otherwise barred by a legal but not a moral rule restitution is not available.[65]

Conscious ignorance must be distinguished from mistake. For example, where both the insured and the insurer act under a mistaken belief that a given death or casualty has occurred, the payment made is recoverable,[66] but if there is conscious doubt whether the death or casualty loss has occurred the settlement stands.[67] Also to be distinguished is the rule discussed in the previous section with respect to payments made under a mistaken belief of law that payment is owed and payment is demanded in good faith by the payee.

 WESTLAW REFERENCES
"mistake in performance"

this is usually treated as sufficient evidence of duress in this context.

59. Restatement, Restitution § 18; see generally, 13 Williston §§ 1574–1575; Woodward, supra note 48, § 179; Foulke, Mistake in the Formation and Performance of a Contract (Part II), 11 Colum.L. Rev. 299, 303–319 (1911).

60. McDonald's Corp. v. Moore, 237 F.Supp. 874 (W.D.S.C.1965); Restatement, Restitution § 20.

61. Restatement, Restitution §§ 39–40; Annot. 10 A.L.R.4th 524 (1984) (mistaken payments by banks).

62. Some of the difficulties involved in calculating "value" in this context are suggested by Findlay v. State, 113 Tex. 30, 250 S.W. 651 (1923) (conveyance of excess land).

63. Restatement, Restitution § 59.

64. Restatement, Restitution § 61; see Equilease Corp. v. Hentz, 634 F.2d 850 (5th Cir.1981).

65. On the legal meaning of moral obligation in the law of contracts, see ch. 5 supra.

66. Continental Cas. Co. v. Van Deventer, 277 App.Div. 553, 101 N.Y.S.2d 342 (1st Dep't 1950).

67. New York Life Ins. Co. v. Chittenden & Eastmen, 134 Iowa 613, 112 N.W. 96 (1907); Sears v. Grand Lodge AOUW, 163 N.Y. 374, 57 N.E. 618, 50 L.R.A. 204 (1900); contra, Phoenix Indemnity Co. v. Steiden Stores, 267 S.W.2d 733 (Ky.1954), 40 Cornell L.Q. 618 (1955).

mistak! /s perform! /s restitution recover!

agreement contract*** /s "mistaken belief" /s relief recover!
     restitution

equilease +s hentz

§ 9–30. Defenses—Change of Position, Ratification, Assumption of the Risk

Suppose because of mistake in formation of a contract or mistaken overpayment one party has clearly been unjustly enriched, but has subsequently spent the money or otherwise disposed of what he has received. Should not the payor be estopped from claiming restitution? The answer in general terms is that a detrimental change of position by the payee in reliance upon the overpayment may raise such an estoppel,[68] but merely spending the money may not be a detrimental change of position if it is not shown that the expenditure would not have been made from other funds. For example, where the payee used funds paid to her by mistake to pay off the mortgage on her house, she was not deemed to have engaged in a detrimental change of position.[69]

Other defenses to avoidance for mistake include affirmance of the transaction after knowledge of the mistake [70] and undue delay in manifesting an intent to rescind the transaction.[71] The need by the avoiding party to offer to restore what he has received is governed by essentially the same principles as in the case of avoidance for misrepresentation.[72]

As previously indicated, the underlying rationale for avoidance for mistake is that the risk of the particular unknown fact was not consciously assumed by, and is not reasonably allocable to, the party upon whom the consequences of the mistake will fall if the contract is not avoided.[73] The parties can expressly allocate the risk of mistake in the contract.[74] For example, it has been held that an "as is" clause allocated to the purchaser the risk of mutual mistake as to the usability and legality of the vendor's sewerage system.[75]

 WESTLAW REFERENCES

"change of position" /s overpaid overpay!

contract*** agreement /s mistak! /s defense defend*** /s
     chang! +2 position

---

68. Alden Auto Parts v. Dolphin Equipment Leasing, supra note 83; Lake Gogebic Lumber Co. v. Burns, 331 Mich. 315, 49 N.W.2d 310, 40 A.L.R.2d 993 (1951); Restatement, Restitution § 69; see Scott, Restitution from an Innocent Transferee who is Not a Purchaser for Value, 62 Harv.L. Rev. 1002 (1949).

69. Ohio Co. v. Rosemeier, 32 Ohio App. 2d 116, 288 N.E.2d 326 (1972).

70. Restatement, Restitution § 68.

71. Restatement, Restitution § 64.

72. Restatement, Restitution §§ 65–66; see § 9–23 supra.

73. See § 9–26 supra.

74. Restatement, Second, Contracts § 154(a).

75. Lewanee County Board of Health v. Messerly, supra note 94.

F. REFORMATION

Table of Sections

§ 9–31. Introduction to Reformation for Mistake

Reformation is the remedy by which writings are rectified to conform to the actual agreement of the parties.[76] At the simplest level it is the mechanism for the correction of typographical and other similar inadvertent errors in reducing an agreement to writing. There was no common law writ for such redress and reformation was developed as the quintessential equitable remedy, although now in a merged court it is sometimes available at law.[77] Reformation is available on grounds of mistake or misunderstanding [78] as well as duress and related misconduct. The substantive requisites vary with the basis. Reformation is not available except on clear and convincing evidence, a higher standard of proof than is normal in civil cases.[79]

Contracts are not reformed for mistake; writings are. The distinction is crucial. With rare exceptions, courts have been tenacious in refusing to remake a bargain entered into because of mistake.[80] They will, however, rewrite a writing which does not express the bargain.

---

76. See generally, 3 Palmer on Restitution §§ 13.1–13.19 (1978). In England the remedy is known as "rectification." See Powell-Smith, Rectifying Written Agreements, 120 New L.J. 330 (1970).

77. Restatement, Second, Contracts § 155, Comment a; Wilhide v. Keystone, Ins. Co., 195 F.Supp. 659 (M.D.Pa.1961).

78. On misunderstanding, see Palmer, The Effect of Misunderstanding on Contract Formation and Reformation Under the Restatement of Contracts Second, 65 Mich.L.Rev. 33, 51–56 (1966).

79. Restatement, Second, Contracts § 155, Comment c; Akkerman v. Gersema, 260 Iowa 432, 149 N.W.2d 856, 859 (1967); Housing Equity Corp. v. Joyce, 265 Md. 570, 290 A.2d 769 (1972); Amend v. Hurley, 293 N.Y. 587, 59 N.E.2d 416 (1944); Pepsi-Cola Bottling Co. v. Peerson, 471 P.2d 924 (Okl.1970). This standard of proof is often relaxed when there is a confi-

dential relationship between the parties. Hardy v. Hendrickson, 27 Utah 2d 251, 495 P.2d 28 (1972). See § 9–9 supra.

80. Mutual of Omaha Ins. Co. v. Russell, 402 F.2d 339 (10th Cir.1968), certiorari denied 394 U.S. 973, 89 S.Ct. 1456, 22 L.Ed. 2d 753 (1969), noted in 21 Ala.L.Rev. 389 (1969), 29 Md.L.Rev. 237 (1969); Japhe v. A–T–O Inc., 481 F.2d 366 (5th Cir.1973); Sardo v. Fidelity & Deposit Co., 100 N.J.Eq. 332, 134 A. 774 (1926).

Deviations from this principle are to be found in the U.S. Court of Claims. See National Presto Indus., Inc. v. United States, 167 Ct.Cl. 749, 338 F.2d 99 (1964), discussed at § 13–17 infra; Chernick v. United States, 178 Ct.Cl. 498, 372 F.2d 492 (1967) (reformation for mistake in bidding); Annot., 19 A.L.R.Fed. 645 (1974).

Where reformation is sought on grounds of unconscionability, the court can reshape the bargain. See § 9–35 infra.

Stated another way, courts give effect to the expressed wills of the parties; they will not second-guess what the parties would have agreed to if they had known the facts.

At times the distinction is very difficult to apply. Suppose X owns Blackacre including 100% of the mineral interests therein, but mistakenly believes that he owns but 50% of the mineral interests. He informs a prospective purchaser that he has a 50% mineral interest and that he will convey his entire interest with the land. Acting under this mutual mistake as to the extent of his ownership, he conveys Blackacre together with all his mineral rights in Blackacre to the purchaser.[81] Upon discovery of the mistake, may he have reformation? Was the agreement to convey his entire interest or to convey a 50% mineral interest in Blackacre? Courts have reached contradictory results in cases such as this, some being of the opinion that the mistake was one which induced the bargain and others that the mistake is in articulating the bargain.[82]

The requisites for reformation on grounds of mistake are three, although four are often stated.[83] First, there must have been an agreement between the parties. Second, there must have been an agreement to put the agreement into writing. Third, there is a variance between the prior agreement and the writing. The often-stated fourth requisite is that the mistake be mutual. However, except in cases of fraud, every variance between the prior agreement and the writing is deemed to constitute a mutual mistake.[84] Consequently the fourth element is included in the third. When courts speak of mutuality of the mistake, they usually have in mind that a mistaken belief by one party alone that the writing will contain a given provision is not a ground for reformation.[85] This, however, is encompassed in the requisite that there be a prior agreement that the provision be included in the writing. Thus, the mutual-unilateral mistake dichotomy adds nothing to the analysis of reformation problems. This fact has received judicial and scholarly recognition.[86]

Privity is not a requirement. A third party beneficiary may obtain reformation [87] even under circumstances where he is mistakenly excluded from the writing.[88]

---

81. This hypothetical is digested from Malone, The Reformation of Writings for Mutual Mistake of Fact, 24 Geo.L.J. 613, 634 (1936). For a similar dilemma, see Yeargan v. Bank of Montgomery, 268 Ark. 752, 595 S.W.2d 704 (1980).

82. Malone, supra note 81, at 634. In addition, see Metzler v. Bolen, 137 F.Supp. 457 (D.N.D.1956) (reformation denied); Continental Oil Co. v. Doornbos, 386 S.W.2d 610 (Tex.Civ.App.1964), reversed 402 S.W.2d 879 (1966).

83. The analysis which follows owes a large debt to Malone, supra note 81.

84. Malone, supra note 81, at 618.

85. See, e.g., American Family Mutual Ins. Co. v. Bach, 471 S.W.2d 474 (Mo.1971).

86. Alaska Foods, Inc. v. American Mfrs. Mut. Ins. Co., 482 P.2d 842 (Alaska 1971); Travelers Ins. Co. v. Bailey, 124 Vt. 114, 197 A.2d 813 (1964); Palmer, Mistake and Unjust Enrichment 78–79 (1962); 3 Palmer on Restitution § 13.5; but see Restatement, Second, Contracts § 155.

87. Wilhide v. Keystone Ins. Co., 195 F.Supp. 659 (M.D.Pa.1961).

88. Line Lexington Lumber & Millwork Co. v. Pennsylvania Pub. Corp., 451 Pa. 154, 301 A.2d 684 (1973).

WESTLAW REFERENCES

di reformation

nature content quality /s mistak! /s "subject matter"

reform! /s "actual agreement of the parties"

to(328) /p typographical inadverten! scrivener

reformation /s misunderstand! misunderstood

reformation /s "clear and convincing"

reformation /s express! /s writing /s mistak! /s party

requisite /s reformation /s agreement contract***

§ 9–32. The Prior Agreement

It is not a prerequisite to an action for reformation that the antecedent agreement be a contract. It may have merely been an agreement to the effect that if a contract is made and reduced to writing it will contain a particular provision.[89] It may have been a provision contained in a tentative agreement of the type that will not bind the parties until an integration is executed.[90] If by error, rather than by subsequent modification,[91] the writing is at variance with the prior agreement, the writing may be reformed.

 WESTLAW REFERENCES

reformation /s "prior agreement"

§ 9–33. The Agreement to Reduce to Writing: Intentional Omissions and Misstatements

With some frequency, for a multitude of reasons, usually unsound, parties knowingly fail to include an agreed term in their writing. Under some circumstances the parol evidence rule will not bar evidence of that term in an action at law and there is no need for reformation.[92] There is grave danger, however, that the court will deem the writing to be an integration that bars extrinsic evidence of the term.[93] Although the parol evidence rule is not a defense in an action for reformation, reformation is not available for an intentional omission because there was no agreement to put the term into writing.[94] The only possible hope of reformation is if a case for fraud conceivably can be made out.[95] Similarly, if the parties intentionally misstate a term of their agreement, reformation is not available,[96] although if the parties agreed that

89. Restatement, Second, Contracts § 155, Comment a; Joscelyne v. Nissen, [1970] 2 W.L.R. 509, (C.A.), noted in 120 New L.J. 330.

90. 3 Corbin § 614, at 724.

91. See Mid-States Underwriters, Inc. v. Leonhard, 48 Wis.2d 176, 179 N.W.2d 914 (1970).

92. See ch. 3 supra.

93. See § 3–3 supra.

94. Frantl Industries, Inc. v. Maier Constr., Inc., 68 Wis.2d 590, 229 N.W.2d 610 (1975); see Abbott, Mistake of Fact as a Ground for Affirmative Equitable Relief, 23 Harv.L.Rev. 608, 618 (1910); Palmer, Reformation and the Parol Evidence Rule, 65 Mich.L.Rev. 833, 842–44 (1967).

95. See § 9–35 infra.

96. Grubb v. Rockey, 366 Pa. 592, 79 A.2d 255 (1951) criticized in Palmer, supra note 94, at 840–42, 849–50.

the writing would be inoperative a declaratory judgment that the agreement is a sham and therefore a nullity may be available.[97]

 WESTLAW REFERENCES
reformation /s misstat! omit! omission /s intentional! kn*w!
328k21

§ 9–34. The Variance

The variance between the original agreement and the writing may take any one of an infinity of conceivable forms. Typically, there "is the insertion of an incorrect description of the subject matter; street numbers, survey numbers, boundary lines," etc.[98] Computational errors are frequent.[99] Often, the mistake is as to the legal effect of the writing; the parties' agreement called for a particular legal result. The writing, if enforced, produces a different result. Reformation is available.[1]

At times the parties disagree as to the meaning of a writing. One of them takes the position that either his interpretation is the correct one, properly restating the prior agreement, or, if his interpretation is incorrect, the writing ought to be reformed. Such pleading in the alternative is generally permitted under modern practice.[2] While parol evidence is freely admitted on the reformation count,[3] it must satisfy rules excluding parol evidence for purposes of interpretation.[4]

 WESTLAW REFERENCES
mistak! /s "legal effect" /s reformation
"subject matter" /s describ! description /s reformation
reformation /s "parol* evidence rule"
reformation /s "parol* evidence" /s interpret!

§ 9–35. Reformation for Misrepresentation, Non-disclosure or Duress

Where, because of mistake, a writing fails accurately to state the agreement of the parties, reformation is the exclusive remedy. If the

97. See § 3–7 supra.

98. 3 Corbin § 614, p. 714.

99. Covington, Reformation of Contracts of Personal Insurance, 1964 U.Ill. L.F. 548, 552–53.

1. Pasotex Petroleum Co. v. Cameron, 283 F.2d 63 (10th Cir.1960); Franz v. Franz, 308 Mass. 262, 32 N.E.2d 205, 135 A.L.R. 1448 (1941); 3 Corbin § 619; Restatement, Second, Contracts, Comment a; Thompson, Reformation of Written Instruments in Iowa, 23 Drake L.Rev. 327, 334 (1974).

2. Metro Office Parks Co. v. Control Data Corp., 295 Minn. 348, 205 N.W.2d 121 (1973). See Thompson, supra note 1, at

337–38; Comment, Reformation of Written Instruments in Missouri, 37 Mo.L.Rev. 54, 57 (1972); cf. General Discount Corp. v. Sadowski, 183 F.2d 542 (6th Cir.1950) where reformation was granted after plaintiff had lost an action at law based upon his interpretation. Such trial strategy runs into the danger in some jurisdictions of running afoul of the plea of res judicata. See 3 Corbin § 615, p. 735; Annot., 49 A.L.R. 1513 (1927).

3. Restatement, Second, Contracts § 214(d). On the question of the Statute of Frauds and reformation, see § 19–28 infra.

4. See Palmer, supra note 94, at 840 n. 27.

writing is inaccurate because of fraud, the alternative remedies of reformation and rescission are available.[5] It is not every fraud that gives rise to a right of reformation. The misrepresentation must relate to the content or legal effect of the writing.[6] Misrepresentations concerning the qualities of the subject matter or other factors which affect the desirability of the bargain or the economic equivalence of the exchange are not grounds for reformation. Such relief would require the court to remake the agreement itself. Deviations from this principle have been few.[7]

One case, Brandwein v. Provident Mutual Life Ins. Co., has been singled out for such alleged deviation.[8] Plaintiff signed a written agreement on the fraudulent promise that additional promises omitted from the writing would be recorded in the corporate promisor's records. Plaintiff's complaint requesting reformation was upheld. Although this may be fraud in the inducement rather than fraud as to the content of the writing, it does not go to desirability of the bargain, rather, it goes towards its transcription. Thus it appears to be sound.

Non-disclosure is treated as the equivalent of misrepresentation where one party knows that the writing does not express the intention of the other and knows the other's intention.[9]

Duress is normally a ground only for setting a transaction aside. Where, however, because of duress a party is forced, for example, to assent to a mortgage on terms different from those that had earlier been contractually agreed upon, reformation of the mortgage to conform to the prior contract is an appropriate alternative.[10]

  WESTLAW REFERENCES
reformation /s duress
reformation /s misrepresentation

§ 9–36. Defenses to Reformation

Reformation will not be granted if its effect would be to curtail the rights of a bona fide purchaser for value or others who have relied upon

5. Restatement, Second, Contracts § 166, Comment b. Reformation was coupled with an award of punitive damages in Hedworth v. Chapman, 135 Ind.App. 129, 192 N.E.2d 649 (1963).

6. Restatement, Second, Contracts § 166, Comment b; International Milling Co. v. Hachmeister, Inc., 380 Pa. 407, 110 A.2d 186 (1955).

7. Brandwein v. Provident Mut. Life Ins. Co., 3 N.Y.2d 491, 168 N.Y.S.2d 964, 146 N.E.2d 693 (1957), criticised in Note, 44 Cornell L.Q. 124 (1958); Comment, 37 Mo. L.Rev. 54, 68–69 (1972).

8. See Note 27 Fordham L.Rev. 125 (1958). Other cases alleged to deviate from the general rule are cited in McClintock, Equity § 100 (2d ed. 1948). McClintock's analysis is challenged in Comment, 37 Mo. L.Rev. 54, 69 n. 89 (1972).

9. Line Lexington Lumber & Millwork Co. v. Pennsylvania Pub. Corp., 451 Pa. 154, 301 A.2d 684 (1973); Restatement, Contracts § 505; cf. Palmer, Mistake and Unjust Enrichment 76 (2d ed. 1962).

10. Leben v. Nassau Sav. & Loan Ass'n, 40 A.D.2d 830, 337 N.Y.S.2d 310 (2d Dep't 1972), affirmed 34 N.Y.2d 671, 356 N.Y.S.2d 46, 312 N.E.2d 180 (1974).

the writing.[11] Normally reformation will not be given against a donor of a gratuitous conveyance or other instrument of gift.[12]

Many tortured opinions have been written on the question of the negligence of the claimant to reformation. Where one party carelessly believes that a writing contains a certain clause or produces a given result and this belief is neither shared nor induced by the other, the temptation is to deny relief on the ground of the petitioner's negligence.[13] A sounder ground is that the writing does not counterfeit the prior agreement. The weight of authority is that if the requisites of reformation are met, negligence is not a bar to reformation unless the negligence has in some way harmed the other, non-negligent, party.[14]

As is the case with avoidance, the right to reformation can be lost by ratification.[15] And, since reformation is an equitable remedy, equitable defenses such as unclean hands and laches are, of course, applicable. As in the case of equity decrees generally, the court may impose such conditions upon its decree as it deems equitable.[16]

WESTLAW REFERENCES

328k29

reformation /s gratuitous!

reformation /s negligen! /s bar barred barring

328k25

ratif! /s reformation

328k32

G. UNCONSCIONABILITY

Table of Sections

11. Holton State Bank v. Greater Milwaukee Food Merchants Ass'n, Inc., 9 Wis. 2d 95, 100 N.W.2d 322, 79 A.L.R.2d 1176 (1960); Restatement, Second, Contracts § 155, Comment f.

12. Restatement, Second, Contracts § 155, Comment b; Clark, Equity §§ 258–59 (1954).

13. E.g., Harris v. Uhlendorf, 24 N.Y.2d 463, 301 N.Y.S.2d 53, 248 N.E.2d 892 (1969).

14. Anderson, Clayton & Co. v. Farmers Nat. Bank, 624 F.2d 105 (10th Cir.1980);

Maland v. Houston Fire & Cas. Ins. Co. of Fort Worth, Tex., 274 F.2d 299, 81 A.L.R.2d 1 (9th Cir.1960); Woodriff v. Ashcraft, 263 Or. 547, 503 P.2d 472 (1972); Restatement, Contracts § 508; cf. Restatement, Second, Contracts § 157; Clark, Equity § 271 (1954); Comment, Reformation of Written Instruments in Missouri, 37 Mo. L.Rev. 54, 85–90 (1972).

15. Clark, Equity § 274 (1954).

16. Mader v. Hintz, 186 N.W.2d 897 (N.D.1971).

§ 9–37. The Uniform Commercial Code Provision on Unconscionability

Few, if any, sections of the Uniform Commercial Code [17] have attracted more attention than its provision on unconscionability.[18] The provision reads as follows:

> (1) If the court as a matter of law finds the contract or any clause of the contract to have been unconscionable at the time it was made the court may refuse to enforce the contract, or it may enforce the remainder of the contract without the unconscionable clause, or it may so limit the application of any unconscionable clause as to avoid any unconscionable result.

> (2) When it is claimed or appears to the court that the contract or any clause thereof may be unconscionable the parties shall be afforded a reasonable opportunity to present evidence as to its commercial setting, purpose and effect to aid the court in making the determination.

The legislative purpose of the section is illuminated by the following language in the official comment.

> "This section is intended to make it possible for the courts to police explicitly against the contracts or clauses which they find to be unconscionable. In the past such policing has been accomplished by adverse construction of language, by manipulation of the rules of offer and acceptance or by determinations that the clause is contrary to public policy or to the dominant purpose of the contract. This section is intended to allow the court to pass directly on the unconscionability of the contract or particular clause therein and to make a conclusion of law as to its unconscionability. The basic test is whether, in the light of the general commercial background and the commercial needs of the particular trade or

---

17. U.C.C. § 2–302. The concept of unconscionability is also operative in U.C.C. §§ 2–309(3) (termination) and 2–719(3) (limitations on consequential damages). A substantially similar provision has been enacted in New York applicable to real property leases. McKinney's N.Y. Real Prop.Law § 235–c.

18. The most recent law review literature centers upon Leff, Unconscionability and the Code: The Emperor's New Clause, 115 U.Pa.L.Rev. 485 (1967), an intensive study of the various drafts of this Code provision and an often brilliant analysis of the problems of its interpretation and application, but often idiosyncratic in its "value judgments, lamentations, and prophecies of doom." Braucher, The Unconscionable Contract or Term, 31 U.Pitt. L.Rev. 337, 338 (1970). Among the more helpful articles are Davenport, Unconscionability and the Uniform Commercial Code, 22 U.Miami L.Rev. 121 (1967); Ellinghaus, In Defense of Unconscionability, 78 Yale L.J. 757 (1969); Epstein, Unconscionability: A Critical Reappraisal, 18 J.Law & Ec. 293 (1975); Fort, Understanding Unconscionability: Defining the Principle, 9 Loy.U.Chi.L.J. 765 (1978); Hillman, Debunking Some Myths About Unconscionability: A New Framework for U.C.C. § 2–302, 67 Cornell L.Rev. 1 (1981); Schwartz, A Reexamination of Nonsubstantive Unconscionability, 63 Va.L.Rev. 1053 (1977); Spanogle, Analyzing Unconscionability Problems, 117 U.Pa.L.Rev. 931 (1969); Speidel, Unconscionability, Assent and Consumer Protection, 31 U.Pitt.L.Rev. 359 (1970). An acute but rather narrow reading of the intent of the section is Murray, Unconscionability: Unconscionability, 31 U.Pitt.L.Rev. 1 (1969). The balance of the literature, much of very high quality, is vast.

case, the clauses involved are so one-sided as to be unconscionable under the circumstances existing at the time of the making of the contract. Subsection (2) makes it clear that it is proper for the court to hear evidence upon these questions. *The principle is one of the prevention of oppression and unfair surprise* (Cf. Campbell Soup Co. v. Wentz, 172 F.2d 80 (3d Cir.1948)) and not of disturbance of allocation of risks because of superior bargaining power." (Emphasis supplied).

"Oppression" is quite distinct from "surprise." Professor Leff labelled the two kinds of unconscionability as "substantive" and "procedural," distinguishing the content of the contract from the process by which the allegedly offensive terms found their way into the agreement.[19] Many authorities adopted this terminology. Professor Schwartz has suggested that the word, "nonsubstantive," be substituted for "procedural," because some non-procedural factors, such as the status of the parties, are often decisive on the issue of unconscionability.[20] We adopt his suggestion.

An understanding of the U.C.C. condemnation of unconscionability is best understood against the historical background of the concept.

 WESTLAW REFERENCES

unconscionab! /s u.c.c. "uniform commercial code" /s 2–302

"uniform commercial code" u.c.c. /p "prevention of oppression" leff
   /p unconscionab!

unconscionab! /s substantive! /s nonsubstantive! procedural!

§ 9–38. Historical Background

The concept of unconscionability has deep roots in our legal system both in law and equity, but primarily in equity. Indeed, Chief Justice Stone exaggerated only a bit when he described the concept of unconscionability as underlying "practically the whole content of the law of equity." [21] On the ground that a contrary result would involve the "unconscionable exercise of a legal right," mortgagees were and are enjoined from insisting upon a default when the mortgagor tenders late payment.[22] Holders of legal title to land who agree to hold it for the benefit of another were and are enjoined from utilizing the land for their own benefit, for such utilization would involve the unconscionable exercise of legal title.[23] The enforcement of penalty clauses was enjoined by equity on the ground that such remedial relief would be the

19. Leff, note 18 supra, at 487.

20. Schwartz, note 18 supra, at 1054–55.

21. Stone, Book Review, 12 Colum.L. Rev. 756, 756 (1912).

22. Osborne, Mortgages 12–15 (2d ed. 1970). For application of unconscionability doctrine in such a case beyond the general rules developed in this area, see Domus Realty Corp. v. 3440 Realty Co., 179 Misc. 749, 40 N.Y.S.2d 69 (1943), affirmed 266 App.Div. 725, 41 N.Y.S.2d 940 (1st Dep't 1943). Equity doctrine and U.C.C. unconscionability provisions were applied to relieve from an automobile forfeiture in Urdang v. Muse, 114 N.J.Super. 372, 276 A.2d 397 (1971).

23. Bogert, Trusts 9–10 (5th ed. 1973); Scott, Abridgment of the Law of Trusts §§ 1.1–1.6 (1960).

result of unconscionable insistence upon one's legal remedy.[24] Thus equity has a long history of concern with the *substantive* conscionability of the exercise of rights given by agreement.[25] With the passage of time each of the categories alluded to above became a recognized doctrine with general rules, exceptions and variations. This hardening of the categories was never complete and to the time of enactment of the Uniform Commercial Code equity continued, and doubtless will continue, to exercise its generalized power to refuse to enforce oppressive bargains on grounds of substantive unconscionability even outside of distinct doctrines relating to mortgages, trusts, penalties and other matters of special equitable cognizance.[26] Where equitable relief is denied on the generalized doctrine of unconscionability the right to enforce the contract at law is frequently preserved,[27] although often this right is of little use.[28]

Equity has through the centuries also been concerned with *nonsubstantive* conscionability. Agreements are set aside or enforcement is refused in the presence of undue influence,[29] misrepresentation,[30] and other kinds of nonsubstantive unconscionability. Indeed, in one of the more frequently cited cases involving a discussion of unconscionability,[31] the equitable doctrine was adopted in a law case and helped establish the doctrine of relief for unilateral palpable mistake.[32] The case is an excellent illustration of how certain categories of relief originally based upon the generalized concept of unconscionability emerge and are subsequently discussed without regard for their origin. Despite the emergence of such categories, equity continues to apply the original generalized concept of unconscionability when circumstances warrant, refusing to enforce a contract unless it "is fair and open, and in regard to which all material matters known to each have been communicated to the other." [33]

24. The rule of non-enforcement of penalty clauses has been borrowed by law from equity and equitable relief from such a clause is now unnecessary. See § 14–31 infra; 1 Pomeroy, Equity Jurisprudence §§ 72, 434 (4th ed. 1918). Pre-U.C.C. cases at law expressly placing non-enforcement of penalties on grounds of unconscionability include Marshall Milling Co. v. Rosenbluth, 231 Ill.App. 325, 336 (1924); Greer v. Tweed, 13 Abb.Pr., N.S. 427 (N.Y.C.P.1872).

25. See Julius Stone, Human Law and Human Justice, ch. 3 § 10 (1965).

26. Campbell Soup v. Wentz, 172 F.2d 80 (3d Cir.1948) (noted in several law reviews); Weeks v. Pratt, 43 F.2d 53 (5th Cir. 1930); Clark v. Rosario Min. & Mill. Co., 99 C.C.A. 534, 176 Fed. 180 (9th Cir.1910); Marks v. Gates, 83 C.C.A. 321, 154 Fed. 481 (9th Cir.1907); Nevada Nickel Syndicate v. National Nickel Co., 96 Fed. 133 (D.Nev. 1899); Chewning v. Brand, 230 Ga. 255, 196 S.E.2d 399 (1973); McKinnon v. Benedict, 38 Wis.2d 607, 157 N.W.2d 665 (1968),

and see Comment, 44 Can.Bar Rev. 142 (1966).

27. Pope Mfg. Co. v. Gormully, 144 U.S. 224, 12 S.Ct. 632, 36 L.Ed. 414 (1892). See also Kleinberg v. Ratett, 252 N.Y. 236, 169 N.E. 289 (1929). Equity, however, would and will frequently order the rescission of contracts on grounds of fraud and the like, rendering the contract unenforceable even at law.

28. See Frank and Endicott, Defenses in Equity and "Legal Rights," 14 La.L.Rev. 380 (1954).

29. See §§ 9–9 to 9–12 supra.

30. See §§ 9–13 to 9–24 supra.

31. Hume v. United States, 132 U.S. 406, 10 S.Ct. 134, 33 L.Ed. 393 (1889).

32. See § 9–27 supra.

33. Rothmiller v. Stein, 143 N.Y. 581, 592, 38 N.E. 718, 721 (1894); see also West Kentucky Coal Co. v. Nourse, 320 S.W.2d 311 (Ky.1959).

The use and definition of unconscionability at law has been quite different. On rare occasions courts of law have explicitly refused to grant normal contractual enforcement on grounds of unconscionability, stating that an unconscionable agreement is one "such as no man in his senses and not under delusion would make on the one hand, and as no honest and fair man would accept on the other."[34] In general, however, courts of law have not directly condemned a contract as unconscionable but have resorted to imaginative flanking devices to defeat the offending contract.[35] The law courts searched for and found (even though not present under ordinary rules) failure of consideration,[36] lack of consideration,[37] lack of mutual assent,[38] duress or fraud,[39] inadequacy of pleading,[40] lack of integration in a written contract[41] or a strained interpretation after finding ambiguity where little or no ambiguity existed.[42] These approaches, although producing justice in individual cases were highly unreliable and unpredictable.

34. Hume v. United States, 132 U.S. 406, 10 S.Ct. 134, 33 L.Ed. 393 (1889), quoting Earl of Chesterfield v. Janssen, 2 Ves. Sen. 125, 155, 28 Eng.Rep. 82, 100 (Ch. 1750). For other instances of findings of unconscionability at law, see 1 Page, The Law of Contracts § 636 (2d ed. 1920).

35. See Note, 45 Iowa L.Rev. 843 (1960).

36. See Laitner Plumbing & Heating Co. v. McThomas, 61 S.W.2d 270, 272 (Mo. App.1933), in which the court said the seller of refrigeration equipment which broke down several times a month would not be permitted to recover the price of the equipment, not because a disclaimer of warranties was ineffective, but because the jury could find equipment to have no value other than the material of which it was composed.

37. Faced with a contract which required that a borrower pay the lender, a bank president, $100 monthly so long as the borrower remained in business in addition to 8% interest, an Indiana court was able to discard the unconscionable provision by finding that the $5000 loan was consideration for the interest and that there was no consideration for the promise to pay the $100 monthly. Stiefler v. McCullough, 97 Ind.App. 123, 174 N.E. 823 (1931).

38. We have previously seen the general rule that in the absence of fraud one who does not choose to read a contract before signing it is bound by the contract. See § 9–42 infra; Moreira Construction Co., Inc. v. Moretrench Corp., 97 N.J.Super. 391, 235 A.2d 211 (1967), affirmed 51 N.J. 405, 241 A.2d 236 (1968). We have also seen that this rule has been circumvented at times by a finding that there was no mutual consent to a contract or to the terms of a contract. See §§ 9–43 to 9–46 infra. This finding has been made most often in contracts of adhesion. See § 9–44 infra.

39. In McCoy v. Gas Engine & Power Co., 135 App.Div. 771, 119 N.Y.S. 864 (2d Dep't 1909), reargument denied 136 App. Div. 922, 120 N.Y.S. 1133, the court had to assume that a legal fraud had been perpetrated because of a lawyer's unexplained $153,000 contingent fee, due to the lack of a doctrine of unconscionability to which to turn.

40. See Davis Motors, Dodge and Plymouth Co. v. Avett, 294 S.W.2d 882 (Tex.Civ. App.1956).

41. In V. Valente, Inc. v. Mascitti, 163 Misc. 287, 295 N.Y.S. 330, 335 (Rochester City Ct.1937), a buyer of a shortwave radio who was told by the plaintiff's salesman that it "could get Rome easily," was not compelled to pay for the radio despite the lack of any warranty as to the radio's capabilities in the written contract which generally would be considered integrated.

42. See Patterson, The Delivery of a Life Insurance Policy, 33 Harv.L.Rev. 198, 222 (1919), which indicates prime examples of the way language in insurance contracts is occasionally strained "out of its meaning." The rule of interpretation to the effect that language in contracts placing one party at the mercy of the other is not favored by the courts, Tibbetts Contracting Corp. v. O & E Contracting Co., 15 N.Y.2d 324, 258 N.Y.S.2d 400, 206 N.E.2d 340 (1965), can be used to reach the same result.

The conflict between what courts said they were doing and what it was sometimes obvious they were in fact doing has had an unsettling effect on the law, giving the sensitive a feeling of lawlessness, the logician a feeling of irrationality and the average lawyer a feeling of confusion.[43] The tension "produced by the contrary pulls of dogmatic prescriptions and the inherent requirements of individual cases"[44] made unpredictable which of the competing pulls would prevail. "Covert tools," said Karl Llewellyn, principle architect of the Uniform Commercial Code, "are never reliable tools."[45] The Code provision on unconscionability is designed to do two things: (1) encourage courts to openly strike down provisions of the type which had previously been denied enforcement at law largely through covert means; (2) achieve a substantive merger[46] of equity doctrine into law.[47] This twofold purpose is made apparent by the official comment which refers specifically to the prior covert activities of law courts in achieving conscionable results by indirection, followed by citation to a recent and celebrated equity case denying specific performance of an unconscionable contract. The further fact that the Uniform Commercial Code defines a large number of terms, but refrains from a definition of unconscionability, points to a legislative intent to utilize a term in the same general sense in which it has been employed in the legal system in the past.[48] The substantive merger of law and equity is long overdue.[49]

43. The statement of an Eastern sage may here be apposite:

"Now if names of things are not properly defined, words will not correspond to facts. When words do not correspond to facts, it is impossible to perfect anything. Where it is impossible to perfect anything, the arts and institutions of civilization cannot flourish. When the arts and institutions of civilization cannot flourish, law and justice do not attain their ends; and when law and justice do not attain their ends, the people will be at a loss to know what to do."

Confucius, The Analects, xiii, 3. We are indebted for this reference to Jackson, The Scope of the Term "Contract," 53 L.Q.Rev. 525, 536 (1937).

44. Von Mehren & Trautman, The Law of Multistate Problems 78 (1965).

45. Llewellyn, The Common Law Tradition 365 (1960).

46. Procedural merger of law and equity has taken place in many jurisdictions since 1848. Nevertheless, the tendency has been to keep the substantive doctrines separate and apart. See McClintock on Equity § 78 (2d ed. 1948).

47. At least two scholars have argued that there is no intent to adopt the equity approach at law. Murray on Contracts § 78 (1974); Leff, supra note 18, at 528–41. Professor Murray's insistence on divorcing equity unconscionability and U.C.C. unconscionability is tied to his reading the U.C.C. provision in a narrow fashion, tying it to the idea of assent. See Murray §§ 350–354. His analysis shows an awareness that equity unconscionability doctrine goes far beyond what he is willing to grant to the U.C.C. Professor Leff argues that equity is primarily concerned with "presumptive sillies like sailors and heirs and farmers and women" and others who if not crazy are "pretty peculiar." Leff at 532–33. This is simply not so. See, e.g., Weeks v. Pratt, 43 F.2d 53 (5th Cir.1930) (inventive genius). He also argues that equity is concerned with "only one form of substantive unconscionability—overall imbalance." Leff at 533. This is simply not so. Consider equity's treatment of penalty clauses and mortgages. Also consider equity's treatment of employees' covenants not to compete. See §§ 16–19 to 16–22 infra. Equity will relieve against unconscionability of specific clauses as well as gross overall imbalance.

48. Indeed, the evidence is overwhelming that this was the legislative intent. Leff, supra note 18, at 528 n. 166.

49. Newman, The Renaissance of Good Faith in Contracting in Anglo-American Law, 54 Cornell L.Rev. 553, 561–565 (1969).

It may be true that the draftsmen of the U.C.C. had foremost in their mind problems surrounding the taming of the unbridled excesses of a new animal, the contract of adhesion, an animal with which equity has had limited experience.[50] It is also true that equity has had little to do with cases involving the sale of goods. Yet, more than law, equity has stressed principle instead of precedent and the principles developed over the centuries in unconscionability cases are adaptable to sales contracts, of adhesion, or otherwise.

 WESTLAW REFERENCES

unconscionab! /s enjoin! injuncti! /s default! mortgag!

unconscionab! /s enjoin! injuncti! /s equit!

unconscionab! /s penalty

unconscionab! /s relief /s deny! deni**

35k16 /p unconscionab!

§ 9–39. The Emerging Law of Unconscionability

Since the general enactment of the Uniform Commercial Code, several lines of development of the unconscionability concept have become discernable. First, and perhaps most significant, the provision has been applied to numerous transactions outside the coverage of Article 2 of the Code. It has entered the general law of contracts.[51] It has been deemed applicable or, at least, persuasive, in cases involving a contract to construct asphalt plants,[52] home improvement contracts,[53] equipment leases,[54] real estate brokerage contracts,[55] hiring a hall for a Bar Mitzvah,[56] a contract opening a checking account,[57] an apartment house lease,[58] a security transaction,[59] a filling station lease,[60] the

50. Leff, supra note 18, at 537; Murray, supra note 47, at § 78.

51. It has been accepted as a general doctrine of contract law by the American Law Institute. Restatement, Second, Contracts § 208.

52. County Asphalt, Inc. v. Lewis Welding & Engineering Corp., 444 F.2d 372 (2d Cir.1971), certiorari denied 404 U.S. 939, 92 S.Ct. 272, 30 L.Ed.2d 252.

53. American Home Imp., Inc. v. MacIver, 105 N.H. 435, 201 A.2d 886, 14 A.L.R.3d 324 (1964).

54. Fairfield Lease Co. v. Pratt, 6 Conn. Cir. 537, 278 A.2d 154 (1971); Industralease Automated & Scientific Equipment Corp. v. R.M.E. Enterprises, Inc., 58 A.D.2d 482, 396 N.Y.S.2d 427 (2d Dep't 1977); Electronics Corp. of America v. Lear Jet Corp., 55 Misc.2d 1066, 286 N.Y.S.2d 711 (1967).

55. Ellsworth Dobbs, Inc. v. Johnson, 50 N.J. 528, 236 A.2d 843 (1967); cf. Kaye v.

Coughlin, 443 S.W.2d 612 (Tex.Civ.App. 1969).

56. Lazan v. Huntington Town House, Inc., 69 Misc.2d 1017, 332 N.Y.S.2d 270 (Dist.Ct.1969), affirmed 69 Misc.2d 591, 330 N.Y.S.2d 751 (App.Term 1972).

57. David v. Manufacturers Hanover Trust Co., 59 Misc.2d 248, 298 N.Y.S.2d 847 (App.Term 1969).

58. Seabrook v. Commuter Housing Co., 72 Misc.2d 6, 338 N.Y.S.2d 67 (Civ.Ct.1972).

59. Unico v. Owen, 50 N.J. 101, 232 A.2d 405 (1967); but see In re Advance Printing & Litho Co., 277 F.Supp. 101 (W.D.Pa.1967), affirmed 387 F.2d 952 (3d Cir.1967); Hernandez v. S.I.C. Finance Co., 79 N.M. 673, 448 P.2d 474 (1968).

60. Weaver v. American Oil Co., 257 Ind. 458, 276 N.E.2d 144, 49 A.L.R.3d 306 (1971).

settlement of a will contest dispute,[61] and, coming full circle to its equitable origins, to a problem relating to a spendthrift trust.[62]

Second, although it has become quite apparent that consumers will be the primary beneficiaries of the unconscionability doctrine, and that businessmen are expected to be able to look out for their own interests to a far greater extent than consumers,[63] it is equally clear that businesses, particularly small businesses, can be victimized by unconscionable contracts and will receive judicial protection.[64] Of course the unconscionability provision of U.C.C. § 2–309(3) is primarily intended to protect businesses.

Third, subdivision (2) of U.C.C. § 2–302 has been a principal focus of judicial attention. Its admonition that the parties shall be afforded a reasonable opportunity to present evidence as to the commercial setting, purpose and effect of the contract or clause alleged to be unconscionable has been heeded. Many cases have held that the provision mandates an evidentiary hearing or a full fledged trial on the merits.[65] Clearly, however, the section should be understood to mandate such a hearing only if real issues of fact are raised by the parties in their motion papers.[66] Otherwise the unconscionability defense will become the primary dilatory defense in contract litigation.

Fourth, the Uniform Commercial Code makes clear that the issue of unconscionability is to be decided by the court and not to be left to a jury.[67] It has been upheld as constitutional on the ground that the

---

61. Abbott v. Abbott, 188 Neb. 61, 195 N.W.2d 204 (1972).

62. In re Estate of Vought, 70 Misc.2d 781, 334 N.Y.S.2d 720 (Sur.Ct.1972), affirmed 45 A.D.2d 991, 360 N.Y.S.2d 199.

63. Dow Corning Corp. v. Capitol Aviation, Inc., 411 F.2d 622 (7th Cir.1969); Vitex Manufacturing Corp. v. Caribtex Corp., 377 F.2d 795 (3d Cir.1967); County Asphalt, Inc. v. Lewis Welding & Engineering Corp., 323 F.Supp. 1300 (S.D.N.Y.1970), affirmed 444 F.2d 372 (2d Cir.1971); In re Elkins-Dell Manufacturing Co., 253 F.Supp. 864 (E.D.Pa.1966); Architectural Aluminum Corp. v. Macarr, Inc., 70 Misc. 2d 495, 333 N.Y.S.2d 818 (1972); K & C, Inc. v. Westinghouse Elec. Corp., 437 Pa. 303, 263 A.2d 390 (1970); cf. Kaye v. Coughlin, 443 S.W.2d 612 (Tex.Civ.App. 1969) (lawyer).

64. Luick v. Graybar Electric Co., 473 F.2d 1360 (8th Cir.1973); Fairfield Lease Co. v. Pratt, 6 Conn.Cir. 537, 278 A.2d 154 (1971); Architectural Cabinets, Inc. v. Gaster, 291 A.2d 298 (Del.Super.1971); Weaver v. American Oil Co., 257 Ind. 458, 276 N.E.2d 144, 49 A.L.R.3d 306 (1971); Steele v. J.I. Case Co., 197 Kan. 554, 419 P.2d 902 (1966) (large farm); Wilson Trading Co. v. David Ferguson, Ltd., 23 N.Y.2d

398, 297 N.Y.S.2d 108, 244 N.E.2d 685 (1968); Electronics Corp. of America v. Lear Jet Corp., 55 Misc.2d 1066, 286 N.Y.S.2d 711 (1967); United States Leasing Corp. v. Franklin Plaza Apartments, 65 Misc.2d 1082, 319 N.Y.S.2d 531 (Civ.Ct. 1971). See Goldberg, Unconscionability in a Commercial Setting: The Assessment of Risk in a Contract to Build Nuclear Reactors, 58 Wash.L.Rev. 343 (1983); Jordan, Unconscionability at the Gas Station, 62 Minn.L.Rev. 813 (1978).

65. Luick v. Graybar Electric Co., 473 F.2d 1360 (8th Cir.1973); Williams v. Walker-Thomas Furniture Co., 350 F.2d 445, 18 A.L.R.3d 1297 (D.C.Cir.1965); Zicari v. Joseph Harris Co., 33 A.D.2d 17, 304 N.Y.S.2d 918 (4th Dep't 1969), appeal denied 26 N.Y.2d 610, 309 N.Y.S.2d 1027, 258 N.E.2d 103 (1970); see also Wilson Trading Co. v. David Ferguson, Ltd., 23 N.Y.2d 398, 297 N.Y.S.2d 108, 244 N.E.2d 685 (1968) (leaving question open); Central Ohio Co-op Milk Producers, Inc. v. Rowland, 29 Ohio App.2d 236, 281 N.E.2d 42, 58 O.O.2d 421 (1972).

66. Architectural Aluminum Corp. v. Macarr, Inc., 70 Misc.2d 495, 333 N.Y.S.2d 818 (1972).

67. U.C.C. § 2–302(1).

issue of conscionability is an equitable issue for which no constitutional right to a jury trial exists.[68]

Fifth, the flexibility which the Code has endowed the courts in granting remedies to an aggrieved party has been fully exercised and, indeed, may have been expanded. The Code permits the court to refuse to enforce the contract, to excise an unconscionable clause or to limit the application of an unconscionable clause. In most of the cases in which unconscionability has been found, nonenforcement of a clause has been the result.[69] In others, the contract was not enforced.[70] An earlier draft of the Code had expressly permitted courts to reform contracts by remaking the bargain for the parties.[71] Although this provision was deleted from the final draft, courts have been remaking bargains by reducing price terms,[72] increasing a duration term,[73] and reducing interest rates.[74] Most significantly, unconscionability has been held to constitute "fraud" within the meaning of consumer protection legislation empowering the state attorney-general to sue to enjoin the offering of contracts on unconscionable terms.[75]

 WESTLAW REFERENCES

unconscionab! /s "evidentiary hearing" "trial on the merits"

unconscionab! /s enforc! unenforc! nonenforc! /s clause

di(unconscionab! /p "confession of judgment" indemni! (disclaim! /
   s warranty) "limitation of damage" (waiv! /s defense))

to(328) /p unconscionab!

consumer /s fraud! /s unconscionab!

---

68. County Asphalt, Inc. v. Lewis Welding & Engineering Corp., 444 F.2d 372 (2d Cir.1971), certiorari denied 404 U.S. 939, 92 S.Ct. 272, 30 L.Ed.2d 252 (1971).

69. A & M Produce Co. v. FMC Corp., 135 Cal.App.3d 473, 186 Cal.Rptr. 114 (1982) (disclaimer of warranty and consequential damages); Architectural Cabinets, Inc. v. Gaster, 291 A.2d 298 (Del.Super. 1971) (confession of judgment); Weaver v. American Oil Co., 257 Ind. 458, 276 N.E.2d 144, 49 A.L.R.3d 306 (1971) (indemnity clause); Steele v. J.I. Case Co., 197 Kan. 554, 419 P.2d 902 (1966) (limitation of damages); Unico v. Owen, 50 N.J. 101, 232 A.2d 405 (1967) (waiver of defenses); Industralease Automated & Scientific Equipment Corp. v. R.M.E. Enterprises, Inc., (disclaimer of warranty), supra note 54.

70. A lease was cancelled in Seabrook v. Commuter Housing Co., 72 Misc.2d 6, 338 N.Y.S.2d 67 (Civ.Ct.1972). Suits for deficiency judgments were dismissed in Fairfield Lease Co. v. Pratt, 6 Conn.Cir. 537, 278 A.2d 154 (1971); Urdang v. Muse, 114 N.J.Super. 372, 276 A.2d 397 (1971).

71. 63 Yale L.J. 560 (1953).

72. Toker v. Westerman, 113 N.J.Super. 452, 274 A.2d 78 (1970); Jones v. Star Credit Corp., 59 Misc.2d 189, 298 N.Y.S.2d 264 (1969). Further developments in the Star Credit case are in Star Credit Corp. v. Ingram, 75 Misc.2d 299, 347 N.Y.S.2d 651 (Civ.Ct.1973) ($15,000 punitive damages assessed on plaintiff for continued fraudulent and unconscionable conduct).

73. Shell Oil Co. v. Marinello, 120 N.J. Super. 357, 294 A.2d 253 (1972) (franchise cannot be cancelled without just cause), modified 63 N.J. 402, 307 A.2d 598 (1973).

74. In re Elkins-Dell Mfg. Co., 253 F.Supp. 864 (E.D.Pa.1966) (dictum).

75. Kugler v. Romain, 58 N.J. 522, 279 A.2d 640 (1971). Some state legislation explicitly grants this authority to the attorney-general in cases of unconscionability. E.g., McKinney's N.Y.Exec. Law § 63(12). The Uniform Consumer Sales Practices Act would grant similar power to state officials as well as the power to sue for damages on behalf of injured consumers. U.C.S.P.A. § 9.

§ 9–40.   What Is Unconscionable?

"Unconscionable" is a word that defies lawyer-like definition.[76] It is a term borrowed from moral philosophy and ethics. As close to a definition as we are likely to get is "that which 'affronts the sense of decency.' "[77] The purpose of the doctrine is twofold: *prevention of oppression and unfair surprise."* [78] This twofold purpose has led to a distinction between "substantive" (oppression) and "nonsubstantive" (unfair surprise) unconscionability.[79] The cases do not, however, neatly fall into these two divisions. More frequently elements of both are present. Nonetheless, the courts have clearly ruled that gross excessiveness of price is itself unconscionable.[80] Significantly, however, in these cases it was clear that the purchaser was not aware that the price was exorbitant. Consequently they may be viewed as examples of oppressive terms combined with unfair surprise. A number of scholars have suggested several analytic frameworks for analyzing unconscionability cases.[81] These theories appear to have had little impact on the courts. Jeffrey Fort, whose essay is most thoroughly grounded in what the courts have done, has isolated what may be the present content of the unconscionability cases.[82] Certain cases involve exchanges that are unconscionable per se. These include cases where the exchanges are grossly unequal.[83] Holdings along this line are extremely rare because contracts involving grossly unequal exchanges almost always involve some impropriety in the negotiating process or disability of a party. Outside of the unconscionable *per se* cases are cases "[W]here an aggrieved party is ignorant of the risk involved, ignorant of the contract terms which transfer or allocate that risk and/or lacks alternative terms for that risk allocation, the contract or clause may be unconscionable and unenforceable. ＊ ＊ ＊ Stated simply, contract terms which transfer risks or the burdens of a transaction from that which might be expected in an exchange, absent a written agreement, are unenforce-

---

76. The great 17th century lawyer, John Selden, was as troubled by this in his day as some lawyers are troubled today. "One Chancellor has a long foot, another, a short foot, a third an indifferent foot: 'tis the same thing in the Chancellor's conscience." Selden, Table Talk, under the heading "Equity." See also id., under the heading "Conscience."

77. Gimbel Bros., Inc. v. Swift, 62 Misc. 2d 156, 307 N.Y.S.2d 952 (Civ.Ct.1970). The dictionary has little to add: " ＊ ＊ ＊ lying outside the limits of what is reasonable or acceptable: shockingly unfair, harsh, or unjust ＊ ＊ ＊." Webster's Third Unabridged. Other judicial definitions include "an absence of meaningful choice on the part of one of the parties together with contract terms which are unreasonably favorable to the other party." Williams v. Walker-Thomas Furniture Co., 350 F.2d 445, 449 (D.C.Cir.1965). See also text at note 34 supra.

78. U.C.C. § 2–302, Comment 1 (emphasis supplied).

79. Leff, supra note 18, at 487.

80. American Home Imp., Inc. v. McIver, 105 N.H. 435, 201 A.2d 886, 14 A.L.R.3d 324 (1964); Kugler v. Romain, 58 N.J. 522, 279 A.2d 640 (1971); Central Budget Corp. v. Sanchez, 53 Misc.2d 620, 279 N.Y.S.2d 391 (Civ.Ct.1967); but see, Morris v. Capitol Furniture & Appliance Co., Inc., 280 A.2d 775 (D.C.App.1971); Patterson v. Walker-Thomas Furniture Co., 277 A.2d 111 (D.C.App.1971).

81. See notes 18, 47 supra.

82. Fort, Understanding Unconscionability: Defining the Principle, 9 Loy.U. Chi.L.J. 765 (1978).

83. Fort, note 82 supra, at 771–75.

able unless intelligently, knowingly and voluntarily assumed." [84] The term "voluntarily" must be broadly construed. For example, where an experienced promoter knowingly signs a contract with a musician containing a substantively unconscionable term, he will be relieved from it where it is shown that all professional musicians are forbidden by their union to use any contract form other than that prepared by the union and containing the unconscionable term.[85]

Typically the cases in which unconscionability is found involve gross overall one-sidedness or gross one-sidedness of a term disclaiming a warranty, limiting damages, or granting procedural advantages. In these cases one-sidedness is often coupled with the fact that the imbalance is buried in small print and often couched in language unintelligible to even a person of moderate education. Often the seller deals with a particularly susceptible clientele.[86] In what may prove to be a leading case the court indicated that if a clause places great hardship or risk upon the party in the weaker bargaining position it must be shown that "the provisions were explained to the other party and came to his knowledge and there was in fact *a real and voluntary meeting of the minds and not merely an objective meeting.*" [87] A Code comment states that U.C.C. § 2–302 is not intended to cause a "disturbance of allocation of risks because of superior bargaining power," [88] but cases such as the one just quoted make it clear that inequality of bargaining power is an important element in an unconscionability determination. Superior bargaining power is not in itself a ground for striking down a resultant contract as unconscionable. There must be additional elements, as for example, a lack of meaningful choice as in the case of an industry wide form contract heavily weighted in favor of one party and offered on a take it or leave it basis,[89] or a situation where freedom of contract is exploited by a stronger party who has control of the negotiations due to the weaker party's ignorance, feebleness, unsophistication as to interest rates or similar business concepts or general naivete.[90]

---

84. Fort, note 82 supra, at 798.

85. Graham v. Scissor-Tail, Inc., 28 Cal. 3d 807, 171 Cal.Rptr. 604, 623 P.2d 165 (1981) (arbitration clause whereby executive board of union would arbitrate); see Katsoris, The Arbitration of a Public Securities Dispute, 53 Fordham L.Rev. 279, 306–309 (1984).

86. See Kugler v. Romain, 58 N.J. 522, 279 A.2d 640 (1971) ("sales solicitations were consciously directed toward minority group consumers and consumers of limited economic means ∗ ∗ ∗. Sales among these people were thought to be "easier.")

87. Weaver v. American Oil Co., 257 Ind. 458, 464, 276 N.E.2d 144, 49 A.L.R.3d 306 (1971) (emphasis in original).

88. U.C.C. § 2–302, Comment 1. For an argument that inequality of bargaining power should never be a consideration in

an unconscionability determination, see Schwartz, Seller Unequal Bargaining Power and the Judicial Process, 49 Ind.L.J. 367 (1974).

89. See, e.g., Campbell Soup v. Wentz, 172 F.2d 80 (3d Cir.1948); Graham v. Scissor-Tail, Inc., supra note 85; Henningsen v. Bloomfield Motors, Inc., 32 N.J. 358, 161 A.2d 69, 75 A.L.R.2d 1 (1960).

90. See note 84 supra; see also Williams v. Walker-Thomas Furniture Co., 350 F.2d 445, 18 A.L.R.3d 1297 (D.C.Cir.1965), 51 Cornell L.Q. 768 (1966), in which the Court of Appeals for the District of Columbia indicated that relief might be owing to a consumer who had entered into an extremely harsh installment sales contract with a furniture company. The contract had a tie-in clause which the company hoped would permit it to repossess all

It is clear, however, that unconscionability may exist even where the parties are on "about equal footing" or even where the oppressor is inexperienced compared to the oppressed.[91]

Section 2–302 should be considered in conjunction with the obligation of good faith imposed at several places in the Code. For example § 1–203 of the Code provides that "every contract or duty within this Act imposes an obligation of good faith in its performance or enforcement."[92] Despite the fact that § 1–203 relates specifically to the performance of a contract rather than its formulation it has been suggested that good faith should be considered in determining unconscionability.[93]

The Uniform Consumer Sales Practices Act, released in 1970, and as yet not widely adopted, also condemns unconscionable contracts. In addition, it provides six illustrative circumstances which the court should consider in an unconscionability determination. Certainly, these circumstances should be considered in an unconscionability determination under the Uniform Commercial Code. These circumstances are that the supplier has reason to know:[94]

> "(1) that he took advantage of the inability of the consumer reasonably to protect his interests because of his physical infirmity, ignorance, illiteracy, inability to understand the language of an agreement, or similar factors;

> "(2) that when the consumer transaction was entered into the price grossly exceeded the price at which similar property or services were readily obtainable in similar transactions by like consumers;

items purchased over a number of years on default in payment of the price of any one of them.

In Frostifresh Corp. v. Reynoso, 52 Misc. 2d 26, 274 N.Y.S.2d 757 (Nassau County Dist.Ct.1966) reversed in part 54 Misc.2d 119, 281 N.Y.S.2d 964 (App.Term 2d Dep't 1967), a poor Spanish speaking person was persuaded into promising to pay $1145 for a $348 appliance.

See also State by Lefkowitz v. ITM, Inc., 52 Misc.2d 39, 275 N.Y.S.2d 303 (1966), in which the defendant company, which received up to $658 for $80 broilers by selling them on time, was warned to tell consumers of the contract terms "in language the least educated person can understand." Compare Lundstrom v. Radio Corp. of America, 17 Utah 2d 114, 405 P.2d 339, 14 A.L.R.3d 1058 (1965).

91. Miller v. Coffeen, 365 Mo. 204, 280 S.W.2d 100 (1955); see also Pope Mfg. Co. v. Gormully, 144 U.S. 224, 12 S.Ct. 632, 36 L.Ed.2d 414 (1892).

92. § 1–201(19) defines good faith as "honesty in fact in the conduct or transaction concerned." In the case of a merchant it "means honesty in fact and the observance of reasonable commercial standards of fair dealing in the trade." § 2–103(1)(b).

93. Llewellyn, The Common Law Tradition 369 (1960); cf. 1955 N.Y.Law Rev. Comm'n, vol. 1, 658; see Standard Oil Co. of Texas v. Lopeno Gas Co., 240 F.2d 504 (5th Cir.1957); Kugler v. Romain, 58 N.J. 522, 279 A.2d 640 (1971); Flash v. Powers, 99 N.Y.S.2d 765 (1950), which in attempting to define unconscionability have dwelled upon the element of lack of good faith.

94. Uniform Consumer Sales Practices Act § 4. A similar listing appears in McKinney's N.Y. Administrative Code § 2203d–2.0(b), which adds: "the degree to which terms of the transaction require consumers to waive legal rights."

"(3) that when the consumer transaction was entered into the consumer was unable to receive a substantial benefit from the subject of the transaction;

"(4) that when the consumer transaction was entered into there was no reasonable probability of payment of the obligation in full by the consumer;

"(5) that the transaction he induced the consumer to enter was excessively one-sided in favor of the supplier; or

"(6) that he made a misleading statement of opinion on which the consumer was likely to rely to his detriment."

Another guide is found in the Uniform Consumer Credit Code of 1974 which states: "The competence of the buyer, leasee, or debtor, any deception or coercion practiced upon him, the nature and extent of the legal advice received by him, and the value of the consideration are relevant to the issue of unconscionability." [95] In addition, this Code lists a series of factors that must be considered in consumer credit transactions. These are similar to those found in the Uniform Consumer Sales Practices Act.[96]

 WESTLAW REFERENCES

di unconscionab!

unconscionab! /s price /s excess! exceed!

"unconscionab! per se"

unconscionab! /s inequality unequal!

unconscionab! /s risk /s distribut! alloca!

unconscionab! /s "one sided!"

unconscionab! /s arbitra!

unconscionab! /s "meaningful choice"

unconscionab! /s weak!

"uniform consumer sales practices act"

to(92h) /p unconscionab!

H. DUTY TO READ [97]

Table of Sections

95. Uniform Consumer Credit Code § 1.107 (the context is unconscionable settlement agreements regarding disputes arising under the Code).

96. Uniform Consumer Credit Code § 6.111(3); see Hersbergen, The Improvident Extension of Credit as an Unconscionable Contract, 23 Drake L.Rev. 225 (1974).

97. This material is based upon Calamari, Duty to Read—A Changing Concept, 43 Fordham L.Rev. 341 (1974).

§ 9–41. Introduction

This topic could have been discussed under the heading of Offer and Acceptance.[98] However, since it is also directly related to some of the topics discussed immediately above—misrepresentation, mistake, unconscionability—it was determined that coverage here would permit more comprehensive treatment.

§ 9–42. The Traditional Rule

If A sends an offer to B who, without opening it and without suspecting that it is an offer, decides to confuse A by sending a letter which states "I accept," there is a contract because A reasonably believed that B assented to the deal.[99] It is not important to decide whether B has acted intentionally or negligently, because under the objective theory of contracts a party is bound by the reasonable impression he creates.[1] The same principle supplies the basic rule relating to questions of duty to read:[2] a party who signs an instrument manifests assent to it and may not later complain that he did not read the instrument or that he did not understand its contents.[3] A leading case has stated that "one having the capacity to understand a written document who reads it, or, without reading it or having it read to him, signs it, is bound by his signature."[4] The thought is that no one could rely on a signed document if the other party could avoid the transaction by saying that he had not read or did not understand the writing.[5]

---

98. See ch. 2 supra.

99. See ch. 2 supra.

1. Ricketts v. Pennsylvania R.R. Co., 153 F.2d 757, 760 (2d Cir.1946) (L. Hand, J.); Restatement, Second, Contracts § 20, Comment d; 1 Williston § 35; see Whittier, The Restatement of Contracts and Mutual Assent, 17 Calif.L.Rev. 441 (1929).

2. Strictly speaking, the "duty" to read is not an obligation. Rather, a party may be bound by what he fails to read. The theory of the recording acts is based on analogous reasoning. But see Fli-Back Co. v. Philadelphia Mfrs. Mut. Ins. Co., 502 F.2d 214, 217 (4th Cir.1974) which indicates that a failure to read may, in certain contexts, support claims of contributory negligence and failure to mitigate damages.

3. Richardson Greenshield Securities, Inc. v. Metz, 566 F.Supp. 131 (S.D.N.Y.

1983); Colburn v. Mid-State Homes, Inc., 289 Ala. 255, 260, 266 So.2d 865, 868 (1972); Smith v. Standard Oil Co., 227 Ga. 268, 272–73, 180 S.E.2d 691, 693–94 (1971); Prudential Ins. Co. of America v. Holliday, 191 Neb. 144, 145–147, 214 N.W.2d 273, 275 (1974); Pioneer Credit Co. v. Medalen, 326 N.W.2d 717 (N.D.1982); National Bank of Washington v. Equity Investors, 81 Wn. 2d 886, 912–13, 506 P.2d 20, 36 (1973), appeal after remand 83 Wn.2d 435, 518 P.2d 1072 (1974); Lien v. Pitts, 46 Wis.2d 35, 46, 174 N.W.2d 462, 468 (1970); see Belew v. Griffis, 249 Ark. 589, 591, 460 S.W.2d 80, 82 (1970). At times, the rule is stated in terms of estoppel. 1 Williston § 35, at 99.

4. Rossi v. Douglas, 203 Md. 190, 192, 100 A.2d 3, 7 (1953).

5. For a detailed discussion of the policy considerations behind the rule see Ma-

The same rule applies even without a signature if the acceptance of a document which purports to be a contract implies assent to its terms.[6] Thus, for example, the acceptance of documents such as bills of lading, passenger tickets, insurance policies, bank books and warehouse receipts may give rise to contracts based upon the provisions contained therein.[7]

 WESTLAW REFERENCES

"duty to read" /s estop!

"duty to read" /s accept! assent!

"duty to read" /s sign!

95k93(2)

§ 9–43. Traditional Exceptions to the Traditional Rule

There has been a wide variety of qualifications to the traditional duty to read rule. Most of the qualifications are not truly exceptions because they are based upon the conclusion that there was in fact no intentional or apparent manifestation of assent to the document or the term or terms in question.[8] These qualifications will now be discussed.

(a) Document or Provision Not Legible

If the document is not legible it is easy to conclude that there was no assent.[9] Thus the cases generally agree that a party is not bound by fine print [10] or by other conditions which would make the document or clause in question illegible.[11] Describing such a document, one court stated: "The compound, if read by him, would, unless he were an extraordinary man, be an inexplicable riddle, a mere flood of darkness

caulay, Private Legislation and the Duty to Read—Business Run by IBM Machine, The Law of Contracts and Credit Cards, 19 Vand.L.Rev. 1051 (1966).

6. Regan v. Customcraft Homes, Inc., 170 Colo. 562, 565, 463 P.2d 463, 464 (1970).

7. 1 Williston §§ 90A–B. The word "may" is used because the cases are far from harmonious. Compare George v. Bekins Van & Storage Co., 33 Cal.2d 834, 205 P.2d 1037 (1949) and D'Aloisio v. Morton's, Inc., 342 Mass. 231, 234, 172 N.E.2d 819, 821 (1961) with Voyt v. Bekins Moving & Storage Co., 169 Or. 30, 127 P.2d 360 (1942) (all warehouse receipt cases). See U.C.C. §§ 7–203, 7–204; Ruud, Warehouse Receipts, Bills of Lading, and Other Documents of Title: Article VII, 16 Ark.L.Rev. 81 (1961).

The rule stated generally applies to bills of lading. 1 Williston § 90B. Bills of lading and receipts are often covered by statute. 1 Williston § 90BB; U.C.C. § 7–309. Although bank depositors generally are held bound by conditions stated on signature cards and passbooks, Chase v. Waterbury Sav. Bank, 77 Conn. 295, 299–300, 59

A. 37, 39 (1904), it has been held that this does not apply to unusual conditions. Los Angeles Inv. Co. v. Home Sav. Bank, 180 Cal. 601, 182 P. 293, 298 (1919). See Annot., 5 A.L.R.Fed. 394 (1970) (passenger tickets); 30 Tex.L.Rev. 634 (1952) (insurance policies).

8. Cf. note 7 supra.

9. Compare this statement with the rules relating to blind and illiterate persons discussed infra at text accompanying notes 39 and 40 infra.

10. Lisi v. Alitalia-Linee Aeree Italiane, S.P.A., 370 F.2d 508, 513–14 (2d Cir.1966), affirmed by an equally divided Court 390 U.S. 455, 88 S.Ct. 1193, 20 L.Ed.2d 27 (1968) (per curiam); Dessert Seed Co. v. Drew Farmers Supply, Inc., 248 Ark. 858, 861, 454 S.W.2d 307, 309 (1970); Baker v. Seattle, 79 Wn.2d 198, 484 P.2d 405 (1971); Note, Contract Clauses in Fine Print, 63 Harv.L.Rev. 494 (1950).

11. 1 Williston § 90C; see, e.g., Silvestri v. Italia Societa Per Azioni Di Navigazione, 388 F.2d 11 (2d Cir.1968), noted in 30 Ohio St.L.J. 609 (1969).

and confusion. ＊ ＊ ＊ [I]t was printed in such small type, and in lines so long and so crowded, that the perusal of it was made physically difficult, painful, and injurious." [12] Frequently, statutes make provision with respect to the size of the type to be used in certain clauses of common contracts.[13]

(b) Provisions Not Sufficiently Called to the Attention of One Party

Even when the provision in question is legible it may be placed in such a way that it is not likely to come to the attention of the other party. When this occurs a party should not be bound by such a provision.[14] This situation occurs frequently in cases involving printed notices on letterheads, catalogues, or tags,[15] and on the merchandise itself.[16] In a similar vein a number of recent cases have suggested that a party is not bound by clauses printed on the reverse side of a document which he signs unless they are called to his attention.[17] Similar problems arise when the document attempts to incorporate other provisions by reference.[18]

Closely related are cases in which a purported contractual provision is posted on a desk or wall. For example, in one case, a sign containing such a provision was posted at the reception desk of a garage. The court held the provision not binding on the customer unless, prior to contracting, the customer had actually observed the

---

12. De Lancey v. Rockingham Farmers' Mut. Fire Ins. Co., 52 N.H. 581, 588 (1873). As a result of decisions such as this, standardized drafts of certain insurance policies have become common. See Vance, Insurance 56–62 (3d ed. Anderson 1951); Kimball & Pfennigstorf, Legislative and Judicial Control of the Terms of Insurance Contracts: A Comparative Study of American and European Practice, 39 Ind.L.J. 675 (1964).

13. See, e.g., Md.Code 1957, art. 83, §§ 129(c), 131(b) (repl. vol. 1969); Mich. Comp.Laws Ann. § 24–10310; McKinney's N.Y.Pers.Prop.Law §§ 46–c(a), 402(1)–(2), 402A(5)(a), 403(3)(a); see U.C.C. §§ 2–316(2), 1–201(10); McKinney's N.Y.C.P.L.R. 4544.

14. Egan v. Kollsman Instrument Corp., 21 N.Y.2d 160, 168–69, 287 N.Y.S.2d 14, 19, 234 N.E.2d 199, 202–03 (1967), certiorari denied 390 U.S. 1039, 88 S.Ct. 1636, 20 L.Ed.2d 301 (1968) (a passenger ticket case).

15. 1 Williston § 90D. However, here again, the cases are not harmonious.

16. Even here, if the provision is plainly stamped, it may be binding on the buyer. 1 Williston § 90E. But see Willard Van Dyke Productions, Inc. v. Eastman Kodak Co., 16 A.D.2d 366, 369–70, 228 N.Y.S.2d 330, 334–35 (1st Dep't 1962), affirmed 12 N.Y.2d 301, 239 N.Y.S.2d 337, 189 N.E.2d 693 (1963) (print on film package limiting liability held not binding on buyer).

17. Allstate Ins. Co. v. La Perta, 42 A.D.2d 104, 108, 345 N.Y.S.2d 138, 141–42 (2d Dep't 1973); Tri-City Renta-Car & Leasing Corp. v. Vaillancourt, 33 A.D.2d 613, 304 N.Y.S.2d 682 (3d Dep't 1969); Cutler Corp. v. Latshaw, 374 Pa. 1, 97 A.2d 234 (1953). The notion that a particular clause must be brought to the attention of the other party is gaining currency and is consistent with the cases discussed in § 9–44 infra; see also § 9–40 supra; see, e.g., Birmingham Television Corp. v. Water Works, 292 Ala. 147, 290 So.2d 636 (1974) (warehouse receipt); Kushner v. McGinnis, 289 Mass. 326, 194 N.E. 106 (1935) (amusement park ticket).

18. Compare Level Export Corp. v. Wolz, Aiken & Co., 305 N.Y. 82, 86–87, 111 N.E.2d 218, 220 (1953) (incorporation by reference held enforceable) with Riverdale Fabrics Corp. v. Tillinghast-Stiles Co., 306 N.Y. 288, 118 N.E.2d 104 (1954), reargument denied 307 N.Y. 689, 120 N.E.2d 859 (1954) (incorporation by reference held unenforceable).

sign, or the sign was posted so prominently that the customer must have known of its existence and assented to its terms.[19] Lachs v. Fidelity & Casualty Co.[20] went even further. In Lachs an air traveler purchased from a vending machine an insurance policy which limited coverage to flights on "scheduled airlines." A large sign posted in the area listed the names of non-scheduled airlines. The passenger bought a ticket on a non-scheduled flight and was killed when it crashed. In the subsequent action by the beneficiary of the policy, the majority of the court held that it was a question of fact for the jury whether the passenger had been given sufficient notice of the limitation,[21] but that the sign was of little or no significance in making this determination.[22]

Another fact pattern in which the question of whether the contractual provisions are sufficiently called to the attention of a party occurs where a person accepts an instrument in which he would not reasonably expect to find contractual provisions.[23] The most common illustration is a parcel room check which contains a limitation of liability. The majority of courts have held that the average person would consider such a check merely as evidence of the right to a return of goods and would not expect it to contain contractual provisions.[24] This result is actually a corollary of the more fundamental rule that if a person, without fault on his part, assents to a document believing that it is something other than what it is, the instrument is void.[25] Obviously no attempt has been made to state a rule which would determine when consent is deemed to be present. No such rule can be stated. All that can be said is that whether a contractual provision is sufficiently called to the attention of a party depends upon whether a reasonable man, considering all circumstances of the case, would know that the terms in question were intended to be part of the proposed agreement.[26] As one court noted, "failure to read an instrument is not negligence per se but

---

19. Mendelssohn v. Normand, Ltd., [1969] 3 W.L.R. 139 (C.A.); accord, Brummett v. Jackson, 211 Miss. 116, 51 So.2d 52 (1951).

20. 306 N.Y. 357, 118 N.E.2d 555 (1954).

21. Id. at 365, 118 N.E.2d at 558–559.

22. Id. at 364, 118 N.E.2d at 558. Other insurance cases requiring exclusions to be conspicuous and clear: Daburlos v. Commercial Ins. Co., 521 F.2d 18 (3d Cir. 1975); Ponder v. Blue Cross, 145 Cal.App. 3d 709, 193 Cal.Rptr. 632 (1983).

23. 1 Williston, § 90B, at 301–02.

24. Kergald v. Armstrong Transfer Express Co., 330 Mass. 254, 113 N.E.2d 53 (1953); Klar v. H. & M. Parcel Room, Inc., 270 App.Div. 538, 542–43, 61 N.Y.S.2d 285, 289 (1st Dep't 1946), affirmed 296 N.Y. 1044, 73 N.E.2d 912 (1947) (mem.). Tickets

issued by a parking lot often are treated the same way. Parkrite Auto Park, Inc. v. Badgett, 242 S.W.2d 630 (Ky.1951), noted in 44 Ky.L.J. 233 (1956); cf. Ellish v. Airport Parking Co. of America, 42 A.D.2d 174, 345 N.Y.S.2d 650 (2d Dep't 1973), affirmed 34 N.Y.2d 882, 359 N.Y.S.2d 280, 316 N.E.2d 715 (1974) (mem.). The cases are divided on the issue of whether contract provisions on an ordinary baggage check are binding. 1 Williston § 90B, at 301. On questions of limiting liability by filing tariffs, see Annot., 68 A.L.R.2d 1350, 1359–1363 (1959); Shirazi v. Greyhound Corp., 145 Mont. 421, 401 P.2d 559 (1965).

25. 1 Williston § 95A.

26. Mellinkoff, How to Make Contracts Illegible, 5 Stan.L.Rev. 418, 430–31 (1953); see also § 9–22 supra.

must be considered in light of all surrounding facts and circumstances." [27]

(c) Fraud and Mistake

There is a relationship between the duty to read and fraud or mistake, and the related issue of assent.[28] For example, if a party misrepresents the terms of a writing and the other party, relying on the misrepresentation, signs without having read the document, what is the result? [29] Some courts have bound the deceived party on the theory that, given the facts of the particular case, he had no right to rely on the misrepresentation.[30] Other courts have taken the position either that there is a lack of mutual assent or that the party who misrepresents is guilty of fraud.[31] Those courts which follow the fraud theory have allowed the defrauded party to avoid the contract or, at times, on a theory of estoppel or reformation, to claim that there is a contract based upon the terms as they were represented to the innocent party.[32] The Restatement Second adopts the latter view.[33] Both Restatements give this illustration: "A says to B, 'I offer to sell you my horse for $100.' B, knowing that A intends to offer to sell his cow, not his horse for that price, and that the use of the word 'horse' is a slip of the tongue, replies, 'I accept.' " [34] The first Restatement concludes that "[t]here is no contract for the sale of either the horse or the cow." [35] The Restatement Second concludes "[t]here is a contract for the sale of the cow and not of the horse." [36]

What explanation can be offered for the different results? The Restatement Second expresses the view that B's conduct is fraudulent and that, even if A is negligent, a fraudulent party is more guilty than

---

27. Chandler v. Aero Mayflower Transit Co., 374 F.2d 129, 136 (4th Cir. 1967) (bill of lading).

28. Duress, which also relates to the issue of assent, seems irrelevant in a discussion of the duty to read. As to undue influence, see Dauer, Contracts of Adhesion in Light of the Bargaining Hypothesis: An Introduction, 5 Akron L.Rev. 1, 29–30 (1972).

29. The discussion here is without reference to the parol evidence rule which is considered infra at notes 42 to 45.

30. Sanger v. Yellow Cab Co., 486 S.W.2d 477, 481 (Mo.1972). The rule generally has been condemned. In the words of one court: "Is it better to encourage negligence in the foolish, or fraud in the deceitful? Either course has most obvious dangers. But judicial experience exemplifies that the former is the least objectionable, and least hampers the administration of pure justice." Western Mfg. Co. v. Cotton & Long, 126 Ky. 749, 754, 104 S.W. 758, 760 (1907); see § 9–14 supra; Comment, Contracts—Misunderstanding—Misrepre-

sentation of the Contents of a Written Offer, 34 Mich.L.Rev. 705 (1936).

31. E.g., Quillen v. Twin City Bank, 253 Ark. 169, 485 S.W.2d 181 (1972); Toker v. Perl, 103 N.J.Super. 500, 247 A.2d 701 (1968), affirmed 108 N.J.Super. 129, 260 A.2d 244 (App.Div.1970); see Phillips Petroleum Co. v. Roth, 186 Minn. 173, 242 N.W. 629 (1932), noted in 31 Mich.L.Rev. 568 (1933); Whipple v. Brown Bros. Co., 225 N.Y. 237, 121 N.E. 748 (1919). See also Bixler v. Wright, 116 Me. 133, 100 A. 467 (1917); Cameron v. Estabrooks, 73 Vt. 73, 50 A. 638 (1901).

32. See note 31 supra.

33. Restatement, Second, Contracts § 20.

34. Restatement, Contracts § 71. illus. 2; Restatement, Second, Contracts § 20, illus. 5.

35. Restatement, Contracts § 71, illus. 2.

36. Restatement, Second, Contracts § 20, illus. 5.

a negligent party; consequently, there should be a contract based upon the understanding of the more innocent party.[37] The original Restatement, however, either refused to weigh one fault (negligence) against the other (fraud), or relies upon the rule: "If either party knows that the other does not intend what his words or other acts express, this knowledge prevents such words or other acts from being operative as an offer or an acceptance." [38]

A good and recurring illustration of the problem involves a person who is blind, illiterate or unfamiliar with the language in which the contract is written and who has signed a document which was not read to him.[39] There is all but unanimous agreement that he is bound by the general rule previously stated. Therefore, except possibly in the case of an emergency, he must protect himself by procuring someone to read it for him. However, if the other party deceives him as to its contents, the problem is the one discussed above—the effect of fraud on a failure to read. Most of the cases have held that such a contract may at least be avoided.[40] Under the theory of the Restatement Second,[41] the defrauded party also would have the option to sue on the contract as it was described to him.

The problem of a party misrepresenting the contents of the writing to one who has failed to read is more complicated when one takes into account the parol evidence rule. For example, if a party signs a document which contains a merger clause to the effect that no representations have been made other than those stated in the writing (so that the instrument is presumably integrated), may the party who has failed to read show that the prior oral agreement: (1) contained a misrepresentation upon which he relied and which was intended to be included in the writing; and (2) that the other party fraudulently represented that the writing contained this representation? [42] There are cases which, in effect, state that a failure to read the integration precludes a party from introducing a representation made to him

---

37. See id. § 20, Comment d. There is also a suggestion that A may avoid the contract if he so desires. See also Restatement, Second, Contracts § 157, Comment b.

38. Restatement, Contracts § 71(c) & Comment a; see §§ 3–11, 3–12 supra.

39. Gaskin v. Stumm Handel GMBH, 390 F.Supp. 361 (S.D.N.Y.1975) (contract in German); Smith v. Standard Oil Co., 227 Ga. 268, 180 S.E.2d 691 (1971); Ellis v. Mullen, 34 N.C.App. 367, 238 S.E.2d 187 (1977); Roberd v. First Fed. Sav. & Loan Ass'n, 490 S.W.2d 243 (Tex.Civ.App.1973); see Gesualdi v. Miranda, 110 R.I. 694, 296 A.2d 676 (1972). See also Comment, "No Hablo Ingles," 11 San Diego L.Rev. 415

(1974). British Commonwealth cases may be more flexible. See Date-Bah, Illiterate Parties and Written Contracts, 3 Rev. of Ghana Law 181 (1971).

40. Pimpinello v. Swift & Co., 253 N.Y. 159, 170 N.E. 530 (1930); 3A Corbin § 607; 1 Williston § 35.

41. See text accompanying notes 32 and 33 supra.

42. It has been said that when a party presents a document for signature he represents that its contents conform to the terms of the agreement previously reached. See, e.g., Bixler v. Wright, 116 Me. 133, 136, 100 A. 467, 469 (1917).

despite an allegation of fraud in the execution of the instrument.[43]   A better view, however, is repeated in an Arkansas case [44] as follows:

> "There is a well-recognized exception to the rule that a party is bound to know the contents of a paper which he signs; and that is where one party procures another to sign a writing by fraudulently representing that it contains the stipulations agreed upon, when, in fact, it does not, and where the party signing relies on the faith of these representations, and is thereby induced to omit the reading of the writing which he signs.   It is well settled that a written contract which one party induced another to execute by false representations as to its contents is not enforceable, and the party so defrauded is not precluded from contesting the validity of the contract, by the fact that he failed to read it before attaching his signature." [45]

When a party signs an instrument without reading it, it is clear that in a loose (but not legal) sense he is operating under a mistake as to the contents of the document.[46]   Under the rules previously stated, however, he is not ordinarily allowed to avoid the contract.[47]   Nonetheless, the situation is different if the writing does not reflect the agreement previously made and the term was not omitted by agreement.   In such a situation most courts have granted reformation for mutual mistake despite the negligence involved in failing to read the document,[48] the parol evidence rule,[49] and the Statute of Frauds.[50]

---

43. Knight & Bostwick v. Moore, 203 Wis. 540, 234 N.W. 902 (1931).

44. Belew v. Griffis, 249 Ark. 589, 460 S.W.2d 80 (1970); see also Estes v. Republic Nat'l Bank of Dallas, 462 S.W.2d 273 (Tex. 1970).

45. 249 Ark. at 591–92, 460 S.W.2d at 82, quoting Massachusetts Mut. Life Ins. Co. v. Brun, 187 Ark. 790, 794, 62 S.W.2d 961, 963 (1933), quoting Tanton v. Martin, 80 Kan. 22, 24, 101 P. 461, 462 (1909).   The discussion here relates primarily to fraud in the execution of the contract rather than to fraud in the inducement of the contract.   The general rule is that proof of fraud in the inducement may be shown, even if it contradicts an integration.   See 3 Corbin § 580; Restatement, Second, Contracts § 214(d).   See also § 9–21 supra.

Other courts have taken the position that a promise which contradicts the integration may not be shown upon a theory of promissory fraud, i.e., a promise made without an intent to perform which could be considered the equivalent of a fraudulent misrepresentation.   See Sweet, Promissory Fraud and the Parol Evidence Rule,

49 Calif.L.Rev. 877 (1961) and cases cited therein.

It has been suggested that by virtue of U.C.C. §§ 2–202 and 2–316, an express warranty which contradicts an integration may be shown.   Broude, The Consumer and the Parol Evidence Rule: Section 2–202 of the Uniform Commercial Code, 1970 Duke L.J. 881.   See also Associated Hardware Supply Co. v. Big Wheel Distributing Co., 355 F.2d 114 (3d Cir.1965).

Both law review articles cited in this note make it clear that it is often difficult to distinguish among representations, warranties and promises.

46. 3 Corbin § 607.

47. Id.

48. See §§ 9–31 to 9–36 supra; Annot., 81 A.L.R.2d 7, 37–39 (1962); Restatement, Second, Contracts § 157, Comment b.

49. Restatement, Second, Contracts § 214(d).   See also Restatement, Second, Contracts § 157, Comment b.

50. See generally Palmer, Reformation and the Statute of Frauds, 65 Mich.L.Rev. 421 (1967); see also § 19–28 infra.

Assuming a case where there is no mistake or wrongdoing on the part of the other party,[51] a claim of mistake of fact might still exist in favor of the party who signs an instrument thinking that he knows its contents when in fact he does not. In such a case, however, rescission for unilateral mistake ordinarily would be denied.[52] Today, rescission will be allowed in some jurisdictions, even though the mistake is unilateral, if two conditions concur: (1) enforcement of the contract against the mistaken party would be oppressive (or at least result in an unconscionably unequal exchange of values); and (2) rescission would impose no substantial hardship on the other.[53] Some courts have refused to grant a decree of specific performance against a party who has failed to read.[54]

 WESTLAW REFERENCES

(a) *Document or Provision Not Legible*

document /s "fine print" legib! illegib!

(b) *Provisions Not Sufficiently Called to the Attention of One Party*

clause /s "reverse side"

fail! duty +2 read /s negligen!

fail! duty +2 read /s conspicuous!

(c) *Fraud and Mistake*

fail! duty +2 read /s fraud! mistak!

fail! duty +2 read /s represent! misrepresent!

fail! duty +2 read /s right /s rely reli****

duty fail! +2 read /s "parol* evidence"

duty fail! +2 read /s valid! invalid! unenforc!

duty fail! +2 read /s content

duty fail! +2 read /s reform!

duty fail! +2 read /s adhesion

duty fail! +2 read /s disclaim! warranty

duty fail! +2 read /s avoid! void!

duty fail! +2 read /s exception

weaver +s "american oil" /p unconscionab!

unconscionab! /p "public servant" "common carrier"

unconscionab! /s exculpat!

---

51. If one party is mistaken as to the contents of the document and the other has actual knowledge of this fact, the mistaken party may avoid the contract. 3 Corbin § 607, at 663; Restatement, Second, Contracts § 157, Comment a.

52. See Sanger v. Yellow Cab Co., 486 S.W.2d 477, 481 (Mo.1972) (mutual mistake distinguished from unilateral failure to read); Hampshire v. Hampshire, 485 S.W.2d 314, 316 (Tex.Civ.App.1972) (failure to read sales contract held not to justify rescission, absent fraud).

53. Gethsemane Lutheran Church v. Zacho, 258 Minn. 438, 443, 104 N.W.2d 645, 649 (1960); cf. Beatty v. Depue, 78 S.D. 395, 103 N.W.2d 187 (1960); Annot., 1 A.L.R.3d 531 (1960). See § 9–27 supra; 13 Williston §§ 1577–78; 3 Corbin § 607.

54. 13 Williston § 1577.

§ 9–44. The Modern View—Contracts of Adhesion

There has been a tendency, particularly in recent years, to treat contracts of adhesion or standard form contracts differently from other contracts.[55] This is particularly true with respect to the duty to read.[56] There is a growing body of case law which subverts the traditional duty to read concept either upon a theory that there was not true assent to a particular term, or that, even if there was assent, the term is to be excised from the contract because it contravenes public policy or is unconscionable.[57] At times, the same decision may employ all three rationales. This modern approach to the problem and the meaning of true assent may be shown best by a brief examination of three of the leading cases on the subject.

Perhaps the most significant case is Weaver v. American Oil Co.,[58] which considered a lease by an oil company to an individual. The lessee signed without reading the lease under which he agreed, inter alia, to indemnify the lessor as a result of damages caused by the lessor's negligence. The majority opinion first stated that the duty to read rule had no application to the case because "the clause was in fine print and contained no title heading * * *."[59] This conclusion would have ended the matter under the rules discussed above, but the court seemed anxious to break new ground for it hastened to add:

> "When a party show[s] that the contract, which is * * * to be enforced, was * * * an unconscionable one, due to a prodigious amount of bargaining power on behalf of the stronger party, which is used to the stronger party's advantage and is unknown to the lesser party, the contract provision, or the contract as a whole, if the provision is not separable, should not be enforceable on the grounds that the provision is contrary to public policy. The party seeking to enforce such a contract has the burden of showing that the provisions were explained to the other party and came to his knowledge and there was in fact a real and voluntary meeting of the minds and not merely an objective meeting."[60]

55. Kessler, Contracts of Adhesion—Some Thoughts About Freedom of Contract, 43 Colum.L.Rev. 629 (1943). In the Kessler article, as here, the terms "contract of adhesion" and "standardized contract" are used interchangeably, but the two concepts are not always treated as coextensive. See Sheldon, Consumer Protection and Standard Contracts: The Swedish Experiment in Administrative Control, 22 Am.J.Comp.L. 17, 18 (1974).

56. Ehrenzweig, Adhesion Contracts in the Conflict of Laws, 53 Colum.L.Rev. 1072 (1953); Note, Contract Clauses in Fine Print, 63 Harv.L.Rev. 494 (1950); see Wilson, Freedom of Contract and Adhesion Contracts, 14 Int'l & Comp.L.Q. 172 (1965).

57. The notion of condemning clauses as illegal or contrary to public policy is hardly new. However, it is being used today more often and in a wider variety of circumstances. See, e.g., von Hippel, The Control of Exemption Clauses—A Comparative Study, 16 Int'l & Comp.L.Q. 591 (1967). Unconscionability is discussed in §§ 9–37 to 9–40 supra.

58. 257 Ind. 458, 276 N.E.2d 144 (1971); Annot., 49 A.L.R.3d 306 (1973). See also Frame v. Merrill Lynch, Pierce, Fenner & Smith, Inc., 20 Cal.App.3d 668, 97 Cal.Rptr. 811 (1st Dist.1971).

59. 257 Ind. at 462, 276 N.E.2d at 147.

60. Id. at 464, 276 N.E.2d at 148.

Although the above quotation combines three different concepts (unconscionability, violation of public policy, and lack of true assent),[61] the court's ultimate approach appears to be that the contract is unconscionable because an objective assent which flows from a duty to read is not sufficient (despite the objective theory of contracts) to bind a party to clauses which are unusual or unfair unless the clauses are at least brought to his attention and explained.[62] The theory is that since such clauses impose a great hardship or risk on the weaker party, who is otherwise unable to protect himself, an informed and voluntary consent should be required.[63] A party might be considered to be otherwise able to protect himself if he has a bargaining power relatively equal to that of the other party, or if he were able to obtain insurance at a reasonable rate to protect against a known risk being imposed upon him.

The same approach was employed by the court in the well known case of Henningsen v. Bloomfield Motors, Inc.[64] which arose under the Uniform Sales Act rather than the Uniform Commercial Code.[65] In

61. The Weaver opinion also proceeded upon a warranty analogy when it stated: "The burden should be on the party submitting such 'a package' in printed form to show that the other party had knowledge of any unusual or unconscionable terms contained therein. The principle should be the same as that applicable to implied warranties, namely, that a package of goods sold to a purchaser is fit for the purposes intended and contains no harmful materials other than that represented." Id., 276 N.E.2d at 147–48. See also C. & J. Fertilizer, Inc. v. Allied Mut. Ins. Co., 227 N.W.2d 169 (Iowa 1975).

62. See § 9–40. Under this approach a party who carefully reads the proposed contract is in a worse position than one who does not. Carr v. Hoosier Photo Supplies, Inc., 441 N.E.2d 450 (Ind.1982).

63. See, e.g., Vitex Mfg. Corp. v. Caribtex Corp., 377 F.2d 795, 799–800 (3d Cir. 1967); Johnston, The Control of Exemption Clauses: A Comment, 17 Int'l & Comp.L.Q. 232 (1968).

64. 32 N.J. 358, 161 A.2d 69 (1960); Annot., 75 A.L.R.2d 39 (1961).

65. If the case had arisen under the U.C.C., the court could have noted the Code provision that, in the case of a disclaimer of the warranty of merchantability, the word merchantability must be used and the disclaimer must be conspicuous. U.C.C. § 2–316(2). The term "conspicuous" is defined in id. § 1–201(10). What is or is not conspicuous still appears to be a matter of controversy. A disclaimer in the smallest type preceded by the word "NOTE" printed in the largest type was held to be conspicuous in Velez v. Craine &

Clark Lumber Corp., 41 A.D.2d 747, 341 N.Y.S.2d 248 (2d Dep't 1973), reversed on other grounds 33 N.Y.2d 117, 305 N.E.2d 750, 350 N.Y.S.2d 67 (1973). But see Tennessee Carolina Transp., Inc. v. Strick Corp., 283 N.C. 423, 196 S.E.2d 711 (1973), appeal after remand 286 N.C. 235, 210 S.E.2d 181 (1974). Even more to the point is U.C.C. § 2–719(3) which provides: "Consequential damages may be limited or excluded unless the limitation or exclusion is unconscionable. Limitation of consequential damages for injury to the person in the case of consumer goods is prima facie unconscionable but limitation of damages where the loss is commercial is not." See also U.C.C. §§ 2–316(1), 2–718, 2–719(1) & (2).

Professor Murray takes the position that even if the disclaimer is conspicuous it must, in addition, be negotiated, and comprehensible to the buyer. See Murray, Unconscionability: Unconscionability, 31 U.Pitt.L.Rev. 1, 48–49 (1969). Contra, Leff, Unconscionability and the Code—The Emperor's New Clause, 115 U.Pa.L.Rev. 485, 523–24 (1967). There are, as usual, cases which support each position. Compare Belden-Stark Brick Corp. v. Morris Rosen & Sons, Inc., 39 A.D.2d 534, 331 N.Y.S.2d 59 (1st Dep't 1972), affirmed 31 N.Y.2d 884, 292 N.E.2d 321, 340 N.Y.S.2d 186 (1972) (mem.) with Dobias v. Western Farmers Ass'n, 6 Wn.App. 194, 491 P.2d 1346 (1971). Professor Broude suggests that under §§ 2–202 and 2–316 printed form disclaimers of warranties, even though they are contained in an integration, should not be considered to be part of the agreement because they are not truly assented to. Broude, The Consumer and the Parol Evi-

Henningsen, a consumer brought an action for personal injuries against both the vendor and manufacturer of his automobile. Relying upon a provision in the contract of sale that an express warranty contained therein was in lieu of all other warranties express or implied, the defendants argued that the plaintiff's action should be limited to a claim for defective parts. The heart of the Henningsen decision appears in a paragraph near the end of the opinion:

> "True, the Sales Act authorizes agreements between buyer and seller qualifying the warranty obligations. But quite obviously the Legislature contemplated lawful stipulations (which are determined by the circumstances of a particular case) arrived at freely by parties of relatively equal bargaining strength. The lawmakers did not authorize the automobile manufacturer to use its grossly disproportionate bargaining power to relieve itself from liability and to impose on the ordinary buyer, who in effect has no real freedom of choice, the grave danger of injury to himself and others that attends the sale of such a dangerous instrumentality as a defectively made automobile. In the framework of this case, illuminated as it is by the facts and the many decisions noted, we are of the opinion that Chrysler's attempted disclaimer of an implied warranty of merchantability and of the obligations arising therefrom is so inimical to the public good as to compel an adjudication of its invalidity." [66]

Although there was some discussion about mutual assent, the ultimate holding was based upon the conclusion that such a clause, under the circumstances of the case (clause on reverse side, small print, disparity of bargaining power, clause on a take-it-or-leave-it basis and included by all major car manufacturers), was invalid as being contrary to public policy. This was made clear when the court further stated that it was not required to consider whether a particular charge which related to mutual assent was correct because "the disclaimer is void as a matter of law." [67]

Another leading case illustrating the same approach is Williams v. Walker-Thomas Furniture Co.[68] There, an installment sales agreement had a provision which resulted in "a balance due on every item purchased until the balance due on all items, whenever purchased, was liquidated." [69] As a result, in the event of a default on any one item, all items could be repossessed. The court in concluding that the fairness of the clause needed to be tested at trial stated:

---

dence Rule: Section 2–202 of the Uniform Commercial Code, 1970 Duke L.J. 881. Professor Rakoff goes further, arguing that all non-dickered terms in an adhesion contract be treated as presumptively invalid. Rakoff, Contracts of Adhesion: An Essay in Reconstruction, 96 Harv.L.Rev. 1173 (1983).

66. 32 N.J. at 404, 161 A.2d at 95.

67. Id. at 405, 161 A.2d at 95.

68. 350 F.2d 445 (D.C.Cir.1965), noted in 79 Harv.L.Rev. 1299 (1966).

69. 350 F.2d at 447. See also Uniform Consumer Credit Code § 3.302; U.C.C. § 9–204.

"Ordinarily, one who signs an agreement without full knowledge of its terms might be held to assume the risk that he has entered a one-sided bargain. But when a party of little bargaining power, and hence little real choice, signs a commercially unreasonable contract with little or no knowledge of its terms, it is hardly likely that his consent, or even an objective manifestation of his consent, was ever given to all the terms. In such a case the usual rule that the terms of the agreement are not to be questioned should be abandoned and the court should consider whether the terms of the contract are so unfair that enforcement should be withheld.[70]

The three cases discussed above do not expunge the duty to read rule, but create an exception if the terms (or a term) of the contract are unfair under the circumstances. In such a case, the ordinary manifestation of assent implicit in a signature or acceptance of a document is insufficient because the assent is not reasoned and knowing. Such consent involves an understanding of the clause in question [71] and a reasonable opportunity to accept or decline.[72] Even then, if the clause is sufficiently odious, it will be struck down as unconscionable or contrary to public policy.

Having established the nature of the new approach the question becomes how it has been applied. A discussion of cases relating to promises to indemnify a person against the consequences of his own negligence, and to exculpate another for his own negligence, serve as excellent illustrations.

While Weaver [73] holds that a promise to indemnify was not binding under the circumstances of the case it can hardly be said that there is a general rule that promises to indemnify are objectionable.[74] On a similar set of facts, a New York case, Levine v. Shell Oil Co.,[75] seems to have reached a conclusion directly opposite to that of Weaver.[76] The court paid lip service to the rules announced in the cases discussed above when it stated:

"Lastly, there has been no showing that the agreement involved herein is either a contract of adhesion or an unconscionable agreement and we need not now pass upon the question whether an

70. 350 F.2d at 449–50 (footnotes omitted).

71. See, e.g., Henningsen v. Bloomfield Motors, Inc., 32 N.J. 358, 399–400, 161 A.2d 69, 92 (1960).

72. Id. at 390, 161 A.2d at 87. But what is the choice being discussed? In the Henningsen case it was clear that a person could not buy a new car from a major manufacturer without submitting to the clause in question. But in Weaver there was no evidence that the lessee could not have obtained a similar lease from another oil company without the offending clause. How important should this be on the issue of true assent?

By now it should be clear that the assent discussed in § 9–42 hereof is not the same type of assent being discussed here under the label "true assent."

73. See notes 58 to 63 supra and accompanying text.

74. Messersmith v. American Fidelity Co., 232 N.Y. 161, 133 N.E. 432 (1921); Annot., 19 A.L.R. 879 (1921); Corbin §§ 1471, 1472; Restatement, Contracts § 572.

75. 28 N.Y.2d 205, 269 N.E.2d 799, 321 N.Y.S.2d 81 (1971).

76. A reading of the briefs tends to reinforce this conclusion.

indemnification clause in a contract of that nature would be void for those reasons. * * * In this arm's length transaction the indemnification provision was a part of [sic] business relationship between the parties. If Visconti [the lessee] had reservations as to the scope of the agreement, he should have insisted on a different indemnification clause or refused to give his assent to the contract. * * * Since he apparently elected not to do so and has not demonstrated to this court that Shell was guilty of fraud or overreaching conduct, he is bound by the expression of intent in the lease." [77]

Notice, however, that while the Levine court emphasized that it was not dealing with a contract of adhesion, the dissenting opinion in Weaver criticized the majority for incorrectly relying upon cases involving adhesion contracts instead of following the more traditional rule.[78] One has the feeling that the facts in Weaver and Levine are not dissimilar but an opposite result is being reached.

The intermediate appellate court in Weaver held that a provision in a contract by which one party agreed not to hold the other liable for his negligence is contrary to public policy in the absence of an understanding of the provision and true assent to it.[79] Although, this cannot be considered to be the traditional view,[80] that view does recognize an

---

77. 28 N.Y.2d at 213, 321 N.Y.S.2d at 86–87, 269 N.E.2d at 803, (citation omitted).

78. This raises the problem of what is a contract of adhesion. A standardized agreement has been described as one which is dictated by a predominant party to cover transactions with many people rather than with an individual, and which resembles an ultimatum or law rather than a mutually negotiated contract. Siegelman v. Cunard White Star, Ltd., 221 F.2d 189, 206 (2d Cir.1955). It is characterized by a lack of negotiation. Cohen, The Basis of Contract, 46 Harv.L.Rev. 553, 588–90 (1933); Llewellyn, What Price Contract?—An Essay in Perspective, 40 Yale L.J. 704, 731–34 (1931); Meyer, Contracts of Adhesion and the Doctrine of Fundamental Breach, 50 Va.L.Rev. 1178, 1179–86 (1964); Oldfather, Toward a Usable Method of Judicial Review of the Adhesion Contractor's Lawmaking, 16 U.Kan.L.Rev. 303, 305–07 (1968); Slawson, Standard Form Contracts and Democratic Control of Lawmaking Power, 84 Harv.L.Rev. 529, 531 (1971); Note, The Form 50 Lease: Judicial Treatment of an Adhesion Contract, 111 U.Pa.L.Rev. 1197, 1205–06 (1963). See also K & C, Inc. v. Westinghouse Elec. Corp., 437 Pa. 303, 308–09, 263 A.2d 390, 393 (1970).

The New York court in Levine assumed that the lessee had a choice and could

bargain with respect to the clause. Would the Weaver court agree? See notes 58–63 supra. It should also be noted that the plaintiffs in the Henningsen and Williams cases are consumers in the accepted sense of the word while the lessee in Weaver probably is not. See, e.g., 15 U.S.C.A. § 1602(a)–(h); Uniform Consumer Credit Code § 1.301(11); Model Consumer Credit Act § 1.410. How important this factor should be is still unclear. Certainly as a matter of fact, it may usually be assumed that a consumer has little or no bargaining power. In any event, there are other cases which have taken the Weaver approach even though consumers were not involved. See, e.g., Chandler v. Aero Mayflower Transit Co., 374 F.2d 129 (4th Cir.1967); Standard Oil Co. of Cal. v. Perkins, 347 F.2d 379 (9th Cir.1965).

79. Weaver v. American Oil Co., 261 N.E.2d 99, 104 (Ind.App.1970), modified 262 N.E.2d 663 (1970), modified 257 Ind. 458, 276 N.E.2d 144 (1971).

Exculpatory clauses are often circumvented by a process of interpretation. See e.g., Willard Van Dyke Productions, Inc. v. Eastman Kodak Co., 12 N.Y.2d 301, 189 N.E.2d 693, 239 N.Y.S.2d 337 (1963).

80. Johnston, The Control of Exemption Clauses: A Comment, 17 Int'l & Comp.L.Q. 232 (1968); von Hipple, The Control of Exemption Clauses: A Compara-

exception in the case of public servants involved in the performance of their public duties for compensation.[81] The primary illustration of such public servants is a common carrier.[82]

Cases involving private voluntary transactions, however, are not harmonious. While the lower court in the Weaver case held an exculpation clause invalid,[83] a number of recent cases have indicated the contrary.[84] Here again, the problem is discussed not only from the perspective of public policy, but also from the point of view of mutual assent.[85] For example, in Ciofalo v. Vic Tanny Gyms, Inc.,[86] a patron of a gymnasium operated by the defendant agreed in a membership contract to assume the risk of injuries arising out of the defendant's negligence. The court did not find the clause in opposition to public policy, adding: "Here there is no special legal relationship and no overriding public interest which demand that this contract provision, voluntarily entered into by competent parties, should be rendered ineffectual." [87] Although the court stated that the plaintiff had voluntarily assented, the facts here were not sufficiently delineated to allow

---

tive Study, 16 Int'l & Comp.L.Q. 591 (1967); Note, 42 Chi.-Kent L.Rev. 82 (1965). However there is a different rule for willful, wanton, reckless, gross or intentional negligence. Winterstein v. Wilcom, 16 Md. App. 130, 136, 293 A.2d 821, 824 (1972). It might be observed that the courts have shown a greater hostility to exculpatory clauses than to indemnification agreements. See Jamison v. Ellwood Consol. Water Co., 420 F.2d 787, 789 (3d Cir.1970); Diamond Crystal Salt Co. v. Thielman, 395 F.2d 62, 65 (5th Cir.1968); Haynes v. County of Missoula, 163 Mont. 270, 280–282, 517 P.2d 370, 377 (1973).

81. Tunkl v. Regents of the Univ. of Calif., 60 Cal.2d 92, 98–102, 383 P.2d 441, 445, 447, 32 Cal.Rptr. 33, 37–39 (1963).

82. There also have been a number of statutes dealing with the topic of exculpation. See e.g., 6 Del.Code § 2704; Ill.— Smith-Hurd Ann. ch. 80, ¶ 91; McKinney's N.Y.Gen.Obli.Law §§ 5–321 to 5–325 (concerning leases; caterers; building service and maintenance contracts; architects; engineers; surveyors; garages and parking lots).

83. See 261 N.E.2d at 101; accord, Dixilyn Drilling Corp. v. Crescent Towing & Salvage Co., 372 U.S. 697, 83 S.Ct. 967, 10 L.Ed.2d 78 (1963), on remand 324 F.2d 272 (5th Cir.1963); Bisso v. Inland Waterways Corp., 349 U.S. 85, 75 S.Ct. 629, 99 L.Ed. 911 (1955); Kansas City Power & Light Co. v. United Tel. Co., 458 F.2d 177, 179 (10th Cir.1972); Fitzgerald v. Newark Morning Ledger Co., 111 N.J.Super. 104, 267 A.2d 557 (1970) (such a clause not favored but question is one of public policy and answer

depends upon position of the parties). See also Rogers v. Dorchester Associates, 32 N.Y.2d 553, 564, 347 N.Y.S.2d 22, 30, 300 N.E.2d 403, 409 (1973).

84. Royal Typewriter Co., Division Litton Business Systems, Inc. v. M/V Kulmerland, 346 F.Supp. 1019 (S.D.N.Y.1972), affirmed 483 F.2d 645 (2d Cir.1973); Cree Coaches, Inc. v. Panel Suppliers, Inc., 384 Mich. 646, 186 N.W.2d 335 (1971); Great Northern Oil Co. v. St. Paul Fire & Marine Ins. Co., 291 Minn. 97, 189 N.W.2d 404 (1971); Stamp v. Windsor Power House Coal Co., 154 W.Va. 578, 177 S.E.2d 146 (1970). See also Restatement, Contracts § 574. These authorities do not necessarily conflict with the cases cited in note 83 supra, since the underlying rationale of all these cases is that the question is one of assent and public policy.

85. The leading case is probably Tunkl v. Regents of Univ. of Calif., 60 Cal.2d 92, 32 Cal.Rptr. 33, 383 P.2d 441 (1963).

86. 10 N.Y.2d 294, 177 N.E.2d 925, 220 N.Y.S.2d 962 (1961). See also Empress Health & Beauty Spa, Inc. v. Turner, 503 S.W.2d 188 (Tenn.1973).

87. 10 N.Y.2d at 297–98, 177 N.E.2d at 927, 220 N.Y.S.2d at 965. There has been much discussion concerning the language required for an exculpatory clause to be effective irrespective of any question of public policy. See Levine v. Shell Oil Co., 28 N.Y.2d 205, 269 N.E.2d 799, 321 N.Y.S.2d 81 (1971); Cason v. Geis Irrigation Co. of Kansas, Inc., 211 Kan. 406, 507 P.2d 295 (1973).

a determination of whether there was the true, voluntary, understanding assent required by Weaver and a number of other cases.[88]

The indemnity and exculpation cases are in a process of development. A gradual but perceptible change is occurring.[89] Freedom of contract, laissez-faire, and black letter law are giving way to notions of what is fair under the particular circumstances of the case, even if the result is not strictly in compliance with the objective theory of contract.[90] These cases also illustrate the modern attack on the duty to read rule—(1) a finding of a lack of true mutual assent; or (2) a conclusion that even if there were true assent, the challenged clause should be stricken as unconscionable or contrary to a rule of public policy that a party should not be permitted to shift the burden of his wrongdoing to a weaker party or to deprive the injured party of his right to recover for the wrong done to him.[91]

A Minnesota court has summarized the recent trend as follows:

An examination of the cases demonstrates the emergence of a two-prong test used by the courts in analyzing the policy considerations. Before enforcing an exculpatory clause, both prongs of the test are examined, to-wit: (1) whether there was a disparity of bargaining power between the parties (in terms of a compulsion to sign a contract containing an unacceptable provision and the lack of ability to negotiate elimination of the unacceptable provision) and (2) the types of services being offered or provided (taking into consideration whether it is a public or essential service).[92] (Citations omitted)

The summary is largely accurate but fails to take into account more radical cases that emphasize the presence or absence of true assent.[93]

§ 9–45. Duty to Read and Restatement Second

Somewhat curiously the Restatement Second does not state a general rule with respect to the duty to read as did the original Restatement.[94] Rather it sets forth a rule primarily for standardized

---

88. Winterstein v. Wilcom, 16 Md.App. 130, 293 A.2d 821 (1972); Van Noy Interstate Co. v. Tucker, 125 Miss. 260, 87 So. 643 (1921); Joseph v. Sears Roebuck & Co., 224 S.C. 105, 77 S.E.2d 583, 40 A.L.R.2d 742 (1953); Dodge v. Nashville, C. & St. L.R.R. Co., 142 Tenn. 20, 215 S.W. 274 (1919).

89. See, e.g., Smith v. Kennedy, 43 Ala. App. 554, 195 So.2d 820 (1966), certiorari denied 280 Ala. 718, 195 So.2d 829 (1967), which according to the casenote in 19 Ala. L.Rev. 484, 486 (1967) makes a substantial change in the law of Alabama. See also 4 Duq.U.L.Rev. 475 (1966).

90. W. Friedmann, Law in a Changing Society 93–94 (1959).

91. See notes 55 to 72 supra and accompanying text.

92. Schlobohm v. Spa Petite, Inc., 326 N.W.2d 920, 923 (Minn.1982).

93. See Krohnert v. Yacht Systems Hawaii, Inc., ___ Hawaii App. ___, 664 P.2d 738 (1983) where true assent is made a third prong.

94. The rule of the original Restatement is set forth in § 70 which is in basic conformity with the general rule discussed in § 9–41 supra. The Restatement, Second, Contracts § 211, Comment b, suggests some recognition of the general rule and Comment d covers to some extent the same ground as § 9–42 hereof.

agreements in the chapter on interpretation.[95] Section 211 provides as follows:

> "(1) Except as stated in Subsection (3), where a party to an agreement signs or otherwise manifests assent to a writing and has reason to believe that like writings are regularly used to embody terms of agreements of the same type, he adopts the writing as an integrated agreement with respect to the terms included in the writing.

> "(2) Such a writing is interpreted wherever reasonable as treating alike all those similarly situated, without regard to their knowledge or understanding of the standard terms of the writing.

> "(3) Where the other party has reason to believe that the party manifesting such assent would not do so if he knew that the writing contained a particular term, the term is not part of the agreement."

The rule obviously has a dual thrust. First, it recognizes that standardized agreements serve a useful purpose because most contracts are concluded between a party who bargains, if at all, only with respect to certain limited terms, and by an agent of a business who has limited understanding of the terms and limited authority to vary them.[96] Secondly, it follows the lead of cases such as Weaver v. American Oil Co.[97] by stating that parties "are not bound to unknown terms which are beyond the range of reasonable expectation." [98] The rationale is that if the drafter of the form knows or has reason to know that "the adhering party would not have accepted the agreement if he had known that the agreement contained the particular term" then the adhering party should not be deemed to assent.[99]

Although the Restatement Second speaks of assent it seems that it is not using the word assent in its ordinary connotation for it indicates that all persons who sign a standardized agreement should be treated alike, even though a more sophisticated individual customer might give the type of informed assent required by some of the cases discussed above. Thus what the Restatement appears to be saying is that if the ordinary reasonable man would not expect such a clause it should be read out of the contract.[1] The Restatement in essence is talking about unconscionability based upon "unfair surprise." [2] It recognizes this

95. There is no definition of standardized agreement. See note 78 supra; see also Restatement, Second, Contracts § 157, Comment b.

96. Restatement, Second, Contracts § 211, Comments a & b.

97. 257 Ind. 458, 276 N.E.2d 144 (1971); see notes 17–19 supra and accompanying text.

98. Restatement, Second, Contracts § 211, Comment f.

99. Id.

1. Id. at § 211(2). However, in Comment f it is stated that one of the factors to be considered is whether the adhering party ever had an opportunity to read the term.

2. U.C.C. § 2–302, Comment 1. Professor Leff treats unfair surprise as procedural unconscionability. See § 9–40 supra; cf. Clark, Equity 247 (1954).

when it states that the rule set forth in Section 211 "is closely related to the policy against unconscionable terms." [3]

Two of the factors to be considered in determining whether a reasonable man would expect a particular provision in the agreement are: (1) whether "the term is bizarre or oppressive," [4] and (2) whether "it eviscerates the non-standard terms explicitly agreed to, or * * * eliminates the dominant purpose of the transaction." [5]

The Restatement Second thus recognizes the utility of standard agreements but refuses to allow them to be used unfairly. This seems a reasonable resolution of the problem and is in general accord with the rule of some of the cases discussed above that even an objective manifestation of assent stemming from a failure to read should not preclude consideration of whether there is true assent to unfair or unexpected terms.

 WESTLAW REFERENCES
"restatement second" /p "standard! agreement" (duty fail! +2 read)

§ 9–46. Conclusion

The underlying philosophy of the objective theory of contracts is to enshrine a writing as sacrosanct and inviolate. This result is achieved by rules that exclude or minimize the true subjective intention of the parties. The policy is that a party to a written agreement may safely rely upon the written document.[6] These results are achieved, for example, under the traditional parol evidence rule and traditional rules of interpretation including the plain meaning rule. It might be noted that all of these rules are presently under serious attack.[7]

The duty to read rule is yet another fortification thrown up by the objective theory of contracts to make a writing impregnable.[8] It is based on the realities of the bargaining practices of the past, when the

---

3. Restatement, Second, Contracts § 211, Comment f; see § 9–40 supra.

4. Restatement, Second, Contracts § 211, Comment f.

5. Id.; see Meyer, Contracts of Adhesion and the Doctrine of Fundamental Breach, 50 Va.L.Rev. 1178 (1964). See also Fairbanks, Morse & Co. v. Consolidated Fisheries Co., 190 F.2d 817 (3d Cir.1951); Weisz v. Parke-Bernet Galleries, Inc., 67 Misc.2d 1077, 325 N.Y.S.2d 576 (N.Y.C.Civ. Ct.1971); reversed 77 Misc.2d 80, 351 N.Y.S.2d 911 (App.Term 1974); Karsales (Harrow), Ltd. v. Wallis [1956] 2 All E.R. 866 (C.A.).

6. D. Hume, A Treatise of Human Nature 523–26 (Silby-Bigge ed. 1888); Whittier, The Restatement of Contracts and Mutual Assent, 17 Calif.L.Rev. 441 (1929); cf. 1 Williston §§ 21 & 35.

7. See, e.g., Restatement, Second, Contracts ch. 9.

8. The Weaver case recognized the relationship between the objective theory of contracts and the duty to read when it stated: "The parole evidence rule states that an agreement or contract, signed by the parties, is conclusively presumed to represent an integration or meeting of the minds of the parties. This is an archaic rule from the old common law. The objectivity of the rule has as its only merit its simplicity of application which is far outweighed by its failure in many cases to represent the actual agreement, particularly where a printed form prepared by one party contains [sic] hidden clauses unknown to the other party is submitted and signed. The law should seek the truth or the subjective understanding of the parties in this more enlightened age. The burden

self-reliance ethic was strong and standardized agreements were rare. Under such circumstances, it may have been realistic to expect each party to read and understand his agreement. However, in the current era of mass marketing, a party may reasonably believe that he is not expected to read a standardized document and would be met with impatience if he did. In such circumstances an imputation that he assents to all of the terms in the document is dubious law. An assertion that he is bound by them would place a premium upon an artful draftsman who is able to put asunder what the salesman and the customer have joined together.[9]

Thus, some of the more modern cases search not only for apparent objective assent but also for a true assent. Under this view true assent does not exist unless there is a genuine opportunity to read the clause in question and its impact is explained by the dominant party and understood by the other party who has a reasonable choice, under the circumstances, of accepting or rejecting the clause.[10] Thus the printed form which implicitly suggests that it should not be challenged or even read loses some of its apparent authority.[11] The Restatement Second goes one step further when it indicates that what is important, at least in contracts of adhesion, is whether a reasonable man would have expected to find such a clause in the contract. If not, the clause is considered to be oppressive, unfair or indecent.[12] This, of course, carries one into the doctrine of substantive unconscionability which in turn is related to the question of whether a particular clause should be struck down as contrary to public policy.[13] The Restatement Second seems to be suggesting a new kind of objective approach to standardized agreements. Rather than seeking out true assent on a case by case basis it places the duty upon the courts to consider the essential fairness of the printed terms, both from the viewpoint of surprise and inherent one-sidedness.

Not only is there inconsistency in the authorities regarding which theory should be applied, but apparently opposite results are being reached in cases with substantially similar fact patterns.[14] This should not come as a surprise to any student of the law. The plain fact is that

should be on the party submitting such 'a package' in printed form to show that the other party had knowledge of any unusual or unconscionable terms contained therein," 257 Ind. at 463–64, 276 N.E.2d at 147 (emphasis deleted).

It also has been suggested that the party who prepared the standardized form should shoulder the burden of proving that an opportunity for bargaining existed. Wilson, Freedom of Contract and Adhesion Contracts, 14 Int'l & Comp.L.Q. 172, 186 (1965).

9. See generally Dauer, Contracts of Adhesion in Light of the Bargain Hypothe-

sis: An Introduction, 5 Akron L.Rev. 1 (1972); Mellinkoff, How to Make Contracts Illegible, 5 Stan.L.Rev. 418 (1953); Slawson, Standard Form Contracts and Democratic Control of Lawmaking Power, 84 Harv.L.Rev. 529 (1971).

10. See § 9–44 supra.

11. Shuchman, Consumer Credit by Adhesion Contracts, 35 Temp.L.Q. 125 (1962).

12. K. Llewellyn, The Common Law Tradition: Deciding Appeals 370 (1960).

13. See § 9–44 supra.

14. See § 9–44 supra.

new law is evolving in this area and it will be many years, if ever, before any semblance of uniformity will be achieved.[15]

The ultimate result may be a radically different set of rules for transactions in which all major aspects of the agreement are negotiated and those in which standard forms are used. If the industries that employ standard forms do not police themselves so as to insure inherent fairness of forms, it is likely that the courts will increasingly refuse legal effect to non-negotiated terms of a contract and that standardized forms, as in the case of insurance policies, will be dictated by legislatures or administrative agencies.

15. Perhaps what is called for is an administrative approach to the problem.

See, e.g., Sales, Standard Form Contracts, 16 Mod.L.Rev. 318, 337–38 (1953); Sheldon, Consumer Protection and Standard Contracts: The Swedish Experiment in Administrative Control, 22 Am.J.Comp. L. 17 (1974); Comment, Administrative Regulation of Adhesion Contracts in Israel, 66 Colum.L.Rev. 1340 (1966). See also Speidel, Unconscionability, Assent and Consumer Protection, 31 U.Pitt.L.Rev. 359 (1970).

Chapter 10

CONSUMER PROTECTION

Table of Sections

§ 10–1. Introduction

Much of the law of contracts is based upon an ethic of self-reliance. When negotiating an agreement, each individual is charged with the burden of looking out for his own self-interest. Under the common law, the State will normally refuse to police the content or the process of formation of a bargain. Exceptions to this proposition have existed where contract formation is contaminated by fraud, undue influence and the like; or where the bargain is unconscionable, illegal or against public policy.[1] Even in these cases, however, the protective rules of law must normally be actuated by the aggrieved party by bringing a court action or raising an affirmative defense.

The self-reliance ethic presupposes, as a model, parties who understand the legal consequences of the agreement and who have equal bargaining power or, at least, who are equally free to refuse to bargain unless their terms are met. Today however, the realities of the market often are at variance with that presupposition.[2] Very often, the consumer, whether poor, middle class or rich, is placed in the position of accepting or rejecting, without possibility of alteration, the terms proposed by a large institution or industry. Very often the terms are not understood or even read.[3] The analogy of the automobile warranty to law-making by the automotive giants is irresistible.[4] In particular

1. See chs. 9 and 22. See also Hamilton, the Ancient Maxim Caveat Emptor, 40 Yale L.J. 1133 (1931).

2. W. Magnuson & J. Carper, The Dark Side of the Marketplace: the Plight of the American Consumer (1969); D. Caplovitz, The Poor Pay More (1963); cf. K. Llewellyn, The Common Law Tradition 401–41 (1960); Rothschild & Throne, Criminal

Consumer Fraud: A Victim-Oriented Analysis, 74 Mich.L.Rev. 661 (1976).

3. A. La France, M. Schroeder, R. Bennett, W. Boyd, Law of the Poor § 101 (1970). See ch. 9H supra.

4. Slawson, Standard Form Contracts and Democratic Control of Lawmaking Power, 84 Harv.L.Rev. 529 (1971); Oldfather, Toward a Usable Method of Ju-

instances such law-making may be benign rather than despotic, but it is never democratic.

Another difficulty with the model presupposed by contract law is that very often the amount involved in any consumer grievance may be less than the cost of implementing the processes of law through bringing a private law suit or raising a defense.[5] And yet the grievance may be meritorious and shared by a multitude of others similarly situated. Moreover, successful litigation by a single consumer will seldom deter continuation of the conduct about which the consumer grieved.

Nineteenth century concepts of *laissez-faire* and freedom of contract have never found absolute acceptance by the legal system. Usury statutes, which relate to the imposition of a maximum price for the use of money, have long been a part of the American scene.[6] Late in the nineteenth century larger assaults upon freedom of contract began to be legislated. These assaults had as characteristics the imposition of governmental controls upon parties with great economic power to attempt to redress imbalances in bargaining power. A second characteristic has been a partial shift in the policing of contracts from private to public law; from aggrieved individuals to public officials. Some early illustrations of this change of philosophy are the regulation of carriers by the I.C.C.,[7] the regulation of the insurance industry and the terms of the insurance contract [8] and statutes regulating labor relations.[9] The limitations of litigation by a single aggrieved consumer have been overcome in part by a more liberal allowance of class actions.

In recent decades there has been broader recognition that there are differences between consumer and other commercial transactions and that the consumer needs to be protected.[10] The result is a massive

dicial Review of the Adhesion Contractor's Lawmaking, 16 U.Kan.L.Rev. 303 (1968).

5. Mueller, Contracts of Frustration, 78 Yale L.J. 576 (1969); Comment, Translating Sympathy for Deceived Consumers into Effective Programs for Protection, 114 U.Pa.L.Rev. 395 (1966); Jones & Boyer, Improving the Quality of Justice in the Marketplace: The Need for Better Consumer Remedies, 40 Geo.Wash.L.Rev. 357 (1972); Mussehl, The Neighborhood Consumer Center: Relief for the Consumer at the Grass-Roots Level, 47 Notre Dame Law. 1093 (1972).

6. See Oeltjen, Usury; Utilitarian or Useless?, 3 Fla.St.U.L.Rev. 167 (1975).

7. See e.g., The Interstate Commerce Act, 49 U.S.C.A. § 1 et seq.

8. See J. Vance on Insurance 56–59 (3d ed.1951).

9. See for example the Taft-Hartley Act, 29 U.S.C.A. § 141 et seq.

10. See ch. 9 G supra. A very important question is who is a consumer? In general, a consumer transaction is one in which a natural person buys or borrows for family, personal or household reasons. Elaborate definitions are contained, for example, in the Truth in Lending Act, 15 U.S.C.A. § 1601 et seq. See also § 1.301(11) of the U.C.C.C.; § 1.301(8) of the Nat'l Consumer Act; and § 1.410 of the Model Consumer Credit Act. The Uniform Commercial Code does not have a definition of consumers and does not give any special treatment to them. See, e.g., §§ 9–505 and 9–507. However, the U.C.C. does have sections which were drafted with the consumer in mind (e.g., §§ 9–201, 9–203) and others which were drafted to limit the advantage of a person with superior bargaining power (e.g., §§ 1–201(3), 1–203 and 2–302) and sections which make distinctions based upon whether both parties are merchants or not (e.g., § 2–207). It also contains special rules relating to security interests in "consumer goods." U.C.C. § 9–109(1). See Skilton & Helstad, Protection of the Installment Buyer of

array of statutes, federal and state, that have been enacted to protect the consumer.[11]

WESTLAW REFERENCES

contract /s "laissez faire"

usury /s statut! /s protect! /s contract

statut! /s "bargaining power" /s unequal! inequality imbalance

ci((49 +4 1) (29 +4 141))

"consumer transaction" /5 define* definition

§ 10–2. Scope of the Discussion

Consumer protection legislation has various kinds of impact on contract law, often by indirection only. For example, a statute or regulation may penalize certain kinds of conduct without effecting the validity of the consumer transaction. For reasons such as this, consumer protection has become a subject matter and a discipline of its own.[12] The purpose of this chapter is merely to acquaint the reader in a general way with what has been occurring in this area in recent decades.

§ 10–3. Consumer Credit Protection Act

The most significant federal statute is the Consumer Credit Protection Act which is known as the Truth In Lending Law.[13] Title I requires that a creditor disclose to the consumer the important credit terms so that the borrower may make an informed decision.[14] What must be disclosed and when depends on a number of factors.[15] The

Goods Under the Uniform Commercial Code, 65 Mich.L.Rev. 1465 (1967).

11. Consumer transactions are generally limited to situations where a party acquires property or services "primarily for a personal, family, household or agricultural purpose." See U.C.C. § 9–109(1) and U.C. C. § 2.104(1)(b).

12. General works include Epstein & Nickles, Consumer Law in a Nutshell (2d ed.1981); Feldman, Consumer Protection: Problems and Prospects (2d ed.1980); Hemphill, The Consumer Protection Handbook (1981).

13. 15 U.S.C.A. § 1601 et seq. Significant changes in this act were made by the Truth In Lending Simplification and Reform Act of 1980. Most of the amendments became effective in 1982. Regulation Z, implementing Truth In Lending, was promulgated by the Federal Reserve Board at 12 C.F.R. § 226–1.

14. 15 U.S.C.A. § 1601. The notion is that a knowledge of unit pricing enables the consumer to shop around. See generally Davis, Revamping Consumer Credit Contract Law, 68 Va.L.Rev. 1333 (1982);

Jordan & Warren, Disclosure of Finance Charges: A Rationale, 64 Mich.L.Rev. 1285 (1966). Recently nutrition labeling, ingredient labeling and dating of perishable commodities and quality standards have been regulated. See, e.g., 21 U.S.C.A. §§ 341, 343G; 7 U.S.C.A. § 1622. See generally, Whitford, The Functions of Disclosure Regulation in Consumer Transactions, 1973 Wis.L.Rev. 400. See 1 CCH Consumer Credit Guide, §§ 4080–4140; see also B. Curran, Trends in Consumer Legislation 91–92, 95–97, 117–19, 293–300 (1965). The Uniform Commercial Credit Code is generally in conformity with the disclosure provisions of the Consumer Credit Protection Act. The Uniform Commercial Credit Code is mentioned below.

15. 15 U.S.C.A. §§ 1636–1639. See also Fed.Reserve Bd.Reg. Z § 226.2(r), 34 Fed. Reg. 2003; id. § 226.7, 34 Fed.Reg. at 2006; id. § 226.8, 34 Fed.Reg. at 2007; Upshaw, Banking in the Consumer Protection Age, 5 U.C.C.L.J. 232 (1973). See also R. Jordan & W. Warren, Manual on the Federal Truth In Lending Law (1969); Kintner, Henneberger & Neill, A Primer on Truth in Lending, 13 St. Louis U.L.J. 501 (1969).

Consumer Credit Protection Act also regulates consumer credit advertising.[16]

Subchapter III places restrictions on the garnishment of wages.[17] A National Commission on Consumer Finances was created to investigate the consumer finance industry and make recommendations.

In time, a number of additions were made to the statute. In 1970 and 1974 provisions with respect to credit cards were introduced.[18] One important provision establishes a fifty dollar limitation of liability when a credit card is used without the authority of the cardholder even if the cardholder fails to give notice of the fact that the card has been lost.[19] Also passed in 1970 was the Fair Credit Reporting Act. It regulates credit reports prepared by "Consumer Reporting Agencies" and users of said reports.[20]

In 1974 three additional provisions were added to the Consumer Credit Protection Act. The Fair Credit Billing Act is designed to protect consumers against unfair practices of issuers of open-end credit (e.g. credit cards) and it requires a creditor to set up and inform the debtor of procedures with respect to billing errors.[21] The second is the Equal Credit Opportunity Act. This act prohibits discrimination against one seeking credit on the basis of sex or marital status.[22] In the same year the Consumer Credit Protection Act created a right to rescind. The power to rescind relates only to a consumer credit sale in which a security interest (lien) is or will be retained or acquired in real property used or intended to be used by the consumer as his principal residence. The section does not apply to a first lien or equivalent security in connection with financing the acquisition of a dwelling in which the customer expects to reside.[23]

In 1977 the Fair Debt Collection Practices Act was added. It places a number of stringent restrictions on the process of debt collection. It relates only to debt collectors who regularly collect debts.[24] Another addition to the Consumer Credit Protection Act is the Interstate Land Sales Full Disclosure Act[25] which relates to "federally related mortgage

---

On the question of timing of disclosures, see Timing of Truth-in-Lending Disclosures; 58 Iowa L.Rev. 389 (1972).

16. 15 U.S.C.A. § 1661 et seq.

17. 15 U.S.C.A. §§ 1671–1677. Wage assignments are not covered by the act and are governed by state law.

18. 15 U.S.C.A. §§ 1642–1646. There are also state statutes governing credit cards. See, e.g., Ill.—S.H.A. ch. 121½, ¶ 381 (1976); McKinney's N.Y.Gen.Bus. Law § 512 et seq.; Wis.Stat.Ann. 421.101 et seq. See also Nat'l Consumer Act §§ 2.601–2.605; Model Consumer Credit Act § 2.408; West's Ann.Cal.Civ.Code § 1747 et seq.

19. 15 U.S.C.A. § 1643(a).

20. 15 U.S.C.A. §§ 1681–1681(t). See Comment, An Analysis of the Fair Credit Reporting Act, 1 Fordham Urban L.J. 48 (1972). There are a number of states that have passed similar statutes. See 1 CCH Consumer Credit Guide § 680 collecting statutes.

21. 15 U.S.C.A. §§ 1666–1666(j).

22. 15 U.S.C.A. §§ 1691–1691(f).

23. 15 U.S.C.A. § 1635(a). There are state laws granting a right to rescind but for the most part these statutes relate to home solicitation sales. See Sher, the "Cooling-Off" Period in Door-to-Door Sales, 15 U.C.L.A.Rev. 717 (1968).

24. 15 U.S.C.A. § 1692 et seq.

25. 15 U.S.C.A. § 1701 et seq.

loans". It is patterned after the Securities Act of 1933. Some states have similar legislation.[26]

WESTLAW REFERENCES
"consumer credit protection act"
to(92b)
"truth in lending simplification and reform act"
"finance charge" /s disclos! /s consumer
"national commission on consumer finance"
"credit card" /s state /s statut!
"fair credit" +1 reporting billing
"equal credit opportunity act"
ci(15 +4 1635)

§ 10–4. Other Federal Statutes

Another important consumer protection statute is of the Federal Trade Commission Act of 1914 pursuant to which the Federal Trade Commission was created to prevent "unfair methods of competition in commerce".[27] In 1938 Section 5 of the Federal Trade Commission Act was amended to condemn in addition "unfair or deceptive acts or practices in commerce".[28] Title II of the Magnuson-Moss Warranty Federal Trade Commission Improvement Act passed in 1975 significantly increased the jurisdiction and power of the F.T.C.[29] Title I of the Magnuson-Moss Act governs warranties made by warrantors in writing in relation to the sale of consumer products. The act contains disclosure requirements. Warranties must be designated as either "full" or "limited". In addition the act curtails the right to limit or disclaim implied warranties. Finally the act provides for various enforcement procedures.[30]

Another important Federal Statute is the Real Estate Settlements Procedures Act of 1974.[31] The primary purpose of this act is to protect buyers and sellers of residential real estate from unreasonably high settlement costs by requiring advance disclosure of such costs and by outlawing certain 'kickbacks'.[32]

26. See e.g., McKinney's N.Y.Gen.Bus. Law, Art. 29H, § 600 et seq.

27. 15 U.S.C.A. § 45.

28. 52 Stat. 111 (1938). As to what is unfair see Comment, Unfairness Without Deception: Recent Positions of the Federal Trade Commission, 5 Loyola U.Chi.L.J. 537 (1974). The purpose is to protect even gullible or credulous consumers. Exposition Press, Inc. v. F.T.C., 295 F.2d 869 (2d Cir. 1961), certiorari denied 370 U.S. 917, 82 S.Ct. 1554, 8 L.Ed.2d 497 (1962). See also Gellhorn, Proof of Consumer Deception Before the Federal Trade Commission, 17 U.Kan.L.Rev. 559 (1969); Loevinger, The Politics of Advertising, 15 Wm. & Mary L.Rev. 1 (1973).

29. 15 U.S.C.A. §§ 45, 53 and 56. Many states have a statute or statutes which prohibit unfair or deceptive trade practices. See generally 2 C.C.H. Poverty L.Rep. §§ 3015, 3200.

30. 15 U.S.C.A. § 230 et seq. Obviously this material must be considered in connection with the warranty provisions of the Uniform Commercial Code.

31. 12 U.S.C.A. § 2601.

32. See D. Epstein & S. Nickles, Consumer Law In A Nutshell, 149–51 (2d ed. 1981).

In addition there are a whole host of other federal statutes that may be considered to be consumer protection statutes.[33]

WESTLAW REFERENCES

"unfair methods of competition in commerce"

"magnuson moss warranty"

"door to door" /s "cooling off"

§ 10–5. State Statutes

Related state statutes have been mentioned in connection with our discussion of federal statutes. Here we shall only make more explicit mention of two "uniform" statutes that have been prepared. One is the Uniform Commercial Credit Code which was proposed in 1968 and revised in 1974. To-date it has been adopted with some revisions by a number of states.[34] The other Model Act is the Model Consumer Credit Act (originally the National Consumer Act) which was promulgated by the National Consumer Law Center at Boston College. It is much more consumer oriented than the U.C.C.C. It is not yet law in any jurisdiction. It has, however, influenced legislation in some states.[35] These statutes have a whole host of provisions that place serious limitations on freedom of contract.

WESTLAW REFERENCES

"model consumer credit act" "uniform commercial credit code"

---

33. Nor can consideration be given to statutes such as the Consumer Product Safety Act, 15 U.S.C.A. § 2051 et seq. discussed in 34 Fed.B.J. 139 (1975); The Federal Hazardous Substances Act, 15 U.S. C.A. § 1261 et seq.; discussed in 13 B.C. Ind. & Com.L.Rev. 504 (1972); The Poisonous Prevention Packaging Act, 15 U.S.C.A. § 1471 et seq.; The Flammable Fabrics Act, 15 U.S.C.A. § 1191 et seq.; The Federal Food, Drug and Cosmetic Act, 21 U.S. C.A. § 301 et seq.; The Clean Air Act of 1970, 42 U.S.C.A. § 1857 et seq.; The National Traffic and Motor Vehicle Safety Act, 15 U.S.C.A. § 1381 et seq.; The Fur Products Labeling Act, 15 U.S.C.A. § 69 et seq.; The Textile Fiber Products Act, 15 U.S.C.A. § 70 et seq.; The Wool Products Labeling Act, 15 U.S.C.A. § 68 et seq.; The Fair Packaging and Labeling Act, 15 U.S. C.A. § 1451 et seq.; Civil Rights Legislation such as the Civil Rights Act of 1964, 42 U.S.C.A. § 2000(e) et seq.; The Child Protection and Toy Safety Act of 1969, 15 U.S.C.A. § 1261 et seq.; The Interstate Land Sales Full Disclosure Act, 15 U.S.C.A. § 1701 et seq., discussed in 48 St. John's L.Rev. 947 (1974); The Motor Vehicle Information and Cost Savings Act, 15 U.S. C.A. § 1901 et seq.; The Automobile Information Disclosure Act, 15 U.S.C.A. § 1231 et seq.; The Cigarette Labeling and Advertising Act, 15 U.S.C.A. § 1331 et seq.; Fair Resale Price Act, 15 U.S.C.A. § 1; The Hobby Protection Act, 15 U.S.C.A. § 2101 et seq.

34. E.g., Indiana, Utah, Oklahoma, Wyoming and Idaho. See Jordon & Warren, The Uniform Consumer Credit Code, 68 Colum.L.Rev. 387 (1968).

35. The Nat'l Consumer Act, which was promulgated in 1970, covers generally the matters dealt with in the U.C.C.C. and in addition, topics such as Debt Collection and Credit Reporting Agencies which are not covered in the U.C.C.C. The Model Consumer Credit Actions promulgated in 1973 and is more liberal than the Nat'l Consumer Act. Reference should also be made to the Wisconsin Consumer Act which is a synthesis of the Nat'l Consumer Act and the U.C.C.C. and the Uniform Consumer Sales Practices Act. See Recent Developments in Consumer Law: A Symposium, 1973 Wis.L.Rev. 333–531.

Chapter 11

CONDITIONS

Table of Sections

Table of Sections

A. INTRODUCTION

B. CONSTRUCTIVE CONDITIONS AND RELATED TOPICS

A. INTRODUCTION

Table of Sections

§ 11–1. The Relationship of This Chapter to Offer and Acceptance

This chapter relates primarily to the *performance* of a contract rather than *formation* of a contract.[1] In a bilateral contract there is a clear distinction between the formation and the performance of a contract. As we have seen, a bilateral contract arises when the offeree makes the promise requested of him whether by act or promise.[2] It is obvious that, in a sense, offer and acceptance are conditions precedent to the performance of the contract because if the contract is not formed, there is no need to perform it. But this is not the terminology used here. Rather the terminology of offer and acceptance is used to determine if there is a bilateral contract. Once this is decided, questions relating to the performance of a bilateral contract arise, and it is in this context that the word condition is used.[3]

Above we limited the discussion to bilateral contracts. The reason is that the situation is somewhat different in the case of a unilateral contract. If A says to B, "If you walk across the Brooklyn Bridge, I'll pay you $10," it is clear that walking the Bridge creates a unilateral contract.[4] In the terminology of this chapter, it could be said that walking the Bridge is an express condition precedent to A's duty to

---

1. Restatement, Second, Contracts § 224, Comment c.

2. See § 2–10 supra.

3. See § 2–10 supra and note 1 supra.

4. See § 2–10 supra.

perform his promise to pay $10. The result is the same no matter which approach is taken.[5]

It is clear that this chapter on conditions relates primarily to bilateral contracts. However, at times illustrations based on unilateral contracts will be used because they make the point under discussion more clearly.

§ 11–2. Definition of a Condition

The basic concept of a condition is that it is an act or event that affects a promised performance. Thus in the Brooklyn Bridge case above, B's failure to walk the bridge (condition) relieves A of his promise to pay.

Traditionally, a condition is defined as an act or event other than a lapse of time, which, unless it is excused, affects a duty to render a promised performance.[6] The Restatement Second defines a condition as "an event, not certain to occur which must occur unless its nonoccurrence is excused, before performance under a contract becomes due."[7]

Let us compare the two definitions. The phrases "not certain to occur" and "other than a lapse of time" are synonomous. Both definitions refer to excuse of condition. This is a matter that will be discussed below.[8]

The major difference in the two formulations is that the first definition uses the words *affects* a duty to render a promised performance. The second definition talks in terms of an event which must occur "*before* performance under a contract becomes due." The point is that the Restatement Second definition is limited to what is referred to below as a condition precedent.[9] The first definition is broad enough to include both a condition precedent and a condition subsequent.[10]

A better definition may be that a condition is an act or event, other than a lapse of time, which, unless the condition is excused, must occur before a duty to perform a promise in the agreement arises (condition precedent), or which discharges a duty of performance that has already arisen (condition subsequent).

This definition has two merits. It covers both conditions precedent and conditions subsequent and suggests the basis for the distinction. Secondly, it makes it clear that a condition affects in some way a promise that has been made in the agreement.

A particular promise in an agreement may, by definition, be unconditional (independent, absolute) or conditional. If on July 1, A promises to pay B $10 on July 15, A's promise is, by definition,

5. It should be noted that even under the rule of § 45 of the Restatement the offeree must completely perform within the time stated. See § 2–22 supra.

6. Restatement, Contracts § 250.

7. Restatement, Second, Contracts § 224; First Nat. Bank of Dekalb County v. National Bank of Georgia, 249 Ga. 216, 290 S.E.2d 55 (1982).

8. See ch. 11C infra.

9. See § 11–5 infra.

10. See § 11–5 and § 11–7 infra.

unconditional because the duty to perform arises after the time stated has elapsed and lapse of time is not treated as a condition because it is looked upon as an event certain to occur.[11] A promise made on July 1, to pay $10 on July 15, if it rains on July 2, is by definition conditional.

§ 11–3. Classification of Conditions

Conditions may be classified in at least two different ways. A classification is frequently made based upon the time when the conditioning event is to happen in relation to the promisor's duty to perform a promise. Under this classification, conditions are labelled as conditions precedent, conditions concurrent and conditions subsequent. A second classification is based upon the manner in which the condition arises; that is, whether it is imposed by the parties or whether it is created by law. Under this division conditions are divided into express conditions and constructive conditions.

§ 11–4. The Time Classification

When conditions are divided into conditions precedent, concurrent and subsequent, it is clear that these terms are used in relation to a particular point of time. The point of time selected relates to when a duty to perform a particular promise in the agreement arises.[12] With this thought firmly in mind, we shall now briefly discuss each of the three categories.

§ 11–5. Conditions Precedent

A condition precedent is an act or event, other than a lapse of time, which must exist or occur before a duty to perform a promised performance arises.[13] If the condition does not occur and is not excused, the promised performance need not be rendered.[14] For example, if A has promised for a consideration to pay B $100 if a specified ship arrives in

---

11. Corbin, Conditions in the Law of Contract, 28 Yale L.Rev. 739, 742 (1919), Selected Readings 871, 874. This rationale is not entirely convincing. The writers are seemingly unanimous in this view that a mere lapse of time cannot be a condition. It is said that a condition must be "future and uncertain." Ashley, Conditions in Contract, 14 Yale L.J. 424, 425 (1905), Selected Readings 866, 867; see also Restatement, Second, Contracts § 224, Comment b; 5 Williston § 663. Why this should be so does not seem to be explained adequately by Professor Corbin's reasoning. If a duty is not to be performed until a certain day in the future, the duty is for most purposes treated as conditional. (In the law of negotiable instruments, however, the characterization of such a promise as unconditional is meaningful.) For example, in the absence of a repudiation an action brought prior to the due date to enforce the promise will be dismissed.

One suspects that the requirement of "future and uncertain" was borrowed from rules governing conditional estates in land where major substantive distinctions exist between estates conditioned on uncertain events and estates limited by definite time periods. See 2 W. Blackstone, Blackstone's Commentaries ch. 10.

12. Harnett & Thompson, The Insurance Condition Subsequent: A Needle In a Semantic Haystack, 17 Fordham L.Rev. 220 (1948).

13. Internatio–Rotterdam, Inc. v. River Brand Rice Mills, Inc., 259 F.2d 137 (2d Cir.1958), certiorari denied 358 U.S. 946, 79 S.Ct. 352, 3 L.Ed.2d 352 (1959); Ross v. Harding, 64 Wn.2d 231, 391 P.2d 526 (1964); Partlow v. Mathews, 43 Wn.2d 398, 261 P.2d 394 (1953); Restatement, Contracts § 250(a).

14. Restatement, Second, Contracts § 225(2).

port before a certain date, A's duty to pay does not arise unless and until the ship arrives. If the ship does not arrive within the time specified A need not keep his promise.

It should again be stressed that in this chapter the term "condition" is ordinarily used to describe acts or events which must occur before a party is obliged to perform a promise made in an *existing contract*.[15] This situation must be distinguished from a condition precedent to the existence of a contract usually called a condition precedent to the formation of a contract.[16] In that situation the contract itself does not arise unless and until the condition occurs.[17] This means that the parties are free to terminate their arrangement until the condition occurs.[18] This concept of a condition precedent to the formation of a contract has already been mentioned in connection with the parol evidence rule.[19] It is difficult in a concrete case to distinguish a condition precedent to the formation of a contract from a condition precedent to the performance of a contract.[20]

It is also possible that in the case of a condition precedent to the performance of a contract, the event that operates as a condition may have occurred before or at the time of the formation of the contract.[21] For example, this could occur in the case of a marine policy that insures against a loss that already occurred at the time of contracting.[22]

WESTLAW REFERENCES

"condition precedent" /3 define* definition

"condition precedent" /s "existing contract"

95k221(2)

"condition precedent" /s formation

"condition precedent" /s performance

§ 11–6. Concurrent Conditions

Concurrent conditions exist where the parties are to exchange performances at the same time.[23] It is conceivable that if neither party performed at the appointed time each could sue the other. However, although this was the law initially, it was soon changed by virtue of the doctrine of constructive conditions—a topic to be discussed below.[24]

An illustration will help clarify the existing law. S agrees to sell and B agrees to buy a certain book at a fixed time and place. Under these circumstances, in the absence of an agreement to the contrary, payment and delivery are often looked upon as concurrent conditions.

15. See § 11–1 supra.

16. Hicks v. Bush, 10 N.Y.2d 488, 225 N.Y.S.2d 34, 180 N.E.2d 425 (1962).

17. Hicks v. Bush, 10 N.Y.2d 488, 225 N.Y.S.2d 34, 180 N.E.2d 425 (1962).

18. Edmund J. Flynn Co. v. Schlosser, 265 A.2d 599 (D.C.App.1970).

19. See § 3–7 supra.

20. M.K. Metals, Inc. v. Container Recovery Corp., 645 F.2d 583 (8th Cir.1981).

21. Restatement, Second, Contracts § 224, Comment b.

22. Restatement, Second, Contracts § 224, Comment b.

23. Restatement, Contracts § 251.

24. See ch. 11B infra.

As a result for S to put B in default, he must make conditional tender of the book or show that tender is excused, and in order for B to put S in default, he must make conditional tender of the price or show that tender is excused.[25] For this reason a concurrent condition is in reality a particular kind of condition precedent.[26] In other words in the illustration given, a party must perform or tender his performance *before* he has a claim unless tender is excused.[27] It should be noted that concurrent conditions principally occur in contracts for the sale of goods [28] and contracts for the conveyance of land.[29]

 WESTLAW REFERENCES
"concurrent condition"

§ 11–7. Conditions Subsequent

A condition subsequent is any event the existence of which, by agreement of the parties, operates to discharge a duty of performance that has arisen.[30] The key to understanding a condition subsequent is the notion that a duty to perform a promised performance has already arisen and is discharged because it was agreed that it would be discharged if a certain event occurs. That event is called a condition subsequent.

For example, assume that an insurance company promises to make payments if a fire occurs and if the insured files proof of loss with the insurer within sixty days after the loss. It is clear that the occurrence of the fire and the proof of loss are conditions precedent to the company's performance of its promise to pay.[31] Let us assume that these

25. Vidal v. Transcontinental & Western Air, 120 F.2d 67 (3d Cir.1941); Rubin v. Fuchs, 1 Cal.3d 50, 81 Cal.Rptr. 373, 459 P.2d 925, (1969); Restatement, Contracts (2d) § 238 and Comment a; see Ocean Air Tradeways, Inc. v. Arkay Realty Corp., 480 F.2d 1112 (9th Cir.1973); McFadden v. Wilder, 6 Ariz.App. 60, 429 P.2d 694 (1967); 3A Corbin § 629; § 11–21 infra. Under the traditional notion of tender the parties must be face to face. See Petterson v. Pattberg, 248 N.Y. 86, 161 N.E. 428 (1928). Under a more modern version tender "as used in this connection means" a readiness and willingness to perform in case of *concurrent* performance by the other party, with present ability to do so, and notice to the other party of such readiness. 6 Williston, Contracts § 833 quoted in Monroe Street Properties, Inc. v. Carpenter, 407 F.2d 379 (9th Cir.1969). See also U.C.C. § 2–503(1). On excuse of tender see Owens v. Idaho First Nat. Bank, 103 Idaho 465, 649 P.2d 1221 (App.1982).

26. Restatement, Contracts § 251.

27. Vidal v. Transcontinental & Western Air, 120 F.2d 67 (3d Cir.1941).

28. U.C.C. §§ 2–503(1), 2–507, 2–511, 2–709.

29. It is possible for concurrent conditions to exist in a unilateral contract. For example A says to B, "If you pay me $10.00 I promise to hand you my watch." B may condition his tender of the $10 upon the conditional tender of the watch. See Turner v. Goodwin, 92 Eng.Rep. 796 [K.B. 1711].

30. Restatement, Contracts § 250(b).

31. Lawson v. American Motorists Ins. Corp., 217 F.2d 724 (5th Cir.1954); Harris v. North British & Mercantile Ins. Co., 30 F.2d 94 (5th Cir.1929), certiorari denied 279 U.S. 852, 49 S.Ct. 348, 73 L.Ed. 995 (1929). For such a provision in an employment contract, see Inman v. Clyde Hall Drilling Co., 369 P.2d 498 (Alaska 1962), noted in 14 Syracuse L.Rev. 109 (1963).

are the only two conditions precedent to the insurance company's obligation to pay. With this assumption, if these conditions are met it is clear that the company is obliged to keep its promise to pay at this point in time and that a failure to pay amounts to a breach.

However if there is a provision to the effect that the insurance company's obligation to pay is discharged if the insured fails to sue within one year of the filing of proofs of loss, we are dealing with a condition subsequent because the failure to sue within the time specified discharges a duty that has already arisen.[32]

In the law of contracts conditions precedent are quite common while true conditions subsequent are very rare.[33] From a substantive point of view the characterization of a condition as precedent or subsequent is not important. However, the distinction is procedurally important because it controls the issue of burden of proof.[34] The plaintiff ordinarily will be obliged to prove conditions precedent while the defendant will have the burden of proof on conditions subsequent. More accurately, the party who wishes to sue on a promise has the burden of proving that the conditions precedent attached to that promise arose, otherwise there would be no breach of that promise.[35] So also if a party seeks to discharge a duty that has already arisen, he has the burden of proof on that issue.[36]

32. Berman v. Palatine Ins. Co., 379 F.2d 371 (7th Cir.1967); Barza v. Metropolitan Life Ins. Co., 281 Mich. 532, 275 N.W. 238 (1937). Although this characterization is made by the writers of law books and Restatements, the courts have not always labelled such a condition as a condition subsequent. E.g., Graham v. Niagra Fire Ins. Co., 106 Ga. 840, 32 S.E. 579 (1899) (characterized as condition precedent); see Harnett and Thornton, note 12 supra. A condition subsequent is in many respects similar to an affirmative defense and the particular provision under discussion is similar to the defense of statute of limitations.

In some jurisdictions contractual clauses curtailing the statute of limitations are invalid, see Annot., 112 A.L.R. 1288 (1938), or regulated by Statute. E.g., McKinney's N.Y.Ins.Law §§ 164(3)(A)(11), 168(6). But such clauses frequently are utilized even outside the insurance field and are generally upheld. Soviero Bros. Contracting Corp. v. New York, 286 App.Div. 435, 142 N.Y.S.2d 508 (1st Dep't 1955), affirmed 2 N.Y.2d 924, 161 N.Y.S.2d 888, 141 N.E.2d 918 (1957); Restatement, Contracts § 218; Williston § 183. The U.C.C. specifically validates such clauses in § 2–725(1).

33. Kindler v. Anderson, 433 P.2d 268 (Wyo.1967).

34. Holmes, The Common Law, 316–318 (1881).

35. That this is sometimes a matter of great importance is demonstrated by the case of McGowin v. Menken, 223 N.Y. 509, 119 N.E. 877 (1918), in which the executor of the wife was unable to show that the wife survived when the husband and wife perished in a common disaster. Formerly, the party to whom the duty is owed (usually the plaintiff) also had the burden of alleging the occurrence of all conditions precedent. Shipman, Common Law Pleading 246–49 (3d ed.1923). Under Code pleading, a general allegation of due compliance with all conditions precedent is generally sufficient. Clark, Code Pleading 280–82 (2d ed.1947); 5 Williston § 674. Under recent procedural enactments even this requirement is dispensed with. The simplification of pleading requirements does not, however, change the burden of proof. Although the burden is placed on the defendant to deny the occurrence of a condition precedent, once he has made the denial, the burden is placed on the plaintiff to prove its occurrence. McKinney's N.Y. C.P.L.R. 3015.

36. Gray v. Gardner, 17 Mass. 188 (1821).

Thus in the illustration above relating to insurance, the insured would have the burden of proving that a fire occurred and that notice of loss was given within sixty days. The insurance company would have the burden on the question of whether the action has been duly commenced within one year.

We have already seen that true conditions subsequent are very rare. However, there are many cases that have treated what is by definition a condition precedent as a condition subsequent because the language used is subsequent in form. A good illustration is the case of Gray v. Gardner.[37] In that case defendant promised to pay 60 cents per gallon for oil that had been delivered. At the same time he promised to pay an additional 25 cents per gallon in the future with the proviso that this second promise would be void if a greater quantity of oil should arrive in whaling vessels at Nantucket and New Bedford on or before the first day of April and the first day of October both inclusive, than had arrived at the said place within the same time the previous year.

The first promise was clearly unconditional and it is equally clear that the second promise was not to be performed if a greater quantity of oil arrived during the specified period. In other words the non-arrival of a greater quantity of oil during the specified period was by definition a condition precedent to defendant's obligation to perform his second promise.[38]

The court decided that the condition was a condition subsequent primarily because of the use of the word void which suggests that a duty that has already arisen is being discharged.

Whether this was a condition precedent or a condition subsequent was very important in the case on the issue of burden of proof. This is so because there was a conflict in the evidence on the issue of whether a certain vessel arrived at Nantucket on October 1, 1819. Since the court found that the condition was subsequent, the burden of proof on this issue was placed upon the defendant.

Conditions subsequent in form but precedent by definition are particularly common in insurance policies and surety bonds. In these cases, perhaps more often than not, courts will, for purposes of pleading and burden of proof, treat the condition as if it were a condition subsequent. There is no universal consistency and a good deal of sublety has gone into the refinements of the problem,[39] without, however, resulting in any satisfactory resolution of the basic problem.[40]

37. 17 Mass. 188 (1821).

38. Restatement, Second, Contracts § 227, Comment d and ill. 13.

39. 5 Williston §§ 667, 667A, 674; see Clark, Code Pleading 280–83 (2d ed.1947). It has recently been stated that whether a condition is a condition precedent or subsequent cannot be determined simply by looking at the words of the clause involved, but that many other factors should be considered. Loyal Erectors, Inc. v. Hamilton & Sons, Inc., 312 A.2d 748 (Me.1973).

40. Compare 3A Corbin §§ 749–51 with the authorities in the preceding note. Corbin appears to argue that, unless social policy dictates another conclusion, the burden of proof should be allocated in accordance with whether or not the condition is a true condition subsequent and that the form in which the condition is couched

At times what is by definition a condition precedent is treated as a condition subsequent, so that the burden of proof is placed upon the party with knowledge of facts.[41]

Although the Restatement Second disapproves of the term "condition subsequent" as confusing, the basic notions but not the vocabulary conveyed here are followed.[42]

WESTLAW REFERENCES
95k226

"condition subsequent" /s duty

358k59 /p "condition subsequent"

"condition subsequent" /s oblig!

"true condition subsequent"

"condition subsequent" /s burden +2 proof proving

condition +1 subsequent precedent /s insurance surety

§ 11–8. The Other Classification of Conditions

In section 11–3 we saw that there are two classification of conditions. One is a time classification. This has already been covered. The other is based upon how the condition arises. If it is placed there by the parties, it is an express (true) condition.[43] If the condition is imposed by law to do justice, it is a constructive condition, sometimes called a condition implied in law.[44]

In addition to a condition implied in law (constructive condition) there are also conditions implied in fact. A condition implied in fact is an express (true) condition. It is not spelled out in so many words but rather is "gathered from the terms of the contract as a matter of interpretation." [45]

should be disregarded. Compare with this argument Anson, Contract 434 (Corbin's ed. 1924), wherein it is stated:

"Thus it is evident, in spite of very general assumptions to the contrary, that the burden of allegation and the burden of proof cannot be determined by the test of such descriptive adjectives as precedent and subsequent. It is no doubt true that the law on this subject needs entire reconstruction and restatement, that there is no existing test capable of logical definition, and that the rules are largely arbitrary as well as conflicting. Such rules as now exist will frequently be found to be based on false logic and on more or less ill-defined notions of public policy."

41. Buick Motor Co. v. Thompson, 138 Ga. 282, 75 S.E. 354 (1912). But see Tallman Pools of Georgia, Inc. v. Fellner, 160 Ga.App. 722, 288 S.E.2d 46 (1982).

42. Restatement, Second, Contracts § 224, Comment e & ill. 8. The Restatement adds that as a matter of interpretation there should be a preference in favor of a condition precedent rather than a condition subsequent. Restatement, Second, Contracts § 227(3) and Comment.

43. Restatement, Contracts § 252; Corbin, Conditions in the Law of Contracts, 28 Yale L.J. 739 (1919).

44. Restatement, Contracts § 253; Restatement, Second, Contracts § 226, Comment c.

45. Costigan, The Performance of Contracts 50 (2d ed. 1927). For an illustration of an implied in fact condition see Caldwell v. Blake, 6 Gray 402 (Mass.1856) wherein an obligation to instruct in the art of making paper was treated as an implied in fact condition to the duty to pay in paper.

In a given agreement it may be difficult to determine whether a condition has been expressed in so many words or whether it is implied in fact by virtue of the words and conduct of the parties. It is not important that this determination be made since the same general rule applies to both, that is, a true condition must be literally complied with.[46] Since there is no difference in consequences, implied in fact conditions and conditions set forth in so many words are both denominated as express (true) conditions.[47]

The dividing line between an express condition (especially implied in fact conditions) and constructive conditions is often quite indistinct.[48] Yet, the distinction is often of crucial importance. The general rule governing an express condition, is that it must be literally performed. The general rule as to constructive conditions is that substantial compliance is sufficient.[49]

This distinction and its ramifications are pursued in the sections that follow.

 WESTLAW REFERENCES
"express condition" /s party
"constructive condition"
"condition implied by law"
"condition implied in fact"
contract agreement /s literal! +1 comply! compli**** /s
    condition
"substantial! perform!" /s "constructive condition"

§ 11–9.   Distinction Between an Express Condition and a Promise

We have already seen that the general rule is that an express condition must be literally complied with.[50] For example if A says to B, "If you walk across the Brooklyn Bridge I will pay you $10." B's walking the Bridge is an express condition precedent to A's obligation to pay. In other words, if B does not literally perform (and his performance is not excused), A will not be obliged to pay. If B does not walk the Bridge, he will not be liable because he has not made a promise to walk.[51] It is important to keep in mind that one cannot be liable for breach of contract unless he breaches a *promise* he has made.

If, however, A had said to B, I promise to pay you $10 if you promise to walk the Bridge and if you in fact walk the Bridge and B so promises. Here we have the same express condition but in addition

---

46. Jungmann & Co. v. Atterbury Bros., 249 N.Y. 119, 163 N.E. 123 (1928); Ram Development Corp. v. Siuslaw Enterprises, Inc., 283 Or. 13, 580 P.2d 552 (1978).

47. Restatement, Contracts § 258.

48. 5 Williston, § 668.

49. See § 11–18(b) infra.

50. See § 11–8 supra.

51. United States v. O'Brien, 220 U.S. 321, 31 S.Ct. 406, 55 L.Ed. 481 (1911); Hale v. Finch, 104 U.S. (14 Otto) 261, 26 L.Ed. 732 (1881); Arizona Land Title & Trust Co. v. Safeway Stores, Inc., 6 Ariz.App. 52, 429 P.2d 686 (1967), appeal after remand 10 Ariz.App. 225, 457 P.2d 938 (1969), vacated 105 Ariz. 329, 464 P.2d 612 (1970).

here B has made a promise to walk the Bridge. In this case if B does not walk, A need not pay the $10 because B has failed to perform the express condition precedent to A's promise to pay. In addition, since B has made a promise to walk the Bridge, he will be liable for breach of his promise.

In these illustrations, the conditions and the promises are clearly labeled. However, there are many situations in which it is difficult to tell whether particular language is language of promise or language of condition. The result in a particular case is a matter of the intention of the parties,[52] and all of the rules of interpretation previously discussed apply.[53]

However, in this area it is clear that the courts, in a doubtful case prefer the interpretation that particular language is language of promise rather than language of condition.[54] In one case [55] the parties entered into an agreement whereby plaintiff agreed to do certain work for the defendant and defendant agreed to pay a fixed amount and to reimburse plaintiff for labor costs over 4 cents per square foot. There were provisions in the contract stating that plaintiff would furnish defendant with an itemized cost breakdown. This was not done. Had furnishing the cost breakdown been looked upon as an express condition precedent to defendant's promise to pay additional labor costs, it is clear that defendant would not have been obliged to pay these costs because the express condition was not performed. If the language was a promise on the part of plaintiff to furnish itemized costs, it is clear that the plaintiff would be guilty of a breach of this promise but that this would not defeat plaintiff's claim because the breach would be immaterial.[56]

The court relied upon the presumption in favor of finding that the language in question is language of promise and added that this is particularly true when a finding that there is a condition and not a

52. Cramer v. Metropolitan Sav. & Loans Ass'n, et al., 401 Mich. 252, 258 N.W.2d 20 (1977), certiorari denied 436 U.S. 958, 98 S.Ct. 3072, 57 L.Ed.2d 1123 (1978); Partlow v. Mathews, 43 Wn.2d 398, 261 P.2d 394 (1953).

53. Restatement, Second, Contracts §§ 226, Comment b and 227; Restatement, Contracts § 258; Chirichella v. Erwin, 270 Md. 178, 310 A.2d 555 (1973).

54. Sahadi v. Continental Ill. Natl. Bank & Trust Co. of Chicago, 706 F.2d 193 (7th Cir.1983); Howard et al. v. Federal Crop. Ins. Corp., 540 F.2d 695 (4th Cir. 1976); Home Sav. Assoc. v. Tappan Co., 403 F.2d 201 (5th Cir.1968); O'Neal v. George E. Breece Lumber Co., 38 N.M. 492, 35 P.2d 314 (1934); Restatement, Contracts § 261; Restatement, Second, Contracts § 227(2) and Comment d. The First Re-

statement also set forth a presumptive test based upon whose words are being interpreted. If they purport to be the words of the party to do the act they are presumed to be language of promise. If they purport to be the words of the party who is not to do act then they are language of condition. Restatement, Contracts § 260. This rule, which is not very helpful, was not included in the Second Restatement. Restatement, Second, Contracts § 227.

55. Pacific Allied v. Century Steel Products, Inc., 162 Cal.App.2d 70, 327 P.2d 547 (1958).

56. In the case the result was based on the doctrine of constructive conditions and the rule that constructive conditions need only be substantially performed. See § 11–18(b) infra.

promise would lead to a forfeiture on the part of a party who had done the work.[57]

In a recurring fact pattern, a prime contractor agrees to make payment to a sub-contractor as money is received from the owner or language to that effect. The cases arise when the subcontractor sues the general contractor for payment after he has completed his work but before the owner has paid the general contractor. The question is whether the quoted language is language of express condition or language of promise.[58] If it is language of condition then it is clear that the subcontractor may not sue at this point in time because the condition has not been met. Some courts have concluded it is language of condition.[59] Others have concluded that it is language of promise. In other words, according to these courts, the language is put into the contract as a convenient time for payment and if that event does not occur then there is promise to pay within a reasonable time.[60]

The question is one of interpretation. Most of the modern cases lean to the view that this is not an express condition and some have even applied the plain meaning rule and excluded extrinsic evidence thus reaching the conclusion that this is language of promise as a matter of law.[61]

The notion behind the modern view is that when personal services are rendered it will not lightly be assumed that payment was contingent upon the happening of an event outside the control of the party rendering services. If, however, the services are of a kind that are frequently rendered on a contingent fee basis, the result will be otherwise. Thus a promise to pay a brokerage commission "on closing of title" will be held to be expressly conditioned upon the closing of title.[62]

A large number of cases are concerned with the interpretation of a promise to pay "when able." Although there is said to be a "majority rule", interpreting this language as language of condition [63] and a "minority rule" interpreting such language as a promise that payment

---

57. Forfeiture as used here goes beyond the concept of unjust enrichment. It also includes a situation where a party loses "his right to an agreed exchange after he has relied substantially on the expectation of that exchange, as by preparation for performance." Restatement, Second, Contracts § 227, Comment b.

58. See Restatement, Second, Contracts § 227. However the language is not likely to be interpreted as language of promise if under the facts it would be impractical to assess damages or if the event in question is not within the control of the party upon whom the duty to perform would be placed. See Farnsworth, Contracts § 8.4 at 551.

59. Mascioni v. I.B. Miller, Inc., 261 N.Y. 1, 184 N.E. 473 (1933).

60. North American Graphite Corp. v. Allan, 184 F.2d 387 (D.C.Cir.1950); DeWolf v. French, 51 Me. 420 (1864); Grossman Steel and Aluminum Corp. v. Samson Window Corp. 54 N.Y.2d 653, 442 N.Y.S.2d 769, 426 N.E.2d 176 (1981).

61. Thos. J. Dyer Co. v. Bishop Int'l Eng'r Co., 303 F.2d 655 (6th Cir.1962); Kalwell Corporation v. K. Capolino Design and Renovation et al., 54 A.D.2d 941, 388 N.Y.S.2d 346 (2d Dep't 1976); Mignot v. Parkhill, 237 Or. 450, 391 P.2d 755 (1964); Restatement, Second, Contracts § 227, Comment b, ills. 1 and 2.

62. Amies v. Wesnofske, 255 N.Y. 156, 174 N.E. 436 (1931) (collecting cases).

63. Zane v. Mavrides, 394 So.2d 197 (Fla.Dist.Ct.App.1981).

will be made in a reasonable time,[64] it is likely that many of the seemingly conflicting cases can be reconciled if it is realized that in each case the language must be interpreted in its verbal and factual context. If, as is often the case, the promise to pay "when able" is a new promise to pay a debt that otherwise would be barred by bankruptcy or the statute of limitations, it is gratuitous and interpretation of the language as a condition would seem to be justified.[65] Similarly, if a major stockholder renders services to the corporation on the understanding that he will be paid "as the financial condition of the corporation permits out of profits" it can readily be inferred from the relationship of the parties that the corporation's promise was intended to be conditional.[66] Where, however, the promise is to pay for services rendered, goods delivered, or property conveyed, in the absence of special circumstances, it would be reasonable to assume that the promisee intended no more than to allow the promisor a reasonable time in which to effectuate payment.[67]

A draftsman who wishes to obtain the benefits of the rule of strict compliance with an express condition should use clear language of express condition. Thus, a provision of a contract stating that filing of a notice of claim with the other contracting party within thirty days after any claim arises "shall be a condition precedent to recovery" creates an express condition precedent in the most explicit fashion.[68] As a rule of thumb, provisions which commence with words such as "if",[69] "on condition that,"[70] "subject to"[71] and "provided"[72] create conditions precedent.[73] However, this result cannot be guaranteed because of the presumption in favor of language of promise and because courts are free to interpret language.[74]

 WESTLAW REFERENCES
"express** condition**" /s intent! intend! /s party

64. See 5 Williston § 804; Annot., 94 A.L.R. 721 (1935). A promise to pay "when able to effect a sale" requires the promisor to bring the event about or pay within a reasonable time. Duncan Box & Lumber Co. v. Sargent, 126 W.Va. 1, 27 S.E.2d 68 (1943); see 3A Corbin § 641. Some cases take an intermediate position, holding that the promisor is obligated at least to use reasonable efforts to become able to pay.

65. Tebo v. Robinson, 100 N.Y. 27, 2 N.E. 383 (1885).

66. Booth v. Booth & Bayliss Commercial School, 120 Conn. 221, 180 A. 278 (1935).

67. Sanford v. Luce, 245 Iowa 74, 60 N.W.2d 885 (1953) (construction work); Mock v. Trustees of First Baptist Church of Newport, 252 Ky. 243, 67 S.W.2d 9 (1934) (architectural services).

68. Inman v. Clyde Hall Drilling Co., 369 P.2d 498 (Alaska 1962). The court also discussed questions of unconscionability and public policy.

69. Guerrette v. Cheetham, 289 Mass. 240, 193 N.E. 836 (1935).

70. Hale v. Finch, 104 U.S. (14 Otto) 261, 26 L.Ed. 732 (1881); Simpson, Contracts 305.

71. Rubin v. Fuchs, 1 Cal.3d 50, 81 Cal. Rptr. 373, 459 P.2d 925 (1969); Barbara Oil Co. v. Patrick Petroleum Co.; 1 Kan.App. 2d 437, 566 P.2d 389 (1977).

72. Goodwin v. Jacksonville Gas Corp., 302 F.2d 355 (5th Cir.1962); Hamilton Constr. Co. v. Board of Pub. Instruction of Dade County, 65 So.2d 729 (Fla.1953).

73. Restatement, Second, Contracts § 226, Comment a.

74. See, e.g., Southern Surety Co. v. MacMillan Co., 58 F.2d 541 (10th Cir.1932).

"express** condition***" /s promis!

condition! /s promis! /s pay*** payment paid repaid repay! /s
  able soon

---

§ 11–10. Express Language of Condition May Be Implied Language of Promise

Not only is it difficult to determine whether particular language is language of condition or language of promise (discussed immediately above) but the problem is further complicated by the fact that express language of condition may in addition be implied language of promise [75] (discussed in this section) and conversely express language of promise may give rise to an implied in fact or a constructive condition (to be discussed in the next three sections).

To illustrate, A and B enter into a contract for the sale and purchase of real property. The contract contains a clause that performance is "contingent upon B obtaining" a described mortgage.[76] The phrase in the quotation is obviously language of condition so that B [77] is not obliged to perform unless he obtains the mortgage loan.[78] In addition, however, B has impliedly promised to use reasonable efforts to obtain mortgage financing.[79] Stated in other terms, he has impliedly

---

75. Restatement, Second, Contracts § 225(3), Comment d; Restatement, Contracts § 257; Stewart v. Griffith, 217 U.S. 323, 30 S.Ct. 528, 54 L.Ed. 782 (1910); Green County v. Quinlan, 211 U.S. 582, 29 S.Ct. 162, 53 L.Ed. 335 (1909); Skakey's Inc. v. Covalt, 704 F.2d 426 (9th Cir.1983); Western Hills, Oregon, Ltd. v. Pfau, 265 Or. 137, 508 P.2d 201 (1973).

76. If the mortgage is not sufficiently described there could be an indefiniteness problem. See, e.g., Aiken, "Subject to Financing" Clauses in Interim Contracts For Sale of Realty, 43 Marq.L.Rev. 265 (1960).

77. Although, as indicated, the clause is a condition precedent to B's obligation to proceed with the underlying contract it is not a condition precedent to A's obligation to proceed if B was ready, willing and able to tender the money even though he did not obtain the mortgage. De Freitas v. Cote, 342 Mass. 474, 477, 174 N.E.2d 371 (1961). In other words the condition is for the benefit of B only and he alone may waive it. Restatement, Second, Contracts § 226, ill. 4; see § 11–30 infra.

A slightly different question is presented in such a case if, when B is unable to obtain a mortgage loan, A offers to take a purchase money mortgage from B to enable him to proceed with the deal. In one case the vendee was held to be under a duty to accept the purchase money mort-

gage financing. Marino v. Nolan, 24 A.D.2d 1005, 266 N.Y.S.2d 65 (2d Dep't 1965), affirmed 18 N.Y.2d 627, 272 N.Y.S.2d 776, 219 N.E.2d 291 (1966). In another case the vendee was held not to be obliged to accept such a mortgage because the contract language referred to obtaining a mortgage from a "lending institution." Glassman v. Gerstein, 10 A.D.2d 875, 200 N.Y.S.2d 690 (2d Dep't 1960). See also Simms Co. v. Wolverton, 232 Or. 291, 375 P.2d 87 (1962). But see Kovarick v. Vesely, 3 Wis.2d 573, 89 N.W.2d 279 (1958).

78. Sheldon Builders, Inc. v. Trojan Towers, 255 Cal.App.2d 781, 63 Cal.Rptr. 425 (1968); Mecham v. Nelson, 92 Idaho 783, 451 P.2d 529 (1969); cf. Lane v. Elwood Estates, Inc., 28 N.Y.2d 620, 320 N.Y.S.2d 79, 268 N.E.2d 805 (1971). It should be noted that in this situation the vendor does not suffer a forfeiture as that term is defined in § 11–35 infra. Although the vendor may be deprived of an expectancy interest there is no unjust enrichment and there is no reliance injury on his part. See note 57 supra.

79. Lach v. Cahill, 138 Conn. 418, 85 A.2d 481 (1951); Eggan v. Simonds, 34 Ill. App.2d 316, 181 N.E.2d 354 (1962); Carlton v. Smith, 285 Ill.App. 380, 2 N.E.2d 116 (1936). But see Paul v. Rosen, 3 Ill.App.2d 423, 122 N.E.2d 603 (1954).

promised to use reasonable efforts to cause the condition to occur and if he does not do this he is guilty of a breach of that promise.[80]

In the same transaction, however, if B conditioned his promise upon the Dow Jones average reaching 3000 at some point between the time of the signing of the contract and the time for performance, it is obvious that B would not be bound to perform if the condition did not arise and in addition, he is not impliedly promising to use reasonable efforts to cause the condition to occur.[81]

No simple rule can be set forth which explains when express language of condition will or will not give rise to implied language of promise. One of the important factors to be considered is whether the conditioning event is within the control of the party who is alleged to have made an implied promise. Thus in the mortgage illustration it was within B's control to use reasonable efforts to obtain a mortgage; but in the case relating to the Dow Jones average, it was not within B's power to cause the Dow Jones average to reach 3000. A related question is discussed in § 11–28.

WESTLAW REFERENCES
"language of promise" "promissory language" /s contract***
agreement transact!

§ 11–11. Express Language of Promise Giving Rise to Implied or Constructive Conditions

In the preceding section we examined the problem of express language of condition giving rise to an implied promise. The converse question is presented here. However, here we must distinguish whether the condition which arises from language of promise is constructive or implied in fact.[82] This can best be explained through an historical approach.

§ 11–12. The History of Constructive Conditions

At early common law the English courts were very literal minded. If they looked at an instrument and it contained only language of promise, the court would say that no conditions were present. Thus, at early common law, if S agreed to sell and B agreed to buy 100 cases of apples, S without tendering performance could sue B for breach and

---

80. Internatio-Rotterdam, Inc. v. River Brand Rice Mills, Inc., 259 F.2d 137 (2d Cir.1958), certiorari denied 358 U.S. 946, 79 S.Ct. 352, 3 L.Ed.2d 352 (1959). See generally Patterson, Constructive Conditions in Contracts, 42 Colum.L.Rev. 903, 928–42 (1942).

81. Connor v. Rockwood, 320 Mass. 360, 69 N.E.2d 454 (1946); Simpson, Contracts 307.

82. See § 11–8 supra. At times a constructive condition may be imposed by law unrelated to language of promise. See Hadden v. Consolidated Edison Co., 34 N.Y.2d 88, 356 N.Y.S.2d 249, 312 N.E.2d 445 (1974), appeal after remand 58 A.D.2d 154, 396 N.Y.S.2d 210 (1977), modified 45 N.Y.2d 466, 410 N.Y.S.2d 274, 382 N.E.2d 1136 (1978).

conversely B without tendering performance could sue S.[83] In time the courts held that such express mutual promises gave rise to constructive concurrent conditions.[84] This means that although neither party expressly conditions his promise on performance by the other, the law, to do justice, constructs a condition that performance, or tender of performance, by one party is a condition precedent to the liability of the other party.[85] Constructive conditions are discussed in more detail below.[86]

§ 11–13. Constructive Conditions Distinguished From Implied in Fact Conditions

In section 11–8 supra, we saw that implied in fact conditions are true conditions and therefore the general rule with respect to these conditions is that they must be literally performed. We also saw that constructive conditions need only be substantially performed. For this reason the courts prefer to find constructive conditions rather than implied in fact conditions.[87] In other words the doctrine of substantial performance is a more flexible instrument for justice than a rule that requires literal performance of an express condition.

Since constructive conditions and implied in fact conditions both ordinarily arise from language of promise, they are difficult to distinguish. The theoretical difference is that in the case of an implied in fact condition, the parties have impliedly agreed to the condition, whereas in the case of a constructive condition the court constructs a condition in the interests of justice even though the condition was not put into the contract by the parties either expressly or impliedly.[88] For the reasons stated above, the courts are reluctant to find implied in fact conditions. Thus the courts are becoming more and more inclined to limit implied in fact conditions to situations involving cooperation. This involves a situation where A's promise by the terms of the contract is incapable of performance unless there is performance by B. In such a case, B's performance is an implied in fact condition to A's duty to perform.[89] For example, if A promised to paint B's house and B promised to supply the paint, since, by the terms of the contract A cannot perform without B keeping his promise to supply the paint, B's supplying the paint is an implied in fact condition to A's duty to paint even though this is not expressly stated in the contract.

83. Nichols v. Raynbred, 80 Eng.Rep. 238 (K.B. 1615). It is clear that only one of two parties was likely to sustain damages.

84. See § 11–6 supra which anticipated this discussion.

85. Kingston v. Preston, Lofft 194, 2 Doug. 684 (K.B. 1773). See § 11–6 supra.

86. See 11B infra.

87. Gold Bond Stamp Co. v. Gilt-Edge Stamps, 437 F.2d 27 (5th Cir.1971); Orkin

Exterminating Co. v. Harris, 224 Ga. 759, 164 S.E.2d 727 (1968).

88. Restatement, Second, Contracts § 226, Comment c.

89. 3A Corbin § 640; Restatement, Second, Contracts § 226, Comment c.; Mainieri v. Magnuson, 126 Cal.App.2d 426, 272 P.2d 557 (1954); Caldwell v. Blake, 72 Mass. (6 Gray) 402 (1856).

§ 11–14.   Constructive Promises—Omitted Terms

Immediately above we have seen that constructive conditions are created by the courts to do justice. We have already alluded elsewhere to the fact that in addition to express and implied in fact promises, there are also constructive promises.[90]

The distinction between an implied in fact and a constructive promise has already been discussed.[91]

In addition the topic of omitted terms was discussed in Chapter Three [92] and in the area of indefiniteness [93] and will also be mentioned in the chapter relating to Impossibility of Performance and Frustration of the Venture.[94] All of these matters, including constructive conditions, can be subsumed under the heading of "omitted terms" which is designed to convey the notion that when parties fail to cover a term the court, in the interests of justice, may supply the term that is omitted.[95]

An illustration of a constructive promise should be given. A wrote a book and sold the right to use the book to B as the basis of a play. Before the play was produced talking pictures were invented and A was negotiating to sell his rights to use the book as the basis of a movie. The court constructed a promise that A would not grant "talkie" rights.[96]

Even though a constructive promise is created by a court to do justice, once it is created by the court it is a full fledged promise—that is to say it is not in any way diminished by the fact that it is a constructive promise.

The material in this section does not relate to the topic of this chapter—conditions. It was placed here particularly to note that there are constructive promises as well as constructive conditions. We return now to the subject matter of this chapter.

 WESTLAW REFERENCES

"omitted term"   /s   court   /s   supply! supplied

95k143(3)   /p   "omitted term" insert! supply! supplied

kirke   +1   "lashelle" "la shelle"   /p   implied** imply! supplied
     supply! insert!

---

90. See § 4–12.

91. See § 4–12.

92. See § 3–18 supra.

93. See § 2–9 supra.

94. See Ch. 13 infra.

95. See Farnsworth, Disputes over Omission in Contracts, 68 Colum.L.Rev. 860 (1968).

96. Kirke La Shelle Co. v. Paul Armstrong Co., 263 N.Y. 79, 188 N.E. 163 (1933). According to Restatement, Second, Contracts § 204, Comment d, when constructing an omitted promise "the court should supply a term which comports with community standards of fairness and policy rather than analyze a hypothetical model of the bargaining process."

§ 11–15. Importance of Distinguishing Between Express and Constructive Conditions: Substantial Performance and Material Breach

We have already adverted to the importance of the distinction between an express (including an implied in fact condition) and a constructive condition. An express condition must be literally performed while a constructive condition need only be substantially performed.[97] We have also adverted to the fact that very often it is difficult to determine whether particular language is language of express condition or language of promise or both language of express condition and implied language of promise.[98]

The purpose of this section is to show the results that follow in a concrete case once this determination has been made. It also serves to introduce the concepts of material breach and substantial performance.

Assume that A is the owner in possession of a vessel in England who agreed in a bilateral contract to charter the vessel to B who was in the United States. By the terms of the agreement, A was to supply the vessel and B was to pay for it when it arrived. The critical clause in the agreement stated: "The vessel to sail from England on or before the 4th day of February." The vessel in fact did not sail by the 4th but actually sailed on February 5th.[99]

It is clear that the quoted language is ambiguous and that therefore there is a question of interpretation. The clause in question could be interpreted in three possible ways, 1) as an express condition to B's obligation to pay, 2) as a promise by A to cause the vessel to sail on or before the 4th, and 3) both as an express condition to B's obligation to pay and as a promise by A to cause the vessel to sail by the 4th.[1]

If the clause is interpreted as an express condition to B's obligation to pay, B is free not to proceed with the contract if he so desires because as a general proposition a true condition must be literally performed.[2] A is not liable for breach of contract because by hypothesis he has not made a promise to cause the vessel to sail.[3]

If the language is looked upon as language of promise and that promise was breached by the late sailing, there are at least two ways in which a case could arise. B could sue A for breach in which event the issue would be the materiality of the breach. If the breach is material,

---

97. See § 11–8 supra.

98. See §§ 11–9 and 11–10 supra.

99. The fact pattern is suggested by Glaholm v. Hayes, 133 Eng.Rep. 743 (C.P.1841).

1. As suggested above, the preferred interpretation would be that this was language of promise. However, for reasons we need not now consider, the court decided that sailing by the 4th was an express condition; therefore B was justified in cancelling the contract.

2. Actually B could elect to continue with the contract if he so chooses. See § 11–32 infra.

3. It is important to remember that a party is liable only when he breaches a promise that he made. However the failure to perform a condition has other effects. For example, it may discharge the duty of the other party to the contract.

B would be free not to proceed and could sue for a total breach or he could elect to continue with the contract and sue for a partial breach.[4] If the breach is immaterial, B would still be required to perform and could only assert a claim for a partial breach.[5]

But what if A sued B for breach when B refused to take the vessel because it was one day late? Under the assumption that A made a promise, the case should be approached under the doctrine of constructive conditions. Even though there is no express condition, it is clear that A is to perform before B is to perform and, therefore, A's performance is a constructive condition precedent to B's obligation to pay.[6] The question, then, is whether A has tendered substantial performance of the constructive condition. If he has, he is entitled to recover his damages less any damages A may have caused B by the late sailing.[7]

It is important to note that substantial performance and material breach are opposite sides of the same coin. If a party has substantially performed, it follows that any breach he may have committed is immaterial. Conversely, if a party has committed a material breach, his performance cannot be substantial. Thus, the way in which the issue is stated may not be of great importance, but clarity of thought is promoted by drawing the distinction.[8] Generally, speaking, if the plaintiff claims that he has performed, the issue is substantial performance, but if he claims that he has not performed because of a breach by the defendant, the issue is whether the defendant is guilty of a material breach.[9]

The third possibility based upon the illustration set forth is that the quoted language is both language of express condition and implied language of promise. As stated above, the failure of A to perform the express condition would allow B not to proceed with the contract. If B follows that course, the question remains whether B would have a cause of action for total breach or only for partial breach by virtue of A's breach of his promise. There is very little law on this subject. One view is that he may sue for total breach. This would be upon the theory that since he may rightfully terminate the contract because of the condition, he should be able to sue for his losses under the contract.[10] The other view is that he need not terminate the contract because of the failure of condition and that if he chooses to do so, he should be permitted to sue only for a partial breach.[11]

The doctrines of constructive conditions, substantial performance, material breach and some related topics are discussed immediately below.

4. See § 11–18(a) infra.

5. Phillips & Colby Constr. Co. v. Seymour, 91 U.S. (1 Otto) 646, 23 L.Ed. 341 (1875). This is the terminology adopted by the Restatement Second. See Reporter's Notes to § 236. See 11–18(a) infra.

6. See § 11–18(b) infra.

7. See § 11–18(b) infra.

8. Restatement, Second, Contracts § 237, Comment d.

9. Austin v. Parker, 672 F.2d 508 (5th Cir.1982).

10. Simpson, Contracts 305.

11. Farnsworth, Contracts § 8.3 at 548.

B. CONSTRUCTIVE CONDITIONS AND RELATED TOPICS

Table of Sections

§ 11–16. Introduction

We have already seen that constructive conditions are created by courts in order to do justice.[12] We have also seen that constructive conditions are found only in bilateral contracts.[13] In most bilateral contracts, the parties exchange not only promises but also performances. That is to say that the parties exchange promises with the understanding that there will also be an exchange of performances.[14] This is true even when the performances are not to be exchanged simultaneously.[15] As the Restatement Second says, bilateral contracts are presumed to involve promises exchanged for an exchange of performance and thus involve constructive conditions of exchange.[16]

---

12. See § 11–8 supra.

13. See § 11–1 supra. The fact that express conditions are also present in the contract does not prevent constructive conditions from arising. Restatement, Second, Contracts § 231, Comment c.

14. Restatement, Second, Contracts Ch. 10 Introductory Note.

15. Restatement, Second, Contracts § 231, Comment b.

16. Restatement, Second, Contracts § 231, Comment a and Ch. 10 Introductory

The ultimate point being made above is in the case of promises exchanged for an exchange of performances the failure of one party to perform may have an effect on the obligation of the other party to perform. This notion of constructive conditions of exchange becomes important in many areas. For example, it relates to the order of performance in a bilateral contract, whether one party's performance of some but not all of the promises undertaken by him entitles him to performance by the other party, what effect failure or delay in performing by one party has upon the rights and duties of the other party and the effect of present or prospective inability or unwillingness to perform.[17]

WESTLAW REFERENCES

"promise of an agreed exchange"

§ 11–17. Required Order of Performance in a Bilateral Contract

In a bilateral contract the parties often neglect to state the order in which their promises are to be performed. These gaps are supplied under the doctrine of constructive conditions.[18] Fortunately the way in which these gaps are filled is based upon common sense, or at least the average person is familiar with them by reason of business experience.

The first and simplest rule is that unless otherwise indicated by the agreement,[19] a party who is to perform work over an extended period of time must substantially perform before he becomes entitled to payment.[20] In other words, performance of the work is a constructive condition precedent to the duty to pay. Periodic payments are not implied.[21]

If, however, periodic payments have been agreed upon, a different situation is presented. In such a case, a series of alternating constructive conditions precedent exist. Performance is a constructive condi-

Note. The Restatement used the term "promises of an agreed exchange." Restatement, Contracts § 266.

17. Most of these matters and others are discussed in the sections that follow and will help clarify the concepts discussed in this section. The question of prospective inability or unwillingness is discussed in Ch. 12.

18. Rochester Distilling Co. v. Geloso, 92 Conn. 43, 101 A. 500 (1917).

19. Clark v. Gulesian, 197 Mass. 492, 84 N.E. 94 (1908).

20. Bright v. Ganas, 171 Md. 493, 189 A. 427 (1937) (for years of faithful performance plaintiff was to receive $20,000 out of employer's estate, but with employer on his death bed plaintiff wrote a love letter to employer's wife, i.e., was unfaithful and

thus there was not substantial performance); Coletti v. Knox Hat Co., 252 N.Y. 468, 472, 169 N.E. 648, 649 (1930) ("when the performance of a contract consists in doing (faciendo) on one side, and in giving (dando) on the other side, the doing must take place before the giving."); Restatement, Second, Contracts § 234(2) and Comment e. This rule arises primarily in service contracts such as employment and construction contracts. Id. § 234, Comment f; Restatement, Contracts, § 270.

21. Smoll v. Webb, 55 Cal.App.2d 456, 130 P.2d 773 (1942); LeBel v. McCoy, 314 Mass. 206, 49 N.E.2d 888 (1943); Kelley Constr. Co. v. Hackensack Brick Co., 91 N.J.L. 585, 103 A. 417 (1918); Stewart v. Newbury, 220 N.Y. 379, 115 N.E. 984 (1917).

tion precedent to the first periodic payment and the first payment is a condition precedent to the next stage of the work, and so on.[22] Assume a case where defendant made a contract with plaintiff for the erection of 19 houses on property owned by the defendant. There was an agreement for progress payments according to a stated formula. Plaintiff finished a portion of the work and defendant, without any justification, failed to pay the amount alloted to the installment.

The first question is whether plaintiff is entitled to suspend performance upon the failure to make payment. The earlier cases generally held that plaintiff was justified in suspending performance.[23] The Restatement Second indicates that he may suspend performance only if the breach is sufficiently serious to warrant this response.[24]

Assuming that plaintiff did suspend performance and was justified in so doing, at what point would he be justified in declaring the contract at an end. The answer in general terms is when there is a material breach.[25] The point in time at which a failure to pay becomes a material breach is ordinarily a question of fact.[26]

Where the promised acts are capable of simultaneous performance, each duty of performance is constructively conditioned upon conditional tender of the other unless otherwise agreed.[27] The primary application of this rule is in contracts for the sale of personal or real property.[28] In such cases, constructive concurrent conditions will normally be imposed in the following circumstances:

> "(a) the same time is fixed for the performance of each promise; or
>
> "(b) a fixed time is stated for the performance of one of the promises and no time is fixed for the other; or
>
> "(c) no time is fixed for the performance of either promise; or

---

22. Guerini Stone Co. v. P.J. Carlin Constr. Co., 248 U.S. 334, 39 S.Ct. 102, 63 L.Ed. 275 (1919); K & G Constr. Co. v. Harris, 223 Md. 305, 164 A.2d 451 (1960); Turner Concrete Steel Co. v. Chester Constr. & Contracting Co., 271 Pa. 205, 114 A. 780 (1921); Pelletier v. Masse, 49 R.I. 408, 143 A. 609 (1928). The same is true of a divisible contract. Restatement, Contracts § 272, ill. 2. But see Palmer v. Watson Constr. Co., 265 Minn. 195, 121 N.W.2d 62 (1963); Zulla Steel, Inc. v. A. & M. Gregos, Inc., 174 N.J.Super. 124, 415 A.2d 1183 (App.Div.1980).

23. Restatement, Contracts § 276, ill. 5; Harton v. Hildebrand, 230 Pa. 335, 79 A. 571 (1911).

24. Restatement, Second, Contracts § 237 and Comment a.

25. See § 11–18(a) infra.

26. 3A Corbin § 692; Darrell J. Didericksen & Sons v. Magna Water, 613 P.2d 1116 (Utah 1980).

27. Restatement, Second, Contracts § 234(1). The rule also applies where simultaneous performances are possible in part. Id. §§ 233(2), 234 and Comment b.

28. Rubin v. Fuchs, 1 Cal.3d 50, 81 Cal. Rptr. 373, 459 P.2d 925 (1969). The Uniform Commercial Code is explicit on the point. U.C.C. § 2–507(1) provides: "Tender of delivery is a condition to the buyer's duty to accept the goods and, unless otherwise agreed, to his duty to pay for them. Tender entitles the seller to acceptance of the goods and to payment according to the contract." U.C.C. § 2–511(1) provides: "Unless otherwise agreed tender of payment is a condition to the seller's duty to tender and complete any delivery." Restatement, Second, Contracts § 234, Comment a. As to Real Property, see McFadden v. Wilder, 6 Ariz.App. 60, 429 P.2d 694 (1967).

"(d) the same period of time is fixed within which each promise shall be performed." [29]

Where each party is to perform an act which takes time, the performances are concurrent at least in the sense that one need not proceed with his performance unless the other performance is proceeding apace.[30]

 WESTLAW REFERENCES

faciendo /s dando

"substantial! perform!" /s entitl! /s pay*** paid payment

harton +s hildebrand

"suspen! perform!" /s breach! pay paying payment paid

material! /3 breach! /s question /2 fact!

simultaneous! /s duty /s perform! /s condition

"concurrent condition" /s perform!

"uniform commercial code" u.c.c. /p 2–507

tender! /s deliver! payment /s condition /s duty

§ 11–18. Material Breach and Substantial Performance

(a) Material Breach

As we have seen, where a party fails to perform a promise, it is important to determine if the breach is material.[31] If the breach is material, the aggrieved party may cancel the contract.[32] He may sue also for a total breach if he can show that he would have been ready, willing and able to perform but for the breach.[33] However he also has the option of continuing with the contract and suing for a partial breach.[34] If the breach is immaterial, the aggrieved party may not cancel the contract [35] but he may sue for a partial breach.[36] The Restatement Second speaks in terms "of a claim for a partial or a total breach" rather than a breach that is a material breach.[37] The change is not significant because the concepts are not changed.

When an aggrieved party has a right to cancel a contract and does so, it is clear that there is to be no further performance under the contract and thus his damages are assessed upon the premise that the breaching party will not perform. In other words, he is permitted to recover all of his damages under the contract. When the aggrieved party sues for a partial breach, the contract continues. Since that is so,

29. Restatement, Contracts § 267; See also Restatement, Second, Contracts § 234, Comment b.

30. Murray, Contracts § 165.

31. See § 11–15 supra.

32. See § 11–18(a) supra. Until he does this the contract remains in effect. Bocchetta v. McCourt, 115 Ill.App.3d 297, 71 Ill.Dec. 219, 450 N.E.2d 907.

33. Malani v. Clapp, 56 Hawaii 507, 542 P.2d 1265 (1975).

34. Cities Service Helex, Inc. v. United States, 543 F.2d 1306 (Ct.Cl.1976).

35. See § 11–15 supra.

36. See § 11–15 supra.

37. Compare Restatement, Second, Contracts § 236, Reporter's Note, with Restatement, Contracts § 313.

he may recover only for whatever damages were caused by the breach that occurred.[38]

The Second Restatement has also made other changes in terminology. It uses the term "material" breach to cover a breach that justifies the aggrieved party in suspending his performance and uses the term "total" breach to cover a situation where the breach is sufficient to justify the aggrieved party in cancelling the contract. The Restatement Second then goes on to say that after the aggrieved party has suspended his performance, the breaching party may cure his breach by remedying the defect until there is a "total" breach that the injured party has used to cancel the contract.[39]

The Reporter's Note to § 237 of the Restatement Second tells us that this terminology is introduced into general contract law in part because the word "cure" is used, albeit in a different sense, in the Uniform Commercial Code. It seems to us that this is not a sufficient reason to change the orthodox terminology that has been used in this chapter. In the terms of the orthodox terminology even though there is an "immaterial" breach, it is possible for the aggrieved party to suspend his performance and, of course, the breaching party is free to correct (cure) that breach before there is a "material" breach and the aggrieved party elects to cancel the contract. As indicated above, this text does not employ the new terminology because we believe that the new terminology only results in confusion.

Certain it is that the new terminology does not change the result in any case. Let us re-examine a case that was analyzed in terms of the orthodox terminology.[40] In that case the defendant made a contract with the plaintiff for the erection of 19 houses on property owned by defendant. There was an agreement for progress payments according to a stated formula. Plaintiff finished a portion of the work and defendant, without any justification, failed to pay the amount allotted to this installment on the due date. Assuming that plaintiff suspended his performance and the suspension was justified,[41] it is clear that the net the result is that defendant may make that payment until the breach has become "material" (terminology used in this text) or "total" (modern terminology) and the injured party elects to cancel the contract.

There is no simple test to ascertain whether or not a breach is material.[42] Among the factors to be considered are:

38. Restatement, Second, Contracts § 236; Restatement, Contracts § 313.

39. Restatement, Second, Contracts § 237. For a criticism of this section see Lawrence, Cure After Breach of Contract Under the Restatement, Second, Contracts: An Analytical Comparison With the Uniform Commercial Code. 70 Minn.L.Rev. 713 (1986).

40. See § 11–17 supra.

41. See § 11–17 supra.

42. See 4 Corbin §§ 945–46; 6 Williston §§ 812–86(2).

1) to what extent, if any, the contract has been performed at the time of the breach.[43] The earlier the breach the more likely it will be regarded as material.[44] 2) A willful breach is more likely to be regarded as material than a breach caused by negligence or by fortuitous circumstances.[45] 3) A quantitatively serious breach is more likely to be considered material.[46] In addition, the consequences of the determination must be taken into account. The degree of hardship on the breaching party is an important consideration particularly when considered in conjunction with the extent to which the aggrieved party has or will receive a substantial benefit from the promised performance and the adequacy with which he may be compensated for partial breach by damages.[47] Materiality of breach is ordinarily a question of fact.[48]

43. The more a party has performed the more likely it is that he will suffer a forfeiture. The less he has performed the more likely it is that the injured party will be deprived of the benefit which he reasonably expected. Restatement, Second, Contracts § 241(a) and (c) and Comments b and d.

44. A breach which occurs at the very beginning is more likely to be deemed material even if it is relatively small. See Note, The Breach in Limine Doctrine, 21 Colum.L.Rev. 358 (1921); Leazzoo v. Dunham, 95 Ill.App.3d 847, 51 Ill.Dec. 437, 420 N.E.2d 851 (1981). The reason for this is that it is fair in determining the materiality of the breach, to consider what has been done and the benefits which the non-breaching party has received. At times the same problem arises in another form where there is in fact a breach which is excused. Thus, if a school teacher is absent for five weeks at the beginning of school due to illness, although her performance is excused under the doctrine of impossibility of performance, nevertheless the employer is free to discharge her if the employer is deprived of an important part of what it bargained for. Hong v. Independent School Dist. No. 245, 181 Minn. 309, 232 N.W. 329, Annot., 72 A.L.R. 280 (1930); Poussard v. Spiers, 1 Q.B.D. 410 (1876); cf. Bettini v. Gye, 1 Q.B.D. 183 (1876). See also Restatement, Second, Contracts § 237, Comment a.

45. Since the basic question in determining materiality of the breach is one of fairness, it is obvious that whether the breaching party was guilty of willful or negligent behavior is relevant. Thus where an employee absented himself from his employer's business for one day to care for his own business where permission has been denied by the employer the breach was deemed willful and material. Jerome v. Queen City Cycle Co., 163 N.Y. 351, 57 N.E. 485 (1900). But see Midway School Dist. of Kern County v. Griffeath, 29 Cal.2d 13, 172 P.2d 857 (1946). The result would have been different if the employee had been sick and undoubtedly, even if he had been sick, as a result of intoxication. Insubordination by an employee amounts to a material breach. Rudman v. Cowles Communications, Inc., 35 A.D.2d 213, 315 N.Y.S.2d 409 (1st Dep't 1970), modified on the facts 30 N.Y.2d 1, 330 N.Y.S.2d 33, 280 N.E.2d 867 (1972).

46. It is apparent that the ratio of the part performed to the part to be performed is an important question in determining substantial performance and so also an important question in determining material breach. However, it is equally true that a breach which might ordinarily be insignificant could be deemed material if it prevents the other party from obtaining what he bargained for. However, in the case of a sale of goods under a non-installment contract the buyer need not take any number less than called for in the contract. See § 11–20(e) infra.

47. Restatement, Second, Contracts § 241(b) and Comment c. The same section adds that the likelihood that the breaching party will perform should be taken into account as well as whether he is acting in good faith and dealing fairly. Restatement, Second, Contracts § 241(d) & (e) and Comments e & f. Also to be taken into account is the difficulty of calculating damages for a total breach. Restatement, Second, Contracts § 243, Comment d. See generally, Restatement, Contracts § 275; 4 Corbin §§ 945–46; 3A Corbin §§ 700–12.

48. Coxe v. Mid–America Ranch & Recreation Corp., 40 Wis.2d 591, 162 N.W.2d 581 (1968); Coleman v. Shirlen, 53 N.C. App. 573, 281 S.E.2d 431 (1981). A breach

Perhaps the most frequent question raised in this area is whether delay in performance constitutes a material breach.[49] It is generally agreed that a party need not perform on the precise day stated in the contract unless time is made of the essence.[50] If time is not of the essence, reasonable delay in performing does not constitute a material breach of promise, however, unreasonable delay constitutes a material breach.[51] If time is of the essence, the breach of that promise will constitute a material breach.[52]

The key question is when is time of the essence. The general answer is that in making this determination, the trier of fact should not use a mechanical test, but should determine the intention of the parties in the light of the instrument itself and all the surrounding circumstances, including the parties' words, actions and interpretation of their agreement.[53]

One might conclude that the easiest way in which to make time of the essence is to put a clause in the contract that states, "Time is of the essence." When this has been done most cases have concluded that time is of the essence.[54] There is a growing school of thought that indicates that "such stock phrases" do not necessarily have this effect, although they are to be considered along with other circumstances in determining the effect of delay.[55]

The rules stated above apply to all types of contracts with the exception of contracts for the sale of goods which are discussed in the next section.[56]

(b) Substantial Performance

Substantial performance is the antithesis of material breach. If it determined that a breach is material, it follows that substantial per-

may be material even if the breaching party is unaware of the facts which give rise to the breach. Restatement, Second, Contracts § 237, Comment c; Pots Unlimited, Ltd. v. United States, 600 F.2d 790 (Ct.Cl. 1979).

49. Restatement, Second, Contracts § 242 and Comments a, b, c and d.

50. Leavitt v. Fowler, 118 N.H. 541, 391 A.2d 876 (1978); Tator v. Salem, 81 A.D.2d 727, 439 N.Y.S.2d 497 (3d Dep't 1981). But see Pinewood Realty Ltd. Partnership v. United States, 617 F.2d 211 (Ct.Cl.1980).

51. Keller v. Hummel, 334 N.W.2d 200 (N.D.1983).

52. E.E.E. Inc. v. Hanson, 318 N.W.2d 101 (N.D.1982). A "time of the essence" clause could be looked upon as a condition or a promise, or, what is probably more likely, express language of condition plus implied language of promise.

53. Blaustein v. Weiss, 409 So.2d 103 (Fla.App.1982); Allard & Geary, Inc. v.

Faro, 122 N.H. 573, 448 A.2d 377 (1982); Cahoon v. Cahoon, 641 P.2d 140 (Utah 1982). In other words it is possible for time to be of the essence even though this is not specifically so stated. Barber v. Johnson, 591 P.2d 886 (Wyo.1979).

54. Freeman v. Boyce, 66 Hawaii 327, 661 P.2d 702 (1983); Goldston v. Ami Investments, Inc., 98 Nev. 567, 655 P.2d 521 (1982); Corbray v. Stevenson, 98 Wn.2d 410, 656 P.2d 473 (1982) (en banc).

55. Restatement, Second, Contracts § 242, Comment d; Nash v. Superior Court of Los Angeles County, 86 Cal.App.3d 690, 150 Cal.Rptr. 394 (1978); Vermont Marble Co. v. Baltimore Contractors, Inc., 520 F.Supp. 922 (D.D.C.1981); Pederson v. McGuire, 333 N.W.2d 823 (S.D.1983).

56. 3A Corbin §§ 719–20; 6 Williston 849; Walton v. Denhart, 226 Or. 254, 359 P.2d 890 (1961).

formance has not been rendered. Just as the question of materiality of breach depends upon many factors so also the question of substantial performance depends to a large extent on the same factors.[57] The question of substantial performance is also ordinarily a question of fact.[58]

The doctrine of substantial performance is a natural outgrowth of the doctrine of constructive conditions. If a constructive condition had to be literally performed, as does a true condition, the doctrine of constructive conditions which was developed as an instrument for justice would have been a vehicle for injustice. Therefore, it was soon held that a constructive condition requires only substantial performance.[59] As one court has stated, "The 'substantial performance doctrine' provides that where a contract is made for an agreed exchange of two performances, one which is to be rendered first, substantial performance rather than exact, strict or literal performance by the first party of the terms of the contract is adequate to entitle the party to recover on it." [60]

As indicated in this quotation the doctrine is applicable to all bilateral contracts for an agreed exchange of performances.[61] One exception is a contract for the sale of goods.[62] The doctrine has been applied with particular emphasis to building contracts where a considerable default is sometimes treated as immaterial.[63]

For the doctrine of substantial performance to apply, the part unperformed must not destroy the value or the purpose of the contract.[64] However, if more than one promise is made, each promise does not have to be substantially performed. Overall substantial performance is sufficient.[65]

---

57. 3A Corbin § 700; Restatement, Second, Contracts § 237, Comment d. Nordin Constr. Co. v. Nome, 489 P.2d 455 (Alaska 1971); Hadden v. Consolidated Edison Co. of New York, Inc., 34 N.Y.2d 88, 356 N.Y.S.2d 249, 312 N.E.2d 445 (1974), appeal after remand 58 A.D.2d 154, 396 N.Y.S.2d 210 (1977), modified 45 N.Y.2d 466, 410 N.Y.S.2d 274, 382 N.E.2d 1136 (1978).

58. Litle Thompson Water Ass'n v. Strawn, 171 Colo. 295, 466 P.2d 915 (1970); Wm. G. Tannhaeuser, Co., Inc. v. Holiday House, Inc., 1 Wis.2d 370, 83 N.W.2d 880 (1957).

59. Boone v. Eyre, 126 Eng.Rep. 160 (K.B.1777).

60. Brown-Marx Associates, Ltd. v. Emigrant Sav. Bank, 703 F.2d 1361 (11th Cir. 1983).

61. See § 11–16 supra.

62. See § 11–20 infra.

63. Chinigo v. Ehrenberg, 112 Conn. 381, 152 A. 305 (1930) (default involved about one-third of the value of the promised performance); Jardine Estates, Inc. v. Donna Brook Corp., 42 N.J.Super. 332, 126 A.2d 372 (1956). But see Schieven v. Emerick, 220 App.Div. 468, 221 N.Y.S. 780 (1927) (five per cent deviation; no substantial performance). Nor is there substantial performance where there is a structural defect. Spence v. Ham, 163 N.Y. 220, 57 N.E. 412 (1900). That there is no simple solution to the problem based upon a ratio between monetary loss to the injured party and the contract price, see Restatement, Second, Contracts § 241, Comment b.

64. Mac Pon Co., Inc. v. Vinsoni Painting & Decorating Co., 423 So.2d 216 (Ala. 1982); E. Martin Schaeffer v. Kelton, 95 N.M. 182, 619 P.2d 1226 (1980); Klug & Smith Co. v. William Sommer and Richard Gebhardt, 83 Wis.2d 378, 265 N.W.2d 269 (1978).

65. Restatement, Second, Contracts § 232, Comment b.

There is a great deal of authority to the effect that substantial performance does not apply where the breach is willful. "The willful transgressor must accept the penalty of his transgression."[66] The word willful in this context is not easily defined.[67] An intentional variation from the contract, even if made with good motives, is deemed by some courts to be willful.[68] However, there are contrary cases.[69] In recent years this strict approach to the doctrine of willful breach has been softened by a number of authorities. The notion is that a willful breach does not prevent substantial performance—it is only one of the factors to be considered.[70] As stated in Vencenzi v. Cerro,[71] "[t]he contemporary view, however, is that even a conscious and intentional departure from the contract specifications will not necessarily defeat recovery, but may be considered as one of the several factors involved in deciding whether there has been full performance. The pertinent inquiry is not simply whether the breach was 'willful' but whether the behavior of the party in default 'comports with the standards of good faith and fair dealing.' Even an adverse conclusion on this point is not decisive but is to be weighed with other factors, such as the extent to which the owner will be deprived of a reasonably expected benefit and the extent to which the builder may suffer forfeiture, in deciding whether there has been substantial performance." (Citations omitted). Under any view trivial defects, even if willful, are to be ignored under the doctrine of de minimis non curat lex.[72]

It must be remembered that substantial performance is not full performance and that the party who relies on the doctrine has breached his contract. Consequently, he is liable in damages to the aggrieved party.[73] Thus, the party who has substantially performed is limited to the contract price less appropriate allowance "for cost of completing omissions and correcting defects."[74] Under the majority view, the burden of proof on this issue is upon the party who claims to have rendered substantial performance.[75]

---

66. Jacobs & Youngs, Inc. v. Kent, 230 N.Y. 239, 244, 129 N.E. 889, 891 (1921).

67. 3A Corbin § 707; 6 Williston § 842.

68. Shell v. Schmidt, 164 Cal.App.2d 350, 330 P.2d 817, Annot., 76 A.L.R.2d 792 (1958), certiorari denied 359 U.S. 959, 79 S.Ct. 799, 3 L.Ed.2d 766 (1959).

69. See Annot., 76 A.L.R.2d 792 (1958).

70. Restatement, Second, Contracts § 241 ill. 7 (based upon Mathis v. Thunderbird Village, Inc. 236 Or. 425, 389 P.2d 343 (1964)); Hadden v. Consolidated Edison Co. of New York, Inc., 34 N.Y.2d 88, 356 N.Y.S.2d 249, 312 N.E.2d 445 (1974), appeal after remand 58 A.D.2d 154, 396 N.Y.S.2d 210 (1977), modified 45 N.Y.2d 466, 410 N.Y.S.2d 274, 382 N.E.2d 1136 (1978).

71. 186 Conn. 612, 442 A.2d 1352, 1354 (1982).

72. 3A Corbin § 707; Van Clief v. Van Vechten, 130 N.Y. 571, 29 N.E. 1017 (1892).

73. Cox v. Freemont County Pub. Bldg. Auth., 415 F.2d 882 (10th Cir.1969); Reynolds v. Armstead, 166 Colo. 372, 443 P.2d 990 (1968).

74. Mirisis v. Renda, 83 A.D.2d 572, 441 N.Y.S.2d 138 (2d Dep't 1981).

75. Treiber v. Schaefer, 416 S.W.2d 576 (Tex.Civ.App.1967). There are many cases that place the burden of proof on the other party. See, e.g., Hopkins Constr. Co. v. Reliance Ins. Co., 475 P.2d 223 (Alaska 1970); Silos v. Prindle, 127 Vt. 91, 237 A.2d 694 (1967). Assuming substantial performance, some courts say that the measure of damages is the difference between the value of the house as built and the value it would have had had it been constructed according to the contract. White v. Mitch-

There are situations where a party is not proceeding with performance in accordance with the terms of the contract but is not yet guilty of a material breach. Under these circumstances, the other party may, by a proper notice set a reasonable time for performance and specify that time is of the essence. If a reasonable period of time is provided in the notice, it will be effective to make failure to perform by the specified date a material breach of contract.[76]

 WESTLAW REFERENCES

(a) *Material Breach*

breach! /s "ready willing and able"

material! immaterial! /s breach! /2 partial!

"right to cancel!" /s contract /s perform!

"partial! breach!" /s recover! damage

95k320 /p breach!

"total! breach!" /s rescission rescind! cancel! relief remedy

breach! /s cure

willful! wilful! /s material! /3 breach!

material! /3 breach! /s hardship

material! /3 breach! /s test

95k261(2)

delay! /3 perform! /s breach!

95k261(7)

time +4 essence /s delay! breach!

time +4 essence /s intend! intent! /s party

(b) *Substantial Performance*

"substantial! perform!" /s "material! breach!"

"substantial! perform!" /s question /2 fact!

digest(doctrine theory /3 "substantial performance")

di("substantial! perform!" /p "building contract!")

"substantial! perform!" /s value purpose /s contract

95k323(3) /p "substantial! perform!"

"substantial! perform!" /s willful! wilful!

"substantial! perform!" /s deviat!

95k320 /p "substantial! perform!"

"substantial! perform!" /s burden /2 proof proving /s remedy
recover! damage

---

ell, 123 Wash. 630, 213 P. 10 (1923); Venzke v. Magdanz, 243 Wis. 155, 9 N.W.2d 604 (1943). On the other hand there are jurisdictions which hold that ordinarily the defaulting party will be allowed to recover the contract price less the cost of correction of the defects of the unfinished work. Bellizzi v. Huntley Estates, Inc., 3 N.Y.2d 112, 164 N.Y.S.2d 395, 143 N.E.2d 802 (1957). But where this measurement would be unfair, as where correction of a usable structure containing no structural defect would require substantial tearing down of the structure and its rebuilding, the deduction will be for the difference between the value of the structure had it been built according to specifications and its value as constructed. Jacob & Youngs, Inc. v. Kent, 230 N.Y. 239, 129 N.E. 889 (1921); see Annot., 76 A.L.R.2d 805 (1961); § 14–29 infra. It should also be noted that these formulae are also used in determining whether there is substantial performance.

76. 3A Corbin § 723; Blaustein v. Weiss, 409 So.2d 103 (Fla.App.1982); 4200 Ave. K Realty Corp. v. 4200 Realty Co., 89 A.D.2d 978, 454 N.Y.S.2d 137 (2d Dep't 1982).

```
95k234   /p   "substantial! perform!"
95k322(1)   /p   "substantial! perform!"
```

§ 11–19. Successive Actions for Breach—Risk of Splitting a Claim

An illustration will help clarify the problem under discussion. A agrees to build five cottages at staggered intervals for B who agrees to pay $100,000 upon completion of the entire contract. Periodic payments are not provided for in the contract. The first cottage is completed several months after the date provided for in the contract. (Assume the breach was not material.) B sues and recovers for a partial breach as he has a right to do.[77] A subsequently abandons the work. At this point there is a material breach.[78] The question presented is whether B's prior action for a partial breach precludes a second action for total breach upon a theory of splitting an indivisible cause of action.

Logically, B should be permitted to institute another action for his additional damages. He should not be barred from recovery of those damages which he could not have recovered in the initial action.[79] There is another view, based upon the theory of splitting an indivisible cause of action. Under this view, there can be only one claim for the breach of one indivisible contract[80] and as a practical matter, the aggrieved party should defer bringing the action until the consequences of the breach are clear because if it should turn out that the breaching party will not perform his contract, the plaintiff will be precluded from bringing a second action. Under this approach the exercise of a legal right in bringing an action for partial breach becomes a snare for the innocent. However, there are some cases that have reached this conclusion.[81]

A word about the theoretical basis of the doctrine of splitting and indivisible claim appears to be in order. The reason for the rule against splitting an indivisible claim is that multiple actions on the same claim would be unjust and vexatious to the defendant.[82] The theoretical basis for the rule is found in the law of judgments. The effect of a judgment is to extinguish the claim upon which the judgment was based. In other words, the claim is merged in the judgment

77. See § 11–18(a) supra.

78. See § 11–18(a) supra.

79. Restatement, Contracts § 449, Comment e; Restatement, Judgments § 62, Comment h; cf. Clark, Code Pleading § 74 (2d ed. 1947).

80. 11 Williston § 1293. None of the cases cited by this authority supports this broad a proposition. With the exception of Pakas v. Hollingshead, see note 87 infra, all of the cited cases involve either dictum or a clear repudiation by the breaching

party. As stated hereafter in the case of a repudiation there is no right to elect to continue performance and sue for partial breach. See § 12–8 infra. However there is an exception to this rule stated in § 12–9 infra.

81. See note 80 supra.

82. 4 Corbin § 950; Clark, Code Pleadings § 73 (2d ed. 1947); Clark, Joinder and Splitting of Causes of Action, 25 Mich.L. Rev. 393 (1926).

with the result that the judgment creditor is precluded from bringing a second action on the same claim.[83]

It is obvious that what is critical is the definition of the term "claim" or "cause of action." [84] However, it is clear that there is no "consistent and commonly accepted definition that * * * can be used to advantage." [85]

In any event, a problem exists under the minority view stated above. The same type of problem exists when there is a material breach and the non-breaching party elects to treat it as a partial breach. There is also the same split of authority.[86] The same type of problem also occurs in installment contracts which are entire rather than divisible.[87] However, when the contract is divisible, it seems generally to be agreed that a breach of the severable portion gives rise to a separate cause of action.[88]

Closely related in policy to the rule against splitting a cause of action is the rule that even though there are successive breaches, the plaintiff must sue for all of the breaches that have occurred prior to the commencement of his action or lose his right to any cause of action not included.[89] This rule is not generally deemed to apply to separate and distinct contracts.[90] However, if separate and distinct contracts constitute a running account,[91] then the general rule stated above applies so that a suit on less than all of the breaches which have occurred will result in the loss of those claims not joined in the action.[92]

 WESTLAW REFERENCES

permit! permissibl* impermissibl! /s split! /s "cause of action"

indivisib! divisib! /s "cause of action"

"indivisible claim"

"indivisible contract" /s "cause of action" split!

83. 11 Williston § 1293.

84. Sometimes this problem is referred to as splitting a claim. At other times it is referred to as splitting a cause of action.

85. 4 Corbin § 955; cf. Restatement, Judgments, Ch. 3 Introductory Note Topic 2, Title D (1942) which indicates that the meaning of these terms varies with the context.

86. See also Restatement, Second, Contracts § 243, Comment d. Compare Restatement, Contracts § 449, Comment e and Restatement, Judgments § 62, Comment h with 11 Williston § 1294.

87. The leading case espousing the minority view is Pakas v. Hollingshead, 184 N.Y. 211, 77 N.E. 40 (1906); cf. Perry v. Dickerson, 85 N.Y. 345 (1881). The case of Goodwin v. Cabot, 129 Me. 36, 149 A. 574 (1930), is representative of the majority view. The Uniform Commercial Code appears to have adopted the majority view as

to installment contracts. U.C.C. § 2–612(3) and Comment 6.

88. 4 Corbin § 949.

89. Thomas v. Carpenter, 123 Me. 241, 122 A. 576 (1899); See v. See, 294 Mo. 495, 242 S.W. 949, Annot., 24 A.L.R. 880 (1922); 11 Williston § 1294.

90. Lozier Automobile Exch. v. Interstate Cas. Co., 197 Iowa 935, 195 N.W. 885 (1923). Negotiable bills and notes have long been regarded as separate contracts. 4 Corbin § 952.

91. Whether or not there is a running account appears to be a question of intent, often manifested by submission and acceptance of a consolidated bill for multiple purchases or services rendered. Corey v. Jaroch, 229 Mich. 313, 200 N.W. 957 (1924).

92. Kruce v. Lakeside Biscuit Co., 198 Mich. 736, 165 N.W. 609 (1917).

digest(contract*** agreement /p judgement judgment /s claim /s merg!)

228k582

"cause of action" /2 definition define*

"successive! breach!"

---

§ 11–20. Contracts for the Sale of Goods—The Perfect Tender Rule

In an earlier section it was stated that the doctrine of substantial performance which is almost universally applied [93] does not apply to contracts for the sale of goods. [94] During the nineteenth century, the perfect tender rule developed with respect to contracts for the sale of goods. Under that rule the buyer was free to reject the goods unless the tender conformed in every respect to the contract. This includes not only quantity and quality but also the details of shipment. [95] In the words of Learned Hand, "There is no room in commercial contracts for the doctrine of substantial performance." [96] The rule has been criticized [97] and is particularly unfair when it is impractical for the seller to resell the rejected goods, for example, because the goods were specially manufactured. [98]

Despite these criticisms, it appears that the Uniform Commercial Code has retained the perfect tender rule. [99] Section 2–601 of the Code specifically states, unless otherwise agreed, [1] "if the goods or the tender of the delivery fail in any respect to conform to the contract, the buyer may

    (a) reject the whole; or

    (b) accept the whole; or

    (c) accept any commercial unit or units and reject the rest."

93. At times a rule equivalent to the perfect tender rule has been applied to contracts for the sale of realty where the action is for damages at law. Smyth v. Sturges, 108 N.Y. 495, 15 N.E. 544 (1888).

94. See § 11–18(b) supra.

95. Norrington v. Wright, 115 U.S. 188, 6 S.Ct. 12, 29 L.Ed.2d 366 (1885); Filley v. Pope, 115 U.S. 213, 6 S.Ct. 19, 29 L.Ed. 372 (1885).

96. Mitsubishi Goshi Kaisha v. J. Aron & Co., 16 F.2d 185, 186 (2d Cir.1926).

97. Honnold, Buyer's Right of Rejection, 97 U.Pa.L.Rev. 457 (1949). Some more modern common law cases refused to follow this strict doctrine. See, e.g., LeRoy Dyal Co. v. Allen, 161 F.2d 152 (4th Cir. 1947).

98. Ellison Furniture & Carpet Co. v. Langever, 52 Tex.Civ.App. 50, 113 S.W. 178 (1908). Another objection to the perfect tender rule is that "buyers in a declining market would reject goods for minor nonconformities and force the loss on surprised sellers." Ramirez v. Autosport, 88 N.J. 277, 440 A.2d 1345 (1982).

99. See Priest, Breach and Remedy for the Tender of Nonconforming Goods under the Uniform Commercial Code: An Economic Approach, 91 Harv.L.Rev. 960 (1978).

1. For example, if the contract provides that the seller's obligations are limited to replacement of defective items or if a trade usage is inconsistent with the perfect tender rule.

However, the Code has limited the perfect tender rule by engrafting upon the rule a number of exceptions to be discussed below.[2] It has been suggested that these exceptions, in fact, represent a new rule, supplanting the perfect tender rule, and that despite § 2–601, the intent of the Code is to apply the doctrine of substantial performance to sales contracts.[3] The cases are generally in accord with the notion that the perfect tender rule is still alive but that the Code, through its exceptions, "strikes a different balance."[4] These exceptions will now be briefly discussed.[5]

(a) Cure

As we have seen above, the general notion of the perfect tender rule is that the buyer may reject goods if they are non-conforming in any respect.[6] Although the right to reject continues under the Code,[7] the buyer's rejection does not necessarily discharge the contract because the Code grants to the seller a right to cure in two specific situations.[8]

(1) When the Time for Performance Has Not Expired

Assume, for example, that the buyer rejects a defective tender of the seller before the time for performance has expired. In such a case the seller has an unconditional right to cure by making a conforming delivery within the contract time.[9] There is some question as to whether the cure may consist of repair of the defective goods.[10] It has

---

2. Section 2–503(1) of the Code states: "[t]ender of delivery requires that the seller put and hold conforming goods at the buyer's disposition and give the buyer any notification reasonably necessary to enable him to take delivery." Section 2–504 limits the perfect tender rule in a shipment contract when it provides that a failure to give notice is not a grounds for rejection if no material delay or loss results.

3. J. White & R. Summers, Uniform Commercial Code § 8–3 at 303–5. In addition Professor Murray suggests that the good faith provisions of the Code modify the perfect tender rule. See Murray, Contracts § 176.

4. Ramirez v. Autosport, 88 N.J. 277, 440 A.2d 1345 (1982); Restatement, Second, Contracts § 241, Comment b.

5. There is no intent to cover these exceptions in great detail and much less to cover all the provisions of Article 2 that may in some way relate to the topic under discussion.

6. See generally Schwartz, Private Law Treatment of Defective Products in Sales Situations, 49 Ind.L.J. 8 (1983); Whaley, Tender, Acceptance, Rejection and Revocation, the U.C.C.'s "Tarr" baby, 24 Drake L.Rev. 52 (1974).

7. There has been an occasional suggestion that because some defects can be cured under the rules stated below, rejection is not justified. Gindy Mfg. Corp. v. Cardinale Trucking Corp., 111 N.J.Super. 383, 268 A.2d 345 (1970). This suggestion was rejected in Ramirez v. Autosport, 88 N.J. 277, 440 A.2d 1345 (1982).

8. If the cure takes place before the rejection the right to reject is lost although buyer retains his right to sue under U.C.C. § 2–714.

9. U.C.C. § 2–508(1). See Note, Uniform Commercial Code—Sales—Section 2–508 and 2–608—Limitations on the Perfect Tender Rule, 69 Mich.L.Rev. 130 (1970).

10. Note, Uniform Commercial Code: Minor Repairs or Adjustments Must Be Permitted by a Buyer When the Seller Attempts To "Cure" a Non-conforming Tender of Merchandise, 52 Minn.L.Rev. 937 (1968). Compare Zabriskie Chevrolet v. Smith, 99 N.J.Super. 441, 240 A.2d 195 (1968), with Newmaster v. Southeast Equip., Inc., 231 Kan. 466, 646 P.2d 488 (1982). There is also some question as to whether a seller is entitled to cure non-conforming goods after acceptance or after the buyer has revoked acceptance. Lin-

been stated that the right to cure should not be extended to defects that substantially impair value.[11]

(2) When the Time for Performance Has Expired

When the buyer rejects a non-conforming tender, the seller also has a right to cure after the time for performance has passed if (1) the seller had reasonable grounds to believe that the tender would be accepted "with or without money allowance;"[12] (2) "the seller * * * seasonably notifies the buyer" of his intention to cure and cures the non-conforming tender within "a further reasonable time."[13] The statute is not limited to situations where the seller knowingly makes a defective tender. The overall aim of the Uniform Commercial Code is to encourage the parties to amicably resolve their own problems.[14]

(b) Rejection and Acceptance of Goods

Ordinarily when non-conforming goods are tendered, the buyer has a choice between accepting the goods or rejecting them.[15] It is obvious that he loses the right to reject the goods if he accepts them.[16] Even if he does not accept them, the buyer loses the right to reject if he does not reject them "within a reasonable time after their delivery or tender" or fails to "seasonably" notify the seller of their rejection.[17]

After rejection is properly notified, it is to be remembered that the seller often has a right to cure.[18] Consequently, the Code provides that when a buyer rejects, he must state all defects discoverable by reasonable inspection. If he does not do this, he may not justify his rejection

scott v. Smith, 3 Kan.App.2d 1, 587 P.2d 1271 (1978).

11. Linscott v. Smith, 3 Kan.App.2d 1, 587 P.2d 1271 (1978); Johannsen v. Minnesota Valley Ford Tractor Co., 304 N.W.2d 654 (Minn.1981); Pavesi v. Ford Motor Co., 155 N.J.Super. 373, 382 A.2d 954 (1978); cf. Zabriskie Chevrolet, Inc. v. Smith, 99 N.J. Super. 441, 240 A.2d 195 (1968); Oberg v. Phillips, 615 P.2d 1022 (Okl.App.1980).

12. Reasonable grounds include course of dealing, course of performance, usage of trade, and the particular circumstances of the contract itself. For a more elaborate explanation see Comment 2 to U.C.C. § 2–508. For a more complete discussion see White & Summers, Uniform Commercial Code § 8–4.

13. U.C.C. § 2–508(2). There is also some question as to whether a price adjustment given by the seller amounts to a cure. See White & Summers, Uniform Commercial Code § 8–4.

14. T.W. Oil, Inc. v. Consolidated Edison Co., 57 N.Y.2d 574, 457 N.Y.S.2d 458, 443 N.E.2d 932 (1982).

15. U.C.C. § 2–601. The buyer's duties as to properly rejected goods are set forth in U.C.C. § 2–602(2) and the duties of the merchant buyer are set forth in U.C.C. § 2–603. U.C.C. § 2–604 states what the buyer may do if the seller does not take any such action after rejection and the goods are already in the buyer's possession.

16. It should be noted that this is not a problem of offer and acceptance; rather what is being discussed is the acceptance of the goods being bought and sold.

17. U.C.C. § 2–602(1); Bead Chain Mfg. Co. v. Saxton Products, Inc., 183 Conn. 266, 439 A.2d 314 (1981); G & H Land & Cattle v. Heitzman & Nelson Inc., 102 Idaho 204, 628 P.2d 1038 (1981); Axion Corp. v. G.D.C. Leasing Corp., 359 Mass. 474, 269 N.E.2d 664 (1971); Southeastern Steel Co. v. Burton Block and Concrete Co., 273 S.C. 634, 258 S.E.2d 888 (1979). If the buyer pays against documents without reserving his rights and there are "defects apparent on the face of the documents," the buyer may not recover payment because of the existence of such defects. U.C.C. § 2–605(2) and Comment 4.

18. See § 11–20(a) supra.

upon any unstated claim that the seller could, if he had seasonable notice of the defect, have cured. Between merchants, a more drastic rule prevails. When a seller requests in writing a full and final statement of all defects on which buyer prepares to rely upon as grounds for rejection, the buyer cannot rely upon unstated defects (irrespective of their curability) that reasonably could have been discovered.[19] This discussion involves a rejection that is for some reason "ineffective" and thus results in an acceptance. If a rejection is wrongful (e.g. rejection of conforming goods), there is no acceptance but there is liability for the wrongful rejection.[20]

The Code states that there are three ways in which a buyer accepts goods. One is where he fails to make an effective rejection—discussed immediately above. The second arises where there is an express acceptance. In the language of the Code, there is an acceptance "when the buyer after a reasonable opportunity to inspect the goods [21] signifies to the seller that the goods are conforming or that he will take or retain them in spite of their non-conformity".[22]

In addition the buyer accepts if he "does any act inconsistent with the seller's ownership; but if such act is wrongful as against the seller it is an acceptance only if ratified by him." [23] What is consistent or inconsistent with the seller's ownership is a difficult question.[24] Use after rejection or revocation is wrongful.[25] The words "ratified by him" indicate that an act inconsistent with the seller's ownership is an acceptance if the seller treats it as an acceptance. In other words, the seller also has the option of treating it as a conversion.[26]

Acceptance not only precludes rejection but requires the buyer to pay at the contract rate.[27] In addition, acceptance of the goods shifts the burden of proof to the buyer "to establish any breach with respect to the goods accepted." [28] Even though the buyer is required to pay at

---

19. U.C.C. § 2–605(1).

20. White & Summers, Uniform Commercial Code § 8–3 at 314 (2d ed. 1980).

21. For example, a buyer who signs a seller's form stating he has inspected the goods and found them conforming has not accepted under this rule unless he genuinely has a reasonable opportunity to perform more than a cursory inspection. See also T.J. Stevenson & Co. v. 81,193 Bags of Flour, 629 F.2d 338 (5th Cir.1980), rehearing denied 651 F.2d 779 (5th Cir.1981); Jakowski v. Carole Chevrolet, 180 N.J. Super. 122, 433 A.2d 841 (1981). The basic section of the Code that relates to inspection is § 2–513. See also §§ 2–310(b) and 2–321(3).

22. U.C.C. § 2–606(1)(a); Plateau Corp. v. Matchlett Lab., 189 Conn. 433, 456 A.2d 786 (1983). Subdivision (2) of this section also provides, "acceptance of part of a commercial unit is acceptance of that entire unit."

23. U.C.C. § 2–606(1)(c).

24. See White & Summers, Uniform Commercial Code, § 8–2 at 297–301; Jacobs v. Rosemount Dodge-Winnebago South, 310 N.W.2d 71 (Minn.1981); Steinmetz v. Robertus, 196 Mont. 311, 637 P.2d 31 (1981).

25. U.C.C. § 2–602(2)(a).

26. See § 2–19 supra.

27. U.C.C. § 2–607(1); Unlaub Co. v. Sexton, 568 F.2d 72 (8th Cir.1977); Borges v. Magic Valley Foods, Inc., 101 Idaho 494, 616 P.2d 273 (1980); Montana Seeds, Inc. v. Holliday, 178 Mont. 119, 582 P.2d 1223 (1978).

28. U.C.C. § 2–607(4); Miron v. Yonkers Raceway, Inc., 400 F.2d 112 (2d Cir. 1968) noted in 31 Ohio St.L.J. 151 (1970). It is even possible to have an acceptance after a revocation. Cardwell v. International Housing, Inc., 282 Pa.Super. 498, 423 A.2d 355 (1980).

the contract price after acceptance, if the goods are non-conforming, he is still entitled to recover damages for breach provided that the buyer gives proper notice of non-conformity.[29]

(c) Revocation of Acceptance

Even though the goods have been accepted, the buyer may in a proper case revoke the acceptance.[30] Under the terms of U.C.C. § 2–608(1) the first requirement for revocation of an acceptance of a lot or commercial unit is that its non-conformity substantially impairs its value to the buyer. This is a question of fact.[31] The question may be phrased in terms of the seller's substantial performance. If the seller has substantially performed, the buyer may not revoke.[32] The question could also be phrased in terms of whether the seller was guilty of a material breach. If the seller is guilty of a material breach, the buyer may revoke.[33] As previously suggested, the result will be the same under either formulation.[34] The words "impairs its value to him" seems to suggest a subjective test. Comment 2 seems to be in accord with this suggestion when it states, "The question is whether the non-conformity is such as will in fact cause a substantial impairment of the value to the buyer though the seller had no advance knowledge as to the buyer's particular circumstances." [35]

When it has been found that the seller has not substantially performed or has materially breached, the buyer may revoke only if he satisfies one of two requisites set forth in section 2–608. He must show either that he has accepted (a) "on the reasonable assumption that its non-conformity would be cured and it has not been seasonably cured;" or (b) even if he did not discover such non-conformity at the time of acceptance, "if his acceptance was reasonably induced either by the difficulty of discovery before acceptance or by the seller's assurances." [36]

29. U.C.C. § 2–607(3) provides: When a tender has been accepted (a) "[T]he buyer must within a reasonable time after he discovers or should have discovered any breach notify the seller of breach or be barred from any remedy." See Note, Notification of Breach under U.C.C. § 2–607(3)(a): A Conflict, A Resolution, 70 Cornell L.Rev. 525 (1985); see also U.C.C. § 2–714; Maybank v. S.S. Kresge, 302 N.C. 129, 273 S.E.2d 681 (1981); Note, Notice of Breach and the Uniform Commercial Code, 25 U.Fla.L.Rev. 520 (1973).

30. See Phillips, Revocation of Acceptance and the Consumer Buyer, 75 Comm. L.J. 354 (1970). See also Annot., 65 A.L.R.3d 388 (1975); Annot., 65 A.L.R.3d 354 (1975).

31. Erling v. Homera, Inc., 298 N.W.2d 478 (N.D.1980).

32. See Note, Uniform Commercial Code—Sales—Sections 2–508 and 2–608; Limitations on the Perfect Tender Rule, 69 Mich.L.Rev. 130 (1970).

33. White & Summers, Uniform Commercial Code § 8–3 at 305–06 (2d ed. 1980).

34. See § 11–18 supra.

35. See White & Summers, supra note 33, at 308–09. The cases are not all precisely in accord. See, e.g., Black v. Don Schmid Motor, Inc., 232 Kan. 458, 657 P.2d 517 (1983); Champion Ford Sales, Inc. v. Levine, 49 Md.App. 547, 433 A.2d 1218 (1981); Bergenstock v. LeMay's G.M.C. Inc., 118 R.I. 75, 372 A.2d 69 (1977); see also Note, Revocation of Acceptance: The Test For Substantial Impairment, 32 U.Pitt.L.Rev. 439 (1971); Annot., 98 A.L.R.3d 1183 (1980).

36. U.C.C. § 2–608(1)(a), (b); Four Sons Bakery, Inc. v. Dulman, 542 F.2d 829 (10th Cir.1976); Lynx, Inc. v. Ordnance Products, Inc., 273 Md. 1, 327 A.2d 502 (1974).

Even if the buyer has satisfied the rules stated above in order to revoke effectively, he must revoke "within a reasonable time after the buyer discovers or should have discovered the ground for it (revocation) and before any substantial change in condition of the goods which is not caused by their own defects." [37] When the statute talks about "should have discovered" these words are directed to the requirement that the buyer make a reasonable inspection.[38] The revocation is not effective until the buyer notifies the seller of the revocation of acceptance.[39] No particular form of notice is required.[40] The effect of a valid revocation of acceptance is that the buyer has the same rights and duties with regard to the goods involved as if he had rejected them.[41]

Continued possession and reasonable use of property after buyer has notified seller of revocation of acceptance does not necessarily amount to a waiver of the right to revoke acceptance.[42]

(d) Installment Contracts

The perfect tender rule does not apply to an installment contract with the result that the installment buyer may not reject a tender merely because it is not perfect. Where a non-conformity with respect to one or more installments substantially impairs the value of the whole contract, the buyer is justified in rejecting the delivery in question and cancelling the whole contract because there is a material breach.[43] However, if the non-conformity of an installment impairs the value only of that installment, the buyer must accept the installment if it can be cured and the seller gives adequate assurance of its cure.[44]

For example, in one case,[45] B contracted to buy 20 carloads of plywood from S. Nine percent of the first carload consisted of non-conforming sheets of plywood. B cancelled the contract. S sued. The court held that B was liable for breach of contract because the non-conformity did not substantially impair the value of the entire contract. Moreover, it is doubtful whether B could have rejected the first carload. Even if the value of that installment was impaired, S would still be entitled to attempt a cure. As Professor Quinn points out: "It is tough

---

37. U.C.C. § 2–608(2); Conte v. Dwan Lincoln Mercury, Inc., 172 Conn. 112, 374 A.2d 144 (1976); Michigan Sugar Co. v. Jebavy Sorenson Orchard, 66 Mich.App. 642, 239 N.W.2d 693 (1976); Desilets Granite Co. v. Stone Equalizer Corp., 133 Vt. 372, 340 A.2d 65 (1975).

38. Lynx, Inc. v. Ordnance Products, Inc., 273 Md. 1, 327 A.2d 502 (1974).

39. U.C.C. § 2–608(2).

40. Peckham v. Larsen Chevrolet-Buick-Oldsmobile, 99 Idaho 675, 587 P.2d 816 (1978).

41. U.C.C. § 2–608(3). See (b) supra in this section on the question of the rights

and duties of the parties when the goods are rejected. Volkswagen of America, Inc. v. Novak, 418 So.2d 801 (Miss.1982).

42. O'Shea v. Hatch, 97 N.M. 409, 640 P.2d 515 (1982).

43. U.C.C. § 2–612(3); see Note, Breach of Installment Contracts Under the Uniform Commercial Code, 7 Willamette L.J. 107 (1971).

44. U.C.C. § 2–612(2); Kirkwood Agri-Trade v. Frosty Land Foods, 650 F.2d 602 (5th Cir.1981).

45. Continental Forest Products v. White Lumber Sales, Inc., 256 Or. 466, 474 P.2d 1 (1970).

to reject any single installment under an installment contract and even tougher to get rid of the rest of the whole contract." [46]

An installment contract is one in which separate lots are to be delivered and these lots are to be separately paid for.[47] There is a presumption that goods are to be delivered in one lot.[48] However, this presumption may be rebutted by the express language of the contract or may be inferred from the circumstances.[49] When it is clear that the parties intended an installment contract this will not be changed by a clause to the effect that " 'each delivery is a separate contract' or its equivalent." [50]

(e) The Perfect Tender Rule and the Buyer

The rules stated above related to what is the effect of a non-conforming tender by the seller. Here the question is the effect of a non-conforming tender by the buyer. It is clear in the case of an installment contract that when the buyer fails to make a conforming payment, the perfect tender rule does not apply and the issue is material breach.[51] However, if literally interpreted, the Uniform Commercial Code would seem to regard late payment of a non-installment contract as a material breach.[52] The buyer may also breach by failing to accept goods pursuant to the terms of the contract even though payment is not yet due.[53]

It is interesting to note that the Code provides that payment ordinarily need not be made in cash and that a check will suffice. It provides: "Tender of payment is sufficient when made by any means or in any manner current in the ordinary course of business unless the seller demands payment in legal tender and gives any extension of time reasonably necessary to procure it." [54]

 WESTLAW REFERENCES

"perfect tender rule"

2–601 /s "uniform commercial code" u.c.c.

remedy breach! /s conform! non-conform! /4 good

(a) *Cure*

conform! nonconform! /4 good /s cure

"right to cure"

    (1) *When the Time for Performance Has Not Expired*

2–508 /s u.c.c. "uniform commercial code"

---

46. T. Quinn, Uniform Commercial Code Commentary and Digest, § 2–612[A][5].

47. U.C.C. § 2–612(1).

48. U.C.C. § 2–307; see also Restatement, Second, Contracts § 233(2) and ill. 3 and Reporter's Note.

49. U.C.C. § 2–307 and Comment 2.

50. U.C.C. § 2–612(1).

51. Cherwell-Ralli, Inc. v. Rytman Grain Co., 180 Conn. 714, 433 A.2d 984 (1980). This was also the rule prior to the Code. See Helgar Corp. v. Warner Features, 222 N.Y. 449, 119 N.E. 113 (1918).

52. U.C.C. § 2–703.

53. U.C.C. § 2–703.

54. U.C.C. § 2–511(2).

"right to cure" /s accept! /s reject!

"right to cure" /s impair!

(2) When the Time for Performance Has Expired

"right to cure" /s expir!

"right to cure" /s reasonabl*

(b) Rejection and Acceptance of Goods

"right to reject!" /s "reasonable time"

343k168(4)

reject! /s good /s ineffective!

reject! /s good /s wrongful!

reject! /s good /s dominion

reject! /s good /s tender! /s fail!

reject! /s good /s inconsisten!

"reasonable opportunity" /s inspect! /s accept!

343k178(3)

reject! /s ratif! /s wrongful!

(c) Revocation of Acceptance

2–608 /p revoc! revok!

revoc! revok! /s impair! /s question /2 fact!

"material! breach!" "substantial! perform!" /s revok! revoc!

(d) Installment Contracts

"perfect tender" non-conform! /s installment

"material! breach!" /s installment

reject! /s installment /s cure

deliver! /s separate! /s installment /s pay*** payment paid

"installment contract" /s "separate lot"

installment /s each /2 delivery /4 contract

(e) The Perfect Tender Rule and the Buyer

late untimel! delinquen! /2 payment paid pay*** /s breach! /s buyer

400k335

2–511(2) /s "uniform commercial code" u.c.c.

---

§ 11–21. A Note on Terminology: "Failure of Consideration"

The term "failure of consideration" is not related to the term consideration as used in Chapter 4. It does not relate to the formation of a contract but rather to the performance of a contract.[55] An illustration will help indicate how the term is used. If C promises to build a structure for O and O promises to make payment when the work is completed, it is clear that there is consideration on both sides of this contract and that therefore a contract was *formed* upon the exchange of promises.[56] If C fails to perform, the result is sometimes

55. Lord Simon in Fibrosa Spolka Akcyjna v. Fairbairn Lawson Combe Barbour, Ltd., 1943 A.C. 32, [1942] 2 All E.R. 122 (H.L.); Converse v. Zinke, 635 P.2d 882 (Colo.1981); Franklin v. Carpenter, 309 Minn. 419, 244 N.W.2d 492 (1976).

56. See § 4–2 supra.

described as a "failure of consideration." "Failure of consideration" simply means a failure to perform and as used covers both a material breach of constructive conditions and a failure to perform an express condition.[57]

The use of the term "failure of consideration" in this sense appears to be an unnecessary invitation to confusion because the word consideration is being used in two different senses. Fortunately, the use of this phrase has gradually fallen into disuse. It is, however, still sufficiently widespread to be mentioned here. This volume nowhere utilizes "failure of consideration" as an operative concept.

 WESTLAW REFERENCES

fail*** lack inadequate   /3   consideration   /s   "material! breach!"

fail*** lack inadequate   /3   consideration   /s   fail!   +2   perform!

95k83

§ 11–22. Recovery for Less Than Substantial Performance: Quasi-Contractual and Statutory Relief

As we have seen a defaulting plaintiff who has substantially performed is ordinarily entitled to a recovery based upon the terms of the contract.[58] The question here is whether a defaulting plaintiff who has not substantially performed is entitled to a quasi-contractual recovery (restitution) as a means of avoiding unjust enrichment.

Two early cases involving employment contracts have forcefully stated the opposite approaches that have been taken to this problem. In Stark v. Parker,[59] an early Massachusetts case, the plaintiff was hired to work for one year for the sum of $120. Before the end of this agreed upon period, the plaintiff without cause left the defendant's employment. He framed his complaint for services rendered in the quasi-contractual form of action known as indebitatus assumpsit. The Supreme Judicial Court found the plaintiff's complaint "strange" and "repugnant" saying:

> "The law indeed is most reasonable in itself. It denies only to a party an advantage from his own wrong. It requires him to act justly by a faithful performance of his own engagement before he exacts the fulfillment of dependent obligation on the part of others. It will not admit of the monstrous absurdity that a man may voluntarily and without cause violate his agreement and make the very breach of that agreement the foundation of an action which he could not maintain under it."[60]

57. Murray, Contracts § 168; Restatement, Second, Contracts § 237, Comment a. But see Williston § 814.

58. See § 11–18(b) supra. There are other instances where a defaulting plaintiff, who has not substantially performed, is entitled to a contractual recovery. See §§ 11–22 to 11–26 infra.

59. 19 Mass. (2 Pick.) 267 (1824).

60. Id. at 275.

Although this case probably still constitutes the weight of authority,[61] the contrary reasoning of another old and still widely cited case continues to make converts and to influence legislation. In a nearly identical fact pattern, the Supreme Court of Judicature of New Hampshire in Britton v. Turner [62] ruled that the defaulting plaintiff, although unable to recover on the contract, could recover under a quasi-contractual theory for the reasonable value of his services less any damages suffered by defendant. The Court laid stress on the injustice of the defendant's retention without payment of benefits received under the contract.[63] It also took note that the general understanding of the community is that payment should be made for services actually rendered.

The conflict of authority extends beyond employment contracts to all kinds of contracts. Some jurisdictions permit quasi-contractual relief under a building or other service contract, even where the performance is less than substantial, less damages for breach.[64] The same split of authority is found when a defaulting purchaser of land seeks to recover his down payment.[65] In the case of a buyer of goods, the Uniform Commercial Code permits a defaulting buyer to obtain restitution of payments made by him to the extent that these exceed $500 or 20% of the buyer's obligation, whichever is smaller.[66] The buyer's claim for restitution is subject to an offset in the amount of the seller's actual damages and the value of benefits received by the buyer

---

61. 1 G. Palmer, Law of Restitution § 5.13 (1978); see Lee, The Plaintiff in Default, 19 Vand.L.Rev. 1023 (1966).

62. 6 N.H. 481 (1834).

63. See Ashley, Britton v. Turner, 24 Yale L.J. 544 (1915); Corman, The Partial Performance Interest of the Defaulting Employee, (pts. I & II) 38 Marq.L.Rev. 61, 139 (1954–55); Laube, The Right of An Employee Discharged for Cause, 20 Minn. L.Rev. 597 (1936); Laube, The Defaulting Employee—Britton v. Turner Re-Viewed, 83 U.Pa.L.Rev. 825 (1935); Laube, The Defaulting Employee—No Retraction 84 U.Pa.L.Rev. 68, 69 (1935); Williston, The Defaulting Employee—A Correction, id. at 68.

64. Mills v. Denny Wiekhorst Excavating, Inc., 206 Neb. 443, 293 N.W.2d 112 (1980); Lynn v. Seby, 29 N.D. 420, 151 N.W. 31 (1915) (contract to thresh grain); Kirkland v. Archbold, 113 N.E.2d 496 (Ohio App.1953); Burke v. McKee, 304 P.2d 307 (Okl.1956) (contract to clear land of timber); see Nordstrom & Woodland, Recovery by Building Contractor in Default, 20 Ohio St.L.J. 193 (1959). Although

generally where substantial performance is rendered, recovery is allowed on the contract, in some jurisdictions only quasi-contractual relief is permitted. Allen v. Burns, 201 Mass. 74, 87 N.E. 194 (1909).

65. Lawrence v. Miller, 86 N.Y. 131 (1881); Beechwood Corp. v. Fisher, 19 N.Y.2d 1008, 228 N.E.2d 823, 281 N.Y.S.2d 843 (1967) (majority); Freedman v. Rector, 37 Cal.2d 16, 230 P.2d 629, Annot., 31 A.L.R.2d 1 (1951) (minority). The minority view is supported by Corbin, The Right of a Defaulting Vendee to Restitution of Installments Paid, 40 Yale L.J. 1013 (1931). A recent case has stated that where there is a provision in the contract allowing seller to retain the downpayment the issue is whether there is a forfeiture or such unfairness as shocks the conscience of the court. Huckins v. Ritter, 99 N.M. 560, 661 P.2d 52 (1983); see also Ponderosa Pines Ranch, Inc. v. McBride, 197 Mont. 301, 642 P.2d 1050 (1982) (stating that claimant is not entitled to restitution where he has been grossly negligent or his conduct is willful or fraudulent).

66. U.C.C. § 2–718(2)(b).

as a result of the contract.[67]   The buyer's rights may be curtailed or expanded by a valid liquidated damages clause.[68]

For example, B contracts to purchase living room furniture from S for $2,100, paying $700 of the purchase price.   B repudiates and sues for restitution of the down payment.   B obtains restitution of $700 minus the lesser of $500 or 20% of the price ($420).   Since $420 is less than $500, B is entitled to $700–$420; that is $280.   This sum will be reduced to the extent of the seller's damages and the value of benefits received by the buyer.

The modern trend in the law is that a party in substantial default should not be treated as an outlaw.   This is being accomplished by virtue of case law,[69] legislation [70] and the provisions of the Restatement Second which states in the Reporter's Note that it "is more liberal in allowing recovery" than the first Restatement.[71]

There is a substantial question as to whether a willful breach should prevent the granting of restitution.[72]

Despite the inroads of statutes and fairly wide acceptance of the doctrine of Britton v. Turner, the majority of jurisdictions appear to adhere to the general principle that a defaulting party has no remedy notwithstanding the degree of hardship and forfeiture he may suffer. The general principle is punitive, but is not rational in meting out punishment.   The penalty is not fashioned to meet the specific wrong. Rather, the amount of penalty depends upon the fortuitous circumstances of the transaction.   Paradoxically, the more the defaulting party has performed, the greater his forfeiture and the greater the unearned enrichment of the other party.[73]

   WESTLAW REFERENCES
"unjust! enrich!"   /s   "substantial! perform!"
95k320   /p   "substantial! perform!"

67.   U.C.C. § 2–718(3).

68.   U.C.C. § 2–718(2)(a).   On the validity of liquidated damages clauses, see §§ 14–15—14–17, infra.

69.   5A Corbin § 1123; see Judge Clark's able discussion in Amtorg Trading Corp. v. Miehle Printing Press & Mfg. Co., 206 F.2d 103 (2d Cir.1953) (prophesying a change in New York law.   The prophesy has not been fulfilled); see also Kitchin v. Mori, 84 Nev. 181, 437 P.2d 865 (1968) (asserting that the weight of authority now permits a party in default to recover the value of his performance less the aggrieved party's damages).

70.   In addition to the U.C.C. provision most states have labor legislation requiring the payment of wages to workmen at periodic intervals, and the payment of accrued wages at the termination of employment regardless of any contractual provision to the contrary.   Restatement, Second, Contracts § 265, Comment a.

71.   Restatement, Second, Contracts § 374 Reporter's Note.

72.   Compare Harris v. The Cecil N. Bean, 197 F.2d 919 (2d Cir.1952) with Begovich v. Murphy, 359 Mich. 156, 101 N.W.2d 278 (1960) and Restatement, Second, Contracts § 374 and Comment b.

73.   In Freedman v. Rector, 37 Cal.2d 16, 230 P.2d 629, 31 A.L.R.2d 1 (1951), the court in granting restitution to a defaulting purchaser of land stated that the majority rule, in effect, grants punitive damages to the non-breaching party.   But this award has no "rational relationship to its purpose. * * * It not only fails to take into consideration the degree of culpability but its severity increases as the seriousness of the breach decreases." 37 Cal.2d at 22, 230 P.2d at 632.

"substantial! perform!" /s quasi-contract***

"substantial! perform!" /s breach! /s recover!

"reasonable value" /s quasi-contract***

"substantial! default!" /s recover!

willful! wilful! /s breach! /s restitution

§ 11–23. Recovery by a Party in Default: Divisibility

Some contracts are said to be "entire" while others are said to be "divisible." A contract is said to be divisible if "performance by each party is divided into two or more parts" and "performance of each part by each party is the agreed exchange for a corresponding part by the other party." [74] It is often said that whether a contract is divisible is a question of interpretation or one of the intention of the parties. [75] However, the process of interpretation and the search for intention appear to be result-oriented. [76] It is easier to understand the distinction between divisible and entire contracts if one understands the consequences of the determination.

If A and B agree that A will act as B's secretary for one year at a salary of $100 per week, the contract is said to be divisible. [77] Once the secretary has worked one week he becomes entitled to $100 irrespective of any subsequent events. [78] Thus, even if the secretary breaches the contract by wrongfully leaving B's employment, he is nonetheless entitled to $100 less whatever damages were caused by A's material breach. [79] In effect, for the purpose of payment, the contract is deemed

74. Howard University v. Durham, 408 A.2d 1216 (D.C.1979); Restatement, Second, Contracts § 240 and Comments a & d; Restatement, Contracts § 266, Comment e; 6 Williston § 860; see also 3A Corbin § 694.

75. Blakesley v. Johnson, 227 Kan. 495, 608 P.2d 908 (1980); Gaspar v. Flott, 209 Neb. 260, 307 N.W.2d 500 (1981); Matter of Estate of Wilson, 50 N.Y.2d 59, 427 N.Y.S.2d 977, 405 N.E.2d 220 (1980); Management Services Corp. v. Development Associates, 617 P.2d 406 (Utah 1980).

76. It is also often stated that a contract should be treated as entire when by a consideration of its terms, nature and purposes each and all of the parts appear to be interdependent and common to one another and to the consideration. Singleton v. Foreman, 435 F.2d 962 (5th Cir.1970); First Sav. & Loan Ass'n v. American Home Assurance Co., 29 N.Y.2d 297, 327 N.Y.S.2d 609, 277 N.E.2d 638 (1971). Custom and usage are important in making the determination as are the background and the surrounding circumstances. George v. School Dist. No. 8R of Umatilla County, 7 Or.App. 183, 490 P.2d 1009 (1971); see also Restatement, Second, Contracts § 240,

Comment e; Village Inn Pancake House of Mobile, Inc. v. Higdon, 294 Ala. 378, 318 So.2d 245 (1975). At times it is said that the question is one of law. L.D.A. Inc. v. Cross, ___ W.Va. ___, 279 S.E.2d 409 (1981). Other courts have indicated that it is a question of fact. Studzinski v. Motor Car Ins. Co., 180 N.J.Super. 416, 434 A.2d 1160 (1981).

77. Yeargin v. Bramblett, 115 Ga.App. 862, 156 S.E.2d 97 (1967) (physicians' services over a period of years to patient afflicted with chronic diseases held to be severable for purposes of statue of limitations); White v. Atkins, 62 Mass. (8 Cush.) 367 (1851); Wrightsman v. Brown, 181 Okl. 142, 73 P.2d 121 (1937).

78. As a matter of fact if the secretary substantially performed a divisible part of the contract he would be entitled to $100 less whatever damages were caused by the failure to work a full week. See Lowy v. United Pac. Ins. Co., 67 Cal.2d 87, 60 Cal. Rptr. 225, 429 P.2d 577 (1967).

79. However there are cases holding that even though the employee is entitled to be paid for the severable performance rendered, nevertheless if he breaches, the

to be divided into 52 exchanges of performance. However, if it be assumed that the secretary failed, without justification, to work for four days out of a particular week and the employer wished to discharge him, the question would be materiality of the breach. On this issue the divisibility of the contract would be immaterial since the question of materiality of the breach would be decided on the ratio of four days to a year rather than four days to a week.[80]

Not only must one inquire for *what purposes* a contract is divisible, one must also ascertain *how* the contract is divisible. A good illustration is the case of Gill v. Johnstown Lumber Co.[81] In that case plaintiff agreed to drive logs and cross-ties for the defendant. We shall limit our discussion to the logs. The contract provided that plaintiff would receive $1.00 per thousand feet for logs of oak and 75 cents per thousand for all other logs. In each case the logs were to be delivered to the Johnstown Boom. Here the contract is divisible according to 1000 feet. In other words the plaintiff was entitled to be paid $1.00 each time he delivered 1000 feet of logs of oak or whatever amounted to substantial performance of 1000 feet. If plaintiff drove 1000 feet of said logs very close to the Boom could he recover if, without his fault, at the last moment the goods were swept away by a flood? The court answered in the negative. In other words, the contract was not divisible by the distance traversed.

In another case [82] the plaintiff agreed to make extensive alterations to the defendant's property for $3,075 to be payable in installments, $150 upon signing the contract, $1,000 on delivery of the material and starting to work, $1,500 upon completion of the rough carpentry and $425 upon the completion of the work. The contract was held to be entire. In this situation what would happen if the plaintiff completed the rough carpentry and then repudiated? If the contract were divisible it is clear that plaintiff would be entitled to $1,500. Since the contract is entire however, plaintiff is not entitled to a contractual recovery unless there is substantial performance of the contract. Since there is not substantial performance and the contract is not divisible he is not entitled to a contractual recovery and therefore is not entitled to the $1,500 payment provided in the contract.[83] In other words the provision for payments amounts to nothing more than progress payments [84] because the payment was not provided as an equivalent for the

employer would not be guilty of a breach in failing to pay this sum at least as long as he does not retain an amount in excess of his damages. McGowan, The Divisibility of Employment Contracts, 21 Iowa L.Rev. 50, 56–58 (1935); see also Restatement, Second, Contracts § 240, Comment a, which points out that state statutes requiring frequent periodic payment of wages have reduced the importance of the doctrine of divisibility in employment contracts.

80. Restatement, Second, Contracts § 240, Comment b.

81. 151 Pa. 534, 25 A. 120 (1892).

82. New Era Homes Corp. v. Forster, 299 N.Y. 303, 86 N.E.2d 757, Annot., 22 A.L.R.2d 1338 (1949).

83. See § 11–18(b) supra.

84. See the discussion that follows. In particular see note 91 infra.

work.[85] That is to say the $1,500 is not an "agreed exchange" for the rough carpentry. Nor is the plaintiff entitled to a quasi-contractual recovery under the majority view.[86]

In the same case what would be the result if the plaintiff completed the rough carpentry and the owner without justification refused to pay the third installment? More specifically is plaintiff entitled to recover the $1,500 at this point? Under the majority view the answer is in the affirmative.[87] Under the minority view he is entitled only to his damages as a result of the failure to pay.[88] Under either view he most probably may suspend his performance [89] and wait until there is a material breach and then sue for damages for a total breach.[90]

It is rare that the parties express an intention on the issue of divisibility. The test ultimately appears to be whether, had the parties thought about it as fair and reasonable people, they would be willing the exchange the performance in question irrespective of what transpired subsequently or whether the divisions made are merely for the purpose of requiring periodic payments as the work progresses.[91] The results reached depend largely upon the kind of contract involved. Building contracts are generally deemed to be entire [92] while employment contracts are generally held to be divisible.[93] The rules of the Uniform Commercial Code relating to installment contracts are discussed above.[94]

   WESTLAW REFERENCES

di(divisible /s contract /s intend! intent!)

distinguish! distinct! /s entire /s divisible /s contract

"entire contract" /s severable

"divisible contract" /s breach!

85. City of Bridgeport v. T.A. Scott Co., 94 Conn. 461, 109 A. 162 (1920); Pennsylvania Exch. Bank v. United States, 170 F.Supp. 629 (D.Ct.Cl.1959).

86. See § 11–22 supra.

87. 3A Corbin § 697; Rich v. Arancio, 277 Mass. 310, 178 N.E. 743, Annot., 82 A.L.R. 313 (1931).

88. New Era Homes Corp. v. Forster, 299 N.Y. 303, 86 N.E.2d 757, Annot., 22 A.L.R.2d 1338 (1949).

89. See § 11–18(a) supra.

90. 3A Corbin § 697; cf. Shapiro Engineering, Corp. v. Francis O. Day Co., 215 Md. 373, 137 A.2d 695 (1958). Undoubtedly even at this point plaintiff could elect to sue for a partial breach. See § 11–18(a) supra. However, he could be creating a problem relating to splitting an indivisible cause of action. See § 11–19 supra.

91. Tipton v. Feitner, 20 N.Y. 423 (1859).

92. City of Bridgeport v. Scott Co., 94 Conn. 461, 109 A. 162 (1920); New Era

Homes Corp. v. Forster, 299 N.Y. 303, 86 N.E.2d 757, Annot., 22 A.L.R.2d 1338 (1949). But cf. Lowy v. United Pac. Ins. Co., 67 Cal.2d 87, 60 Cal.Rptr. 225, 429 P.2d 577 (1967), which combined the doctrines of divisibility and substantial performance. The contract provided that contractor was to do excavation work and street improvement work and a unit price was allocated to each phase. The contract was held to be divisible and the contractor was permitted to recover for substantial performance of the first phase, although he defaulted entirely on the second phase and in part as to the first phase. In the case of the construction of 35 houses each house was deemed to be divisible. See Carrig v. Gilbert-Varker Corp., 314 Mass. 351, 50 N.E.2d 59 (1943).

93. This is not necessarily so. For example, a contract to teach a course in Contracts could be looked upon as an entire contract.

94. See § 11–20(d) supra.

```
severable divisible  /s  contract  /s  "statute of limitation"
severable divisible  /s  "substantial! perform!"
divisible severable  /s  contract  /s  purpose
"progress payment"  /s  divisible
default! fail!  /s  pay***  paid payment  /s  divisible severable
"building contract"  /s  divisible indivisible severable
"employment contract"  /s  divisible indivisible severable
```

§ 11–24. Divisibility: Other Use of the Concept

The concept of divisibility is, perhaps, employed primarily in connection with the problem of whether a party in default may recover as discussed in the section immediately above. However, it is also used in other contexts. It is often used to determine whether a contract tainted with illegality can be severed into a legal and enforceable portion and an illegal and unenforceable portion.[95] The concept is also used to determine allocation of risks where performance of contractual duties in part becomes impossible.[96] The question of divisibility may be raised in connection with the running of the Statute of Limitations [97] and the applicability of the Statute of Frauds,[98] as well as with the question of whether the aggrieved party has one cause of action or several.[99]

Given the wide variety of contexts in which the question of divisibility is raised, it is fairly obvious that the contours of the concept will be reshaped to provide a just result in the particular context in which the concept is raised.[1]

 WESTLAW REFERENCES

```
contract*** agreement  /s  illegal! unlawful!  /s  divisib! indivisib!
    severab!
di("statute of limitation"  /p  contract*** agreement  /3  indivisib!
    divisib! severab! entire)
"statute of fraud"  /s  contract*** agreement  /3  indivisib! divisib!
    severab!
to(185)  /p  contract*** agreement  /3  indivisib! divisib! severab!
```

§ 11–25. Independent Promises

As we have seen, a promise is independent [2] (unconditional) if it is unqualified or if nothing but the lapse of time is necessary to make the

---

95. See § 22–6 infra. However, as we shall see, the word is not necessarily used in the same sense in which it is used here.

96. See Restatement, Contracts § 463; ch. 13 infra.

97. See Rich v. Arancio, 277 Mass. 310, 178 N.E. 743, Annot., 82 A.L.R. 313 (1931).

98. See United States Rubber Co. v. Bercher's Royal Tire Serv., Inc., 205 F.Supp. 368 (W.D.Ark.1962).

99. See Armstrong v. Illinois Bankers Life Ass'n, 217 Ind. 601, 29 N.E.2d 415, Annot., 131 A.L.R. 769 (1940), rehearing denied 217 Ind. 601, 29 N.E.2d 953 (1940).

1. Restatement, Second, Contracts § 240, Comment e.

2. The Restatements prefer not to use the term "independent promise." See Restatement, Second, Contracts § 231 Reporter's Note.

promise presently enforceable.[3] If a party makes an independent promise he must perform that promise even though the other party has not performed his part of the bargain.[4]

For example, A promises to build a house for B and B promises to pay X dollars when the house is completed. On this set of facts B's promise is constructively conditioned on A's performance. A must perform first.[5] He must perform before B is required to do anything. Thus, A's promise is, by definition, independent (unconditional) with the result that if A is guilty of a material breach, B may cancel and sue for a total breach despite his own non-performance. B need only prove that he would have been ready, willing and able to pay had A performed.[6] Even though A's promise is by definition independent, events may occur which would relieve him of his duty to perform his promise. For example, if B repudiated the contract A would not be obliged to perform.[7] In addition, promises which were originally independent may become conditional with the passage of time. For example, in a transaction for the sale and purchase of real property B agrees to pay the purchase price in three installments and S agrees to convey at the time of the payment of the final installment. It is clear that the buyer's promises to pay the first two installments are unconditional (independent) but that his promise to pay the last installment is concurrently conditional with the tendering of the deed.[8] However, if B has not paid the first two installments when the third installment becomes due, S may not, under the majority view, sue for the first two installments without tendering his deed or showing that such tender is excused.[9] Thus a promise which was originally unconditional, by definition becomes conditional, presumably in an attempt to do justice.[10]

Except in the type of case discussed above where one party by the terms of the contract must perform before the other, there is a strong presumption that a promise in a contract is not intended to be an independent promise "unless a contrary intention is clearly manifest-

---

3. See § 11–2 supra.

4. Orkin Exterminating Co. v. Harris, 224 Ga. 759, 164 S.E.2d 727 (1968); Orkin Exterminating Co. v. Gill, 222 Ga. 760, 152 S.E.2d 411 (1966); Guglielmi v. Guglielmi, ___ R.I. ___, 431 A.2d 1226 (1981); Hanks v. Gab Business Servs., Inc., 644 S.W.2d 707 (Tex.1982), reversing 626 S.W.2d 564 (Tex.App.1981). But cf. Kaye v. Orkin Exterminating Co., 472 F.2d 1213 (5th Cir. 1973); Associated Spring Corp. v. Roy F. Wilson & Avnet, 410 F.Supp. 967 (D.S.C.1976).

5. See § 11–17 supra.

6. See § 11–17. B's promise is constructively conditional upon A's substantial performance.

7. See § 12–8 infra.

8. Kane v. Hood, 30 Mass. (13 Pick.) 281 (1832).

9. See § 11–6 supra.

10. Jozovich Mfg. Co. v. Central California Berry Growers Ass'n, 183 Cal.App.2d 216, 6 Cal.Rptr. 617 (1960); Beecher v. Conradt, 13 N.Y. (3 Kern.) 108 (1855). But cf. Gray v. Meek, 199 Ill. 136, 64 N.E. 1020 (1902) (all but last installment may be recovered without tender). See also Restatement, Second, Contracts § 234, Comment d & ill. 8.

ed." [11] The result is that very few promises are looked upon as being independent.[12]

At times courts talk about a promise being "independent of" another promise. When they use this expression it does not relate to the definition of independent promises as discussed above. A few illustrations will make the point.

Williston [13] suggests a situation where A promises to deliver to B an automobile and to change a flat tire for B in exchange for B's promise to pay $3,500. It is clear that B's promise is conditional (not independent) because B's promise is constructively conditioned upon A's performance. However, since changing the tire is relatively trivial, delivery of the automobile would undoubtedly amount to substantial performance of the constructive condition.[14] If this is so then, in a sense, B's promise is "independent of" (not conditioned upon) A's promise to repair the tire. As indicated, this statement is unrelated to the definition of independent promise discussed above.[15]

Similarly the promise of an insurance company is always conditioned upon the insured event (e.g. fire) and thus its promise is conditional and not independent. At times the insured will make a promise to pay premiums. If the doctrine of constructive conditions applied, one would expect that the insurance company's obligation would be constructively conditioned on the payment of the premiums so that the insured could not recover if he did not pay the premium. However under the cases, the insured may recover even though he has not paid the premium because the promise of the insurance company is deemed to be "independent of" the payment of premiums.[16] It should be noted

---

11. Restatement, Second, Contracts § 232 and Comment a; K & G Constr. Co. v. Harris, 223 Md. 305, 164 A.2d 451 (1960).

12. Restatement, Second, Contracts § 232; Gold Bond Stamp Co. v. Gilt-Edge Stamps, 437 F.2d 27 (5th Cir.1971).

13. 6 Williston § 822.

14. It should again be pointed out that in determining substantial performance the question is not whether each promise is substantially performed but whether there is overall substantial performance. Restatement, Second, Contracts § 232, Comment b.

15. For a case with a similar problem that is decided differently, see Palmer v. Fox, 274 Mich. 252, 264 N.W. 361, Annot., 104 A.L.R. 1057 (1936); accord, on similar facts, De Bisschop v. Crump, 24 F.2d 807 (5th Cir.1928); Horowitz v. Bergen Assocs., Inc., 162 Misc. 430, 295 N.Y.S. 33 (1937) (purchasers were permitted to rescind and obtain restitution).

Contrary to the modern approach expressed in Palmer v. Fox, supra, the traditional view was that breach of a covenant which "goes only to part of the consideration on both sides" would not be deemed a failure of constructive condition. This was Rule 3 of the famous "Sergeant Williams' Rules" first published in an annotation to Pordage v. Cole, 1 Wm. Saund. 319 (1798). These rules are reprinted in 6 Williston § 820. Also illustrative of the modern approach is Tichnor Bros. v. Evans, 92 Vt. 278, 102 A. 1031 (1918) (sale of postcards to defendant with collateral promise not to sell similar cards to defendant's competitors; held breach of collateral promise did not "go to the essence" of the contract); cf. Brown v. Fraley, 222 Md. 480, 161 A.2d 128 (1960). Compare Specialties Dev. Corp. v. C–O–Two Fire Equip. Co., 207 F.2d 753 (3d Cir.1953), certiorari denied 347 U.S. 919, 74 S.Ct. 519, 98 L.Ed. 1074 (1954) (licensor of patent breached covenant to prosecute infringers; breach held to be material).

16. Dwelling-House Ins. Co. v. Hardie, 37 Kan. 674, 16 P. 92 (1887); Restatement, Contracts § 293. The Restatement Second achieves the same result on totally different reasoning. It states that the insurance company may terminate for non-payment

that this is not a question of substantial performance, but rather the courts simply refuse to apply the doctrine of constructive conditions, and thus the insured may sue the insurer upon its promise even though the insured has not paid the premiums. To avoid this result the insurance company may and does expressly condition its promise upon payment of the premium or includes a clause providing for cancellation in the event of nonpayment.

It is often stated that a lease is an illustration of a true independent promise.[17] A lease is a peculiar instrument. It acts as a conveyance of a leasehold interest in real property. Usually it also is a bilateral contract in which the tenant agrees to pay rent and the landlord agrees to make repairs. Courts have generally focused on the property rather than the contract aspects of the lease.[18] As a result of this orientation it has generally been held that the tenant's duty to pay is independent of the landlord's promise to repair or to provide services,[19] a result which contributed to the decay of urban housing and to the phenomenon of the "rent strike".[20] The rule is mitigated by holding that if the landlord's non-performance is extreme it may amount to a "constructive eviction" justifying cancellation of the lease by the tenant, and in recent years a number of courts have applied the contract rules of constructive conditions to leases.[21]

 WESTLAW REFERENCES

independent unconditional unqualif!	+ 1	promise agreement	/s	qualif!
independent unconditional	+ 1	promise agreement	/s	breach!
independent unconditional intent!	+ 1	promise agreement	/7	intend!
independent unconditional	+ 1	promise agreement	/s	lease

§ 11–26. Dependency of Separate Contracts

The discussion here relates to a situation where the parties have executed two contracts at substantially the same time. The question is whether the two agreements are unrelated or part of the same ex-

---

of premium but it must do so before the insured event occurs otherwise it will be deemed to have elected to continue the contract. Restatement, Second, Contracts § 379; see § 11–32 infra.

17. Restatement (Second) of Property, (Landlord & Tenant) § 7.1 Reporter's Note (1977) and Ch. 7 Introductory Note.

18. Rock County Sav. & Trust Co. v. Yost's, Inc., 36 Wis.2d 360, 153 N.W.2d 594 (1967); see also Restatement, Second, Contracts § 231, Comment e.

19. Restatement, Contracts § 290; Means v. Dierks, 180 F.2d 306 (10th Cir. 1950); Thomson-Houston Elec. Co. v. Durant Land Improvement Co., 144 N.Y. 34, 39 N.E. 7 (1894). This conclusion does not

prove that the tenant's promise is unconditional (independent) because tenant need not pay if the landlord does not have title.

20. See Simmons, Passion and Prudence: Rent Withholding under New York's Spiegel Law, 15 Buffalo L.Rev. 572 (1966).

21. Charles E. Burt, Inc. v. Seven Grand Corp., 340 Mass. 124, 163 N.E.2d 4 (1959); see McKinney's N.Y. Real Prop. Law § 235–b (providing that every lease contains a warranty of habitability); Quinn & Phillips, The Law of Landlord-Tenant: A Critical Evaluation of the Past With Guidelines For the Future, 38 Fordham L.Rev. 225 (1969).

change. If the two contracts are not part of the same exchange, a breach of one will have no effect on the other. If they are part of the same exchange, the question will be the over all materiality of the breach.[22] The cases state that this is a question of intention but normally lean to the notion that the making of two separate contracts ordinarily indicates an intent that a failure to perform one contract will have no effect on the other contract.[23]

 WESTLAW REFERENCES
separate /s independen! /s agreement contract***

C. EXCUSE OF CONDITION

Table of Sections

§ 11–27. Introduction

We have already seen that in an action for breach of contract a plaintiff has the burden of proving that he has performed all of the conditions precedent to the promise which plaintiff says was breached.[24] We have also seen that the very definition of condition embodied the notion that there are situations when a condition is excused.[25] This

---

22. Restatement, Contracts § 231, Comment d.

23. Rudman v. Cowles Communications, Inc., 30 N.Y.2d 1, 330 N.Y.S.2d 33, 280 N.E.2d 867 (1972). But see Bethea v. Investors Loan Corp., 197 A.2d 448

(D.C.1964); Star Credit Corp. v. Molina, 59 Misc.2d 290, 298 N.Y.S.2d 570 (Civ.Ct. 1969).

24. See § 11–7 supra.

25. See § 11–2 supra.

subdivision relates to that problem. In a general way it can be said that a condition will be excused when it would be unjust to insist upon the fulfillment of a condition, express or constructive.[26] Some of the reasons why a condition may be excused will now be discussed.[27]

§ 11–28. Wrongful Prevention and Wrongful Substantial Hindrance as an Excuse of Condition

The basic question presented here is may a plaintiff who has failed to perform a condition precedent to defendant's obligation recover on the contract when his failure to perform has been wrongfully prevented or wrongfully substantially hindered by the conduct of the defendant? Only the law of the jungle would say under such circumstances that plaintiff's failure to perform should not be excused.[28] Thus the major question here relates to what is wrongful conduct.[29] A single illustration will help clarify the problem under discussion.

In a well known case [30] plaintiff agreed to care for his granduncle until the uncle died in exchange for a payment to be made when his uncle died. Plaintiff was prevented from doing so when without cause he was ordered to leave. Plaintiff obviously could not prove that he had fulfilled the constructive condition precedent to the uncle's obligation to pay. However, he did rely upon a theory of excuse of condition and succeeded because the conduct of the uncle was clearly wrongful and prevented the condition from occurring.

The case raises a number of questions, some actual, some potential. The first is what does it mean when one says that a condition is excused? It means that even though the condition did not take place, the plaintiff may recover *on the contract* provided he can show that he would have been ready, willing and able to perform but for the prevention.[31] A recovery on the contract does not mean that the plaintiff will receive the amount called for by the contract. Thus, in the case involving the uncle the plaintiff would obtain a recovery diminished by what he could reasonably have earned by being freed from performing the remainder of the contract. However, if the condition which is excused is only an incident of performance, as for example, where a contractor is excused from producing an architect's certificate then, if the contractor has otherwise performed he is entitled to recover the amount called for in the contract.[32]

26. Hubler Rentals, Inc. v. Roadway Exp., Inc., 637 F.2d 257 (4th Cir.1981).

27. Propst Constr. Co. v. North Carolina Dep't of Transp., 56 N.C.App. 759, 290 S.E.2d 387 (1982). It might be observed that when a party elects to cancel the contract and sue for a total breach his failure to perform any further is excused by the material breach. The same is true of a repudiation. See § 12–3 infra.

28. Rohde v. Massachusetts Mutual Life Ins., 632 F.2d 667 (6th Cir.1980); Re-

statement, Second, Contracts § 245 and Comment a.

29. Restatement, Contracts § 315.

30. Barron v. Cain, 216 N.C. 282, 4 S.E.2d 618 (1939).

31. Restatement, Second, Contracts § 225, Comment c.

32. See § 11–37(c) infra.

Another potential question is when does wrongful conduct actually prevent the condition from occurring. Since this is not a problem in the case involving the uncle, a different problem will be used for purposes of illustration. H and W entered into an ante-nuptial agreement. H promised W that H's executor would pay her $20,000 at H's death, if she survived him. H killed W intentionally and deliberately. H is now dead. Is W's executor entitled to the $20,000?[33] It is clear that W's survival is an express condition precedent to the obligation to pay. It is equally clear that H's conduct was wrongful. The question raised is whether H's wrongful conduct was the proximate cause of W's failure to survive H. In other words would W, in the normal course of events, have survived H? Under the First Restatement the test was whether "the condition would have occurred * * * except for such prevention or hindrance."[34] The Restatement Second applies a more liberal approach. It states that the condition will be excused if the wrongful conduct "substantially contributed to the non-occurrence of the condition" and puts the burden of proof on this issue upon the defendant.[35]

As stated earlier in this section one of the difficult questions is what constitutes *wrongful* prevention or *wrongful* substantial hindrance.[36] A discussion of the two cases involving real estate brokers will help develop the problem. In Amies v. Wesnofske[37] plaintiff's right to a brokerage commission from the vendor was, by agreement conditioned "upon closing of title."[38] The vendee defaulted under the contract but the vendor took no legal action against the defaulting vendee and agreed with the vendee that the vendee was discharged from his duties under the contract in consideration of the vendor being permitted to retain the down payment. The broker insisted that he was entitled to the commission, arguing that the occurrence of the condition was excused because of the vendor's failure to bring an action for specific performance against the vendee. Such an action was incumbent upon the vendor, he argued, because the seller was obliged to bring an action for specific performance. This would bring about the

---

33. These are the basic facts in the case of Foreman State Trust Sav. Bank v. Tauber, 348 Ill. 280, 180 N.E. 827 (1932).

34. Restatement, Contracts § 295.

35. Restatement, Second, Contracts § 245, Comment b and ill. 5. The actual case did not discuss this problem.

36. The Restatement Second states the rule of this section in terms of a wrongful failure to cooperate. As a practical matter there does not appear to be any difference between wrongful prevention and wrongful failure to cooperate. In other words wrongful prevention implies a wrongful failure to cooperate. See St. Louis Dressed Beef & Provision Co. v. Maryland Cas. Co., 201 U.S. 173, 26 S.Ct. 400, 50 L.Ed. 712 (1906).

37. 255 N.Y. 156, 174 N.E. 436, Annot., 73 A.L.R. 918 (1931).

38. When this condition is not imposed by the contract the broker is entitled to his commission when the buyer and seller execute a contract in which all of the terms customarily encountered in such a transaction are agreed upon and the broker's efforts are the efficient cause of the sale; that is to say, when the broker produces a buyer who is ready, willing and able to buy. Turner v. Minasian, 358 Mass. 425, 265 N.E.2d 371 (1970); Kaelin v. Warner, 27 N.Y.2d 352, 267 N.E.2d 86, 318 N.Y.S.2d 294 (1971). The purchaser is not ordinarily liable to the broker. Geller v. New England Indus., Inc., 535 F.2d 1381 (2d Cir. 1976); Annot., 30 A.L.R.3d 1395 (1970).

closing of title. The court held that the seller was not guilty of wrongful conduct in failing to bring an action for specific performance.[39] Under the terminology of the Second Restatement seller's duty to cooperate did not extend to bringing an action for specific performance. The broker would be entitled to his commission, however, if the seller agreed with the buyer to rescind the contract when there had been no breach on the part of the buyer.[40] In other words this would amount to wrongful conduct.

When a court will say that there is wrongful prevention does not depend upon any mechanical rule. Rather the court's instinct for the commercial setting, the ethical position of the parties, the probable understanding that they would have reached had they considered the matter and many other factors enter into the determination.[41]

Let us compare two other cases which raise some of the same problems discussed above with some additional wrinkles.

In Patterson v. Meyerhofer,[42] plaintiff agreed to sell real property to the defendant. Plaintiff informed defendant that he did not have title to the property and expected to acquire it at a foreclosure sale. The defendant outbid the plaintiff at the foreclosure sale. Two results followed from the wrongful prevention of the defendant. First plaintiff was excused from his inability to convey because of wrongful prevention; and second since his inability to convey was excused he could force the defendant to respond in damages.[43]

The other case to be discussed is Iron Trade Products Co. v. Wilkoff Co.[44] In that case plaintiff entered into a contract with the defendant for the purchase of 2600 tons of section relaying rails. Defendant failed to deliver and alleges as a defense that the supply of such rails was very limited and that the plaintiff during the term of the contract bought and agreed to buy large quantities of rails from the two parties from whom defendant was obliged to buy thus enhancing the price. The defendant was seeking to be excused from his promise to sell the rails

---

39. Ellsworth Dobbs, Inc. v. Johnson, 50 N.J. 528, 236 A.2d 843 (1967); Beattie-Firth, Inc. v. Colebank, 143 W.Va. 740, 105 S.E.2d 5, Annot., 74 A.L.R.2d 431 (1958); see also Barbetta Agency v. Sciaraffa, 135 N.J.Super. 488, 343 A.2d 770 (App.Div. 1975). Contra, Tarbell v. Bomes, 48 R.I. 86, 135 A. 604, Annot., 51 A.L.R. 1386 (1927). A seller will normally be liable to the broker when he refuses to convey without cause. Westhill Exports, Ltd. v. Pope, 12 N.Y.2d 491, 240 N.Y.S.2d 961, 191 N.E. 2d 447 (1963).

40. Cf. Levy v. Lacey, 22 N.Y.2d 271, 292 N.Y.S.2d 455, 239 N.E.2d 378 (1968).

41. Patterson, Constructive Conditions in Contracts, 42 Colum.L.Rev. 903, 928–42 (1942).

42. 204 N.Y. 96, 97 N.E. 472 (1912).

43. Kehm Corp. v. United States, 93 F.Supp. 620 (Ct.Cl.1950) (the government failed to supply the proper tail assemblies for bombs to be made by the plaintiff); Suburban Land Co. v. Brown, 237 Mass. 166, 129 N.E. 291 (1921); Bruson Heights Corp. v. State, 281 App.Div. 371, 120 N.Y.S.2d 73 (3d Dep't 1953) (owner was to select fixtures for the building); Levicoff v. Richard I. Rubin & Co., 413 Pa. 134, 196 A.2d 359 (1964) (lessee neglected to provide plans for store which lessor was to build). So also it is generally held that a general contractor must take reasonable measures to insure that his subcontractor is not delayed. McGrath v. Electrical Constr. Co., 230 Or. 295, 364 P.2d 604 (1961).

44. 272 Pa. 172, 116 A. 150 (1922).

and was arguing that the wrongful prevention gave him a defense that excused his promise.[45] The court held that the defendant did not have a defense because plaintiff's conduct was not wrongful since this was a foreseeable commercial risk which the defendant assumed.[46] If the defendant assumed this risk plaintiff's conduct could not be wrongful.[47]

The result would be different if plaintiff, buyer, exhausted what he knows to be the seller's only source of supply. In that situation, as in the Patterson case supra, defendant would have a defense and also, as in that case could compel the plaintiff to respond in damages.

 WESTLAW REFERENCES
perform! /s wrongful! /2 hinder! hindrance prevent!
95k303(4) /p excus!
wrongful! /s excus! /2 condition
recover! /s excus! /2 condition
di("wrongful! prevent!" /s contract*** agreement)
patterson meyerhofer /s prevent!

§ 11–29. Excuse of Condition by Waiver, Estoppel and Election

(a) Introduction

These three concepts arise in many contexts in the fabric of the law. Here we are concerned with these concepts only as they relate to excuse of contractual conditions. We also briefly consider here the topic of renunciation of a right to damages for partial or total breach.[48]

(b) Estoppel Defined

The doctrine being discussed here is equitable estoppel which is also known as estoppel *in pais*. It is in fact a progenitor of the doctrine of promissory estoppel discussed above.[49] In its traditional form the doctrine of equitable estoppel states that a party (1) who is guilty of a misrepresentation of existing fact including concealment, (2) upon which the other party justifiably relies, (3) to his injury, is estopped from denying his utterances or acts to the detriment of the other party.[50]

The courts have struggled with the meaning of the word misrepresentation in this context. There is a substantial body of law to the effect that not only must the representation be false but that the party to be estopped must be shown to have known that the representation was false. In addition, under this view it must be shown that the party to be estopped must have intended that the representation be acted

---

45. See Ch. 13 infra.

46. See also United States v. Fidelity & Deposit Co. of Maryland, 152 Fed. 596 (2d Cir.1907); 6 Corbin § 1264; 5 Williston §§ 677–77A.

47. Restatement, Second, Contracts § 245, Comment a.

48. See § 11–33 infra.

49. See Ch. 6 supra.

50. 1 Williston § 139.

upon or at least must so act that the party asserting the estoppel has a right to believe that it was so intended.[51]

Contrary to the traditional view of equitable estoppel some of the more modern cases are stating that a misrepresentation of fact is not necessary for the doctrine to apply.[52] A promise is sufficient to form the basis of an equitable estoppel.[53] Under this view actual fraud, bad faith or intent to deceive is not essential.[54]

Once it is decided that a promise may be the basis of an equitable estoppel it becomes more difficult to distinguish equitable estoppel from promissory estoppel. For example, if a party promised before breach to accept a late payment he would be estopped from asserting the lateness of the payment unless the promise was withdrawn in time.[55] It should be observed that here a promise is being enforced even though there is no consideration for it.[56] This is a species of promissory estoppel except that the term promissory estoppel is ordinarily used in reference to the *formation* of a contract and not to the *performance* of a contract.[57] The ultimate point being made is that this promise is effective upon a theory of estoppel whether it be denominated equitable or promissory.[58]

It is often stated that equitable estoppel is an affirmative defense that must be established by clear and convincing evidence and that its

51. Beverage v. Harvey, 602 F.2d 657 (4th Cir.1979); Strong v. County of Santa Cruz, 15 Cal.3d 720, 125 Cal.Rptr. 896, 543 P.2d 264 (1975); Bettendorf Education Ass'n v. Bettendorf Community, 262 N.W.2d 550 (Iowa 1978); County of Scott's Bluff v. Hughes, 202 Neb. 551, 276 N.W.2d 206 (1979); Albuquerque National Bank v. Albuquerque Ranch Estates, Inc., 99 N.M. 95, 654 P.2d 548 (1982).

52. A misrepresentation of fact includes admission and silence when there is a duty to speak. Stratmann v. Stratmann, 6 Kan. App.2d 403, 628 P.2d 1080 (1981); Wynn v. Farmers Ins. Group, 98 Mich.App. 93, 296 N.W.2d 197 (1980); Cheqer, Inc. v. Painters and Decorators Joint Committee, Inc., 98 Nev. 609, 655 P.2d 996 (1982); In re Allstate Ins. Co., 179 N.J.Super. 581, 432 A.2d 1366 (1981); Williams v. Stansbury, 649 S.W.2d 293 (Tex.1983). See § 9–20 supra.

53. Novelty Knitting Mills, Inc. v. Siskind, 500 Pa. 432, 457 A.2d 502 (1983).

54. Arctic Contractors, Inc. v. State, 564 P.2d 30 (Alaska 1977) appeal after remand 573 P.2d 1385 (Alaska 1978); Town of West Hartford v. Rechel, 190 Conn. 114, 459 A.2d 1015 (1983); Pino v. Maplewood Packing Co., 375 A.2d 534 (Me.1977); Addressograph—Multigraph Corp. v. Zink, 273 Md. 277, 329 A.2d 28 (1974); Triple Cities Const. Co. v. Maryland Cas. Co., 4 N.Y.2d 443, 176 N.Y.S.2d 292, 151 N.E.2d 856 (1958).

55. Dreier v. Sherwood, 77 Colo. 539, 238 P. 38 (1925); see U.C.C. § 2–209(5).

56. The explanation for this result and the limitations placed upon it are explained in § 11–31 infra.

57. Williams v. FNBC Acceptance Corp., 419 So.2d 1363 (Ala.1982); B.F. Goodrich Co. v. Parker, 282 Ala. 151, 209 So.2d 647 (1967); Morgan v. Maryland Cas. Co., 458 S.W.2d 789 (Ky.1970); Leonard v. Sav-a-Stop Services, Inc., 289 Md. 204, 424 A.2d 336 (1981); Perkins v. Kerby, 308 So. 2d 914 (Miss.1975); Clark & Enerson v. Schimmel Hotels, 194 Neb. 810, 235 N.W.2d 870 (1975); Commonwealth, Dep't of Public Welfare v. School Dist. of Philadelphia, 49 Pa.Cmwlth. 316, 410 A.2d 1311 (1980); Klinke v. Famous Recipe Fried Chicken Inc., 94 Wn.2d 255, 616 P.2d 644 (1980).

58. Moline I.F.C. Finance Inc. v. Soucinek, 91 Ill.App.2d 257, 234 N.E.2d 57 (1968); Arrow Lathing & Plastering Inc. v. Schaulat Plumbing Supply Co., 83 Ill.App. 2d 394, 228 N.E.2d 209 (1967); Dart v. Thompson, 261 Iowa 237, 154 N.W.2d 82 (1967); American Bank & Trust Co. v. Trinity Universal Ins. Co., 251 La. 445, 205 So.2d 35 (1967); Triple Cities Const. Co. v. Maryland Cas. Co., 4 N.Y.2d 443, 176 N.Y.S.2d 292, 151 N.E.2d 856 (1958).

existence is ordinarily a question of fact.[59] In addition it should be observed that the rules of equitable estoppel are applied somewhat differently to a government.[60]

(c) Waiver and Election

A waiver is defined as a voluntary and intentional relinquishment of a known right.[61] The general notion is that the party waiving must have actual knowledge of the facts giving rise to the right he waives.[62] His knowledge of the law is immaterial.[63] Whether and to what extent a waiver is effective is the subject matter of the next three sections. These sections examine waiver contemporaneous with the formation of the contract, waiver after formation of the contract but before failure of condition and waiver after failure of condition. It is a waiver after failure of condition that is referred to as an election. Waiver is also ordinarily a question of fact.[64] A waiver may be express or implied.[65]

 WESTLAW REFERENCES

(b) *Estoppel Defined*

di estop!

"equitable estoppel" /2 define* definition

156k52 /p "estoppel in pais"

"equitabl! estop!" /s misrepresent!

"equitabl! estop!" /s promise* promising

"equitabl! estop!" /s "duty to speak"

"equitabl! estop!" /s "promissor! estop!"

"promissor! estop!" /s formation

"equitabl! estop!" /s question /2 fact***

"equitabl! estop!" /s affirmative! /2 defense defend** defending

(c) *Waiver and Election*

di waiver

waiv! /s voluntar! /s relinquish!

waiv! /s question /2 fact***

59. Coachmen Indus., Inc. v. Security Trust & Sav. Bank, 329 N.W.2d 648 (Iowa 1983); Stevan v. Brown, 54 Md.App. 235, 458 A.2d 466 (1983); Mundy v. Arcuri, 165 W.Va. 128, 267 S.E.2d 454 (1980). However there are recent cases saying that equitable estoppel may be the basis of a cause of action as is true of promissory estoppel. Janke Construction Co. v. Vulcan, 527 F.2d 772 (7th Cir.1976).

60. See, e.g., Saltzman, Estoppel Against the Government: Have Recent Decisions Rounded the Corners of the Agent's Authority Problem In Federal Procurements, 45 Fordham L.Rev. 497 (1976).

61. Realty Growth Investors v. Council of Unit Owners, 453 A.2d 450 (Del.1982); Babb's, Inc. v. Babb, 169 N.W.2d 211 (Iowa 1969); Cohler v. Smith, 280 Minn. 181, 158 N.W.2d 574 (1968).

62. Mobley v. Estate of Parker, 278 Ark. 37, 642 S.W.2d 883 (1982); Realty Growth Investors v. Council of Unit Owners, 453 A.2d 450 (Del.1982); Alsen's Americal Portland Cement Works v. Degnon Constr. Co., 222 N.Y. 34, 118 N.E. 210 (1917). The Restatement states that the promisor must know or have reason to know. Restatement, Second, Contracts § 93.

63. Restatement, Second, Contracts § 93.

64. Riverside Development Co. v. Ritchie, 103 Idaho 515, 650 P.2d 657 (1982); Travelers Indem. Co. v. Fields, 317 N.W.2d 176 (Iowa 1982).

65. Goldenberg v. Corporate Air, Inc. 189 Conn. 504, 457 A.2d 296 (1983); James v. Mitchell, 159 Ga.App. 761, 285 S.E.2d 222 (1981).

§ 11–30. Waiver Contemporaneous With the Formation of the Contract

If an insurance policy provides that the policy is void if the same property is covered by other insurance and an authorized agent "waives" this condition by a statement contemporaneous with the issuance of the policy it is clear that the issue is one of the admissibility of evidence of this promise (waiver) under the parol evidence rule. There is no consideration problem because that promise is supported by the same consideration as supports the other promises of the insurance company.   Under the parol evidence rule it would appear that the policy was a total integration and that the oral promise contradicts the integration.   A minority of the courts have followed this logic.[66]   A majority, however, on a variety of theories, especially on the grounds of equitable estoppel have held that the parol evidence rule does not bar proof of the "waiver".[67] Other cases have proceeded on the theory that reformation of the instrument is available even in an action at law.[68]

Whatever the analytic grounds which may be advanced to support these cases, it is clear that the courts have been influenced by the relative bargaining positions of the parties and have attempted to mitigate the "take it or leave it" nature of printed form policies.[69] Statutory enactments in a number of states have put this problem on a new basis. The power of the insurer is reduced by requiring the policy to conform to statutory standard; at the same time, the insured's right to rely on oral waivers is removed or severely restricted.[70]

This theory of "waiver" has also been applied in non-insurance cases but much more sparingly. A good illustration is the case of Ehret Co. v. Eaton, Yale & Towne, Inc.[71] In that case a franchisee (A) is presented by B (franchisor) with a written franchise agreement that contains a 30 day termination clause. A balked at the termination provision but signed it after B orally promised A that A could rely on

66. Lumber Underwriters of New York v. Rife, 237 U.S. 605, 35 S.Ct. 717, 59 L.Ed. 1140 (1915); Northern Assurance Co. v. Grand View Bldg. Ass'n, 183 U.S. 308, 22 S.Ct. 133, 46 L.Ed. 213 (1902); see 5 Williston §§ 748–49.

67. See 5 Williston § 750 (collecting cases). Note that the estoppel here is promissory in nature. This once again demonstrates that promissory estoppel is not merely a substitute for consideration, since the "waiver" is supported by consideration.

68. Wilhide v. Keystone Ins. Co., 195 F.Supp. 659 (M.D.Pa.1961); Grand View Bldg. Ass'n v. Northern Assurance Co., 73 Neb. 149, 102 N.W. 246 (1905), affirmed

203 U.S. 106, 27 S.Ct. 27, 51 L.Ed. 109 (1906). For the availability of reformation at law, see Restatement, Contracts § 507.

69. See 5 Williston § 747.

70. Metropolitan Life Ins. Co. v. Alterovitz, 214 Ind. 186, 14 N.E.2d 570, Annot., 117 A.L.R. 770 (1938); Johnson v. Mutual Benefit Health & Accident Ass'n, 5 A.D.2d 103, 168 N.Y.S.2d 879 (3d Dep't 1957), resettled 6 A.D.2d 947, 176 N.Y.S.2d 250 (3d Dep't 1958), modified 5 N.Y.2d 1031, 185 N.Y.S.2d 552, 158 N.E.2d 251 (1959); see 5 Williston § 750A.

71. 523 F.2d 280 (7th Cir.1975), certiorari denied 425 U.S. 943, 96 S.Ct. 1683, 48 L.Ed.2d 186.

fair treatment in this respect. Under the parol evidence rule this evidence would be excluded except possibly under the doctrine of promissory fraud. The court allowed the evidence upon a theory of "waiver". Again, however, the basis of the decision is estoppel, whether equitable or promissory.[72]

§ 11–31. Waiver Before Failure of Condition but After Formation of the Contract

In the case of an express condition in this context one is talking about a waiver before an express condition fails to occur. A constructive condition fails only when it is no longer possible to render substantial performance. Thus while substantial performance is still possible a constructive condition has not failed.

There are three important rules to remember with respect to a waiver of a condition before failure of condition. The most important rule is that a waiver of a material part of the agreed exchange is ineffective.[73] In other words only an immaterial part of the agreed exchange may be waived. Examples of an immaterial part of the agreed exchange are conditions which merely fix the time or manner of performance or provide for giving notice or the supplying of proofs.[74] Thus if A agreed to paint B's house and B promised to pay $1,000 and immediately after the promise was made B promised to pay $1,000 even if A did not perform, the waiver would not be effective because there is an attempt to waive a material part of the agreed exchange. Any other result would completely subvert the policy underlying the doctrine of consideration—a matter to be discussed in more detail below. So also if A for a consideration promises to pay $1,000 if B's house burns and then promises to pay even if B's house does not burn, there is an attempted waiver of a condition which is material to the risk, that is to say a material part of the agreed exchange and thus the waiver is ineffective.[75]

The second rule is that even if an immaterial part of the agreed exchange is waived the waiver may be withdrawn or modified if the withdrawal or modification does not operate unfairly.[76] Thus, if A agrees to complete a structure for B by Jan. 1 and time is made of the essence and B, before there is a failure of condition, waives the Jan. 1 deadline by a promise that the work may be completed later, such a waiver is effective because for this purpose the completion date is not

72. See, e.g., Miller v. Lawlor, 245 Iowa 1144, 66 N.W.2d 267 (1954).

73. Restatement, Second, Contracts § 84, Comment c; Restatement, Contracts § 297, Comment c; Rennie & Laughlin, Inc. v. Chrysler Corp., 242 F.2d 208 (9th Cir.1957); Industrial Machinery, Inc. v. Creative Displays, 344 So.2d 743 (Ala. 1977).

74. Restatement, Second, Contracts § 84, Comment d; Spaulding v. McCaige, 47 Or.App. 129, 614 P.2d 594 (1980).

75. Restatement, Second, Contracts § 84, ill. 1.

76. 3A Corbin § 752; Restatement, Second, Contracts § 84, Comment f; Imperator Realty Co. v. Tull, 228 N.Y. 447, 127 N.E. 263 (1920).

deemed to be a material part of the agreed exchange.[77] As a matter of fairness the limitation once waived may be reimposed if there has been no change of position in reliance upon the waiver; and even if there has been such reliance a new limitation may be set by B, provided that a reasonable time is allowed.[78] Even if B sets no time limit, performance within a reasonable time from the time of the waiver is still required.[79]

The third rule is that the condition being waived must be solely for the benefit of the party waiving it.[80] At times it is difficult to determine whether the condition is for the benefit of the party waiving it or is for the benefit of the other party or what is more likely for the benefit of both parties. If it is for the benefit of both parties then it cannot be unilaterally waived by either party.[81]

As indicated above, a word should be said about the relationship between a waiver and a modification. As we have seen a modification requires offer and acceptance and consideration or a statutory equivalent of consideration or injurious reliance.[82] A waiver, as indicated above, is ordinarily unilateral in character. However, to be effective a waiver of an immaterial part of the agreed exchange need not be supported by consideration, etc.[83] Thus the doctrine of waiver is an exception to the doctrine of consideration but it is a very limited exception because the exception relates only to an immaterial part of the agreed exchange. It should also be pointed out that if there is a binding modification the parties are not free to terminate the modification except by mutual agreement, whereas in the case of an effective waiver the party waiving may withdraw the waiver if the withdrawal does not operate unfairly.

77. 3A Corbin § 756. It is, of course, true that failure to perform on time when there is a time of the essence clause would amount to a material breach. However, for the purpose of waiver, time, as we have seen, is an immaterial part of the agreed exchange. In other words in waiving the time of the essence clause B is not waiving any of the work agreed upon.

78. Restatement, Second, Contracts § 84 and Comment f; U.C.C. § 2–209(5). "A party who has made a waiver effecting an executory portion of the contract may retract the waiver by reasonable notification received by the other party that strict performance will be required of any term waived, unless the retraction would be unjust in view of a material change of position in reliance on the waiver." See also Salvatore v. Trace, 109 N.J.Super. 83, 262 A.2d 409 (1969), affirmed 55 N.J. 362, 262 A.2d 385 (1970).

79. 3A Corbin § 756. It should be noted that ordinarily a waiver of condition does not amount to a renunciation of a right to damages for breach. See § 11–33 infra.

80. Brotman v. Raelofs, 70 Mich.App. 719, 246 N.W.2d 368 (1976). Bliss v. Carter, 26 Mich.App. 177, 182 N.W.2d 54 (1970); Goebel v. First Federal Sav. & Loan Ass'n of Racine, 83 Wis.2d 668, 266 N.W.2d 352 (1978).

81. Wallstreet Properties, Inc. v. Gassner, 53 Or.App. 650, 632 P.2d 1310 (1981).

82. See Chs. 4, 5 and 6 supra.

83. Nassau Trust Co. v. Montrose Concrete Products, 56 N.Y.2d 175, 451 N.Y.S.2d 663, 436 N.E.2d 1265 (1982), reargument denied 57 N.Y.2d 674, 454 N.Y.S. 2d 1032, 439 N.E.2d 1247 (1982); Wachovia Bank & Trust Co., N.A. v. Rubish, 306 N.C. 417, 293 S.E.2d 749 (1982), rehearing denied 306 N.C. 753, 302 S.E.2d 884 (1982).

Another problem in this area is the effect of repeated waivers. It has been held that repeated progress payments made by the owner to the contractor prior to performance of the condition requiring payment will not prevent the owner from insisting upon fulfillment of the condition precedent to the next progress payment.[84] At times, however, the repeated waivers may be such as to cause the contractor justifiably to change his position so that a demand for compliance with future conditions would be manifestly unjust. In such a case an estoppel will be raised against the owner and he will be held to have effectively waived his right to insist upon compliance with future conditions of the same kind, unless a reasonable period of notice is granted that strict compliance will be demanded.[85]

Ultimately, the question of whether repeated waivers are effective as to future performances depends upon whether the other party justifiably believes that subsequent performances will be accepted in spite of similar defects.[86] Another question is how repeated waivers are effected by a "no waiver" clause. In such a case it would appear that the issue would still be justifiable reliance.[87]

It should also be noted that repeated waivers may constitute a course of performance and thus operate as a modification.[88] In most cases there would not be consideration to support the modification.[89] However under the Code a modification is binding without consideration.[90]

 WESTLAW REFERENCES

waiv! /s executory /s contract*** agreement /s retract!

contract /s condition /s waiv! /s benefit!

"repeat! waiv!" /s contract*** agreement perform!

§ 11–32. Waiver After Failure of Condition: Election

The word election implies making a choice between two inconsistent courses of action. Here we are discussing a right of election when there has been a material breach of a constructive condition or a failure

---

84. Cases are collected in 3A Corbin § 754 n. 13. Waiver by a road commission of a condition in one contract with the plaintiff does not estop the commission from insisting upon compliance with a similar condition in another contract. W.P. Harlin Const. Co. v. Utah State Road Commission, 19 Utah 2d 364, 431 P.2d 792 (1967). Making payments on the purchase of an interest in real property prior to delivery of a deed does not waive the condition of delivery as to future payments. Gail v. Gail, 127 App.Div. 892, 112 N.Y.S. 96 (4th Dep't 1908).

85. Kummli v. Myers, 400 F.2d 774 (D.C.Cir.1968) (mortgagee who has consistently waived lateness of payments may

not without prior reasonable notice refuse a late payment and institute foreclosure proceedings); Fox v. Grange, 261 Ill. 116, 103 N.E. 576 (1913); Stinemeyer v. Wesco Farms, Inc., 260 Or. 109, 487 P.2d 65 (1971). Additional cases are collected in 3A Corbin § 754 n. 15.

86. Restatement, Second, Contracts § 247; Iversen v. Kiger, 480 Or.App. 873, 617 P.2d 1386 (1980).

87. 5 Williston, § 765.

88. See § 3–17 supra.

89. See § 4–2 supra.

90. See § 5–14 supra; U.C.C. § 2–209(1).

to literally perform an express condition. Two illustrations will help to explain the concept.

Assume first a case in which A, in England, promises to charter a vessel to B who is in the United States and who promises to pay when the vessel arrives in the United States. B insists that the vessel must sail from England "on or before Feb. 4" and causes an express condition precedent to that effect to be included in the agreement. The vessel sails on Feb. 5th. Since the express condition has not been literally performed, A may elect to terminate the contract. On the other hand, he may elect to pay the money and continue with the contract.[91]

The second illustration relates to a constructive condition that arises out of a bilateral contract. A, a contractor, who has promised to erect a structure for B at some point is no longer able to render substantial performance and thus simultaneously is guilty of a material breach. B may elect to terminate the contract and sue for a total breach or continue with the contract and sue for a partial breach.[92]

An election may be shown by promise or by conduct.[93] Conduct basically will take one of two forms. One, where the innocent party continues his own performance after failure of condition (e.g. the Feb. 4th case above), the other where he allows the other party to continue his performance after there has been a material breach (e.g. the construction case).[94]

An important question is whether an election once made may be withdrawn. Under the majority view an election once made may not be withdrawn and this is so even though the other party has not relied on the choice made.[95] Many of cases included in the majority view are cases involving insurance companies.[96] Under a minority view (which is consistent with the rule on waiver discussed above) the election may be withdrawn if it would be fair to do so.[97]

In the case involving the contractor above if the contractor failed to perform on time and this amounted to a material breach and the owner elected to continue the contract it is clear that the contractor would still have to perform within a reasonable time or that the owner could reimpose a reasonable time or in a proper case set a reasonable date and make time of the essence.[98] Note the similar discussion in the topic of waiver before failure of condition.[99]

91. See § 11–18(a) supra.

92. § 11–18(a) supra.

93. Stephens v. West Pontiac-GMC, Inc., 7 Ark.App. 275, 647 S.W.2d 492 (1983), appeal after remand ___ Ark.App. ___, ___ S.W.2d ___ (1985), Restatement, Contracts § 309; 3A Corbin § 755.

94. S.S. Steiner Inc. v. Hill, 191 Or. 391, 230 P.2d 537 (1951); Restatement, Second, Contracts § 84.

95. Restatement, Second, Contracts § 84.

96. Restatement, Second, Contracts § 84, Comment d.

97. Restatement, Contracts § 309. Schenectady Steel Co. v. Bruno Trimpoli General Const. Co., 43 A.D.2d 234, 350 N.Y.S.2d 920 (3d Dep't 1974), affirmed 34 N.Y.2d 939, 359 N.Y.S.2d 560, 316 N.E.2d 875 (1974).

98. See § 11–31 supra.

99. See § 11–31 supra.

In the topic of waiver we discussed the effect of repeated waivers.[1] A similar problem arises in the area of an election where a party makes repeated elections to continue the contract when he could elect otherwise. The results in the election cases parallel the results in the waiver cases.[2] This is also true of a "no-election" clause.[3]

In the case of a waiver of condition *before* failure of condition we saw that the rule is that all that can be waived is an immaterial part of the agreed exchange. In the case of an election after a material breach may the non-breaching party "elect" to perform, for example, pay, despite the material breach? Professor Farnsworth suggests that the answer to this question is in the affirmative, "since the injured party will be compensated for the breach" in an action for partial breach.[4] What the injured party is doing is electing to pay even though there is not substantial performance. In any event, since the injured party can collect damages for partial breach for the unperformed portion he is not "electing" to eliminate a material part of the agreed exchange by way of gift. An election to eliminate a material part of the agreed exchange by way of gift should be ineffective in the absence of consideration or its equivalent because if this could be done it would subvert the doctrine of consideration.[5]

An illustration of this situation arises when a party elects to pay despite a material breach in a case when a builder contracts to build a structure on the owner's property. Assume a case where the owner, despite a material breach known to him, moves into the structure. In such a case, unlike a case involving the sale of goods,[6] the owner does not lose his right to sue for a total breach because in moving in he does not concede that there is substantial performance simply by the retention of the defective performance. He is still able to sue for a material breach. This is so because the defective performance is attached to the owner's property and cannot be removed without material injury.[7] The situation is somewhat different if the owner manifests an intent to pay the contract price despite the existence of these known defects. In that event he is electing to pay despite the material breach and is limited to an action for partial breach. The owner is still free to show that

1. See § 11–31 supra.

2. 3A Corbin § 754; W.P. Harlin Const. Co. v. Utah State Road Commission, 19 Utah 2d 364, 431 P.2d 792 (1967); Porter v. Harrington, 262 Mass. 203, 159 N.E. 530 (1928). This is so even though time is of the essence. Heinzman v. Howard, 348 N.W.2d 147 (S.D.1984), appeal after remand 366 N.W.2d 500 (S.D.1985).

3. See, e.g., Westinghouse Credit Corp. v. Shelton, 645 F.2d 869 (10th Cir.1981); Porter v. Harrington, 262 Mass. 203, 159 N.E. 530 (1928).

4. Farnsworth, Contracts § 8.19 at 621.

5. See the discussion of the parallel problem in the preceding section. But see § 11–33 and § 21–12 infra.

6. In a case involving sale of goods if the buyer accepts them knowing of the defects that would entitle him to reject them he must pay the price and is limited to his action for partial breach. See § 11–20 supra.

7. Cawley v. Weiner, 236 N.Y. 357, 140 N.E. 724 (1923); Nees v. Weaver, 222 Wis. 492, 269 N.W. 266 (1936); Restatement, Second, Contracts § 246(2).

defects of which he was justifiably not aware [8] gave rise to a material breach so as to allow an action for total breach.[9]

 WESTLAW REFERENCES

di(waiv! /s elect*** /s breach! /s contract)

porter +2 harrington

build! property /s agreement contract /s breach! /s elect***
    /s pay*** payment paid

---

§ 11–33. Election to Continue Contract Despite Material Breach Does Not Amount to a Renunciation of Damages

We have seen that an immaterial breach does not justify the non-breaching party in terminating the contract but that he is entitled to sue for a partial breach.[10] We have also seen that in the case of a material breach one option open to the aggrieved party is to elect to continue the contract and sue for a partial breach.[11]

The point being made here is that a material failure to perform a constructive condition also amounts to a material breach and an election to continue with the contract does not foreclose a suit for a partial breach. For example, if a building contract contains a promise by the contractor that the structure will be completed by January 1 and time is made of the essence, failure to complete by January 1 is a failure of an express condition and simultaneously is a material breach. If the work is not finished on January 1, and the owner allows the contractor to continue with the work and he subsequently finishes the work within a reasonable time from the time of the election, the owner is still entitled to sue for a partial breach because of the late completion.[12] It should be pointed out, however, that the language or conduct of the aggrieved party may indicate not only an election to continue the contract but also a renunciation of rights to damages.[13]

The Uniform Commercial Code has two provisions that apply to the issue being analyzed. One provision requires a buyer to give notice of

---

8. Ting Wan Liang v. Malawista, 70 A.D.2d 415, 421 N.Y.S.2d 594 (2d Dep't 1979).

9. Restatement, Second, Contracts § 246, ill. 7.

10. See § 11–18(a) supra.

11. See § 11–18(a) supra.

12. Phillips & Colby Const. Co. v. Seymour, 91 U.S. (Otto) 646, 23 L.Ed. 341 (1875); Federal Welding Serv., Inc. v. Dioguardi, 295 F.2d 882 (2d Cir.1961); Glen Cove Marina, Inc. v. Vessel Little Jennie, 269 F.Supp. 877 (E.D.N.Y.1967); Barton v. Morin, 281 Mass. 98, 183 N.E. 170 (1932); Dunn v. Steubing, 120 N.Y. 232, 24 N.E. 315 (1890). Contra Minneapolis Threshing Mach. Co. v. Hutchins, 65 Minn. 89, 67 N.W. 807 (1896). The distinction between waiver of condition and discharge of a right to damages is sometimes lost sight of. See Western Transmission Corp. v. Colorado Mainline, Inc., 376 F.2d 470 (10th Cir. 1967), where the court, although reaching a correct result, assumed that plaintiff's continued acceptance of defendant's performance after breach ordinarily results in a waiver of a right to damages. The court found a supposed exception to this supposed rule. For sounder analyses, see Sitlington v. Fulton, 281 F.2d 552 (10th Cir.1960); Robberson Steel Co. v. Harrell, 177 F.2d 12 (10th Cir.1949).

13. See § 21–12 infra.

breach or "be barred from any remedy."[14]   This has already been discussed.[15]   The other permits a renunciation of damages without any consideration provided that the renunciation is "signed and delivered by the aggrieved party".[16]   This section has already been mentioned.[17] Whether or not it represents a codification of common law or a departure from common law will be discussed subsequently.[18]

WESTLAW REFERENCES

elect*** /s continu! /s contract agreement /s renounc! renunciation

"material! breach!" /s continu! /s elect*** renunciation renounc! foreclos!

di(continu! /s accept! /s breach! /s waiv!)

§ 11–34. Giving Incomplete Reasons for Refusing to Perform as an Excuse of Condition

Ordinarily a party is not required to give reasons for rejecting or objecting to the other party's performance.   However, if he gives one or more reasons and fails to state other reasons which he knows or should know[19] and the other party reasonably understands that the reasons stated are exclusive, then the party who has failed to state all of the reasons will be estopped from asserting the unstated reasons if the other party has relied to his injury upon the exclusivity of the reasons stated.[20]   Thus, if an owner lists defects in construction and a contractor cures these defects, the owner may not rely upon known unstated defects that could be cured in claiming that the contractor did not substantially perform or was guilty of a material breach.[21]

WESTLAW REFERENCES

"new england" +s loranger

§ 11–35. Excuse of Conditions Involving Forfeiture

It is obvious that the rule that an express condition must be literally performed can lead to a forfeiture (loss of property or denial of compensation for something done, in other words loss of reliance interest) and to unjust enrichment (improperly permitting a party to

---

14. See, e.g., U.C.C. § 2–607(3)(a): "the buyer must within a reasonable time after he discovers or should have discovered any breach notify the seller of breach or be barred from any remedy. * * *" This provision applies to accepted goods. For the rule as to rejected goods, see U.C.C. § 2–605.

15. See § 11–20 supra.

16. U.C.C. § 1–107.

17. See § 5–16 supra.

18. See § 21–12 infra. According to the Restatement of Contracts, a renunciation of damages resulting from a partial breach does not require consideration. The same is true of a total breach unless there has been full performance on the other side so that a debt has arisen. Restatement, Contracts, §§ 410–411.

19. In re Nagel, 278 Fed. 105 (2d Cir. 1921). The U.C.C. rules on this point were discussed in § 11–20 supra. See generally, 5 Williston §§ 743–744.

20. Restatement, Second, Contracts § 248.

21. New England Structures, Inc. v. Loranger, 354 Mass. 62, 234 N.E.2d 888 (1968).

obtain a benefit and not pay for it—a restitutionary interest.) [22] Although it has recently been stated [23] that "virtually all contemporary American contract decisions refuse to give effect" to the rule that express conditions must be literally performed, this is undoubtedly a significant overstatement.[24]

In any event, one way in which this rule is evaded is by an excuse of condition on the grounds of forfeiture. The first Restatement [25] stated a broad generalized rule as follows:

"A condition may be excused without other reason if its requirement

(a) will involve extreme forfeiture or penalty, and

(b) its existence or occurrence forms no essential part of the exchange for the promisor's performance."[26]

In addition before the condition is excused, the courts will balance the equities. In other words, the courts will take into account the ethical position of the party who seeks to have the condition excused (e.g. was he guilty of mistake or willful conduct?) and the injury suffered by the other party.[27] Even though few courts have explicitly relied on this Restatement rule, the Second Restatement adopts the same rule except that it speaks in terms of an excuse to the extent that there would be a "disproportionate forfeiture." [28] It also points out the relationship of this rule to the doctrine of unconscionability.[29] Unconscionability relates to the time of the formation of the contract. This rule relates to a forfeiture that would arise "because of ensuing events." [30]

Many of the cases involving excuse of condition as a result of forfeiture have been option cases. A leading case is Holiday Inns of

22. Restatement, Second, Contracts § 227, Comment b and § 229, Comment b.

23. Childres, Conditions In the Law of Contracts, 45 N.Y.U.L.Rev. 33 (1970).

24. See, e.g., Inman v. Clyde Hall Drilling Co., 369 P.2d 498 (Alaska 1962).

25. Restatement, Contracts § 302.

26. This statement parallels one of the requirements listed for a "waiver" before failure of condition. See § 11–31 supra. The Section is undoubtedly based upon the notion that "equity abhors a forfeiture". Jefferson Chemical Co. v. Mobay Chemical Co., 267 A.2d 635 (Del.1970). In a jurisdiction where there is a merger of law and equity the relief may be given at law. Sharp v. Holthusen, 189 Mont. 469, 616 P.2d 374 (1980); Jackson v. Richards 5 & 10 Inc., 289 Pa.Super. 445, 433 A.2d 888 (1981). One of the illustrations under the Section, based upon Jacob & Young v. Kent, 230 N.Y. 239, 129 N.E. 889 (1921), seems to excuse a material part of the

agreed exchange. However, as pointed out above, there would be a corresponding right to damages for a partial breach. See Restatement, Second, Contracts § 229, ill. 1. See § 11–32 supra.

27. See, e.g., Xanthakey v. Hayes, 107 Conn. 459, 140 A. 808 (1928).

28. Restatement, Second, Contracts § 229, Comment b explains the meaning of "disproportionate forfeiture." "In determining whether the forfeiture is 'disproportionate', a court must weigh the extent of the forfeiture by the obligee against the importance to the obligor of the risk from which he sought to be protected and the degree to which that protection will be lost if the non-occurrence of the condition is excused to the extent required to prevent forfeiture."

29. Restatement, Second, Contracts § 229, Comment a.

30. Id.

America v. Knight.[31] Plaintiff entered into a contract with the defendant for an option to purchase certain real property for the sum of $198,633. The option could be exercised at any time but not later than April 1, 1968. The contract was signed on September 30, 1963, when an initial payment of $10,000 was made as consideration for the option. Under the terms of the option if plaintiff wished to keep the option open he was required to make additional payments of $10,000 on or before July 1, 1964, 1965, 1966 and 1967. Time was stated to be of the essence. These payments were not to be applied to the purchase price. On June 30, 1966, plaintiff mailed a check for $10,000. The check was received on July 2. Defendant refused to accept the late payment. Plaintiff sought a declaration that the option was still effective. The court granted the relief sought based upon a California statute[32] relating to forfeitures. The court pointed to the "economic realities of the transaction. * * *" It stated, "On the basis of risk allocation, it is clear that each payment of $10,000 was partially for an option to buy the land during that year and partially for the renewal of the option for another year up to a total of five years. With the passage of time, plaintiffs have paid more and more for the right to renew, and it is this right that would be forfeited by requiring payment strictly on time. At the time the forfeiture was declared, plaintiff had paid the sum of $30,000 for the right to exercise the option during the last two years. Thus, they have not received what they bargained for and they have lost more than the benefit of their bargain. In short, they will suffer a forfeiture of that part of the $30,000 attributable to the right to exercise the option during the last two years."[33]

It should be noted that the case relates to a late installment payment rather than a late exercise of an option to purchase realty. In the latter situation the court makes it clear that the time within which an option must be exercised "cannot be extended beyond" the time stated in the contract.[34] The Restatement Second appears to be in accord on the theory that if the condition were excused, the optionee would receive "a more extensive option than that on which the parties agreed."[35]

A failure to exercise an option to extend a lease on time has been placed on a more liberal footing. The main reasons for this result are that realistically the lessee pays more rent during the term of the lease because of the option to renew and very often the lessee in reliance on

31. 70 Cal.2d 327, 74 Cal.Rptr. 722, 450 P.2d 42 (1969).

32. There is no reason to believe that the result in the case would be different if the statute (Civil Code of California § 3275) had not existed.

33. Id. at 331–32, 75 Cal.Rptr. at 725, 450 P.2d at 45.

34. Id. at 330, 74 Cal.Rptr. at 724, 450 P.2d 44.

35. Restatement, Second, Contracts § 229, ill. 5. In other words if the relief is granted the optionee would have additional time to speculate at the expense of the optionor. See, e.g., Cummings v. Bullock, 367 F.2d 182 (9th Cir.1966).

his right to renew makes substantial improvements that would revert to the landlord.[36]

 WESTLAW REFERENCES
excus! /2 condition /s forfeit!
"disproportionate forfeiture"
"holiday inn" +5 knight
forfeit! penal! /s fail! /s exercis! /s option /s extend!
　　extension /s lease

§ 11–36.　Other Bases for Excusing Conditions

As we have seen, conditions may be excused by a tortured interpretation of particular language, that is to say, by reading express language of condition as language of promise.[37]　A condition may also be excused if it is contrary to public policy,[38] unconscionable[39] or if there is no duty to read the particular provision.[40]　A condition may also be excused on a theory of impossibility.　Discussion of an excuse of condition based upon impossibility is best reserved for later consideration when the doctrine of impossibility is considered in all of its aspects.[41]

§ 11–37.　The Satisfaction Cases

(a) Introduction

The satisfaction cases are discussed here because for the most part they relate to the excuse of an express condition.[42]　To some extent they also relate to excuse of conditions because of forfeiture.[43]　The cases relating to satisfaction are treated in a separate section because there are a significant number of cases under this heading.　One of the key issues in most cases is whether the provision in the contract calls for personal (actual) satisfaction or only reasonable satisfaction.[44]　The

36. Xanthakey v. Hayes, 107 Conn. 459, 140 A. 808 (1928); Donovan Motorcar Co. v. Niles, 246 Mass. 106, 140 N.E. 304 (1923); J.N.A. Realty Corp. v. Cross Bay Chelsea, 42 N.Y.2d 392, 397 N.Y.S.2d 958, 366 N.E.2d 1313 (1977); Sy Jack Realty Co. v. Pergament Syosset Corp., 27 N.Y.2d 449, 318 N.Y.S.2d 720, 267 N.E.2d 462 (1971).

37. § 11–9 supra.

38. Inman v. Clyde Hall Drilling Co., 369 P.2d 498 (Alaska 1962); see also ch. 22.

39. Inman v. Clyde Hall Drilling Co., 369 P.2d 498 (Alaska 1962); see also §§ 9–37 to 9–40 infra.

40. C & J Fertilizer, Inc. v. Allied Mutual Ins. Co., 227 N.W.2d 169 (Iowa 1975); see also §§ 9–41 to 9–46 infra.

41. See § 13–10 infra.

42. It is possible to have a case where a party promises satisfaction and there is no express condition of satisfaction.　In such a case the promise to satisfy gives rise to a constructive condition of satisfaction.　3A Corbin § 645.　In Fursmidt v. Hotel Abbey Holding Corp., 10 A.D.2d 447, 200 N.Y.S.2d 256 (1st Dep't 1960), reargument denied 11 A.D.2d 649, 203 N.Y.2d 1012 plaintiff promised to give personal satisfaction and there was no express condition.　Plaintiff sued when defendant cancelled but lost his case because of his failure to fulfill the constructive condition of personal satisfaction.　On the defendant's counterclaim the court suggested that the issue should be objective satisfaction.

43. See § 11–35.

44. Restatement, Second, Contracts § 228.

discussion is divided into two parts—the satisfaction of a party to the contract and the satisfaction of a third party.

(b) Satisfaction of a Party to the Contract

Assume a case where the plaintiff promised to paint a portrait and the defendant promised to pay for it only if he is personally satisfied with the portrait. In this case it is clear that the contract calls for the personal satisfaction of the defendant. However, where there is doubt or ambiguity, the preferred interpretation is that the contract calls for a performance which is objectively satisfactory.[45] The Restatement Second is in accord, but makes it clear that personal satisfaction is required if the "agreement leaves no doubt that it is only honest satisfaction that is meant" [46] or if it is the type of case in which it is impracticable to apply a reasonable man test.[47]

There is no question that in the case of the satisfaction of a party most of the courts tend to group the cases into two categories. "(1) Those which involve taste, fancy or personal judgment, the classical example being a commission to paint a portrait. In such cases the promisor is the sole judge of the quality of the work, and his right to reject, if in good faith, is absolute and may not be reviewed by court or jury.[48] (2) Those which involve utility, fitness or value, which can be measured against a more or less objective standard. In these cases, although there is some conflict, we think the better view is that performance need only be 'reasonably satisfactory,' and if the promisor refuses the proferred performance, the correctness of his decision and the adequacy of his grounds are subject to review." [49]

This statement seems to say that there are two categories of cases and once it is decided into which category the case fits, the problem is solved. This is not true. For example, in the portrait case, although it involves taste, etc., the parties could agree that the defendant was entitled only to reasonable satisfaction and the agreement would be honored,[50] unless the fact pattern is looked upon as one in which it is impracticable to apply a reasonable man test.

45. Handy v. Bliss, 204 Mass. 513, 90 N.E. 864 (1910); Hawkins v. Graham, 149 Mass. 284, 21 N.E. 312 (1889); Restatement, Contracts § 265.

46. Restatement, Second, Contracts § 228, Comment a.

47. Western Hills Oregon, Ltd. v. Pfau, 265 Or. 137, 508 P.2d 201 (1973).

48. Illustrations of this type of case include contracts to provide a work of art, Davis v. General Foods Corp., 21 F.Supp. 445 (S.D.N.Y.1937); valet services, Fursmidt v. Hotel Abbey Holding Corp., 10 A.D.2d 447, 200 N.Y.S.2d 256 (1st Dep't 1960), reargument denied 11 A.D.2d 649, 203 N.Y.S.2d 1012 (1960) and household services, Scott v. Erdman, 9 Misc.2d 961, 173 N.Y.S.2d 843 (App.Term.1957), appeal

denied 5 A.D.2d 849, 172 N.Y.S.2d 542 (1958). Also subject to the good faith test are contracts conditioned upon one party's satisfaction with the financial status or credit rating of another, Jackson v. Roosevelt Fed. Sav. & Loan Ass'n, 702 F.2d 674 (8th Cir.1983), and a lease satisfactory to the purchaser, Mattei v. Hopper, 51 Cal. 2d 119, 330 P.2d 625 (1958). The distinction is not always easily applied in a particular fact pattern.

49. Johnson v. School Dist. No. 12, 210 Or. 585, 590–91, 312 P.2d 591, 593 (1957); see also Action Engineering v. Martin Marietta Aluminum, 670 F.2d 456 (3d Cir. 1982).

50. Fitzmaurice v. Van Vlaanderen Mach. Co., 110 N.J.Super. 159, 264 A.2d

Would a promise to paint a barn to the personal satisfaction of the promisee also be honored? There are many cases which have responded to this question in the negative.[51] The court's tendency to remake the contract for the parties in cases involving mechanical fitness, utility or marketability can be criticized on the ground that under the guise of interpretation the courts ignore the manifest intention of the parties.[52] In many of the cases such interference with freedom of contract is based upon the notion that literal compliance with the contract would result in unjust enrichment and/or forfeiture.[53] If this is the basis of the decisions, it is submitted forthright recognition should be given to this underlying rationale and a distinction drawn between cases involving unjust enrichment and/or forfeiture on the one hand, and cases in which these elements are not present.

As we have seen, once it is decided that personal satisfaction is called for, the issue is the good faith of the party to be satisfied.[54] This does not mean that a party's statement with respect to his satisfaction must be accepted. If such were the agreement, it would be illusory.[55] The dissatisfaction must be actual and not merely simulated.[56] Under the good faith test, it is difficult for the plaintiff to prevail. He must show that the defendant is, in fact, satisfied with the performance rendered or tendered and has other motives for testifying to his dissatisfaction. He may establish defendant's true state of mind by evidence showing that that defendant made statements giving other reasons for his rejection of the performance,[57] that he refused to examine performance,[58] or that he has a motive to simulate dissatisfaction, for example, because there has been a change of circumstances.[59] According to some authorities, evidence of the unreasonableness of the

---

740 (1970), certification granted 56 N.J. 476, 267 A.2d 58 (1971).

51. Loma Linda Univ. v. District-Realty Title Ins. Corp., 443 F.2d 773 (D.C.Cir. 1971); American Oil Co. v. Carey, 246 F.Supp. 773 (E.D.Mich.1965) ("obtain * * * permits satisfactory to Purchaser," id. at 774); Alper Blouse Co. v. E.E. Connor & Co., 309 N.Y. 67, 127 N.E.2d 813, (1955) (sale of goods); Doll v. Noble, 116 N.Y. 230, 22 N.E. 406 (1889) (rubbing and staining woodwork); Duplex Safety Boiler Co. v. Garden, 101 N.Y. 387, 4 N.E. 749 (1886) (remodernization of a boiler). Contra Thompson-Starrett Co. v. La Belle Iron Works, 17 F.2d 536 (2d Cir.1927) (contract to build houses—reasonableness of honest dissatisfaction immaterial); Gerisch v. Herold, 82 N.J.L. 605, 83 A. 892 (1912) (taste or fancy of owner may be an important element in satisfaction involving a dwelling house).

52. Murray, Contracts § 152.

53. Handy v. Bliss, 204 Mass. 513, 90 N.E. 864 (1910).

54. The burden of proof is upon the party asserting bad faith. Hortis v. Madison Golf Club, Inc., 92 A.D.2d 713, 461 N.Y.S.2d 116 (4th Dep't 1983).

55. See § 4–12(4) supra. However, it is possible for the contract language to mean that one party has absolute discretion and that good faith is irrelevant. McDougold Const. Co. v. State Highway Dep't, 125 Ga. App. 591, 188 S.E.2d 405 (1972).

56. Tow v. Miner's Memorial Hosp. Ass'n, 305 F.2d 73 (4th Cir.1962); Mattei v. Hopper, 51 Cal.2d 119, 330 P.2d 625 (1958).

57. Restatement, Contracts § 265, ill. 1.

58. Restatement, Contract § 265, ill. 2; Frankfort Distilleries, Inc. v. Burns Bottling Mach. Works, 174 Md. 12, 197 A. 599 (1938).

59. Thompson-Starrett Co. v. La Belle Iron Works, 17 F.2d 536, 541 (2d Cir.1927), certiorari denied, 274 U.S. 748, 47 S.Ct. 763, 71 L.Ed. 1330 (1927).

defendant's expressed dissatisfaction is admissible to justify an inference of bad faith.[60]

(c) Satisfaction of a Third Party

In the construction industry it is quite common to have a provision in the contract expressly conditioning the owner's promise to make progress payments, or at least the final payment, upon the personal satisfaction or approval of a named architect or engineer, evidenced by his certificate. Although the third person whose personal approval is made a condition precedent is usually retained by the party for whom the structure is to be built, the parties have agreed to rely on his professional integrity.[61]

Generally, courts have applied the same standard to this type of express condition precedent that has been applied to other express conditions.[62] Strict compliance with the condition is the rule.[63] The court will not substitute the approval or satisfaction of judge or jury for that of the chosen expert.[64] Nevertheless, if it can be established that the expert acted dishonestly or in bad faith the condition that he express his approval in a certificate or otherwise will be excused.[65] Under the modern view this is also true of gross mistake unless this risk has been assumed.[66] The expert's misconduct is a question of fact and the burden of proof is on the party who alleges it. Although unreasonableness may be circumstantial evidence of dishonesty,[67] in most jurisdictions the mere fact that the refusal is unreasonable is insufficient grounds for excusing the condition.[68]

There is, however, a contrary minority view. There are a number of cases, especially in New York, which go far in remaking the contract of the parties. The leading case is Nolan v. Whitney.[69] In that case

60. 6A Corbin § 645. Sometimes it is said that the plaintiff should prevail if he can prove that the promisor is dissatisfied with his bargain rather than with the performance. Thompson-Starrett Co. v. La Belle Iron Works, 17 F.2d 536 (2d Cir.1927), certiorari denied 274 U.S. 748, 47 S.Ct. 763, 71 L.Ed. 1330 (1927). Nor may he base his dissatisfaction on facts of which he was aware on the signing of the contract. Western Hills, Oregon, Ltd. v. Pfau, 265 Or. 137, 508 P.2d 201 (1973).

61. Devoine Co. v. International Co., 151 Md. 690, 136 A. 37 (1927); Grobarchik v. Nasa Mortgage & Inv. Co., 117 N.J.L. 33, 186 A. 433 (1936).

62. Restatement, Second, Contracts § 228, Comment b. In the usual case the third party is not in the employ of the owner. Some courts have followed the same notion even though the third party is in fact an employee of the employer. See, e.g., Frankfort Distilleries v. Burns Bottling Mach. Works, 174 Md. 12, 197 A. 599 (1938).

63. Pope v. King, 108 Md. 37, 69 A. 417 (1908); cf. Restatement, Contracts § 303. See generally 3A Corbin §§ 647–652; 5 Williston §§ 675–675B.

64. Second Nat'l Bank v. Pan Am. Bridge Co., 183 F. 391 (6th Cir.1910).

65. Rizzolo v. Poysher, 89 N.J.L. 618, 99 A. 390 (1916); Zimmerman v. Marymor, 290 Pa. 299, 138 A. 824 (1927) (collusion); Restatement, Contracts § 303.

66. Restatement, Second, Contracts § 227, Comment c.

67. 3A Corbin § 645.

68. Herbert v. Dewey, 191 Mass. 403, 77 N.E. 822 (1906); Gerisch v. Herold, 82 N.J.L. 605, 83 A. 892 (1912); see also Childres, Conditions in the Law of Contracts, 45 N.Y.U.L.Rev. 33, 42–44 (1970).

69. 88 N.Y. 648 (1882); accord, Coplew v. Durand, 153 Cal. 278, 95 P. 38 (1908); Richmond College v. Scott-Nuckols Co., 124 Va. 333, 98 S.E. 1 (1919). For an extended criticism see Mehler, Substantial Perform-

plaintiff, builder, sued for $2700, the final payment in a building contract. An express condition to the payment of the final instalment was the issuance of an architect's certificate of satisfaction. The architect refused to issue the certificate because some of the plastering was defective. The evidence showed that it would cost $200 to remedy this condition.

Under the majority view, discussed above, the condition calling for personal satisfaction would be excused only if the architect acted in bad faith or the like. The court did not discuss the issue of good faith but instead examined the question of whether the architect acted unreasonably. The court decided that the architect acted unreasonably and stated "an unreasonable refusal to give the certificate dispenses with its necessity." [70] The court concluded that since the plaintiff had substantially performed, he could recover the final payment less $200.

This is a decision that defies logic. Why was the architect unreasonable in refusing to issue a certificate when the work was defective? However, even if the architect acted unreasonably, this is not the issue. Under the terms of the contract, the architect was entitled to personal satisfaction. Therefore, as the majority view states, he is entitled to personal satisfaction rather than reasonable satisfaction. Thus, the issue of substantial performance is irrelevant in the case of an express condition.

The Court of Appeals in this case was manipulating concepts in order to achieve a fair result. [71] The case was subsequently explained by the Court of Appeals as resting "upon the basis that enforcement of the contract according to its strict terms would cause forfeiture of compensation for work done or materials furnished." [72] Since the basis of the decision is forfeiture (and if the plaintiff was working on defendant's property unjust enrichment) it seems clear that the same court would apply the majority view to a case involving the sale of ordinary goods where the contract made the sale subject to the personal satisfaction of a named expert.

The minority view is obviously limited to situations where there is a potential for forfeiture and/or unjust enrichment. It should also be noted that the Nolan case involved "mechanical fitness." How would the New York Court of Appeals decide a case involving approval of a portrait by a third party? We believe that since what is involved here is "personal judgment", the Court would apply the majority rule. [73] The

ance Versus Freedom of Contract, 33 Brooklyn L.Rev. 196 (1967); see also Ashley, Should There Be Freedom of Contract, 4 Colum.L.Rev. 423, 425 (1904).

70. Id. at 650.

71. It might be pointed out that a quasi-contractual recovery would be permitted in this type of case in some jurisdictions. However, this is not true in New York. See § 11–22 supra. There are also cases where the problem is avoided by interpret-

ing the language as calling for the reasonable satisfaction of the third party. Vought v. Williams, 120 N.Y. 253, 24 N.E. 195 (1890).

72. Van Iderstine Co. v. Barnet Leather Co., 242 N.Y. 425, 434, 152 N.E. 250, 252 (1926).

73. These are terms used in the preceding section where different rules are stated in relation to the satisfaction of a party to the contract. We use them here because

rule of the Nolan case was further restricted by an Appellate Division case which stated that:

> "Substantial performance might make compliance with an express condition unnecessary, but only when the departure from full performance is an inconsiderable trifle having no pecuniary importance." [74]

We have just discussed the effect of a clause in a contract making payment expressly conditional on the personal satisfaction of an architect or engineer, etc. Very often the same contract will contain a provision that any finding of fact by the named party is final. The question is to what extent can the findings of fact made by the third party be reviewed by a court? The answer to this question has been formulated in many ways.[75] However under federal procurement law, a statute provides that a court may review to see if the third party is "capricious or arbitrary or so grossly erroneous as necessarily to imply bad faith or is not supported by substantial evidence." [76] Under this statute a court may review the findings to see if the third party was guilty of fraud.[77]

 WESTLAW REFERENCES

(a) *Introduction*

satisfaction /s condition /4 excus!

fursmidt +s "hotel abbey"

(b) *Satisfaction of a Party to the Contract*

"personal! satisf!" /s contract

"honest! satisf!" /s contract

reasonable +1 man person /s satisf! /s perform! /s contract

satisf! /s perform! service /s "good faith" /s contract

"objective standard" /s satisf! /s contract

95k282

actual! /s dissatisf! /s contract

"bad faith" /s dissatisf! /s contract

(c) *Satisfaction of a Third Person*

"condition precedent" /s satisf! approv! /s (third +1 party person) architect engineer /s contract

95k284(3)

they help convey the distinction being made.

74. Witherell v. Lasky, 286 App.Div. 533, 536, 145 N.Y.S.2d 624, 627 (4th Dep't 1955).

75. See discussion below.

76. 41 U.S.C.A. §§ 321–322 is referred to as the Wunderlich Act because the statute was in response to the restrictive decision in United States v. Wunderlich, 342 U.S. 98, 72 S.Ct. 154, 96 L.Ed. 113 (1951). See Annot., 2 A.L.R.Fed. 691 (1969).

77. Most courts will review the third party's determination for fraud. In a state that limits the review to fraud the courts may evade the rule by finding that there is constructive fraud. Anthony P. Miller, Inc. v. Wilmington Hous. Auth., 179 F.Supp. 199 (D.Del.1959); see also Restatement, Second, Contracts § 227, ill. 8. Under some views the court may also reverse the third party if his determinations are based upon an "error of law." J.J. Finn Elec. Serv., Inc. v. P. & H. Gen. Contractors, Inc., 13 Mass.App. 973, 432 N.E.2d 116 (1982).

gerisch +s herold

"certificate of satisfaction" /s architect engineer inspect! contractor

"substantial! perform!" /s "express! condition!"

D. GOOD FAITH

Table of Sections

§ 11–38. Good Faith

(a) Introduction

Despite a promising beginning in the eighteenth century, "the common law has traditionally been reluctant to recognize, at least as overt doctrine, any generalized duty to act in good faith toward others in social intercourse".[78] This approach was solidified with the development, "during the nineteenth century, of the pure theory of contract characterized by notions of volition, *laissez-faire,* freedom of contract, judicial nonintervention and bargained-for-exchange."[79] In recent years doctrines of promissory estoppel, unconscionability and modern theories of quasi-contracts have changed these rigid notions.[80] As part of the same development "modern contract law appears to support and promote good faith conduct based on reasonable standards in the formation, performance and discharge of contracts."[81] The Uniform Commercial Code and Second Restatement have been influential in bringing about this result.[82]

(b) Relationship to Other Portions of Text

The concept of good faith has been mentioned in many areas of this text. A few illustrations will suffice. In the area of indefiniteness we have seen that where "a contract confers on one party a discretionary power affecting the rights of the other, a duty is imposed to exercise the discretion in good faith and in accordance with fair dealing".[83] The concept of good faith is used in the chapter on consideration with respect to the termination of an agreement,[84] illusory promises,[85] the

---

78. Holmes, A Contextual Study of Commercial Good Faith: Good-Faith Disclosure In Contract Formation, 39 University Pittsburg Law Review 381, 384 (1978).

79. Id. at 384–5.

80. Id. at 389–90.

81. Id. at 381. But see notes 95 and 3 infra.

82. Id. at 384.

83. Perdue v. Crocker Nat. Bank, 38 Cal.3d 913, 216 Cal.Rptr. 345, 702 P.2d 503 (1985), appeal dismissed ___ U.S. ___, 106 S.Ct. 1170, 89 L.Ed.2d 290 (1986). See § 2–9 note 63 supra.

84. See § 4–12 supra.

85. See § 4–12 supra.

surrender of an invalid claim [86] and output and requirements contracts.[87] The concept is also used in the area of duress.[88] In the area of promissory estoppel the notion of culpa in contrahendo is based upon a duty to bargain in good faith.[89]

Perhaps the largest number of cases involving the topic of good faith arise in the context of an implied in fact or a constructive promise to act in good faith.[90] A much quoted phrase is "that in every contract there exists an implied covenant of good faith and fair dealing." [91] Normally, a violation of such a duty is treated as a breach of contract. There is a tendency, however, in violations of insurance contracts of insurers [92] and in abusive discharges of at-will employees [93] to treat violations of the duty of good faith and fair dealing as torts. The distinction is not purely of academic interest. Characterization of the violation as a tort opens the door to punitive damages and difficulties in choosing the applicable statute of limitations.

(c) The Meaning of Good Faith

Immediately above it was mentioned that the Uniform Commercial Code has specific provisions relating the concept of good faith.[94] U.C.C. § 1–203 states "Every contract or duty within this Act imposes an obligation of good faith in its performance or enforcement." [95] The comment adds: "This section sets forth a basic principle running throughout this Act. The principle involved is that in commercial transactions good faith is required in the performance and enforcement of all agreements or duties."

Section 1–203 does not define "good faith". However, there are two sections that do. Section 1–201(19) defines "good faith" as "honesty in fact in the conduct or transaction concerned." [96] Since the section is in Article 1 it applies to the entire Code. Professor Braucher points out that definition "makes negligence irrelevant to good faith." He also points out that the test is "subjective" and that the test is known

---

86. See § 4–8 supra.

87. See § 4–13 supra.

88. See § 5–15 supra and ch. 9 supra.

89. Kessler and Fine, Culpa in Contrahendo, Bargaining in Good Faith, and Freedom of Contract, 77 Harv.L.Rev. 401 (1964). See also § 6–5 supra.

90. This discussion relates back to § 11–14 and involves constructive promises and omitted terms.

91. Kirke La Shelle Co. v. Paul Armstrong Co., 263 N.Y. 79, 87, 188 N.E. 163, 167 (1933). Restatement, Second, Contracts § 205. The concept of good faith is embodied in both the U.C.C. (§ 1–203) and the Restatement Second (§ 205). It has been pointed out that "there is an express mention of 'good faith' in some fifty of the four hundred sections of the Code." Farnsworth, Good Faith Performance and Com-

mercial Reasonableness under the Uniform Commercial Code, 30 U.Chi.L.Rev. 666, 667 (1963).

92. See Louderback & Juriska, Standards for Expanding the Tort of Bad Faith Breach of Contract, 16 U.S.F.L.Rev. 187 (1982); Speidel, The Borderland of Contract, 10 N.Ky.L.Rev. 163 (1983).

93. See Murphy v. American Home Products Corp., 58 N.Y.2d 293, 461 N.Y.S.2d 232, 448 N.E.2d 86 (1983) (Meyer, J., dissenting and collecting authorities)

94. See note 82 supra.

95. Note that this does not apply to contract formation, but it applies to a modification because a modification relates to the performance of a contract.

96. See also Wendling v. Cundall, 568 P.2d 888 (Wyo.1977).

as the rule of "the pure heart and the empty head." [97] The subjective nature of this test has been severely criticized. There is a strong feeling that the test should have an objective component.[98]

However, for sales of goods, the Code has a different definition in the case of a merchant. Section 2–103 states: "Good faith" in the case of a merchant means honesty in fact and the observance of reasonable commercial standards of fair dealing in the trade. This definition includes the subjective test supplied by § 1–203, but adds an objective standard.

The Restatement provides that: "Every contract imposes upon each party a duty of good faith and fair dealing in its performance and its enforcement." [99] In Comment a to the section, the U.C.C. definitions of "good faith" are repeated. The Comment goes on to say that the meaning of the phrase "varies somewhat with the context". According to the Comment, "Good faith performance or enforcement of the contract emphasizes faithfulness to an agreed common purpose and consistency with the justified expectations of the other party; it excludes a variety of types of conduct characterized as involving "bad faith because they violate community standards of decency, fairness, or reasonableness."

Comment d elaborates on what is "good faith" and what is "bad faith". It states: "Subterfuges and evasions violate the obligation of good faith in performance even though the actor believes his conduct to be justified. But the obligation goes further: bad faith may be overt or may consist of inaction, and fair dealing may require more than honesty. A complete catalogue of types of bad faith is impossible, but the following types are among those which have been recognized in judicial decisions; evasion of the spirit of the bargain, lack of diligence and slacking off, willful rendering of imperfect performance, abuse of power to specify terms, and interference with or failure to cooperate in the other party's performance". This catalog contains both subjective and objective criteria.

It should be noted that Comment b states that this section does not relate to the formation of a contract. *A fortiori* it does not relate to preliminary negotiations. Pre-contractual bad faith may, however, be redressed under rules regulating fraud,[1] duress [2] and promissory estoppel.[3]

97. Braucher, The Legislative History of the Uniform Commercial Code, 58 Colum.L.Rev. 798 (1958).

98. See, for example, Farnsworth, Good Faith Performance and Commercial Reasonableness under the Uniform Commercial Code, 30 U.Chi.L.Rev. 666 (1963); Summers, Good Faith in General Contract Law

and the Sales Provision of the Uniform Commercial Code, 54 Va.L.Rev. 195 (1968).

99. Restatement, Second, Contracts § 205.

1. See Ch. 9D supra.

2. See Ch. 9B supra.

3. See Ch. 6, supra.

The Restatement section has been quoted in detail to show that the concept of good faith is amorphous.[4] A wide variety of attempts to give it flesh and substance can be found in the literature.[5] What is or is not good faith is ordinarily a question of fact.[6]

As we have seen, closely related to the topic under discussion is the doctrine of tortious bad faith breach of contract.[7] The Silberg case cited in note 7 states that the insurer's duty is "to give the interests of the insured at least as much consideration as it gives to its own interests."[8] However, another case has stated that a "duty of good faith does not mean that a party vested with a clear right is obligated to exercise the right to his own detriment for the purpose of benefiting another party to the contract."[9]

An interesting application of the concept of good faith is found in the case of Fortune v. National Cash Register Co.,[10] involving a hiring at will. The contract actually reserved to the parties an explicit power to terminate the contract without cause. The facts indicated that the employer terminated the contract to prevent the salesman from collecting bonuses on goods already sold.

The court found that there was a violation of an implied duty of good faith, stating:

> "We do not question the general principles that an employer is entitled to be motivated by and to serve its own legitimate business interests; that an employer must have wide latitude in deciding whom it will employ in the face of the uncertainties of the business world; and that an employer needs flexibility in the face of changing circumstance. We recognize the employer's need for a large amount of control over its work force. However, we believe that where, as here, commissions are to be paid for the work performed by the employee, the employer's decision to terminate its at will employee should be made in good faith. NCR's right to

4. Burton, Good Faith Performance of a Contract within Article 2 of the Uniform Commercial Code, 67 Iowa L.Rev. 1 (1981); Eisenberg, Good Faith Under the Uniform Commercial Code—A New Look at an Old Problem, 54 Marq.L.Rev. 1 (1971).

5. Burton, Breach of Contract and the Common Law Duty to Perform in Good Faith, 94 Harv.L.Rev. 369 (1980); Burton, Good Faith Performance of a Contract within Art. 2 of the Uniform Commercial Code, 67 Iowa L.Rev. 1 (1981).

6. Eisenberg, supra note 4 at 15.

7. See notes 92 and 93 supra and Silberg v. California Life Insurance Co., 11 Cal.3d 452, 113 Cal.Rptr. 711, 521 P.2d 1103 (1974).

8. Id. at 460, 521 P.2d at 1109, 113 Cal. Rptr. at 716–717. See also Holmes, Is There Life After Gilmore's Death of Contract—Introductions from a Study of Commercial Good Faith in First Party Insurance Contracts, 65 Cornell L.Rev. 330, 360–7 (1980).

9. Rio Algom Corp. v. Jimco Ltd., 618 P.2d 497 (Utah 1980). It has been held that the concept of good faith "may not be used to override explicit contractual terms". Grand Light & Supply Co., Inc. v. Honeywell, Inc., 771 F.2d 672, 679 (2d Cir. 1985). But see Wakefield v. Northern Telecom, Inc., 769 F.2d 109 (2d Cir.1985).

10. 373 Mass. 96, 364 N.E.2d 1251 (1977).

make its decisions in its own interest is not, in our view, unduly hampered by a requirement of adherence to this standard." [11]

This case goes beyond the at will cases discussed in section 2–9. In that section it was pointed out that the traditional view in a hiring at will is that the agreement may be terminated "for good cause, for no cause, or even for a cause morally wrong." [12] We also saw that many recent cases have made an exception where the discharge is in retaliation for the use by the employee of a statutory right.[13] The Fortune case is somewhat similar to the case of Monge v. Beebe Rubber Co.[14] also discussed in chapter 2.[15]

It is apparent that the concept of "good faith" can be used in any situation to right a wrong that would be created if the traditional rule were applied.[16]

 WESTLAW REFERENCES

(a) *Introduction*

di good faith

"good faith" /s unconscionab! "promissor! estop!"

(b) *Relationship to Other Portions of Text*

"good faith and fair dealing" /s tort

(c) *The Meaning of Good Faith*

"good faith" /s 1–203

"good faith" /2 definition define*

"good faith" /s subjective! /s test

"good faith" /s fact*** /2 question

tort tortious! /s "bad faith" /s breach! /s contract

---

11. 373 Mass. at 101, 364 N.E.2d at 1256.

12. § 2–9 infra.

13. Id.

14. 114 N.H. 130, 316 A.2d 549, 62 A.L.R.3d 264 (1974). See Blades, Employ-ment at Will v. Individual Freedom: On Limiting the Abusive Exercise of Employer Power, 60 Colum.L.Rev. 1404 (1967).

15. See § 2–9 supra.

16. Restatement, Second, Contracts § 205.

Chapter 12

BREACH AND PROSPECTIVE NON-PERFORMANCE

Table of Sections

§ 12–1.   Introduction

Any failure to perform a contractual duty which has arisen constitutes a breach.[1] This is so even if the party who was to have received the performance had benefited by its non-performance.[2] The topic of breach has already been discussed in Chapter 11. It is not our purpose to repeat that material here.

Our main goal in this chapter is to discuss two types of non-performance—prospective inability or unwillingness to perform and anticipatory repudiation.[3] Prospective inability and unwillingness to

---

1. Seybold v. Magnolia Land Co., 376 So.2d 1083 (Ala.1979); Restatement, Second, Contracts § 235(2); Restatement, Contracts § 312. The original Restatement in § 312 also indicates that a breach may take place "by prevention or hindrance, or by repudiation." Conversely, full performance of a duty discharges a duty. Restatement, Second, Contracts § 235(1). If the non-performance is justified, there is no breach. Restatement, Second, Contracts § 235, Comment b. Restatement, Contracts § 312, Comment a.

2. Beattie v. New York, N.H. & H.R.R. Co., 84 Conn. 555, 80 A. 709 (1911).

3. A few words will also be said about present inability and unwillingness and a present repudiation.

perform should really have been discussed in Chapter 11 because it relates to constructive conditions.[4] However, the two types of prospective non-performance under discussion are closely related and therefore it seems preferable to discuss them in the same chapter. A repudiation is a particular kind of breach and is not in all respects the same type of breach discussed in Chapter 11.[5] These two types of prospective non-performance will now be discussed.

 WESTLAW REFERENCES
"fail! to perform! a contractual duty"

§ 12–2. Prospective Inability and Unwillingness to Perform as Constructive Conditions

When the First Restatement discusses this topic it seems clear that it is concerned with inability or unwillingness which arises before the party who is unable or unwilling to perform is obliged to perform.[6] In such a situation what the other party may do depends upon how serious the prospective inability or unwillingness is. Under some circumstances where there is prospective non-performance the other party may be justified only in suspending his performance; at other times he may be justified in regarding the contract as cancelled or in changing his position.[7] The course which may be taken ultimately depends upon whether there is reasonable probability that a party will not or cannot substantially perform.[8] If substantial performance is still possible the most that the other party can do is suspend his performance.

Prospective inability, or unwillingness to perform may be manifested by word or by conduct,[9] destruction of the subject matter,[10] death or illness of a person whose performance is essential under the contract,[11] encumbrance or lack of the title in a contract vendor at the time of the making of the contract, or a sale of the property by him subsequent to the making of the contract,[12] existing or supervening illegality of a promised performance,[13] insolvency of a party [14] and under the Uniform Commercial Code defective performances rendered under other contracts between the parties or even a contract with third parties.[15] A

---

4. See § 11–13 supra.

5. Contractors, Lab., Teamsters & Eng'rs v. Harkins Construction, 733 F.2d 1321 (8th Cir.1984); Bill's Coal Co. v. Board of Pub. Utilities, 682 F.2d 883 (10th Cir. 1982). The differences are pointed out in § 12–8 infra.

6. If there is a serious prospective inability or unwillingness to perform coupled with a present breach, it is all but certain that there would be a material breach. See § 12–3 infra. The question of up to what point of time may a prospective inability or unwillingness to perform be withdrawn or cured will be discussed below in connection with the topic of repudiation. See § 12–7 infra.

7. See generally Restatement, Contracts §§ 280–87; 6 Corbin §§ 1259–1261; 6 Williston §§ 875–79; 5 Williston § 699.

8. At times in the subsequent discussion, this is referred to as "serious" prospective inability or unwillingness.

9. Restatement, Contracts § 280.

10. Id. § 281.

11. Id. § 282.

12. Id. §§ 283–84.

13. Id. §§ 285–86.

14. Id. § 287.

15. U.C.C. § 2–609, Comment 3.

few words will now be stated concerning each of these topics as well as the more recent topic of demanding assurances when there is prospective inability or unwillingness.

Assume that S agrees to sell and B agrees to buy a specific second hand car, delivery to be made and title to pass on June 1, and B agrees to pay the purchase price on May 1. If the car is destroyed by fire on April 25th, B could not successfully enforce the contract against S, for as we shall see S would have the defense of impossibility of performance.[16] Although B's promise is originally independent of any performance on the part of S, B's performance is excused because S's apparent ability to perform his part of the agreed exchange is a constructive condition precedent to B's duty to perform.[17] In other words S has the defense of impossibility and B has the defense of prospective inability to perform.

But suppose that in the same case there is no fire but rather S on April 26 unconditionally sells his car to X, and B on April 26th buys a different car. (Here there is no impossibility of performance). The authorities agree that B, by virtue of S's prospective non-performance, was justified in changing his position by buying a different car and therefore was not obliged to buy on May 1 and was discharged from his obligations under the contract by virtue of S's prospective inability and unwillingness to perform.[18] B in addition would have a cause of action for a total breach of the contract. However, he could not bring an action for the breach until June 1, unless S's conduct amounted to a repudiation.[19]

If it be assumed, however, that B did not buy another car on April 26th but merely told S that B's duties under the contract were terminated and S on April 27 re-obtained the auto in question a more difficult question is presented.[20] Some authorities indicate that B was justified in stating that he would not proceed and that he is no longer bound despite the fact that S re-obtained the auto.[21] In other words B is relieved of his obligations even though he has not actually changed his position. The First Restatement is explicit that there must be change of position for this result to obtain. However, it does not indicate whether it considers B's notification a change of position.[22]

In the same illustration, if S instead of selling the car on April 25 tells B that he positively will not perform and B immediately buys a

---

16. Dexter v. Norton, 47 N.Y. 62 (1871). See § 13–3 infra.

17. Restatement, Contracts § 282, ill. 4.

18. Brimmer v. Salisbury, 167 Cal. 522, 140 P. 30 (1914); Fort Payne Coal & Iron Co. v. Webster, 163 Mass. 134, 39 N.E. 786 (1895); James v. Burchell, 82 N.Y. 108 (1880).

19. See the discussion in § 12–8 infra wherein this rule is compared with the doctrine of anticipatory repudiation. See also § 12–4 infra.

20. If S did not reacquire the automobile, there can be no doubt that his probable non-performance would justify B in not paying the purchase price on May 1 even if he had not stated that he would not proceed with the transaction.

21. Sommerville v. Epps, 36 Conn.Supp. 323, 419 A.2d 909 (1980); Simpson 340–41.

22. Restatement, Contracts § 284; cf. U.C.C. § 2–611(1).

different automobile (change of position), B would not be bound to pay on May 1 and would be discharged from his obligations under the contract.[23] All of the prior discussion would relate equally well to a contract involving real property.[24]

As previously indicated another way in which the topic of prospective inability to perform may arise is as a result of death or illness of a person whose performance is essential under the contract. A good illustration is the well known English case of Poussard v. Spiers.[25] In that case D (defendant) agreed to employ P (plaintiff) to play the lead in a particular opera for a period of three months at a specified salary. The first performance was to take place on November 28th. On November 23rd P became ill during a rehearsal. At this time the length of her incapacity was indefinite and unknown. D hired the only other available substitute performer to take P's place. The substitute insisted on being hired for the entire performance. P was ready to perform on Dec. 4th at which time she tendered her services. These were refused. The jury found as a fact that the engagement of the substitute was reasonable.

Clearly there was prospective inability to perform of an unknown duration. D changed his position which would terminate D's obligation under the contract if the change of position was justified. Whether the change of position was justified depends upon how serious the prospective inability was. The finding of fact made by the jury was the equivalent of a finding that there was reasonable probability that P will not or cannot substantially perform. Therefore, the prospective inability was serious and D was justified in changing his position and D's obligations under the contract were terminated. P was not guilty of any breach because P had the defense of impossibility of performance.[26]

Some of the cases in this area involve contracts for the sale of realty where the vendor does not have title to the property at the time the contract of sale was entered into. This obviously involves serious prospective inability to perform. The rule formulated to cover this situation is that the vendee may invoke the doctrine of prospective inability (change position, etc.) unless the vendor has the right to become owner or has a justifiable expectation of becoming owner in time to perform under the terms of the contract [27] or unless the vendee had knowledge of the lack of title when the contract was signed.[28]

A similar problem arises when the vendor has title to the property but the title is encumbered by a defect that would render title unmarketable. The Restatement announces the same rule with respect to

23. Windmuller v. Pope, 107 N.Y. 674, 14 N.E. 436 (1887). Not only would there be a discharge but B could sue immediately under a theory of anticipatory repudiation. See § 12–3 infra.

24. See Restatement, Contracts § 284.

25. 1 Q.B.D. 410 (1876); See also Restatement, Second, Contracts § 262, Comment a; cf. Bettini v. Gye, 1 Q.B.D. 183 (1876).

26. See § 13–7 infra.

27. Clark v. Ingle, 58 N.M. 136, 266 P.2d 672 (1954); Restatement, Contracts § 283.

28. Tague Holding Corp. v. Harris, 250 N.Y. 422, 165 N.E. 834 (1929).

this situation as it does when the vendor does not have title.[29]   However, there is another view, probably a majority view, which takes a different approach.   It states that when time is not of the essence and the vendor has the power to remedy the defect within a reasonable time after the deed should have been given, the vendee does not have the right to change his position and cancel his duties under contract.[30]   As has been stated, "The question must resolve itself into one of degree and probability." [31]   It should be pointed out that in this situation the vendee must advise the seller of curable title defects—that is, defects which can be cured within a reasonable time.[32]

Obviously insolvency will also raise the question of prospective inability to perform.   It does not involve prospective unwillingness to perform or repudiation because it is not voluntarily caused and thus it can amount only to prospective inability to perform.[33]   For example, if S agrees to sell and deliver certain goods to B on May 1, for which B is to pay on August 1, and on April 30 B is insolvent, must S deliver the goods according to terms of the contract?

The question of what makes a party insolvent must be addressed. U.C.C. § 1-201(23) lists three situations that constitute insolvency: (1) ceasing to pay debts in the ordinary course of business; (2) inability to pay debts as they mature; (3) insolvency within the meaning of the Federal Bankruptcy Act—that is to say where a party's debts are greater than his assets.   The Restatement Second is in accord.[34]   Although mere doubts as to insolvency are not enough, if a reasonable man would conclude that a party is insolvent that is sufficient.   For example, unsatisfied judgments would lead a reasonable man to such a conclusion.[35]

Assuming that the buyer,[36] in the illustration given, is insolvent, what may the seller do because of the insolvency?   U.C.C. § 2-702 lists four courses that seller may follow.   Of these, the course that relates most directly is subdivision (1) which states, "where the seller discovers the buyer to be insolvent he may refuse delivery except for cash including payment for all goods theretofore delivered under the contract, * * *." [37]   The Restatement, Second, however, allows the buyer to give security rather than pay cash and thus become entitled to the

29.   Restatement, Contracts § 283, Comment a.

30.   Schilling v. Levin, 328 Mass. 2, 101 N.E.2d 360 (1951); Cohen v. Kranz, 12 N.Y.2d 242, 238 N.Y.S.2d 928, 189 N.E.2d 473 (1963) (vendor could have cured title by moving a fence; vendee not justified in cancelling contract.)

31.   6 Williston § 879.

32.   First Nat'l Bank v. Ron Rudin Realty Co., 97 Nev. 20, 623 P.2d 558 (1981); Ilemar Corp. v. Krochmal, 44 N.Y.2d 702, 405 N.Y.S.2d 444, 376 N.E.2d 917 (1978).

33.   See § 12-6 infra.

34.   Restatement, Second, Contracts § 252(2).

35.   Leopold v. Rock-Ola Mfg. Corp., 109 F.2d 611 (5th Cir.1940).

36.   In this fact pattern if the seller was insolvent, the insolvency would be immaterial because the rules being discussed relate only to the insolvency of a party receiving credit.   Restatement, Contracts § 287, ill. 3.

37.   Subdivision (1) ends with the words "and stop delivery under this article." The section continues: "(2) Where the seller discovers that the buyer has received goods on credit while insolvent he may

delivery of the goods.[38]   In either case, under the majority view the failure of the insolvent party to make the necessary tender within a reasonable time discharges the duty of the solvent party altogether.[39]

The First Restatement appears to indicate that the solvent party may reasonably and materially change his position and thus discharge his obligation without any necessity for waiting a reasonable time for the insolvent party to tender cash or security.[40]

U.C.C. § 2–609 introduced into the law the notion that where a party to a contract is guilty of serious prospective inability or unwillingness to perform, the other party may make a demand for "adequate assurances of due performance."   There was no such common law procedure.[41]   This section reads as follows:

"Right to Adequate Assurance of Performance

"(1) A contract for sale imposes an obligation on each party that the other's expectation of receiving due performance will not be impaired.   When reasonable grounds for insecurity arise with respect to the performance of either party the other may in writing demand adequate assurance of due performance and until he receives such assurance may if commercially reasonable suspend any performance for which he has not already received the agreed return.

"(2) Between merchants the reasonableness of grounds for insecurity and the adequacy of any assurance offered shall be determined according to commercial standards.

"(3) Acceptance of any improper delivery or payment does not prejudice the aggrieved party's right to demand adequate assurance of future performance.

"(4) After receipt of a justified demand failure to provide within a reasonable time not exceeding thirty days such assurance of due performance as is adequate under the circumstances of the particular case is a repudiation of the contract."

reclaim the goods upon demand made within ten days after the receipt, but if misrepresentation of solvency has been made to the particular seller in writing within three months before delivery the ten day limitation does not apply.   Except as provided in this subsection the seller may not base a right to reclaim goods on the buyer's fraudulent or innocent misrepresentation of solvency or of intent to pay. (3) The seller's right to reclaim under subsection (2) is subject to the rights of a buyer in ordinary course or other good faith purchaser under this Article (section 2–403).   Successful reclamation of goods excludes all other remedies with respect to them."   See In re Federal's, Inc., 402 F.Supp. 1357 (E.D.Mich.1975).

38. Restatement, Second, Contracts § 252(1).

39. Leopold v. Rock-Ola Mfg. Corp., 109 F.2d 611 (5th Cir.1940); Hanna v. Florence Iron Co., 222 N.Y. 290, 118 N.E. 629 (1918); but cf. Keppelon v. W. M. Ritter Flooring Corp., 97 N.J.L. 200, 116 A. 491 (1922) (the solvent party must tender or at least inquire whether the insolvent party can furnish the required security or cash).

40. Restatement, Contracts § 287.

41. McCloskey & Co. v. Minweld Steel Co., 220 F.2d 101 (3d Cir.1955); 1973 ALI Proc. 232 (1974).

The Code innovation in this section is to impose an obligation on each party to the contract to provide assurances to the other when there is reasonable ground for insecurity. According to Comment 1 there is reasonable grounds for insecurity when the willingness or the ability of a party to perform materially declines between the time of contracting and the time for performance.[42] Implicit in this is the notion that the insecurity must be based on matters not known to the party demanding assurances at the time of contracting and as to which he did not assume the risk.[43] Under the Code the insecurity may be based upon defaults under other contracts between the parties and even upon defaults with third parties.[44]

Three remedies have been provided under this section. First, in a proper case the aggrieved party is permitted to suspend his performance. Second, he is given the right to require adequate assurance. Third, under subdivision 4, failure to supply adequate assurances may create an anticipatory repudiation and thus give rise to all of the remedies available for such a repudiation.[45] In other words this section creates a new form of repudiation.

Although the term "adequate assurance" is left intentionally vague, the Code Comment indicates that standards of commercial reasonableness are involved, and depending upon the nature of the insecurity and the reputation of the parties, these standards may at one extreme be satisfied by a simple letter stating an intention to perform, and at the other extreme may require posting of guaranty.[46] When a party has reasonable grounds for insecurity is ordinarily a question of fact.[47]

U.C.C. § 2–609 applies only to a contract involving sale of goods unless it is extended by analogy. The Restatement Second adopts a similar rule and applies it to all types of contracts in § 251. The two sections are not in all respects the same. Some differences do not appear to be very important. For example, the Restatement Second

---

42. The Restatement, Second, which has a provision that is similar to U.C.C. § 2–609, provides on this point, "In any case, in order for the section to apply, the ground for insecurity must call into question the obligor's willingness or ability to perform without a breach that would so substantially impair the value of the contract as to the obligee as to give him a claim for total breach." Restatement, Second, Contracts § 251, Comment c. It has been suggested that the U.C.C. provision is not that limited. Rosett, Contracts Performances Promises, Conditions and the Obligations to Communicate, 22 U.C.L.A. L.Rev. 1083, 1087, n. 5. (1975).

43. Field v. Golden Triangle Broadcasting, Inc., 451 Pa. 410, 305 A.2d 689 (1973),

certiorari denied 414 U.S. 1158, 94 S.Ct. 916, 39 L.Ed.2d 110 (1974); U.C.C. § 2–609, Comment 3; Restatement, Second, Contracts § 251, Comments a and c.

44. U.C.C. § 2–609, Comment 3; accord Restatement, Second, Contracts § 251, Comment c.

45. U.C.C. § 2–609, Comment 2. See § 12–8 infra.

46. For a more detailed discussion, see Comment, The Right to Assurance of Performance Under U.C.C. § 2–609 and Restatement, Second, Contracts § 251: Toward a Uniform Rule of Contract Law, 50 Fordham L.Rev. 1292, 1306 (1982).

47. AMF, Inc. v. McDonald's Corp., 536 F.2d 1167 (7th Cir.1976).

does not require that the demand for assurances be in writing.[48] Again, while the Code requires assurances to be given within thirty days the Restatement speaks of supplying assurances within a reasonable time.[49]

However, there are also some significant differences between the two sections. A most important question is whether the procedure for demanding assurances where there is prospective inability or unwillingness supplants the prior common law which, for example, permitted the insecure party to change his position, or whether it is in addition to the responses previously permitted by the common law which was incorporated into the First Restatement.

The Restatement Second has rejected the approach of the First Restatement and has replaced all of that learning with the section on assurances. In other words under the Second Restatement the insecure party may no longer, for example, change his position. He must proceed by way of a demand for assurances.[50] The Code appears to be silent on this point. However, it has been suggested that the procedure of demanding assurances is merely authorized by the Code and not required.[51] If this is so the insecure party may, if he wishes, still resort to the responses previously discussed.

Another important difference is that the Restatement Second gives the insecure party the choice of treating a failure to provide assurances as a repudiation or as a material breach.[52] The significance of this point is discussed below.[53]

It seems that it is generally felt that this new approach of demanding assurances has rescued the insecure party from a difficult choice.[54] It is undoubtedly true that the insecure party had to make a perilous choice. For example, if he changed his position and was correct he would be protected from liability. If however, a jury determined that the prospective inability was not sufficiently serious to permit a change of position then he would be subjected to an action for a total breach either upon a theory of repudiation or material breach.

Does this new approach of demanding assurances spare him from this unhappy choice? For example, assume that a party deems himself to be insecure when in fact he is not correct. He suspends performance and makes a demand for assurance which the other party properly refuses to give the party who is asserting his insecurity: the party who feels insecure refuses to proceed. Is he not guilty of a repudiation?

 WESTLAW REFERENCES
prospective! /s inability fail! unable /s perform! /s suspend! suspension

48. Restatement, Second, Contracts § 251, Comment d. Under the Code, asking for oral assurances does not bring the section into operation.

49. Restatement, Second, Contracts § 251, Comments e and f.

50. Reporter's Note to § 251.

51. J. White & R. Summers, § 6–2, note 11.

52. Restatement, Second, Contracts § 251(2).

53. See § 12–8 infra.

54. Farnsworth, Contracts § 8:23 at 643.

prospective! /s inability fail! unable unwilling! /s perform! /s discharg! cancel!

inability fail! unable unwilling! /s chang! /s position /s prospective! /s perform!

clark +s ingle

vend** /s "reasonable time" /s title /s (chang! /s position) cancel! rescission rescind!

future prospective! /s solven! insolven! /s inability unable fail! /s perform!

1–201 /s solven! insolven!

"adequate assurance" /s demand!

assurance /s repudiat! /s breach!

---

§ 12–3. Anticipatory Repudiation—History and Analysis

Where a party repudiates his obligations under the contract before the time for his performance arises under the terms of the contract the issue of anticipatory repudiation is presented.[55] The problem is that in this situation it is difficult to find a breach precisely because no promise made by the promisor has as yet been breached since no promised performance on his part is owing. The effect of such a repudiation has received a great deal of attention by the courts and writers.[56]

All discussion of the problem revolves around the case of Hochster v. De La Tour.[57] In April 1852 the plaintiff and the defendant entered into a contract by the terms of which plaintiff was to work for a fixed period commencing on June 1, 1852. On May 11, 1852 defendant positively stated that he would not perform (a repudiation). The plaintiff brought an action for breach of contract on May 22 at which time defendant had not breached any promise. The defendant resisted the suit on the grounds that the action was premature since there was no breach on his part.

The court disagreed. It reasoned erroneously that unless plaintiff was free to sue immediately he would have to wait for an actual breach (which under the court's analysis could not possibly occur before June 1)[58] before suing or even before changing his position by, for example,

---

55. CCE Fed. Credit Union v. Chesser, 150 Ga.App. 328, 258 S.E.2d 2 (1979). It is clear that anticipatory repudiation is related to prospective inability and more particularly to prospective unwillingness to perform discussed in the preceding section. A repudiation is a particular kind of prospective unwillingness. See § 12–4 infra.

56. Leading articles are Ballantine, Anticipatory Breach and the Enforcement of Contractual Duties, 22 Mich.L.Rev. 329 (1924); Limburg Anticipatory Repudiation of Contracts, 10 Cornell L.Rev. 135 (1925); Vold, The Tort Aspect of Anticipatory Repudiation of Contracts, 41 Harv.L.Rev. 340 (1928); Vold, Withdrawal of Repudiation

after Anticipatory Breach of Contract, 5 Tex.L.Rev. 9 (1926); Wardrop, Prospective Inability in the Law of Contracts, 20 Minn. L.Rev. 380 (1936); Williston, Repudiation of Contracts, 14 Harv.L.Rev. 317, 421 (1901); Rosett, Partial, Qualified and Unequivocal Repudiation of Contract, 81 Colum.L.Rev. 93 (1981).

57. 118 Eng.Rep. 922 (1853).

58. Under the facts it might be argued that the defendant would not commit a present breach until he was required by the contract to make the first payment. However, it is clear that a breach would have occurred on June 1, if the defendant

getting another position.   As the court saw the problem unless the plaintiff were permitted to sue immediately he would be caught in a dilemma: to remain idle and hope in the future for a favorable court judgment or to obtain other employment thereby forfeiting his rights against defendant since he could not show that he was ready, willing and able to perform at the agreed time.   The court overlooked the doctrine of prospective unwillingness to perform, discussed in the preceding section.   Under that doctrine although the plaintiff could not have sued on May 22 he was free to change his position, as for example by obtaining other employment.   In any event on the facts, as previously explained, he could have successfully sued on June 1 if he could show not that he *was* ready, willing and able to perform at that time but that he *would have been* ready, willing and able to perform *but for* the repudiation.[59]

Although based on erroneous premises, the doctrine of anticipatory breach, or more properly, breach by virtue of anticipatory repudiation, has been followed in England and in the United States.[60]   Since the case which introduced the doctrine was based on erroneous premises, it has been hostilely received by many influential writers.   Partially as a result of this academic hostility a number of limitations which are not inherent in the nature of the doctrine have been accepted by the courts.

To illustrate the depth of this hostility, the following quotation from Professor Terry of Columbia will suffice.   In a book review complimenting Professor Williston's treatment of the doctrine, he states that the "fearlessness with which the author stamps in no uncertain terms and with clearness of logic and irrefutable argument those vicious errors which have crept in, in one way or another, but which should be extirpated for the everlasting good of the science, can be illustrated in no better way than by his attack upon the false doctrine of 'anticipatory breach.'   That doctrine, as the author well demonstrates, is not and never has been defensible * * *.   There can be no fine-spun reasoning which will successfully make that a breach of promise which, in fact, is not a breach of promise * * *.   To say that it may be broken by anticipation is to say that which, in the nature of things, cannot be so." [61]

Is it indeed possible that a doctrine which in a few generations swept practically the entire common law world is so illogical as to

on that date refused to permit the plaintiff to perform the services for which he was engaged as this would have been a breach of the defendant's duty of cooperation.   Indeed, it could be argued that a repudiation may constitute a breach of a duty of cooperation even before any performance is due.   See 11 Williston § 1316.   For a suggestion that a repudiation always has this effect, see Equitable Trust Co. v. Western Pac. Ry., 244 Fed. 485, 501–02 (S.D.N.Y. 1917), affirmed 250 Fed. 327 (2d Cir.1918), certiorari denied 246 U.S. 672, 38 S.Ct. 423,

62 L.Ed. 932 (1918).   This question is discussed in more detail below in this section.

59.   See the preceding section.   The meaning of the "but for" clause is explored in § 12–7 infra.

60.   See Holiday Inns of America, Inc. v. Peck, 520 P.2d 87 (Alaska 1974); Restatement, Second, Contracts § 253(1), Comment a; 4 Corbin § 959; 11 Williston § 1312.

61.   Book Review, 34 Harv.L.Rev. 891, 894 (1921), Selected Readings, 1259, 1263.

violate the "nature of things?" On the contrary, it is submitted the doctrine does not offend logic and is supported by practical wisdom. As far as logic goes, a contract is usually formed by promises, but the obligation of a contract is the sum of duties thrust by law on the promisor or promisors by virtue of the promises. There is no lack of logic in the law's imposition of a duty not to repudiate, as, for example, it has imposed constructive conditions and duties of cooperation on the contracting parties. This duty not to repudiate imposed by law may be breached although no express promise has been breached.[62] Whether this duty is articulated in terms of an implied promise that neither party "will do anything to the prejudice of the other inconsistent with that [contractual] relation"[63] or in terms that "the promisee has an inchoate right to performance of the bargain * * * he has a right to have the contract kept open as a subsisting and effective contract,"[64] there is no lack of power in a common law court to develop the law by imposing duties. The exercise of this power is no offense to logic, much less to "the nature of things." As far as the wisdom of imposing a duty not to repudiate, there is much to say for it. Very often a repudiation is made because the repudiator believes he is justified in so doing. The sooner this issue is resolved, the better. Let it be resolved when memories are fresh and witnesses available. From a more substantive point of view, a right to a future performance is of present economic value. Usually, it may be dealt with in the market as an asset, either by outright assignment or by assignment as security for a loan. Apart from this possibility, its presence or absence on a balance sheet affects credit standings. A repudiated right, however, is of little value on the market or on an honest financial statement since the statement usually must indicate that the right in question is contested. Moreover, a promisee has a valuable interest, trite as it may seem, in peace of mind. Will his expectation of a future benefit materialize? The sooner the community enables him to obtain an answer, the sooner it will have performed one of the most valuable functions the law can serve.

A repudiation that occurs simultaneously with or subsequent to a breach (hereinafter referred to as a "present repudiation" as opposed to an "anticipatory repudiation") is not necessarily governed by the same rules that relate to an anticipatory repudiation. For example, where there is a "present repudiation," as defined above, there is actually a breach and that breach is treated as is any other breach. That is to say the breach may be considered total or partial, but ordinarily the breach will be total.[65] An anticipatory repudiation is treated in a different fashion.[66] As we proceed we shall also point out some of the other

---

62. See Ballantine, supra note 56.

63. Hochester v. De La Tour, 118 Eng. Rep. 922, 926 (1853).

64. Frost v. Knight, L.R., 7 Ex. 111 (1872).

65. Restatement, Second, Contracts § 253, Comment b; Restatement, Second,

Contracts § 317, Comment b. "The breach will be considered partial only if it does not substantially impair "the value of the contract to the injured party." Restatement, Second, Contracts § 243(4).

66. See § 12–8 infra.

areas wherein the rules governing "anticipatory repudiation" and "present repudiation" are different.

 WESTLAW REFERENCES

hochster +s "de la tour"

anticipatory +1 breach! repudiat! /s "united states" england

"doctrine of anticipatory" +1 breach! repudiat!

§ 12–4. What Constitutes a Repudiation?

In the preceding section the emphasis was on the anticipatory phase of the doctrine of an anticipatory repudiation. Here the stress is on the word repudiation.[67] As already pointed out not every prospective unwillingness to perform amounts to a repudiation.[68]

The first Restatement of Contracts, in discussing the doctrine of anticipatory repudiation as a total breach, lists three actions which constitute repudiation.[69] These are "(a) a positive statement to the promisee or other person having a right under the contract [70] indicating that the promisor will not or cannot substantially perform his contractual duties; [71] (b) transferring or contracting to transfer to a third person an interest in specific land, goods or in any other thing essential for the substantial performance of his contractual duties; [72] (c) any voluntary affirmative act which renders substantial performance of his contractual duties impossible or apparently impossible." [73]

(a) A Positive Statement, etc.

A great deal of learning has gone into the question of what constitutes a "positive statement." The traditional rule is that the statement must be so positive that the intent not to be bound by the terms of the contract must be beyond question. Thus a statement to the effect that "I doubt that I will perform" is not a repudiation.[74] In addition, under the traditional rule, if the promisor states that he will

---

67. The word "repudiation" carries with it the connotation that the party is not justified in taking the position that he takes. If the other party has been guilty of a material breach, the "repudiation" would be justified and would not be wrongful.

68. See § 12–2 supra note 19.

69. Restatement, Contracts § 318.

70. This refers to a third party beneficiary or an assignee, Restatement, Second, Contracts § 250, Comment b.

71. U.C.C. § 2–610 has a similar provision as does Restatement, Second, Contracts § 250. See City of Fairfax v. Washington Metropolitan Area Transit Authority, 582 F.2d 1321 (4th Cir.1978), certiorari denied 440 U.S. 914, 99 S.Ct. 1229, 59 L.Ed.2d 463 (1979); Fredonia Broadcasting Corp., Inc. v. RCA Corp., 481 F.2d 781 (5th Cir.1973), appeal after re-

mand 569 F.2d 251 (5th Cir.1978), rehearing denied 572 F.2d 320 (5th Cir.1978).

72. See also Restatement, Second, Contracts § 250, Comment a.

73. Gilman v. Pedersen, 182 Conn. 582, 438 A.2d 780 (1981); see also Restatement, Second, Contracts § 250, Comment a. As we have seen, the Uniform Commercial Code has added to this list a type of constructive repudiation. See § 12–2 supra. It might also be noted that for some purposes an adjudication of bankruptcy is treated as the equivalent of a repudiation. See § 12–6 infra.

74. Restatement, Second, Contracts § 250, Comment b. However, it should be recalled that this language amounts to prospective unwillingness to perform and would justify a demand for assurances. See § 12–2 supra. A suggestion for a mod-

not perform unless a specified event occurs this is not deemed to be a positive statement even though the event is not likely to occur.[75] The more modern notion is found in the Second Restatement. It states that the statement "must be sufficiently positive to be reasonably interpreted that a party will not or cannot substantially perform." The Restatement adds: "However, language that under a fair reading 'amounts to an intention not to perform except on conditions which go beyond the contract' constitutes a repudiation."[76] The rule of the Uniform Commercial Code in this respect is generally in accord with the Restatement Second. It contains the language of the "However" clause above and states, "Repudiation can result from action which reasonably indicates a rejection of the continuing obligation."[77]

It should be stressed that, subject to the rules stated below, when a party cannot perform he is not thereby guilty of a repudiation.[78] The point here is that there must be positive language that he will not or cannot substantially perform. Even though the language used is not sufficiently positive to amount to a repudiation, if the language is accompanied by non-performance, there may still be a repudiation.[79] This statement relates to "present repudiation" rather than an "anticipatory repudiation."[80] As we have seen, "a present repudiation" ordinarily amounts to a material breach and is treated as such.[81]

(b) Transferring or Contracting to Transfer Specific Property, etc.

At the beginning of the preceding section an illustration relating to the sale of goods was discussed. It related to a case where S agrees to sell and B agrees to buy a specific second hand car, delivery to be made and title to pass on June 1, and B agrees to pay the price on May 1. This illustration was used as the basis for an extended discussion of the doctrine of prospective inability or unwillingness to perform. Under

---

ification does not amount to a repudiation. Unique Systems Inc. v. Zotos Int'l, Inc., 622 F.2d 373 (8th Cir.1980).

75. Dingley v. Oler, 117 U.S. 490, 6 S.Ct. 850, 29 L.Ed. 984 (1886); McCloskey & Co. v. Minweld Steel Co., 220 F.2d 101 (3d Cir.1955).

76. Restatement, Second, Contracts § 250, Comment b. By way of illustration what the Restatement seems to have in mind is a statement by a party that he will not perform unless the other party advances money to him in a case where there is no duty under the contract to make such an advance. See also Created Gemstones, Inc. v. Union Carbide Corp., 47 N.Y.2d 250, 417 N.Y.S.2d 905, 391 N.E.2d 987 (1979), appeal after remand 89 A.D.2d 545, 453 N.Y.S.2d 14 (1982).

77. U.C.C. § 2–610, Comment 2. Some of the cases do not appear to have taken the comment too seriously. See, e.g., Tenavision, Inc. v. Neuman, 45 N.Y.2d 145, 408 N.Y.S.2d 36, 379 N.E.2d 1166 (1978). The Code does not attempt a formal definition of repudiation. However, as we have seen, the Code has added an additional form of repudiation to those known under prior law by virtue of its provisions for a demand for assurances contained in U.C.C. § 2–609. See the discussion in § 12–2 supra.

78. Restatement, Contracts § 318, Comment h.

79. Restatement, Second, Contracts § 250, Comment b.

80. See § 12–3 supra.

81. See § 12–3 supra, note 65.

526 BREACH & PROSPECTIVE NON-PERFORMANCE   Ch. 12

one version of this illustration it was assumed that S sold his car to a third party. At that point the question of prospective inability and unwillingness was stressed.[82] In this section what is being stressed is that by virtue of the sale B has an immediate cause of action against S upon a theory of anticipatory repudiation.[83]

(c) Voluntary Affirmative Act Which Renders Performance Substantially Impossible

As the First Restatement stated a "voluntary affirmative act" by a party "which renders substantial performance of his contractual duties impossible, or apparently impossible," amounts to a repudiation. One illustration will suffice. If A agrees to work for B for one year starting on June 1, in exchange for B's promise to pay and on May 25th A embarks on a voyage around the world there is not only prospective inability and unwillingness to perform, but there is also a repudiation.[84]

WESTLAW REFERENCES

di repudiat!

repudiat! /p "positive statement"

(a) *Positive Statement, Etc.*

repudiat! /s intend! intent! /s bind binding bound

repudiat! /s "substantial! perform!"

repudiat! /s statement /s manifest!

repudiat! /s statement /s restatement

to(95) /p repudiat! /p language writing

(b) *Transferring or Contracting to Transfer Specific Property, Etc.*

anticipatory +1 breach! repudiat! /s transfer!

(c) *Voluntary Affirmative Act Which Renders Performance Substantially Impossible*

95k313(2)

repudiat! /s "voluntary affirmative act"

repudiat! /s perform! /s impossib!

§ 12–5. Repudiation and Good Faith

Frequently a party states that he will not perform or takes some action which objectively constitutes a repudiation and does so with the most honorable of motives. In good faith he believes that his contract entitles him to act as he did or that he has a lawful excuse for his

---

82. See § 12–2 supra.

83. Miller v. Baum, 400 F.2d 176 (5th Cir.1968); Wilson Sullivan Co. v. International Paper Makers Realty Corp., 307 N.Y. 20, 119 N.E.2d 573 (1954); Pappas v. Crist, 223 N.C. 265, 25 S.E.2d 850 (1943); Lazarov v. Nunnally, 188 Tenn. 145, 217 S.W.2d 11 (1949); Petersen v. Intermountain Capital Corp., 29 Utah 2d 271, 508 P.2d 536 (1973); Allen v. Wolf River Lumber Co., 169 Wis. 253, 172 N.W. 158, 9 A.L.R. 271 (1919).

84. Restatement, Contracts § 318, ill. 6. For a case in which the death of a contracting party, coupled with the inability of the representatives of the decedent to perform, constituted a repudiation, see Bonebrake v. Cox, 499 F.2d 951 (8th Cir. 1974); Taylor v. Johnston, 15 Cal.3d 130, 123 Cal.Rptr. 641, 539 P.2d 425 (1975); Board of Supervisors of Fairfax County v. Ecology One, Inc., 219 Va. 29, 245 S.E.2d 425 (1978).

action. There is respectable authority to the effect that a good faith refusal to perform is not a repudiation.[85] The prevailing view, however, is that the test should be objective and that good faith is immaterial.[86]

WESTLAW REFERENCES

"new york life" +5 viglas

repudiat! /s motiv! faith /s immaterial!

§ 12–6. Bankruptcy as the Equivalent of Repudiation

We have already seen that insolvency, although it gives rise to the application of the doctrine of prospective inability, does not amount to a repudiation because it is not voluntarily caused.[87] However it is well established that filing a petition in bankruptcy does amount to an anticipatory repudiation if the trustee in bankruptcy does not adopt the contract within a reasonable time.[88] However, this conclusion is not based on the definition of repudiation. The rule was adopted so that unmatured claims would be "provable claims" under the Bankruptcy Act and thus be discharged by virtue of the bankruptcy proceedings.[89] Since this is so the failure of the promisee to prove his claim in the bankruptcy proceedings will terminate his rights against the bankrupt.[90]

It should also be pointed out that if a petition in bankruptcy is filed but does not result in an adjudication of bankruptcy, the legal effect is similar to that of a withdrawal of a repudiation [91]—to be discussed immediately below.

WESTLAW REFERENCES

repudiat! /s bankrupt!

85. New York Life Ins. Co. v. Viglas, 297 U.S. 672, 56 S.Ct. 615, 80 L.Ed. 971 (1936); Peter Kiewit Sons Co. v. Summit Construction Co., 422 F.2d 242 (8th Cir. 1969); Grismore § 184.

86. Walker & Co. v. Harrison, 347 Mich. 630, 81 N.W.2d 352 (1957); Restatement, Second, Contracts § 250, Comment d; Restatement, Contracts § 318; 4 Corbin § 973; 11 Williston § 1323. However good faith does appear to be important on the issue of material breach. See § 11–18(a) supra.

87. See the discussion in § 12–2 supra; see also Restatement, Contracts § 324; 4 Corbin § 985.

88. Central Trust Co. of Illinois v. Chicago Auditorium Ass'n, 240 U.S. 581, 36 S.Ct. 412, 60 L.Ed. 811 (1916); In re Marshall's Garage, 63 F.2d 759 (2d Cir.1933); Restatement, Second, Contracts § 250, Comment c; Restatement, Contracts § 324, Comment a.

89. 4 Corbin § 985; 11 Williston § 1325. As the Court said with respect to the prior Bankruptcy Act: "Possible doubts as to the meaning of the section should be resolved in the light of the purpose of the act 'to convert the assets of the bankrupt into cash for distribution among creditors and then to relieve the honest debtor from the weight of oppressive indebtedness and permit him to start afresh free from the obligations and responsibilities consequent upon business misfortunes.'" Maynard v. Elliott, 283 U.S. 273, 277, 51 S.Ct. 390, 391, 75 L.Ed. 1028 (1931).

90. Restatement, Contracts § 324, ill. 3. But cf. Restatement, Contracts § 324, ill. 2 (relating to certain obligations which are not discharged in bankruptcy).

91. Restatement, Contracts § 324, Comment a.

§ 12–7. Retraction of an Anticipatory Repudiation Rule With Respect to a "Present Repudiation"

Section 2–611(1) of the U.C.C. entitled "Retraction of Anticipatory Repudiation" states: "Until the repudiating party's next performance is due he can retract his repudiation unless the aggrieved party has since the repudiation cancelled or materially changed his position or otherwise indicated that he considers the repudiation final." This is in general accord with the common law rule that an anticipatory repudiation may be retracted until the other party has commenced an action thereon or has otherwise changed his position.[92] The Code is explicit that no other act of reliance is necessary where the aggrieved party indicates "that he considers the repudiation final."[93]

Retraction of a repudiation is ordinarily written or verbal;[94] but where the repudiation consists of an act (or failure to act) inconsistent with the contract the retraction may consist in the repudiator's regaining his ability to perform.[95] However to be effective this fact must come to the attention of the other party.[96]

At common law it is generally held, somewhat anomalously, that if an anticipatory breach is withdrawn in time there is no breach.[97] The Uniform Commercial Code has changed this rule. It provides: "Retraction reinstates the repudiating party's rights under the contract with due excuse and allowance to the aggrieved party for any delay occasioned by the repudiation."[98]

92. See generally, Squillante, Anticipatory Repudiation and Retraction, 7 Val. U.L.Rev. 373 (1973); Roehm v. Horst, 178 U.S. 1, 20 S.Ct. 780, 44 L.Ed. 953 (1900); Guerrieri v. Severini, 51 Cal.2d 12, 330 P.2d 635 (1958). The change of position need not be communicated. Lumbermens Mutual Casualty Co. v. Klotz, 251 F.2d 499 (5th Cir.1958); Bu-Vi-Bar Petroleum Corp. v. Krow, 40 F.2d 488, 69 A.L.R. 1295 (10th Cir.1930). The same rule is applied in the area of prospective inability and unwillingness.

93. U.C.C. § 2–611. The majority of the common law cases appear to be in accord with this position. United States v. Seacoast Gas Co., 204 F.2d 709 (5th Cir. 1953), certiorari denied 346 U.S. 866, 74 S.Ct. 106, 98 L.Ed. 377 (1953); Restatement, Second, Contracts § 256(1) and Comment c. As we have seen similar rules apply to a cure of prospective inability or unwillingness to perform. See § 12–2 supra and 12–7 infra and Restatement, Second, Contracts § 251, Comment b.

94. Restatement, Second, Contracts § 256, Comment b.

95. Restatement, Second, Contracts § 256(2); 11 Williston § 1335.

96. Restatement, Second, Contracts § 256(2); Restatement, Contracts § 319. The Code provides: "Retraction may be by any method which clearly indicates to the aggrieved party that the repudiating party intended to perform, but must include any assurance justifiably demanded under the provisions of this Article (§ 2–609)." U.C.C. § 2–611(2). It has been held that a repudiation is effective when and where mailed. Auglaize Box Board Co. v. Kansas City Fibre Box Co., 35 F.2d 822 (6th Cir. 1929), certiorari denied 281 U.S. 730, 50 S.Ct. 247, 74 L.Ed. 1147 (1930); see Restatement, Contracts § 321.

97. Restatement, Contracts § 319, Comment a. The result is different if there is a present repudiation. Restatement, Second, Contracts § 256, Comment a. Another peculiarity of the anticipatory breach doctrine is that the courts hold that the statute of limitations does not begin to run until there is a failure to perform. Brewer v. Simpson, 53 Cal.2d 567, 2 Cal.Rptr. 609, 349 P.2d 289 (1960); Ga Nun v. Palmer, 202 N.Y. 483, 96 N.E. 99 (1911); Restatement, Contracts § 322; 4 Corbin § 989.

98. U.C.C. § 2–611(3). See generally, Wallach, 13 U.C.C.L.J. 48 (1980). The Restatement Second does not appear to be in

Up until what point of time may an anticipatory repudiation be withdrawn? Professor Farnsworth states: "The repudiating party can prevent the injured party from treating the contract as terminated by retracting before the injured party has acted in response thereto." [99] He obviously has in mind the injured party's change of position, or his indicating that the repudiation is final or his commencement of a law suit. Notice that as Professor Farnsworth states the rule there is no specific time limit during which retraction must take place. In other words retraction may take place *at any time* until there is a change of position or an indication that the repudiation is final.[1]

The Uniform Commercial Code section quoted at the beginning of this section is not in accord because it limits the retraction of an anticipatory repudiation "until the repudiating party's next performance is due." The Uniform Commercial Code does not explain why it used this phrase. One could speculate that what it has in mind is the notion that once the repudiating party's next performance is due the repudiation is no longer anticipatory and that therefore there is now a breach accompanied by a repudiation with the result that there is a material breach that ordinarily justifies an action for total breach.[2] If this thought is not pursued further it is because it is not particularly significant. However, as we shall see in the next section there is an important distinction between a material breach and a repudiation.[3]

 WESTLAW REFERENCES

repudiat! /s retract! withdr*w! /s chang! /s position

contract*** agreement /s repudiat! /s oral! verbal! wr*te writing
   written

riess +s murchison

§ 12–8. Responses to an Anticipatory Repudiation

Basically there are three possible responses to an anticipatory repudiation. One has already been discussed. The injured party may bring an immediate action for a total breach if he can show that he would have been ready, willing and able to perform but for the repudiation.[4] By virtue of this action in response to the repudiation his duties under the contract are discharged.[5] Of course he need not sue immediately but if he does not he runs the risk of the repudiation being retracted.[6] Whenever he sues, even if it is after the time for perform-

accord with the U.C.C. See Restatement, Second, Contracts § 256, Comment a.

99. Farnsworth, Contracts § 8.22, at 638.

1. The Restatement Second seems to be in accord. Restatement, Second, Contracts § 256, Comment c.

2. Riess v. Murchison, 329 F.2d 635 (9th Cir.1964), certiorari denied 383 U.S. 946, 86 S.Ct. 1196, 16 L.Ed.2d 209 (1966); Restatement, Second, Contracts § 243(2).

3. See § 12–8 infra; Stocker v. Hall, 269 Ark. 468, 602 S.W.2d 662 (1980).

4. See § 12–3 supra.

5. In re Estate of Weinberger, 203 Neb. 674, 279 N.W.2d 849 (1979).

6. See § 12–7 supra; Space Center, Inc. v. 451 Corp., 298 N.W.2d 443 (Minn.1980). However, as we have seen, the repudiation may not be retracted if there is a change of position or a statement by the innocent

ance arrives, he must still show that he would have been ready, willing and able to perform but for the repudiation.[7]

Another possible response by the aggrieved party is to urge or insist that the other party perform—in other words to urge the repudiating party to undo his repudiation. The effect of this response is tied into the topic of election. Some of the early English cases interpreted the doctrine as granting the promisee the power to elect to keep the contract in force or to terminate it.[8] The modern and better view is that there is no right of election in the face of repudiation.[9]

An illustration of the problem under discussion will help to clarify it. In Bernstein v. Meech,[10] plaintiff had contracted to perform in December at the defendant's theater. In August plaintiff wrote that he would not honor the engagement unless the promised remuneration was increased. Defendant replied insisting the plaintiff comply with the contract. Defendant heard nothing further from the plaintiff and booked other entertainers for the period in question. In December plaintiff appeared at the theater and tendered his services which, because a substitute had been hired, were refused.

The court, applying the election theory, held that defendant by insisting upon performance had elected to keep the contract alive and therefore was liable for breach of contract. The case and the election theory have been strongly criticized. Fortunately, the weight of authority,[11] the Restatements,[12] and the Uniform Commercial Code take a position contrary to this decision. The Code specifically states that the non-repudiating party may "resort to any remedy for breach * * * even though he has notified the repudiating party that he would await the latter's performance and had urged retraction.[13] The theory is that

---

party that his duties under the contract are discharged.

7. Restatement, Second, Contracts § 255, Comments a and b. For example, assume in Hochster v. De La Tour, § 12–3 supra, that after the repudiation plaintiff suffered a severe injury that prevented him from serving any part of the period provided for by the contract. On this set of facts plaintiff is not able to show that he would have been ready, willing and able to perform but for the repudiation. In other words it was not the repudiation that caused his non-performance and thus he may not recover. If he obtained another position after the repudiation then the repudiation would be the cause of his non-performance and he could recover. See also Iowa-Mo Enterprises, Inc. v. Avren, 639 F.2d 443 (8th Cir.1981); Hospital Mortgage Group v. First Prudential Dev. Corp., 411 So.2d 181 (Fla.1982), on remand 412 So.2d 409 (1982).

8. See, e.g., Johnstone v. Milling, 16 Q.B.D. 460, 472 (1886).

9. 4 Corbin § 981.

10. 130 N.Y. 354, 29 N.E. 255 (1891). Subsequent New York cases have overruled this case by implication. See, e.g., De Forest Radio Tel. & Tel. Co. v. Triangle Radio Supply Co., 243 N.Y. 283, 153 N.E. 75 (1926).

11. Renner Co. v. McNeff Bros., 102 F.2d 664 (6th Cir.1939), certiorari denied 308 U.S. 576, 60 S.Ct. 92, 84 L.Ed. 483 (1939); Tri-Bullion Smelting & Dev. Co. v. Jacobsen, 233 F. 646 (2d Cir.1916); Canda v. Wick, 100 N.Y. 127, 2 N.E. 381 (1885); Carvage v. Stowell, 115 Vt. 187, 55 A.2d 188 (1947); 11 Williston §§ 1333–34.

12. Restatement, Second, Contracts § 257 and Comment a; Restatement, Contracts § 320.

13. U.C.C. § 2–610(b) and Comment 4. This rule can on occasion be rather harsh on the repudiating party. See Duesenberg & King, § 14.06[2][a]. It may be pointed out, however, that the repudiator is responsible for his own plight.

a party by demanding performance which is his right under the contract should not lose his right to terminate the contract and sue for damages unless the repudiating party retracts his repudiation in time.[14]

The topic of election is also related to the third possible response. The question is may the aggrieved party elect to ignore the repudiation and proceed with his performance or does the repudiation prevent him from exercising the normal election that he has when there is a material breach?[15]

For example, if the promisor contracts to pay for the construction of a bridge and repudiates in advance of any performance by the promisee, may the promisee elect to proceed with his performance? Under the election theory a number of earlier American cases reached the conclusion that the promisee may elect to perform.[16] The modern cases representing the weight of authority hold that the duty to mitigate damages overrides the concept of election.[17] In other words the promisee may not continue his performance if the effect of performance would be to enhance damages. Conversely, if the contractor repudiated, the one for whom the bridge is being built must mitigate damages, for example, by securing another contractor.[18]

The question arises as to how soon the non-repudiating party must act to mitigate damages. Section 2–610(a) of the Uniform Commercial Code, which by its terms applies to an anticipatory repudiation, provides that the aggrieved party may "for a commercially reasonable time await performance by the repudiating party." Comment 1 to this section adds: "But if he awaits performance beyond a commercially reasonable time he cannot recover resulting damages which he should have avoided." This rule was apparently placed in the Code to overcome the rule employed by some cases that in case of an anticipatory repudiation the aggrieved party may ignore the anticipatory repudia-

14. Lagerloef Trading Co. v. American Paper Products Co., 291 F. 947 (7th Cir. 1923); Sawyer Farmers Coop. Assn. v. Linke, 231 N.W.2d 791 (N.D.1975).

15. As we have seen, when there is a material breach the non-breaching party may elect to continue with the contract if he so desires. See § 11–18(a) supra. As indicated below there is a different rule as to a repudiation. The same is true of a present repudiation. See § 12–3 supra; Restatement, Second, Contracts § 243(2), Comment b.

16. Reliance Cooperage Corp. v. Treat, 195 F.2d 977 (8th Cir.1952); John A. Roebling's Sons Co. v. Lock-Stitch Fence Co., 130 Ill. 660, 22 N.E. 518 (1889). Many of the cases relying on this reasoning are sustainable on other grounds. See e.g., Barber Milling Co. v. Leichthammer Baking Co., 273 Pa. 90, 116 A. 677, 27 A.L.R. 1227 (1922) (dealer in goods need not sell at time of buyer's repudiation to minimize damages; this rule is explained in the chapter on Damages at §§ 14–15 to 14–17 infra.).

17. Bu-Vi-Bar Petroleum Corp. v. Krow, 40 F.2d 488, 69 A.L.R. 1295 (10th Cir.1930); Fowler v. A & A Co., 262 A.2d 344 (D.C.1970); Cameron v. White, 74 Wis. 425, 43 N.W. 155 (1889). Other cases are collected in 4 Corbin § 983; 11 Williston §§ 1301–1303. Problems concerning mitigation and anticipatory breach are also considered in the chapter on Damages at § 14–15 to 14–17 infra.

18. See the authorities cited in the previous note. The rules stated here apply equally well to a "present repudiation." See § 12–3 supra and Restatement, Second, Contracts § 243(2). Comment b to this section points out that if the repudiator agrees the other party may continue to perform.

tion until there was a breach by non-performance.[19]   However, the general common law rule appears to be that the injured party must act promptly after he learns of the repudiation.[20]

WESTLAW REFERENCES

di(repudiat! /s elect*** /s perform!)

johnstone +s milling

repudiat! /s "material! breach!" /s elect***

repudiat! /s elect*** /s contractor

minimiz! mitigat! /2 damage /s repudiat!

repudiat! /s "commercial! reasonabl!"

§ 12–9.   Exception to Rule That Anticipatory Repudiation Gives Rise to an Action for Total Breach

It has been made clear that an anticipatory repudiation gives rise to an action for total breach.[21]   However there is one exception to that rule.   An illustration will aid in understanding the exception.   A lends B $12,000 and B promised to pay $1,000 per month starting one month from the making of the loan.   Before the time for the first payment arrives, B repudiates.   There is obviously an anticipatory repudiation and under the rule allowing an action for a total breach A should be entitled to $12,000 (plus interest) minus an adjustment if there is an early payment.   However, in this situation, the courts do not permit such an action and permit A to sue for an installment only after that particular installment becomes due.[22]   It should be noted that there are two factors in this case.   One, the plaintiff has completely performed and two, the plaintiff is entitled to a fixed payment of money at one time or in installments.[23]   For the exception to apply, the first factor

19. Reliance Cooperage Corp. v. Treat, 195 F.2d 977 (8th Cir.1952).

20. Farnsworth, Contracts § 12–12, at 862.

21. See § 12–3 and § 12–4 supra.

22. Restatement, Contracts § 318 (amended in 1946); 4 Corbin §§ 962–969; 1 Williston §§ 1326–1330.   There is a distinct minority to the contrary.   See Placid Oil Co. v. Humphrey, 244 F.2d 184 (5th Cir. 1957); Pitts v. Wetzel, 498 S.W.2d 27 (Tex. Civ.App.1973).   The majority rule does not mean that A must bring twelve suits. Rather he may wait and sue for all of the installments at one time.   In this type of situation it is common to find an acceleration clause in the contract.   Such a clause states that one default makes all installments due and payable.   This effectively does remove the exception.

23. This relates not only to performance of all promises but also to conditions. For example, in a life insurance policy the insured is not normally required to pay premiums.   However, his payment of premiums is a condition.   In such a situation if the insurance company repudiates the insured has not fully performed and thus he may sue for a total breach because the exception does not apply.   American Ins. Union v. Woodward, 118 Okl. 248, 247 P. 398, 48 A.L.R. 102 (1926).   But there is a minority view which refuses to permit an action for total breach because the insured's rights can be protected in an action in equity for a declaratory judgment. However, even under the minority view an action for restitution would be available. Kelly v. Security Mut. Life Ins. Co., 186 N.Y. 16, 78 N.E. 584 (1906).   Some courts have held that the insured may sue for a total breach or for a declaratory judgment. Stephenson v. Equitable Life Assurance Soc., 92 F.2d 406 (4th Cir.1937).   Courts at times have ordered defendant to continue to make periodic payments.   John Hancock Mut. Life Ins. Co. v. Cohen, 254 F.2d 417 (9th Cir.1958); Equitable Life Assurance Soc. v. Goble, 254 Ky. 614, 72 S.W.2d

must always be present. Some courts have diluted the second requirement by not insisting that the obligor's promise involve an obligation to pay.[24]

It is sometimes difficult to make a determination as to whether a party has completely performed. For example, in a disability policy, the insured must periodically furnish proof of continued disability. In theory this should permit an action for total breach since the exception by its terms does not apply because plaintiff has not completely performed; but there are contrary cases.[25]

Another interesting case on this point is Long Island R.R. v. Northville Industry Corp.[26] In that case the plaintiff gave the defendant a license to install and use an oil pipeline along the Railroad's right of way. The defendant agreed to pay plaintiff a minimum of $20,000 per year for twenty years plus additional sums based upon use.[27] The defendant repudiated the agreement and the repudiation was anticipatory. The issue in the case was whether the exception being discussed here applied or whether the general rule applied. The case turned upon whether there had been full performance by the plaintiff.[28] The court decided that the plaintiff had not fully performed. In the language of the court, "analysis of this agreement leads to the inescapable conclusion that the railroad is obligated to future performance." The court points out that railroad had continuing obligations under the contract because it was under a duty not to abandon the property and not to sell to one who would use the property in such a way as to prevent the construction of the pipeline.[29]

35 (1934); Amend v. Hurley, 293 N.Y. 587, 59 N.E.2d 416 (1944); contra, Brotherhood of Locomotive Firemen & Enginemen v. Simmons, 190 Ark. 480, 79 S.W.2d 419 (1935).

24. See Diamond v. University of S. California, 11 Cal.App.3d 49, 89 Cal.Rptr. 302 (1970).

25. Cobb v. Pacific Mut. Life Ins., 4 Cal. 2d 565, 51 P.2d 84 (1935).

26. 41 N.Y.2d 455, 393 N.Y.S.2d 925, 362 N.E.2d 558 (1977).

27. This clause relating to additional sums was not important in the case because the court, before attacking the repudiation problem held the defendant's obligation was limited to the guaranteed minimum because defendant was not obliged to build the pipeline.

28. Notice that the case involves a bilateral contract. There is some question as to whether the exception applies in the case of a unilateral contract. See 11 Williston § 1305. Compare 4 Corbin § 962 with Sodus Mfg. Corp. v. Reed, 94 A.D.2d 932, 463 N.Y.S.2d 952 (4th Dep't. 1983).

29. The Court concludes that since there was "dependency of performance" (in other words plaintiff continued to have obligations under the contract) plaintiff could sue for a total breach in order to be relieved from these continuing obligations. Had the case involved a lease, under some authorities, the result would be different because a lease is looked upon as having completely performed when the lease is executed. In other words in the case of a lease there is no dependency of performance and the exception rather than the rule applies. In the language of the court, "Perhaps for this reason, the courts of this state have held that 'no suit can be brought for future rent in the absence of a clause permitting acceleration'." The court points out that other jurisdictions treat a lease as involving continuing obligations and thus apply the rule rather than the exception being discussed in this section.

The discussion above should not be confused with a situation where one party repudiates and the other party has made an independent promise that he breaches. For example, A and B enter into an em-

At times the element of the exception that is missing is the fixed payment of money either at one time or in installments. For example, A transfers a farm to B in consideration of B's promise to support A for life and prior to the time for performance B repudiates. A may bring an action for total breach based upon the anticipatory repudiation. Although A has completely performed there is no fixed amount for each payment to be made.[30]

The discussion above related to an "anticipatory repudiation." When there is a breach by non-performance coupled with a repudiation, the non-repudiating party has an action for a partial or a material breach depending on circumstances.[31] In the case of a material breach ordinarily justifying an action for total breach Professor Farnsworth indicates the same exception applies. In other words, "If at the time of the breach, the injured party has fully performed and the only remaining duty of performance of the party in breach is to pay money in independent installments, the failure to pay one or more installments does not amount to a total breach that will accelerate the time for payment of the balance of the debt."[32] This is true whether or not the material breach is based upon a present repudiation.[33]

 WESTLAW REFERENCES
di(repudiat! /s installment)

---

ployment contract for five years. A (employee) promises not to engage in the same business for a designated period after the termination of his employment. The parties agree that this promise is independent. After A starts to perform B repudiates the contract. A is still liable on his promise and if A breaches his promise B may sue for breach of this covenant even though B has repudiated. Restatement, Contracts (2d) § 232, ill. 3.

30. Restatement, Contracts § 317, ill. 6; see 4 Corbin § 970; 11 Williston § 1326.

31. Restatement, Second, Contracts § 243, Comment b; see § 12–3 supra for a definition of present repudiation.

32. Farnsworth, Contracts § 8–18 at 619; Restatement, Second, Contracts § 243(3); Restatement, Contracts § 313. Not all of the cases are in accord.

33. Hermitage Co. v. Levine, 248 N.Y. 333, 162 N.E. 97 (1928). But see Sagamore Corp. v. Willcutt, 120 Conn. 315, 180 A. 464 (1935) (allowing an action for a total breach).

Chapter 13

IMPOSSIBILITY OR IMPRACTICABILITY OF PERFORMANCE, FRUSTRATION OF THE VENTURE AND RISK OF CASUALTY LOSSES

Table of Sections

535

§ 13–1. Impossibility of Performance: Introduction

This chapter relates to a situation where an event occurs subsequent to the formation of a contract which makes it impossible to perform a promise that was made in a contract.[1]

The traditional common law rule was "Pacta Sunt Servanda";[2] promises must be kept even if they are impossible to perform.[3] In other words although an Equity Court will not grant specific performance of such a promise, the breaching party must still respond in damage.[4] The theory was that the breaching party should protect himself by a provision in the contract.[5]

Despite this absolute statement of the rule, from early times an exception was made in the case of performance of a promise of personal services made impossible by death or unavoidable illness.[6] A second exception was made where there was a supervening change in the law which made performance unlawful and therefore impossible.[7]

Since the middle of the last century the courts of England and the United States have expanded the exceptions to the doctrine and much of impetus for this liberalization of the doctrine is attributed to case of Taylor v. Caldwell[8] to be discussed below.[9] This expansion was articulated in the terms of implied or constructive conditions.[10] The parties are said to have contemplated the continued existence of a particular state of facts. If these facts change so as to render impossible a party's performance, it is often said that the continued existence of the contemplated state of facts is a condition precedent to the promisor's duty under the contract.[11] Another more recent development is that there

---

1. The topic of existing impossibility is discussed in § 13–11.

2. Sharp, Pacta Sunt Servanda, 41 Colum.L.Rev. 783 (1941).

3. 6 Corbin § 1322; Paradine v. Jane (1647) Aleyn 26, 82 Eng.Reprint 897; Silverman v. Charmac, Inc., 414 So.2d 892 (Ala.1982).

4. Restatement, Second, Contracts, Introductory Note to ch. 11.

5. Paradine v. Jane (1647) Aleyn 26, 28 Eng.Rep. 897 (K.B.1647).

6. 6 Williston § 1931.

7. 6 Williston § 1931.

8. 122 Eng.Rep. 309 (K.B.1863); Page, The Development of the Doctrine of Impossibility of Performance, 18 Mich.L.Rev. 589 (1920); Annot., 84 A.L.R.2d 12 (1962).

9. See § 13–3 infra.

10. See § 13–20 infra.

11. This is the basic approach taken by the Uniform Commercial Code and the Restatement Second. See § 13–20 infra. There has been some tendency to treat questions of impossibility and frustration as questions of law rather than fact. Restatement, Contracts (2d), Introductory Note to ch. 11; Mitchell v. Ceazan Tires, Ltd., 25 Cal.2d 45, 153 P.2d 53 (1944). But

has been a tendency to talk in terms of impracticability rather than impossibility.[12]

A modern statement of the impossibility doctrine appears in a leading case.[13]

> "The doctrine of impossibility of performance has gradually been freed from the earlier fictional and unrealistic strictures of such tests as the 'implied term' and the parties' contemplation.' [citations omitted]. It is now recognized that 'A thing is impossible in legal contemplation when it is not practicable; and a thing is impracticable when it can only be done at an excessive and unreasonable cost.' [citations omitted]. The doctrine ultimately represents the ever-shifting line, drawn by courts hopefully responsive to commercial practices and mores, at which the community's interest in having contracts enforced according to their terms is outweighed by the commercial senselessness of requiring performance. When the issue is raised, the court is asked to construct a condition of performance based on changed circumstances, a process which involves at least three reasonably definable steps. First, a contingency—something unexpected—must have occurred. Second, the risk of the unexpected occurrence must not have been allocated either by agreement or by custom. Finally, occurrence of the contingency must have rendered performance commercially impracticable.

The requirement that the contingency be unexpected relates to foreseeability and is discussed below.[14] This case stresses the two main hurdles that a party seeking to employ the defense of impossibility of performance must overcome in order to have the defense of impossibility under the modern case law. Not only must he show impossibility or impracticability but he must show that he did not assume the risk of the event that occurred.[15] This synthesis has been somewhat changed by the U.C.C. and the Restatement Second—a matter discussed immediately below.

 WESTLAW REFERENCES

"pacta sunt servanda"

impossib! /3 perform! /s formation

impossib! /3 perform! /s "specific performance"

see Oosten v. Hay Haulers, Dairy Employees & Helpers Union, 45 Cal.2d 784, 291 P.2d 17 (1955), certiorari denied 351 U.S. 937, 76 S.Ct. 833, 100 L.Ed. 1464 (1956); Mishara Constr. Co. v. Transit-Mixed Concrete Corp., 365 Mass. 122, 310 N.E.2d 363, 14 U.C.C.Rep. 556 (1974); Housing Authority of Bristol v. East Tennessee Light & Power Co., 183 Va. 64, 31 S.E.2d 273 (1944).

12. Both the Uniform Commercial Code and the Restatement Second speak in terms of impracticability rather than impossibility. See § 13–9 infra.

13. Transatlantic Financing Corp. v. United States, 363 F.2d 312, 315 (D.C.Cir. 1966); 41 Tul.L.Rev. 709 (1967); 8 Wm. & Mary L.Rev. 679 (1967).

14. See § 13–18 infra.

15. See 6 Corbin §§ 1320–72; Patterson, The Apportionment of Business Risks Through Legal Devices, 24 Colum.L.Rev. 335 (1924). Restatement, Second, Contracts, Introductory Note to ch. 11.

```
impossib!  /3  perform!  /s  "personal service"
impossib!  /3  perform!  /s  death illness
to(95)  /p  impossib!  /3  perform!
impossib!  /3  perform!  /s  exception
di(impossib!  /3  perform!  /s  lawful! unlawful! illegal!)
doctrine theory  /3  impossib!  /3  perform!
impossib!  /3  perform!  /s  impractica!
impossib!  /3  perform!  /s  commercial!
impossib!  /3  perform!  /s  contingen!
impossib!  /3  perform!  /s  risk
```

§ 13–2. The Rule of the U.C.C. and the Restatement Second

U.C.C. § 2–615 states in part as follows:

> "*Except so far as a seller may have assumed a greater obligation * * *.* (emphasis supplied). (a) Delay in delivery or non-delivery in whole or in part by a seller who complies with paragraphs (b) and (c) is not a breach of his duty under a contract for sale if performance as agreed has *become impracticable* by the occurrence of a contingency the non-occurrence of which was a basic assumption on which the contract was made * * *." (emphasis supplied).

A careful reading shows that the underlined portions refer to impracticability and assumption of the risk—the two "hurdles" that a party seeking to use the defense of impossibility must overcome. It is equally clear that a new element has been introduced by the words "by the occurrence of a contingency the non-occurrence of which was a basic assumption on which the contract was made."

Dean Murray suggests that this new element is "a somewhat complicated way of putting" the question of assumption of the risk.[16] However it is clear that the introductory language ("Except so far as a seller may have assumed a greater obligation) also relates to assumption of the risk. How do the two provisions relating to assumption of risk mesh? Apparently the answer is that one provision relates to an assumption of the risk under the law and the other (the introductory language) relates to an assumption of risk by virtue of the facts of a particular case.

Thus under this section there are three questions to be asked before a party may successfully assert the defense of impossibility of performance. These three questions are as follows:

(1) Was there an event that changed a basic assumption (common to both parties) on which the contract was made? If this event was not a basic assumption of both parties then the defen-

16. Murray, § 204, at 412; United States v. Wegematic Corp., 360 F.2d 674, 676 (2d Cir.1966).

dant does not have the defense of impossibility under the existing law.

(2) If so, did that event in fact make performance impossible or at least impracticable. A performance is rendered impracticable if it can be accomplished only with extreme and unreasonable difficulty.[17]

(3) Even if questions (1) and (2) are answered affirmatively, one must still inquire whether the party who seeks to utilize the defense of impossibility assumed this risk as a matter of fact. If he did he does not have the defense of impossibility.

The Restatement Second takes exactly the same approach except it makes explicit, what the Code leaves implicit, that a party may not avail himself of the doctrine of impossibility of performance if he is guilty of contributory fault.[18]

It is clear that it is not essential in every case to ask all of these questions or to ask them in this particular order. For example, if the contingency is covered by the contract or an operative custom there is no need to look beyond these sources.[19] However, this is not ordinarily true in cases which are litigated. In these it is better to proceed by ascertaining if there is impossibility or impracticability and, if there is not, the promisor is bound by his promise unless a contrary intent is implied. If there is impossibility or impracticability, then the question remains upon whom should the risk in question be visited? In other words did the party who is seeking to assert the defense of impossibility assume this risk either legally or factually? This decision is undoubtedly based upon what appears to be just under the circumstances. As stated above, "the doctrine ultimately represents the ever shifting line, drawn by courts hopefully responsive to commercial practices and mores, at which the community's interest in having contracts enforced according to their terms is outweighed by the commercial senselessness of requiring performance."

Although impossibility or impracticability of performance may arise in many different ways, the tendency has been to classify the cases into several categories. These are: 1) Destruction, deterioration or unavailability of the subject matter or the tangible means of performance; 2) Failure of the contemplated mode of delivery or payment; 3) Supervening prohibition or prevention by law; 4) Failure of the intangible means of performance; and 5) Death or illness. Closely related to the doctrine of impossibility is the doctrine of excuse of performance by reasonable apprehension of impossibility or reasonable apprehension of danger to life or health and also the doctrine of frustration of the venture. With the understanding that these catego-

---

17. See § 13–9 infra.

18. Restatement, Second, Contracts § 261. See § 13–15 infra.

19. On operative custom, see § 3–17 supra.

ries are convenient groupings rather than conceptually distinct classification,[20] they will be discussed in order.

WESTLAW REFERENCES

"uniform commercial code" u.c.c. /s 2–615

impossib! /3 perform! /s fault

§ 13–3. Destruction, Deterioration or Unavailability of the Subject Matter or Tangible Means of Performance

As previously stated the modern doctrine of impossibility can be traced to Taylor v. Caldwell.[21] In this case the defendant promised, for a consideration, to permit the plaintiff to use his Music Hall for the giving of concerts. Prior to the time for performance a fire destroyed the Music Hall. The court held that the defendant was excused from performance; that is, his failure to perform did not constitute a breach of contract.[22] Of course, the plaintiff in such a situation is also excused from performance under the doctrine of prospective or present inability to perform.[23] Since this case was decided, it has rather consistently been held that impossibility is an excuse for non-performance when there has been a fortuitous destruction, material deterioration, or unavailability of the subject matter [24] or tangible means of performance of the contract.

If we apply the analysis of the previous section to this case it is clear that the court says that the continued existence of the Music Hall was a basic assumption on which the contract was made and defendant did not assume the risk of the destruction of the Music Hall under the law. The court also decided that there was in fact impossibility and that defendant had not on the facts of the case assumed the risk of the destruction of the Music Hall. If the defendant had promised to be liable even though the Music Hall burned down, the result would be different under question (3). Since this is a complicated approach quite often in the ensuing discussion we will combine elements (1) and (3) and simply speak of assumption of the risk.

A good illustration of the topic under discussion is the numerous crop failure cases that have been decided.[25] If A promises to deliver

---

20. U.C.C. § 2–615, Comment 2; Restatement, Second, Contracts § 261, Comment a.

21. See note 8 supra.

22. An excuse from performance should be distinguished from an excuse of condition. The former discharges a duty so that a party under a duty is not liable for his failure of performance. An excuse of condition operates to transform a conditional duty into an absolute duty notwithstanding the non-occurrence of the condition to the duty. See § 13–10 infra.

23. See § 12–2 supra.

24. Restatement, Second, Contracts § 263 and Comment a. It is important to note that in the Music Hall case the plaintiff had a license rather than a lease to use the Music Hall. There are certain rules of property or sales law which may lead to a different result where the subject matter of the contract is destroyed. This is discussed in §§ 13–24 to 13–28 infra.

25. See Comment, Crop Failures and Section 2–615 of The Uniform Commercial Code, 22 S.D.L.Rev. 529 (1977).

2000 tons of Regent potatoes to be delivered from his farm in Elmira, New York, he would be excused from performance if, without any fault on his part, a pestilence destroyed his crop.[26] The case is somewhat different if A simply promised to deliver 2000 tons of Regent potatoes without specifying where they were to be grown. In this type of case if the parties assumed as a matter of course that the crops were to be grown on this farm, the majority of cases would allow the defense of impossibility because the parties by implication agreed that the potatoes were to come from this farm.[27] This is particularly true where the parties made the contract while they were at the farm of the seller.[28] Other courts have taken the absolute language of the contract at face value and have concluded that since the parties did not contract with respect to a particular source of supply, destruction of a source does not excuse performance.[29]

The situation is somewhat different if the contract is made for the delivery of potatoes but not with a farmer. What if both parties assume as a matter of course that the potatoes are to come from a specific area (e.g., a 100 mile radius) and that entire crop in that area is destroyed. Again there are conflicting cases but the cases seem to be a

26. Ontario Deciduous Fruit-Growers' Ass'n v. Cutting Fruit-Packing Co., 134 Cal. 21, 66 P. 28 (1901); accord, Bruce v. Indianapolis Gas Co., 46 Ind.App. 193, 92 N.E. 189 (1910) (oil or gas from named well); Ward v. Vance, 93 Pa. 499 (1880) (water from named well); Howell v. Coupland, 1 Q.B.D. 258 (1876), 46 L.J.Q.B. 147 (1876).

27. Restatement, Contracts § 460; U.C.C. § 2–615, Comments 5 and 9; Restatement, Second, Contracts § 263, ill. 7.

28. Squillante v. California Lands, 5 Cal.App.2d 89, 42 P.2d 81 (1935); Unke v. Thorpe, 75 S.D. 65, 59 N.W.2d 419 (1953); Snipes Mountain Co. v. Benz Bros. & Co., 162 Wash. 334, 298 P. 714 (1931).

29. Bunge Corp. v. Miller, 381 F.Supp. 176, 15 U.C.C.Rep. 384 (W.D.Tenn.1974); accord Whitman v. Anglum, 92 Conn. 392, 103 A. 114 (1918) (failure of milk supply caused by death of cows); Oakland Elec. Co. v. Union Gas & Elec. Co., 107 Me. 279, 78 A. 288 (1910) (failure of electricity supply caused by injury to dam); Anderson v. May, 50 Minn. 280, 52 N.W. 530 (1892) (failure of bean crop). Overall shortages of supply of a given product can constitute a defense. U.C.C. § 2–615, Comment 4; Mansfield Propane Gas Co. v. Folger Gas Co., 231 Ga. 868, 204 S.E.2d 625 (1974); G.W.S. Serv. Stations, Inc. v. Amoco Oil Co., 75 Misc.2d 40, 346 N.Y.S.2d 132 (1973); Note, The Liability of Natural Gas Pipeline Companies for Breach of Contract Due to F.P.C.-Ordered Curtailment, 1973 Duke L.J. 867. For the burden of proof which

the seller ought to meet, see Ohio Turnpike Comm'n v. Texaco, Inc., 35 Ohio Misc. 99, 297 N.E.2d 557 (1973). This result is sometimes based upon the parol evidence rule if there is an integrated writing. See, e.g., Bunge Corp. v. Recker, 519 F.2d 449 (8th Cir.1975); Ralston Purina Co. v. M.S. Rooker, 346 So.2d 901 (Miss.1977). Other courts have not considered the parol evidence rule as important upon the theory that you cannot tell whether a contract is impossible unless one knows the basis upon which the parties contracted. Krell v. Henry (1903) 2 K.B. 740, a "frustration" case, appears to have taken this approach. See also Canadian Indus. Alcohol Co. v. Dunbar Molasses Co., 258 N.Y. 194, 179 N.E. 383 (1932). It is clear that this problem may also be approached from the point of view of interpretation. See, e.g., International Paper Co. v. Rockefeller, 161 App. Div. 180, 146 N.Y.S.2d 371 (3d Dep't 1914) and Restatement, Second, Contracts § 263, Comment b, which states: "In proving such an understanding, prior negotiations may be used to show the meaning of a writing even though it takes the form of a completely integrated writing."

If the parties actually orally agreed that the subject matter of the contract was to come from a particular source, a different parol evidence problem would arise if there was an integrated writing. Under these facts the evidence should be excluded if it contravenes the parol evidence rule. See Paymaster Oil Mill Co. v. Mitchell, 319 So. 2d 652 (Miss.1975).

little more reluctant to reach the conclusion that the defense of impossibility should be granted.[30]

The same problem exists in cases stemming from the destruction of factories. Here the question is whether the parties agreed that the goods were to come from the particular factory destroyed or could come from other factories. The same confusion can be found in the factory cases as in the crop cases.[31]

The method of allocating risks is also illustrated in the building contract field. In a common factual pattern a contractor agrees to construct a building on land owned by the other party to be completed and delivered on May 5. On April 30, the nearly completed building is destroyed by fire without fault on the part of the contractor.[32] It would appear that as a practical matter performance is impossible. Yet although the Restatement of Contracts accepts extreme "impracticability" as the equivalent of "impossibility",[33] it deals with this situation under the heading of "unanticipated difficulty" which does not provide an excuse for non-performance.[34] In this analysis it is in accord with the great weight of authority.[35] How can this situation be distinguished from Taylor v. Caldwell?[36] One could say that in Taylor v. Caldwell,[37] the contract related to the existing Music Hall, while in the

30. Compare Pearce-Young-Angel Co. v. Charles R. Allen, Inc., 213 S.C. 579, 50 S.E.2d 698 (1948) (allowing a defense of impossibility) and Mitchell Canneries v. United States, 77 F.Supp. 498 (D.Fed.Ct.Cl. 1948) with Huntington Beach v. Continental Info System, 621 F.2d 353 (9th Cir.1980) ("Under California law, the seller's inability to acquire the contract item from a third party is no defense to an action for breach unless both parties contemplated that the item would be obtained from a particular source."); Holly Hill Fruit Products Co. v. Bob Staton, Inc., 275 So.2d 583 (Fla.App.1973) (even if no particular source is contemplated "Statons obligation was not to buy fruit wherever one could find it in order to fulfill the contract. His obligation was to find fruit, if possible, even at greater expense than anticipated in Highland and Hardee Counties.") and United Sales Co. v. Curtis Peanut Co., 302 S.W.2d 763 (Tex.Civ.App.1957).

31. See Stewart v. Stone, 127 N.Y. 500, 28 N.E. 595 (1891); Annot., 12 A.L.R. 1273 (1921); Annot., 74 A.L.R. 1289 (1931); Restatement, Contracts (2d) § 263, ill. 1. Compare Booth v. Spuyten Duyvil Rolling Mill Co., 60 N.Y. 487 (1875) with Canadian Indus. Alcohol Co. v. Dunbar Molasses Co., 258 N.Y. 194, 198–99, 179 N.E. 383, 387 (1932).

32. The fact pattern is suggested by School Dist. No. 1 v. Dauchy, 25 Conn. 530 (1857).

33. Restatement, Second, Contracts § 261. Compare Restatement, Contracts § 454.

34. Restatement, Contracts § 467, ill. 1; The Restatement, Contracts (2d) § 263, ill. 4 reaches the same result. Compare id. at § 1957. However, there is authority that where the house was essentially completed at the time of the fire, risk of loss shifted to the owner. Baker v. Aetna Ins. Co., 274 S.C. 231, 262 S.E.2d 417 (1980). Often it is provided that the risk of loss is upon the contractor until the project is "accepted." Hartford Fire Ins. v. Riefolo Const. Co., 81 N.J. 514, 410 A.2d 658 (1980). See also Halmar Const. Corp. v. New York State Environmental Facilities Co., 76 A.D.2d 978, 429 N.Y.S.2d 51 (3d Dep't 1980), appeal denied 51 N.Y.2d 705, 432 N.Y.S.2d 1028, 411 N.E.2d 798 (1980).

35. School Dist. v. Dauchy, 25 Conn. 530 (1857); Rowe v. Peabody, 207 Mass. 226, 93 N.E. 604 (1911); Tompkins v. Dudley, 25 N.Y. 272 (1862); see Note, 54 Harv. L.Rev. 106 (1940). The concept of "an act of God" is irrelevant in a discussion of "impossibility of performance." See 6 Williston § 1936 (rev'd ed. 1938). As a legal concept, "act of God" involves excuse for non-performance by common carriers of duties imposed by law. Page, supra note 5, at 592–94.

36. 122 Eng.Rep. 309 (K.B.1863) (the Music Hall case).

37. Id.

construction case the contract related to a completed building constructed on the site, not necessarily the first. It is much more realistic
to say, however, that the risk should be allocated to the builder because
this is what the parties would probably have agreed upon if they had
paused to consider the matter.[38] In other words the contractor assumed this risk with the consequence that he is not only bound to
return progress payments received but is also liable for damages for
total breach of contract.[39]

The foregoing situation is further complicated if the building is
destroyed or rendered less valuable because of defective plans and
specifications supplied by the owner. Earlier cases took the position
that the builder by accepting the owner's plans promises to produce the
result called for by the plans and accepts the risks attendant upon
using the owner's specifications.[40] It was believed that the owner relied
upon the builder's technical knowledge. The modern cases, however,
generally hold that where plans which the contractor must follow are
prepared by professionals hired by the owner, unless the language of
the contract or the circumstances otherwise indicate,[41] the owner warrants that the plans are adequate to produce the desired result [42] unless
the builder has reason to know of the inadequacy.[43] As indicated in
this statement of the rule the parties are free to allocate the risks by

38. Cf. Parker & Adams, The A.I.A.
Standard Contract Forms and the Law 45–
48, 131–34 (1954) (owner's obligation under
standard forms to procure insurance).

39. 6 Williston § 1964. The result is
based upon the superior knowledge of the
contractor who has custody of the premises. The contractor may, of course, protect himself by obtaining insurance. See
R. Posner, Economic Analysis of Law 78–79
(2d ed. 1977).

40. Stees v. Leonard, 20 Minn. 494
(1894); Superintendent & Trustees of Public School v. Bennett, 27 N.J.L. 513 (1859);
Dobler v. Malloy, 214 N.W.2d 510
(N.D.1973).

41. Compare Faber v. New York, 222
N.Y. 255, 118 N.E. 609 (1918), with Application of Semper, 227 N.Y. 151, 124 N.E.
743 (1919).

42. United States v. Spearin, 248 U.S.
132, 39 S.Ct. 59, 63 L.Ed. 166 (1918); J.L.
Simmons Co. v. United States, 412 F.2d
1360 (Fed.Cir.Ct.Cl.1969); Simpson Timber
Co. v. Palmberg Const. Co., 377 F.2d 380
(9th Cir.1967); North American Philips Co.
v. United States, 358 F.2d 980 (Fed.Cir.Ct.
Cl.1966); State v. Commercial Cas. Ins. Co.,
125 Neb. 43, 248 N.W. 807 (1933);
MacKnight Flintic Stone Co. v. Mayor of
New York, 160 N.Y. 72, 54 N.E. 661 (1899);
see Burke County Public School v. Juno
Const., 50 N.C.App. 238, 273 S.E.2d 504

(1981), appeal after remand 64 N.C.App.
158, 306 S.E.2d 557 (1983), review denied
310 N.C. 152, 311 S.E.2d 290 (1984); 5
Okla.L.Rev. 480 (1930). Some courts appear to proceed upon a negligence rather
than a warranty theory. In either case it
would be relevant to ascertain whether the
plans were the proximate cause of the failure to complete. Kinser Const. Co. v.
State, 204 N.Y. 381, 97 N.E. 871 (1912).
The defective specifications provide not only an excuse for non-performance, but also
a basis for an action for recovery of increased expenses involved in producing the
desired result. Montrose Contracting Co.
v. County of Westchester, 80 F.2d 841 (2d
Cir.1936), certiorari denied 298 U.S. 662, 56
S.Ct. 746, 80 L.Ed. 1387 (1936), second appeal 94 F.2d 580 (2d Cir.1938); see Simpson
Timber Co. v. Palmberg Const. Co., 377
F.2d 380 (9th Cir.1967).

43. Montrose Contracting Co. v. County
of Westchester, 94 F.2d 580 (2d Cir.1938),
certiorari denied 304 U.S. 561, 56 S.Ct. 943,
82 L.Ed. 1529 (1938); Lewis v. Anchorage
Asphalt Paving Co., 535 P.2d 1188 (Alaska
1975), appeal after remand 629 P.2d 65
(Alaska 1981); Banducci v. Frank T. Hickey, Inc. 93 Cal.App.2d 658, 209 P.2d 398,
399 (1949); Marine Colloids, Inc. v. M.D.
Hardy, 433 A.2d 402 (Me.1981); Mayville
Portland School v. C.L. Linfoot, 261
N.W.2d 907 (N.D.1978).

their agreement. Thus, if the builder expressly warrants that the owner's plans are adequate, he may not claim the excuse that they are inadequate.[44] If the parties agree upon contingency plans or payments in the event of unexpected soil conditions, the agreement will be given effect despite any alleged inadequacy of the specifications, and whether or not the unexpected conditions were grossly outside the reasonable contemplation of the parties.[45]

The situation is completely different where the owner supplies plans which show the desired end result without indicating the method of completion. In such cases the contractor, as in the early cases, is deemed to promise the result called for by the plans and to shoulder the risks of completion.[46]

Construction contracts with the federal government now routinely include a "changed conditions" clause which provides for an equitable adjustment in price or in time for performance in the event unknown physical conditions occur or are discovered after the contract is entered into.[47] As a result much of the litigation in government contracts cases concerning the issues discussed herein now centers upon the applicability of standard contract provisions.

A contract to repair or alter an existing building is not treated in the same way as a contract to construct a building. That is to say a different allocation of risk is made. The continued existence of the building is deemed to be a basic assumption on which the parties contracted and it is impossible to repair a non-existing building. Thus, unless the contractor in fact assumed this risk, he is excused from performance of his duty to repair or alter under the doctrine of impossibility of performance.[48] As discussed later, once the contract is discharged because of impossibility justice may require that the rights of the parties be adjusted.[49] Here the contractor is entitled to a quasi-contractual recovery.[50] The same concepts have been applied to excuse subcontractors from their duty of performance when a building is

44. Philadelphia Housing Authority v. Turner Constr. Co., 343 Pa. 512, 23 A.2d 426 (1942).

45. Simpson Timber Co. v. Palmberg Constr. Co., 377 F.2d 380 (9th Cir.1967); Depot Const. Co. v. State, 19 N.Y.2d 109, 278 N.Y.S.2d 363, 224 N.E.2d 866 (1967). But see note 10, p. 567 infra.

46. See Coto-Matic, Inc. v. Home Indem. Co., 354 F.2d 720 (10th Cir.1965). See also § 13–17 infra.

47. Cf. Fattore Co. v. Metropolitan Sewerage Comm'n, 505 F.2d 1 (7th Cir.1974); 35 Geo.Wash.L.Rev. 978 (1967).

48. The analysis is based upon the explanation offered in § 13–2 supra.

49. See § 13–23 infra.

50. Bell v. Carver, 245 Ark. 31, 431 S.W.2d 452, 28 A.L.R.3d 781 (1968). The

measure of damages under the theory of quasi-contract has varied. Under one view, the contractor's recovery is limited to the value of the fixtures incorporated into the building. Young v. Chicopee, 186 Mass. 518, 72 N.E.2d 63 (1904). Other cases allow, in addition, the value of materials destroyed at the job site. Haynes, Spencer & Co. v. Second Baptist Church, 88 Mo. 285 (1885). Still other cases have allowed, in addition, expenses in preparation for performance. Albre Marble & Tile Co. v. John Bowen Co., 338 Mass. 394, 155 N.E.2d 437 (1959). Some courts have allowed a "cost avoided" approach rather than a test based on net enrichment. Under such a test, the contractor's recovery is measured by what it would have cost the owner to procure similar labor and material. Angus v. Scully, 176 Mass. 357, 57 N.E. 674 (1900). See also § 13–23 infra.

destroyed. Here, too, quasi-contractual relief will be awarded to sub-contractors.[51] By extension of the reasoning in the repair and the sub-contractor cases a construction contractor has been excused from performance when the structure being erected was destroyed without his fault where the owner was cooperating in the project by supplying some labor.[52] A different result has been reached where the owner merely supplies materials.[53]

WESTLAW REFERENCES

95k309(2) /p impossib! impractica!

taylor +2 caldwell

impossib! /3 perform! /s excus!

impossib! impractica! /s perform! /s fortuit! destroy! destruction deteriorat!

impossib! impractica! /s perform! /s crop /3 fail!

di(contract /s excus! /s perform! /s destruction destroy!)

impossib! impractica! /s perform! /s "parol* evidence"

impossib! impractica! /s perform! /s source

impossib! impractica! /s perform! /s defense

impossib! impractica! /s perform! /s "act of god"

impossib! impractica! /s perform! excus! /s "unanticipated difficulty"

impossib! impractica! /s perform! excus! /s defect!

defect! +2 specification

"changed condition clause"

§ 13–4. Failure of the Contemplated Mode of Performance

In the preceding sections the impossibility or impracticability went to the heart of the contract. Here we are discussing impossibility with respect to a matter which, although important, is incidental to the main obligations of each party, for example, mode of payment and mode of delivery. It would seem to be axiomatic that if it becomes impossible to perform an incidental obligation and a commercially reasonable substitute is available, that substitute should be used and accepted.[54]

This approach could have been used in a number of cases involving the closing of the Suez Canal in 1956 and again in 1967. A leading case is American Trading and Production Corp. v. Shell Int'l Marine Ltd.[55] However, the court decided the case in accordance with the rules stated in § 13–2 above by concluding that the closing of the Canal was not an

51. M. Ahern Co. v. John Bowen Co., 334 Mass. 36, 133 N.E.2d 484 (1956); Hayes v. Gross, 9 App.Div. 12, 40 N.Y.S. 1098 (3d Dep't 1896), affirmed 162 N.Y. 610, 57 N.E. 1112 (1900).

52. Butterfield v. Byron, 153 Mass. 517, 27 N.E. 667 (1891).

53. Vogt v. Hecker, 118 Wis. 306, 95 N.W. 90 (1903).

54. E.g., Meyer v. Sullivan, 40 Cal.App. 723, 181 P. 847 (1919); Iasigi v. Rosenstein, 141 N.Y. 414, 36 N.E. 509 (1894).

55. 453 F.2d 939 (2d Cir.1972); see also Transatlantic Fin. Corp. v. United States, 363 F.2d 312 (D.C.Cir.1966) and Schlegel, Of Nuts, and Ships, and Sealing Wax, Suez, and Frustrating Things—The Doctrine of Impossibility of Performance, 23 Rutgers L.Rev. 419 (1969).

event that changed a basic assumption on which the contract was made and in addition the closing of the Canal did not involve impossibility or even impracticability. What the court should have decided was that although it was impossible to use the Canal the trip around the Cape of Good Hope was a commercially reasonable substitute and consequently the owner was obliged to use that route and the charterer was obliged to pay the contract price.[56]

The U.C.C.[57] has a provision that specifically relates to cases involving failure of the contemplated mode of delivery or payment. This section provides:

(1) Where without fault of either party the agreed berthing, loading, or unloading facilities fail or an agreed type of carrier becomes unavailable or the agreed manner of delivery otherwise becomes commercially impracticable but a commercially reasonable substitute is available, such substitute performance must be tendered and accepted.

(2) If the agreed means or manner of payment fails because of domestic or foreign governmental regulation, the seller may withhold or stop delivery unless the buyer provides a means or manner of payment which is commercially a substantial equivalent. If delivery has already been taken, payment by the means or in the manner provided by the regulation discharges the buyer's obligation unless the regulation is discriminatory, oppressive or predatory.

Subdivision 1 contains a provision that would apply to the Suez Canal case if the case involved sale of goods. An interesting question is whether the owners in the Suez Canal cases not only did not have the defense of impossibility of performance but in addition would be liable because they did not perform on time. Comment 7 to U.C.C. Section 2–615 indicates that the additional time taken should not amount to a breach,[58] but it is not applicable to a ship charter agreement except by analogy.

---

56. If the contract specifically calls for a Suez passage or a trip around the Cape of Good Hope, then the promise made is alternative. In that situation, both alternatives must become impossible or impracticable before the defense of impossibility is available. Glidden Co. v. Hellenic Lines, 275 F.2d 253 (2d Cir.1960), on remand 207 F.Supp. 262 (S.D.N.Y.1962). As a matter of fact, the Transatlantic Fin. Corp. case specifically states that "the Cape route is generally regarded as an alternative means of performance." See note 55 supra. If the agreement contained an express condition precedent that the obligation of the owner to deliver would cease if the Canal was closed, the owner's duty to deliver would end, not because of the im-

possibility doctrine, but because an express condition precedent did not occur. Compare Northern Corp. v. Chugach Electric Assoc., 518 P.2d 76 (Alaska 1974).

57. U.C.C. § 2–614.

58. "The failure of conditions which go to convenience or collateral values rather than to commercial practicability of the main performance does not amount to a complete excuse. However, good faith and the reason of the present section and of the preceding one may properly be held to justify and even to require any needed delay involved in a good faith inquiry seeking a readjustment of the contract terms to meet the new conditions."

Subdivision 2 relates to the mode of payment. The first part relates to a case where delivery has not yet been made and payment in accordance with the terms of the agreement becomes illegal under the applicable foreign or domestic regulations. In such a case in the language of the statute "the seller may withhold or stop delivery unless the buyer provides a means or manner of payment which is commercially a substantial equivalent." Under this provision it appears that the contract is discharged unless the buyer chooses to proceed. The second part of the subdivision relates to the same situation except that the goods have already been delivered. Here the statute provides for "payment by the means or in the manner provided by the regulation * * * unless the regulation is discriminatory, oppressive or predatory." [59]

WESTLAW REFERENCES

impossib! impractica! /s "commercially reasonable substitute"

impossib! impractica! /s "substitut! performance"

§ 13–5.　Supervening Prohibition or Prevention by Law

If an agreement is illegal when made the problem is illegality.[60] If an agreement that is legal when made later becomes illegal the issue is not illegality but supervening impossibility of performance. Lawful performance becomes impossible. It is well settled that supervening prohibition of performance by law or administrative regulation of the United States, a state or municipality provides an excuse for nonperformance,[61] provided, of course, that all of the other requisites of the doctrine are met.[62]

For example, if the law intervenes because of the fault of the promisor he is denied the defense of impossibility because he is guilty of contributory fault and the impossibility is only subjective.[63] The problem arises typically in a case where a promisor is enjoined from

---

59. Exceedingly complex problems have arisen in regard to currency regulations of foreign countries. Treaty obligations are often applicable. In the absence of a treaty, traditionally, domestic courts have refused to recognize foreign restrictive regulations on the movement of currency. See Banco Do Brasil v. A.C. Israel Commodity Co., 12 N.Y.2d 371, 239 N.Y.S.2d 872, 190 N.E.2d 235 (1963), certiorari denied 376 U.S. 906, 84 S.Ct. 657, 11 L.Ed.2d 605 (1964); A. Ehrenzweig, Conflict of Laws § 191 (1962). The Code's recognition of these regulations is potentially a radical innovation. The provision is open to various interpretations, however, on the question of when the restrictive currency regulation is applicable to the case. This is a question of conflicts of law, not clearly answered by the Code. Cf. U.C.C. § 1–105.

60. See Chapter 22 infra.

61. Restatement, Second, Contracts § 284; see Horowitz v. United States, 267 U.S. 458, 45 S.Ct. 344, 69 L.Ed. 736 (1925); In re Kramer & Uchitelle, Inc., 288 N.Y. 467, 43 N.E.2d 493 (1942), reargument denied 289 N.Y. 649, 44 N.E.2d 622 (1942); Cinquergrano v. T.A. Clarke Motors, Inc., 69 R.I. 28, 30 A.2d 859 (1943); see also McNair & A. Watts, The Legal Effects of War 156–202 (4th ed. 1966); Blair, Breach of Contract Due to War, 20 Colum.L.Rev. 413 (1920).

62. Restatement, Second, Contracts § 264, Comment a; Harwell v. Growth Programs, Inc., 451 F.2d 240 (5th Cir.1971).

63. Klauber v. San Diego Street Car Co., 95 Cal. 353, 30 P. 555 (1892); Peckham v. Industrial Sec. Co., 31 Del. 200, 113 A. 799 (1921). See 13–15 infra.

performing. If he is at fault for the issuance of the injunction he is denied the defense of impossibility.[64] Where, however, the order is not caused by the promisor's fault, there is no reason why it should not provide as much an excuse for non-performance as any other kind of legal prohibition.[65] Indeed non-judicial action by a governmental agency which affects a particular party rather than the public generally has been held to excuse performance: for example the requisition of a factory for war production has been held to excuse performance of civilian contracts for production at the factory.[66] There is no reason why judicial action affecting a party should not equally be an excuse. The Uniform Commercial Code is in accord with the views stated here.[67]

A promisor is not only denied the defense of impossibility when he is guilty of contributory fault but also when he has in fact assumed the risk of the change in the law.[68]

The early cases generally took the position that prevention or prohibition by foreign law was not an excuse for non-performance.[69] Although this rule has been discarded in most modern cases,[70] some courts have continued arbitrarily to distinguish between domestic and foreign law.[71] The Uniform Commercial Code explicitly equates foreign law with domestic law as an excuse for non-performance.[72]

 WESTLAW REFERENCES

perform! /s illegal! unlawful! prohibit! /s impractica! impossib!

impractica! impossib! /s perform! /s superven!

impractica! impossib! /s contract*** /s assum! /s risk

contract*** /s impractica! impossib! /s "foreign law"

---

64. Peckham v. Industrial Sec. Co., 31 Del. 200, 113 A. 799 (1921).

65. Boston Plate & Window Glass Co. v. John Bowen Co., 335 Mass. 697, 141 N.E.2d 715 (1957); Kuhl v. School Dist. No. 76, 155 Neb. 357, 51 N.W.2d 746 (1952); People v. Globe Mut. Life Ins. Co., 91 N.Y. 174 (1883).

66. Israel v. Luckenbach S.S. Co., 6 F.2d 996 (2d Cir.1925), certiorari denied 268 U.S. 691, 45 S.Ct. 510, 69 L.Ed. 1159 (1924) (vessel commandeered); Mawhinney v. Millbrook Woolen Mills, Inc., 231 N.Y. 290, 132 N.E. 93 (1921) (output of factory requisitioned); see Note, 28 Yale L.J. 399 (1919). Informal governmental pressure was held to excuse late performance in Eastern Airlines v. McDonnell Douglas Corp., 532 F.2d 957 (5th Cir.1976).

67. U.C.C. § 2–615(a). The Restatement, Second, Contracts § 264, Comment b, is in accord. The comment adds that it is not necessary that the order be valid, but a party may have a duty to test its validity. Ordinarily if performance is simply made more burdensome, this will not suffice as an excuse. See § 13–9 infra.

68. Fast Bearing Co. v. Precision Development Co., 185 Md. 288, 44 A.2d 735 (1945); Restatement, Second, Contracts § 264, Comment a.

69. Jacobs, Marcus & Co. v. Credit Lyonnais, 12 Q.B.D. 589 (1884).

70. Texas Co. v. Hogarth Shipping Co., 256 U.S. 619, 41 S.Ct. 612, 65 L.Ed. 1123 (1921) (ship requisitioned by British Government); Rothkopf v. Lowry & Co., 148 F.2d 517 (2d Cir.1945); Held v. Goldsmith, 153 La. 598, 96 So. 272 (1919) (contract by German to ship goods to U.S. on British vessel discharged by outbreak of war between Germany and Britain); Restatement, Second, Contracts § 264.

71. Central Hanover Bank & Trust Co. v. Siemens & Halske AG, 15 F.Supp. 927 (S.D.N.Y.1936), affirmed 84 F.2d 993 (2d Cir.1936), certiorari denied 299 U.S. 585, 57 S.Ct. 110, 81 L.Ed. 431 (1936); Vanetta Velvet Corp. v. Kakunaka & Co., 256 App. Div. 341, 10 N.Y.S.2d 270 (1st Dep't 1939).

72. U.C.C. § 2–615(a).

§ 13–6.   Failure of the Intangible Means of Performance

This topic was covered in the First Restatement in a section entitled "Non-Existence of Essential Facts Other Than Specific Things or Person." [73] The Second Restatement does not appear to distinguish between tangible and intangible means of performance [74] and even the First Restatement took the position that the same basic rules should apply although the fact patterns may create a different type of problem.[75]

This distinction was important during the evolution of the doctrine of impossibility when the courts limited the defense of impossibility to situations "where performance is rendered impossible by an act of God, the law, or the other party." [76] This formulation was intended to include the destruction of a specified thing and death or incapacitating illness of a promisor in a contract which has for its object the rendering of personal services. The formulation did not include failure of the intangible means of performance.[77]

The chief illustrations of the failure of the intangible means of performance are prevention under foreign law, which has already been discussed, and strikes. Illustrative of the traditional rule with respect to the failure of the intangible means of performance is the case of Fritz-Rumer-Cooke Co. v. United States.[78] The plaintiff agreed to remove certain railroad tracks from an area around a gaseous diffusion plant. The contract specifically provided that the work was to be completed in one month and did not contain any provision protecting the contractor against a delay caused by strike. Employees of the gaseous diffusion plant went on strike and the employees of the plaintiff, although not on strike, refused to cross the picket line set up by the strikers. The strike lasted for 30 days. The government granted an extension of time. Plaintiff seeks to recover damages sustained because of the interruption in the work caused by the strike. The court disposed of the problem by stating what it termed "a well settled rule of law that if a party by a contract charges himself with an obligation possible to be performed, unforeseen difficulties, however great, will not excuse him, unless performance is rendered impossible by act of God, the law, or the other party." [79]

---

73. Restatement, Contracts § 461.

74. See Restatement, Second, Contracts § 261.

75. Restatement, Contracts § 461, Comments a, b, and c.

76. Fritz-Rumer-Cooke Co. v. United States, 279 F.2d 200 (6th Cir.1960).

77. Wischhusen v. American Medicinal Spirits Co., 163 Md. 565, 163 A. 685 (1933); Browne & Bryan Lumber Co. v. Toney, 188 Miss. 71, 194 So. 296 (1940); Ellis Gray Milling Co. v. Sheppard, 359 Mo. 505, 222 S.W.2d 742 (1949); see also Elsemore v. Inhabitants of Hancock, 137 Me. 243, 18

A.2d 692 (1941) (which also includes the act "of a public enemy").

78. 279 F.2d 200 (6th Cir.1960); see also Restatement, Contracts § 461, ill. 7.

79. 279 F.2d at 201. The same result has been reached where it is the promisor's employees who are on strike. The theory is that he must yield to the demands of the employees and if he does not, he is guilty of contributory fault. 6 Corbin § 1340; McGovern v. New York, 234 N.Y. 377, 138 N.E. 26 (1923); cf. Richland S.S. Co. v. Buffalo Dry Dock Co., 254 Fed. 668 (2d Cir. 1918), certiorari denied 248 U.S. 582, 39 S.Ct. 133, 63 L.Ed. 432 (1918); Empire

The more modern approach is exemplified by the case of Mishara Construction Co. v. Transit-Mixed Concrete Corp.[80] The plaintiff was a general contractor and the defendant, a sub-contractor, promised to supply ready-mixed concrete. Deliveries were to be made "as required" by plaintiff. In time there was a labor dispute, which disrupted work on the site for a month or so and even though work resumed "a picket line was maintained on the site until the completion of the project in 1969." Defendant failed to make deliveries and plaintiff purchased elsewhere and sued for damages.

Plaintiff sought to exclude any evidence relating to the picket line and sought an instruction that defendant "was required to comply with the contract regardless of picket lines, strikes or labor difficulties." The court analyzed the impossibility problem in more modern terms and concluded that plaintiff's request to charge to the effect that there was no impossibility as a matter of law was incorrect and that the issue was properly submitted to the jury.[81] The court repeats Professor Williston's conclusion that there are "many variables" that bear on the question and that the trend is "toward recognizing strikes as excuses for non-performance."[82] The Second Restatement omits reference to strikes. The Reporter's Note to § 261 and Comment d to the Restatement Second state that it "is omitted, because the parties often provide for this eventuality and, where they do not, it is particularly difficult to suggest a proper result without a detailed statement of all the circumstances." As suggested by the quotation it has become customary to include strike clauses in the agreement with the result that there has been a substantial amount of litigation relating to the interpretation of these clauses.[83] The Uniform Commercial Code does not appear to specifically refer to the subject of strikes.[84]

WESTLAW REFERENCES

delay! /s contract /s fail! /s perform! /s strike

"unforesee! difficulty" /s perform! /s contract

Transp. Co. v. Philadelphia & R. Coal & Iron Co., 77 Fed. 919 (8th Cir.1896); 6 Williston § 1951 A (rev. ed. 1938).

80. 365 Mass. 122, 310 N.E.2d 363, Annot. 70 A.L.R.3d 1259 (1974); see also City of New York v. Local 333, 79 A.D.2d 410, 437 N.Y.S.2d 98 (1st Dep't 1981), reversing 106 Misc.2d 888, 433 N.Y.S.2d 527 (1980), affirmed 55 N.Y.2d 898, 449 N.Y.S.2d 24, 433 N.E.2d 1277 (1982).

81. More often than not a question of impossibility is looked upon as a question of law. See § 13–1, note 11 supra.

82. 6 Williston § 1951 A (rev. ed. 1938).

83. See, e.g., Corona Coal Co. v. Robert P. Hyams Coal Co., 9 F.2d 361 (5th Cir. 1925); Davis v. Columbia Coal Min. Co., 170 Mass. 391, 49 N.E. 629 (1898); J.M. Rodriguez & Co. v. Moore-McCormack Lines, Inc., 32 N.Y.2d 425, 345 N.Y.S.2d 993, 299 N.E.2d 243 (1973); Normandie Shirt Co. v. J.H. & C.K. Eagle Inc., 238 N.Y. 218, 144 N.E. 507 (1924); see also § 13–19 infra.

84. But see U.C.C. § 2–615, particularly Comment 4. This states that an "unforeseen shutdown of major sources of supply" may give rise to impossibility.

§ 13–7. Death or Illness

We have already seen that ordinarily the death of the offeror terminates the power of acceptance created by his offer.[85] But death does not necessarily terminate a contract.[86] However, if a contract calls for personal performance by the promisor [87] or a third person [88] and the person who is to render the performance becomes so ill [89] as to make performance by him impossible or seriously injurious to his health, the promisor's duty is excused unless the risk was assumed by the promisor.[90] If the act to be performed is delegable, however, the death or illness of the promisor or of a third party who is expected to perform the act does not excuse performance.[91]

The personal representative of the deceased employee is entitled to quasi-contractual recovery for the reasonable value of the services rendered. The contract rate is evidence of this value but is not conclusive, except that it sets the upward limit on recovery.[92] Although the death of the employee who is to render personal services is not a breach, a number of jurisdictions have permitted the employer to set off his damages for non-performance of the contract against the

---

85. See § 2–20(c) supra.

86. Thomas Yates & Co. v. American Legion Dep't of Mississippi, 370 So.2d 700 (Miss.1979). Thus a promise to pay money is not made impossible because of the death or illness of either the debtor or creditor. Hasemann v. Hasemann, 189 Neb. 431, 203 N.W.2d 100 (1972).

87. Herren v. Harris, Cortner & Co., 201 Ala. 577, 78 So. 921 (1918); Buccini v. Paterno Const. Co., 253 N.Y. 256, 170 N.E. 910 (1930); Peaseley v. Virginia Iron, Coal & Coke Co., 12 N.C.App. 226, 182 S.E.2d 810 (1971), certiorari denied 279 N.C. 512, 183 S.E.2d 688 (1971). Conversely, the promisee need not accept a performance tendered by the deceased promisor's personal representative. Smith v. Preston, 170 Ill. 179, 48 N.E. 688 (1897); cf. 6 Corbin § 1335.

88. Spalding v. Rosa, 71 N.Y. 40 (1877); Phillips v. Alhambra Palace Co., 1 Q.B. 59 (1901).

89. Strader v. Collins, 280 App.Div. 582, 116 N.Y.S.2d 318 (1st Dep't 1952) (football coach). Of course, if the illness is relatively minor, there may be only temporary or partial impossibility. See § 13–13 and 13–14 infra. On the effect of supervening mental illness of a client on the attorney-client relationship, see Donnelly v. Parker, 486 F.2d 402 (D.C.Cir.1973). Supervening disabling illness of a student has been held to be grounds for entitlement to a refund of tuition. Dubrow v. Briansky Saratoga Ballet Center, Inc., 68 Misc.2d 530, 327 N.Y.S.2d 501 (Civ.Ct.1971). The case appears to be an instance of frustration rather than impossibility.

90. Mullen v. Wafer, 252 Ark. 541, 480 S.W.2d 332 (1972); Restatement, Contracts (2d) § 262 and Comment a.

91. Chamberlain v. Dunlop, 126 N.Y. 45, 26 N.E. 966 (1891). Restatement, Contracts § 459, Comment c makes this clear when it states:

Whether performance can be rendered only by a particular person is the same question, put in another form, as whether performance can be delegated to another. A question of this sort is involved not only in cases where a contractor dies or becomes ill, but in those where he voluntarily delegates the performance to another person and his power to do this is undisputed. If a contractor without violation of duty can go abroad and perform by means of another, his death or illness will not make subsequent performance of his contract impossible.

Compare Restatement, Second, Contracts § 262, Comment a. See §§ 18–28 infra.

92. Buccini v. Paterno Const. Co., 253 N.Y. 256, 170 N.E. 910 (1930). Difficult problems arise where the deceased was to be paid a contingent fee. See Rowland v. Hudson County, 7 N.J. 63, 80 A.2d 433 (1951); see also Morton v. Forsee, 249 Mo. 409, 155 S.W. 765 (1913) (death of attorney); City of Barnsdall v. Curnutt, 198 Okl. 3, 174 P.2d 596 (1945) (architect to receive percentage of construction costs; plans were incomplete; building never built).

estate's claim for quasi-contractual recovery for part performance.[93] Such results appear to be sound inasmuch as the parties' own risk allocations ought to be considered a principal guide towards reallocations of the risks necessitated by the doctrine of impossibility of performance.[94]

The same principles should govern the death or serious illness of an employer. If the employee was to work under the personal direction and supervision of the employer, the employer's incapacity makes supervision in accordance with the contract impossible. The employer is discharged because of impossibility and the employee because of employer's prospective inability to perform.[95] Thus, the question is whether the employer's duty and right of supervision are delegable and assignable.[96] Although perhaps most of the cases are reconcilable with this test, too often courts have indulged in sweeping generalizations and have indicated that a rule of mutuality is applied to the effect that since the employee's duties are personal, death of the employer discharges both parties.[97]

WESTLAW REFERENCES

contract /s personal /s terminat! /s death

excus! discharg! /s perform! duty /s contract /s death

risk /s assum! /s promisor /s health ill illness death disab!

95k311

burka +s patrick

death deceased /s employee /s "personal service"

§ 13–8. Reasonable Apprehension of Impossibility or Danger

Closely related to the doctrine of impossibility of performance is a doctrine that states reasonable apprehension of impossibility excuses beginning or continuing performance.[98] The most frequent application of the rule is to situations where the apprehension of impossibility relates to danger to life or health.[99] The rule applies not only when there is a threatened harm to the promisor but also where the threatened harm relates to others.[1] The doctrine is not ordinarily applied

---

93. Clark v. Gilbert, 26 N.Y. 279 (1863); Patrick v. Putnam, 27 Vt. 759 (1855); 46 Mich.L.Rev. 401, 421 (1948); see 69 Yale L.J. 1054 (1960).

94. See Burka v. Patrick, 34 Md.App. 181, 366 A.2d 1070 (1976); Perillo, Restitution in a Contractual Context, 73 Colum.L. Rev. 1208, 1224–25 (1973).

95. See Lacy v. Getman, 119 N.Y. 109, 23 N.E. 452 (1890); 6 Corbin § 1335. Although it is not impossible for the employer to pay, it is impossible for him to supervise. Perhaps it could also be said that there is frustration of the purpose.

96. See Kelley v. Thompson Land Co., 112 W.Va. 454, 164 S.E. 667 (1932); see also § 18–31.

97. See 6 Williston § 1941 (rev. ed. 1938). A mixture of sound analysis and sweeping over-generalizations is often found. See, e.g., Minevitch v. Puleo, 9 A.D.2d 285, 193 N.Y.S.2d 833 (1st Dep't 1959).

98. Restatement, Contracts § 465, Comment a.

99. Restatement, Contracts § 465, Comment b.

1. Restatement, Contracts § 465, Comment f.

where the danger to be apprehended relates to land or goods because ordinarily that situation will not involve impossibility.[2] "Nevertheless, where the risk of pecuniary loss or harm to land or goods is great and the harm to the promisee caused by failure to perform is not, the risk need not be taken if there is good ground for apprehending that performance will be impossible."[3] Thus, an actor is excused from performing if he has symptoms of what may be a serious disease and enters a hospital for an examination. It matters not that the examination reveals that his illness is not serious.[4] A ship is excused from sailing into submarine infested waters and the ship owner is excused from his failure to deliver its cargo, although it subsequently is shown that the ship could have arrived at its destination several hours prior to the outbreak of hostilities.[5] An employee is discharged from his duty to work in an area where an epidemic of a serious contagious disease appears to be in progress.[6]

The Restatement Second no longer treats cases in this category as representing a separate doctrine, but rather as examples of impracticability of performance.[7] However, it states the same general rules.[8] The Restatement Second adds that the promisor must use reasonable efforts to overcome the obstacles to performance.[9]

WESTLAW REFERENCES
"wasserman theatrical" +s harris
"reasonable effort" /s perform! /s impossib! impractica! sick
   sickness illness

§ 13–9. Impracticability

Under the more traditional rule performance was required to be literally impossible.[10] Under the more modern view, impracticability is sufficient.[11] This trend is due to the first Restatement which equated extreme impracticability with impossibility.[12] This trend has continued and has been fortified by the Uniform Commercial Code which utilizes

2. Restatement, Contracts § 465, Comment d.

3. Restatement, Contracts § 465, Comment e.

4. Wasserman Theatrical Enterprise v. Harris, 137 Conn. 371, 77 A.2d 329 (1950).

5. The Kronprinzessin Cecilie, North German Lloyd v. Guaranty Trust Co., 244 U.S. 12, 37 S.Ct. 490, 61 L.Ed. 960 (1917).

6. Lakeman v. Pollard, 43 Me. 463 (1857); see also Hanford v. Connecticut Fair Ass'n, 92 Conn. 621, 103 A. 838 (1918). In all of these cases there may be additional questions such as assumption of the risk, contributory fault and whether the impossibility is temporary. See §§ 13–16 & 13–13 infra.

7. Restatement, Second, Contracts § 261.

8. Restatement, Second, Contracts § 261, Comment a, and ill. 7. Compare Restatement, Second, Contracts § 262, ill. 5.

9. Restatement, Second, Contracts § 261, Comment d.

10. Hudson v. D & V Mason Contractors, Inc., 252 A.2d 166 (Del.Super.1969).

11. Portland Section of Council of Jewish Women v. Sisters of Charity, 266 Or. 448, 513 P.2d 1183 (1973); F.J. Busse, Inc. v. Dep't of Gen. Servs., 47 Pa.Cmwlth. 539, 408 A.2d 578 (1979).

12. Restatement, Contracts § 454.

the term "impracticable" to encompass "impossible" [13] and the Restatement Second which follows the lead of the Code.[14]

Professor Williston used the term in his 1920 edition as meaning "not obtainable except by means and with an *expense* impracticability in a business sense." [15] The Restatement Second also speaks of impracticable because of "extreme or unreasonable difficulty, expense, injury or loss * * *." It adds that "impracticability means more than impracticality." [16]

How much difficulty amounts to impracticability? It is generally held that a mere increase in the expense of performing does not give rise to a defense of impossibility. For example increase in costs in the amount of 33⅓%, 100%, and 300% have been held to be insufficient.[17] Both Restatements state that a party assumes the risk of increased cost within a normal range but might not assume the risk of "extreme and unreasonable difficulty." [18]

The Uniform Commercial Code is less explicit. An official comment to the Commercial Code states that "increased cost alone does not excuse performance unless the rise in cost is due to some unforeseen contingency which *alters the essential nature of the performance.* Neither is a rise or a collapse in the market in itself a justification, for that is exactly the type of business risk which business contracts made at a fixed price are intended to cover. But a severe shortage of raw materials or of supplies due to a contingency such as war, embargo, local crop failure, unforeseen shutdown of major sources of supply or the like, which causes a marked increase in cost is within the contemplation of this section." [19]

Illustrative of a contingency that alters the essential nature of the performance is the California case of Mineral Park Land Co. v. Howard.[20] The defendant agreed to fulfill his requirements of gravel needed on a bridge building project by removing it from plaintiff's land and to pay for it at a rate of five cents per yard. The defendant removed all of the gravel above water level but refused to take gravel below water level on the grounds that the cost of removal would be ten to twelve times the usual cost of removing gravel. The court held that the defendant was excused from performing. It reasoned that although it was not impossible to remove additional gravel, for practical purposes no additional gravel was available and therefore, performance was

---

13. U.C.C. § 2–615.

14. Chapter 11 of the Second Restatement is entitled, "Impracticability of Performance and Frustration of Purpose."

15. 3 Williston § 1963 (1920).

16. Restatement, Second, Contracts § 261, Comment d.

17. American Trading & Production Corp. v. Shell Int'l Marine, 453 F.2d 939 (2d Cir.1972); Publicker Indus. v. Union Carbide Corp., 17 U.C.C.Rep. 989 (E.D.Pa.

1975); International Paper Co. v. Rockefeller, 161 App.Div. 180, 146 N.Y.S. 371 (3d Dep't 1914).

18. Restatement, Second, Contracts § 261, Comment d. Restatement, Contracts §§ 454, 460, ill. 2 and 3; J. Murray, § 199. The First Restatement mentions an abrupt ten fold increase.

19. U.C.C. § 2–615, Comment 4.

20. 172 Cal. 289, 156 P. 458 (1916), critically noted in 4 Calif.L.Rev. 407 (1916).

excused because of the non-existence, for practical purposes, of the subject matter of the contract. A good number of cases [21] in accord concerning mineral leases had previously been decided on a variety of grounds, mostly as a matter of interpretation of the lease but also on grounds of mutual mistake of fact.[22] The case actually involves existing impossibility rather than supervening impossibility.[23]

There are a number of cases that have used impracticability as the basis for applying the defense of impossibility of performance where the cost of performance is considerably increased as a result of the necessity of performing in a manner radically different than was originally contemplated.[24] There are relatively few cases where impracticability was the foundation of a defense of impossibility solely on the basis of increased costs. A large number of recent cases dealing with inflationary rises in cost have reiterated the traditional notion that increased costs alone do not give rise to the defense of impracticability.[25]

Cases relating to reasonable apprehension of impossibility, which under the modern view are treated under the heading of impracticability, are discussed above.[26]

WESTLAW REFERENCES

impractica! /s williston

di impracticab!

restatement /s perform! /s impractica! /s impossib!

perform! /s impractical! /s impracticab! impossib!

increas! /s expense /s impractica! impossib! /s perform!

"alter the essential nature of the performance"

shortage /s perform! /s impossib! impractica!

contract /s perform! /s defense defend*** /s impossib! /s
    impractica!

---

21. E.g., Swiss Oil Corp. v. Riggsby, 252 Ky. 374, 67 S.W. 30 (1934); Carozza v. Williams, 190 Md. 143, 57 A.2d 782 (1948); Brick Co. v. Pond, 38 Ohio St. 65 (1882).

22. Petrey v. John F. Buckner & Sons, 280 S.W.2d 641 (Tex.Civ.App.1955); Paddock v. Mason, 187 Va. 809, 48 S.E.2d 199 (1948).

23. See § 13–11 infra.

24. City of Vernon v. Los Angeles, 45 Cal.2d 710, 290 P.2d 841 (1955); see also Northern Corp. v. Chugach Elec. Ass'n, 518 P.2d 76 (Alaska 1974).

25. Neal-Cooper Grain Co. v. Texas Gulf Sulphur Co., 508 F.2d 283 (7th Cir. 1974); Hudson v. D. & V. Mason Contractors, Inc., 252 A.2d 166 (Del.Super.1969); Maple Farms, Inc. v. City School District of Elmira, 76 Misc.2d 1080, 352 N.Y.S.2d 784 (Sup.Ct.1974); Portland Section of Council of Jewish Women v. Sisters of Charity of Providence in Oregon, 266 Or. 448, 513 P.2d 1183 (1973); cf. Northern Corp. v. Chugach Electric Ass'n, 518 P.2d 76 (Alaska 1974). There has been a flood of publication on this point in recent years. See Eagan, The Westinghouse Uranium Contracts. Commercial Impracticability and Related Matters, 18 Am.Bus.L.J. 281 (1980); Jaskow, Commercial Impossibility, The Uranium Market and the Westinghouse Case, 6 J. Legal Studies 119 (1976); Schwartz, Sales Law and Inflations, 50 S.Cal.L.Rev. 1 (1976); Wallach, The Excuse Defense in the Law of Contracts: Judicial Frustration of the U.C.C. Attempt to Liberalize the Law of Commercial Impracticability, 55 Notre Dame Law. 203 (1979); Note, U.C.C. § 2–615: Sharp Inflationary Increases in Cost As Excuse From Performance of Contract, 50 Notre Dame Law. 297 (1974). See also § 13–16 infra.

26. See § 13–8 supra.

§ 13–10. Impossibility as an Excuse of Condition

In the preceding sections the discussion concerned the defense of impossibility as an excuse for a failure to perform a promise. The concept of impossibility is being used defensively. Here the discussion relates to the possibility of using the concept affirmatively. The plaintiff seeks to use the concept to excuse an express condition which is impossible to perform so that he may recover on the contract despite his inability to perform the condition. For example, in the Music Hall case the defendant's promise to give a license was excused.[27] What would be the result if defendant argued that his failure to perform (constructive condition) was excused because of impossibility and therefore he should be entitled to a contractual recovery? Such an argument outrages common sense. If accepted, the plaintiff would be obliged to pay the license fee even though he has not received what he bargained for. However, there are cases where a condition (express) has been excused because of impossibility. The problem is closely related to § 11–35 supra entitled "Excuse of Conditions Involving Forfeiture."

In that section we discussed the Restatement rule that an express condition "may be excused without other reason" if (a) the failure to excuse the condition will result in extreme forfeiture and (b) the condition being excused is not a material part of the agreed exchange.[28] Examples of an immaterial part of the performance are conditions which merely fix the time or manner of performance or provide for giving notice or the supplying of proofs.[29] The same basic rule applies to excusing an express condition on the basis of impossibility except that the Restatement Second indicates that the forfeiture need not be extreme.[30]

It should be obvious by now that this doctrine may not be used to excuse a constructive condition because, by definition, a constructive condition of performance is a material part of the agreed exchange. Thus in the second version of the Music Hall case, assumed above, the condition would not be excused because no forfeiture is involved and the condition is not an immaterial part of the agreed exchange.

Both elements of the rule are satisfied in a case where a building contractor who has at least substantially performed cannot produce the certificate of a named architect because of the architect's death or incapacity. In such a case the failure to produce the certificate (an express condition) is excused and the contractor may recover on the contract.[31] If the contractor had not substantially performed prior to

---

27. See § 13–3 supra.

28. Restatement, Contracts § 302; Restatement, Second, Contracts § 271.

29. See § 11–35 supra; Restatement, Second, Contracts § 88, Comment d.

30. Restatement, Second, Contracts § 271, Comment a. The Comment seems

to indicate that the rule may apply even if the party seeking excuse assumed the risk of the condition but then he must show extreme forfeiture. Compare Murray § 192.

31. Restatement, Second, Contracts § 271, ill. 1.

the death of the architect, presumably the contract would be discharged and he would be limited to a quasi-contractual recovery.[32]

Another instance of excuse of condition is where an insured, because of impossibility, fails to furnish proofs of loss or fails to give notice within the time stated. Some courts have so held but others have disagreed.[33] However, the situation is different if the insured fails to pay a premium within a stipulated time. The condition relating to the premium is a material part of the agreed exchange and therefore is not excused.[34] There is some contrary authority.[35]

Similar problems may also arise in cases involving the sale of goods. Prior to the enactment of the Uniform Commercial Code, if goods were to be sold at a price to be fixed by an appraiser, the buyer was excused from performance if the price was not so fixed.[36] If the goods were delivered and accepted, however, the buyer's duty of performance was not discharged, rather the condition to his duty of performance was excused. He was required to pay a reasonable value.[37] The Code puts cases of this kind on a somewhat different basis.[38] If the price is not fixed in the manner agreed, the contract will be construed to mean that a reasonable price must be paid upon delivery. If, however, the parties intended not to be bound unless the price is fixed in the manner agreed upon, as when they rely on the unique expertise of the appraiser, the contract is discharged if the appraiser is unable to set the price even though the goods have been delivered. The buyer must return the goods already received. If this is not possible, he must pay reasonable value.

 WESTLAW REFERENCES

contract*** /s condition! /s excus! /s impossib! impractica!

fail! /s perform! /s excus! /s impossib! impractica!

clements +s "preferred accident"

insured /s impossib! /s "proof of loss"

"uniform commercial code" u.c.c. /s 2–305

§ 13–11. Existing Impossibility

We have been discussing impossibility that occurs after the agreement was made—so called supervening impossibility. It is equally

32. See § 13–23 infra.

33. Compare Restatement, Second, Contracts § 271, ill. 2 with Clements v. Preferred Accident Ins. Co., 41 F.2d 470 (8th Cir.1930). See Comment, Impossibility as an Excuse for Failure to Perform Conditions in Insurance Policies Requiring Notice of Loss, 34 Mich.L.Rev. 257 (1935).

34. Restatement, Second, Contracts § 271, ill. 3.

35. See Mulligan, Does War Excuse the Payment of Life Insurance Premiums?, 17 Fordham L.Rev. 63, 85 (1948).

36. Louisville Soap Co. v. Taylor, 279 Fed. 470 (6th Cir.1922), certiorari denied 259 U.S. 583, 42 S.Ct. 586, 66 L.Ed. 1075 (1922) (price to be that prevailing on Savannah market; market was inactive); Stern v. Farah Bros., 17 N.M. 516, 133 P. 400 (1913); Turman Oil Co. v. Sapulpa Refining Co., 124 Okl. 150, 254 P. 84 (1926); see U.C.C. § 2–305, Comment 4.

37. Hood v. Hartshorn, 100 Mass. 117 (1868).

38. U.C.C. § 2–305; see § 2–9 supra.

possible that impossibility may exist at the time of the agreement. The rules stated above generally apply equally well to existing impossibility.[39] There are two major differences. One is that the party seeking to use the doctrine must show that he did not know or have reason to know the facts that made performance impossible.[40] In addition existing impossibility results in a void contract whereas supervening impossibility discharges a contract that has already arisen.[41]

Knowledge of existing impossibility creates an assumption of risk. A party may assume the risk of existing impossibility in other ways.[42] One illustration is a case involving technological break-through which is discussed below.[43] These cases show that the problem of existing impossibility is closely related to the topic of mistake.[44]

 WESTLAW REFERENCES

"existing impossibility"

inception beginning /s knew know! /s perform! /s impossib!
     /s contract

risk /s assum! /s contract /s impossib!

§ 13–12. Frustration of the Venture

The doctrine of frustration of the venture had its origin in what are generally known as the coronation cases. In Krell v. Henry,[45] the plaintiff has granted the defendant a license to use his apartment for two days to view the coronation procession of King Edward VII and defendant agreed to pay £ 75 for this privilege. After the agreement was made the coronation was cancelled because the King was stricken by perityphlitis. It was held that the defendant was excused from his duty of payment under the doctrine of frustration.

What is the difference between impossibility and frustration? A person who is to supply lands, goods or services and finds that he

39. Faria v. Southwick, 81 Idaho 68, 337 P.2d 374 (1959); Housing Authority of Bristol v. East Tenn. Light & Power Co., 183 Va. 64, 31 S.E.2d 273 (1944); Restatement, Second, Contracts § 266, Comment a.

40. Reid v. Alaska Packing Ass'n, 43 Or. 429, 73 P. 337 (1903); Restatement, Contracts § 455; Restatement, Second, Contracts § 266, Comment a.

41. Mariani v. Gold, 13 N.Y.S.2d 365 (Sup.Ct.1939); Restatement, Second, Contracts § 266, Comment a.

42. Restatement, Second, Contracts § 266, Comment b.

43. See § 13–17 infra.

44. As to mistake see ch. 9 infra and § 13–20 infra.

45. [1903] 2 K.B. 740. As is often the case with doctrines believed to be innova-
tive, there were prior decisions in accord which were not perceived as having broken new ground. A perfect example is Miles v. Stevens, 3 Pa. 21, 45 Am.Dec. 621 (1846), where a contract for the sale of lots was premised on the construction of a canal to a particular point. The canal route was shifted. Deciding that the contract was discharged because of mistake, the court said: "We perceive no distinction either in principle or authority, where the parties contract, either with a view to existing facts, or facts merely in contemplation between the parties dependent on future events or contingencies. In either case, when the basis of the contract fails without the assent of the parties, to attempt to enforce the agreement is inequitable." Id. at 37, 45 Am.Dec. at 624–5.

cannot perform will attempt to use the impossibility defense. A buyer or any party who is obliged to pay will ordinarily attempt to use the defense of frustration. For example, if A agreed to supply B with a number of barges to carry a finished product from B's plant and B promises to pay a fixed sum per barge, A would attempt to use the defense of impossibility of performance if he was unable to supply the barges. If B had no product to ship he would attempt to use the frustration doctrine. Impossibility does not apply to B's promise because it is still perfectly possible for B to pay. The problem is that B is getting nothing for his money. It should also be observed that on this assumption performance on A's part is also possible. What is said here is equally true in the coronation case above. At times the courts confuse the two concepts when they conclude that it is impracticable for a party who has promised to pay to be obliged to respond in damages when nothing is received unless that risk has been assumed by him.[46]

The Restatement Second [47] sets forth the same rule for frustration as it does for impossibility. In essence a party must comply with four requirements before he has the defense of frustration of the venture. These requirements are as follows: (1) The object of one of the parties in entering into the contract must be frustrated. (2) The other party must also have contracted on the basis of the attainment of this object. In other words the attainment of this object was a basic assumption common to both parties.[48] (3) The frustration must be total or nearly total—in more modern terminology the principal purpose of the promisor (the one seeking to use the defense) must be either totally or substantially frustrated.[49] This distinction is akin to the distinction between impossibility or impracticability. (4) The party seeking to use the defense must not have assumed a greater obligation than the law imposes. In addition, as in the case of impossibility, the party seeking to use the defense must not be guilty of contributory fault.

The answers to each of these questions are as much in doubt as the corresponding questions in the impossibility area. Particularly troublesome in the frustration area is the second question listed above. Let us compare two cases. In Holton v. Cook [50] a pupil was enrolled in school for the year 1927–28. The charge was $1800 for the year payable $900

46. Downing v. Stiles, 635 P.2d 808 (Wyo.1981).

47. Restatement, Second, Contracts § 265.

48. See Restatement, Second, Contracts § 265; 6 Corbin §§ 1353–61. It should be noted that as used in England, the term "frustration" today encompasses both frustration of the venture and impossibility of performance.

49. Lloyd v. Murphy, 25 Cal.2d 48, 153 P.2d 47 (1944). North American Capital Corporation v. McCants, 510 S.W.2d 901

(Tenn.1974); Chicago, Milwaukee, St.P. & Pacific R. Co. v. Chicago & N.W., 82 Wis.2d 514, 263 N.W.2d 189 (1978). This is the same as saying under the doctrine of impossibility that there must be impossibility or extreme impracticability. See Restatement, Second, Contracts § 265, Comment a, which says that the frustration must be substantial and the fact that the transaction became less profitable is insufficient.

50. 181 Ark. 806, 27 S.W.2d 1017, Annot. 69 A.L.R. 709 (1930).

per semester. The pupil completed the first semester but did not return to school for the second semester because she developed defective eyesight during the break. The school sued for the second semester tuition and lost. This means that both parties contracted on the basis of the continued good health of the child.

In the second case defendant promised to pay $400 for a wedding dress to be made by P. Between the time of the agreement and the wedding D's husband-to-be (H) was killed in an accident. This occurred after the dress was ready but before it was delivered. It has been suggested that the continued existence of H was not the basis on which both parties entered into the agreement.[51] This result seems to contradict the previous case. In any event if it were held that defendant had the defense of frustration the rights of the parties would have to be adjusted to prevent P from losing the value of the materials and his services.

Before a party may assert the frustration defense he must overcome another difficult hurdle—that the principal purpose was substantially frustrated.[52] This proposition is well illustrated in the cases involving leases.[53] For example, in Doherty v. Monroe Eckstein Brewing Co.,[54] the defendant was in possession under a lease which provided: "It being expressly agreed that the only business to be carried on in said premises is the saloon business." [55] During the term of the lease Congress passed a national prohibition law which made the sale of alcoholic beverages illegal. It is obvious that this is not a case of supervening illegality of the lease; it is not illegal for the tenant to pay rent on unused premises. Rather, the courts have held that there is frustration even though the defendant could still have used the premises to sell cigars, cigarettes, soft drinks and the like. Thus the holding is that the principal purpose (the sale of alcoholic beverages) was totally frustrated.[56] As previously indicated the net result is that where the principal use is completely frustrated the frustration will be deemed to

51. See problem 2, p. 849 Casebook, Farnsworth, Young and Jones (2d ed. 1972) and the corresponding portion of the Teacher's Manual.

52. See note 49 supra.

53. It should be observed that some cases have doubted whether a lease can ever be discharged by frustration. Viewed as a matter of property law, a lease is a conveyance of an estate in land, performance being complete on the execution of the lease. In Paradine v. Jane, 82 Eng. Rep. 897 (K.B.1647), it was held that a lessee was required to pay rent although the premises were allegedly occupied by alien enemies. It is rather clear today, however, that the doctrine applies to leases as well as other kinds of contracts. See Perry v. Champlain Oil Co., 101 N.H. 97, 134 A.2d 65 (1957); 2814 Food Corp. v. Hub Bar Building Corp., 59 Misc.2d 80, 297 N.Y.S.2d 762 (Sup.Ct.1969). It would appear that in England the doctrine has not been extended to leases. See Ramaseshan, Doctrine of Frustration and Leases, 14 J.Indian L.Inst. 90 (1972).

54. 198 App.Div. 708, 191 N.Y.S. 59 (1st Dep't 1921).

55. Id. at 708, 191 N.Y.S. 59. Such a restrictive covenant is often deemed essential to give rise to a question of frustration of a lease.

56. See also The Stratford v. Seattle Brewing & Malting Co., 94 Wash. 125, 162 P. 31 (1916). Contra, Proprietors' Realty Co. v. Wohltmann, 95 N.J.L. 303, 112 A. 410 (1921). Some courts despite what is said above speak in terms of supervening illegality.

be total or nearly total, but where the principal use is not completely frustrated the defense of frustration is not available.[57]

In another case, not involving a lease S, a Canadian seller, agreed to sell a quantity of lamb pelts to B. Delivery was to be made in Toronto for delivery to Philadelphia. Prior to the delivery date, United States government regulations were promulgated under which the importation of lamb pelts of this type was prohibited. The defendant then refused to take delivery and asserted the defense of frustration. The court stated in part that under the contract the goods could be shipped anywhere else in the world since shipping instructions are not an essential part of the agreement. Thus the purpose of the buyer was not substantially frustrated even though the buyer may suffer a loss as a result.[58]

It seems to be widely believed that the courts are more inclined to sustain a defense of impossibility than one based upon frustration.[59] It has been asserted that there is no valid reason why this should be. One law review article states that "neither sense nor justice would be served by allowing seller to use a section 2–615 (U.C.C.) defense and simultaneously deny it to the buyer in the same situation."[60] In the language of another article, "Buyers and sellers should have the opportunity to claim a section 2–615 excuse when faced with an unduly burdensome and commercially senseless contract. Equity and mutuality of remedies support this view."[61]

It is true that both of these articles relate to the U.C.C. and that the U.C.C. may not contain an explicit provision relating to frustration.[62] If so, it is clear that the Code intends that the common law of frustration should apply.[63] Thus the point made in these articles would appear to be valid as a universal. A good illustration is the hypothetical case involving the hiring of the barges mentioned at the beginning of this section. If the supplier of barges could have the defense of impossibility for failure to supply barges why couldn't the hirer of the barges have a defense of frustration if without any fault on his part he had nothing to ship on the barges he hired? Mississippi seems to have

57. Lloyd v. Murphy, 25 Cal.2d 48, 153 P.2d 47 (1944) (auto dealership); Wood v. Bartolino, 48 N.M. 175, 146 P.2d 883 (1944) (gasoline station); Colonial Operating Corp. v. Hannan Sales & Service, Inc., 265 App.Div. 411, 39 N.Y.S.2d 217 (2d Dep't 1943), appeal granted 266 App.Div. 742, 41 N.Y.S.2d 953 (1943) (auto dealership).

58. Swift Canadian Co. v. Banet, 224 F.2d 36 (3d Cir.1955); Bardons & Oliver, Inc. v. Amtorg Trading Corp., 123 N.Y.S.2d 633 (Sup.Ct.1948), affirmed 275 App.Div. 748, 88 N.Y.S.2d 872 (1st Dep't 1949), affirmed 301 N.Y. 622, 93 N.E.2d 915 (1950).

59. Sections 2–615 and 2–616 of The Uniform Commercial Code: Partial Solutions To The Problem of Excuse, 5 Hofstra L.Rev. 167 (1976); Uniform Commercial

Code Section 2–615; Commercial Impracticability from the Buyer's Perspective, 51 Temp.L.Q. 518 (1978).

60. Uniform Commercial Code Section 2–615. Commercial Impracticability from the Buyer's Perspective, 51 Temple L.Q. 518, 548 (1978).

61. Sections 2–615 and 2–616 of The Uniform Commercial Code: Partial Solutions To The Problem of Excuse, 5 Hofstra L.Rev. 167, 183 (1976). See also Comment 9.

62. See § 13–22 infra.

63. See § 13–22 infra. See also Nora Springs Coop Co. v. Brandau, 247 N.W.2d 744 (Iowa 1976).

recognized the problem. It has added an additional provision to the U.C.C. which has been designated as U.C.C. § 2–617.

Just as there are cases of existing impossibility, there are also cases of existing frustration. The rules are the same. A good illustration of the problem can be found in another one of the coronation cases.[64] In that case there was also an agreement to hire a room to view the coronation procession, but it was made one hour after the decision to operate on the king was made.

 WESTLAW REFERENCES

frustration +3 venture

doctrine theory /s frustration /s perform!

frustration /s defense /s contract

krell +s henry

superven! /s frustrat! /s purpose

di(frustrat! /s impossib! /s perform!)

frustrat! /s "basic assumption"

frustrat! /s total entire /s contract

purpose /s contract /s substantial! /s frustrat!

frustrat! /s discharg! /s leasing lease

frustrat! /s "principal purpose"

frustrat! /s "restrictive covenant"

frustrat! /s contract /s principal +1 use purpose

§ 13–13. Temporary Impossibility or Frustration

One cannot state rules governing temporary impossibility without recognizing that temporary impossibility gives rise to prospective inability to perform.[65] In other words although the promisor is excused by temporary impossibility[66] the prospective inability will normally give the other party a right to suspend his performance. However, if the prospective inability created by the temporary impossibility is so serious that there is reasonable probability that substantial performance will not be forthcoming the other party may terminate contract despite the impossibility.[67]

If the other party does not have a right to terminate the contract or chooses not to, what rules govern the conduct of the party in whose favor the defense of temporary impossibility runs? Obviously he may suspend his performance and later when the impossibility ceases he is usually expected to perform in full and is entitled to an appropriate extension of time for performance.[68] Is he always obliged to begin or resume performance? The answer is the negative. Whether he must depends upon whether the delay will make his performance substan-

64. Griffith v. Brymer, 19 T.L.R. 434 (K.B.1903).

65. Restatement, Contracts § 462, Comment a.

66. Colorado Coal Furnace Distribs. v. Prill Mfg., 605 F.2d 499 (10th Cir.1979).

67. See § 12–2 supra.

68. Restatement, Second, Contracts § 269, Comment a.

tially more burdensome. When this is true the temporary impossibility not only suspends but discharges his obligation.[69]

Two illustrations will serve to clarify these rules. A promised to sing the leading female role in a new opera being produced by B. The first performance was to take place on November 28th. On November 23rd A became ill during a rehearsal. At this time the length of her illness was indefinite and unknown. B hired the only other available substitute performer to take A's place. The substitute insisted on being hired for the entire performance and was hired. A was ready to perform on December 4th at which time she tendered her services. They were refused. The jury found as a fact that the engagement of the substitute was reasonable.[70]

It is clear that A's illness was a defense to any action for breach of contract that B might bring relating to the period of illness. B undoubtedly could suspend his own performance during the period of illness. However, B did more than suspend his performance, he chose to terminate the contract. The question in the case was whether B was justified. In technical language there was a finding that there was serious prospective inability to perform which justified B in terminating the contract. The result, probably would be different if it were clear on November 23 that A's illness would have lasted only two or three days.[71]

As already stated, the party who has the defense of temporary impossibility may also terminate the contract if the delay will make his performance substantially more burdensome. In one case [72] a well known movie star was drafted into the army. Not only was he excused from performing while he was in the army but he was relieved of all obligations under the contract because the delay made his performance substantially more burdensome.[73] There is some authority that if the impossibility actually extends beyond the contract period there is automatic termination.[74] The same rules apply to temporary frustration.[75] Again the rules stated are over-ridden if one party has assumed the risk in question by agreement or otherwise.[76]

 WESTLAW REFERENCES
"temporary impossibility"

69. Restatement, Second, Contracts § 269, Comment a; 6 Corbin § 1348; 6 Williston 1957–58 (rev. ed. 1938); Patterson, Temporary Impossibility of Performance of Contract, 47 Va.L.Rev. 798 (1961).

70. These are the facts in Poussard v. Spiers & Pond, 1 Q.B.D. 410 (1876). This case was previously discussed in § 12–2 infra.

71. See, for example, Bettini v. Gye, 1 Q.B.D. 183 (1876).

72. Autry v. Republic Products, 30 Cal. 2d 144, 180 P.2d 888 (1947).

73. See also Village of Minnesota v. Fairbanks, Morse & Co., 226 Minn. 1, 31 N.W.2d 920 (1948). But see Peerless Cas. Co. v. Weymouth Gardens, 215 F.2d 362 (1st Cir.1954).

74. 6 Corbin § 1348.

75. Restatement, Second, Contracts § 269; see Patch v. Solar Corp., 149 F.2d 558 (7th Cir.1945), certiorari denied 326 U.S. 741, 66 S.Ct. 53, 90 L.Ed. 442 (1945).

76. Restatement, Second, Contracts § 269, Comment a.

§ 13–14. Partial Impossibility

If a promisor has the defense of impossibility (impracticability) as to part of his performance he is excused from performing that part [77] except that if he can render a reasonable substitute performance he is obliged to do so.[78] If substantial performance is still practicable (taking into account any reasonable substitute performance he is required to render) he is required to perform the remainder of the contract.[79] His performance is considered to be impracticable if the partial impossibility has made the remainder of his performance substantially more burdensome.[80] Even though substantial performance is no longer possible he is still obliged to continue performance if the other party within a reasonable time promises to perform in full or, if he has already performed in part, promises to perform the balance.[81]

The other question is the effect of the partial impossibility on the other party. The answer is that he has a right to terminate the contract if the part that is unperformed due to impossibility involves a failure to perform a material part of the agreed exchange or, to say it in another way, prevents the possibility of substantial performance.[82]

If the failure to perform the part that is partially impossible does not prevent substantial performance, both parties are obliged to perform the other part of the contract.[83] The party who has a defense is excused as to the partially impossible part and the other party may have a claim for restitution.[84] The various ways in which the rights of the parties may be adjusted after a contract has been terminated by impossibility (including partial impossibility) are discussed below.[85]

  WESTLAW REFERENCES
"partial impossibility"

§ 13–15. Subjective Impossibility—Contributory Fault

The First Restatement contained a specific section to the effect that a defense of impossibility may not be based upon subjective impossibility; objective impossibility was required.[86] It describes the difference between the two as the difference between "the thing cannot be done"

---

77. Restatement, Contracts § 463.

78. Meyer v. Sullivan, 40 Cal.App. 723, 181 P. 847 (1919); Restatement, Second, Contracts § 270 and Comment a; U.C.C. § 2–614, Comment 1.

79. Restatement, Second, Contracts § 270(a).

80. Restatement, Second, Contracts § 270, Comment a.

81. Restatement, Second, Contracts § 270(b) and Comment c; see also Van Dusen Aircraft Supplies v. Massachusetts Port Authority, 361 Mass. 131, 279 N.E.2d 717 (1972).

82. See § 11–18(b) supra.

83. Restatement, Second, Contracts § 270, Comment b.

84. Restatement, Second, Contracts § 270, Comment b.

85. See § 13–23 infra.

86. Restatement, Contracts § 455; Ballou v. Basic Const. Co., 407 F.2d 1137 (4th Cir.1969); Phillips v. Marcin, 162 Ga.App. 202, 290 S.E.2d 546 (1982); Roundup Cattle Feeders v. Horpestad, 184 Mont. 480, 603 P.2d 1044 (1979); Sachs v. Precision Products Corp., 257 Or. 273, 476 P.2d 199 (1970); Williams v. Carter, 129 Vt. 619, 285 A.2d 735 (1971).

and "I cannot do it." [87] As we have seen if a party is to perform a personal obligation and he dies, his obligation is discharged by impossibility.[88] In such a case the impossibility is not only subjective but it is also objective because he is the only one who can perform the duty since a personal performance is non-delegable.[89]

The Second Restatement recognizes, that subjective impossibility involves assumption of the risk or contributory fault.[90] We have already seen that a person who is guilty of contributory fault or assumes the risk is denied the defense of impossibility of performance.[91] For example, a person who is enjoined by a court from performing a promise may be allowed to use the defense of impossibility. However, if his wrongful conduct was responsible for the injunction he will be denied the defense because of his contributory fault.[92] If a party is to deliver specific goods on Feb. 1 and fails without good cause to deliver them on that date and the goods are subsequently destroyed, he will be denied the defense of impossibility because of his contributory fault.[93]

Perhaps the most common illustration of assumption of the risk is an impossibility that arises because a promisor is insolvent and is unable to make scheduled payment. In these circumstances the promisor is not excused irrespective of the reason for the promisor's insolvency.[94]

The burden of proof is upon the party who asserts impossibility.[95] He must show that the thing to be done could not be achieved by any means including substitute performances.[96] A fortiori if a party creates the impossibility by his own voluntary act he is not excused.[97]

87. Restatement, Contracts § 455, Comment a; White Lakes Shopping Center v. Jefferson Standard Life Ins. Co., 208 Kan. 121, 490 P.2d 609 (1971); Stone v. Stone, 34 Md.App. 509, 368 A.2d 496 (1977).

88. See § 13–7 supra.

89. Restatement, Contracts § 455, ill. 4; see § 13–7 supra and § 18–12 infra.

90. Restatement, Second, Contracts § 261, Comment e.

91. See § 13–2 supra.

92. See § 13–5 supra. As a matter of fact some courts have held that if an injunction is granted against a promisor, he is automatically guilty of contributory fault. South Memphis Land Co. v. McLean Hardwood Lumber Co., 179 Fed. 417 (6th Cir.1910).

93. International Paper Co. v. Rockefeller, 161 App.Div. 180, 146 N.Y.S. 371 (1914).

94. Central Trust Co. v. Chicago Auditorium Ass'n, 240 U.S. 581, 591, 36 S.Ct.

412, 60 L.Ed. 811 (1916); Christy v. Pilkinton, 224 Ark. 407, 273 S.W.2d 533 (1954); Baldi Const. Eng., Inc. v. Wheel Awhile, Inc., 263 Md. 670, 284 A.2d 248 (1971); 407 East 61st Garage, Inc. v. Savoy Fifth Ave. Corp., 23 N.Y.2d 275, 296 N.Y.S.2d 338, 243 N.E.2d 37 (1968); Title & Trust Co. v. Durkheimer Inv. Co., 155 Or. 427, 451, 63 P.2d 909, 919 (1936); Restatement, Contracts (2d) § 281, Comment b.

95. Ocean Air Treadways, Inc. v. Arkay Realty Corp., 480 F.2d 1112 (9th Cir.1973); 18 Williston § 1978B.

96. Lowenchuss v. Kane, 520 F.2d 255 (2d Cir.1975), on remand 72 F.R.D. 498 (S.D.N.Y.1976); Kama Rippa Music, Inc. v. Schekeryk, 510 F.2d 837 (2d Cir.1975); Miller v. Titeca, ___ Mont. ___, 628 P.2d 670 (1981).

97. Omni Investment Corp. v. Cordon International Corp., 603 F.2d 81 (9th Cir. 1979).

WESTLAW REFERENCES
subjective objective +1 impossibility
burden +2 proof proving /s impossib! /s contract
95k99(1) 95k322(1) /p impossib!

§ 13–16. Assumption of the Risk

One of the key issues in any impossibility or frustration case is which party assumed the risk in question. Under the recent formulation of the Restatement Second and the U.C.C. a party not only assumes a risk that the law imposes but in addition he may assume a risk that the law does not impose upon him.[98] In other words the facts of a particular case may show that said party assumed this risk.

The courts have never clearly revealed how they conclude that a particular risk should be imposed by law upon a particular party. However a little light is shed on the matter by the case of Transatlantic Financing Corp. v. United States,[99] wherein it is stated, "The doctrine ultimately represents the evershifting line, drawn by courts hopefully responsive to commercial practices and mores at which the communities' interest in having contracts enforced according to their terms is outweighed by the commercial senselessness of requiring performance."[1] As one court has stated the question is who the community would normally expect to assume this risk.[2]

The way in which this approach is employed in the concrete is well illustrated by considering the facts in the case of Canadian Industrial Alcohol Co. v. Dunbar Molasses[3] and some variations thereon. The plaintiff agreed to buy and the defendant, a middleman, agreed to sell approximately 1,500,000 gallons of molasses of the usual run from the National Sugar Refinery, Yonkers, N.Y., to test around 60% Sugars.[4] The output of the factory fell below its capacity when the refinery voluntarily curtailed its output and as a result defendant was able to deliver only 344,083 gallons. When sued the defendant employed the defense of impossibility. The court held, inter alia, that the defendant could not avail itself of that defense because it was guilty of contributory fault in failing to enter into a contract with the refinery.[5]

If the refinery had burned down and there was still no contract between the defendant and the refinery, the court indicates that the

---

98. See § 13–2 supra.

99. 363 F.2d 312, 315 (D.C.Cir.1966).

1. Id.; 41 Tul.L.Rev. 709 (1967); 8 Wm. & Mary L.Rev. 679 (1967).

2. Quick v. Stuyvesant, 2 Paige 84, 93 (N.Y.1830).

3. 258 N.Y. 194, 179 N.E. 383 (1932). A similar case reaching the same result is Barbarossa & Sons, Inc. v. Iten Chevrolet, Inc., 265 N.W.2d 655 (Minn.1978).

4. It is clear that the court assumes that this is not merely language of description but that the molasses must come from a particular factory.

5. Contributory fault has already been discussed in § 13–15 infra. The words contributory fault "are used if the promisor is in some way responsible for the event which makes performance of his promise impossible. In that case justice dictates that he not be excused." Appalachian Power Co. v. John Stewart Walker, Inc., 214 Va. 524, 201 S.E.2d 758 (1974); cf. Lowenschuss v. Kane, 367 F.Supp. 911 (S.D.N.Y.1973), judgment reversed 520 F.2d 255 (2d Cir.1975), on remand 72 F.R.D. 498 (S.D.N.Y.1976); Restatement, Contracts § 261, Comment d and § 265, Comment b.

defendant would have the defense of impossibility of performance. Here the fault of the defendant in not entering into the contract did not contribute to defendant's failure to perform. Rather the proximate cause of non-performance was the destruction of the refinery. The court concluded that the defendant did not assume the risk of the destruction of the refinery.[6] In other words, in the language of the Restatement Second and the U.C.C., the continued existence of the refinery was the basis on which both parties entered into the agreement and defendant did not in fact assume this risk. This seems fair, because on this assumption the defendant would not have a cause of action against the refinery even if he had entered into a contract with the refinery.

If it were assumed that the defendant entered into contract with the refinery and the refinery nevertheless voluntarily curtailed its output, should the defendant have the defense of impossibility? The answer suggested in the case is that the defendant would not have the defense. The reason is that both parties did not enter into the agreement on the basis of the voluntary continued output of the refinery. In other words the defendant assumed the risk of a voluntary diminution in the refinery's output. This is particularly true because the defendant is a middleman and it is logical that a middleman should assume just such a risk. In any event the result is just because defendant, in turn, would have a cause of action against the refinery.[7]

The result would be different if the parties had agreed that defendant's performance was contingent upon the refinery's performance.[8] Here, although the risk of voluntary curtailment is imposed by law upon defendant, that risk is imposed by agreement upon plaintiff by virtue of the condition in the contract.[9] There are other cases that conclude that surrounding circumstances may show that a party assumed a risk that was not imposed upon him by law.[10]

 WESTLAW REFERENCES

contract /s assum! /s risk /s impossib! impractica!

"canadian industrial" +s "dunbar molasses"

assum! /s risk /s perform! /s contingen!

output /s impossib! impractica! /s perform! agreement contract

circumstan! /s contract /s assum! /s risk

---

6. Center Garment Co. v. United Refrigerator Co., 369 Mass. 633, 341 N.E.2d 669 (1976); cf. Sunseri v. Garcia & Maggini Co., 298 Pa. 249, 148 A. 81 (1929).

7. U.C.C. § 2–615, Comment 5 seems to say the defendant should have the defense of impossibility of performance in this case but on the condition that he turns over to the plaintiff "his rights against the defaulting source of supply * * *."

8. Mosby v. Smith, 194 Mo.App. 20, 186 S.W. 49 (1916); Scialli v. Correale, 97

N.J.L. 165, 117 A. 255 (1922); Restatement, Contracts § 460, ill. 12.

9. See also § 13–17 infra relating to technological impossibility. A custom or usage that forms part of the agreement is also obviously important.

10. Wills v. Shockley, 52 Del. 295, 157 A.2d 252 (1960); Savage v. Peter Kiewit Sons' Co., 249 Or. 147, 432 P.2d 519 (1967), modified 249 Or. 147, 437 P.2d 487 (1968); see also U.C.C. § 2–615, Comment 8.

§ 13–17. Assumption of the Risk—Technological Impossibility

Another good illustration of assumption of the risk are the cases involving a technological breakthrough. In a number of cases, mostly involving government contracts for the manufacture of new products, or the use of new processes, the manufacturer has contended that compliance with the contract has proved impossible, at least under existing technology. The cases relate to existing rather than supervening impossibility.[11] Generally, the cases have held that the contractor has assumed the risk that production was possible because he knew or should have known of the limits of existing technology.[12]

On the other hand, where detailed plans of manufacturing processes, as opposed to goals which the end product must meet, are provided by the government, it has been held that the government assumes the risk because it warrants that the plan will produce the desired result.[13]

Cases involving existing impossibility are somewhat related to the topic of mistake and this is equally true of the cases involving technological impossibility.[14]

In an interesting and unprecedented case,[15] a contractor agreed to produce artillery shells for the government using a new process. In the course of negotiations the contractor argued that the process would not produce the result desired unless certain machinery were used to remove excess steel. The government, however, insisted that such equipment was not needed. The plaintiff succumbed to the government's insistence and agreed to produce the shells pursuant to the process at a fixed price. After costly experimentation the government agreed that the process would not work without equipment such as plaintiff had originally urged and permitted the plaintiff to make use of such equipment. The plaintiff sued for extra compensation based upon the losses sustained as a result of the added expenses incurred in attempting to make the original specifications work. The court rightly

---

11. See § 13–11 supra.

12. J.A. Maurer, Inc. v. United States, 485 F.2d 588 (Ct.Cl.1973); United States v. Wegematic Corp., 360 F.2d 674 (2d Cir. 1966) (applying the U.C.C. as "federal common law"); Austin Co. v. United States, 314 F.2d 518 (Ct.Cl.1963), certiorari denied 375 U.S. 830, 84 S.Ct. 75, 11 L.Ed.2d 62 (1963); Rolin v. United States, 160 F.Supp. 264 (Ct.Cl.1958). Contra, Smith Engineering v. Rice, 102 F.2d 492 (9th Cir.1939), certiorari denied 307 U.S. 637, 59 S.Ct. 1034, 83 L.Ed. 1519 (1939) (applying Mont. Law).

13. Coto-Matic, Inc. v. The Home Indem. Co., 354 F.2d 720 (10th Cir.1965); Helene Curtis Indus. v. United States, 312 F.2d 774 (Ct.Cl.1963). Where the government merely suggests rather than requires a given production process, the government does not warrant that the process will produce the desired result. Clark Grave Vault Co. v. United States, 371 F.2d 459 (Ct.Cl.1967). For a case in which both parties were held to be at fault, see Admiral Plastics Corp. v. Trueblood, Inc., 436 F.2d 1335 (6th Cir.1971).

14. The topic of mistake is discussed below. See ch. 9 infra.

15. National Presto Indus. v. United States, 338 F.2d 99 (Ct.Cl.1964), certiorari denied 380 U.S. 962, 85 S.Ct. 1105, 14 L.Ed. 2d 153 (1965).

held that the plaintiff could not recover under breach of implied warranty. The specific negotiations concerning the adequacy of the specifications negated any justifiable reliance on them. The court, however, held that the plaintiff was entitled to reformation of the contract on grounds of mutual mistake. The plaintiff and the defendant were required by the court to share the losses as if they had been engaged in a joint venture rather than in a fixed price contract. The decision has received less than favorable comment in the law reviews [16] and the court clearly and admittedly departed from principles ordinarily governing mutual mistake and reformation. Although impossibility of performance was not discussed, it is clear that performance in the manner agreed was in fact impossible. Under traditional analysis, however, impossibility would not have excused performance because the plaintiff foresaw and even complained about the risk. Either the decision will be deemed "wrong" and ignored in the future or it will help point the way to a more flexible allocation of the parties' risks without reference to their agreement [17]—a further move from contract to status.

WESTLAW REFERENCES

impossib! impractica! /p (maurer +s "united states") ("united
    states" +s wegematic) ("austin company" +s "united
    states")

government! /s assum! /s risk /s impossib! impractica!

adequa! inadequa! /s specification /s justif! /s rely! relied
    reliance

impossib! impractica! /s excus! /s perform! /s foresee! foresaw

§ 13–18. Foreseeability

There is abundant authority that if the event which is the basis of a claim of impossibility or frustration is reasonably foreseeable the defense will be lost because the promisor should have provided for said contingency in the contract.[18] Failure to provide for the foreseeable

16. 65 Colum.L.Rev. 542 (1965); 33 Fordham L.Rev. 507 (1965).

17. See Cuneo & Cromwell, Impossibility of Performance—Assumption of the Risk or Act of Submission?, 29 Law & Contemp. Prob. 531, 533 (1964), where the authors state: "Neither the common law nor the restatement furnish the necessary tools for an adequate analysis of space age impossibility under fixed-price contracts."

18. Bernina Distributors, Inc. v. Bernina Sewing Machine Co., 646 F.2d 434 (10th Cir.1981); Associated Grocers of Iowa v. West, 297 N.W.2d 103 (Iowa 1980); Meyer v. Diesel Equipment Co., 1 Kan.App.2d 574, 570 P.2d 1374 (1977); Barbarossa & Sons, Inc. v. Iten Chevrolet, Inc., 265 N.W.2d 655 (Minn.1978); Helms Const. & Development Co. v. State, 97 Nev. 500, 634 P.2d 1224

(1981); Brenner v. Little Red School House, Ltd., 302 N.C. 207, 274 S.E.2d 206 (1981), appeal after remand 59 N.C.App. 68, 295 S.E.2d 607 (1982), review denied 307 N.C. 468, 299 S.E.2d 220 (1983); see also Annot., 89 A.L.R.3d 329 (1979). What is and is not reasonably foreseeable is not an easy question to answer. As Williston says, any kind of impossibility or frustration is more or less capable of anticipation. Nevertheless it is generally held that death, illness or destruction of the subject matter is not reasonably foreseeable. Williston § 1953, at 5475. Yet it has been held that the closing of the Suez Canal, America's entry into World War II and OPEC price increases were all reasonably foreseeable. Transatlantic Fin. Corp. v. United States, 363 F.2d 312 (D.C.Cir.1966),

contingency is deemed to demonstrate that the promisor assumed the risk.

However there are a few authorities that argue that this rule should be abandoned or at least modified.[19] The Restatement Second argues that foreseeability is only one of the factors to be considered in determining whether the defense of impossibility is available.[20] It is also stated that the promisor should be free to explain why there was no clause in the contract covering the contingency; for example, that the other party was the dominant party and therefore he was forced to sign a standard form contract.[21] It also states that in a complicated contract failure to deal with an improbable or insignificant contingency, even though foreseen should not be deemed to amount to an assumption of the risk.[22]

An even more liberal view has been espoused by a few cases and a thought provoking law review article.[23] The notion is that foreseeability is of no importance when it is clear that the parties did not intend that the risk of the occurrence should be assumed by the promisor.

A leading case helps to clarify the point being made.[24] Defendant contracted to sell certain real property to the plaintiff and to lease it back. As the plaintiff was a tax-exempt charitable institution, the parties believed that certain very substantial tax benefits would accrue to defendant. Plaintiff assured the defendant that these tax advantages would accrue.[25] Under the evidence it is clear that plaintiff knew that the defendant would not have entered into the transaction but for the prospective tax advantages and that the transaction was premised

---

noted in 41 Tul.L.Rev. 709 (1969) and 6 Wm. & Mary L.Rev. 679 (1967); Glidden Co. v. Hellenic Lines, Ltd., 275 F.2d 253 (2d Cir.1960), on remand 207 F.Supp. 262 (S.D. N.Y.1962), judgment affirmed 315 F.2d 162 (2d Cir.1963); Lloyd v. Murphy, 25 Cal.2d 48, 153 P.2d 47 (1944); Publicker Industries, Inc. v. Union Carbide Corp., 17 U.C.C.Rep.Serv. 989 (E.D.Pa.1975).

19. Glen R. Sewell Sheet Metal, Inc. v. Loverde, 70 Cal.2d 666, 75 Cal.Rptr. 889, 451 P.2d 721 (1969); Wills v. Shockley, 52 Del. 295, 157 A.2d 252 (1960); Mishara Const. Co. v. Transit-Mixed Concrete Corp., 365 Mass. 122, 310 N.E.2d 363 (1974); Restatement, Contracts § 457. U.C.C. § 2–615, Comment 8 states, "Thus the exemptions of this section do not apply when the contingency in question is sufficiently foreshadowed at the time of contracting to be included among the business risks which are fairly to be regarded as part of the dickered terms, either consciously or as a matter of reasonable, commercial interpretation from the circumstances."

20. Restatement, Second, Contracts § 261, Comment b.

21. L.N. Jackson & Co. v. Royal Norwegian Gov't, 177 F.2d 694 (2d Cir.1949), certiorari denied 339 U.S. 914, 70 S.Ct. 574, 94 L.Ed. 1340 (1950).

22. L.N. Jackson & Co. v. Royal Norwegian Gov't, 177 F.2d 694 (2d Cir.1949), certiorari denied 339 U.S. 914, 70 S.Ct. 574, 94 L.Ed. 1340 (1950); Restatement, Contracts (2d) § 261.

23. West Los Angeles Institute for Cancer Research v. Mayer, 366 F.2d 220 (9th Cir.1966), certiorari denied 385 U.S. 1010, 87 S.Ct. 718, 17 L.Ed.2d 548 (1967); Edward Maurer Co. v. Tubeless Tire Co., 285 Fed. 713 (6th Cir.1922); Glen R. Sewell Sheet Metal, Inc. v. Loverde, 70 Cal.2d 666, 75 Cal.Rptr. 889, 896 n. 13, 451 P.2d 721 (1969). Smit, Frustration of Contract. A Comparative Attempt at Consolidation, 58 Colum.L.Rev. 287 (1958); see also Aubrey, Frustration Reconsidered, 12 Int'l. & Comp.L.Q. (1963).

24. West Los Angeles Institute for Cancer Research v. Mayer, note 23 supra.

25. The word "assured" here is not the equivalent of "promised." What it means is that this was his prediction or opinion.

upon these advantages. The IRS subsequently issued a revenue ruling disallowing the kinds of tax advantages foreseen by the parties. Defendant refused to perform upon a theory of frustration of the venture.

The court agreed with the defendant that tax advantage is the basis on which both parties contracted. However plaintiff argued that defendant did not have the defense of frustration because it was foreseeable that the IRS might disapprove the transaction. Despite this, the court held that the defense was available because it was clear that the parties intended that neither party should assume this risk.[26]

WESTLAW REFERENCES

impossib! impractica! /s assum! /s risk /s foresee! foresaw

fail! /s provision provid! /s contingen! /s foresee! foresaw

frustrat! /s contract /s foresee! foresaw

agreement contract*** perform! /s foresee! foresaw unforesee! /s
      defense defend*** /s impossib! impractica!

§ 13–19. Force Majeure Clauses

Since most cases have held that failure to cover a foreseeable risk in the contract deprives a party of the defense of impossibility, it is obvious that the best way to protect a client from this rule is to provide against foreseeable risks in the agreement. Such a clause in the writing is often referred to as a *force majeure* clause or an excusable delay clause.[27]

Drafting such a clause involves the draftsman in a number of intricate problems. Many courts have concluded that "Exculpatory provisions which are phrased merely in general terms have long been construed as excusing only *unforeseen* events which make performance impracticable * * *. Courts have often held, therefore, that if a promisor desires to broaden the protections available under the impossibility doctrine he should provide for the excusing contingencies with particularity and not in general language." [28]

If the risk is unforeseen and unforeseeable then the exculpatory clause that enlarges upon excuses provided by law may be phrased in general terms. Even here the draftsman faces a number of problems. One illustration will suffice.[29] The force majeure clause reads, "*Neither party shall be liable for its failure to perform hereunder* if said performance is made *impracticable due to any occurrence* beyond its reasonable control, including acts of God, fires, floods, wars, sabotage, accidents, labor disputes or shortages, governmental laws, ordinances, rules and regulations."

26. See also Krell v. Henry, [1903] 2 K.B. 740 (C.A.).

27. See Publicker Industries, Inc. v. Union Carbide Corp., 17 U.C.C.Rep.Serv. 989 (E.D.Pa.1975) and Eastern Air Lines, Inc. v. McDonnell Douglas Corp., 532 F.2d 957 (5th Cir.1976).

28. Eastern Airlines, Inc. v. McDonnell Douglas Corp., 532 F.2d 957, 990–91 (5th Cir.1976).

29. The illustration is based upon Publicker Industries, Inc. v. Union Carbide Corp., 17 U.C.C.Rep.Serv. 989 (E.D.Pa. 1975).

Assume that the event upon which the claimed impossibility is based is an act of the OPEC cartel. The underlined introductory language is broad enough to cover any contingency. However under a rule of interpretation that passes under the Latin name of *ejusdem generis* the broad introductory language is cut down by the specific language that follows so that if the particular risk (cartel) is not indicated in the listing it shall not serve as an excuse unless it is very similar to the specified events.[30] There is some authority that the rule of ejusdem generis may be avoided by using the phrase "including but not limited to" rather than simply "including".[31]

Another problem with the force majeure clause in this case is its use of underlined word "impracticable". If performance is impracticable under existing law the clause is not needed. If the performance is not impracticable, then the use of the word prevents the clause from applying.[32]

The U.C.C. expresses some limitations on broad exculpatory clauses when it states "Generally, express agreements as to exemptions designed to enlarge upon or supplant the provisions of this section are to be read in the light of mercantile sense and reason, for this section itself sets up the commercial standard for normal and reasonable interpretation and provides a minimum beyond which the agreement may not go."[33] This language is far from clear. A recent case rejected the notion that it means that any attempt by a seller to enlarge upon the provisions of the statute must be in clear and specific language since such an intent may also be found by virtue of trade usage of surrounding circumstances.[34] It is clear that any exemption clause which is manifestly unreasonable, in bad faith, or unconscionable will not be enforced.[35]

 WESTLAW REFERENCES

di force majeure

"force majeure clause"

"force majeure" /s liab!

to(95) /p "force majeure"

"force majeure" /s impossib! impractica!

"force majeure" /s unforesee! foresee! foresaw! unexpected
    unpredict!

§ 13–20. Underlying Rationale

Contract liability is no-fault liability. The fundamental maxim is *pacta sunt servanda*—agreements must be kept. Even if performance

30. Id.

31. Eastern Airlines v. McDonnell Douglas Corp., 532 F.2d 957 (5th Cir.1976).

32. Publicker Industries, Inc. v. Union Carbide Corp., 17 U.C.C.Rep.Serv. 989 (E.D. Pa.1975).

33. U.C.C. § 2–615, Comment 8. See also Northern Indiana Pub. Serv. v. Carbon County Coal, 799 F.2d 265 (7th Cir.1986).

34. Eastern Airlines v. McDonnell Douglas Corp., 532 F.2d 957 (5th Cir.1976).

35. U.C.C. §§ 1–102(3), 1–203, and 2–302.

is impossible or senseless, the assessment of damages for non-perform-ance remains a possibility. What policy judgments have been made to create the limited excuses for non-performance discussed in this chap-ter? There appear to be several. The first stems from one of the underpinnings of contracts obligations. Contract liability stems from consent.[36] If an event occurs which is totally outside the contemplation of the parties and which drastically shifts the nature of the risks ostensibly consented to, is consent real? [37]

Second, the doctrines of impossibility and frustration are closely allied to the doctrine of mutual mistake.[38] The distinction is that mutual mistake as a doctrine is applicable only if the parties are mistaken as to a vital existing fact, while ordinarily frustration and impossibility relate to future events. As was stated in the discussion of mistake, ideas of unjust enrichment are heavily involved. Before applying the doctrine one must search the facts for unexpected, unbar-gained for gain on the one hand and unexpected, unbargained for loss on the other.[39]

Third, notions of conscionability and fairness tend to support the doctrines. The law deems it to be unconscionably sharp practice to take advantage of the mistake of another. It may equally be deemed unconscionable to take advantage of a mistake as to the course of future events.[40]

From the point of view of legal analysis, the doctrine of impossibili-ty and frustration have been explained by a number of conceptual models. The earlier cases talked in terms of the existence of an implied (in fact) term. Thus in the Music Hall case [41] the court spoke of "an implied condition that the parties shall be excused in case, before breach, performance becomes impossible from the perishing of the thing" that formed the foundation of the contract. Other cases have talked about the "contemplation of the parties." [42] The notion is that one can infer from the facts that the parties did not intend that performance would have to be rendered if an unexpected event would create a radical change in the nature of the performance. This is the prevailing view in England.[43]

36. See § 2-1 supra.

37. See Sharp, The Ethics of Breach of Contract, 45 Int'l J. of Ethics 27, 42-44 (1934).

38. See United States v. General Doug-las MacArthur Senior Village, Inc., 508 F.2d 377 (2d Cir.1974), where the majority discusses frustration and the dissent ar-gues mistake; Cook v. Kelley, 352 Mass. 628, 227 N.E.2d 330 (1967), where the court discusses mistake when the case involved an unexpected future event.

39. See § 9-26(b) supra. See also Sharp, supra note 37, at 42-44.

40. See Newman, The Renaissance of Good Faith in Contracting in Anglo-Ameri-can Law, 54 Cornell L.Rev. 553, 561 (1969); Note, The Fetish of Impossibility in the Law of Contracts, 53 Colum.L.Rev. 94 (1953).

41. Taylor v. Caldwell, 122 Eng.Rep. 309 (K.B.1863).

42. Transatlantic Financing Corp. v. United States, 363 F.2d 312, 315 (D.C.Cir. 1966).

43. See Nicholas, Rules and Terms, 48 Tul.L.Rev. 946 (1974).

Later cases speak of the excuse being based upon a constructive condition—that is one imposed by law in the interests of justice. In other words the excuse stems from a rule of law rather than inferences drawn from the facts.[44] However, as we have seen, the circumstances or the agreement may indicate that a party has assumed a risk greater than the risk imposed upon him by law.[45]

The most recent explanation is that even though the promise in the agreement is in terms absolute, it was not intended to cover the situation that in fact arose and therefore the court is free to supply a term that will do justice.[46] In the words of the Second Restatement, "since it is the rationale of this chapter that, in a case of impracticability or frustration, the contract does not cover the case that has arisen, the court's function can be viewed generally as that * * * of supplying a term to deal with the omitted case." [47]

§ 13–21. Effect of Impossibility Upon a Prior Repudiation

If A and B enter into an agreement under which A is to serve B for a year and B repudiates before the time for performance arrives and A dies within that time, as we have seen, although A had a cause of action for the repudiation, his estate could not recover, because it would be necessary to show that A would have been ready, willing and able to perform but for the repudiation.[48]

The converse of this situation exists where, after a party repudiates, events occur which make his own performance impossible. Should the subsequent impossibility be taken into account in adjusting the rights of the parties? Some have taken the position that it should not because the rights of the parties became fixed by the repudiation.[49] The better rule appears to be that subsequent impossibility will discharge an anticipatory breach and will ordinarily limit damages in the case of a non-anticipatory breach.[50]

Thus, under the better rule in the illustration previously given, if A repudiated before the time for performance and died before the time for

---

44. See Quotation from Quick v. Stuyvesant, 2 Paige Ch. 84, 91–92 (N.Y.1830), and Transatlantic Financing Corp. v. United States, 363 F.2d 312, 315 (D.C.Cir.1966); see also Farnsworth, Disputes Over Omission in Contracts, 68 Colum.L.Rev. 860 (1968); Patterson, Constructive Conditions in Contracts, 42 Colum.L.Rev. 903, 946–50 (1942); Smit, Frustration of Contract: A Comparative Attempt at Consolidation, 58 Colum.L.Rev. 287 (1958).

45. See § 13–2 supra.

46. Watson v. Kenlick Coal Co., 498 F.2d 1183, 1190–91 (6th Cir.1974), certiorari denied 422 U.S. 1012, 95 S.Ct. 2639, 45 L.Ed.2d 677 (1975); see also Kirke La Shelle Co. v. Paul Armstrong Co., 263 N.Y. 79, 188 N.E. 163 (1933) discussed in § 11–12 supra.

47. Restatement, Second, Contracts § 272, Comment c and Introductory Note to Ch. 11.

48. See §§ 12–2 and 13–7 supra.

49. Papaioannou v. Sirocco Supper Club, Inc., 75 Misc.2d 1001, 349 N.Y.S.2d 590 (App.Term 1973); Simpson § 175.

50. Jones v. Fuller-Garvey Corp., 386 P.2d 838 (Alaska 1963); Model Vending, Inc. v. Stanisci, 74 N.J.Super. 12, 180 A.2d 393 (1962); Fratelli Pantanella, S.A. v. International Commercial Corp., 89 N.Y.S.2d 736 (Sup.Ct.1949). See generally 6 Corbin § 1341; 6 Williston § 1967A (rev'd ed. 1938).

performance, B would not be entitled to any recovery.[51] If A repudiated before the time for his performance and died one month after performance was to begin, B would be entitled to damages for only one month.[52] So also if A performed for two weeks and then repudiated and A died two weeks later, B would be entitled to damages for only two weeks.[53]

WESTLAW REFERENCES

"prior repudiation"

"subsequen! impossib!"

jones +s "fuller garvey"

breach! /s "superven! impossib!"

superven! subsequen! /s impossib! /s repudiat!

§ 13–22. Impossibility and Frustration Under the Uniform Commercial Code

There are three sections in the Code relating to the subject matter of this chapter. Reference has been made to section 2–614 which governs failure of the contemplated means of delivery or payment.[54] Section 2–613 entitled "casualty to Identified Goods" is discussed below.[55]

The basic section of the Code relating to this topic is § 2–615. This section has been mentioned a number of times in the prior discussion. This material will not be repeated here except where it is necessary to understand the new material in this section. It reads as follows:

Excuse by Failure of Presupposed Conditions

Except so far as a seller may have assumed a greater obligation and subject to the preceding section on substituted performance:

    (a) Delay in delivery or non-delivery in whole or in part by a seller who complies with paragraphs (b) and (c) is not a breach of his duty under a contract for sale if performance as agreed has been made impracticable by the occurrence of a contingency the non-occurrence of which was a basic assumption on which the contract was made or by compliance in good faith with any applicable foreign or domestic governmental regulation or order whether or not it later proves to be invalid.

    (b) Where the causes mentioned in paragraph (a) affect only a part of seller's capacity to perform, he must allocate production and deliveries among his customers but may at his option include regular customers not then under contract

51. Restatement, Contracts § 457, Commend d.

52. Id., ill. 4.

53. Id., Comment 4.

54. See § 13–4 supra.

55. See §§ 13–24 to 13–28 infra.

as well as his own requirements for further manufacture. He may so also allocate in any manner which is fair and reasonable.

(c)   The seller must notify the buyer seasonably that there will be delay or non-delivery and, when allocation is required under paragraph (b), of the estimated quota thus made available for the buyer.

The introductory language and the material in paragraph (a) have already been discussed. Together they contain the three-fold test set up in § 13–2. Although the introductory language makes it clear that the seller may assume a greater burden than that imposed by law it is equally clear that, within limits, the seller may diminish his obligation by agreement. This is demonstrated by an examination of the legislative history of the Code.[56]

If all of the elements of subsection (a) are met and the seller has not assumed a greater obligation, the seller is excused for a delay in delivery or non-delivery in whole or in part if he complies with paragraphs (b) and (c) and is not in breach of his duty under the contract.

Subsection (b) relates primarily to a situation where the impossibility found under paragraph (a) affects only a part of the seller's capacity to perform. In that case the section requires the seller to allocate what is available among his customers in "any manner which is fair and reasonable."[57] The seller in allocating may include regular customers not under contract as well as his own requirements for further manufacture. In addition under sub-division (c) the seller must notify the buyer in writing of the "estimated quota thus made available to the buyer." When the buyer receives notice of allocation that is justified under the rules stated above he may under U.C.C. § 2–616 as to any delivery concerned, modify the contract by agreeing to take his available quota in substitution or terminate and discharge the unexecuted portion of the contract.[58]

Not all cases under this section involve an allocation problem. There may be cases that involve a material or indefinite delay that is excused under subdivision (a). In that case the seller must still give notice and the buyer still has the option set forth above.

56. See Eastern Airlines, Inc. v. McDonnell Douglas Corp., 532 F.2d 957 (5th Cir. 1976); Hawkland, The Energy Crisis and Section 2–615 of the Uniform Code, 79 Com.L.J. 75 (1974). See also Comment 8 to U.C.C. § 2–615 which indicates that there is a point beyond which such agreements may not go.

57. See U.C.C. § 2–615, Comment 11; see also Harvey v. Fearless Farris Wholesale, Inc., 589 F.2d 451 (9th Cir.1979); Terry v. Atlantic Richfield Co., 72 Cal.App.3d 962, 140 Cal.Rptr. 510 (1977).

58. J. White & R. Summers, § 3–9, at 134. This rule in the U.C.C. appears to be in substantial accord with the present law. County of Yuba v. Mattoon, 160 Cal.App.2d 456, 325 P.2d 162 (1958); Mawhinney v. Millbrook Woolen Mills, Inc., 234 N.Y. 244, 137 N.E. 318 (1922) (government requisitioned much, but not all, of manufacturer's output); 6 Corbin § 1342; Restatement, Contracts § 464; see also U.C.C. § 2–615, Comment 11; cf. Hudson, Prorating in the English Law of Frustrated Contracts, 31 Mod.L.Rev. 535 (1968).

In U.C.C. § 2–616 there is a particular provision with respect to any installment contract which gives the buyer the option to terminate or modify where the prospective deficiency caused by a material or indefinite delay or an allocation as to that installment substantially impairs the value of the whole contract. If the value of the whole contract is not impaired the buyer would not have that option as to the whole contract but only as the installment or installments involved.[59]

Subdivision (3) of U.C.C. § 2–616 provides, "The provisions of this section may not be negated by agreement except in so far as the seller has assumed a greater obligation under the preceding section." This subdivision is designed to protect the buyer not the seller.[60]

It should be observed that U.C.C. §§ 2–615 and 2–616 facially set up a rule that gives an excuse only to the seller. Despite this, there is at least one case that states the section does apply to a buyer.[61] Even if the Code section is deemed not to apply to buyers it is clear that the pre-Code law would be consulted to supplement the Code in case of a buyer's claim of excuse which most likely would relate to frustration of the venture.[62]

 WESTLAW REFERENCES
"uniform commercial code" u.c.c. /s 2–615

§ 13–23. Effect of Impossibility and Frustration—Adjusting the Rights of the Parties

The effect of total supervening impossibility or frustration is to discharge the excused party with respect to his remaining duties.[63] Simultaneously the other party is discharged because the performance of the excused party will not be forthcoming.[64] If the supervening impossibility or frustration is only prospective the other party has the same options as in a case where the non-performance would be a breach, except that he will not have a cause of action for breach.[65] We have already discussed the rules relating to temporary impossibility and partial impossibility.[66]

Even though the contract has been discharged for impossibility or frustration it is often necessary, in the interests of justice, to adjust the rights of the parties.[67] For example, if the excused party has rendered part of his performance before the impossibility arose he should be entitled to recover on the contract for what he has done if the contract

59. See § 11–20(d) supra.

60. U.C.C. § 2–616, Comment.

61. Nora Springs Corp. Co. v. Brandau, 247 N.W.2d 744 (Iowa 1976).

62. U.C.C. § 2–615, Comment 9; Note, 105 U.Pa.L.Rev. 880, 904 (1957); see G. Gilmore, Security Interests § 41.7 at 1104–6 (1965); see also U.C.C. § 1–103.

63. Restatement, Second, Contracts § 261.

64. See § 11–18(b) supra.

65. See § 12–12 supra.

66. See §§ 13–13 to 13–14 supra.

67. For a detailed discussion of this problem, see Dawson, Judicial Revision of Frustrated Contracts, 64 B.U.L.Rev. 1 (1984). Mullen v. Wafer, 252 Ark. 541, 480 S.W.2d 332 (1972). See § 11–28 supra.

is divisible.[68] The Restatement Second suggests that a court may sever a contract in the interests of justice although the normal tests for divisibility are not met.[69]

If the arrangement is deemed not to be divisible or severable another possibility is restitution. The courts have had difficulty in applying the concept of restitution in an impossibility or frustration context. This was demonstrated by the coronation cases. While in Krell v. Henry [70] it was held that the defendant was excused from paying for use of the premises, in the related case of Chandler v. Webster,[71] it was held that a defendant who had made a substantial down payment and had agreed to pay the balance in advance of the coronation was not entitled to restitution and furthermore was liable to pay the balance. The rule was simply that the parties should be placed in the position they would have been in at the occurrence of the frustrating event. Chandler v. Webster was subsequently overruled by the Fibrosa case [72] which, however, produced an equally arbitrary rule. In a case involving supervening impossibility, restitution of a down payment was granted, placing the parties in the position they enjoyed prior to contracting. This ruling was not flexible enough to take into account the relative extent to which the parties might be out of pocket by reason of action in reliance on the contract. At the suggestion of the Law Lords in the Fibrosa case, the English Parliament enacted legislation [73] permitting recovery under a contract discharged by reason of impossibility or frustration for the value of benefits received, "if it considers it just to do so, having regard for all the circumstances." Pursuant to this enactment, the court may deduct for expenses incurred in reliance on the contract, taking into consideration the circumstances giving rise to the frustration or impossibility.

In the United States, courts have generally taken the view that when a contract is discharged by impossibility or frustration the parties must make restitution for the benefits conferred upon them. At times the concept of "benefit" is stretched to include expenses incurred in preparation for performance (reliance) but this is not generally true.[74] However, there is increasing recognition that restitution, when employed to unwind a contract that cannot be performed, is concerned with equitable adjustment of gains and losses sustained by the parties and not merely the redressing of unjust enrichment.[75] In this respect

68. Mullen v. Wafer, 252 Ark. 541, 480 S.W.2d 332 (1972).

69. Restatement, Second, Contracts § 272, Comment c; see id., ill. 3.

70. [1903] 2 K.B. 740.

71. [1904] 2 K.B. 493.

72. Fibrosa Spolka Akeyjna v. Fairbarn Lawson Combe Barbour, Ltd., H.L., [1943] A.C. 32 (1942), 2 All E.R. 122; Annot., 144 A.L.R. 1298; 91 U.Pa.L.Rev. 262 (1942).

73. Law Reform (Frustrated Contracts) Act, 1943, 6 & 7 Geo. 6, ch. 40. For a suggested American statute, see Comment, 69 Yale L.J. 1054 (1960).

74. The American cases are ably analyzed in Comment, 69 Yale L.J. 1054 (1960). A landmark case has recognized explicitly that "reliance" expenses incurred by the promisee may be recoverable when the equities are on his side. Albre Marble & Tile Co. v. John Bowen Co., 338 Mass. 394, 155 N.E.2d 437 (1959), modified 343 Mass. 777, 179 N.E.2d 321 (1962).

75. See Restatement, Second, Contracts § 272, Comment b; Perillo, Restitution in

the Restatement Second states that the court may grant relief on such terms "as justice requires including protection of the parties' reliance interests."[76] The notion is that gains and losses should be apportioned without concern for conceptual barriers.

It is even possible to reshape the contract so that the duties of the parties will continue. This may be done by allocation,[77] by the rules governing temporary or partial impossibility[78] or by supplying a term that "is reasonable in the circumstances."[79] The party to whom performance is owed has the power to reshape the contract by waiving restrictive clauses,[80] or substantial non-performance[81] and other obstacles, thereby reinstating the duty of performance, albeit on somewhat different terms.[82] This power demonstrates that one of the bases of the doctrine of impossibility is the unconscionability of insisting on strict performance in the light of radically changed circumstances. There is even some authority for the proposition that a party who has a defense of impossibility may waive it and perform by virtue of a source of supply not contemplated by the contract.[83]

WESTLAW REFERENCES

digest(impossib! frustrat! /s perform! duty /s discharg! excus! /s contract)

impossib! frustrat! /s perform! /s recover! /s part partly partial!

impossib! frustrat! /s restitution /s contract agreement

di(impossib! frustrat! /s reform! modif! /s agreement contract)

di(frustrat! impossib! /s perform! /s chang!)

§ 13–24. Risk of Casualty Losses: Introduction

This material is only tangentially related to the topic of impossibility of performance. When goods or real property are in the process of being sold, or are under lease or bailment, frequently the question arises as to which of the parties must bear the risk of damage or destruction of the subject matter. Unlike the problems presented earlier in this chapter the primary question is not whether a promise is being excused because of impossibility of performance. At times, however, this problem may incidently arise by virtue of the destruction of the subject matter. A good illustration is presented by the real property cases discussed immediately below.

a Contractual Context, 73 Colum.L.Rev. 1208 (1973).

76. Restatement, Second, Contracts § 272(2).

77. See Restatement, Second, Contracts § 272, ill. 5; see § 13–22 supra.

78. See Restatement, Second, Contracts § 272, ill. 4; see §§ 13–13 and 13–14 supra.

79. Restatement, Second, Contracts § 272, Comment c.

80. Lloyd v. Murphy, 25 Cal.2d 48, 153 P.2d 47 (1944); 33 Colum.L.Rev. 397, 423.

81. Restatement, Second, Contracts § 272, ill. 1.

82. Cf. Northern Corp. v. Chugach Elec. Ass'n, 518 P.2d 76 (Alaska 1974), judgment affirmed 562 P.2d 1053 (Alaska 1977) (defendant's refusal to modify the contract after performance proved impossible enhanced defendant's liability).

83. International Paper Co. v. Rockefeller, 161 App.Div. 180, 146 N.Y.S. 371 (3d Dep't 1914). ("We need not say that defendant could not have furnished live wood of equal quality from other lands").

§ 13–25. Risk of Loss: Sale of Real Property

The question of risk of loss is presented when real property is fortuitously destroyed between the time a contract is signed and the time for the closing of title. There are three views on this problem. The majority view places the risk of loss on the purchaser. The result is based on the theory of equitable conversion: once the contract is made the purchaser is regarded by a court of equity as the owner. Under this view "risk of loss" means that the buyer must pay for the property even though he had not received legal title to it at the time of the casualty. Under a minority view the buyer does not assume this risk. The seller as legal owner of a property simply loses his own property and is not entitled to look to the buyer for payment.[84] In a sense the seller suffers the risk of loss. Under this view an additional question arises which does relate to the doctrine of impossibility of performance. Must the seller respond in damages for his failure to convey the property? The answer is in the negative because he has the defense of impossibility based upon the destruction of the subject matter of the contract.[85] A third view, embodied in the Uniform Vender and Purchaser Risk Act, enacted in about ten states, places the risk of loss upon a purchaser only if he is in possession or has legal title.[86]

WESTLAW REFERENCES

"risk of loss" /s realty (real +1 estate property)

realty (real +1 estate property) /s destroy! destruction /s seller
vendor buyer purchaser vendor /s insurance

400k203 /p loss destruction destroy!

§ 13–26. Risk of Loss: Sale of Goods

(a) Introduction

The problem under discussion arises in a case involving sale of goods, only where the goods are identified to the contract.[87] When this

---

84. Ross v. Bumstead, 65 Ariz. 61, 173 P.2d 765 (1946) (majority); Rector v. Alcorn, 241 N.W.2d 196 (Iowa 1976); Skelly Oil Co. v. Ashmore, 365 S.W.2d 582 (Mo. 1963) (minority). See generally, J. Cribbet, Principles of the Law of Property, 149–154 (2d ed.1975).

85. Potts Drug Co. v. Benedict, 156 Cal. 332, 104 P. 432 (1909). However, the down payment must be returned. See also Dixon v. Salvation Army, 142 Cal.App.3d 463, 191 Cal.Rptr. 111 (1983).

86. See, e.g., McKinney's N.Y.Gen.Oblig.Laws § 5–1311. As to how insurance relates to this problem, see Brownell v. Board of Educ. of Inside Tax Dist. of Saratoga Springs, 239 N.Y. 369, 146 N.E. 630, Annot. 37 A.L.R. 13, 19 (1925); Gilles v. Sprout, 293 Minn. 53, 196 N.W.2d 612

(1972); Long v. Keller, 104 Cal.App.3d 312, 163 Cal.Rptr. 532 (1980). See generally McCord, Allocation of Loss, and Property Insurance, 39 Ind.L.J. 647 (1964); Comment, 28 Albany L.Rev. 253 (1964). On related problems arising where the land is taken by condemnation, see, e.g., Lucenti v. Cayuga Apartments, Inc., 48 N.Y.2d 530, 423 N.Y.S.2d 886, 399 N.E.2d 918 (1979); Chester Litho v. Palisades Interstate Park Comm'n, 27 N.Y.2d 323, 317 N.Y.S.2d 761, 266 N.E.2d 229 (1971); Annot., 27 A.L.R.3d 572 (1969).

87. The manner of identification of goods to the contract is governed by U.C.C. § 2–501, or by contract. See id. § 1–102; see also Martin Marietta Corp. v. N.J. Nat. Bank, 612 F.2d 745 (3d Cir.1979), on remand 505 F.Supp. 946 (1981); Servbest

happens the U.C.C. has a set of rules which determines which party bears the risk of fortuitous destruction. Prior to the enactment of the Uniform Commercial Code the risk of loss was placed on the party who had title to the goods. This turned out to be a most confused and confusing problem.[88] The Code has shifted from a property (title) approach to a contractual approach.[89] Under the Code the parties are free to allocate the risk of loss in their contract.[90]

In the absence of agreement,[91] the basic U.C.C. sections which determine risk of loss are sections 2–509 and 2–510. The Code starts with the principle that risk of loss is upon the seller until some event occurs to shift the risk to the buyer. These events are set out in section 2–509. Section 2–510 considers the effect of a breach by the buyer or seller on the issue of risk of loss.

Foods, Inc. v. Emessee Industries, Inc., 82 Ill.App.3d 662, 37 Ill.Dec. 945, 403 N.E.2d 1 (1980); Holstein v. Greenwich Yacht Sales, Inc., 122 R.I. 211, 404 A.2d 842 (1979).

88. See White & Summers, § 5–1 pp. 175–177 (1972).

89. U.C.C. § 2–509, Comment 1. This is not to say that the Code does not employ the title concept for any purpose and does not have rules relating to title. The rules relating to passage of title are covered in § 2–401. They were included in the Code to help solve problems which were not foreseen by the drafters of the Code. Also there is a considerable body of non-sales law where the title concept is still important; for example, taxation of personalty. Even in the Code there are references to title in §§ 2–106 (definition of a sale), 2–312 (warranty of title), 2–326 (goods are deemed to be on sale or return even though the person delivering the goods has reserved title), 2–327 (title does not pass in a sale on approval), 2–403 (a person with a voidable title has power to transfer title to a good faith purchaser for value), 2–501 (the seller retains an insurable interest as long as he returns title to the goods), and 2–722 (a person with title can sue third persons for injury to the goods). R. Nordstrom, Law of Sales § 125 (1970).

90. U.C.C. § 2–509(4).

91. As stated immediately above, the parties may agree as they wish on the question of risk of loss. Sometimes the agreement as to risk of loss is established by the use of terms which have a particular meaning. For example: (1) In the case of a "sale on approval", the goods are delivered primarily for use as opposed to resale and so the goods may be returned at the seller's expense even if they conform and the risk of loss remains on the seller until acceptance. U.C.C. §§ 2–326(1)(a), 2–327(1) (a). (2) If the agreement is a "sale or return", (here the goods are delivered for resale) again the buyer may return the goods even if they are conforming; but he does so at his own expense, and risk of loss passes to him on delivery and remains with him until the goods are returned to the seller. Id. § 2–327(2)(b). (3) In a "sale on consignment" the buyer (consignee) is an agent, and the risk of loss is on the seller-principal. (4) In an F.O.B. contract the seller must get the goods to the point named in the contract at his own expense and risk. Id. § 2–319(1). (5) In an F.A.S. contract the seller, at his own expense and risk, is required to deliver alongside a named vessel. Thereafter the risk is on the buyer. Id. § 2–319(2). (6) A C.I.F. contract is one where the seller must pay for the cost of insurance and freight. In a C & F contract he must pay only for the freight. In either case the risk passes to the buyer at the point of shipment. Id. § 2–320. (7) In an "ex ship" contract the risk of loss is not on the buyer "until the goods leave the ship's tackle or are otherwise properly loaded." Id. § 322. (8) In a "no arrival no sale agreement", the risk of loss is on the seller but he is protected from an action in damages by the buyer. Id. § 2–324. This matter is discussed in subsection (c) of this section below.

(b) U.C.C. § 2–509

(1) Subdivision 1

Section 2–509 does not state an all inclusive rule, but rather states a rule for three types of cases. The first rule relates to situation where the contract requires or authorizes the seller to ship goods by carrier.[92] Here a distinction is made between a shipment and destination contract.[93] In a shipment contract "the risk of loss passes to the buyer when the goods are duly delivered to the carrier."[94] In a destination contract the risk of loss passes to the buyer when the goods arrive at the destination and are there duly tendered while in the possession of the carrier so as to enable the buyer to take delivery.[95] The word "duly" is used in each case to incorporate into section 2–509 the tender requirements of a shipment contract.[96] In either a shipment or a destination contract, where the risk of loss has passed to the buyer, if the buyer wrongfully refuses the goods and returns them to the control of the seller, the seller assumes the risk of loss after a commercially reasonable time.[97]

(2) Subdivision 2

Subdivision 2 of section 2–509 deals with a situation where goods are in possession of a bailee (for example, goods stored in a warehouse) and are sold without any intention to move the goods. The risk of loss passes to the buyer in such a case: "(a) on his receipt of a negotiable document of title covering the goods; or (b) an acknowledgment by the bailee of the buyer's right to possession of the goods; or (c) after his receipt of a non-negotiable document of title or other written direction to deliver, as provided in subsection (4)(b) of section 2–503." The relevant part of section (4)(b) of section 2–503 adds, "risk of loss of the goods and of any failure by the bailee to honor the non-negotiable document of title or to obey the direction remains on the seller until the buyer has had a reasonable time to present the document or direction." This means that in the case of a non-negotiable document of title or other written direction even receipt by the buyer does not shift the risk of loss. Risk of loss remains on the seller until the buyer has a reasonable time to present the document, and even then the risk does not shift if the bailee refuses to honor the document.

(3) Subdivision 3

Section 2–509(3) is designed to cover cases which do not come within subsection (1) or (2). It states "that the risk of loss passes to the

---

92. This authority is given to the seller whenever he is to send goods to the buyer. See U.C.C. §§ 2–310(b), 2–319, 2–320, 2–504.

93. See § 11–20 supra.

94. U.C.C. § 2–509(1)(a); Eberhard Manufacturing Company v. Brown, 61 Mich.App. 268, 232 N.W.2d 378 (1975).

95. U.C.C. § 2–509(1)(b).

96. U.C.C. § 2–509, Comment 2. These tender requirements are set forth in U.C.C. § 2–504. See § 11–20 supra.

97. R. Nordstrom, Law of Sales, § 136 (1970).

buyer on his receipt of the goods if the seller is a merchant; otherwise the risk passes to the buyer on tender of delivery ＊ ＊ ＊." [98] Receipt of goods is defined to mean "taking physical possession of them." [99]

(c) Risk of Loss in the Event of Breach: U.C.C. § 2-510

(1) Breach by Seller

Under subdivision 1 the effect of a breach by the seller is to cause the risk of loss to remain on him "if the tender or delivery is so defective as to give a right of rejection." [1] If the seller cures or the buyer accepts then the risk of loss will pass to the buyer. [2] So also if the buyer rightfully revokes [3] his acceptance, "he may to the extent of any deficiency in his effective insurance treat the risk of loss as having rested on the seller from beginning." This provision in effect amounts to an anti-subrogation provision. [4]

(2) Breach by Buyer

If the buyer repudiates or is otherwise in breach, the risk of loss is placed on the buyer if the goods are conforming and have been identified to the contract. In this event the risk of loss is on the buyer for a commercially reasonable time "to the extent of any deficiency in his effective insurance coverage." This provision also amounts to an anti-subrogation provision. [5]

(d) U.C.C. § 2-613: Casualty to Identified Goods

This section does not strictly speaking relate to risk of loss but rather relates to the topic of impossibility of performance. In effect it states that where goods have been identified to a contract and are destroyed without the fault of either party before the risk of loss passes to the buyer the contract is ended. This means that the buyer need not pay for the goods and he may not recover for breach of contract. [6] If the loss is partial or the goods have deteriorated so as not to conform to the contract, the buyer has the option of avoiding the contract or of accepting the goods with due allowance. [7] Again, the buyer may not maintain an action for breach of contract. The same is true in the case of a "No Arrival No Sale" contract. [8]

As previously stated, the question of risk of loss does not arise unless and until goods have been identified to the contract. Nor does the mere fact that the particular goods the seller intends to deliver are destroyed (before identification) give the seller the defense of impracticability. If he does not offer replacement goods he will be liable although under appropriate circumstances he may be excused under the doctrine of temporary impossibility.

98. See Centurian Corp. v. Cripps, 624 P.2d 706 (Utah 1981).

99. U.C.C. § 2-103(1)(c).

1. See § 11-20 supra.

2. See § 11-20 supra.

3. See § 11-20 supra.

4. White & Summers, § 5-6.

5. Id. at § 5-5.

6. U.C.C. § 2-613(a).

7. U.C.C. § 2-613(b).

8. U.C.C. § 2-324.

WESTLAW REFERENCES

(a) *Introduction*

"risk of loss" /s u.c.c. "uniform commercial code"

(b) *U.C.C. § 2–509*

(1) *Subdivision 1*

"uniform commercial code" u.c.c. /p 2–509 /p carrier

(2) *Subdivision 2*

"uniform commercial code" u.c.c. /p 2–509(2)

(3) *Subdivision 3*

"uniform commercial code" u.c.c. /p 2–509(3)

(c) *Risk of Loss in the Event of Breach: U.C.C. 2–510*

(1) *Breach by Seller*

"uniform commercial code" u.c.c. /p 2–150

(d) *U.C.C. § 2–613: Casualty to Identified Goods*

"uniform commercial code" u.c.c. /p 2–613

§ 13–27. Risk of Loss: Leases

Under the common law with respect to leases, which regards the lessor as having completely performed when the lease is given, risk of loss is placed upon the lessee.[9] This rule has been changed in many states by statute or judicial decision.[10]

WESTLAW REFERENCES

di("risk of loss" /s lessee)

di("risk of loss" /s lease)

§ 13–28. Risk of Loss: Bailments

If a bailee does not return the bailed articles a prima facie case is made out against him,[11] but if he can show that the goods were fortuitously destroyed and that he exercised the requisite degree of care he will not be liable because he has the defense of impossibility of performance.[12] There have been some recent cases that have interpreted the language of the agreement as imposing the duty of an insurer upon a bailee.[13]

WESTLAW REFERENCES

bail! /s good /s impossib!

"risk of loss" /s bail!

bail! /s care /s destruction destroy!

---

9. See 1 Friedman on Leases, ch. 9 (2d ed.1983).

10. Id. See J. Cribbet, Principles of the Law of Property, 205–09 (2d ed.1975).

11. R. Brown, On Personal Property, § 11.8, 291–296 (3d ed.1975).

12. Atlanta Limousine Airport Services, Inc. v. Rinker, 160 Ga.App. 494, 287 S.E.2d 395 (1981); R. Brown, On Personal Property § 11.81, 291–296 (3d ed.1975).

13. R. Brown, On Personal Property, § 11.5, 275–276 (3d ed.1975).

Chapter 14

DAMAGES

Table of Sections

Table of Sections

A. INTRODUCTION

Sec.
14–1.   Damages Defined.

B. NON–COMPENSATORY DAMAGES

14–2.   Nominal Damages.
14–3.   Punitive Damages.

C. COMPENSATORY DAMAGES

14–4.   The General Standard.

D. FORESEEABILITY

14–5.   The Rule of Hadley v. Baxendale.
    (a) Economic Injury.
    (b) Mental Distress.
14–6.   Application of the Rule in Carrier and Telegraph Cases.
14–7.   Application of the Rule in Other Cases.

A. INTRODUCTION

Table of Sections

§ 14-1. Damages Defined

In the later stages of the system of common law pleading in an action to enforce a contract, two basic writs were available.[1] If the plaintiff had fully performed all or a severable part of his contractual obligation and if the agreed exchange for his performance was the payment of money, the writ of *general assumpsit* was available to him. The plaintiff's recovery was the agreed price, or, if no price had been agreed upon, the reasonable value of the labor or services he had rendered or the property which he had transferred to the defendant. Although such recovery was sometimes referred to as "damages,"[2] it is conceptually and practically different from an award of damages as that term is generally understood.

When the defendant breached his contract prior to a completed performance by the plaintiff, the appropriate writ was *special assumpsit*. In this case the plaintiff was not entitled to recover the agreed price, but only the amount of the pecuniary injury, if any, he had suffered. It is sometimes said that the plaintiff's contract rights are primary rights and upon breach by the defendant, these primary rights are discharged and in substitution the law grants the plaintiff secondary rights.[3] The law of remedies defines the scope of these secondary rights.

Modern law has kept the distinction made in these common law writs. This is not necessarily because the common law writs continue to rule us from the grave; rather the distinction makes good economic sense. When the plaintiff has fully performed, he has earned the agreed price. The Uniform Commercial Code labels a lawsuit seeking this kind of recovery an "action for the price."[4] When the plaintiff has

---

1. A common law pleader would find this statement and ensuing discussion greatly over-simplified. For a discussion of the writs formerly available in contract cases, see Shipman, Common Law Pleading 132–169 (3d ed. Ballantine 1923).

2. E.g., Stephen, Principles of Pleading in Civil Actions 361 (2d ed. Andrews 1901).

3. 5 Corbin § 995. The First Restatement, looking at the right-duty relationship from the perspective of the obligor's duty, states that the obligor's contractual

duty is discharged and in substitution a duty to make compensation is placed upon him. Restatement, Contracts § 399(1). The Second Restatement distinguishes between "rights to performance" (Restatement, Second, Contracts § 236, Comment b) and "rights to damages." Id. § 346, Comment a.

4. U.C.C. § 2–709. Unlike the rule under the common law writs, in an action for the price, incidental damages may sometimes be recovered in addition to the price.

not fully performed it would often be unduly generous to him and unduly harsh on the defendant to award him the price. Rather, the inquiry should be and is: what was the extent of his economic injury?[5] Usually, this will be less than the agreed exchange; but sometimes it will be more. Compensation allowed by law for this injury is known as damages. In addition, two categories of recoveries—nominal damages and punitive damages—have other non-compensatory functions. These play a rather small role in contract actions and will be discussed briefly at the outset of this chapter.

 WESTLAW REFERENCES

di damage

damage /s "general assumpsit"

"special assumpsit" /s breach! /s perform!

"primary right" /s "secondary right"

"action for the price" /s u.c.c. "uniform commercial code"

B. NON–COMPENSATORY DAMAGES

Table of Sections

§ 14–2. Nominal Damages

For every legal wrong there is a legal remedy.[6] Thus, for every breach of contract a cause of action exists. If the aggrieved party has suffered no damage he is entitled to a judgment for nominal damages,[7] usually in the amount of six cents or one dollar,[8] to symbolize vindication of the wrong done to him.

As a practical matter an award of nominal damages in a contract action may serve either of two functions. First, the plaintiff may bring an action knowing that he will at best obtain nominal damages in order to establish a precedent in a test case or in a dispute that is likely to recur in a continuing relationship.[9] Today, under modern statutes, he is more likely to bring an action for a declaratory judgment. Second, and more frequently, the plaintiff is likely to institute his action in the

---

See § 14–25 infra; 5 Corbin § 995; U.C.C. § 2–709.

5. Two kinds of economic harm are usually non-compensable and thus excluded from an award of damages. These are attorneys' fees (§ 14–35 infra) and attrition of the real value of the amount recovered because of inflation. See Hauser, Breach of Contracts Damages During Inflation, 33 Tul.L.Rev. 307 (1959).

6. Ashby v. White, 92 Eng.Rep. 126 (Q.B. 1703).

7. Freund v. Washington Square Press, 34 N.Y.2d 379, 357 N.Y.S.2d 857, 314 N.E.2d 419 (1974); Cook v. Lawson, 3 N.C. App. 104, 164 S.E.2d 29 (1968); Restatement, Second, Contracts § 346(2).

8. Hasselbusch v. Mohmking, 76 N.J.L. 691, 73 A. 961 (1909); Manhattan Sav. Institution v. Gottfried Baking Co., 286 N.Y. 398, 36 N.E.2d 637 (1941).

9. McCormick, Damages 95–96 (1935) [hereinafter McCormick, Damages].

belief that he is entitled to substantial damages. At trial he establishes that the contract was breached, but fails to establish that he has suffered actual damages. He thus is entitled to a judgment for nominal damages.[10] Traditionally, since he has established his cause of action he is also entitled to the costs of the action. It is sometimes said that nominal damages is a "peg to hang costs on." [11] In recent years this function of nominal damages has been somewhat curtailed. Statutory provisions frequently provide that if the action could have been brought in a court of inferior jurisdiction costs will not be recovered unless a specified minimum judgment is entered.[12] These statutes are designed to relieve congestion in the major trial courts.

 WESTLAW REFERENCES

di(breach! /s contract /s award! /s nominal /2 damage)

di nominal damage

actual substantial +1 damage /s "nominal damage"

§ 14–3. Punitive Damages

Punitive damages are granted to punish malicious or willful and wanton conduct.[13] The purpose of such an award is to deter the wrongdoer from similar conduct in the future as well as to deter others from engaging in such conduct. Punitive damages awards are of growing importance in tort litigation. Traditionally, however, punitive damages are not awarded in contract actions, no matter how malicious the breach.[14]

Where, however, the breach constitutes or is accompanied by an independent malicious or wanton tort, punitive damages are available.[15]

---

10. Beattie v. New York, N.H. & Hartford Ry., 84 Conn. 555, 80 A. 709 (1911); Asibem Associates, Ltd. v. Rill, 264 Md. 272, 286 A.2d 160 (1972); Freund v. Washington Square Press, Inc., 34 N.Y.2d 379, 357 N.Y.S.2d 857, 314 N.E.2d 419 (1974). On the additional question involved in such cases of whether a judgment for the defendant will be reversed and remanded when it appears that the plaintiff is entitled to merely nominal damages, see Note, 25 Colum.L.Rev. 963 (1925).

11. Stanton v. New York & E. Ry., 59 Conn. 272, 282, 22 A. 300, 303 (1890).

12. E.g., McKinney's N.Y.C.P.L.R. 8102; see McCormick, Damages 94–95.

13. See McCormick, Damages 275–299. Punitive damages are also known as exemplary damages.

14. J.J. White, Inc. v. Metropolitan Merchandise Mart, 48 Del. 526, 107 A.2d 892 (1954); American Ry. Exp. Co. v. Bailey, 142 Miss. 622, 107 So. 761 (1926); U.C.C. § 1–106(1); Restatement, Contracts § 342. See 11 Williston § 1340; Farns-

worth, Legal Remedies for Breach of Contract, 70 Colum.L.Rev. 1145, 1145–46 (1970); Simpson, Punitive Damages for Breach of Contract, 20 Ohio St.L.J. 284 (1959); Comment, Exemplary Damages in Contract Cases, 7 Willamette L.Rev. 137 (1971); Annot., 84 A.L.R. 1345 (1933). To the effect that an arbitrator has no power to award punitive damages for breach of contract, see Garrity v. Lyle Stuart, Inc., 40 N.Y.2d 354, 386 N.Y.S.2d 831, 353 N.E. 2d 793 (1976).

15. Klingbiel v. Commercial Credit Corp., 439 F.2d 1303 (10th Cir.1971) (breach of contract constituted a conversion); El Ranco, Inc. v. First Nat'l Bank, 406 F.2d 1205 (9th Cir.1968), certiorari denied 396 U.S. 875, 90 S.Ct. 150, 24 L.Ed.2d 133 (1969); Nader v. Allegheny Airlines, Inc., 365 F.Supp. 128 (D.D.C.1973) reversed 512 F.2d 527 (D.C.Cir.1975); General Motors v. Piskor, 281 Md. 627, 381 A.2d 16 (1977) (breach of contract involved false imprisonment and assault); I.H.P. Corp. v. 210 Central Park South Corp., 12 N.Y.2d 329, 239 N.Y.S.2d 547, 189 N.E.2d 812

They are also awarded where the breach also involves the malicious or wanton violation of a fiduciary duty even where the violation does not constitute an independent tort.[16] Some jurisdictions go beyond the independent tort and fiduciary violation cases and permit an award of punitive damages where elements of fraud, malice, gross negligence or oppression "mingle" with the breach.[17]

A recent trend has allowed punitive damages against insurance companies for bad faith refusals to settle claims; the breach of the implied covenant of good faith and fair dealing being treated as if it were a tort.[18] At this writing, California has carried this one step further beyond insurance cases, holding that a breach of a covenant of good faith and fair dealing in any contract is tortious and therefore a predicate for punitive damages.[19]

 WESTLAW REFERENCES

di("punitive damage" /s conduct /s contract /3 breach)

contract /s "punitive damage" /s deter deterrent deterred deterring

to(115) /p contract /s "punitive damage" /s breach! /3 recover! availab!

di("punitive damage" /s fiduciary)

"punitive damage" /s insur****

"punitive damage" /s "good faith and fair dealing"

"punitive damage" /s "exemplary damage" /s willful! wilful! wanton! malic!

C. COMPENSATORY DAMAGES

Table of Sections

(1963) (breach of lease constituted tort of forcible entry and detainer). For additional cases see Simpson, note 14 supra.

16. Brown v. Coates, 253 F.2d 36 (D.C. Cir.1958), noted in 33 N.Y.U.L.Rev. 878 (1958) (real estate broker); cf. International Brotherhood of Boilermakers v. Braswell, 388 F.2d 193 (5th Cir.1968), certiorari denied 391 U.S. 935, 88 S.Ct. 1848, 20 L.Ed. 2d 854 (1968) (union wrongfully expelled member); Hoche Productions, S.A. v. Jayark Films Corp., 256 F.Supp. 291 (S.D. N.Y.1966) (film distributor fraudulently accounted for gross receipts); Wagman v. Lee, 457 A.2d 401 (D.C.App.1983), certiorari denied 464 U.S. 849, 104 S.Ct. 158, 78 L.Ed.2d 145.

17. Boise Dodge, Inc. v. Clark, 92 Idaho 902, 453 P.2d 551 (1969); Art Hill Ford, Inc. v. Callender, 423 N.E.2d 601 (Ind. 1981); Sullivan, Punitive Damages in the Law of Contract: The Reality and Illusion of Legal Change, 61 Minn.L.Rev. 207 (1977); Note, Punitive Damages for Breach of Contract, 10 S.C.L.Rev. 444 (1958).

18. Gruenberg v. Aetna Ins. Co., 9 Cal. 3d 566, 108 Cal.Rptr. 480, 510 P.2d 1032 (1973); Smith v. American Family Mut. Ins. Co., 294 N.W.2d 751 (N.D.1980); see Creedon, Punitive Damages for Breach of Contract—Does the Punishment Fit the Crime?, 1983 Det.C.L.Rev. 1149; Holmes, Is There Life after Gilmore's Death of Contracts?—Induction from a Study of Commercial Good Faith in First-Party Insurance Contracts, 65 Cornell L.Rev. 330 (1980); Notes, 45 Fordham L.Rev. 164 (1976); 46 U.Cin.L.Rev. 170 (1977).

19. Seaman's Direct Buying Service v. Standard Oil Co. of California, 36 Cal.3d 752, 206 Cal.Rptr. 354, 686 P.2d 1158 (1984).

§ 14-4. The General Standard

For breach of contract the law of damages seeks to place the aggrieved party in the same economic position he would have had if the contract had been performed.[20] This involves an award of both the "losses caused and gains prevented by the defendant's breach, in excess of savings made possible."[21] An illustrative case is Lieberman v. Templar Motors Co.[22] The plaintiff contracted to manufacture a number of specially designed automobile bodies. The contract was repudiated by the defendant after production had commenced and about one-quarter of the bodies had been delivered. Since there was no market for auto bodies of this special design, the plaintiff could not mitigate his damages by completing the manufacture of the remaining bodies and selling them on the market. It was held that the plaintiff could recover his gains prevented calculated by the difference of what would have been the cost of performance and the contract price; in other words, the profit the plaintiff would have made if the contract had been fully performed. In addition, the plaintiff was permitted to recover the amount of his losses sustained. These consisted of payments for labor and material, reasonably made in part performance of the contract, to the extent that these were wasted; that is, to the extent that the labor product and materials could not be salvaged. Also included are "overhead expenses" such as an allocated share of the cost of management, plant, electric power, etc.[23]

There are many rules of damages for particular kinds of contracts; for example, for contracts for the sale of goods,[24] construction contracts,[25] employment contracts,[26] etc. With only a few exceptions, mainly in the real property area,[27] these specialized rules implement the general standard of gains prevented and losses sustained. It sometimes happens that because of the particular facts of a case the specialized rule usually applicable does not fulfill its purpose of providing an accurate formula for determining the gains prevented and losses sustained. In such a case the courts will turn to the general standard.[28]

Recently, a new analysis of the elements of contract damages has been made.[29] It has been pointed out that a contracting party has

---

20. U.C.C. § 1-106; 5 Corbin § 992; McCormick, Damages 561; 11 Williston § 1338.

21. Restatement, Contracts § 329, see also Restatement, Second, Contracts § 347.

22. 236 N.Y. 139, 140 N.E. 222, 29 A.L.R. 1089 (1923). The same result would be reached today under U.C.C. § 2-708(2). See § 14-27 infra.

23. See Conditioned Air Corp. v. Rock Island Motor Transit Co., 253 Iowa 961, 114 N.W.2d 304, 3 A.L.R.3d 679 (1962), certiorari denied 371 U.S. 825, 83 S.Ct. 46, 9 L.Ed.2d 64 (1962); accord, U.C.C. § 2-708(2).

24. See §§ 14-20 to 14-27 infra.

25. See §§ 14-28 to 14-29 infra.

26. See §§ 14-18 to 14-19 infra.

27. See § 14-30 infra.

28. See, e.g., Great Atlantic & Pacific Tea Co. v. Atchison, T. & S.F. Ry., 333 F.2d 705 (7th Cir.1964), cert. denied 379 U.S. 967, 85 S.Ct. 661, 13 L.Ed.2d 560 (1965); Liberty Navig. & Trading Co. v. Kinoshita & Co., Ltd., 285 F.2d 343 (2d Cir.1960), cert. denied 366 U.S. 949, 81 S.Ct. 1904, 6 L.Ed. 2d 1242 (1961); DeWaay v. Muhr, 160 N.W.2d 454 (Iowa 1968); Abrams v. Reynolds Metals Co., 340 Mass. 704, 166 N.E.2d 204 (1960).

29. Fuller & Perdue, The Reliance Interest in Contract Damages (Parts I and II),

three legally protected interests: a restitution interest, a reliance interest, and an expectation interest. The first of these represents his interests in the benefits he has conferred upon the other. The reliance interest represents the detriment he may have incurred by changing his position. The expectation interest represents the prospect of gain from the contract. This analysis does not conflict with the gains prevented and losses sustained analysis; it merely represents a different breakdown of the same economic harm suffered. The use of this newer analysis is gaining acceptance as it often permits a clearer way of determining the actual economic harm.

Our legal system starts with the premise that the expectation interest of contracting parties deserves protection. In order to protect it to the fullest; that is, in order to put the aggrieved party in the same economic position he would have attained upon full performance of the contract, the restitution and reliance interests need to be protected as well. The following hypothetical is illustrative:

P contracts to purchase Blackacre from V for $100,000, subject to obtaining a mortgage loan, paying V $10,000 as a down payment on contracting. An appraisal commissioned by P's bank shows that Blackacre has a market value of $120,000. Upon learning of the appraisal, V repudiates. Prior to repudiation, P expended $500 for a survey of Blackacre and $500 for banking fees for his loan application, and, as was foreseen by V, $1,000 for an option to purchase adjoining land which he intended to use to provide additional parking for the structure on Blackacre. P's expectancy of profit is $20,000. His restitution interest is the $10,000 down payment. His reliance interest is $2,000. His recovery will be $31,000, his expectancy and restitution interests and that part of his reliance interest (the option money) that would not have to be expended toward earning his expectancy.

At times the expectancy interest is unavailable, because of a lack of probative evidence [30] or for policy reasons.[31] In such instances the aggrieved party may have recovery based on one or both of the other interests.

WESTLAW REFERENCES

to(95 115) /p "compensatory damage" /s breach! /5 contract

"compensatory damage" /s economic

lieberman +s "templar motor"

"compensatory damage" /s gain** /s loss

"compensatory damage" /s "full* perform!"

to(115) /p contract /p "compensatory damage"

46 Yale L.J. 52, 373 (1936–37). See Hudec, Restating the "Reliance Interest," 67 Cornell L.Rev. 704 (1982).

30. See § 14–9 infra.

31. E.g., certain promissory estoppel decisions, discussed in ch. 6 supra; certain cases where a vendor breaches a contract to convey real property (§ 14–30); certain non-commercial contracts, such as a plastic surgeon's breach of promise to achieve a given result. Sullivan v. O'Connor, 363 Mass. 576, 296 N.E.2d 183 (1973). See Restatement, Second, Contracts § 351(3).

```
expense  /s  contract  /s  "compensatory damage"
restitution reliance expecta!  +1  interest  /s  damage
115k40(2)  /p  compensat!
restitution reliance expecta!  +1  interest  /s  recover!
```

D. FORESEEABILITY

Table of Sections

§ 14–5. The Rule of Hadley v. Baxendale

(a) Economic Injury

Prior to 1854 there were almost no rules of contract damages. The assessment of damages was for the most part left to the unfettered discretion of the jury.[32] Such broad discretion, however, was unsuited to the now mature commercial economy of England. In that year the case of Hadley v. Baxendale[33] was decided. It has won universal acceptance in the common law world and remains the leading case in the field.

The plaintiffs operated a grist mill which was forced to suspend operations because of a broken shaft. An employee of the plaintiff brought the broken shaft to the defendants for shipment to an engineering company which was to manufacture a new shaft, using the broken one as a model. The defendants unexcusably delayed the shipment for several days. As a result the mill was shut down for a greater period of time than it would have been had the shipment been seasonably dispatched.[34] A judgment entered upon a jury verdict for

---

32. McCormick, Damages 562–563; Washington, Damages in Contract at Common Law, 47 Law Q.Rev. 345 (1931), 48 Law Q.Rev. 90 (1932).

33. 156 Eng.Rep. 145 (1854). It has been argued persuasively that the decision of the case represents a borrowing from the French writer, Pothier. Washington, supra note 32 at 103; see also Danzig, Hadley v. Baxendale: A Study in the Industrialization of the Law, 4 J.Leg.Studies 249, 257–59 (1975). The decision in this celebrated case had been preceded by a number of American cases in which the court borrowed from and cited this great French author. See, e.g., Blanchard v. Ely, 21 Wend. 342 (N.Y.1839). Pothier's analysis was well known to early American writers. See, e.g., Chipman, An Essay on the

Law of Contracts for the Payment of Specific Articles 122 (1822).

34. There has been confusion as to the facts of the case. According to the reporter's statement of the facts the plaintiff's servant told the clerk that the mill was stopped and the shaft was to be sent immediately. But the opinion of the court states: "We find that the only circumstances here communicated by the plaintiffs to the defendants at the time the contract was made were that the article to be carried was the broken shaft of a mill, and the plaintiffs were millers of that mill." Even as careful a scholar as McCormick uncritically accepted the reporter's statement of the facts. McCormick, Damages 564; McCormick, The Contemplation Rule as a Limitation upon Damages for

the plaintiff which included an award of damages for the lost profits of the mill was reversed.

The decision was clearly based on the policy of protecting enterprises in the then burgeoning industrial revolution.[35] The court laid down two rules. First, the aggrieved party may recover those damages "as may fairly and reasonably be considered * * * arising naturally, i.e., according to the usual course of things, from such breach of contract itself." Second, he may recover damages "such as may reasonably be supposed to have been in the contemplation of both parties, at the time they made the contract, as the probable result of the breach of it." [36] A several days delay in the shipment of a shaft does not "in the usual course of things" result in catastrophic consequences. Usually, delay in shipment of a chattel results in a loss of the value of its use for the period of delay; that is, its rental value.[37] Liability for damages in excess of that value, according to the second rule of Hadley v. Baxendale, will only be awarded if such additional damages were in the contemplation of both parties as a probable consequence of a breach. As applied in this case and subsequent cases, this means that such consequences must be foreseeable.[38] Thus, if the shipper had known that the mill was shut down because of the want of the shaft and that no substitute shaft was available, the shipper would have been liable for consequential damages consisting of the lost profits of the mill.

When parties enter into a contract their minds are usually fixed on performance rather than on breach. To the extent that this is true, it is fictional to speak in terms of the damages which are in the subjective

---

Breach of Contract, 19 Minn.L.Rev. 497, 509 (1935). A subsequent English case has pointed out the error of reliance on the reporter's statement insofar as it conflicts with the court's analysis of the facts. Victoria Laundry (Windsor) Ltd. v. Newman Industries, Ltd., [1949] 2 K.B. 528, 537; see Danzig, supra note 33, at 262–63. In this case the court indicated that if the reporter's headnote were correct, the decision would have gone the other way. Unfortunately some cases have relied on the headnote, thereby reaching erroneous results. E.g., Moss Jellico Coal Co. v. American Ry. Exp. Co., 198 Ky. 202, 248 S.W. 508 (1923).

35. Danzig, supra note 33; McCormick, The Contemplation Rule as a Limitation upon Damages for Breach of Contract, 19 Minn.L.Rev. 497 (1935).

36. 156 Eng.Rep. at 151.

37. New Orleans & N.E.R.R. v. J.H. Miner Saw Mfg. Co., 117 Miss. 646, 78 So. 577 (1918); Chapman v. Fargo, 223 N.Y. 32, 119 N.E. 76 (1918). If, however, the goods are shipped for the purpose of sale, the aggrieved party may recover any depreciation in the market value of the goods which may have occurred between the time the goods should have arrived and the time of their arrival. Ward v. New York Cent. R.R., 47 N.Y. 29 (1871); The Heron II (Koufos v. C. Czarnikow, Ltd.) [1967] 3 All E.R. 686 (H.L.). But cf. Great Atlantic & Pacific Tea Co. v. Atchison, T. & S.F. Ry., 333 F.2d 705 (7th Cir.1964), certiorari denied 379 U.S. 967, 85 S.Ct. 661, 13 L.Ed.2d 560 (1965) (no damages awarded where wholesale price declined but goods were resold at price originally contemplated).

38. Restatement, Second, Contracts § 351. For the intimate relationship between the doctrine of foreseeability and the doctrine of avoidable consequences, see § 14–15 infra. For an argument to the effect that knowledge of the consequences of a breach acquired after contracting should also be relevant, see Samek, The Relevant Time of Foreseeability of Damage in Contract, 38 Austl.L.J. 125 (1964). Such an approach appears to have been adopted by the U.C.C. See § 14–22 infra. On the rule of foreseeability, see generally Farnsworth, supra note 14 at 1199–1210; Note, An Economic Approach to Hadley v. Baxendale, 62 Neb.L.Rev. 157 (1983).

contemplation of the parties.[39]   When courts speak in terms of the "contemplation of the parties," they use this terminology within the framework of the objective theory of contracts.   Under the first rule of Hadley v. Baxendale, certain damages will so naturally and obviously flow from the breach that every one is deemed to contemplate them. Frequently such damages are known as "general" damages.   Under the second rule, less obvious kinds of damages are deemed to be contemplated if the promisor knows or has reason to know the special circumstances which will give rise to such damages.   Such damages are frequently known as "special" or "consequential" damages.

A number of English cases subsequently applied a stricter rule than that announced in Hadley v. Baxendale.   According to these cases, mere notice of special circumstances is an insufficient basis for imposing liability for consequential damages.   These decisions required that the knowledge of special circumstances "must be brought home to the party to be charged under such circumstances that he must know that the person he contracts with reasonably believes that he accepts the contract with the special condition attached to it." [40]   In other words there must be an express or implied manifestation of intent to assume the risk of forseeable consequential damages.   This "tacit agreement" test was adopted by Mr. Justice Holmes for the United States Supreme Court as Federal common law,[41] but has attracted few followers among the state courts.[42]   This additional qualification of the Rule of Hadley v. Baxendale appears to have been abandoned in England [43] and has been repudiated by the Uniform Commercial Code [44] and the Restatement Second.[45]   The "tacit agreement" test was based on the dubious assump-

39.   Leonard v. New York, Albany and Buffalo Electro-Magnetic Tel. Co., 41 N.Y. 544, 567 (1870).

40.   British Columbia Saw-Mill Co. v. Nettleship, L.R., 3 C.P. 499, 500 (1868); accord, Horne v. Midland R.R., L.R., 7 C.P. 583 (1872), L.R., 8 C.P. 131 (1873).

41.   Globe Ref. Co. v. Landa Cotton Oil Co., 190 U.S. 540, 23 S.Ct. 754, 47 L.Ed. 1171 (1903).   See also Hooks Smelting Co. v. Planters' Compress Co., 72 Ark. 275, 79 S.W. 1052 (1904).   With the general abandonment of Federal common law, in diversity cases the Federal courts must now apply state law in such cases. Krauss v. Greenbarg, 137 F.2d 569 (3d Cir.1943), certiorari denied 320 U.S. 791, 64 S.Ct. 207, 88 L.Ed. 477 (1943).

42.   See McCormick, Damages 579–80. It has also been attacked by writers on contracts.   5 Corbin § 1010; 11 Williston § 1357.   It is supported by Bauer, Consequential Damages in Contract, 80 U.Pa.L. Rev. 687 (1931).   While, from time to time, the test has been articulated in modern decisions, it is usually in contexts where the particular item of damage could not be

recoverable under any test because of availability of a substitute performance. E.g., Keystone Diesel Engine Co. v. Irwin, 411 Pa. 222, 191 A.2d 376 (1963).

43.   Victoria Laundry (Windsor) Ltd. v. Newman Industries Ltd., [1949] 2 K.B. 528, seems to have slightly liberalized the Hadley v. Baxendale test.   Consequential damages were allowed where the defendant had "reason to know" the special circumstances although these were not communicated by the plaintiff.   Accord, Appliances, Inc. v. Queen Stove Works, Inc., 228 Minn. 55, 36 N.W.2d 121 (1949).

44.   U.C.C. § 2–715, Comment 2.   It seems no longer to be followed by Federal courts in the application of federal statutes, such as the Carmack Amendment, 49 U.S.C.A. § 20(11), concerning the liability of land carriers in interstate commerce. See, e.g., L.E. Whitlock Truck Serv. v. Regal Drilling Co., 333 F.2d 488 (10th Cir. 1964).

45.   Restatement, Second, Contracts § 351, Comment a, and Reporter's Notes thereto.

tion that damages for breach of contract are based upon the contracting parties' implied or express promise to pay damages in the event of breach, rather than based upon a secondary duty imposed by law as a consequence of the breach.[46]

(b) Mental Distress

It is well established that, as a general rule, no damages will be awarded for the mental distress or emotional trauma that may be caused by a breach of contract.[47] While some courts have concluded that this result is reached because such damages are too remote to have been within the contemplation of the parties,[48] it seems apparent that the courts have forged "a rule of policy defining the limits of business risk." [49]

Exceptions have been made in situations where "the plaintiff's interests of personality are involved. * * * These are cases of actions for breach of contract for expulsions of guests from hotels, or passengers from trains, or expulsion or refusal of admission to ticket holders in places of public resort or entertainment." [50] Contracts for funeral arrangements are also well within this class,[51] while employment contracts are generally outside it.[52]

Although there seems to be no tendency of the courts to enlarge the kinds of cases in which damages for mental distress are given, the recent enlargement of the categories of cases in which punitive damages are granted may be seen as an indirect way of redressing such injuries.[53]

 WESTLAW REFERENCES

(a) *Economic Injury*

    hadley +s baxendale /s foresee!

    recover! /s damage /s contract /s party /s contemplat!

    contract /s damage /s "probable consequence"

    contract /s consequence /s breach! /s foresee!

    115k23

    contract /s foresee! /s los* /2 profit

    foresee! /s "consequential damage"

    "general damage" /s contemplat! /s contract

    special consequential +1 damage /s "reason to know"

46. See 5 Corbin § 1010; 11 Williston § 1357.

47. Restatement, Second, Contracts § 353; Corbin § 1076; McCormick on Damages § 145; Williston §§ 1338, 1341.

48. E.g., Addis v. Gramaphone Co., [1909] A.C. 488; Redgrave v. Boston Symphony Orchestra, 557 F.Supp. 230 (D.Mass. 1983); Westwater v. Rector, etc. of Grace Church, 140 Cal. 339, 735 P. 1055 (1903).

49. McCormick on Damages 593.

50. Ibid. (Footnotes omitted).

51. Hirst v. Elgin Metal Casket Co., 438 F.Supp. 906 (D.Mont.1977); Lamm v. Shingleton, 231 N.C. 10, 55 S.E.2d 810 (1949). See B & M Homes & Co. v. Hogan, 376 So. 2d 667 (Ala.1979) (faulty construction of home).

52. See cases cited in note 48 supra. In England there is a trend toward including employment contracts. See Comment, 55 Can.B.Rev. 169, 333 (1977).

53. See discussion in Zimmerman v. Michigan Hospital Service, 96 Mich.App. 464, 292 N.W.2d 236 (1980).

special consequential   +1   damage   /s   "special circumstance"   /s
   contract

special consequential   +1   damage   /s   assum!   /s   risk

(b) *Mental Distress*

"mental distress"   /s   breach!   /s   contract

emotional mental   +1   distress anguish   /s   contract   /s   damage

§ 14–6. Application of the Rule in Carrier and Telegraph Cases

Hadley v. Baxendale itself was a carrier case. It indicated that a carrier will be liable for consequential damages if it is on notice of the particular purpose the cargo will serve and the fact that there is no available substitute for the cargo which is delayed, lost or injured in transit. If there were an available substitute the aggrieved party, by virtue of the doctrine of avoidable consequences, would not be able to recover those damages which could have been avoided by employment of the substitute.[54]

Applying this test, a carrier is not liable for consequential damages consisting of lost profit when it delays shipment of motion picture film to a theater if it has no notice that the theater could not procure a substitute film.[55] Similarly a carrier was held not liable for a lost engagement suffered by a vaudeville artist caused by delay in shipment of his baggage where, although the carrier knew the contents of baggage, it did not know that the artist was engaged for a performance at the point of destination.[56]

On the other hand, if the shipment is of such a character that its purpose is obvious and the consequences of non-delivery equally obvious, the carrier will be held liable for consequential damages. Thus, when a carrier undertakes to transport scenery for a road show and knows the date of the scheduled theatrical performance it will be liable for consequential damages suffered by the road company as the carrier should be aware that no substitute scenery will be available.[57] In a decision perhaps more liberal than most a carrier was held liable for loss of a herd of hogs caused by its delay in the shipment of hog cholera serum.[58] The Court indicated that the carrier should be aware of the probable use and probable consequences of the delay although it did not know, for example, that the consignee was a farmer. A stronger case is made out when the carrier is actually told the special circumstances. Thus, if the carrier is told that an oil well drilling rig is the only one the consignor has and the consequent importance of timely delivery, it is liable for the loss of profit attributable to the lack of prompt

---

54. See § 14–15 infra.

55. Chapman v. Fargo, 223 N.Y. 32, 119 N.E. 76, 1918F L.R.A. 1049 (1918).

56. Rives v. American Ry. Exp. Co., 227 App.Div. 375, 237 N.Y.S. 429 (1st Dep't 1929).

57. Weston v. Boston & M. R.R., 190 Mass. 298, 76 N.E. 1050, 4 L.R.A.(n.s.) 569 (1906).

58. Adams Exp. Co. v. Allen, 125 Va. 530, 100 S.E. 473 (1919).

delivery.[59] If, however, other rigs were available on a short term basis on the rental market, the decision would go the other way.

Decisions involving the liability of telegraph companies are closely aligned to those involving carriers. Telegraph companies share with common carriers a duty to serve everyone on an equal basis. In addition, they both receive a relatively small compensation for services which, if not duly performed, could result in catastrophic financial losses to their clients. The courts have been highly reluctant to shift these losses to the carrier in view of the disproportion between the compensation received and the potentially large burden of damages. Thus, the courts have tended towards particular strictness in these classes of cases in applying the test of foreseeability. If a telegraph message clearly indicates the nature of the transaction, the telegraph company is liable for consequential damages flowing from negligence in failing to transmit the message or in transmitting it erroneously.[60] If the message conveys nothing to the company as to the nature of the transaction, clearly there is no liability for consequential damages.[61] Where, as is often the case, the message is obviously a business message, but the nature of the transaction is not clear, there is not a sufficient basis for recovery of consequential damages. "Notice of the business, if it is to lay the basis for special damages, must be sufficiently informing to be notice of the risk." [62]

In any modern case involving a common carrier or telegraph company, an additional factor to be considered is limitations of the carrier's liability under applicable state and federal regulatory legislation.[63] While these statutes do not overrule the contemplation of the parties test, they frequently curtail the amount of recovery by setting a maximum limit, or permit the parties to set such a limit by agreement.

 WESTLAW REFERENCES

"consequential damage" /s mail "common carrier" telegraph

70k135

372k209

---

59. L.E. Whitlock Truck Serv., Inc. v. Regal Drilling Co., 333 F.2d 488 (10th Cir. 1964).

60. Leonard v. New York, Albany and Buffalo Electro-Magnetic Tel. Co., 41 N.Y. 544 (1870) (message as transmitted read, "Send 5,000 casks of salt immediately," instead of "send 5,000 sacks of salt immediately."); Allen v. Western Union Tel. Co., 209 S.C. 157, 39 S.E.2d 257, 167 A.L.R. 1392 (1946). Contra, Daughtery v. American Union Tel. Co., 75 Ala. 168 (1883) (rejecting rule of Hadley v. Baxendale).

61. Primrose v. Western Union Tel. Co., 154 U.S. 1, 14 S.Ct. 1098, 38 L.Ed. 883 (1894) (message in private code).

62. Kerr S.S. Co. v. Radio Corp. of America, 245 N.Y. 284, 288, 157 N.E. 140, 141, 55 A.L.R. 1139 (1927); accord, EVRA Corp. v. Swiss Bank Corp., 673 F.2d 951 (7th Cir.1982), certiorari denied 459 U.S. 1017, 103 S.Ct. 1017, 74 L.Ed.2d 511 (1982) (bank negligently handled telex message); Einbinder v. Western Union Tel. Co., 205 S.C. 15, 30 S.E.2d 765, 154 A.L.R. 704 (1944).

63. Cf. U.C.C. § 7–309 as to carriers' limitations of liability, with citations in the official comments to other legislation. On the question of preemption of state law by federal legislation, see Western Union Tel. Co. v. Priester, 276 U.S. 252, 48 S.Ct. 234, 72 L.Ed. 555 (1928); Western Union Tel. Co. v. Abbott Supply Co., 45 Del. 345, 74 A.2d 77, 20 A.L.R.2d 754 (1950).

372k280

"common carrier" telegraph /s liab! /s loss

70k108

70k135

"common carrier" telegraph /s limit! /s liable liablity /s statut!

u.c.c. "uniform commercial code" /s 7–309

§ 14–7.   Application of the Rule in Other Cases

The doctrine of foreseeability is applicable not only in carrier cases but in all contract cases. The discussion in this chapter dealing with damages in particular kinds of contract actions (§§ 14–18—14–30) will consider both general and consequential damages in such actions.

It should be noted that the rule is not applied blindly and mechanically. Courts must be aware of the transactional context in which the transactions occur. Notions of disproportionality between the agreed price and the ensuing loss, relative fault, and the willfulness or innocence of the breach are some of the factors that guide the decisions in a concrete case.[64]

 WESTLAW REFERENCES
digest(doctrine theory /2 foreseeability /s contract)

E.   CERTAINTY

Table of Sections

§ 14–8.   Certainty as a Limitation Upon Recovery of Damages

Ordinarily, prior to rendering its verdict a jury is charged by the judge to render a decision based on the "preponderance of the evidence."[65] The jury's verdict may be set aside only if the court concludes "that no reasonable man would solve the litigation in the way the jury has chosen to do."[66] Frequently, however, a different standard is applied in cases involving contract damages. The jury's verdict will be set aside if the standard of "certainty" is not met. It has been said that the damages "must be certain, both in their nature and in

---

64. Restatement, Second, Contracts § 351(3); see Stone, Recovery of Consequential Damages for Product Recall Expenditures, 1980 B.Y.U.L.Rev. 485, 528–38.

65. McCormick, Evidence § 319 (1954).

66. Rapant v. Ogsbury, 279 App.Div. 298, 109 N.Y.S.2d 737 (3rd Dep't 1952).

respect to the causes from which they proceed." [67] It seems to be generally recognized that absolute certainty is not required; "reasonable certainty" will suffice.[68]

Courts do not as a rule impose the requirement of certainty except where the damages in issue involve lost profits on transactions other than the transaction on which the breach occurred.[69] To illustrate, if there is a contract for the delivery of sugar at six cents a pound and at the time the buyer learns of the breach the market price is seven cents, the purchaser has suffered gains prevented in the amount of one cent per pound. The courts generally do not insist upon a standard of certainty in establishing this loss even though market price may be in fact uncertain or fictitious.[70] If, however, the seller has reason to know that the sugar will be used by the buyer for the baking of cakes for resale and no other supply of sugar will seasonably be available to the buyer, the seller may be liable for the profits which would have been made upon resale of the cakes.[71] It is to profits such as these that the standard of certainty most frequently is applied. The baker must show with certainty that he would have made profits on the sale of the cakes as not all bakery operations necessarily result in profits. Although there are cases holding that the amount of such profits must be established with certainty, the trend is clearly in the direction of holding that once the fact of damage is established, its amount need not be shown with precision.[72]

There is no satisfactory way of defining what is meant by "certainty" or "reasonable certainty." It means, however, that the quality of the evidence must be of a higher caliber than is needed to establish most other factual issues in a lawsuit. Although the courts have been using more or less the same language for well over a century, the stringency of its application has tended to vary in different decades dependent upon the makeup and philosophy of the bench in a particular jurisdiction at a particular time.[73]

67. Griffin v. Colver, 16 N.Y. 489 (1858). See generally Farnsworth, supra note 14, at 1210–15.

68. Restatement, Second, Contracts § 352; McCormick, Damages 401.

69. Corbin §§ 1020–1028; McCormick, Damages 104–106.

70. See § 14–12 infra. For a case in which the standard of certainty was applied to a question of the value of property, see Asibem Associates, Ltd. v. Rill, 264 Md. 272, 286 A.2d 160 (1972). See also Wenzler & Ward Plumbing & Heating Co. v. Sellen, 53 Wn.2d 96, 330 P.2d 1068 (1958), where the court assumed that the doctrine was applicable in determining the value of services.

71. See § 14–20 infra.

72. Typographical Service, Inc. v. Itek Corp., 721 F.2d 1317 (11th Cir.1983); Mann v. Weyerhaeuser Co., 703 F.2d 272 (8th Cir. 1983); A to Z Rental, Inc. v. Wilson, 413 F.2d 899, 908 (10th Cir.1969); El Fredo Pizza, Inc. v. Roto-Flex Oven Co., 199 Neb. 697, 261 N.W.2d 358 (1978).

73. Compare the liberal attitude and the relaxed standard of certainty in Wakeman v. Wheeler & Wilson Mfg. Co., 101 N.Y. 205, 4 N.E. 264 (1886), with the stringent standard of Judge Cardozo in Broadway Photoplay Co. v. World Film Corp., 225 N.Y. 104, 121 N.E. 756 (1919), and the return to a relaxed standard in Duane Jones Co. v. Burke, 306 N.Y. 172, 117 N.E.2d 237 (1954); Spitz v. Lesser, 302 N.Y. 490, 99 N.E.2d 540 (1951), noted in 9 Wash. & Lee L.Rev. 75 (1952) and a shift to an antedeluvian standard in Kenford Co. v. Erie County, 67 N.Y.2d 257, 502 N.Y.S.2d 131, 493 N.E.2d 234 (1986).

It has usually been held that lost profits caused by a breach of contract to produce a sporting event,[74] theatrical performance or other form of entertainment,[75] are too uncertain for recovery. Evidence of profits made by other performances of a similar kind or by the same performance in a different city has been deemed insufficiently probative of whether profits would have been made and, in any event, of the amount which would have been made. Similarly, new businesses have not generally been successful in establishing with certainty what their profits, if any, would have been in cases where the defendant's breach prevented or delayed their opening for business. This has been the result, despite evidence of earnings subsequent to their opening or earnings of similar businesses elsewhere.[76] It is interesting to note, however, that in actions based upon antitrust law violations, new businesses have been awarded damages based upon lost profits.[77] The difference in treatment accorded to contract actions reveals rather clearly that the standard of certainty, like the rule of foreseeability, is based at least partly upon a policy of limiting contractual risks.[78]

As a rule, established businesses can prove lost profits on transactions of a kind in which the particular business has traditionally engaged with sufficient certainty.[79] Even here, however, a verdict for

74. Chicago Coliseum Club v. Dempsey, 265 Ill.App. 542 (1932); Carnera v. Schmeling, 236 App.Div. 460, 260 N.Y.S. 82 (1st Dep't 1932).

75. Narragansett Amusement Co. v. Riverside Park Amusement Co., 260 Mass. 265, 157 N.E. 532 (1927); Bernstein v. Meech, 130 N.Y. 354, 29 N.E. 255 (1891); Willis v. Branch, 94 N.C. 142 (1886). But see Contemporary Mission, Inc. v. Famous Music Corp., 557 F.2d 918 (2d Cir.1977); compare Orbach v. Paramount Pictures Corp., 233 Mass. 281, 123 N.E. 669 (1919) with Broadway Photoplay Co. v. World Film Corp., 225 N.Y. 104, 121 N.E. 756 (1919).

76. Benham v. World Airways, Inc., 432 F.2d 359 (9th Cir.1970); Central Coal & Coke Co. v. Hartman, 111 Fed. 96 (8th Cir. 1901); Thrift Wholesale, Inc. v. Malkin-Illion Corp., 50 F.Supp. 998 (E.D.Pa.1943); Marvell Light & Ice Co. v. General Elec. Co., 162 Ark. 467, 259 S.W. 741 (1924); California Press Mfg. Co. v. Stafford Packing Co., 192 Cal. 479, 221 P. 345, 32 A.L.R. 114 (1923); Paola Gas Co. v. Paola Glass Co., 56 Kan. 614, 44 P. 621 (1896); Evergreen Amusement Corp. v. Milstead, 206 Md. 610, 112 A.2d 901 (1955); Cramer v. Grand Rapids Show Case, 223 N.Y. 63, 119 N.E. 227, 1 A.L.R. 154 (1918); Brenneman v. Auto-Teria, 260 Or. 513, 491 P.2d 992 (1971); Barbier v. Barry, 345 S.W.2d 557 (Tex.Civ.App.1961). But see Excelsior Motor Mfg. & Supply Co. v. Sound Equip., 73 F.2d 725 (7th Cir.1934); Lakota Girl Scout

Council, Inc. v. Harvey Fund-Raising Management, Inc., 519 F.2d 634 (8th Cir.1975); Upjohn Co. v. Rachelle Labs, Inc., 661 F.2d 1105 (6th Cir.1981). See Wallach, The Buyer's Right to Monetary Damages, 14 U.C.C. L.J. 236, 265–71 (1982).

77. William Goldman Theatres v. Loew's, 69 F.Supp. 103 (E.D.N.Y.1946), review denied 163 F.2d 241 (3d Cir.1947).

78. Botto v. Brunner, 42 N.J.Super. 95, 126 A.2d 32 (1956), certification granted 23 N.J. 139, 128 A.2d 309 (1958); cf. McCormick, Damages 105; Fuller & Perdue, supra note 29, at 373–77. Indeed, courts have on occasion intermingled the foreseeability and certainty tests into a single doctrine. See Archer-Daniels-Midland Co. v. Paull, 293 F.2d 389 (8th Cir.1961), on remand 199 F.Supp. 319 (W.D.Ark.1961), judgment affirmed 313 F.2d 612 (8th Cir. 1963), 48 Iowa L.Rev. 147 (1962); Witherbee v. Meyer, 155 N.Y. 446, 50 N.E. 58 (1898).

79. Natural Soda Prod. Co. v. Los Angeles, 23 Cal.2d 193, 143 P.2d 12 (1943), certiorari denied 321 U.S. 793, 64 S.Ct. 790, 88 L.Ed. 1594 (1944). The cases which are perhaps most cited on the point today are cases involving private actions to recover treble damages under the antitrust laws. Bigelow v. RKO Radio Pictures, Inc., 327 U.S. 251, 66 S.Ct. 574, 90 L.Ed. 652 (1946), rehearing denied 327 U.S. 817, 66 S.Ct. 815, 90 L.Ed. 1040 (1946); Eastman Kodak Co. v. Southern Photo Materials Co., 273

the plaintiff will be set aside if the court is not convinced that the record contains the best available evidence upon which an informed verdict can be based.[80]

There are said to be several modifying doctrines of the rule of certainty. Leading among these is the statement that "where the defendant's wrong has caused the difficulty of proof of damage, he cannot complain of the resulting uncertainty."[81] If this statement were literally true, no verdict could be set aside on the ground of uncertainty except in the case where plaintiff's counsel has failed to produce the best available evidence of the fact and amount of lost profits. Yet courts frequently rely on this supposed modifying doctrine.[82] It is also clear that they frequently do not.[83] It has been suggested that there is a tendency to relax the rule of certainty and to apply this modifying doctrine where the breach is willful.[84] What is clear is that there is no universal application of the rule of certainty, and that, within a given jurisdiction, case authority which applies a stringent test often exists along with other cases which, in express terms[85] or, in effect, hold that certainty is not a requirement. More commonly than is the case in other fields of contract law, the decision as to a particular set of facts cannot be predicted by the application of abstract legal rules. Official comments to the Uniform Commercial Code indicate that in Code governed cases the standard of proof must be flexibly applied and certainty will not be insisted upon where the facts of the case do not permit more than an approximation.[86]

U.S. 359, 47 S.Ct. 400, 71 L.Ed. 684 (1927). Reliance on the relatively relaxed standard applied in these cases, particularly in the Bigelow case, has had a notably liberalizing effect upon contract decisions.

A small number of decisions take the position that lost profits on resale are inherently too speculative for proof and refuse to allow any evidence on the point. See Paris v. Buckner Feed Mill, 279 Ala. 148, 182 So.2d 880 (1966).

80. Center Chem. Co. v. Avril, Inc., 392 F.2d 289 (5th Cir.1968); Alexander's Dep't Stores, Inc. v. Ohrbach's Inc., 269 App.Div. 321, 56 N.Y.S.2d 173 (1st Dep't 1945); Allen, Heaton & McDonald, Inc. v. Castle Farm Amusement Co., 151 Ohio St. 522, 86 N.E.2d 782, 17 A.L.R.2d 963 (1949); McCormick, Damages 107–10. For an excellent summary of the kind of evidence deemed acceptable, see 14 Minn.L.Rev. 820 (1930). See also Commonwealth Trust Co. v. Hachmeister Lind Co., 320 Pa. 233, 181 A. 787 (1935).

81. McCormick, Damages 101.

82. Bigelow v. RKO Radio Pictures, Inc., 327 U.S. 251, 66 S.Ct. 574, 90 L.Ed. 652 (1946), rehearing denied 327 U.S. 817, 66 S.Ct. 815, 90 L.Ed. 1040 (1946) (antitrust case); Milton v. Hudson Sales Corp., 152 Cal.App.2d 418, 313 P.2d 936 (1957); Wakeman v. Wheeler & W. Mfg. Co., 101 N.Y. 205, 4 N.E. 264 (1886).

83. Broadway Photoplay Co. v. World Film Corp., 225 N.Y. 104, 121 N.E. 756 (1919); and see the cases cited at notes 74–76 supra.

84. Bauer, The Degree of Moral Fault as Affecting Defendant's Liability, 81 U.Pa. L.Rev. 586, 592 (1931). See Jaffe v. Alliance Metal Co., 337 Pa. 449, 12 A.2d 13 (1940); Restatement, Second, Contracts, Comment a.

85. Cases which have expressly stated that certainty is not a requirement include Hacker Pipe & Supply Co. v. Chapman Valve Mfg. Co., 17 Cal.App.2d 265, 61 P.2d 944 (1936) (standard of reasonable probability); Tobin v. Union News Co., 18 A.D.2d 243, 239 N.Y.S.2d 22 (4th Dep't 1963), affirmed 13 N.Y.2d 1155, 247 N.Y.S.2d 385, 196 N.E.2d 735 (1964). ("A reasonable basis for the computation of approximate result is the only requisite"). Such cases in the present state of the law should be viewed skeptically.

86. U.C.C. § 1–106, Comment 1; id. § 2–715, Comment 4.

If the aggrieved party is unable to prove his damages with sufficient certainty it does not follow that he may not have any recovery. The next three sections will consider alternative measures of recovery where lost profits cannot be established.

 WESTLAW REFERENCES

contract /s damage /s "reasonabl! certain!"

115k40(2)

los* /2 profit /s damage /s certain!

115k190

los* /2 profit /s uncertain! speculat! /s contract

di(business /s breach /s los* /2 profit)

"rule of certainty"

willful! wilful! /s breach /s damage /s certainty

115k189 /p certain! establish!

"standard of proof" /s contract /s damage

---

§ 14–9.   Alternative Recovery: Reliance Interest Protected Where Expectation Interest Is Uncertain or Non-existent

When the aggrieved party cannot establish his loss of profits with sufficient certainty, he is permitted to recover his expenses of preparation and of part performance, as well as other foreseeable expenses incurred in reliance upon the contract.[87] This relief is awarded on "the assumption that the value of the contract would at least have covered the outlay." [88]

Thus, for example, where the defendant's breach of contract prevents the staging of a theatrical event, it is very unlikely that the plaintiff can establish with sufficient certainty the amount of profits he would have made had the performance taken place, but he will be permitted to recover his expenses in preparation for performance.[89] A farmer who purchases and plants defective seed, may or may not be able to prove what the value of his crop would have been if the seed had been of merchantable quality.[90] If not, he is permitted to recover the amount paid for the seed, the rental value of the land on which it was sown and the cost of preparing the land and sowing the seed.[91] A distributor whose franchise is wrongfully terminated may or may not

---

87. Restatement, Second, Contracts § 349; Anglia Television, Ltd. v. Reed, 3 All E.R. 690 (C.A.1971).

88. McCormick, Damages 586. This rationale is also expressed in Holt v. United Security Life Ins. and Trust Co., 76 N.J.L. 585, 72 A. 301, 21 L.R.A.,N.S., 691 (1909).

89. Chicago Coliseum Club v. Dempsey, 265 Ill.App. 542 (1932) (promoter's expenses in preparing for boxing match); Bernstein v. Meech, 130 N.Y. 354, 29 N.E. 255 (1891).

90. In many cases the farmer has been successful in proving the value the crop would have had. E.g., Gore v. Ball, Inc., 279 N.C. 192, 182 S.E.2d 389 (1971), noted in 7 Wake Forest L.Rev. 669 (1971); Haner v. Quincy Farm Chemicals, 97 Wn.2d 753, 649 P.2d 828 (1982); but see Albin Elevator Co. v. Pavlica, 649 P.2d 187 (Wyo.1982).

91. Crutcher & Co. v. Elliott, 13 Ky.L. Rep. 592 (1892); 5 Corbin § 1026.

be able to prove his lost profits; if not, he may elect to claim his reliance expenditures. It is to be noted that such expenditures include not only expenses incurred in part performance and in preparation for performance, but also such foreseeable collateral expenses as amounts expended in advertising the manufacturer's product.[92] The owner of a plant who incurs expenses by building a foundation on which to install machinery may recover these expenses if the machines are not delivered.[93] Of course, to the extent that the reliance expenditures are salvageable no recovery will be allowed.[94]

Since the allowance of recovery for reliance expenditures is based on the assumption that the aggrieved party would at least have broken even if the contract had been performed, if it can be shown that the contract would have been a losing proposition for him, an appropriate deduction should be made for the loss which was not incurred. It has been held that the burden of proof that a loss would have occurred is upon the wrongdoer.[95]

Not all contracting parties contemplate a direct and identifiable profit from the contract. A manufacturer may contract to have a product shipped to a convention for display in the hopes of attracting interest in its product, rather than immediate sales. If the shipper is aware of the manufacturer's purpose, it can foresee that in reliance upon the contract the manufacturer will rent exhibition space and incur other expenses. In the event of breach such reliance expenditures are recoverable.[96]

The new Restatement suggests that reliance recovery is limited to the contract price, apparently on the theory that if reliance expenditures exceed the contract price, full performance would have resulted in a losing contract.[97] This reasoning ignores consequential expenditures that could have been recouped if the contract had fully been performed.[98]

---

92. Hardin v. Eska Co., 256 Iowa 371, 127 N.W.2d 595 (1964); accord, Las Colinas, Inc. v. Banco Popular, 453 F.2d 911 (1st Cir.1971), certiorari denied 405 U.S. 1067, 92 S.Ct. 1502, 31 L.Ed.2d 797 (1972) (expenditures in reliance upon a promise of financing); Sperry & Hutchinson Co. v. O'Neill-Adams Co., 185 Fed. 231 (2d Cir. 1911) (advertising and other expenses in connection with promotion of trading stamps).

93. L. Albert & Son v. Armstrong Rubber Co., 178 F.2d 182, 17 A.L.R.2d 1289 (2d Cir.1949).

94. Royce Chem. Co. v. Sharples Corp., 285 F.2d 183 (2d Cir.1960); Gruber v. S–M News Co., 126 F.Supp. 442 (S.D.N.Y.1954).

95. On the burden of proof of non-salvageability, see L. Albert & Son v. Armstrong Rubber Co., 178 F.2d 182, 17

A.L.R.2d 1289 (2d Cir.1949); Matter of Yeager, 227 F.Supp. 92 (N.D.Ohio 1963); Brenneman v. Auto-Teria, Inc., 260 Or. 513, 491 P.2d 992 (1971); Restatement, Second, Contracts § 349, Comment a; see 5 Corbin § 1033.

96. Security Store & Mfg. Co. v. American Ry. Exp. Co., 227 Mo.App. 175, 51 S.W.2d 572 (1932).

97. Restatement, Contracts § 349, Comment a.

98. See, e.g., Security Store & Mfg. Co. v. American Rys. Exp. Co., 227 Mo.App. 175, 51 S.W.2d 572 (1932) ($1000 reliance damages; contract price $147); Anglia Televisions, Ltd. v. Reed, 3 All E.R. 690 (C.A.1971) (£ 2,750 reliance damages; contract price £ 1,050); see also Hudec, Restating the Reliance Interest, 67 Cornell L.Rev. 704 (1982).

§ 14–10.   Alternative Recovery: Value of a Chance or Opportunity

In Chaplin v. Hicks [99] the plaintiff was one of fifty semifinalists in a beauty contest in which twelve finalists would receive prizes. The defendant, promoter of the contest, breached the contract by failing properly to notify the plaintiff of the time and place of the competition. The jury assessed the damages at £100, about one quarter of the value of the lowest prize. The judgment entered upon the jury's verdict was affirmed on appeal. It is obvious that not only was the amount of damages uncertain, but also the fact of damage. The court, nonetheless, indicated that the chance of winning had value which could be assessed by the law of averages. The Restatement of Contracts has accepted the rationale of this decision but only under circumscribed conditions. In general the Restatement allows recovery for the value of a chance only if the promised performance is aleatory; that is, conditioned upon an event that is not within the control of the parties.[1] As such, its primary fields of applicability are in the cases of contests [2] and in cases of wrongful cancellation of insurance contracts by the insurer.[3] It has also been applied in some cases to contracts to drill exploratory oil or gas wells.[4]

One may well question the wisdom of the limitation imposed upon the doctrine by the Restatement. If damages based upon a theory of probability is a sound approach to aleatory contracts, why is it unsound as to other contracts?[5] For example, if a manufacturer wrongfully terminates a distributorship, it will frequently be impossible to prove

99. [1911] 2 K.B. 786.

1. Restatement, Contracts § 332; Restatement, Second, Contracts § 348(3).

2. Recovery for the value of a chance in contest cases has been granted in Mange v. Unicorn Press, Inc., 129 F.Supp. 727 (S.D. N.Y.1955); Wachtel v. National Alfalfa Journal Co., 190 Iowa 1293, 176 N.W. 801 (1920); Kansas City, M. & O. Ry. v. Bell, 197 S.W. 322 (Tex.1917). Contra, Phillips v. Pantages Theatre Co., 163 Wash. 303, 300 P. 1048 (1931); Collatz v. Fox Wis. Amusement Corp., 239 Wis. 156, 300 N.W. 162 (1941).

3. Caminetti v. Manierre, 23 Cal.2d 94, 142 P.2d 741 (1943); Commissioner of Ins. v. Massachusetts Acc. Co., 314 Mass. 558, 50 N.E.2d 801 (1943); People v. Empire Mut. Life Ins. Co., 92 N.Y. 105 (1883).

4. Because of the speculative nature of exploratory drilling, a wide variety of approaches have been taken toward the assessment of damages. See Ballem, Some Second Thoughts on Damages for Breach of a Drilling Commitment, 48 Can.B.Rev. 698 (1970); Scott, Measure of Damages for Breach of a Covenant to Drill a Test Well for Oil and Gas, 9 U.Kan.L.Rev. 281 (1961); 5 Corbin § 1093; Annot., 4 A.L.R.2d 284 (1949).

5. For discussions relating legal theory to probability theory, see Schaefer, Uncertainty and the Law of Damages, 19 Wm. & Mary L.Rev. 719 (1978); Comment, Damages Contingent Upon Chance, 18 Rutgers L.Rev. 875 (1964).

that the distributorship would have made a profit and the amount, if any, of such profits. Aside from the possibility of electing to claim merely reliance damages, the distributor in such a case faces an all or nothing prospect: full recovery for the profits he would have made or merely nominal damages. If, as an alternative, he were permitted to recover the value of the lost opportunity to strive for the profit, the hazards and possible injustice of the all or nothing approach would be reduced. Recovery would be allowed on the basis of the price that a reasonable businessman would pay for the opportunity.[6] Despite authority for such an approach in an excellently reasoned old American case,[7] counsel in this country seem seldom to have made this argument,[8] although this approach is now well accepted in England.[9] Interestingly, it has been applied in a negligence case in which the plaintiff suffered slight permanent damage of her voice which deprived her of the opportunity of commencing a career as an opera singer, a field of endeavor in which the chances of success are speculative and remote.[10]

 WESTLAW REFERENCES

chaplin +s hicks

damage /s contingen! /s chance

chance opportunity valu! /s damage recover! /s probability

§ 14–11. Alternative Recovery: Rental Value of Property That Might Have Produced Profits

If the evidence in Hadley v. Baxendale had established that the defendants had sufficient notice to be able to foresee the prolonged shut-down of the mill as a consequence of their breach, it nevertheless might have been impossible for the plaintiff to establish the fact and amount of his loss with sufficient certainty. The plaintiff would, however, be able to obtain recovery under an alternative theory, formulated in the Restatement in the following language: "[i]f the breach is one that prevents the use and operation of property from which profits would have been made, damages may be measured by the rental value of the property or by interest on the value of the property." [11] The Restatement rule is based upon ample authority.[12]

6. See Kessler, Automobile Dealer Franchises: Vertical Integration by Contract, 66 Yale L.J. 1135, 1188–89 (1957); Comment, The Elusive Measure of Damages for Wrongful Termination of Automobile Dealership Franchises, 74 Yale L.J. 354 (1964); Annot., 54 A.L.R.3d 324 (1973).

7. Taylor v. Bradley, 39 N.Y. 129 (1868) where the court said: " * * * he is deprived of his adventure; what was this opportunity which the contract had apparently secured to him worth?" 39 N.Y. at 144. See also Mechanical Wholesale, Inc. v. Universal-Rundle Corp., 432 F.2d 228 (5th Cir.1970); Locke v. United States, 283 F.2d 521 (Ct.Cl.1960); Air Technology

Corp. v. General Elec. Co., 347 Mass. 613, 199 N.E.2d 538 (1964).

8. The argument is, however, persuasively put forth in McCormick Damages 117–23.

9. Hall v. Meyrick, [1957] 2 Q.B. 455, rev'd on other grounds 2 Q.B. 473; Domine v. Grimsdall, [1937] 2 All E.R. 119 (K.B.).

10. Grayson v. Irvmar Realty, 7 A.D.2d 436, 184 N.Y.S.2d 33 (1st Dep't 1959).

11. Restatement, Contracts § 331(2); Restatement, Second, Contracts § 348(1). Hadley v. Baxendale is discussed in § 14–5 supra.

12. See note 12 on page 607.

F.   THE CONCEPT OF VALUE

Table of Sections

§ 14–12.   Market Value as the Usual Standard

One of the most pervasive concepts of our law is that of "value." In practically every tort and contract case in which damages are to be assessed there is some reference to value. The concept also is widely used in cases of condemnation, taxation, quasi contract, administrative rate making, and even in criminal law.

By and large in contract cases the standard of valuation considered is market value in contradistinction to any peculiar value the object in question may have had to the owner.[13] This standard offers no particular problems as to goods and securities which are actively traded upon stock and commodity exchanges. As to these there is in the literal sense a market place and a market price.[14] When the standard is applied to other objects, such as commodities and shares of stock which are not actively traded, land, unique chattels, and professional services, the determination of a market value involves something of a fiction. What is sought is the sum of money which a willing buyer would pay to a willing seller,[15] although some courts refuse to engage in the use of

---

12. New York & Colorado Mining Syndicate & Co. v. Fraser, 130 U.S. 611, 9 S.Ct. 665, 32 L.Ed. 1031 (1889) (defective machinery rendered silver mill inoperative; rental value of mill calculated at the rate of legal interest on the cost of the mill in absence of other competent testimony of rental value); Witherbee v. Meyer, 155 N.Y. 446, 50 N.E. 58 (1898) (failure to provide sufficient waterpower to a mill; damages awarded for diminution in rental value); Dixon-Woods Co. v. Phillips Glass Co., 169 Pa. 167, 32 A. 432 (1895) (defective furnace installed; damages awarded for rental value of glass factory); Livermore Foundry & Mach. Co. v. Union Compress & Storage Co., 105 Tenn. 187, 58 S.W. 270 (1900) (rental value of compressing plant for entire season); see 5 Corbin § 1029; but cf. Natural Soda Prod. Co. v. Los Angeles, 23 Cal.2d 193, 143 P.2d 12 (1943), certiorari denied 321 U.S. 793, 64 S.Ct. 790, 88

L.Ed. 1082 (1944), rehearing denied 322 U.S. 768, 64 S.Ct. 942, 88 L.Ed. 1594 (1944).

13. See McCormick, Damages § 44.

14. But even as to shares of stock listed on stock exchanges, the current price is not necessarily the value if special circumstances exist. Seas Shipping Co. v. Commissioner of Internal Revenue, 371 F.2d 528 (2d Cir.1967), certiorari denied 387 U.S. 943, 87 S.Ct. 2076, 18 L.Ed.2d 1330 (1967) (large block of shares in a corporation whose shares were traded rather inactively); Kahle v. Mt. Vernon Trust Co., 22 N.Y.S.2d 454 (Sup.Ct.1940).

15. Standard Oil Co. v. Southern Pac. Co., 268 U.S. 146, 45 S.Ct. 465, 69 L.Ed. 890 (1925); Heiman v. Bishop, 272 N.Y. 83, 4 N.E.2d 944 (1936) reargument denied 273 N.Y. 497, 6 N.E.2d 422 (1937); Allen v. Chicago & N.W. R.R., 145 Wis. 263, 129 N.W. 1094 (1911).

the fiction and speak of "real" value where there is no market.[16] The main issues which arise in making this factual determination involve the kind of evidence which may be admitted. When market value does not compensate fully for the peculiar use of the property by the owner, "value to the owner" is used as a standard.[17] At times the courts reject any single standard.[18]

 WESTLAW REFERENCES

contract /s "market value" /s standard /s valu! /s damage

"market value" /s unique! /s contract

digest(market-place (market +1 price) /s "market value")

market +1 value price /s stock /s breach! /s contract /s damage

"market value" /s willing /s buyer /s seller /s contract

contract /s "real value" /s breach! damage

"value to the owner" /s contract

§ 14–13. Proof of Value

Publications reporting the price of goods regularly bought and sold in any established commodity market are admissible.[19] If goods of the kind in issue have not been traded at the relevant time or place, evidence is admissible of prices prevailing at any reasonable times prior or subsequent to the relevant time and at any place which could reasonably serve as a substitute, with due allowance for transportation costs to that place.[20]

Other relevant evidence includes the opinions of qualified experts as to value,[21] original cost less depreciation,[22] reproduction cost less an allowance for depreciation,[23] and sales of comparable personalty or realty.[24] Also admissible is the sale price of the property if it was

16. See Airight Sales, Inc. v. Graves Truck Lines, Inc., 207 Kan. 753, 486 P.2d 835 (1971).

17. See Alfred Atmore Pope Found., Inc. v. New York, N.H. & H. Ry., 106 Conn. 423, 138 A. 444 (1927) (negligence action; forest attached to forestry school was destroyed by fire).

18. See McAnarney v. Newark Fire Ins. Co., 247 N.Y. 176, 159 N.E. 902, 56 A.L.R. 1149 (1928) (action on a fire insurance policy; structure destroyed was a brewery rendered obsolete by national prohibition).

19. U.C.C. § 2–724.

20. Id § 2–723.

21. Standard Oil Co. v. Southern Pac. Co., 268 U.S. 146, 45 S.Ct. 465, 69 L.Ed. 890 (1925). This is said to be the most common sort of evidence of value. McCormick, Damages 175.

22. Standard Oil Co. v. Southern Pac. Co., 268 U.S. 146, 45 S.Ct. 465, 69 L.Ed. 890

(1925) (ship); Thornton v. Birmingham, 250 Ala. 651, 35 So.2d 545, 7 A.L.R.2d 773 (1948) (price paid for land two years previously). Original cost of goods some years prior to the wrong, standing alone, is not sufficient evidence of value. Some evidence as to depreciation must also be introduced. Rauch v. Wander, 122 Misc. 650, 203 N.Y.S. 553 (App.Term 1924), as well as evidence of changes in market values, Watson v. Loughran, 112 Ga. 837, 38 S.E. 82 (1901).

23. Standard Oil Co. v. Southern Pac. Co., 268 U.S. 146, 45 S.Ct. 465, 69 L.Ed. 890 (1925); Alabama G. S. R.R. v. Johnston, 128 Ala. 283, 29 So. 771 (1901); Missouri Pac. R.R. v. Fowler, 183 Ark. 86, 34 S.W.2d 1071 (1931).

24. Redfield v. Iowa State Highway Comm'n, 251 Iowa 332, 99 N.W.2d 413, 85 A.L.R.2d 96 (1959); Amory v. Commonwealth, 321 Mass. 240, 72 N.E.2d 549, 174 A.L.R. 370 (1947); Village of Lawrence v.

resold to another soon after the breach.[25] Offers to purchase the property are inadmissible on the grounds that the fabrication of such evidence would be too easy.[26] Offers to sell the property however, may be introduced in evidence but only as evidence against the offeror.[27] On the realistic ground that tax assessments of real property are notoriously unreliable as indicia of value, the overwhelming weight of authority is to the effect that such evidence is inadmissible.[28] The owner's statements to the tax assessing authorities are admissible against him, however, as admissions.[29]

WESTLAW REFERENCES

"uniform commercial code" u.c.c. /s 2–724

"reasonable time" /s eviden! /s admit! admiss! /s price

admit! admiss! /s opinion /s "qualified expert" /s value

contract /s value /s expert /s opinion

contract /s valu! /s comparable

offer! +2 purchas! /s admiss! admit! /s valu!

157k113(16)

371k348(3)

"tax assess!" /s admission

§ 14-14. Value a Variable Concept

It is obvious that property may have more than one market value. There is a wholesale and a retail market for most products. The appropriate market is the one in which the aggrieved party may obtain replacement of the property. Thus, for the consumer the retail market is normally the appropriate standard, while for the dealer it is the wholesale market.[30] Less obvious is the fact that a given object can have different market values dependent upon various uses which it may have.[31] A cow may be used for beef production, milk production or

Greenwood, 300 N.Y. 231, 90 N.E.2d 53 (1949). In a substantial minority of jurisdictions, however, such evidence is not admissible as to real property and unique chattels. Walnut Street Fed. Sav. & Loan Ass'n v. Bernstein, 394 Pa. 353, 147 A.2d 359 (1959).

25. Louis Steinbaum Real Estate Co. v. Maltz, 247 S.W.2d 652, 31 A.L.R.2d 1052 (Mo.App.1952) (fraud case); Wolff v. Meyer, 75 N.J.L. 181, 66 A. 959 (1907); Triangle Waist Co. v. Todd, 223 N.Y. 27, 119 N.E. 85 (1918) (breach by employee; salary paid by new employer evidence of value of employee's services).

26. Sharp v. United States, 191 U.S. 341, 24 S.Ct. 114, 48 L.Ed. 211 (1903); Thornton v. Birmingham, 250 Ala. 651, 35 So.2d 545, 7 A.L.R.2d 773 (1948); City of Fort Worth v. Beaupre, 617 S.W.2d 828, 25 A.L.R.4th 562 (Tex.Civ.App.1981), writ ref. n.r.e.

27. Kalb v. Int'l Resorts, Inc., 396 So.2d 199, 25 A.L.R.4th 977 (Fla.App.1981), review denied 407 So.2d 1104 (Fla.1981); Cotton v. Boston Elevated R.R., 191 Mass. 103, 77 N.E. 698 (owner's listing price); McAnarney v. Newark Fire Ins. Co., 247 N.Y. 176, 159 N.E. 902, 56 A.L.R. 1149 (1928).

28. Comm. of Kentucky v. Gilbert, 253 S.W.2d 264, 39 A.L.R.2d 205 (1952).

29. San Diego Land & Town Co. v. Jasper, 189 U.S. 439, 23 S.Ct. 571, 47 L.Ed. 892 (1903).

30. Illinois Cent. R.R. v. Crail, 281 U.S. 57, 50 S.Ct. 180, 74 L.Ed. 699, 67 A.L.R. 1423 (1930); Wehle v. Haviland, 69 N.Y. 448 (1877).

31. "A loblolly pine tree at sixty years that would produce a fifty-foot piling would be worth fifty dollars peeled and loaded on a truck, for saw timber it would be worth $4.80." Shirley and Graves, Forest Ownership for Pleasure and Profit 32 (1967); cf.

primarily for breeding. The aggrieved party is entitled to an evaluation based upon the most profitable use to which he reasonably could have put the object.[32]

 WESTLAW REFERENCES

contract /s "market value" /s retail

343k418(3)

"wholesale market value" /s damage contract

damage /s contract /s wholesale retail /s "market value"

343k442(6)

G. AVOIDABLE CONSEQUENCES

Table of Sections

§ 14–15. The "Duty" to Mitigate Damages

As an almost inflexible proposition a party who has been wronged by a breach of contract may not unreasonably sit idly by and allow damages to accumulate. The law does not permit him to recover from the wrongdoer those damages which he "could have avoided without undue risk, burden, or humiliation." [33] This absence of a right of recovery for enhanced damages, often improperly called a "duty to mitigate," [34] is at the root of many of the rules of the law of damages. Thus, for example, the rule of Hadley v. Baxendale [35] becomes clearer when viewed in terms of the doctrine of avoidable consequences. Under that decision the defendant would have been liable for the lost profits of the mill if it had had reason to know that no substitute shaft was available. In other words, liability for consequential damages stems from reason to know that the plaintiff will be unable to mitigate

Spink v. New York, N.H. & H.R.R., 26 R.I. 115, 58 A. 499 (1904) (standing timber destroyed in fire may be valued on the basis of prices for poles and piles rather than cordwood).

32. Campbell v. Iowa Central Ry., 124 Iowa 248, 99 N.W. 1061 (1904) (brood mare); Southwestern Tel. & Tel. Co. v. Krause, 92 S.W. 431 (Tex.Civ.App.1906) (milk cows not valued on basis of value of beef cattle).

33. Restatement, Second, Contracts § 350; see Goetz & Scott, The Mitigation Principle: Toward a General Theory of Contractual Obligation, 69 Va.L.Rev. 967 (1983).

34. McClelland v. Climax Hosiery Mills, 252 N.Y. 347, 358–59, 169 N.E. 605, 614 (1930) (Cardozo, C.J., concurring).

In an attempt to employ the legal classifications developed by Hohfeld, others have referred to a "disability" to recover damages which could have been avoided, rather than the more accurate "no right" to recover. Rock v. Vandine, 106 Kan. 588, 189 P. 157 (1920); Comment, Does Breach of Contract Destroy Duty to Perform?, 32 Yale L.J. 380 (1923); 28 Yale L.J. 827 (1920); cf. 5 Corbin § 1039; Farnsworth, supra § 14–3 n. 14, at 1183–99.

35. See § 14–5 supra.

his damages. The doctrine of avoidable consequences is also an unspoken premise in most rules of general damages. Thus, the rule in sales contracts that damages for breach by the seller are measured by the difference between the market price and the contract price is based on the thought that in the event of breach the plaintiff can minimize his damages by purchasing similar goods on the open market.

In addition to its role as an implied premise in many other rules and doctrines, the doctrine of avoidable consequences is frequently used as an independent basis for a decision. For example, where a municipality breaches a contract to fill in waterfront land, the aggrieved party may not sit idle for many years and then recover the rental value the filled land would have had during the period the land was unfilled. Rather, he may have such recovery measured by a reasonable period of time, as it was incumbent upon the plaintiff, if feasible, to have the land filled by other means.[36] Likewise where an experienced farmer is supplied patently defective seed he will not be permitted to enhance his damages by planting the seed and losing a crop.[37] Similarly, the doctrine is employed in every manner of contract including contracts of employment,[38] sale,[39] construction,[40] and in the United States, even in cases of breach by anticipatory repudiation.[41] Only in rare instances does continuation of performance cut down damages. In such a case the aggrieved party may continue without jeopardizing his recovery.[42]

The doctrine merely requires reasonable efforts to mitigate damages. Thus, if reasonable, the efforts need not be successful.[43] Under the rule of reasonableness, the wronged party need not act if the cost of avoidance would involve unreasonable expense.[44] He need not commit a wrong, as by breaching other contracts, in order to minimize damages,[45] nor need he jeopardize his credit rating.[46] He need not take action where the breaching party assures him that performance, though late, will be forthcoming.[47]

One troublesome issue has vexed and divided the courts. Must the aggrieved party accede to a wrongful demand by the wrongdoer if his accession would minimize damages? The problem is illustrated in its extreme form in a case where a water company unjustifiably asked for

36. Losei Realty Corp. v. New York, 254 N.Y. 41, 171 N.E. 899 (1930).

37. Wavra v. Karr, 142 Minn. 248, 172 N.W. 118 (1919).

38. See §§ 14–18 to 14–19 infra.

39. See generally §§ 14–20 to 14–27 infra.

40. See §§ 14–28 to 14–29 infra.

41. See § 14–23 infra; § 12–8 supra.

42. F. Enterprises v. Kentucky Fried Chicken Corp., 47 Ohio St.2d 154, 351 N.E.2d 121 (1976); see also § 14–27 infra.

43. Ninth Ave. & Forty-Second St. Corp. v. Zimmerman, 217 App.Div. 498, 217 N.Y.S. 123 (1st Dep't 1926) (unsuccessful suit against third party to clear title); Restatement, Second, Contracts § 350(2).

44. Taylor v. Steadman, 143 Ark. 486, 220 S.W. 821 (1920); Chambers v. Belmore Land Co., 33 Cal.App. 78, 164 P. 404 (1917); 5 Corbin § 1041.

45. Leonard v. New York, Albany and Buffalo Electro-Magnetic Tel. Co., 41 N.Y. 544 (1870); McCormick, Damages 141 (1935). Contra, Western Union Tel. Co. v. Southwick, 214 S.W. 987 (Tex.Civ.App. 1919), noted in 33 Harv.L.Rev. 728 (1920).

46. Audiger, Inc. v. Hamilton, 381 F.2d 24 (5th Cir.1967).

47. S.J. Groves & Sons Inc. v. Warner Co., 576 F.2d 524 (3d Cir.1978).

the yearly payment of $58.00 in installments in advance instead of at the end of contract period as provided in the contract. The plaintiff, an owner of an irrigated vineyard, refused to accede to this change of company policy. As a consequence the water supply was shut off and the plaintiff lost his crop. The court ruled that the trivial extra cost (interest on the advance payments) amounting to less than $2.00, viewed in relation to the large amount of injury foreseeably ensuing, was such that the plaintiff should have acceded to the unjustified demand.[48] On similar facts other courts have disagreed,[49] while still others have let the jury decide whether the plaintiff's refusal was reasonable.[50] On the other hand, where the demand is not trivial in relation to the ensuing damages, most courts have ruled that the plaintiff need not bend his will to that of the wrongdoer even if it would have the effect of minimizing damages.[51]

Frequently, the aggrieved party does accede to the demands of the other often because any other course of action would result in a major disruption of his business or personal affairs. When this is done, it may be held that the aggrieved party is without remedy because he has entered into a substituted agreement discharging the prior contract.[52] This result may be avoided under the Uniform Commercial Code by surrendering to the demand while indicating that accession is under protest.[53] If this is not done and the elements of duress are present it may be possible for the aggrieved party to set aside the discharge of his rights under the earlier contract.[54]

An exception to the doctrine of avoidable consequences exists, under the orthodox view, as to leases of real property. Upon the tenant's abandonment of the premises the landlord may elect to termi-

---

48. Severini v. Sutter-Butte Canal Co., 59 Cal.App. 154, 210 P. 49 (1922). The decision was distinguished in a subsequent case involving similar facts except that the water company's unjustified demand was in the amount of about $100. The court deemed this to be a substantial rather than trivial demand. Schultz v. Lakeport, 5 Cal.2d 377, 54 P.2d 1110, 108 A.L.R. 1168 (1936).

49. Southwestern Gas & Elec. Co. v. Stanley, 45 S.W.2d 671 (Tex.Civ.App.1931), affirmed 123 Tex. 157, 70 S.W.2d 413 (1934).

50. Key v. Kingwood Oil Co., 110 Okl. 178, 236 P. 598 (1925).

51. Coppola v. Marden, Orth & Hastings, 282 Ill. 281, 118 N.E. 499 (1918); Schatz Distributing Co., Inc. v. Olivetti Corp. of America, 7 Kan.App.2d 676, 647 P.2d 820 (1982); Seeley v. Peabody, 139 Wash. 382, 247 P. 471 (1926), rehearing denied 141 Wash. 696, 250 P. 469 (1926); see 5 Corbin § 1043; McCormick, Damages § 39 (1935). This point is further illustrat-

ed by the rule that an employee whose employment is pursuant to an employment contract need not mitigate damages by accepting an offer from his employer for employment in a different position or on other different terms. Billetter v. Posell, 94 Cal.App.2d 858, 211 P.2d 621 (1949); and see § 14–18 infra.

52. Stanspec Corp. v. Jelco, Inc., 464 F.2d 1184 (10th Cir.1972); see Comment, Effect of Second Contract With Defaulter upon Rights for Breach of First, 19 N.C.L. Rev. 59 (1940). Compare the sound result in Dreyfuss v. Board of Educ., Etc., 76 Misc.2d 479, 350 N.Y.S.2d 590 (Sup.Ct. 1973), affirmed 45 A.D.2d 988, 359 N.Y.S.2d 871 (2d Dep't 1974) (no discharge by accepting substitute position).

53. U.C.C. § 1–207.

54. Austin Instrument, Inc. v. Loral Corp., 29 N.Y.2d 124, 324 N.Y.S.2d 22, 272 N.E.2d 533 (1971), reargument denied 29 N.Y.2d 749, 326 N.Y.S.2d 1027, 276 N.E.2d 238 (1971); see § 9–7 supra.

nate the tenancy and sue for damages, or to continue the tenancy. If he elects to continue the tenancy he may sue for the agreed rent although he makes no effort to secure a substitute tenant. This is based on the property concept that the landlord has conveyed a lease-hold to the tenant, therefore performing the agreed exchange.[55]

WESTLAW REFERENCES

"mitigation principle"

breach! /s contract /s "duty to mitigate"

liab! /s "duty to mitigate"

contract /s "doctrine of avoidable consequence"

contract*** /s mitigat! /s "consequential damage"

to(343) /p breach! /p seller vendor /p "market price" /p "contract price"

343k418(7)

prevent! mitigat! /3 damage /s contract /s employ**** construction (anticipatory +1 breach! repudiation)

contract /s "reasonable effort" /s mitigat! prevent! /3 damage

di(mitigat! prevent! minimiz! /3 damage /p contract /p duty)

inferior similar different /s employ**** /s contract /s mitigat! prevent! minimiz! /3 damage

breach! /s contract /s lease /s mitigat! prevent! minimiz! /3 damage

---

§ 14–16. Non-exclusive Contracts—An Apparent Exception to the Doctrine of Avoidable Consequences

A full time employee owes a duty to his employer to devote all his working hours to his employer's business. If the employee is wrongfully discharged, his damages are reduced by any earning from employment he secures or could with reasonable diligence secure during the contract period.[56] If it were not for the breach such employment could not lawfully be obtained.

If the relation between the parties is such that the wronged party was legally free to enter into similar contracts with others, the fact that subsequent to the breach the wronged party could have or actually has made similar contracts in no way reduces the damages to which he is entitled. Thus, for example, if the lessee of automobiles from a car rental company breaches the lease, damages will not be reduced by the fact that the lessor leases, or could have leased, the automobiles to another.[57] The lessor was free to obtain as many customers as it was

---

55. Enoch C. Richards Co. v. Libby, 136 Me. 376, 10 A.2d 609, 126 A.L.R. 1215 (1940); Sancourt Realty Co. v. Dowling, 220 App.Div. 660, 222 N.Y.S. 288 (1st Dep't 1927). A strong contrary trend is developing. Sommer v. Kridel, 74 N.J. 446, 378 A.2d 767 (1977); see Wright v. Baumann, 239 Or. 410, 398 P.2d 119, 21 A.L.R.3d 527 (1965), appeal after remand 254 Or. 175, 458 P.2d 674 (1969); but see Spohn v. Fine, 124 Misc.2d 1075, 479 N.Y.S.2d 139 (County Ct.1984).

56. See § 14–18 infra.

57. Mount Pleasant Stable Co. v. Steinberg, 238 Mass. 567, 131 N.E. 295, 15 A.L.R. 749 (1921) (teams of horses and wagons); Locks v. Wade, 36 N.J.Super. 128, 114 A.2d 875 (1955) (juke box).

willing and able to secure, provided that as a practical matter it could secure additional automobiles for such customers. On the other hand, if the lease is of a unique chattel such as an ocean going freighter, the lessor's damages will be reduced by any amount earned or earnable by chartering the ship to another, each ship being regarded as unique.[58] Similar considerations exist where a purchaser breaches a contract for sale.[59] Construction contracts are non-exclusive and a construction contractor's damages are not normally reduced by any earnings attributable to contracts made subsequent to the breach.[60] Similarly a publisher's damages resulting from breach of an advertising contract are not to be reduced under the doctrine of avoidable consequences,[61] unless the publication has limited space for advertising, in which case it would be incumbent upon the publisher to attempt to secure additional advertisers to fill the space vacated as a result of the breach.[62]

 WESTLAW REFERENCES
locks +s wade

§ 14–17. Recovery of Expenses Sustained in Avoiding Consequences of a Breach

The doctrine of avoidable consequences is a two edged sword. That it may reduce the aggrieved party's damages has been considered in the preceding discussion. It may, also, act to provide recovery for certain kinds of expenses not otherwise recoverable. This aspect of the doctrine is best illustrated by the leading tort case.[63] The plaintiff, a steamship company flying the neutral flag of Norway during World War I, was accused by the defendant newspaper publisher of carrying

---

58. Liberty Navigating & Trading Co. v. Kinoshita & Co., Ltd., 285 F.2d 343 (2d Cir. 1960), certiorari denied 366 U.S. 949, 81 S.Ct. 1904, 6 L.Ed.2d 1242 (1961).

59. See generally §§ 14–23 to 14–27 infra.

60. Koplin v. Faulkner, 293 S.W.2d 467 (Ky.1956); M. & R. Contractors and Builders, Inc. v. Michael, 215 Md. 340, 138 A.2d 350 (1958); Olds v. Mapes-Reeve Const. Co., 177 Mass. 41, 58 N.E. 478 (1900). In a celebrated case the court seems inappropriately to have applied the general rule. The plaintiff contracted with X corporation to install certain apparatus in X's plant. X, because of insolvency, repudiated the contract. X's receivers sold the plant to Y corporation. Y contracted with the plaintiff to make the same installation. This contract was performed. Nevertheless, on the ground that it was not a contract for personal services, plaintiff was permitted to recover damages against X's receivers for breach of the first contract without a deduction for the profit made on the second contract despite the fact that but for

the breach of the first contract plaintiff could not have entered into the second. Grinnell Co. v. Voorhees, 1 F.2d 693 (3rd Cir.1924), noted in 34 Yale L.J. 553 (1925); accord, Olds v. Mapes-Reeve Constr. Co., 177 Mass. 41, 58 N.E. 478 (1900). Contra, Canton-Hughes Pump Co. v. Llera, 205 Fed. 209 (6th Cir.1913); cf. Kunkle v. Jaffe, 71 N.E.2d 298 (Ohio App.1946).

61. Western Grain Co. v. Barron G. Collier, Inc., 163 Ark. 369, 258 S.W. 979 (1924); Western Advertising Co. v. Mid-West Laundries, 61 S.W.2d 251 (Mo.App.1933); J.K. Rishel Furniture Co. v. Stuyvesant Co., 123 Misc. 208, 204 N.Y.S. 659 (Mun.Ct. 1924).

62. Barron G. Collier, Inc. v. Women's Garment Store, 152 Minn. 475, 189 N.W. 403 (1922).

63. Den Norske Ameriekalinje Actiesselskabet v. Sun Printing & Publishing Ass'n, 226 N.Y. 1, 122 N.E. 463 (1919); accord, Restatement, Second, Contracts § 347, Comment c; see 5 Corbin § 1044; McCormick, Damages § 42.

on illegal activities for the benefit of the German war effort. In order to protect its reputation it placed paid advertisements in other newspapers refuting the defendant's libel. It was held that the plaintiff could recover these expenses as a reasonable effort, whether or not successful, to mitigate damages.

The same principle finds wide application in cases involving breach of contract,[64] and is implicitly recognized by the Uniform Commercial Code in its provisions regarding "cover"[65] and "incidental" damages.[66] A common law example is the holding that the cost of procuring a substitute outlet for water is recoverable where the defendant breached his contract to allow the use of his ditch.[67] Such reasonable expenditures are recoverable even if hindsight shows that the expenditure made is in excess of the amount by which damages are diminished.[68]

WESTLAW REFERENCES

"doctrine of avoidable consequence" /s expense cost

contract breach! /s mitigat! reduc! minimiz! prevent! /3 damage
    /s recover! /s expense cost

343k418(7) /p substitute

H. DAMAGES IN PARTICULAR ACTIONS

Table of Sections

64. See, e.g., Audiger v. Hamilton, 381 F.2d 24 (5th Cir.1967).

65. See § 14–20 infra.

66. See §§ 14–22, 14–25 infra.

67. Hoehne Ditch Co. v. John Flood Ditch Co., 76 Colo. 500, 233 P. 167 (1925); Spang Indus., Inc., Fort Pitt Div. v. Aetna Cas. and Sur. Co., 512 F.2d 365 (2d Cir. 1975) (overtime labor and other expenses in crash program to pour concrete before freezing weather where supplier delayed delivery of steel); Apex Mining Co. v. Chi-

cago Copper & Chem. Co., 306 F.2d 725 (8th Cir.1962) (defendant failed to deliver ore; plaintiff purchased jaw crusher to process substitute ore of a different type); see also Northwestern Steam Boiler & Mfg. Co. v. Great Lakes Engineering Works, 181 Fed. 38 (8th Cir.1910).

68. Apex Mining Co. v. Chicago Copper & Chem. Co., 306 F.2d 725 (8th Cir.1962); Hogland v. Klein, 49 Wn.2d 216, 298 P.2d 1099 (1956).

§ 14–18. Wrongful Discharge of Employee

When an employee is wrongfully discharged he is entitled to the salary [69] that would have been payable during the remainder of the term reduced by the income which he has earned, will earn, or could with reasonable diligence earn during the unexpired term.[70] This rule takes into consideration the employee's burden of mitigation. In carrying out this burden, however, the employee need not seek or accept a position of lesser rank,[71] or at a reduced salary,[72] or at a location unreasonably distant from his former place of employment,[73] or a position necessitating a residence apart from the employee's spouse.[74] The authorities agree that an employee has properly mitigated his damages by going into business for himself with the knowledge that the prospects for earning from the business are minimal in its initial stages.[75] It was wisely held in one such case, however, that his

69. The problem of the valuation of fringe benefits as an element of salary has yet to be explored thoroughly by the courts. For one discussion, see McAleer v. McNally Pittsburgh Mfg. Co., 329 F.2d 273 (3rd Cir.1964) (no recovery for loss of group life insurance protection); Wyatt v. School Dist., 148 Mont. 83, 417 P.2d 221, 22 A.L.R.3d 1039 (1966) (value of teacher's rent free quarters).

70. Sutherland v. Wyer, 67 Me. 64 (1877); Hollwedel v. Duffy-Mott Co., 263 N.Y. 95, 188 N.E. 266 (1933); Godson v. MacFadden, 162 Tenn. 528, 39 S.W.2d 287 (1931); Galveston H. & S.A. R.R. v. Eubanks, 42 S.W.2d 475 (Tex.Civ.App.1931). If the unexpired term is of lengthy duration, the recovery is to be discounted at a reasonable rate of interest inasmuch as the plaintiff will recover well in advance of the dates on which future salary payments would have been payable. Hollwedel v. Duffy-Mott Co., supra; Dixie Glass Co. v. Pollak, 341 S.W.2d 530, 91 A.L.R.2d 662 (Tex.Civ.App.1960), affirmed 162 Tex. 440, 347 S.W.2d 596 (1961).

A small minority of jurisdictions permit the discharged employee to recover damages suffered only up to the time of trial. The authorities on this question are collected in Dixie Glass Co. v. Pollak, supra, where the minority view is repudiated.

71. Parker v. Twentieth Century-Fox Film Corp., 3 Cal.3d 176, 89 Cal.Rptr. 737, 474 P.2d 689 (1970) (actress engaged as lead in musical film need not accept in substitution a role as lead in a western film); Cooper v. Stronge & Warner Co., 111 Minn. 177, 126 N.W. 541, 27 L.R.A.,N.S., 1011, 20 Ann.Cas. 663 (1910) (department manager need not accept position as sales clerk at same salary); State ex rel. Freeman v. Sierra County Bd. of Ed., 49 N.M. 54, 157 P.2d 234 (1945) (principal need not accept post as teacher at reduced salary); Rudman v. Cowles Communications, Inc., 30 N.Y.2d 1, 330 N.Y.S.2d 33, 280 N.E.2d 867 (1972); Mitchell v. Lewensohn, 251 Wis. 424, 29 N.W.2d 748 (1947).

72. Billetter v. Posell, 94 Cal.App.2d 858, 211 P.2d 621 (1949); Crabtree v. Elizabeth Arden Sales Corp., 105 N.Y.S.2d 40 (Sup.Ct.1951), affirmed 279 App.Div. 992, 112 N.Y.S.2d 494 (1st Dep't 1952), affirmed 305 N.Y. 48, 110 N.E.2d 551 (1953).

73. American Trading Co. v. Steele, 274 Fed. 774 (1st Cir.1921) (resident of China need not seek employment in U.S.); San Antonio & A.P. R.R. v. Collins, 61 S.W.2d 84 (Tex.Comm.App.1933) (resident of Houston need not accept employment in San Antonio).

74. Jackson v. Wheatley School Dist. No. 28 etc., 464 F.2d 411 (8th Cir.1972), appeal after remand 489 F.2d 608 (8th Cir. 1973).

75. Ransome Concrete Machinery Co. v. Moody, 282 Fed. 29 (2d Cir.1922); Cornell v. T.V. Dev. Corp., 17 N.Y.2d 69, 268

recovery should be reduced by the value of his services in building up the business.[76]

In tort cases involving personal injuries a doctrine known as the "collateral source rule" has evolved. Generally, damages assessed against a tortfeasor are not diminished by any payments received by the injured party from medical insurance, pension and disability plans, or other sources other than the tortfeasor or the tortfeasor's insurer.[77] The question has less often arisen in litigation based upon breach of contract. Should recovery awarded to a wrongfully discharged employee be diminished by the amount he receives from unemployment insurance [78] or from his social security pension? [79] No consistent answer has been given.[80] There seems to be no justification, however, for the cases allowing for recovery of more money than required to compensate him for the injury done.

Generally speaking a public officer's right to compensation is not dependent upon contract, but on public law. If he is wrongfully denied his office the doctrine of avoidable consequences is inapplicable. Therefore, his recovery is not diminished by the amount he has earned or could have earned during his term of office.[81] Most persons on the public payroll, however, are employees rather than officers [82] and are subject to the doctrine of avoidable consequences.[83]

Rarely are special damages awarded for wrongful discharge. Damages for injury to the employee's reputation are ordinarily said to be too remote and not in the contemplation of the parties,[84] but expenses

N.Y.S.2d 29, 215 N.E.2d 349 (1966), on remand 50 Misc.2d 422, 270 N.Y.S.2d 45 (1966); see Note, Measure of Damages on a Contract When the Discharged Employee Goes to Work for Himself, 15 Harv.L.Rev. 662 (1902).

76. Kramer v. Wolf Cigar Stores Co., 99 Tex. 597, 91 S.W. 775 (1906).

77. Helfend v. Southern Cal. Rapid Transit Dist., 2 Cal.3d 1, 84 Cal.Rptr. 173, 465 P.2d 61 (1970).

78. Diminution was not permitted in Billetter v. Posell, 94 Cal.App.2d 858, 211 P.2d 621 (1949); Pennington v. Whiting Tubular Products, Inc., 370 Mich. 590, 122 N.W.2d 692 (1963). Contra, Meyers v. Director of Employment Security, 341 Mass. 79, 167 N.E.2d 160 (1960); Dehnart v. Waukesha Brewing Co., 21 Wis.2d 583, 124 N.W.2d 664 (1963).

79. Recovery was diminished in United Protective Workers Local No. 2 v. Ford Motor Co., 223 F.2d 49 (7th Cir.1955).

80. Restatement, Second, Contracts § 347, Comment c; Fleming, The Collateral Source Rule and Contract Damages, 71 Calif.L.Rev. 56 (1983); Note, 48 B.U.L.Rev. 271 (1968).

81. Gentry v. Harrison, 194 Ark. 916, 110 S.W.2d 497 (1937); Corfman v. McDevitt, 111 Colo. 437, 142 P.2d 383, 150 A.L.R. 97 (1943).

82. For the distinction between public office and public employment, see C.J.S. Officers § 5; Annot., 140 A.L.R. 1076 (1942). See also Punke, Breach of Teacher Contracts, and Damages, 26 Ala.Law. 243, 265–74 (1965).

83. White v. Bloomberg, 501 F.2d 1379 (4th Cir.1974) (postal employee); Stockton v. Department of Employment, 25 Cal.2d 264, 153 P.2d 741 (1944); People ex rel. Bourne v. Johnson, 32 Ill.2d 324, 205 N.E.2d 470 (1965); Spurck v. Civil Service Bd., 231 Minn. 183, 42 N.W.2d 720 (1950); Wyatt v. School Dist. No. 104, 148 Mont. 83, 417 P.2d 221, 22 A.L.R.3d 1039 (1966).

84. Mastoras v. Chicago, M. & St.P. Ry., 217 Fed. 153 (D.C.Cir.1914); Skagway City School Board v. Davis, 543 P.2d 218 (Alaska 1975); Gary v. Central Georgia Ry., 37 Ga.App. 744, 141 S.E. 819 (1928); Tousley v. Atlantic City Ambassador Hotel Corp., 25 N.J.Misc. 88, 50 A.2d 472 (1947); Amaducci v. Metropolitan Opera Ass'n, 33 A.D.2d 542, 304 N.Y.S.2d 322 (1st Dep't 1969).

incurred in an attempt to mitigate damages by securing other employment are recoverable.[85] There is considerable authority in England [86] and some in the United States for an award of consequential damage where the contract contemplates that performance will enhance the employee's reputation, as where a script writer is promised screen credits[87] and where a disc jockey is promised exposure to a large audience.[88] Such holdings are consistent with the related rule that if the services to be rendered will be of benefit to the employee as by enhancing his skill or reputation, the employer is obliged not only to pay his salary but also to provide work of the kind contemplated.[89]

 WESTLAW REFERENCES

wrong! +1 discharg! terminat! /s mitigat! prevent! reduc! minimiz!
  /3 damage

255k42(2) /p mitigat! prevent! minimiz! reduc! /3 damage

"reasonabl! diligen!" /s wrongful! +1 terminat! discharg!

di(employ**** /p accept! /p mitigat! reduc! minimiz! prevent! /3
  damage)

"collateral source" /s breach! /s contract

"special damage" /s wrongful! +1 discharg! terminat!

damage /s reputation /s wrongful! +1 terminat! discharg!

"consequential damage" /s wrongful! +1 discharg! terminat!

§ 14–19. Wrongful Termination by Employee

When an employee wrongfully terminates his employment, the employer's recovery is measured by the additional market cost of obtaining substitute help for the unexpired contract term; that is, the difference between the market value of such services and the contract rate of compensation.[90] Although courts do not generally deny the possibility of an award of consequential damages against the employee, the rules of foreseeability, mitigation and certainty have been so strictly applied as to indicate a strong policy against such awards against employees.[91]

85. Wyatt v. School Dist., 148 Mont. 83, 417 P.2d 221, 22 A.L.R.3d 1039 (1966).

86. Tolnay v. Criterion Film Prods., 2 All E.R. 1225 (1936); Marbe v. George Edwards, Ltd., 1 K.B. 269, 56 A.L.R. 888 (1928).

87. Paramount Productions v. Smith, 91 F.2d 863 (9th Cir.1937), certiorari denied 302 U.S. 749, 58 S.Ct. 266, 82 L.Ed. 579 (1937).

88. Colvig v. RKO General, Inc., 232 Cal.App.2d 56, 42 Cal.Rptr. 473 (1965). See Annot., 96 A.L.R.3d 437 (1979).

89. Sigmon v. Goldstone, 116 App.Div. 490, 101 N.Y.S. 984 (1st Dep't 1906); Restatement, Second, Agency § 433. See

Comment, The Loss of Publicity as an Element of Damages for Breach of Contract to Employ an Entertainer, 27 U.Miami L.Rev. 465 (1973).

90. Roth v. Speck, 126 A.2d 153, 61 A.L.R.2d 1004 (D.C.App.1956); Triangle Waist Co. v. Todd, 223 N.Y. 27, 119 N.E. 85 (1918); 5 Corbin § 1096; 11 Williston § 1362A.

91. See Riech v. Bolch, 68 Iowa 526, 27 N.W. 507 (1886); Peters v. Whitney, 23 Barb. 24 (N.Y.1856); Winkenwerder v. Knox, 51 Wn.2d 582, 320 P.2d 304 (1958). For a rare case awarding such damages, see Stadium Pictures, Inc. v. Walker, 224 App.Div. 22, 229 N.Y.S. 313 (1928).

WESTLAW REFERENCES
roth +s speck

§ 14–20. Total Breach of Sales Contracts—Buyer's General Damages

The traditional measure of general damages for a total breach of contract by the seller is the difference between the market price and the contract price. This rule has been retained by the Uniform Commercial Code [92] but the Code has added an alternative measure. The buyer may cover; that is, he may make a good faith purchase or contract to purchase substitute goods without unreasonable delay.[93] He may then recover the difference between the cost of cover and the contract price.[94] While this measure of damages will often produce the same result as the traditional market price minus contract price rule, this will not always be so. When notified of a breach the purchaser may be forced to go outside his normal sources of supply and to pay more than the normal price which constitutes the "market."[95] Or he may pay a higher than market price unaware that the goods were available at the market price from some suppliers. He may find that goods of the same quality and specifications are not readily available and procure as a reasonable substitute goods of a somewhat higher quality and cost.[96] In all of these circumstances the cover price minus contract price result produces a more reasonable result.[97] In addition the often difficult, expensive and time consuming task of proving market price at trial can be obviated. This provision, although one of the simplest, is yet one of the most useful innovations to appear in the Commercial Code. The provision creates some new problems, however. It might appear that if the buyer covers at less than the market price, the buyer's sagacity will redound to the benefit of the seller. The buyer's recovery may be limited to the difference between the cost of cover and the market price plus incidental damages.[98] A real difficulty

92. U.C.C. § 2–713(1). The Code speaks of this as the remedy "for non-delivery or repudiation." The same measure would apply in case the buyer "rightfully rejects or justifiably revokes acceptance." U.C.C. § 2–711.

93. U.C.C. § 2–712(1).

94. U.C.C. § 2–712(2).

95. For example, an article in the Financial Section of the New York Times, dated January 1, 1967, discussing the tight supply of sulphur, points out that while two large producers charged $28.50 per ton, "Demand is so strong that some consumers have been paying more than $50 a ton for spot supplies. * * * Authorities said overseas markets had been chaotic and prices had been hard to catalogue. They were reported to have ranged recently from $40 to $65 a ton."

96. Thorstenson v. Mobridge Iron Works Co., 87 S.D. 358, 208 N.W.2d 715, 64 A.L.R.3d 242 (1973).

97. Cf. 3 Williston, Sales § 599 (rev.ed. 1948) where the rationale for the older view is expressed; "[I]f the buyer pays more than the market price, it is not the seller's wrong but his own error of judgment which was the cause of the excessive payment."

98. U.C.C. § 2–713, Comment 5; see White & Summers, Uniform Commercial Code 233–34 (2d ed.1980). Trenchant criticism of the notion of giving the breaching party the benefit of the aggrieved party's actions cutting losses to below market levels appears in Simon, A Critique of the Treatment of Market Damages in the Restatement (Second) of Contracts, 81 Colum. L.Rev. 80 (1981); Simon & Novak, Limiting the Buyer's Market Damages to Lost Prof-

that is bound to arise is that it may be difficult to determine if and when a buyer has covered. A buyer may have many active accounts with suppliers of similar goods. In the event of breach by one of them it may be quite difficult to establish that any particular contract entered into after the buyer learns of the breach is the "cover" contract.[99] The potential for vexatious problems in a case of this sort is immense if the market is a fluctuating one.[1]

Although the buyer has an option to cover or not, the choice is not altogether a free one. The buyer cannot recover consequential damages which could have been avoided by cover.[2] Moreover, replevin[3] and specific performance[4] are not available remedies if the disappointed purchaser could have obtained substitute goods elsewhere.

In the event that the buyer does not cover, and utilizes instead the market price minus contract price rule, the relevant price is that which is in effect at the time the buyer learned of the breach.[5] The majority view under prior law was to the contrary, holding that the applicable market price was that of the date on which delivery should have been made.[6] The Commercial Code rule arguably makes two significant changes in prior law. First, (and this is non-controversial), it *postpones* the date on which damages are assessed in cases where the buyer is unaware of the breach until after performance is due; for example, where defective goods are shipped and defects are discovered later.[7] The buyer can cover only when he learns of the breach and if he fails to cover, the principle of avoidable consequences does not allow him to enhance damages by standing idly by. Thus, damages are measured as of the time he could have covered. Second, (and this is controversial), the Code *accelerates* the date on which damages are assessed in cases where there is a breach by anticipatory repudiation.[8] The literal meaning of § 2–713(1) so provides: "[T]he measure of damages for non-

its: A Challenge to the Enforceability of Market Contracts, 92 Harv.L.Rev. 1395 (1979). Totally contrary to these two articles is Childres, Buyer's Remedies: The Danger of Section 2–713, 72 Nw.U.L.Rev. 837 (1978) (market price minus contract price never an appropriate measure). See also Wallach, The Buyer's Right to Monetary Damages, 14 U.C.C.L.J. 236, 238–42 (1982); Carroll, A Little Essay in Partial Defense of the Contract—Market Differential as a Remedy for Buyers, 57 S.Cal.L. Rev. 667 (1984).

99. See Jamestown Farmers Elevator, Inc. v. General Mills, Inc., 552 F.2d 1285 (8th Cir.1977) (seller must prove buyer's purchases were intended as "cover").

1. Nordstrom, The Law of Sales 444 (1970).

2. U.C.C. § 2–715(2); see § 14–22 infra.

3. U.C.C. § 2–716(3).

4. See U.C.C. § 2–716, Comment 2.

5. U.C.C. § 2–713(1). It is important to note that in the event of a breach by the buyer the rule is different and the applicable market price is that in effect at the date of delivery. See § 14–23 infra.

6. Reliance Cooperage v. Treat, 195 F.2d 977 (8th Cir.1952); Acme Mills & Elevator Co. v. Johnson, 141 Ky. 718, 133 S.W. 784 (1911); Segall v. Finlay, 245 N.Y. 61, 156 N.E. 97 (1927); McCormick, Damages § 175; Restatement, Contracts § 338. This still appears to be the law in England. See George, Damages for Anticipatory Breach of Contract, 1971 J.Bus.L. 109.

7. Cf. Perkins v. Minford, 235 N.Y. 301, 139 N.E. 276 (1923) (under prior law).

8. Contrary to the analysis herein is White & Summers, Uniform Commercial Code 242–49 (2d ed.1980). Essentially in accord, but urging amendment of the Code, is Nordstrom, The Law of Sales 453–57 (1970). Also in accord is Jackson, "Anticipatory Repudiation" and the Temporal El-

delivery or repudiation by the seller is the difference between the market price at the time when the buyer learned of the breach and the contract price. * * * " An initial difficulty with accepting a literal interpretation of this section is that this language requires some creative interpretation when read with § 2–610, which permits the aggrieved party after the repudiation to await performance "for a commercially reasonable time." A logical solution of the difficulty is to conclude that if the buyer exercises such patience, he has "learned of the breach" at the expiration of a commercially reasonable time.[9] Other difficulties are (1) that early analysts of the Code did not read § 2–713 as overturning precedent in the anticipatory repudiation field,[10] and (2) that there is a conflict between the literal meaning of § 2–713 and a cross reference to § 2–713 in the evidentiary rule of § 2–723.[11] Such arguments and other arguments based upon textual exegesis will not solve the problem. What ought to be determinative is whether the result reached achieves internal consistency with the economic results achievable by other remedies available to the buyer under the Code. Primary among these remedies is the buyer's option to cover and recover any amount paid in excess of the contract price. Under a literal reading, § 2–713(1) measures the difference between contract price and market price as of the time the buyer would reasonably cover if he wished to. Such a reading has the principle of avoidable consequences built into it. If the buyer does not cover, he cannot enhance damages by remaining idle until the time for delivery under the contract. The same economic harm ought to be measured in essentially the same way no matter which remedial choice is made by the buyer. Consequently, the literal meaning of § 2–713 ought to be and has generally been followed.[12]

 WESTLAW REFERENCES

"uniform commercial code" u.c.c. /s 2–712 /s cover

"market price" /s "contract price" /s damage /s buyer vendee purchas!

ement of Contract Law: An Economic Inquiry into Contract Damages in Cases of Prospective Non Performance, 31 Stan.L. Rev. 69 (1978) (forward, not spot, price a reasonable time after learning of the repudiation); Leibson, Anticipatory Breach and Buyer's Damages—A Look into How the U.C.C. Has Changed the Common Law, 7 U.C.C.L.J. 272 (1975).

9. First Nat'l Bank of Chicago v. Jefferson Mortgage Co., 576 F.2d 479 (3d Cir. 1978).

10. For pre-U.C.C. Law, see Beale, Damages Upon Repudiation of a Contract, 17 Yale L.J. 443 (1908); Note, Measure of Damages for Anticipatory Breach of a Contract for Sale, 24 Colum.L.Rev. 55 (1924).

11. The villain of the piece, § 2–723(1) provides: "If an action based on anticipatory repudiation comes to trial before the time for performance with respect to some or all of the goods, any damages based on market price (Section 2–708 or Section 2–713) shall be determined according to the price of such goods prevailing at the time when the aggrieved party learned of the repudiation." A literal reading of § 2–713(1) would require that the cross-reference in § 2–723 to § 2–713 be treated as inadvertent surplusage and that § 2–723 is applicable only to a case involving a buyer's repudiation. See § 14–23 infra.

12. See Palmer v. Idaho Peterbilt, Inc., 102 Idaho 800, 641 P.2d 346 (1982) (collecting cases); Wallach, Anticipatory Repudiation and the U.C.C., 13 U.C.C.L.J. 48 (1980); Restatement, Second, Contracts § 350, ill. 17.

"contract price" /s cover! /s recover!

"substitute good" /s cover!

400k330

buyer /s "general damage"

"market price" /s "incidental damage"

"market price" /s "contract price" /s breach! /s know! knew
learn!

343k418(2)

§ 14–21. Buyer's General Damages for Seller's Breach of Warranty or Fraud

The Commercial Code adopts the measure of general damages which previously prevailed for breach of warranty. The measure is the difference between the value of the goods accepted and the value they would have had if they had been as warranted.[13] In routine cases, the difference in value is established by showing the reasonable cost of repair.[14] Value normally is determined, however, at the time and place of acceptance,[15] rather than, as under the Sales Act, the time and place of delivery.[16] As indicated in the discussion of the concept of value, barring very special circumstances, an objective "market" standard of value is employed by the legal system.[17] It has been suggested, however, that a subjective standard of value to the buyer should be applied in connection with breach of warranty where the buyer is able to show that the goods are less valuable to him in the light of his special needs.[18] Such a suggestion seems to be an unnecessary invitation to further confusion of the concept of value. Rather, in such circumstances, the buyer's recourse is under the last clause of § 2–714(2), which permits recovery where "special circumstances show proximate damages in a different amount."[19] In addition § 2–715 specifically takes into account the buyer's special needs in allowing for consequential damages, provided the seller has reason to know of those needs—a complex subjective-objective test. Purely subjective tests ought not to be favored. Recovery of "proximate damages of a different amount" has been allowed in a case in which a painting was sold and there was a breach of warranty of title. It was held that damages should be assessed as of the time the true owner reclaimed the painting from the disappointed buyer—a time at which the painting had greatly enhanced in value.[20]

13. U.C.C. § 2–714(2).

14. Bendix Home Systems, Inc. v. Jessop, 644 P.2d 843 (Alaska 1982); White & Summers, Uniform Commercial Code 377–80 (2d ed. 1980).

15. U.C.C. § 2–714(2).

16. Uniform Sales Act § 69(7).

17. See §§ 14–12 to 14–14 supra. On proof of value of a unique computer system, see Chatlos Systems, Inc. v. NCR Corp., 670 F.2d 1304 (3d Cir.1982), certiora-

ri dismissed 457 U.S. 1112, 102 S.Ct. 2918, 73 L.Ed.2d 1323 (1982).

18. Peters, Remedies for Breach of Contracts Relating to the Sale of Goods Under the Uniform Commercial Code: A Roadmap for Article Two, 73 Yale L.J. 199, 269 (1963).

19. See White & Summers, Uniform Commercial Code 383 (2d ed. 1980).

20. Menzel v. List, 24 N.Y.2d 91, 298 N.Y.S.2d 979, 246 N.E.2d 742 (1969).

The Uniform Commercial Code provides that remedies for material misrepresentation or fraud shall be the same as for breach of contract.[21] In an action for damages, therefore, it would seem that the measure of damages would be the same as for breach of warranty. This has the almost unnoticed effect of repealing, at least in the context of sales of goods, the "out of pocket" rule previously applicable to actions for fraud in a number of jurisdictions.[22] Pursuant to this rule the defrauded purchaser was permitted to recover only the difference between the amount paid and the value of the goods received rather than the difference between the value of the goods would have had if they were as represented and actual value which may now be recovered.

 WESTLAW REFERENCES

"general damage" /s "breach of warranty"

2–714 /s value

warrant! /s "reasonable cost of repair"

"time and place of acceptance" /s valu!

§ 14–22. Buyer's Consequential and Incidental Damages for Seller's Breach

In the ordinary case the buyer is made whole by application of the rules of general damages. Thus, if the buyer contracted to purchase sugar at four cents per pound and the seller breaches when the market price is seven cents the purchaser is entitled to damages of three cents per pound. This ordinarily provides full compensation because the purchaser may go out into the market and purchase the sugar at no cost except the original unpaid contract price plus the damages to which he is entitled. Suppose, however, there is no sugar on the market or no sugar available for delivery in time for the purchaser to keep his commitments for resale to retail outlets or for keeping his bakery in operation. The lost profits and other proximate damages, as, for example, damages he must pay to aggrieved retailers, are recoverable by him only if these were foreseeable to the seller. Prior to the Uniform Commercial Code many cases held that such consequential damages were awardable only if the seller knew two things at the time of contracting: first, the buyer's purpose in making the purchase and, second, that no substitute would be available to the purchaser in the

21. U.C.C. § 2–721; cf. Hill, Breach of Contract as a Tort, 74 Colum.L.Rev. 40 (1974), where this provision appears to have gone unnoticed; and Restatement, Second, Torts § 549, where the reporter's notes do not refer to the Code. See, however, Hill, Damages for Innocent Misrepresentation, 73 Colum.L.Rev. 679 n. 255 (1973).

22. The leading cases establishing this rule are Peek v. Derry, L.R., 37 Ch.Div. 541 (1887); and Reno v. Bull, 226 N.Y. 546, 124

N.E. 144 (1919), noted in 5 Cornell L.Q. 167. See McCormick, Damages 448. The contrary "benefit of the bargain" rule adopted by the Uniform Commercial Code has support in prior law in a good number of jurisdictions. Hartwell Corp. v. Bumb, 345 F.2d 453, 13 A.L.R.3d 868 (9th Cir. 1965), certiorari denied 382 U.S. 891, 86 S.Ct. 182, 15 L.Ed. 148 (1965). A compromise position is taken in Restatement, Second, Torts § 549.

event of a breach by the seller.[23] The Code seems to have relaxed the requirement of foreseeability considerably. Section 2–715(2) provides that consequential damages include:

> "any loss resulting from general or particular requirements and needs of which the seller at the time of contracting had reason to know and which could not reasonably be prevented by cover or otherwise ∗ ∗ ∗."

Under the Code it would seem not to be necessary that the seller have reason to know at the time of contracting that no substitute will be available to the buyer.[24] It is sufficient that at the time of the breach no substitute is reasonably available[25] and that the seller had reason to know the buyer's needs. It does not follow, however, that if the seller has such knowledge he will be liable for all consequential losses. For example, where the seller knows that the buyer is purchasing for resale to a sub-vendee, the seller has reason to know that the buyer will suffer a loss of resale profits if the seller breaches and the buyer cannot seasonably replace the goods on the market. Ordinarily he does not have reason to know that the sub-vendee will cancel his account with the buyer. Absent knowledge of special circumstances tending to show that such a cancellation will occur, the seller will neither be liable for damages caused by the cancellation,[26] nor for a general loss of good will.[27] While an occasional case allows recovery for loss of good will, generally the tests of foreseeability and certainty are applied so stringently as to preclude recovery.[28]

In addition to obvious cases of market shortages,[29] a seller has reason to know that the buyer cannot obtain substitute goods when the goods are brand name goods and the seller controls the supply of goods

---

23. Marcus & Co. v. K.L.G. Baking Co., 122 N.J.L. 202, 3 A.2d 627 (1939); Czarnikow-Rionda Co. v. Federal Sugar Ref. Co., 255 N.Y. 33, 173 N.E. 913, 88 A.L.R. 1426 (1930); Thomas Raby, Inc. v. Ward-Meehan Co., 261 Pa. 468, 104 A. 750 (1918).

24. Sun Maid Raisin Growers of Calif. v. Victor Packing Co., 146 Cal.App.3d 787, 194 Cal.Rptr. 612 (1983); accord under prior law, Lukens Iron & Steel Co. v. Hartmann-Greiling Co., 169 Wis. 350, 172 N.W. 894 (1919) (steel shortage occurred after the contract was formed); cf. Samek, The Relevant Time of Foreseeability of Damage in Contract, 38 Austl.L.J. 135 (1964). The Restatement (Second) appears to take the position that the Code has not changed the common law as stated above. Restatement, Second, Contracts § 351, Comment d.

25. As to "reasonable availability," see Oliver-Electrical Mfg. Co. v. I.O. Teigen Const. Co., 177 F.Supp. 572 (D.Minn.1959),

motion denied 183 F.Supp. 768 (D.Minn. 1960) (defendant proved that a substitute supplier was available but failed to prove that plaintiff should have known this).

26. Harbor Hill Lith. Corp. v. Dittler Bros., 76 Misc.2d 145, 348 N.Y.S.2d 920 (Sup.Ct.1973).

27. Neville Chem. Co. v. Union Carbide Corp., 422 F.2d 1205 (3d Cir.1970), cert. denied 400 U.S. 826, 91 S.Ct. 51, 27 L.Ed.2d 55 (1970).

28. See Comment, Consequential Damages: The Loss of Goodwill, 23 Baylor L.Rev. 106 (1971); Comment, Loss of Goodwill and Business Reputation as Recoverable Elements of Damages Under Uniform Commercial Code § 2–715—The Pennsylvania Experience, 75 Dick.L.Rev. 63 (1970); Annot., 96 A.L.R.3d 299 (1980).

29. Lukens Iron & Steel Co. v. Hartmann-Greiling Co., 169 Wis. 350, 172 N.W. 894 (1919).

bearing that brand [30] or when the goods are made pursuant to a patent exclusively controlled by one of the parties.[31]

Where a seller delivers goods to a manufacturer knowing they are to be used in the manufacturing process, the seller has reason to know that defective goods may cause a disruption of production and a consequent loss of profits. Under the Code it is clear that the seller is liable for such lost profits.[32] He also has reason to know that if a component supplied is defective it may result in an expensive process of product recall and component replacement.[33]

As under prior law, consequential damages for breach of warranty also include foreseeable injury to person or property proximately resulting from the breach.[34]

The Code expressly permits the parties to limit or exclude consequential damages by agreement, unless the limitation or exclusion is unconscionable. An attempt to limit damages for injury to the person in connection with a sale of consumer goods is, however, "prima facie unconscionable but limitation of damages where the loss is commercial is not." [35] Frequently warranties are limited and consequential damages are excluded by agreement. In substitution for the broader warranties and damages, the seller promises to repair defects for a given period of time. Such agreements are permitted by the Code. If the seller breaches the promise to repair, however, consequential damages may flow from the breach, as the remedy contractually substituted for Code remedies has failed of its essential purpose.[36] The material breach of the contractual substitute entitles the purchaser to cancel the remedies clause of the contract and utilize the remedies provisions of the Code.

The Code had adopted a category of damages known as incidental damages. Included in this category are "expenses reasonably incurred in inspection, receipt, transportation and care and custody of goods rightfully rejected * * *." [37] Under prior law such damages would

---

30. Orester v. Dayton Rubber Mfg. Co., 228 N.Y. 134, 126 N.E. 510 (1920).

31. Booth v. Spuyten Duyvil Rolling Mill Co., 60 N.Y. 487 (1875).

32. Southern Illinois Stone Co. v. Universal Engineering Corp., 592 F.2d 446 (8th Cir.1979); Lewis v. Mobil Oil Corp., 438 F.2d 500 (8th Cir.1971).

33. Taylor & Gaskin, Inc. v. Chris-Craft Industries, 732 F.2d 1273 (6th Cir.1984).

34. U.C.C. § 2–715(2)(b); see Prosser & Keeton, Torts § 97 (5th ed.1984).

35. U.C.C. § 2–719(3). A case considering the conscionability of a limitation of consequential damages to commercial losses is Luick v. Graybar Elec. Co., 473 F.2d 1360 (8th Cir.1973), holding that a trial was needed to determine the question.

36. U.C.C. § 2–719(2); RRX Industries, Inc. v. Lab-Con, Inc., 772 F.2d 543 (9th Cir. 1985) (inability to de-bug software); Lewis Refrigeration Co. v. Sawyer Fruit, Vegetable and Cold Storage Co., 709 F.2d 427 (6th Cir.1983); Adams v. J.I. Case Co., 125 Ill. App.2d 388, 261 N.E.2d 1 (1970), noted in 22 Case W.L.Rev. 349 (1971); Jones & McKnight Corp. v. Birdsboro Corp., 320 F.Supp. 39 (N.D.Ill.1970). See Note, 36 Okla.L.Rev. 669 (1983); but see Keystone Diesel Engine Co. v. Irwin, 411 Pa. 222, 191 A.2d 376 (1963).

37. U.C.C. § 2–715(1).

have been recoverable but often would have been characterized as direct or consequential damages.[38]

Also included in the Code category of incidental damages are "any commercially reasonable charges, expenses or commissions in connection with effecting cover ∗ ∗ ∗."[39] Such damages were also available under prior law as damages incurred in a proper attempt to mitigate damages.[40] In addition "any other reasonable expense incidental to the delay or other breach" are recoverable as incidental damages.[41]

 WESTLAW REFERENCES

lost loss +2 profit /s know! knew foresee! unforesee! /s seller vendor

343k418(17)

damage /s seller vendor /s foresee! know! knew /s contract***

good-will /s loss lost /s damage /s contract***

192k7 /p contract***

booth +s spuyten

"consequential damage" /s "breach of warranty" /s injur!

limit! /s "consequential damage" /s unfair! unconscionab!

"prima facie unconscionable"

"uniform commercial code" u.c.c. /s "incidental damage"

---

§ 14–23. Seller's General Damages for Non-acceptance or Repudiation

The seller's general damages for non-acceptance or repudiation by the buyer is the difference between the market price and the unpaid contract price.[42] It is quite clear, however, that very often the seller will not be placed in as good a position by this measure of damages as performance would have. For example, if a dealer contracts to sell an automobile at the retail market price of $10,000, upon a breach by the

---

38. Messmore v. New York Shot & Lead Co., 40 N.Y. 422 (1869) (direct). Often such damages were permitted to be recovered without any characterization. Taylor v. Saxe, 134 N.Y. 67, 31 N.E. 258 (1892).

39. U.C.C. § 2–715(1).

40. See § 14–17 supra.

41. U.C.C. § 2–715(1).

42. U.C.C. § 2–708(1). In a highly sophisticated series of articles, Professor Harris has formulated a rule for the measurement of seller's damages in terms differing from that of the Code and conventional analyses. "The rule is: Plaintiff should recover (minuend minus subtrahend) plus incidental damages. The 'minuend' is always the value to plaintiff of the difference between what defendant promised to do and what he in fact actually did

in the way of performance. The 'subtrahend' is always the value to plaintiff of being relieved by defendant's breach from all or part of plaintiff's scheduled performance." Harris, A Radical Restatement of the Law of Damages: New York Results Compared, 34 Fordham L.Rev. 23, 28 (1965); see Harris, A General Theory for Measuring Seller's Damages for Total Breach of Contract, 60 Mich.L.Rev. 577 (1962); Harris, A Radical Restatement of the Law of Seller's Damages: Michigan Results Compared, 61 Mich.L.Rev. 849 (1963); Harris & Graham, A Radical Restatement of the Law of Seller's Damages: California Results Compared, 18 Stan.L. Rev. 553 (1965); Harris, A Radical Restatement of the Law of Seller's Damages: Sales Act and Commercial Code Results Compared, 18 Stan.L.Rev. 66 (1965).

buyer recovery on the basis of the difference between retail market price and contract price would result in a recovery of only nominal damages.[43] But in fact the dealer has lost the profit on the sale measured by the difference between the cost to him of the automobile and the contract price. In order to give full compensation in such cases § 2–708(2) of the Uniform Commercial Code provides that if the difference between market price and contract price provides inadequate recovery, "the measure of damages is the profit (including reasonable overhead) which the seller would have made from full performance by the buyer."[44] Recovery of the lost profit would be appropriate in any case in which the seller has, for practical purposes, an unlimited supply of goods of the kind involved in the transaction.[45] The seller's lost profits can be calculated by subtracting the cost (so-called variable costs) to the dealer of the automobile from the contract price. This will give the seller his gross profit which includes both his net profit and an allocation calculated in the contract price for a share of his overhead.[46] Section 2–708(2) ends by stating that the seller is to allow "due credit for payments or proceeds of resale." Legislative history clarifies this confusing clause, which on its face, appears to undercut the entire thrust of the subsection. "Proceeds of resale" refers not to the proceeds of resale of the subject matter but, in a manufacturing contract, to proceeds of the sale of any components for junk.[47]

43. This was the result in a number of jurisdictions under the Sales Act. Charles Street Garage Co. v. Kaplan, 312 Mass. 624, 45 N.E.2d 928 (1942).

44. U.C.C. § 2–708(2). For a definitive analysis of this provision, see Childres & Burgess, Seller's Remedies: The Primacy of UCC 2–708(2), 48 N.Y.U.L.Rev. 833 (1973), which contradicts much of the analysis contained in Speidel & Clay, Seller's Recovery of Overhead Under UCC Section 2–708(2); Economic Cost Theory and Contract Remedial Policy, 57 Cornell L.Rev. 681 (1972). The latter analysis is also characterized as "incorrect" in Posner, Economic Analysis of Law 59 n. 7 (1972). Also sound is Schlosser, Construing U.C.C. Section 2–708(2) to Apply to the Lost-Volume Seller, 24 Case W.L.Rev. 686 (1973). An alternative analysis, rejecting in this context the general principle that an aggrieved party is entitled to protection of his expectation interest, is Shanker, The Case for a Literal Reading of UCC Section 2–708(2) (One Profit for the Reseller), 24 Case W.L.Rev. 697 (1973); cf. U.C.C. § 1–106 (expectation interest protected). A critical economic analysis of this provision is made in Goetz & Scott, Measuring Seller's Damages: The Lost-Profits Puzzle, 31 Stan.L. Rev. 323 (1979), which is reviewed critically in Sebert, Remedies under Article 2 of the U.C.C.: An Agenda for Review, 130

U.Pa.L.Rev. 360, 386–93 (1981). See, for synthesis, Schlosser, Damages for a Lost Volume Seller: Does an Efficient Formula Already Exist?, 17 U.C.C.L.J. 238 (1985); Note, 9 Wm.Mitchell L.Rev. 266 (1984). To the effect that an award of lost profits in this context is unfair and unnecessary, see Cooter & Eisenberg, Damages for Breach of Contract, 72 Cal.L.Rev. 1432, 1471–77 (1985).

45. Teradyne, Inc. v. Teledyne Industries, Inc., 676 F.2d 865 (1st Cir.1982); Neri v. Retail Marine Corp., 30 N.Y.2d 393, 334 N.Y.S.2d 165, 285 N.E.2d 311 (1972).

46. Murray On Contracts 491 (1974); Nordstrom, The Law of Sales § 177 (1970). Alternatively, net profit would have to be calculated and added to a pro rata share of the seller's fixed overhead. A trial on this basis would involve an expensive and cumbersome clash between the accountants of the parties. See White & Summers, Uniform Commercial Code § 7–13 (2d ed.1980); Shanker, supra note 44, at 707–10. For a particularly difficult case, see Automated Medical Labs. v. Armour Pharmaceutical Co., 629 F.2d 1118 (5th Cir.1980).

47. See authorities collected in Neri v. Retail Marine Corp., 30 N.Y.2d 393, 399 n. 2, 334 N.Y.S.2d 165, 169 n. 2, 285 N.E.2d 311, 314, n. 2 (1972).

Generally, the appropriate market price is the price at the "time and place for tender." [48] The relationship between this rule and the doctrines of anticipatory breach and avoidable consequences is complex. The Code provisions have been described as "curiously inconsistent and almost incoherent in places." [49] The inconsistencies must be resolved by following the Code's guiding remedial principle: "that the aggrieved party may be put in as good a position as if the other party had fully performed * * *," [50] and its guiding philosophy of requiring commercially reasonable conduct. If the goods are of the kind that the seller normally deals in, and in which there is an active market, e.g., grains, it would be commercially reasonable for the seller to take no action, await the time for performance, and seek damages measured by the contract price minus market price differential as of that date. Of course, he will have actual damages only if his prognosis as to grain prices was correct. Equally reasonable, on learning of the repudiation the seller might enter into a forward contract to sell grain and charge the breaching party with the difference between this resale price and the contract price.[51] If the contract involves the transfer of used machinery which would decline in value merely by aging, and the seller is not a dealer in such machinery, a prompt resale (or action for the price) would seem incumbent upon the seller. The variations are many, but the key goals of protecting the seller's expectancy interest and protecting the breaching party from predatory or other commercially unreasonable retaliation must guide the outcome.

 WESTLAW REFERENCES

"market price" /s "unpaid contract price"

damage /s 2–708

"market price" /s "time and place for tender"

"contract price" /s "re-sale price"

di("contract price" /p "market price" /p minus subtract! differen! reduc!)

§ 14–24. Seller's General Damages Following Resale

In the event of a breach by the buyer, whether by wrongful non-acceptance of the goods, repudiation, or failure to make a payment when due,[52] the seller may identify the goods to the contract [53] and resell them at a private or public sale. He may then recover from the buyer the difference between the resale price and contract price,[54]

48. U.C.C. § 2–708(1). If the case comes to trial prior to the date for performance, damages will be determined at the time the seller learned of the breach. U.C.C. § 2–723(1).

49. Jackson, "Anticipatory Repudiation" and the Temporal Element of Contract Law: An Economic Inquiry into Contract Damages in Cases of Prospective Nonperformance, 31 Stan.L.Rev. 69, 103 (1978).

50. U.C.C. § 1–106(1).

51. On "resale" as a remedy see § 14–24 infra.

52. U.C.C. § 2–703.

53. Id. § 2–704.

54. Id. § 2–706(1); see Shuchman, Profit on Default: An Archival Study of Automobile Repossession and Resale, 22 Stan.L. Rev. 20 (1969).

provided the sale is conducted in a commercially reasonable manner.[55] This, of course, is the counterpart of the buyer's remedy of cover.[56] The seller need not account to the buyer for any profit made on the resale.[57] The Code is unclear, however, as to how any part payment made by the buyer is to be allocated. In fairness such payment ought to be credited to the buyer.[58]

The resale remedy is not exclusive, however. Seller's remedies under the U.C.C. are cumulative[59] in the sense that, although the same economic harm is not to be compensated more than once, recovery under all remedial provisions of the Code can be had until the aggrieved party is made whole. Thus, for example, if a retailer has an unlimited supply of a given product, the resale of goods at the market price does not make him whole: he has been deprived of profit on a lost sale. As discussed in connection with damages under U.C.C. § 2–708(1),[60] in such a case the seller may recover "the profit (including reasonable overhead) which the seller would have made from full performance by the buyer."[61]

 WESTLAW REFERENCES
2–703 /s code u.c.c.

§ 14–25. Seller's Consequential and Incidental Damages

According to Section 1–106 of the Uniform Commercial Code consequential damages are not available unless specifically provided for by the Code or other rule of law and none of the provisions of the Code dealing with seller's damages allow for the recovery of consequential damages.[62] In the last analysis almost every breach by the buyer involves a failure or refusal to pay the contract price.[63] Even under prior case law the buyer's failure to pay the price or indeed his failure to pay any liquidated indebtedness was never a sufficient basis for the award of consequential damages no matter how foreseeable the injury to the creditor. The only recovery allowable was the sum of money owed with interest.[64] Thus, a seller's claim for consequential damages faces difficult obstacles indeed. There is one well recognized exception to the common law view precluding consequential damages to an

55. California Airmotive Corp. v. Jones, 415 F.2d 554 (6th Cir.1969).

56. See § 14–20 supra.

57. U.C.C. § 2–706(6).

58. See Nordstrom, Seller's Damages Following Resale Under Article Two of the Uniform Commercial Code, 65 Mich.L.Rev. 1299 (1967).

59. U.C.C. § 2–703, Comment 1.

60. See § 14–23 supra.

61. Neri v. Retail Marine Corp., 30 N.Y.2d 393, 334 N.Y.S.2d 165, 285 N.E.2d 311 (1972); Childres & Burgess, supra note 44, at 870–874.

62. Northern Helex Co. v. United States, 524 F.2d 707 (Ct.Cl.1975), cert. denied 429 U.S. 866, 97 S.Ct. 176, 50 L.Ed.2d 146 (1976).

63. For an exceptional situation, see text at notes 70–74 infra.

64. Loudon v. Taxing Dist., 104 U.S. (14 Otto) 771, 26 L.Ed. 923 (1881); 11 Williston § 1410. Recently departing from this rule by way of dictum is Salem Engineering & Const. Corp. v. Londonderry School District, 122 N.H. 379, 445 A.2d 1091 (1982).

aggrieved creditor. Where payment is to be made to a third person, the creditor has been allowed to recover special damages suffered by him, often consisting of injury to his credit and reputation.[65]

The Code expressly, however, permits recovery for incidental damages suffered by the seller. These "include any commercially reasonable charges, expenses or commissions incurred in stopping delivery, in the transportation, care and custody of goods after the buyer's breach, in connection with return or resale of the goods or otherwise resulting from the breach." [66] Incidental damages are recoverable whether he sues for damages following resale,[67] for damages without reference to resale,[68] or if he sues for the price.[69]

Occasionally the buyer's breach may involve misconduct other than a failure to pay, as where a buyer breaches his duty of cooperation in providing specifications, resulting in delayed production and additional cost to the seller.[70] While the Code permits the seller to cancel,[71] or to perform in any reasonable manner such as providing his own specifications,[72] it is silent on the situation where the seller exercises patience, awaits the buyer's specifications and thereby suffers a loss. It would seem that the buyer's breach could be deemed a breach of a "collateral" obligation,[73] remedial rights from which are not abrogated by the U.C.C.[74]

 WESTLAW REFERENCES

"consequential damage" /s buyer vendee purchaser /2 breach!

purchaser buyer vendee /2 breach! /s interest /s recover!
    damage /s money debt indebtedness

to(219) /p breach! /2 purchaser buyer vendee

4–402 /s u.c.c. "uniform commercial code" /s credit! dishonor!

"uniform commercial code" u.c.c. /s purchaser buyer vendee /2
    breach! /s "incidental damage"

"incidental damage" /s resale

§ 14–26. Seller's Action for the Price

Although an action by the seller for the price is not an action for damages,[75] brief consideration of the circumstances under which such an action is available seems appropriate to round out the discussion of

65. Cf. U.C.C. § 4–402 (liability of bank to depositor for wrongful dishonor). See also Dillon v. Lineker, 266 F. 688 (9th Cir. 1920) (damages of $28,000 sustained by failure of defendant to pay off creditor's mortgage of $3,000); Miholevich v. Mid-West Mut. Auto Ins. Co., 261 Mich. 495, 246 N.W. 202, 86 A.L.R. 633 (1933) (liability insurer failed to pay judgment recovered against insured, held liable for damages as a result of a body execution levied on insured).

66. U.C.C. § 2–710.

67. Id. § 2–706(1).

68. Id. § 2–708(1), (2).

69. Id. § 2–709(1).

70. Kehm v. United States, 93 F.Supp. 620 (Ct.Cl.1950).

71. U.C.C. § 2–711.

72. U.C.C. § 2–311.

73. U.C.C. § 2–701.

74. Semble: Holmgren v. Rogers Bros. Co., 94 Idaho 267, 486 P.2d 278 (1971).

75. See § 14–23 supra.

the various kinds of money judgments available to an aggrieved seller. Such an action is available if the goods have been accepted by the buyer.[76] It is also available if the seller identifies the goods to the contract and the seller is unable after reasonable effort to resell them at reasonable price, or if the circumstances reasonably indicate that such effort will be unavailing.[77] In this event the seller must hold the goods for the buyer, but if resale subsequently becomes practicable the seller may resell them at any time prior to collection of a judgment for the price.[78]

The seller also has an action for the price if the goods are lost or damaged within a commercially reasonable time after risk of their loss has passed to the buyer.[79] Analysis of this provision would require discussion of the complexities of when risk of loss passes [80] and the relation of these complexities to the question of insurance coverage.[81] This is best left to works on Sales.[82]

 WESTLAW REFERENCES

seller vendor /s "action for the price"
"action for the price" /s damaged damaging los* destroy!
destruction theft stolen

§ 14–27. Seller's Damages for Contracts to Manufacture Special Goods Under the Code

There is no explicit provision in the Code measuring damages for repudiation by the buyer of a contract to manufacture special goods. It is clear that if the manufacture is completed the seller may maintain an action for the price if the goods are not reasonably resaleable [83] and if resaleable, he may utilize the resale remedy [84] or maintain an action for damages.[85]

The problem arises where the repudiation occurs prior to completion of manufacture. The Code has an express provision as to mitigation in this eventuality. The seller "in the exercise of reasonable commercial judgment for the purposes of avoiding loss and of effective realization" has two options.[86] He may complete the manufacture, appropriate the goods to the contract and then exercise his remedy of

76. U.C.C. § 2–709(1)(a). It is unclear whether this includes the situation where the buyer accepts the goods and subsequently wrongfully purports to revoke his acceptance because of alleged defects. See White & Summers, Uniform Commercial Code § 7–3 (2d ed.1980) (such situations are included); Peters, Remedies for Breach of Contracts Relating to the Sale of Goods Under the Uniform Commercial Code; A Roadmap for Article Two, 73 Yale L.J. 199, 241–43 (1963) (such situations are not included; revocation is equivalent of rejection by buyer).

77. U.C.C. § 2–709(1)(b); see Annot., 90 A.L.R.3d 1146.

78. Id. § 2–709(2).

79. Id. § 2–709(1)(a).

80. Id. § 2–509; see § 13–2 supra.

81. U.C.C. § 2–510.

82. See Nordstrom, The Law of Sales § 178 (1970); White & Summers, Uniform Commercial Code §§ 7–3, 7–4, 7–5 (2d ed. 1980).

83. See § 14–26 supra.

84. See § 14–24 supra.

85. See § 14–23 supra.

86. U.C.C. § 2–704(2).

resale or of an action for the price. His second option is to "cease manufacture and resell for scrap or salvage value or proceed in any other reasonable manner." If he exercises this option, the Code does not indicate his remedy. It seems clear, however, that he may, under the Code, sue for damages measured by the difference between the market price and contract price plus incidental damages, or for the profit which he would have made.[87] Recovery of profit alone, however, would not compensate him for his losses sustained. Under prior law in addition to his gains prevented he would have been entitled to his losses sustained measured by the expenditures made pursuant to the contract to the extent that the product of such expenditures are not salvageable.[88] The Code appears to continue to permit such recovery in addition to lost profits by requiring "due allowance for costs reasonably incurred." [89]

 WESTLAW REFERENCES
special! /s manufactur! /s good /s repudiat!

§ 14–28. Construction Contracts: Measure of Recovery by Contractor

The construction contractor is in many respects in the position of a seller of goods. The major difference is that his performance is affixed to land of another. Thus, such remedies as resale or replevin are unavailable. If he has completely performed he is unquestionably entitled to the agreed price.[90] If, however, the contract is repudiated by the owner or if the contractor justifiably cancels the contract because of a breach by the owner, the contractor's remedy is in damages.[91] If no work has been done the contractor is entitled to the profit he would have made measured by the difference between the contract price and the prospective cost of performance.[92] If the contractor is delayed by the breach, he may recover at least the rental value of the equipment tied up during the period of the delay [93] plus increased overhead costs,[94] and higher labor costs. If the work has commenced the contractor is

87. Anchorage Centennial Dev. Co. v. Van Wormer & Rodrigues, Inc., 443 P.2d 596 (Alaska 1968); Detroit Power Screwdriver Co. v. Ladney, 25 Mich.App. 478, 181 N.W.2d 828, 42 A.L.R.3d 173 (1970), appeal after remand 39 Mich.App. 629, 197 N.W.2d 857 (1972); see § 14–23 supra.

88. Lieberman v. Templar Motor Co., 236 N.Y. 139, 140 N.E. 222, 29 A.L.R. 1089 (1923); see § 14–25 supra.

89. U.C.C. § 2–708(2). For discussions of damages for breach of manufacturing contracts, see Duesenberg & King § 13.07[4]; Peters, supra note 76, at 273–75.

90. McCormick, Damages § 640.

91. He also has a remedy in restitution, discussed in § 15–3 infra.

92. McCormick, Damages § 164; 11 Williston § 1363. For a thorough discussion of the rules discussed in this section, see Patterson, Builder's Measure of Recovery for Breach of Contract, 31 Colum.L. Rev. 1286 (1934).

93. W.G. Cornell Co. v. Ceramic Coating Co., Inc., 626 F.2d 990 (D.C.Cir.1980); Mullinax Eng. Co. v. Platte Valley Const. Co., 412 F.2d 553 (10th Cir.1969); Studer v. Rasmussen, 80 Wyo. 465, 344 P.2d 990 (1959).

94. Walter Kidde Constructors, Inc. v. State, 37 Conn.Sup. 50, 434 A.2d 962 (1981); Higgins v. Fillmore, 639 P.2d 192 (Utah 1981).

entitled for a total breach to the unpaid contract price less the amount it would have cost him to complete his performance.[95] The measure of recovery is sometimes expressed in a somewhat different formula. Under this second formula the contractor is entitled to the profit he would have made plus the cost of work actually performed, less any progress payments he may have received.[96] A third formula has also found judicial approval. This permits the builder to recover "such proportion of the contract price as the cost of the work done bears to the total cost of doing the job, plus, for the work remaining, the profit that would have been made on it." [97] In most cases each of these formulas yields the same result. Where the contract would have been performed at a loss to the contractor, however, each of the formulas may produce a different result.[98] It should be noted, however, that on a losing contract, the contractor would frequently find that his recovery would be greater in an action for restitution than in an action for damages.[99]

WESTLAW REFERENCES

contractor /s cancel! repudiat! /s owner /s damage

contractor /s "contract price" /s "cost of perform!"

contractor /s rent! /s delay! /s breach!

115k122 /p contractor

---

§ 14–29. Construction Contracts: Measure of Recovery by the Owner

When a building contract is defectively performed, as a general rule the owner is entitled to damages measured by the cost of remedying the defect.[1] There are a number of controversial cases where this measure is arguably overly generous to the owner. Consider these facts:

95. Guerini Stone Co. v. P.J. Carlin Const. Co., 240 U.S. 264, 280, 36 S.Ct. 300, 307, 60 L.Ed. 636 (1916); Peter Kiewet Sons Co. v. Summit Const. Co., 422 F.2d 242 (8th Cir.1969); Millen v. Gulesian, 229 Mass. 27, 118 N.E. 267 (1917).

96. United States v. Behan, 110 U.S. 338, 344, 4 S.Ct. 81, 83, 28 L.Ed. 168, 170 (1884); Warner v. McLay, 92 Conn. 427, 103 A. 113 (1918). For a discussion of the similarity of result usually achieved by the application of this and the previous formula, see Petropoulos v. Lubienski, 220 Md. 293, 152 A.2d 801 (1959).

97. McCormick, Damages § 641. Cases utilizing this formula include McGrew v. Ide Estate Inv. Co., 106 Kan. 348, 187 P. 887 (1920); Kehoe v. Borough of Rutherford, 56 N.J.L. 23, 27 A. 912 (1893).

98. The following illustration is given in McCormick, Damages 642. "Assume an extreme case: The contract price is $10,000, the work already done has cost $5,000, and the unfinished part would cost $10,000 to complete. Here under the three formulas the builder would recover (1) zero, (2) $5,000, and (3) $3,333.33."

99. See § 15–4 infra; Guittard, Building Contracts: Damages and Restitution, 32 Texas B.J. 91 (1969).

1. Shell v. Schmidt, 164 Cal.App.2d 350, 330 P.2d 817, 76 A.L.R.2d 792 (1958); Jackson v. Buesgens, 290 Minn. 78, 186 N.W.2d 184 (1971); Bellizzi v. Huntley Estates, 3 N.Y.2d 112, 164 N.Y.S.2d 395, 143 N.E.2d 802 (1957); Prier v. Refrigeration Engineering Co., 74 Wn.2d 25, 442 P.2d 621 (1968); 5 Corbin § 1089; McCormick, Damages § 168; 11 Williston § 1363. Caveat: if the owner has not fully paid the price and performance by the builder is not substantial in many jurisdictions the owner need pay nothing, or nothing further, on the contract. See § 11–22 supra.

Case I. The contractor inadvertently installs Cohoes instead of Reading brand wrought iron pipe into a new house, contrary to the contract specifications. The two brands are regarded in the trade as of equal quality. The owner discovers the breach only after the walls are plastered. The cost of removing the Cohoes pipe, installing Reading pipe and replastering the walls would be $35,000. The house, as is, is worth $250,000. If the defect is remedied, its value would be precisely the same.

On facts such as these, courts have refused to apply the usual measure of damages and have held that the owner is entitled to merely the difference between the value of the structure if built to specifications and the value it has as constructed.[2] On the facts of Case I the owner is, therefore, entitled only to nominal damages. It has been said that the rationale for such cases is to avoid "unreasonable economic waste."[3] The matter, however, is more complex than a simple matter of avoiding economic waste. It seems clear that if the owner had, and had communicated, an idiosyncratic value he attached to Reading pipe (e.g., he was an executive of the Reading Company), he ought to be awarded a judgment in the amount required to replace the plumbing, regardless of economic waste.[4] Similarly, if the breach were willful (e.g., Cohoes pipe was purchased more cheaply at a distributor's distress sale), many courts would award replacement cost rather than difference in value.[5] In Case I these elements are absent. In the event the owner were to receive replacement cost he would doubtlessly pocket the money rather than replace the pipes. Such enrichment appears unjust in relationship to the cost to the innocent, albeit breaching, contractor.

Case II. A strip miner contracts to lease 60 acres of farmland, mine it, and restore the surface to specified grades and conditions. The land is mined and not restored. Restoration would cost $29,000, but the land is worth only $300 less than it would be worth if restored.

The court adjudicating Case II restricted the owners' recovery to $300.[6] There are cases to the contrary[7] and the appropriate result is in

2. Jacob & Youngs v. Kent, 230 N.Y. 239, 129 N.E. 889, 23 A.L.R. 1429 (1921).

3. 5 Corbin § 1090 at p. 493.

4. Groves v. John Wunder Co., 205 Minn. 163, 286 N.W. 235, 123 A.L.R. 502 (1939) (dissent); Chamberlain v. Parker, 45 N.Y. 569 (1871) (A man may choose "to erect a monument to his caprice or folly on his premises. * * *"). See also Linzer, On the Amorality of Contract Remedies— Efficiency, Equity, and the Second Restatement, 81 Colum.L.Rev. 111, 117–20, 131–34 (1981); Note, Breach of a Covenant to Restore, 39 S.Cal.L.Rev. 309 (1966); Muris, Cost of Completing or Diminution in Market Value: The Relevance of Subjective Value, 12 J.Leg.Stud. 379 (1983).

5. Shell v. Schmidt, 164 Cal.App.2d 350, 330 P.2d 817, 76 A.L.R.2d 792 (1958), cert. denied 359 U.S. 959, 79 S.Ct. 799, 3 L.Ed.2d 766 (1959); City School District v. McLane Const. Co., 85 A.D.2d 749, 445 N.Y.S.2d 258 (3d Dep't 1981), appeal denied 56 N.Y.2d 504, 451 N.Y.S.2d 1026, 436 N.E.2d 1345 (1982); see generally Marschall, Willfulness: A Crucial Factor in Choosing Remedies for Breach of Contract, 24 Ariz.L.Rev. 733 (1982).

6. Peevyhouse v. Garland Coal Mining Co., 382 P.2d 109 (Okl.1962), cert. denied 375 U.S. 906, 84 S.Ct. 196, 11 L.Ed.2d 145 (1963).

7. Groves v. John Wunder Co., 205 Minn. 163, 286 N.W. 235, 123 A.L.R. 502

dispute among the scholars.[8] Note that the breach is willful and the strip miner keeps $29,000 in his pocket that he had committed himself to expend. As one commentator has written:

"While one might argue for a damage system that neither encourages nor discourages performance, it is difficult to advance reasoned argument in favor of a damage system that affirmatively encourages non performance." [9]

Arguments based on what is the most economically efficient result seem to cancel each other out.[10] The decision in Case II appears plainly wrong when approached from the perspective of the moral obligation created by contractual promises, the policy of discouraging contract breaches and the prevention of unjust enrichment.

> *Case III.* L, a municipality, owned a pier which it leased to T for a ten year term at an annual rental of $200,000. T agreed to keep the pier in good repair at T's expense. At the expiration of the leasehold, L discovered that T had failed to maintain the pier in good repair and that the cost of repair would be about $200,000. Soon thereafter, L, pursuant to plan known to T at the time of entering into the lease, demolished the pier for replacement by a containership terminal. In an action by L for damages, T argues that L suffered no damages as the pier had been scheduled for demolition and was, in fact, demolished.

Case III is much like Case II. The primary difference is that it is absolutely clear that repairs will be valueless not only in terms of market value but in terms of any subjective or idiosyncratic value repair might have to L. Repair would be economically inefficient. Nonetheless, judgment was awarded to L for the cost of repairs.[11] While it is clear that L suffered no economic injury by the failure to repair, a judgment for T would have validated T's unjust enrichment. Part of T's bargained-for return was the cost of repairs. There is no economic inefficiency in allocating to L, rather than T, the savings caused by the lack of repair. If T had acted honorably and rationally it would have offered, during the leasehold period, to renegotiate the lease, offering, perhaps, an additional payment of $5,000 per year in exchange for a release from the covenant to repair. If L acted rational-

(1939) (performance of promise to grade gravel and sand pit would cost $80,000; land as restored would be worth $12,000); Emery v. Caledonia Sand and Gravel, Inc., 117 N.H. 441, 374 A.2d 929 (1977); American Standard v. Schectman, 80 A.D.2d 318, 439 N.Y.S.2d 529 (1981), appeal denied, 54 N.Y.2d 604, 443 N.Y.S.2d 1027 (1981) (contract to demolish and remove foundations to depth of one foot; land levelled but no foundation removed; court awards $90,000 cost of completion rather than $3,000 diminution in value).

8. The discussions are many. For recent thorough discussions, see Linzer, supra note 4; Marschall, supra note 5; Yorio, In Defense of Money Damages for Breach of Contract, 82 Colum.L.Rev. 1365, 1388–1424 (1982).

9. Vernon, Expectancy Damages for Breach of Contract: A Primer and Critique, 1976 Wash.U.L.Q. 179, 228.

10. See Yorio, supra note 8, at 1388–97.

11. Farrell Lines, Inc. v. New York, 30 N.Y.2d 76, 330 N.Y.S.2d 358, 281 N.E.2d 162 (1972); contra, Associated Stations, Inc. v. Cedars Realty and Dev. Corp., 454 F.2d 184 (4th Cir.1972).

ly it would have accepted that offer, or at least made a counter-offer for, say, $10,000 per year. Rather than award L the full cost of repair in Case III the court could have split the windfall between the parties, although few cases have done so.[12]

> *Case IV.* The United States chartered a ship from plaintiff, agreeing that, at the end of World War II, it would restore the ship to its original condition. At the end of the War there was a glut of ships and labor and materials costs had risen. As a result of these two factors restoration would cost $4,000,000, but would result in a ship that would be worth only $2,000,000. Unrestored, the ship is valueless except as scrap.

The court, stating that if plaintiff were awarded $4,000,000, the ship "would still rust at anchor," [13] awarded plaintiff the loss in value ($2,000,000). It deprived plaintiff of what it regarded as a $2,000,000 windfall. In a sense, however, the United States received a $2,000,000 windfall by not having to undertake the costs of repair to which it had contractually committed itself. There seems to be no clear-cut answer to the dilemma posed by Case IV. Neither party is dishonorable. They are caught up in a set of circumstances that they did not foresee.

It has been suggested that the court split the difference,[14] but there is little authority for splitting either losses or windfalls.[15] It has been suggested that in Cases II, III and IV, the best solution is to order the breaching party to specifically perform.[16] Because the owner prefers money to performance in each of the cases, the parties would then negotiate an economically efficient solution. While this would cut through the conflicting vectors, it faces formidable traditional obstacles against the award of specific performance in construction cases.[17]

It cannot usually be said that there is unreasonable economic waste or windfall recovery if the structure is unusable or unsafe in its present condition. Thus, the owner's measure of damages in such a case is the cost of remedying the defect.[18]

In the event the builder abandons the construction prior to completion, normally the measure of damages is the reasonable cost of completion,[19] plus any damages suffered by the consequent delay in completion.[20] Damages for delay normally consist of the rental or use

---

12. Restatement, Second, Contracts § 351(3) suggests that the court has the power to limit recovery. See Young, Half Measures, 81 Colum.L.Rev. 19 (1981).

13. Eastern S.S. Lines, Inc. v. United States, 112 F.Supp. 167, 175 (Ct.Cl.1953).

14. See Yorio, supra note 8, at 1365, 1417–18.

15. See Young, supra note 12.

16. See Linzer, supra note 4.

17. See § 16–5 infra. The obstacles are recognized by the proponent. See Linzer, supra note 4, at 126–30.

18. Bellizzi v. Huntley Estates, Inc., 3 N.Y.2d 112, 164 N.Y.S.2d 395, 143 N.E.2d 802 (1957).

19. State, etc. Randolph County v. R.M. Hudson Paving & Const. Co., 91 W.Va. 387, 113 S.E. 251 (1922); McCormick, Damages § 169.

20. Noonan v. Independence Indem. Co., 328 Mo. 706, 41 S.W.2d 162 (1931).

value the premises would have had during the period of delay.[21] If the requisite foreseeability and certainty exist, special damages are also recoverable.[22]

WESTLAW REFERENCES

built build! /s defect! /s perform! /s damage /s cost

"unreasonable economic waste"

115k123 /p contractor construction

"unjust! enrich!" /s contractor /s breach!

los* /2 valu! /s breach! /s build! built contractor home house office

"reasonable cost of complet!" /s abandon!

delay! /s abandon! /s complet! /s construct! contractor

delay! abandon! /s build! built construct! contractor /s "special damage"

---

§ 14–30.   Contracts to Sell Realty: Measure of Damages for Total Breach

Among the earliest rules of damages laid down in England were those relating to real property.[23] In 1776 it was held in Floreau v. Thornhill[24] that upon a vendor's breach of a contract because of an inability to convey good title the vendee may not recover for his loss of bargain. About half of the American states have accepted this English rule.[25] In such jurisdictions the vendee generally may recover only his down payment plus the reasonable expenses in examining title.[26] In its inception the limitation on vendee's recovery was based upon the difficulty besetting a vendor in ascertaining whether his title was marketable in view of the lack of adequate land registries.[27] In those

21. Wing & Bostwick Co. v. United States Fidelity & Guar. Co., 150 Fed. 672 (W.D.N.Y.1906); Standard Oil Co. v. Central Dredging Co., 225 App.Div. 407, 233 N.Y.S. 279 (3d Dep't 1929), affirmed 252 N.Y. 545, 170 N.E. 137 (1929); McCormick, Damages § 170; Lande, Uncle Sam's Right to Damages for Delay in the Wonderland of Government Contract, 10 Santa Clara Law. 2 (1969). The owner, however, under the doctrine of avoidable consequences may not enhance damages by prolonging the period of delivery. See Losei Realty Corp. v. New York, 254 N.Y. 41, 171 N.E. 899 (1930), a case which pushes the requirement of mitigation to extreme limits, holding that although the defendant did not expressly repudiate the contract and manifested an intention of eventually performing, the plaintiff as a reasonable man should have mitigated damages by putting an end to the contract.

22. Olson v. Quality-Pak Co., 93 Idaho 607, 469 P.2d 45 (1970); Reilly v. Connors,

65 App.Div. 470, 72 N.Y.S. 834 (2d Dep't 1901); J.T. Stark Grain Co. v. Harry Bros. Co., 57 Tex.Civ.App. 529, 122 S.W. 947 (1909). Normally, consequential damages will not include injury to one's credit rating. Raymond Le Chase, Inc. v. Vincent Buick, Inc., 77 Misc.2d 1024, 353 N.Y.S.2d 151 (Sup.Ct.1974).

23. Other early rules limiting damages, not here considered, relate to breaches of covenants in conveyances. See McCormick, Damages § 185.

24. 96 Eng.Rep. 635 (1776).

25. McCormick, Damages §§ 177, 179 (lining up the jurisdictions).

26. Id. § 182.

27. See Oakley, Pecuniary Compensation for Failure to Complete a Contract for the Sale of Land, 39 Cambridge L.J. 58 (1980).

jurisdictions in which the limitation is accepted, despite the presence of adequate land registries, the rule is so well established and known to the legal profession and to land-owners that any judicial overturning of the rule would be unwarranted.[28] Nevertheless, the original rationale must be strictly borne in mind in applying the rule. If the vendor has good title but refuses to convey he will be liable for ordinary contract damages, measured by the difference between the value of the land and the contract price,[29] together with consequential damages.[30] Similarly, he will be so liable if he was aware of the defect in title at the time of contracting [31] or if a previously unknown curable defect is discovered and the vendor fails to utilize his best efforts to remove the defect.[32] All of these cases are frequently said to come within a "bad faith" exception to the English rule, although in many such cases the question of whether or not the vendor was in bad faith is not so much in issue as is the question of whether the vendor knowingly assumed the risk that he would acquire marketable title.[33] In cases where the vendee is permitted to recover for his loss of bargain, he may not also recover his expenses in examining title,[34] but in a proper case consequential damages will be awarded.[35]

In jurisdictions following the "American rule," the vendee is entitled to recover in all cases his loss of bargain together with consequential damages pursuant to the general principles of contract damages.[36]

In the event of breach by the vendee, it seems to be the rule everywhere that the vendor may recover standard contract damages: the difference between the contract price and the market value of the land.[37] In an appropriate case the vendor may recover consequential

---

28. The English rule was overturned in Donovan v. Bachstadt, 91 N.J. 434, 453 A.2d 160, 28 A.L.R.4th 1062 (1982).

29. Soloman v. Western Hills Development, 110 Mich.App. 257, 312 N.W.2d 428 (1981).

30. Ocean Air Tradeways, Inc. v. Arkay Realty Corp., 480 F.2d 1112 (9th Cir.1973); Pearce v. Hubbard, 223 Ala. 231, 135 So. 179 (1931); Donovan v. Bachstadt, note 28 supra (increased mortgage interest). Of course, as a prerequisite to the recovery of consequential damages the vendee must meet the tests of foreseeability and certainty. Gilmore v. Cohen, 95 Ariz. 34, 386 P.2d 81, 11 A.L.R.3d 714 (1963).

31. Stone v. Kaufman, 88 W.Va. 588, 107 S.E. 295 (1921); Arentsen v. Moreland, 122 Wis. 167, 99 N.W. 790 (1904). See also Potts v. Moran's Ex'rs, 236 Ky. 28, 32 S.W.2d 534 (1930), which collects many of the cases and adopts a somewhat different view. See Carnahan, The Kentucky Rule of Damages for Breach of a Contract to Convey, 20 Ky.L.J. 304 (1932).

If the vendee is aware of the vendor's lack of marketable title at the time of

contracting, as where the vendor merely has a contract to purchase the realty, some cases take the position that since there is a lack of bad faith, the vendor will not be liable for loss of bargain where he cannot perfect his title. Northridge v. Moore, 118 N.Y. 419, 23 N.E. 570 (1890). Contra, Edgington v. Howland, 111 Neb. 171, 195 N.W. 934 (1923).

32. Braybrooks v. Whaley, [1919] 1 K.B. 435.

33. See Hammond v. Hannin, 21 Mich. 374, 386–87 (1970); Arentsen v. Moreland, 122 Wis. 167, 99 N.W. 790 (1904); McCormick, Damages 689–91.

34. Schultz & Son v. Nelson, 256 N.Y. 473, 177 N.E. 9 (1931).

35. Petrie-Clemons v. Butterfield, 122 N.H. 120, 441 A.2d 1167 (1982).

36. Doherty v. Dolan, 65 Me. 87 (1876); McCormick, Damages § 177; Annots., 48 A.L.R. 12 (1927); 68 A.L.R. 137 (1930).

37. McCormick, Damages § 186.

damages measured by the profit which the vendor would have made on the transaction.[38]

If the breach takes the form of a vendor's delay in conveying, the vendee may recover the rental value of the premises during the period of delay, plus, if the prerequisites exist,[39] consequential damages.[40]

WESTLAW REFERENCES

"good title" /s loss +4 bargain

400k351(8) /p title

"good title" /s convey! /s damage

"good title" /s refus! /s convey!

400k343(3)

400k334(5)

"bad faith" /s title /s realty (real +1 estate property) land

"american rule" /s realty (real +1 estate property) land /s damage

vendee /s breach! /s "contract price" /s "market value"

vendor /s breach! /s delay! /s convey!

I. AGREED DAMAGES

Table of Sections

§ 14–31. Liquidated Damages Distinguished From Penalties

Historically, a rule developed in Equity that penalties agreed upon by the parties would not be enforced. This equitable rule, designed to prevent over-reaching and to give relief from unconscionable bargains, was later adopted by courts of law.[41] Given the deeply rooted principle

---

38. Tague Holding Corp. v. Harris, 250 N.Y. 422, 165 N.E. 834 (1929) (vendor had a contract to purchase from the owner).

39. See §§ 14–5 to 14–8 supra.

40. Christensen v. Slawter, 173 Cal. App.2d 325, 343 P.2d 341, 74 A.L.R.2d 567 (1959); Bumann v. Maurer, 203 N.W.2d 434 (N.D.1972).

41. Liquidated damages are discussed in McCormick, Damages §§ 146–157, and the historical development of the doctrine in § 147. See generally Crowley, New York Law of Liquidated Damages Revisited, 4 N.Y.Cont.Leg.Ed. No. 1, 59 (1966); Macneil, Power of Contract and Agreed Remedies, 47 Cornell L.Q. 495 (1962); Sweet, Liquidated Damages in California, 60 Cal.L.Rev. 84 (1972); Comment, Liquidated Damages in Illinois Contracts, 45 Chi.-Kent L.Rev. 183 (1968); Comment, Liquidated Damages: A Comparison of the Common Law and the Uniform Commercial Code, 45 Fordham L.Rev. 1349 (1977)

of freedom of contract and the reluctance of courts to inquire into the wisdom of a bargain except when fraud or something like it is proved, it has seemed somewhat anomalous that common law courts have continued assiduously to refuse enforcement of penalty clauses. The answer seems to be that in general parties are free to enter into a contract containing whatever terms they wish regarding the establishment of primary rights, but except within narrow limits they are not free to determine that remedial rights will be provided.[42] Remedies are provided by the state and are defined by public rather than private law. Therefore, for example, a contractual clause providing that in the event of breach specific performance will be granted will not be given effect.[43] In addition, the traditional equitable doctrine of unconscionability survived in this area as a foundation for the rule against the enforcement of contractual penalties.[44]

While parties are not empowered to provide for penalties in the event of a breach, they are permitted under certain conditions to determine in advance what damages will be assessed in the event of a breach.

A penalty is designed to deter a party from breaching his contract and to punish him in the event the deterrent is ineffective.[45] Courts ritualistically list three criteria by which a valid liquidated damages clause may be distinguished from a penalty: first, the parties must intend to provide for damages rather than for a penalty; second, the injury caused by the breach must be uncertain or difficult to quantify; third, the sum stipulated must be a reasonable pre-estimate of the

(hereinafter Fordham Comment). Differing analyses of the economic efficiency of rules regarding penalties are given in Rea, Efficiency Implication of Penalties and Liquidated Damages, 13 J.Leg.Stud. 147 (1984); Goetz & Scott, Liquidated Damages, Penalties and the Just Compensation Principle: Some Notes on an Enforcement Model and a Theory of Efficient Breach, 77 Colum.L.Rev. 554 (1977); Clarkson, Miller & Morris, Liquidated Damages v. Penalties: Sense or Nonsense, 1978 Wis.L.Rev. 351; Comment, Liquidated Damages and Penalties Under the Uniform Commercial Code and the Common Law: An Economic Analysis of Contract Damages, 72 Nw.U.L. Rev. 1055 (1978) (hereinafter Northwestern Comment); Note, A Critique of the Penalty Limitation on Liquidated Damages, 50 S.Cal.L.Rev. 1055 (1977).

42. Garrity v. Lyle Stuart, Inc., 40 N.Y.2d 354, 386 N.Y.S.2d 831, 353 N.E.2d 793 (1976). For a somewhat similar analysis, predicated, however, on the premise that the rule against penalties is not an abridgment of freedom of contract, see Macneil, supra note 41. Cf. Leff, Contract as Thing, 19 Am.U.L.Rev. 131, 148 n. 61 (1970).

43. But the clause may be influential in determining how the court will exercise its discretion. The cases are collected in Macneil, supra note 41, at 521–22.

44. Fridman, Freedom of Contract, 2 Ottawa L.Rev. 1, 10–11 (1967).

45. Muldoon v. Lynch, 66 Cal. 536, 6 P. 417 (1885); Berger v. Shanahan, 142 Conn. 726, 118 A.2d 311 (1955); Shields v. Early, 132 Miss. 282, 95 So. 839 (1923). Compare the function of punitive damages and the general lack of availability of such damages in contract actions. See § 14–3 supra. Special situations: Continental Turpentine & Rosin Co. v. Gulf Naval Stores Co., 244 Miss. 465, 142 So.2d 200 (1962) (trade association "fine"); Garrett v. Coast & Southern Federal Sav. & Loan Ass'n, 9 Cal.3d 731, 108 Cal.Rptr. 845, 511 P.2d 1197 (1973), appeal after remand 136 Cal.App.3d 266, 186 Cal.Rptr. 178 (1982) ("late charges"); City of Rye v. Public Service Mut. Ins. Co., 34 N.Y.2d 470, 358 N.Y.S.2d 391, 315 N.E.2d 458 (1974) (penal bond extracted by municipality).

probable loss. The Uniform Commercial Code and the Restatement Second have reshaped these criteria somewhat. Under both the traditional and newer formulations the third criterion is generally determinative.[46]

(a) Intention

That intention is of little moment is indicated by decisions upholding clauses that the parties have labelled as penalty clauses [47] and striking down clauses which parties have labelled as providing for liquidated damages.[48] Moreover, even if it be shown that the parties conscientiously intended to provide for liquidated damages, the clause will be struck down if the amount stipulated is out of proportion to the probable injury.[49] Significantly, neither U.C.C. § 2–718 nor Section 356 of the new Restatement considers the question of intention to be relevant on the issue.

(b) Injury Uncertain or Difficult to Quantify

Traditionally courts have stated that as a prerequisite to upholding a liquidated damages clause, damages must be uncertain. Professor MacNeill has isolated five kinds of uncertainty: [50]

> (1) Difficulty of *producing proof* of damages from a breach after it has occurred. (2) Difficulty of determining what damages were caused by the breach. (3) Difficulty of ascertaining what damages were contemplated when the contract was made. (4) Absence of any standardized measure of damages for a certain breach. (5) Difficulty of forecasting, when the contract was made, all the *possible* damages which may be caused (or occasioned) by any of the possible breaches.

Despite the wealth of potential suggested by this analysis, the criterion of uncertainty has been little explored and been seldom decisive. Frequently, liquidated damages clauses have been upheld although actual damages are readily calculable.[51] The language of the U.C.C. and of the Second Restatement speaks not of uncertainty but of "the difficulties of proof of loss." [52] Whether this represents a substantive

---

46. This is convincingly demonstrated in McCormick, Damages §§ 148–149; Crowley, supra note 41, at 60–66.

47. United States v. Bethlehem Steel Corp., 205 U.S. 105, 27 S.Ct. 450, 51 L.Ed. 731 (1907); Pierce v. Fuller, 8 Mass. 223 (1811); Tode v. Gross, 127 N.Y. 480, 28 N.E. 469, 13 L.R.A. 652 (1891). But see Berger v. Shanahan, 142 Conn. 726, 118 A.2d 311 (1955), where intention is heavily emphasized.

48. Caesar v. Rubinson, 174 N.Y. 492, 67 N.E. 58 (1903); Seeman v. Biemann, 108 Wis. 365, 84 N.W. 490 (1900).

49. J. Weinstein & Sons v. New York, 264 App.Div. 398, 35 N.Y.S.2d 530 (1st Dep't), affirmed 289 N.Y. 741, 46 N.E.2d 351 (1942); Corbin § 1058.

50. Macneil, supra note 41, at 502 (emphasis in original; footnote omitted).

51. Callanan Road Improvement Co. v. Colonial Sand & Stone Co., 190 Misc. 418, 72 N.Y.S.2d 194 (Sup.Ct.1947) (excellent discussion). For additional cases see McCormick, Damages 605–06; Clarkson, Miller & Muris, supra note 41, at 354–55; Northwestern Comment, supra note 41, at 1064–65.

52. Restatement, Second, Contracts § 356(1); U.C.C. § 2–718(1).

change from pre-existing law is uncertain.[53] Although not many cases have appeared to turn on the criterion of uncertainty,[54] it is nonetheless true that a liquidated damages clause is most useful to the parties and most likely to be upheld in cases where actual damages are most difficult to prove, as in the case of a covenant not to compete ancillary to the sale of a business.[55]

(c) Reasonableness

A provision containing an unreasonably high liquidated damages clause is void as a penalty. Until enactment of the U.C.C. there was almost general agreement that reasonableness ordinarily must be judged as of the time of contracting rather than as of the time of the breach. The Uniform Commercial Code and the new Restatement take the view that reasonableness should be tested "in the light of the anticipated or actual" loss.[56] Thus, contrary to prior doctrine, there are two moments at which the liquidated damages clause may be judged rather than just one.[57] This change clearly works in favor of more frequent enforceability of agreed damages clauses.

Under both the more traditional and newer views it would appear that if a substantial penalty clause was a reasonable pre-estimate of the harm likely to be caused by a breach, it should be enforced even if no damage ensues. Some cases have so held.[58] Others have ruled that under such extreme circumstances the general rule should not be followed.[59] The new Restatement indicates that the latter cases are sound because the actual loss (or rather absence of loss) can be readily proved.[60] This indicates that to the restaters the difficulty of proof is to be examined at the time of trial rather than at the time of contracting.

---

53. See Fordham Comment, supra note 41, at 1358–63; Northwestern Comment, supra note 41, at 1063–65. See text at notes 58–60 infra.

54. See note 51 supra.

55. Jaquith v. Hudson, 5 Mich. 123 (1858), which contains one of the better discussions of the relative significance of intention, uncertainty and disproportion, is such a case; Henshaw v. Kroenecke, 656 S.W.2d 416 (Tex.1983), on remand 671 S.W. 2d 117 (Tex.App.1984) (ancillary to partnership agreement); Robbins v. Finlay, 645 P.2d 623 (Utah 1982) (covenant not to use customer leads).

56. U.C.C. § 2–718(1); Restatement, Second, Contracts § 356(1).

57. Equitable Lumber Corp. v. IPA Land Development Corp., 38 N.Y.2d 516, 381 N.Y.S.2d 459, 344 N.E.2d 391 (1976).

58. Gaines v. Jones, 486 F.2d 39 (8th Cir.1973), cert. denied 415 U.S. 919, 94 S.Ct. 1418, 39 L.Ed.2d 474 (1974) (dictum); Southwest Eng'r Co. v. United States, 341 F.2d 998 (8th Cir.1965), cert. denied 382

U.S. 819, 86 S.Ct. 45, 15 L.Ed.2d 66 (1965); Frick Co. v. Rubel Corp., 62 F.2d 765 (2d Cir.1933) (evidence of lack of any actual damages was excluded, an erroneous decision because under any view such evidence should be admissible as bearing on what losses were foreseeable); Blackwood v. Liebke, 87 Ark. 545, 113 S.W. 210 (1908); McCarthy v. Tally, 46 Cal.2d 577, 297 P.2d 981 (1956), noted in 9 Stan.L.Rev. 381 (1957).

59. Massman Const. Co. v. Greenville, 147 F.2d 925 (5th Cir.1945) (one factor in decision); Rispin v. Midnight Oil Co., 291 Fed. 481, 34 A.L.R. 1331 (9th Cir.1923); Norwalk Door Closer Co. v. Eagle Lock & Screw Co., 153 Conn. 681, 220 A.2d 263 (1966); McCann v. Albany, 158 N.Y. 634, 53 N.E. 673 (1899). Such cases are criticized in Crowley, supra note 41, at 64; and are discussed with approval in Macneil, supra note 41, at 504–509.

60. Restatement, Second, Contracts § 356, ill. 4; but see Reporter's Notes to Comment b.

Prior law has been in conflict as to the proper moment for testing uncertainty of damages, although the prevailing view appears to be that the proper moment is the time of contracting.[61]

The phrases "actual harm" or "actual loss" are ambiguous. Do they include injury not compensable as damages because of the rules of foreseeability, certainty and mitigation? There is no definitive answer.[62] It is submitted that "actual harm" means all harm, whether or not compensable in the absence of an agreed damages clause.[63]

Even if no actual harm flows from the breach the facts should be scrutinized to determine if the breaching party would be unjustly enriched by the breach,[64] as where a seller has been paid a premium price for prompt delivery, but delivers tardily with no actual injury to the buyer.[65]

It is not a requirement that the liquidated damages clause be expressed by a liquidated sum. A formula for its calculation is sufficient.[66]

When the parties' agreement sets damages at a sum disproportionately *lower* than the foreseeable or actual harm the clause is not viewed as a penalty. It may, however, be struck down as unconscionable.[67]

It is generally held that the burden of proof that the agreed damages clause is disproportionate to the foreseeable (or actual) harm is on the defendant.[68]

 WESTLAW REFERENCES

contract agree**** /s penal! /s equity /s enforc! unenforc!
    void! avoid!

"liquidated damage" /s penal! /s distinct! distinguish!

115k163(3)

"liquidated damage clause" /s unenforc!

61. Northwestern Comment, supra note 41, at 1065–69.

62. See Fordham Comment, supra note 41, at 1357.

63. So held in Wassenaar v. Panos, 111 Wis.2d 518, 331 N.W.2d 357 (1983).

64. Berger v. Shanahan, 142 Conn. 726, 118 A.2d 311 (1955).

65. United States v. Bethlehem Steel Co., 205 U.S. 105, 27 S.Ct. 450, 51 L.Ed. 731 (1907). It should be noted that although it is common to speak of penalty clauses and penalty bonds in government contracts, such clauses are valid in the absence of a specific statute, only if they conform to the requirements of liquidated damage clauses generally. Priebe & Sons, Inc. v. United States, 332 U.S. 407, 68 S.Ct. 123, 92 L.Ed. 32 (1947); City of Rye v. Public Service Mut. Life Ins. Co., 34 N.Y.2d 470, 358 N.Y.S.2d 391, 315 N.E.2d 458 (1974); see Gantt & Breslauer, Liquidated Damages in Federal Government & Contracts, 47

B.U.L.Rev. 71 (1967); Peckar, Liquidated Damages in Federal Construction Contracts: Time or a New Approach, 5 Public Contract L.J. 129 (1972).

66. Dave Gufstafson & Co. v. State, 83 S.D. 160, 156 N.W.2d 185 (1968); see Sweet, supra note 41, at 120–24.

67. U.C.C. § 2–718, Comment 1; Morgan Co. v. Minnesota M. & M., 310 Minn. 305, 246 N.W.2d 443 (1976); Wedner v. Fidelity Security Systems, Inc., 228 Pa. Super. 67, 307 A.2d 429 (1973); Restatement, Second, Contracts § 356, Comment 1; but see Bonhard v. Gindin, 104 N.J.L. 599, 142 A. 52 (1928). See generally Fritz, "Underliquidated Damages as Limitation of Liability," 33 Texas L.Rev. 196 (1954); Sweet, supra note 41, at 92–93.

68. Continental Ins. Co. v. Hull, 98 Nev. 542, 654 P.2d 1024 (1982); Wasenaar v. Panos, supra note 63; contra, Utica Mut. Ins. Co. v. Didonato, 187 N.J.Super. 30, 453 A.2d 559 (1982).

"penalty clause" /s refus!

"liquidated damage" /s penal! /s law statut! legislat!

"liquidated damage" /s penal! /s unconscionab!

penal! /s breach! /s deter deterred deterring deterrence

(a) *Intention*

"penalty clause" /s intend! intent!

"liquidated damage clause" /s intend! intent!

"liquidated damage clause" /s disproportion! proportion! injur!

(b) *Injury Uncertain or Difficult to Quantify*

"liquidated damage clause" /s ascertain! unascertain! certain! uncertain! quantif! determin!

"liquidated damage clause" /s proof prove* proving

(c) *Reasonableness*

"liquidated damage clause" /s reasonabl! unreasonabl!

di("liquidated damage clause" /s time moment harm loss)

penalty "liquidated damage" +1 clause /s formula

§ 14–32. Two Pitfalls of Draftsmanship: The Shotgun Clause and the Have Cake and Eat It Clause

Many contracts contain a number of covenants of varying importance. Damages for breach of each of these covenants may vary greatly. Thus a lessee may promise to pay rent, maintain fire insurance, keep the corridors lighted, etc. A clause which stipulates that in the event the lessee breaches the lease a given sum will be paid as liquidated damages (or that a given security deposit will be forfeited), cannot be a reasonable pre-estimate of the loss for breach of each of the lessee's covenants and thus will be deemed a penalty.[69] If such holdings are pressed to their logical conclusions, no liquidated damages clause would be valid because even as to the major covenant a breach may take varying forms.[70] It will often be possible to interpret such a clause so as to confine it to breach of the major covenant in which event if the stipulated sum is a reasonable pre-estimate of the loss for the breach of that covenant the clause will be upheld.[71] It is possible, however, to liquidate damages for specific kinds of harm with a provision for actual damages for other kinds of harm.[72] Under the flexible formulation of the U.C.C. the reasonableness of the clause is to be tested by the anticipated *or* actual harm. Thus, such a clause can be

---

69. Seach v. Richards, Dieterle & Co., 439 N.E.2d 208 (Ind.App.1982); H.J. Mc-Grath Co. v. Wisner, 189 Md. 260, 55 A.2d 793 (1947); Wilt v. Waterfield, 273 S.W.2d 290 (Mo.1954); Lenco, Inc. v. Hirschfeld, 247 N.Y. 44, 159 N.E. 718 (1928); Jolley v. Georgeff, 92 Ohio App. 271, 110 N.E.2d 23 (1952); Management, Inc. v. Schassberger, 39 Wn.2d 321, 235 P.2d 293 (1951).

70. Macneil, supra note 41, at 509–13.

71. Hungerford Const. Co. v. Florida Citrus Exposition, Inc., 410 F.2d 1229 (5th

Cir.1969), cert. denied 396 U.S. 928, 90 S.Ct. 263, 24 L.Ed.2d 276 (1969); Ward v. Haren, 183 Mo.App. 569, 167 S.W. 1064 (1914); Hackenheimer v. Kurtzmann, 235 N.Y. 57, 138 N.E. 735 (1923); Hathaway v. Lynn, 75 Wis. 186, 43 N.W. 956 (1889); cf. Ann Arbor Asphalt Const. Co. v. Howell, 226 Mich. 647, 198 N.W. 195 (1924).

72. Hathaway & Co. v. United States, 249 U.S. 460, 39 S.Ct. 346, 63 L.Ed. 707 (1919).

upheld if it bears a reasonable relationship to the actual consequences of the breach.[73]

Another pitfall into which contract draftsmen have plunged involves an attempt to fix damages in the event of a breach with an option on the part of the aggrieved party to sue for such additional actual damages as he may establish. These have been struck down as they do not involve a reasonable attempt definitively to estimate the loss.[74]

WESTLAW REFERENCES

"shotgun clause"

"liquidated damage" /s breach! /s leas! less**

"liquidated damage" penalty +1 clause /s additional

§ 14–33. Availability of Specific Performance When Damages Are Liquidated

Despite the presence in a contract of a valid liquidated damages clause, if the criteria for equitable relief are met, the court will issue a decree for specific performance. The fact that damages have been liquidated does not give the party who has promised to pay liquidated damages an option to perform the basic agreement or to pay damages at his discretion.[75] In issuing its decree for specific performance a court of equity may also award damages for injury sustained between the period of the breach and the issuance of the decree.[76]

WESTLAW REFERENCES

penalty "liquidated damage" +1 clause /s "specific! perform!"

wirth +s hamid

§ 14–34. Liquidated Damages and Penalties Distinguished From Alternative Promises

If a builder promises to build two houses by a specified day or pay the other $4,000, several interpretations of the agreement are possible. The parties may have regarded their agreement as calling for a firm commitment to build the houses, and on default, the builder is to pay $4,000 as (1) damages or (2) as a penalty. A third interpretation is also

---

73. See Fordham Comment, supra note 41, at 1358.

74. Jarro Building Indus. Corp. v. Schwartz, 54 Misc.2d 13, 281 N.Y.S.2d 420 (Sup.Ct.1967); cf. In re Plywood Co., 425 F.2d 151 (3d Cir.1970), where the court permitted the aggrieved party to retain the agreed amount but disallowed additional damages for the breach of lease. See discussion in Fordham Comment, note 41 supra, at 1369–71.

75. Southeastern Land Fund, Inc. v. Real Estate World, Inc., 237 Ga. 227, 227

S.E.2d 340 (1976); Bauer v. Sawyer, 8 Ill.2d 351, 134 N.E.2d 329 (1956); Rubenstein v. Rubenstein, 23 N.Y.2d 293, 296 N.Y.S.2d 354, 244 N.E.2d 49 (1968); Bradshaw v. Millikin, 173 N.C. 432, 92 S.E. 161, 1917E L.R.A. 880 (1917); 11 Williston § 1444; Fordham Comment, supra note 41, at 1371–72.

76. Wirth & Hamid Fair Booking Co. v. Wirth, 265 N.Y. 214, 192 N.E. 297 (1934).

possible. The parties may have meant that the builder was to have the privilege of not building; the price of this privilege was fixed at $4,000. Thus interpreted the agreement would be an option contract, with a price fixed for the exercise of an option to terminate.[77] Such options are sustained,[78] but the form of the agreement is not controlling. The court must determine whether the parties actually bargained for an option.[79] If the clause was inserted at the request of the party who wishes to terminate the contract, it is likely that an option was intended.[80]

WESTLAW REFERENCES

"liquidated damage" "penalty clause" /s alternative! /s promise

§ 14–35. Additional Agreed Damages: Attorney's Fees

In the United States an award of damages does not ordinarily include reimbursement of the successful party's attorney's fees. The apparent rationale is that a contrary rule would discourage impecunious plaintiffs from prosecuting meritorious claims.[81] It has become common practice for leases, notes and contracts for sale on credit to contain an agreement that if legal fees are incurred in the collection of payments due under the instrument, reasonable attorney's fees will also be payable. The majority of jurisdictions uphold such agreements,[82] thereby permitting recovery of an agreed amount in excess of the damages that would accrue by operation of law.

WESTLAW REFERENCES

di("attorney fee" /s breach! /s contract /s damage)

default! /s pay paying payment paid /s "attorney fee" /s
   collection

default! /s attorney legal +1 fee /s leas!

233k285(9)

"attorney fee" /s reimburs! /s contract breach! default!

77. This was the holding in the fact pattern discussed in the text. Pearson v. Williams' Adm'rs, 24 Wend. 244 (N.Y.1840), which, however, was later affirmed on the theory that the promise to pay was a valid liquidated damages clause. 26 Wend. 630 (N.Y.1841).

78. Pennsylvania Re-Treading Tire Co. v. Goldberg, 305 Ill. 54, 137 N.E. 81 (1922), noted in 32 Yale L.J. 618 (1924) (promise to deliver shares of stock or pay $50,000); Edward G. Acker, Inc. v. Rittenberg, 255 Mass. 599, 152 N.E. 87 (1926) (defendant to give leasehold or pay $4,000); Chandler v. Doran Co., 44 Wn.2d 396, 267 P.2d 907 (1954).

79. Bradford v. New York Times Co., 501 F.2d 51 (2d Cir.1974).

80. Fordham Comment, supra note 41, at 1373.

81. See Note, Attorney's Fees: Where Shall the Ultimate Burden Lie? 20 Vand. L.Rev. 1216 (1967).

82. Steele v. Vanderslice, 90 Ariz. 277, 367 P.2d 636 (1961); Wilson v. Wilson, 54 Cal.2d 264, 5 Cal.Rptr. 317, 352 P.2d 725 (1960); Puget Sound Mut. Sav. Bank v. Lillions, 50 Wn.2d 799, 314 P.2d 935 (1957), cert. denied 357 U.S. 926, 78 S.Ct. 1373, 2 L.Ed.2d 1371 (1958); Restatement, Second, Contracts § 356, Comment d.

Chapter 15

RESTITUTION AS A REMEDY
FOR BREACH

Table of Sections

§ 15–1. Introduction

While the aim of the law of contract damages is generally to place the aggrieved party in the same economic position he would have had if the contract had been performed, the aim of restitution is to place both of the parties in the position they had prior to entering into the transaction. Throughout this volume reference has been made to the availability in particular circumstances of a quasi-contractual or other restitutionary recovery. The availability of such remedies has been discussed or alluded to in the context of performance pursuant to agreements that are too indefinite to constitute contracts,[1] agreements made by persons lacking full contractual capacity,[2] contracts that are avoided because of duress, undue influence, misrepresentation or mistake,[3] contracts that are unenforceable because of the Statute of Frauds,[4] contracts that are discharged because of impossibility of performance or frustration of the venture,[5] agreements that are illegal,[6] and situations in which a defaulting plaintiff seeks to recover for part performance.[7]

1. See § 2–9 supra.

2. See §§ 8–8, 8–13 supra.

3. See ch. 9 supra.

4. See §§ 19–40 to 19–45 infra.

5. See § 13–23 supra.

6. See ch. 22 infra.

7. See § 11–22 supra.

This chapter has a twofold objective: first, to discuss briefly the common principles which underlie the law of restitution; and second, to discuss restitution as an alternative remedy for breach of contract.

§ 15–2. What Is Meant by Restitution? The Concept of Unjust Enrichment

As the term is generally used today, "restitution" has a very flexible meaning.[8] It encompasses recovery in quasi contract in which form of action the plaintiff recovers a money judgment.[9] It is also used to encompass equitable remedies for specific relief such as decrees which cancel deeds [10] or impose constructive trusts or equitable liens as well as some recoveries in equity for sums of money.

The common thread which draws these actions together is that "one person is accountable to another on the ground that otherwise he would unjustly benefit or the other would unjustly suffer loss." [11] At the core of the law of restitution is the principal that "A person who has been unjustly enriched at the expense of another is required to make restitution to the other. * * *" [12] It should be emphasized, however, that this is a principle which underlies many particular rules rather than an operative rule.[13] Taken as a rule it would at the same time be too broad and too narrow. Too broad, because there are situations in which one's sense of justice would urge that unjust enrichment has occurred, yet no relief is available. Too narrow, because very often restitution is available where there has been no enrichment of the defendant but the plaintiff has suffered a loss. For example, where the plaintiff seeks restitution for the value of his performance pursuant to a contract unenforceable under the Statute of Frauds, the measure of recovery is ordinarily the losses sustained by the plaintiff (but not the gains prevented) as a result of the breach.[14] Not infrequently, however, this result is articulated in manipulative terms by artificially labelling the losses sustained by the plaintiff as benefits conferred upon the defendant.[15] In other contexts, however, such as in those limited areas where the plaintiff may recover for benefits conferred upon another without request, courts are rather

---

8. See Comment, Restitution: Concept and Terms, 19 Hastings L.J. 1167 (1968). Modern general works on restitution are Douthwaite, Attorney's Guide to Restitution (1977); Goff 8c Jones, Law of Restitution (2d ed. 1978); Palmer, The Law of Restitution (4 vols. 1978).

9. See § 1–12 supra.

10. See § 15–5 infra.

11. See Restatement, Restitution p. 1 (1937); see also Restatement, Second, Restitution Ch. 1 (Tent.Draft No. 1, 1983).

12. Restatement, Restitution p. 1 (1937).

13. Restatement, Restitution p. 11 (1937).

14. See § 19–44 infra.

15. See Childres & Garamella, The Law of Restitution and The Reliance Interest in Contract, 64 Nw.U.L.Rev. 433 (1969); Dawson, Restitution without Enrichment, 61 B.U.L.Rev. 563, esp. 577–85 (1981); Perillo, Restitution in a Contractual Context, 73 Colum.L.Rev. 1208 (1973); Sullivan, The Concept of Benefit in the Law of Quasi-Contract, 64 Geo.L.J. 1 (1975).

strict in seeking to limit recovery to the amount by which the defendant has actually been enriched.[16]

WESTLAW REFERENCES

digest(restitution /s quasi /s "unjust! enrich!")

205hk4

di restitution

restitution /s define* definition

restitution /s unjust! /2 benefit! suffer!

restitution /s "statute of frauds"

§ 15–3. Restitution as an Alternative Remedy for Breach

Restitution is not available as a remedy for partial breach.[17] In the event of total breach of contract, the aggrieved party may cancel the contract and pursue his remedies, one of which is restitution. In former times, if he sued for damages he was deemed to be seeking to enforce the contract. If he decided to obtain restitution it was deemed that he elected to rescind the contract and pursue a quasi-contractual remedy not based on the contract. Although for a considerable number of decades it has been recognized that the right to damages or restitution are both remedial rights based on the contract,[18] the older view that an action for restitution is not based on the contract has left its imprint on the rules governing the availability, and measure, of recovery under this remedy. Thus, for restitution to be available, it was the rule that the plaintiff must give prompt notice that he cancels (under older terminology, "rescinds" or "disaffirms") the contract.[19] He may cancel only if the breach may be characterized as a total breach.[20]

16. Discussion of recovery for benefits conferred without request is outside the scope of this volume. An illustration of such a recovery is restitution awarded against a parent to one who unofficiously supplies necessaries to an infant. Greenspan v. Slate, 12 N.J. 426, 97 A.2d 390 (1953); Note, 39 Cornell L.Q. 337 (1954). See generally, Wade, Restitution for Benefits Conferred Without Request, 19 Vanderbilt L.Rev. 1183 (1966); 2 Palmer on Restitution §§ 10–1 to 10–11.

17. United States for the use of Building Rentals Corp. v. Western Casualty & Surety Co., 498 F.2d 335 (9th Cir.1974); Rudd Paint & Varnish Co. v. White, 403 F.2d 289 (10th Cir.1968); 5 Corbin § 1104.

18. See 5 Corbin § 1106; Woodward, Quasi Contracts § 260 (1913). The argument whether an action for restitution based on breach is a contract remedy or a quasi-contractual action is not devoid of practical significance. For example, the United States has not waived its immunity under the Tucker Act as to quasi-contractual actions. Knight Newspapers, Inc. v.

United States, 395 F.2d 353 (6th Cir.1968). An action for restitution based on breach may, however, be brought under the Act, Acme Process Equip. Co. v. United States, 171 Ct.Cl. 324, 347 F.2d 509 (1965), cert. granted 384 U.S. 917, 86 S.Ct. 1367, 16 L.Ed.2d 438 (1966), on the theory that the action is on the contract. Rev'd on other grounds 385 U.S. 138, 87 S.Ct. 350, 17 L.Ed. 2d 249 (1966), reh. denied 385 U.S. 1032, 87 S.Ct. 738, 17 L.Ed.2d 680 (1967). For the confused state of the law with respect to restitutionary claims against the government, see Wall & Childres, The Law of Restitution and the Federal Government, 66 Nw.U.L.Rev. 587 (1971).

19. 12 Williston § 1469; Woodward, supra note 18, at 429; accord, U.C.C. § 2–602(1) (notice of rejection by buyer); U.C.C. § 2–608(2) (notice of revocation of acceptance).

20. Buffalo Builder's Supply Co. v. Reeb, 247 N.Y. 170, 159 N.E. 899 (1928); Sidney Stevens Imp. Co. v. Hintze, 92 Utah 264, 67 P.2d 632, 111 A.L.R. 331 (1937); Harris v. Metropolitan Mall, 112 Wis.2d

Such notice is now required, however, only if the plaintiff retains some tangible benefit from the contract,[21] or failure to give notice operates as a waiver of condition.[22] Indeed, some courts have gone further. Judge Cardozo put the rule in this fashion: "notice may be given at any time within the period of the Statute of Limitations unless delay would be inequitable."[23] The standard imposed by the Uniform Commercial Code appears to be stricter; goods must be rejected "within a reasonable time after their delivery or tender"[24] and a revocation of acceptance "must occur within a reasonable time after the buyer discovers or should have discovered the ground for it."[25]

The use of the term "rescission" to describe the notice of cancellation of the contract should be avoided. The legal relations resulting from a mutual rescission and from a decision by an aggrieved party to cancel the contract are quite distinct, but have often been confused because of the semantic trap caused by utilization of the same term to describe distinct concepts. The Uniform Commercial Code avoids this difficulty by adopting the term "cancel."[26]

As a prerequisite to an action for restitution, at common law the plaintiff was required to tender[27] back all tangible benefits he had received pursuant to the contract as a condition to commencement of the action.[28] In equity, however, actual tender was not always required, as a court of equity could condition its decree upon restitution by the plaintiff or offset the value of the benefits retained.[29] Today, in a good number of jurisdictions the equity rule has now been adopted at law.[30] Although the Restatement (Second) § 384 continues to require an offer (but not a tender) by the plaintiff to make restoration, it provides for a number of exceptions.

487, 334 N.W.2d 519 (1983); cf. Rosenwasser v. Blyn Shoes, Inc., 246 N.Y. 340, 159 N.E. 84 (1927); 5 Corbin § 1104; Woodward, supra note 18 at, § 263.

For a discussion of total breach, see § 11–18 supra.

21. Ripley v. Hazelton, 3 Daly (N.Y.) 329 (1870).

22. United States for Use and Benefit of Harkol v. Americo Constr. Co., 168 F.Supp. 760 (D.Mass.1958); Crofoot Lumber, Inc. v. Thompson, 163 Cal.App.2d 324, 329 P.2d 302 (1958); Restatement, Contracts § 353; 5 Corbin § 1104.

23. Richard v. Credit Suisse, 242 N.Y. 346, 351, 152 N.E. 110, 111, 45 A.L.R. 1041, 1044 (1926). On the question of inequitable delay, see Schwartz v. National Computer Corp., 42 A.D.2d 123, 345 N.Y.S.2d 579 (1st Dep't 1973).

24. U.C.C. § 2–602(1).

25. U.C.C. § 2–608(2).

26. U.C.C. §§ 2–106(4), 2–703(f), 2–711(1); see also § 21–2 infra.

27. The Restatement, Contracts § 349, avoids the technical term "tender" and requires merely an offer to return. The Uniform Commercial Code requires neither a tender nor an offer to return. The buyer must merely hold the goods at the seller's disposition. U.C.C. § 2–602(2)(b).

28. Woodward, supra note 18, at § 265. As a corollary to this rule a plaintiff who had received intangible benefits, such as services, could not bring an action at law for restitution. This is no longer the prevailing view. Timmerman v. Stanley, 123 Ga. 850, 51 S.E. 760 1, L.R.A.,N.S., 379 (1905); Brown v. Woodbury, 183 Mass. 279, 67 N.E. 327 (1903); Bollenback v. Continental Casualty Co., 243 Or. 498, 414 P.2d 802 (1966).

29. See Holdeen v. Rinaldo, 28 A.D.2d 947, 281 N.Y.S.2d 657 (3d Dep't 1967); Sneed v. State, 683 P.2d 525 (Okl.1983); 5 Corbin §§ 1102–1103, 1115–1116; 12 Williston §§ 1460, 1460A, 1463.

30. See 5 Corbin §§ 1102–1103, 1115–1116; 12 Williston § 1460.

WESTLAW REFERENCES

restitution /s partial! total! +1 breach!

restitution /s remedy! /s breach! /s contract

notice notif! /s 2–602 2–608 /s "uniform commercial code" u.c.c.

di(restitution /s tender!)

di(restitution /s restor! /s contract)

restitution /s off-set! set-off

restitution /s equit! /s contract

§ 15–4. Measure of Recovery in an Action for Restitution Based on Breach

The basic aim of restitution is to place the plaintiff in the same economic position as he enjoyed prior to contracting. Thus, unless specific restitution is obtained, the plaintiff's recovery is for the reasonable value of services rendered, goods delivered, or property conveyed less the reasonable value of any counter-performance received by him.[31] The plaintiff recovers the reasonable value of his performance whether or not the defendant in any economic sense benefited from the performance.[32] The quasi-contractual concept of benefit continues to be recognized by the rule that the defendant must have received the plaintiff's performance. Traditionally it has been said that acts merely preparatory to performance will not justify an action for restitution.[33] "Receipt," however, is a legal concept rather than a description of physical fact. If what the plaintiff has done is part of the agreed exchange, it is deemed to be "received" by the defendant.[34]

As stated elsewhere, the trend of the law is to go beyond the benefit concept:

> When the plaintiff has expended funds, rendered services, or otherwise diminished his own estate in performing or preparing to perform an agreement that has since failed, but has not conferred a benefit on the defendant, the cutting edge of the case law has allowed recovery of these expenses. Often courts have accomplished this by legal alchemy, transmuting reliance damages into "benefits conferred" simply by so labelling them. Other courts have, with greater candor, expressly protected the reliance interest in restitution actions.[35] (Citations omitted).

31. Woodward, supra note 18, at § 268. When an insured sues for restitution of premiums because his insurer wrongfully refuses to pay a claim, the cases are divided on the question of whether a deduction should be made for the value of coverage the insured has had. See Bollenback v. Continental Cas. Co., 243 Or. 498, 414 P.2d 802 (1966) (collecting cases).

32. United States v. Zara Contracting Co., 146 F.2d 606 (2d Cir.1944); Schwasnik v. Blandin, 65 F.2d 354 (2d Cir.1933); Rogers v. Becker-Brainard Milling Mach. Co., 211 Mass. 559, 98 N.E. 592 (1912); Mooney v. York Iron Co., 82 Mich. 263, 46 N.W. 376 (1890); Robertus v. Candee, ___ Mont. ___, 670 P.2d 540 (1983); see Restatement, Second, Contracts § 371.

33. Restatement, Contracts § 348; Restatement, Second, Contracts § 370.

34. Farash v. Sykes Datatronics, Inc., 59 N.Y.2d 500, 465 N.Y.S.2d 917, 452 N.E.2d 1245 (1983); Restatement, Contracts § 348, Comment a; Restatement, Second, Contracts § 370, Comment a.

35. Perillo, Restitution in the Second Restatement of Contracts, 81 Colum.L.Rev.

By the weight of authority the plaintiff is not restricted to the contract rate of payment although the contract price is admissible as evidence of the value of his performance.[36] Thus, in Boomer v. Muir,[37] the plaintiff on a construction project justifiably cancelled because of the defendant's breach. Had he completed the work he would have been entitled to an additional payment of $20,000. Rather than sue for damages, however, the plaintiff elected at trial to sue for restitution. Judgment entered upon a verdict in the amount of $257,965.06 was affirmed on appeal. Some observers have regarded results such as this as an unwarranted disturbance of the risks assumed by the parties and argue that the contract rate should set an upper limit [38] or that the claimant be relegated to obtaining expectancy damages.[39] Others have justified such results by pointing out either that the wrongdoer must take the consequences of his own wrongdoing,[40] or that the party who has breached should not be permitted to seek the protection of the contract.[41]

The Restatement (Second) states that restitution is available only if the benefit is conferred by the plaintiff. "It is not enough that it was simply derived from the breach." [42] The comments offer the illustration of an employee, A, who in violation of his obligation to his employer, B, not to work for anyone else, takes a part-time job with C. B cannot recover from A the salary paid by C, "because it [is] not a benefit conferred by B." [43] While the illustration is sound, the rule must be supplemented by exceptions existing beyond the borderland of traditional contract scholarship, such as those contained in the Restatements of Agency and Restitution. Three sections of the Restatement of Agency deal with such exceptions.[44] The rule is that an employer may recover a bribe received by an employee.[45] Employees and others in fiduciary or confidential relationships must disgorge any other benefits

37, 39 (1981). A more recent example of legal alchemy is Petrie-Clemons v. Butterfield, 122 N.H. 120, 441 A.2d 1167 (1982).

36. United States for the use of Building Rentals Corp. v. Western Cas. & Surety Co., 498 F.2d 335 (9th Cir.1974). See Palmer, The Contract Price as a Limit on Restitution for Defendant's Breach, 20 Ohio St. L.J. 264 (1959).

37. 24 P.2d 570 (Cal.App.1933), hearing dismissed.

38. Childres & Garamella, The Law of Restitution and the Reliance Interest in Contract, 64 Nw.U.L.R. 433 (1969); Perillo, Restitution in the Second Restatement of Contracts, 81 Colum.L.Rev. 37, 44–45 (1981).

39. Mather, Restitution as a Remedy for Breach of Contract: The Case of the Partially Performing Seller, 92 Yale L.J. 14 (1982).

40. Palmer supra note 36, at 269–73.

41. Gegan, In Defense of Restitution: A Comment on Mather, Restitution as a Remedy for Breach of Contract: The Case of the Partially Performing Seller, 57 S.Cal.L.Rev. 723 (1984).

42. Restatement, Second, Contracts § 370, Comment a.

43. Restatement, Second, Contracts § 370, ill.4.

44. Restatement, Second, Agency §§ 403, 404, 404A.

45. Lamdin v. Broadway Surface Advertising, 272 N.Y. 133, 5 N.E.2d 66 (1936) (restitution at law); Fuchs v. Bidwill, 31 Ill.App.3d 567, 334 N.E.2d 117 (1975), reversed on other grounds 63 Ill.2d 503, 3 Ill. Dec. 748, 359 N.E.2d 158 (1976) (constructive trust in equity); Restatement, Second, Agency § 403; Restatement, Restitution § 197.

received by them in breach of trust.[46] Other exceptions to the Restatement "source of benefit" rule exist and, though sporadic, arise frequently enough to suggest that there are a residuum of cases in which the most appropriate remedy is restitution by the breaching party of ill gotten gains obtained from the breach.[47]

WESTLAW REFERENCES

restitution /s "reasonabl! valu!"

prepar! /s perform! /s restitution

restitution /s contract +1 rate price

restatement /s restitution /s confer! /s benefit

restitution /s fiduciary /s benefit

§ 15–5. Specific Restitution

At times an equitable decree for specific restitution is available for breach of contract. All the requisites of an action at law for restitution must be present except that it is not a precondition to a suit that the plaintiff have offered to restore what he has received under the contract.[48] In addition to the prerequisites for an action of law, the traditional rule has been that the plaintiff must show the inadequacy of the legal remedy.[49] The new Restatement dispenses with this requirement,[50] but there is little or no authority for this dispensation.

Inadequacy of the legal remedy may exist because property transferred by the plaintiff is unique. While in an action for specific performance, real property is treated as unique, it is not normally so treated in an action for specific restitution. Since the plaintiff was willing to part with the property, it normally cannot be said that it has unique value to him.[51] Therefore specific restitution in the form of cancellation of a deed is not normally available [52] against a defaulting purchaser. Another reason commonly given for denial of such relief is that the grantor could have protected himself by a condition in the deed or by taking back a purchase money mortgage.[53] Nevertheless, if special circumstances exist, such relief is available. Thus, if real

46. Raestle v. Whitson, 119 Ariz. 524, 582 P.2d 170 (1978); Meinhard v. Salmon, 249 N.Y. 458, 164 N.E. 545, 62 A.L.R. 1 (1928); 4 Palmer on Restitution § 21.7.

47. Snepp v. United States, 444 U.S. 507, 100 S.Ct. 763, 62 L.Ed.2d 704 (1980); 4 Palmer on Restitution § 4.9; Farnsworth, Your Loss or My Gain? The Dilemma of the Disgorgement Principle in Breach of Contract, 94 Yale L.J. 1339 (1985); Jones, The Recovery of Benefits Gained from Breach of Contract, 99 L.Q.Rev. 443 (1983). An economic justification for such results is given in Kronman, Specific Performance, 45 U.Chi.L.Rev. 351, 376–82 (1978).

48. Restatement, Contracts § 354(b); see § 15–3 supra.

49. Restatement, Contracts § 354.

50. Restatement, Second, Contracts § 372, but see Comment b as to land transactions. See Perillo, Restitution in the Second Restatement of Contracts, 81 Colum.L.Rev. 37, 47–49 (1981).

51. Restatement, Contracts § 354, Comment b; 5 Corbin § 1120.

52. 12 Williston § 1456.

53. City of Cleveland v. Herron, 102 Ohio St. 218, 131 N.E. 489 (1921); see Comment, Specific Restitution of the Title to Land upon Failure of Consideration in a Contract for the Sale of Land, 46 Chi.-Kent L.Rev. 197 (1969). Similarly a purchaser is usually denied restitution on a real property transaction for failure of title on the ground he should have protected himself by insisting on warranties. Comment,

property is transferred in exchange for a life support promise, specific restitution has generally been permitted for total breach of the promise.[54] Where there has been an agreement to exchange parcels of land, and the legal remedy has been shown to be inadequate, restitution has been granted.[55] Also, mineral leases have been cancelled where the lessee has breached its promise to develop the tract.[56] In one case, land was transferred in exchange for a promise that the land would be subdivided and developed and a portion of the land would be reconveyed to the original grantor. Specific restitution was ordered.[57] In most of these cases the legal remedy is deemed inadequate because of the speculative nature of the damages suffered.

Specific restitution of personalty is also available where the legal remedy is inadequate. Thus, where the holder of a patent assigns it to another in consideration of a share of profits to be earned from its exploitation, he may have specific restitution for total breach by the assignee.[58] The remedy of damages would be inadequate because damages cannot be proved with sufficient certainty. Although monetary restitution for the value of the patent is more susceptible to proof, the seller evinced no intent to transfer his patent for a cash price. A denial of specific restitution would transmute the contract to a cash sale. Restitution of shares of stock issued under a stock option plan has been ordered when a contrary result would destroy the purpose of the stock option plan.[59] Such restitution has also been permitted where the transfer of stock has resulted in a change of corporate control.[60] Of course, here, as elsewhere, the breach must go to the essence of the contract. The Uniform Commercial Code is silent on the question of whether a seller may reclaim goods for a breach other than insolvency. When payment is due on delivery of goods and payment is demanded, the buyer's "right as against the seller to retain or dispose of them is conditional upon his making the payment due." [61] Consequently, it has been suggested that under this provision if the seller is given a check which is dishonored, he may have specific restitution by replevying the

Remedies for Failure of Title Other Than a Suit on the Covenants, 18 Baylor L.Rev. 92 (1966).

54. Restatement, Second, Contracts § 372, ill. 3; Caramini v. Tegulias, 121 Conn. 548, 186 A. 482, 112 A.L.R. 666 (1936); Yuhas v. Schmidt, 434 Pa. 447, 258 A.2d 616 (1969). An equitable lien has sometimes been imposed instead of cancellation of the deed. See Coykendall v. Kellogg, 50 N.D. 857, 198 N.W. 472 (1924).

55. Restatement, Second, Contracts § 372, ill. 2; Graves v. White, 87 N.Y. 463 (1882); Piper v. Queeney, 282 Pa. 135, 127 A. 474 (1925).

56. Sauder v. Mid-Continent Petroleum Corp., 292 U.S. 272, 54 S.Ct. 671, 78 L.Ed.

1255, 93 A.L.R. 454 (1934); Leonard v. Carter, 389 S.W.2d 147 (Tex.Civ.App.1965), error dismissed.

57. Benassi v. Harris, 147 Conn. 451, 162 A.2d 521 (1960); see also Sneed v. State, 683 P.2d 525 (Okl.1983).

58. Alder v. Drudis, 30 Cal.2d 372, 182 P.2d 195 (1947); Restatement, Contracts § 354, ill. 7.

59. Maytag Co. v. Alward, 235 Iowa 455, 112 N.W.2d 654, 96 A.L.R.2d 162 (1962).

60. Callanan v. Powers, 199 N.Y. 268, 92 N.E. 747 (1910). See also Restatement, Second, Contracts § 372, ill. 5.

61. U.C.C. § 2–507(2).

goods.[62] Whether, in transactions governed by the U.C.C., specific restitution is available based on the inadequacy of the legal remedy because the goods are unique is an open question.[63]

Often the inadequacy of the legal remedy is predicated upon the insolvency of the defendant and the consequent inability to obtain satisfaction of a money judgment. Equity will grant specific restitution in such cases provided, however, that the interests of other creditors will not be adversely affected.[64] As to sales of goods, the Uniform Commercial Code contains specific provisions with respect to insolvency. Section 2–702(2) provides, in part, that:

> Where the seller discovers that the buyer has received goods on credit while insolvent he may reclaim the goods upon demand made within ten days after the receipt, but if misrepresentation of solvency has been made to the particular seller in writing within three months before delivery the ten day limitation does not apply.

Both under common law [65] and under the Uniform Commercial Code,[66] rights of specific restitution are cut off by a sale of property to a bona fide purchaser for value. If the proceeds can be traced, however, to other property, the court may impose a constructive trust or equitable lien upon the other property.[67]

WESTLAW REFERENCES

"specific restitution" /s breach!

"specific restitution" /s tender! return! restor!

"specific restitution" /s land realty (real +1 estate property) deed

"specific restitution" /s "bona fide" bonafide "equitable lien" "constructive trust"

---

§ 15–6. Restitution at Law Not Available if a Debt Has Been Created: Severability

It is an anomaly of the law of restitution that if the plaintiff in Boomer v. Muir, discussed in section 15–4, had completed the performance and was aggrieved by the defendant's failure to pay, his maximum recovery would have been $20,000. It is firmly established that if the plaintiff's performance has created a contract debt in money because of

---

62. Nordstrom, Sales § 166; see also White & Summers, Uniform Commercial Code § 7–15.

63. A negative view is expressed in Nordstrom, Sales § 165 n. 86, apparently on the ground that U.C.C. § 2–703 and related sections contain considered policy decisions as to the rights of sellers, particularly with respect to the rights of other creditors. There is, however, a residuum of special situations that fall outside such considered policy decisions and which can be decided under U.C.C. § 1–103. See, e.g., Alder v. Drudis, 30 Cal.2d 372, 182 P.2d 195 (1947) (restitution of patent rights and

patent models; certainly the models are goods and specific restitution appears to be the most rational remedy).

64. Restatement, Contracts § 354(a), ills. 6, 7.

65. Restatement, Contracts § 354(a).

66. See Nordstrom, Sales § 170.

67. Clark v. McCleery, 115 Iowa 3, 87 N.W. 696 (1901); Matthews v. Crowder, 111 Tenn. 737, 69 S.W. 779 (1902); cf. Restatement, Contracts § 354, ill. 4 (subrogation); cf. Restatement, Second, Contracts § 372, Comment a.

the plaintiff's full performance of his obligations,[68] he may not have restitution.[69] He is restricted to an action for recovery of the debt. No explanation for this rule appears to exist other than such a result appears to have been established early in the history of the writ of indebitatus assumpsit.[70]

An interesting case pointing up the anomaly is Oliver v. Campbell,[71] in which plaintiff, an attorney, was retained as counsel in a divorce action for the agreed fee of $750. At the conclusion of the divorce trial, but before judgment, plaintiff was discharged. The court found that the reasonable value of his services was $5,000. The majority of the court, however, took the position that plaintiff had fully performed and thus could recover only $750, while the dissenting judges were of the opinion that he had not fully performed and was therefore entitled to $5,000.

It also has been stated to be the rule that if any severable portion of the contract has been performed the plaintiff may not obtain restitution as to that portion, but only the apportioned price.[72] Conversely, if the contract is severable, the plaintiff may obtain restitution of the materially breached portions without cancelling those portions which are performed.[73]

It should be noted, however, that the criteria for severability developed in other contexts have not been mechanically applied in this connection. The mere fact that a unit price has been established by contract per ton of coal delivered or per unit of earth excavated should not result in a finding of severability if it appears that the contract price is based on an average of the estimated future market price which fluctuates seasonally or an average value per unit of excavation of ground of varying difficulty, and the plaintiff's deliveries were made during the period when the market price was highest [74] or the ground

---

68. Lynch v. Stebbins, 127 Me. 203, 142 A. 735 (1928); Farron v. Sherwood, 17 N.Y. 227 (1858); 5 Corbin § 1110; Comment, Restitution-Availability as an Alternative Remedy Where Plaintiff Has Fully Performed a Contract to Provide Goods or Services, 57 Mich.L.Rev. 268 (1958).

69. Siebler Heating & Air Conditioning, Inc. v. Jenson, 212 Neb. 830, 326 N.W.2d 182 (1982); Restatement, Second, Contracts § 373(2).

70. Keener, Quasi Contracts 301–02 (1893); Woodward, supra note 18, at 415; cf. 5 Corbin § 1110.

71. 43 Cal.2d 298, 273 P.2d 15 (1954); Matter of Montgomery's Estate, 272 N.Y. 323, 6 N.E.2d 40, 109 A.L.R. 669 (1936) (plaintiff attorney was promised $5,000 for agreed services; after completing five-sixths of the agreed services he was discharged; recovery of $13,000 was sustained).

72. Dibol v. Minott, 9 Iowa 403 (1859); Restatement, Contracts § 351.

73. Czarnikow-Rionda Co. v. West Market Grocery Co., 21 F.2d 309 (2d Cir.1927) cert. denied 275 U.S. 558, 48 S.Ct. 118, 72 L.Ed. 425 (1927); Portfolio v. Rubin, 233 N.Y. 439, 135 N.E. 843 (1922); cf. U.C.C. §§ 2–703, 2–711.

74. Wellston Coal Co. v. Franklin Paper Co., 57 Ohio St. 182, 48 N.E. 888 (1897) (coal has a higher market value in winter); accord, Clark v. Manchester, 51 N.H. 594 (1872) (contract of employment for one year at $25 per month; plaintiff discharged after working during season when wages were generally highest); see also Davidson v. Laughlin, 138 Cal. 320, 71 P. 345, 5 L.R.A.,N.S., 579 (1903); Williams v. Bemis, 108 Mass. 91 (1871).

excavated was of more than average difficulty.[75] The mere fact that a debt has been created will not bar restitution if the claimant was owed other duties under the contract, such as the continuation of a partnership [76] or a reasonable opportunity to be considered for admission to a partnership.[77]

 WESTLAW REFERENCES
restitution /s "indebitatus assumpsit"

§ 15–7. May the Plaintiff Recover Both Damages and Restitution? Common Law Contrasted With U.C.C.

As a general rule a plaintiff may not have both restitution and damages for breach of contract.[78] At some stage he must elect his remedies; [79] the time at which such an election must be made varies with local practice, but the modern tendency is to dispense with the earlier requirement that an election be made in the pleadings.[80]

It should carefully be noted, however, that in an award for damages, the plaintiff's restitutionary interest is usually protected.[81] He is entitled to losses sustained (benefits conferred on the other as well as reliance expenditures) as well as gains prevented. Until the advent of the Uniform Commercial Code, however, in an action for restitution the plaintiff's expectation interest usually received no protection. If defective machinery were delivered to the buyer and if he elected to return the machinery, he was entitled to restitution of payments made and often certain reliance expenditures,[82] but he received no compensation

75. Scaduto v. Orlando, 381 F.2d 587 (2d Cir.1967); Clark v. Mayor of N.Y., 4 N.Y. 338 (1850); Restatement, Contracts § 347, ill. 3. Cf. Palmer, The Contract Price as a Limit on Restitution for Defendant's Breach, 20 Ohio St.L.J. 264, 276 (1959).

76. Nelson v. Gish, 103 Idaho 57, 644 P.2d 980 (1982); Bailey v. Interstate Airmotive, Inc., 358 Mo. 1121, 219 S.W.2d 333, 8 A.L.R.2d 710 (1949). Not all jurisdictions accept this view. See Comment, 57 Mich. L.Rev. 268 (1958).

77. Kovacic, Applying Restitution to Remedy a Discriminatory Denial of Partnership, 34 Syracuse L.Rev. 743 (1983).

78. Downs v. Jersey Central Power & Light Co., 117 N.J.Eq. 138, 174 A. 887 (1934); Pickinpaugh v. Morton, 268 Or. 9, 519 P.2d 91 (1974).

79. For a discussion of what election is most favorable to a plaintiff in one context, see Guittard, Building Contracts: Damages and Restitution, 32 Tex.B.J. 91 (1969).

80. See, e.g. Barron & Holtzoff, Federal Practice and Procedure § 282 (1960); Clark, Code Pleading § 77 (2d ed. 1937); Moore, Federal Practice § 2.06[3] (1967);

Weinstein, Korn and Miller, New York Civil Practice § 3002–04 (1968); Restatement, Second, Contracts § 378.

81. See generally, Fuller & Perdue, The Reliance Interest in Contract Damages, 46 Yale L.J. 52, 373 (1936–37).

82. Freight charges were recovered in International Harvester Co. v. Olson, 62 N.D. 256, 243 N.W. 258 (1932); Houser & Haines Mfg. Co. v. McKay, 53 Wash. 337, 101 P. 894, 27 L.R.A.,N.S., 925 (1909); but see American Paper & Pulp Co. v. Denenberg, 233 F.2d 610 (3d Cir.1956). Expenses incurred in attempting to utilize defective purchases were recovered in Granette Products Co. v. Arthur H. Newmann & Co., 200 Iowa 572, 203 N.W. 935 (1925), modified 200 Iowa 572, 205 N.W. 205 (1925), affirmed 208 Iowa 24, 221 N.W. 197 (1928); National Sand & Gravel Co. v. R.H. Beaumont Co., 9 N.J.Misc. 1026, 156 A. 441 (1931). Consequential damages resulting from personal injuries were recovered in Russo v. Hochschild Kohn & Co., 184 Md. 462, 41 A.2d 600, 157 A.L.R. 1070 (1945). See 12 Williston § 1464; Anderson, Quasi Contractual Recovery in the Law of Sales, 21 Minn.L.Rev. 529 (1937); Rooge, Damages upon Rescission for

for any additional cost of replacing the machinery. Under the Uniform Commercial Code, however, the buyer may exercise the remedy of restitution and recover damages as well.[83] For example, a purchaser of goods may revoke his acceptance upon discovery of a breach of warranty, offer to return the goods, and recover the purchase price plus damages measured by his expectation and reliance interests.[84] It would also appear, although not explicitly, that a seller may recover in restitution for the value of goods delivered and also damages for breach as well.[85]

 WESTLAW REFERENCES

elect*** /s damage /s restitution /s breach!

damage /s "restitution! interest"

2–711 /s "uniform commercial code" u.c.c.

Breach of Warranty, 28 Mich.L.Rev. 26 (1929); Notes, 21 Minn.L.Rev. 111 (1936); 45 Yale L.J. 1313 (1936).

83. U.C.C. § 2–711(1); see Grandi v. Le-Sage, 74 N.M. 799, 399 P.2d 285 (1965).

84. See Nordstrom, Restitution on Default and Article Two of the Uniform Com-

mercial Code, 19 Vand.L.Rev. 1143, 1175 (1966); 1 Palmer on Restitution § 4.15.

85. See Nordstrom supra note 84, at 1151–68; 1 Palmer on Restitution § 4.16.

Chapter 16

SPECIFIC PERFORMANCE AND INJUNCTIONS

Table of Sections

Table of Sections

A. SUBSTANTIVE BASES FOR EQUITABLE RELIEF

B. DEFENSES

C. COVENANTS NOT TO COMPETE

A. SUBSTANTIVE BASES FOR EQUITABLE RELIEF

Table of Sections

§ 16–1. Inadequacy of the Legal Remedy

A legal system can provide redress of various kinds for breach of contract. It can choose to compel a defaulting promisor to perform. While a number of legal systems regard a decree for specific performance to be the ideal and preferred choice, the common law has evolved differently. The primary relief offered in the Anglo-American legal system is substitutionary relief.[1] The primary remedy is damages. Instead of mandating performance of the promise, the value of the promise is substituted. The next preferred remedy is restitution where the value of what has been given in exchange for the promise is substituted for the performance of the promise.[2]

---

1. See Dawson, Specific Performance in France and Germany, 57 Mich.L.Rev. 495 (1959); Farnsworth, Legal Remedies for Breach of Promise, 70 Colum.L.Rev. 1145, 1145–60 (1970); J. Weingarten, Inc. v. Northgate Mall, Inc., 404 So.2d 896 (La. 1981).

2. Delivery Service and Transf. Co. v. Heiner Equip. & Supply Co., 635 P.2d 21 (Utah 1981); but see Restatement, Second, Contracts § 359(3) and Comment c.

The remedy of specific performance is an extraordinary remedy developed in Courts of Equity to provide relief when the legal remedies of damages and restitution are inadequate.[3] A decree for specific performance takes the form of a decree ordering a party affirmatively to carry out his contractual duties or enjoining him from acting where he has a duty of forbearance. At times, a party will merely be enjoined from violating a contract rather than ordered to perform. For example, a seller under an output contract may be enjoined from selling to anyone other than the plaintiff.[4] The court will not be burdened with supervision of performance, but the seller will have every economic incentive to perform. Although there is a variety of methods of enforcing such a decree, its ultimate force derives from the ability of a court of equity to punish violations of its decrees by fines and imprisonment for contempt of court.[5]

Economic analysts have analyzed whether equitable relief produces efficient results. While some analysts stress that specific performance exactly protects the expectancy interest and thus avoids overcompensation and undercompensation,[6] others have warned that the routine grant of specific performance would be inadvisable. They argue that where the cost of full performance exceeds its value to the claimant, the claimant would be in a position to exact "bribe" money for settling the case or, at any rate, that the cost of negotiating a settlement would be excessive and inefficient.[7] They tend to ignore that, in the situation where cost of performance exceeds its value, the breaching party is unjustly enriched if he is relieved of the duty of performance. Why the breaching party's savings should not inure to, or be shared by, the aggrieved party is not at all clear. Whatever the merits of those economic analyses that support the routine grant of equitable relief, the restrictions on equitable relief are so ingrained in our legal system that only a very gradual removal of them is foreseeable.

In those situations where specific performance is routinely given, the claimant's interest in the subject matter is very much akin to a

---

3. Maryland and Massachusetts by statute have broadened the test of equity jurisdiction, permitting specific performance in some cases where, under traditional tests, the legal remedy is adequate. See Van Hecke, Changing Emphases in Specific Performance, 40 N.C.L.Rev. 1, 9–11 (1961).

4. See Restatement, Second, Contracts § 357, ill. 1; but see Florida Jai Alai, Inc. v. Southern Catering Services, Inc., 388 So. 2d 1076 (Fla.App.1980).

5. See McClintock, Handbook of the Principles of Equity § 17 (2d ed. 1948) [hereinafter McClintock].

6. Schwartz, The Case for Specific Performance, 89 Yale L.J. 271 (1979); Linzer, On the Amorality of Contract Remedies— Efficiency, Equity, and the Second Restate- ment, 81 Colum.L.Rev. 111 (1981); Ulen, The Efficiency of Specific Performance, Toward a Unified Theory of Contract Remedies, 83 Mich.L.Rev. 341 (1984); compare Yorio, In Defense of Money Damages for Breach of Contract, 82 Colum.L.Rev. 1365 (1982).

7. Posner, Economic Analysis of Law 95–96 (2d ed. 1977); Kronman, Specific Performance, 45 U.Chi.L.Rev. 351 (1978); Muris, The Cost of Freely Granting Specific Performance, 1982 Duke L.J. 1053. Economic, moral and administrative factors that inform a decision to grant or deny equitable relief are analyzed in Rendleman, The Inadequate Remedy at Law Prerequisite for an Injunction, 33 U.Fla.L.Rev. 346 (1981).

property interest.[8] The other party is not merely subject to a liability to pay damages but must turn over precisely the thing or service promised. The rules pertaining to real property have long recognized this phenomenon, developing the doctrine of equitable conversion to account for the contract purchaser's interest in realty.[9]

The next four sections of this chapter discuss the inadequacy of the legal remedy in contexts where the issue most frequently arises. It should be noted, however, that the legal remedy may be inadequate in any context. For example, a breach of contract to give a film maker screen credits on the film may be redressed by enjoining further release of the film without such credits, partly because the loss of publicity is most difficult to quantify and, if quantified, does not fully repair the injury done.[10] A breach of a unilateral obligation to pay money in installments is best redressed by a decree ordering payments to be made as they mature [11] because the legal remedy redresses only past due breaches of such an obligation.[12] A pre-marital agreement to appear before a rabbinical tribunal in the event of a civil divorce, in order to release the spouse from the religious tie of marriage, has been specifically enforced.[13] Without such appearance the spouse cannot, consistent with religious conscience, remarry. No adequate legal remedy for breach exists.

WESTLAW REFERENCES

"specific! perform!" /s inadequa! /s remedy

358k5

di(contract /p breach! /p equit! /p "specific! perform!") and
  sy(breach /s contract)

contempt /s "specific! perform!"

"specific! perform!" /s "unjust! enrich!"

---

§ 16–2. Inadequacy of the Legal Remedy—Real Property

In Medieval England where one's rank in society was often derived from the nature and quality of one's land holdings, it became established doctrine that each parcel of land and every interest in land was unique. Consequently, the remedy of damages for breach of a contract to convey an interest in land was deemed inadequate. Today, despite the frequently non-unique character of parcels in housing subdivisions, the medieval doctrine still holds. Every interest in land is conclusively presumed to be unique and a contract to convey will be specifically

---

8. See Kronman, supra Note 7.

9. See Cunningham, Stoebuck & Whitman, The Law of Property § 10.13 (1984).

10. Tamarind Lithography Workshop v. Sanders, 143 Cal.App.3d 571, 193 Cal.Rptr. 409 (1983).

11. Tuttle v. Palmer, 117 N.H. 477, 374 A.2d 661 (1977); Teague v. Springfield Life Ins. Co., Inc., 55 N.C.App. 437, 285 S.E.2d 860 (1982).

12. See 12–9 supra.

13. Minkin v. Minkin, 180 N.J.Super. 260, 434 A.2d 665 (1981); Avitzur v. Avitzur, 58 N.Y.2d 108, 459 N.Y.S.2d 572, 446 N.E.2d 136 (1983), cert. denied 464 U.S. 817, 104 S.Ct. 76, 78 L.Ed.2d 88 (1983), noted in 49 Albany L.Rev. 131 (1984), 33 Cath.U.L.Rev. 219 (1983).

enforced,[14] even where the presumptive unique value of the land is rebutted as when the vendee has in turn contracted to resell the interest to a third party.[15] The availability of specific performance is so well established that the law of property has come to look at the contract purchaser as the owner under the doctrine of equitable conversion, a doctrine having numerous practical consequences.[16]

When the vendor's title is discovered to be encumbered, the vendee may nonetheless elect to enforce the contract. The court will decree specific performance with an abatement in price.[17] Although it has been charged that such a decree involves the remaking of the contract, in fact the court is merely tailoring the remedy for breach of contract to fit the situation by enforcing the contract and offsetting damages from the purchase price.[18] Frequently, however, the court will refuse an abatement where the vendee knew of the defect at the time of contracting [19] (on a theory of assumption of the risk or estoppel) or where the nature of the defect is such that only a radically different kind of estate can be conveyed from that contracted for.[20]

WESTLAW REFERENCES

digest((real + 1 property estate) realty land /s inadequa! /s
   remedy)

(real + 1 property estate) realty land /s unique! /s specific!
   + 1 enforc! perform!

specific! + 1 perform! enforc! /s abat! /s price /s title

abat! /s price /s title /s know! knew

§ 16–3. Inadequacy of the Legal Remedy—Personal Property

The Uniform Commercial Code provides in Section 2–716 that "specific performance may be decreed where the goods are unique or in

---

14. Kitchen v. Herring, 42 N.C. (7 Ired Eq.) 190 (1851); Restatement, Contracts § 360(a) and Comment a; Restatement, Second, Contracts § 360, Comment e; DeFuniak, Contracts Enforceable in Equity, 34 Va.L.Rev. 637, 643 (1948); Annot., 65 A.L.R. 7, 40 (1930). Contra, Suchan v. Rutherford, 90 Idaho 288, 410 P.2d 434 (1966); Centex Homes Corp. v. Boag, 128 N.J.Super. 385, 320 A.2d 194 (1974) (condominium apartment deemed not unique), noted in 6 St. Mary's L.Rev. 766 (1975), 9 Suffolk L.Rev. 922 (1975); 48 Temple L.Q. 847 (1975); 43 U.Cin.L.Rev. 935 (1974).

15. Justus v. Clelland, 133 Ariz. 381, 651 P.2d 1206 (1982); Restatement, Contracts § 360, Comment a; Restatement, Second, Contracts § 360, Comment e. De Funiak, supra note 4 at 643. Contra, Marthinson v. King, 150 Fed. 48 (5th Cir.1906).

16. See Cunningham, Stoebuck & Whitman, supra note 9.

17. Wooster Republican Printing Co. v. Channel Seventeen, Inc., 682 F.2d 165 (8th Cir.1982); Fleenor v. Church, 681 P.2d 1351 (Alaska 1984); Atkin v. Cobb, 663 S.W.2d 48 (Tex.App.1983); See Annot. 143 A.L.R. 555 (1943); 5A Corbin § 1160; 11 Williston § 1436; Note, 24 Okl.L.Rev. 495 (1971); Restatement, Contracts § 365. On rare occasions a *vendor* has been granted specific performance with an abatement in an action against a vendee. See Dobbs, Remedies 862 (1973); McClintock at 174–75. See also § 9–26 supra.

18. McClintock at 175.

19. Hughes v. Hadley, 96 N.J.Eq. 467, 126 A. 33 (1924).

20. In re Estate of Hayhurst, 478 P.2d 343 (Okl.1970), 24 Okla.L.Rev. 495 (1971) (vendor had life estate instead of fee); Reid v. Allen, 216 Va. 630, 221 S.E.2d 166 (1976).

other proper circumstances." [21] This rule represents a departure from the more circumscribed rule previously in effect under the Uniform Sales Act. Clearly goods are unique if they are "family heirlooms or priceless works of art," [22] or a stereo system assembled over a period of fifteen years.[23] In addition goods may be deemed "unique" or "other proper circumstances" exist if there is an inability to cover.[24] Inability to cover may exist because of market shortages [25] or because of a monopoly on the part of the defendant.[26] Normally, however, goods are available in the market and damages is an adequate remedy.[27]

Requirements and output contracts have been specifically enforced with some frequency. One reason why this is so is that damages are very difficult to ascertain when goods are to be delivered in installments over a long term.[28]

Contracts for the sale of unique personalty other than goods are also specifically enforceable as the purchaser cannot obtain a substitute performance on the market. Consequently contracts for the transfer of patents,[29] copyrights,[30] or shares in a closely held corporation [31] or sufficient shares to assure control of a corporation whose shares are publicly traded have been specifically enforced.[32] Contracts for the sale

21. On the background and application of this provision, see Axelrod, Specific Performance of Contracts for Sales of Goods: Expansion or Retrenchment in the 1980's, 7 Vt.L.Rev. 249 (1982); Greenberg, Specific Performance under Section 2–716 of the Uniform Commercial Code: "A More Liberal Attitude" in the "Grand Style," 17 New Eng.L.Rev. 321 (1982), reprinted in 87 Comm.L.J. 583 (1982).

22. U.C.C. § 2–716, Comment 1. See 11 Williston § 1419 n. 2.

23. Cumbest v. Harris, 363 So.2d 294 (Miss.1978).

24. U.C.C. § 2–716, Comment 2.

25. Laclede Gas Co. v. Amoco Oil Co., 522 F.2d 33 (8th Cir.1975), appeal after remand 531 F.2d 942 (8th Cir.1976); Mitchell-Huntley Cotton Co., Inc. v. Waldrep, 377 F.Supp. 1215 (D.Ala.1974) (Court orders defendant to pick, gin and deliver cotton crop during market shortage); Kaiser Trading Co. v. Associated Metals & Minerals Corp., 321 F.Supp. 923 (N.D.Cal. 1970), appeal dismissed 443 F.2d 1364 (9th Cir.1971); Glick v. Beer, 263 App.Div. 599, 33 N.Y.S.2d 833 (1st Dep't 1942); see Comment, Remedies—The High Price of Cotton and the Breaching Farmer, 53 N.C.L.Rev. 579 (1975).

26. 11 Williston § 1419. On the right of the seller to sue for the price (a form of specific performance at law), see § 14–26 supra.

27. Pierce-Odom, Inc. v. Evenson, 5 Ark.App. 67, 632 S.W.2d 247 (1982).

28. Laclede Gas Co. v. Amoco Oil Co., 522 F.2d 33 (8th Cir.1975), appeal after remand 531 F.2d 942 (8th Cir.1976); Griffin v. Oklahoma Nat. Gas Corp., 37 F.2d 545 (10th Cir.1930); Hunt Foods v. O'Disho, 98 F.Supp. 267 (N.D.Cal.1951); Eastern Rolling Mill Co. v. Michlovitz, 157 Md. 51, 145 A. 378 (1929); Adalex Laboratories v. Krawitz, 270 P.2d 346 (Okl.1954) (exclusive territorial franchise); 5A Corbin §§ 1147, 1149; 11 Williston § 1419B; Van Hecke, Changing Emphases in Specific Performance, 40 N.C.L.Rev. 1, 4–9 (1961); see U.C.C. § 2–716, Comment 2.

29. Conway v. White, 9 F.2d 863 (2d Cir.1925).

30. Benziger v. Steinhauser, 154 Fed. 151 (2d Cir.1907).

31. Caldwell v. English, 652 P.2d 310 (Okl.App.1982); Owen v. Merts, 240 Ark. 1080, 405 S.W.2d 273, 28 A.L.R.3d 1390 (1966); see 5a Corbin § 1148; Van Hecke, supra note 14, at 1–3.

32. Armstrong v. Stiffler, 189 Md. 630, 56 A.2d 808 (1948). As to the seller's ability to sue for the price of securities, see U.C.C. § 8–107 and the greatly liberalized New York and California versions of the section.

of a business are also often specifically enforced as each business may be deemed unique.[33]

The remedy of replevin is a legal rather than an equitable remedy. When employed as a remedy for breach of contract the result is a form of specific enforcement. The Uniform Commercial Code permits a buyer to replevy goods as a remedy for breach in rather limited circumstances. The goods must have been identified to the contract. In addition the buyer must show either that an attempt to cover has been or will be unavailing or that the goods have been shipped to him under reservation (i.e. the seller has reserved a security interest to help assure payment) and he has made or tendered satisfaction of the security interest.[34]

Although the Code liberalizes the availability of specific relief,[35] it should be stressed that such relief remains the extraordinary rather than the ordinary remedy. In a market economy, the very existence of a market in most kinds of personalty affords a breaching party an opportunity to cover.[36] This includes a situation in which a lender breaches a contract to lend money.[37] Our legal system will almost always withhold specific relief when the opportunity to cover is present. Yet, the entire picture must be considered. In one striking case the court granted specific performance of a stock option agreement, although the plaintiff could have purchased equivalent shares on the market. The court ruled that the special treatment granted by the Internal Revenue Code to securities purchased under stock options made the remedy at law inadequate.[38] The decision is thought-provoking and could, if extended, provide a new basis for equitable relief as the tax consequences of a damages recovery will often be quite different from the tax consequences of specific performance.

 WESTLAW REFERENCES

    specific! +1 enforc! perform! /s unique! /s good

    specific! +1 perform! enforc! /s "uniform sales act"

33. Wooster Republican Printing Co. v. Channel Seventeen Inc., supra Note 17; Leasco Corp. v. Taussig, 473 F.2d 777 (2d Cir.1972); Cochrane v. Szpakowski, 355 Pa. 357, 49 A.2d 692 (1946); Van Hecke, supra note 14, at 3–4; Annot. 82 A.L.R.2d 1102.

34. U.C.C. § 2–716(3); see White & Summers, Uniform Commercial Code 239–240 (2d ed. 1980).

35. For some ingenious hypotheticals, see Comment, 33 U.Pitt.L.Rev. 243 (1971).

36. See generally Farnsworth, supra note 1.

37. Annot., 41 A.L.R. 357 (1926). But see First Nat'l Bank v. Commonwealth Federal S. & L. Ass'n, 610 F.2d 164 (3d Cir. 1979); Vandeventer v. Dale Constr. Co., 271 Or. 691, 534 P.2d 183, 82 A.L.R.3d 1108 (1975), appeal after remand 277 Or. 817,

562 P.2d 196 (1977). For a debate on the question of whether a lender should be permitted to obtain specific performance of a loan commitment, compare Groot, Specific Performance of Contracts to Provide Permanent Financing, 60 Cornell L.Rev. 718 (1975), with Draper, The Broker Commitment: A Modern View of the Mortgage Lender's Remedy, 59 Cornell L.Rev. 418 (1974); see also Brannon, Enforceability of Mortgage Loan Commitments, 18 Real Prop.Prob. & T.J. 724 (1983); Mehr & Kilgore, Enforcement of the Real Estate Loan Commitment: Improvement of the Borrower's Remedies, 24 Wayne L.Rev. 1011 (1978).

38. Kentucky Fried Chicken Corp. v. Thuermer, an unreported case discussed in 22 Vand.L.Rev. 416 (1969).

stock patent copyright business corporat! /4 sale sell selling sold
/s specific! +1 enforc! perform!

2–716 2.716 /s u.c.c. "uniform commercial code"

§ 16–4. Inadequacy of the Legal Remedy—Insolvency of the Defendant

There is a current of authority to the effect that specific performance will be ordered against an insolvent because the legal remedy of
damages is inefficacious against a person who is judgment proof.[39]
Before the remedy is granted, it is necessary that care be given to
assure that rights of other creditors not be infringed.[40] The specific
enforcement of an insolvent's contract does not necessarily curtail the
rights of other creditors. For example, a contract by an insolvent to
transfer his stock in trade for a fair price will not prejudice other
creditors as the decree will be conditioned on the price being paid.[41]
The result would be otherwise if the buyer had already paid for the
stock in trade. In this case delivery to the buyer would give him a
preference over other creditors.[42] Although in some instances insolvency may be the basis for the decree of specific performance in other
instances the defendant's insolvency may be grounds for denying specific performance, as where the decree would give the plaintiff a preference over other creditors.[43] As we shall see below the interests of third
parties is a factor to be considered in granting or withholding equitable
relief.[44]

 WESTLAW REFERENCES
specific! +1 relief perform! enforc! /s insolven!

specific! +1 relief perform! enforc! /s creditor /s prefer!

§ 16–5. Service Contracts

It is clear that no court will order an employee or other person who
is to render personal services to perform.[45] Such an order may well
violate the involuntary servitude clause of the thirteenth amendment.[46]
Additional reasons given for such refusal are the difficulty of supervi-

---

39. Restatement, Contracts § 362; Restatement, Second, Contracts § 360, Comment d. There is also strong authority to
the contrary. See generally, Horack, Insolvency and Specific Performance, 31 Harv.
L.Rev. 702 (1918); Note, Specific Performance and Insolvency—A Reappraisal, 41 St.
John's L.Rev. 577 (1967); 5A Corbin
§ 1156.

40. See Restatement, Contracts § 362,
Comments b, c, d and ills. 1, 2; Restatement, Second, Contracts § 365, Comment b
and ill. 4.

41. Restatement, Second, Contracts
§ 360, ill. 9.

42. Restatement, Contracts § 362, ill. 1.

43. Jamison Coal & Coke Co. v. Goltra,
143 F.2d 889, 154 A.L.R. 1191 (8th Cir.
1944), cert. denied 323 U.S. 769, 65 S.Ct.
122, 89 L.Ed.2d 615 (1944).

44. See § 16–13 infra.

45. Restatement, Second, Contracts
§ 367(1), although the lower Court did so
order in Pingley v. Brunson, 272 S.C. 421,
252 S.E.2d 560 (1979). The law was not
always thus. See Dalton, The Countrey
Justice 68–75 (1622 ed.).

46. See People v. Lavender, 48 N.Y.2d
334, 422 N.Y.S.2d 924, 398 N.E.2d 530
(1979); Stevens, Involuntary Servitude by
Injunction, 6 Corn.L.Q. 235 (1921). Contracts of military enlistment are, however,

sion of the decree and an unwillingness to force individuals into an unwanted personal association.[47]

Courts have on occasion "indirectly enforced by injunction"[48] contracts to render personal services by restraining the defendant from working for a competitor.[49] The theory is that the court is merely enforcing an express or implied negative covenant not to work for competitors during the contract term.[50] Although there is some authority for the proposition that no injunction will issue unless the plaintiff employer will suffer irreparable harm from breach of the negative covenant (as by luring his clientele to a competitor)[51] the weight of authority is less restrictive. Injunctions have been granted against working for another where the employee's services are unique and extraordinary.[52] The main applications of the rule have been in the entertainment industry,[53] and in professional sports.[54] The recent tendency is to regard all professional athletes as possessing unique and extraordinary skills.[55] Injunctive relief frequently appears to be granted against breaching players to preserve the organizational structure of professional athletics, without reference to the question of the degree of injury to the employer by breach of the negative covenant not to work for another.

On occasion an employee has sought specific performance of an employment contract against an employer. Such relief has almost invariably been denied.[56] Such enforcement would not involve questions of involuntary servitude, but would involve difficulty of supervision and, often, forcing the continuance of a distasteful personal rela-

specifically enforced. See Baldwin v. Cram, 522 F.2d 910 (2d Cir.1975); Dilloff, A Contractual Analysis of The Military Enlistment, 8 U.Richmond L.Rev. 121, 147–48 (1974).

47. 5A Corbin § 1204.

48. Restatement, Contracts § 380(2).

49. The leading case is Lumley v. Wagner, 42 Eng.Rep. 687 (1852).

50. For a discussion of covenants not to compete after the contract term expires, see §§ 16–19 to 16–22 infra.

51. De Pol v. Sohlke, 30 N.Y.S. 280 (1867); 5A Corbin § 1206; 11 Williston § 1450 ("In general it is not the mere taking of new employment but unfair competition which equity enjoins"); Stevens, supra note 32, at 265–68.

52. Since in most cases the purpose of the injunction is to coerce the individual into returning to work, it has been argued that the constitutional provision against involuntary servitude is violated. Stevens, supra note 46. Contra, McClintock, Equity § 65 (2d ed. 1948). Without taking a position on involuntary servitude, The Restatement, Second, Contracts § 367, Comment c,

opposes injunctions that are designed to coerce performance.

53. See Tannenbaum, Enforcement of Personal Service Contracts in the Entertainment Industry, 42 Cal.L.Rev. 18 (1954); Berman & Rosenthal, Enforcement of Personal Service Contracts in the Entertainment Industry, 7 J.Beverly Hills B.A. 49 (1973).

54. See Brennan, Injunction against Professional Athletes Breaching their Contracts, 34 Brooklyn L.Rev. 61 (1967); Notes and Comments 43 Conn.B.J. 538 (1969); 77 Dick.L.Rev. 352 (1973); 6 Tulsa L.J. 40 (1969).

55. See e.g., Central N.Y. Basketball, Inc. v. Barnett, 181 N.E.2d 506 (Ohio C.P.1961); Dallas Cowboys Football Club, Inc. v. Harris, 348 S.W.2d 37 (Tex.Civ.App. 1961); Cf. Brennan, supra note 54, at 70; but see Connecticut Professional Sports Corp. v. Heyman, 276 F.Supp. 618 (S.D. N.Y.1967).

56. Kaplan v. Kaplan, 98 Ill.App.3d 136, 53 Ill.Dec. 449, 423 N.E.2d 1253 (1981); see 5A Corbin § 1204.

tionship. Arbitration awards ordering reinstatement have, however, been specifically enforced,[57] and reinstatements have been ordered under civil service and similar legislation.[58] In view of these developments, the reasons behind the traditional bar against a court decree ordering an employer to perform are questionable.[59]

Courts have been reluctant to enforce even non-personal services contracts on grounds of difficulty of supervision.[60] For example, normally courts have not granted specific performance of construction contracts.[61] Such relief has, however, been granted where particularly compelling circumstances have made the remedy at law particularly inadequate. For example, where a defendant agreed to construct and lease a building in a shopping center to the plaintiff, specific performance was granted.[62] Plaintiff's damages would have been entirely speculative and the land site was unique in the ordinary, as well as the legal, sense of the word. In the ordinary building or repair contract where construction is to be on plaintiff's land, a substitute contractor can be called in and damages ascertained with relative certainty; consequently, specific performance normally will be denied. No matter what the nature of the construction contract, however, arbitration awards of specific performance will be enforced.[63]

Service contracts other than for construction or personal services may be specifically enforced if grounds for equitable intervention exist. The remedy at law must be inadequate. If the service is unique so that a substitute performance would not make the plaintiff whole, specific performance will be granted.[64] There are cases not involving uniqueness where damages are inadequate. For example the promisee in a

57. Staklinski v. Pyramid Elec., 6 N.Y.2d 159, 188 N.Y.S.2d 541, 160 N.E.2d 78 (1959) (reinstatement of production manager).

58. See, e.g., McKinney's N.Y.Civ.Serv. Law. § 75.

59. So held in A.A.U.P. v. Bloomfield College, 136 N.J.Super. 442, 346 A.2d 615 (App.Div.1975); State ex rel. Wright v. Weyandt, 50 Ohio St.2d 194, 363 N.E.2d 1387 (1977).

60. See § 16–10 infra.

61. Northern Delaware Indus. Dev. Corp. v. E.W. Bliss Co., 245 A.2d 431 (Del. Ch.1968); Bissett v. Gooch, 87 Ill.App.3d 1132, 42 Ill.Dec. 900, 409 N.E.2d 515 (1980) (contract to build and convey); London Bucket Co. v. Stewart, 314 Ky. 832, 237 S.W.2d 509 (1951). See 5A Corbin § 1172; 11 Williston § 1422A; Axelrod, Judicial Attitudes toward Specific Performance of Construction Contracts, 7 U.Dayton L.Rev. 33 (1981); Barnicle, Expediting Construction by Enjoining Performance, 21 Prac. Law (No. 5) 59 (1975); Note, 47 Notre Dame Law. 1025 (1972).

62. City Stores Co. v. Ammerman, 266 F.Supp. 766 (D.D.C.1967), affirmed 394 F.2d 950 (D.C.Cir.1968); accord, O'Neil v. Lipinski, 173 Mont. 339, 567 P.2d 909 (1977); cf. Besinger v. National Tea Co., 75 Ill.App.2d 395, 221 N.E.2d 156 (1966); see also McDonough v. Southern Oregon Mining Co., 177 Or. 136, 159 P.2d 829, rehearing denied 161 P.2d 786, 164 A.L.R. 788 (1945).

63. Grayson-Robinson, Inc. v. Iris Constr. Corp., 8 N.Y.2d 133, 202 N.Y.S.2d 303, 168 N.E.2d 377 (1960), reargument denied 8 N.Y.2d 1099, 209 N.Y.S.2d 1025, 171 N.E.2d 465 (1960), noted in numerous law reviews.

64. See American Brands, Inc. v. Playgirl, Inc., 498 F.2d 947 (2d Cir.1974) (is the back cover of "Playgirl" unique as an advertising medium?); Wilson v. Sandstrom, 317 So.2d 732 (Fla.1975), cert. denied 423 U.S. 1053, 96 S.Ct. 782, 46 L.Ed.2d 642 (1976) (contract to furnish greyhounds for racing).

contract made for a third party donee beneficiary ordinarily will suffer no pecuniary injury by the breach. Consequently, the remedy of specific performance is open to him.[65] Insurance policies that are wrongfully cancelled before the insured event occurs may be specifically enforced because of the speculative nature of damages in such a case.[66]

WESTLAW REFERENCES

specific! +1 relief perform! enforc! /s personal! +1 serve*
    service serving

358k75 358k74

358k73

specific! +1 relief perform! enforc! /s "involuntary servitude"

specific! +1 relief perform! enforc! /s supervis!

enjoin! injuncti! /s "personal service" /s contract competit!

lumley +s wagner

negative +1 promise covenant /s enjoin! injuncti! specific! /s
    competit!

212k61(2)

enjoin! injuncti! specific! /s employ**** /s unique! extraordinary

212k128(5)

enjoin! injuncti! specific! /s contract /s entertain! actor actress
    athlete

specific! +1 perform! enforc! relief /s "construction contract"

§ 16–6. Mutuality as a Basis for Equitable Relief

For considerable time a doctrine known as "mutuality of remedy" was in vogue in equity jurisprudence. The most important use of the doctrine was to deny specific performance in certain cases. This will be discussed below.[67] The doctrine also had an affirmative side which was to the effect that a plaintiff may obtain specific performance if the defendant could have obtained specific performance if the plaintiff were the breaching party. Consequently, a vendor of land was permitted to obtain specific performance although the vendee's performance (payment) is not unique. Also, a seller of a unique chattel was able to obtain specific performance against a purchaser. The affirmative rule of mutuality seems not to have been applied to service contracts.

Today the doctrine of mutuality as a basis for denying relief has been exploded.[68] Yet the rule remains that a vendor of real property or a seller of unique goods may obtain specific performance. Scholarly attempts have been made to base this rule on the inadequacy of the legal remedy.[69] Yet it cannot be said in each such case that the legal

---

65. Drewen v. Bank of Manhattan, 31 N.J. 110, 155 A.2d 529, 76 A.L.R.2d 221 (1959). See § 17–11 infra. If the remedy at law is inadequate, the beneficiary has an action for specific performance. 5A Corbin § 1200.

66. Burnet v. Wells, 289 U.S. 670, 53 S.Ct. 761, 77 L.Ed. 1439 (1933); see Annot., 34 A.L.R.3d 245, § 8.

67. See § 16–11 infra.

68. See § 16–11 infra.

69. Walsh, Equity § 68 (1930).

remedy is inadequate.[70]   The availability of specific performance in such instances continues to be based on precedents formulated under the mutuality doctrine.[71]

 WESTLAW REFERENCES

"mutuality of remedy"

mutuality /s (specific! +1 enforc! perform!) equit!

358k6

B. DEFENSES

Table of Sections

§ 16–7. Discretionary Nature of Equitable Relief

Historically, an appeal to equity was a petition to the chancellor. It was normally a request for grace based on "reason and conscience," rather than for the implementation of a rule of law.[72]   The historical foundation of equity has left its residue on today's equitable jurisprudence.   Equitable discretion is based no longer on the chancellor's conscience, but consists of a sound discretion, based upon precedents, principles and doctrines that have to a large extent hardened over the last two centuries.[73]   These will be considered in the discussion which follows.

---

70. Inadequacy on specific facts was shown in Shuptrine v. Quinn, 597 S.W.2d 728 (Tenn.1979).

71. McClintock at 185.   The Restatement regards mutuality as one factor to consider in granting specific performance. Restatement, Contracts § 372 and Comment e.   Restatement, Second, Contracts § 360, Comment c, regards the doctrine as discarded.   While Corbin regards the doctrine as innocuous (5A Corbin § 1179), Richards urges its abolition.   Richards,

Mutuality of Remedy—A Call for Reform, 13 Memphis St.L.Rev. 1 (1982).

72. For a history of equity, see Walsh, Equity §§ 1–7 (1930).   On equitable discretion, see 5A Corbin § 1136; 11 Williston §§ 1425, 1425A; Restatement, Second, Contracts § 357, Comment c.

73. Van Wagner Advertising Corp. v. S & M Enterprises, 67 N.Y.2d 186, 501 N.Y.S.2d 628, 492 N.E.2d 756 (1986); County of Lincoln v. Fischer, 216 Or. 421, 339

16–8.   Validity, Enforceability, and Definiteness of the Contract

For the equitable remedy of specific performance to be granted there must be a valid and enforceable contract.[74] The one exception to this rule is that if a contract for the sale of real property does not satisfy the Statute of Frauds, equity may grant specific performance under the part performance doctrine,[75] although traditionally there has been no legal enforcement remedy.[76] Promissory estoppel also can be invoked to compel specific performance of an otherwise unenforceable contract.[77]

Equity requires that a contract be more definite than is necessary at law for enforcement.[78] Since a violation of an equitable decree may be punishable by contempt, the parties must know with reasonable certainty what is expected of them. Before a contract is denied specific enforcement on grounds of indefiniteness, all applicable gap fillers should be used [79] and parol evidence considered to clarify any indefinite provisions.[80]

The law has of late adopted a more flexible attitude towards the validity of contracts containing some indefiniteness of terms; [81] so too have courts of equity in determining whether to grant specific performance. A standard of reasonable certainty has replaced an earlier standard of precision.[82]

WESTLAW REFERENCES

"statute of fraud" /s doctrine /4 part partly partial** +1
    perform! /s realty (real +1 estate property) land

185k129(3) /p (part partly partial** +1 perform!) (promissor!
    +1 estop!)

"specific! enforc!" /s "valid and enforceable contract"

equit! /s definite definiteness /s contract /s enforc!

equit! /s "reasonabl! certain!" /s contract /s enforc!

P.2d 1084 (1959); Restatement, Contracts § 359, Comment a; Restatement, Second, Contracts § 357, Comment c; 5A Corbin § 1136; 11 Williston §§ 1425, 1425A.

74. Restatement, Contracts § 358, Comment e.

75. See § 19–15 infra.

76. Restatement, Second, Contracts § 129, Comment c. See § 19–15 infra.

77. See § 19–48 infra.

78. Sweeting v. Campbell, 8 Ill.2d 54, 132 N.E.2d 523, 60 A.L.R.2d 247 (1956); Restatement, Second, Contracts § 362.

79. See Squillante, Specific Performance of Indefinite Contracts, 72 Com.L.J. 12 (1967).

80. McClintock § 56.

81. See § 2–9 supra; Restatement, Second, Contracts § 362, Comment b.

82. Restatement, Second, Contracts § 362; Scott v. Stoulil, 138 Cal.App.3d 786, 188 Cal.Rptr. 289 (1982); Furuseth v. Olson, 297 Minn. 491, 210 N.W.2d 47 (1973); Van v. Fox, 278 Or. 439, 564 P.2d 695 (1977); see Note, 5 UCLA-Alaska L.Rev. 122 (1975); but see Plantation Land Co. v. Bradshaw, 232 Ga. 435, 207 S.E.2d 49 (1974).

§ 16–9. Consideration in Equity

The rules for the presence or absence of consideration are basically the same in equity as in law.[83] Nonetheless specific performance will generally be denied if the consideration is merely nominal.[84] The question of whether nominal consideration is sufficient to support a contract is controversial.[85] Assuming its sufficiency, equity will generally refuse specific performance. Similarly equity will not enforce a promise if its validity is based solely on the fact that it is under seal or in writing.[86] Such refusals are often stated in maxims such as "equity disregards the form" and "equity will not aid a volunteer." [87] There are important exceptions to this rule.

Where a contract, such as an option contract, is supported by nominal consideration, a seal, or a writing, and looks to a further performance which constitutes a fair exchange as a condition to the defendant's duty, equity will enforce it.[88] Moreover, if past consideration has been given, a new promise supported by a statutory writing, a seal, or nominal consideration, or rules dispensing with consideration will be specifically enforced.[89]

The degree to which equity will examine the adequacy of the consideration is discussed below.[90]

WESTLAW REFERENCES

equit! "specific! enforc!"   /s   nominal   /s   consideration

sufficien**   /s   contract   /s   "nominal consideration"

"equity disregards the form"   "equity will not aid a volunteer"

"new promise"   "past consideration"   /s   equit!   "specific! enforc!"

---

§ 16–10. Difficulty of Supervision

In many cases, courts have refused to grant specific performance on grounds that supervision of performance would involve an undue investment of judicial time and effort.[91] This has particularly been true in cases seeking specific performance of construction contracts [92] but also in contracts requiring continuing services of various kinds and

83. This has not always been so. See Pound, Consideration in Equity, 13 Ill.L. Rev. 667 (1919).

84. George W. Kistler, Inc. v. O'Brien, 464 Pa. 475, 347 A.2d 311 (1975).

85. See § 4–6 supra.

86. George W. Kistler, Inc. v. O'Brien, supra note 84; Restatement, Contracts § 366; Restatement, Second, Contracts § 364, Comment b.

87. McClintock § 55.

88. Restatement, Contracts § 366 and Comment b; 5A Corbin § 1165. Cf. Restatement, Second, Contracts § 87(1)(a) and Comment b, § 88(a) and Comment a. See § 4–6 supra.

89. McCrilles v. Sutton, 207 Mich. 58, 173 N.W. 333 (1919); accord, Speelman v. Pascal, 10 N.Y.2d 313, 222 N.Y.S.2d 324, 178 N.E.2d 723 (1961), reargument denied 10 N.Y.2d 1011, 224 N.Y.S.2d 1025, 180 N.E.2d 272 (1961) (not a contract but an assignment; statutory writing coupled with past consideration).

90. See § 16–14 infra.

91. Peachtree on Peachtree Investors, Ltd. v. Reed Drug Co., 251 Ga. 692, 308 S.E.2d 825 (1983).

92. See § 16–5 supra.

in contracts requiring long term delivery of goods. This last category clearly appears to have been overturned by the Uniform Commercial Code,[93] where it had not already been overturned by judicial decision.[94] Indeed, there is an increasing realization that in many cases the difficulties have been overstated.[95] Indeed, the willingness of courts of equity in recent decades to take on supervision of complex school desegregation and legislative reapportionment plans would indicate that supervision of contract performance is a burden that courts can deal with.

 WESTLAW REFERENCES
"specific! enforc!" /s supervis!
358k74

§ 16–11. Mutuality of Remedy—Will the Defendant Get His Side of the Bargain?

In 1858 an English scholar, Fry, published a treatise on specific performance, stating a rule of mutuality of remedy to the effect that specific performance will not be granted unless from the outset (in the event of breach) the remedy is available against both parties.[96] He listed several exceptions. Subsequent scholars added to the list of exceptions.[97] Except in states that have adopted the rule by statute,[98] the requirement of mutuality generally has been abandoned.[99]

An important core of the doctrine, however, has been preserved. If there was ever a common sense rationale to the doctrine it was that a defendant should not be compelled to perform if he is not assured that the plaintiff will perform. That rationale is stated in the Restatement Second as follows:[1]

93. See § 16–3 supra.

94. See, e.g., Fleischer v. James Drug Stores, Inc., 1 N.J. 138, 62 A.2d 383 (1948).

95. See 5A Corbin §§ 1171–1172; Van Hecke, supra note 28, at 13–16; Restatement, Contracts § 371, Comment a; Restatement, Second, Contracts § 366.

96. Fry, Specific Performance § 460 (1858). For earlier statements of a rule of mutuality, see Parkhurst v. Van Cortlandt, 1 Johns.Ch. *273, *280 (N.Y.Ch.1814) reversed 14 Johns. 15 (dictum by Chancellor Kent); Hutcheson v. Heirs of McNutt, 1 Ohio 14, 20 (1821).

97. 11 Williston § 1434 lists seven exceptions to the former rule.

98. Note, Mutuality of Remedy in California under Civil Code Section 3386, 19 Hastings L.J. 1430 (1968).

99. Stamatiades v. Merit Music Service, Inc., 210 Md. 597, 124 A.2d 829 (1956);

Vanzandt v. Heilman, 54 N.M. 97, 214 P.2d 864, 22 A.L.R.2d 497 (1950). For its rise and fall in one typical jurisdiction, see Austin, Mutuality of Remedy in Ohio: A Journey from Abstraction to Particularism, 28 Ohio St.L.J. 629 (1967); see also Walsh, Equity § 70 (1930). Where the doctrine has not been abandoned "it has been practically nullified by exceptions." McClintock, at 181. Its final abandonment is urged in Richards, Mutuality of Remedy—A Call for Reform, 13 Memphis St.L.Rev. 1 (1982).

1. Restatement, Second, Contracts § 363. This appears to be the core of what Cardozo, C.J., meant when he wrote that, "What equity exacts today as a condition of relief is the assurance that the decree, if rendered, will operate without injustice or oppression either to plaintiff or defendant." Epstein v. Gluckin, 233 N.Y. 490, 494, 135 N.E. 861, 862 (1922).

> Specific performance or an injunction may be refused if a substantial part of the agreed exchange for the performance to be compelled is unperformed and its performance is not secured to the satisfaction of the court.

Thus, for example, a vendor who has contracted to convey on deferred payment terms can be compelled to convey, but the court may condition relief on the purchaser's execution of a mortgage to secure payment.[2] In cases where the performances of the parties are to be concurrent, the defendant is protected by the rules concerning concurrent conditions.[3] In other cases, the respective rights of the parties can be protected by the great flexibility of the equitable decree. It can be conditioned not only on some performance or security to be rendered by the plaintiff,[4] but also upon acts of persons not parties to the litigation.[5] There are cases where the decree cannot assure the defendant that return performance will be rendered.[6] This is particularly true in cases where the plaintiff is to render personal services in the future in exchange for a conveyance or other immediate performance. More often than not specific performance is denied in such circumstances.[7]

 WESTLAW REFERENCES
stamatiades +s merit
"concurrent condition" /s perform!

§ 16–12. Plaintiff in Default—Relief From Forfeiture

In an action at law, whenever there has been a failure of express condition to the defendant's obligation or a material breach by the plaintiff, there can be no successful action for breach of contract[8] although quasi-contractual relief is available in some jurisdictions.[9] Generally, the same rule prevails in equity.[10] There is, however, a different rule with respect to the plaintiff's readiness, willingness and ability to perform. In an action at law, plaintiff must prove that he would have been ready, willing and able to perform but for the defendant's breach. In an action for specific performance, the plaintiff must instead show that he was ready, willing and able to perform at the time of the breach and continues to be ready, willing and able.[11]

2. Restatement, Second, Contracts § 363, ill. 1. See Carman v. Gunn, 198 So. 2d 76 (Fla.App.1967) (court imposes an equitable lien as security; see also Rego v. Decker, 482 P.2d 834 (Alaska 1971).

3. Walsh, Equity 349 (1930). See §§ 11–6, 11–17 supra.

4. See Dillon v. Cardio-Kinetics, Inc., 52 Or.App. 627, 628 P.2d 1269 (1981) (conditions of decree not complied with).

5. Safeway System, Inc. v. Manual Bros., Inc., 102 R.I. 136, 228 A.2d 851 (1967).

6. Stenehjem v. Kyn Jin Cho, 631 P.2d 482 (Alaska 1981).

7. See 5A Corbin § 1184.

8. See §§ 11–9, 11–12, 11–18 supra.

9. See § 11–22 supra.

10. Restatement, Second, Contracts § 369.

11. Allen v. Nissley, 184 Conn. 539, 440 A.2d 231 (1981); Haddock Motors v. Metzger, 92 A.D.2d 1, 459 N.Y.S.2d 634 (4th Dep't 1983). While some cases require a formal tender to put the defendant into breach, Derosia v. Austin, 115 Mich.App.

There is one other major difference in the treatment of conditions in law and equity. The difference is expressed by the maxim "equity abhors a forfeiture." The main application of the maxim has been in contracts for the sale of land where a plaintiff in default has made substantial payments toward the purchase price. Such a plaintiff may obtain specific performance on condition that future payments are well secured to the satisfaction of the court and on condition that damages be paid to the defendant.[12] In a number of jurisdictions where the practice of selling real property for installment payments is ingrained, statutes have been enacted to regulate the matter.[13] Another application of the doctrine has been in the area of options to renew or to purchase ancillary to a lease. Courts have permitted late acceptance of such options where the tenants would otherwise forfeit fixtures, and good will built up during the leasehold period.[14]

 WESTLAW REFERENCES

equit! (specific! +1 enforc! perform!) /s "material! breach!"
  "express** condition!"

equit! (specific! +1 enforc! perform!) /s "ready willing and able"

358k87

di("equity abhors a forfeiture")

§ 16–13. Impracticability or Adverse Effect on Third Persons or the Public Interest

Under certain circumstances, a party's contractual duty is discharged when its performance becomes impossible or impractical.[15] There are many circumstances, however, where impossibility does not discharge a duty; for example, where the impossibility has been caused by the obligor himself.[16] When this occurs, the obligor is liable at law, but no decree of specific performance will be issued.[17] For example,

647, 321 N.W.2d 760 (1982); Century 21 v. Webb, 645 P.2d 52 (Utah 1982), others excuse tender even in the absence of repudiation. Fleenor v. Church, 681 P.2d 1351 (Alaska 1984); Tantillo v. Janus, 87 Ill. App.3d 279, 42 Ill.Dec. 291, 408 N.E.2d 1000 (1980).

12. Restatement, Contracts §§ 374(2), 375(3); see Reporter's Notes to Restatement, Second, Contracts § 369; McClintock §§ 75, 117; 5A Corbin § 1177; 11 Williston § 1425B; Dillingham Commercial Co. v. Spears, 641 P.2d 1 (Alaska 1982); Berry v. Crawford, 237 Ark. 380, 373 S.W.2d 129 (1963); MacFadden v. Walker, 5 Cal.3d 809, 97 Cal.Rptr. 537, 488 P.2d 1353 (1971) (despite wilfulness of the breach), noted in 5 Loyola U.L.Rev. 435 (1972); Kaiman Realty, Inc. v. Carmichael, 65 Hawaii 637, 655 P.2d 872 (1982); Christiansen v. Griffin, 398 So.2d 213 (Miss. 1981); see Annot., 55 A.L.R.3d 10 (1974).

13. See Lee, Remedies for Breach of the Installment Land Contract, 19 U.Miami L.Rev. 550, 562 (1965); Annot., 55 A.L.R.3d 10, § 5b (1974).

14. Xanthakey v. Hayes, 107 Conn. 459, 140 A. 808 (1928); Holiday Inns of America v. Knight, 70 Cal.2d 327, 74 Cal.Rptr. 722, 450 P.2d 42 (1969); J.N.A. Realty Corp. v. Cross Bay Chelsea, 42 N.Y.2d 392, 397 N.Y.S.2d 958, 366 N.E.2d 1313 (1977); see also Schlegal v. Hansen, 98 Idaho 614, 570 P.2d 292 (1977) (lessee in arrears exercised option to purchase).

15. See ch. 13 supra.

16. See § 13–15 supra.

17. Brand v. Lowther, 168 W.Va. 726, 285 S.E.2d 474 (1981); Restatement, Contracts § 368; Restatement, Second, Contracts § 364, Comment a.

where a contract vendor of land breaches his contract by conveying to a bona fide purchaser for value, he is liable for damages but a decree for specific performance will not be granted.[18]

The effect of specific performance on third persons is an appropriate factor to be considered by the court in determining whether the discretionary relief of specific performance is to be granted.[19] Persons on an equal footing will be treated alike. Suppose, for example, a seller contracts to sell 500 bushels of seed to X and 500 bushels to Y and is able to deliver only a total of 500 bushels because of a market shortage under conditions that do not excuse him. In a suit by X for specific performance, the court may properly limit X's relief to a decree requiring delivery of 250 bushels plus compensatory damages.[20]

The public interest is also a factor to be considered in granting or denying relief.[21] This concept has primarily been applied to deny relief in cases where railroads have contracted to maintain grade crossings or railroad stations at places inconvenient to the public[22] and to grant relief, despite the difficulty of supervision, of a contract by a railroad to elevate its tracks.[23] Specific performance of a contract to sell land has also been denied because of the public interest in the esthetic appearance of an art museum.[24] It has also been refused where enforcement would cause employees of the defendant to go out on strike, thereby inconveniencing the public.[25] An oil supplier was enjoined from breaching its contract to supply a public power company with fuel, despite the availability of cover at a substantially higher price, because of the adverse effect any power interruption would have on the public.[26]

18. Flackhamer v. Himes, 24 R.I. 306, 53 A. 46 (1902); see also Restatement, Contracts § 368, ill. 1.

19. Thus specific performance with an abatement was denied where the rights of contingent remaindermen would be adversely affected. Hawks v. Sparks, 204 Va. 717, 133 S.E.2d 536 (1963), 5 Wm. & Mary L.Rev. 290 (1964).

20. Cf. Restatement, Contracts § 368, ill. 1.

21. City of London v. Nash, 3 Atk. 512 (Ch. 1747); Peachtree on Peachtree Investors, Ltd. v. Reed Drug Co., supra note 91.

22. See Restatement, Contracts § 369 and ills. 1 & 2; Restatement, Second, Contracts § 365 and ill. 2; see also Seaboard Air Line Ry. v. Atlanta, B. & C.R.R., 35 F.2d 609 (5th Cir.1929), cert. denied 281 U.S. 737, 50 S.Ct. 333, 74 L.Ed. 1152 (1930), 14 Minn.L.Rev. 580 (1930); City of N.Y. v.

N.Y. Central R.R., 275 N.Y. 287, 9 N.E.2d 931 (1937), 38 Colum.L.Rev. 914 (1938).

23. Pennsylvania R.R. v. Louisville, 277 Ky. 402, 126 S.W.2d 840 (1939), 26 Va.L. Rev. 116 (1939). See also Laclede Gas Co. v. Amoco Oil Co., 522 F.2d 33 (8th Cir. 1975), appeal after remand 531 F.2d 942 (8th Cir.1976) (public interest in requirements contract for propane gas); Wilson v. Sandstrom, 317 So.2d 732 (Fla.1975).

24. Rockhill Tennis Club v. Volker, 331 Mo. 947, 56 S.W.2d 9 (1932), 18 Minn.L. Rev. 90 (1933); 47 Harv.L.Rev. 141 (1932).

25. Gulf, M. & N.N.R. v. Illinois Cent. R.R., 21 F.Supp. 282 (W.D.Tenn.1937), appeal dismissed 109 F.2d 1016 (6th Cir. 1940).

26. Orange & Rockland Util., Inc. v. Amerada Hess Corp., 67 Misc.2d 560, 324 N.Y.S.2d 494 (1971).

WESTLAW REFERENCES

(equit! /s remedy! relief) (specific! +1 enforc! perform!) /s "public interest"

brand +s lowther

public /s convenien! inconvenien! /s specific! +1 enforc! perform!

§ 16–14. Harshness, Inequitable Conduct and Other Forms of Unconscionability; Balancing

As indicated in an earlier chapter,[27] the foundation stone of much of equitable doctrine is the concept of unconscionability. Although in some areas of the law of contracts, such as mistake and penalty clauses, where the concept has been used to set aside contracts or contractual clauses, elsewhere it has frequently been used merely as a basis for denying the remedy of specific performance while leaving the contract intact.[28] Few rules can be stated in the area. Refusal of enforcement, states the Restatement, depends "upon the moral standards of enlightened judges." [29]

As indicated elsewhere, equity generally requires as a prerequisite to specific performance that there be free and open disclosure of all pertinent facts.[30] For example, in one case specific performance was denied because the vendor failed to inform the vendee of an underground water course. In the same case, however, the vendee was not permitted to avoid the contract with the result that the vendor was permitted to retain the down payment and seek damages.[31] Similarly, to obtain specific performance, the purchaser of land must have disclosed the existence of mineral deposits known to him on the land he contracts to purchase,[32] or that the value of the land exceeds the purchase price [33] but he need not have disclosed that he proposes to make improvements in the area which will enhance the value of the land.[34]

Only recently has unilateral mistake been recognized at law as grounds for avoidance of a contract.[35] Equity, however, long refused to grant specific performance where one party was under a material mistake. Such refusal is by no means automatic. The mistake must be viewed in the light of the harshness of enforcement, any change of position by the other party, any hint of unfair conduct by that party

---

27. See §§ 9–37 to 9–40 supra.

28. For an argument that equity should not refuse enforcement of valid contracts, despite the case law to the contrary, see Patterson, Equitable Relief for Unilateral Mistake, 28 Colum.L.Rev. 859, 899 (1928).

29. Restatement, Contracts § 367, Comment b; see Restatement, Second, Contracts § 364; 5A Corbin § 1164.

30. See § 9–20 supra.

31. Kleinberg v. Ratett, 252 N.Y. 236, 169 N.E. 289 (1929). The double standard of morality in law and equity is criticized in Newman, The Renaissance of Good Faith in Contracting in Anglo-American Law, 54 Cornell L.Rev. 553 (1969).

32. Schlegel v. Moorhead, 170 Mont. 391, 553 P.2d 1009 (1976). The rule is stated and criticized as based on "sentiment." McClintock at 201. See also 11 Williston § 1426.

33. Margraf v. Muir, 57 N.Y. 155 (1874).

34. See § 9–20 supra.

35. See § 9–27 supra.

and the nature and degree of any negligence by the mistaken party.[36] Although unilateral mistake is now grounds for avoidance at law, a mistake of a kind that would not permit avoidance of the contract may permit denial of specific performance.[37]

Equity does examine the adequacy of consideration.[38] Many cases state that inadequacy of consideration standing alone is not a basis for denying specific performance,[39] but is only a factor to be considered to determine if the agreement was obtained inequitably.[40] Others have said that inadequacy of consideration is some evidence of fraud, over-reaching, sharp practice, lack of mental capacity, undue influence or the like.[41] Other courts have indicated that gross inadequacy of consideration, standing alone, is sufficient to deny specific enforcement.[42] It is difficult to assess where the weight of authority lies as it is a rare case indeed where inadequacy of consideration is not the fruit of inequitable dealing.[43]

Such cases do, however, exist. In one fascinating case, the court found that the defendant had invented a device and fuel which would enable an automobile to run 400 miles to the gallon. The fuel could be manufactured for 1 cent per gallon. The defendant in a complicated transaction, stripped to its essentials, agreed to transfer a 49% interest in the process and control over its marketing for a sum of $50,000. Plaintiff's experts testified that the process was worth from $20,000,000 to $1,000,000,000. Specific performance was denied on the grounds of inadequacy of consideration.[44]

Apart from the adequacy of the consideration the court will examine the entire transaction to determine whether it is so grossly one-sided as to be oppressive.[45] Thus in one case a carrot farmer contracted to sell carrots. Under the contract the purchaser was free, under certain circumstances, to refuse to accept the carrots. In such event the seller was not permitted to sell the carrots to others without the purchaser's consent. This clause coupled with other one-sided clauses

---

36. See 11 Williston § 1427; McClintock § 74; Restatement, Contracts § 367(c) and Comment a; Restatement, Second, Contracts § 364, Comment a; Annot., 65 A.L.R. 7, 97–102 (1930).

37. See Clayburg v. Whitt, 171 N.W.2d 623 (Iowa 1969) (seller's action for specific performance dismissed; counter-claim based on "rescission" denied).

38. See Annot., 65 A.L.R. 7, 86–96 (1930).

39. Ligon v. Parr, 471 S.W.2d 1 (Ky. 1971).

40. See, e.g., Schiff v. Breitenbach, 14 Ill.2d 611, 153 N.E.2d 549 (1958).

41. Musser v. Zurcher, 180 Neb. 882, 146 N.W.2d 559 (1966); 5A Corbin § 1165.

42. Margraf v. Muir, 57 N.Y. 155 (1874); Hodge v. Shea, 252 S.C. 601, 168 S.E.2d 82 (1969). In some jurisdictions this rule is codified. See O'Hara v. Lynch, 172 Cal. 525, 157 P. 608 (1916); Moody v. Mendenhall, 238 Ga. 689, 234 S.E.2d 905 (1977) (plaintiff must show that contract is fair).

43. 11 Williston § 1428; McClintock § 71; Restatement, Second, Contracts § 364(1)(c) ("grossly inadequate").

44. Weeks v. Pratt, 43 F.2d 53 (5th Cir. 1930), cert. denied 282 U.S. 892, 51 S.Ct. 106, 75 L.Ed. 786 (1930). Anyone having information about the whereabouts of this process, please contact the authors!

45. McKinnon v. Benedict, 38 Wis.2d 607, 157 N.W.2d 665 (1968).

in a contract of adhesion led the court to a finding of unconscionability.[46]

There is considerable, but not unanimous, authority to the effect that a contract fair and conscionable when made will not be specifically enforced if supervening events have rendered the contract so unfair as to shock the conscience.[47] A sharp increase or decrease in the market value of the subject matter, however, standing alone should not be grounds for denying specific performance.[48]

Equity will balance the hardship to the defendant against the benefit to the plaintiff that would ensue from the enforcement of the contract. If the benefit to the plaintiff will be slight and the hardship to the defendant relatively great, specific enforcement will be refused.[49]

WESTLAW REFERENCES

specific specifically + 1 enforc! perform! /s balanc! /s equit!

"equitable relief" (specific specifically + 1 enforc! perform!) /s
    "unilateral! mistak!"

"equitable relief" (specific specifically + 1 enforc! perform!) /s
    hardship unconscionab! /p 358k16

358k52

negligen! /s mistak! /s "equitable relief" (specific specifically + 1
    enforc! perform!)

"equitable relief" (specific specifically + 1 enforc! perform!) /s
    adequa! inadequa! /s consideration

"equity /s adequa! inadequa! /s consideration /s fraud!
    overreach! "undue influence"

equit! /s one-sided!

equit! /s balanc! /s hardship /s benefit!

---

§ 16–15. Laches—Prejudicial Delay

Equity will not allow a party to sleep on his rights, at least where such slumber is prejudicial to the other party. Specific performance will be denied where such prejudicial delay occurs. The prejudice may involve a change of position by the defendant,[50] the loss of evidence or the death of witnesses.[51] Similarly, a court of equity will not grant specific performance to a plaintiff who bides his time until the subject

46. Campbell Soup v. Wentz, 172 F.2d 80 (3d Cir.1948).

47. Jensen v. Southwestern States Management, 6 Kan.App.2d 437, 629 P.2d 752 (1981); Hart v. Brown, 6 Misc. 238, 27 N.Y.S. 74 (1893); Bergstedt v. Bender, 222 S.W. 547 (Tex.1920); 5A Corbin § 1162; 3 Pomeroy Specific Performance 452, 457 (3d ed. 1926); Annot., 65 A.L.R. 7, 72–75 (1930).

48. County of Lincoln v. Fischer, 216 Or. 421, 339 P.2d 1084 (1959); see Annot., 11 A.L.R.2d 390 (1950).

49. Restatement, Contracts § 367(b); Restatement, Second, Contracts § 364(1)(b);

Patel v. Ali, [1984] 1 All.E.R. 978, noted in 134 New L.J. 927 (1984); Kakalik v. Bernardo, 184 Conn. 317, 439 A.2d 1016 (1981); Smith v. Meyers, 130 Md. 64, 99 A. 938 (1917); Miles v. Dover Furnace Co., 125 N.Y. 294, 26 N.E. 261 (1891); Parolisi v. Beach Terrace Improvement Ass'n Inc., ___ R.I. ___, 463 A.2d 197 (1983).

50. Brandenburg v. Country Club Bldg. Corp., 332 Ill. 136, 163 N.E. 440 (1928); Seifert v. Seifert, 173 Mont. 501, 568 P.2d 155 (1977).

51. Hungerford v. Hungerford, 223 Md. 316, 164 A.2d 518 (1960).

matter significantly increases or decreases in value.[52]   Delay that is nonprejudicial, however, does not bar equitable relief.[53]

 WESTLAW REFERENCES

di(prejudic! non-prejudic! un-prejudic! /s delay! /s equit!)

§ 16–16. Unclean Hands

A plaintiff will be denied equitable relief if he comes into court with "unclean hands." [54]   This principle has been used very broadly to encompass cases where the plaintiff has been guilty of inequitable conduct such as misrepresentation and nondisclosure.[55]   More narrowly the doctrine applies to conduct bordering on illegality.   For example, plaintiff conveys real property to defendant on the defendant's promise to reconvey at a later date.   The purpose of the contract is to defraud plaintiff's creditors.   Plaintiff may not obtain specific performance because he comes into court with unclean hands.[56]   In cases of this kind, as in cases of illegal conduct,[57] the rationale is not injury to the defendant, but rather a policy of keeping the courts respectable.[58]

The doctrine is flexible and often difficult to apply.   For example, a collegiate sports star is signed up by a professional team and in violation of collegiate rules it is agreed that the contract is to be kept secret until the end of the season and he will continue to play collegiate ball until that time.   While one court has found this to be a classic example of unclean hands,[59] another has disagreed.[60]

The doctrine of unclean hands cannot be invoked unless the inequitable conduct relates to the same transaction.   Thus, in a partnership accounting action, the trial judge ascertained that the partnership books were intentionally inaccurate to evade taxes and dismissed the case with the statement: "why should this court give aid to crooks?"   The illicit conduct was not directly related to the subject matter of the litigation, ruled the appellate court, reversing the trial court.[61]

52. Welborne v. Preferred Risk Ins. Co., 232 Ark. 828, 340 S.W.2d 586 (1960); Commonwealth v. Pendleton, 480 Pa. 107, 389 A.2d 532 (1978); Gaglione v. Cardi, 120 R.I. 534, 388 A.2d 361 (1978); Crawford v. Workman, 64 W.Va. 10, 61 S.E. 319 (1908); cf. Amoco Oil Co. v. Kraft, 89 Mich.App. 270, 280 N.W.2d 505 (1979) ("unclean hands").

53. Shell v. Strong, 151 F.2d 909 (10th Cir.1945); Hochard v. Deiter, 219 Kan. 738, 549 P.2d 970 (1976); McClintock § 28.

54. See McClintock § 26.

55. So used in 5A Corbin § 1168, and in many cases. E.g., Merimac Co. v. Portland Timber & Land Holding Co., 259 Or. 573, 488 P.2d 465 (1971).

56. MacRae v. MacRae, 37 Ariz. 307, 294 P. 280 (1930); cf. Seagirt Realty Corp. v. Chazanof, 13 N.Y.2d 282, 246 N.Y.S.2d

613, 196 N.E.2d 254 (1963), 66 W.Va.L.Rev. 333 (1964).

57. See § 22–1 infra.

58. See Stringfellow, Who Comes into Equity Must Come with Clean Hands, 1 Ala.Lawyer 248 (1940); but see the critical article, Chafee, Coming into Equity with Clean Hands, 47 Mich.L.Rev. 877, 1065 (1949).

59. New York Football Giants, Inc. v. Los Angeles Chargers F. Club, 291 F.2d 471 (5th Cir.1961).

60. Houston Oilers, Inc. v. Neely, 361 F.2d 36 (10th Cir.1966), cert. denied 385 U.S. 840, 87 S.Ct. 92, 17 L.Ed.2d 74 (1966).

61. Dinerstein v. Dinerstein, 32 A.D.2d 750, 300 N.Y.S.2d 677 (1st Dep't 1969); see McClintock at 163–64.

It has been held that inequitable conduct after the contract has been entered into does not give rise to the doctrine,[62] but there is no unanimity on this point.[63] At any rate, even if the doctrine is technically inapplicable, the new emphasis of the Uniform Commercial Code [64] and the Restatement Second [65] on good faith in the performance of a contract is of course applicable in equity and in law.

 WESTLAW REFERENCES

digest(equitable +1 remedy relief /s "unclean hand")

to(150) /p doctrine theory /2 "unclean hand" & sy ("unclean hand")

150k65(2)

"clean hand" /s illegal! misrepresent! nondisclos!

unclean clean +1 hand /s same similar /s transaction

150k65(3)

§ 16–17. Effect of Denial of Specific Performance or Injunctions

A denial of specific performance, whether on the ground that the legal remedy is adequate or on the basis of the plaintiff's inequitable conduct, does not void the contract. The plaintiff may still enforce the contract in an action for damages or seek restitution. Frequently, however, this option is of little comfort to the plaintiff because damages may be merely nominal [66] or may be too speculative to be susceptible to proof.[67] Under many modern procedural codes the court is empowered, when denying specific performance, to grant damages thereby avoiding the necessity of commencing a new action.[68]

If specific performance is denied on a ground that would bar an action for damages as well, (e.g., invalidity of the contract), a subsequent action at law would be barred on grounds of res judicata.[69]

 WESTLAW REFERENCES

(specific specifically +1 enforc! perform!) "equitable relief" /s "res judicata"

---

62. Meis v. Sanitas Service Corp., 511 F.2d 655 (5th Cir.1975).

63. Myers v. Smith, 208 N.W.2d 919 (Iowa 1973).

64. U.C.C. §§ 1–201(19), 1–203, 2–103(1)(b).

65. Restatement, Second, Contracts § 205.

66. Margraf v. Muir, supra note 33.

67. See Frank & Endicott, Defenses in Equity and "Legal Rights," 14 La.L.Rev. 380 (1954).

68. Sundstrand Corp. v. Standard Kollsman Industries, Inc., 488 F.2d 807 (7th Cir. 1973); Charles County Broadcasting Co. v. Meares, 270 Md. 321, 311 A.2d 27 (1973); Lane v. Mercury Record Corp., 21 A.D.2d 602, 252 N.Y.S.2d 1011 (1st Dep't 1964), affirmed 18 N.Y.2d 889, 276 N.Y.S.2d 626, 223 N.E.2d 35 (1966), 31 Brooklyn L.Rev. 428 (1965).

69. Restatement, Judgments § 65, Comment e. See Annot., 38 A.L.R.3d 323 (1971).

§ 16–18. Relationship to Damages; Agreed Remedies

Clearly, a decree for specific performance is generally inconsistent with a judgment for damages. If the plaintiff receives what he has bargained for he should not also be compensated for the value of the defendant's promise. There are occasions, however, where the award of some damages is proper. Where there is a breach of a valid covenant not to compete, an injunction will issue coupled with damages incurred during the period between the breach and the issuance of the injunction.[70] Where a conveyance is decreed, damages for delay may be awarded.[71] So also, where personalty is ordered to be delivered, delay damages may be awarded.[72]

As discussed elsewhere, the existence of a liquidated damages clause is no bar to an action for specific performance.[73]

Clauses providing for specific performance in the event of breach are rare. Generally the courts have ruled that such a clause is ineffective but may be influential in determining how the court will exercise its discretion.[74] Clauses providing that specific performance will not be an available remedy are given effect,[75] but are narrowly construed.[76]

 WESTLAW REFERENCES

injuncti! enjoin! (specific specifically +1 enforc! perform!) "equitable relief" /s award! /s damage /s covenant! convey! delay!

covenant! /s compet! /s breach! /s equit! /s damage

convey! /s breach! /s delay! /s damage

115k89(2) /p covenant! equit! (specific specifically +1 enforc! perform!) enjoin! injuncti!

358k129

---

70. See § 14–33 supra.

71. Reis v. Sparks, 547 F.2d 236 (4th Cir.1976) (Hadley v. Baxendale not applicable to damages from higher interest rate); Turley v. Ball Associates, Ltd., 641 P.2d 286 (Colo.App.1981) (damages from higher interest rate); Bostwick v. Beach, 103 N.Y. 414, 9 N.E. 41 (1886) (accounting for rents and profits or value of use and occupation); Brockel v. Lewton, 319 N.W.2d 173 (S.D.1982); cf. Pirchio v. Noecker, 226 Ind. 622, 82 N.E.2d 838, 7 A.L.R.2d 1198 (1948) (loss of resale opportunity not compensable).

72. Winchell v. Plywood Corp., 324 Mass. 171, 85 N.E.2d 313 (1949); cf. Owen v. Merts, 240 Ark. 1080, 405 S.W.2d 273, 28

A.L.R.3d 1390 (1966); Virginia Pub. Service Co. v. Steindler, 166 Va. 686, 187 S.E. 353, 105 A.L.R. 1413 (1936) (depreciation in value not compensable).

73. See § 14–33 supra.

74. The cases are analyzed in Macneil, Power of Contract and Agreed Remedies, 47 Cornell L.Q. 495, 520–23 (1962).

75. Sun Bank of Miami v. Lester, 404 So.2d 141 (Fla.App.1981), review denied 412 So.2d 467 (Fla.1982); Ashley v. Metz, 49 Or.App. 1105, 621 P.2d 671 (1980).

76. S.E.S. Importers, Inc. v. Pappalardo, 53 N.Y.2d 455, 442 N.Y.S.2d 453, 425 N.E.2d 841 (1981).

C. COVENANTS NOT TO COMPETE

Table of Sections

§ 16–19. Agreement Not to Compete

Although agreements not to compete are not exclusively of equitable cognizance, most of the litigation concerning them has arisen in equitable actions to enjoin violations of such agreements and, in general, the rules concerning these agreements preserve an equitable flavor. An agreement by a person to refrain from exercising his trade or calling, standing alone, is viewed as being illegal and contrary to public policy because it is inimical to the interests of society in a free competitive market and to the interests of the person restrained in earning a livelihood.[77] Thus such agreements are viewed from the perspectives of both illegality and unconscionability. But if a covenant not to compete forms part of a legitimate transaction a different problem is presented. Such a covenant is often described as an "ancillary restraint" to indicate its connection with a legitimate transaction. The legitimate transactions to which such restraints are most frequently connected are sales of business and employment contracts.[78]

(a) *Agreement by a Seller of a Business Not to Compete With a Buyer*

It is common in the purchase of a business as a going concern to buy along with the other assets of the business its "good will" in the hope that the customers of the concern will patronize the new owners. To protect this expectation it is common to provide that the seller shall not reopen his business in competition with the business sold.

77. Restatement, Second, Contracts § 187; United States v. Addyston Pipe & Steel Co., 85 Fed. 271 (6th Cir.1898), modified and affirmed 175 U.S. 211, 20 S.Ct. 96, 44 L.Ed. 1361 (1899); 6A Corbin §§ 1379–1384; Handler & Lazaroff, Restraint of Trade and the Restatement, Second, Contracts, 57 N.Y.U.L.Rev. 669, (1982).

78. This chapter discusses covenants not to compete ancillary to sales of going businesses and ancillary to employment contracts. Rules similar to those applicable to these transactions have been forged for other ancillary restraints, such as restraints ancillary to the sale of corporate shares (6A Corbin § 1388), ancillary to the sale or lease of real property (6A Corbin § 1389; 14 Williston § 1642), ancillary to partnership agreements (14 Williston § 1644), and ancillary to stock option agreements. Fox v. Avis Rent-A-Car Systems, Inc., 223 Ga. 571, 156 S.E.2d 910 (1967). Some of these are discussed in depth in Handler & Lazaroff, supra note 77, at 678–714.

English cases made the question of legality depend upon whether the restraint imposed was "general" or "limited." [79]   In some of the early cases in the United States a restraint that covered an entire state was deemed to be per se illegal [80] and in others a restraint that did not cover the entire country was deemed to be limited and therefore legal.[81] This test has now generally been abandoned and the test is whether the restraint of trade is unreasonable.[82]   Thus, if the business is national in extent, a covenant not to compete anywhere in the nation may be upheld if otherwise reasonable.[83]

"A promise by a seller not to compete with the buyer is illegal and unenforceable insofar as the restraint is in excess of the extent of the good will purchased." [84]   Thus, if the restraint covers territory in which the seller has no good will, it is an unreasonable restraint of trade and the same is true if the restraint covers lines of trade in which the seller was not engaged.[85]   Many cases however have held or intimated that the covenant may validly embrace the area of probable expansion of the business sold.[86]

Although there are a number of cases to the effect that the duration of the restrictive covenant is immaterial,[87] the better view appears to be that a restraint is invalid if it is to continue "for a longer time than the good will built up by the seller and sold to the buyer can reasonably be expected to continue." [88]

(b) Agreements by an Employee Not to Compete After the Termination of His Employment

Frequently an employee promises his employer that upon the completion of the employment he will not compete with his employer either in his own business or by working for another.[89]   Even where

79. Mitchel v. Reynolds, 24 Eng.Rep. 347 (Ch. 1711).

80. Parish v. Schwartz, 344 Ill. 563, 176 N.E. 757, 78 A.L.R. 1032 (1931).

81. Diamond Match Co. v. Roeber, 106 N.Y. 473, 13 N.E. 419 (1887).

82. Coffee System of Atlanta v. Fox, 226 Ga. 593, 176 S.E.2d 71 (1970), appeal after remand 227 Ga. 602, 182 S.E.2d 109 (1971); Grempler v. Multiple Listing Bur., 258 Md. 419, 266 A.2d 1 (1970); Jewel Box Stores Corp. v. Morrow, 272 N.C. 659, 158 S.E.2d 840 (1968); Restatement, Second, Contracts § 188.

83. Voices, Inc. v. Metal Tone Mfg. Co., 119 N.J.Eq. 324, 182 A. 880 (1936), affirmed 120 N.J.Eq. 618, 187 A. 370 (1936), cert. denied 300 U.S. 656, 57 S.Ct. 433, 81 L.Ed. 866 (1937); Diamond Match Co. v. Roeber, 106 N.Y. 473, 13 N.E. 419 (1887) (where, however, Nevada and Montana were excluded from the restraint.)

84. 6A Corbin § 1387. "When a business is sold with its good will, but without

any express promise not to compete, the seller is privileged to open up a new business in competition with the buyer; but he is under obligation not to solicit his former customers or to conduct his business under such a name and in such a manner as to deprive the buyer of the 'good will' that he paid for."   6A Corbin § 1386.

85. Schultz v. Johnson, 110 N.J.Eq. 566, 160 A. 379 (Ct.Err. & App.1932); Purchasing Associates Inc. v. Weitz, 13 N.Y.2d 267, 246 N.Y.S.2d 600, 196 N.E.2d 245 (1963), reargument denied 14 N.Y.2d 584, 248 N.Y.S.2d 1027, 198 N.E.2d 270 (1964).

86. Schnucks Twenty-Five, Inc. v. Bettendorf, 595 S.W.2d 279 (Mo.App.1979); See Handler, Blake, Pitofsky, Goldschmid, Trade Regulation—Cases and Materials 46 (1975).

87. Beatty v. Coble, 142 Ind. 329, 41 N.E. 590 (1895).

88. 6A Corbin § 1391.

89. See generally, Blake, Employee Covenants Not to Compete, 73 Harv.L.Rev.

there is consideration for the covenant,[90] if the employee learns no secrets and does not have any contact with the customers of the employer there is no reason for enforcing such a restrictive covenant and the covenant should be struck down as imposing an undue hardship upon the person restricted.[91] It is generally agreed that, if an employee learns a trade secret or confidential information, a promise not to disclose it or use it will be enforced.[92] Indeed, even in the absence of an express covenant, employees may not, even after termination of employment, disclose or make use of trade secrets, including secret customer lists.[93] Enforcement by injunctions of reasonable covenants not to compete where the former employee has learned trade secrets goes one step beyond this rule as it eliminates the *potential* for misuse or wrongful disclosure.[94]

Another class of cases in which covenants not to compete are frequently upheld is the difficult area where the former employee has had contact with the employer's customers under circumstances where he may have obtained the good will of the customers—a good will that is likely to follow him. The present tendency is to enforce the covenant only in cases where the customers were developed over a period of time with great effort. If the customers were such as are listed in standard directories, enforcement is refused.[95] However, there are many cases to the contrary.[96] In short, the customer list must be akin to a trade secret. In addition, as in the cases involving the sale of a business, if the restraint in space and time is greater than is necessary to protect the employer it will be deemed overbroad.[97] Similarly the restraint is

625 (1960); Hutter, Drafting Non-Competition Agreements to Protect Confidential Business Information, 45 Albany L.Rev. 311 (1981); Wetzel, Employment Contracts and Non-competition Agreements, 1969 U.Ill.L.F. 61.

90. Hollingsworth Solderless Terminal Co. v. Turley, 622 F.2d 1324 (9th Cir.1980); Environmental Products Co. v. Duncan, 168 W.Va. 349, 285 S.E.2d 889 (1981).

91. E.L. Conwell & Co. v. Gutberlet, 429 F.2d 527 (4th Cir.1970); Crowell v. Woodruff, 245 S.W.2d 447 (Ky.1951); Restatement, Contracts § 515(b); Restatement, Second, Contracts § 188.

92. McCall Co. v. Wright, 198 N.Y. 143, 91 N.E. 516 (1910); J. & K. Computer Systems, Inc. v. Parrish, 642 P.2d 732 (Utah 1982).

93. Mixing Equipment Co. v. Philadelphia Gear, Inc., 436 F.2d 1308 (3d Cir. 1971); Town & Country House & Home Serv. v. Newbery, 3 N.Y.2d 554, 170 N.Y.S.2d 328, 147 N.E.2d 724 (1958). Cf. In re Uniservices, 517 F.2d 492 (7th Cir. 1975) (implied contract theory).

94. Business Intelligence Services, Inc. v. Hudson, 580 F.Supp. 1068 (S.D.N.Y. 1984).

95. American Hardware Mut. Ins. Co. v. Moran, 705 F.2d 219 (7th Cir.1983); Columbia Ribbon & Carbon Mfg. v. A–1–A Corp., 40 N.Y.2d 496, 398 N.Y.S.2d 1004, 369 N.E.2d 4 (1977); Microbiological Research Corp. v. Muna, 625 P.2d 690 (Utah 1981); Fields Foundation, Ltd. v. Christensen, 101 Wis.2d 465, 309 N.W.2d 125 (1981); see Rubin & Shedd, Human Capital and Covenants Not to Compete, 10 J.Leg.Stud. 93 (1981).

96. Murray v. Lowndes County Broadcasting Co., 248 Ga. 587, 284 S.E.2d 10 (1981); Dana F. Cole & Co. v. Byerly, 211 Neb. 903, 320 N.W.2d 916 (1982); Rental Uniform Service of Florence, Inc. v. Dudley, 278 S.C. 674, 301 S.E.2d 142 (1983); Roanoke Engineering Sales Co., Inc. v. Rosenbaum, 223 Va. 548, 290 S.E.2d 882 (1982).

97. Purchasing Assoc. v. Weitz, 13 N.Y.2d 267, 246 N.Y.S.2d 600, 196 N.E.2d 245 (1963), reargument denied 14 N.Y.2d 584, 248 N.Y.S.2d 1027, 198 N.E.2d 270 (1964); Eastern Business Forms, Inc. v. Kistler, 258 S.C. 429, 189 S.E.2d 22 (1972).

overbroad if it covers a line of endeavor not engaged in by the employer.[98]

A number of cases have intimated that there is a third circumstance in which a covenant not to compete will be upheld; that is, where the employee's services are "unique" or "extraordinary." [99] Such intimations are believed to be unsound and have been uncritically borrowed from cases in which an employee has been enjoined from competing during his term of employment.[1] After the employment term is terminated the general principle of free competition supersedes any interest the employer has in preventing competition from unique and extraordinary individuals.[2] It is only where the employer has a legitimate interest in protecting himself from the possibility of tortious or near tortious conduct by his former employee that a restraint should be upheld. It is primarily to protect this legitimate interest that injunctions are issued in the trade secret and customer contact cases despite the principle of free competition.[3] Although the cases generally fall into the categories discussed above, the modern approach is to utilize an overall standard of reasonableness. Among the factors to be considered, for example, is whether the employee has received adequate additional compensation for the non-competition covenant.[4] As put by the Texas court:

> "A determination of the reasonableness of territorial restraints upon non-competition contracts requires a balance of the interests of the employer, the employee, and the public while being mindful of the basic policies of individual liberty, freedom of contract, freedom of trade, protection of business, encouragement of competition and discouragement of monopoly." [5]

Matlock v. Data Processing Security, Inc., 618 S.W.2d 327 (Tex.1981). A restraint unlimited in time may be valid if otherwise reasonable. Karpinski v. Ingrasci, 28 N.Y.2d 45, 320 N.Y.S.2d 1, 268 N.E.2d 751 (1971); Note, 40 Fordham L.Rev. 430 (1971).

98. Thus a covenant not to practice dentistry in a given area is too broad where the employment related only to oral surgery. Karpinski v. Ingrasci, 28 N.Y.2d 45, 320 N.Y.S.2d 1, 268 N.E.2d 751 (1971); 40 Fordham L.Rev. 430 (1971).

99. E.L. Conwell & Co. v. Gutberlet, 429 F.2d 527 (4th Cir.1970); Purchasing Associates v. Weitz, 13 N.Y.2d 267, 246 N.Y.S.2d 600, 196 N.E.2d 245 (1963), reargument denied 14 N.Y.2d 584, 248 N.Y.S.2d 1027, 198 N.E.2d 270 (1964).

1. See § 16–5 supra.

2. See Kniffen, Employee Noncompetition Covenants: The Perils of Performing Unique Services, 10 Rutgers-Camden L.J. 25 (1978).

3. See Diaz v. Indian Head, Inc., 402 F.Supp. 111 (N.D.Ill.1975), affirmed 525 F.2d 694 (7th Cir.1975). For discussions of covenants not to compete from the viewpoint of legal policies furthering competition, see, Goldschmid, Antitrust's Neglected Stepchild: A Proposal for Dealing with Restrictive Covenants under Federal Law, 73 Colum.L.Rev. 1193 (1973); Sullivan, Revisiting the "Neglected Stepchild:" Antitrust Treatment of Postemployment Restraints of Trade, 1977 U.Ill.L.F. 621.

4. Bradford v. New York Times Co., 501 F.2d 51 (2d Cir.1974).

5. Matlock v. Data Process Security, Inc., supra note 97.

Covenants not to compete contained in contracts employing lawyers or in law partnership agreements are violation of professional ethics and void because they deprive clients of freedom of choice.[6]

 WESTLAW REFERENCES

ancillary /s agree! contract /s compet! /s refrain! restrain!

"ancillary restraint"

(a) *Agreement by a Seller of a Business Not to Compete With a Buyer*

restrain! refrain! /s compet! /s goodwill "good will"

212k61(2) /p restrain* refrain restrict! /s compet!

192k6(1)

illegal! unreasonabl! /s covenant! /s "restraint of trade"

di("restrictive covenant" /s duration)

(b) *Agreements by an Employee Not to Compete After the Termination of His Employment*

headnote("restrictive covenant" /s terminat! /s employ****)

agree! contract /s employ**** /s terminat! /s compet!

"restrictive covenant" /s terminat! /s secret /s "customer list"

employ**** /s "customer contact" /s enjoin! injuncti! specific
restrain! refrain! terminat!

255k60 /p restrain! refrain! restrict! /s compet! covenant non-
compet!

employ**** /s covenant! restrain! /s overbroad unique!
extraordinary

---

§ 16–20. Equitable Discretion and Remedy at Law

Even if the covenant meets the standards of validity, equity may nonetheless refuse injunctive relief if such relief will result in disproportionate hardship to the defendant[7] or failure to issue the injunction will cause no irreparable harm to the plaintiff.[8] Where injunctive relief is sought the entire array of equitable defenses is of course available.[9] As Corbin states, "Before granting an injunction preventing an employee from earning his living in his customary trade or employment, the court should make sure, not only that he contracted to forbear and is guilty of a breach, but also that the former employer is suffering substantial harm, that the employee is soliciting former customers or otherwise depriving his employer of business good will that he has paid wages for helping to create, and that the employee will not be deprived of opportunity to support himself and his family in

---

6. Dwyer v. Jung, 137 N.J.Super. 135, 348 A.2d 208 (1975). As to Physicians, see Annots., 62 A.L.R.3d 918, 970, 1014 (1975).

7. Mixing Equipment Co. v. Philadelphia Gear, Inc., 436 F.2d 1308 (3d Cir.1971) (dissenting opinion); Cogley Clinic v. Martini, 253 Iowa 541, 112 N.W.2d 678 (1962);

48 Iowa L.Rev. 159 (1962); Standard Oil Co. v. Bertelsen, 186 Minn. 483, 243 N.W. 701 (1932).

8. Menter Co. v. Brock, 147 Minn. 407, 180 N.W. 553, 20 A.L.R. 857 (1920).

9. See §§ 16–7 to 16–18 supra.

reasonable comfort." [10]   As usual all of the facts and circumstances should be considered in making this determination of unreasonable hardship.[11]

Because there is likely to be greater hardship on an employee than on the seller of a business, courts have stated on a number of occasions that they are more reluctant to uphold and to enforce covenants not to compete entered into by employees than those agreed to by sellers of businesses.[12] The cases are divided on the question whether covenants not to compete attached to partnership agreements are to be treated on a par with employment agreements or sales of businesses.[13]

Where an injunction is denied on equitable principles despite the validity of the agreement, damages may be awarded the plaintiff.[14] Damages are also available in addition to an injunction for injury done between the time of the breach and the time the injunction is issued.[15]

WESTLAW REFERENCES

equit! specific /s unreasonable disproportionate + 1 hardship

headnote("irreparabl! harm***" /s equit! specific)

§ 16–21. Limited Enforcement of Overbroad Restraints

In the past the standard approach to an unreasonable covenant not to compete was to strike the entire covenant.[16] The rule of total invalidity was mitigated by the "blue pencil" rule under which the courts would, if grammatically feasible, sever some words of the covenant, leaving intact those parts of the covenant which were reasonable. For example, in one case the employee agreed not to compete in 46 named counties. The court granted an injunction against competing in

10. 6A Corbin § 1394; see Taylor Freezer Sales Co. v. Sweden Freezer Eastern Corp., 224 Ga. 160, 160 S.E.2d 356 (1968).

11. Solari Indus. Inc. v. Malady, 55 N.J. 571, 264 A.2d 53 (1970); Note, 17 Drake L.Rev. 69 (1967).

12. Day Companies, Inc. v. Patat, 403 F.2d 792 (5th Cir.1968), cert. denied 393 U.S. 1117, 89 S.Ct. 993, 22 L.Ed.2d 122 (1969); H & R Block, Inc. v. Lovelace, 208 Kan. 538, 493 P.2d 205 (1972); Morgan's Home Equip. Corp. v. Martucci, 390 Pa. 618, 136 A.2d 838 (1957).

13. Compare Millet v. Slocum, 4 A.D.2d 528, 167 N.Y.S.2d 136 (4th Dep't 1957), affirmed 5 N.Y.2d 734, 177 N.Y.S.2d 716, 152 N.E.2d 672 (1958) (employment) with Scott v. McReynolds, 36 Tenn.App. 289, 255 S.W.2d 401 (1952) (business); cf. Brad-

ford v. Billington, 299 S.W.2d 601 (Ky.1957) (sui generis).

14. Tull v. Turek, 38 Del.Ch. 182, 147 A.2d 658 (1958); see Comment, 15 So.Tex. L.J. 289 (1974).

15. See § 16–18 supra.

16. Some examples are Welcome Wagon, Inc. v. Morris, 224 F.2d 693 (4th Cir. 1955); Rector-Phillips-Morse, Inc. v. Vroman, 253 Ark. 750, 489 S.W.2d 1 (1973); Weatherford Oil Tool Co. v. Campbell, 161 Tex. 310, 340 S.W.2d 950 (1960); 40 Tex.L. Rev. 152 (1961).

In one case, the consideration for the covenant was found to be so interwoven with the entire agreement that the agreement as a whole was deemed invalid. Alston Studios, Inc. v. Lloyd V. Gress & Assoc., 492 F.2d 279 (4th Cir.1974).

31 of the named counties.[17] The blue pencil rule has its basis in the doctrine of severability as applied to illegal contracts.[18]

A more modern approach that represents the weight of recent authority is that an overbroad covenant will be enforced by the issuance of an injunction limited to the area, time, or calling as to which the covenant is reasonable, regardless of whether a grammatical severance is possible.[19] This modern approach is based upon a realization that an equitable decree is a flexible instrument and that such flexibility need not be based on a theory of severability.[20] While this approach has much to commend it, it doubtless has the effect of encouraging employers to draft overbroad covenants not to compete which have *in terrorem* effect on employees who can only ascertain their rights by costly litigation.[21] Therefore, it has been held that enforcement will be totally denied where the employer has made no effort to protect the legitimate interests of the employee.[22]

 WESTLAW REFERENCES

"blue pencil"

limit! /3 enforc! /s covenant! /s reasonabl!

§ 16–22. Anti-competition Conditions Distinguished From Covenants

Although covenants not to compete must meet the standards of reasonableness, the weight of authority automatically upholds anti-competition conditions without regard to reasonableness. In the typical case a pension plan or other form of deferred compensation provides that rights under the plan are conditioned upon the ex-employee's refraining from entering into competitive employment. On the dubious ground that the employee is not restrained from entering into competing employment but has a choice whether to compete or not, such conditions have generally been upheld.[23] It would appear, however,

17. Thomas v. Coastal Industries Services, Inc., 214 Ga. 832, 108 S.E.2d 328 (1959). Georgia has subsequently abandoned the "blue pencil" rule and has refused to adopt the concept of limited enforcement. Rollins Protective Services Co. v. Palermo, 249 Ga. 138, 287 S.E.2d 546 (1982), but accepts limited enforcement as to covenants ancillary to sales of businesses. Jenkins v. Jenkins Irrigation, Inc., 244 Ga. 94, 259 S.E.2d 47 (1979).

18. See § 22–6 infra.

19. Solari Indus., Inc. v. Malady, supra note 11; Karpinski v. Ingrasci, 28 N.Y.2d 45, 320 N.Y.S.2d 1, 268 N.E.2d 751 (1971); Jacobson & Co. v. International Environment Corp., 427 Pa. 439, 235 A.2d 612 (1967); Weatherford Oil Tool Co. v. Campbell, 161 Tex. 310, 340 S.W.2d 950 (1960), 40 Tex.L.Rev. 152 (1961); see 6A Corbin §§ 1390, 1394; 14 Williston §§ 1659, 1660.

20. For an interesting example of such flexibility, see Electronic Data Systems Corp. v. Kinder, 497 F.2d 222 (5th Cir. 1974).

21. See Blake, supra note 89 at 683–84; Rector-Phillips-Morse, Inc. v. Vroman, 253 Ark. 750, 489 S.W.2d 1, 61 A.L.R.3d 391 (1973) (adhering to traditional view).

22. Insurance Center, Inc. v. Taylor, 94 Idaho 896, 499 P.2d 1252 (1972); see Comment, Partial Enforcement of Post-Employment Restrictive Covenants, 15 Columb. J.L. & Soc. Problems 181, 222–31 (1979); Restatement, Second, Contracts § 184(2) and Comment b.

23. Rochester Corp. v. Rochester, 450 F.2d 118 (4th Cir.1971). The vitality of a leading case, Kristt v. Whelan, 4 A.D.2d 195, 164 N.Y.S.2d 239 (1st Dep't 1957), affirmed 5 N.Y.2d 807, 181 N.Y.S.2d 205,

that Federal law now severely restricts the validity of such pension forfeitures.[24]

 WESTLAW REFERENCES

anti-compet! non-compet!   /s   pension "deferred compensation"

---

155 N.E.2d 116 (1958), was questioned in Bradford v. New York Times Co., 501 F.2d 51 (2d Cir.1974). For a critical appraisal of the covenant-condition distinction, see Goldschmid, Anti-trust's Neglected Stepchild: A Proposal for Dealing with Re-

strictive Covenants Under Federal Law, 73 Colum.L.Rev. 1193, 1196–1200 (1973).

24. See Note, Erisa's Restrictions on the Use of Postemployment Anticompetition Covenants, 45 Albany L.R. 410 (1981).

Chapter 17

THIRD PARTY BENEFICIARIES

Table of Sections

§ 17–1. History and Introduction

It was firmly established in the nineteenth century that a person not in "privity" could not sue on the contract.[1] Although the word "privity" is used in several senses, in this context it refers to those who exchange the promissory words or those to whom the promissory words are directed.[2]

Some earlier cases had been to the contrary. In Dutton v. Poole,[3] the defendant had promised his father to pay defendant's sister £1000 if the father would forbear from selling certain property. Defendant's sister sued on this promise. Defendant took the position that plaintiff could not succeed because plaintiff was not in privity. The court

---

1. Price v. Easton, 110 Eng.Rep. 518 (K.B.1833); Tweedle v. Atkinson, 121 Eng. Rep. 762 (Q.B.1861); Dunlop Pneumatic Tyre Co. v. Selfridge & Co., [1915] A.C. 847; Beswick v. Beswick [1968] A.C. 58.

2. 4 Corbin § 778.

3. 83 Eng.Rep. 523 (K.B.1677), aff'd 83 Eng.Rep. 156 (Ex.Ch. 1679).

sustained the action even though there was no privity because of the close relationship between the father and the plaintiff, his daughter.

In the language of this chapter the defendant is the promisor, the father is the promisee, and the plaintiff is the alleged beneficiary.[4] On the facts of Dutton v. Poole the relationship that was important was the relationship between the promisee (father) and the beneficiary (daughter).

In the terminology of this chapter the plaintiff is a donee beneficiary.[5] This means that the father by virtue of the contract he made with his son intended to and did confer upon his daughter a gift in the form of a promise. This gift does not require delivery because it was purchased by the consideration furnished by the father.[6]

As indicated above this case was repudiated by the later English cases cited in footnote one. English courts have often avoided the rigidity of this view by being "very ready to torture such a contract into a trust." [7]

The third party beneficiary doctrine has received a much warmer reception in the United States. This is exemplified by the well known case of Lawrence v. Fox.[8] In this case Holly, the promisee, owed $300 to Lawrence. Holly loaned $300 to Fox in exchange for Fox's promise to pay $300 to Lawrence. Since the agreement was between Holly (promisee) and Fox (promisor), Lawrence was not in privity. Although there was some discussion of trusts and agency [9] in the decision, ultimately the case held that Lawrence could recover as a third party beneficiary because it was manifestly just that he should.

This case is somewhat different than Dutton v. Poole even though in both cases the plaintiff prevailed. Here the plaintiff is referred to as

---

4. It is obvious that in the case of a bilateral contract there are two promisors. Why then should the defendant be called the promisor? The simple answer is that he has made the promise on which suit is being brought. Another answer is that in most cases only one of the promisors has made a promise that benefits the third party. However, it is conceivable that both parties could make a promise beneficial to the beneficiary. In such a case, as indicated above, the promisor would be the party against whom suit is brought.

5. See § 17–2 infra.

6. Bryon Chamber of Commerce, Inc. v. Long, 92 Ill.App.3d 864, 48 Ill.Dec. 77, 415 N.E.2d 1361 (1981); In re Estate of Sheimo, 261 Iowa 775, 156 N.W.2d 681 (1968); Continental Bank of Pennsylvania v. Barclay Riding Academy, Inc., 93 N.J. 153, 459 A.2d 1163 (1983), cert. denied 464 U.S. 994, 104 S.Ct. 488, 78 L.Ed.2d 684 (1983).

7. 1 A. Scott on Trusts § 14.4, at 152 (3d ed. 1967). The English decisions are analyzed in 4 Corbin § 836–55; Comment,

Third Party Beneficiary Contracts in England, 35 U.Chi.L.Rev. 544 (1968). That the state of English law is unsatisfactory is perhaps demonstrated by the enactment of legislation in at least one commonwealth country overturning the English precedents. See S.K. Date-Bah, The Enforcement of Third Party Contractual Rights in Ghana, 8 U.Ghana L.J. 76 (1971).

8. 20 N.Y. 268 (1859).

9. The concurring judges preferred to rest the decision on an agency theory; that is to say, that Holly was acting as an agent for Lawrence. On the facts this theory was of doubtful applicability. See Restatement, Second, Contracts § 302, Comment f. Until recently this was the approach taken in Massachusetts which refused to recognize the third party beneficiary doctrine. See Green v. Green, 298 Mass. 19, 9 N.E.2d 413 (1937). This approach was overturned in the case of Choate, Hall & Stewart v. SCA Serv., 378 Mass. 535, 392 N.E.2d 1045 (1979), on remand 22 Mass.App. 522, 495 N.E.2d 562 (1986).

a creditor beneficiary because the plaintiff is a creditor of the promisee.[10] It should be observed that in a case such as Lawrence v. Fox, whether the plaintiff is a third party beneficiary is often not important. This is true because the plaintiff may sue the promisee Holly who in turn may implead the defendant.

 WESTLAW REFERENCES
dutton +3 poole

§ 17–2. The First Restatement

Based upon Dutton v. Poole and Lawrence v. Fox and other similar precedents the First Restatement formulated an approach under which there are three types of third party beneficiaries. Creditor beneficiaries, donee beneficiaries and incidental beneficiaries. Under this approach if the third party is a creditor or a donee beneficiary he will qualify as a third party beneficiary; if he is an incidental beneficiary his action is doomed to failure.[11]

What is critical under the First Restatement is the purpose of the promisee. If the purpose of the promisee in obtaining the promise of the promisor is to confer a gift upon the beneficiary, the beneficiary is a donee beneficiary. It is made clear that in making this determination the terms of the agreement and the surrounding circumstances should be taken into account.[12]

If the purpose of the promisee in obtaining the promise is to discharge "an actual or supposed or asserted duty of the promisee to the beneficiary," the beneficiary is a creditor beneficiary.[13] As stated above if a beneficiary does not fall into either of these two categories, he is called an incidental beneficiary and may not enforce the promise.[14]

 WESTLAW REFERENCES
"creditor beneficiary" /s restatement
"donee beneficiary" /s restatement
"incidental beneficiary" /s restatement

§ 17–3. The Test of Intent to Benefit

Many of the more modern cases have refused to employ the approach of the First Restatement. For these courts the first question

10. See § 17–2 infra.

11. See Restatement, Contracts § 133; Williams v. Fenix & Scisson, Inc., 608 F.2d 1205 (9th Cir.1979).

12. See Restatement, Contracts § 133(a); People ex rel. Resnik v. Curtis & Davis, 78 Ill.App.2d 381, 36 Ill.Dec. 338, 400 N.E.2d 918 (1980).

13. Restatement, Contracts § 133(b). The effect of a supposed obligation is also discussed in sections 17–4 and 17–6 infra.

In addition this provision states that a person may qualify as a creditor beneficiary even though his claim against the promisee "has been barred by the Statute of Limitations or by a discharge in bankruptcy, or which is unenforceable because of the Statute of Frauds." Id. This question is discussed in § 17–4 infra.

14. See Restatement, Contracts § 133(c).

to be discussed in a third party beneficiary situation is the question of "intent to benefit" the alleged third party beneficiary. If there is no such intent the alleged third party beneficiary is an incidental beneficiary.[15]

The phrase "intent to benefit" is not necessarily used in the same sense by all of the courts that employ it. There are two key questions that often receive different answers. Of whose intent do we speak and what evidence is admissible on the issue of intent? We shall proceed to say a few words about each of these two questions.

Some cases stress the intent of the promisee[16] whereas others have indicated that the intention of both parties is equally important.[17] When we speak of the admissibility of evidence we should recall that the intention of the parties relates to the topic of interpretation[18] and that all of the questions discussed there again become relevant. Thus, we are again confronted with the plain meaning rule[19] and its opposite ambiguity,[20] the admissibility of extrinsic evidence[21] including evidence of subjective intent.[22] Again there is the problem of whether one is dealing with a question of fact or question of law.[23]

The Pennsylvania courts had announced a most restrictive rule. They stated that both parties must intend to benefit the third party and that such intention must be found in the contract.[24] Pennsylvania has, however, recently adopted the approach of the Second Restatement.[25]

15. See, e.g., H.R. Moch Co. v. Rensselaer Water Co., 247 N.Y. 160, 159 N.E. 896 (1928).

16. See Norfolk & Western Co. v. United States, 641 F.2d 1201 (6th Cir.1980); Insurance Co. of North America v. Waterhouse, 424 A.2d 675 (Del.1980).

17. See Holbrook v. Pitt, 643 F.2d 1261, 1270–1271 n. 17 (7th Cir.1981), appeal after remand 748 F.2d 1168 (7th Cir.1984); Hylte Bruks Aktiebolag v. Babcock & Wilcox Co., 399 F.2d 289, 292 (2nd Cir.1968).

18. See ch. 3 supra.

19. See First Hartford Realty Corp. v. Corporate Property Investors, 12 Mass. App. 911, 423 N.E.2d 1020 (1981).

20. Wilson v. General Mortgage Co., 638 S.W.2d 821 (Mo.App.1982).

21. See Garcia v. Truck Ins. Exchange, 36 Cal.3d 426, 682 P.2d 1100, 204 Cal.Rptr. 435 (1984); Lane v. Aetna Cas. & Sur. Co., 48 N.C.App. 634, 269 S.E.2d 711 (1980), review denied 302 N.C. 219, 276 S.E.2d 916 (1981).

22. See Local 80 v. Tishman Constr. Corp., 103 Mich.App. 784, 303 N.W.2d 893 (1981); Kary v. Kary, 318 N.W.2d 334 (S.D.1982).

23. See Hylte Bruks Aktiebolag v. Babcock & Wilcox Co., 399 F.2d 289 (2d Cir. 1968), noted in 37 Fordham L.Rev. 291 (1968); Clarke v. Asarco, Inc., 124 Ariz. 8, 601 P.2d 612 (1978), vacated 123 Ariz. 587, 601 P.2d 587 (1979); Concrete Contractors v. E.B. Roberts Const. Co., 664 P.2d 722 (Colo.App.1982), judgment affirmed 704 P.2d 859 (Colo.1985); Cutler v. Hartford Life Ins. Co., 22 N.Y.2d 245, 292 N.Y.S.2d 430, 239 N.E.2d 361 (1968).

24. See Jett v. Phillips & Associates, 439 F.2d 987 (10th Cir.1971); Austin v. Seligman, 18 F. 519 (2d Cir.1883); Spires v. Hanover Fire Ins. Co., 364 Pa. 52, 70 A.2d 828 (1950); O'Boyle v. Dubose-Killeen Properties, Inc., 430 S.W.2d 273 (Tex.Civ. App.1968). For an opposite extreme, see Beardsley v. Stephens, 134 Okl. 243, 273 P. 240 (1928), which seems to indicate that the writing itself is always insufficient to establish an intention to benefit. But see Apex Siding & Roofing Co. v. First Fed. Sav. & Loan Ass'n, 301 P.2d 352 (Okl.1956).

25. Guy v. Liederbach, 501 Pa. 47, 459 A.2d 744 (1983).

The presumption is that the parties contract for their own benefit and not for the benefit of a third party.[26] However, if the parties explicitly agree that the third party shall have an enforceable right, their express agreement on this point will ordinarily be given effect.[27] So also if it is clear that the performance promised by the promisor is to run directly to the beneficiary.[28] This test of to whom is the performance to run has been used in many cases even though, at times, it is not clear to whom the performance is to run.[29] Under this test if it is decided that the performance is to run directly to the promisee, the third party is ordinarily an unprotected incidental beneficiary,[30] but if it runs to the third party he is ordinarily an intended beneficiary.[31] Thus, for example, if a bank promised A a loan with which to pay his creditors, under the test being discussed, the creditors would be deemed incidental beneficiaries,[32] but if the bank's promise was to pay the money directly to the creditors they would be classified as intended beneficiaries.[33]

However, this is not the only test employed. For example, in Lucas v. Hamm,[34] a lawyer (promisor) promised to draft a will for the testator (promisee) and the plaintiffs (third parties) were distributees under the will. Because the will was improperly drawn, the plaintiffs received

26. See Brown v. Summerlin Associates, Inc., 272 Ark. 298, 614 S.W.2d 227 (1981).

27. See Seaboard Const. Co. v. Continental Mortgage Investors, 298 F.Supp. 579 (S.D.Ga.1969). The same is true if the contract reserves enforcement to the promisee. See Moosehead Sanitary District v. S.G. Phillips Corp., 610 F.2d 49 (1st Cir.1979); Borough of Brooklawn v. Brooklawn Housing Corp., 124 N.J.L. 73, 11 A.2d 83 (1940).

28. See Fourth Ocean Putnam Corp. v. Interstate Wrecking Co., 108 A.D.2d 3, 487 N.Y.S.2d 591 (2d Dept.1985) affirmed 66 N.Y.2d 38, 495 N.Y.S.2d 1, 485 N.E.2d 208 (1985); Lenz v. Chicago & N.W. Ry. Co., 111 Wis. 198, 86 N.W. 607 (1901); Vikingstad v. Baggott, 46 Wn.2d 494, 282 P.2d 824 (1955).

29. See, e.g., La Mourea v. Rhude, 209 Minn. 53, 295 N.W. 304 (1940); H.R. Moch Co. v. Rensselaer Water Co., 247 N.Y. 160, 159 N.E. 896 (1928); Apex Siding & Roofing Co. v. First Fed. Sav. & Loan Ass'n., 301 P.2d 352 (Okl.1956); see also Heyer v. Flaig., 70 Cal.2d 223, 74 Cal.Rptr. 225, 449 P.2d 161 (1969).

30. See McConnico v. Marrs, 320 F.2d 22 (10th Cir.1963); Tomaso, Feitner and Lane, Inc. v. Brown, 4 N.Y.2d 391, 175 N.Y.S.2d 73, 151 N.E.2d 221 (1958).

31. See Fidelity & Deposit Co. v. Rainer, 220 Ala. 262, 125 So. 55 (1929); Carson Pirie Scott & Co. v. Parrett, 346 Ill. 252, 178 N.E. 498 (1931); Lenz v. Chicago & N.W. Ry. Co., 111 Wis. 198, 86 N.W. 607 (1901) ("Payment direct to the third person is, of course, a benefit to him, and, if that is required by a contract, the intent to so benefit is beyond question."); Vikingstad v. Baggott, 46 Wn.2d 494, 282 P.2d 824 (1955).

32. See Mortgage Associates, Inc. v. Monona Shores, Inc., 47 Wis.2d 171, 177 N.W.2d 340 (1970). Compare Hamill v. Maryland Cas. Co., 209 F.2d 338 (10th Cir. 1954).

33. See Apex Siding & Roofing Co. v. First Fed. Sav. & Loan Ass'n., 301 P.2d 352 (Okl.1956).

34. 56 Cal.2d 583, 15 Cal.Rptr. 821, 364 P.2d 685 (1961), cert. denied 368 U.S. 987, 82 S.Ct. 603, 7 L.Ed.2d 525 (1962); cf. Cutler v. Hartford Life Ins. Co., 22 N.Y.2d 245, 239 N.E.2d 361, 292 N.Y.S.2d 430 (1968); Weiner v. Physicians News Serv., 13 A.D.2d 737, 214 N.Y.S.2d 474 (1st Dep't 1961). See also United States v. Carpenter, 113 F.Supp. 327 (E.D.N.Y.1949) (agreement between exporters and U.S. importer to restrict use of potatoes imported into U.S. for seed purposes, the U.S. Government held to be an intended beneficiary); TSS Sportswear, Ltd. v. The Swank Shop (Guam) Inc., 380 F.2d 512 (9th Cir.1967) (agreement between seller and buyer of stock that corporate debtor would no longer owe any money to seller or firms controlled by him).

$75,000 less from the testator's estate than the testator had intended. The court recognized that the performance (drawing the will) was to run to the testator but rejected this test. It stated, "Insofar as intent to benefit a third person is important in determining his right to bring an action under a contract, it is sufficient that the promisor must have understood that the promisee had such intent." [35]

Notice that this test stresses the intent of the promisee but also indicates that the promisor must also have reasonably understood this intent. On the facts it is clear that although the will was being drawn for the testator, the ultimate beneficiaries of a will are the distributees named in the will.

It is clear that a different result can be reached on a set of facts depending on which of the two tests set forth above is used. It is equally clear that the test of to whom is the performance to run is a more mechanical test while the other test is better because it is based upon the intention of the parties. The more modern cases are heading in the direction of the test in Lucas v. Hamm.[36]

This approach has been used, for example, in cases where a party has made a promise to obtain liability insurance for another party. For example, O, the owner of property, obtained a mortgage loan from B Bank. As part of the mortgage agreement B promised to obtain liability insurance to cover the premises. B failed to keep this promise. Plaintiff was injured as a result of O's negligence in the maintenance of the property. May plaintiff successfully sue B as a result of B's failure to keep its promise made to O? A number of cases have given an affirmative answer even though B's promised performance (to obtain the insurance) ran to O.[37]

Enough has been said to show that the test of intent to benefit is not easily or uniformly applied.[38] However, the courts do not always decide cases solely on the basis of the intent of the parties. In making decisions the courts openly or covertly have employed policy considerations to advance social and economic policies.[39] A good illustration is a provision for the support of a child living with his mother under a separation agreement. It has been stated that it would be poor public policy to have the payment made directly to the child.[40] However, if

35. Lucas v. Hamm, 56 Cal.2d 583, 15 Cal.Rptr. 821, 825, 364 P.2d 685, 689 (1961), cert. denied 368 U.S. 987, 82 S.Ct. 603, 7 L.Ed.2d 525 (1962).

36. See Guy v. Liederbach, 501 Pa. 47, 459 A.2d 744 (1983); Matter of Gosmire's Estate, 331 N.W.2d 562 (S.D.1983). According to some authorities the action may be brought on either a tort or a contract theory. See Heyer v. Flaig, 70 Cal.2d 223, 226, 74 Cal.Rptr. 225, 449 P.2d 161 (1969).

37. See Johnson v. Holmes Tuttle Lincoln-Mercury, Inc., 160 Cal.App.2d 290, 325 P.2d 193 (1958); Khalaf v. Bankers & Shipper's Ins. Co., 404 Mich. 134, 273 N.W.2d

811 (1978); Pappas v. Jack O.A. Nelsen Agency, 81 Wis.2d 363, 260 N.W.2d 721 (1978). The case of Schell v. Knickelbein, 77 Wis.2d 344, 252 N.W.2d 921 (1977), reaches an opposite result.

38. See Note, Third Party Beneficiaries and the Intention Standard: A Search for Rational Contract Decision-Making, 54 Va. L.Rev. 1166 (1968).

39. See note 38 supra.

40. See Forman v. Forman, 17 N.Y.2d 274, 270 N.Y.S.2d 586, 217 N.E.2d 645, 34 A.L.R.3d 1351 (1966); cf. Astle v. Wenke, 297 A.2d 45 (Del.Super.1972); Ferro v.

the mother refuses to take the money and the children are not being supported that is a different matter.[41]

Often it is quite clear that a decision rests primarily on policy grounds. For example, a Delaware Court ruled that a federal prisoner kept in a Delaware state prison under a contract between the state and the United States is a third party beneficiary of that contract, permitting him to recover for injuries suffered in an assault in the prison. The decision, circumventing Delaware's rule of sovereign immunity in the tort area,[42] was based in part on giving the prisoner rights similar to those in federal prisons, by virtue of which rights a prisoner may sue the federal government under the Federal Torts Claim Act.[43] Third party beneficiary theory has also been employed as the basis for the advancement of a social policy of racial equality.[44] However, tenants in a federally subsidized housing project were not held to be third party beneficiaries when it was alleged that private defendants were illegally siphoning federal funds and the United States was acquiescing in this illegal conduct.[45]

At times recognition of a right of action by a third party beneficiary has no real effect upon the promisor's burden. For example, if A is actually indebted to B and C agrees with A, for a consideration, to pay this debt directly to B, B is held to be a third party beneficiary. This does not change C's burden because if B were not a third party beneficiary he could still sue A and A could in turn sue C. In such a case the efficiency of judicial administration may be slightly increased by permitting B to sue C.[46] Thus, in this type of case the court must really decide whether the parties intend that the obligation of the promisee should be discharged by virtue of the promisor's performance to the beneficiary or whether the intent is to render performance to the

Bologna, 31 N.Y.2d 30, 334 N.Y.S.2d 856, 286 N.E.2d 244 (1972).

41. E.C. Ernst, Inc. v. Manhattan Const. Co., 551 F.2d 1026 (5th Cir.1977); Bethune v. Bethune, 96 Misc.2d 507, 413 N.Y.S.2d 800 (1976), reinstated 46 N.Y.2d 897, 414 N.Y.S.2d 905, 387 N.E.2d 1220 (1979). But see Percival v. Luce, 114 F.2d 774 (9th Cir. 1940).

42. Another case in which the doctrine of sovereign immunity was a prime factor in extending third party beneficiary recovery is Visintine & Co. v. New York, C. & St. L.R.R., 169 Ohio St. 505, 160 N.E.2d 311 (1959), affirmed 168 Ohio St. 470, 155 N.E.2d 682 (1958).

43. See Blair v. Anderson, 325 A.2d 94 (Del.Super.1974).

44. See Olzman v. Lake Hills Swim Club, Inc., 495 F.2d 1333 (2d Cir.1974) (statute forbidding discrimination in con-

tracting on racial grounds forbids discrimination against contracting party's guest at swimming pool; guest is a third party beneficiary); see also Bossier Parish School Board v. Lemon, 370 F.2d 847 (5th Cir.), cert. denied 388 U.S. 911, 87 S.Ct. 2116, 18 L.Ed.2d 1350 (1967).

45. Falzarano v. United States, 607 F.2d 506 (5th Cir.1979); Martinez v. Socoma Companies, 11 Cal.3d 394, 113 Cal. Rptr. 585, 521 P.2d 841 (1974). Where a person claims a right under a statute the question often is whether the statute was intended to create individual rights. See Chaplin v. Consolidated Edison Co., 579 F.Supp. 1470 (S.D.N.Y.1984). See also Waters, The Property in the Promise: A Study of the Third Party Beneficiary Rule, 98 Harv.L.Rev. 1109 (1985).

46. See Shingleton v. Bussey, 223 So.2d 713 (Fla.1969).

promisee so that the third party may proceed only against the promisee.[47]

This situation is quite different in a donee beneficiary situation. In that situation the donee beneficiary ordinarily has no claim against the promisee and the promisee ordinarily has little or no financial incentive to sue the promisor.[48] In such a case it would seem to be fair that an intended donee beneficiary should have a direct claim against the promisor.[49]

However, there are cases where the third party beneficiary doctrine could be used to impose a crushing burden in a donee beneficiary situation. A good illustration is the case of H.R. Moch Co. v. Rensselaer Water Co.[50]

In that case defendant promised the City of Rensselaer, inter alia, to supply water at fire hydrants. Plaintiff's building caught fire and was destroyed because of the breach of defendant's promise. Plaintiff was not a creditor beneficiary[51] and the court treated him as a potential donee beneficiary. The court, however, concluded that he was not an intended beneficiary in part because the defendant could have been destroyed financially if, for example, the entire city had been destroyed by this fire.

Again this involves a policy consideration. However, in this type of situation the law of contracts overlaps the law of torts.[52] As a matter of fact in the Moch case a cause of action based upon common law tort was also rejected. In this type of case extensive attention to policy considerations that underlie tort law in general and to the economic and social impact of extended liability in the particular area of the economy involved will produce sounder analysis than an attempt to fathom the intention of the parties.[53]

The difficulty of fathoming the intention of the parties in the construction industry has lead courts to conclude that it should not be lightly concluded that one who is not in privity should be considered to be a third party beneficiary. This is so, according to these courts "because of the multiple contractual relationships involved and because performance ultimately, if indirectly, runs to each party of the several contracts."[54]

---

47. See United States v. Ogden Technology Laboratories, Inc. 406 F.Supp. 1090, (E.D.N.Y.1973); Restatement, Second, Contracts § 302, Comment b.

48. See §§ 17–13 to 17–14 infra.

49. See, e.g., Seaver v. Ransom, 224 N.Y. 233, 120 N.E. 639 (1918).

50. 247 N.Y. 160, 159 N.E. 896 (1928).

51. See discussion in § 17–5 infra.

52. See, e.g., McDonald v. Amtel, Inc., 633 P.2d 743 (Okl.1981).

53. For sophisticated analyses of such considerations as to one profession, see Katsoris, Accountants' Third Party Liability—How Far Do We Go?, 36 Fordham L.Rev. 191 (1967); Comment, Title Abstractor's Liability in Tort and Contract: A Right of Action for Injured Third Persons, 22 Am.U.L.Rev. 455 (1973).

54. Port Chester Elec. Const. Corp. v. Atlas, 40 N.Y.2d 652, 655–56, 357 N.E.2d 983, 986, 389 N.Y.S.2d 327, 330, (1976).

In construction projects owners, tenants, prime contractors, sub-contractors and suppliers are enmeshed in a network of contracts. For example, should an owner be deemed to be a third party beneficiary of a contract between a general contractor (promisee) and a sub-contractor (promisor)? Should a sub-contractor be treated as a beneficiary of the owner's promise (promisor) to pay the general contractor (promisee)? Most cases have answered both questions in the negative.[55] Recent cases indicate a trend toward permitting such actions thus indicating disagreement with the basis for the conclusion of the earlier cases.[56] Undoubtedly each view is based in part on the courts' feeling of what is good for the construction industry and society in general.

Another potentially important factor in the third party beneficiary area is the element of reliance.[57]

It is important to observe that it is possible that in a contract where the promisor makes a number of promises, the third party may be the beneficiary of one promise but not of another. For example in the Moch [58] case although the plaintiff was not a third party beneficiary of the defendant's promise to supply water at fire hydrants, he was a third party beneficiary of the promise specifying maximum rates to be charged.[59]

It is also possible that both the promisee and the third party beneficiary could suffer consequential damages as a result of a breach of one promise. For example, in Exercycle of Michigan v. Wayson [60] plaintiff was a distributor of Exercycle. He had an exclusive right to sell a certain kind of Exercycle machine within a certain area but not in any other area. A, another distributor who signed a similar contract for a different territory, sold 123 machines in the territory which was exclusively assigned to the plaintiff. When plaintiff sued on A's promise made to Exercycle not to compete, the court concluded that he qualified as a third party beneficiary. The point is that Exercycle would also have an action for consequential damages if for example, plaintiff, because of A's conduct, gave up his dealership to the injury of Exercycle.[61]

---

55. See Safer v. Perper, 569 F.2d 87 (D.C.Cir.1977); A.R. Moyer, Inc. v. Graham, 285 So.2d 397 (Fla.1973); Boyd v. Bunkelman Pub. Housing Authority, 188 Neb. 69, 195 N.W.2d 230 (1972); Vogel v. Reed Supply Co., 277 N.C. 119, 177 S.E.2d 273 (1970); Comment, Contracts for the Benefit of Third Parties in the Construction Industry, 40 Fordham L.Rev. 315 (1971).

56. See Sears, Roebuck & Co. v. Jardel Co., 421 F.2d 1048 (3d Cir.1970); Comment, supra note 55, at 326–32 (1971). For two more recent cases holding that an architect could be sued by a party not in privity, see Seiler v. Levitz Furniture Co., 367 A.2d 999 (Del.Super.1976) and Davidson & Jones Inc. v. County of New Hanover, 41 N.C.App.

661, 255 S.E.2d 580 (1979), cert. denied 298 N.C. 295, 259 S.E.2d 911 (1979).

57. See Straus v. Belle Realty Co., 65 N.Y.2d 399, 482 N.E.2d 34, 492 N.Y.S.2d 555 (1985); Comment, Third Party Beneficiaries and the Intention Standard: A Search for Rational Contract Decision-Making, 54 Va.L.Rev. 1166 (1968); Restatement, Second, Contracts § 302, Comment d discussed in § 17–4 infra.

58. See note 50 supra.

59. See § 17–7 infra; Northwest Airlines, Inc. v. Crosetti Bros., Inc., 483 P.2d 70 (Or.1971).

60. 341 F.2d 335 (7th Cir.1965).

61. See § 17–14 infra; Roehrs v. Lees, 178 N.J.Super. 399, 429 A.2d 388 (1981).

A third party may qualify as a third party beneficiary even if the beneficiary is not named, identifiable or even in being at the time of contracting. It is sufficient that he be identifiable when the time arrives for the performance of the promise made for the benefit of the third party.[62] The Restatement, Second adds, however, that this is one of the factors to be considered in determining whether the beneficiary is an intended or incidental beneficiary.[63]

At the beginning of this section it was stated that many courts have emphasized the test of "intent to benefit." Some courts have used this test as a sole test [64] but others have looked to see, in addition, if the third party qualifies as a creditor or a donee beneficiary.[65]

The Restatement, Second on this point is discussed in the next section.

A good number of states have enacted statutes governing the question of third party beneficiaries. By and large, the questions which arise and the solutions reached are the same as those in non-statutory states.[66]

 WESTLAW REFERENCES

"third party beneficiary" /s "intent to benefit"

95k187(1) /p intent! intend! /2 benefit

find 449 a2d 666

lucas +3 hamm /p "intended beneficiary"

moch +5 rensselaer

§ 17–4. The Second Restatement

The Restatement, Second has produced a new formulation of the doctrine of third party beneficiary but it certainly has its roots in the past. It avoids the use of the terms "donee" and "creditor" beneficiaries because they "carry overtones of obsolete doctrinal difficulties" and adopts the test of intent to benefit which we have just explored.[67]

---

62. See Beverly v. Macy, 702 F.2d 931 (11th Cir.1983); United States v. State Farm Mut. Automobile Ins. Co., 455 F.2d 789 (10th Cir.1972); Keith v. Schiefen-Stockham Ins. Agency, Inc., 209 Kan. 537, 498 P.2d 265 (1972); Associated Teachers of Huntington, Inc. v. Board of Ed., 33 N.Y.2d 229, 306 N.E.2d 791, 351 N.Y.S.2d 670 (1973). Restatement, Contracts § 139; but see Data Proc. Fin. & Gen. Corp. v. I.B.M. Corp., 430 F.2d 1277 (8th Cir.1970).

63. Restatement, Second, Contracts § 308, Comment a.

64. Whether the third person is a creditor or donee beneficiary is relevant primarily in determining the issue of intent to benefit. See Broadway Maintenance Corp. v. Rutgers, 90 N.J. 253, 447 A.2d 906 (1982).

65. See e.g. Seavers v. Ransom, 224 N.Y. 233, 120 N.E. 639 (1918) (court stressed that there was not only an intent to benefit but also a close family relationship between the promisee and the beneficiary.)

66. A table of statutes appears in 2 Williston § 367. For a discussion see id. § 365; Note, The Third Party Beneficiary Concept; A Proposal, 57 Colum.L.Rev. 406, 414–15 (1957).

67. Restatement, Second, Contracts Introductory Note to Ch. 14 and Reporter's Note to § 302. See § 17–3 supra. It should be recalled that the First Restatement did not employ the test of intent to benefit but rather decided cases based on three categories—creditor, donee and incidental beneficiaries. See § 17–2 supra.

However, in order to qualify as an intended beneficiary the third party must meet two requirements otherwise he is only an incidental beneficiary.[68]

These two requirements are listed in § 302. (1) The third party must show that recognition of a right to performance in the beneficiary "is appropriate to effectuate the intention of the parties." (2)(a) "[T]he performance of the promise will satisfy an obligation of the promisee to pay money to the beneficiary" *or* (b) "the circumstances indicate that the promisee intends to give the beneficiary the benefit of the promised performance."

The first requirement clearly relates to intent to benefit. It does not attempt to solve the many problems, already discussed, that are inherent in these words.[69]

It should be noted that the second requirement is in the alternative. As previously stated the Restatement, Second avoids the use of the terms "donee" and "creditor" beneficiary. Thus, one is somewhat surprised when one reads the alternatives set forth in the second requirement. The first one certainly relates to creditor beneficiaries and the second to donee beneficiaries. Instead of using the words "creditor" and "donee" beneficiaries the Restatement, Second refers to a promise under (a) as a "promise to pay the promisee's debt" and a promise under (b) as a "gift promise".[70]

In the case of a promise "to pay the promisee's debt" (creditor beneficiary) the Restatement, Second makes some significant changes. Contrary to the First Restatement which stated that a third party qualified as a third party beneficiary even if there was only a *supposed* obligation owing from the promisee to the beneficiary,[71] the Second Restatement requires an *actual* obligation owing from the promisee to the beneficiary.[72] In addition the performance of the promise of the promisor must satisfy an obligation of the promisee to pay money or its equivalent.[73] Thus, a case that was looked upon as involving a creditor beneficiary under the First Restatement may be looked upon as involving a donee situation under the Second Restatement.[74]

Subdivision (b) relates to a "gift promise" or under the old terminology a donee beneficiary. Notice that there are no restrictions on a

---

68. See Restatement, Second, Contracts § 302(2); Reidy v. Macauley, 57 N.C.App. 184, 290 S.E.2d 746 (1982), review denied 306 N.C. 386, 294 S.E.2d 211 (1982).

69. See § 17–3 supra.

70. Restatement, Second, Contracts § 302, Comments (b) and (c).

71. See § 17–2 supra.

72. Restatement, Second, Contracts § 302, Comment (b). However, a "suretyship relation may exist even though the duty of the promisee is voidable or unenforceable by reason of the statute of limita-

tions, the Statute of Frauds, or a discharge in bankruptcy." See § 17–2 note 13 supra.

73. Restatement, Second, Contracts § 302, Comment b. In this comment it is stated that the equivalent of money is something that is easily converted into money, "as in cases of obligations to deliver commodities or securities which are actively traded in organized markets." Id.

74. See Restatement, Second, Contracts § 302, Comment b; Rae v. Air–Speed, Inc., 386 Mass. 187, 435 N.E.2d 628 (1982).

donee beneficiary, as for example, the requirement of a close family relationship between the promisee and the beneficiary.[75]

The Restatement, Second also states that a third party who does not qualify as an intended beneficiary under the rules stated above may qualify as an intended beneficiary "if the beneficiary would be reasonable in relying on the promise as manifesting an intention to confer a right upon him * * *."[76] The comment does not speak in terms of actual reliance but rather in terms of whether reliance would be reasonable. The illustrations used, however, do involve actual reliance.[77]

Parenthetically, it may be noted that the Restatement, Second agrees that the parties may agree as they wish on the issue of third party beneficiaries so long as the agreement is not contrary to public policy.[78]

 WESTLAW REFERENCES
"third party beneficiary" /p second 2d /1 restatement

§ 17–5. Relationship of Third Party Beneficiary to the Statute of Wills

Under the Statute of Wills and its modern descendants a testamentary disposition must usually be in writing, signed and witnessed in a rather rigidly specified manner. If a contract for the benefit of a third party makes the beneficiary's rights conditional upon his surviving the promisee, some courts have held that he acquires no rights because of non-compliance with the Statute of Wills.[79] This is clearly incorrect. The promisee is not disposing of an existing right by will but is creating a present conditional right by contract.[80] If compliance with the Statute of Wills were required, no life insurance policy would be enforceable.

---

75. Restatement, Second, Contracts § 302. See note 65 supra.

76. Restatement, Second, Contracts § 302, Comment d. See Aronowicz v. Nalley's, Inc., 30 Cal.App.3d 27, 106 Cal.Rptr. 424 (1972). The reliance referred to here is the reliance of the beneficiary and not the reliance of the promisee. See Overlock v. Central Vt. Pub. Serv. Corp., 126 Vt. 549, 237 A.2d 356 (1967); Loews Corp. v. Sperry Corp., 86 A.D.2d 221, 449 N.Y.S.2d 715 (1st Dept.1982). See Note, "Should a beneficiary be allowed to invoke promisee's reliance to enforce promisor's gratuitous promise?", 6 Val.U.L.Rev. 353 (1972).

77. See Restatement, Second, Contracts § 302 ill. 11, 12.

78. Restatement, Second, Contracts § 302.

79. See Coley v. English, 235 Ark. 215, 357 S.W.2d 529 (1962); McCarthy v. Pieret,

281 N.Y. 407, 24 N.E.2d 102 (1939), reargument denied 282 N.Y. 800, 27 N.E.2d 207 (1940). But see Freer v. J.G. Putman Funeral Home, Inc., 195 Ark. 307, 111 S.W.2d 463 (1937); In re Estate of Hillowitz, 22 N.Y.2d 107, 291 N.Y.S.2d 325, 238 N.E.2d 723 (1968).

80. See Murray on Contracts § 278, at 567–68. If, however, the promisor undertakes by contract to provide for the beneficiary by will, in some jurisdictions the Statute of Frauds provides that his promise must be in writing. See McKinney's N.Y. E.P.T.L. 13–2.1(2). A number of peculiar rules govern contracts to make wills. See Marosites v. Proctor, 59 N.C.App. 353, 296 S.E.2d 526 (1982); Note, Separation Agreements to Make Mutual Wills for the Benefit of Third Parties, 18 Hastings L.J. 423 (1967).

WESTLAW REFERENCES
"statute of wills"　/s　"third party beneficiary"

§ 17–6. The Mortgage Assumption Cases and Vrooman v. Turner

A mortgage is a security interest in real property typically given in exchange for a loan. The loan is usually evidenced by a bond or note.[81] Suppose that A in exchange for a loan gives a bond and mortgage to B and sells the mortgaged property to C. The transaction in the past could be negotiated in two ways.[82] C could "assume" the mortgage, which in common usage means that he promises A that he will pay the mortgage indebtedness to B. In such a case the situation is in essence the same as Lawrence v. Fox.[83] It is generally agreed that B is a third party beneficiary of C's promise made to A.[84] Continuing with this illustration, if C conveyed the property to D who validly assumed the mortgage, B would be a third party beneficiary of D's promise to C.[85]

If, in the conveyance, C had merely taken subject to the mortgage, that is, recognized that there was a security interest in the land but assumed no personal obligation in regard to the indebtedness, B clearly would not be a third party beneficiary since C has not made any promise with respect to payment of indebtedness.[86] Suppose, however, C, despite the absence of any personal obligation on his part, in a subsequent conveyance to D causes D to assume the mortgage. This was the situation in the well known case of Vrooman v. Turner.[87]

The court ruled that D's promise to pay the indebtedness was not enforceable by B. It stated that before a party may qualify as a third party beneficiary two requirements must be met. First, there must be an intent to benefit, which the court apparently found to exist, and, second, there must be an obligation owing from the promisee to the beneficiary. The second requisite was missing because C, the promisee, had not made any promise with respect to the indebtedness.[88]

---

81. The bond represents a personal obligation and the mortgage a security interest.

82. In modern days what is said here has been changed by "a due on sales" clause inserted in the mortgage. Under this clause when the property is sold the entire amount due becomes due and payable. For the most part these clauses have been sustained as written. See Income Realty & Mortgage, Inc. v. Columbia Savings & Loan Ass'n, 661 P.2d 257 (Colo. 1983); First Federal Savings & Loan Ass'n v. Wick, 322 N.W.2d 860 (S.D.1982). Annot., What Transfers Justify Acceleration under "Due-on-Sales" Clause of Real-Estate Mortgage", 22 A.L.R.4th 1266 (1983).

83. 20 N.Y. 268 (1859). This case was discussed in § 17–1 supra.

84. See Burr v. Beers, 24 N.Y. 178 (1861); 4 Corbin § 796; 2 Williston § 383. Notice that this is a case where the promise is to pay directly to the third party. See § 17–3 supra.

85. See The Home v. Selling, 91 Or. 428, 179 P. 261 (1919). On the facts B would have a cause of action for breach against A, C and D but would be entitled to only one satisfaction. See § 17–13 infra.

86. See Schewe v. Bentsen, 424 F.2d 60 (5th Cir.1970) (nor may the vendor sue the vendee for failing to pay the mortgage debt as the vendee has made no promise).

87. 69 N.Y. 280 (1877).

88. Notice that in this case the Court posits a second requirement in addition to intent to benefit. See § 17–4 supra.

An interesting question with respect to cases such as Vrooman v. Turner, is why did C, who was under no personal liability to B, extract a promise of assumption from D? It is generally agreed that there is no basis for a finding that C's purpose was to confer a gift upon B.[89] Nor will it usually be concluded that the assumption clause was included inadvertently or by mistake.[90] Rather, generally it will be deemed that C's purpose was to guard against a supposed liability upon his part.[91]

What the court in Vrooman v. Turner actually decided was that B was not a third party beneficiary because an *actual* obligation owing from the promisee to the beneficiary is required to create a creditor beneficiary. A large number of cases are in accord with this conclusion.[92] As we have seen, however, the First Restatement disagrees.[93] It takes the position that a *supposed* obligation is sufficient.[94] The Second Restatement seems to conclude that the plaintiff in Vrooman v. Turner qualifies as a third party donee beneficiary. It indicates that the plaintiff is in fact an intended beneficiary or at least should be treated as an intended beneficiary under the theory of reliance.[95] Plaintiff cannot qualify as a creditor beneficiary under the Restatement Second because it requires an *actual* obligation owing from the promisee to the beneficiary to qualify as a third party beneficiary.[96]

WESTLAW REFERENCES
vrooman +3 turner
95k187(1) /p mortgag!

§ 17–7. Public Contracts

The primary question presented here is whether an inhabitant of a governmental unit is a third party beneficiary of a contract made by the governmental unit (promisee) with a promisor.[97] In a sense every

89. In some cases such a motive can be found. See Schneider v. Ferrigno, 110 Conn. 86, 147 A. 303 (1929); Federal Bond & Mortgage Co. v. Shapiro, 219 Mich. 13, 188 N.W. 465 (1922) (promisee wished to protect his second mortgage on the premises).

90. Parol evidence is admissible to strike out an assumption clause on grounds of mistake, to reform the instrument, or to show that the clause was inserted in the deed without the assent of the promisor. See Blass v. Terry, 156 N.Y. 122, 50 N.E. 953 (1898) (no assent); Kilmer v. Smith, 77 N.Y. 226 (1879) (clause stricken out); cf. Ross v. Warren, 196 Iowa 659, 195 N.W. 228 (1923) (insufficient evidence to justify reformation).

91. See 2 Williston § 386A.

92. See 4 Corbin § 796, at 151.

93. See § 17–2 supra. A large number of cases are also in accord with the First Restatement.

94. Restatement, Second, Contracts § 302, Comment d; Restatement, Second, Contracts § 304, Comment c, ill. 2.

95. Restatement, Second, Contracts § 302, Comment d. See discussion in § 17–6 supra.

96. See § 17–4 supra.

97. See Restatement, Second, Contracts § 313. "The rules stated in this Chapter apply to contracts with a government or governmental agency except to the extent that application would contravene the policy of the law authorizing the contract or prescribing remedies for its breach." Restatement, Second, Contracts § 313(1). It has been held that a non-inhabitant of the political unit in question may qualify as a third party beneficiary. Wilson v. Oliver Costich Co., 231 App.Div. 346, 247 N.Y.S. 131 (1931), affirmed 256 N.Y. 629, 177 N.E. 169 (1931).

contract made by a governmental unit is made for the benefit of its inhabitants. If a city contracts to have a police station, fire house, tax office, or park built, it does so to enhance the general welfare and, thus, to benefit the public. The ultimate question is whether there was an intent to benefit the inhabitants in the sense that individual inhabitants have the right to enforce the contract. In such an action, contrary to a taxpayers' action, the recovery goes to the individual rather than to the public treasury. Although for the most part the courts often purport to employ the same rules as are applied to private contracts, they are reluctant to find that such rights exist in this type of case.[98]

There are, nevertheless, situations where an individual inhabitant may be deemed to be a third party beneficiary. The first arises where the promisor agrees to perform services for the governmental unit which the unit is under a legal duty to perform to individual members of the public. In such a case it is held that the individuals may recover from the promisor if the promisor fails to perform his promise. Obviously the key question is when is a governmental unit under a duty to an individual member of the public? When or whether such a duty exists involves questions of tort law, the doctrine of sovereign immunity and, at times, questions of interpretation of statutes.[99]

The discussion immediately above related to plaintiffs who have been traditionally called creditor beneficiaries.[1] There are also situations where an individual has been held to be an intended donee beneficiary of the contract between the governmental unit and the promisor. A good illustration is the case of La Mourea v. Rhude.[2] In that case the defendant contractor promised the City of Duluth "to do certain work of sewer construction." The contract contemplated "the use of heavy charges of explosives." In consequence in the contract defendant was made "liable for any damages done to the work or other structure or public or *private property* and injuries sustained by persons." (emphasis supplied) Plaintiff's property was injured by the blasting. The court treats the plaintiff as a donee beneficiary and decides that the language manifests an intent to benefit plaintiff directly because damages were to be paid directly to him. In other words the promised performance ran directly to the plaintiff.[3]

---

98. See Restatement, Contracts § 145; Restatement, Second, Contracts § 313(2) which is also discussed in the next section.

99. New Hampshire Insurance Co. v. Madera, 144 Cal.App.3d 298, 192 Cal.Rptr. 548 (5th Dist.1983); St. Joseph Light & Power Co. v. Kaw Valley Tunneling, Inc., 589 S.W.2d 260 (Mo.1979), appeal after remand 660 S.W.2d 26 (Mo.App.1983) (en banc); see W. Prosser, Law of Torts 625–626 (4th ed. 1971).

1. See § 17–2 supra. However, whether these plaintiffs would be considered to be creditor beneficiaries under the Second

Restatement is a more difficult matter. Under the Second Restatement to qualify as a creditor beneficiary there must be an actual obligation on the part of the promisee to pay *money* or its equivalent to the beneficiary. See § 17–4 supra. Is a breach of a duty that results in a money judgment a duty to pay money within the meaning of the Second Restatement? See the specific language of Restatement, Second, Contracts § 313.

2. 209 Minn. 53, 295 N.W. 304 (1940).

3. See the discussion of to whom is the performance to run in § 17–3 supra.

This case should be carefully compared with a case such as H.R. Moch Co. v. Rensselaer Water Co.,[4] previously discussed.[5] Defendant, Water Company, had promised the City of Rensselaer to furnish the City with water at its hydrants. Plaintiff, an inhabitant sued when his house was destroyed by the failure to have sufficient water pressure at the hydrant. Again the issue was whether the plaintiff was an intended donee beneficiary. The court concluded that the promised performance ran to the City and that therefore the plaintiff was an incidental beneficiary. Clearly part of the reason for the decision was one grounded in public policy. In the words of the court if plaintiff were permitted to recover the defendant's "field of obligation would be expanded beyond reasonable limits." [6] The majority of the cases are in accord.[7] As previously indicated, in the area of the public contracts, courts are reluctant to find that an inhabitant qualifies as a third party beneficiary.[8]

In the Moch case there was also a promise the defendant made to the City to limit the prices that could be charged by the Water Company. The court indicated that the performance was to run to the individual and that therefore the plaintiff could qualify as a third party beneficiary. There are many cases in accord.[9] Notice that in this situation there was no possibility of the crushing burden as there was in the branch of the case relating to the fire hydrant.

 WESTLAW REFERENCES
"la mourea" +3 rhude

§ 17–8. Promises of Indemnity

Indemnification is a vast and complicated problem. Here we are concerned only with the question of whether a third party qualifies as a third party beneficiary of a promise of indemnification against loss or a promise of indemnification against liability.[10]

---

4. 247 N.Y. 160, 159 N.E. 896 (1928).

5. See § 17–3 supra.

6. H.R. Moch Co. v. Rensselaer Water Co., 247 N.Y. 160, 164, 159 N.E. 896, 897 (1928).

7. See Farnsworth, Contracts § 10.4 (1982).

8. This is illustrated by the cases where contractors have promised a governmental unit to repair or maintain highways. See Davis v. Nelson-Deppe, Inc., 91 Idaho 463, 424 P.2d 733 (1967). See also Kornblut v. Chevron Oil Co., 88 Misc.2d 651, 389 N.Y.S. 2d 232 (1976), reversed 62 A.D.2d 831, 407 N.Y.S.2d 498 (2d Dep't 1978), affirmed 48 N.Y.2d 853, 424 N.Y.S.2d 429, 400 N.E.2d 368 (1979). Contra, Potter v. Carolina Water Co., 253 N.C. 112, 116 S.E.2d 374 (1960); but see, Matternes v. Winston-Sa-

lem, 286 N.C. 1, 209 S.E.2d 481 (1974). But see the discussion in § 17–8 infra.

9. See, e.g., Bush v. Upper Valley Telecable Co., 96 Idaho 83, 524 P.2d 1055 (1973); Rochester Tel. Co. v. Ross, 195 N.Y. 429, 88 N.E. 793 (1909); Pond v. New Rochelle Water Co., 183 N.Y. 330, 76 N.E. 211 (1906). So also a contract with a municipality and a tract developer as to compliance with subdivision regulations has been held to give enforceable rights to a purchaser of a house within the tract. Town of Ogden v. Earl R. Howarth & Sons, Inc., 58 Misc.2d 213, 294 N.Y.S.2d 430 (1968).

10. The distinction is well set out in the case of Sorenson v. Overland Corp., 142 F.Supp. 354 (D.Del.1956), affirmed 242 F.2d 70 (3d Cir.1957); Restatement, Security § 82, Comment l.

In essence a promise of indemnity against loss is a promise by the indemnitor to reimburse the indemnitee after the indemnitee has paid the third party. For example, A Corp. (indemnitee) obtained a policy of fidelity insurance from I (indemnitor) under which I agreed to reimburse (indemnify) A against any loss which A might sustain through the fraudulent or dishonest acts of any of its own employees. C, a third party, has a claim against A for the dishonest acts of an employee. The question is may C successfully sue I on a third party beneficiary theory? The answer is clearly in the negative because it is clear that I need not perform until A has paid. Clearly the promised performance runs to A and not C.[11]

The situation is somewhat different in the case of indemnity against liability—a situation in which I (indemnitor) promises A (indemnitee) that he will discharge A's legal liability in the event that A becomes liable to the third party. This is the situation presented under a liability insurance policy.

In this type of situation it is often held that the third party may not recover from the indemnitor until a valid judgment has been obtained against the indemnitee.[12] Under this holding in effect the third party is not a third party beneficiary until a judgment has been obtained. This conclusion is often bolstered by specific language in the insurance contract providing that no action shall be brought against the insurer[13] but also often as a result of a policy against having the jury be aware that an insurer will ultimately pay the damages the jury assesses.[14]

Despite the discussion above wherein it is stated that a promise of indemnity against loss does not give rise to a third party beneficiary situation, there are a significant number of municipality cases to the contrary. A typical illustration will suffice. A, a municipality, owes a duty to the public to keep its streets in good repair.[15] B promises A to keep the streets in good repair and also promises to indemnify A

11. Ronnau v. Caravan Int'l Corp., 205 Kan. 154, 468 P.2d 118 (1970).

12. See Jefferson v. Sinclair Ref. Co., 10 N.Y.2d 422, 223 N.Y.S.2d 863, 179 N.E.2d 706 (1961); Snyder Plumbing & Heating Corp. v. Purcell, 9 A.D.2d 505, 195 N.Y.S.2d 780 (1st Dep't.1960); Smith v. King, 52 N.C.App. 158, 277 S.E.2d 875 (1981). There are cases to the contrary. See Annot., 64 A.L.R.3d 1207 (1975).

13. Litigation concerning the validity and effect of such language has been especially prolific in conflict of laws cases. For discussions of the problems of contract law and conflict of laws, see MacDonald, Direct Action Against Liability Insurance Companies, 1957 Wis.L.Rev. 612; Note, Foreign Application of Louisiana's Direct Action Statute: Two Views, 57 Colum.L.Rev. 256 (1957); Note, Direct-Action Statutes: Their

Operational and Conflict-of-Law Problems, 74 Harv.L.Rev. 357 (1960). For a decision holding that such contractual language is void because it impedes the effectiveness of the remedies of an injured party, see Shingleton v. Bussey, 223 So.2d 713 (Fla.1969).

14. See Morton v. Maryland Cas. Co., 1 A.D.2d 116, 148 N.Y.S.2d 524 (2d Dep't 1955), affirmed 4 N.Y.2d 488, 176 N.Y.S.2d 329, 151 N.E.2d 881 (1958). This policy has been somewhat relaxed in New York, but only as to cases in which the law of another jurisdiction is applicable. See Oltarsh v. Aetna Ins. Co., 15 N.Y.2d 111, 256 N.Y.S.2d 577, 204 N.E.2d 622 (1965).

15. See § 17–7 note 8 supra wherein it is noted that in the majority of jurisdictions a promise by a contractor to keep streets in repair does not create a third party beneficiary situation.

against loss if it fails to keep the streets in good repair. B breaches its promise to keep the streets in good repair and as a result C is injured.

Under the rule relating to indemnity against loss, discussed above, C should not be considered a third party beneficiary. As indicated above in this type of case there are a number of cases that have held that C is a third party beneficiary.[16] This is in part due to the original Restatement which did not employ the test of intent to benefit but rather allowed third parties to sue if they were creditor or donee beneficiaries.[17] The point of the illustration is that although there is no intent to benefit C, under the facts asserted he is a creditor beneficiary. Thus, under the analysis of the First Restatement C is an intended creditor beneficiary and as we have seen courts have followed this analysis.[18]

The Restatement, Second takes pains to indicate its disapproval of this result. Instead it sets forth a more flexible rule. It states that where, as here, the municipality is under a duty to C, C may bring an action against the promisor if the action "is consistent with the terms of the contract and with policy of the law authorizing the contract and prescribing remedies for its breach".[19] The Restatement, Second lists as factors which may make an action against the promisor inappropriate: "arrangements for governmental control over the litigation and settlement of claims, the likelihood of impairment of service or of excessive financial burden, and the availability of alternatives such as insurance." [20]

 WESTLAW REFERENCES
indemnity /s "third party beneficiary"

§ 17–9. The Surety Bond Cases

When a general contractor undertakes substantial construction for a private owner or a public works project for the United States or other political body it is common to require the general contractor to obtain a surety bond from a bonding company. In third party beneficiary terms the general contractor and the surety company are the promisors, the owner is the promisee and the potential beneficiaries are those named in the bond.[21]

---

16. See O'Connell v. Merchants' & Police Dist. Tel. Co., 167 Ky. 468, 180 S.W. 845 (1915); Rigney v. New York Cent. & Hudson River R.R. Co., 217 N.Y. 31, 111 N.E. 226 (1916); Stewart v. Sullivan County, 196 Tenn. 49, 264 S.W.2d 217 (1953); cf. Coley v. Cohen, 169 Misc. 933, 9 N.Y.S.2d 503 (1939), affirmed 258 App.Div. 292, 17 N.Y.S.2d 101 (4th Dep't 1939), affirmed 289 N.Y. 365, 45 N.E.2d 913 (1942). But see Silton v. Kansas City, 446 S.W.2d 129 (Mo. 1969) (indemnity against loss provision held to be solely for the benefit of the promisee).

17. See § 17–2 supra.

18. See § 17–7 note 8 supra and Blair v. Anderson, 325 A.2d 94 (Del.1974).

19. Restatement, Second, Contracts § 313(2)(b).

20. Restatement, Second, Contracts § 313, Comment a; see also id. ill. 5.

21. The language of the bond must be read with great care. See, e.g. Home Indem. Co. v. Daniels Const. Co., 285 Ala. 68, 228 So.2d 824 (1969) (language of the bond held to include all of the subcontractors of

There are various types of bonds that may be used singly or in conjunction with one another. The one that is most likely to create a third party beneficiary situation is a payment bond. Such a bond, in technical terms is "conditioned to be void" upon payment by the contractor to those named in the bond. In other words if the principal does not pay, the surety company will pay.[22]

The question is whether these parties are third party beneficiaries of the payment bond. As a practical matter the situation is quite different if the owner is a private owner or the owner is the United States or a political subdivision. In the case of a private owner these parties, if not paid, will have a mechanics' lien against the owner.[23] In the public works situation this is not true since public property is generally exempt from a mechanics' lien. As a result, the United States and other political subdivisions have passed statutes requiring a payment bond in favor of these parties.[24] Since the purpose of the statutes is to protect these parties because they do not have mechanics' liens in public property it has generally been held that they are third party beneficiaries of bonds given pursuant to these statutes.[25]

The situation is a little more complicated in the case of a private owner. In this case it has often been concluded that the owner's intent is to protect against mechanics' liens and therefore these parties are incidental beneficiaries.[26] However, other courts have recognized that the owner is protected if these parties are looked upon as third party beneficiaries because, in such a case, the promisors will be bound to pay

---

the general contractor but not subcontractors of subcontractors). Ordinarily the bond will include subcontractors of subcontractors and laborers of materialmen. See note 24 infra.

22. Since the courts are reluctant to conclude that parties not in privity are third party beneficiaries of a construction contract, the parties named in the bond ordinarily will not be third party beneficiaries of any other contract. See Superior Glass Co., Inc. v. First Bristol County Nat'l Bank, 380 Mass. 829, 406 N.E.2d 672 (1980). See § 17–3 supra. In suretyship terms the general contractor is the principal debtor, the binding company is the surety and the parties named in the bond are the creditors.

23. This means that even if there is no personal obligation on the part of the owner to pay these parties there is a lien on his property that may be foreclosed.

24. See, e.g., Miller Act, 40 U.S.C.A. §§ 270a–270e (West Supp.1986); Graybar Elec. Co. v. John A. Volpe Constr. Co., 387 F.2d 55 (5th Cir.1967). A Miller Act payment bond covers only (1) those material-

men, laborers and contractors who deal directly with a prime contractor and (2) those materialmen, laborers and contractors who have a direct relationship with a subcontractor. Those in the second category must give written notice to the contractor within 90 days after the date on which such claimant performed the last of the labor or delivered the last of the material for which the claim is made. See MacEvoy v. United States, 322 U.S. 102, 64 S.Ct. 890, 88 L.Ed. 1163 (1944); Cushman, Surety Bonds on Federal Construction Contracts: Current Decisions Reviewed, 25 Fordham L.Rev. 241, 249 (1956).

25. Acoustics, Inc. v. Hanover Ins. Co., 118 N.J.Super. 361, 287 A.2d 482 (1971); Neenah Foundry Co. v. Nat'l Sur. Corp., 47 Ill.App.2d 427, 197 N.E.2d 744 (1964); Socony-Vacuum Oil Co. v. Continental Cas. Co., 219 F.2d 645 (2d Cir.1955). Carolina Builders Corp. v. AAA Dry Wall, Inc., 43 N.C.App. 444, 259 S.E.2d 364 (1979).

26. Ross v. Imperial Const. Co., 572 F.2d 518 (5th Cir.1978); Fidelity & Deposit Co. of Baltimore v. Rainer, 220 Ala. 262, 125 So. 55 (1929).

them and that payment will extinguish the possibility of a mechanics' lien.[27]

The problem is further complicated when a subcontractor furnishes the general contractor with a payment bond. The question again is whether the parties named are third party beneficiaries of this bond.[28]

Much has been said as to whether the beneficiaries under a payment bond are creditor or donee beneficiaries.[29] Where a statute requires the delivery of a payment bond, it is clear that the situation is *sui generis* and does not fit within the categories previously developed. This is so because a private owner does not owe a personal obligation to the alleged beneficiary but his land is burdened by their lien. The situation is more analagous to a creditor beneficiary situation.[30] This situation is not the same as Vrooman v. Turner discussed above because in that case not only did the promisee not owe a personal obligation to the beneficiary, in addition, when he conveyed the property to the party who assumed, he was no longer concerned with the lien of the mortgage.[31] It has been suggested that no point is served in pursuing this discussion.[32]

A different situation arises in the case of a performance bond. This type of bond is ordinarily designed to assure payment of damages to the owner in the event of the contractor's non-performance. It seems clear that the parties in question are not third party beneficiaries of a performance bond.[33] However, the argument is often made that what is labeled as a performance bond is by virtue of the language therein also a payment bond.[34]

27. See Ogden Development Corp. v. Federal Insurance Co., 508 F.2d 583 (2d Cir.1974); Socony-Vacuum Oil Co. v. Continental Cas. Co., 219 F.2d 645 (2d Cir.1955); Daniel-Morris Co. v. Glens Falls Indem. Co., 308 N.Y. 464, 126 N.E.2d 750 (1955); 2 Williston § 372; Restatement, Second, Contracts § 302, ill. 12; Mungall, The Jacobs Case: Pennsylvania Contract Bond Law Goes Modern, 11 Vill.L.Rev. 41, 42–43 (1965).

28. An intent to benefit the named beneficiaries was found in Daniel Morris Co. v. Glens Falls Indem. Co., 308 N.Y. 464, 126 N.E.2d 750 (1955). If the named parties are already protected under another bond there is a split of authority as to whether the named parties are protected. Compare Socony-Vacuum Oil Co. v. Continental Cas. Co., 219 F.2d 645 (2nd Cir.1955) with Treasure State Indus., Inc. v. Welch, 173 Mont. 408, 567 P.2d 947 (1977) and McGrath v. American Sur. Co., 307 N.Y. 552, 122 N.E.2d 906 (1954).

29. Compare 2 Williston § 372 with 4 Corbin § 802 (1951).

30. See Holiday Development Co. v. J.A. Tobin Const. Co., 549 Kan. 701, 549 P.2d 1376 (1976). Under the Restatement, Second is there an actual obligation to pay money or its equivalent when a lien exists? See Restatement, Second, Contracts § 302, Comment d, ill. 12.

31. See discussion in § 17–6 supra.

32. L. Simpson, Annual Survey of American Law (Contracts), 31 N.Y.U.L. Rev. 471, 474 (1956).

33. See Frommeyer v. L. & R. Constr. Co., 139 F.Supp. 579 (D.N.J.1956); Scales-Douwes Corp. v. Paulaura Realty Corp., 24 N.Y.S.2d 724, 301 N.Y.S.2d 980, 249 N.E.2d 760 (1969); Restatement, Security § 166.

34. See, e.g. Cretex Companies v. Const. Leaders, 342 N.W.2d 135 (Minn.1984); Novak & Co. v. Travelers Indemnity Co., 56 A.D.2d 418, 392 N.Y.S.2d 901 (2d Dep't 1977), appeal denied 42 N.Y.2d 806, 398 N.Y.S.2d 1027, 367 N.E.2d 660 (1977).

There are also bonds that are expressly labeled as a joint performance—payment bond. The decisions in this situation have not been harmonious.[35] A leading case has indicated that where there is a performance—payment bond, at least presumptively, the bond is intended to inure solely to the benefit of the promisee owner; otherwise the bond might be dissipated in paying the third party beneficiaries without paying the promisee.[36]

 WESTLAW REFERENCES
"surety bond" /s "third party beneficiary"
390k136 /p "third party beneficiary"
find 387 f2d 55
170bk408
393k67(4)
di("miller act" /p surety)

§ 17–10. May the Promisor Assert Against the Beneficiary a Defense or Claim That He Has Against the Promisee?

In all of the preceding sections the issue has been who qualifies as a third party beneficiary. The main point being made here is that even though a party not in privity qualifies as a third party beneficiary he may still lose the case. This is so because the rights of the beneficiary stem from the contract between the promisor and the promisee.[37] For this reason the general rule is that the promisor may assert against the beneficiary any defense which he could assert against the promisee.[38]

35. See 4 Corbin §§ 799–803; 2 Williston § 372.

36. Fosmire v. National Sur. Co., 229 N.Y. 44, 127 N.E. 472 (1920) remit. amend. & rearg. denied 229 N.Y. 564, 128 N.E. 130 (1920). But cf. Johnson Serv. Co. v. E.H. Monin, 253 N.Y. 417, 171 N.E. 692 (1930). These and subsequent New York cases are discussed in Note, Third Party Beneficiaries: Test for Materialmen's Suit on Contractor's Surety Bond, 41 Cornell L.Q. 482 (1956); Comment, Third Party Beneficiaries on a Contractor's Surety Bond, 27 Fordham L.Rev. 262 (1958). Contra, Byram Lumber and Supply Co. v. Page, 109 Conn. 256, 146 A. 293 (1929); Neenah Foundry Co. v. National Sur. Corp., 47 Ill. App.2d 427, 197 N.E.2d 744 (1964). The presumption discussed in Fosmire may be rebutted if the bond specifically states that it is for the benefit of these third parties or if the bond is given pursuant to a statute which permits such suits. Even in these cases, however, the third party is obliged to show that the promisee has received substantial performance or that the bond is sufficient to cover the claims of the promisee and the beneficiaries. It is also possible

that the promisee has a cause of action on behalf of the third parties as a trustee but the question remains whether he is obligated to bring such an action. See Comment, Third Party Beneficiaries on a Contractor's Surety Bond, 27 Fordham L.Rev. 262 (1958); see also Scale-Douwes Corp. v. Paulaura Realty Corp., 24 N.Y.S.2d 724, 301 N.Y.S.2d 980, 249 N.E.2d 760 (1969).

37. See Rotermund v. United States Steel Corp., 474 F.2d 1139 (8th Cir.1973); Willis v. Hamilton Mut. Ins. Co., 614 S.W.2d 251 (Ky.App.1981).

38. See Punikaia v. Clark, 720 F.2d 564 (9th Cir.1983), cert. denied 469 U.S. 816, 105 S.Ct. 83, 83 L.Ed.2d 30 (1984). This general rule applies to both creditor and donee beneficiaries. See Restatement, Second, Contracts § 309; Blue Cross, Inc. v. Ayotte, 35 A.D.2d 258, 315 N.Y.S.2d 998 (3d Dep't 1970). Here we are talking about a defense that the promisor has against the promisee. It goes without saying that the promisor may assert any wrongful conduct on the part of the beneficiary against the beneficiary. Restatement, Second, Contracts § 309; Dorman v. Pan-American In-

Thus, for example, if A (promisee) promises not to cut down certain timber in exchange for B's promise (promissor) to pay C $1,000 and A cuts down the timber, C, although he qualifies as a third party beneficiary, may not successfully sue B, because B has the defense of non-performance against A.[39] The same would be true, for example, if the defense of the promisor against the promisee is fraud,[40] mistake,[41] lack of consideration[42] and illegality.[43]

There are a number of exceptions to the general rule stated here. The first is where the parties agree that the beneficiaries will have an enforceable right despite any defense which the promisor has against the promisee.[44] This situation arises most frequently in fire insurance contracts containing "the standard mortgagee clause" which provides that a mortgagee (3rd party) may recover on the policy despite any act or neglect of the mortgagor-promisee. Under this clause it is possible for the mortgagee to recover from the insurer despite fraud or non-payment of premium by the promisee.[45]

There are occasional cases that violate the general rule presumably on a policy basis. Thus, in collective bargaining agreements it has been held that the employer may not use against its employees a defense that it has against the union.[46] At times it has been held that a beneficiary under a payment bond[47] has rights against the surety even though the surety would have a defense against the owner.[48]

Another exception to the general rule occurs when the doctrine of estoppel applies. In other words at times the promisor will be estopped

---

vestments, Inc., 625 F.2d 605 (5th Cir. 1980).

39. See Kyner v. Clark, 29 F.2d 545 (8th Cir.1928); Sedgwick v. Blanchard, 170 Wis. 121, 174 N.W. 459 (1919).

40. While the beneficiary's rights are subject to the defense of fraud, the promisor may not retain the benefits of the transaction if he wishes to rely on the defense. See Arnold v. Nichols, 64 N.Y. 117 (1876).

41. See Page v. Hinchee, 174 Okl. 537, 51 P.2d 487 (1935).

42. See Western Farm Bureau Mut. Ins. Co. v. Barela, 79 N.M. 149, 441 P. 2d 47 (1968). But see Bass v. John Hancock Mut. Life Ins. Co., 10 Cal.3d 792, 518 P.2d 1147, 112 Cal.Rptr. 1950 (1974); Lawhead v. Booth, 115 W.Va. 490, 177 S.E. 283 (1934).

43. See Burns Jackson Miller Summit & Spitzer v. Lindner, 59 N.Y.2d 314, 464 N.Y.S.2d 712, 451 N.E.2d 459 (1983); Lawhead v. Booth, 115 W.Va. 490, 177 S.E. 283 (1934).

44. See Schneider Moving & Storage v. Robbins, 466 U.S. 364, 104 S.Ct. 1844, 80 L.Ed.2d 366 (1984) cert. granted, 464 U.S. 813, 104 S.Ct. 66, 78 L.Ed.2d 81 (1983).

45. General Credit Corp. v. Imperial Cas. & Indem. Co., 167 Neb. 833, 95 N.W.2d 145 (1959); Goldstein v. Nat'l Liberty Ins. Co., 256 N.Y. 26, 175 N.E. 359 (1931), reversed 134 Misc. 90, 234 N.Y.S. 40 (1928); Prudential Ins. Co. v. Franklin Fire Ins. Co., 180 S.C. 250, 185 S.E. 537 (1936).

46. See Lewis v. Benedict Coal Corp., 361 U.S. 459, 80 S.Ct. 489, 4 L.Ed.2d 442 (1960); Western Washington Cement Masons Health & Security Trust Funds v. Hillis Homes, 26 Wn.App. 224, 612 P.2d 436 (1980). A collective bargaining agreement is not a typical third-party beneficiary situation and policy considerations should prevail.

47. See § 17–9 supra.

48. See School Dist. of Kansas City ex rel. Koken Iron Works v. Livers, 147 Mo. 580, 49 S.W. 507 (1899); Doll v. Crume, 41 Neb. 655, 59 N.W. 806 (1894). But see Rumsey Elec. Co. v. Univ. of Delaware, 358 A.2d 712 (Del.Super.1976); Camelot Excavating Co. v. St. Paul Fire & Marine Ins. Co., 410 Mich. 118, 301 N.W.2d 275 (1981); Haakinson & Beaty Co. v. Inland Insurance Co., 216 Neb. 426, 344 N.W.2d 454 (1984).

from asserting defenses that he has against the promisee by virtue of reliance on the part of the beneficiary.[49]

Still another exception to this rule exists under the confusing label of vesting, the subject of the next section.

There are very few cases dealing with the question of whether the promisor may assert counterclaims against the beneficiary which he might assert against the promisee. The general answer appears to be that he may by way of counterclaim assert claims that arise out of the same transaction but not a claim arising out of other transactions.[50]

 WESTLAW REFERENCES
promisor /s assert*** /s defense /s beneficiary
95k328(4)
find 492 f2d 772

§ 17–11. Vesting—Attempted Discharge or Modification of the Rights of a Third Party Beneficiary

This section assumes that A is a third party beneficiary of a contract between B (promisee) and C (promisor). The question here is whether B and C by an agreement subsequent to the contract that created the rights of the third party, may destroy or modify these rights. It is agreed that after a certain point this may not be done. The technical language is that this may not be done if the rights of the beneficiary vest before he learned of the second agreement.[51] The question then becomes at what point in time the rights of the beneficiary vest.

According to the original Restatement the rights of a creditor beneficiary vest when he brings an action to enforce the contract or otherwise materially changes his position before he knows of the discharge or the modification. This view requires injurious reliance on the part of the beneficiary before his rights vest.[52] Another view is that

49. See Levy v. Empire Ins. Co., 379 F.2d 860 (5th Cir.1967) (beneficiary who purchased debentures in reliance on terms of written contract permitted to recover although the written contract was subject to conditions precedent not stated in the writing); Simmons v. Western Assurance Co., 205 F.2d 815 (5th Cir.1953); Aetna Ins. Co. v. Eisenberg, 188 F.Supp. 415 (E.D.Ark. 1960), affirmed 294 F.2d 301 (8th Cir.1961) (insurance policy covering furs stored by customers of furrier where furrier and insured cooperated in advertising coverage not avoidable against customers although furrier failed to comply with policy conditions); but see United States Pipe and Foundry Co. v. United States Fidelity and Guar. Co., 505 F.2d 88 (5th Cir.1974).

50. See Restatement, Second, Contracts § 309, Comment c; United States v. Indus.

Crane & Mfg. Corp., 492 F.2d 772 (5th Cir. 1974).

51. See Restatement, Second, Contracts § 311(2).

52. See Sears, Roebuck & Co. v. Jardel Co., 421 F.2d 1048 (3d Cir.1970); Morstain v. Kircher, 190 Minn. 78, 250 N.W. 727 (1933); Restatement, Contracts §§ 142–143; accord, Crowell v. Currier, 27 N.J.Eq. 152, aff'd sub nom. Crowell v. Hospital of St. Barnabas, 27 N.J.Eq. 650 (1876) (rescission permitted; no change of position); cf. Hartman v. Pistorius, 248 Ill. 568, 94 N.E. 131 (1911) (rescission permitted; court indicated that creditor beneficiary's rights do not vest while the performances running between promisee and promisor are still executory, unless the beneficiary changes his position in reliance upon the contract).

the rights of a creditor beneficiary vest upon learning of the initial contract and assenting to it.[53] The second view seems preferable in that once the creditor beneficiary has assented to the contract he is likely to rely in subtle ways, not easily provable, upon the security of the contract.[54]

When the beneficiary is a donee, according to the original Restatement, the rights of the beneficiary vest immediately upon the making of the contract.[55] This view is supported by a good number of life insurance cases [56] and a few other decisions.[57] A large number of cases have questioned the soundness of the original Restatement's position upon the theory that a donee beneficiary should not have greater rights than a creditor beneficiary.[58] Thus, the trend today is to apply the rules originally applied to creditor beneficiary to donee beneficiaries.[59] The Restatement, Second has noted these criticisms and has set forth a rule which applies equally well to all intended beneficiaries.[60]

Under the rule of the Second Restatement the rights of a beneficiary vest when the beneficiary "materially changes his position in justifiable reliance on the promise or brings suit on it or manifests assent to it at the request of the promisor or promisee." [61]

It is generally agreed that the parties may by agreement determine the issue of vesting. They may by agreement create a right in the beneficiary that may not be varied by a subsequent agreement without the beneficiaries' consent.[62] Conversely the parties may by agreement

53. See Palmer v. Radio Corp., 453 F.2d 1133 (5th Cir.1971); Copeland v. Beard, 217 Ala. 216, 115 So. 389 (1928) (on theory that creditor's assent makes him a party to the contract); Gifford v. Corrigan, 117 N.Y. 257, 22 N.E. 756 (1889). Sometimes assent is presumed. See Lawrence v. Fox, 20 N.Y. 268 (1859) (dictum; presumption of assent); Annot., 44 A.L.R.2d 1266 (1955). This is especially true if the beneficiary is an infant. See Rhodes v. Rhodes, 266 S.W.2d 790 (Ky.1953); Plunkett v. Atkins, 371 P.2d 727 (Okl.1962): But see Spates v. Spates, 267 Md. 72, 296 A.2d 581 (1972); Restatement, Second, Contracts § 311, Comment d.

54. See Gifford v. Corrigan, 117 N.Y. 257, 22 N.E. 756 (1889); Restatement, Second, Contracts § 311, Comment h (analogy to the law of offer and acceptance).

55. Restatement, Contracts § 142.

56. See, e.g., Ford v. Mutual Life Ins. Co., 283 Ill.App. 325 (1936); Whitehead v. New York Life Ins. Co., 102 N.Y. 143, 6 N.E. 267 (1886); Vance, The Beneficiary's Interest in a Life Insurance Policy, 31 Yale L.J. 343 (1922).

57. See Plunkett v. Atkins, 371 P.2d 727 (Okl.1962); Logan v. Glass, 136 Pa.

Super. 221, 7 A.2d 116 (1939) (following Restatement), affirmed 338 Pa. 489, 14 A.2d 306 (1940); Tweeddale v. Tweeddale, 116 Wis. 517, 93 N.W. 440 (1903).

58. See, e.g., McCulloch v. Canadian Pac. Ry. Co., 53 F.Supp. 534 (D.Minn.1943) (reliance required); Lehman v. Stout, 261 Minn. 384, 112 N.W.2d 640 (1961); Salesky v. Hat Corp., 20 A.D.2d 114, 244 N.Y.S.2d 965 (1st Dep't 1963); see Page, The Power of the Contracting Parties to Alter a Contract for Rendering Performance to a Third Person, 12 Wis.L.Rev. 141 (1937).

59. See e.g. Blackard v. Monarch's Mfrs. and Distribs., 131 Ind.App. 514, 169 N.E.2d 735 (1960); Comment, The Third Party Beneficiary Concept: A Proposal, 57 Colum.L.Rev. 406, 418–420 (1957).

60. Restatement, Second, Contracts § 311.

61. Restatement, Second, Contracts § 311(1), Comments a and b. Notice that this is a blending of the two rules originally applied to creditor beneficiaries.

62. See Restatement, Second, Contracts § 311. This broad statement is limited by considerations of fairness. Restatement, Second, Contracts § 311, Comment j.

reserve "a power to discharge or modify the promisor's duty".[63] This is nearly always done in modern life insurance policies,[64] employee death benefits plans [65] and the like.

The rights of the named irrevocable beneficiary in a life insurance policy may also be defeated by a provision in the contract that allows the insured promisee to borrow against it. In such a case the beneficiary may not complain if the promisee reduces or destroys his rights by borrowing pursuant to the terms of the contract.[66]

The doctrine of vesting forms an exception to the general rule that the promisor may assert against the beneficiary any defense which he could assert against the promisee.[67] After the rights of the beneficiary vest he is not subject to any defenses which the promisor has against the promisee which purports to vary or discharge the beneficiary's rights. In this connection it is important to stress that the question of vesting arises only where the promisor and the promisee purport to vary or discharge the rights of the beneficiary. When this is not the case the topic of vesting is irrelevant. Assume a case where the promisee agrees not to cut down certain timber and the promisor in exchange promises to pay $1000 to the beneficiary and the promisee does not perform. Assume also that the law of the jurisdiction is that the rights of the beneficiary vest immediately. On the facts the last statement is irrelevant because the case does not involve a situation where the promisee and the promisor attempt to vary or discharge their rights of the promisee. Since the topic of vesting is irrelevant it is clear that this case is governed by the general rule stated in the preceding section, that is that the promisor may assert against the beneficiary any defense that he could assert against the promisor.

Another interesting question is whether and up to what point of time a third party beneficiary may disclaim the rights created for him by the contract between the promisor and the promisee. The rule is that he may within a reasonable time after learning of the contract for his benefit "render any duty to himself inoperative from the beginning by disclaimer".[68] However, "once the beneficiary has manifested assent, disclaimer is operative only if the requirements are met for the discharge of a contractual duty." [69] There are complicated questions as to the effect of a disclaimer by the beneficiary upon the rights of the promisee and third parties.[70]

63. Restatement, Second, Contracts § 311, Comments c and e; New York Life Ins. Co. v. Cook, 237 Mich. 303, 211 N.W. 648 (1927).

64. See New York Life Ins. Co. v. Cook, 237 Mich. 303, 211 N.W. 648 (1927).

65. See Salesky v. Hat Corp., 20 A.D.2d 114, 244 N.Y.S.2d 965 (1st Dep't 1963).

66. Fankuchen v. Fankuchen, 63 Misc. 2d 348, 311 N.Y.S.2d 704 (Civ.Ct.1970).

67. See Restatement, Second, Contracts § 309.

68. Restatement, Second, Contracts § 306.

69. Restatement, Second, Contracts § 306, Comment b. This means that there must be consideration or its equivalent.

70. See Restatement, Second, Contracts § 306, Comments c and d. See also Restatement, Contracts § 356.

§ 17–12. May a Promisor Assert Against a Third Party Beneficiary a Defense Which the Promisee Has Against the Beneficiary?

In section 17–10 supra the discussion related to whether the *promisor* may assert against the beneficiary a defense the *promisor* has against the promisee. Here the question is whether the promisor may assert against the beneficiary a defense which the *promisee* has against the beneficiary.

A typical illustration of this problem is the well known case of Rouse v. United States.[71] In the Rouse case the plaintiff's assignor sold an oil burner to B on credit pursuant to a conditional sales contract. When B sold the house, the defendant, purchaser, agreed to assume the payments still due on the oil burner contract. The defendant failed to pay and sought to interpose as a defense that plaintiff's assignor had breached a warranty made to B.

As indicated above the issue is whether the promisor (defendant) may assert against the beneficiary (plaintiff) a defense (breach of warranty) which B has against the plaintiff. The court held that the issue was one of interpretation and states that there are two possible interpretations. One that the promisor promises to pay whatever the promisee owes. Under this interpretation the promisor is permitted to use the defense.

The other possible interpretation is that the promisor promises to pay irrespective of the liability of the promisee to the beneficiary. Under this view clearly the defendant may not assert the defense that the promisee has against the beneficiary. The court then concludes that a promise to assume amounts is a promise to pay irrespective of the liability of the promisee.[72]

In the Rouse case the court assumed that the plaintiff was a third party beneficiary.[73] Would this be true in a jurisdiction that followed the rule of Vrooman v. Turner? The rule of that case is that the third party does not qualify as a third party beneficiary unless there is an actual obligation owing from the promisee to the beneficiary. In the Rouse case was the promisee under an obligation to the plaintiff within the meaning of the Vrooman case? The answer appears to be in the

---

71. 215 F.2d 872 (D.C.Cir.1954).

72. See Restatement, Second, Contracts § 312.

73. Under the two Restatements, as we have seen, a plaintiff, situated as was the plaintiff in the Vrooman case qualifies as a third party beneficiary. Both make the

point that this result is not changed if the promisee has a defense of Statute of Limitations, Statute of Frauds or discharge in bankruptcy against the promisee. See §§ 17–2 and 17–4 supra. Should the Restatements have limited the rule stated to these specific defenses?

affirmative.[74] This does not mean that Vrooman v. Turner has been overruled on its own facts because in the Rouse case the promisee made a voidable promise; in Vrooman the promisee, having taken subject to the mortgage, made no promise whatsoever.

 WESTLAW REFERENCES
find 215 f2d 872
95k328(4)

§ 17–13. Rights of the Beneficiary Against the Promisee

The assumption here is that under the rules stated above a third party beneficiary has a cause of action against the promisor. The question here is whether the beneficiary also has a claim against the promisee. In this context the distinction between a creditor and a donee beneficiary is important.

Assume a case in which C is indebted to A and C for a consideration causes B to assume this indebtedness.[75] It is clear that A is an intended creditor beneficiary and as such has a cause of action against B.[76] A does not, however, thereby lose his rights against C. The original obligation continues unimpaired.[77] The net result is that A may obtain a judgment against both C and B but is entitled to only one satisfaction.[78]

As between C and B the relationship is principal-surety. B is the principal and C the surety.[79] The main consequence of this relationship is that if C is compelled to pay the indebtedness, he may proceed against B for reimbursement.[80]

In contrast to a creditor beneficiary a donee beneficiary ordinarily has no rights against the promisee. By definition there is no antecedent obligation owing from the promisee to the beneficiary and he undertakes no obligation by virtue of the third party beneficiary contract. However, there is authority to the effect that where the

74. See Bennett v. Bates, 94 N.Y. 354 (1888); 4 Corbin, §§ 821–822; 2 Williston § 399.

75. If there was no consideration from C for B's promise B could assert the lack of consideration against A. See § 17–10 supra.

76. See § 17–6 supra.

77. See § 18–25 infra. If A releases C in exchange for B's assumption of the obligation there is a novation, that is to say that B becomes liable and C is discharged. Notice that the release arises by virtue of an agreement between A and C. See § 21–8 infra. If there were only a promise to release there would not be a novation but rather an executory bilateral contract of accord. See § 21–8 infra. Some courts have erroneously held that when B as-

sumes the obligation A releases C if he proceeds against B. Conversely if he proceeds against C he will release B. See, e.g., Henry v. Murphy, 54 Ala. 246 (1875).

78. See Copeland v. Beard, 217 Ala. 216, 115 So. 389 (1928); Vulcan Iron Works v. Pittsburgh-Eastern Co., 144 A.D. 827, 129 N.Y.S. 676 (3d Dep't 1911); Erickson v. Grande Ronde Lumber Co., 162 Or. 556, 94 P.2d 139 (1939); see also Restatement, Contracts (2d) § 310(1). It will generally be possible for the beneficiary to join the original debtor and the assuming promisor as defendants in the same action.

79. See Restatement, Second, Contracts § 314; id. § 310, Comments a & b.

80. See 4 Corbin § 825. Generally speaking a surety is also entitled to exoneration and subrogation.

promisee receives consideration for a promise to discharge or modify the promisor's duty a donee beneficiary may have an interest in the consideration received by the promisee. According to the First Restatement the beneficiary was required to elect whether he would assert a right against the consideration so received or whether he would pursue his right against the promisor.[81] Under the Restatement, Second the requirement for an election is eliminated [82] and substituted therefor is a rule of what is equitable under the circumstances.[83]

 WESTLAW REFERENCES
right /s beneficiary /s claim action /s promisee

§ 17-14. Rights of the Promisee Against the Promisor

The question posed here is whether the promisee may sue the promisor for breach even though the beneficiary has a cause of action against the promisor based upon the same breach. The majority view is that the promisee may maintain such an action and this is logically correct because the promise breached was made to the promisee.[84]

The problem is not significant in a donee beneficiary situation because ordinarily the promisee will not suffer any compensatory damages [85] and if he does they will not duplicate the damages suffered by the beneficiary.[86] Since the action for damages in this situation is ordinarily inadequate the promisee may bring an action for specific performance.[87] An action for restitution may also be available.[88]

The situation is substantially different in a creditor beneficiary situation. Under the majority view the failure of the promisor to perform his promise to pay the debt permits the promisee to recover the amount of the debt.[89] Since the beneficiary may do the same, the possibility of a double recovery exists. To avoid this possibility, some courts have ruled that the promisee may recover the debt only if he has paid it.[90] Of course, the promisor may protect himself against double recovery by paying the creditor beneficiary prior to judgment. In addition, he may ordinarily insure that both the promisee and the

---

81. Restatement, Contracts § 142.

82. Restatement, Second, Contracts § 311(4).

83. Id. § 311(4), Comment j.

84. See In re Spong, 661 F.2d 6 (2d Cir. 1981); Heins v. Byers, 174 Minn. 350, 219 N.W. 287 (1928); Restatement, Contracts §§ 135(b), 136(1)(b). The Restatement, Second continues the same rule in § 305.

85. See Restatement, Second, Contracts § 305; Restatement, Contracts § 345.

86. See discussion in § 17-3 supra. See also Vineyard v. Martin, 29 N.Y.S.2d 935 (Sup.Ct.1941).

87. See Drewen v. Bank of Manhattan Co., 31 N.J. 110, 155 A.2d 529 (1959);

Croker v. New York Trust Co., 245 N.Y. 17, 156 N.E. 81 (1927).

88. See Restatement, Contracts § 136, Comment c; id. § 356.

89. See 11 Williston § 1408; Restatement, Second, Contracts § 305.

90. See White v. Upton, 255 Ky. 562, 74 S.W.2d 924 (1934) (promisee, however, may sue the promisor to compel him to pay the debt). Other courts have held that the promisee holds the proceeds in trust for the creditor and that the promisor can compel the promisee to pay the money to the beneficiary. See Gustafson v. Koehler, 177 Minn. 115, 224 N.W. 699 (1929).

creditor participate in the same action by utilizing interpleader procedure or other procedural techniques. In the event this is not done, the remote possibility of a double recovery can be avoided by the flexibility possessed by a modern court in which law and equity are merged; for example, the court may order the judgment be payable to the creditor even if the action is brought by the promisee,[91] or the court may accept payment into court to be held until the rights of the parties can be sorted out.[92]

WESTLAW REFERENCES
find 219 nw 287

---

91. See Heins v. Byers, 174 Minn. 350, 219 N.W. 287 (1928). It has also been suggested that the promisor may enjoin the action by the promisee but the injunction will be conditioned on payment of the debt to the creditor. Simpson, Suretyship 202.

92. See Lewis v. Germantown Ins. Co., 251 Md. 535, 248 A.2d 468 (1968).

Chapter 18

ASSIGNMENT AND DELEGATION

Table of Sections

Table of Sections

A. INTRODUCTION

Sec.

18–1.   Terminology—Relationship to Prior Chapter.

18–2.   History.

B. ASSIGNMENTS—GENERAL BACKGROUND

18–3.   Nature of an Assignment.

18–4.   What Assignments Are Covered in This Chapter—Impact of U.C.C.

18–5.   Formalities.

C. DEVIANTS FROM THE NORM

18–6.   Introduction.

18–7.   Gratuitous Assignments.

18–8.   Voidable Assignment and Conditional Assignments of Rights.

18–9.   Assignment of Future Rights.

720

D. ARE THERE RIGHTS WHICH ARE NOT ASSIGNABLE?

E. DEFENSES OF THE OBLIGOR

F. COUNTERCLAIMS, SET OFF, AND RECOUPMENT

G. OTHER POSSIBLE LIMITATIONS ON THE RIGHTS OF THE ASSIGNEE

H. RIGHTS OF THE ASSIGNEE AGAINST THE ASSIGNOR

I. DELEGATION

A. INTRODUCTION

Table of Sections

§ 18–1. Terminology—Relationship to Prior Chapter

Just as the chapter on third party beneficiaries employs the terminology of promisor, promisee and beneficiary, here there is a similar terminology.[1]

Assume a case where A promises to pay B $1000 if B paints A's house (unilateral) and assume B assigns his right to payment to C. Before B paints the house A is only a promisor but after B paints the house A is an obligor because B has performed and A now must pay what he promised. Thus in this problem A could be referred to as a promisor or an obligor depending upon when performance occurred. For the balance of the chapter we shall ignore the distinction made here and simply refer to A as the obligor. Thus in the problem A is the obligor, B is the obligee-assignor (hereafter the term obligee will not be employed) and C is the assignee.

The illustration above involves a unilateral arrangement. It is clear that it could just as easily involve a bilateral contract. In such a case who is the obligor? The answer is the party being sued.[2]

A little should be said about the words employed in the chapter heading—assignment and delegation. An assignment involves the transfer of rights.[3] A delegation involves the appointment of another to perform one's duties.[4] The courts and lawyers generally are not always careful to make this distinction and are prone to use the word "assignment" (a word of art) inartfully, frequently intending to encompass within the term the distinct concepts of assignment and delegation.[5]

Our discussion of delegation will, to some extent, overlap a situation that was discussed in the chapter relating to third party beneficiaries. In that chapter we spoke of a situation where A owes B $100 and C for a consideration agrees to assume A's obligation. As discussed in the chapter on third party beneficiaries, B is a third party beneficiary of C's promise made to A.[6] In terms of this chapter A has

---

1. See § 17–1 supra.

2. The point is that although there are two obligors, we are concerned only with the obligation of the party being sued. This is the same approach that was taken in the area of third party beneficiaries. See note 1 supra.

3. See § 18–3 infra.

4. See § 18–25 infra.

5. A classic article which has helped to unsnarl the terminological confusion in this area is Corbin, Assignment of Contract Rights, 74 U.Pa.L.Rev. 207 (1926), Selected Readings on The Law of Contracts 718. See also Restatement, Second, Contracts § 328, Comment a and § 316, Comment c.

6. See § 17–6 supra.

delegated his duty to pay $100 to C.[7] Because C assumed this duty, B is a third party beneficiary of C's promise made to A.[8]

Students sometimes confuse the concepts of assignment and third party beneficiary. It is true that both involve rights in the hands of a person who was not a party to the contract. The basic distinction is that the rights of a third party beneficiary are created by the contract of the two parties to the contract. The rights of an assignee do not arise by virtue of the creation of the contract. They arise when a party who has rights under a contract, including a third party beneficiary, transfers the rights that have been created to an assignee.

 WESTLAW REFERENCES

di unilateral

di assignment

di delegation

di third party beneficiary

§ 18–2. History

At early common law an attempted assignment of a contract right was ordinarily ineffective.[9] It was believed that the contractual relation was too personal to permit the interjection of a third person into the relationship without the consent of the obligor. This idea was reinforced by the law's policy against maintenance and champerty. It was believed that assignments would be employed to stir up and finance litigation.[10] The rule against assignments was in time circumvented by the use of powers of attorney. The assignee was appointed as agent of the assignor and was in time permitted to sue in the name of the assignor and retain the proceeds.[11] Under this approach the agency of the assignee was terminated by the assignor's revocation of the agency or his death or bankruptcy.[12] In time equity held that such an

---

7. See § 18–25 infra. The terminology relating to delegation is discussed in § 18–31 infra.

8. It is possible to have a delegation of a duty that does not involve a third party beneficiary situation. See § 18–26 infra.

9. The historical background of the law of assignments is traced in Bailey, Assignments of Debts in England from the Twelfth to the Twentieth Century, 47 L.Q. Rev. 516 (1931), 48 L.Q.Rev. 248, 547 (1932); Holdsworth, The History of the Treatment of Choses in Action by the Common Law, 33 Harv.L.Rev. 997 (1920), Selected Readings on The Law of Contracts 706. There were some exceptions to the rule of non-assignability, such as assignments by the government. These are but of historical interest. Under the Law Merchant bills and notes were transferable. These mercantile instruments contin-

ue to be governed by a separate body of law, until recently governed by the Uniform Negotiable Instruments Law and presently, largely by Article 3 of the Uniform Commercial Code. See Gilmore, The Commercial Doctrine of Good Faith Purchase, 63 Yale L.J. 1057 (1954).

10. Lord Coke utilized this rationale to explain the rule against assignments. See Lampet's Case, 77 Eng.Rep. 994, 997 (K.B.1613).

11. See Mallory v. Lane, 79 Eng.Rep. 292 (Ex.Ch.1615). An interesting historical parallel is found in Roman law. The Roman rule against assignments was circumvented in the same manner. M. Radin, Roman Law 53, 290–92 (1927).

12. Potter v. Turner, Winch 7, 124 Eng. Rep. 7 (K.B.1622).

assignment was not terminable.[13]   The law courts eventually followed suit,[14] although it was generally necessary for the assignee to sue in the assignor's name and to make the assignor a party to the action.[15]   This requirement was abolished in most states in the nineteenth century by statutes permitting the assignee to sue in his own name as the real party in interest.[16]

The history of the law of assignments is an interesting illustration of the struggle between commercial needs and the tenacity of legal conceptualism.   The common law developed when wealth was primarily land and, secondarily, chattels.   Intangibles hardly mattered.   In a developed economy, however, wealth is primarily represented by intangibles: bank accounts, securities, accounts receivable, etc.   The free alienability of these assets is essential to commerce.[17]   This is fully recognized by the Uniform Commercial Code.[18]

 WESTLAW REFERENCES

"common law" /s assignment /s "contract right"

B. ASSIGNMENTS—GENERAL BACKGROUND

Table of Sections

§ 18–3. Nature of an Assignment

Ordinarily parties to an assignment have one of two purposes in mind.   They may intend an outright transfer of the right in question, or they may intend that the right be transferred as collateral security for an indebtedness.   An assignment made as collateral security creates

13. Peters v. Soame, 2 Vern. 428, 23 Eng.Rep. 874 (Ch. 1701).

14. See Cook, The Alienability of Choses in Action, 29 Harv.L.Rev. 816 (1916), Selected Readings on The Law of Contracts, 738 (1931); Williston, Is the Right of an Assignee of a Chose in Action Legal or Equitable?, 30 Harv.L.Rev. 97 (1916), Selected Readings on The Law of Contracts, 754, and 31 Harv.L.Rev. 822 (1918), Selected Readings on The Law of Contracts, 790.

15. The equity courts, however, held that the assignee could sue in his own name.   See Cook, The Alienability of Choses in Action, 29 Harv.L.Rev. 816, 820, (1916), Selected Readings on The Law of Contracts, 738, 742 (1931).

16. See Clark & Hutchins, The Real Party in Interest, 34 Yale L.J. 259 (1924). The introductory note to Chapter 15 of the Restatement, Second, Contract contains a list and analysis of the state real party in interest statutes.

17. In this country, the value of receivables which have been assigned to obtain financing amounts to tens of billions of dollars at any given moment. See Coogan & Gordon, The Effect of the Uniform Commercial Code upon Receivables Financing—Some Answers and Some Unsolved Problems, 76 Harv.L.Rev. 1529, 1530 (1963).

18. U.C.C. § 9–318(4), § 2–210(2), discussed at § 18–16 infra.

a security interest in the assignee.[19] We are not concerned in this text with security assignments. Security assignments are covered in works on secured transactions which broadly speaking relates to Article 9 of the Code.

We are, however, concerned with outright assignments. An outright assignment may be defined as a manifestation of intent by the owner to the assignee [20] to make a present transfer of the right to the assignee.[21] For example, if A in a signed writing states, "I sell and transfer this account against David Mead to William Richardson" is there an assignment? There is because there is a manifestation of intent by the assignor (A) to presently transfer a right that he has against David Mead (obligor) to William Richardson (assignee).[22] The fact that the word "assign" was not used is not important.[23] Ordinarily an outright assignment extinguishes the right in the assignor and transfers it to the assignee.[24]

Since an assignment is by definition a present transfer—an executed transaction—it is clear that a promise to do something in the future cannot be an assignment because a promise is by nature executory. Thus, a promise to pay money when the promisor collects it from a specified source is not an assignment.[25] There is no present transfer. The same is true of a promise to assign at some future time a right that the promisor presently owns.[26] However, it has been held that since

19. See International Harvester v. Peoples Bank & Trust, 402 So.2d 856 (Miss. 1981). At times courts have caused decisions to turn upon whether title to the security is in the secured party or whether the secured party merely has a lien. See, e.g., Ralston Purina Co. v. Como Feed & Milling Co., 325 F.2d 844 (5th Cir.1963). The Uniform Commercial Code rejects the notion that the assignee has title by virtue of a security assignment. See the Official Comment to U.C.C. § 9–101.

20. See Restatement, Contracts § 149, Restatement, Second, Contracts § 317. The manifestation may be made to a third person upon the assignee's behalf. Restatement, Second, Contracts § 324.

21. See Matter of Boyd's Estate, 606 P.2d 1243 (Wyo.1980).

22. Richardson v. Mead, 27 Barb. 178 (1858).

23. Farnsworth, Contracts § 11.3, p. 754.

24. See Continental Oil Co. v. United States, 326 F.Supp. 266 (S.D.N.Y.1971); Kelly Health Care, Inc. v. Prudential Ins. Co., 226 Va. 376, 309 S.E.2d 305 (1983). When this result takes place, the assignment is sometimes referred to as an effec-tive assignment. See Restatement, Contracts (2d) § 317, Comment a; Restatement, Contracts § 150. The word "ordinarily" is used in the text because although the definition of assignment is met, the result stated does not necessarily occur where the assignment may be terminated because it is gratuitous (Section 18–7) voidable (Section 18–8) or equitable (18–9). An outright assignment ordinarily carries with it rights, remedies and benefits which are incidental to the thing assigned. See Kintzel v. Wheatland Mut. Ins. Ass'n, 203 N.W.2d 799, 5 A.L.R.3d 1110 (Iowa 1973). For example, the assignment of a bond carries with it a security interest such as a mortgage. See Bryan v. Easton Tire Co., 262 Ark. 731, 561 S.W.2d 79 (1978).

25. See Bass v. Olson, 378 F.2d 818 (9th Cir.1967); Donovan v. Middlebrook, 95 App.Div. 365, 88 N.Y.S. 607 (1st Dep't 1904); 4 Corbin § 877. There may be a contract.

26. See City of Kansas City v. Milrey Development Co., 600 S.W.2d 660 (Mo. 1980); Lauerman Bros. Co. v. Komp, 156 Wis. 12, 145 N.W. 174 (1914). An assignment of a right not presently owned is discussed in § 18–9 infra.

the promises discussed here may be specifically enforced the promisee in such a case has an equitable assignment or an equitable lien.[27]

If D owes C \$1000 and C writes D, "Please pay A for his own use \$100 out of the amount you owe me", does this amount to an assignment? The answer is in the negative because the manifestation of intent is to the obligor and not to the assignee or to a third person on his behalf.[28] Therefore, in the case posed, A acquires no rights by virtue of the order issued by C to D. However, if D paid A, D's debt would be discharged.[29]

The situation is somewhat different if C delivered this order to A. There is authority that the instrument amounts to an assignment because it is conditioned on the duty of D to C and because C manifests an intention that a person other than C is to receive the performance.[30]

 WESTLAW REFERENCES
assignment /s manifestation /s intent
find 606 f2d 1243
38k31
promise /s assign! /s future
assignment /s "present transfer"

§ 18–4. What Assignments Are Covered in This Chapter— Impact of U.C.C.

It has already been stated that coverage here is limited to outright assignments.[31] In addition it is limited to outright assignments of contractual choses in action.[32] Thus we are talking about the assignment of intangible rights that arise by contract.[33] In this chapter we will study the common law rules governing the assignment of these contractual rights as changed by statute.

The statute that is most relevant is Article 9 of the Uniform Commercial Code. It might occur to the reader at this point to inquire how this could be when it already has been stated that Article 9 of the Code relates to security transactions.[34] The point is, however, that

27. See Morrison Flying Serv. v. Deming Nat'l Bank, 404 F.2d 856 (10th Cir. 1968), cert. denied 393 U.S. 1020, 89 S.Ct. 628, 21 L.Ed.2d 565 (1969). But see Monegan v. Pacific Nat'l Bank of Washington, 16 Wn.App. 280, 556 P.2d 226 (1976). See § 18–9 infra.

28. See Restatement, Second, Contracts § 325, Comment a. The situation is similar to the use of a check. A check is not ordinarily an assignment. U.C.C. § 3–409(1).

29. See Edmund Wright Ginsberg Corp. v. C.D. Kepner Leather Co., 317 Mass. 581, 59 N.E.2d 253 (1945).

30. See Delbrueck & Co. v. Manufacturers Hanover Trust Co., 609 F.2d 1047 (2d Cir.1979); Restatement, Contracts (2d) § 325(1).

31. See § 18–3 supra.

32. The words "chose in action," as used here, refer to an intangible right.

33. The Restatement, Second uses the same approach. See Restatement, Second, Contracts § 316, Comment a. It suggests that the rules stated here may apply to non-contractual choses in action. These include intangible property rights (for example, patents and copyrights) and intangible tort rights. See Restatement, Second, Contracts, Introductory Note to Ch. 15; Restatement, Second, Contracts § 316, Comment a.

34. See § 18–3 supra.

Article 9, by its terms, also covers an outright assignment for value [35] of accounts, contract rights and chattel paper.[36] We shall now discuss the Code's definition of these three terms in Article 9.

Under the original definition in the Code " 'Account' means any right to payment for goods sold or leased or for services rendered which is not evidenced by an instrument or chattel paper." [37] " 'Contract right' means any right to payment under a contract not yet earned by performance and not evidenced by an instrument or chattel paper." [38]

Notice that there is an account or a contract right only when there is a right to payment. Thus a right to receive goods or services does not amount to an account or a contract right. Notice also that there is not an account or a contract right if the obligation is evidenced by an instrument or chattel paper. The word instrument refers to a negotiable instrument and certain specialties.[39] " 'Chattel paper' means a writing or writings which evidence both a monetary obligation and a security interest in or a lease of specific goods * * *." [40] Notice also that to have an account the right must have been earned by performance. However, it is not necessary that the amount be due at the time of performance. A "contract right" relates to a right of payment not yet earned.

In 1972 the Code was amended so as to drop the term "contract right." At the same time the term "account" was redefined to mean "any right to payment for goods sold or leased or for services rendered which is not evidenced by an instrument or chattel paper whether or not it has been earned by performance." It is clear that the new definition of "account" was designed to encompass both "accounts" and "contract right" as originally defined.[41]

It is clear that an account can arise only when the right to payment arises as a result of goods being sold or leased or as a result of services rendered. In addition the right to payment must arise out of a contract. If the right does not arise out of contract it is a general intangible [42] and is not covered by Article 9.[43]

---

35. The term "for value" is defined in § 18–7 infra.

36. See U.C.C. § 9–102(1)(b).

37. U.C.C. § 9–106.

38. U.C.C. § 9–106.

39. U.C.C. § 9–105(1)(i).

40. U.C.C. § 9–105(1)(b). Chattel paper is generally used in a consumer sale where the consumer buys goods on credit. In such a situation, the consumer promises to pay for the item purchased by executing a promissory note. In addition, as a result of a security agreement or financing statement, the seller retains a security interest in the goods which, in effect, gives him a lien upon the property.

41. The reason for the change is that the distinction between "contract rights" and "accounts" was important only in § 9–318(2). This section has now been redrafted to reflect the elimination of the term "contract rights." See generally Coogan, The New U.C.C. Article 9, 86 Harv.L.Rev. 477 (1973). The 1972 Amendments have not as yet been adopted by some jurisdictions.

42. " 'General intangibles' means any personal property (including things in action) other than goods, accounts, chattel paper, documents, instruments, and money." U.C.C. § 9–106. The term includes, goodwill, literary rights, copyrights, trademarks and patents. U.C.C. § 9–106, Comment 9.

43. See U.C.C. §§ 9–102(1)(b), 9–106.

Since Article 9 of the U.C.C. applies to outright assignments of accounts, and chattel paper [44] because of their financing character,[45] it is logical that certain outright assignments that fit the definition of an account or chattel paper would be eliminated from the coverage of Article 9 because they do not have a financing character. These include wage assignments; [46] any outright assignment in connection with the sale of a business from which the rights assigned arose; assignments for the purposes of collection only, a transfer of rights to an assignee who is also to perform under the contract; and "a transfer of a single account to an assignee in whole or partial satisfaction of a pre-existing indebtedness." [47] It should be pointed out that U.C.C. § 9–104 excludes a variety of other transactions from the coverage of Article 9.

When a transaction is excluded from the coverage of Article 9 it is clear that such a transaction will be governed by common law rules although other statutory enactments must also be consulted in appropriate cases.[48]

There is also a provision relating to assignments in Article 2 of the Code which applies only if the assignment arises out of a sales transaction.[49]

WESTLAW REFERENCES

```
ucc   /5   9–106   /s   account
ucc   /5   9–106   /s   "contract right"
ucc   /5   9–106   /s   "chattel paper"
ucc   /5   9–106   /s   "general intangible"
ucc   /5   9–106
ucc   /5   9–104
ucc   /5   2–210
```

§ 18–5.   Formalities

In the absence of an applicable statute, the manifestation of intent required for an assignment need not be in writing.[50] In Article 9 of the Uniform Commercial Code the requirement of a writing is heavily emphasized. A "security interest" governed by Article 9 of the Commercial Code is not enforceable against the debtor or third persons

---

44. The term "contract rights" is not included here because it was eliminated by the 1972 amendments to the Code. See note 36 supra.

45. See 1 G. Gilmore, Security Interests in Personal Property § 10.5 (1965).

46. See U.C.C. § 9–104(d).

47. U.C.C. § 9–104(f).

48. For example, in most states wage assignments are covered by statute.

49. See U.C.C. § 2–210. This section is discussed in many of the sections that fol-

low. See particularly § 18–16 where a potential conflict between the Article 9 provision and the Article 2 provision is raised.

50. See Anaconda Aluminum Co. v. Sharp, 243 Miss. 9, 136 So.2d 585, 99 A.L.R.2d 1307 (1962); Jemison v. Tindall, 89 N.J.L. 429, 99 A. 408 (1916); Brown v. Fore, 12 S.W.2d 114 (Tex.App.1929); Restatement, Second, Contracts § 324, Comment a; Restatement, Contracts § 157; 4 Corbin § 879.

unless the debtor has signed a "security agreement" [51] or unless the assignee has possession of the collateral.[52] The statute performs the function of a Statute of Frauds.[53]

This rule applies to a security assignment but as previously stated security assignments are not our concern.[54] However, the same rule applies to an outright assignment of accounts, contract rights and chattel paper.[55] It follows that an outright assignment of an account, contract right or chattel paper is unenforceable unless it is evidenced by a security agreement signed by the assignor.[56]

WESTLAW REFERENCES

38k34

find 136 so2d 585

u.c.c. "uniform commercial code" /5 9–203

di("security interest" /s signed /s "security agreement")

u.c.c. "uniform commercial code" /5 9–105

u.c.c. "uniform commercial code" /5 9–302(1)(e) (9–302 +s
  (1)(e))

349ak84

C. DEVIANTS FROM THE NORM

Table of Sections

§ 18–6. Introduction

We have already seen that ordinarily an assignment terminates a right in the assignor and transfers it to the assignee.[57] There are, however, situations where there is an assignment and yet the assignment may be terminable or revocable. In these situations, in effect, the

---

51. See U.C.C. §§ 9–203 and 9–105(1)(*l*).

52. See U.C.C. § 9–203(1)(a). In other words when the creditor has possession of collateral, a signed security agreement is not necessary. Collateral is defined in U.C.C. § 9–105(1)(c).

53. See Comments to § 9–203. The Code contains other sections that relate to the Statute of Frauds, but these will be discussed in Chapter 19.

54. See § 18–3 supra.

55. See U.C.C. §§ 9–105(1)(b) and 1–201(37). It is impossible to possess an account or a contract right or chattel paper

and thus the requirement of a writing may not be avoided in this way. See note 47 supra.

56. Under Article 9 a writing must ordinarily be filed to protect the assigned against third parties. Annot., 58 A.L.R.3d 1050. There is an exception to the filing requirement where an assignment of accounts do not alone or in conjunction with other assignments transfer a significant part of the outstanding accounts. See U.C.C. § 9–302(1)(e).

57. See § 18–3 supra.

right of the assignee for a period of time is in limbo. In other words to what extent the assignee may use the right assigned depends upon events subsequent to the assignment. We cover here three of these typical situations.

 WESTLAW REFERENCES
di assignment

§ 18–7. Gratuitous Assignments

A gratuitous (gift) assignment illustrates what is said immediately above because a gratuitous assignment is terminable by the death of the assignor, by a subsequent assignment of the same right or by a notice of termination communicated by the assignor to the assignee or to the obligor.[58] However, a gratuitous assignment need not remain terminable in perpetuity. The gift of the right may be completed in a variety of ways. Thus whether the gratuitous assignee will have rights under the assignment depends upon which occurs first, the terminating event or the completion of the gift. What events or occurrences complete the gift of the assignment?

The law of gifts of chattels requires that a gift be completed by delivery.[59] Since a right cannot be physically delivered, the law has validated certain substitutes for delivery. The assignee can complete the gift by obtaining payment from or a judgment against the obligor or by entering into a substituted contract with the obligor—that is to say an agreement with the obligor that he will pay the assignee.[60]

The gift is also deemed to be completed if the right assigned is evidenced by a writing which the creditor is required to surrender upon payment (what the Second, Restatement refers to as a symbolic writing) and the writing is delivered to the assignee.[61] Writings in this class include bonds and mortgages, savings account books, life insurance policies and stock certificates.[62] The Restatement, Second adds that this rule should be extended to include the delivery of an evidentiary writing—a writing that embodies an integrated writing.[63] A number of cases have adopted the same basic position in holding that the delivery

---

58. Restatement, Second, Contracts § 332.

59. See Adams v. Merced Stone Co., 176 Cal. 415, 178 P. 498 (1917); Biehl v. Biehl's Adm'x, 263 Ky. 710, 93 S.W.2d 836 (1936); Cook v. Lum, 55 N.J.L. 373, 26 A. 803 (1893); Williston, Gifts of Rights under Contracts in Writing by Delivery of the Writing, 40 Yale L.J. 1 (1930). See also Bruton, The Requirement of Delivery as Applied to Gifts of Choses in Action, 39 Yale L.J. 837 (1930).

60. Restatement, Contracts § 158; Restatement, Second, Contracts § 332. However, a gratuitous assignment bars action by the assignor unless and until he effectively terminates the assignment.

61. See Restatement, Contracts § 158(1)(b); Restatement, Second, Contracts § 332(1)(b); Farrell v. Passaic Water Co., 82 N.J.Eq. 97, 88 A. 627 (1913).

62. See Brooks v. Mitchell, 163 Md. 1, 161 A. 261 (1932) (delivery of suitcase containing savings bank book sufficient delivery to create assignment of bank account); 4 Corbin §§ 915–920; 3 Williston §§ 438A–440.

63. See Restatement, Second, Contracts § 332, Comment d.

of the contract embodying a right is sufficient delivery even though it is not a symbolic writing.[64]

In jurisdictions that continue to recognize the efficacy of a seal an assignment may be completed by a deed of gift, that is a written instrument under seal.[65] In other states it has generally been held that a gratuitous assignment is made irrevocable by the delivery of a signed writing expressing an intent to assign.[66] This result is obtained in New York by a statute which provides: "An assignment shall not be denied the effect of irrevocably transferring the assignor's rights because of the absence of consideration if such an assignment is in writing and signed by the assignor, or by his agent."[67] For the most part in these cases it has been held that delivery of the writing is necessary.[68]

A gift assignment may also be made irrevocable under the doctrine of estoppel. If the assignor should reasonably foresee that the assignee will change his position in reliance on the assignment and such detrimental reliance does occur, the assignment is irrevocable.[69]

Assignments for this purpose are divided into two categories— gratuitous assignments and assignments for value. Both the Restatement, Second and the Uniform Commercial Code state that an assignment is for value if the assignee parts with consideration or if the assignment is taken as security for or in total or partial satisfaction of a pre-existing debt.[70] If the assignment is not for value then it is gratuitous and the rules stated above apply.[71]

64. See In re Huggins' Estate, 204 Pa. 167, 53 A. 746 (1902) (gift of rights under a contract for the sale of real property effected by delivery of the written contract); Restatement, Second, Contracts § 332, Comment d. Contra, Restatement, Contracts § 158, ill. 2. See Reporter's Note to Restatement, Second, Contracts § 332.

65. See Sweeney v. Veneziano, 70 N.J. Super. 185, 175 A.2d 241 (1961). Restatement, Second, Contracts § 332(1)(a); Restatement, Contracts § 158(1)(a).

66. See Berl v. Rosenberg, 169 Cal.App. 2d 125, 336 P.2d 975 (1959); Smith v. Smith, 313 S.W.2d 753 (Mo.App.1958); Thatcher v. Merriam, 121 Utah 191, 240 P.2d 266 (1952); 4 Corbin § 921, 3 Williston § 438A.

67. McKinney's N.Y.Gen.Oblig.L. § 5–1107; see Speelman v. Pascal, 10 N.Y.2d 313, 222 N.Y.S.2d 324, 178 N.E.2d 723 (1961).

68. See Biehl v. Biehl Adm'x, 263 Ky. 710, 93 S.W.2d 836 (1936); Cooney v. Equitable Life Assur. Soc., 235 Minn. 377, 51 N.W.2d 285 (1952). See generally Williston, Gifts of Rights under Contracts in Writing by Delivery of the Writing, 40 Yale L.J. 1 (1930).

Another interesting question is whether delivery of such a writing is sufficient to complete the gift when the right to be transferred is embodied in a symbolic writing. In other words, in such a case should not the symbolic writing be transferred? In Thatcher v. Merriam, 121 Utah 191, 240 P.2d 266 (1952) the court held that the symbolic writing need not be delivered. This decision is to be applauded. The delivery of the informal writing is a sufficient evidentiary base for a finding of a completed gift.

69. See Restatement, Second, Contracts 332(4); Restatement, Contracts § 158(1)(c).

70. See Restatement, Second, Contracts § 332(5); U.C.C. § 1–201(44); Abramson v. Boedeker, 379 F.2d 741 (5th Cir.1967), cert. denied 389 U.S. 1006, 88 S.Ct. 563, 19 L.Ed. 2d 602 (1967).

71. It is important to observe that it is possible to have a gratuitous assignment because an assignment is an executed transaction and therefore there is no requirement that an assignment be supported by consideration. See United States v. Currency Totalling $48,318.08, 609 F.2d 210 (5th Cir.1980); Restatement, Contracts § 150.

WESTLAW REFERENCES

gratuitous gift /3 assignment /s terminat***

assigned /2 right /s writing

38k31 /p right /3 assigned

gift /2 assignment /s seal

find 379 f2d 741

38k53

38k55

§ 18–8. Voidable Assignments and Conditional Assignments of Rights

Just as a contract may be voidable [72] an assignment may also be voidable. For example, an assignment may be voidable because of infancy, insanity, duress and fraud.[73] In the case of a voidable assignment the assignment does not necessarily extinguish the right of the assignor because the assignor has a right to avoid it according to the rules stated elsewhere.[74]

However, in the case of a voidable assignment the obligor's duty to the assignor is discharged if the obligor pays the assignee in good faith without notice of the defect that made the assignment voidable. If the obligor pays the assignee with reason to know that the assignment is voidable, he does so at his peril.[75] The voidable assignment bars an action by the assignor until he avoids it.

A conditional assignment of a right is another situation where the rights of the assignor are not extinguished by the assignment.[76] The Restatement gives the following illustration. A has a right to $400 against B and assigns the right to C in payment for an automobile delivered by C on condition that the car runs 1000 miles without needing repairs. Although there is an assignment under the terms of the assignment the $400 belongs to A and not to C until the condition occurs or is excused.[77] Thus in this situation the rights of A are not extinguished upon the occurrence of the assignment. They are extinguished only when the event specified occurs or is excused.[78]

WESTLAW REFERENCES

assignment /s voidable /s minor infan**

assignment /s voidable /s insan***

assignment /s voidable /s duress

assignment /s voidable /s fraud

38k115

---

72. See Chapters 8 and 9 supra.

73. See Restatement, Second, Contracts § 338, Comment g.

74. See Chapters 8 and 9 supra.

75. See Restatement, Second, Contracts § 338, Comment g.

76. See Restatement, Second, Contracts § 331.

77. See Restatement, Second, Contracts § 331, ill. 1.

78. See Restatement, Second, Contracts § 331, Comment b.

§ 18–9. Assignment of Future Rights

Here we are concerned with an assignment of a future right as opposed to the assignment of a present right.[79] The cases have been in confusion as to the distinction between the two. An illustration will help clarify the problem.

Suppose a builder under an existing contract is to be paid progress payments of $1,000 per month, conditioned upon his performance of a specified amount of work each month. There is no question that an assignment by the contractor at the end of the first month amounts to a present assignment.[80] The question that has created the greatest problem is whether an assignment at the end of the first month of the money to be earned in the second month amounts to the assignment of a present or future right? The modern cases lean strongly to the view that this is a present assignment because the right being assigned is to arise out of an existing contract. Under this prevailing view an assignment of a future right arises only when a party assigns a right under a contract which is not in existence but which he expects to enter into.[81]

The notion of assignment of a future right has presented a conceptual difficulty. As a philosophical proposition it has often been stated that it is impossible for a person to transfer a right that is not yet in existence.[82] In time it was held that the assignment of a right under a contract not yet in existence amounted to an equitable assignment from the time that the assignor enters into the future contract[83] provided that the assignee has a right of specific performance against the assignor.[84] This would ordinarily be the case.[85] Thus the assignee would ordinarily have rights superior to the assignor and the obligor.[86]

79. It will be recalled that the word assignment carries the connotation of a present transfer. See § 18–3 supra. Here we are concerned with a present transfer of a future right. Thus, an assignment of a future right fits the definition of an assignment and the only issue is what is the effect of an attempted transfer of a future right. This situation must be distinguished from a promise by the obligee to assign a present right or a promise by the obligee to transfer proceeds that he will collect. We have already seen that these promises do not amount to an assignment because a promise does not amount to a present transfer. See § 18–3 supra. However, as we have seen, such a promise may create an equitable assignment or an equitable lien. See § 18–3 supra. Thus, the discussion with respect to the results stated in this section will apply to the promises discussed above. Compare Restatement, Second, Contracts § 321, with Restatement, Second, Contracts § 330.

80. See Restatement, Second, Contracts § 321, Comment a. However, in the case

of a continuing relationship where there is no contract, for example, a hiring at will, the situation is often treated as involving a present transfer. See Restatement, Second, Contracts § 321, Comment c.

81. See Restatement, Contracts § 154(2); Restatement, Second, Contracts § 321(2); Comment, The New York Law Governing the Relative Rights of Assignees and Third Party Claimants to a Future Fund, 27 Ford.L.Rev. 579 (1959).

82. See Restatement, Second, Contracts § 331, Comment b. The same philosophical problem arose with respect to a mortgage on after acquired property. See G. Osborne, Mortgages § 39 (2d ed. 1970).

83. Before this occurs, the assignment is terminable. See Murray, Contracts § 298, at 612.

84. Restatement, Second, Contracts § 330, Comment c and § 321, Comment d.

85. Murray, Contracts § 298.

86. See Speelman v. Pascal, 10 N.Y.2d 313, 222 N.Y.S.2d 324, 178 N.E.2d 723

However, the assignee of a future right has rights inferior to a number of potential third party claimants. Thus, in the case of a double assignment the second assignee who obtained a legal assignment with the attributes of a purchaser for value would prevail over the equitable assignee.[87] In addition it has been held that an attaching creditor of the assignor prevails over the equitable assignee if the rights of the creditors attach after the right has arisen and before the assignor has made a present assignment.[88] In addition the equitable assignee will be subordinated to the rights of the assignor's trustee in bankruptcy.[89]

These common law rules have been changed by the U.C.C. and generally speaking if the assignee files a notice of his assignment he will prevail.[90]

WESTLAW REFERENCES

assignment /s ''future right''

38k48 /p ''future right''

find 296 nys2d 2

u.c.c. ''uniform commercial code'' /4 9–204

u.c.c. ''uniform commercial code'' /4 9–402

u.c.c. ''uniform commercial code'' /4 9–205

D. ARE THERE RIGHTS WHICH ARE NOT ASSIGNABLE?

Table of Sections

(1961); Restatement, Second, Contracts § 321, Comment d; Farnsworth, Contracts § 11.5, at p. 770.

87. See State Factors Corp. v. Sales Factors Corp., 257 A.D. 101, 12 N.Y.S.2d 12 (1st Dep't 1939).

88. See Harold Moorstein & Co. v. Excelsior Ins. Co., 31 A.D.2d 177, 296 N.Y.S.2d 2 (1st Dep't 1968), affirmed 25 N.Y.2d 651, 254 N.E.2d 766, 306 N.Y.S.2d 464 (1969); Restatement, Second, Contracts § 330, Comment d. There are contrary cases. See 1 G. Gilmore, supra note 45 at § 7–12.

89. See Manchester Nat'l Bank v. Roche, 186 F.2d 827 (1st Cir.1951).

90. See U.C.C. §§ 9–204, 9–402. In addition U.C.C. § 9–205 expressly validates a floating lien on a shifting account and on a shifting stock of goods. Under this section a creditor is permitted to obtain from his debtor a lien in his shifting stock in trade (merchandise) and a security interest in his shifting accounts receivable. To achieve this result, the agreement should provide that the creditor's lien should automatically attach to newly acquired stock in trade and should automatically attach to newly created accounts. In addition, the creditor must file a financing statement. If this section is followed, it is clear that an assignment of a future right will effectively operate as the assignment of a present right.

§ 18–10.   Introduction

In contrast with the earlier law [91] the modern view is emphatically to the effect that ordinarily rights are assignable.[92] Both Restatements [93] and Article 2 of the Uniform Commercial Code,[94] however, provide that a right is not assignable in the following circumstances: (1) if the assignment would materially change the duty of the obligor; (2) if the assignment would increase materially the burden or risk imposed on the obligor by his contract; or (3) if the assignment would impair the obligor's chance of obtaining return performance or, according to the Second Restatement, if the assignment would materially reduce the value of the return performance to the obligor.[95] In addition, on various policy grounds, the law restricts the assignability of certain kinds of rights.[96]

WESTLAW REFERENCES
find 152 cal rptr 446

§ 18–11.   When Does an Assignment Materially Change the Duty of the Obligor?

Almost any assignment changes, to a degree, the duty of the obligor. Nevertheless, it is generally recognized that in practically every case a right to payment of money is assignable.[97] So too is a right

91. See § 18–2 supra.

92. See Macke Co. v. Pizza of Gaithersburg, Inc., 259 Md. 479, 270 A.2d 645 (1970); S. & L. Vending Corp. v. 52 Thompkins Ave. Restaurant, Inc., 26 A.D. 2d 935, 274 N.Y.S.2d 697 (2d Dep't 1966); Willow City v. Vogel, Vogel, Brantner & Kelly, 268 N.W.2d 762 (N.D.1978); Weathers v. M.C. Lininger & Sons, Inc., 68 Or.App. 30, 682 P.2d 770 (1984), review denied 297 Or. 492, 683 P.2d 1372 (1984). Free assignability is deemed to be good public policy. See Augusta Med. Complex v. Blue Cross of Kansas, 230 Kan. 361, 634 P.2d 1123 (1981). The problem is purely pragmatic. If a right to payment could not be assigned, the credit system employed in our civilization could not exist. See H. Macleod, Principles of Economical Philosophy 481 (2d ed. 1972). See also § 18–2 note 17 supra.

93. See Restatement, Second, Contracts § 317(2)(a); Restatement, Contracts § 151(a).

94. See U.C.C. § 2–210(2).

95. See Restatement, Second, Contracts § 317(2)(a).

96. This matter is discussed in § 18–15 infra. See also § 18–16 infra which relates to the extent that an agreement may prevent the assignment of an otherwise assignable right, and § 18–32 infra which relates to the assignability of an option contract.

97. See American Lithographic Co. v. Ziegler, 216 Mass. 287, 103 N.E. 909 (1914); Booker v. Everhart, 294 N.C. 146, 240 S.E.2d 360 (1978). But see Bondanza v. Peninsula Hospital & Med. Ctr., 23 Cal.3d 260, 152 Cal.Rptr. 446, 590 P.2d 22 (1979).

to delivery of goods.[98] But if A agreed to paint B's portrait for a fee B could not by assignment of the right to C obligate A to paint C's portrait. A's duty would be materially changed.[99] What is and what is not a material change of duty is obviously a question of degree with the result that there may be some difficult problems in this area.[1]

A good illustration of this problem arises in the area of requirements contracts. It was frequently held that the contract right to receive one's requirements were not assignable.[2] However, there were cases which reached a contrary result.[3] These cases are not necessarily in conflict because of factual differences in the cases.[4]

The Code has a provision which bears on the problem.[5] With respect to a requirement contract it states the "requirements in the hands of the new owner continue to be measured by the actual good faith * * * requirements under the normal operation of the enterprise prior to sale." [6] The "good faith" mentioned in the comment is that of the assignee and this would appear to grant to the assignee an element of personal discretion. However, this element of personal discretion is carefully circumscribed by supplying the objective criterion of "the normal operations of the enterprise prior to sale." This provision apparently will make most rights to requirements assignable.

 WESTLAW REFERENCES

assignment /s chang*** /s duty /s obligor

find 220 p2d 864

u.c.c. "uniform commercial code" /4 2–306

§ 18–12. Where the Assignment Would Increase Materially the Burden or Risk of the Obligor

In this situation the assumption is that there is no material change in the obligor's duty as a result of the assignment but that there is a material increase in the obligor's burden or risk.

The typical illustration under this heading is a purported assignment of a fire insurance policy. If A owns a building which is insured by X insurance company against loss due to fire and A sells the property to B, may A without the assent of the insurer assign his right to the insurance coverage to B?

98. See Rochester Lantern Co. v. Stiles & Parker Press Co., 135 N.Y. 209, 31 N.E. 1018 (1892).

99. The situation would be different if B gave C a right to receive B's portrait after it was painted.

1. Some of these problems are discussed in § 18–12 infra.

2. See Crane Ice Cream Co. v. Terminal Freezing & Heating Co., 147 Md. 588, 128 A. 280, 39 A.L.R. 1184 (1925); Kemp v. Baerselman, 2 K.B. 604 (1906).

3. See Matson v. White, 122 Colo. 79, 220 P.2d 864 (1950); C.H. Little Co. v. Cadwell Transit Co., 197 Mich. 481, 163 N.W. 952 (1917).

4. The key issue in each case seems to be whether the requirements of the assignee would approximate the requirements of the assignor.

5. See U.C.C. § 2–306, Comment 4.

6. U.C.C. § 2–306, Comment 4.

It is clear that the assignment does not change the obligor's duty. The insurer is still obliged to pay in the event of fire. It is equally clear that the insurer's risk will be increased if B is a less careful person than A. However, as business is conducted, the insurer is not required to deal with B even if B could prove that he is the most careful person in the world. In other words the insurance company may reject the assignment because the risk *may* be different.[7] Any other result would force the insurer to weigh in every case the care that would be used by the assignor and the assignee.[8]

 WESTLAW REFERENCES
assignment /s increas*** /s burden risk /s obligor
find 52 f2d 823

§ 18–13. Where the Assignment Would Impair Materially the Other Party's Chance of Obtaining Return Performance

It is self evident that when an assignor assigns his rights under a contract to an assignee in exchange for a consideration from the assignee he loses some of his incentive to perform because the consideration that was to come to him from the obligor is now to go to the assignee. However, it is generally held that this elimination in incentive would not impair the other party's chance of obtaining his return performance. One illustration will suffice.

S agrees to sell and deliver 1,000 bushels of potatoes to B in exchange for B's promise to pay $1,000 on delivery. S, for a consideration, prior to delivery assigns his right to payment to T. As a result of the assignment S undoubtedly loses some of his incentive to perform because upon performance the $1,000 goes to T. Nevertheless as indicated above, the courts generally have held that the assignment is effective.[9] S has a sufficient incentive to perform because if he fails to perform he will be liable to both B and the assignee.[10]

There are cases where the incentive of the assignor is deemed to be more seriously impaired. In one case the owner of a patent entered into agreement with a licensee on a royalty basis. In the agreement the patentee promised to cooperate in the exploitation of the patent. The patentee assigned his rights to money for the balance of the term to an assignee. The assignment was held to be improper.[11]

7. See Central Union Bank v. New York Underwriters' Ins. Co., 52 F.2d 823, 78 A.L.R. 494 (4th Cir.1931). This is the same approach that has been taken in the prior editions of this book and criticized by Professors Murray and Farnsworth without any direct authority to support their positions. See Murray, Contracts § 295 and E. Farnsworth, Contracts § 11.4, at 764. See also Vance On Insurance § 128 (3rd ed. 1951).

8. This also conforms to the general notion that an insurance contract is deemed to be personal in nature.

9. See Rockmore v. Lehman, 129 F.2d 892 (2d Cir.1942), cert. denied 317 U.S. 700, 63 S.Ct. 525, 87 L.Ed. 559 (1943).

10. See 4 Corbin § 869.

11. See Paper Prods. Mach. Co. v. Safepack Mills, 239 Mass. 114, 131 N.E. 288 (1921), criticized in 4 Corbin § 865 nn. 13 and 14.

WESTLAW REFERENCES
assignment /s impair*** /s "return performance"
find 129 f2d 892

§ 18–14. Effect of an Attempted Transfer of a Non-assignable Right

It is readily apparent that the attempted assignment of a right that is not assignable need not be honored by the obligor.[12] However, the obligor may waive the fact of non-assignability if he so desires and the assignor may not object.[13] It is generally held that the assignment of a non-assignable right does not amount to a material breach unless the assignor makes it clear that he would proceed with the deal only if the improper assignment were accepted.[14]

The assignor does not warrant that the right he purports to assign is assignable. Therefore the assignee does not have a claim against the assignor if the right assigned is not assignable.[15]

WESTLAW REFERENCES
transfer**** /s non-assignable /2 right
u.c.c. "uniform commercial code" /4 2–609
find 528 f.supp. 768

§ 18–15. Assignment Prohibited by Statute or Contrary to Public Policy

Many states have statutes that outlaw or restrict certain types of assignments.[16] For example, most states have statutes that regulate wage assignments by outright prohibition or by limiting their duration or effect.[17] These are designed to prevent a wage earner from, in effect, mortgaging his entire wage earning capacity.[18] Federal statutes and

---

12. Under U.C.C. § 2–609 discussed in § 11–28 supra, the obligor has a right to demand assurances against the assignor before he asserts his right not to honor the assignment. This right is one of the factors to be considered in determining whether the assignment impairs the obligor's chance of obtaining return performance. In addition in making this determination, any security which the obligor has should be taken into account. Farnsworth, Contracts § 11.4, at 764. U.C.C. § 2–210(5) which also relates to security will be discussed below.

13. See Citibank, N.A. v. Tele/Resources Inc., 724 F.2d 266 (2d Cir.1983); Metropolitan Life Ins. Co. v. Dunne, 2 F.Supp. 165 (S.D.N.Y.1931); Sillman v. Twentieth Century-Fox Film Corp., 3 N.Y.2d 395, 165 N.Y.S.2d 498, 144 N.E.2d 387 (1957); Restatement, Contracts (2d)

§ 322(2) and Comment d; Restatement, Contracts § 176. An assignor may not complain the right assigned is not assignable. State Farm Fire & Cas. Ins. Co. v. Farmers Ins. Exch., 489 P.2d 480 (Okl. 1971).

14. See Mitsui & Co., Inc. v. Puerto Rico Water Resources Authority, 528 F.Supp. 768 (D.C.Puerto Rico 1981); 3 Williston § 420.

15. Farnsworth, Contracts § 11.4, n. 6.

16. See Restatement, Second, Contracts § 317(2)(b), Comment e; Restatement, Contracts § 547.

17. See Restatement, Second, Contracts Chapter 15, Introductory Note.

18. See In re Nance, 556 F.2d 602 (1st Cir.1977).

some state statutes forbid with some exceptions, the assignability of a right to payment that arises under a public contract.[19]

Even though the assignment of a right is not prohibited by statute it may still be ineffective because it violates public policy.[20] The most common illustrations are the non-assignability in most jurisdictions of the salary or other remuneration of a public officer [21] which has not yet been earned; [22] the non-assignability of government pensions; [23] and unmatured alimony claims.[24] The securing of assignments for the purpose of stirring up litigation is also against public policy.[25] This is especially true if the assignee is a lawyer.[26] However, this is not true if the attorney has a legitimate business interest in acquiring the assignment.[27]

WESTLAW REFERENCES

di(assignment /s prohibit*** restrict** outlaw** /s statute %
    criminal)

assignment /s contrary /s "public policy"

restatement /3 contract +8 217

find 556 f2d 602

38k11

§ 18–16. Effect of Contractual Prohibition or Authorization of an Assignment

The parties to a contract sometimes include in their contract a provision against assignment. The question here is the validity and effect of such a provision. Some cases have held that a contractual provision prohibiting the assignment of rights created by the contract is an unlawful restraint on alienation.[28] The great majority of cases, however, have refused to interfere with the parties' freedom of contract in so explicit a manner. Rather, they have indicated that a provision of

19. See 31 U.S.C.A. § 3727; 41 U.S.C.A. 15. See also Poorvu v. United States, 420 F.2d 993 (Ct.Cl.1970) and 44 A.L.R.Fed. 775 (1979).

20. Restatement, Second, Contracts § 317(2)(b), Comment e.

21. There is no unanimity on the question of who is a "public officer." Compare Bliss v. Lawrence, 58 N.Y. 442 (1874) with Kimball v. Ledford, 13 Cal.App.2d 602, 57 P.2d 163 (1936).

22. Kaminsky v. Good, 124 Or. 618, 265 P. 786 (1928); 3 Williston § 417. The reason for this rule is the protection of the public by protecting those engaged in performing public duties. See Bliss v. Lawrence, 58 N.Y. 442 (1874). Compare Community State Bank of Independence, La. v. United States, 493 F.2d 908 (5th Cir.1974) (held that there was a question of fact as to whether the assignment deprived the public officer of his means of support).

23. See 5 U.S.C.A. § 8346(a).

24. See Welles v. Brown, 226 Mich. 657, 198 N.W. 180 (1924).

25. See Kenrich Corp. v. Miller, 377 F.2d 312 (3d Cir.1967) (in form, involved a power of attorney rather than an assignment). The obligor's defense of champerty was sustained.

26. Cf. Ellis v. Frawley, 165 Wis. 381, 161 N.W. 364 (1917).

27. Capobianco v. Halebass Realty, Inc., 72 A.D.2d 804, 421 N.Y.S.2d 924 (2d Dep't 1979).

28. Portuguese-American Bank v. Welles, 242 U.S. 7, 37 S.Ct. 3, 61 L.Ed. 116 (1916), criticized in 26 Yale L.J. 304 (1917).

this kind is effective.[29]   At the same time, however, they have tended to find that the particular provision before the court was not drafted with sufficient clarity to accomplish its purpose of prohibiting assignment. They have often emasculated the provision by holding it to be merely a promise not to assign.[30]   Under such a construction an assignment is effective but the obligor has a cause of action against the assignor for breach of contract.[31]   Since damages for such a breach ordinarily will be merely nominal, the anti-assignment provision is of no practical value.   If, however, the provision expressly states that any assignment shall be void, or uses other equivalent language, the courts have generally held that the purported assignment is ineffective,[32] unless the obligor consents to the assignment.[33]

The Uniform Commercial Code has two provisions that limit the effectiveness on an anti-assignment clause.   One is in Article 2 (sale of goods) and the other is in 9–318(4).   Section 2–210(2) provides that an anti-assignment clause will not render ineffective an assignment for damages caused by a total breach.   It also provides that such a clause does not prohibit the assignment of a right arising out of the assignor's due performance.

Section 9–318(4) has adopted the rule that an anti-assignment clause is ineffective to prohibit the assignment of an "account" or a "contract right." [34]

It should be observed that both the Article 2 provision and the Article 9 provision make ineffective a clause that seeks to prevent the assignment of an "account." [35]   The Article 9 provision also relates to a

29. See Hanigan v. Wheeler, 19 Ariz. App. 49, 504 P.2d 972, 59 A.L.R.3d 239 (1972); Masterson v. Sine, 68 Cal.2d 222, 65 Cal.Rptr. 545, 436 P.2d 561 (1968); Dobitz v. Oakland, 172 Mont. 126, 561 P.2d 441 (1977).

See also Goddard, Non Assignment Provisions in Land Contracts, 31 Mich.L.Rev. 1 (1932). See generally Grismore, Effect of a Restriction on Assignment in a Contract, 31 Mich.L.Rev. 299 (1933).

30. See Randal v. Tatum, 98 Cal. 390, 33 P. 433 (1893); Grigg v. Landis, 21 N.J. Eq. 494 (1870); Portland Electric & Plumbing v. Vancouver, 29 Wn.App. 292, 627 P.2d 1350 (1981).

31. See Hull v. Hostettler, 224 Mich. 365, 194 N.W. 996 (1923). It has been held that there is no breach of an anti-assignment clause when the assignment is made because of a change in the assignor's business, as where an individual proprietor forms a corporation and assigns his contractual rights to the corporation. See Ruberoid Co. v. Glassman Const. Co., 248 Md. 97, 234 A.2d 875 (1967); Note, Effect of Corporate Reorganization on Nonassignable Contracts, 74 Harv.L.Rev. 393 (1960).

32. See Allhusen v. Caristo Const. Corp., 303 N.Y. 446, 103 N.E.2d 891 (1952); Restatement, Second, Contracts § 317(2)(c) and Comment c. Restatement, Contracts § 151(c). However, the clause does not prohibit an assignment of a claim for damages for breach of contract. See Paley v. Cocoa Masonry, Inc., 433 So.2d 70 (Fla. App.1983).

33. See Grady v. Commers Interiors, Inc., 268 N.W.2d 823 (S.D.1978). See § 18–14 supra.

34. See Mississippi Bank v. Nickles & Wells Construction Co., 421 So.2d 1056 (Miss.1982). These terms are defined and explained in § 18–4 supra. Notice that both terms relate to a right of payment. It should also be recalled that 1972 amendments to the Code eliminated the term "contract right" and redefined the term account to also include a contract right. Thus under the 1972 amendments, § 9–318(4) refers only to an account.

35. The word "account" is used here in its pre-1972 sense, that is a "right to payment for goods sold or leased or for services rendered." In other words, it refers to a right earned by performance.

"contract right."[36] The Article 2 provision obviously covers an "account" but does not include a "contract right".[37] This appears to create a potential conflict.[38] As one writer has stated it appears that the two provisions "were drafted by different groups for different purposes." [39]

The Code also contains a provision relating to interpretation which bears on the problem. The Code provides that in a sales situation a clause prohibiting assignment of "the contract" should be, unless the circumstances indicate the contrary, construed as barring only the delegation of duties.[40] In other words such a clause is to be read as not relating to an assignment but rather as forbidding only delegation of duties.[41]

If the contract contains a provision permitting assignment it will be honored (except in the case of an illegal assignment) [42] even if the rights under the contract would be otherwise non-assignable.[43] However, very often a clause appears in a contract to the effect that the contract shall inure to the benefit of the heirs and assigns of the parties. Such a clause normally is not directed at the issue of assignability and unless there is some other manifestation of intent of assignability it will not be taken into account on this issue.[44]

WESTLAW REFERENCES

di(contract /s prohibit*** /s assignment) & sy(contract /s assign!)

"anti-assignment clause"

u.c.c. "uniform commercial code" /4 2–210(2) (2–210 +s (2))

u.c.c. "uniform commercial code" /4 9–318(4) (9–318 +s (4))

---

36. The word "contract right" is used here in its pre-1972 sense, that is to say a "right to payment under a contract not yet earned by performance."

37. Again the words are used with their pre-1972 meaning.

38. In other words in the case of a "contract right" (in its original sense), Article 9 would say that an anti-assignment is ineffective but that such a clause would be effective under Article 2.

39. See R. Nordstrom, Law of Sales, § 45 (1970). See generally Jackson and Peters, Quest for Uncertainty: A Proposal for Flexible Resolution of Inherent Conflicts Between Articles 2 and 9 of the Uniform Commercial Code, 87 Yale L.J. 907 (1978).

40. See U.C.C. § 2–210(3); accord Restatement, Contracts (2d) § 322(a); see also Union Bond & Trust Co. v. M & M Wood Working Co., 256 Or. 384, 474 P.2d 339 (1970).

41. See § U.C.C. § 2–210(3).

42. See § 18–15 supra.

43. See Restatement, Second, Contracts § 323(1); Restatement, Contracts § 162(1); 3 Williston § 423.

44. See Standard Chautauqua Sys. v. Gift, 120 Kan. 101, 242 P. 145 (1926); Paige v. Faure, 229 N.Y. 114, 127 N.E. 898 (1920); Restatement, Second, Contracts § 323, Comment b. But see Baum v. Rock, 106 Colo. 567, 108 P.2d 230 (1940).

E. DEFENSES OF THE OBLIGOR

Table of Sections

§ 18–17. Defenses of the Obligor Against the Assignee

We saw in the previous chapter the general rule that a promisor may assert against a third party beneficiary any defense which he may assert against the promisee.[45] A similar rule prevails here. That is, the obligor may generally assert against the assignee the defenses he could have asserted against the assignor.[46] For example, S and B enter into a contract for the sale and purchase of goods. S, before delivery, assigns his rights under the contract to A. A gives notice of the assignment to B. S fails to deliver. In an action by A against B, B has the defense of non-performance.[47]

However, just as in a third party beneficiary context there is an exception discussed under the doctrine of "vesting",[48] a related exception exists in the area of assignments. The assignee is not bound by any defense resulting from an agreement reached between the obligor and the assignor or payment made to the assignor after the obligor has notice of the assignment.[49] In other words, notice received by the obligor of the assignment vests the rights of the assignee in the sense that after notice his rights are not defeasible by agreement of the

45. See § 17–10 supra.

46. See Sponge Divers' Ass'n v. Smith, Kline & French Co., 263 Fed. 70 (1st Cir. 1920); Jones v. Martin, 41 Cal.2d 23, 256 P.2d 905 (1953); Fajen v. Powlus, 98 Idaho 246, 561 P.2d 388 (1977); McIntyre v. Ilb Inv. Corp., 172 N.J.Super. 415, 412 A.2d 810 (1979). This is true even if the assignee did not know of the defenses at the time of assignment and even if the defenses came into existence subsequent to the assignment. See James Talcott, Inc. v. H. Corenzwit & Co., 76 N.J. 305, 387 A.2d 350 (1978). The Uniform Commercial Code has adopted this rule. See U.C.C. § 9–318(1).

47. See Sponge Divers' Ass'n v. Smith, Kline & French Co., 263 F. 70 (3d Cir.1920); First Inv. Co. v. Andersen, 621 P.2d 683 (Utah 1980). By way of illustration, the same rule applies to lack of consideration, illegality, Statutes of Frauds, incapacity and duress.

48. See § 17–11 supra.

49. See Welch v. Mandeville, 14 U.S. (1 Wheat.) 233, 4 L.Ed. 79 (1816) (assignor may not release obligor after notice of the assignment); Terino v. LeClair, 26 A.D.2d 28, 270 N.Y.S.2d 51 (4th Dep't 1966); Continental Purchasing Co. v. Van Raalte Co., 251 App.Div. 151, 295 N.Y.S. 867 (4th Dep't 1937) (obligor may not pay assignor after notice of assignment); Cooper v. Holder, 21 Utah 2d 40, 440 P.2d 15 (1968). Until the obligor has received notice, he is, of course, free to deal with the assignor. See Van Keuren v. Corkins, 66 N.Y. 77 (1876) (payment after assignment of bond and mortgage, recording is not notice to obligor); Restatement, Second, Contracts § 338(1); U.C.C. § 9–318(3). A gratuitous release (one not supported by consideration or its equivalent, see § 21–10 infra) given by the assignor to the obligor even prior to notice does not affect the rights of the assignee unless the assignment is terminable or voidable. If the assignment is revocable or voidable, the gratuitous release would revoke or avoid the assignment. See §§ 18–7 and 18–8 supra.

original contracting parties or by payment made by the obligor to the assignor.[50]

It should be reiterated that the doctrine of vesting becomes relevant only when notice has been given and the defense in question is based upon a subsequent agreement between the obligor and the assignor or payment made by the obligor to the assignor. For example, if S and B enter into a contract for the sale of goods and S assigns his rights under the contract to A who gives notice of the assignment, a subsequent modification of the agreement by S and B will not be effective against A.[51]

In the illustration used in the first paragraph of this section it should be observed that although notice vested A's rights the topic of vesting is irrelevant because the defense in question is failure to perform and does arise by virtue of an agreement between the obligor and the assignor or by payment made by the obligor to the assignor.

The Uniform Commercial Code has some provisions relating to the doctrine of vesting. Some of these provisions continue the common law rules, others clarify it and others make radical changes. Article 9 of the Code provides that the obligor may continue to pay the assignor until he receives notice of the assignment and his duty to pay the assignee.[52] This is in accord with the previously discussed common law rule. The Code has clarified the question of the kind of notice required. First, the notice must "reasonably identify" the rights assigned.[53] Moreover, if requested by the obligor the assignee must furnish proof that the assignment was made and if he fails to do so the obligor may pay the assignor.[54]

---

50. See Equilease Corp. v. State Federal S. & L. Ass'n, 647 F.2d 1069 (10th Cir. 1981); Citizens & Southern Nat'l Bank v. Bruce, 562 F.2d 590 (8th Cir.1977). It is often said that notice is not necessary to the validity of an assignment. Broyles v. Iowa Dep't of Social Services, 305 N.W.2d 718 (Iowa 1981); Commonwealth v. Baldassari, 279 Pa.Super. 491, 421 A.2d 306 (1980). The statement is correct. It means that an assignment is effective without notice. However, the failure to give notice may destroy the rights of the assignee in the sense that his rights will not vest and that therefore he will be subject to defenses based upon an agreement between the obligor and the assignor or payment by the obligor to the assignor.

51. See Brice v. Bannister, 3 Q.B.D. 569 (1878). This does not prevent the obligor and the assignor from making a new agreement if the assignor was guilty of a material breach.

52. See U.C.C. § 9–318(3). See also Annot., 100 A.L.R.3d (1980); § 1–201(26) which defines notice as involving actual receipt. In other words, a person receives notification under this section when it comes to his attention or is duly delivered at a place held out by him as a place for receipt of such communication. However, the assignor will be liable to the assignee upon a theory of breach of warranty. This topic is discussed in § 18–24 infra.

53. See U.C.C. § 9–318(3); Uniform Commercial Credit Code § 3.406 (1968); National Consumer Act § 2.408; Bank of Salt Lake v. Corporation of Pres. of Church of Jesus, 534 P.2d 887 (Utah 1975).

54. U.C.C. § 9–318(3), Comment 5 provides "if there is doubt as to the adequacy either of the notification or of the proof submitted after request, the account debtor may not be safe in disregarding it unless he has notified the assignee with commercial promptness as to the respects in which proof is considered negative." At common law no specific kind of notice or proof was required. A rule of reasonableness prevailed. See 3 Williston § 437. The Code has adopted a more stringent notice and proof requirement, such as had been adopted by judicial decision for the protection of banks in cases involving assignment of

The significant change in the Code is a provision that despite notification of the assignment to the obligor, if the assigned contract right has not become an account,[55] the original contracting parties may agree to modify or substitute [56] the contract in good faith and in accordance with reasonable commercial standards.[57] Under this provision, the assignee is bound by the modification but acquires rights under the modified or substituted contract.[58] These provisions constitute a radical departure from the traditional common law rule.

The drafters of the Uniform Commercial Code obviously felt that the traditional common law rule on vesting was too rigid and not suited to the realities of business. In promulgating its rule the Code had in mind decisions involving necessary advances. In one case [59] a canning company agreed to buy a farmer's crop. The farmer assigned its rights to payment to an assignee who gave notice of the assignment to the canning company. The canning company made advances to the farmer and claimed that it should be able to deduct these advances from what it owed to the assignee. The court agreed because the advance was "necessary to enable the assignor to perform the contract" and the advances were used for this purpose.

The section of the Uniform Commercial Code under discussion obviously would consider that the advance payment was made in good faith and in accordance with reasonable commercial standards and therefore the payments were effective.

Another illustration of the Code rule is furnished by a hypothetical case. A County (R) contracted with C for the construction of a new county courthouse for the sum of $25,000,000. C assigned its rights under the contract to A, a bank, which agreed to extend to C a line of credit to be drawn upon as C purchases supplies and meets his payroll. Because of complaints by its citizens, R renegotiated the contract with C. The modification agreement called for a smaller courthouse at a price of $18,000,000. It would seem that the modification was made in good faith and according to reasonable commercial standards.[60] Thus

bank accounts. See Gibraltar Realty Corp. v. Mt. Vernon Trust Co., 276 N.Y. 353, 12 N.E.2d 438 (1938). On the question of bank deposits and commercial instruments, see also Restatement, Second, Contracts § 339, Comment c.

55. The word "account" is not used in the latest version of U.C.C. § 9–318(2), but it is clear that the section is saying that it does not apply to an account in the pre-1972 definition of that term.

56. It is generally believed that the words "modifying or substitute" include the concept of "termination." See Restatement, Second, Contracts § 338, ill. 6.

57. Comment 2 to U.C.C. § 9–318 states that this change is needed to cover a situation where a government agency finds it necessary to terminate or amend an ex-

isting contract with a general contractor. Under this section the general contractor may make appropriate arrangements with his subcontractors without getting the permission of the assignees of the subcontractor.

58. See U.C.C. § 9–318(2). The Restatement, Second adopts the rule of this section. See Restatement, Second, Contracts § 338(2). For a detailed discussion of this section, see Gilmore, The Assignee of Contract Rights and His Precarious Security, 74 Yale L.J. 217 (1964).

59. Fricker v. Uddo & Taormina Co., 48 Cal.2d 696, 312 P.2d 1085 (1957).

60. See, for example, Babson v. Village of Ulysses, 155 Neb. 492, 52 N.W.2d 320 (1952).

A's rights were effectively curtailed. It should be noted, however that A was not injured by the change if it could locate other creditworthy borrowers at the same rate of interest.

There are two provisions in the Code by which the assignee may be protected against the rule under discussion. If the obligor and assignor have agreed that the Code rule should not apply then the common law rule applies.[61] In addition, the assignee may obtain as part of the assignment a promise by the assignor that a modification or rescission of the original contract will constitute a breach by the assignor.[62]

It obviously will take many years before we have some idea how the courts will apply the Code provisions discussed herein in a concrete case. Although the provision destroys the symmetry of prior law, its flexibility allows for a just result on the facts of a particular case. When a case arises it would be wise to consult the excellent article of Professor Gilmore on this topic.[63]

Since it is a general rule that the obligor may assert against the assignee any defense which he can assert against the assignor, it is often stated that "an assignee stands in the shoes of his assignor",[64] that is, the assignee does not have any better rights than his assignor.[65] This is another way of saying that an assignee does not qualify as a good faith purchaser for value even though he has the attributes of a purchaser for value.[66]

We have already seen that the doctrine of vesting is an exception to the general rule that the assignee stands in the shoes of his assignor.[67] There are other exceptions. One occurs under the ubiquitous doctrine of estoppel.[68] Suppose that A assigns and delivers his savings bankbook to C. C in turn assigns to D, but D allows C to retain the book. The bank pays C in good faith before notice of assignment from D but does not require surrender of the book. Subsequently, C assigns and delivers the book to E who has the attributes of a bona fide purchaser for value. The bank is liable to E because of its failure to require production of a symbolic writing.[69] In other words its failure to do this estops it from asserting its payment to C against E.[70] Finally there are

61. See U.C.C. § 9–318(2). In theory the assignee is a third party beneficiary.

62. See U.C.C. § 9–318(2).

63. Gilmore, The Assignee of Contract Rights and His Precarious Security, 74 Yale L.J. 217 (1964).

64. James Talcott, Inc. v. H. Corenzwit & Co., 76 N.J. 305, 387 A.2d 350 (1978); Pioneer State Bank v. Johnsrud, 284 N.W.2d 292 (N.D.1979); Aird Ins. Agency v. Zions First Nat. Bank, 612 P.2d 341 (Utah 1980).

65. See Fox Greenwald Sheet Metal Co. v. Markowitz Bros., Inc., 452 F.2d 1346 (D.C.Cir.1971); Morse Electro Prods. v.

Beneficial Indus. Loan Co., 90 Wn.2d 195, 579 P.2d 1341 (1978).

66. See Gilmore, The Commercial Doctrine of Good Faith Purchase, 63 Yale L.J. 1057 (1954).

67. See § 18–17 supra.

68. See Dimmitt & Owens Financial v. Realtek Ind., Inc., 90 Mich.App. 429, 280 N.W.2d 827 (1979).

69. On the meaning of "symbolic writings" see § 18–7 supra.

70. Assets Realization Co. v. Clark, 205 N.Y. 105, 98 N.E. 457 (1912); See Restatement, Second, Contracts § 338, Comment h and ill. 12.

statutes under which an assignee may have greater rights than his assignor.[71]

Financial institutions which received assignments from retailers became most unhappy with the rule that they were bound by the defenses that the consumer had against the retailer. One vehicle of escape was the use of a negotiable instrument under which the institutions could qualify as a holder in due course and thus be, in a general way, in the equivalent position of a purchaser for value.[72]

The financial institutions also devised another way to circumvent the rule that the obligor may assert against the assignee any defense that he had against the assignor. They did this by having the retailer include in his contract with the consumer a provision which reads substantially as follows:

> "Buyer hereby acknowledges notice that the contract may be assigned and that the assignees will rely upon the agreements contained in this paragraph, and agrees that the liability of the Buyer to any assignee shall be immediate and absolute and not affected by any default whatsoever of the Seller signing this contract; and in order to induce assignees to purchase this contract, the Buyer further agrees not to set up any claim against such Seller as a defense, counterclaim or offset to any action by any assignee for the unpaid balance of the purchase price or for possession of the property." [73]

It is obvious that if such a clause is valid it effectively eliminates the rule that the obligor may assert against the assignee any defense which the obligor has against the assignor. Under such a clause the rights of the assignee would resemble those of a holder in due course.[74] There are jurisdictions which have held, as a common law proposition, that such clauses are invalid [75] but the majority of courts have sustained them.[76]

The Uniform Commercial Code validates such clauses where the assignee takes in good faith for value without notice of the defense but

71. For example, the Real Property Recording Act.

72. If an instrument is negotiable and negotiated to a transferee (holder), he will qualify as a holder in due course if he takes the instrument in good faith and without notice that it is overdue, or has been dishonored, or that there is a defense against it or claim to it. In that event the holder in due course takes free of personal defenses (e.g. breach of warranty) but subject to real defenses (e.g. illegality). See U.C.C. §§ 3–302 – 2–305.

73. This is the language of the instrument in Unico v. Owen, 50 N.J. 101, 106, 232 A.2d 405, 408 (1967).

74. See note 72 supra. The argument in favor of the effectiveness of such a clause is the policy of free assignability. The argument on the other side is that the consumer must pay even though he has a defense against the assignor and this is unfair particularly when the assignor has become insolvent.

75. Fairfield Credit Corp. v. Donnelly, 158 Conn. 543, 264 A.2d 547, 39 A.L.R.3d 509 (1969); Quality Fin. Co. v. Hurley, 337 Mass. 150, 148 N.E.2d 385 (1958); Motor Contract Co. v. Van Der Volgen, 162 Wash. 499, 298 P. 705, 79 A.L.R. 29 (1931).

76. See United States ex rel. Adm'r of F.H.A. v. Troy-Parisian, Inc., 115 F.2d 224 (9th Cir.1940), cert. denied 312 U.S. 699, 61 S.Ct. 739, 85 L.Ed. 1133 (1941).

not with respect to defenses which would be denominated as real defenses to a negotiable instrument [77] except that this provision is subordinated "to any statute or decision which establishes a different rule for buyers or lessees of consumer goods." [78]

As to the issues of good faith and without notice there are cases that have held that these do not exist when there is a close or continuing relationship between the assignor and the assignee.[79] In addition there are statutes that make the waiver of defense clause a nullity.[80] Other statutes have provided that the buyer (obligor) may preserve his defenses by giving notice within a specified time.[81]

This problem has also been addressed by the Federal Trade Commission. The Federal Trade Commission has promulgated a trade regulation rule which abolishes the holder in due course rule in the case of consumer paper and prohibits retail installment sales, agreements and leases which contain provisions destroying the consumer's rights against either the seller or his assignee.[82]

WESTLAW REFERENCES

obligor /s assert*** /s defense /s assignor

38k100

"third party beneficiary" /s vesting

obligor /s notice /4 assignment /s assignor

38k1

find 305 nw2d 718

38k71

38k72

38k57

u.c.c. "uniform commercial code" /s 9–318(3) (9–318 +s (3))

u.c.c. "uniform commercial code" /s 1–201(26) (1–201 +s (26))

u.c.c. "uniform commercial code" /s 3–302

u.c.c. "uniform commercial code" /s 3–305

77. See U.C.C. § 9–206(1); Holt v. First Nat'l Bank of Minneapolis, 297 Minn. 457, 214 N.W.2d 698 (1973); General Elec. Credit Corp. v. Tidenberg, 78 N.M. 59, 428 P.2d 33 (1967); see also Littlefield, Preserving Consumer Defenses: Plugging the Loophole in the New U.C.C.C., 44 N.Y.U.L.Rev. 272 (1969).

78. U.C.C. § 9–206(1); see also U.C.C. §§ 9–201, 9–203, Comment 6, (relating to the possibility of estoppel against an obligor even though the agreement not to assert a defense is invalid). See generally Restatement, Second, Contracts § 336, Comment f and Hogan, A Survey of State Retail Installment Sales Legislation, 44 Cornell L.Q. 38 (1958); cf. President and Directors of Manhattan Co. v. Monogram Associates, Inc., 276 App.Div. 766, 92 N.Y.S.2d 579 (2d Dep't 1949). In general, "Goods are 'consumer goods' if they are used or bought for use primarily for per-

sonal, family or household purposes." U.C.C. § 9–109(1).

79. See Rehurek v. Chrysler Credit Corp., 262 So.2d 452 (Fla.App.1972), cert. denied 267 So.2d 833 (Fla.1972); Massey-Ferguson, Inc. v. Utley, 439 S.W.2d 57 (Ky. 1969); Unico v. Owen, 50 N.J. 101, 232 A.2d 405 (1967); Murphy, Another "Assault Upon the Citadel": Limiting the Use of Negotiable Notes and Waiver-of-Defense Clauses in Consumer Sales, 29 Ohio St.L.J. 667 (1968).

80. See 1 CCH Consumer Credit Guide ¶ 4380 (1969).

81. See, e.g., U.C.C.C. § 3.406 (1968); Nat'l Consumer Act § 2.406; Model Consumer Credit Act § 2–601 (1973); Meyers v. Postal Finance Co., 287 N.W.2d 614 (Minn.1979).

82. See 16 C.F.R. 433.2 (1973). Consumer is defined in note 78 supra.

u.c.c. "uniform commercial code" /s 9–206(1) (9–206 +s (1))
u.c.c. "uniform commercial code" /s 9–201
u.c.c. "uniform commercial code" /s 9–203
find 287 nw2d 614

§ 18–18. Defenses of the Assignor Against the Assignee

This topic has been covered in a number of prior sections—18–5, which relates to an assignment that contravenes the Statute of Frauds; gratuitous assignments (18–7); voidable assignments and conditional assignments of rights (18–8); assignment of future rights (18–9).

None of these sections involve a void assignment. However, it seems clear that generally speaking a void assignment should be governed by the rules relating to void contracts.[83]

 WESTLAW REFERENCES
38k109
38k105

F. COUNTERCLAIMS, SET OFF, AND RECOUPMENT

Table of Sections

§ 18–19. To What Extent May an Obligor Use a Counterclaim That He Has Against the Assignor

In § 18–17 above we discussed the question of whether the obligor may assert against the assignee a defense that he has against the assignor. Here the same question is presented in relation to counterclaims. In this situation there is a distinction drawn between a counterclaim in the nature of a recoupment and a counterclaim in the nature of a set-off.[84]

In the case of a counterclaim in the nature of a recoupment (a claim that arises out of the assigned contract) the common law rule is that the obligor may use the breach of the assignor against the assignee whether or not the claim arose prior to the notice of assignment.[85] The claim of the obligor may only be used in diminution of the claim of the assignee. That is to say that the obligor may not use the claim to

---

83. See Sections 1–11 and 4–12 supra.

84. See First Nat. Bank of Louisville v. Master Auto Service Corp., 693 F.2d 308 (4th Cir.1982).

85. American Bridge Co. v. Boston, 202 Mass. 374, 88 N.E. 1089 (1909); Cronkleton v. Hastings Theatre & Realty Corp., 134 Neb. 168, 278 N.W. 144 (1938); Seibert v. Dunn, 216 N.Y. 237, 110 N.E. 447 (1915). The assignor's failure to perform would amount to a breach of warranty. See § 18–24 infra.

obtain a judgment against the assignee.[86] This would not be true where the obligor has a claim directly against the assignee himself.[87] The rule of the Code is in accord.[88]

A counterclaim in the nature of a set-off involves a claim that does not arise out of the agreement that gives rise to the assignment. It may arise out of another agreement between the same parties or even more likely a claim that a third person has against the assignor. Before the Code this topic was covered for the most part by statute. These statutes varied in different jurisdictions. The Uniform Commercial Code takes the position that if the set-off accrues before the obligor receives notice of assignment it may be used against the assignee. Conversely if the claim matured after notice of the assignment it may not be used.[89] The Restatement, Second has adopted the Code rule. Again, the obligor may only utilize the set-off by way of subtraction from the assignee's claim and may not obtain a judgment against the assignee for any excess over the assignee's claim.[90] The obligor may obtain a judgment against the assignor only if he has a claim against the assignee himself.[91]

The rule of the Uniform Commercial Code, discussed above, also applies to sub-assignees—that is, subsequent assignees of the original assignee.[92] The same is true of the rule of the Second Restatement.[93] A contrary rule stated in the original Restatement [94] was eliminated to bring the Restatement into harmony with the U.C.C.[95]

WESTLAW REFERENCES
obligor /s counter-claim /s assignor
obligor /s set-off /s assignor
38k100
u.c.c. "uniform commercial code" /s 9–318(1)(a) (9–318 +s
  (1)(a))
349ak185
u.c.c. "uniform commercial code" /s 9–318(1)(b) (9–318 +s
  (1)(b))

---

86. Restatement, Second, Contracts § 336.

87. This would occur when the assignee has assumed the duty of the assignor. See § 18–26 infra. There are cases that hold if the obligor pays the assignee before he learns of the defense he is entitled to restitution even if he acts negligently provided the assignee has not changed his position in reliance on the payment. Farmers Acceptance Corp. v. Delozier, 178 Colo. 291, 496 P.2d 1016 (1972). Contra, Daniels v. Parker, 209 Or. 419, 306 P.2d 735 (1957).

88. U.C.C. § 9–318(1)(a).

89. U.C.C. § 9–318(1)(b) and Comment 1. The word accrues means when a cause of action accrues. Seattle-First Nat'l Bank v. Oregon Pac. Indus., Inc., 262 Or. 578, 500 P.2d 1033 (1972). The Restatement, Second is in accord with the U.C.C. section. Restatement, Second, Contracts § 336(2).

90. U.C.C. § 9–318(1)(b); Restatement, Second, Contracts 336, Comment d.

91. The obligor's right to counterclaim on an unrelated transaction may be limited for trial convenience by procedural rules. See Restatement, Second, Contracts 336, Comment c.

92. U.C.C. § 9–318(1)(b).

93. Restatement, Second, Contracts § 336.

94. Restatement, Contracts § 167(3).

95. See Restatement, Second, Contracts § 336, Comment e and reporter's note.

G. OTHER POSSIBLE LIMITATIONS ON THE RIGHTS OF THE ASSIGNEE

Table of Sections

§ 18–20. Latent Equities

A "latent equity" is an equity that exists in a party other than the obligor or the assignor. Although the phrase "latent equity" is used, the issue is who owns the assigned right, the assignee or some third party. This in turn depends upon whether the assignee takes subject to "latent equities."

An illustration will help clarify the discussion. A is obligated to B and B assigns to C as a result of C's fraud. C then assigns to D who takes in good faith, for value and without notice of the right that B had to avoid the assignment in the hands of C. The question is whether or not D takes subject to B's latent equity.[96]

The result depends on whether D qualifies as a purchaser for value. We have already seen that an assignee does not usually qualify as a purchaser for value.[97] The reason for this is that historically an assignee was looked upon as having an equitable right and to qualify as a purchaser for value one had to receive a legal title.[98]

If this approach is followed, it is clear in the illustration given, that B will prevail.[99] However, in this situation, the modern approach is to consider an assignment as vesting a legal interest in the assignee. Under this approach, in the illustration given D would qualify as purchaser for value and defeat the claim of B.[1]

---

96. The illustration is based upon illustration 1 of § 174 of the original Restatement.

97. We have already seen that the assignee stands in the shoes of the assignor and that this means that the assignee does not qualify as a purchaser for value. See § 18–17 supra.

98. Holt v. American Woolen Co., 129 Me. 108, 150 A. 382 (1930); McClintock, Equity 69–71 (1948). As between two competing equities the rule is that prior in time is prior in right. Id. at 52. On the meaning of "value" see § 18–7 supra.

99. See Owen v. Evans, 134 N.Y. 514, 31 N.E. 999 (1892). This view is strongly supported by 3 Williston § 447, where he

states that it is supported by the weight of authority. See also 3 Williston § 438. His policy rationale, stated in § 447, ("it is to be observed that intangible choses in action are not primarily intended for merchandising, as chattels are") is no longer an accurate statement of commercial practice.

1. See Glass v. Springfield L.I. Cemetery Soc'y., 252 App.Div. 319, 299 N.Y.S. 244 (1st Dep't 1937), appeal denied 13 N.E.2d 479 (1938); Restatement, Second, Contracts § 343; Restatement, Contracts § 174. Corbin describes this as the prevailing view. 4 Corbin § 900. See Comment, 20 U.Chi.L.Rev. 692 (1953). This rule is not applied where the protection of

§ 18–21. Priorities Between Successive Assignees of the Same Claim

Suppose A assigns to B a right of payment of $1,000 which is owed to A by X. If A subsequently assigns the same right to C, who prevails? A has obviously acted unlawfully in making the second assignment, and if solvent and brought to justice, can be made to pay for his wrongful act.[2] As between the two innocent assignees there are essentially three views on the question of priority. The English view is that as between successive assignees the second will prevail if he is the first to give notice and acts without notice of the first assignment and pays value.[3] The rule is designed to encourage assignees to give prompt notice to the obligor so that the obligor is in a position to answer inquiries as to who owns the claim. The failure to give such notice is looked upon as negligence.[4]

The New York rule is that first in time is first in right. Under this rule if the obligor pays the second assignee who was first to give notice the first assignee may still recover from the second assignee.[5] Under this rule, however, the obligor is discharged by his payment to the second assignee.[6] The rationale of the New York rule is that as between two competing equities first in time is first in right.[7] It is based on the philosophical axiom, *"Nemo dat quod non habet"*—no one gives what he does not have. In other words, having assigned once, there is nothing left for the assignor to assign.[8]

The Restatements have adopted a third view—the so called "Massachusetts" or "four horsemen" rule. Under this rule the first assignee prevails unless a second assignee who pays value in good faith without notice (a) obtains payment from the obligor; (b) recovers judgment; (c) enters into a new contract with the obligor—in other words the obligor promises to pay the second assignee; or (d) receives delivery of a

the purchaser would impair the rights of the obligor. Restatement, Second, Contracts § 343, Comment b.

2. See § 18–24 infra relating to the warranties of the assignor. The second assignment may even constitute larceny. People v. Schwartzman, 24 N.Y.2d 241, 299 N.Y.S.2d 817, 247 N.E.2d 642 (1969).

3. Graham Paper Co. v. Pembroke, 124 Cal. 117, 56 P. 627 (1899); Anaconda Aluminum Co. v. Sharp, 243 Miss. 9, 136 So.2d 585, 99 A.L.R.2d 1307 (1962). On the meaning of "value" see § 18–7 supra.

4. Dearle v. Hall, 38 Eng.Rep. 475 (Ch. 1827).

5. Superior Brassiere Co., Inc. v. Zimetbaum, 214 App.Div. 525, 212 N.Y.S. 473 (1st Dep't 1925).

6. This is so because the obligor has not received any notice from the first assignee. See § 18–20 supra.

7. Salem Trust Co. v. Manufacturers' Fin. Co., 264 U.S. 182, 44 S.Ct. 266, 68 L.Ed. 628 (1924).

8. See note 5 supra.

tangible token or writing, the surrender of which is required by the obligor's contract (a symbolic writing).[9]

Even in states which adopt the New York rule it is clear that the second assignee will prevail if the first assignment was gratuitous and not at the time of the second agreement a completed gift or is voidable.[10] So also, if the necessary elements are present, the first assignee may be estopped from asserting priority as, for example, where he has failed to take possession of a symbolic writing.[11] The second assignee may also prevail under certain statutes, as for example, the Real Property Recording Act. The same is true in the case of an assignment of a future right if the second assignment is legal and the assignee pays value and takes without notice.[12]

The problem of successive assignments is not extremely important in itself, since such conduct is rare. Yet there has been a highly dramatic side effect of the rule governing successive assignments. In Corn Exchange National Bank & Trust Co. v. Klauder, the United States Supreme Court ruled that assignments of accounts receivable in Pennsylvania, where the English rule prevailed, were not "perfected" liens within the protection of the Bankruptcy Act.[13] This was because it was possible that a second hypothetical assignee could, under the Pennsylvania law, obtain priority over the bankrupt first assignee. This means that the first assignee was not protected under the Bankruptcy Act and thus he became an unsecured creditor. The legislative response was prompt and a majority of states enacted legislation to protect the security interest that the assignee received by virtue of the outright assignment. In some, the New York rule was enacted; in some, a system of marking the debtor's books was adopted; and in others a filing system was instituted.[14]

Against this background the Commercial Code (in Article 9) provided for a filing system. The filing system was also made applicable to the outright assignment of an account as defined in the 1972 amendments.[15] However, as we have seen, certain outright assignments are

9. Restatement, Second, Contracts §§ 342, 332, Comment c; Restatement, Contracts § 173(b); see Rabinowitz v. People Nat'l Bank, 235 Mass. 102, 126 N.E. 289 (1920). According to the Restatement, Second, the justification for the rule is that the second assignee takes a legal title and qualifies as a purchaser for value. Restatement, Second, Contracts § 342, Comment e. The rule relating to a symbolic writing is based on the doctrine of estoppel. Restatement, Second, Contracts § 342, Comment f. As to symbolic writings, see § 18–7 and § 18–17 supra.

10. See McKnight v. Rice, Hoppner, Brown & Brunner, 678 P.2d 1330 (Alaska 1984); Restatement, Second, Contracts § 342, Comment d; cf. Perkins v. City Nat'l Bank, 253 Iowa 922, 114 N.W.2d 45 (1962).

11. See note 9 supra.

12. See § 18–20 supra.

13. 318 U.S. 434, 63 S.Ct. 679, 87 L.Ed. 884 (1943). The "four horsemen" rule, however, was held to perfect the assignment within the meaning of the Bankruptcy Act. In re Rosen, 157 F.2d 997 (3d Cir. 1946), cert. denied 330 U.S. 835, 67 S.Ct. 972, 91 L.Ed. 1282 (1947).

14. The statutes are analyzed in Comment, Multistate Accounts Receivable Financing: Conflicts in Context, 67 Yale L.J. 402 (1958).

15. See § 18–4 supra.

excluded from the coverage of Article 9.[16]   In addition, the filing provisions of Article 9 are inapplicable "to an assignment of accounts which does not alone or in conjunction with other assignments to the same assignee transfer a significant part of the outstanding accounts of the assignor." [17]

If the filing provision of Article 9 is applicable, as between two assignees for value the one who first files a financing statement will prevail.[18]   This allows a party to rely on the filing system.   The assignment of an account excluded from Article 9 will be covered by the common law rules discussed above as will be true of an assignment other than the assignment of an account.[19]   Where the right assigned is covered by the Code but is excluded from the filing provision of the Code, the assignee's right is perfected without filing and thus he will prevail if the formalities described in § 18–5 are met.[20]

 WESTLAW REFERENCES

priority /s assignment /s successive innocent /3 assignee

english /2 rule /s successive /3 assignee

dearle +3 hall

"new york" /2 rule /s assign!

"four horseman" massachusetts /3 rule /s assign!

"corn exchange" +s klauder

u.c.c. "uniform commercial code" /s 9–302(1)(e) (9–302 +s (1)(e))

349ak84

349ak144

u.c.c. "uniform commercial code" /s 9–315(5) (9–315 +s (5))

349ak145

---

§ 18–22. Rights of the Assignee Against an Attaching Creditor of the Assignor

An assignee clearly has rights superior to the general creditors of the assignor. A general creditor does not have a security interest in any property of the debtor. An assignee has a specific interest in the right assigned. Thus an assignee will always prevail over a general creditor. However, a general creditor may in a variety of ways obtain a security interest in specific property of the debtor. One of these ways is by attaching an asset of the debtor (obligor).

The discussion here relates to a situation where a creditor attaches the same right that is assigned to the assignee. If the creditor attached this right prior to the assignment the attaching creditor has priority

16. See § 18–4 supra.

17. U.C.C. § 9–302(1)(e). See § 18–4 supra.

18. U.C.C. § 9–312(5). If the statute is taken literally, this is true even though the second assignee has knowledge of the first assignment. This allows a party to rely on the filing system.

19. See § 18–4 supra.

20. See U.C.C. § 9–203(1) and § 9–302. See generally Annot., 85 A.L.R.3d 1050 (1978).

over the claim of the assignee.[21] The converse is usually true. An assignment which precedes an attachment will have priority over the attachment.[22]

The rule last stated, if absolute, could work to the prejudice of the debtor (obligor). It is therefore held that under certain circumstances the assignee is estopped from asserting his priority.[23] The issue arises in relation to the failure of the assignee to give timely notice.[24] There are two versions as to what is timely notice. One version bars the claim of the assignee unless notice is received in time to call the assignment to the attention of the court in the attachment proceeding and thus prevent a judgment in favor of the attaching creditor in those proceedings.[25] Other cases have held that even though judgment has been entered in the attachment proceedings in favor of the attaching creditor, the rights of the assignee will not be barred if he gives notice to the debtor prior to payment of the judgment entered as a result of the attachment proceedings provided the obligor could still use the assignment to defeat the claim of the attaching creditor.[26]

The Uniform Commercial Code, to a large extent, resolves the priority problem discussed here by its filing system. Thus if the assignment is of the kind which comes under the filing provisions, and the assignment is filed prior to the attachment the assignment takes priority over the lien of the subsequent attachment.[27] Conversely, if the attachment arises before the filing occurs, the attaching creditor (lien creditor) will prevail.[28] If the assignment is covered by Article 9 but is excluded from the filing provisions of the Code, the assignment is perfected without filing and thus the assignee will prevail over a subsequent lien creditor if the formalities described in § 18–5 are met.[29] If the assignment is excluded from Article 9 then the common law rules discussed above will apply.

21. Restatement, Second, Contracts § 341(1).

22. Stathos v. Murphy, 26 A.D.2d 500, 276 N.Y.S.2d 727 (1st Dep't 1966), affirmed 19 N.Y.2d 883, 281 N.Y.S.2d 81, 227 N.E.2d 880 (1967); 4 Corbin § 903; 3 Williston § 434. For the rule in the case of an assignment of future rights, see § 18–21 supra.

23. Restatement, Second, Contracts § 341, Comment b.

24. Since a creditor does not qualify as a purchaser for value by virtue of his attachment, he can obtain priority over an assignee only by virtue of the doctrine of estoppel or by the terms of a particular statute. Restatement, Second, Contracts § 341, Comment a. However, an attaching creditor who is subsequent to an assignee will have superior rights if the assignment is terminable or voidable. Restatement,

Second, Contracts § 341, Comment b; cf. Restatement, Contracts § 172(1).

25. Restatement, Contracts § 172(2).

26. See McDowell, Pyle & Co. v. Hopfield, 148 Md. 84, 128 A. 742, 52 A.L.R. 105 (1925); Goldfarb v. C & K Purchasing Corp., 170 Misc. 90, 9 N.Y.S.2d 952 (App. Term 1939); see also Restatement, Second, Contracts § 341(2).

27. Dubay v. Williams, 417 F.2d 1277 (9th Cir.1969). In the terminology of the Code, an attaching creditor is a "lien creditor." U.C.C. § 9–301(3).

28. U.C.C. § 9–301(1)(b). In technical language, a person who becomes a lien creditor before the assignment interest is perfected has priority. Farnsworth, Contracts § 11.9, at 794.

29. See U.C.C. §§ 9–203(1), 9–302(1).

WESTLAW REFERENCES

digest(assignee /s priority prevail*** prefer! /s creditor) &
  sy(assign! /s creditor)

349ak138 /p creditor /s assignee

find 276 nys2d 727

38k71

38k86

assignee /s timely /2 notice /s creditor

u.c.c. "uniform commercial code" /s 9–301(3) (9–301 +s (3))

u.c.c. "uniform commercial code" /s 9–301(1)(b) (9–301 +s
  (1)(b))

u.c.c. "uniform commercial code" /s 9–203(1) (9–201 +s (1))

u.c.c. "uniform commercial code" /s 9–302(1) (9–302 +s (1))

349ak84

349ak144

§ 18–23. Partial Assignments

At common law a partial assignment was unenforceable over the objection of the obligor because of the rule against splitting a cause of action.[30] Moreover, because procedure at law limited any suit to two parties, the obligor would be subject to multiplicity of suits.[31] In time, however, partial assignments were recognized in equity because the obligor could join all of the partial assignees in one law suit.[32] Today, the majority view, often as a result of Code procedure, is that the equity rule applies not only in equity but also at law.[33] In other words, the partial assignee may sue at law provided that all of the interested parties have been joined, or the assignee complies with procedural rules that dispense with the necessity of joining other partial assignees because it is fair to do so under the circumstances.[34]

WESTLAW REFERENCES

sy,di("partial assignment")

find 270 nys2d 51

30. Standard Discount Co. v. Metropolitan Life Ins. Co., 321 Ill.App. 220, 53 N.E.2d 27 (1944).

31. Andrews Elec. Co. v. St. Alphonse Catholic Total Abstinence Soc'y, 233 Mass. 20, 123 N.E. 103 (1919).

32. See National Exch. Bank v. McLoon, 73 Me. 498 (1882); see also Annot., 80 A.L.R. 413 (1932).

33. See Schwartz v. Horowitz, 131 F.2d 506 (2d Cir.1942); Zurcher v. Modern Plastic Mach. Corp., 24 N.J.Super. 158, 93 A.2d 778 (1952), affirmed 12 N.J. 465, 97 A.2d 437 (1953); Prudential Fed. Sav. & Loan Ass'n v. Hartford Acc. & Indem. Co., 7 Utah 2d 366, 325 P.2d 899 (1958); see 4 Corbin § 889; cf. 3 Williston §§ 442–43; Terino v. LeClair, 26 A.D.2d 28, 270 N.Y.S.2d 51 (4th Dep't 1966) (obligor who continued to pay assignor after notice of the partial assignment held liable to the assignee); Geo. V. Clark Co. v. New York, N.H. & H.R. Co., 279 App.Div. 39, 107 N.Y.S.2d 721 (1st Dep't 1951) (specific performance of partial assignment of right to purchase land).

34. Staples v. Rush, 99 So.2d 502 (La. App.1957); In re Fine Paper Litigation State of Washington, 632 F.2d 1081 (3d Cir. 1980); Restatement, Second, Contracts § 326(2).

38k7 /p partial** /s assign!
38k30

H. RIGHTS OF THE ASSIGNEE
AGAINST THE ASSIGNOR

Table of Sections

Sec.
18–24. Warranties of the Assignor.

§ 18–24. Warranties of the Assignor

If the assignee has rights against the assignor it is ordinarily upon a theory of breach of warranty. Thus the question is what does an assignor warrant when he makes an assignment to the assignee. As in other areas the warranty may be expressed or implied. If an express warranty is made it will be enforced.[35] Conversely, it may be agreed that the assignment is without warranty, express or implied.[36]

Where the parties are silent on the subject, the law in the case of an assignment for value[37] is that certain warranties are implied. According to the Restatements an assignor makes three implied warranties.[38] (1) The right exists and is subject to no defenses or limitations except as stated or apparent.[39] (2) He will do nothing to defeat or impair the value of the assignment and has no knowledge of any fact that would do so. (3) Any document delivered as part of the transaction is genuine (not a forgery).

The assignor does not warrant that the obligor is solvent or that he will perform.[40] In the absence of a contrary manifestation of intention, the warranties (express or implied) of an assignor to an assignee do not run to a sub-assignee.[41]

 WESTLAW REFERENCES
express /2 warranty /s assignor
implied /2 warranty /s assignor

35. Warner v. Seaboard Fin. Co., 75 Nev. 470, 345 P.2d 759 (1959); Restatement, Second, Contracts § 333(3).

36. Brod v. Cincinnati Time Recorder Co., 82 Ohio App. 26, 77 N.E.2d 293 (1947); Restatement, Second, Contracts § 333, Comment b.

37. The distinction between an assignment "for value" and a gratuitous assignment is drawn in § 18–7 supra.

38. Lonsdale v. Chesterfield, 99 Wn.2d 353, 662 P.2d 385 (1983); Restatement, Second, Contracts § 333(1); Restatement, Contracts § 175.

39. In the absence of a binding disclaimer, this warranty is violated if the obligor has a defense or a counterclaim against the assignor that may be used against the assignee. See §§ 18–17 and 18–19 supra.

40. Restatement, Second, Contracts § 333; Restatement, Contracts § 175. In other words, the assignor is not a guarantor unless he agrees to be one.

41. Restatement, Second, Contracts § 333(4).

38k97

find 662 p2d 385

38k95

I.   DELEGATION

Table of Sections

§ 18–25.   Introduction

We have already adverted to the importance of the distinction between assignment and delegation. Rights are assigned; duties are delegated.[42] When a right is assigned, the assignor ordinarily no longer has any interest in the claim.[43] When a duty is delegated, however, the delegating party (delegant) continues to remain liable.[44] If this were not so, every solvent person could obtain freedom from his debts by delegating them to an insolvent. Delegation involves the appointment by the obligor-delegant of another to render performance on his behalf. It does not free the obligor-delegant from his duty to see to it that performance is rendered,[45] unless there is a novation.[46] These thoughts are pursued further in the next section.

 WESTLAW REFERENCES
find 309 se2d 770
38k114

---

42. See § 18–1 supra.

43. See § 18–3 supra. As we have seen, if the assignment is revocable, voidable, unenforceable or conditional, the assignor may retain some interest in the right assigned. See §§ 18–6, 18–7, 18–8 and 18–9 supra.

44. Callon Petroleum Co. v. Big Chief Drilling Co., 548 F.2d 1174 (5th Cir.1977), rehearing denied 552 F.2d 369 (5th Cir. 1977); Cuchine v. H. O. Bell, Inc., ___

Mont. ___, 682 P.2d 723 (1984); Baker v. Weaver, 279 S.C. 479, 309 S.E.2d 770 (1983).

45. U.C.C. § 2–210(1) restates the common law when it says: "No delegation of performance relieves the party delegating of any duty to perform or any liability for breach." See also 3 Williston § 419; Restatement, Contracts § 160(4).

46. See § 17–13 supra and § 18–26 infra.

§ 18–26.　Liability of the Delegate

The concept of delegation was actually involved in the chapter relating to third party beneficiaries.[47]　If A owes B $1,000 and C, for a consideration, agrees with A to assume that duty, there are a number of consequences that flow from the transaction.　1) There is a delegation of A's duty to C (the delegate) because A has appointed C to pay the money on his behalf.　2) B is a third party beneficiary of the agreement between C and A.[48]　3) Since A continues to remain liable and C is liable to B under a third party beneficiary theory, it follows that B has a claim against both A and C but is entitled to only one satisfaction.[49]　4) In this situation the delegate (C) is liable to B on a third party beneficiary theory and is also liable to A because his promise to assume was made to A.[50]　5) As indicated above A continues to remain liable in the absence of a novation.[51]　A novation would occur in the illustration above if B expressly discharged A in consideration of C's assumption of A's duty.[52]

In the situation discussed above there is a delegation of a duty and the delegate (C) assumes the duty.　This is only one of the ways in which delegation can take place.

In the situation above, as we have seen, C becomes liable to both A and B.　It is certainly possible for A and C to agree in such a way that C's promise to A with respect to the delegated duty runs only to A and not B.　In the language of the preceding section B would at most be an incidental beneficiary of the delegation.[53]

It is also possible for A to delegate the duty to C by giving C the option of performing the duty if he wishes.　Clearly in such a case C is not liable to either A or B if he does not perform.[54]

In the illustration given at the beginning of this section, C *expressly* assumed A's duty.　It is also possible to have an *implied* assumption of a duty by conduct.　For example, in Epstein v. Gluckin,[55] the New York Court of Appeals held that the assignee of a right to purchase property, who had not assumed the duty at the time of the assignment, assumed it subsequently by bringing an action for specific performance.　In a later case the same court held that the purchaser of a building who has taken subject to a lease of air conditioners impliedly assumed the

---

47.　See chapter 17.

48.　See § 17–6 supra.

49.　See § 17–13 supra.

50.　See § 17–14 supra.

51.　See § 17–13 supra.

52.　See § 17–13 supra and § 21–8 infra; Tony & Leo, Inc. v. United States Fidelity and Guaranty Co., 281 N.W.2d 862 (Minn. 1979).　The point is that the assumption of a duty, standing alone, does not give rise to a novation.　Mount Wheeler Power, Inc. v.

Gallagher, 98 Nev. 479, 653 P.2d 1212 (1982).

53.　See § 17–2 supra; 4 Corbin §§ 779D and 779E.

54.　Restatement, Second, Contracts § 318, Comment b; Restatement, Contracts § 160(2).

55.　233 N.Y. 490, 135 N.E. 861 (1922); cf. Kneberg v. H. L. Green Co., 89 F.2d 100 (7th Cir.1937) (no implied assumption where assignee sues for restitution).

obligation by refusing to allow the lessor of air conditioners to remove them.[56]

 WESTLAW REFERENCES

di(delegat! /s liab! /s contract)

95k280(2)

assum! /s duty /s novation

278k5

find 213 ne2d 884

§ 18–27. Problems of Interpretation

At times it is difficult to tell whether a party intends to assign his rights or delegate his duties or both.[57] The issue often becomes one of interpretation.

A common question of interpretation arises when a party to a bilateral contract uses general language such as, "I assign this contract to T." Although the question should be treated as a question of interpretation of the language in the light of the particular circumstances of the case,[58] it has frequently been treated as if it were governed by the mechanics of *stare decisis*. Some courts have adhered to the rule that such phraseology creates merely an assignment of rights.[59] A more modern view is that the probable intention is to create not only an assignment of rights but also a delegation and assumption of duties.[60] The sales article of the Commercial Code

56. Conditioner Leasing Corp. v. Sternmor Realty Corp., 17 N.Y.2d 1, 266 N.Y.S.2d 801, 213 N.E.2d 884 (1966), reargument denied 17 N.Y.2d 730, 269 N.Y.S. 2d 1025, 216 N.E.2d 844 (1966); cf. Fleming v. Wineberg, 253 Or. 472, 455 P.2d 600 (1969).

57. In a situation where there is both an assignment of a right and a delegation of a duty, a word on terminology is in order. For example, assume a situation where A promises to deliver goods to B in exchange for B's promise to pay $1000, and A assigns his rights and delegates his duties to C. When A assigns his rights, he is the assignor and C is the assignee. B is the obligor because he has the duty of paying $1000. As to A's duty to deliver the goods, A is the delegant, and C is the delegate. In this phase of the transaction, B is often referred to as the other party. See also § 18–31 infra.

58. This was admirably done in Chatham Pharmaceuticals, Inc. v. Angier Chemical Co., 347 Mass. 208, 196 N.E.2d 852 (1964).

59. Loegler v. C. V. Hill & Co., 238 Ala. 606, 193 So. 120 (1940); Pumphrey v. Kehoe, 261 Md. 496, 276 A.2d 194 (1971); Meyer v. Droegemueller, 165 Minn. 245,

206 N.W. 391 (1925); State ex rel. Hoyt v. Shain, 338 Mo. 1208, 93 S.W.2d 992 (1936); Langel v. Betz, 250 N.Y. 159, 164 N.E. 890 (1928). See generally Grismore, Is the Assignee of a Contract Liable for the Non-Performance of Delegated Duties? 18 Mich.L.Rev. 284 (1920); 4 Corbin § 906; 3 Williston § 418A; Selected Readings on the Law of Contracts 802.

60. Newton v. Merchants & Farmers Bank, 11 Ark.App. 167, 668 S.W.2d 51 (1984); Rose v. Vulcan Materials Co., 282 N.C. 643, 194 S.E.2d 521, 67 A.L.R.3d 1 (1973). See Art Metal Const. Co., for Use of McCloskey & Co. v. Lehigh Structural Steel Co., 116 F.2d 57 (3d Cir.1940) but compare the decision after trial, where it was found as a fact that no assumption was intended. 126 F.2d 134 (1942) cert. denied 316 U.S. 694, 62 S.Ct. 1296, 86 L.Ed. 1764 (1942); Restatement, Contracts § 164. The Restatement, Second, Contracts § 328, which is generally in accord, points out, however, that the overwhelming weight of authority in land contract cases is in accord with Langel v. Betz, 250 N.Y. 159, 164 N.E. 890 (1928), and therefore it takes no position with respect to land contracts. For a rationalization of an exception for

adopts the latter presumption.[61] The presumption can, of course, be overcome if the language or the circumstances indicate the contrary.[62] This would certainly be true in the case of a security assignment.[63]

WESTLAW REFERENCES

find 116 f2d 57

38k107

u.c.c. "uniform commercial code" /s 2–210

§ 18–28. Non-delegable Duties

Just as there are rights which are not assignable, there are duties which are not delegable. Here again the modern law has come a long way from the era when contractual relations were deemed strictly personal. *Delectus Personae* was the Law Latin catch-phrase to indicate that a party had a right to choose with whom he would deal. Today, however, the general proposition is that, subject to exceptions, duties are delegable. A duty is non-delegable where performance by the delegate would vary materially from performance by the obligor.[64] In other words the test is whether performance by the delegating party (delegant) or under his personal supervision has been bargained for.[65] The Uniform Commercial Code expresses the same thought in the following language: "A party may perform his duty through a delegate * * * unless the other party has a substantial interest in having his original promisor (delegant) perform or control the acts required by the contract."[66] The same formulation is found in the Restatement Second.[67]

The test is most imprecise. Equally imprecise is a phrase that is often used a "personal service contract."[68] The phrase implies that the "other party" to the contract relies on the personality of the delegant and that therefore any attempted delegation is improper. Personality comprises many ingredients including honesty, skill, reputation, character, ability, wisdom and taste.[69] Thus, if the contract is premised on the artistic skill or unique abilities of a party, the duties are not delegable. There is no objective standard by which the performance of the delegate can be determined to be the equivalent of the delegant if

land contracts see Restatement, Second, Contracts § 328, Comment c.

61. U.C.C. § 2–210(4). According to the Code and the Restatement, Second, the same rule applies in the case of an assignment of "all my rights under the contract." Since the word "rights" is used here, it is certainly arguable that the language refers only to an assignment of rights. Restatement, Second, Contracts § 328.

62. U.C.C. § 2–210(4).

63. U.C.C. § 2–210, Comment 5.

64. Overseas Development Disc Corp. v. Sangamo Const. Co., 686 F.2d 498 (7th Cir. 1982); Boswell v. Lyon, 401 N.E.2d 735 (Ind.App.1980); Devlin v. Mayor, 63 N.Y. 8 (1875); Restatement, Contracts § 160.

65. Devlin v. Mayor, 63 N.Y. 8 (1875).

66. U.C.C. § 2–210(1).

67. Restatement, Second, Contracts §§ 318(2) and 319(2).

68. Loftus v. American Realty Co., 334 N.W.2d 366 (Iowa App.1983).

69. 4 Corbin § 866.

the performance is to paint a portrait [70] or to produce an entertainment.[71] Also non-delegable are duties which involve a close personal relationship, such as the duties owed by an attorney to his client,[72] or a physician to his patient.[73] In addition it is often held that a party to a contract who has expressly or impliedly promised to act in "good faith" or to use his "best efforts" may not delegate that duty even though the duty might otherwise be delegable.[74]

It is generally held that duties under a construction contract are delegable because it is contemplated that the work will be performed by a person other than the obligor. This result has been placed on the well known custom of general contractors to delegate to subcontractors.[75] So, too, duties under other contracts calling for mechanical skills which can be tested by objective standards are generally delegable [76] at least where it is not contemplated that a given individual perform or supervise the work.[77] A seller's duty to deliver goods is also generally delegable.[78]

A duty to pay money is also generally delegable. It is immaterial if the delegate is less creditworthy than the delegant because as we have seen the delegant continues to remain liable.[79] If, however, one of the duties sought to be delegated is the execution of a promissory note or other instrument of credit, the delegation is ineffective [80] unless the delegate is willing and able to tender cash in place of the instrument of the delegant (delegating party).[81]

It has been intimated that the duty of a corporation is always delegable because a corporation necessarily performs by delegation of

70. See Taylor v. Palmer, 31 Cal. 240 (1866) ("[a]ll painters do not paint portraits like Sir Joshua Reynolds, nor landscapes like Claude Lorraine, nor do all writers write dramas like Shakespeare or fiction like Dickens. Rare genius and extraordinary skill are not transferable, and contracts for their employment are therefore personal, and cannot be assigned [correction, delegated]. But rare genius and extraordinary skill are not indispensable to the workmanlike digging down of a sand hill or the filling up of a depression to a given level, or the construction of brick sewers with manholes and covers, and contracts for such work are not personal, and may be assigned [delegated])."

71. Standard Chautauqua Sys. v. Gift, 120 Kan. 101, 242 P. 145 (1926). A song publisher's duties to publish and promote a song has, however, been held to be delegable. Nolan v. Williamson Music, Inc., 300 F.Supp. 1311 (S.D.N.Y.1969), judgment affirmed 499 F.2d 1394 (2d Cir.1974).

72. Corson v. Lewis, 77 Neb. 446, 109 N.W. 735 (1906).

73. Deaton v. Lawson, 40 Wash. 486, 82 P. 879 (1905).

74. Wetherell Bros. Co. v. United States Steel Co., 200 F.2d 761 (1st Cir.1952); Paper Prods. Mach. Co. v. Safepack Mills, 239 Mass. 114, 131 N.E. 288 (1921).

75. New England Iron Co. v. Gilbert Elec. R.R., 91 N.Y. 153 (1883); 4 Corbin § 865; Whether a general contractor could delegate to another is more doubtful.

76. Devlin v. Mayor, 63 N.Y. 8 (1875) (duty to clean streets); British Waggon Co. v. Lea & Co., 5 Q.B.D. 149 (1880) (duty to keep railway cars in repair).

77. Restatement, Second, Contracts § 318, Comment c and ill. 7; Swarts v. Narragansett Elec. Lighting Co., 26 R.I. 388, 59 A. 77 (1904), rehearing denied 26 R.I. 436, 59 A. 111 (1904); Johnson v. Vickers, 139 Wis. 145, 120 N.W. 837 (1909).

78. U.C.C. § 2–210(1).

79. See § 18–25 supra.

80. E. M. Loews, Inc. v. Deutschmann, 344 Mass. 765, 184 N.E.2d 55 (1962).

81. Cochran v. Taylor, 273 N.Y. 172, 7 N.E.2d 89 (1937); see discussion on option contracts in § 18–32 infra.

duties to individuals.[82] This is perhaps too broad a statement. It is possible to conceive of a contract under which the basis of the bargain is the personal performance of particular individuals within the corporate structure and delegation to another corporation or person would be ineffective.[83]

If the delegant has a right or a duty to control or supervise the performance of the delegate, this may in a close case lead to a decision in favor of delegability.[84] Conversely, if the delegant dissolves his business, this will ordinarily lead to the conclusion that the duty is nondelegable.[85] In such a case it is clear that the delegant is no longer in a position to supervise. In addition this may lead to a situation where the delegant, who is still liable despite the delegation, is no longer in a position to fulfill that obligation.[86]

A delegation of particular duties may be prohibited by statute or by a rule of public policy.[87] In addition the contract itself may contain a provision against delegation. In contrast with rules favoring free alienation of rights which limit the validity of clauses purporting to prohibit assignments,[88] there seems to be no restriction on the parties' ability to provide in their contract that duties are non-delegable.[89] Once more it should be recalled that it is common for contract draftsmen to utilize the word "assignment" where "delegation" is meant. Taking notice of this proclivity, the Commercial Code provides: "Unless the circumstances indicate the contrary, a prohibition of assignment of 'the contract' is to be construed as barring only the delegation to the assignee of the assignor's performance." [90]

---

82. New England Iron Co. v. Gilbert Elec. R.R., 91 N.Y. 153, 167 (1883).

83. For example, a corporation producing motion pictures for a distribution company could not delegate its duties to another corporation producing motion pictures if the effect of the delegation is to deprive the other party to the contract of the contemplated performance of famous "stars", directors, or key figures within the delegating corporation's structure. cf. Emerald Christmas Tree Co. v. Bedortha, 66 Or.App. 425, 674 P.2d 76 (1984). But see New York Bank Note Co. v. Hamilton Bank Note Engraving & Printing Co., 180 N.Y. 280, 73 N.E. 48 (1905); Note, 74 Harv.L.Rev. 393 (1960).

84. Arnold Productions Inc. v. Favorite Films Corp., 298 F.2d 540 (2d Cir.1962).

85. New England Cabinet Works v. Morris, 226 Mass. 246, 115 N.E. 315 (1917).

86. Wetherell Bros. Co. v. United States Steel Co., 200 F.2d 761 (1st Cir.1952); New York Bank Note Co. v. Hamilton Bank Note Engraving & Printing Co., 180 N.Y. 280, 293, 73 N.E. 48, 52 (1905). Both cases involve the liquidation of a corporation. This situation is quite similar to the cases

discussed in § 18–30 infra, where the delegating party repudiates. However this rule may not apply to a transaction that amounts to a consolidation or a merger or where the purchasing corporation is merely a continuation of the selling corporation. Fisher v. Berg, 158 Wash. 176, 290 P. 984 (1930).

87. Restatement, Second, Contracts §§ 318(1) and 319(1); Restatement, Contracts § 160(3)(b).

88. See § 18–16 supra.

89. U.C.C. § 2–210(1); Restatement, Second, Contracts §§ 318(1), 319(1); Restatement, Contracts § 160(3)(c). They may also provide by agreement that the duties are delegable. Baum v. Rock, 106 Colo. 567, 108 P.2d 230 (1940). However, a routine provision to the effect that a party's successor is bound by the contract does not make a duty delegable. Standard Chautauqua Sys. v. Gift, 120 Kan. 101, 242 P. 145 (1926). There is a similar rule with respect to assignments of rights. See § 18–16 supra.

90. U.C.C. § 2–210(3); accord, Restatement, Second, Contracts § 322(a).

WESTLAW REFERENCES

di(non-delega! /6 duty /s contract)

u.c.c. "uniform commercial code" /s (2–210 +s (1)) 2–210(1)

"personal service contract" /s non-delegable delega!

95k280(2)

taylor +3 palmer

38k19 /p personal

corson +3 lewis

deaton +3 lawson

di(contractor /s delega! /s sub-contractor)

find 674 p2d 76

38k18 /p contract /s personal

§ 18–29. Effect of Attempted Delegation of a Non-delegable Duty

It is clear that if the delegant delegates a delegable duty to a delegate and the delegate performs, the duty of the delegant will be discharged. This also implies that the other party must accept the performance of the delegate and that if he refuses to do so he is guilty of a repudiation.[91]

If the duty is non-delegable the other party may refuse to proceed. This does not mean that the attempted delegation of a non-delegable duty amounts to a repudiation. An attempted delegation of a non-delegable duty in reality amounts to nothing more than an offer to waive non-delegability.[92] This offer will be accepted if the other party assents, as for example, by dealing with the delegate. If the other party refuses to accept the offer and the delegant indicates that he refuses to honor the contract unless the other party assents to the delegation, the delegant is guilty of a repudiation.[93]

WESTLAW REFERENCES

devlin +3 mayor

§ 18–30. Effect of Repudiation by Delegating Party

In the preceding section we saw that an attempted delegation of a non-delegable duty does not amount to an offer of novation.[94] Here the question is whether a repudiation by the delegating party may amount to an offer of novation.

As we have seen, when the delegating party delegates his duty his liability continues unless he is discharged by the other party in consid-

---

91. Devlin v. Mayor, 63 N.Y. 8 (1875).

92. 4 Corbin, § 867. This does not amount to an implied offer of novation. Clark v. General Cleaning Co., 345 Mass. 62, 185 N.E.2d 749 (1962).

93. American Colortype Co. v. Continental Colortype Co., 188 U.S. 104, 23 S.Ct.

265, 47 L.Ed. 404 (1903); Restatement, Second, Contracts § 329(2).

94. Crane Ice Cream Co. v. Terminal Freezing & Heating Co., 147 Md. 588, 128 A. 280, 39 A.L.R. 1184 (1925).

eration of the delegate's assumption of the delegant's duty.[95] But what if the delegating party delegates his duty and asserts that he refuses to remain liable? For example, A and B enter into a bilateral contract. B delegates his duty to C who agrees to assume B's duty. As part and parcel of the same transaction, B tells A that he regards his liability at an end. B's statement is regarded as an offer of novation—an offer to A to substitute the liability of C for that of B.[96] A need not accept the offer. If he does not accept and B insists on his position, B becomes guilty of a repudiation.[97]

But what if A deals with C with knowledge of the delegation and opportunity to reject performance? There is substantial authority to the effect that B's offer of novation has been accepted when A deals with C.[98] Even if this is considered to be a logical approach, it seems unfair that B should be released by his repudiation when there is no actual agreement to release him.

The Restatements has softened the rigor of this rule by indicating that A may defeat the occurrence of a novation by notifying either B or C that he intends to retain unimpaired his contract rights.[99]

 WESTLAW REFERENCES
u.c.c. "uniform commercial code" /s 2–609

§ 18–31. Some Additional Animadversions on What Rights Are Assignable and What Duties Are Delegable

As this text is structured we first discussed what rights are assignable and later covered what duties are delegable. In many cases, however, a party will do both. That is to say he will simultaneously assign his rights and delegate his duties. This section is designed to show how such a problem should be approached. This will be done by analyzing a number of concrete cases. In addition some questions not previously mentioned will be introduced into the discussion. In this discussion the terminology used is based on Section 18–1 supra.

In a well known case,[1] defendant (Pizza) entered into an arrangement with Virginia under which Virginia was to supply cold drink vending machines to defendant's pizza parlors. Virginia also agreed to keep machines in good repairs and stocked with merchandise and to pay a percentage of income to Pizza. During the term of the contract Virginia assigned its rights and delegated its duties to the plaintiff,

---

95. See § 18–26.

96. See § 18–26 supra.

97. 4 Corbin § 870; 3 Williston § 420.

98. Western Oil Sales Corp. v. Bliss & Wetherbee, 299 S.W. 637 (Tex.App.1927). A similar problem arises when the delegating party is a corporation and is dissolved. See § 18–28, note 86 supra; 4 Corbin § 865. As to the effect of the insolvency of

the assignor, see U.C.C. § 2–609; 3 Williston § 420; 6 Williston § 880.

99. Restatement, Second, Contracts § 329(2) (particularly Comment c which states that A must affirmatively reserve his rights); Restatement, Contracts § 165.

1. Macke Co. v. Pizza of Gaithersburg, Inc., 259 Md. 479, 270 A.2d 645 (1970).

Macke. When this occurred defendant terminated the contract. It argued that the duty was non-delegable.

The first step to take in such a case is to analyze what the rights and duties of Virginia are.[2] Here Virginia's right was to get money and this right as we have seen, is assignable.[3] Virginia's duty was to install and leave the machines, stock them with merchandise, make repairs and pay a percentage of the gross to Pizza. As indicated the issue is whether the duty is delegable.

The court analyzed the case in terms of whether this was "a personal service contract"[4] and concluded that it was not since the duties of Virginia were mechanical in nature and performance by Macke was not significantly different than performance by Pizza.[5] This conclusion was not changed by the fact that Pizza had dealt with Macke before and had chosen Virginia because they liked the way in which Virginia did business.[6] The plaintiff prevailed because of the repudiation of the defendant.[7]

The court also mentions U.C.C. § 2–210(5) which has not previously been discussed.[8] This section provides that the "other party may treat any assignment which delegates performance as creating reasonable grounds for insecurity and may without prejudice to his rights against the assignor[9] demand assurances against the assignee."[10]

On the facts of the case under discussion Virginia was an assignor-delegant referred to in the statute as the assignor. Macke was the assignee-delegate referred to in the statute as the assignee. Pizza is "the other party". The point is that Pizza could have demanded assurances against Macke even if the duty was delegable. But no such demand was made in this case.

2. Naturally, we are not concerned with whether the rights of Pizza are assignable or its duties delegable because there was no transfer of rights and duties by Pizza. If Pizza had assigned rights and duties, the situation would be reversed and the discussion would relate to whether Pizza's rights were assignable and its duties delegable.

3. See § 18–11 supra.

4. See § 18–28 supra.

5. See § 18–28 supra.

6. This seems to be the generally accepted view. C.H. Little Co. v. Caldwell Transit Co., 197 Mich. 481, 163 N.W. 952 (1917). An opposite view has been reached by the much criticized case of Boston Ice Co. v. Potter, 123 Mass. 28 (1877). In determining the issue of delegability, it is clear that the nature of the duty is important. However, in some cases it has been held that the "personality" of the delegant is also important. See § 18–28 supra.

7. It should be recalled that an attempt to delegate a non-delegable duty amounts only to an offer to waive the non-delegability. However, if the delegant persists in the delegation after the other party refuses, there is a repudiation. See § 18–29 supra.

8. We, however, previously discussed U.C.C. § 2–609 (demanding assurances) as it relates to the question of assignments. See § 18–14 supra.

9. Presumably "the other party" would have rights against the assignee under U.C.C. § 2–609 which is the basic section in the Code relating to a demand for assurances. See § 12–2 supra.

10. There is no requirement in the statute that "the other party" must proceed by way of demanding assurances.

In another case [11] plaintiff entered into a contract with the defendant, Bates Studio, for dance lessons. Bates, in time assigned its rights and delegated its duties to the Dale Studio. Again we must differentiate the rights from the duties. Bates' right was to receive money and this right is normally assignable. The duty was to give dance lessons. Again the question is whether this duty was delegable. This court again inquires whether this was a "personal service contract" and concludes that it was. Therefore, the plaintiff was not required to take lessons from Dale and Bates would have been guilty of a repudiation if it continued to insist on the delegation of this non-delegable duty.[12]

However, on the facts, after the delegation the plaintiff took lessons for a period of time at the Dale Studios. According to the court this amounted to a waiver of non-delegability and thus plaintiff was bound to continue to take lessons from Dale.[13] However, there was no novation and Bates continued to remain liable.[14]

A case that shows the importance of clearly distinguishing between the rights and duties is the case of Paige v. Faure.[15] The defendant gave Paige and Linder an exclusive agency in return for their best efforts to promote the defendant's product. Subsequently Linder assigned his rights and delegated his duties under the contract to Paige. The court held the assignment ineffective stating broadly: "Rights arising out of a contract cannot be transferred if they are coupled with liabilities." [16] The courts reasoning was defective because, as we have seen in the cases above, the assignment of an assignable right is not rendered ineffective even if it is coupled with the delegation of a duty if the duty is delegable. Here the court actually held that the duty was non-delegable at least in part because of the duty to use "reasonable efforts." [17]

The cases discussed thus far have related primarily to issues of delegation of duties. Let us discuss one case [18] that can be discussed in terms of assigning rights. In this case the defendant Sisco entered into a contract of employment with Gas & Chemicals (Employer). The

11. Seale v. Bates, 145 Colo. 430, 359 P.2d 356 (1961).

12. If, as here, the right is assignable and the duty non-delegable and the plaintiff objected and Bates acquiesced, it would seem clear, that, in the absence of contrary indications, not only would there be no delegation of duty but also that the assignment would fail because it would be linked to the delegation in a package deal.

13. See § 18–30 supra.

14. See § 18–30 supra.

15. 229 N.Y. 114, 127 N.E. 898 (1920).

16. 229 N.Y. at 118, 127 N.E. at 899 (1920).

17. See § 18–28 supra wherein it is stated that if there is a duty to act in "good faith" or to use "reasonable efforts," a court will very often hold the duty to be non-delegable. This approach should be compared with U.C.C. § 2–306, Comment 4. This comment relates in part to an output contract. It says that if an output contract continues after the sale of the plant, the output is "to be measured by the actual good faith output * * * under the normal operation of the enterprise prior to sale." Does this mean that it is the delegate who is to exercise his good faith after sale? If so, the section seems to take an approach that is different from the normal approach.

18. Sisco v. Empiregas, Inc., 286 Ala. 72, 237 So.2d 463 (1970).

employment contract contained a provision that the employee would not compete with the employer for 5 years after the termination of the contract within a 50 mile radius. There was also a provision that permitted the employer to terminate the contract by giving 30 days notice. At some point Gas & Chemicals assigned its rights and delegated its duties to Empire Gas, the plaintiff. The plaintiff seeks to enjoin Sisco from working for his new employer relying upon the non-competition clause.

According to the court the first issue in the case is whether Gas & Chemicals could effectively assign its rights to Sisco's services to Empire.[19] The court held that the contract was a personal service contract. However, it did not say that a right to an employee's services is never assignable. It reached the conclusion that this was a personal service contract based upon the facts of the case. It pointed to the non-competition clause coupled with the notice provision.[20]

As suggested above there are cases where it has been held that the right to an employee's services may be assigned even if there is a non-competition clause.[21] The factual setting of each case is all important including whether the assignee is in a loose sense an *alter ego* of the assignor, as for example as a result of a consolidation or a merger.[22]

The previous discussion of the Sisco case would indicate that the employee would prevail. However, there were additional facts showing that Sisco worked for Empire for a period of time after the improper assignment. The court said that this evidence gave rise to the possibility that Sisco consented to and adopted the assignment or that as a result of his continued work Empire entered into a contract that contained all of the terms of the contract between Sisco and the original employer.[23]

One of the reasons for this section is to lead the reader to conclude that there is no simple answer to the question of what rights are assignable and what duties are delegable.

 WESTLAW REFERENCES
find 270 a2d 645

19. Some cases would have looked at the problem by asking whether Gas & Chemicals could delegate its duty of supervision. There is no question that the duty to pay wages could be delegated.

20. The court argued that no employee would sign such an agreement unless he placed great trust and confidence in the employer. In addition Sisco had worked for this employer for a period of time before signing this contract.

21. Torrington Creamery, Inc. v. Davenport, 126 Conn. 515, 12 A.2d 780 (1940); Sickles v. Lauman, 185 Iowa 37, 169 N.W. 670 (1918).

22. E. Farnsworth, Contracts § 11.4 at 763. But see Evening News Ass'n v. Peterson, 477 F.Supp. 77 (D.C.Cir.1979) where it was held that the services of a newscaster-anchorman were assignable even though the new owner was not an alter ego of the delegant. See also Munchak Corp. v. Cunningham, 457 F.2d 721 (4th Cir.1972) 4 Corbin § 865. Notice that there is a similar rule with respect to delegation. See § 18–28 supra.

23. The same thought could possibly be expressed by saying that there was a waiver of the fact that the right was non-assignable. The same type of problem arose in Seale v. Bates (the dance studio case) except in that case the issue was delegation rather than assignment.

38k18

u.c.c. "uniform commercial code" /s 2–609

38k19

38k98

paige +3 faure

§ 18–32.   Option Contracts

In the previous edition of this text this section was entitled, "The Assignability of Option Contracts" and was included in the portion of the book relating to assignments. However, since the issue of delegation arises in the discussion of this topic, it was concluded that it would be better to cover this topic after the material on delegation.

The rule of law that an offer may be accepted only by the person or persons for whom it is intended has previously been discussed.[24] It follows that an offer is not assignable. The prohibition is based, at least in part, on the notion that everyone has the privilege of choosing with whom he wishes to contract.[25] This is true whether the offer looks to a bilateral or a unilateral contract, and even though the offeree is only to pay money. Thus, if A offers to sell his car to B for $100, the offer cannot be accepted by C. But once an offer has ripened into a contract, the rights created are usually assignable.[26] This seeming anomaly is at least partially explainable. An assignor by his assignment divests himself of rights; but he cannot divest himself of his duties. While he may sometimes delegate his duties he remains liable for their due performance.[27] The other contracting party is thus not frustrated from having the right to enforce his contract against the person on whose credit and reputation he relied in entering into the contract.[28]

In discussing the assignability of an option contract it must be recalled that an option contract gives the optionee the option of accepting or rejecting the terms of the underlying contract.[29] Whether the optionee may assign his rights in the underlying contract to a third party depends upon a number of factors including whether the underlying contract is unilateral or bilateral in nature.[30] Suppose, for example, A offers to sell property to B in exchange for B's promise to pay $10,000 (underlying contract). A asks B for $100 to keep the offer open for 10 days, which B pays creating an option contract. The offer in the underlying contract is an offer looking to a bilateral contract and can be accepted only by B's promise. If B does not make the promise there is no possibility of the underlying contract being effectively assigned

---

24.   See § 2–14 supra.

25.   This privilege is not absolute. In some cases, antitrust and civil rights legislation, forbid discriminatory refusals to deal.

26.   See § 18–10 supra.

27.   See § 18–25 supra.

28.   This rule also explains the liability of an agent who does not disclose his principal. See Seavey, Agency § 123 (1964). However, it does not explain why an offer is not assignable if all that is required of the offeree is payment in cash.

29.   See § 2–25 supra.

30.   1 Corbin § 57.

because A is entitled to B's promise because he relied on B's credit.[31]   If B makes that promise, then, whether the underlying contract may be assigned and/or delegated depends upon the rules already discussed. In this situation, under these rules the right to receive a deed would be assignable and the duty to pay money would be delegable.[32]

The situation is obviously different if the underlying contract is unilateral.   Here B need not make a promise in order to make any attempted assignment effective.   The only issue is whether the right is assignable and/or whether the act is delegable.   Thus, in the illustration above, let us assume that A promised to convey on receipt of $10,000 within 10 days and, as before, $100 was paid to keep the offer open and B assigned his rights and delegated his duties to C.   B's right is still assignable.   Technically, B has no duty because he has the option of buying or not buying.   The question, then, is not whether the *duty* is delegable but rather whether the *act* called for is delegable. The rules as to delegability are the same in this situation as when there is duty.[33]   On the other hand if B was to pay by rendering personal services, the act would be non-delegable although the right would be assignable.[34]   In other words, A is not required to accept C's services in substitution because they are personal.[35]   C may, however, enforce the underlying contract if B performs the services.[36]

WESTLAW REFERENCES
find 7 ne2d 89
95k19 /p option (offer** /3 open)

---

31. 1 Corbin § 57; see also Restatement, Second, Contracts § 152 and Comment a; Restatement, Contracts § 155.

32. Another issue to be confronted is whether the parties intended the option to be limited to the optionee. Masterson v. Sine, 68 Cal.2d 222, 65 Cal.Rptr. 545, 436 P.2d 561 (1968); Campbell v. Campbell, 313 Ky. 249, 230 S.W.2d 918 (1950).

33. See § 18–28.

34. Restatement, Second, Contracts § 319.

35. Franklin v. Jordan, 224 Ga. 727, 164 S.E.2d 718 (1968); Lojo Realty Co. v. Estate of Johnson, 253 N.Y. 579, 171 N.E. 791 (1930).

36. Cochran v. Taylor, 273 N.Y. 172, 183, 7 N.E.2d 89, 92–93 (1937); 1 Corbin § 57; 4 Corbin § 883.

Chapter 19

STATUTE OF FRAUDS

Table of Sections

I. WHEN A WRITING IS NECESSARY

I. WHEN A WRITING IS NECESSARY

§ 19–1. Introduction

At early common law, oral promises were generally not enforced by the King's courts, but this changed with the advent and gradual expansion of the writ of assumpsit.[1] When oral promises became enforceable, perjury and subornation of perjury appear to have become commonplace.[2] In 1677 Parliament enacted an Act for the Prevention of Fraud and Perjuries.[3] This Statute contained twenty-five sections

---

1. See 2 Corbin § 275; Teeven, Seventeenth Century Evidentiary Concerns and the Statute of Frauds, 9 Adelaide L.Rev. 252 (1983–85).

2. See 6 Holdsworth, A History of English Law 379–97 (1927).

3. 29 Car. II, c. 3, 8 Stat. at Large 405.

which dealt with conveyances, wills, trusts, judgment and execution in addition to contracts.[4] Only two sections, the fourth and the seventeenth are important for contract purposes. These sections read as follows:

> "Sec. 4.   And be it further enacted by the authority aforesaid, That from and after the said four and twentieth day of June no action shall be brought [(1)] whereby to charge any executor or administrator upon any special promise, to answer damages out of his own estate; (2) or whereby to charge the defendant upon any special promise to answer for the debt, default, or miscarriage of another person; (3) or to charge any person upon any agreement made upon consideration of marriage; (4) or upon any contract [f]or sale of lands, tenements or hereditaments, or any interest in or concerning them; (5) or upon any agreement that is not to be performed within the space of one year from the making thereof; (6) unless the agreement upon which such action shall be brought, or some memorandum or note thereof, shall be in writing, and signed by the party to be charged therewith, or some other person thereunto by him lawfully authorized.

> "Sec. 17.   And be it further enacted by the authority aforesaid, That from and after the said four and twentieth day of June no contract for the sale of any goods, wares and merchandizes, for the price of ten pounds sterling or upwards, shall be allowed to be good, except the buyer shall accept part of the goods so sold, and actually receive the same, or give something in earnest to bind the bargain, or in part of payment, or that some note or memorandum in writing of the said bargain be made and signed by the parties to be charged by such contract, or their agents thereunto lawfully authorized."

While the writing requirement is imposed in large part to obviate perjury, it is clear that other policy bases for the requirement exist. An agreement reduced to writing promotes certainty; false testimony stems from faulty recollection as well as from faulty morals. In addition, the required formality of a writing "promotes deliberation, seriousness, . . . and shows that the act was a genuine act of volition." [5] While all will agree that to a lesser or greater extent these are desirable goals, it is obvious that the carrying out of these goals may well frustrate honesty and fair dealing. As with the case of a strict application of the parol evidence rule, the quest for certainty and deliberation involves the exclusion of evidence of what the parties may have actually agreed upon. Oral agreements are made and are performed. If the oral agreement is within the Statute of Frauds and the Statute is enforced with vigor, the expectations of the person who had performed would be frustrated and the person who had breached the

4. See Hamburger, The Conveyancing Purposes of the Statute of Frauds, 27 Am. J.Legal Hist. 354 (1983).

5. Rabel, The Statute of Frauds and Comparative Legal History, 63 L.Q.Rev. 174, 178 (1947).

oral agreement would be unjustly enriched. If such were the result, the Statute would encourage fraud and sanction unethical conduct.

The ability of the Statute to cause injustice has had a strong impact on judicial decisions. Often the courts have viewed the Statute with disfavor and have tended to give it a narrow construction as to the kinds of contracts covered. In addition, they have developed devices for "taking the contract outside" the Statute. Finally, a variety of legal and equitable remedies have been forged to grant relief to a party who has performed an oral agreement within the statutory terms. Other courts have tended to view the basic policy of the Statute as sound and have given it a broad construction. It is not surprising that the decisions rendered throughout its 300 year history are not entirely harmonious. In 1954 the British Parliament repealed all but the provisions with respect to real property and suretyship.[6] Similar repeal in the United States is, however, not considered likely within the foreseeable future. Indeed, in the United States the policy of requiring a writing has been extended by legislation to other areas. For example, the policy of the statute has been extended in some jurisdictions to contracts to leave property by will, contracts to pay a broker a commission, and a promise to pay a debt contracted during infancy.[7]

Writing requirements serve numerous important functions.[8] Many observers have suggested, however, that the tri-centenarian Statute of Frauds in its present form has outlived its usefulness.[9] The kinds of transaction selected to be put in writing do not seem to constitute a rational catalog of transactions which ought to be singled out for formalization. The consequences of non-compliance appear too drastic. Most importantly, the volume of litigation involving questions of whether the transaction is within the Statute and if it is, whether it fits within one of the judge-made exceptions is enormous. Also, in many cases, there is written evidence of the contract and the litigation focuses on the sufficiency of the writing rather than on the crux of the dispute between the parties.[10] Reform is needed. Recently, the Uniform Commercial Code adopted a modernized version of the Statute of Frauds for sales and certain other transactions.[11] The Code eliminates many of the dysfunctional aspects of the original statute and could provide a guide for modernization of the Statute as a whole.[12]

---

6. 2 & 3 Eliz. II, c. 34.

7. See Restatement, Second, Contracts, Statutory Note to Ch. 5; Note, The Statute of Frauds' Lifetime and Testamentary Provisions: Safeguarding Decedents' Estates, 50 Fordham L.Rev. 239 (1981). In addition, many statutes and regulations requiring government contracts to be in writing are deemed to be in the Statute of Frauds tradition. See United States v. American Renaissance Lines, Inc., 494 F.2d 1059 (D.C.Cir.1974), cert. denied 419 U.S. 1020, 95 S.Ct. 495, 42 L.Ed.2d 294 (1974).

8. See Fridman, The Necessity for Writing in Contracts Within the Statute of Frauds, 35 U. Toronto L.Rev. 43 (1985); Perillo, The Statute of Frauds in the Light of the Functions and Dysfunctions of Form, 43 Fordham L.Rev. 39, 43–68 (1974).

9. Id. at n. 232.

10. See §§ 19–26 to 19–39 infra.

11. See § 19–34 infra.

12. But see Cunningham, A Proposal to Repeal Section 2–201: The Statute of

WESTLAW REFERENCES
"act for the prevention of frauds and perjuries"

A. SURETYSHIP AGREEMENTS

§ 19–2. Promise by Executor or Administrator

A promise by an administrator or executor "to answer damages out of his own estate" is "within" the Statute of Frauds. The term "within the Statute of Frauds" means that the Statute requires a writing for this kind of transaction. The clause is somewhat unclear because it does not state what or whose damages the executor or administrator is promising to pay. The cases have made it clear, however, that the Statute applies only where the executor or administrator promises to pay out of his own property a debt of the deceased.[13] It does not apply to promises to pay debts of the deceased out of the assets of the estate.[14]

Since this is the accepted view of the meaning of this section, this provision is merely a particular application of the second subdivision relating to promises to answer for the debt, default or miscarriage of another and that what is said with reference to that subdivision is applicable here.[15]

WESTLAW REFERENCES
mackin +3 dwyer

§ 19–3. Special Promises to Answer for the Debt, Default or Miscarriage of Another [16]

The task here is to determine which oral promises [17] contravene this section of the Statute and which promises are not condemned by the Statute even though they are oral. When a promise contravenes this section because it is not in writing, it is said to be collateral; when it does not, it is called original. These words are generally used to

---

Frauds Section of Article 2, 85 Com.L.J. 361 (1980).

13. Mackin v. Dwyer, 205 Mass. 472, 91 N.E. 893 (1910); Bellows v. Sowles, 57 Vt. 164 (1884).

14. Piper v. Goodwin, 23 Me. (10 Shop) 251 (1843); Norton v. Edwards, 66 N.C. 367 (1872).

15. Bellows v. Sowles, 57 Vt. 164 (1884); 2 Corbin § 346; Restatement, Second, Contracts § 111 and Comment a.

16. Much of this discussion is based upon Calamari, The Suretyship Statute of Frauds, 27 Fordham L.Rev. 332 (1958). Although the word "special" may have had a particular meaning when the statute was originally passed, see Hening, A New and

Old Reading on the Fourth Section of the Statute of Frauds, 57 U.Pa.L.Rev. 611 (1909), today it is used "to restrict the statutory provision to promises in fact made." 2 Corbin § 347.

17. A number of states have extended the Statute of Frauds by providing that there shall be no liability for a misrepresentation as to the credit of a third person unless the representation is in a signed writing. See Tenna Mfg. Co. v. Columbia Union Nat. Bank & Trust Co., 484 F.Supp. 1214 (W.D.Mo.1980); Taylor, The Statute of Frauds and Misrepresentations as to the Credit of Third Persons: Should California Repeal its Lord Tenterden's Act? 16 U.C. L.A. L.Rev. 603 (1969).

express a result and do not help in ascertaining which promises are enforceable.[18]

It is apparent from the wording of the section that almost all of the factual situations governed by it will be tripartite. One party has made the promise and now pleads the Statute as a defense. We will refer to him as the promisor, and since he is invariably the defendant in these cases, by the letter D. The person to whom the promise is made we will refer to as the creditor (C). Invariably he will be the plaintiff in the action. The person for whom the promisor promises we shall refer to as the third party (TP). This terminology is used rather than P (principal) and S (surety) to minimize the possibility of begging the question by assuming that one of the parties is the principal and another the surety.[19]

At the outset a distinction must be drawn between cases where there is no prior obligation owed by the third party (TP) to the creditor (C) to which D's promise relates, and cases where there is such a prior obligation.[20] This distinction is of extreme importance, since, as we shall see, there are different rules governing the two situations. We shall discuss first the cases where there is no prior obligation. The word "obligation" is used to include all duties recognized by law, whether contractual or not.

WESTLAW REFERENCES
find 484 f.supp 1214
185k17

§ 19–4. Cases Where There Is No Prior Obligation Owing From TP to C to Which D's Promise Relates

An illustration will serve to bring this category of cases into focus. D says to C, "Deliver these goods to TP and I will see that you are paid." C delivers the goods. Is D's promise enforceable? This depends upon the answers to a number of questions, some of contract, some of suretyship. In a case where there is no prior obligation owing from TP to C, for the promise to be collateral TP must come under at least a voidable obligation to C; there must be a principal-surety relationship between TP and D; and C must know or have reason to know of the principal-surety relationship.[21] In addition some courts hold that the promise must not be joint.[22] Moreover the main purpose rule must not apply. Each of these facets of the problem will now be explored.

---

18. 3 Williston § 463; 2 Corbin § 348. See Kutilek v. Union Nat'l Bank of Wichita, 213 Kan. 407, 516 P.2d 979 (1973).

19. See note 33 infra.

20. 2 Corbin § 350; 3 Williston § 462.

21. Restatement, Second, Contracts § 112.

22. Id. § 113(b) and Comment b.

(a) TP Must Come Under at Least a Voidable Obligation to C

D's promise can be collateral only where TP eventually [23] comes under an obligation to C. If TP does not come under an obligation to C, it is reasoned that the promise must be original because D is not promising to pay the debt of another, there being no other debt. It would appear, then, that the first inquiry which must be made is whether TP eventually came under at least a voidable obligation to C. For the purposes of this rule a voidable obligation is an obligation, but a void obligation is not.[24]

In the illustration given, did TP come under any such obligation to C? The first requisite for any contract is that the offeror manifest a contractual state of mind,[25] and this is true in determining whether TP came under obligation to C. This explains why the courts place so much emphasis on the question of whether C extended credit to TP,[26] for this is merely another way of inquiring whether C manifested an intention to contract with TP. In other words if credit is extended only to D, his promise is original.[27] Charging TP as a debtor upon C's book is strong evidence that credit was extended to TP [28] but is not conclusive.[29] The question is ordinarily one of fact.[30] The fact that C did not charge TP is some evidence that credit was not extended to TP, but is not considered strong evidence.

If C has extended credit to TP, obviously the only remaining question to determine whether TP came under an obligation to C is to ascertain whether TP accepted C's offer. In many of the reported cases [31] there is no discussion of what transpired after D made his promise to C. In such a case, however, whether TP accepted C's offer must be determined under the already discussed rules relating to acceptance by silence or exercise of dominion, as well as other forms of manifestation of assent by conduct.[32]

An instructive case on the question of who is TP is Mease v. Wagner.[33] The defendant (D), a friend of the deceased, Mrs. Bradley, told the plaintiff (C), an undertaker, to bury Mrs. Bradley in a certain

---

23. Of course it is arguable that D's promise has to be original since at the time he makes his promise there is no obligation owing from TP to C. This contention was rejected in the early case of Jones v. Cooper, 98 Eng.Rep. 1058 (K.B.1774). See 2 Corbin § 350; 3 Williston § 461.

24. 2 Corbin § 356; Simpson, Suretyship 126–27 (1950); 3 Williston § 454.

25. 1 Williston §§ 22–27.

26. See General Elec. Co. v. Hans, 242 Miss. 119, 133 So.2d 275 (1961).

27. See J. J. Brooksbank Co. v. American Motors Corp., 289 Minn. 404, 184 N.W.2d 796 (1971), noted in 56 Minn.L.Rev. 281 (1971).

28. Lusk v. Throop, 189 Ill. 127, 59 N.E. 529 (1901); Wood v. Dodge, 23 S.D. 95, 120 N.W. 774 (1909); Simpson, Suretyship 124 (1950).

29. Hammond Coal Co. v. Lewis, 248 Mass. 499, 143 N.E. 309 (1924); Annot., 99 A.L.R. 79, 83 (1935).

30. Lawrence v. Anderson, 108 Vt. 176, 184 A. 689 (1936); 2 Corbin § 352; Burdick, Suretyship and the Statute of Frauds, 20 Colum.L.Rev. 153, 155 (1920).

31. For example, this is true of all of the cases in Simpson, Cases on Suretyship 1–10 (1942) which deal with this problem.

32. See Restatement, Contracts §§ 72–73 (1932). See §§ 2–18, 2–19 supra.

33. 5 S.C.L. (1 McCord) 395 (1821).

manner and to charge the estate of Dr. Bradley (TP) (the husband of Mrs. Bradley who had predeceased her) or a certain nephew (also TP) of Mrs. Bradley and "if they don't pay I will." It may be assumed that the plaintiff extended credit to the estate of Dr. Bradley and to the nephew. However the estate of Dr. Bradley never became liable because it did nothing to manifest an acceptance and would not otherwise be liable. The estate of a deceased husband is not ordinarily liable even for the necessaries of a wife. His death, generally speaking, terminates his duty to support.[34] Although the nephew promised to pay after the services were rendered, he never became liable because of the familiar doctrine that past consideration is not consideration.[35] However, under long established principles of quasi contract the estate of a decedent is liable for burial expenses.

The court concluded that since neither the estate of Dr. Bradley nor the nephew came under an obligation to the plaintiff, the promise of the defendant had to be original and therefore was enforceable notwithstanding the absence of a writing. The court did not consider whether the estate of Mrs. Bradley became liable.[36] The theory was that it is "settled doctrine that when no action will lie against the party undertaken for, it is an orignal [sic] promise."[37] Here the third parties were the estate of Dr. Bradley and the nephew. Since they did not come under an obligation the promise is original,[38] irrespective of whether the estate of Mrs. Bradley became liable. In a word, for the purpose of the Statute of Frauds,[39] TP is the person for whom the defendant undertakes.

To summarize: In the category of cases under discussion, the courts reason that if TP does not come under an obligation (at least voidable) to C, the promise is original. If TP does come under obligation, *so far as we know now,* the promise is collateral.[40] The emphasized words are meant to indicate that although TP comes under an obligation to C, the promise, due to factors discussed below, may still be original.

There is another contract question which must be considered. It can perhaps best be introduced by a simple illustration. D says to C, "Deliver these goods to TP and, provided you extend credit to TP, I will

---

34. Wilson v. Hinman, 182 N.Y. 408, 75 N.E. 236 (1905).

35. See 1 Williston § 142.

36. Cape Girardeau Bell Tel. Co. v. Hamil, 160 Mo.App. 521, 140 S.W. 951 (1911); Annots., 35 A.L.R.2d 1399 (1954); 82 A.L.R.2d 873 (1962). This liability would exist even if the undertaker did not specifically intend to charge her estate but only whomever proved ultimately responsible. Restatement, Restitution § 113, Comment e.

37. Mease v. Wagner, 5 S.C.L. (1 McCord) 395, 396 (1821); cf. Crawler Parts, Inc. v. Hill, 441 So.2d 1357 (Miss.1983); Four Winds Hospital v. Keasbey, 59 N.Y.2d 943, 466 N.Y.S.2d 300, 453 N.E.2d 529 (1983) (question of fact).

38. Simpson, Suretyship 125 (1950).

39. On the assumptions made, the defendant would be a non-consensual surety in relation to the estate of Mrs. Bradley. Mathews v. Aikin, 1 N.Y. (1 Const.) 595 (1848); Campbell, Non-Consensual Suretyship, 45 Yale L.J. 69 (1935).

40. Fendley v. Dozier Hardware Co., 449 So.2d 1236 (Ala.1984); Drummond v. Pillsbury, 130 Me. 406, 156 A. 806 (1931); Builders Supply Co., Inc. v. Carr, 276 N.W.2d 252 (S.D.1979); Johnson Co. v. City Cafe, 100 S.W.2d 740 (Tex.Civ.App.1936).

pay if he does not." Assume that the goods are delivered to TP but that C extends no credit to TP. Is D liable to C?

It is clear under the rules previously considered that D's promise is original because TP never came under an obligation to C. Yet this question can only be of academic interest. D should not be liable to C since, in failing to extend credit to TP, C has not accepted D's offer. In the logical order, of course, this question should be considered before adverting to whether the promise is original or collateral, for if there is no contract between C and D the question of whether the promise is original or collateral under the Statute of Frauds can only be of academic interest.

This simple illustration makes clear that in every case it is important to determine whether C has accepted D's offer and performed.[41] Some authorities do not emphasize this in the least and seem to imply that C in every case is free to extend or not extend credit as he sees fit.[42] The better view, however, is that in the ordinary case whether D has insisted as a condition precedent to his liability that credit be extended to TP or that TP come under an obligation to C is a question of interpretation and very often a jury question.[43]

In summary, the first inquiry to be made in this type of case (one where TP is not under a prior obligation to C at the time D makes his promise to C) is whether TP eventually comes under an obligation to C. If he does not, the promise is original. If he does, the promise is collateral unless it is rendered original for one of the reasons now to be discussed.

(b) There Must Be a Principal-Surety Relationship Between TP and D

Even though TP comes under an obligation to C, D's promise will still be original if there is not a principal-surety relationship[44] between TP and D.[45] To illustrate, assume that TP makes a purchase from C and at the same time D guarantees payment and credit is extended to TP who becomes obligated. The case is still within the first category, for if TP and D became bound at the same time, there was no prior obligation on the part of TP to C at the time that D made his promise. Under the rules thus far considered D's promise would be collateral. But if it were established that TP was acting as D's agent in this transaction, would D's promise be collateral? The answer is in the negative.[46] As pointed out above, for D's promise to be collateral there must not only be an obligation on the part of TP but there must also be

41. 3 Williston § 454.

42. See Simpson, Suretyship 125 (1950); 2 Corbin § 353. See also Lawrence v. Anderson, 108 Vt. 176, 184 A. 689 (1936).

43. Duca v. Lord, 331 Mass. 51, 117 N.E.2d 145 (1954); Simpson, Suretyship 273–77 (1950); 3 Williston § 454.

44. Restatement, Second, Contracts § 112. Restatement, Security § 82 (1941) defines suretyship.

45. 2 Corbin § 349.

46. Lesser-Goldman Cotton Co. v. Merchants & Planters' Bank, 182 Ark. 150, 30 S.W.2d 215 (1930); cf. Bartolotta v. Calvo, 112 Conn. 385, 152 A. 306 (1930).

a principal-surety relationship between TP and D. Here that relation-ship does not exist. Here under the assumption made, TP would be liable to C as an agent who has not disclosed his principal.[47] TP is the agent and D is the principal. Though it is probably true that as between the two, D should ultimately pay,[48] so that there may be additionally a principal and surety relationship under the Restatement definition, still the relationship between TP and D is not principal and surety but surety and principal. When the rule states that there must be a principal-surety relationship between TP and D it means that TP must be the principal and D the surety and not vice versa.

(c) C Must Know or Have Reason to Know of the Principal-Surety Relationship

Even if TP comes under an obligation to C and there is in fact a principal-surety relationship between TP and D, D's promise will still be original if C does not know or have reason to know of the relation-ship.[49] One illustration will suffice.[50] When goods are being purchased from C, D promises to pay and TP states he will guarantee D's payment. C is informed that the goods are to be delivered to D. As a matter of fact the arrangement between TP and D is that D shall turn the goods over to TP and this is done. Credit is extended to both. Though TP came under an obligation to C and there is a principal-surety relationship between TP and D, D's promise is still original because C did not know or have reason to know of the principal-surety relationship between TP and D. In the illustration, TP would also be liable to C, but TP is the principal debtor because the goods came to him and as between him and D he should ultimately pay.

C knows that there is a principal-surety relationship but he thinks TP is the surety and that the defendant (D) is the principal. The rule means that before the promise of the defendant (D) can be collateral, the creditor must know, or have reason to know, that the defendant (D) is the surety. This only is fair, otherwise the creditor, even if he knew of the Statute of Frauds, might not require a writing. This result is at times explained by saying that the sale to D makes him the principal, "[a]nd ordinarily it makes no difference what he did with the goods after conveyance to him; he may have destroyed, sold or given them away, yet he remains a debtor notwithstanding." [51]

47. Ferson, Principles of Agency § 170 (1954).

48. Thomas J. Nolan, Inc. v. Martin & William Smith, Inc., 193 Misc. 877, 85 N.Y.S.2d 380 (New York City Mun.Ct. 1949), affirmed 85 N.Y.S.2d 387 (App.Term 1949).

It might also be noted that an agent who does not disclose his principal does not have the defense of Statute of Frauds. Savoy Record Co. v. Cardinal Export Corp., 15 N.Y.2d 1, 254 N.Y.S.2d 521, 203 N.E.2d 206, (1964); Salzman Sign Co. v. Beck, 10 N.Y.2d 63, 217 N.Y.S.2d 55, 176 N.E.2d 74 (1961).

49. Restatement, Second, Contracts § 112; 2 Corbin § 362; 3 Williston § 475.

50. Restatement, Contracts § 112, ill. 11; Corbin § 355 (1950), particularly Colbath v. Everett D. Clark Seed Co., 112 Me. 277, 91 A. 1007 (1914).

51. 2 Corbin § 355. This is undoubtedly what the author of the Restatement of Contracts means when, after giving the illustration, he states that D's promise is not subject to the Statute of Frauds, "since

(d) The Promise Must Not Be Joint

By the great weight of authority,[52] even though TP comes under an obligation to C and there is a principal-surety relationship between TP and D and C knows of this relationship, D's promise is still original if his promise and TP's promise are joint.[53] The theory of these cases is that since the promise is joint there is only one obligation (a joint one) and that, therefore, the obligation *in toto* must be original.[54] The rule does not apply where the obligation is joint and several because in such a case more than one obligation results.[55]

(e) Summary

From what has been said it is concluded that where there is no prior obligation on the part of TP to C to which D's promise relates at the time that D's promise is made, the promise will be original unless all of the following conditions concur:

1. TP comes under an obligation at least voidable to C.

2. There is a principal-surety relationship between TP and D.

3. C knows or has reason to know of the principal-surety relationship between TP and D.

4. The promise is not joint (in jurisdictions which posit this requirement).

5. The main purpose rule is not satisfied.

If all of these conditions concur the promise is collateral; otherwise it is original. The main purpose rule will be discussed in § 19–6 infra.

 WESTLAW REFERENCES

find 441 so2d 1357

185k25

find 203 ne2d 206

find 405 f2d 859

§ 19–5. Cases Where There Is a Prior Obligation Owing From TP to C to Which D's Promise Relates

In the previous section consideration was directed to the cases where there is no obligation owing from TP to C at the time that D makes his promise. Here the rules covering the situation where TP is obligated to C at that time will be discussed.

the duty to pay is in truth his." Restatement, Second, Contracts § 112, ill. 11; see also id. § 112, ill. 10.

52. Fluor Corp. v. United States, 405 F.2d 823 (9th Cir.1969), cert. denied 394 U.S. 1014, 89 S.Ct. 1632, 23 L.Ed.2d 40 (1969); Boyce v. Murphy, 91 Ind. 1 (1883); Restatement, Contracts § 181; 2 Corbin § 361; 2 Williston § 466.

53. The rules which establish when a promise is joint, joint and several, or several, are discussed in 4 Corbin §§ 923–42; 2 Williston §§ 316–46; § 20–2 infra.

54. The joint nature of the promise does not prevent a surety relationship from arising. Simpson, Contracts §§ 136–43 (2d ed. 1965). On the question of joint and joint several obligations, see § 20–2 infra.

55. Simpson, Suretyship 132 (1950).

It is readily apparent that the words of the Statute clearly apply to such a situation. It is not surprising, therefore, to find that where TP is obligated to C at the time of D's promise, the promise will be held to be collateral [56] and therefore subject to the requirement of a writing, unless it falls within one of a number of recognized exceptions to the Statute which will not be discussed.

(a) Novation

The first exception which is universally recognized arises where there is a novation.[57] This is so whether the novation be denominated legal or equitable.[58] A practical reason for the exception is that if the promise of D causes TP's obligation to be discharged and if D's promise were held to be collateral, C would be in the unfortunate position of being unable to collect the obligation from either TP or D. The legal reason usually given is that advanced by Lord Mansfield in Anstey v. Marden: [59] "I did not see how one person could undertake for the debt of another, when the debt, for which he was supposed to undertake, was discharged by the very bargain." [60]

(b) Where the Promise to Pay Is Made to TP

The second exception arises where D makes his promise to TP rather than to C.[61] A typical illustration is the situation where the assuming grantee (D) promises the grantor (TP) that he will pay a mortgage debt according to its terms to the mortgagee (C). In that case, C may ordinarily enforce D's promise made to TP under the theory of third party beneficiary [62] or, in some jurisdictions, under the theory of equitable subrogation.[63] The Statute of Frauds provision under discussion is not a defense to D.[64] The best reason given as to why this should be is that as a result of the promise D becomes the

56. Colpitts v. L. C. Fisher Co., 289 Mass. 232, 193 N.E. 833 (1935); 2 Corbin § 350; 3 Williston § 469.

57. Hill v. Grat, 247 Mass. 25, 141 N.E. 593 (1923); Annot., 74 A.L.R. 1025 (1931); 2 Corbin § 365. For example, if D says to C, "release TP and I will pay," and C releases TP, D's promise is original. But if C does not release TP other problems arise. If the arrangement between C and D were bilateral, D undoubtedly could sue for specific performance and TP might have rights as a third party beneficiary.

58. 3 Williston § 477. See § 21–8 infra.

59. 1 Bos. & Pul. (N.R.) 124, 127 Eng. Rep. 406 (C.P.1804).

60. Id. at 131, 127 Eng.Rep. at 409; Henry C. Beck Co. v. Fort Wayne Structural Steel Co., 701 F.2d 1221 (7th Cir.1983).

61. People's State Sav. Bank v. Cross, 197 Iowa 750, 198 N.W. 70 (1924); Restatement, Second, Contracts § 123; 2 Corbin § 357; 3 Williston § 460.

62. Osborne, Mortgages § 261 (2d ed. 1970); see § 17–6 supra. Of course, under the orthodox view (§ 4–9) there must be consideration for the assumption. Trans-State, Inc. v. Barber, 170 Ga.App. 372, 317 S.E.2d 242 (1984).

63. Osborne, Mortgages § 262 (2d ed. 1970).

64. Walter E. Heller & Co. v. Video Innovations, Inc., 730 F.2d 50 (2d Cir.1984); Campbell v. Hickory Farms, 258 S.C. 563, 190 S.E.2d 26 (1972). In some states a promise to assume a mortgage must be in writing because of a different statute. See, e.g., McKinney's N.Y.Gen'l Obl.Law § 5–705.

principal debtor and is, therefore, merely promising to pay his own debt.[65]

(c) Where the Promise Is Made to C but Is Co-extensive with D's Obligation to C

The question then arises as to what extent a promise made by D to C, after D's promise to TP, is enforceable. Assume a situation in which C is an employee of TP under a hiring at will. TP owes C wages of $1000. TP enters into an agreement with D whereby TP agrees to turn the business over to D in consideration *inter alia* of D's promise to pay TP's obligation to C. As we have seen, D's promise made to TP to pay C is enforceable by C.

But suppose that one week later D personally promises C to pay him. Is this promise enforceable? So far as the Statute of Frauds is concerned the promise is original.[66] Since D is already the principal debtor [67] he is merely promising to pay his own debt. The courts do not usually consider whether there is consideration for D's promise, but this is a situation where his promise is enforceable without consideration.[68]

Suppose in the illustration given that D's promise to TP was that he would pay TP's debt to C out of profits and that D makes the same promise to C later. Both of these promises are enforceable despite the absence of a writing.[69] When D makes his promise to TP he becomes the principal, and when he makes the same promise to C he is merely promising to pay his own debt. For the same reason, where one of several co-partners promises personally to pay the whole debt of the partnership, the promise is not within the Statute of Frauds.[70]

Suppose further in the illustration given that when D makes his promise to TP, he promises to pay C out of proceeds. Subsequently, D says to C, "If you agree to continue the work that you were doing for TP for six months, I promise to pay you $100 per week and to pay TP's debt to you after one month." [71] There is consideration for D's promises. Though there may be other reasons why there is consideration, it is clear that C, in promising to work six months when the original hiring by TP was at will, is suffering detriment. Is the promise to pay TP's debt after one month original? If not, is the other promise to pay $100 per week enforceable, or must both promises stand or fall together?

---

65. Aldrich v. Ames, 75 Mass. (9 Gray) 76 (1857); Restatement, Security § 100, Comment a (1941).

66. Restatement, Second, Contracts § 114.

67. Restatement, Second, Contracts § 119.

68. 1 Williston §§ 143–44; 2 Corbin § 363; see § 5–3 supra.

69. Contra, Ackley v. Parmenter, 98 N.Y. 425 (1885). Cases where TP has not consented to D's promise to pay from property of TP under D's control have not been uniform. See 2 Corbin § 363.

70. For this and other cases where this principle applies, see 2 Corbin § 391.

71. These facts are suggested by the facts in the case of Belknap v. Bender, 75 N.Y. 446 (1878).

The answer to these questions depends in part upon the so-called main purpose rule which is discussed in the next section.[72]

 WESTLAW REFERENCES

(a) *Novation*

find 141 ne 593

(b) *Where the Promise to Pay is Made to TP*

aldrich +3 ames

(c) *Where the Promise is Made to C but is Co-extensive with D's Obligation to C*

belknap +3 bender

§ 19–6. The Main Purpose (or Leading Object) Rule

The main purpose rule may be stated in substance as follows: "Where the party promising has for his object a benefit which he did not enjoy before his promise, which benefit accrues immediately to himself, his promise is original, whether made before, after or at the time of the promise of the third party, notwithstanding that the effect is to promise to pay or discharge the debt of another."[73]

It should be noted that the main purpose rule applies whether there was or was not a prior obligation owing from TP to C to which the promise relates.[74]

It is also clear that two elements are necessary to cause the main purpose rule to apply: (a) there must be consideration for D's promise and (b) the consideration must be beneficial to him. The benefit to be obtained has been described by adjectives such as personal, immediate, pecuniary and direct.[75]

It is obvious that this rule involves difficult distinctions as to the degree of benefit and as to purpose and motive so that no extended discussion of these matters is possible here.[76] However a few typical situations will be discussed in the next section.

 WESTLAW REFERENCES
nelson +3 boynton

§ 19–7. Some Illustrations

If TP is indebted to C and C has a lien upon TP's property and D promises to pay the debt in order to discharge the lien of the property

---

72. See also § 19–36 infra.

73. Nelson v. Boynton, 44 Mass. (3 Metc.) 396 (1841); accord, Burlington Indus., Inc. v. Foil, 284 N.C. 740, 202 S.E.2d 591 (1974); Austford v. Smith, 196 N.W.2d 413 (N.D.1972).

74. See §§ 19–4 and 19–5 supra.

75. Warner-Lambert Pharmaceutical Co. v. Sylk, 471 F.2d 1137 (3d Cir.1972); Hurst Hardware Co. v. Goodman, 68 W.Va.

462, 69 S.E. 898 (1910); but see General Electric Co. v. Lions Gate, 273 S.C. 88, 254 S.E.2d 305 (1979). Restatement, Second, Contracts § 116 states the rule in terms of whether the promisor desires his own "economic advantage." Yet not every interest or economic advantage will trigger the rule. See Walton v. Piqua State Bank, 204 Kan. 741, 466 P.2d 316 (1970).

76. See 2 Corbin §§ 366–372.

does the main purpose rule apply? The answer is that it depends upon whether D has some interest to protect as would be the case where he had taken subject to a mortgage.[77] It is otherwise however if the lien surrendered is upon property in which D has no interest to protect as, for example, where he is a first mortgagee and has no other reason to promise to pay the second mortgagee.[78]

Another common situation involving the main purpose rule occurs when a stockholder of a corporation makes a promise to a creditor of the corporation which induces action which at least indirectly is beneficial to the stockholder. For example, in one case [79] defendant was a substantial stockholder in a corporation and the plaintiff, a creditor, had been furnishing merchandise to the corporation which had not paid its bills. Defendant thereupon promised to be responsible for these bills and for future deliveries if the plaintiff would continue to supply the corporation, which plaintiff did. The court held that the main purpose rule did not apply because stock ownership is too indirect and remote to satisfy the main purpose rule. This is the orthodox view.[80] Where the defendant was the sole stockholder, the cases are not in harmony but it would appear that the better view is that the main purpose rule should apply.[81]

A number of cases have arisen where D, the owner of unimproved realty, employs TP, a general contractor, to build a house for D on the latter's land. TP orders material from C who makes deliveries for which TP fails to pay. C tells TP that he will not fill further orders but subsequently agrees to fill further orders to TP when D agrees to pay the overdue debt of TP and to pay for subsequent deliveries. C fills the orders. TP does not pay. C sues D who sets up the defense of Statute of Frauds. Is the Statute in whole or in part a defense?

There are three views. One view is that the promise to pay for past deliveries is unenforceable but the promise to pay for future deliveries is enforceable.[82] Under this view the promises are said to be severable. The Restatement of Security rejects the doctrine of severability and carries the main purpose rule to its logical conclusion when

77. Kahn v. Waldman, 283 Mass. 391, 186 N.E. 587, 88 A.L.R. 699 (1933).

78. Griffin v. Hoag, 105 Iowa 499, 75 N.W. 372 (1898).

79. Hurst Hardware Co. v. Goodman, 68 W.Va. 462, 69 S.E. 896 (1910).

80. Richardson Press v. Albright, 224 N.Y. 497, 121 N.E. 362, 8 A.L.R. 1195 (1918); Mid-Atlantic Appliances, Inc. v. Morgan, 194 Va. 324, 73 S.E.2d 385, 35 A.L.R.2d 899 (1952); Note, 54 N.Car.L.Rev. 117 (1975); but see Pravel, Wilson & Matthews v. Voss, 471 F.2d 1186 (5th Cir.1973) (question of fact); Howard M. Schoor Assocs., Inc. v. Holmdel Heights Const. Co.,

68 N.J. 95, 343 A.2d 401 (1975); Nelson v. TMH, Inc., 292 N.W.2d 580 (N.D.1980).

81. To the effect that the main purpose rule does not apply, see Bulkley v. Shaw, 289 N.Y. 133, 44 N.E.2d 398 (1942); Goldie-Klenert Distrib. Co. v. Bothwell, 67 Wash. 264, 121 P. 60 (1912). Contra, Davis v. Patrick, 141 U.S. 479, 12 S.Ct. 58, 35 L.Ed. 826 (1891); Eastern Wood Prods. Co. v. Metz, 370 Pa. 636, 89 A.2d 327 (1952). See 2 Corbin § 372; Simpson, Suretyship § 38 (1950).

82. Peterson v. Paxton-Pavey Lumber Co., 102 Fla. 89, 135 So. 501 (1931).

it holds both promises enforceable because of the benefit conferred.[83] New York, for reasons to be discussed in the next section, hold both promises to be unenforceable.[84]

 WESTLAW REFERENCES
find 289 ny 133
185k33(2)
185k23(1)
185k33(1)

§ 19–8. The Peculiar New York Rule

It is generally agreed that the New York main purpose rule is different from the main purpose rule as it exists elsewhere.[85] A discussion of this difference and its extent may begin with a brief review of the landmark cases [86] which culminated in the decision of White v. Rintoul.[87]

Leonard v. Vredenburgh [88] held that so long as the promisor (D) received new consideration for his promise the promise was original. The fallacy of this position was demonstrated in Mallory v. Gillett.[89] In that case, the plaintiff (C) had made repairs upon the boat of TP and therefore had a lien.[90] D went to C and promised that if C would surrender possession of the boat, he (D) would pay for the repairs. C surrendered possession and when he was not paid brought his action against D. It is clear that under the test of Leonard v. Vredenburgh the promise would be original because D's promise to pay is supported by consideration. The surrender of the boat and the lien is consideration. The court pointed out that to say the new consideration makes the promise original effectively eliminates the Statute of Frauds since consideration is necessary to support the new promise in any event. The court added that for the main purpose rule to apply not only is consideration for D's promise necessary but in addition the consideration must be directly beneficial to the promisor. At this point New

---

83. Restatement, Security § 93, ill. 1 (1941). See Restatement, Second, Contracts § 116, ill. 3; accord, Wilson Floors Co. v. Sciota Park, Ltd., 54 Ohio St.2d 451, 377 N.E.2d 514 (1978) (bank guaranteed that subcontractor would be paid after general contractor defaulted); Haas Drilling Co. v. First Nat'l Bank, 456 S.W.2d 886 (Tex.1970), noted in 2 St. Mary's L.J. 267 (1970); Gulf Liquid Fertilizer Co. v. Titus, 163 Tex. 260, 354 S.W.2d 378 (1962) (incoming partner expressly agrees to pay outstanding debts of partner in order that future deliveries will be made on credit); cf. Abraham v. H. V. Middleton, Inc., 279 F.2d 107 (10th Cir.1960).

84. Witschard v. A. Brody & Sons, Inc., 257 N.Y. 97, 177 N.E. 385 (1931).

85. Conway, Subsequent Oral Promise to Perform Another's Duty and the New York Statute of Frauds, 22 Fordham L.Rev. 119 (1953). Compare Martin Roofing, Inc. v. Goldstein, 60 N.Y.2d 262, 469 N.Y.S.2d 595, 457 N.E.2d 700 (1983), cert. denied 466 U.S. 905, 104 S.Ct. 1681, 80 L.Ed.2d 156 (1984), with White Stag Mfg. Co. v. Wind Surfing, Inc., 67 Or.App. 459, 679 P.2d 312 (1984).

86. Conway, supra note 85, at 124–30 has an extended discussion of these cases.

87. 108 N.Y. 222, 15 N.E. 318 (1888).

88. 8 Johns. 29 (N.Y.1811).

89. 21 N.Y. 412 (1860).

90. McKinney's N.Y. Lien Law § 80.

York had adopted the main purpose rule in its generally accepted form.[91]

In Brown v. Weber [92] the Court of Appeals introduced a third element to the content of the New York law when it stated as dictum:

> The language shows that the test to be applied to every case is, whether the party sought to be charged is the principal debtor, primarily liable, or whether he is only liable in case of the default of a third person; in other words, whether he is the debtor, or whether his relation to the creditor is that of surety to him for the performance, by some other person, of the obligation of the latter to the creditor.[93]

The Court of Appeals explained, or attempted to explain, the meaning of this language in the leading case of White v. Rintoul. In that case, Wheatcroft and Rintoul (TP) made two notes in favor of the plaintiff (C). Before the maturity date of the notes, D, who was the father of one of the members of the firm, requested that C forbear collection and stated that if C would do so he would see that C was paid. D was a secured creditor of the firm. C complied with D's request and sought to recover from D on his promise. It is apparent that the court might simply have stated that the promise was collateral because the consideration for the promise of D was not sufficiently beneficial to him. The benefit was to TP and not D. However, the court reviewed the earlier cases and concluded as follows:

> These four cases, advancing by three distinct stages in a common direction, have ended in establishing a doctrine in the courts of this state which may be stated with approximate accuracy thus, that where the primary debt subsists and was antecedently contracted, the promise to pay it is original when it is founded on a new consideration moving to the promisor and beneficial to him, and such that the promisor thereby comes under an independent duty of payment irrespective of the liability of the principal debtor.[94]

A reading of this language compels the conclusion that three elements must be satisfied before the main purpose rule will apply:

(a) there must be consideration,

(b) it must be beneficial to the promisor, and

(c) the situation must be such that "the promisor thereby comes under an independent duty of payment irrespective of the liability of the principal debtor."

The same thought is expressed in different language in Richardson Press v. Albright,[95] when the Court of Appeals said that D's promise "is regarded as original only where the party sought to be charged clearly

91. Conway, supra note 85, at 125.

92. 38 N.Y. 187 (1868).

93. Id. at 189.

94. 108 N.Y. 222, 227, 15 N.E. 318, 320 (1888).

95. 224 N.Y. 497, 502, 121 N.E. 362, 364 (1918).

becomes, within the intention of the parties (TP and D) a principal debtor primarily liable."

We have seen in the preceding section that in New York the promise of an owner to pay a subcontractor for goods delivered by the general contractor has the defense of Statute of Frauds since the main purpose rule does not apply.[96] The reason is that the court feels that the third element of White v. Rintoul is not satisfied. It is difficult to determine what this requirement means because of the paucity of cases which appear to have decided that this requirement is satisfied.[97]

 WESTLAW REFERENCES
white +3 rintoul
mallory +3 gillett

§ 19–9. Promises of Indemnity

Although the word indemnitor is used in many senses, as used here, indemnitor means one who agrees to save a promisee harmless from some loss or liability irrespective of the liability of a third person.[98] This statement takes into account the distinction between an indemnitor against loss who promises to pay only after a loss and an indemnitor against liability who promises to pay after the promisee becomes liable and before loss.[99] The overwhelming weight of authority is to the effect that a promise of indemnity is not within the Statute of Frauds.[1]

A problem which has divided the court is a four party situation where the defendant requests the plaintiff to become a surety on the obligation of TP to C and orally promises the plaintiff that if he is forced to pay, the defendant will reimburse him. If the plaintiff complies and is compelled to pay, may he sue the defendant upon his oral promise or is the promise collateral? Some courts have concluded that the promise is original, as one of indemnity, because the promise was made to a debtor, the surety.[2] However, as some courts have pointed out the surety is also a creditor for he has a right to reimburse-

96. See note 84 supra.

97. This requirement was held to be satisfied in Raabe v. Squier, 148 N.Y. 81, 42 N.E. 516 (1895) and Rosenkranz v. Schreiber Brewing Co., 287 N.Y. 322, 39 N.E.2d 257 (1942). These cases are analyzed extensively in Calamari, The Suretyship Statute of Frauds, 27 Fordham L.Rev. 332 (1958). See also Biener Contracting Corp. v. Elberon Restaurant Corp., 7 A.D.2d 391, 183 N.Y.S.2d 756 (1st Dep't 1959), noted in 28 Fordham L.Rev. 384 (1959); Leonard Lang, Ltd. v. Birch Holding Corp., 72 A.D.2d 806, 421 N.Y.S.2d 921 (2d Dep't 1979). This last case might better have been decided under the rule stated in § 19–5(b).

98. See Restatement, Security § 82, Comment e (1941).

99. See Sorenson v. Overland Corp., 142 F.Supp. 354 (D.Del.1956), affirmed 242 F.2d 70 (3d Cir.1957).

1. Corbin, Contracts of Indemnity and the Statute of Frauds, 41 Harv.L.Rev. 689 (1928).

2. Restatement, Second, Contracts § 118; see Rosenbloom v. Feiler, 290 Md. 598, 431 A.2d 102, 13 A.L.R.4th 1140 (1981); Tighe v. Morrison, 116 N.Y. 263, 22 N.E. 164 (1889); Newbern v. Fisher, 198 N.C. 385, 151 S.E. 875, 68 A.L.R. 345 (1930). See § 19–5 supra.

ment from the principal and so these courts conclude that the promise is collateral.[3]

We have seen that when a promise is made to a debtor it can be safely concluded that it is not within the Statute of Frauds. However, when a promise is made to a creditor it is very difficult to determine whether the promise is one of indemnity or one of suretyship (a promise to answer for the debt, default or miscarriage of another). Part of the difficulty stems from the fact that the authorities are not in total accord on the test to be used in making this determination. Williston states that there is suretyship and not indemnity where the parties, the plaintiff (C) and defendant (D), expect that a third party (TP) will come under an obligation to C.[4] Professor Corbin states that there is a promise of indemnity where the contract is made solely for the benefit of the promisee (C) and not for the accommodation or benefit of some third person.[5] Professor Corbin, in answering the question of whether a third party was being accommodated, places great weight on whether the third party is an indeterminate third person or a specific third person.[6]

A good illustration of the difference in approach is a case of credit insurance. According to Williston credit insurance involves suretyship and not indemnity because the parties expect that a third party will come under an obligation.[7] Under Corbin's view a contract of credit insurance would be a contract of indemnity because the contract is for the benefit of the promisee and not for the accommodation of a third person.[8] Both agree that a contract of collision insurance involves indemnity[9] and that a contract of fidelity insurance involves suretyship.[10] It might also be noted that if the contract is one of suretyship the premium received by the insurance company does not bring the case within the main purpose rule.[11]

WESTLAW REFERENCES
indemnity /s "statute of fraud"

§ 19–10. The Promise of the Del Credere Agent

A del credere agent is one who receives possession of the goods for sale upon commission and who guarantees to his own principal that those to whom he sells will perform. The Statute of Frauds problem arises when the principal seeks to enforce the oral promise of the del credere agent. In the terminology that has been employed herein, the

---

3. Restatement, Second, Contracts § 118; see Green v. Cresswell, 10 Ad. & El. 453, 113 Eng.Rep. 172 (1839); Restatement, Security § 96.

4. 3 Williston § 482; Restatement, Security § 82, Comment e (1941).

5. 2 Corbin §§ 384, 388.

6. Id.

7. See note 4 supra.

8. See notes 5 & 6 supra.

9. See notes 4–6 supra.

10. 2 Corbin § 371 and note 4 supra.

11. 3 Williston § 472; Restatement, Second, Contracts § 116, Comment c.

agent is D, his principal is the creditor and the third persons are the unknown persons to whom the agent sells.

It is uniformly held that the oral promise of the del credere agent is not within the Statute of Frauds.[12] A variety of reasons are assigned for the holding. Thus, for example, Corbin explains the result on the ground that this is a promise of indemnity because it is not for the accommodation or benefit of the third parties.[13] Williston explains the case by saying that the guaranty is merely incidental to the agency in that it is part and parcel of the arrangement for compensation.[14]

 WESTLAW REFERENCES
di del credere
"statute of fraud" /s "del credere"

---

§ 19–11. The Promise of the Assignor to His Assignee Guaranteeing Performance by the Obligor

It is well settled that the promise of an assignor to his assignee guaranteeing performance by the obligor is not within the Statute of Frauds.[15] Here the obligor is TP, the assignee is C and the assignor is D. Here again Corbin explains the result upon the theory that this is a promise of indemnity,[16] and Williston again explains it by saying that the guaranty is incidental to a larger contract.[17]

 WESTLAW REFERENCES
promise /s guarantee*** /s performance /s "statute of fraud"

---

§ 19–12. A Promise to Buy a Claim

If A owes B one hundred dollars and B promises to assign his right to payment to C and C promises to pay a stated sum for the assignment, it is clear that C's promise to pay is not a promise to answer for the debt, default or miscarriage of another. C is not promising to pay the debt, but rather it is contemplated that the claim will continue with C as the holder of the claim.[18]

 WESTLAW REFERENCES
find 362 nys2d 268
195k4

---

12. 2 Corbin § 389; Restatement, Second, Contracts § 121(2).

13. Id.

14. 3 Williston § 484.

15. 2 Corbin § 390; Restatement, Second, Contracts § 122.

16. Id.

17. See note 14 supra.

18. Chester Nat'l Bank v. Rondout Marine, Inc., 46 A.D.2d 985, 362 N.Y.S.2d 268 (3d Dep't 1974), appeal denied 37 N.Y.2d 706, 375 N.Y.S.2d 1025, 337 N.E.2d 617 (1975); 3 Williston § 480; Restatement, Second, Contracts § 122.

B. AGREEMENTS IN CONSIDERATION OF MARRIAGE

§ 19–13. When the Statute of Frauds Applies

The Statute of Frauds covers "any agreements made upon consideration of marriage." It has consistently been held however that the Statute does not apply to mutual promises to marry.[19] This is not inherent in the language of the Statute but rather appears to be a policy decision,[20] although there is some indication that the draftsmen of the act did not intend to encompass mutual promises to marry within this terminology.[21] However it does apply to promises to give money or property or anything else in exchange for marriage or a promise of marriage,[22] including a promise to support a child of the prospective spouse.[23] It would even apply to a negative covenant given in exchange for the consideration of marriage.[24]

But the courts have held that the Statute does not apply if the promise is made merely in contemplation of marriage, that is to say, if marriage is not truly a consideration for the promise but is merely an occasion for the promise, or a condition of it.[25] The same is true if marriage is merely an incident of the contract and not the end to be attained.[26]

The fact that the marriage ceremony has taken place is not sufficient performance to make the promise enforceable.[27] If there has been additional part performance the unperformed part of the contract may become enforceable.[28] If not, restitutionary remedies may be available.[29] As usual, full performance on both sides eliminates any question of the Statute of Frauds.[30]

---

19. Clark v. Pendleton, 20 Conn. 495 (1850); Blackburn v. Mann, 85 Ill. 222 (1877); Brock v. Button, 187 Wash. 27, 59 P.2d 761 (1936).

20. Short v. Stotts, 58 Ind. 29 (1877); Kellner v. Kellner, 196 Misc. 774, 90 N.Y.S.2d 743 (1949).

21. See Costigan, Has There Been Judicial Legislation in the Interpretation and Application of the "Upon Consideration of Marriage" and Other Contract Clauses of the Statute of Frauds?, 14 Ill.L.Rev. 1 (1919).

22. Chase v. Fitz, 132 Mass. 359 (1882).

23. Byers v. Byers, 618 P.2d 930 (Okl. 1980).

24. Williams v. Hankins, 75 Colo. 136, 225 P. 243 (1924).

25. Riley v. Riley, 25 Conn. 154 (1856); Restatement, Second, Contracts § 124, ill. 5.

A promise made by a third party in consideration of the marriage of two other persons is within this subdivision of the Statute of Frauds. In re Peterson's Estate, 55 S.D. 457, 226 N.W. 641 (1929); Restatement, Second, Contracts § 124.

26. Bader v. Hiscox, 188 Iowa 986, 174 N.W. 565, 10 A.L.R. 316 (1919).

27. Busque v. Marcou, 147 Me. 289, 86 A.2d 873, 30 A.L.R.2d 1411 (1952).

28. Restatement, Second, Contracts § 124, Comment d; see Ferrell v. Stanley, 83 Kan. 491, 112 P. 155 (1910); Thompson v. St. Louis Union Trust Co., 363 Mo. 667, 253 S.W.2d 116 (1952).

29. In re Marriage of Heinzman, 198 Colo. 36, 596 P.2d 61 (1979); see §§ 19–40 to 19–46 infra.

30. McDonald v. McDonald, 215 Ala. 179, 110 So. 291 (1926); Bernstein v. Prudential Ins. Co., 204 Misc. 775, 124 N.Y.S.2d 624 (1953); see Annot. 30 A.L.R.2d 1419 (1953).

Of late, many courts have begun to recognize the validity of express contracts between unmarried cohabitants.[31] Perhaps anomalously such contracts are not subject to this provision of the Statute of Frauds.[32]

 WESTLAW REFERENCES
"statute of fraud" /s marriage
205k247 /p "statute of fraud"
185k103(1) /p marriage

C. AGREEMENTS FOR THE SALE OF LAND OR OF INTERESTS IN LAND

§ 19–14. Contracts for the Sale of Land

(a) Introduction

The original Statute by its terms applied to "any contract or sale of lands, tenements or hereditaments, or any interest in or concerning them." The language used would appear to encompass both the conveyance of an interest in land and an executory contract to transfer an interest in land.[33] However, other sections of the original Statute covered conveyances, and it is common even today to find conveyances governed by a separate statute. The clause under discussion has been interpreted as if it had said "contract for the sale of land" and this is the wording which is commonly adopted today. The phrase "tenements or hereditaments" is not of great significance today and many of the modern Statutes do not use this phraseology.[34]

(b) Is a Promise to Pay for an Interest in Real Property Within the Statute?

Setting aside questions of part performance which are discussed later,[35] one of the most troublesome questions has been whether the Statute, which obviously applies to a promise to transfer an interest in land, also applies to a promise to pay for the interest. There is substantial authority for the proposition that a contract for the purchase and sale of an interest in realty is unenforceable against either the purchaser or the vendor absent a sufficient memorandum signed by the party to be charged.[36] This is because, as we shall see, contracts, rather than promises, are within the Statute of Frauds.[37] However, under the wording of some Statutes, the memorandum to be enforcea-

---

31. See § 22–1 n. 6 infra.

32. Morone v. Morone, 50 N.Y.2d 481, 429 N.Y.S.2d 592, 413 N.E.2d 1154 (1980); see Levin & Spak, Judicial Enforcement of Cohabitation Agreements: A Signal to Purge Marriage from the Statute of Frauds, 12 Creighton L.Rev. 499 (1978).

33. A revocation of an offer to sell land need not be in writing. Board of Control v. Burgess, 45 Mich.App. 183, 206 N.W.2d 256 (1973).

34. 2 Corbin § 396.

35. See § 19–15 infra. See also Hamburger, the Conveyancing Purposes of the Statute of Frauds, 27 Am.J.Legal Hist. 354 (1983).

36. Restatement, Second, Contracts § 125, Comment d; 2 Corbin § 397.

37. See §§ 19–22 and 19–36 infra.

ble must be signed by the "vendor" rather than the "party to be charged". Under such Statutes it would seem clear that the purchaser's promise could be enforced without a memorandum signed by him.[38]

(c) Interests in Land

A difficult question which is presented by the Statute is whether the subject matter of a particular contract constitutes an interest in land.[39] Some of the problems in this area are discussed below.

(1) In General

Not only is a promise to transfer a legal estate in lands covered but also a promise to create, or transfer or assign a lease,[40] or easement,[41] or rent,[42] or according to the majority view, a restriction on land.[43] Unlike an easement, a license is not within the Statute.[44] Also included are promises relating to equitable interests in land including the assignment of a contract to sell.[45] An option to buy an interest in realty is clearly within the Statute.[46] The ultimate answer to the question of what is an interest in land is found generally in the law of property,[47] but policy concerns may dictate deviations. For example, it has been held that shares in a cooperative apartment constitute real property.[48]

(2) Liens

A promise to give a mortgage or other lien as security for money loaned has ordinarily been held to be within this section of the Statute

---

38. Krohn v. Dustin, 142 Minn. 304, 172 N.W. 213 (1919). Some courts have held that in such a case the vendor must introduce a memorandum signed by him and delivered to the purchaser or otherwise accepted by him as a correct memorandum. Geraci v. Jenrette, 41 N.Y.2d 660, 394 N.Y.S.2d 853, 363 N.E.2d 559 (1977). Cf. Thomas v. Dickinson, 12 N.Y. (2 Kern.) 364 (1855).

39. For a listing of interests in land, see 3 Williston § 491.

40. Most statutes exclude a lease of short duration—usually from one to three years—from the operation of this subdivision of the Statute. 2 Corbin § 402; Restatement, Second, Contracts § 125, Comment b. On special problems concerning leases, see Volkmer, The Oral Lease v. Contract for Lease Problem under the Nebraska Statute of Frauds, 6 Creighton L.Rev. 342 (1973); Note, 27 Clev.St.L.Rev. 231 (1978).

41. Canell v. Arcola Housing Corp., 65 So.2d 849 (Fla.1953); Estabrook v. Wilcox, 226 Mass. 156, 115 N.E. 233 (1917).

42. "The common law regarded rent as 'issuing from the land.' Although the con-ception is artificial, an agreement to transfer the right to rent must, in many jurisdictions, be in writing; but a promise by an assignee of a lease to assume payment of rent need not be." 3 Williston § 491 (footnotes omitted).

43. Sargent v. Leonardi, 223 Mass. 556, 112 N.E. 633 (1916); Kincheloe v. Milatzo, 678 P.2d 855 (Wyo.1984) (majority view); Thornton v. Schobe, 79 Colo. 25, 243 P. 617 (1925) (minority). Restatement, Second, Contracts § 127, Comment b is in accord with the majority view.

44. Moon v. Central Builders, Inc., 65 N.C.App. 793, 310 S.E.2d 390 (1984); 2 Corbin § 404; Restatement, Second, Contracts § 127, Comment b.

45. Traiman v. Rappaport, 41 F.2d 336, 71 A.L.R. 475 (3d Cir.1930).

46. Coombs v. Ouzounian, 24 Utah 2d 39, 465 P.2d 356 (1970).

47. Restatement, Second, Contracts § 127, Comment a.

48. Lebowitz v. Mingus, 100 A.D.2d 816, 474 N.Y.S.2d 748 (1st Dep't 1984).

of Frauds even though the Statute refers to the "sale" of land.[49] But the Statute does not apply to an interest in land that arises by operation of law; for example, a grantor's lien or a constructive trust.[50] However, once a mortgage is created a promise to assign it is not considered by most courts as the sale of an interest in land, but rather as the assignment of a chose in action since the assignment is ordinarily in connection with the transfer of the debt which the mortgage secures.[51]

(3) Fructus Industriales

Products of the soil, such as annual crops, obtained by the labor and cultivation of man are not considered an interest in land even though at the time of the making of the contract the crops are attached to the soil. "It has also been held to be true of crops that are gathered annually even though borne on perennial trunks or stems, such as apples, small fruits, and hardy shrubs and bulbs." [52] The Sales Article of the Uniform Commercial Code adopts this approach when it states, "[t]he concept of 'industrial' growing crops has been abandoned, for under modern practices fruit, perennial hay, nursery stock and the like must be brought within the scope of this Article." [53] The code is also specific that "the unborn young of animals" are to be considered goods.[54]

(4) Buildings and Other Things Attached to the Earth Not Included in the Concept Fructus Industriales

Whether a contract to sell any of the above is a contract for the sale of an interest in land is one upon which the decided cases were not in agreement prior to enactment of the U.C.C.[55] The Uniform Commercial Code [56] provides: "A contract for the sale of minerals or the like (including oil and gas) or a structure or its materials to be removed from realty is a contract for the sale of goods within this Article if they

49. Nixon v. Nixon, 100 N.J.Eq. 437, 135 A. 516 (1927); Sleeth v. Sampson, 237 N.Y. 69, 142 N.E. 355, 30 A.L.R. 1400 (1923); Lambert v. Home Fed. Sav. & Loan Ass'n, 481 S.W.2d 770 (Tenn.1972).

50. 2 Corbin § 401; accord, Remmick v. Mills, 165 N.W.2d 61 (N.D.1969) (alfalfa).

51. Osborne, Mortgages § 65 (2d ed. 1970); Citizens United Bank, N.A. v. Pearlstein, 733 F.2d 28 (3d Cir.1984) (agreement to accept substitute performance to discharge mortgage). A promise to release property from the lien of a mortgage has been held not to be within the Statute of Frauds. Nye v. University Dev. Co., 10 N.C.App. 676, 179 S.E.2d 795 (1971), cert. denied 278 N.C. 702, 181 S.E.2d 603 (1971).

But see Eastgate Enterprises, Inc. v. Bank & Trust Co. of Old York Road, 236 Pa.Super. 503, 345 A.2d 279 (1975) (promise not to foreclose is within the Statute).

52. 2 Corbin § 410.

53. U.C.C. § 2–105, Comment 1.

54. Id. § 2–105(1).

55. Compare Baird v. Elliott, 63 N.D. 738, 249 N.W. 894 (1933) with Home Owners' Loan Corp. v. Gotwals, 67 S.D. 579, 297 N.W. 36 (1941) and with Slingluff v. Franklin Davis Nurseries, Inc., 136 Md. 302, 110 A. 523 (1920).

56. See § 1–7 supra.

are to be severed by the seller * * *." [57] "If the buyer is to sever, such transactions are considered contracts affecting land * * *." [58]

The Code further provides: "a contract for the sale apart from land of growing crops or other things attached to realty and capable of severance without material harm thereto but not described in subsection (1) [59] or of timber to be cut is a contract for the sale of goods within this Article whether the subject matter is to be severed by the buyer or by the seller even though it forms part of the realty at the time of contracting, and the parties can by identification effect a present sale before severance." [60]

(5) Miscellaneous Items Deemed Not to Be Within this Section of the Statute of Frauds Relating to Interests in Land

If the subject matter of the contract is not the transfer of an interest in realty it does come within the Statute, although the end result would be an interest in land. For example, a contract to build a building or to do work on land is not within the Statute,[61] and the same would be true of a promise to lend money with which to buy land,[62] and of a contract between partners to buy and sell real estate and to divide the profits.[63] It should also be noted that the fact that the consideration on one side of a contract is an executed interest in land does not bring the agreement within the Statute.[64] Boundary line and partition agreements are generally held to be within this section of the Statute of Frauds.[65]

A promise to pay a broker a commission for finding a purchaser is not within the traditional Statute of Frauds.[66] Several states, however, have enacted a separate statute requiring such a contract to be in writing.[67]

WESTLAW REFERENCES

(a) *Introduction*

find 206 nw2d 256

57. U.C.C. § 2–107(1).

58. Id. § 2–107, Comment 1; see Bell v. Hill Bros. Constr. Co., 419 So.2d 575 (Miss. 1982).

59. Set forth in the preceding paragraph in the text.

60. U.C.C. § 2–107(2).

61. Plunkett v. Meredith, 72 Ark. 3, 77 S.W. 600 (1903); McCaffrey v. Strainer, 81 A.D.2d 977, 439 N.Y.S.2d 773 (3d Dep't 1981), appeal dismissed 55 N.Y.2d 700, 446 N.Y.S.2d 947, 431 N.E.2d 308 (1981); Scales v. Wiley, 68 Vt. 39, 33 A. 771 (1895).

62. Horner v. Frazier, 65 Md. 1, 4 A. 133 (1886).

63. Anderson v. Property Developers, Inc., 555 F.2d 648 (8th Cir.1977); Evanovich v. Hutto, 204 So.2d 477 (Miss.1967); Pace v. Perk, 81 A.D.2d 444, 440 N.Y.S.2d

710 (2d Dep't 1981); see 2 Corbin § 411. A joint venture agreement that contemplates the transfer of land owned by one of the parties is within the Statute. Dobbs v. Vornado, Inc., 576 F.Supp. 1072 (E.D.N.Y. 1983).

64. Byers v. Locke, 93 Cal. 493, 29 P. 119 (1982).

65. Restatement, Second, Contracts § 128(1); but see Norwood v. Stevens, 104 Idaho 44, 655 P.2d 938 (App.1982); Dewitt v. Lutes, 581 S.W.2d 941 (Mo.App.1979); Norberg v. Fitzgerald, 122 N.H. 1080, 453 A.2d 1301 (1982).

66. Atlantic Coast Realty Co. v. Robertson, 240 Fed. 372 (4th Cir.1917).

67. See, e.g., Pine-Wood, Ltd. v. Detroit Mortgage and Realty Co., 95 Mich.App. 85, 290 N.W.2d 86 (1980).

(b) *Is a Promise to Pay for an Interest in Real Property Within the Statute?*

promise /3 pay /4 (real +1 estate property) land /s "statute of fraud"

(c) *Interest in Land*
   (1) *In General*

di(license /s "statute of fraud")

   (2) *Liens*

di(lien /s "statute of fraud")

   (3) *Fructus Industriales*

di fructus industriales

u.c.c. "uniform commercial code" /s 2–105

"fructus industriales" /s "statute of fraud"

   (4) *Buildings and Other Things Attached to the Earth Not Included in the Concept Fructus Industriales*

u.c.c. "uniform commercial code" /s 2–107(1) (2–107 +s (1))

   (5) *Miscellaneous Items Deemed Not to be Within this Section of the Statute of Frauds Relating to Interests in Land*

find 440 nys2d 710

---

§ 19–15. Performance as Causing a Contract Within the Statute to be Enforceable

Prior to enactment of the Statute of Frauds a permissible method of conveyance of land was "livery of seisin", an oral transfer accompanied by a symbolic handing over of a twig or clump of earth in the presence of witnesses.[68] Within a decade of enactment of the Statute, the Chancellor ruled that where a grantee had been put into possession of land the Statute of Frauds was inapplicable as the transaction was "executed".[69] Consequently, the grantee was entitled to specific performance in the face of the grantor's attempt to oust him from possession.

Later courts, losing sight of the historical origins of the part performance doctrine, required more than possession, insisting on some conduct "unequivocally referable" to the alleged oral agreement. In Cardozo's words, there must be "performance which alone and without the aid of words of promise is unintelligible or at least extraordinary unless as an incident of ownership, assured if not existing * * *. [W]hat is done must itself supply the key to what is promised. It is not enough that what is promised may give significance to what is done."[70]

---

68. See 6A Powell on Real Property ¶ 880 (1984).

69. Butcher v. Stapley, 1 Vern. 363, 23 Eng.Rep. 524 (Ch. 1685); see Pound, The Progress of the Law, 1918–1919, Equity, 33 Harv.L.Rev. 929–944 (1920).

70. Burns v. McCormick, 233 N.Y. 230, 232, 135 N.E. 273, 273 (1922). Cardozo may well have been influenced by Pound, supra note 69, at 944. For stringent application of the rule, see Wilson v. Le Van, 22 N.Y.2d 131, 291 N.Y.S.2d 344, 238 N.E.2d 738 (1968), noted in 35 Brooklyn L.Rev. 301 (1969); Gilbride, The Part Performance Exception in New York, 26 Brooklyn L.Rev. 1 (1959). For analyses in other states, see Comment, Oral Land Contracts and the Doctrine of Part Performance in Idaho, 8

In short, the conduct must convincingly evidence the existence of the agreement. This occurs in some jurisdictions where there is payment and the making by the vendee of valuable improvements upon the land with the consent of the vendor.[71] But in other jurisdictions these elements are not necessary [72] although it is clear that these are always important factors to be considered.[73] A very small number of states do not recognize the doctrine of part performance.[74]

The doctrine is strictly a doctrine of equity, the available remedy being specific performance and not damages.[75] Under the equitable notion of mutuality, if the circumstances are such that the purchaser might obtain specific performance under the part performance doctrine, the vendor is entitled to demand specific performance.[76]

It is well settled that if the vendor fully performs by conveying to the vendee, the oral promise of the vendee is enforceable unless payment is to be by transfer of an interest in land.[77] On the other hand, full payment by the purchaser does not justify enforcement of the contract because the purchaser has the quasi-contractual remedy of restitution.[78]

As discussed later in this chapter [79] the doctrine of promissory estoppel is fast making inroads upon enforcement of oral contracts within the Statute of Frauds. As this doctrine gains greater acceptance, the various technical requirements of the part performance

Idaho L.Rev. 205 (1971); Comment, The Statute of Frauds and Part Performance in Kansas, 14 Kan.L.Rev. 647 (1966); Note, The Doctrine of Part Performance as Applied to Oral Land Contracts in Utah, 9 Utah L.Rev. 91 (1964). For its application to leases, see Comment, 28 Baylor L.Rev. 413 (1976).

71. Pfeifer v. Raper, 253 Ark. 438, 486 S.W.2d 524 (1972); [but see Langston v. Langston, 3 Ark. 286, 625 S.W.2d 554 (App. 1981)]; Baker v. Rice, 37 So.2d 837 (Fla. 1948); Weale v. Massachusetts Gen'l Housing Corp., 117 N.H. 428, 374 A.2d 925 (1977); Sharp v. Stacy, 535 S.W.2d 345 (Tex.1976); Bradshaw v. McBride, 649 P.2d 74 (Utah 1982); Jasmin v. Alberico, 135 Vt. 287, 376 A.2d 32 (1977). Two requisites are considered in Note, Property—The Problem of Part Payment in Removal from the Statute of Frauds, 22 Baylor L.Rev. 588 (1970); Note, Character of Possession Necessary to Satisfy the Rules of Hooks v. Bridgewater, 22 Baylor L.Rev. 361 (1970).

72. Zukowski v. Dunton, 650 F.2d 30 (4th Cir.1981); Smith v. Cox, 247 Ga. 563, 277 S.E.2d 512 (1981); Recker v. Gustafson, 279 N.W.2d 744 (Iowa 1979); Powers v. Hastings, 93 Wn.2d 709, 612 P.2d 371 (1980). See 2 Corbin § 434.

73. Stackhouse v. Cook, 271 S.C. 518, 248 S.E.2d 482 (1978).

74. Mississippi, North Carolina and Tennessee. See 2 Corbin § 443. But see Baliles v. Cities Service Co., 578 S.W.2d 621 (Tenn.1979) (estoppel).

75. McKinnon v. Corporation of the President of the Church of Jesus Christ of Latter-Day Saints, 529 P.2d 434 (Utah 1974); 2 Corbin § 419; Restatement, Second, Contracts § 129, Comment c; Comment, 47 Can.B.Rev. 644 (1969). For a break-through case holding that because of the merger of law and equity, damages are now available, see Miller v. McCamish, 78 Wn.2d 821, 479 P.2d 919 (1971), noted in 47 Wash.L.Rev. 524 (1972); see also Clay v. Bradley, 74 Wis.2d 153, 246 N.W.2d 142 (1976) (damages awarded; no discussion of remedy).

76. Walter v. Hoffman, 267 N.Y. 365, 196 N.E. 291, 101 A.L.R. 919 (1935). See § 16–6 supra.

77. Restatement, Second, Contracts § 125(3); Wiggins v. White, 157 Ga.App. 49, 276 S.E.2d 104 (1981); Dangelo v. Farina, 310 Mass. 758, 39 N.E.2d 754 (1942); Allen v. Allen, 550 P.2d 1137 (Wyo.1976).

78. Restatement, Second, Contracts § 129, ill. 1; Pugh v. Gilbreath, 571 P.2d 1241 (Okl.App.1977); but see Kartes v. Kartes, 195 Mont. 383, 636 P.2d 272 (1981).

79. See § 19–48 infra.

doctrine applied in many states are giving way to a broader principle of promissory estoppel.

WESTLAW REFERENCES

di("livery by seisin")

find 135 ne 273

185k129(12)

185k129(3)

358k39

di(doctrine theory /2 "part performance" /s contract)

D. AGREEMENTS FOR THE SALE OF GOODS: THE UNIFORM COMMERCIAL CODE

§ 19–16. Contracts for the Sale of Goods

(a) Introduction

Prior to enactment of the Uniform Commercial Code, the Uniform Sales Act was the law of sales prevailing generally throughout the United States. Section 2–201 of the Uniform Commercial Code is to a large extent a restatement of the Sales Act provision with modifications and clarifications.[80] To a large extent, therefore, cases decided under the Sales Act continue to be authoritative.

---

80. Section 2–201 of the U.C.C. provides:

Formal Requirements; Statute of Frauds

(1) Except as otherwise provided in this section a contract for the sale of goods for the price of $500 or more is not enforceable by way of action or defense unless there is some writing sufficient to indicate that a contract for sale has been made between the parties and signed by the party against whom enforcement is sought or by his authorized agent or broker. A writing is not insufficient because it omits or incorrectly states a term agreed upon but the contract is not enforceable under this paragraph beyond the quantity of goods shown in such writing.

(2) Between merchants if within a reasonable time a writing in confirmation of the contract and sufficient against the sender is received and the party receiving it has reason to know its contents, it satisfies the requirements of subsection (1) against such party unless written notice of objection to its contents is given within ten days after it is received.

(3) A contract which does not satisfy the requirements of subsection (1) but which is valid in other respects is enforceable

(a) if the goods are to be specially manufactured for the buyer and are not suitable for sale to others in the ordinary course of the seller's business and the seller, before notice of repudiation is received and under circumstances which reasonably indicate that the goods are for the buyer, has made either a substantial beginning of their manufacture or commitments for their procurement; or

(b) if the party against whom enforcement is sought admits in his pleading, testimony or otherwise in court that a contract for sale was made, but the contract is not enforceable under this provision beyond the quantity of goods admitted; or

(c) with respect to goods for which payment has been made and accepted or which have been received and accepted (Section 2–606).

This statute is also discussed in § 19–34 infra.

(b) Price or Value

The Sales Act applied to goods "of the *value* of five hundred dollars or upwards," while the Code refers to "the *price* of $500 or more." To what extent the codifiers intended a substantive change is unclear. In ordinary speech "price" is far less vague a term than "value" and thus it may be that the codifiers intended to eliminate problems of (1) whether the Statute of Frauds applies when goods are sold for a price less than their value [81] and (2) when, in addition to a monetary consideration, other benefits are conferred on the seller.[82] The resolution of the second of these problems, however, is complicated by § 2–304(1) which provides that: "the price can be made payable in money or otherwise." This definition makes clear that the Statute of Frauds continues to apply if goods are exchanged not for money but for other property or services of a value of five hundred dollars or more.[83] The gray area in which the Code is unclear, then, is in the case of a sale of goods for basically a monetary consideration coupled with incidental benefits conferred on the seller.

The Code offers no solution to a frequently recurring problem under pre-existing law. Often parties contract for the exchange of a number of chattels having an aggregate value in excess of five hundred dollars but which individually have a value below this statutory amount. The test, often difficult to apply, is whether there is one contract or several.[84]

(c) Goods

Prior to enactment of the Sales Act there were wide divergencies among the authorities on the applicability of the Statute of Frauds to contracts for the manufacture of goods.[85] The Commercial Code provision is largely based on the compromise solution enacted in the Sales Act. A contract for sale of goods to be manufactured is within the Statute, unless "the goods are to be specially manufactured for the buyer and are not suitable for sale to others in the ordinary course of the seller's business and the seller, before notice of the repudiation is received and under circumstances which reasonably indicate that the goods are for the buyer, has made either a substantial beginning of their manufacture or commitments for their procurement." [86] This exception to the writing requirement contains two significant innovations. Under the Sales Act, the writing requirement was dispensed with for contracts for sale of specially manufactured goods only if the

---

81. See Duesenberg and King, Sales and Bulk Transfers § 202[2] (1966).

82. See Hawkland, Sales and Bulk Sales 33 (1958).

83. This was the weight of authority under the Sales Act. Misner v. Strong, 181 N.Y. 163, 73 N.E. 965 (1905).

84. See Williston, Sales § 70 (rev. ed. 1948); Duesenberg and King, supra note 81, at § 2.20[2].

85. Compare Goddard v. Binney, 115 Mass. 450, 15 Am.R. 112 (1874) with Bingham v. Wells, Rich, Greene, Inc., 34 A.D.2d 924, 311 N.Y.S.2d 508 (1st Dep't 1970) (per curiam).

86. U.C.C. § 2–201(3)(a). On the distinction between stock items and specially manufactured goods, see Annot., 45 A.L.R.4th 1126 (1981).

seller was also the manufacturer. Under the Code it is clear that the seller need not be the manufacturer, but may be a third party. The Sales Act exempted all contracts for sale of specially manufactured goods from coverage of the Statute of Frauds. The Code exemption applies, however, only if the seller has acted in reliance upon the contract by making a substantial beginning toward manufacturing or has made commitments for the procurement of the goods.

It is of course obvious that items which are considered realty or interests in realty are not included in the term "goods." This matter has been discussed sufficiently in section 19–14 supra. A vexatious problem is the mixed contract involving the sale of goods and transfer of real property, the rendition of services, or the transfer of intangibles. It is well established that a contract to furnish labor and materials in erecting a structure or repairing a chattel is not within the Statute unless there is a transfer of title to goods prior to annexation.[87] Some courts have sought to find the "essence" of the transaction, and to classify the transaction as "essentially" a sales transaction or a service transaction.[88]

Others have looked to the dominant purpose of the transaction.[89] Others have sought to allocate a percentage of the transaction as coming under the Uniform Commercial Code.

(d) Choses in Action

The Statute of Frauds provision of the Uniform Sales Act specifically encompassed choses in action as well as goods. Section 2–201 of the Uniform Commercial Code is restricted solely to contracts for the sale of goods. Three sections of the Code govern writing requirements in connection with transfer of choses in action. Section 8–319 relates to investment securities and Section 9–203 relates to the creation of security interests and the assignment of contract rights.[90]

Section 1–206 governs all contracts for the sale of personal property not specifically governed by the other three Statute of Frauds provisions of the Code.[91] It requires a writing signed by the party to be

---

87. 2 Corbin § 476; Marshall, The Applicability of the Uniform Commercial Code to Construction Contracts, 28 Emory L.J. 335 (1979); Annot., 5 A.L.R.4th 501 (1981).

88. Robertson v. Ceola, 255 Ark. 703, 501 S.W.2d 764 (1973); see generally Note, Dual Nature Contracts and the Uniform Commercial Code, 28 Md.L.Rev. 136 (1968).

89. United Industrial Syndicate, Inc. v. Western Auto Supply Co., 686 F.2d 1312 (8th Cir.1982); Colorado Carpet Installation, Inc. v. Palermo, 668 P.2d 1384, 45 A.L.R.4th 1113 (Colo.1983).

90. A security interest which is not evidenced by a signed writing is subordinate to the claims of a subsequent attaching creditor although the secured creditor has filed a financing statement. Mid-Eastern Electronics, Inc. v. First Nat'l Bank, 380 F.2d 355 (4th Cir.1967), appeal after remand 455 F.2d 141 (4th Cir.1970).

Section 5–104(1) & (2) contains provisions in the nature of a Statute of Frauds for certain credits or letters of credit.

91. Many problems in the interpretation of this Section are discussed in Comment, The Uniform Commercial Code, Section 1–206—A New Departure in the Statute of Frauds?, 70 Yale L.J. 603 (1961). The Section reads as follows:

(1) Except in the cases described in subsection (2) of this section a contract for the sale of personal property is not

charged in the case of a contract relating to the sale of a chose in action if the amount sought to be enforced in court exceeds $5000. Principally this section is intended to govern the assignment of rights (e.g. patent rights)[92] that are not governed by Article 8 or 9 of the Code. Since outright assignments of general intangibles are not covered by Article 9 they are covered by this section.

(e) Part Performance

The original sales Statute of Frauds provided that no writing was required if the buyer accepted or received the goods or gave something in earnest to bind the bargain or made a part payment. The Sales Act reenacted these exceptions.[93] The Code, however, has made significant departures from preexisting law. The Code provision with respect to specifically manufactured goods is discussed above.[94]

(1) Accept and Receive

Prior to the Code the entire oral contract was enforceable if the buyer had accepted and received part of the goods.[95] Acceptance related to title[96] and receipt had to do with possession.[97] The Code continues preexisting law only in part. The writing requirement is dispensed with only as to those items which have been received and accepted.[98] Receipt continues to mean the taking of physical possession of the goods.[99] Acceptance, however, has a somewhat different meaning under the Code. It is not a question of whether the buyer accepted title to the goods but whether he has indicated an intention to keep the goods.[1] This represents a shift in emphasis from a legal conclusion to a

---

enforceable by way of action or defense beyond five thousand dollars in amount or value of remedy unless there is some writing which indicates that a contract for sale has been made between the parties at a defined or stated price, reasonably identifies the subject matter, and is signed by the party against whom enforcement is sought or by his authorized agent.

(2) Subsection (1) of this section does not apply to contracts for the sale of goods (Section 2–201) nor of securities (Section 8–319) nor to security agreements (Section 9–203).

See Olympic Junior, Inc. v. David Crystal, Inc., 463 F.2d 1141 (3d Cir.1972).

92. Goldsmith v. Income Properties, Inc., 3 N.Y.2d 1023, 341 N.Y.S.2d 898, 294 N.E.2d 657 (1973).

93. See Uniform Sales Act § 4.

94. See text at notes 80–83 supra.

95. Uniform Sales Act § 4(1). This was true although the buyer denied contracting for any quantity beyond what he had accepted and received. John Thallon & Co.

v. Edsil Trading Corp., 302 N.Y. 390, 98 N.E.2d 572 (1951).

96. See Restatement, Contracts § 201.

97. See id. § 202.

98. U.C.C. § 2–201(3)(c); see Bagby Land & Cattle Co. v. California Livestock Comm'n Co., 439 F.2d 315 (5th Cir.1971); In re Nelsen's Estate, 209 Neb. 730, 311 N.W.2d 508 (1981); Gardner & Beedon Co. v. Cooke, 267 Or. 7, 513 P.2d 758 (1973).

99. U.C.C. § 2–103(1)(c) provides: " 'Receipt' of goods means taking physical possession of them." However, it is possible for the buyer to "receive" goods even though there has been no change in the physical possession of the goods. See e.g., James Mack Co. v. Bear River Milling Co., 63 Utah 565, 277 P. 1033, 36 A.L.R. 643 (1924). But a conversion is not a receipt. Nelson v. Hy-Grade Constr. & Materials, Inc., 215 Kan. 631, 527 P.2d 1059 (1974).

1. The concept of acceptance is disclosed in § 11–20 supra. For a typical Statute of Frauds acceptance case, see Pride Lab., Inc. v. Sentinel Butte Farmers Elevator Co., 268 N.W.2d 474 (N.D.1978).

factual one. The rationale for the "accept and received" exception as well as for the exception discussed in the next paragraph is that "[r]eceipt and acceptance either of goods or of the price constitutes an unambiguous overt admission by both parties that a contract actually exists."[2] It should be noted, however, unlike the exception to the real property Statute of Frauds, there is no requirement that the part performance be "unequivocally referable" to the alleged contract.[3]

(2) Payment or Earnest

"Something in earnest," a phrase used in the original Statute of Frauds and in the Sales Act, sounds rather remote from modern commercial practice. The phrase has reference to an old custom of giving a sum of money or some tangible object to cement a bargain. "Earnest" is not part payment as it is not applied to the price.[4] Because of the disappearance or, at least, rarity of this practice, the Code has abolished this exception to the writing requirement.

Under prior law if payment in whole or in part was made by the buyer and accepted by the seller, the entire contract was enforceable.[5] The Code, if taken literally, seems to have significantly changed this rule by providing that the contract is enforceable only as to "goods for which payment has been made and accepted."[6] Part payment, therefore, would seem to give rise only to partial enforcement.[7] However, the commentators and some decisions take the position that if a just apportionment can be made it should be made; if not, part payment should make the entire contract enforceable.[8] The Code also indicates that the part payment may be made by money, check, goods or services so long as the money, check, goods or services have been accepted.[9]

One authority argues that the Code definition of "acceptance" does not apply to the Statute of Frauds provision and that more flexible pre-Code decisions should continue to be applied in this context. Duesenberg and King, supra note 81, at § 2.04[4][a]. This argument is difficult to accept in view of the express cross-reference to U.C.C. § 2–606 found in U.C.C. § 2–201(3)(c).

The question of whether a revocation of acceptance on grounds of non-conformity of the goods (U.C.C. § 2–608) revives the writing requirement is discussed in Duesenberg and King, supra note 81. The Code is silent on the point.

2. U.C.C. § 2–201, Comment 2.

3. Hofmann v. Stoller, 320 N.W.2d 786 (N.D.1982); Gerner v. Vasby, 75 Wis.2d 660, 250 N.W.2d 319, 97 A.L.R.3d 897 (1977).

4. See 2 Corbin § 494; 3 Williston § 564. Some cases have held that "earnest" and part payment are the same thing. Scott v. Mundy & Scott, 193 Iowa 1360, 188 N.W. 972, 23 A.L.R. 460 (1922).

5. 2 Corbin § 495; 3 Williston § 565; Restatement, Contracts § 205.

6. U.C.C. § 2–201(3)(c); see Huyler Paper Stock Co. v. Information Supplies Corp., 117 N.J.Super. 353, 284 A.2d 568 (1971).

7. Williamson v. Martz, 11 Pa.D. & C.2d 33 (1956).

8. Hawkland, A Transactional Guide to the Uniform Commercial Code § 1.1202, at 28–29 (1964); Nordstrom, Sales § 27, at 69–72 (1970); see Lockwood v. Smigel, 18 Cal.App.3d 800, 96 Cal.Rptr. 289 (1971); Thomaier v. Hoffman Chevrolet, Inc., 64 A.D.2d 492, 410 N.Y.S.2d 645 (2d Dep't 1978) (both cases hold that a small down payment permitted proof that a contract was made for the sale of a car). See, Beane, The Partial Payment Exception to the U.C.C. Sale of Goods Statute of Frauds, 13 U.C.C. L.J. 135 (1980); Note, 20 U.Kan. L.Rev. 538 (1972). See also U.C.C. § 2–201, Comment 2.

9. U.C.C. § 2–201, Comment 2; see Kaufman v. Solomon, 524 F.2d 501 (3d Cir. 1975) (receipt and retention of a check).

(f) Admission in Court

The Uniform Commercial Code expressly provides that a contract is enforceable "if the party against whom enforcement is sought admits in his pleading, testimony or otherwise in court that a contract for sale was made, but the contract is not enforceable under this provision beyond the quantity of goods admitted." [10]

This provision is new, although to some extent the problems it concerns itself with were raised in prior case law.[11] The principal question the Code provision raises is whether and to what extent the party against whom enforcement is sought can be compelled to admit the existence of the oral contract either during the trial or in pre-trial proceedings. That is, may he object to the question on the grounds that he is asserting the Statute of Frauds as an affirmative defense or must he answer the question under oath as to whether the oral contract was made? It has been held that, under the U.C.C., it is no longer possible to dismiss a complaint that on its face alleges an oral contract within the Statute of Frauds because the defendant may conceivably admit the existence of the contract at trial, and such holdings appear to be quite consistent with the legislative intention behind the U.C.C. provision.[12] For this exception to apply, it is essential that the person testifying be, at the time of testifying, the party to be charged or an agent still having authority to bind the principal.[13]

(g) Sufficiency of the Memorandum, Written Confirmations and Estoppel

These topics are discussed below.[14]

10. Id. § 2–201(3)(b). There is a similar provision in § 8–319(d). Cf. Martocci v. Greater New York Brewery, Inc., 301 N.Y. 57, 92 N.E.2d 887 (1950), motion denied 301 N.Y. 662, 93 N.E.2d 926 (1950). U.C.C. § 2–201, Comment 7 adds: "Under this section it is no longer possible to admit the contract in court and still treat the statute as a defense. However, the contract is not thus conclusively established. The admission so made by a party is itself evidential against him of the truth of the facts so admitted and of nothing more, as against the other party, it is not evidential at all." See also, Blankenfeld v. Smith, 290 Minn. 475, 188 N.W.2d 872 (1971); Restatement, Second, Contracts § 133, Comment d; Stevens, Ethics and the Statute of Frauds, 37 Cornell L.Q. 355 (1952).

(1966); Lewis v. Hughes, 276 Md. 247, 346 A.2d 231, 88 A.L.R.3d 406 (1975); Weiss v. Wolin, 60 Misc.2d 750, 303 N.Y.S.2d 940 (1969); contra, Triangle Marketing, Inc. v. Action Industries, Inc., 630 F.Supp. 1578 (N.D.Ill.1986). See, Duesenberg, The Statute of Frauds in its 300th Year: The Challenge of Admissions in Court and Estoppel, 33 Bus.Law. 1859 (1978); Yonge, The Unheralded Demise of the Statute of Frauds Welsher in Oral Contracts for the Sale of Goods and Investment Securities: Oral Sales Contracts are Enforceable by Involuntary Admissions in Court under U.C.C. §§ 2–201(3)(b) and 8–319(d), 33 Wash. & Lee L.Rev. 1 (1976); Notes, 65 Cal.L.Rev. 150 (1977); 3 J.L. & Com. 167 (1983); 56 Tex.L.Rev. 915 (1978); 32 U.Fla.L.Rev. 486 (1980); Annot., 88 A.L.R.3d 416 (1978).

11. See 2 Corbin §§ 317–320; Note, 38 Cornell L.Q. 604 (1953).

13. Miller v. Sirloin Stockade, 224 Kan. 32, 578 P.2d 247 (1978).

12. Roth Steel Prod. v. Sharon Steel Corp., 705 F.2d 134 (6th Cir.1983); Garrison v. Piatt, 113 Ga.App. 94, 147 S.E.2d 374

14. See § 19–34 infra (sufficiency of the memorandum and written confirmations), §§ 19–47, 19–48 infra (estoppel).

WESTLAW REFERENCES

(a) *Introduction*

u.c.c. "uniform commercial code" /s 2–201

(b) *Price or Value*

u.c.c. "uniform commercial code" /s price value /s 500 $500
  five-hundred

u.c.c. "uniform commercial code" /s 2–304(1)

(c) *Goods*

u.c.c. "uniform commercial code" /s 2–201(3)(a) (2–201 +s
  (3)(a))

find 501 sw2d 764

185k84

(d) *Choses in Action*

u.c.c. "uniform commercial code" /s 8–319

u.c.c. "uniform commercial code" /s 9–203

u.c.c. "uniform commercial code" /s 1–206

u.c.c. "uniform commercial code" /s 5–104

(e) *Part Performance*
  (1) *Accept and Receive*

u.c.c. "uniform commercial code" /s 2–201(3)(c) (2–201 +s
  (3)(c))

u.c.c. "uniform commercial code" /s 2–606

u.c.c. "uniform commercial code" /s 2–608

  (2) *Payment or Earnest*

sy,di("something in earnest")

u.c.c. "uniform commercial code" /s 2–201(3)(c) (2–201 +s
  (3)(c))

(f) *Admission in Court*

u.c.c. "uniform commercial code" /s 2–201(3)(b) (2–201 +s
  (3)(b))

185k144

E. CONTRACTS NOT TO BE PERFORMED
WITHIN ONE YEAR

§ 19–17. Computation of the One Year Period

Subdivision 5 of Section 4 of the original Statute of Frauds provided that a writing is required for "an agreement that is not to be performed within the space of one year from making thereof." The test is not how long the performance will take, but when will it be complete. Thus, if on January 10, 1987, A in a bilateral contract promises to make a one hour television appearance on February 1, 1988, the contract is within the Statute.[15]

It is generally accepted that if A contracts to work for B for one year, his work to begin more than one day after making the agreement,

---

15. See Lund v. E.D. Etnyre & Co., 103 Ill.App.2d 158, 242 N.E.2d 611 (1968). Special problems dealing with unilateral contracts are discussed in § 19–24 infra.

the contract is within the one year section;[16] but if the work is to begin the very next day the contract is not within the Statute on the theory that the law disregards fractions of a day.[17] If the contract is restated at the beginning of the work and the restatement can be regarded as the making or remaking of the contract, the year starts to run from that time. "Courts have been very liberal in holding that the restatement was itself a contract."[18]

It is difficult to discern a rationale for the one year provision of the Statute of Frauds.[19] Some have thought that its purpose was "not to trust to the memory of witnesses for a longer time than one year."[20] However, it has been pointed out that "[t]here is no necessary relationship between the time of the making of the contract, the time within which its performance is required and the time when it might come to court to be proven."[21] Because of the lack of discernable rationale, the tendency has been to give the provision a narrow construction.[22]

 WESTLAW REFERENCES
find 202 ne2d 516
185k53

§ 19–18.   Possibility of Performance Within One Year

The one year section of the Statute of Frauds has never been a favorite of the courts and so it has been interpreted in such a way as to narrow its scope as much as possible. Thus it is has been interpreted to mean that it only applies to a promise or agreement[23] which by its terms does not admit of performance within one year from the time of its making. If by its terms performance is possible within one year, however unlikely or improbable that may be, the agreement or promise is not within this subdivision of the Statute of Frauds.[24] Thus a promise made in October 1920 to cut down and deliver certain timber on or before April 1, 1922 is not within the Statute.[25] It is immaterial

16. Sinclair v. Sullivan Chevrolet Co., 31 Ill.2d 507, 202 N.E.2d 516 (1964); Jennings v. Ruidoso Racing Ass'n, 79 N.M. 144, 441 P.2d 42 (1968).

17. Restatement, Contracts § 198, Comment d; 2 Corbin § 447; 3 Williston § 502.

18. 2 Corbin § 448. See also 3 Williston § 503; Restatement, Second, Contracts § 130, Comment c.

19. It has been speculated that "as in the case of the other subdivisions the draftsmen had in mind a transaction type: employment and similar relationships, such as apprenticeships and fiduciary retainers. The common law rule was that a general hiring was presumed to be for a one year term." Perillo, The Statute of Frauds in the Light of the Functions and Dysfunctions of Form, 43 Fordham L.Rev. 39, 77 n. 214 (1974).

20. Smith v. Westall, 1 Ld. Raym. 316, 317, 91 Eng.Rep. 1106, 1107 (1697).

21. D & N Boening, Inc. v. Kirsch Beverages, Inc., 63 N.Y.2d 449, 454, 483 N.Y.S.2d 164, 165, 472 N.E.2d 992, 993 (1984).

22. Explicitly so stated in, e.g., Ohanian v. Avis Rent A Car System, 779 F.2d 101, 106 (2d Cir.1985).

23. The question of whether "promises" or "agreements" are within this subdivision of the Statute of Frauds is discussed in § 19–22 infra.

24. Howarth v. First Nat'l Bank, 540 P.2d 486 (Alaska 1975), affirmed 551 P.2d 934 (1976); Adams v. Wilson, 264 Md. 1, 284 A.2d 434 (1971).

25. Gallagher v. Finch, Pruyn & Co., 211 App.Div. 635, 207 N.Y.S. 403 (3d Dep't 1925), amended 212 A.D. 847 (1925). Nu-

whether or not the actual period of performance exceeded one year.[26] The same is true of a promise to build a house within fifteen months.[27] A promise to perform upon completion of a dam is not within the Statute although it is contemplated that the dam will be completed in three years and in fact completion takes three years.[28] In general, contracts of indefinite duration are not within this provision of the Statute.[29] A distinct minority of cases have taken into account how the parties intended and expected that the contract would be performed and if they expect performance to endure beyond a year from the making of the contract it is held to be within the Statute.[30]

There are contracts that by general agreement would be deemed to be within the Statute of Frauds. A promise by A to work for B for a period in excess of one year [31] or a promise not to compete for two years is within the Statute,[32] as is a promise by B to pay in monthly installments extending over a period of two years.[33]

It has generally been held that a contract whereby an employee is to be paid a bonus or commission on an annual basis but which cannot be calculated and paid until after the books have been closed is not within the Statute although the bonus cannot be calculated until after the end of the year.[34]

merous cases in accord are collected in 2 Corbin § 444.

26. In re Estate of Hargreaves, 201 Kan. 57, 439 P.2d 378 (1968).

27. Plimpton v. Curtiss, 15 Wend. 336 (N.Y.1836); Restatement, Second, Contracts § 130, Comment a.

28. Gronvold v. Whaley, 39 Wn.2d 710, 237 P.2d 1026 (1951); accord, Walker v. Johnson, 96 U.S. (6 Otto) 424, 24 L.Ed. 834 (1877); Augusta Bank & Trust v. Broomfield, 231 Kan. 52, 643 P.2d 100 (1982); Swain v. Harmount & Woolf Tie Co., 226 Ky. 823, 11 S.W.2d 940 (1928); Chesapeake Fin. Corp. v. Laird, 289 Md. 594, 425 A.2d 1348 (1981); Thompson v. Stuckey, ___ W.Va. ___, 300 S.E.2d 295 (1983).

29. Joe Regueira, Inc. v. American Distilling Co., 642 F.2d 826 (5th Cir.1981); Weiner v. McGraw-Hill, Inc., 57 N.Y.2d 458, 457 N.Y.S.2d 193, 443 N.E.2d 441, 33 A.L.R.4th 110 (1982); Restatement, Second, Contracts § 130, Comment a.

30. Krueger v. Young, 406 S.W.2d 751 (Tex.Civ.App.1966); 2 Corbin § 446; 3 Williston § 500. On the peculiar line of New York cases in agency situations see § 19–24 infra.

31. Carroll v. Palmer Mfg. Co., 181 Mich. 280, 148 N.W. 390 (1914); Feiner-

man v. Russ Togs, Inc., 37 A.D.2d 805, 324 N.Y.S.2d 855 (1st Dep't 1971) (per curiam); Chase v. Hinkley, 126 Wis. 75, 105 N.W. 230 (1905).

32. Higgins v. Gager, 65 Ark. 604, 47 S.W. 848 (1898); McGirr v. Campbell, 71 App.Div. 83, 75 N.Y.S. 571 (1st Dep't 1902). Contra, Doyle v. Dixon, 97 Mass. 208 (1867); Restatement, Second, Contracts § 130, ill. 4; see 2 Corbin § 453; 3 Williston § 497. The theory of the authorities cited as contra is that although the contract cannot by its terms be performed or even terminated within a year, nonetheless its purpose is attained within a year if the promisor dies. See § 19–20 infra.

33. Sophie v. Ford, 230 App.Div. 568, 245 N.Y.S. 470 (4th Dep't 1930); Thompson v. Ford, 145 Tenn. 335, 236 S.W. 2 (1921). But see Restatement, Second, Contracts § 130, Comment d.

34. White Lighting Co. v. Wolfson, 68 Cal.2d 336, 66 Cal.Rptr. 697, 438 P.2d 345 (1968); Dennis v. Thermoid Co., 128 N.J.L. 303, 25 A.2d 886 (1942); John William Costello Associates, Inc. v. Standard Metals Corp., 99 A.D.2d 227, 472 N.Y.S.2d 325 (1st Dep't 1984); Robertson v. Pohorelsky, 583 S.W.2d 956 (Tex.Civ.App. 1979).

§ 19–19. Promises Performable Within One Year but Conditional Upon an Uncertain Event

If A promises to pay B $10,000 upon the sale of certain property, A's promise is not within the Statute because the act of payment obviously can be performed within a year and it is possible that the condition will occur within a year.[35] Insurance contracts for more than one year are generally not within the one year section because the contingency upon which payment is promised may occur within the year.[36] A warranty that a pressure cooker will not explode is not within the one year provision even if the explosion upon which suit is brought occurs two years after the making of the warranty.[37] Also it has been held that an oral promise made by a railroad to maintain a switch so long as the plaintiff needed it is enforceable twenty-two years after it was made.[38]

So too, the one year provision does not bar enforcement of a contract to leave a bequest by will [39] or to pay a sum at the death of a named person.[40] The contingency of death could occur within the year and therefore it is immaterial whether it occurred within the year or many years later. It should be noted, however, that legislation in some jurisdictions has extended the Statute of Frauds to contracts which are not performable before the end of a lifetime and to contracts to make a testamentary disposition.[41]

---

35. Sullivan v. Winters, 91 Ark. 149, 120 S.W. 843 (1909); Bartlett v. Mystic River Corp., 151 Mass. 433, 24 N.E. 780 (1890).

36. Sanford v. Orient Ins. Co., 174 Mass. 416, 54 N.E. 883 (1899); International Ferry Co. v. American Fidelity Co., 207 N.Y. 350, 101 N.E. 160 (1913); Struzewski v. Farmers' Fire Ins. Co., 179 App.Div. 318, 166 N.Y.S. 362 (4th Dep't 1917) reversed on other grounds 226 N.Y. 338, 123 N.E. 661 (1919); 2 Corbin § 445; Hollman, Insurance and the Statute of Frauds, [1977] Ins. L.J. 143. But if there is a promise by a person to pay premiums over a number of years, this promise is within the one year section of the Statute of Frauds. Hummel v. Hummel, 133 Ohio St. 520, 14 N.E.2d 923 (1938).

37. Joseph v. Sears, Roebuck & Co., 224 S.C. 105, 77 S.E.2d 583, 40 A.L.R.2d 742 (1953).

38. Warner v. Texas and P. Ry., 164 U.S. 418, 17 S.Ct. 147, 41 L.Ed. 495 (1896).

39. Dixon v. Lamson, 242 Mass. 129, 136 N.E. 346 (1922); Carlin v. Bacon, 322 Mo. 435, 16 S.W.2d 46, 69 A.L.R. 1 (1929). Such an agreement may, however, be within the real property provision. See § 19–14 supra.

40. Riddle v. Backus, 38 Iowa 81 (1874).

41. See Note, The Statute of Frauds' Lifetime and Testamentary Provisions: Safeguarding Decedents' Estates, 50 Fordham L.Rev. 239 (1981).

§ 19–20. A Promise of Extended Performance That Comes to an End Upon the Happening of a Condition That May Occur Within A Year

If A promises to supply B with goods for the duration of the war, A's promise is not within the Statute because the war may end within a year.[42] So too if A promises to support X for life or to employ X for life, the promise is not within the Statute because it is not for a fixed term and the contract by its terms is conditioned upon the continued life of X and the condition may cease to exist within a year because X may die within a year.[43] These cases should be compared with cases cited at note 31 supra. There it is said that if A promised to work for B for two years, the contract is within the Statute of Frauds. It is quite possible that A might die within a year and the contract discharged under the doctrine of impossibility of performance.[44] Nonetheless, the courts hold that where the contract is phrased in terms of a number of years rather than in terms of a lifetime, death operates as a *defeasance* of the contract rather than as its fulfilment.[45] Where the contract is phrased in terms of a specific number of years with an express provision for termination at death, the authorities are not harmonious as to the proper result.[46]

In Duncan v. Clarke [47] a promise was made to pay for the support of the illegitimate child by paying sixty dollars per month until the child became twenty-one. At the time of the promise the child was four years of age. The majority opinion held that if the child were to die the agreement would be fully performed and since the child could have died within a year the promise by its terms could be performed within a year.[48] The contrary argument, that appears to have been accepted by the Court below, is death would have resulted in the defeasance of the contract and not the attainment of its essential purpose.

 WESTLAW REFERENCES
find 308 ny 282

185k50(2)

---

42. Canister Co. v. National Can Corp., 63 F.Supp. 361 (D.Del.1945), motion denied 71 F.Supp. 45 (D.Del.1974).

43. Quirk v. Bank of Commerce & Trust Co., 244 F. 682 (6th Cir.1917); Kitsos v. Mobile Gas Service Corp., 404 So.2d 40 (Ala.1981), appeal after remand 431 So.2d 1150 (Ala.1983); Hobbs v. Brush Elec. Light Co., 75 Mich. 550, 42 N.W. 965 (1889); Bussard v. College of Saint Thomas, Inc., 294 Minn. 215, 200 N.W.2d 155 (1972); Fidelity Union Trust Co. v. Reeves, 96 N.J. Eq. 490, 125 A. 582 (1924), affirmed 98 N.J. Eq. 412, 129 A. 922 (1925).

44. See 13–7 supra.

45. See 2 Corbin § 447.

46. Compare Gilliam v. Kouchoucos, 161 Tex. 299, 340 S.W.2d 27, 88 A.L.R.2d 693 (1960) with Silverman v. Bernot, 218 Va. 650, 239 S.E.2d 118 (1977); see Restatement, Second, Contracts § 130, Comment b.

47. 308 N.Y. 282, 125 N.E.2d 569, 49 A.L.R.2d 1287 (1955); accord In re Marriage of Strand, 86 Ill.App.3d 827, 42 Ill. Dec. 37, 408 N.E.2d 415 (1980).

48. 2 Corbin § 446; see Restatement, Second, Contracts § 130, Comment b.

§ 19–21. Contracts for Alternative Performances and Contracts With Option to Terminate, Renew or Extend

Where a contractor promises one of two or more performances in the alternative the promise is not within the one year section if any of the alternatives can be performed within one year from the time of the making thereof. It does not matter which party has the right to name the alternative.[49]

If A and B enter into an oral contract by the terms of which A promises to perform services for B for five years and B promises to pay for the services at a fixed rate over that period and one or both have the right by the terms of the contract to terminate the contract as for example by giving 30 days notice within the year, is the one-year section a defense? The majority view is that the Statute is a defense because although *defeasance* is possible within a year *performance* is not.[50]

The other view is that the contract is not within the Statute of Frauds.[51] It is reasoned that alternative promises are provided: (1) either to perform for the full period or (2) to perform up to the time of election and then exercise that option to cancel.[52] As we have seen the general rule is that if one of the alternative promises may be performed within a year the one year section does not apply. A peculiar variation on this approach has been made by the New York courts. It is held that the Statute does not apply if the option of termination is bilateral or if the option is in the defendant but that the Statute would be defense if the option of termination is only in the plaintiff. "For in such cases defendant's liability endures indefinitely subject only to the uncontrolled voluntary act of the party who seeks to hold the defendant. Under such circumstances it is illusory, from the point of view of the defendant, to consider the contract terminable or performable within one year."[53]

Options to extend or renew present similar problems. The same split of authority evidenced in the option to terminate cases also

49. 2 Corbin § 454. But see § 19–36 infra, which states a different rule for the other subdivisions of the Statute of Frauds.

50. Coan v. Orsinger, 265 F.2d 575 (D.C. Cir.1959); Barth v. Women's City Club, 254 Mich. 270, 236 N.W. 778 (1931); Deevy v. Porter, 11 N.J. 594, 95 A.2d 596 (1953); see 3 Williston §§ 498A–498B; Restatement, Second, Contracts § 130, Comment b. However, comment b goes on to say that the "distinction between performance and non-performance is sometimes tenuous; it depends on the terms and the circumstances, particularly on whether the essential purpose of the parties will be at-

tained." Illustrations 6 and 7 appear to be contradictory.

51. Fothergill v. McKay Press, 361 Mich. 666, 106 N.W.2d 215 (1960); see 2 Corbin § 449.

52. Hopper v. Lennen & Mitchell, Inc., 146 F.2d 364 (9th Cir.1944); Johnston v. Bowersock, 62 Kan. 148, 61 P. 740 (1900); Blake v. Voight, 134 N.Y. 69, 31 N.E. 256 (1892).

53. Harris v. Home Indem. Co., 6 A.D.2d 861, 175 N.Y.S.2d 603 (1st Dep't 1958).

appears here.[54]   Again New York takes a peculiar position.   If the option to extend or renew that could require performance for more than one year is held by the plaintiff alone, the contract is within the Statute.   If the option is bilateral or is held by the defendant alone, the contract is outside the reach of the Statute.[55]

WESTLAW REFERENCES
find 265 f2d 575

185k51

§ 19–22.   Is a Promise or a Contract Within the One Year Section of the Statute of Frauds?

It appears to be settled that where any of the promises on either side of a bilateral contract cannot be fully performed within one year from the time of the formation of the contract, all of the promises in the contract are within the one year section of the Statute of Frauds.[56] This means that the contract is unenforceable by either party in the absence of a sufficient memorandum or in the absence of performance, the effect of which is discussed in the next section.

WESTLAW REFERENCES
promise /s performance /s "one year" /s "statute of fraud"

§ 19–23.   Effect of Performance Under the One Year Section

Courts have had to deal with the question of part and full performance on one side under each subdivision of the Statute of Frauds. Different doctrines have been forged for many of these subdivisions. Under the majority view, full performance on one side renders a contract within the one year section enforceable.[57] Some of the jurisdictions adopting this view, however, qualify this position by requiring that the performance must have actually taken place within one year from the making of the contract.[58] A minority of jurisdictions, howev-

54. Hand v. Osgood, 107 Mich. 55, 64 N.W. 867 (1895) (holding that the Statute is a defense).   Contra, Ward v. Hasbrouch, 169 N.Y. 407, 62 N.E. 434 (1902).   See generally 2 Corbin § 450.

55. See Belfert v. Peoples Planning Corp. of America, 22 Misc.2d 753, 199 N.Y.S.2d 839 (1959), affirmed 11 A.D.2d 760, 202 N.Y.S.2d 101 (1st Dep't 1960), affirmed 11 N.Y.2d 755, 226 N.Y.S.2d 693, 181 N.E.2d 630 (1962).

56. 2 Corbin § 456; Restatement, Contracts § 198; Restatement, Second, Contracts § 130(1) and Comment d.   However,

see the rule stated for alternative promises in § 19–21 supra and § 19–36 infra.

57. Ortega v. Kimbell Foods, Inc., 462 F.2d 421 (10th Cir.1972); Emerson v. Universal Prods., Inc., 35 Del. 277, 162 A. 779 (1932); Glass v. Minnesota Protective Life Ins. Co., 314 N.W.2d 393 (Iowa 1982); Coker v. Richtex Corp., 261 S.C. 402, 200 S.E.2d 231 (1973); Lambousis v. Johnston, 657 P.2d 358 (Wyo.1983); 2 Corbin § 456; Restatement, Second, Contracts § 130 and Comment d; Annot., 6 A.L.R.2d 1111 (1949).

58. See 2 Corbin § 457.

er, hold that performance is ineffective to render the contract enforceable, restricting the performing party to his quasi-contractual remedy.[59]

It seems everywhere to be agreed that part performance on one side does not entitle either party to sue to enforce the contract,[60] unless according to some authorities, the contract is divisible.[61] Quasi-contractual recovery is available to the performing party.[62] There are also a number of cases in which enforcement has been granted on the basis of estoppel.[63]

 WESTLAW REFERENCES
find 657 p2d 358
185k139(1)

§ 19–24.   Unilateral Contracts

There is a great deal of authority to the effect that unilateral contracts are enforceable without reference to the one year Statute of Frauds.[64] This stems in part from the majority rule that where the plaintiff has fully performed his side of the bargain the one year provision of the Statute is not a defense.[65]

Even in jurisdictions adopting the minority view, however, it is still arguable that a unilateral contract, would not ordinarily be within the Statute of Frauds. If A said to B, "if you walk across Brooklyn Bridge three years from today, I promise to pay you $100 immediately after you walk," the promise logically would not be within the one year provision of the Statute because by its terms its performance is to take place immediately after the contract is made.[66] The result would logically be different if A's promise was to pay more than one year after B performed the act which created the contract.[67]

A series of decisions in New York, a minority jurisdiction, are of interest in this context. Among the more interesting of these cases is Martocci v. Greater N.Y. Brewery, Inc.[68] The defendant had promised

59. Montgomery v. Futuristic Foods, Inc., 66 A.D.2d 64, 411 N.Y.S.2d 371 (2d Dep't 1978).

60. Advocate v. Nexus Indus., Inc., 497 F.Supp. 328 (D.Del.1980); Chevalier v. Lane's Inc., 147 Tex. 106, 213 S.W.2d 530, 6 A.L.R.2d 1045 (1948); Restatement, Second, Contracts § 130, Comment e.

61. Blue Valley Creamery Co. v. Consolidated Prods. Co., 81 F.2d 182 (8th Cir. 1936) (installment sales of dairy products); but see § 19–36 infra.

62. See §§ 19–40 to 19–46 infra.

63. See §§ 19–47, 19–48 infra.

64. Hartung v. Billmeier, 243 Minn. 148, 66 N.W.2d 784 (1954) ("You boys stick with me for five years and I will give you a hundred dollars a year bonus"); John William Costello Associates, Inc. v. Standard

Metals Corp., 99 A.D.2d 227, 472 N.Y.S.2d 325 (1st Dep't 1984); Auerbach's Inc. v. Kimball, 572 P.2d 376 (Utah 1977). Restatement, Second, Contracts § 130, Comment a; 2 Corbin § 457.

65. See § 19–23 supra.

66. This is logical where the Statute speaks in terms of an "agreement", but not necessarily so when it speaks in terms of a "promise". That is to say the issue is whether in the case of a unilateral contract the year is to be measured from the making of the promise or the making of the contract.

67. See Simpson, Contracts 172 (2d ed. 1965); Restatement, Second, Contracts § 130, Comment c.

68. 301 N.Y. 57, 92 N.E.2d 887 (1950), motion denied 301 N.Y. 662, 93 N.E.2d 926

to pay the plaintiff a 5% commission on all sales made by the defendant to P. Lorillard & Co., if the plaintiff introduced P. Lorillard & Co. to the defendant. The plaintiff performed and the defendant set up the defense of the one year provision of the Statute of Frauds.

There are a number of preliminary observations to be made. First the plaintiff had completely performed, and, therefore, under the majority view the Statute of Frauds would have been satisfied. Second, the contract was unilateral as it did not arise until the plaintiff had performed.

The Court of Appeals held, however, that the defendant's promise was within the Statute, stating:

"If the terms of the contract here had included an event which might end the contractual relationship of the parties within a year, defendant's possible liability beyond that time would not bring the contract within the [S]tatute. Since, however, the terms of the contract are such that the relationship will continue beyond a year, it is within the [S]tatute, even though the continuing liability to which defendant is subject is merely a contingent one. The endurance of the defendant's liability is the deciding factor. The mere cessation of orders from Lorillard to defendant would not alter the contractual relationship between the parties; it would not constitute performance; plaintiff would still be in possession of his contractual right, though it may have no monetary value, immediately or ever." [69] The contract was treated as of perpetual rather than of indefinite duration.[70]

The court here distinguished the kind of case typified by a promise to deliver goods for the duration of the war. In such a case the contingency is expressed in the contract and the contingency terminates the contractual relationship; thus the promise by its terms may be performed within a year. In a case such as Martocci, the promise endures continuously into the future. The court does not take into account the possibility that P. Lorillard may cease to exist within a year. We have previously seen that if a promise is limited by the life of a person, or even if the essential purpose of the contract for a period of years is attained upon the death of a person, it is not within the one year section.[71] In the Martocci case, however, it is quite clear that by

(1950). This and subsequent New York cases are discussed in Comment, The Cohen Case and the One Year Provision of the Statute of Frauds, 25 Fordham L.Rev. 720 (1957).

69. 301 N.Y. at 62–63, 92 N.E.2d at 889; accord, Zupan v. Blumberg, 2 N.Y.2d 547, 161 N.Y.S.2d 428, 141 N.E.2d 819 (1957) (commission payable to salesman on any account he brought in so long as account remained active); Nurnberg v. Dwork, 12 A.D.2d 612, 208 N.Y.S.2d 799 (1st Dep't 1960), affirmed 12 N.Y.2d 776, 234 N.Y.S. 721, 186 N.E.2d 568 (1962) (commission on

percentage of sales if at any future times plaintiff obtains concessions for defendant at designated stores).

70. The distinction under Florida law is discussed in Joe Regueira, Inc. v. American Distilling Co., 642 F.2d 826 (5th Cir.1981).

71. See § 19–20 supra. To be distinguished are cases where there is an offer looking to a series of contracts. Here each contract should be treated individually to see if it violates the one year section of the Statute of Frauds. See Nat Nal Serv. Stations, Inc. v. Wolf, 304 N.Y. 332, 107 N.E.

its terms the performance of the defendant was not limited by the life of the customer, P. Lorillard & Co. Had it been, the problem would be that stated in § 19–22. It would also appear that the essential purpose of the parties would not be achieved if the corporation ceased to exist.

In a more recent Court of Appeals case,[72] the plaintiff, pursuant to an oral agreement entered into in October of 1960, was promised the exclusive distributorship of the defendant's beer in a specified area for as long as defendant sold beer in the area.[73] The defendant designated a new distributor in 1962. Plaintiff sued for breach and defendant set up as a defense the one year section of the Statute of Frauds. The Court of Appeals held that the Statute was not a defense. The Court indicates that since by the terms of the contract the defendant could at any time discontinue its beer sales in the area, the defendant under the New York view could perform in less than a year by withdrawing its products from the market in the area.

The Court distinguished the Martocci case by saying that there the plaintiff had completely performed and therefore there was greater opportunity for fraud in that type of case, and, secondly, that in the Martocci case the agreement by its terms could not be terminated by either party to the contract, whereas here at least, as pointed out above, the defendant had a right to terminate the arrangement. The court treated the defendant's right to discontinue doing business in the locality as an option to terminate and it then followed the traditional New York rule that a right held by a defendant to terminate within a year takes the contract outside of the Statute of Frauds.[74]

 WESTLAW REFERENCES

"unilateral contract" /s "statute of fraud"

185k139(1) /p "unilateral contract"

185k44(1) /p "unilateral contract"

185k74(1) /p "unilateral contract"

martocci +3 greater

---

§ 19–25. Relationship of the One Year Provision to Other Subdivisions of the Statute

The one year section applies to all contracts no matter what their subject matter.[75] Thus, for example, a contract for the sale of goods must comply with both the one year and the sale of goods provisions of the Statute.[76] According to the weight of authority, mutual promises to

2d 473 (1952); Restatement, Second, Contracts § 130, ill. 10.

72. North Shore Bottling Co. v. C. Schmidt & Sons, Inc., 22 N.Y.2d 171, 292 N.Y.S.2d 86, 239 N.E.2d 189 (1968).

73. The language would seem to raise a consideration problem but this was not discussed. See § 4–12(c)(4) supra.

74. See § 19–21 supra.

75. Restatement, Second, Contracts § 130, Comment f; see Haire v. Cook, 237 Ga. 639, 229 S.E.2d 436 (1976) (apply the more rigorous one year provision to real property contract); but see § 19–39 infra.

76. Seaman's Direct Buying Service v. Standard Oil Co., 36 Cal.3d 752, 206 Cal. Rptr. 354, 686 P.2d 1158 (1984); Bryant v. Credit Serv., Inc., 36 Del. 360, 175 A. 923 (1934); contra, Roth Steel Prod. v. Sharon

marry not performable within one year are within the one year provision,[77] although not within the consideration of marriage subdivision.[78]

 WESTLAW REFERENCES
find 686 p2d 1158

II. WHAT IS A SUFFICIENT WRITING OR MEMORANDUM AND THE EFFECT THEREOF

Table of Sections

§ 19–26. Introduction

Assuming that a contract is within the Statute of Frauds, it is clear that it is enforceable if there is a sufficient writing or memorandum. This was spelled out in Section 4 of the English Statute which made the contract enforceable if "the agreement * * *, or some memorandum or note thereof, shall be in writing, and signed by the party to be charged therewith, or some other person thereunto by him lawfully

Steel Corp., 705 F.2d 134 (6th Cir.1983) (need satisfy only U.C.C.).

77. 2 Corbin §§ 455, 461.

78. See § 19–13 supra.

authorized." This language in substance has been adopted by most of the states. However, there are variations from state to state. All that can be said is the variations are not so great as to prevent general discussion but that in every case the words of the particular statute should be considered.

 WESTLAW REFERENCES
"english statute" /s writing memorandum

§ 19–27. Parol Evidence and the Memorandum

The relationship between the parol evidence rule and the Statute of Frauds is wrapped in much the same controversy and confusion as the parol evidence rule itself.[79] It is clear that a memorandum sufficient to satisfy the Statute of Frauds need not be an integrated writing.[80] Yet the distinction between an integrated writing and a nonintegrated writing is important in at least one respect.

Where the writing is not integrated it may be shown that the oral agreement made contained essential terms different from or additional to those stated in the memorandum. When the memorandum is thus exposed as inaccurate, the party sought to be charged may obtain a dismissal of the case against him because the memorandum does not contain the essential terms of the agreement [81]—one of the more bizarre results of the often criticized Statute of Frauds.[82] However, if there is a total integration, the writing may not be varied, contradicted or supplemented in order to show that it is inaccurate.[83]

The situation is quite different when a party seeks to introduce oral evidence in order to establish terms not found in the memorandum for the purpose of enforcing those terms. Here whether the memorandum is integrated or not makes no difference, because for this purpose the Statute of Frauds has its own built-in exclusionary rule which excludes oral evidence offered to supply essential terms. But here, as above, consistent additional non-essential oral terms may be shown unless there is a total integration.[84] However, extrinsic evidence should be admissible in aid of interpretation unless it is excluded by the rules of interpretation set forth in Chapter 3.[85]

79. See Ch. 3 supra.

80. See Drury v. Young, 58 Md. 546 (1882) where the memorandum was made by defendant for his records without plaintiff's knowledge.

81. 2 Corbin § 498; 4 Williston § 575; Restatement, Second, Contracts § 131, Comment g. The statement does not take into account the possibility of a court of equity granting reformation, a question which is discussed in § 19–28 infra.

82. See 2 Corbin § 275. See also 4 Williston § 599 at 275 n. 12 (urging a uniform liberalized statute).

83. Lyon v. Big Bend Dev. Co., 7 Ariz. App. 1, 435 P.2d 732 (1968); N.E.D. Holding Co. v. McKinley, 246 N.Y. 40, 157 N.E. 923 (1927); Restatement, Contracts § 131, ill. 11. The possibility of reformation is considered at § 19–28 infra.

84. See Lynch v. Davis, 181 Conn. 434, 435 A.2d 977 (1980); 4 Williston § 575; cf. 2 Corbin § 527; A. B. C. Auto Parts, Inc. v. Moran, 359 Mass. 327, 268 N.E.2d 844 (1971).

85. See, e.g., § 3–10 supra; Koedding v. Slaughter, 634 F.2d 1095 (8th Cir.1980); Marsico v. Kessler, 149 Conn. 236, 178 A.2d 154 (1962); Stanley v. A. Levy & J.

WESTLAW REFERENCES

di("parol* evidence rule" /s "statute of fraud")

157k417(9) /p "parol* evidence" /s "statute of fraud"

185k84 /p "parol* evidence"

390k88

390k109

185k139(1) /p "parol* evidence"

185k106(1) /p "parol* evidence"

185k142 /p "parol* evidence"

185k158(3) /p "parol* evidence"

§ 19–28. Does the Statute of Frauds Preclude Reformation?

The great majority of cases have held that if the equitable relief of reformation is sought, the Statute of Frauds does not exclude parol evidence tending to prove that a written agreement or conveyance is at variance with the parties' prior oral agreement.[86]

A minority of jurisdictions have refused to admit such evidence on the ground that the admission of such evidence would fly in the face of the statutory ban against the enforcement of oral agreements.[87] The majority answers, however, that by the process of reformation the court is not enforcing an oral agreement but is rectifying the writing to conform it to what the parties thought they were writing. "The correction of erroneous instruments therefore does not rest necessarily upon any assumption that a prior completed oral contract is being enforced."[88]

It is very important to remember that if the alleged contract is within the Statute of Frauds, the writing as reformed must satisfy the statutory requirements. It should also be recalled that terms intentionally omitted may not be added by a decree of reformation.[89] In addition, reformation is not permitted except upon clear and convincing evidence.[90] With these three safeguards in mind, it would be incorrect to state that the policy of the Statute is violated by permitting reformation.

Zentner Co., 60 Nev. 432, 112 P.2d 1047 (1941); see also § 19–29 infra. For purposes of interpretation Williston treats a memorandum under the Statute of Frauds as if it were an integration. See § 3–11 supra.

86. World of Sleep, Inc. v. Seidenfeld, 674 P.2d 1005 (Colo.App.1983); Restatement, Second, Contracts § 156; see Palmer, Reformation and the Statute of Frauds, 65 Mich.L.Rev. 421 (1967). Such a result has even been reached under a statute requiring contracts hiring school superintendents to be in writing and filed with the county treasurer. Hampton School Dist. No. 1 v. Phillips, 251 Ark. 90, 470 S.W.2d 934 (1971).

87. The minority position had been accepted in part by Restatement, Contracts § 509. The Restatement, Second, Contracts § 156 embraces the majority view.

88. 9 Wigmore, Evidence § 2417 (Chadbourn rev. 1981).

89. See § 9–33 supra; Restatement, Second, Contracts § 156, Comment a.

90. See § 9–31 supra.

In New York a peculiar distinction has been made. Although a written contract may be reformed,[91] a written memorandum of a contract may not be reformed.[92] This rule apparently stems from confusion between the exclusionary rules of the Statute of Frauds and the parol evidence rule.[93]

WESTLAW REFERENCES

"statute of fraud" /s reformation

328k44 /p "statute of fraud"

§ 19–29. The Contents of the Memorandum

The memorandum [94] must state with reasonable certainty: (a) the identity of both contracting parties; however, the party need not be named if he is sufficiently described since extrinsic evidence to clarify the description is admissible; [95] (b) the subject matter of the contract so that it can be identified either from the writing or if the writing is not clear by the aid of extrinsic evidence; [96] (c) the essential "terms and conditions of all the promises constituting the contract and by whom and to whom the promises are made." [97] If the consideration is executed (e.g., payment has been made) it is still in dispute whether the consideration must be stated.[98]

It should be repeated that the "essential terms"—a term of considerable flexibility itself—must be stated with only "reasonable" certain-

91. Brandwein v. Provident Mut. Life Ins. Co., 3 N.Y.2d 491, 168 N.Y.S.2d 964, 146 N.E.2d 693 (1957).

92. Friedman & Co. v. Newman, 255 N.Y. 340, 174 N.E. 703, 73 A.L.R. 95 (1931).

93. See Palmer, supra note 86, at 437–40.

94. If the Statute reads that the contract must be in writing, a memorandum is insufficient. Restatement, Second, Contracts § 131, Comment a.

95. Restatement, Contracts § 207(a); Restatement, Second, Contracts § 131(b) adds that the memorandum should indicate that a contract has been made or that the signer has made an offer. See Restatement, Second, Contracts § 131, Comment f and ill. 10; Arcuri v. Weiss, 198 Pa.Super. 506, 184 A.2d 24 (1962).

96. Restatement, Contracts § 131(a); 2 Corbin § 505; Clark v. Larkin, 172 Kan. 284, 239 P.2d 970 (1952); Kidd v. Early, 289 N.C. 343, 222 S.E.2d 392 (1976); Malin v. Ward, 21 A.D.2d 926, 250 N.Y.S.2d 1009 (3d Dep't 1964), appeal denied 15 N.Y.2d 482, 255 N.Y.S.2d 1025, 203 N.E.2d 800 (1964); Owen v. Hendricks, 433 S.W.2d 164, 30 A.L.R.3d 929 (Tex.1968); Wozniak

v. Kuszinski, 352 Mich. 431, 90 N.W.2d 456 (1958); ("your 960 acres in Dallam County" may be a sufficient description for recovery under statute requiring a writing for real estate brokerage commissions, if seller owned no other land in that county). But see for a strict view, White v. Rehn, 103 Idaho 1, 644 P.2d 323 (1982); Martin v. Seigel, 35 Wn.2d 223, 212 P.2d 107, 23 A.L.R.2d 1 (1949) (street address of premises an insufficient description in an action for specific performance of contract to convey).

97. Restatement, Contracts § 207(c); Restatement, Second, Contracts § 131(c); Slotkin v. Willmering, 464 F.2d 418 (8th Cir.1972); Botello v. Misener-Collins Co., 469 S.W.2d 793 (Tex.1971). Terms implied in law are deemed to be in the memorandum. This is true even if the implied term has been agreed to. Restatement, Second, Contracts § 131, Comment g. But see Morris Cohon & Co. v. Russell, 23 N.Y.2d 569, 297 N.Y.S.2d 947, 245 N.E.2d 712 (1969).

98. 2 Corbin § 501. See Restatement, Second, Contracts § 131, particularly Comment h and the reporter's notes to Comments a & h.

ty.[99] A leading case which illustrates this rule is Marks v. Cowdin.[1] In 1911 the plaintiff was employed under a written contract for two years as "sales manager". When this period expired the parties made an oral agreement for further employment. The memorandum, signed some time later read: "It is understood . . . that the arrangements made for employment of L. Marks in our business on January 1, 1913 for a period of three years from that date at a salary of $15,000 per year plus 5 percent of the gross profits earned in our business which we agree shall not be less than $5,000 per year—continues in force until Jan. 1, 1916."

It is apparent that the memorandum did not state the nature of the employment to be performed by Marks, the plaintiff. The court held that the memorandum was sufficient to permit the plaintiff to show that he had been employed as a "sales manager" and that the employment had been continued. The court stated that "the statute must not be pressed to the extreme of a literal and rigid logic * * *. The memorandum which it requires, like any other memorandum, must be read in the light of reason." In addition the nature of the employment was stated in a notice sent during the first period of employment to salesmen describing him as "sales-manager".[2]

WESTLAW REFERENCES
memorandum /s identi** /2 party
185k107(2)
185k113(2)
185k106(1)
185k115(1)
di(memorandum /s "subject matter" /p contract)
di(memorandum /s "essential term" /p contract)
marks +3 cowdin

---

§ 19–30. The Form of the Memorandum and When It Is to Be Prepared—Necessity for Delivery

(a) Writing

The memorandum that satisfies the Statute may be in any written form.[3] It may be a receipt[4] or a telegram[5] or an exchange of correspondence[6] or the record books of a business,[7] or a check,[8] or a letter

---

99. Restatement, Contracts § 207; Restatement, Second, Contracts § 131, Comment g. See Morris Cohon & Co. v. Russell, 23 N.Y.2d 569, 297 N.Y.S.2d 947, 245 N.E.2d 712 (1969); Pick v. Bartel, 659 S.W.2d 636 (Tex.1983).

1. 226 N.Y. 138, 123 N.E. 139 (1919).

2. Accord, Lloyd v. Grynberg, 464 F.2d 622 (10th Cir.1972); Jennings v. Ruidoso Racing Ass'n, 79 N.M. 144, 441 P.2d 42 (1968).

3. Restatement, Second, Contracts § 131, Comment d.

4. Goetz v. Hubbell, 66 N.D. 491, 266 N.W. 836 (1936).

5. Brewer v. Horst & Lachmund Co., 127 Cal. 643, 60 P. 418 (1900).

6. United States v. New York, 131 F.2d 909 (2d Cir.1942), cert. denied 318 U.S. 781, 63 S.Ct. 858, 87 L.Ed. 1149 (1943); Aragon

7.–8. See notes 7 and 8 on page 821.

which acknowledges the contract and repudiates it,[9] or even a suicide note.[10] It may be in the form of a written statement addressed to a stranger to the contract,[11] or a last will and testament.[12] For the memorandum to be sufficient it must "amount to acknowledgment by the party to be charged that he has assented to the contract that is asserted by the other party."[13]

The memorandum need not be prepared with the purpose of satisfying the Statute,[14] nor at the same time that the contract is made; but, according to the first Restatement, it must be made before the suit is instituted.[15] It is also generally agreed that the memorandum need not be delivered.[16] Of course a deed must be delivered to be effective as a deed but there is no such requirement for it to be effective as a memorandum. It is also clear that the memorandum need not be in existence at the time of suit; it is sufficient that it existed at one time.[17]

(b) Recordings and Oral Stipulations

Whether a tape recording of a conversation in which an oral contract is made can be deemed a writing has not received a uniform response.[18] It seems to be well settled that an oral stipulation made in open court satisfies the Statute of Frauds even though the record is not signed by the party to be charged.[19]

(c) Admissions

As we have seen, an admission in pleadings or in court satisfies the sale of goods writing requirements even if the admission is compelled

v. Boyd, 80 N.M. 14, 450 P.2d 614 (1969) (correspondence subsequent to oral agreement).

7. Al-Sco Realty Co. v. Suburban Apt. Corp., 138 N.J.Eq. 497, 48 A.2d 838 (1946), affirmed 141 N.J.Eq. 40, 55 A.2d 296 (1947).

8. See Annot., 9 A.L.R.4th 1009 (1981).

9. See Restatement, Contracts § 209; Restatement, Second, Contracts § 133 and Comment c; Schmoll Fils & Co. v. Wheeler, 242 Mass. 464, 136 N.E. 164 (1922); Webb v. Woods, 176 Okl. 306, 55 P.2d 959 (1936).

10. In the Matter of Doran, 96 Misc.2d 846, 410 N.Y.S.2d 44 (1978).

11. Morris Cohon & Co. v. Russell, 23 N.Y.2d 569, 297 N.Y.S.2d 947, 245 N.E.2d 712 (1969); Bunbury v. Krauss, 41 Wis.2d 522, 164 N.W.2d 473 (1969).

12. See Annot., 94 A.L.R.2d 921 (1964).

13. 2 Corbin § 517. See § 19–29 supra and § 19–33 infra.

14. Annot., 85 A.L.R. 1184, 1215 (1933); see Restatement, Second, Contracts § 133 which makes an exception in the case of a contract in consideration of marriage.

15. Restatement, Contracts §§ 214, 215; accord, Watson v. McCabe, 527 F.2d 286 (6th Cir.1975); The Restatement Second omits § 215 of the original Restatement "as procedural, and as contrary to the spirit of modern procedural reforms" (§ 136 Reporter's Note).

16. Drury v. Young, 58 Md. 546 (1882); Restatement, Second, Contracts § 133, Comment b; see Kludt v. Connett, 350 Mo. 793, 168 S.W.2d 1068, 145 A.L.R. 1014 (1943). Contra, Main v. Pratt, 276 Ill. 218, 114 N.E. 576 (1916).

17. Hiss v. Hiss, 228 Ill. 414, 81 N.E. 1056 (1907); 2 Corbin § 529; Restatement, Second, Contracts § 137.

18. Ellis Canning v. Bernstein, 348 F.Supp. 1212 (D.Colo.1972) (yes); Sonders v. Roosevelt, 64 N.Y.2d 869, 487 N.Y.S.2d 551, 476 N.E.2d 996 (1985) (no); see Misner, Tape Recordings, Business Transactions Via Telephone, and the Statute of Frauds, 61 Iowa L.Rev. 941 (1976).

19. Szymkowski v. Szymkowski, 104 Ill. App.3d 630, 60 Ill.Dec. 310, 432 N.E.2d 1209 (1982); Fuchs v. Fuchs, 65 A.D.2d 595, 409 N.Y.S.2d 414 (2d Dep't 1978).

by cross-examination.[20] Of late a number of courts have applied the same rule to other provisions of the Statute of Frauds.[21]

(d) Usage, Course of Dealing and Course of Performance

A number of cases have confronted the question of whether a trade usage, a course of dealing or a course of performance can override the writing requirements of the Statute of Frauds.[22] As an abstract proposition the Statute of Frauds cannot be waived by an actual or imputed agreement,[23] however, a consistent usage or course of dealing can be the basis of an estoppel [24] and a course of performance may modify a contract.[25]

WESTLAW REFERENCES

(a) *Writing*

di(check /s "statute of fraud") & sy("statute of fraud")

find 410 nys2d 44

185k113(2)

(b) *Recordings and Oral Stipulations*

find 348 f.supp. 1212

(c) *Admissions*

find 768 f2d 217

§ 19–31. Signed by the Party to Be Charged

The term "signature" includes any memorandum, mark or sign, written, printed, stamped, photographed, engraved, or otherwise placed upon any instrument or writing with intent to execute or authenticate such instrument or writing.[26] The important thing is that the instrument be authenticated by the party to be charged.[27] Authentication

20. See § 19–16(f) supra.

21. Strotzel v. Continental Textile Corp., 768 F.2d 217 (8th Cir.1985); Anchorage-Hynning & Co. v. Moringiello, 697 F.2d 356 (D.C.Cir.1983); Wolf v. Crosby, 377 A.2d 22 (Del.Ch.1977) (real property); Adams-Riker, Inc. v. Nightingale, 119 R.I. 862, 383 A.2d 1042 (1978). The traditional and contrary view is expressed in Pierce v. Gaddy, 42 N.C.App. 622, 257 S.E.2d 459 (1979), cert. denied 298 N.C. 569, 261 S.E.2d 124 (1979); see also Haskins v. Loeb Rhoades & Co., 76 A.D.2d 751, 429 N.Y.S.2d 874 (1st Dep't 1980) (dissenting opinions), affirmed 52 N.Y.2d 523, 438 N.Y.S.2d 989, 421 N.E.2d 109 (1981); See Sheed, Statute of Frauds: Judicial Admission Exception—Where has it Gone? Is It Coming Back?, 6 Whittier L.Rev. 1 (1984); see also Note, 67 Iowa L.Rev. 551 (1982) as to an exceptional statute in Iowa.

22. Wholesale Materials Co., Inc. v. Magna Corp., 357 So.2d 296 (Miss.1978),

cert. denied 439 U.S. 864, 99 S.Ct. 188, 439 L.Ed.2d 174 (1978) (course of dealing); Farmers Coop. Ass'n of Church's Ferry v. Cole, 239 N.W.2d 808 (N.D.1976) (usage).

23. See U.C.C. § 1–205, Comment 4.

24. Northwest Potato Sales, Inc. v. Beck, ___ Mont. ___, 678 P.2d 1138 (1984); H.B. Alexander & Son, Inc. v. Miracle Recreation Equipment Co., 314 Pa.Super. 1, 460 A.2d 343 (1983).

25. Farmers Elevator Co. v. Anderson, 170 Mont. 175, 552 P.2d 63 (1976).

26. See McKinney's N.Y. Gen.Constr. Law § 46 which restates the common law. 2 Corbin § 522; Restatement, Second, Contracts § 134 and Comment a; U.C.C. § 1–201(39); Hillstrom v. Gosnay, 188 Mont. 388, 614 P.2d 466 (1980) (typewritten signature on telegram); Hansen v. Hill, 215 Neb. 573, 340 N.W.2d 8 (1983) (same).

27. Scheck v. Francis, 26 N.Y.2d 466, 311 N.Y.S.2d 841, 260 N.E.2d 493 (1970).

means that the signer assents to and adopts the writing as his own.[28] If the name is inscribed at the end, that constitutes prima facie evidence of authentication. "If the name is inscribed elsewhere * * * the contrary presumption may arise, making other evidence requisite to convince the court that the inscribed name was intended to be a signature."[29] Some states, as to some or all provisions of the Statute of Frauds, have imposed the requirement that the writing be "subscribed" rather than "signed". Some courts have held that because of this language the writing must be signed at the end.[30] Others, however, have held that "subscribed" and "signed" are basically synonymous.[31]

The memorandum need not be signed by both parties, it need only be signed by the party to be charged.[32] The party to be charged is ordinarily the defendant, but in case of a counterclaim it is the plaintiff.[33] Since the memorandum need be signed only by the party to be charged it is apparent that there will be situations where the contract is enforceable against one party and not the other as, for example, where one party sends a signed written offer and the other party orally accepts.[34] Some statutes do not use the phrase signed "by the party to be charged" but rather use the phrase "signed by the vendor or lessor". Under such statutes it would appear that the vendee's promise could be enforced without a memorandum;[35] but some courts have held that the vendor must introduce a memorandum signed by him and delivered to the purchaser or otherwise accepted by the purchaser as a correct memorandum.[36]

The original Statute of Frauds expressly provided that a memorandum is sufficient if signed by an authorized agent of the party to be charged. Generally the American statutes have expressly or implicitly continued this rule.[37] By the great weight of authority, the agent's power to sign a written instrument need not be vested in him by a written instrument.[38] Thus an oral grant of authority is sufficient. A

---

28. Restatement, Second, Contracts § 134.

29. 2 Corbin § 521.

30. 300 West End Ave. Corp. v. Warner, 250 N.Y. 221, 165 N.E. 271 (1929); see R.C. Durr Co. v. Bennett Indus., Inc., 590 S.W.2d 338 (Ky.App.1979).

31. California Canneries Co. v. Scatena, 117 Cal. 447, 49 P. 462 (1897); Butler v. Lovoll, 96 Nev. 931, 620 P.2d 1251 (1980); see 2 Corbin § 521.

32. Ullsperger v. Meyer, 217 Ill. 262, 75 N.E. 482 (1905); but see Hemingway v. Gruener, 106 Idaho 422, 679 P.2d 1140 (1984).

33. Restatement, Second, Contracts § 135, Comment a.

34. Hagan v. Jockers, 138 Ga.App. 847, 228 S.E.2d 10 (1976); Tymon v. Linoki, 16 N.Y.2d 293, 266 N.Y.S.2d 357, 213 N.E.2d 661 (1965); Kitchen v. Stockman Nat'l Life Ins. Co., 192 N.W.2d 796 (Iowa 1971).

35. Western Land Ass'n v. Banks, 80 Minn. 317, 83 N.W. 192 (1900); see Annot., 46 A.L.R.3d 619 (1972) (leases).

36. Schwinn v. Griffith, 303 N.W.2d 258 (Minn.1981); Geraci v. Jenrette, 41 N.Y.2d 660, 394 N.Y.S.2d 853, 363 N.E.2d 559 (1977). Restatement, Second, Contracts § 133, Comment b.

37. Restatement, Second, Contracts § 135, Comment b; Vickers v. North American Land Dev., 94 N.M. 65, 607 P.2d 603 (1980).

38. See 2 Corbin § 526; Seavey, Agency § 19F (1964); but see Cincinnati Ins. Co. v. Talladega, 342 So.2d 331 (Ala.1977). The problem of the relationship between rules governing agents for undisclosed principals, the Statute of Frauds and the parol evidence rule are not considered in this

number of states, however, have by statute provided that if the contract is within the Statute of Frauds, the agent's authority must be evidenced by a writing.[39] Often, however, this requirement is limited to the real property Statute of Frauds.[40]

WESTLAW REFERENCES

find 614 p2d 466

185k103(1) /p sign** signature
185k115(2) /p sign** signature
185k115(3) 185k115(4) 95k35 /p "statute of fraud"
185k113(2) & sy("statute of fraud")

§ 19–32. The Memorandum in Auction Sales

If goods having a price of $500 or more, or real property, are sold at auction, the Statute of Frauds must be satisfied. It is well established that the auctioneer is authorized to sign a memorandum of sale on behalf of both parties.[41] This authority is limited and expires soon after the sale has been made.[42] According to some authorities, the buyer or seller has the power to terminate the auctioneer's authority to sign a memorandum on his behalf between the time of the fall of the hammer and the signing of the memorandum.[43] The Restatement, however, regards the auctioneer's authority as irrevocable.[44]

If the auctioneer is himself the seller, he cannot satisfy the Statute of Frauds by signing on the purchaser's behalf.[45] His clerk, however, can satisfy the statute by signing on behalf of the buyer.[46] The memorandum must meet the requisites of a sufficient writing.[47]

WESTLAW REFERENCES

auction /s "statute of frauds"

---

book. On the subject, see Dodge v. Blood, 299 Mich. 364, 300 N.W. 121, 138 A.L.R. 322 (1941), noted in 42 Colum.L.Rev. 475 (1942) and 40 Mich.L.Rev. 900 (1942); cf. Jaynes v. Petoskey, 309 Mich. 32, 14 N.W.2d 566 (1944).

39. See 2 Corbin § 526.

40. E.g., McKinney's N.Y.Gen.Oblig. Law § 5–703; see Commission on Ecumenical Mission v. Roger Gray, Ltd., 27 N.Y.2d 457, 318 N.Y.S.2d 726, 267 N.E.2d 467 (1971); Ripple v. Pittsburgh Outdoor Adv. Corp., 280 Pa.Super. 121, 421 A.2d 435 (1980).

41. Schwinn v. Griffith, 303 N.W.2d 258 (Minn.1981); Restatement, Second, Contracts § 135, Comment b; Restatement, Second, Agency § 30, Comment f; 4 Williston § 588; Note, 9 U.W.Austl.L.Rev. 70 (1969).

42. The cases quoted in 4 Williston § 588 speak in terms of signing "immediately" after the sale. The Restatement, Second, Agency § 30, Comment f, speaks of "a reasonable time during the day of the sale." Cf. 2 Corbin § 525 (reasonable time).

43. 4 Williston § 588 and cases therein cited. Restatement, Contracts § 212(2) was in accord.

44. Restatement, Second, Agency § 30, Comment f.

45. Restatement, Second, Agency § 24 and Comment b; 4 Williston § 588. The rule is acknowledged but criticized in 2 Corbin § 525.

46. Romani v. Harris, 255 Md. 389, 258 A.2d 187 (1969).

47. Del Rio Land, Inc. v. Haumont, 118 Ariz. 1, 574 P.2d 469 (1977).

§ 19–33. Problems Presented When the Memorandum Is Contained in More Than One Writing

If there is more than one writing and all of the writings are signed by the party to be charged and it is clear by their contents that they relate to the same transaction, no problems other than those previously discussed are present.[48]

But if the party to be charged has signed only one of the documents comprising the memorandum, the matter becomes a little more complicated. Two issues are present—the connection between the documents and the existence of assent to the unsigned document. When the unsigned document is physically attached to the signed document at the time it is signed, the Statute is satisfied.[49] This is also true when the signed document by its terms expressly refers to the unsigned document.[50]

However the cases are in conflict where the signed document is not attached to or does not expressly refer to the unsigned papers. One view is that in such a situation the unsigned document is not sufficiently authenticated.[51] The other and better view is that even if the signed document does not expressly refer to the unsigned document or is not attached, it is still sufficient if the documents by internal evidence refer to the same subject matter or transaction; and in that event extrinsic evidence is admissible to help show the connection between the documents and the assent of the party to be charged.[52]

Even under this view it is necessary that the signed document evidence a contractual relationship. Thus, a signed cover letter transmitting an unsigned proposed contract is not a sufficient basis for treating the unsigned document as a sufficient memorandum.[53]

---

48. Jennings v. Ruidoso Racing Ass'n, 79 N.M. 144, 441 P.2d 42 (1968); Central Power & Light Co. v. Del Mar Conservation Dist., 594 S.W.2d 782 (Tex.Civ.App.1980).

49. Tallman v. Franklin, 14 N.Y. (4 Kern) 584 (1856).

50. Leach v. Crucible Center Co., 388 F.2d 176 (1st Cir.1968); Tampa Shipbldg. & Eng'r Co. v. General Constr. Co., 43 F.2d 309, 85 A.L.R. 1178 (5th Cir.1930).

51. Ezzell v. S.G. Holland Stave Co., 210 Ala. 694, 99 So. 78 (1924); Young v. McQuerrey, 54 Hawaii 433, 508 P.2d 1051 (1973); Hoffman v. S V Co., Inc., 102 Idaho 187, 628 P.2d 218 (1981), noted in 18 Idaho L.Rev. 133 (1982); Owen v. Hendricks, 433 S.W.2d 164, 30 A.L.R.3d 929 (Tex.1968).

52. Crabtree v. Elizabeth Arden Sales Corp., 305 N.Y. 48, 110 N.E.2d 551 (1953); Greenberg v. Bailey, 14 N.C.App. 34, 187 S.E.2d 505 (1972); Restatement, Second, Contracts § 132, Comments a, b, and c. Unsigned memoranda prepared by the plaintiff do not ordinarily bind the defendant. Karlin v. Avis, 457 F.2d 57 (2d Cir. 1972), cert. denied 406 U.S. 849, 93 S.Ct. 56, 34 L.Ed.2d 90 (1972). But see § 19–34 infra. See also Intercontinental Planning Ltd. v. Daystrom Inc., 24 N.Y.2d 372, 300 N.Y.S.2d 817, 248 N.E.2d 576, 47 A.L.R.3d 125 (1969), reargument denied 25 N.Y.2d 959, 305 N.Y.S.2d 1027, 252 N.E.2d 864 (1969); Morris Cohon & Co. v. Russell, 23 N.Y.2d 569, 245 N.E.2d 712, 297 N.Y.S.2d 947 (1969). At times a writing which is subsequent to the signed writing may be considered part of the memorandum. Restatement, Second, Contracts § 132, Comment d.

53. Scheck v. Francis, 26 N.Y.2d 466, 311 N.Y.S.2d 841, 260 N.E.2d 493 (1970); cf. Pirilla v. Bonucci, 320 Pa.Super. 496, 467 A.2d 821 (1983) (minutes and letter of intent); Tiverton Estates Ltd. v. Wearwell Ltd., [1974] 1 All E.R. 209, noted in [1974] Cambridge L.J. 42 and 37 Mod.L.Rev. 695 (1974). See § 19–29, supra at n. 95.

§ 19–34. The Memorandum Under U.C.C. § 2–201—The Sale of Goods Section

Section 2–201 of the Uniform Commercial Code introduces several innovations with respect to the contents of the memorandum and the necessity of a writing signed by the party to be charged. Only three definite and invariable requirements as to the memorandum are made by this subsection. First, it must evidence a contract for the sale of goods; second, it must be "signed", a word which includes any authentication which identifies the party to be charged;[54] and third, it must specify a quantity.[55]

This represents a significant relaxation of the writing requirement.[56] According to Comment 1 to U.C.C. § 2–201, all that is required is that "there is some writing sufficient to indicate that a contract for sale has been made". Thus, it is not necessary that all essential terms be included. "It need not indicate which party is the buyer and which the seller * * *. The price, time and place of payment or delivery, the general quality of the goods, or all particular warranties may be omitted * * *. Of course if the 'price' consists of goods rather than money the quantity of goods must be stated."[57]

We have already seen that as a general rule it may be shown that the oral agreement contained terms not set forth in the memorandum, with the result that the memorandum is insufficient under the Statute of Frauds unless a court of equity would grant reformation based upon mistake.[58] Under the Code if the memorandum is in error as to any term, other than the quantity term, extrinsic evidence is admissible to correct the error.[59] The Statute explicitly states: "A writing is not insufficient because it omits or incorrectly states a term agreed upon but the contract is not enforceable under this paragraph beyond the quantity of goods shown in such writing." If the quantity term is not accurately stated, recovery is limited to the amount stated, presumably unless the other party is able to get reformation.

54. Southwest Eng'r Co. v. Martin Tractor Co., 205 Kan. 684, 473 P.2d 18 (1970); U.C.C. § 1–201(39).

55. See Southwest Eng'r Co. v. Martin Tractor Co., 205 Kan. 684, 473 P.2d 18 (1970); see White & Summers, Uniform Commercial Code § 2–4 (2d ed. 1980).

56. See generally Comment, 4 U.S.F.L. Rev. 177 (1969).

57. U.C.C. § 2–201, Comment 1; Derden v. Morris, 247 So.2d 838 (Miss. 1971); Harry Rubin & Sons, Inc. v. Consolidated Pipe Co., 396 Pa. 506, 153 A.2d 472 (1959); Julian C. Cohen Salvage Corp. v. Eastern Elec. Sales Co., 205 Pa.Super. 26, 206 A.2d 331 (1965). However, a notation on a check stating: "tentative deposit on tentative purchase," is not a sufficient writing as it shows a lack of commitment to the purchase. Arcuri v. Weiss, 198 Pa. Super. 506, 184 A.2d 24 (1962). See, Restatement, Second, Contracts § 131, Comment b; § 19–29 n. 41 supra.

58. See § 19–27 n. 81. and § 19–28 supra; 2 Corbin § 288.

59. 2 Corbin § 531.

The Code's insistence that the memorandum contain a quantity term creates difficulties in contracts containing open quantity terms, such as requirement or output contracts, distributorships and the like. The Code's substantive provisions encourage flexibility rather than rigidity.[60] It would be unfortunate if a rigid application of the quantity requirement of the Statute of Frauds were to subvert the substance of the Code.[61]

When merchants [62] have concluded an oral contract it is quite common for one to send to the other a letter of confirmation, or perhaps a printed form of contract. Naturally, this confirmation will serve as a memorandum and will be signed only by the party who sent it, thus leaving one party at the mercy of the other. The Code remedies this situation by providing: "Between merchants if within a reasonable time a writing in confirmation of the contract and sufficient against the sender is received and the party receiving it has reason to know its contents, it satisfies the requirement of subsection (1) against such party unless written notice of objection to its contents is given within [ten] days after it is received." [63] This means that under the circumstances provided for in the Code, the receiver of the memorandum is in the equivalent position of having signed the writing so that it may be enforced against him. However the party alleging the contract still has the burden of proving the oral agreement that the memorandum purports to confirm.[64]

Finally this section of the Code provides that the agreement is enforceable despite the absence of a memorandum "if the party against whom enforcement is sought admits in his pleading, testimony or otherwise in court that a contract for sale was made, but the contract is not enforceable under this provision beyond the quantity of goods admitted." [65]

60. E.g., U.C.C. § 2–204 discussed in § 2–9 supra.

61. Rigid cases include Cox Caulking & Insulating Co. v. Brockett Distributing Co., 150 Ga.App. 424, 258 S.E.2d 51 (1979) ("2.62 per bag for the above project," not a sufficient indication of quantity term); Ace Concrete Products Co. v. Charles J. Rogers Constr. Co., 69 Mich.App. 610, 245 N.W.2d 353 (1976). Flexibility is shown in Riegel Fiber Corp. v. Anderson Gin Co., 512 F.2d 784 (5th Cir.1975). For thorough analysis, see Bruckel, The Weed and The Web: Section 2–201's Corruption of the U.C.C.'s Substantive Provisions—The Quantity Problem, 1983 U.Ill.L.Rev. 811.

62. Merchant is defined in § 1–7 supra.

63. U.C.C. § 2–201(2). On the question of what constitutes a notice of objection, see Simmons Oil Corp. v. Bulk Sales Corp., 498 F.Supp. 457 (D.N.J.1980).

64. I.S. Joseph Co., Inc. v. Citrus Feed Co., 490 F.2d 185 (5th Cir.1974), rehearing denied 492 F.2d 1242 (5th Cir.1974); Perdue Farms, Inc. v. Motts, Inc., 459 F.Supp. 7 (N.D.Miss.1978) (thorough discussion); Azevedo v. Minister, 86 Nev. 576, 471 P.2d 661 (1970); but see Shpilberg v. Merrill Lynch, Pierce, Fenner & Smith, 535 S.W.2d 227 (Ky.1976) (confirmation treated as a total integration); contra, Matter of Marlene Indus., 45 N.Y.2d 327, 408 N.Y.S.2d 410, 380 N.E.2d 239 (1978).

65. This matter has already been discussed in § 19–16(f) supra.

WESTLAW REFERENCES

writing memorandum /s u.c.c. "uniform commercial code" /s 1–201

writing memorandum /s u.c.c. "uniform commercial code" /s 2–201

§ 19–35. Is the Oral Contract Which Does Not Comply With the Statute "Unenforceable" or "Void"?

The many Statutes of Frauds which have been adopted have not been uniform in describing the effect of non-compliance with the Statute. The fourth section of the English Statute says "no action shall be brought," the seventeenth section says "no action shall be allowed to be good." The Uniform Commercial Code states that the oral contract "is not enforceable by way of action or defense." [66] Some statutes say that the oral contract is "void" [67] and at least one statute talks in terms of admissibility of evidence.[68]

Partly as a result of the difference in wording above and partly as a result of judicial interpretation the effect of non-compliance has not always been deemed to be the same.[69] Despite the differences in wording, the tendency of the decisions is to avoid literal construction of the Statute. The majority view is to treat the oral contract as unenforceable rather than void, even when the Statute uses the term "void." [70] The vast majority of the cases which have held that the Statute merely makes the contract unenforceable hold that the oral contract is operative for a wide variety of purposes.[71] However, the courts which say that the oral contract is void or that the oral contract is not admissible have held that the oral contract is inoperative at least for some of these purposes.[72]

This difference probably can be best understood in the light of a few illustrations. We have already seen that under the majority view if the memorandum is signed by only one party it is enforceable against him.[73] However under the minority view since the return promise of the unsigned party is not sufficient consideration, being void, the entire contract is unenforceable under the doctrine of mutuality.[74]

---

66. U.C.C. § 2–201(1).

67. E.g., McKinney's N.Y.Gen.Oblig. Law § 5–701. But see n. 72 infra.

68. Iowa Code Ann., § 622.32 (West 1950).

69. See Note, Statute of Frauds: Evaluation of Underlying Theories, 14 Cornell L.Q. 102 (1928).

70. Borchardt v. Kulick, 234 Minn. 308, 48 N.W.2d 318 (1951); Crane v. Powell, 139 N.Y. 379, 34 N.E. 911 (1893).

71. 2 Corbin § 279 lists ten purposes for which the oral contract is effective under this view. See also, U.C.C. § 2–201, Comment 4; Daughtery v. Kessler, 264 Md.

281, 286 A.2d 95 (1972). Under Pennsylvania law the Statute of Frauds applies only to an action for specific performance and not to a suit for damages for breach of oral contract respecting real estate. Polka v. May, 383 Pa. 80, 118 A.2d 154 (1955). On the distinction between void, voidable and unenforceable see § 1–12 supra.

72. 2 Corbin §§ 284, 288.

73. See § 19–31 supra.

74. Wilkinson v. Heavenrich, 58 Mich. 574, 26 N.W. 139 (1886); Burg v. Betty Gay Inc., 423 Pa. 485, 225 A.2d 85 (1966), noted in 71 Dick.L.Rev. 494 (1967).

Again under the majority view the Statute of Frauds must be pleaded as an affirmative defense.[75] However under the minority view since the oral agreement is no contract at all, this may be shown under a general denial,[76] or, if no writing is pleaded, a motion to dismiss for failure to state a cause of action.[77] But even here it cannot be raised for the first time upon appeal.[78]

Again where the contract has been fully performed on both sides it is unanimously agreed that the Statute has no effect, thus indicating that the oral agreement is not void.[79] So also the general rule is that the Statute of Frauds is personal to the party to the contract and those in privity with him, and so a third party may not assert its invalidity, thus indicating that the oral agreement is not void.[80] However, the opposite result has been reached where the Statute was deemed to make the contract void.[81]

Finally, the oral contract is shown to be unenforceable by the rule, previously referred to, that the memorandum may be made at a time other than the time of contracting.[82] However, if the oral contract was "void" the writing would have to come into existence at the same time as the agreement or at least while both parties were still in agreement.[83]

 WESTLAW REFERENCES

"oral contract" /s u.c.c. "uniform commercial code" 2–201

find 48 nw2d 318

185k125(3)

§ 19–36. Effect of Part of a Contract Being Unenforceable Because of the Statute

Where one or more of the promises in a contract are within the Statute and others are not, the general rule is that no part of the contract is enforceable.[84] Any other approach would appear to be

75. Gentile Bros. v. Rowena Homes Inc., 352 Mass. 584, 227 N.E.2d 338 (1967); Raoul v. Olde Village Hall, Inc., 76 A.D.2d 319, 430 N.Y.S.2d 214 (2d Dep't 1980).

76. Jones v. Pettigrew, 25 S.D. 432, 127 N.W. 538 (1910).

77. Leonard v. Martling, 378 Pa. 339, 106 A.2d 585 (1954).

78. Iverson v. Cirkel, 56 Minn. 299, 57 N.W. 800 (1894).

79. E.g., Blackwell v. Blackwell, 196 Mass. 186, 81 N.E. 910 (1907); Restatement, Second, Contracts § 145.

80. Friedman v. Jackson, 266 Cal.App. 2d 517, 72 Cal.Rptr. 129 (1968) (tortious interference with contractual relation); B.D.S., Inc. v. Gillis, 477 A.2d 1121 (D.C.1984); Pasquay v. Pasquay, 235 Ill. 48, 85 N.E. 316 (1908); Blue Valley Turf

Farms, Inc. v. Realestate Marketing and Development, Inc., 424 N.E.2d 1088 (Ind. App.1981); Amsinck v. American Ins. Co., 129 Mass. 185 (1880); Clements v. Withers, 437 S.W.2d 818 (Tex.1969), noted in 21 Baylor L.Rev. 402 (1969); Restatement, Second, Contracts § 144. A party in privity, such as a subsequent contract vendee of real property may invoke the Statute. O'Banion v. Paradiso, 61 Cal.2d 559, 39 Cal.Rptr. 370, 393 P.2d 682 (1964), noted in 5 Santa Clara L.Rev. 87 (1964).

81. Gerndt v. Conradt, 117 Wis. 15, 93 N.W. 804 (1903).

82. See § 19–30 supra.

83. Wilkinson v. Heavenrich, 58 Mich. 574, 26 N.W. 139 (1886).

84. Blanchard v. Calderwood, 110 N.H. 29, 260 A.2d 118 (1969); Restatement, Sec-

unfair. There is, of course, predictable difficulty in determining whether the proffered testimony relates to a part of the contract or a separate contract.[85] A large number of cases have applied the same rule even though the contract might be considered divisible.[86] But there are cases to the contrary which hold that if the contract is divisible and the part which is not within the Statute is performed, the corresponding promise may be enforced.[87] Moreover, there are cases holding that substantial performance takes the contract outside of the Statute.[88]

There are exceptions to the general rule stated above. The first is where all of the promises which are within the Statute have been performed, then all of the other promises become enforceable.[89] The second exception occurs where the party who is to receive the performance under the only promise or promises within the Statute agrees to abandon that part of the performance.[90]

It should also be recalled that under some of the sections of the Statute of Frauds full performance or even part performance may make the contract enforceable.

However, where a promisor makes a promise of alternative performances, one of which is within the Statute and the other without, it is generally held that the promisee may enforce the promise which is without the Statute.[91]

 WESTLAW REFERENCES
find 260 a2d 118
185k75
185k125(2)

---

§ 19–37. Oral Rescission or Modification of a Contract Within the Statute

We have seen that as a general rule a written contract may be rescinded or modified orally and that the only question which is usually

ond, Contracts § 147(3). Contra, White Lighting Co. v. Wolfson, 68 Cal.2d 336, 66 Cal.Rptr. 697, 438 P.2d 345 (1968).

85. Compare Austin v. Montgomery, 336 So.2d 745 (Miss.1976) with Kristinus v. H. Stern Com. E. Ind., S.A., 466 F.Supp. 903 (S.D.N.Y.1979).

86. Hornady v. Plaza Realty Co., Inc., 437 So.2d 591 (Ala.Civ.App.1983); Hurley v. Donovan, 182 Mass. 64, 64 N.E. 685 (1902).

87. Vanston v. Connecticut Gen'l Life Ins. Co., 482 F.2d 337 (5th Cir.1973); Blue Valley Creamery Co., v. Consolidated Prods. Co., 81 F.2d 182 (8th Cir.1936); Belleville Lumber & Supply Co. v. Chamberlain, 120 Ind.App. 12, 84 N.E.2d 60 (1949); 3 Williston § 532 at 766.

88. Vada Corp. v. Harrell, 156 Ga.App. 137, 273 S.E.2d 877 (1980).

89. Restatement, Second, Contracts § 147(2).

90. Restatement, Contracts § 221. Restatement, Second, Contracts § 147(1) states that the exception "does not apply to a contract to transfer property on the promisor's death."

91. Chandler v. Doran Co., 44 Wn.2d 396, 267 P.2d 907 (1954). Other cases are collected in 13 A.L.R. 267 (1921). But see § 19–21 supra which states a different rule for the one year section of the Statute of Frauds that is in effect in some jurisdictions.

presented is one of consideration.[92]   Does the same rule apply when a contract is within the Statute of Frauds and is evidenced by a sufficient memorandum?   The majority rule is that a written executory contract within the Statute of Frauds may be rescinded orally,[93] thus inducing some contracting parties to draft clauses that purport to forbid oral rescissions.[94]

There are some cases which hold that when a contract is within the Statute of Frauds and is in writing, it may not be modified by an oral agreement.[95]   The better rule, however, is that if the new agreement is not within the Statute of Frauds it is not only enforceable without a writing but also serves to discharge the previous written agreement.[96] If the new agreement is within the Statute of Frauds and is unenforceable because it is oral, the former written contract remains enforceable,[97] unless the new agreement takes precedence under the doctrines of waiver and estoppel.[98]   But the waiver may be retracted by reasonable notice that strict performance will be required of any term waived, "unless the retraction would be unjust in view of a material change of position in reliance on the waiver." [99]

This last situation is illustrated by the case of Imperator Realty Co. v. Tull.[1]   There the parties agreed to exchange two pieces of real property.   The contract contained a provision that each seller would clear any violations.   The plaintiff alleged that prior to the time for performance the parties orally agreed that either party instead of clearing a violation could deposit with a third party a sum of money sufficient to clear the violation.   The plaintiff tendered performance under the oral modified agreement; the defendant refused to accept the

---

92.   See §§ 4–9, 5–14 supra.

93.   Annot., 42 A.L.R.3d 242 (1972); Fidelity & Deposit Co. v. Tom Murphy Constr. Co., Inc., 674 F.2d 880 (11th Cir.1982); Strychalski v. Mekus, 54 A.D.2d 1068, 388 N.Y.S.2d 969 (4th Dep't 1976); Investment Properties, Inc. v. Allen, 281 N.C. 174, 188 S.E.2d 441 (1972), vacated on other grounds 283 N.C. 277, 196 S.E.2d 262 (1973); Restatement, Second, Contracts § 148 which adds, "the Statute may, however, apply to a contract to rescind a transfer of property."   Holding to the contrary, that a contract within the Statute may not be rescinded orally.   Givens v. Dougherty, 671 S.W.2d 877 (Tex.1984); Strevell-Paterson Co., Inc. v. Francis, 646 P.2d 741 (Utah 1982).

94.   See § 5–14 supra.

95.   Bradley v. Harter, 156 Ind. 499, 60 N.E. 139 (1901).

96.   Norris, Beggs & Simpson v. Eastgate Theatres, Inc., 261 Or. 56, 491 P.2d 1018 (1971); ABC Outdoor Advertising, Inc. v. Dolhun's Marine, Inc., 38 Wis.2d 457, 157 N.W.2d 680 (1968); Restatement, Contracts § 222; 2 Corbin § 302; 4 Willis-

ton § 592.   As to land contracts, see Restatement, Second, Contracts § 149 and Comment a; Annot., 42 A.L.R.3d 242 (1972).

97.   Lieberman v. Templar Motor Co., 236 N.Y. 139, 140 N.E. 222, 29 A.L.R. 1089 (1923); accord, U.C.C. § 2–209(3).

98.   Van Iderstine Co. v. Barnet Leather Co., 242 N.Y. 425, 152 N.E. 250, 46 A.L.R. 858 (1926); accord, U.C.C. § 2–209(4); Restatement, Second, Contracts § 149(2). This means that the new agreement which contravenes the Statute of Frauds may still have effect under the doctrines of waiver and estoppel.   Cf. Finer v. Loeffler-Green Supply Co., 456 P.2d 534 (Okl.1969) (oral modification fully performed by vendor).

99.   U.C.C. § 2–209(5); Double-E Sportswear Corp. v. Girard Trust Bank, 488 F.2d 292 (3d Cir.1973), noted in 15 Wm. & Mary L.Rev. 699 (1974); see Eisler, Oral Modification of Sales Contracts Under the Uniform Commercial Code: The Statute of Frauds Problem, 58 Wash.U.L.Q. 277 (1980); Note, 21 Drake L.Rev. 593 (1982). See also §§ 19–47, 19–48 infra.

1.   228 N.Y. 447, 127 N.E. 263 (1920).

performance. The court held that although the defendant could have withdrawn his consent to the modification before a change of position by the plaintiff, he could not do so after the plaintiff changed his position.[2] Thus the court, under a theory of estoppel, in effect enforced the oral modified agreement which contravened the real property section of the Statute of Frauds. That is to say, the defendant was estopped from taking advantage of the fact that the plaintiff had not complied with the written agreement,[3] and the oral agreement was enforced despite the Statute of Frauds.

WESTLAW REFERENCES
find 674 f2d 880
95k238(2) /p oral /3 chang*** modif! rescission rescind
bradley +3 harter

§ 19–38. To What Extent May an Oral Contract Which is Not Enforceable Because of the Statute of Frauds Be Used as a Defense?

It is certainly the general rule that a contract which is not enforceable because of the Statute of Frauds may not be used "by way of action or defense."[4] This obviously means that the oral contract may not be used by way of counterclaim, set-off, or recoupment. It is also obvious that if the plaintiff is suing upon an oral contract and has a sufficient memorandum signed by the defendant alone, the defendant may still use any defense arising out of the terms and conditions of the contract.[5]

There are a number of exceptions to the rule, some of which are discussed in the sections which follow. One occurs when the plaintiff is suing in quasi contract but is in default, and the defendant is not in default and has never refused to sign a sufficient memorandum when requested by the plaintiff.[6] This matter is discussed in more detail in § 19–41 infra.

So also an agreement which is unenforceable because of the Statute of Frauds may operate to prevent a tort from occurring.[7] For example, if A has entered into possession under the provisions of an unenforce-

2. Restatement, Second, Contracts § 150. See § 11–31 supra and §§ 19–47, 19–48 infra. But see Callender v. Kalscheuer, 289 Minn. 532, 184 N.W.2d 811 (1971).

3. Accord, Johnston v. Holiday Inns, Inc., 565 F.2d 790 (1st Cir.1977); Ball v. Carlson, 641 P.2d 303 (Colo.App.1981); Thoe v. Rasmussen, 322 N.W.2d 775 (Minn. 1982); North v. Simonini, 142 Vt. 482, 457 A.2d 285 (1983).

4. U.C.C. § 2–201(1); Restatement, Contracts § 217.

5. Oxborough v. St. Martin, 169 Minn. 72, 210 N.W. 854, 49 A.L.R. 115 (1926); Restatement, Second, Contracts § 140.

6. Restatement, Contracts § 217(1)(b); Restatement, Second, Contracts § 138, Comments b and c. On the question of refusing to sign a memorandum see Restatement, Second, Contracts § 141, Comment b.

7. Restatement, Contracts § 217(1)(c); Restatement, Second, Contracts § 142.

able contract or lease, he is not a trespasser until he receives notice of repudiation from the vendor or lessor.[8]

WESTLAW REFERENCES

u.c.c. "uniform commercial code" /s 2–201 /p oral** /3
     contract /s defens! defend***

find 210 nw 284

---

§ 19–39. Some Miscellaneous Rules

The Statute of Frauds does not apply to formal contracts. Included in the concept "formal contracts" are contracts under seal, recognizances and negotiable instruments.[9] In the case of a contract that is within the Statute of Frauds an oral promise to execute a sufficient memorandum is not enforceable for the simple reason that, if it were, the very purpose of the Statute could be circumvented.[10]

It must also be noted that a contract may be within one or more sections of the Statute of Frauds and that ordinarily the various clauses of the Statute of Frauds are considered separately and the most restrictive is applied. However, where a land contract is specifically enforceable under the doctrine of part performance the other clauses of the Statute do not prevent enforcement.[11]

WESTLAW REFERENCES

"statute of fraud" /s seal

185k144 /p seal

III. RESTITUTIONARY REMEDIES

Table of Sections

8. Rosenstein v. Gottfried, 145 Minn. 243, 176 N.W. 844 (1920).

9. 2 Corbin § 280; see Owens v. Lombardi, 41 A.D.2d 438, 343 N.Y.S.2d 978 (4th Dep't 1973), appeal denied 33 N.Y.2d 515, 348 N.Y.S.2d 1026, 302 N.E.2d 554 (1973).

10. McKinnon v. Corporation of the President of the Church of Jesus Christ of Latter-Day Saints, 529 P.2d 434 (Utah 1974); 2 Corbin § 283; Restatement, Second, Contracts § 141, Comment b. However, the Restatement suggests that such a promise may be enforced under the doctrine of promissory estoppel. Restatement, Second, Contracts § 110, Comment d. See also Restatement, Contracts §§ 138, 141, Comment b, and § 19–48 infra.

11. Restatement, Second, Contracts § 129, Comment f. See § 19–15 supra.

§ 19–40. Introduction

It is neither illegal nor against public policy to enter into an oral agreement of the kind governed by the Statute of Frauds. A party who in whole or part performs under such an agreement is not an outlaw. On the contrary, it has been suggested that a defendant's attorney who automatically raises the defense of the Statute in any case in which it is applicable may be guilty of unethical conduct.[12] Thus, as we have seen, the courts have developed doctrines under which the oral agreement will be enforced if sufficient performance has been rendered on one side.[13] As indicated in the prior discussion, the circumstances under which performance will be a sufficient predicate for enforcement of the contract varies with respect to the particular subdivision of the Statute in question and from jurisdiction to jurisdiction.[14]

A plaintiff who has rendered some performance and has not defaulted may recover in quasi contract for the value of the benefits he conferred on the defendant,[15] other expenditures in reliance on the contract,[16] and in some instances he may have specific restitution.[17] The majority of such cases involve a performance which is not sufficient to bring into operation the rules which would permit enforcement of the contract. There is substantial authority to the effect that even in a case in which the plaintiff could secure enforcement of the contract on grounds of performance, he may elect a restitutionary remedy.[18] Restitutionary remedies include quasi-contractual relief in which the recovery is always and solely for a sum of money. Also included are equitable remedies in which specific restitution is granted, such as by cancellation of a conveyance or imposition of a constructive trust, and the legal remedy of replevin.

Apparently very few cases have considered the question of whether a third party beneficiary may recover in quasi contract for the value of the performance rendered by the promisee under an unenforceable contract. Recovery has been denied on the ground that the plaintiff had conferred no benefit on the defendant.[19] The same theory led a

12. Stevens, Ethics and the Statute of Frauds, 37 Cornell L.Q. 355 (1952).

13. See § 19–15 supra, as to real estate transactions; § 19–23 supra, as to the one year section; § 19–16 supra, as to contracts for the sale of goods.

14. Annot., 21 A.L.R.3d 9 (1968).

15. Cato Enterprises Inc. v. Fine, 149 Ind.App. 163, 271 N.E.2d 146 (1971); Hummel v. Hummel, 133 Ohio St. 520, 14 N.E.2d 923 (1938); Ricks v. Sumler, 179 Va. 571, 19 S.E.2d 889 (1942); Restatement, Second, Contracts § 375; 2 Corbin § 321; 3 Williston § 534.

16. See Perillo, Restitution in a Contractual Context, 73 Colum.L.Rev. 1208,

1221–22 (1973); Restatement, Second, Contracts § 139 is in accord but regards such recovery as analytically distinct from the restitutionary remedy of quasi contract. See Perillo, Restitution in the Second Restatement of Contracts, 81 Colum.L.Rev. 37 (1981); see § 19–44 infra.

17. 2 Corbin § 323, 3 Williston § 535; see § 19–46 infra.

18. Id.

19. Pickelsimer v. Pickelsimer, 257 N.C. 696, 127 S.E.2d 557 (1962), noted in 41 N.C.L.Rev. 890 (1963); but see Rowell v. Plymouth-Home Nat. Bank, 13 Mass.App. Ct. 1044, 434 N.E.2d 648 (1982) (dictum).

court to grant restitution to the promisee under an oral contract for the conveyance of land to a third person.[20]

WESTLAW REFERENCES
di restitution

§ 19–41. The Plaintiff Must Not Be in Default

According to the great weight of authority, a plaintiff who is entitled to restitution for his performance under an unenforceable contract must not be in default under the agreement,[21] which of course means that the defendant must have repudiated or otherwise materially breached the agreement.[22] It is obvious that proof of the oral agreement is admissible to establish the obligations of the parties, otherwise a breach could not be proved.

In a minority of jurisdictions, under the doctrine of Britton v. Turner,[23] a defaulting party may have quasi-contractual relief under an unenforceable contract. It logically follows that in such jurisdictions a defaulting party may have quasi-contractual relief under a contract unenforceable under the Statute of Frauds.[24] The same result has been reached in a number of other jurisdictions on the theory that if the decision were made to turn on which party was in default, the court would be indirectly enforcing the contract.[25]

WESTLAW REFERENCES
britton +3 turner
400k335 & sy(forfeit! default!)
343k391(9)

§ 19–42. Effect of Defendant's Restoration of the Status Quo

According to the Restatement,[26] if the defendant tenders restoration of specific property delivered to him pursuant to an unenforceable contract, the plaintiff's right to quasi-contractual relief is divested. This is on the theory that the defendant's obligation is primarily that of

---

20. Graham v. Graham, 134 App.Div. 777, 119 N.Y.S. 1013 (3d Dep't 1909). Cf. Restatement, Contracts § 356.

21. Betnar v. Rose, 259 Ark. 820, 536 S.W.2d 719 (1976); Watkins v. Wells, 303 Ky. 728, 198 S.W.2d 662, 169 A.L.R. 185 (1946); Bendix v. Ross, 205 Wis. 581, 238 N.W. 381 (1931); 2 Corbin §§ 332–34; 3 Williston § 538. See also Keener, Quasi Contracts 234–39 (1893); Woodward, Quasi Contracts § 98 (1913).

22. Restatement, Contracts § 355(4); accord, Restatement, Second, Contracts § 141 (but qualified by § 374).

23. 6 N.H. 481 (1834); see § 11–22 supra.

24. 3 Williston § 538; see Restatement, Second, Contracts § 374.

25. Freeman v. Foss, 145 Mass. 361, 14 N.E. 141 (1887); accord, Reedy v. Ebsen, 60 S.D. 1, 242 N.W. 592 (1932), on the additional ground that in South Dakota an oral contract within the Statute of Frauds is void rather than unenforceable. Contra, Rowell v. Plymouth-Home Nat. Bank, 13 Mass.App. 1044, 434 N.E.2d 648 (1982).

26. Restatement, Contracts § 355(2); accord, Restatement, Second, Contracts § 372(3).

making specific restitution.[27] There is a paucity of case authority on the point and the leading case is to the contrary.[28]

WESTLAW REFERENCES
hawley +3 moody

§ 19–43. Restitution Denied Where Policy of the Statute Would be Thwarted

According to the Restatement, "[t]he remedy of restitution is not available if the Statute that makes the contract unenforceable so provides, or if the purpose of the Statute would be nullified by granting such a remedy." [29] This exception to the general rule does not apply to the original Statute of Frauds nor to the reenactment of its basic provisions.[30] The exception seems to have been confined largely to statutes enacted in a number of jurisdictions requiring a promise to pay a commission for services as a real estate broker to be in writing. The courts in these jurisdictions have generally refused quasi-contractual recovery to the broker who alleges performance under an oral agreement.[31] Although no right to restitution exists, a subsequent promise to pay may be enforced under the moral obligation doctrine.[32]

WESTLAW REFERENCES
baugh +3 darley

§ 19–44. Measure of Recovery

In quasi contract cases it is usually stated that the plaintiff's recovery is the value of "benefits conferred" upon the defendant.[33] As discussed elsewhere in this book,[34] the concept of "benefit" is so flexible as to be misleading. Indeed, the weight of decided cases supports a rule to the effect that the measure of recovery is the injury incurred by the plaintiff in reliance on the contract.[35]

27. Keener, Quasi Contracts 285–89 (1893); 3 Williston § 535.

28. Hawley v. Moody, 24 Vt. 603 (1852); accord, 2 Corbin § 324.

29. Restatement, Contracts § 355(3).

30. 2 Corbin § 324.

31. Baugh v. Darley, 112 Utah 1, 184 P.2d 335 (1947); Hale v. Kreisel, 194 Wis. 271, 215 N.W. 227, 56 A.L.R. 780 (1927); accord, under a statute limited to certain business brokerage contracts, McKinney's N.Y.Gen.Oblig. Law § 5–701(10).

32. See § 5–9 supra.

33. See generally, Jeanblanc, Restitution Under the Statute of Frauds: Measurement of the Legal Benefit Unjustly Retained, 15 Mo.L.Rev. 1 (1950); Jean-

blanc, Restitution Under the Statute of Frauds: What Constitutes an Unjust Retention, 48 Mich.L.Rev. 923 (1950); Jeanblanc, Restitution Under the Statute of Frauds: What Constitutes a Legal Benefit, 26 Ind.L.J. 1 (1950).

34. See § 15–4 supra.

35. Trollope v. Koerner, 106 Ariz. 10, 470 P.2d 91, 64 A.L.R.3d 1180 (1970); Farash v. Sykes Datatronics, Inc., 59 N.Y.2d 500, 452 N.E.2d 1245, 465 N.Y.S.2d 917 (1983); 2 Williston § 536 at 830 n. 6 (collecting cases); Fuller and Perdue, The Reliance Interest in Contract Damages: 2, 46 Yale L.J. 373, 394 (1936); Perillo, Restitution in a Contractual Context, 73 Colum. L.Rev. 1208 (1973).

Typical of the cases which wrestle with the concept of benefit is Fabian v. Wasatch Orchard Co.[36] The plaintiff was employed as a salesman on a commission basis under an oral contract not performable within one year. Acting under the contract the plaintiff procured a number of orders which were filled by the defendant. In an action by the plaintiff for quasi-contractual relief, the defendant argued that the products were sold at a loss and therefore it had not received a benefit. The court, however, ruled that any performance rendered pursuant to agreement and accepted by the defendant constituted a benefit whether or not it resulted in economic enrichment.[37]

Many courts have gone beyond the concept of benefit and have frankly permitted recovery for reliance losses in actions for restitution or on a theory of promissory estoppel.[38] One of the earlier cases in which the reliance interest was openly protected was Riley v. Capital Airlines, Inc.[39] Plaintiff entered into an oral contract to supply defendant's requirements of methanol for a five year period. Upon the defendant's repudiation of the agreement the plaintiff was permitted to recover his losses based on expenditures made as a necessary prerequisite to performance. The plaintiff had purchased special tanks and pumps to produce and store the methanol and was forced by the breach to resell these at a loss. In no sense were these losses a benefit to the defendant. Both of the leading contract treatises assert, without qualification, that in the absence of receipt by the defendant of the plaintiff's property or services, no quasi-contractual relief is possible.[40] Yet, decisions like Riley are now made with some frequency [41] and demonstrate attempts by the courts to prevent the Statute of Frauds from operating as an instrument of injustice.

 WESTLAW REFERENCES

"quasi contract" /s "benefit conferred"

find 185 f.supp 165

185k86

185k125(2)

185k44(4)

§ 19–45. The Contract Price as Evidence of Value: Contrast Between Damages and Restitution

If A orally agrees to perform services for a two year period in return for B's promise to pay $2,000 at the end of the period, the

---

36. 41 Utah 404, 125 P. 860, 1916D L.R.A. 892 (1912). But see Baugh v. Darley, 112 Utah 1, 184 P.2d 335 (1947).

37. Accord, Matousek v. Quirici, 195 Ill. App. 391 (1915) (plaintiff required to pay reasonable rental value of premises orally leased although he never occupied the premises); Randolph v. Castle, 190 Ky. 776, 228 S.W. 418 (1921) (employees may recover for value of their time while on the job site although they performed no services).

38. See §§ 19–47, 19–48 infra.

39. 185 F.Supp. 165 (S.D.Ala.1960).

40. 2 Corbin § 327; 3 Williston § 536 at 832.

41. See authorities cited in note 35 supra.

contract is within the Statute of Frauds. If B discharges A at the end of six months, may A introduce the contract price as evidence of the value of his services? The great weight of authority is to the effect that the price is admissible into evidence [42] despite the fact that in many cases the jury's verdict will often be the equivalent of what it would have been in an action on the contract.

If the preceding sections have not made it clear, however, it should be explicitly stated that in many instances the plaintiff's judgment in an action for quasi contract may differ markedly from the result which would be obtainable if he could have enforced the contract in an action for damages. One illustration may suffice. Suppose an uncle orally promised his nephew to devise to him all of his real property in exchange for the nephew's promise to take care of him for life.[43] Suppose further that several weeks later the uncle repudiated and soon thereafter died. In a quasi-contractual action for the value of his services, the nephew may realistically hope to recover several hundred or perhaps even several thousand dollars. In an action for damages to enforce the contract he would be entitled to the benefit of his bargain; that is, the value of the real property, conceivably millions of dollars, with a deduction for the expenses saved as a result of the repudiation.

On the other hand, in an action for restitution, the plaintiff's recovery may sometimes be greater than would have been available in an action on the contract for damages. Thus, an employee who alleged that he was hired for a three year period under an oral agreement and had been compensated at the rate of $18 to $25 per week before his wrongful discharge was permitted to plead and prove that the value of the services he had rendered was $50 per week.[44]

---

42. Grantham v. Grantham, 205 N.C. 363, 171 S.E. 331 (1933); Bennett Leasing Co. v. Ellison, 15 Utah 2d 72, 387 P.2d 246, 21 A.L.R.3d 1 (1963); Cochran v. Bise, 197 Va. 483, 90 S.E.2d 178 (1955); 2 Corbin § 328; 3 Williston § 536 at 838; Restatement, Contracts § 217(2); Restatement, Second, Contracts § 143. Contra, Blanchard v. Calderwood, 110 N.H. 29, 260 A.2d 118 (1969). The reader is warned to beware of statements couched in terms of "weight of authority." Consider that in one jurisdiction the following cases deem the contract price admissible: Leahy v. Campbell, 70 App.Div. 127, 75 N.Y.S. 72 (1st Dep't 1902); Gall v. Gall, 27 A.D. 173, 50 N.Y.S. 563 (1st Dep't 1898), motion granted and appeal dismissed 160 N.Y. 696, 55 N.E. 1095 (1899); In re Schweizer's Estate, 231 N.Y.S.2d 534 (1962) and the following cases deem it inadmissible: Erben v. Lorillard, 19 N.Y. 299 (1859); Schlanger v. Cowan, 13 A.D.2d 739, 214 N.Y.S.2d 784 (1st Dep't 1961); Parver v. Matthews-Kadetsky Co., 242 App.Div. 1, 273 N.Y.S. 44 (1st Dep't 1934); Black v.

Fisher, 145 N.Y.S.2d 142 (1955). See also Galvin v. Prentice, 45 N.Y. 162 (1871).

43. It is generally held that a promise to leave real property by will is within the real property Statute of Frauds. See 2 Corbin § 398. In addition some jurisdictions have a specific provision of the Statute of Frauds applicable to contracts to make a testamentary disposition. E.g., McKinney's N.Y. Est. Powers & Trusts Law § 13–2.1(2).

Thus, under the majority view to the effect that if any part of the contract is within the Statute, the entire contract must satisfy the Statute (§ 19–36 supra), a promise to leave "all my property" is within the Statute if the promisor owns any real property. Blanchard v. Calderwood, 110 N.H. 29, 260 A.2d 118 (1969).

44. McGilchrist v. F. W. Woolworth Co., 138 Or. 679, 7 P.2d 982 (1932); accord, Schanzenbach v. Brough, 58 Ill.App. 526 (1895) (contract price does not set a maximum); Grossberg v. Double H. Licensing Corp., 86 A.D.2d 565, 446 N.Y.S.2d 296 (1st

§ 19–46. Specific Restitution in Equity

Equity has forged an armory of remedies to aid a deserving petitioner. One recurring fact pattern will be considered to suggest the kind of analysis utilized in equity in cases involving specific restitution.

Very frequently a grantor conveys land to the defendant upon the defendant's *oral* [45] promise to reconvey it to the grantor upon demand or to hold it in trust for the grantor or some third person.[46] The oral promise may be within the Statute of Frauds provision regarding the transfer of interests in land. In addition in most jurisdictions there is a specific provision of the Statute of Frauds requiring a writing for the creation of express trusts.[47] It is obvious that the oral promise cannot be enforced as such without conflicting with the Statute. It is also obvious that the grantee who violates the oral agreement has been unjustly enriched and the grantor unjustly impoverished.

Equity in such a case may impose a constructive trust on the land or the proceeds if the grantee has sold the land. The trust is said to be "constructive" because it is not based on the agreement but is imposed by law to avoid unjust enrichment and inequitable conduct. The conditions under which the constructive trust will be imposed, however, is a matter of dispute among the jurisdictions. The weight of authority supports the imposition of a constructive trust (1) where the conveyance was procured by fraud, misrepresentation, duress, undue influence or mistake, (2) where the transferee is a fiduciary or (3) where the transfer was made as security only.[48] A minority of jurisdictions will construct a trust in any case where there is a violation of an oral agreement to convey.[49] The majority rule is based upon traditional grounds for the

Dep't 1982); Ricks v. Sumler, 179 Va. 571, 19 S.E.2d 889 (1942). For a criticism of this rule, see Perillo, Restitution in the Second Restatement of Contracts, 81 Colum.L.Rev. 37, 44–45 (1981).

45. If the promise is written in a sufficient memorandum, specific restitution is available under the rules discussed in § 15–5 supra.

46. Sometimes this is done to defraud creditors in which case the grantor is faced with the additional difficulty of recovering under an illegal bargain. See Wantulok v. Wantulok, 67 Wyo. 22, 214 P.2d 477 (1950), rehearing denied 67 Wyo. 22, 223 P.2d

1030 (1950), noted in 37 Va.L.Rev. 455 (1951) and 5 Wyo.L.J. 152 (1951).

47. See 2 Corbin § 401.

48. Moses v. Moses, 140 N.J.Eq. 575, 53 A.2d 805, 173 A.L.R. 273 (1947); Restatement, Restitution § 182(c); Restatement, Trusts § 44. On conveyances made for purposes of security, see Straight v. Hill, 622 P.2d 425 (Alaska 1981); Fogelman, The Deed Absolute as a Mortgage in New York, 32 Fordham L.Rev. 299 (1963).

49. Orella v. Johnson, 38 Cal.2d 693, 242 P.2d 5 (1952), noted in 40 Calif.L.Rev. 621 (1952).

existence of equity jurisdiction. Since the merger of law and equity, most jurisdictions have taken the view that merger merely brought procedural unification.[50] Massachusetts appears to stand alone in refusing to construct a trust for violation of an oral promise, relegating the grantor to a quasi-contractual action for the value of the land.[51]

While the Restatement of Restitution states that one of the grounds for the imposition of a constructive trust, where there has been a violation of an oral agreement to reconvey, is the existence of a "fiduciary" relation,[52] many of the cases go well beyond this and hold that any pre-existing confidential relationship is sufficient. This would include such a relationship as husband and wife, father and son, brother and sister, lawyer and client, doctor and patient, priest and parishioner.[53]

It is generally recognized that in order to obtain relief of the kind described here the plaintiff must establish his case by more than the preponderance of the evidence. The cases speak in terms of clear and convincing evidence or of establishing the oral promise beyond a reasonable doubt.[54]

The Restatement (Second) has dramatically enlarged the availability of specific restitution. A party who is entitled to monetary restitution is entitled to specific restitution unless he is in breach or if it would "unduly interfere with the certainty of title to land or otherwise would cause injustice."[55] Since restitution is readily available for performances rendered under unenforceable contracts, acceptance of the rule of the new Restatement would greatly advance the availability of specific restitution.

 WESTLAW REFERENCES
find 242 p2d 5

390k96

---

50. For a convincing argument that a substantive merger of equitable and legal principles ought to extend the range of constructive trusts, see Newman, Some Reflections on the Function of the Confidential Relationship Doctrine in the Law of Trusts, in Perspectives of Law 286, 300–01 (1964).

51. Kemp v. Kemp, 248 Mass. 354, 142 N.E. 779 (1924).

52. Restatement, Restitution § 182.

53. These relationships are specifically enumerated in Fraw Realty Co. v. Natanson, 261 N.Y. 396, 402, 185 N.E. 679 (1933). These are not, however, exclusive. See

generally Newman, supra note 50; Talbott, Restitution Remedies in Contract Cases: Finding a Fiduciary or Confidential Relationship to Gain Remedies, 20 Ohio St.L.J. 320 (1959).

54. E.g., for an especially strong statement, Strype v. Lewis, 352 Mo. 1004, 180 S.W.2d 688, 155 A.L.R. 99 (1944), where it was said that the evidence must be so clear, cogent and convincing as to exclude every reasonable doubt from the chancellor's mind.

55. Restatement, Second, Contracts § 372(1).

IV.　ESTOPPEL

Table of Sections

§ 19–47.　Equitable Estoppel and the Statute of Frauds

Probably all jurisdictions recognize that if the elements of equitable estoppel are present, the party to be charged will not be permitted to avail himself of the defense of the Statute of Frauds.[56] It will be recalled that equitable estoppel requires justifiable injurious reliance upon a factual representation or conduct of the other. Thus, if the Statute of Frauds of a given jurisdiction requires that an agent's authority be granted in writing, the principal will be estopped from asserting this Statute as a defense if he has indicated to the other contracting party that the agent is duly authorized to act on his behalf [57] provided, of course, that the representation produced injurious reliance.[58] So also if the party to be charged, by words or conduct, represents that he has signed a written memorandum of the contract he will be estopped from pleading the Statute.[59]

Some courts have gone far beyond the traditional notion of equitable estoppel and have used the label of equitable estoppel where the claimant has suffered an unconscionable injury by reliance on an oral or insufficiently memorialized contract. Cases such as these have led to the widespread adoption of promissory estoppel as a doctrine under which a plea of the Statute of Frauds may be defeated.

 WESTLAW REFERENCES
di("equitable estoppel" /s "statute of fraud")

§ 19–48.　Promissory Estoppel

The first edition of this hornbook, published in 1970, predicted "a major new approach" towards the interrelationship between promissory estoppel and the Statute of Frauds,[60] basing this prediction on a

---

56. Burdick, A Statute for Promoting Fraud, 16 Colum.L.Rev. 273 (1916); Note, The Doctrine of Equitable Estoppel and the Statute of Frauds, 66 Mich.L.Rev. 170 (1967); But see Ozier v. Haines, 411 Ill. 160, 103 N.E.2d 485 (1952), which requires deceit upon the part of the defendant; Polka v. May, 383 Pa. 80, 118 A.2d 154 (1955), which rejects the notion that the doctrine of estoppel may be invoked against the operation of the Statute of Frauds.

57. Fleming v. Dolfin, 214 Cal. 269, 4 P.2d 776, 78 A.L.R. 585 (1931), noted in 20 Cal.L.Rev. 663 (1932); Levy v. Rothfeld, 271 App.Div. 973, 67 N.Y.S.2d 497 (2d Dep't 1947).

58. Coombs v. Ouzounian, 24 Utah 2d 39, 465 P.2d 356 (1970).

59. Owens v. Foundation for Ocean Research, 107 Cal.App.3d 179, 165 Cal.Rptr. 571 (1980); cf., McKay Prods. Corp. v. Jonathan Logan, Inc., 54 Misc.2d 385, 283 N.Y.S.2d 82 (1967), affirmed 29 A.D.2d 918, 289 N.Y.S.2d 140 (1st Dep't 1968); Restatement, Contracts § 178, Comment f.

60. Calamari & Perillo, Handbook of the Law of Contracts § 327 (1970).

relatively few cases.[61]   Since that time there has been widespread application of promissory estoppel to cases in which it would be inequitable to allow the Statute of Frauds to defeat a meritorious claim.   The older view took the position that "[s]uch a holding is clearly impossible of justification on any theory, in view of the language of the statute." [62] This suggestion appears to be based upon a misunderstanding of the relationship between common law doctrines and legislation.   The doctrine of estoppel, promissory or otherwise, is as much a part of our law as the Statute of Frauds.   It is for the courts to harmonize the Statute and common law doctrine into a coherent and just pattern within our legal system—certainly a difficult task.[63]   Until the Statute of Frauds is reformed so as to take into account the many problems which almost three hundred years of history have shown were unforeseen by its draftsmen, the courts should be encouraged in their creative work of doing justice by utilizing all doctrines available to them.

The First Restatement's only use of the term "promissory estoppel" appears in the context of a promise to make a memorandum which "if * * * relied on, may give rise to an effective promissory estoppel if the Statute would otherwise operate to defraud." [64]   Thus, we find courts which have not fully embraced promissory estoppel have nevertheless applied the doctrine as to such cases.[65]   The Restatement Second had broadly enlarged the availability of the doctrine in Statute of Frauds cases, following the lead of cases such as Alaska Airlines, Inc. v. Stephenson.[66]   The plaintiff had been employed as a pilot with Western Airlines, a position which apparently afforded a good deal of employment security.   He accepted a position as general manager of the defendant airline.   The oral agreement was to the effect that the plaintiff would take a six month leave of absence from his employment with Western to work for the defendant and, if the defendant received a franchise to fly from Seattle to Alaska, the plaintiff would receive a

61. Alaska Airlines v. Stephenson, 15 Alaska 272, 217 F.2d 295 (9th Cir.1954); Monarco v. Lo Greco, 35 Cal.2d 621, 220 P.2d 737 (1950); Boesiger v. Freer, 85 Idaho 551, 381 P.2d 802 (1963); Miller v. Lawlor, 245 Iowa 1144, 66 N.W.2d 267, 48 A.L.R.2d 1058 (1954); Somerset Acres West Homes Ass'n. v. Daniels, 191 Kan. 583, 383 P.2d 952 (1963); Vogel v. Shaw, 42 Wyo. 333, 294 P. 687, 75 A.L.R. 639 (1930), noted in 29 Mich.L.Rev. 1075 (1931).

62. Grismore on Contracts § 284 (rev'd 2d ed. 1965) (this statement does not appear in the current edition known as Murray on Contracts (rev'd ed. 1974).   Compare Ozier v. Haines, 411 Ill. 160, 103 N.E. 2d 485 (1952).   But see Leob v. Gendel, 23 Ill.2d 502, 179 N.E.2d 7 (1961).

63. See Smith v. Ash, 448 S.W.2d 51 (Ky.1969), in which the court refused to invoke an estoppel because of the plaintiff's misrepresentations (coupled with oth-er equities against the plaintiff) despite the plaintiff's extensive acts of reliance on defendant's oral promise. See also Brooks v. Cooksey, 427 S.W.2d 498 (Mo.1968) where an estoppel was denied partly on the ground that defendant did not benefit from plaintiff's change of position; Williams v. Denham, 83 S.D. 518, 162 N.W.2d 285 (1968) where an estoppel was denied because acts in reliance took place after defendant repudiated his oral contract.

64. Restatement, Contracts § 178, Comment f.

65. Johnson v. Gilbert, 127 Ariz. 410, 621 P.2d 916 (App.1980).   Nagle v. Nagle, 633 S.W.2d 796 (Tex.1982); see Klinke v. Famous Recipe Fried Chicken, Inc., 94 Wn. 2d 255, 616 P.2d 644 (1980).

66. 15 Alaska 272, 217 F.2d 295 (9th Cir.1954).

written contract for two years employment. The plaintiff moved his family from California to Alaska, abandoned his tenure rights with his former employer and occupied the position of general manager. When the franchise was obtained, no written contract was forthcoming. The plaintiff was discharged. The court in ruling for the plaintiff explicitly based its decision on promissory estoppel, suggesting that this approach "will generally be followed throughout the country." [67]

The Alaska court's suggestion that the nation's courts would follow its lead has largely proved to be correct,[68] although a few courts have rejected promissory estoppel as a device to overcome the writing requirements of the Statute of Frauds.[69] Although the use of the doctrine for this purpose has been largely accepted, it is marked by what has been labelled as a "remarkably incoherent body of case law." [70] The widespread use of the doctrine in this context is in its infancy, therefore its analytic structure is not yet mature. Factors that go into a finding that the doctrine applies include unconscionable injury, unjust enrichment not fully redressable by restitution, and the extent of which conduct in reliance on the contract corroborates the making of the agreement.[71]

Conduct corroborating the existence of the agreement is, of course, at the root of the part performance doctrine applied mainly in real property cases.[72] These cases, although stemming from different principles, can be looked at as promissory estoppel cases because relief is granted where a party has taken concrete action in reliance upon a promise. Although the part performance doctrine has its own particularized set of rules, there is a tendency to depart from the narrower doctrines of part performance and to base a decision on grounds of estoppel whenever the plaintiff's equities are so great as to make a contrary decision unconscionable.[73] In a few jurisdictions, such as

---

67. 217 F.2d at 298.

68. R.S. Bennett & Co., Inc. v. Economy Mechanical Indus., Inc., 606 F.2d 182 (7th Cir.1979) (Ill. law); Macedward v. Northern Elec. Co., 595 F.2d 105 (2d Cir.1979) (Vt. law); Gray v. Mitsui & Co. (U.S.A.), 434 F.Supp. 1071 (D.Or.1977); Ralston Purina Co. v. McCollum; 271 Ark. 840, 611 S.W.2d 201 (App.1981); Meylor v. Brown, 281 N.W.2d 632 (Iowa 1979); Decatur Co-Op. Ass'n v. Urban, 219 Kan. 171, 547 P.2d 323 (1976); Hickey v. Green, 14 Mass.App. Ct. 671, 442 N.E.2d 37 (1982), review denied 388 Mass. 1102, 445 N.E.2d 156 (1983); Lovely v. Dierkes, 132 Mich.App. 485, 347 N.W.2d 752 (1984); Alpark Distributing, Inc. v. Poole, 95 Nev. 605, 600 P.2d 229 (1979); Jamestown Terminal Elev., Inc. v. Hieb, 246 N.W.2d 736 (N.D.1976); Buddman Distributors, Inc. v. Labatt Importers, Inc., 91 A.D.2d 838, 458 N.Y.S.2d 395 (4th Dep't 1982); T * * * v. T * * *, 216 Va. 867, 224 S.E.2d 148 (1976);

see Annot., 54 A.L.R.3d 715 (1974); Comment, 44 Fordham L.Rev. 114 (1975).

69. Bethune v. Mountain Brook, 293 Ala. 89, 300 So.2d 350 (1974), appeal after remand 336 So.2d 148 (Ala.1976); Sacred Heart Farmers Coop. Elev. v. Johnson, 305 Minn. 324, 232 N.W.2d 921 (1975); Anderson Constr. Co., Inc. v. Lyon Metal Products, Inc., 370 So.2d 935 (Miss.1979); Farmland Service Co-Op. v. Klein, 196 Neb. 538, 244 N.W.2d 86 (1976); Glasgow v. G.R.C. Coal Co., 295 Pa.Super. 498, 442 A.2d 249 (1981).

70. Metzger & Phillips, Promissory Estoppel and Sections 2–201 of the Uniform Commercial Code, 26 Vill.L.Rev. 63, 64 (1980).

71. Restatement, Second, Contracts § 139.

72. See § 19–15 supra.

73. See 2 Corbin § 422A (Supp.1971), § 440; 4 Williston § 533A; Annot., 56

California, the tendency to rely on estoppel is so great as to result in the obliteration of the doctrine of part performance and its incorporation into the more generalized doctrine of estoppel.[74]

Some courts have refused to recognize the applicability of promissory estoppel to cases involving the sale of goods reasoning that U.C.C. § 2–201 provides such a thorough catalog of ways to satisfy the Statute of Frauds that adding to it would be an act of judicial usurpation.[75] In so holding they have seemingly overlooked U.C.C. § 1–203 which provides that "the principles of law and equity, including * * * estoppel * * * shall supplement * * *" the provisions of the Act.

 WESTLAW REFERENCES

"uniform commercial code" u.c.c.   /3   1–203

di("promissory estoppel"   /s   "statute of fraud")

find 217 f2d 295

185k126

A.L.R.3d 1037 (1974). See also Gem Corrugated Box Corp. v. National Kraft Container Corp., 427 F.2d 499 (2d Cir.1970); Boesiger v. Freer, 85 Idaho 551, 381 P.2d 802 (1963) (part performance insufficient, but other actions in reliance raised an estoppel); Somerset Acres West Homes Ass'n v. Daniels, 191 Kan. 583, 383 P.2d 952 (1963); Vogel v. Shaw, 42 Wyo. 333, 294 P. 687, 75 A.L.R. 639 (1930), noted in 29 Mich. L.Rev. 1075 (1931); Summers, The Doctrine of Estoppel Applied to the Statute of Frauds, 79 U.Pa.L.Rev. 440 (1931).

74. Redke v. Silvertrust, 6 Cal.3d 94, 98 Cal.Rptr. 293, 490 P.2d 805 (1971), cert. denied 405 U.S. 1041, 92 S.Ct. 1316, 31 L.Ed.2d 583 (1972); Monarco v. Lo Greco, 35 Cal.2d 621, 220 P.2d 737 (1950); Seymour v. Oelrichs, 156 Cal. 782, 106 P. 88 (1909); but see Itek Corp. v. RCA Corp., 32 N.Y.2d 730, 344 N.Y.S.2d 365, 297 N.E.2d 100 (1973) (applying California law). See also Bunbury v. Krauss, 41 Wis.2d 522, 164 N.W.2d 473 (1969); Steadman v. Steadman, [1974] 3 W.L.R. 56, noted in 90 L.Q.Rev. 433 (1974).

75. E.g., C.R. Fedrick, Inc. v. Borg-Warner Corp., 552 F.2d 852 (1977), noted in 9 Rut.-Cam.L.J. 387 (1977) and 18 Santa Clara L.Rev. 837 (1978); C.G. Campbell & Son v. Comdeq Corp., 586 S.W.2d 40 (Ky. App.1979); contra, Allen M. Campbell Co. v. Virginia Metal Indus., 708 F.2d 930 (4th Cir.1983), noted in 41 Wash. & Lee L.Rev. 588 (1984); Meylor v. Brown, 281 N.W.2d 632 (Iowa 1979); Decatur Co-Op. Ass'n. v. Urban, 219 Kan. 171, 547 P.2d 323 (1976), noted in 26 U.Kan.L.Rev. 327 (1978); Potter v. Hatter Farms, Inc., 56 Or.App. 254, 641 P.2d 628, 29 A.L.R.4th 997 (1982); see generally Metzger & Phillips, Promissory Estoppel and Section 2–201 of the Uniform Commercial Code, 26 Vill.L.Rev. 63 (1980).

Chapter 20

JOINT AND SEVERAL
CONTRACTS

Table of Sections

Table of Sections

A. MULTIPLE OBLIGORS

A. MULTIPLE OBLIGORS

Table of Sections

§ 20–1. Multiple Promisors

This chapter is concerned with rights and duties created by multiple promises of the *same* performance. It is not concerned with multiple promises of *different* performances. Whether or not multiple promises refer to the same performance or to different performances is a question of interpretation.[1] For example, if A and B each promise to pay C $500 they are promising different performances. However, if A and B each promise to pay C a total of $1,000 so that each is liable for $1,000, but C is entitled to collect only once, they are promising the same performance.

We are concerned here with the old common law concepts of joint, joint and several, and several obligations.[2] These concepts are not engaged unless the promises relate to the same performance. The question is whether multiple promisors of the same performance have promised as a unit (jointly), or have promised the same performance separately (severally), or both as a unit and separately (jointly and severally). Having made this determination, the question then is the effect at common law of joint, joint and several, or several obligations, and finally what changes have been made (ordinarily by statute) in the arbitrary and unfortunate common law rules.[3]

 WESTLAW REFERENCES
find 637 f2d 816

1. Restatement, Second, Contracts Ch. 13, Introductory Note; id. § 288. Illustrative of a case involving promises of different performances is Over the Road Drivers, Inc. v. Transport Ins. Co., 637 F.2d 816 (1st Cir.1980).

2. There is a similar problem where a promise is made to multiple promisees. See §§ 20–7 to 20–11 infra.

3. See Werner, Shared Liability: An Alternative to the Confusion of Joint, Several and Joint and Several Obligations, 42 Albany L.Rev. 1 (1977).

di several

di joint

§ 20-2. When Promisors Are Bound Jointly, Severally, or Jointly and Severally

The old common law rule was to the effect that promises of the same performance were joint [4] "unless the promises took a linguistic form appropriate to several duties." [5] Thus if A & B as promisors stated, "we jointly promise to pay the same obligation," there would be nothing to overcome the presumption of a joint obligation. However, if A & B stated "each of us independently promises to pay the obligation," the presumption of a joint obligation would be overcome by the words of severance.[6] If A & B promised by saying, "we and each of us promise to pay," the obligation is joint and several [7] and the same is true where two or more persons promise in the first person singular.[8] In the case of a joint and several obligation involving two promisors there are three obligations, the joint obligation and the two several obligations.

The old common law tended to view the problem "as a deduction from legal concepts." [9] The more modern approach is that the question is one of the intention of the parties and, although the presumption in favor of joint liability continues to exist, it is more easily overcome.[10]

The fact that one of the parties is a principal and the other a surety does not change these rules,[11] and the same is true even where the parties have agreed *inter se,* unknown to the promisee, that each shall be liable to the promisee for an aliquot share of the undertaking.[12]

4. Restatement, Second, Contracts § 289(2); 4 Corbin § 425.

5. Restatement, Second, Contracts § 289, Comment b; see Clayman v. Goodman Properties, Inc., 518 F.2d 1026 (D.C. Cir.1973).

6. Restatement, Second, Contracts § 289, ill. 7. Subscription contracts, that is, promises in one instrument to make individual payments, are held to be several even though reading, "We, the undersigned, subscribe and promise to pay the amounts set opposite our names." 4 Corbin § 927.

7. Lorimer v. Goff, 216 Mich. 587, 185 N.W. 791 (1921); Guynn v. Corpus Christi Bank & Trust, 620 S.W.2d 188 (Tex.Civ. App.1981) ("We or either of us"). Language of joint and several liability creates an "obligation in solido" under the Louisiana Code with consequences which are not quite the same as in other states. Flintkote Co. v. Thomas, 223 So.2d 676 (La. App.1969).

8. U.C.C. § 3–118(e); Restatement, Contracts § 115; Continental Ill. Bank & Trust Co. v. Clement, 259 Mich. 167, 242 N.W. 877 (1932).

9. Restatement, Second, Contracts § 289, Comment b.

10. Restatement, Second, Contracts § 289, Comments b and c; 4 Corbin § 925; Douglas v. Bergere, 94 Cal.App.2d 267, 210 P.2d 727 (1949); Schubert v. Ivey, 158 Conn. 583, 264 A.2d 562 (1969); Falaschi v. Yowell, 24 Wn.App. 495, 601 P.2d 989 (1979). But the vitality of the common law presumption of joint liability should not be underestimated. See Mileasing Co. v. Hogan, 87 A.D.2d 961, 451 N.Y.S.2d 211 (3d Dep't 1982); 2 Williston § 320.

11. Restatement, Second, Contracts § 289, Comment c; City of Philadelphia v. Reeves, 48 Pa. 472 (1865).

12. Knowlton v. Parsons, 198 Mass. 439, 84 N.E. 798 (1908).

Statutes in many states state that promises which would be joint under the common law rules should be treated as if they were joint and several.[13]

 WESTLAW REFERENCES
di(promise /s joint** /s several**)
56k440
56k120

§ 20–3. Consequences of Joint Liability

There are at least five common law doctrines relating to joint obligations that have proved unsatisfactory, indeed, disgracefully so.[14] These are: 1) compulsory joinder of joint promisors; 2) the discharge of other joint promisors by a judgment against one; 3) only a joint judgment can be entered against joint promisors; 4) the rule of survivorship which barred an action against the estate of a deceased joint obligor; and 5) the rule that a discharge of one joint promisor released the others. These doctrines shall now be considered seriatim.

(a) Compulsory Joinder of Joint Promisors

If A & B are joint obligors and C, the obligee, brought a suit against A, at early common law it was held that A could demur to the declaration and the demurrer would be sustained. This was true even though B was insolvent or beyond the jurisdiction. The theory was that A and B had promised as a unit and therefore had to be sued as a unit.[15] In time the rule was modified so that the fact of non-joinder could be raised only by a plea in abatement (motion to dismiss), unless the non-joinder appeared on the face of the declaration,[16] and in the United States at least the plea could be defeated if the joint obligor not joined was not alive or not subject to process.[17] The rule of compulsory joinder continues to be the general rule in the United States today in the absence of a statute,[18] but exceptions have also been made "for

---

13. The statutes are collected in the Restatement, Second, Contracts in the Introductory Note to Chapter 13, as well as in 2 Williston §§ 336–336A; but see Uniform Partnership Act § 15 as to a partner's liability for partnership obligations, which in most instances is joint, but in some instances joint and several.

14. See Braucher, Freedom of Contract and the Second Restatement, 78 Yale L.J. 598, 608 (1969) ("Rules and results * * * outraged both common and commercial sense."). On the general topic, see Griffith, Joint Rights and Liabilities (1897); Williams, Joint Obligations (1949); Evans, Contractual Joint Rights and Duties in

Kentucky and the Restatement, 18 Ky.L.J. 341 (1930).

15. 4 Corbin § 929; 2 Williston § 327; see generally, Reed, Compulsory Joinder of Parties in Civil Actions, 55 Mich.L.Rev. 327 (1927).

16. Rice v. Shute, 96 Eng.Rep. 409 (1770); see Koffler & Reppy, Common Law Pleading § 208 (1969).

17. Camp v. Gress, 250 U.S. 308, 39 S.Ct. 478, 63 L.Ed. 997 (1919); see Koffler & Reppy, Common Law Pleading § 208 (1969).

18. Restatement, Second, Contracts § 290.

dormant partners, bankrupt co-promisors, and promisors against whom a claim is barred by the statute of limitations." [19]

The statutes referred to above have changed the common law rule in a variety of ways. One type of statute allows less than all of the joint obligors to be sued (provided all are named) in the discretion of the court. These statutes further provide that the judgment binds the joint property of all of the joint obligors but the separate property only of those served.[20] A second type of statute is similar to the first except that it eliminates the requirement that all of the joint obligors be named.[21] Another type of statute permits an action against those served without any necessity for naming the other obligors or without any element of discretion in the judge.[22] Many states also have statutes which permit partners to be sued in the firm name irrespective of whether the obligation is joint.[23]

(b) The Discharge of Other Joint Promisors by a Judgment Against One

In subsection (a) we discussed the common law rule whereby a joint obligor could object to the non-joinder of other joint obligors and cause the action to be dismissed. If he did not object, obviously the action would proceed to judgment. We discuss here the result where the judgment is in favor of the plaintiff and against the joint obligor or obligors served. The result reached was that the judgment against the joint obligor or obligors sued merged the entire claim so that no further action could be maintained against the other joint obligors, even though the parties sued proved to be insolvent.[24] In time exceptions came to be made in the case of promisors who were out of the jurisdiction, for foreign judgments, for cases of estoppel, and for judgments on promises given as conditional payment or collateral security.[25]

Today there are many statutes which provide that a judgment against a joint promisor or promisors does not bar an action against other joint promisors, and some have permitted the joint property of those not served to be bound subject to later proceeding wherein they may be required to show cause why they should not be bound.[26]

---

19. Restatement, Second, Contracts § 290, Comment c.

20. This type of statute is now effective in Alaska, Indiana, Nevada, New York, North Carolina, North Dakota, Oklahoma, Oregon, South Carolina, Washington and Wisconsin. See, e.g., McKinney's N.Y.C.P. L.R. 1501.

21. Statutes in Iowa, Kentucky, Mississippi and West Virginia appear to be of this type.

22. California, Georgia, Idaho, Nebraska, New Jersey, Ohio, Utah, Virginia and Wyoming have this type of statute.

23. See Crane and Bromberg, Partnership § 60 (1968); 2 Rowley, Partnerships § 49.3 (2d ed.1960).

24. Ward v. Johnson, 13 Mass. 148 (1816); Mitchell v. Brewster, 28 Ill. 163 (1862).

25. Restatement, Second, Contracts § 292, Comment b; 2 Williston § 327.

26. The statutes are collected in the Introductory Note to § 288 of the Restatement (2d).

(c) Only a Joint Judgment Can Be Entered Against Joint Promisors

In the preceding subsection we discussed the problem presented where the plaintiff obtained a judgment against the joint promisor or promisors served. Here the question is the effects of a judgment in favor of one of the joint obligors served. The common law took the position that as against joint obligors only a joint judgment could be entered. This meant that it was impossible to have a verdict against the plaintiff in favor of one promisor and in favor of the plaintiff against another promisor. In other words if the plaintiff lost to one joint obligor he must lose as to all.[27]

Eventually an exception was made where a defendant won the case because of a defense personal to him as, for example, lack of capacity, discharge in bankruptcy and the statute of limitations.[28]

The Restatement Second in § 291 sets forth the modern rule when it states: "In an action against promisors of the same performance, whether their duties are joint, several, or joint and several, judgment can properly be entered for or against one even though no judgment or a different judgment is entered with respect to another, except that a judgment for one and against another is improper where there has been a determination on the merits and the liability of one cannot exist without the liability of the other."[29]

(d) The Rule of Survivorship

At early common law if a joint obligor died his estate could not be sued. The creditor could proceed only against the surviving co-obligors.[30] If all of the joint obligors died only the estate of the last one to die was liable to the creditor.[31] Obviously this rule worked unfairly particularly where the remaining obligor or obligors were insolvent. The Courts of Chancery did not rigidly apply this doctrine and invented various procedures in order to do justice.[32]

Today whether by statute or by case decisions this rule has been abolished in most states.[33] However, there are still some decisions to

27. Simpson, Contracts § 137 (2d ed. 1965). Although the judgment is joint, a successful plaintiff could levy against the individual assets of any joint obligor who was served.

28. Restatement, Second, Contracts § 291, Comment a; Eastern Elec. Co. v. Taylor Woodrow Blitman Constr. Co., 11 Mass.App.Ct. 192, 414 N.E.2d 1023 (1981), review denied 441 N.E.2d 1042 (Mass.1981).

29. Accord, 4 Corbin § 929. The exception at the end of the statement is based upon principles of res judicata or collateral estoppel by judgment.

30. Davis v. Van Buren, 72 N.Y. 587 (1878); McLaughlin v. Head, 86 Or. 361,

168 P. 614 (1917); 2 Williston § 344; Annot., 67 A.L.R. 608 (1930). The fact the deceased joint obligor or his estate was no longer liable to the creditor did not affect the estate's obligation of contribution to a joint obligor who had been compelled to pay.

31. Restatement, Contracts § 126.

32. 4 Corbin § 930; 2 Williston § 344; Note, 2 Mich.L.Rev. 216 (1903).

33. Restatement, Second, Contracts § 296, Comment b. A statutory table appears in 2 Williston § 344A.

the effect that a surety who is a joint obligor is discharged upon his death.[34]

(e) A Discharge of One Joint Obligor Releases the Others

The joint nature of a joint obligation also led the common law courts to hold that a discharge of one or more joint obligors discharged the other joint obligors.[35] This was true whether the discharge occurred by virtue of release, rescission or accord and satisfaction and irrespective of the intention of the parties.[36] Since the rule was without any rational basis and operated very unfairly, some of the courts held that the rule operated only in the case of a formal release under seal.[37]

The harsh common law was soon circumvented by using a covenant not to sue.[38] While a release is an executed transaction, a covenant not to sue is executory and even when it is breached it is not specifically enforced in favor of the covenantee, and so it is held that a covenant not to sue is not a defense either to the covenantee or the other joint obligors. The covenantee may be sued but he is protected by the court's requiring the creditor to refrain from levying against the property of the covenantee.[39]

Another device to circumvent the rule was a release containing a reservation of rights against the other obligors.[40] Such a reservation of rights caused the release to be interpreted as a covenant not to sue provided that it was concurrent with the purported release and in the same instrument.

The Restatement Second adopts the common law rule but adds: "Modern decisions have converted it from a rule defeating intention to a rule of presumptive intention," and adds that where a contrary intention is manifested the release or discharge should be treated as a

---

34. 4 Corbin § 930.

35. North Pacific Mortgage Co. v. Krewson, 129 Wash. 239, 224 P. 566, 53 A.L.R. 1416 (1924); 4 Corbin § 931; 2 Williston § 333; see generally Havighurst, The Effect of a Settlement With One Co-Obligor upon the Obligations of the Others, 45 Cornell L.Q. 1 (1951); Williston, Releases and Covenants Not To Sue Joint, or Joint and Several Debtors, 25 Harv.L.Rev. 203 (1912), Selected Readings 1179.

36. Restatement, Contracts § 294; Brooks v. Neal, 223 Mass. 467, 112 N.E. 78 (1916); Pacific Southwest Trust & Sav. Bank v. Mayer, 138 Wash. 85, 244 P. 248 (1926); 2 Williston § 333A. Illustrative of the purity of the logic and the barbarity of the results that marked this era is Jenkins v. Jenkins, [1928] 2 K.B. 501, 14 Cornell L.Q. 215 (1928). One of the co-obligors of a

note was appointed executor of the payee's estate. His appointment had the effect of discharging him under the doctrine of merger. (See § 21–13 infra). It was held that other co-obligors who were jointly and severally liable with the executor were also discharged.

37. Deering v. Moore, 86 Me. 181, 29 A. 988 (1893); Line v. Nelson, 38 N.J.L. 358 (1876); 2 Williston § 333A.

38. 4 Corbin § 932; 2 Williston §§ 338, 338C.

39. Restatement, Contracts § 124; Restatement, Second, Contracts § 295. See § 21–10 infra.

40. 4 Corbin § 933; 2 Williston § 338; but see Penza v. Neckles, 340 So.2d 1210 (Fla.App.1976).

covenant not to sue.[41] The requirement that the reservation of rights must be in writing and concurrent stems from the parol evidence rule.[42]

There are also many states which have changed the common law rule by statute. For example, the Model Joint Obligations Act provides that a release or discharge of one or more of joint, joint and several or several obligors does not discharge co-obligors against whom rights are reserved in writing and as part of the same transaction.[43] If there is no reservation of rights, then if the obligee knows or has reason to know "that the obligor released or discharged did not pay so much of the claim as he was bound by his contract or relation with that co-obligor to pay, the obligee's claim against that co-obligor shall be satisfied to the amount which the obligee knew or had reason to know that the released or discharged obligor was bound to such co-obligor to pay." [44]

For example, X, Y and Z are jointly obligated to C in the sum of $18,000 (that is to say each is liable to C for $18,000). Assume that they have agreed *inter se* that X will be liable for ½ and Y for ¼. If C knows this and releases X, then Y and Z will be liable for only $9,000.

The statute goes on to say that, in the illustration given, if C did not know or have reason to know of the agreement of the parties *inter se* then Y and Z will be discharged to the extent of the lesser of two amounts: [45] (1) "the amount of the fractional share of the obligor released or discharged," which on the facts in the illustration is $6,000, that is ⅓ (since there are three co-obligors involved) of $18,000; (2) "the amount that such obligor was bound by his contract or relation with his co-obligor to pay" which on the facts is $9,000.

Since the lesser sum is $6,000, it is obvious that C could still proceed against Y and Z for $12,000 ($18,000–$6,000). It is equally apparent that if Y and Z paid the $12,000 they should still be entitled to collect $3,000 from X.

What has been said does not apply to a suretyship situation. As we have seen, it is possible for a principal and a surety to promise as joint promisors and normally the same rules will apply despite the principal-surety relation.[46] However it is a rule of suretyship law, which has not been changed by statute or by case law, that a creditor who releases a principal with knowledge of the suretyship relation releases the surety in the absence of a reservation of rights.[47] Conversely a discharge of a surety does not discharge a principal debt.[48]

41. Restatement, Second, Contracts § 294, Comment a; accord, Community School Dist. v. Peterson, 176 N.W.2d 169 (Iowa 1970) (collecting cases supporting the modern view); Deblon v. Beaton, 103 N.J. Super. 345, 247 A.2d 172 (1968).

42. Oxford Commercial Corp. v. Landau, 12 N.Y.2d 362, 239 N.Y.S.2d 865, 190 N.E.2d 230, 13 A.L.R.3d 309 (1963); see 4 Corbin § 934.

43. See, e.g., McKinney's N.Y.Gen.Obligations Law § 15–104.

44. See, e.g., McKinney's N.Y.Gen.Obligations Law § 15–105(1); cf. McKinney's N.Y.Gen.Obligations Law § 15–108(a) (applicable to joint tortfeasors).

45. See, e.g., McKinney's N.Y.Gen.Obligations Law § 15–105(2).

46. See § 20–2 supra.

47. Restatement, Security § 122.

48. Restatement, Second, Contracts § 294(1)(a). The principal is ordinarily credited with any consideration which the

WESTLAW REFERENCES

di("compulsory joinder" /p contract)

"compulsory joinder" /p statute /p contract

judgment /s discharg*** /s joint /2 promisor obligor

find 414 ne2d 1023

death died /s joint /2 obligor promisor

discharg*** /s joint /2 obligor promisor

331k28(1) /p joint /2 obligor promisor

331k29(1) /p joint /2 2k52 /p joint /2 obligor promisor

"model joint obligations act"

§ 20–4. Consequences of Joint and Several Liability

As we have seen, if A and B promise jointly and severally there are actually three liabilities, the several liability of A, the several liability of B, and the joint liability of A and B.[49] Therefore, many of the problems which exist with respect to joint liability also exist with respect to joint and several liability.

On the question of joinder, the rule was that the plaintiff could elect to sue one or he could elect to sue all, but he could not elect to sue more than one unless he sued all.[50] Thus, if the creditor sued one of the obligors on his several promise and recovered, there was no merger and separate actions and separate judgments could be obtained against the others.[51] But, if the creditor brought suit against more than one and less than all of the obligors, the rule of merger with respect to joint obligors would apply.[52]

If the creditor sues one of the several obligors without joining the other obligors and loses, the doctrine of merger would not apply and his only problem would be under the doctrine of collateral estoppel by judgment.[53] The result would be otherwise if more than one were sued or if all were sued, in which event the rule with respect to joint obligors would obtain.[54]

The common law doctrine of survivorship which applied to joint obligations did not apply to joint and several obligations in the sense that the creditor could sue the representative of the deceased obligor on

---

surety pays. The surety is entitled to reimbursement for the part payment and upon full payment is in addition entitled to be subrogated. Restatement, Security §§ 104, 141. If there is an agreement that the payment by the surety is not to be credited upon the obligation, the surety loses his right of reimbursement. Restatement, Second, Contracts § 294(3), Comment g.

49. See § 20–2 supra. On the common law of joint and several liability, see generally, Chaney, Liability of Parties Who Are at the Same Time Both Jointly and Severally Liable Ex Contractu, 57 Cent.L.J. 283 (1903).

50. Koenig v. Curran's Restaurant & Baking Co., 306 Pa. 345, 159 A. 553 (1932). This common law rule has been largely eliminated by modern rules of procedure. 4 Corbin § 937.

51. Gruber v. Friedman, 104 Conn. 107, 132 A. 395 (1926).

52. Restatement, Second, Contracts § 291, Comment a.

53. 4 Corbin § 937.

54. Restatement, Second, Contracts § 292, Comment a.

his several obligation.[55]   But, where the creditor sought to sue the representative of the deceased obligor along with other co-obligors, the action could be resisted by the representative.

As we have seen the general common law rule is that a voluntary release of one joint obligor releases the others.[56] Strangely enough the same rule [57] was applied to a joint and several obligation.[58]

Just as the rules with respect to joint obligations have been changed by statute and court decisions,[59] so the rules as to joint and several obligations which followed the joint obligations rules have also been changed.

WESTLAW REFERENCES
joinder /s joint /2 obligor promisor
56k460
merger /s joint /2 obligor promisor
survivorship /s joint /2 obligor promisor

§ 20–5. Consequences of Several Liability

There is very little to be said concerning the consequences of several liability because none of the consequences that arose with respect to joint and joint and several liability arise here except where suretyship principles may be involved.[60] Indeed, since the obligations were considered separate, at common law it was not possible to join the several obligors in one action. If the plaintiff did in fact join several obligors in one action and at trial demonstrated that the defendants were severally liable, judgment would be entered against the plaintiff because only joint or joint and several obligors could be joined as defendants.[61] Under modern procedural statutes several obligors can generally be joined as defendants.[62]

WESTLAW REFERENCES
liab! /s several /2 obligor promisor

---

55. Eggleston v. Buck, 31 Ill. 254 (1863).

56. Fisher v. Chadwick, 4 Wyo. 379, 34 P. 899 (1893).

57. See § 20–3 supra.

58. Dwy v. Connecticut Co., 89 Conn. 74, 92 A. 883 (1915); Deese v. Mobley, 392 So.2d 364 (Fla.App.1981) (rule survives but is affected by Art. 3 of U.C.C.).

59. See § 20–3 supra; see also United Pacific Ins. Co. v. Lundstrom, 77 Wn.2d 162, 459 P.2d 930 (1969) (release of one joint and several obligor does not discharge others unless intention to discharge is manifested.)

60. Simpson, Contracts § 139.

61. Jones and Carlin, Non-Joinder and Misjoinder of Parties—Common Law Actions, 28 W.Va.L.Q. 266, 266–76 (1922); see also Air Engineers, Inc. v. Reese, 283 Ala. 355, 217 So.2d 66 (1968), indicating that this rule prevails in Alabama in attenuated form. If plaintiff alleges joint liability but proves that liability is several he may be non-suited because of a variance between pleading and proof. Wheatley v. Carl M. Halvorson, 213 Or. 228, 323 P.2d 49 (1958).

62. See Clark, Code Pleading §§ 60–61 (2d ed.1947).

§ 20–6. Relation of Co-obligors to Each Other—Contribution

We have discussed the consequences of joint, joint and several, and several liability of co-obligors liable for the same performance from the point of view of their liability to the obligee. The question here is the rights and liabilities of the co-obligors *inter se.* This does not depend upon whether the liability of the co-obligors is joint, joint and several, or several but depends upon suretyship principles.[63]

It is obvious that any payment, whether full or partial, by any co-obligor will inure to the benefit of the other co-obligor in the sense that there is a partial discharge of the obligation.[64] An agreement to the contrary is not effective.[65]

If C builds a house for X and Y at an agreed price of $18,000 and X pays the full $18,000, it is obvious that X should recover $9,000 from Y in the absence of any particular agreement between X and Y. This result is generally stated by saying that a co-obligor who has paid more than his proportionate share is entitled to contribution.[66] What is the proportionate share of a co-obligor depends upon the agreement between or among the co-obligors and, if there is no agreement between or among the parties, upon equitable principles. Thus, in the illustration given, in the absence of an agreement, X and Y as between themselves would be liable for $9,000 each.[67] But if X and Y agreed between themselves that X was responsible for $2/3$ and Y for $1/3$, X would be entitled to only $6,000 from Y.[68]

The situation would be different if C made a loan of $18,000 to X which X and Y agreed to repay. Here although X and Y are still co-obligors, X is the principal and Y the surety,[69] and so when X pays the $18,000 he is not entitled to contribution.[70] The situation would also be different if the loan was to Y, in which event X would be the surety. Here if X paid he would not be entitled to contribution ($9,000), but to reimbursement ($18,000).[71] In addition, he would be entitled to all other rights which a surety has including the right of exoneration,[72]

63. Aspinwall v. Sacchi, 57 N.Y. 331 (1874); 2 Williston § 345.

64. 4 Corbin § 936.

65. Restatement, Second, Contracts §§ 294(3), 295(3). The only exception, as we have seen, is where the payment comes from a surety and it is expressly agreed that the amount paid should not be credited against the obligation. In such an event, the surety loses his right to reimbursement to the extent that he agrees that the amount paid shall not be credited to the obligation. See § 20–3 supra.

66. Thomas v. Diamond, 33 A.D.2d 602, 304 N.Y.S.2d 549 (3d Dep't 1969); Simpson, Contracts § 143 (2d ed.1965).

67. As to C, of course, we are assuming that both X and Y are liable for the full $18,000.

68. 2 Williston § 345; Restatement, Restitution § 81 (1937).

69. The reason why Y is the surety is that as between X and Y, X is the one who should ultimately pay because all of the consideration came to him. Restatement, Security § 82.

70. Obviously the principal debtor does not have rights against the surety.

71. Restatement, Security § 104.

72. Restatement, Security § 112.

which is enforced by an equitable decree compelling the principal to fulfill his obligation to the creditor.[73]

In a sense there is also suretyship involved in the original illustration (where C built a house for X and Y). Here, as between X and Y, X is primarily liable for $9,000 and Y is his surety for that $9,000. Conversely Y is primarily liable for $9,000 and X is his surety for that $9,000.[74] Thus, in the illustration given, X is only entitled to be reimbursed for the $9,000 on which he is a surety; he is not entitled to recover the $9,000 on which he is the principal.[75]

 WESTLAW REFERENCES
digest(contribution /s co-obligor co-promisor)

B. MULTIPLE OBLIGEES

Table of Sections

§ 20–7. Multiple Promisees

Previously we dealt with the question of multiple promisors. In this section we are concerned with multiple promisees. Here again we are not concerned with promises which promise different performances to multiple promisees but rather are concerned with promises which promise the *same* performance to multiple promisees.[76] As is the case with obligations, "rights may be either 'joint' or 'several' or some combination." [77]

Under the modern view, at least, the question is one of intention, and where the intention is not clearly shown the rights of obligees of the same performance are deemed to be joint except where "the interests of the obligee in the performance or in the remedies for

---

73. Glades County v. Detroit Fidelity & Sur. Co., 57 F.2d 449 (5th Cir.1932); D'Ippolito v. Castoro, 51 N.J. 584, 242 A.2d 617 (1968).

74. Lorimer v. Knack Coal Co., 246 Mich. 214, 224 N.W. 362, 64 A.L.R. 210 (1929); Wold v. Grozalsky, 277 N.Y. 364, 14 N.E.2d 437, 122 A.L.R. 518 (1938).

75. See notes 70 and 71 supra.

76. This distinction is drawn in the Restatement, Second, Contracts § 297, Comment a.

77. Restatement, Second, Contracts § 297, Comment a. The Reporter's Note to

§ 128 confusingly states that "[r]eferences to 'several' rights and 'joint and several' rights are omitted." At the same time illustration 3 to the section concludes: "D has a several right." Cf. Braucher, supra note 14, at 610, stating: " * * * the original Restatement provided that co-promisees of the same performance might have a 'joint' right, 'several' rights, or 'joint and several' rights. But nothing of substance seemed to turn on this terminology and the Second Restatement refers only to 'joint' rights."

breach are distinct." [78] This means that the surrounding circumstances will be considered to determine whether or not promisees have distinct interests or a unitary interest in the promised performance.[79] Thus, for example, if A promised to pay B and C $1,000 for work to be done by B and C in the construction of a road, the question of whether B and C are joint promisees is resolved by interpreting the wording of the contract in the light of the nature of the relationship between B and C. If they are partners, they have a community of interest in the profits and losses of the transaction and as a matter of law their rights are joint.[80] If they were not in a formal sense partners, but joined together for this particular project with an intention to share profits and losses, the same result would likely follow.[81] Here too they would be operating as a business organization even if on an ad hoc basis.[82] If, however, B and C were merely employees of A there would be no community of interest between B and C and their rights would be several. In a leading case,[83] A, B, and C promised to care for D's herd of cattle for two years and D promised to pay them one-half of the selling price in excess of $36,000. Although the promise in form might appear to have been made to the promisees jointly, the court took note of the fact that the promisees were but employees and had no community of interest in any capital investment and would not share any losses and held that B could sue separately for his one-sixth interest in the excess over $36,000. Similarly, where a coal merchant in a single document promised to take all of his requirements from three coal companies in equal shares, it was held that each of the coal companies was a several obligee, there being no connection between them other than the contract itself.[84] It should be pointed out, however, that if each of the coal companies desired to join in one action against the merchant, there is little question that the action should be permitted even in the face of a statute which permits joinder of plaintiffs only when they have a "joint" right.[85] If necessary, the rights of the obligees should be classified as "joint" for permitting joint action by them and "several" for the purpose of permitting separate actions by them.

78. Restatement, Second, Contracts § 297; see 4 Corbin §§ 939–940; 2 Williston § 321.

79. St. Regis Paper Co. v. Stuart, 214 F.2d 762 (1st Cir.1954), cert. denied 348 U.S. 915, 75 S.Ct. 296, 99 L.Ed. 717 (1955).

80. Crane and Bromberg, Partnership § 57 (1968).

81. Id. at § 35.

82. Apparently, the intent of the Restatement Second is to reach the same result, but it characterizes cases such as this as involving promises of separate performances. Restatement, Second, Contracts, Reporter's Note to § 297. But see illustration 3 thereto.

83. Beckwith v. Talbot, 95 U.S. (5 Otto) 289, 24 L.Ed. 496 (1877); accord, St. Regis

Paper Co. v. Stuart, 214 F.2d 762 (1st Cir. 1954), cert. denied 348 U.S. 915, 75 S.Ct. 296, 99 L.Ed. 717 (1955) (two salesmen worked as a team and were promised a team commission; despite absence of words of severability, held that one of the salesmen could bring an action for his share of the commission).

84. Shipman v. Straitsville Central Mining Co., 158 U.S. 356 (1895); compare Donzella v. New York State Thruway Authority, 7 A.D.2d 771, 180 N.Y.S.2d 108 (3d Dep't 1958).

85. See 4 Corbin § 940. It should also be observed that almost everywhere several obligees of the same performance are now permitted to join as plaintiffs.

WESTLAW REFERENCES
joint multiple /2 promises

§ 20–8. Compulsory Joinder of Joint Obligees

Where there are multiple promisees and they have a joint right, the promisor has a right to expect that he will not be harassed by a multiplicity of actions.[86] Thus, where less than all of the joint promisees bring an action the defendant as a common law proposition may raise this issue and prevent a judgment.[87] Statutes which have relaxed the rule of compulsory joinder of joint obligors generally also relax the rule as to joint obligees.[88] Even though a joint obligee refuses to join in the action he may be joined as a plaintiff or an additional party defendant.[89] The fact that one of the joint obligees is out of the jurisdiction does not vary the situation because any joint obligee should be able to sue in the name of all of the joint obligees.[90]

 WESTLAW REFERENCES
title(dakin & greer)
find 434 f2d 1027

§ 20–9. Discharge by One Joint Obligee

One joint obligee has the right to act for the others and may discharge the rights of his co-obligees; for example, by accepting payment, by an accord and satisfaction or by release.[91] There is an exception to this rule in the case of negotiable instruments.[92] Another exception occurs where the discharge is in violation of a duty to a co-obligee who may then avoid the discharge to the extent necessary to protect himself "except to the extent that the promisor has given value or otherwise changed his position in good faith and without knowledge or reason to know of the violation."[93]

Inconsistent with the general rule that one joint obligee may discharge a joint obligation, is the holding that a repudiation by one of

86. 4 Corbin § 939; see generally, Reed, supra note 15.

87. Lee v. Ricca, 29 Ariz. 309, 241 P. 508 (1925); Dakin v. Greer, 685 S.W.2d 276 (Mo.App.1985).

88. See, e.g., Fed.R.Civ.P. 19; McKinney's N.Y.C.P.L.R. 1001; § 20–3 supra.

89. Hand v. Heslet, 81 Mont. 68, 261 P. 609 (1927).

90. Jackson Mfg. Co. v. United States, 434 F.2d 1027 (5th Cir.1970). There are exceptions to this rule in the case of negotiable instruments, where the joint obligees have made a contrary agreement, or where bringing the action would amount to the violation of a duty to a co-obligee. Restatement, Second, Contracts § 298(2).

91. Restatement, Second, Contracts § 299; Cayce v. Carter Oil Co., 618 F.2d 669 (1980).

92. U.C.C. § 3–116.

93. Restatement, Second, Contracts § 300(2). Thus if the obligor knows that the obligee he has released is violating his duty to his co-obligees, the release is effective only to the extent of the released obligee's share of the performance. An exhaustive review of the authorities appears in Freeman v. Montague Associates, Inc., 18 Misc.2d 1, 187 N.Y.S.2d 636 (1959) (which, however, reached a contrary conclusion), reversed 9 A.D.2d 936, 195 N.Y.S.2d 392 (2d Dep't 1959), lv. to appeal denied 10 A.D.2d 637, 197 N.Y.S.2d 441 (2d Dep't 1960).

the parties who jointly held rights and obligations under a bilateral contract does not create an anticipatory breach,[94] and that one joint obligee cannot exercise an option to accelerate.[95]

WESTLAW REFERENCES
discharg*** /s joint /2 obligee promisee

§ 20–10. Survivorship of Joint Rights

The rule of survivorship with respect to joint obligors also applied to joint obligees.[96] That is to say that if a joint promisee died his executor no longer had any right to sue the obligor for a money judgment.[97] If all of the joint obligees died the personal representative of the last survivor could alone sue the obligor.[98] Ordinarily, at least, the death of a joint obligee would not deprive his representative of his right to an accounting from the co-obligee who received performance or settled the claim.[99] The rule set forth above has not been changed and is justified as a matter of convenience because "it is unnecessary to join the personal representative of a deceased co-obligee in an action for a money judgment."[1]

WESTLAW REFERENCES
survivorship /s joint /2 obligee promisee

§ 20–11. Multiple Offerees or Optionees

An offer made jointly to a group of six offerees cannot be accepted by two of them.[2] Similarly, an offer made to two joint lessees cannot be accepted by either of them individually.[3] A purported exercise of an option by one of three multiple optionees is not a good acceptance.[4] This is especially true where there is a credit term in the offer.[5] Even in the absence of a credit term, however, an optionor exposes himself to the possibility of litigation if he sells to one of multiple optionees.[6] Of

94. Link v. Weizenbaum, 229 Va. 201, 326 S.E.2d 667 (1985).

95. Lapidus v. Kollel Avreichim Torah Veyirah, 114 Misc.2d 451, 451 N.Y.S.2d 958 (1982).

96. See § 20–3 supra.

97. Israel v. Jones, 97 W.Va. 173, 124 S.E. 665 (1924).

98. Restatement, Second, Contracts § 301.

99. Hill v. Breeden, 53 Wyo. 125, 79 P.2d 482 (1938). Thus, for example, in a partnership, only the surviving partners may enforce partnership claims, but the estate of the deceased partner has a beneficial interest in the proceeds of the litigation. Contrariwise, upon the death of a joint tenant, the estate of the deceased tenant has no such beneficial interest. The result turns on the substantive law of partnership and real property, rather than on merely procedural rules.

1. Restatement, Second, Contracts § 301, Comment b. This comment adds: "Where equitable relief is sought, joinder of such a representative is permitted and when necessary to complete adjudication is required."

2. Meister v. Arden-Mayfair, Inc., 276 Or. 517, 555 P.2d 923 (1976).

3. Spitalnik v. Springer, 59 N.Y.2d 112, 463 N.Y.S.2d 750, 450 N.E.2d 670 (1983), reargument denied 60 N.Y.2d 702, 468 N.Y.S.2d 1027, 455 N.E.2d 1267 (1983).

4. Clayman v. Goodman Properties, Inc., 518 F.2d 1026 (D.C.Cir.1973).

5. Id.

6. Spitalnik v. Springer, note 3, supra.

course, if the one offeree or optionee has authority to bind the others and exercises that authority the result would be different.[7]

7. See, e.g., Crane & Bromberg, Partnership §§ 49–50 on authority of a partner.

Chapter 21

DISCHARGE OF CONTRACTS

Table of Sections

Table of Sections

861

§ 21–1. Introduction

The First Restatement of Contracts listed twenty-two ways in which a contract may be discharged.[1] Some of these have been discussed previously. Included in this category are "occurrence of a condition subsequent";[2] "breach by the other party or failure of consideration, or frustration";[3] "exercise of the power of avoidance if the duty is avoidable";[4] "impossibility";[5] "illegality of a contract or of its enforcement";[6] "the failure of a condition precedent to exist or to occur";[7] "incapacity of the parties to retain the right duty relationship";[8] and "the rules governing joint debtors."[9] Two of the methods of discharge listed, "res judicata" and "the rules governing sureties," are beyond the scope of this treatise. The remaining twelve, some of which have been mentioned elsewhere, will be discussed briefly here.

 WESTLAW REFERENCES
di impossibility
di illegality
di incapacity
di res judicata

I. CONSENSUAL DISCHARGES

A. RESCISSION

Table of Sections

§ 21–2. Mutual Rescission

If A and B enter into an executory bilateral contract they are free to rescind the agreement by a mutual agreement. The surrender of rights under the original agreement by each party is the consideration for the mutual agreement of rescission.[10] Formerly, a sealed instrument could be discharged by a subsequent agreement only if the later agreement was also under seal. Today, however, the prevailing view in jurisdictions which have retained the seal is that an agreement under seal may be modified, rescinded or substituted by an oral agreement or an unsealed written agreement.[11]

---

1. Restatement, Contracts § 385. The Restatement Second contains no such catalog, but see Introductory Note to its Ch. 12.

2. See § 11–7 supra.

3. See § 11–18 and ch. 13 supra.

4. See, e.g., § 8–4 supra.

5. See ch. 13 supra.

6. See ch. 22 infra.

7. See § 11–15 supra.

8. See Restatement, Contracts § 450 (discharge by marriage; an obsolete provision).

9. See ch. 20 supra.

10. Kirk v. Brentwood Manor Homes Inc., 191 Pa.Super. 488, 159 A.2d 48 (1960).

11. Kirk v. Brentwood Manor Homes, Inc., supra; Restatement, Contracts § 407, Comment c; 5A Corbin § 1236; 6 Corbin

Sometimes a contract provides that it cannot be rescinded except in a writing signed by the contracting party. As a common law proposition such a provision is ineffective as the parties cannot restrain their future ability to contract with each other in the future.[12] The U.C.C.[13] and some state statutes of general applicability [14] give efficacy to such provisions however.

If the original agreement has been performed in part by one of the parties before the agreement of mutual rescission, the question frequently presented is whether the performance which has been rendered should be paid for. The question is one of the intention of the parties.[15] Very often, however, the parties have expressed no intention on the matter, expressing themselves in broad terms such as "Let's call the whole deal off." Some courts have ruled that in such a case a promise to pay for the performances rendered should be implied.[16] Others have indulged in the presumption that unless an affirmative agreement to the contrary appears the parties intended that payment need not be made for services rendered prior to rescission.[17] As in any case involving intention, stare decisis should play but a suggestive role and each case should be decided on its facts.[18]

A similar problem arises where a party cancels the contract because of a material breach.[19] Section 2–720 of the Uniform Commercial Code provides that "Unless the contrary intention clearly appears, expressions of 'cancellation' or 'rescission' of the contract or the like shall not be construed as a renunciation or discharge of any claim in damages for an antecedent breach." The Code language and comment make it clear that this provision applies after a breach and is designed to avoid an involuntary loss of a remedy for breach by the use of language by the aggrieved party to the effect that the contract is called off. The Code primarily addresses itself to a number of unsound decisions that have held that, when a contract is cancelled for breach, it is logically impossible to permit an action on the contract since the contract is non-existent; therefore only quasi-contractual relief is available.[20] The Code takes cognizance of the fact that the term "rescission" is often used by lawyers, courts and businessmen in many different

---

§ 1316; 15 Williston §§ 1834–36; see § 7–8 supra and § 21–3 infra.

12. ABC Outdoor Advertising v. Dolhun's Marine, 38 Wis.2d 457, 157 N.W.2d 680 (1968).

13. U.C.C. § 2.209(2), discussed at § 5–14 supra.

14. E.g., Cal.Civ.Code § 1698; McKinney's N.Y.Gen.Oblig.Law § 15–301. As to the effect of the Statute of Frauds, see 19–37 supra.

15. Restatement, Second, Contracts § 283, Comment c; Restatement, Contracts § 409; 5A Corbin § 1236; 15 Williston § 1827.

16. Anderson v. Copeland, 378 P.2d 1006 (Okl.1963); Johnston v. Gilbert, 234 Or. 350, 382 P.2d 87 (1963).

17. Coletti v. Knox Hat Co., 252 N.Y. 468, 169 N.E. 648 (1930).

18. Restatement, Contracts § 409; 5A Corbin § 1236; 15 Williston § 1827; see Montgomery v. Stuyvesant Ins. Co., 393 F.2d 754 (4th Cir.1968); Copeland Process Corp. v. Nalews, Inc., 113 N.H. 612, 312 A.2d 576 (1973).

19. See §§ 11–18, 11–33 supra.

20. Walter-Wallingford Coal Co. v. A. Himes Coal Co., 223 Mich. 576, 194 N.W. 493 (1923); Thackeray v. Knight, 192 P. 263 (Utah 1920); see Woodward, Quasi

senses; for example, termination of a contract by virtue of an option to terminate in the agreement, cancellation for breach and avoidance on the grounds of infancy or fraud.[21] In the interests of clarity of thought—as the consequences of each of these forms of discharge may vary—the Commercial Code carefully distinguishes three circumstances. "Rescission" is utilized as a term of art to refer to a mutual agreement to discharge contractual duties.[22] "Termination" refers to the discharge of duties by the exercise of a power granted by the agreement.[23] "Cancellation" refers to the putting an end to the contract by reason of a breach by the other party.[24] Section 2–720, however, takes into account that the parties do not necessarily use these terms in this way.

To return to the topic of mutual rescission, if one of the parties has fully performed under a bilateral contract or as offeree of a unilateral contract, a mutual agreement to put the contract to an end is ineffective as the party whose duties remain executory has incurred no detriment and therefore the promise of the party who has performed is not supported by consideration. Under some circumstances this purported rescission may be effective as a "release," a concept discussed below.[25] But generally speaking, as we have seen, if a party who has completely performed his part of the contract promises to surrender or purports to surrender his rights under the contract in the absence of consideration or of a statute providing otherwise or in the absence of a completed gift, the transaction is ineffective.[26] Thus it is a general rule that an attempt to discharge a duty that has arisen by complete or substantial performance requires consideration.[27] It must be stressed that we are not talking about a waiver of condition, which is discussed in Chapter 11, or renunciation of a right to damages for breach, which occurs before there has been complete performance, or renunciation of a right to recover for partial performance, which is discussed below.[28]

Rescission also occurs where the parties enter into a new contract which is substituted for the original contract. The old agreement is discharged but the parties are still bound contractually. At times new terms are added to an existing contract. It is obvious that the lines between three situations are indistinct:

Contracts, ch. 19 (1913); 5A Corbin § 1237; see also Annot., 1 A.L.R.2d 1084 (1948).

21. See, e.g., Annot., 1 A.L.R.2d 1084 (1948) ("Notice of Rescission as Irrevocable Election When Other Party Refuses to Assent Thereto"), where the annotator brings together cases involving significantly different issues merely because the court utilized the term "rescission."

22. U.C.C. § 2–209, Comment 3.

23. U.C.C. § 2–106(3).

24. U.C.C. § 2–106(4).

25. See § 5–16 supra and § 21–10 infra.

26. See §§ 4–9, 5–14, 5–16 supra. On the question of the gift of a debt, see also Annot., 63 A.L.R.2d 259 (1959) and § 21–3 infra.

27. It should be reiterated as stated in § 4–10 supra that the question of discharge of duties as an original proposition could have been distinguished and exempted from the requirement of consideration. But this is not the way in which the law developed.

28. See § 21–10 infra.

(1) Unconditional rescission of an existing contract followed by a subsequent entering into of a new agreement.

(2) Rescission of an existing contract contemporaneous with and conditioned on the entering into of a new agreement.

(3) Retention of an existing contract with an agreement as to new terms.

The manner of distinguishing among these situations has not been authoritatively answered and it may be that the variation in factual settings is so extensive that no test can be formulated, yet a good attempt has been made by one court: "An alteration of details of the contract which leaves undisturbed its general purpose constitutes a modification rather than a rescission of the contract." [29] The necessity for distinguishing these categories is not merely academic. For example, the presence or absence of consideration [30] and the necessity of complying with the Statute of Frauds [31] may vary, dependent upon the category into which the transaction falls.

Although rescissions are ordinarily expressed in words there are a good number of cases involving implied rescissions. For example, a mutual failure of the parties to cooperate in the performance of a contract,[32] or concurrent breaches by both parties [33] may be deemed an implied rescission. Where the parties are in dispute as to the mechanics of implementing their contract the failure of one party to reply to the other's offer to rescind may give rise to an implied rescission.[34] An unsuccessful attempt to renegotiate a contract may be found to constitute an implied rescission.[35] In some jurisdictions implied rescissions are classified under a classification known as abandonment,[36] a concept that comes from property rules concerning the relinquishment of leaseholds or other interests in land. The equating of implied mutual rescission and abandonment of a property interest is a source of confusion since distinct rules apply.[37]

WESTLAW REFERENCES
"mutual rescission" /s contract
ucc +s 2–209(2)
find 378 p2d 1006

29. Travelers Ins. Co. v. Workmen's Compensation Appeals Bd., 68 Cal.2d 7, 17, 64 Cal.Rptr. 440, 446, 434 P.2d 992, 998 (1967).

30. See the discussion in § 4–9 supra especially as it refers to Schwartzreich v. Bauman-Basch, Inc., 231 N.Y. 196, 131 N.E. 887 (1921), reargument denied 231 N.Y. 602, 132 N.E. 905 (1921).

31. See § 19–37 supra.

32. Admiral Plastics Corp. v. Trueblood, Inc., 436 F.2d 1335 (6th Cir. 1971); 2 Black, Rescission of Contracts and Cancellation of Written Instruments § 533 (2d ed.1929); 15 Williston § 1826.

33. Gentry v. Smith, 487 F.2d 571 (5th Cir.1973), appeal after remand 538 F.2d 1090.

34. Sweetarts v. Sunline, Inc., 423 F.2d 260 (8th Cir.1970).

35. Minnesota Ltd., Inc. v. Public Utilities Comm'n, 296 Minn. 316, 208 N.W.2d 284 (1973).

36. 2 Black, supra note 32 at § 532; C.J.S. Contracts § 412.

37. See Jakober v. E.M. Loew's Capitol Theater, 107 R.I. 104, 265 A.2d 429 (1970).

ucc   +s   2–720
"implied rescission"

B.   DESTRUCTION OR SURRENDER

Table of Sections

Sec.

§ 21–3.   Cancellation or Surrender, If the Contract Is Formal

At early common law the normal method of discharging a formal obligation was the cancellation of the instrument by its physical destruction or mutilation.[38] The theory was that the instrument itself was the obligation and not merely evidence of the obligation; therefore, cancellation of the instrument discharged the obligation irrespective of the intention of the parties. Surrender without destruction of the formal instrument did not amount to a discharge even if the parties intended a discharge.[39] However, under present law a formal instrument, such as a negotiable instrument,[40] insurance policy or instrument under seal, may be discharged by either cancellation or surrender provided that the party having the right intends to discharge the duty.[41] No consideration is required. Surrender or cancellation of an informal contract may be evidence of an intent to discharge[42] but, in addition, consideration, or one of its substitutes, or the elements of a gift, would be required.[43]

 WESTLAW REFERENCES

cancellation   /s   contract   /s   destroy*** destruction mutilation
ucc   +s   3–605
find 131 ne 887
255k7
95k75
95k253

---

38. Ames, Specialty Contracts and Equitable Defences, 9 Harv.L.Rev. 49 (1895).

39. 15 Williston § 1876.

40. U.C.C. § 3–605(1) (negotiable instruments). But if a negotiable instrument is discharged by surrender, a subsequent holder in due course will be permitted to enforce the instrument. U.C.C. § 3–602.

41. Restatement, Second, Contracts § 274; 15 Williston § 1878; 5A Corbin § 1250. If the formal instrument is bilateral, both parties must join in or consent to cancellation. Restatement, Contracts § 432(2).

42. If the contract is bilateral and executory on both sides, surrender or cancellation joined in by both parties would result in a mutual rescission. See Schwartzreich v. Bauman-Basch, Inc., 231 N.Y. 196, 131 N.E. 887 (1921), reargument denied 231 N.Y. 602, 132 N.E. 905 (1921).

43. See chs. 4, 5, 6 supra; 5A Corbin § 1250; 15 Williston §§ 1876, 1879. See § 21–2 supra.

C. EXECUTORY BILATERAL CONTRACT OF ACCORD—ACCORD AND SATISFACTION— SUBSTITUTED AGREEMENT— UNILATERAL ACCORD

Table of Sections

§ 21–4. Background of the Problem

A bilateral executory accord is "an agreement that an existing claim shall be discharged *in the future* by the rendition of a substituted performance." [44] For example, C (creditor) writes D (debtor), "I promise to discharge the debt you owe me upon delivery of your black mare if you promise to deliver the horse to me within a reasonable time." D promises. Their agreement is a bilateral executory accord.

If D delivers the horse and C accepts it there is an accord and satisfaction. The agreement is the accord. Its performance is the satisfaction.[45] We have already seen that an accord and satisfaction supported by consideration discharges a claim.[46]

Formerly, an executory bilateral accord was without any effect even if, as in the illustration given, it was supported by consideration. An executory accord could not be used as a defense nor did its breach give rise to a cause of action.[47] The reason for the rule is purely historical. Informal contracts supported by consideration were not recognized under the early common law and so it was very often held that an executory bilateral accord was not enforceable. When informal bilateral contracts came to be enforced, apparently the courts failed to recognize that an executory bilateral accord was nothing more nor less

44. Alaska Creamery Products, Inc. v. Wells, 373 P.2d 505, 511 (Alaska 1962); (emphasis supplied); see also Restatement, Second, Contracts § 281(1); 6 Corbin § 1268. See generally, Gold, Executory Accords, 21 Boston U.L.Rev. 465 (1941); Havighurst, Reflections on the Executory Accord, in Perspectives of Law; Essays for Austin Wakeman Scott 190 (1964); Comment, Executory Accord, Accord and Satisfaction, and Novation—The Distinctions, 26 Baylor L.Rev. 185 (1974).

45. Jon-T Chemicals, Inc. v. Freeport Chemical Co., 704 F.2d 1412 (5th Cir.1983); 6 Corbin § 1269. In the cases discussed in § 4–11 the cashing of the check manifests the assent of the creditor to the accord and also simultaneously operates as the satisfaction.

46. See § 4–11 supra.

47. Reilly v. Barrett, 220 N.Y. 170, 115 N.E. 453 (1917); see also Larscy v. T. Hogan & Sons, Inc., 239 N.Y. 298, 146 N.E. 430 (1925).

than a bilateral contract and continued to apply the old rule of unenforceability to them.[48]

An executory bilateral accord must be distinguished from a substituted agreement. Even now, significantly different results stem from the two kinds of transactions. If we change slightly the illustration previously given we can also illustrate a substituted agreement. C (creditor) writes to D (debtor), "If you will promise to deliver your black mare within 30 days I will immediately treat the debt you owe me as satisfied and discharged." D accepts the offer. Here we have a substituted agreement. It operates immediately to discharge C's claim. Because the discharge is immediate, the substituted contract is frequently called an accord and satisfaction. This terminology is not used here because it may prove confusing.[49] This situation is factually distinct from an accord and satisfaction created by the performance of an executory accord.

The two illustrations given above are quite similar. First, we note that both are bilateral and supported by consideration.[50] The essential difference, however, is that in the second case, where a substituted agreement is created, C asks for and accepts D's new promise in satisfaction of the original claim. In the first illustration, however, C made it clear that the original claim will not be discharged until the debtor performs the new agreement.[51] An executory accord is created.

The common law rule making executory accords unenforceable has been overturned by judicial decisions in so many states that today they are generally deemed to be enforceable.[52] In New York the common law rule has been changed by statute but only where such an agreement is in writing and signed by the party "against whom it is sought to enforce the accord," "or by his agent." [53]

48. 6 Corbin § 1271; 15 Williston §§ 1839–40; Gold, supra note 44, at 465–71.

49. Other classifications of such an agreement are "novations," "compromise and settlement" and "accord accepted in satisfaction." As to the use of "novation," see § 21–8 infra.

50. In this context as in others, promissory estoppel may substitute for consideration. Boshart v. Gardner, 190 Ark. 104, 77 S.W.2d 642, 96 A.L.R. 1130 (1935) (an executory accord mistakenly labeled a "novation," but treated as an executory accord; expenses incurred in reliance on the accord a substitute for consideration).

51. 1937 N.Y.Law Rev.Comm.Rep. 214–218.

52. Very v. Levy, 54 U.S. (13 How.) 345, 14 L.Ed. 173 (1851); Markowitz & Co. v. Toledo Met. Housing Auth., 608 F.2d 699 (6th Cir.1979); Union Central Life Ins. Co. v. Imsland, 91 F.2d 365 (8th Cir.1937);

Trenton St. Ry. Co. v. Lawlor, 74 N.J.Eq. 828, 71 A. 234 (Ct.Err. & App.1908); Dobias v. White, 239 N.C. 409, 80 S.E.2d 23 (1954), on appeal after remand 240 N.C. 680, 83 S.E.2d 785 (1954); Ladd v. General Ins. Co., 236 Or. 260, 387 P.2d 572 (1963); Browning v. Holloway, 620 S.W.2d 611 (Tex.Civ.App.1981); Restatement, Second, Contracts § 281; Restatement, Contracts § 417; 6 Corbin §§ 1271–73; 15 Williston § 1845. The common law view retains some adherents. Karvalsky v. Becker, 217 Ind. 524, 29 N.E.2d 560, 131 A.L.R. 1074 (1940); Bartlett v. Newton, 148 Me. 279, 92 A.2d 611 (1952).

53. McKinney's N.Y.Gen.Oblig.Law § 15–501. This statute has been characterized as a provision of the Statute of Frauds. Condo v. Mulcahy, 88 A.D.2d 497, 454 N.Y.S.2d 308 (2d Dep't 1982). Earlier statutes in California and other states adopting a civil code are collected in 1937 N.Y.L.Rev.Comm.Rep. 241–44.

§ 21–5. Differing Consequences of Executory Bilateral Accords and Substituted Contracts

An enforceable executory accord has considerably different effects from a substituted agreement. The original obligations of the parties are, by definition, not satisfied until the bilateral executory accord is performed. Under the view which seems to have gained general acceptance, the executory accord has a suspensive effect on the prior obligations.[54] In the event the debtor breaches the agreement the prior obligation revives and the creditor has the option of enforcing the original claim or the executory bilateral accord.[55] Part performance by the debtor followed by unjustified failure to complete does not prevent an action by the creditor on the original claim.[56]

If the creditor breaches, as by refusing the debtor's tender of his part of the executory accord, a similar rule exists. The debtor may raise the executory accord as a defense against an action by the creditor on the original claim,[57] and may maintain an action for specific performance of the accord.[58] Instead the debtor may seek damages for total or partial breach.[59]

As previously indicated,[60] a substituted contract immediately discharges the prior claim which is merged into the new agreement. Consequently, in the absence of an express agreement to the contrary, the original claim can no longer be enforced. In the event of a breach, any action would have to be brought on the substituted agreement.[61] If, however, the substitute agreement is unenforceable or voidable, the original claim either remains unimpaired or is revived by avoidance of

54. Restatement, Second, Contracts § 281(2). A tripartite accord, although not denominated as such, suspending a mortgagee's right to foreclose, was found in Fairbanks v. Kaye, 16 Alaska 23, 227 F.2d 566 (9th Cir.1955).

55. Markowitz & Co. v. Toledo Met. Housing Auth., 608 F.2d 699 (6th Cir.1979); Mitchell Properties, Inc., v. Real Estate Title Co., Inc., 62 Md.App. 473, 490 A.2d 271 (1985); Ladd v. General Ins. Co., 236 Or. 260, 387 P.2d 572 (1963); Browning v. Holloway, 620 S.W.2d 611 (Tex.Civ.App. 1981). It has been held that the creditor need not elect between the original obligation and the executory accord until after all the evidence has been adduced by both parties. Plant City Steel Corp. v. National Mach. Exch., Inc., 23 N.Y.2d 472, 297 N.Y.S.2d 559, 245 N.E.2d 213 (1969). After judgment has been entered on the executory accord, the creditor is precluded from

suing on the original claim. Coffeyville State Bank v. Lembeck, 227 Kan. 857, 610 P.2d 616 (1980).

56. Stratton v. West States Constr., 21 Utah 2d 60, 440 P.2d 117 (1968).

57. Clark v. Elza, 286 Md.App. 208, 406 A.2d 922 (1979); Bestor v. American Nat'l Stores, Inc., 691 S.W.2d 384 (Mo.App.1985).

58. Union Central Life Ins. Co. v. Imsland, 91 F.2d 365 (8th Cir.1937). See Corbin, Recent Developments in the Law of Contracts, 50 Harv.L.Rev. 449, 466 (1937).

59. Restatement, Second, Contracts § 281(3), Comment c.

60. Section 21–4 supra.

61. Moers v. Moers, 229 N.Y. 294, 128 N.E. 202, 14 A.L.R. 225 (1920); Golden Key Realty, Inc. v. Mantas, 699 P.2d 730 (Utah 1985); see Restatement, Second, Contracts § 279(2); 15 Williston § 1846.

the new agreement.[62] An occasional case has held that upon a material breach of the substitute contract, the aggrieved party may cancel it, reviving the original claim.[63] Such a result is disapproved by the Restatement Second,[64] despite the fact that the result is achieved by normal principles regarding cancellation for material breach followed by restitution. If such a result were to be widely accepted it would, for most practical purposes, erase the distinction between executory accords and substituted contracts. The concept of "substituted contract" was created largely to circumvent the unsatisfactory rules that until recently governed executory accords.[65] Now that these rules have been modernized, the next step should be the reabsorbtion of the substituted contract into the executory accord. Of course, under the general principle of contractual freedom, the parties would continue to be free to articulate the intention that the prior claim is for all purposes and in all circumstances discharged. However, the untidy distinction between executory accords and substituted contracts should not be allowed to complicate litigation about routine claim settlements.

WESTLAW REFERENCES
find 227 f2d 566
278k5
278k7

§ 21–6. Distinguishing an Executory Bilateral Accord From a Substituted Contract

The distinction between executory accords and substituted contracts is often crucial to a determination of the rights of the parties. It is often difficult, however, to classify a given agreement as one or the other. The question is said to be one of the intentions of the parties and is sometimes treated as a question of fact.[66] Where the parties have not expressed themselves on the matter, the courts often emphasize the fact that the burden of proof of discharge of a claim is on the party asserting the discharge.[67] This is the equivalent of holding that the agreement is presumed to be an executory accord which merely suspends the claim. This is sound and not only for formalistic reasons.

62. Restatement, Second, Contracts § 279, Comment b. See also § 19–37 supra.

63. See Publicker Industries, Inc. v. Roman Ceramics Corp., 603 F.2d 1065 (3d Cir. 1979), appeal after remand 652 F.2d 340 (3d Cir.1981) (alternative holding); Christensen v. Hamilton Realty Co., 42 Utah 70, 129 P. 412 (1912); see also 6 Corbin § 1293 at 196; Annot., 94 A.L.R.2d 504 (1964); Gold, supra note 44, at 487–88.

64. Restatement, Second, Contracts § 279(2).

65. See, e.g., 6 Corbin § 1274 n. 55 ("by the device of calling an accord executory a

substituted contract."); Gold, supra note 44, at 475–76.

66. Warner v. Rossignol, 513 F.2d 678 (1st Cir.1975), appeal after remand 538 F.2d 910 (1st Cir.1976); Johnson v. Utile, 86 Nev. 493, 472 P.2d 335 (1970); Moers v. Moers, 229 N.Y. 294, 128 N.E. 202, 14 A.L.R. 225 (1920); Golden Key Realty, Inc. v. Mantas, 699 P.2d 730 (Utah 1985).

67. Publicker Indus., Inc. v. Roman Ceramics Corp., 603 F.2d 1065 (3d Cir.1979), appeal after remand 652 F.2d 340 (3d Cir. 1981); Lipson v. Adelson, 17 Mass.App.Ct. 90, 456 N.E.2d 470 (1983); Rhea v. Marko Constr. Co., 652 S.W.2d 332 (Tenn.1983).

It is usually unlikely that the claimant intended to surrender his claim for a yet unperformed promise. Contrariwise, it is often held that if the claim is disputed or unliquidated the presumption is that there is a substituted agreement.[68] This is because it is assumed that the creditor enters into the new agreement to obtain the certainty of a promise rather than the uncertainty of an unliquidated claim. Even in such a case, however, the determination may turn on the degree of deliberation and formalization which has gone into the agreement. An agreement made with little deliberation and formality is not likely to be deemed to discharge the prior claim.[69] In cases involving a liquidated and undisputed obligation it will generally be presumed that the creditor did not intend to surrender his prior rights unless and until the new agreement is actually performed.[70]

 WESTLAW REFERENCES
"executory bilateral accord"
di("substituted contract")

§ 21–7. An Offer of Accord Looking to a Unilateral Contract

Although most accords are bilateral it is possible to have an offer of accord looking to a unilateral contract. For example, to vary the illustration previously used in § 21–4 supra, C writes to D, "If you deliver your black horse within a reasonable time I promise to discharge your debt." If D tendered the horse and C accepted it, there would be an accord and satisfaction. If D tendered the horse and C refused it, setting aside questions of accord, there would be a unilateral contract.[71] Until quite recently, however, the rule was that C was free to reject the tender without being guilty of any legal wrong.[72] This result has also been changed by the modern authorities [73] and in New York by statute if the offer is in writing and signed by the offeror or by his agent.[74] Under the modern view the debtor could sue for damages for breach of the accord or in a proper case could sue for specific performance of the accord by keeping his tender good. Specific enforcement of the accord would obviously defeat an action upon the original

---

68. Rudick v. Rudick, 403 So.2d 1091 (Fla.App.1981); Restatement, Second, Contracts §§ 279, Comment c, 281, Comment e. But see, McFaden v. Nordblom, 307 Mass. 574, 30 N.E.2d 852 (1941).

69. Goldbard v. Empire State Mut. Life Ins. Co., 5 A.D.2d 230, 171 N.Y.S.2d 194 (1st Dep't 1958). The formality of the proceeding which preceded the settlement agreement was a factor in classifying it as a substituted contract in National American Corp. v. Federal Republic of Nigeria, 597 F.2d 314 (2d Cir.1979).

70. Restatement, Second, Contracts §§ 279, Comment c, 281, Comment e; 15

Williston § 1847; 6 Corbin §§ 1268, 1271, 1293.

71. See ch. 2 supra.

72. Harbor v. Morgan, 4 Ind. 158 (1853); Kromer v. Heim, 75 N.Y. 574, 31 Am.Rep. 491 (1879); see generally 1937 N.Y.Law Rev.Comm.Rep. 212, 233–35.

73. Restatement, Contracts § 417, Comment a.

74. McKinney's N.Y.Gen.Oblig.Law § 15–503.

claim, as would allowance of the accord to be pleaded and proved as an affirmative defense provided the debtor continues ready to perform his part of the bargain.[75]

 WESTLAW REFERENCES
accord /s "unilateral contract"

D. THREE PARTY SITUATIONS

Table of Sections

§ 21–8.   Assignment, Contract for the Benefit of a Third Person and Novation

The common characteristic of the kinds of transactions grouped under this heading is that three parties are involved.

Assignments were discussed in chapter 18. Subject to the qualifications stated in that chapter an effective assignment transfers the assignor's interests to the assignee and thereby discharges the obligor's duty to the assignor.

Contracts for the benefit of a third person were discussed in chapter 17. The making of such a contract creates new duties and often discharges prior duties. If D owes C $100 and they enter into a contract whereby D promises to pay this sum to T, a duty to pay T is substituted for the duty to pay C. C, as promisee, has an interest in the performance of this contract, but this interest now stems not from the original contract but from the substituted contract.[76]

The word "novation" is used in a variety of senses. Courts frequently use it as synonymous with "substituted contract."[77] Most academic writers [78] and both contracts restatements,[79] however, restrict its use to describe a substituted contract involving at least one obligor or obligee who was not a party to the original contract. A contract is a novation in the restricted sense if it does three things: (a) discharges a duty immediately, (b) creates a new duty (or a good faith claim) and (c) includes a new obligor or obligee.[80] An assignment is not a novation

---

75. Cf. Restatement, Contracts § 417(d).

76. Restatement, Contracts § 426; Restatement, Second, Contracts § 280, Comment d.

77. E.g., Capital National Bank of Tampa v. Hutchinson, 435 F.2d 46 (5th Cir. 1970); Mello v. Coy Real Estate Co., 103 R.I. 74, 234 A.2d 667 (1967). Most of the cases in the Decenniel Digests under the heading "Novation" appear to be of this kind. See also Comment, Executory Ac-

cord, Accord and Satisfaction, and Novation—The Distinctions, 26 Baylor L.Rev. 185 (1974).

78. E.g., 6 Corbin § 1297; 15 Williston § 1865.

79. Restatement, Contracts § 424; Restatement, Second, Contracts § 280.

80. Restatement, Contracts § 424; Restatement, Second, Contracts § 280; cf. Kinsella v. Merchants Nat'l Bank & Trust

because it is an executed transaction rather than a contract.[81] A tripartite agreement between the obligor, obligee and prospective assignee is a novation if it discharges a right the assignee has against the obligee, but is not commonly denominated as such.[82] Some third party beneficiary contracts are novations,[83] but are not usually so labeled. Indeed, the utility of the classification of novation is doubtful. Its legal effect is that of a substituted contract.[84] The development of a separate category under the rubric "novation" is doubtless traceable to problems of consideration formerly thought to be present in such contracts because of the former common law rule that consideration must be supplied by the promisee.[85] This rule has long been laid to rest almost everywhere.

It is necessary to distinguish an executory accord from a novation. A novation is a substituted contract which operates immediately to discharge an obligation. If the discharge is to take place upon performance, the tripartite agreement is merely an executory accord.[86] An obligor may be discharged by an actual performance by a third person, accepted by the obligee in full or partial satisfaction of his claim.[87] This is not a novation but an executed accord and satisfaction.

 WESTLAW REFERENCES

find 180 nw2d 613

278k4 /p first previous prior original /3 contract agreement

278k7

Co., 34 A.D.2d 730, 311 N.Y.S.2d 759 (4th Dep't 1970).

81. See § 18–3 supra.

82. Compare Restatement, Contracts § 424, Comment c, with 15 Williston § 1867A.

83. Restatement, Contracts § 426; Restatement, Second, Contracts § 280, Comment d. It should be reiterated that the mere assumption of a duty by a new obligor with the consent of the obligee is not a novation since no duty is discharged by such an assumption unless the obligee also agrees to discharge the original obligor. See United States v. Nill, 518 F.2d 793 (5th Cir.1975); Mansfield v. Lang, 293 Mass. 386, 200 N.E. 110 (1936); Credit Bureaus Adjustment Dep't, Inc. v. Cox Bros., 207 Or. 253, 295 P.2d 1107, 61 A.L.R.2d 750 (1956); and § 18–24 supra. Cf. Navine v. Peltier, 48 Wis.2d 588, 180 N.W.2d 613 (1970).

84. Extensive discussions of novations in 6 Corbin §§ 1297–1302 and 15 Williston

§§ 1865–75 are valuable for their analyses of the variety of factual situations in which a novation has been or is alleged to have been created. For a discussion of one common situation involving the assignment of rights and assumption of duties by a stranger to the contract coupled with a repudiation by the assignor, see § 18–27 supra.

85. See 15 Williston § 1866.

86. See Trudeau v. Poutre, 165 Mass. 81, 42 N.E. 508 (1895) (question of fact whether agreement was to discharge original obligor immediately or only on condition that new obligor perform his promise to execute mortgages); see generally 6 Corbin § 1300.

87. Jackson v. Pennsylvania R.R., 66 N.J.L. 319, 49 A. 730, 55 L.R.A. 87 (1901); Restatement, Contracts § 421; Restatement, Second, Contracts § 278, Comment b. See King, Accord and Satisfaction by a Third Person, 15 Mo.L.Rev. 115 (1950); Gold, Accord and Satisfaction by a Stranger, 19 Can.B.Rev. 165 (1941).

E. ACCOUNT STATED

Table of Sections

§ 21–9.   Account Stated

An account stated arises where there have been transactions between debtor and creditor resulting in the creation of matured debts and the parties by agreement compute a balance which the debtor promises to pay and the creditor promises to accept in full payment for the items of account.[88] The account stated operates as a new contract; a promise to pay a pre-existing debt being binding without new consideration.[89] Few of the reported cases involve express agreements. Many of the cases involve the rendition of a statement of account by the creditor followed by a part payment by the debtor. On these facts some courts find that an account stated is formed as a matter of law;[90] others hold that part payment permits a jury to infer an account stated.[91] More frequently the cases involve an implied agreement arising when the debtor or creditor sends an itemized account to the other who retains it without objection for more than a reasonable time.[92] The debtor's silence is equivocal, however, giving rise to a rebuttable inference of assent which when controverted, as by a prior disagreement between the parties as to the amount of the debt, gives rise to a question of fact.[93] Because of the fiduciary relationship between attorney and client, courts appear reluctant to find assent to an attorney's bill.[94]

88. Restatement, Contracts § 422; Restatement, Second, Contracts § 282; 6 Corbin § 1303; West v. Holstrom, 261 Cal. App.2d 89, 67 Cal.Rptr. 831 (1968).

89. Egles v. Vale, Cro.Jac. 70, 79 Eng. Rep. 59 (1606); see § 5–3 supra.

90. Battista v. Radesi, 112 A.D.2d 42, 491 N.Y.S.2d 81 (4th Dep't 1985).

91. University of South Alabama v. Bracy, 466 So.2d 148 (Ala.Civ.App.1985); Chieffe v. Alcoa Building Products, Inc., 168 Ga.App. 384, 309 S.E.2d 167 (1983).

92. First Commodity Traders, Inc. v. Heinhold Commodities, Inc., 766 F.2d 1007 (7th Cir.1985); Griffith v. Hicks, 150 Ark. 197, 233 S.W. 1086, 18 A.L.R. 882 (1921); R.E. Tharp, Inc. v. Miller Hay Co., 261 Cal. App.2d 81, 67 Cal.Rptr. 854 (1968); Meagher v. Kavli, 251 Minn. 477, 88 N.W.2d 871 (1958); Gerstner v. Lithocraft Studios, Inc., 258 S.W.2d 250 (Mo.App.1953); John-son v. Tindall, 195 Mont. 165, 635 P.2d 266 (1981); Marchi et al. v. All Star Video Corp., 107 A.D.2d 597, 483 N.Y.S.2d 707 (1st Dep't 1985).

93. Sunshine Dairy v. Jolly Joan, 234 Or. 84, 380 P.2d 637 (1963); see also Hunt Process Co. v. Anderson, 455 F.2d 700 (10th Cir.1972); Truestone, Inc. v. Simi West Indus. Park II, 163 Cal.App.3d 715, 209 Cal. Rptr. 757 (1984); Old West Enterprises, Inc. v. Reno Escrow Co., 86 Nev. 727, 476 P.2d 1 (1970).

94. Davis & Cox v. Summa Corp., 751 F.2d 1507 (9th Cir.1985) (presumption of undue influence); Trafton v. Youngblood, 69 Cal.2d 17, 69 Cal.Rptr. 568, 442 P.2d 648 (1968). Compare American Druggists Ins. v. Thompson Lumber Co., 349 N.W.2d 569 (Minn.App.1985) with Roehrdanz v. Schlink, 368 N.W.2d 409 (Minn.App.1985) (attorney and client).

An account stated can not be the origin of a debtor-creditor relationship. There is no duty to reply to a bill from a person with whom one has no debtor-creditor relation.[95]

The chief advantage of an account stated from the plaintiff's point of view is the facility of the requirements of pleading and proof.[96] In an action on the account the creditor need not plead and prove the making and performance of each contract (goods sold and delivered, money loaned, services rendered, etc.) which went into the account.[97] Moreover, since an account stated is a new contract, the statute of limitations commences upon assent to the account.[98]

In its narrowest sense an account stated involves mere computation of liquidated debits and credits. It is not a compromise agreement.[99] No consideration is present in striking such a balance. The account is supported by the survival in this area of the common law rule that a pre-existing debt is consideration for a promise to pay the debt.[1] Such a promise, however, can be avoided for fraud, mistake or other grounds on which a contract may be avoided. Indeed it may be shown that the account contradicts the contractually agreed upon method of computation.[2] If the computation is incorrect the primary effect of an account stated is merely to shift the burden of going forward with the evidence to the party who claims the account is incorrect.[3] If, however, a party has changed his position in reliance upon the account, the other party is estopped from proving that the account was in error.[4] Another effect of an account stated is that it is often held that the account is enforceable even as to items it contains which would otherwise be unenforceable because of the statute of limitations or Statute of Frauds.[5]

95. Big O Tire Dealers, Inc. v. Big O Warehouse, 741 F.2d 160 (7th Cir.1984); Whelan's, Inc. v. Bob Eldridge Const. Co., Inc., 668 S.W.2d 244 (Mo.App.1984) (bill for unrequested services); Free v. Wilmar J. Helric Co., 70 Or.App. 40, 688 P.2d 117 (1984), review denied 298 Or. 553, 695 P.2d 49 (1985) (bill sent to agent of disclosed principal).

96. Cf. Telefunken Sales Corp. v. Kokal, 51 Wis.2d 132, 186 N.W.2d 233 (1971).

97. Karrh v. Crawford-Sturgeon Ins., Inc., 468 So.2d 175 (Ala.Civ.App.1985); Andrews Elec. Co. v. Farm Automation Inc., 188 Neb. 699, 198 N.W.2d 463 (1972); Onalaska Elec. Heating, Inc. v. Schaller, 94 Wis.2d 493, 288 N.W.2d 829 (1980); but see Neil v. Agris, 693 S.W.2d 604 (Tex.App. 1985).

98. Zinn v. Fred R. Bright Co., 271 Cal. App.2d 597, 76 Cal.Rptr. 663, 46 A.L.R.3d 1317 (1969); see Schapiro, Mutual, Open and Current Accounts, Book Accounts, Accounts Stated and the Statute of Limitations, 11 Cal.L.Rev. 12 (1922).

99. 6 Corbin § 1312.

1. See § 5-3 supra.

2. Hopwood Plays, Inc. v. Kemper, 263 N.Y. 380, 189 N.E. 461 (1934); Norfolk Hosiery & Underwear Mills Co. v. Westheimer, 121 Va. 130, 92 S.E. 922 (1917). See 11 A.L.R. 597 (1924); 75 A.L.R. 1287 (1931).

3. Ally & Gargano, Inc. v. Comprehensive Accounting Corp., 615 F.Supp. 426 (S.D.N.Y.1985); Home Health Services of Sarasota, Inc. v. McQuay-Garrett, Sullivan & Co., 462 So.2d 605 (Fla.App.1985); Dodson v. Watson, 110 Tex. 355, 220 S.W. 771, 11 A.L.R. 583 (1920); 6 Corbin §§ 1307, 1308, 1310, 1311.

4. First Nat'l Bank v. Williamson, 205 Iowa 925, 219 N.W. 32 (1928).

5. 6 Corbin § 1309; 15 Williston § 1863; the result in any given jurisdiction is often dependent in part on statutory interpretation. See Boatner v. Gates Bros. Lumber Co., 224 Ark. 494, 275 S.W.2d 627, 51 A.L.R.2d 326 (1955).

Despite its typical inclusion in a chapter on discharge, an account stated does not discharge the antecedent obligations. The creditor may opt to pursue a claim on the original obligations or on the account stated.[6]

 WESTLAW REFERENCES

11k3

11k5

11k6(2)

F.　RELEASE AND COVENANT NOT TO SUE

Table of Sections

§ 21–10.　Release

Historically, the term "release" referred to a formal sealed instrument that expressed in ritual words an intent to discharge an obligation.[7] Because it was under seal, no consideration was necessary to support the discharge.[8] This same result obtains today in jurisdictions that have retained the common law seal.[9] Several jurisdictions that have abolished or downgraded the legal effect of the seal have enacted statutes giving effect to written releases irrespective of the presence or absence of consideration.[10] Most current definitions of "release" indicate that a release must be in writing.[11] Courts, however, not infrequently state that a release supported by consideration may be oral.[12] However, a "release," written or oral, supported by consideration and operative under the laws of a jurisdiction that has abolished the effect of the seal, is an accord and satisfaction.[13] At common law, the release under seal, a species of deed, was ineffective without delivery.[14] Today, a "release" supported by consideration would no more have to be delivered than an accord and satisfaction.[15] A release unsupported by

6. Newburgh v. Florsheim Shoe Co., 200 F.Supp. 599 (D.Mass.1961); 6 Corbin § 1314.

7. Agnew v. Dorr, 5 Whart. 131 (Pa. 1840); Eastman v. Grant, 34 Vt. 387 (1861).

8. See ch. 7 supra.

9. E.g., England. See Guest, Anson's Law of Contracts 429 (26th ed. 1984).

10. See, e.g., U.C.C. §§ 1–107, 3–605; McKinney's N.Y.Gen.Oblig.Law § 15–303; Restatement, Second, Contracts § 284 Reporter's Note.

11. 5A Corbin § 1238; Restatement, Contracts § 402(1); Restatement, Second, Contracts § 284(1).

12. Reserve Ins. Co. v. Gayle, 393 F.2d 585 (4th Cir.1968); Bank of United States v. Manheim, 264 N.Y. 45, 189 N.E. 776 (1934).

13. See §§ 21–4—21–7 supra.

14. See Restatement, Second, Contracts § 284(2). U.C.C. §§ 1–107 and 3–605 impose delivery requirements for releases unsupported by consideration.

15. See the "oral release" cases in note 12, supra.

consideration [16] may be validated by the releasee's injurious reliance upon it.[17] Despite the absence of conceptual differences between many accords and satisfactions, and releases, practitioners tend to use forms entitled "release" for some discharges and contractual documents for other discharges, perhaps more out of habit than necessity.

A release may be conditional.[18] If the condition is precedent, the discharge is effective upon the happening of the condition.[19] If the condition is subsequent the release operates as a covenant not to sue unless and until the condition occurs.[20] A condition precedent which is not contained in the release is also effective. The parol evidence rule does not bar evidence of the condition.[21] A conditional release may be used to circumvent [22] the common law rule that the release of one joint obligor releases the others.[23]

Much litigation centers on the scope of releases, that is, the extent of the claims that are discharged. This is a question of interpretation.[24] The doctrine of mistake is also frequently invoked when a general release discharges claims that were unknown to the releasor.[25]

 WESTLAW REFERENCES
di(release /s seal)
331k31
331k12(2)
331k28(4)
di(release /s support** /s consideration)

§ 21–11. Covenant Not to Sue

A release is an executed transaction. A covenant not to sue is a promise by the creditor not to sue either permanently or for a limited period.[26] If the promise is one never to sue it operates as a discharge

16. Restatement, Second, Contracts § 284 appears to provide that a written unsealed release is valid without consideration. This reading is undercut, however, by Comment b. Cf. 5A Corbin § 1238.

17. Southern Furniture Mfg. Co. v. Mobile County, 276 Ala. 322, 161 So.2d 805 (1963); Fried v. Fisher, 328 Pa. 497, 196 A. 39, 115 A.L.R. 147 (1938).

18. Restatement, Second, Contracts § 284, Comment b.

19. Restatement, Contracts § 404(1); Johnson v. Pickwick Stages System, 108 Cal.App. 279, 291 P. 611 (1930); 19 Geo. L.J. 378 (1931).

20. Restatement, Contracts § 404(2); Robinson v. Thurston, 248 Fed. 420 (9th Cir.1918); but see, 19 Geo.L.J. 378 (1931).

21. Schoeler v. Roth, 51 F.Supp. 518 (S.D.N.Y.1942); Kitchens v. Kitchens, 142 So.2d 343 (Fla.App.1962); see § 3–7 supra.

22. See Johnson v. Pickwick Stages System, 108 Cal.App. 279, 291 P. 611 (1930); 19 Geo.L.J. 378 (1931).

23. See § 20–3 supra.

24. See, e.g., Virginia Impression Prods. Co. v. SCM Corp., 448 F.2d 262 (4th Cir. 1971), cert. denied 405 U.S. 936, 92 S.Ct. 945, 30 L.Ed.2d 811 (1972); Pokorny v. Stastny, 51 Wis.2d 14, 186 N.W.2d 284 (1971); 15 Williston § 1835.

25. See § 9–26 supra.

26. On the manner of distinguishing a release and a covenant not to sue, see Nassif, When is a Release Not a Covenant (Parts I & II), 34 J.Mo.Bar 12, 102 (1978); Sade v. Hemstrom, 205 Kan. 514, 471 P.2d 340 (1970). The Uniform Contribution Among Tortfeasors Act abolishes the distinction between a release and a covenant not to sue. See Ottinger v. Chronister, 13 N.C.App. 91, 185 S.E.2d 292 (1971).

just as does a release.[27] The theory is that should the creditor sue despite his promise not to, the debtor has a counterclaim for damages for breach of the creditor's covenant not to sue which is equal to and cancels the original claim. To avoid circuity of action, despite the promissory form, the promise is given the effect of a discharge of the claim.[28]

The release of one of a number of joint obligors containing a reservation of rights against the others is treated as a covenant not to sue.[29] However, in this situation, and in the case of an express covenant not to sue one joint obligor, the creditor is permitted to sue the "released" obligor despite his covenant not to sue [30] but is precluded from levying execution.[31] The reason for this rule is to be found in the historical and present intricacy of the rules concerning joint obligors, especially the rule that all joint obligors are necessary parties to an action on the obligation.[32]

If the covenant is not to sue for a limited time, the modern view is that the covenant may be raised as an affirmative defense to any action brought in violation of the covenant. The only exception is, as explained above, in the case of joint obligors.[33]

 WESTLAW REFERENCES
331k29(4)
331k37 & sy("covenant not to sue")

G. GIFTS AND REJECTION OF TENDER

Table of Sections

§ 21–12. Executed Gift, Renunciation, and Rejection of Tender

(a) Executed Gift

A gift normally requires delivery of the subject matter and a manifestation of donative intent.[34] If, however, the subject matter is personal property already in the possession of the donee, delivery is not

---

27. Seligman v. Pinet, 78 Mich. 50, 43 N.W. 1091 (1889).

28. Restatement, Contracts § 405, Comment a; 5A Corbin § 1251.

29. See § 20–3.

30. Annot., 53 A.L.R. 1461 (1928).

31. Restatement, Second, Contracts § 285(3); 5A Corbin § 1239.

32. See § 20–3 supra.

33. Restatement, Second, Contracts § 285, Comment a.

34. R. Brown, Personal Property chs. 8 & 9 (3d ed. 1975).

needed.[35] Thus if B pays $5,000 to S for future delivery of an identified automobile, B's subsequent statement to S that S may keep the car as a birthday present perfects the gift.[36] The same result would obtain if S were in possession of a symbolic writing of the kind that ordinarily is deemed to incorporate a debt and B manifested an intention to give the rights symbolized by the writing to S.[37]

A gift of a right not incorporated into a symbolic writing is a more complex issue. As we know, the discharge of an obligation generally requires consideration.[38] There is a vast number of cases holding that part payment of a debt is not consideration for a purported discharge.[39] The purported discharge is not seen as a manifestation of donative intent. Where the purported discharge is manifested in a spirit of liberality rather than settlement, however, there is a completed gift.[40]

(b) Renunciation

A renunciation is a gratuitous statement purporting to surrender a right. Under the majority view a renunciation is generally ineffective because of the absence of consideration.[41]

There is, however, support for the effectiveness of a renunciation in several contexts. The first context merely is a sub-species of gift. When a contract is still executory in whole or in part on both sides, there is authority to the effect that one party may discharge the other from all or part of his obligations under the contract. In essence, despite the absence of consideration he may modify *downwards* the performance owed to him. This rule is supported by both contracts restatements,[42] but does not appear to be supported by much case authority except for cases where the downward modification is actually executed, as in rent reduction cases.[43]

The second context where a renunciation may be effective is where a contract is cancelled for material breach. If the cancellation is accompanied by a renunciation of the right to damages, such a renunciation is effective.[44] U.C.C. § 2–720 adopts the better common law cases when it states:

> "Unless the contrary intention clearly appears, expressions of 'cancellation' or 'rescission' of the contract or the like shall not be

---

35. Restatement, Second, Contracts § 276; Restatement, Contracts § 414.

36. Restatement, Second, Contracts § 276, ill. 1; R. Brown, Personal Property § 7.8 (3d ed. 1975); 5 Williston § 727.

37. Restatement, Contracts § 414; Restatement, Second, Contracts § 276; R. Brown, Personal Property § 8.5 (3d ed. 1975).

38. See § 4–10 supra.

39. See § 4–10 supra.

40. Gray v. Barton, 55 N.Y. 68 (1873); see 5A Corbin § 1247.

41. Burns v. Beeny, 427 S.W.2d 772 (Mo.App.1968); 5A Corbin §§ 1240–1241.

42. Restatement, Second, Contracts § 275; Restatement, Contracts § 416; see 5A Corbin §§ 1248, 1249; 15 Williston §§ 1829–1831.

43. Collected in 5A Corbin § 1249; see also Ottenberg v. Ottenberg, 194 F.Supp. 98 (D.D.C.1961) ("Waiver of contractual duty to support mother").

44. 5 Williston §§ 700–744; Restatement, Contracts § 410. The Restatement, Second § 277 agrees only if the renunciation is in a signed writing.

construed as a renunciation or discharge of any claim in damages for an antecedent breach."

The third context involves a renunciation of damages for partial breach where the renunciation is prior to or upon acceptance of a deficient performance.[45] Under the U.C.C. there are instances where such a renunciation is implied from silence.[46] Last, the Restatement, Second accepts the U.C.C. rule that a written renunciation signed and delivered to the breaching party, even after accepting performance, discharges a claim for damages.[47] In some jurisdictions even broader results are available by utilizing the device of a gratuitous written release.[48]

(c) Rejection of Tender

In the case of a bilateral contract a wrongful refusal of tender is a breach and frequently is so material as to justify cancellation of the contract by the party tendering.[49] If the tendering party's obligation is unilateral, as in the case of services paid for in advance there is authority to the effect that if the services are rejected the obligation is discharged.[50] Such a holding should be made only if material prejudice results from the refusal of tender. At any rate it is clear that a refusal of tender of payment of a debt does not discharge the debt although it may have the effect of cutting off further accrual of interest.[51] For this result to obtain, many authorities hold that the tender must be kept good;[52] i.e., that the amount tendered be segregated from the debtor's other funds. If the debt is governed by Article 3 of the U.C.C. such segregation is not required. A proper tender[53] also has the effect of discharging a mortgage or other lien which secures the debt.[54]

 WESTLAW REFERENCES

(a) *Executed Gift*

di("executed gift")

45. Restatement, Second, Contracts § 277(2); Restatement, Contracts § 411; 5 Williston §§ 700–744. See Schmeck v. Bogatay, 259 Or. 188, 485 P.2d 1095 (1971) (acceptance of a deficient performance without a manifestation of renunciation does not discharge); accord, Aubrey v. Helton, 276 Ala. 134, 159 So.2d 837 (1964).

46. U.C.C. § 2–605. See § 11–34 supra.

47. Restatement, Second, Contracts § 277(2).

48. See §§ 21–10 to 21–11 supra. As to commercial paper see U.C.C. § 3–605.

49. Perlman v. M. Israel & Sons Co., 306 N.Y. 254, 117 N.E.2d 352 (1954); 5 Williston §§ 743–744; 6 Williston §§ 832–833.

50. See 15 Williston §§ 1817–1818; Restatement, Contracts § 415. See the enigmatic reference to § 415 in Restatement, Second Ch. 12 Reporter's Notes, p. 364.

51. See 5A Corbin §§ 1232–1235. The rule is codified in U.C.C. § 3–604.

52. See 5A Corbin § 1235; 15 Williston § 1816.

53. For the requisites of a valid tender of money see 5A Corbin § 1235; 15 Williston §§ 1810–1819. The technical requisites are waived if the creditor does not base his refusal on noncompliance with them. See, e.g., U.C.C. § 2–512(2); Geary v. Dade Dev. Co., 29 N.Y.2d 457, 329 N.Y.S.2d 569, 280 N.E.2d 359 (1972).

54. Kortright v. Cady, 21 N.Y. 343, 78 Am.Dec. 145 (1860); but see Geary v. Dade Dev. Corp., 29 N.Y.2d 457, 329 N.Y.S.2d 569, 280 N.E.2d 359 (1972).

(b) *Renunciation*

di(renunciation /10 contract)

u.c.c. "uniform commercial code" /s 2–720

(c) *Rejection of Tender*

"rejection of tender" /s contract

H. MERGER

Table of Sections

§ 21–13. Merger

The term "merger" may be used in a broad or narrow sense. In a broad sense any time a contract supersedes and incorporates all or part of an earlier agreement it may be said that the earlier agreement is merged into the later. In this sense a substituted contract results in a discharge by merger.[55] Also an earlier tentative agreement is merged into an integration.[56]

In a narrower sense, a common law rule emerged in the 1600's to the effect that a merger occurred if a "lower form" of obligation was superseded by a "higher form." [57] Thus, for example, where an obligation arising under a contract is reduced to judgment the only obligation which remains is the obligation under the judgment; [58] so also where the obligation arising under an informal contract is superseded by a sealed instrument or other specialty.[59] The primary effect of such a discharge of the earlier obligation was an almost total exclusion of parol evidence of the prior contract in an attempt to vary or contradict the higher obligation, or indeed even to explain it.[60] The judgment or specialty was itself the obligation and not merely evidence of it. This early rule of integration preceded the parol evidence rule as applied to informal integrations. Today, the merger of an informal contract into a specialty raises basically the same problem as the merger of an informal contract into an integration; that is, the extent to which the prior expressions of agreement are admissible into evidence. Thus, the existence of a separate heading of "discharge by merger" in Restate-

---

55. See § 21–6 supra.

56. See ch. 3 supra.

57. The historical development and effect of this rule is exhaustively treated in 9 Wigmore, Evidence § 2426 (3d ed.1940); see also 15 Williston §§ 1874–1875C.

58. Restatement, Contracts § 444. The same is true of an arbitration award. Id. § 445.

59. Restatement, Contracts § 446. There is generally stated to be a presumption that a contract is merged in a deed but the question ordinarily is one of intent and a question of fact. Webb v. Graham, 212 Kan. 364, 510 P.2d 1195 (1973); see Dunham, Merger by Deed—Was it Ever Automatic, 10 Ga.L.Rev. 419 (1976).

60. See 9 Wigmore, Evidence § 2426 (3d ed. 1940).

ments, treatises, and texts is largely an anachronism.[61] What is involved is merely a substituted obligation.

Although a negotiable instrument is regarded as a specialty and is a "higher" form of obligation, it has generally been held that the acceptance of a negotiable instrument from the obligor does not discharge the underlying obligation unless it is given and accepted in satisfaction of the underlying obligation. This rule created a good deal of litigation as to the factual question of whether or not the instrument was accepted in satisfaction. The Uniform Commercial Code article on commercial paper makes it clear that in the usual case the instrument acts as an executory accord, suspending the underlying obligation. In the event the instrument is dishonored, the obligee may sue on the instrument or the prior obligation.[62]

Merger by judgment is today largely considered as one aspect of the doctrine of res judicata and treated in depth in works on judgments and civil procedure.

 WESTLAW REFERENCES

di(merger /s contract /p intent! intend! /3 party)

I. UNION OF RIGHT AND DUTY IN THE SAME PERSON

Table of Sections

Sec.
21–14. Acquisition by the Debtor of the Correlative Right.

§ 21–14. Acquisition by the Debtor of the Correlative Right

Closely analogous to merger is a discharge by virtue of a union of right and duty in the same person. The first Restatement stated the general rule as follows: "Where a person subject to a contractual duty, or to a duty to make compensation, acquires the correlative right in the same capacity in which he owes the duty, the duty is discharged." [63] The simplest illustration is where a creditor assigns his claim against a debtor to the same debtor.[64] The Restatement rule, however, is to be disapproved as an overly sweeping generalization. Especially in the field of mortgages, difficult questions arise as to merger of the right-duty relation in the same person and often enough that person's intention to keep the two aspects of the relation separate will be given effect.[65]

---

61. The topic is omitted in the Restatement, Second. See Ch. 12 Reporter's Note, p. 363.

62. U.C.C. § 3–802; see also Id. § 2–511(3).

63. Restatement, Contracts § 451.

64. Wright v. Anderson, 62 S.D. 444, 253 N.W. 484, 95 A.L.R. 81 (1934).

65. See, e.g., Osborne, Mortgages §§ 272–76 (2d ed. 1970).

WESTLAW REFERENCES
"correlative right"   /s   contract

II. DISCHARGES BY OPERATION OF LAW

J. ALTERATION

Table of Sections

Sec.
21–15. Discharge by Alteration.

§ 21–15. Discharge by Alteration

At early common law any material alteration of a written contract whether or not fraudulent and whether caused by the obligee or not, resulted in a discharge.[66] Under modern law an alteration by a third person or by accidental means does not discharge a written contract.[67] The general rule is that a material alteration of a writing by one who asserts a right under it extinguishes his right and discharges the obligation of the obligor if the alteration is made by the obligee with fraudulent intent.[68] An alteration is material if the rights or duties of the obligee would be varied.[69] The Restatements take the position that the rule applies only to sealed instruments, integrations, or memoranda required by the Statute of Frauds.[70] Article 3 of the U.C.C. contains a rule that governs commercial paper much like the general rule stated above.[71]

A discharge caused by an alteration is nullified by a subsequent assent to or forgiveness of the alteration even though the promise to forgive is not supported by consideration.[72] So also, if the contract is bilateral and the innocent party knowing of the alteration asserts his rights under the contract, the duties of both parties are revived.[73] If the arrangement is unilateral, alteration discharges the rights of the party who is guilty of the alteration but does not discharge the rights of the other party who must, however, if he wishes to assert his rights,

---

66. 15 Williston § 1881. For more detailed treatment, see Williston, Discharge of Contracts by Alteration (Pts. I & II), 18 Harv.L.Rev. 105, 165 (1904–05), Selected Readings 1221, 1232.

67. Litton Industries Credit Corp. v. Plaza Super of Malta, Inc., 503 F.Supp. 83 (N.D.N.Y.1980); Kelley v. Kelley, 435 So.2d 214 (Ala.1983).

68. Knapp v. Knapp, 251 Iowa 44, 99 N.W.2d 396 (1959); First Nat'l Bank of McCook v. Hull, 189 Neb. 581, 204 N.W.2d 90 (1973); Restatement, Contracts § 434; Restatement, Second, Contracts § 286(1); cf. Moving Picture Mach. Operators Union

v. Glasgow Theaters, Inc., 6 Cal.App.3d 395, 86 Cal.Rptr. 33 (1970) (voidable at option of innocent party).

69. Restatement, Second, Contracts § 286(2).

70. Restatement, Contracts § 435; Restatement, Second, Contracts § 286(1); 6 Corbin § 1317.

71. U.C.C. § 3–407.

72. Restatement, Second, Contracts § 287.

73. Restatement, Second, Contracts § 287.

perform any acts which he is required to perform under the agreement.[74]

WESTLAW REFERENCES
di(discharg! /s alter! /s contract)

K. BANKRUPTCY

Table of Sections

Sec.
21–16. Bankruptcy.

§ 21–16. Bankruptcy

A bankrupt is discharged by operation of law with respect to his provable debts. The cases sometimes indicate that merely the remedy is barred or suspended by the decree in bankruptcy;[75] but others speak in terms of an actual discharge.[76] The differences in theory are no longer relevant in current law.[77]

WESTLAW REFERENCES
di(discharg! /s contract /s bankruptcy)

L. PERFORMANCE

Table of Sections

Sec.
21–17. Performance of the Duty—To Which Debt Should Payment
　　　　 Be Applied.

§ 21–17. Performance of the Duty—To Which Debt Should Payment Be Applied

A contractual duty is obviously discharged by performance.[78] A very frequent method of performance is payment. Payment is a delivery of money or its equivalent in specific property or services by one from whom it is due to another person to whom it is due.[79] If the contract does not indicate otherwise payment is ordinarily to be made in legal tender. However Section 2–511(2) of the Uniform Commercial Code provides: "Tender of payment is sufficient when made by any means or in any manner current in the ordinary course of business unless the seller demands payment in legal tender and gives any extension of time reasonably necessary to procure it." The giving of

---

74. 6 Corbin § 1317.

75. Zavelo v. Reeves, 227 U.S. 625, 33 S.Ct. 365, 57 L.Ed. 676 (1913).

76. Henry v. Root, 33 N.Y. 526 (1865).

77. See § 5–6 supra.

78. Restatement, Second, Contracts § 235.

79. Sizemore v. E.T. Barwick Indus., Inc., 225 Tenn. 226, 465 S.W.2d 873 (1971).

one's own negotiable instrument does not constitute payment unless the instrument is accepted as payment.[80]

When the debtor owes the creditor more than one debt and a payment is made by the debtor or upon his behalf the question arises, to which debt should the payment be applied? Except as later indicated: (a) if the debtor manifests an intention in this respect at or before the time of payment, the creditor must apply the payment in accordance with the directions manifested by the debtor;[81] (b) if the debtor makes no manifestation, the creditor may within a reasonable time make the application;[82] (c) if neither the creditor nor the debtor makes a seasonable manifestation, the law will apply the payment in the manner which is most equitable.[83]

There is an exception to the rule stated in (a) above where the payor is under a duty to a third person, for example, a surety, to apply the money to a particular debt and the creditor knows or has reason to know of the facts which create the duty. Under these circumstances the creditor must apply the payment in discharge of the debt in which the third party is interested.[84]

There are also exceptions to the rule stated in (b). The creditor may not apply the payment to a claim that is disputed, illegal or unmatured and must apply it to a debt which if not paid by the debtor will result in a forfeiture or violate a duty owed by the debtor to a third party, provided the creditor knows or has reason to know of this duty.[85] Aside from these restrictions, the creditor is permitted to serve its own best interests as by applying a payment to an unsecured rather than secured debt, and to an unenforceable rather than an enforceable debt.[86]

 WESTLAW REFERENCES
find 46 a2d 198
294k39(1)
294k41(1)
294k44
294k43

---

80. United States v. Heyward-Robinson Co., 430 F.2d 1077 (2d Cir.1970), cert. denied 400 U.S. 1021, 91 S.Ct. 582, 27 L.Ed.2d 632 (1971); 15 Williston § 1875A; U.C.C. §§ 3–802(1)(b), 2–511(3).

81. Schreiber v. Armstrong, 70 N.M. 419, 374 P.2d 297 (1962); Restatement, Second, Contracts § 258. A manifestation once made cannot be changed without the consent of the other party.

82. J. & G. Constr. Co. v. Freeport Coal Co., 147 W.Va. 563, 129 S.E.2d 834 (1963); Debelak Bros. Inc. v. Mille, 38 Wis.2d 373, 157 N.W.2d 644 (1968); Restatement, Second, Contracts § 259.

83. Carozza v. Brannan, 186 Md. 123, 46 A.2d 198 (1946); Restatement, Second, Contracts § 260.

84. School District of Springfield v. Transamerica Ins. Co., 633 S.W.2d 238 (Mo. App.1982); Bounds v. Nuttle, 181 Md. 400, 30 A.2d 263 (1943); Restatement, Second, Contracts § 258(2).

85. Restatement, Second, Contracts § 259(2), (3).

86. In re Applied Logic, 576 F.2d 952 (2d Cir.1978); 5A Corbin § 1231; 15 Williston § 1796.

Chapter 22

ILLEGAL BARGAINS

Table of Sections

§ 22-1. What Makes a Bargain Illegal?

The first Restatement of Contracts attempted to define "illegal bargain" with analytic rigor, providing that a bargain is "illegal * * * if either its formation or its performance is criminal, tortious or otherwise opposed to public policy."[1] The Restatement Second avoids the term "illegal" and subsumes all such unenforceable bargains under the concept of "public policy," the "unruly horse"[2] of the law, an amorphous but ubiquitous concept. Under the Restatement Second approach a contract that violates the criminal law is not necessarily against public policy. It is believed that this approach is well supported by the cases.[3] The thrust of new Restatement's rules on the subject is judicial flexibility in weighing the strength of legally recognized policies against the effect on the parties and on the public of declaring a particular bargain to be against public policy.[4]

1. Restatement, Contracts § 512.

2. Richardson v. Mellish, 2 Bing. 229, 252, 130 Eng.Rep. 294, 303 (1824).

3. See, e.g., cases cited at note 33, infra. Also supporting this position are cases that reason that although a particular contract is illegal, it may nevertheless be enforced. See § 22-4 infra.

4. Restatement, Second, Contracts § 178. See Northern Indiana Public Service Co. v. Carbon County Coal Co., 799

As stated by one court, "public policy can be enunciated by the Constitution, the legislature or the courts at any time and whether there is a prior expression or not the courts can refuse to enforce any contract which they deem to be contrary to the best interests of citizens as a matter of public policy." [5]　Public policy has been the announced rationale for striking down contracts or contract clauses on grounds of immorality,[6] unconscionability,[7] economic policy,[8] unprofessional conduct,[9] paternalism,[10] and diverse other criteria.

The various kinds of contracts or contract clauses that have been struck down on grounds of public policy will not be discussed here. This chapter will be limited to considering the consequences of a bargain contaminated in whole or in part by the presence of an actual or contemplated violation of the law of crimes or torts or a collision with other public policies.[11]

The starting point for a discussion of illegality is the maxim, *in pari delicto potior est conditio defendentis* —in a case of equal fault the condition of the defending party is the better one.　In short, the court will leave the parties where it finds them.　Two basic policies underlie this principle.　First, a refusal to enforce a contract that is against public policy will deter the making of such contracts in the future.[12]　A second rationale has been expressed.　"The policy against enforcing a contract calling for an illegal performance is a simple one and does not require extensive comment.　It accomplishes very little in discouraging the performance of illegal acts but it keeps the courts respectable." [13] This policy is often colorfully expressed.　For example, we read "no polluted hand shall touch the pure fountains of justice." [14]　Courts state

F.2d 265, 273–74 (7th Cir. 1986) (Posner, J.).

5. Anaconda Federal Credit Union, # 4401 v. West, 157 Mont. 175, 178, 483 P.2d 909, 911 (1971). See Gellhorn, Contracts and Public Policy, 35 Colum.L.Rev. 679 (1935); Greenhood, The Doctrine of Public Policy in the Law of Contracts— Reduced to Rules (1886); Stone, Social Dimensions of Law and Justice 182–198 (1966); Strong, The Enforceability of Illegal Contracts, 12 Hastings L.J. 347 (1961); Symmons, The Function and Effect of Public Policy in Contemporary Common Law, 51 Aust.L.J. 185 (1977).

6. Casad, Unmarried Couples and Unjust Enrichment: From Status to Contract and Back Again, 77 Mich.L.Rev. 47 (1978); Dwyer, Immoral Contracts, 93 L.Q.Rev. 386 (1977). On the effect of changing attitudes towards sexual morality and their impact on contract law, compare Kozlowski v. Kozlowski, 80 N.J. 378, 403 A.2d 902 (1979), with Hewitt v. Hewitt, 77 Ill.2d 49, 31 Ill. Dec. 827, 394 N.E.2d 1204 (1979).

7. E.g., Rules pertaining to liquidated damages, §§ 14–31 to 14–36 supra.

8. E.g., Restatement, Second, Contracts §§ 186–188 (contracts in restraint of trade).

9. E.g., Rules pertaining to maintenance and champerty. 6A Corbin §§ 1421–1427.

10. See Kronman, Paternalism and The Law of Contracts, 92 Yale L.J. 763 (1983). For the opposite side of paternalism coin, see Kennedy, Distributive and Paternalist Motives in Contract and Tort Law, With Special Reference to Compulsory Terms and Unequal Bargaining Power, 41 Md.L. Rev. 563, 624–649 (1982).

11. For extensive discussion, see 6A Corbin; 14 & 15 Williston.

12. Weil v. Neary, 278 U.S. 160, 173–74, 49 S.Ct. 144, 149, 73 L.Ed. 243 (1929); Sirkin v. Fourteenth St. Store, 124 App. Div. 384, 108 N.Y.S. 830 (1st Dep't 1908).

13. Havighurst, The Nature of Private Contract 53 (1961).

14. Collins v. Blantern, 2 Wils.K.B. 347, 350, 95 Eng.Rep. 850, 852 (1767).

that they refuse to act "as paymasters of the wages of crime." [15] One court pithily put it thus: "[s]traight shooters should always win, but when there are none, bad guys need not look to us for help." [16]

Other policy choices could have been made; for example, confiscation of the proceeds of illegality by the state,[17] restoration of the status quo ante,[18] and a decree ordering payment of illicit proceeds to charity.[19] Nonetheless, the choice made by the common law is in accord with that of many legal systems.[20]

As a general rule an illegal bargain is unenforceable [21] and, often void.[22] This last result has often been described as stemming from the principle that a valid bilateral contract requires that both parties furnish consideration.[23] If A promises to do something lawful and B promises to do something unlawful there can be no action for breach on either side. B may not sue because his illegal promise does not constitute consideration for A's promise and A may not sue, even though he promises to do something lawful, because of the requirement of mutuality of consideration.[24] While this analysis suitably explains cases of hard core illegality (e.g. a promise to pay in exchange for a promise to commit murder), it fails to account for the numerous cases where one of the contracting parties may enforce the agreement despite its illegal taint.[25] As one writer has aptly stated: "contracts are not legal or illegal in the same way that eggs are good or bad." [26] The decision to award or withhold a remedy is based on policy choices and precedents; not only on concepts.

Assuming an agreement involves some actual or contemplated conduct that violates statutory law or other public policy, the courts do not automatically brand the agreement as illegal. There are countless statutes which prohibit criminal activity. There is a vast array of administrative regulations, the violation of which are penalized. If the legislature states the effect of a violation of a criminal statute upon a contract, that expression of intention must of course be followed.[27] Legislatures, however, do not usually provide for the civil consequences of the violation of the criminal law. In such a case the matter is one

---

15. Stone v. Freeman, 298 N.Y. 268, 271, 82 N.E.2d 571, 572, 8 A.L.R.2d 304, 306 (1948).

16. Certa v. Wittman, 35 Md.App. 364, 370 A.2d 573 (1977).

17. See Civil Code of the R.S.F.S.R. Art. 49 (Gray & Stults Trans. 1965); cf. Carr v. Hoy, 2 N.Y.2d 185, 158 N.Y.S.2d 572, 139 N.E.2d 531 (1957).

18. Mexican Civ. Code Art. 2239 (M. Gordon Trans. 1980).

19. Portuguese Civ. Code Art. 692 (1879 ed.).

20. Von Mehren, A General View of Contract § I–42, in VII International Encyclopedia of Comparative Law (1982).

21. Restatement, Second, Contracts § 178.

22. Restatement, Contracts §§ 598, 607.

23. See § 4–12 supra.

24. Restatement, Contracts § 607, Comment a; cf. 6A Corbin § 1523; Buckley, Illegality in Contract and Conceptual Reasoning 12 Anglo-Am.L.Rev. 280 (1983).

25. See § 22–4 infra.

26. Anson's Law of Contract 384 (Guest's 25th ed.).

27. Anderson v. Frandsen, 36 Wn.App. 353, 674 P.2d 208 (1984) (statute provides that unregistered contractor cannot recover).

for judicial determination. An English judge has made sound observations in this regard. Judge Devlin in St. John Shipping Corp. v. Joseph Rank Ltd.,[28] stated: "Caution in this respect is, I think, especially necessary in these times when so much of commercial life is governed by regulations of one sort or another, which may easily be broken without wicked intent * * *. Commercial men who have unwittingly offended against one of a multiplicity of regulations may nevertheless feel that they have not thereby forfeited all right to justice."

Illustrative of the problem are statutes penalizing commercial bribery. New York in 1905 was among the first common law jurisdictions to enact a statute making the bribery of purchasing agents a crime.[29] The penalty was a fine of no more than five hundred dollars and imprisonment for no more than a year. In Sirkin v. Fourteenth Street Store,[30] plaintiff delivered hosiery to the defendant pursuant to a contract plaintiff had obtained by bribing defendant's purchasing agent. The court refused to enter a judgment for the purchase price even though the statute was silent as to the civil effects of its violation. A dissenting opinion accused the majority of judicial legislation and of permitting the unjust enrichment of the defendant.

The debate between the majority and the dissenter is repeated in countless cases. While some cases state the general rule is that the contract will be enforced despite a statutory violation,[31] others state that the general rule provides for non-enforcement.[32] The probability is that the varieties of illegality are too multifarious to be stated in one rule. However where one party has performed under the agreement tainted with illegality he may recover if the offense is merely *malum prohibitum* "and the denial of relief is wholly out of proportion to the requirements of public policy or appropriate individual punishment."[33] While the result is often couched in terms of ascertaining legislative intent, the courts often determine this intent from the degree of hostility manifested by the legislature against the practice it has forbidden.[34] In Sirkin the court made quite clear the legislature's (and its own) hostility to commercial bribery.

28. [1957] 1 Q.B. 267, 288, 289.

29. 1905 N.Y.Laws ch. 136. On commercial bribery, see Note, 108 U.Pa.L.Rev. 848 (1960).

30. 124 App.Div. 384, 108 N.Y.S. 830 (1st Dep't 1908). See Annot., 55 A.L.R.2d 481 (1957).

31. Ets-Hokin & Galvan, Inc. v. Maas Transport, Inc., 380 F.2d 258 (8th Cir.1967), cert. denied 389 U.S. 977, 88 S.Ct. 481, 19 L.Ed.2d 471 (1968).

32. Mascari v. Raines, 220 Tenn. 234, 415 S.W.2d 874 (1967); but see Gene Taylor & Sons Plumbing Co., Inc. v. Corondolet Realty Trust, 611 S.W.2d 572 (Tenn.1981).

33. John E. Rosasco Creameries, Inc. v. Cohen, 276 N.Y. 274, 278, 11 N.E.2d 908,

909, 118 A.L.R. 641, 644 (1937); see also Gates v. Rivers Const. Co., Inc., 515 P.2d 1020 (Alaska 1973); M. Arthur Gensler, Jr. & Assoc., Inc. v. Larry Barrett, Inc., 7 Cal. 3d 695, 103 Cal.Rptr. 247, 499 P.2d 503 (1972), Measday v. Sweazea, 78 N.M. 781, 438 P.2d 525, 26 A.L.R.3d 1386 (1968) (contractor complied with building code but had no building permit); Spadanuta v. Incorporated Village of Rockville Centre, 15 N.Y.2d 755, 257 N.Y.S.2d 329, 205 N.E.2d 525 (1965).

34. See the cases in the prior footnote and United States v. ACME Process Equipment Co., 385 U.S. 138, 87 S.Ct. 350, 17 L.Ed.2d 249 (1966), rehearing denied 385 U.S. 1032, 87 S.Ct. 738, 17 L.Ed.2d 680 (1967); Annot., 55 A.L.R.2d 481 (1957); Ru-

WESTLAW REFERENCES
"illegal bargain"
"st. john shipping corp"   +3   "joseph rank"

---

§ 22–2. Cases Where a Party May Successfully Sue Upon an Illegal Executory Bilateral Contract

Once it is determined that an agreement is illegal, there are a number of situations in which a party may successfully sue upon an illegal executory bilateral contract.

(a) Ignorance of Facts and Law

If a party enters into an illegal bargain and is justifiably ignorant of the facts creating the illegality and the other is not, the innocent party may recover on the contract if he can show that he would have been ready, willing and able to perform but for the illegality.[35] A simple illustration is the case of a man who is already married who promises to marry another woman. She, assuming her ignorance of his marital status, in a state that still recognizes such an action, could bring an action for breach of contract to marry.[36] It has been held that a plaintiff could recover from an unlicensed trucking company for breach of contract of carriage where the plaintiff had no knowledge that the defendant was unlicensed.[37] A seller of land was permitted to recover damages for breach of a contract which was illegal because the purchaser was an enemy alien where the seller was ignorant of the purchaser's nationality.[38]

Cases such as this do not violate the general rule that ignorance of the law is no excuse.[39] There is even an exception to the general rule that ignorance of the law is no excuse where the illegality is minor and the party who is ignorant of the illegality justifiably relies upon an assumed special knowledge of the other of the requirements of law. This usually occurs where the other is in the business to which the contract relates.[40]

pert's Oil Service v. Leslie, 40 Conn.Sup. 295, 493 A.2d 926 (1985) (no recovery for unmetered deliveries of fuel oil).

35. Symcox v. Zuk, 221 Cal.App.2d 383, 34 Cal.Rptr. 462 (1963).

36. Restatement, Second, Contracts § 180.

37. Archbolds (Freightage) Ltd. v. Spanglett Ltd., [1961] 2 W.L.R. 170 (C.A.); accord, Hedla v. McCool, 476 F.2d 1223 (9th Cir.1973) (architect not known to be unlicensed); Commercial Trust & Savings Bank v. Toy Nat'l Bank, 373 N.W.2d 521 (Iowa App.1985) (bank exceeded its lending limits).

38. Branigan v. Saba, [1924] N.Z.L.R. 481 (1923); see also Eastern Expanded

Metal Co. v. Webb Granite & Const. Co., 195 Mass. 356, 81 N.E. 251 (1907); Hoekzema v. Van Haften, 313 Mich. 417, 21 N.W.2d 183 (1946); Millin v. Millin, 36 N.Y.2d 796, 369 N.Y.S.2d 702, 330 N.E.2d 650 (1975). See also the licensing cases at § 22–7 infra.

39. 6A Corbin § 1539.

40. Restatement, Second, Contracts § 180; National Conversion Corp. v. Cedar Building Corp., 23 N.Y.2d 621, 298 N.Y.S.2d 499, 246 N.E.2d 351 (1969) (action on landlord's warranty that lease did not violate zoning requirements); Harrison v. Flushing Nat'l Bank, 83 Misc.2d 658, 370 N.Y.S.2d 803 (Civ.Ct.1975) (bank issued certificates at illegally high rate).

(b) Bargain Illegal by Virtue of Wrongful Purpose

Some bargains are illegal by reason of the wrongful purpose of one or both of the parties. The mere fact that an innocent party knows of the illegal purpose of the other does not bar him from recovering for breach of contract [41] unless the intended purpose involves serious moral turpitude or he takes action to further the illegal purpose of the other. In the leading case the plaintiff, a resident of France, contracted to sell a quantity of tea to the defendant, knowing of defendant's intent to smuggle the tea into England. The English court permitted the plaintiff to recover.[42] Soon thereafter, the court denied recovery where the seller had packed the goods in such a way as to facilitate the smuggling operation.[43]

Penal statutes that have expanded the concept of criminal facilitation broaden the category of illegal agreements in jurisdictions that have enacted them. For example, New York outlaws "conduct which provides [another] with the means or opportunity to commit a crime" when he believes it probable that the other intends to commit a crime.[44] This expansion of criminal liability naturally leads to the expansion of cases where recovery on an agreement is barred.

(c) Where the Parties Are Not In Pari Delicto

Some statutes are designed to protect one class of persons against another. In a case against a lottery-office-keeper, Lord Mansfield stated: "The statute itself * * * *has marked the criminal.* For the penalties are all on one side; upon the office keeper."[45] While most of the civil litigation concerning agreements made in violation of such statutes are actions for restitution [46] there are cases in which damages

41. Gold Bond Stamp Co. v. Bradfute Corp., 463 F.2d 1158 (2d Cir.1972) (trading stamp company supplies prizes for illegal lottery); Watkins v. Curry, 103 Ark. 414, 147 S.W. 43 (1912) (sale of automobile used as prize in illegal lottery); Howell v. Stewart, 54 Mo. 400 (1873) (loan of money to enable defendant to smuggle cattle from Texas to Missouri); San Benito Bank & Trust Co. v. Rio Grande Music Co., 686 S.W.2d 635 (Tex.App.1984) (bank knew of borrower's illegal purpose); Restatement, Second, Contracts § 180.

42. Holman v. Johnson, 1 Cowp. 341, 98 Eng.Rep. 1120 (K.B.1775); accord, Graves v. Johnson, 179 Mass. 53, 60 N.E. 383 (1901) (sale of liquor in Massachusetts knowing the buyer intended to resell in Maine); authorities in note 41 supra.

43. Biggs v. Lawrence, 3 T.R. 454, 100 Eng.Rep. 673 (K.B.1789); accord Hull v. Ruggles, 56 N.Y. 424 (1874) (packaging in aid of a lottery). For variations on this problem, see Williams Mfg. Co. v. Prock, 184 F.2d 307 (5th Cir.1950) (amusement machines offering free plays to winner);

Hart Publications v. Kaplan, 228 Minn. 512, 37 N.W.2d 814 (1949) (contract to print lottery tickets); Carroll v. Beardon, 142 Mont. 40, 381 P.2d 295 (1953) (contract to sell house to be used for prostitution); Fineman v. Faulkner, 174 N.C. 13, 93 S.E. 384 (1917) (contract to sell phonograph to prostitute); Hendrix v. McKee, 281 Or. 123, 575 P.2d 134 (1978) (contract to design illegal gambling machines); see 15 Williston §§ 1754–1756.

44. McKinney's N.Y. Penal Law Art. 115 (the quoted language appears in a number of sections in this article); see Frohlich & Newell Foods, Inc. v. New Sans Souci Nursing Home, 109 Misc.2d 974, 441 N.Y.S.2d 335 (Civ.Ct.1981) (no recovery for sales of food where, at purchaser's request, plaintiff overbilled to enhance purchaser's reimbursement from the State).

45. Browning v. Morris, 2 Cowp. 790, 793, 98 Eng.Rep. 1364, 1365 (K.B.1778) (emphasis supplied).

46. See § 22–7 infra.

for breach have been awarded. Rent control legislation is designed to protect tenants. Consequently, a tenant may bring an action for damages for breach of a lease despite the violation of rent regulations by terms in the lease.[47] A rule designed to protect customers against brokers by limiting the extension of credit does not bar the customer from enforcing the agreement by an action for damages.[48] It has been suggested that an action for specific performance of an agreement that violates a rule designed to protect a class of persons should be available in a proper case to a member of the protected class.[49] An action for damages assuredly is available.[50]

(d) Severance

If an agreement contains an illegal provision that is not central to the agreement and the illegal provision does not involve serious moral turpitude, the illegal portion of the agreement is disregarded and the balance of the agreement is enforceable.[51] We have seen examples of this rule earlier. Thus contracts containing illegal covenants not to compete are enforced. The illegal covenant is disregarded or curtailed.[52] Contracts containing illegal penalty clauses [53] or illegal exculpatory clauses [54] are enforced. The illegal clauses are in effect excised.

Outside of these standardized situations, it has been held that if a contract contained an illegal provision whereunder a party surrenders his right of appeal, the balance of the contract is enforceable.[55] Provisions in a contract unlawfully circumventing the powers of corporate directors have been disregarded where the primary purpose of the contract would not be defeated.[56] A contractual clause which violates state antitrust law by fixing prices to be paid by customers other than the plaintiff may be severed and the plaintiff's promise to purchase enforced.[57] Cases where illegal provisions have been severed or disregarded are many.[58] A difficult question is, what criteria should be used

47. Steinlauf v. Delano Arms, Inc., 15 A.D.2d 964, 226 N.Y.S.2d 862 (2d Dep't 1962).

48. Pearlstein v. Scudder & German, 429 F.2d 1136 (2d Cir.1970) cert. denied 401 U.S. 1013, 91 S.Ct. 1250, 28 L.Ed.2d 550 (1970). This S.E.C. rule has been changed to mark both broker and customer as offenders. See Note, Regulation X, A Complexis, 50 Notre Dame Law. 136 (1974).

49. 6A Corbin § 1540.

50. Bolivar v. Monnat, 232 A.D. 33, 248 N.Y.S. 722 (4th Dep't 1931) (action for breach of implied warranty of bootleg alcohol); State ex rel. American Surety Co. v. Haid, 325 Mo. 949, 30 S.W.2d 100 (1930) (statute forbidding receipt of deposits except at bank does not void a deposit taken elsewhere); see also the licensing cases at note 78 infra.

51. Restatement, Second, Contracts § 184.

52. See § 16–21 supra.

53. See § 14–31 supra.

54. See § 9–44 supra.

55. Marshall v. Wittig, 213 Wis. 374, 251 N.W. 439 (1933); see also Wright v. Robinson, 468 So.2d 94 (Ala.1985) (illegal confession of judgment clause).

56. Jones v. Gabrielan, 52 N.J.Super. 563, 146 A.2d 495 (App.Div.1958); Triggs v. Triggs, 46 N.Y.2d 305, 413 N.Y.S.2d 325, 385 N.E.2d 1254 (1978), rehearing denied 46 N.Y.2d 940, 415 N.Y.S.2d 1027, 388 N.E. 2d 372 (1979).

57. Rose v. Vulcan Materials Co., 282 N.C. 643, 194 S.E.2d 521, 67 A.L.R. 3d 1 (1973).

58. Ferro v. Bologna, 31 N.Y.2d 30, 334 N.Y.S.2d 856, 286 N.E.2d 244 (1972) (note also parties were not in pari delicto); Schue v. Jacoby, 162 N.W.2d 377 (N.D.1968); Osgood v. Central Vt. R.R., 77

to determine whether the primary purpose of the agreement will be defeated by severance of illegal provisions? Primarily the criterion would appear to be whether the parties would have entered into the agreement irrespective of the offending provisions of the contract.[59] This can usually be determined by weighing of the equality of the agreed exchange before and after the proposed severance.[60] Where the illegality permeates the entire agreement, severance is generally not permitted.[61] Even here, however, the degree of forfeiture and unjust enrichment[62] will be taken into consideration to determine whether severance will be granted.[63]

(e) Purposeful Interpretation and Reformation

If an agreement can be read so that either a legal or illegal meaning can be attributed to it, the interpretation giving the agreement a legal meaning will be preferred.[64] In addition to the applicability of this rule of interpretation, the possibility of reformation of a written contract exists, although there are very few cases in which the remedy of reformation has been granted.

In one case, the parties entered into an agreement for a mortgage loan, which was reduced to writing at their request by a title insurance company. The title company made use of a printed form which provided for compound interest in the event of default, a provision that rendered the agreement usurious. It was held that the agreement could be reformed by excision of the offending clause.[65] With the general recognition and gradual expansion of the idea that reformation is available for mistake of law and, in particular, mistake as to the legal effect of a writing,[66] the road is now open to reformation of writing where the parties have inadvertently strayed beyond the boundaries of legality.

De facto reformation often occurs under the doctrines of severance [67] and divisibility.[68] In addition there are cases where the court essentially rewrites the contract to conform to the law relying on no particular doctrine.[69]

Vt. 334, 60 A. 137 (1905); 15 Williston § 1779.

59. Cf. Marsh, The Severance of Illegality in Contract (pts. 1 & 2) 64 L.Q.Rev. 230, 347 (1948).

60. Restatement, Second, Contracts § 184, Comment a.

61. Hall v. Hall, 455 So.2d 813 (Ala. 1984); Hanley v. Savannah Bank & Trust Co., 208 Ga. 585, 68 S.E.2d 581 (1952); Kukla v. Perry, 361 Mich. 311, 105 N.W.2d 176 (1960); Schara v. Thiede, 58 Wis.2d 489, 206 N.W.2d 129 (1973).

62. Murray Walter, Inc. v. Sarkisian Bros., Inc., 107 A.D.2d 173, 486 N.Y.S.2d 396 (3d Dep't 1985).

63. Restatement, Contracts § 603.

64. Restatement, Contracts § 236(a); Restatement, Second, Contracts § 203(a); 4 Williston § 620.

65. First American Title Ins. & Trust Co. v. Cook, 12 Cal.App.3d 592, 90 Cal.Rptr. 645 (1970).

66. See § 9–34 supra.

67. See § 22–2(d) supra.

68. See § 22–6 infra.

69. E.g., Coronet Ins. Co. v. Ferrill, 134 Ill.App.3d 483, 89 Ill.Dec. 691, 481 N.E.2d 43 (1985).

WESTLAW REFERENCES

(a) *Ignorance of Facts and Law*

find 34 cal rptr 462

(b) *Bargain Illegal by Virtue of Wrongful Purpose*

find 463 f2d 1158

(c) *Where the Parties are Not in Pari Delicto*

95k139

"pari delicto" /s illegal

(d) *Severance*

severance /s illegal /2 provision bargain contract

(e) *Purposeful Interpretation*

find 90 cal rptr 645

328k16

328k17(2)

§ 22–3. Effect of Licensing Statutes

The violation of licensing statutes is governed by the same general principles that govern other kinds of illegal conduct. However, certain specific distinctions have been made in this class of cases. Practicing a trade or profession without a license, where a license is required, is ordinarily a criminal offense, but the question remains whether an unlicensed person who performs service is entitled to recover for the services performed. The primary distinction, which seems however, to be eroding, has been between licensing statutes that are merely revenue raising and statutes that are designed to certify the skills or moral fitness of licensees.[70] If it is a revenue raising measure, recovery is permitted.[71] However a person who practices a profession such as law without a license is ordinarily denied a recovery.[72] Even here some cases show flexibility in allowing an out of state attorney to recover where his services in the state are occasional.[73] Substantial compliance

---

70. Cope v. Rowlands, 2 M & W 149, 150 Eng.Rep. 707 (Exch.P.1836) (unlicensed stockbroker; no recovery); 6A Corbin § 1512; Annot., 82 A.L.R.2d 1429 (1962).

71. Colston v. Gulf States Paper Corp., 291 Ala. 423, 282 So.2d 251 (1973); Howard v. Lebby, 197 Ky. 324, 246 S.W. 828, 30 A.L.R. 830 (1923) (licensing fees assessed on building contractors constituted an occupation tax).

72. Lozoff v. Shore Heights, Ltd., 35 Ill. App.3d 697, 342 N.E.2d 475 (1976), affirmed 66 Ill.2d 398, 6 Ill.Dec. 225, 362 N.E.2d 1047 (1977) (out of state attorney); Spivak v. Sachs, 16 N.Y.2d 163, 263 N.Y.S.2d 953, 211 N.E.2d 329 (1965) (California attorney may not recover for services rendered in New York), reversing, 21 A.D.2d 348, 250 N.Y.S.2d 666 (1st Dep't

1964), 33 Fordham L.Rev. 483 (1965); see 11 A.L.R.3d 907 (1967).

73. Spanos v. Skouras Theatres Corp., 364 F.2d 161 (2d Cir.1966), cert. denied 385 U.S. 987, 87 S.Ct. 597, 17 L.Ed.2d 448 (1966) (out of state attorney handling federal antitrust case); see also Food Industries Res. & Eng., Inc. v. Alaska, 507 F.2d 865 (9th Cir.1974) (out of state engineers); Warde v. Davis, 494 F.2d 655 (10th Cir. 1974) (out of state landscape architect); Costello v. Schmidlin, 404 F.2d 87, 32 A.L.R.3d 1139 (3d Cir.1968); Winer v. Jonal Corp., 169 Mont. 247, 545 P.2d 1094, 78 A.L.R.3d 1112 (1976). A contrary result was reached in Marcus & Nocka v. Julian Goodrich Architects, Inc., 127 Vt. 404, 250 A.2d 739 (1969) but note court's close attention to legislative intent.

with a licensing law has been held to permit recovery.[74] The test of revenue raising as opposed to exercise of police power is no longer regarded as an absolute test and today it is regarded as one indicium of legislative intent.[75] Beyond legislative intent, modern courts have been concerned that the windfall to the defendant may be too great and the penalty too high if no recovery is permitted for services rendered by an unlicensed person. There are cases permitting recovery where the lack of a license caused no harm to the defendant and posed no grave threat to the public.[76] Partly on these considerations some courts have allowed recovery where the defendant was not a member of the general public but was engaged in the same line of business as the plaintiff.[77] The Restatement Second encourages the courts to balance the equities in the light of the public policy served.[78]

Because police power licenses are designed to protect the public, the parties are not in pari delicto.[79] Consequently where an unlicensed professional enters into a bargain with a member of the public the professional will be liable for damages in the event of his breach by unskillful performance.[80]

It should be noted that, although the unlicensed professional may be precluded from recovering, once he is paid he can successfully defend an action by the payor for restitution.[81]

 WESTLAW REFERENCES
find 342 ne2d 475

74. Asdourian v. Araj, 38 Cal.3d 276, 211 Cal.Rptr. 703, 696 P.2d 95 (1985).

75. John E. Rosasco Creameries, Inc. v. Cohen, 276 N.Y. 274, 11 N.E.2d 908, 118 A.L.R. 641 (1937) (unlicensed milk dealer permitted recovery); cf. Carmine v. Murphy, 285 N.Y. 413, 35 N.E.2d 19 (1941) (unlicensed liquor dealer not permitted to recover). As to real estate brokers, see Galbreath-Ruffin Corp. v. 40th and 3rd Corp., 19 N.Y.2d 354, 280 N.Y.S.2d 126, 227 N.E.2d 30 (1967), reargument denied 19 N.Y.2d 973, 281 N.Y.S.2d 1028, 228 N.E.2d 421 (1967). For an excellent case attempting to carry out legislative intent and policy, see Keller v. Thornton Canning Co., 66 Cal.2d 963, 59 Cal.Rptr. 836, 429 P.2d 156 (1967) (carrier had no permit, recovery permitted). See also T.E.C. & Assoc., Inc. v. Alberto-Culver Co., 131 Ill.App.3d 1085, 87 Ill.Dec. 220, 476 N.E.2d 1212 (1985) (unlicensed employment agency); Moffit v. Sederlund, 145 Mich.App. 1, 378 N.W.2d 491 (1985) (state securities act).

76. The cases cited in notes 73 and 74 are of this kind. See also Hiram Ricker & Sons v. Students Int'l Meditation Soc., 342 A.2d 262 (Me.1975) appeal dismissed 423 U.S. 1042, 96 S.Ct. 764, 46 L.Ed.2d 631 (1976) (nonrenewal of innkeeper's license

should not result in forfeiture of $65,000); Town Planning & Engineering Associates, Inc. v. Amesbury Specialty Co., Inc., 369 Mass. 737, 342 N.E.2d 706 (1976) (head of engineering firm had no license); Association Group Life, Inc. v. Catholic War Veterans, 120 N.J.Super. 85, 293 A.2d 408 (App.Div.1971) modified 61 N.J. 150, 293 A.2d 382 (1972) (insurance brokerage corporation had no license but employees were duly licensed).

77. Gene Taylor & Sons Plumbing Co., Ins. v. Corondolet Realty Trust, 611 S.W.2d 572 (Tenn.1981); Fillmore Products, Inc. v. Western States Paving, Inc., 561 P.2d 687 (Utah 1977).

78. Restatement, Second, Contracts § 181; Domach v. Spencer, 101 Cal.App.3d 308, 161 Cal.Rptr. 459 (1980); Grenco R.E. I.T. v. Nathaniel Green Dev. Corp., 218 Va. 228, 237 S.E.2d 107 (1977).

79. See § 22–2 supra.

80. Hedla v. McCool, 476 F.2d 1223 (9th Cir.1973); Cohen v. Mayflower Corp., 196 Va. 1153, 86 S.E.2d 860 (1955); see § 22–2 supra. On his liability for non-performance, see § 22–7 infra.

81. Anderson v. Frandsen, 36 Wn.App. 353, 674 P.2d 208 (1984).

§ 22–4. Remoteness of the Illegality

In Sirkin v. Fourteenth Street Store,[82] discussed in § 22–1, the plaintiff's additional argument was that the illegality was too remote. Plaintiff contended that although the agreement between the plaintiff and the purchasing agent was illegal there was nothing illegal in the contract for the sale of hosiery. The court disagreed, pointing out that the illegal bribe was the inducing cause of the hosiery contract and therefore tainted the contract.[83]

According to the first Restatement,[84] without support in the cases,[85] a legal contract could also become illegal if it was *performed* in an illegal manner. The first case of consequence to agree was Tocci v. Lembo.[86] The parties entered into a lawful contract whereby plaintiff would construct a house for defendant. In constructing the house, plaintiff failed to get approval of a federal agency that allocated scarce materials in the period immediately following World War II. Plaintiff's action for the balance of the price was denied. The court relied heavily on Williston's theory that the essential reason for denying recovery on a contract in the context of illegality is the refusal of the courts to reward illegal conduct.[87] Tocci was followed in McConnell v. Commonwealth Pictures Corp.,[88] where defendant retained the plaintiff to obtain certain motion picture distribution rights, promising a commission. Plaintiff obtained the rights by bribing an agent of the motion picture producer. It was held that plaintiff could not recover the promised commission despite the obvious benefits received by the defendant. Assuming these cases are sound, their rationale should be applied only to conduct that is illegal in a major way. A contract to transport goods should not be deemed to have been transmuted into an illegal transaction because the trucker exceeded the speed limit.[89]

There are miscellaneous instances of remote illegality. Where a party gained possession of a ring from its owner under an illegal agreement and pawned it, the true owner was permitted to reclaim it from the pawnbroker. Although the defense of illegality would have applied in litigation between the owner and the other party to the

82. See note 30 supra.

83. See also Thomas v. Ratiner, 462 So. 2d 1157 (Fla.App.1984) appeal denied 472 So.2d 1182 (Fla.1985) (attorney procured retainer in hospital in violation of statute; no recovery of fee).

84. Restatement, Contracts § 512.

85. See Comment, Illegal Performance of a Legal Contract 41 Marq.L.Rev. 34 (1957); Notes, 46 Va.L.Rev. 1601 (1960); 25 Albany L.Rev. 146 (1961); 8 U.C.L.A.L.Rev. 638 (1961) and especially 49 Geo.L.J. 362 (1960). More recently, see Haberman v. Elledge, 42 Wn.App. 744, 713 P.2d 746 (1986).

86. 325 Mass. 707, 92 N.E.2d 254 (1950), noted 31 B.U.L.Rev. 108 (1951).

87. 15 Williston § 1761; see, essentially contra, 6A Corbin § 1529.

88. 7 N.Y.2d 465, 166 N.E.2d 494, 199 N.Y.S.2d 483 (1960). This case is a basis for Restatement, Second, Contracts § 178, ill. 14, a rare instance in which the new Restatement agrees with Williston's rather than Corbin's position.

89. Cf. Reynolds Aluminum Bldg. Prod. Co. v. Leonard, 395 Mass. 255, 480 N.E.2d 1 (1985) (installer of solar panels failed to obtain building permit, recovery allowed); see Annot., 26 A.L.R.3d 1395 (1969).

illegal agreement, it was too remote to be raised by the pawnbroker.[90] Similarly, a purchaser on credit cannot raise as a defense that the seller has entered into illegal contracts with other purchasers but not with it.[91] How remote is "too remote" is obviously a question of degree. "The line of proximity varies somewhat according to the gravity of the evil apprehended." [92]

 WESTLAW REFERENCES
tocci +3 lembo

§ 22–5. Depositaries and Agents

If a person acquires funds by illegal conduct and deposits them in a bank, the bank cannot resist repayment to the depositor. The illegal conduct is simply too remote to be an appropriate defense by the bank.[93]

More difficult to explain are the cases in which *A* pays money to *B*, in *B's* capacity as agent for *C.* If the payment is the fruit of an illegal transaction one would expect that *C* could not recover the amount from *B* as recovery would in effect be the successful culmination of *C's* unlawful conduct. Nonetheless there are numerous cases permitting recovery by *C.*[94] Although various theories have been expressed to explain such holdings, including remoteness, the only tenable explanation is that *B's* fiduciary obligation as agent is regarded as stronger than the policies against enforcement of illegal agreements.[95]

The principle does not apply where the agent or depositary is an active party to the illegal transaction. Thus, where the plaintiff, a clothing jobber, advanced money to the defendant broker to be used to bribe purchasing agents and plaintiff sought restitution of funds which had not been expended, the court held that the defendant was not a mere depositary and therefore could use the defense of illegality.[96]

90. Pelosi v. Bugbee, 217 Mass. 579, 105 N.E. 222 (1914).

91. Roux Laboratories v. Beauty Franchises, Inc., 60 Wis.2d 427, 210 N.W.2d 441 (1973); see also O'Brien v. O'Brien Steel Constr. Co., 440 Pa. 375, 271 A.2d 254 (1970) (failure to report transaction to taxing authority); Seagirt Realty Corp. v. Chazanof, 13 N.Y.2d 282, 246 N.Y.S.2d 613, 196 N.E.2d 254 (1963) (plaintiff lost the deed received in culmination of a successful scheme to defraud creditors; action to quiet title permitted).

92. Restatement, Contracts § 597, Comment b; see also Restatement, Second, Contracts § 178, Comment d; 6A Corbin § 1529; 15 Williston § 1753.

93. An hypothetical case based on Southwestern Shipping Corp. v. National

City Bank, 6 N.Y.2d 454, 190 N.Y.S.2d 352, 160 N.E.2d 836 (1959) cert. denied 361 U.S. 895, 80 S.Ct. 198, 4 L.Ed.2d 151 (1959).

94. E.g., McBlair v. Gibbes, 58 U.S. (17 How.) 232, 15 L.Ed. 132 (1854); Sheahan v. McClure, 199 Mich. 63, 165 N.W. 735 (1917); Murray v. Vanderbilt, 39 Barb. 140, 152 (N.Y.App.Div.1863); see 6A Corbin §§ 1530, 1531; 15 Williston §§ 1785–1786; cf. Restatement, Second, Agency § 412 (1958).

95. 15 Williston § 1785.

96. Stone v. Freeman, 298 N.Y. 268, 82 N.E.2d 571 (1948). As to the doctrine of locus poenitentiae in a case such as this, see § 22–8 infra. Cases to the contrary exist. See annot., 8 A.L.R.2d 307 (1949).

§ 22–6. Divisibility of Illegal Bargains

Earlier we looked at a concept of divisibility pursuant to which a party in material breach of a contract could nonetheless recover for performance of divisible portions of the contract.[97] A similar, but not precisely the same, concept permits recovery where part of the contract is illegal. For example, plaintiff, an unlicensed plumber, entered into a contract with defendant to do certain plumbing work for an agreed sum. Plaintiff performed, but because of his unlicensed status could not recover the price. The court, however, permitted recovery for the materials furnished but not for labor performed.[98] The court thus severed the furnishing of materials from the services rendered although the contract was entire and not divisible in the sense that term is used in § 11–23 supra. This kind of decision tends to show that divisibility is not determined by fixed rules, but by the judicial instinct for justice.[99]

Where a contract is divisible in the sense in which it is used in § 11–23, the rule is that a promise which is legal and has its own separately apportioned consideration is enforceable except where the rest of the bargain is criminal or immoral to a high degree.[1]

§ 22–7. Restitutionary Recovery—Not In Pari Delicto

We have previously considered cases where parties may sue to enforce an illegal bargain.[2] The class of cases in which a party may recover in restitution for performances under illegal bargains is broader than the class of cases in which an illegal executory bargain can be enforced. In particular the doctrine of "not in pari delicto"

---

97. See § 11–24 supra.

98. Lund v. Bruflat, 159 Wash. 89, 292 P. 112 (1930); but see American Store Equip. & Constr. Corp. v. Jack Dempsey's Punch Bowl, Inc., 174 Misc. 436, 21 N.Y.S.2d 117 (1939), affirmed 283 N.Y. 601, 28 N.E.2d 23 (1940); cf. Birnbaum v. Schuler, 56 A.D.2d 556, 391 N.Y.S.2d 601 (1st Dep't 1977). Agreement with respect to illegal cohabitation was severed from the rendition of construction work and business services in Mason v. Rostad, 476 A.2d 662 (D.C.1984) and McCall v. Frampton, 81 A.D.2d 607, 438 N.Y.S.2d 11 (2d Dep't 1981).

99. See 6A Corbin § 1520; Restatement, Second, Contracts § 183.

1. Hill v. Schultz, 71 Idaho 145, 227 P.2d 586 (1951) (mortgage and lease on gambling promises severed; mortgage enforced as it was in consideration of a loan; lease not enforced as it was in consideration of a percentage of gambling revenues); Ingle v. Perkins, 95 Idaho 416, 510 P.2d 480 (1973); Lacks v. Lacks, 39 A.D.2d 485, 336 N.Y.S.2d 874 (1st Dep't 1972), appeal dismissed 32 N.Y.2d 939, 347 N.Y.S.2d 201, 300 N.E.2d 733 (1973); In re Craig's Estate, 298 Pa. 235, 148 A. 83 (1929); Restatement Contracts §§ 606–607; Restatement, Second, Contracts § 183.

2. See § 22–2 supra.

embraces a larger group of claimants than in cases of enforcement of executory agreements. This is appropriate in many cases because denial of relief results in the unjust enrichment of the party who has received the benefit of the performance and the forfeiture of property or services furnished by the other.[3]

A party who has performed under an illegal bargain is entitled to a quasi-contractual recovery if he was not guilty of serious moral turpitude and, although blameworthy, is not equally as guilty as the other party to the illegal bargain.[4] What constitutes serious moral turpitude is obviously a question of degree.[5] A person who bribes or attempts to bribe a public official or agent is usually believed to be guilty of serious moral turpitude.[6] Yet, in a case in which the plaintiff, a Jewish refugee, gave jewels to the defendant to be used in bribing the Portuguese Consul to issue a visa so that plaintiff could escape Hitler's army, it was held that the plaintiff might recover the value of the jewels from the defendant as he was not in pari delicto.[7] The court refused to attach the stigma of moral turpitude to an agreement made by a person in dire necessity and motivated by the instinct of self-preservation.[8]

The second question which must be asked in determining whether the parties are in pari delicto is whether the parties are equally at fault. The cases which allow recovery on the ground that the performing plaintiff is not equally at fault tend to come within several flexible categories. Foremost among these categories are cases in which the transaction is outlawed in order to protect a class of persons of which the plaintiff is a member.[9] Thus, a borrower may recover excess interest paid, and often a penalty as well, from a usurer. Antitrust laws are aimed, in large part, at enterprises enjoying considerable

---

3. See Restatement, Second, Contracts, Introductory Note Ch. 8, Topic 5. See also GMB Enterprises, Inc. v. B-3 Enterprises, Inc., 39 Wn.App. 678, 695 P.2d 145 (1985) (although the parties are in pari delicto, restitution is in the public interest under the facts).

4. Restatement, Second, Contracts § 198(b); Restatement, Contracts § 604; 15 Williston § 1789; see generally, 2 Palmer on Restitution § 8.6 (1978); Grodecki, In Pari Delicto Potior est Conditio Defendentis, 71 L.Q.Rev. 254 (1955); Higgins, The Transfer of Property Under Illegal Transactions, 25 Modern L.Rev. 149 (1962); Wade, Restitution of Benefits Acquired through Illegal Transactions, 95 U.Pa.L. Rev. 261 (1947); Note, The Doctrine of Illegality and Petty Offenders: Can Quasi-Contract Bring Justice?, 42 Notre Dame Law. 46 (1966).

5. William J. Davis, Inc. v. Slade, 271 A.2d 412 (D.C.1970).

6. State v. Strickland, 42 Md.App. 357, 400 A.2d 451 (1979).

7. Liebman v. Rosenthal, 185 Misc. 837, 57 N.Y.S.2d 875 (1945) affirmed 269 App. Div. 1062, 59 N.Y.S.2d 148 (2d Dep't 1945). See 6A Corbin § 1536. Sometimes the doctrine is worded in terms that the plaintiff "is not in particips criminis."

8. Emergency measures to avoid imminent injury may be taken, under modern criminal codes, despite the fact that such measures under ordinary circumstances would constitute a criminal act. See Model Penal Code § 3.02; McKinney's N.Y. Penal Law § 35.05.

9. Stenger v. Anderson, 66 Cal.2d 970, 59 Cal.Rptr. 844, 429 P.2d 164 (1967) (statutes governing pre-paid life care are for the benefit of the aged); Neil v. Pennsylvania Life Ins. Co., 474 P.2d 961 (Okl. 1970); Singh v. Kulubya, [1963] 3 All E.R. 499; 27 Modern L.Rev. 225 (1964); see 6 Corbin § 1540; Wade, supra n. 4, at 270–72. See § 22–2 supra.

market power in order to protect enterprises having a significantly lesser amount of market power. Therefore, it will usually be held that a dealership is not in pari delicto with the manufacturer although the contracts between the manufacturer and its dealers contain illegal provisions in restraint of trade.[10] In some jurisdictions it has been held that a bettor is not in pari delicto with a professional bookmaker as the gambling laws are aimed primarily against organized gambling.[11]

A prominent class of cases in which a party is not in pari delicto exists when "he was induced to participate in the illegality by fraud or duress or by the use of influence derived from superior knowledge, mental power, or economic position."[12] A famous series of cases involving the Buckfoot gang illustrates this proposition. The gang had various operatives whose business it was to lure wealthy westerners to their headquarters at an athletic club in Missouri. One of their techniques was to induce their guests into betting on races allegedly "fixed" in their favor, when actually they were "fixed" for their man to lose. The courts allowed recovery against the gang on the grounds that the parties were not on an equal footing. These highly organized frauds, arranged with consummate skill, were no match for the relatively naive bettors.[13] It has been held that a plaintiff who has paid a marriage brokerage fee may recover it because the transaction inherently involves undue influence.[14] Perhaps a more satisfactory reason is that the rules against marriage brokerage are designed for the protection of the unmarried. Similar considerations provide the foundation for the rule that when an illegal agreement is made between parties in a fiduciary relation such as attorney-client, it will be held that the client is not in pari delicto with the fiduciary,[15] at least where the client

---

10. Perma Life Mufflers, Inc. v. Int'l Parts Corp., 392 U.S. 134, 88 S.Ct. 1981, 20 L.Ed.2d 981 (1968) [overruled on other grounds Copperweld Corp. v. Independence Tube Corp., 467 U.S. 752, 104 S.Ct. 2731, 81 L.Ed.2d 628 (1984)], see Comment, The Demise of In Pari Delicto in Private Actions Pursuant to Regulatory Schemes, 60 Cal.L. Rev. 572 (1972); Note, In Pari Delicto: The Consumer's Best Friend, 30 Ohio St.L.J. 332 (1969). For other examples of legislation designed to protect a class, see Pearlstein v. Scudder & German, 429 F.2d 1136 (2d Cir.1970) cert. denied 401 U.S. 1013, 91 S.Ct. 1250, 28 L.Ed.2d 550 (1971); McAllister v. Drapeau, 14 Cal.2d 102, 92 P.2d 911, 125 A.L.R. 800 (1939) (mortgage in violation of H.O.L.C. Act).

11. Watts v. Malatesta, 262 N.Y. 80, 186 N.E. 210, 88 A.L.R. 1072 (1933); contra, Elias v. Gill, 92 Ky. 569, 18 S.W. 454 (1892) (professional permitted to set off his losses).

12. 6A Corbin § 1537. However it is often urged that this exception should be confined to cases in which the defendant

misled the plaintiff into believing that the transaction would be lawful. 15 Williston § 1791; American Mutual Life Ins. Co. v. Bertram, 163 Ind. 51, 70 N.E. 258 (1904); Cooper v. Gossett, 263 N.Y. 491, 189 N.E. 562 (1934).

13. Stewart v. Wright, 147 Fed. 321 (8th Cir.1906), cert. denied 203 U.S. 590, 27 S.Ct. 777 (1906); Lockman v. Cobb, 77 Ark. 279, 91 S.W. 546 (1905); Hobbs v. Boatright, 195 Mo. 693, 93 S.W. 934 (1906); Falkenberg v. Allen, 18 Okl. 210, 90 P. 415 (1907); see also Catts v. Phalen, 43 U.S. (2 How.) 376, 11 L.Ed. 306 (1844); Grim v. Cheatwood, 208 Okl. 570, 257 P.2d 1049, 39 A.L.R.2d 1209 (1953); see 15 Williston § 1791.

14. Duval v. Wellman, 124 N.Y. 156, 26 N.E. 343 (1891).

15. Singleton v. Foreman, 435 F.2d 962 (5th Cir.1970); Berman v. Coakley, 243 Mass. 348, 137 N.E. 667, 26 A.L.R. 92 (1923); 32 Yale L.J. 745 (1923); Place v. Hayward, 117 N.Y. 487, 23 N.E. 25 (1889);

is acting on the advice of the fiduciary.[16] Intertwined in these cases are considerations of the superior influence which an attorney may exercise on his clients as well as the consideration that an attorney must not be permitted to abuse his quasi public office.

A person entering into an illegal transaction under duress may not be in pari delicto with the party exercising the coercion.[17] Foremost among the cases in which this question arises are those in which a plaintiff seeks restitution of a payment the consideration for which was the defendant's agreement not to press criminal charges against the plaintiff or against a close relative of the plaintiff. The majority of these cases have indicated that, absent special circumstances, the parties are in pari delicto and the plaintiff may have no recovery whether or not the defendant has kept his illegal promise.[18] A number of cases have indicated, however, that if the party was innocent of the crime for which prosecution was threatened, he may have restitution.[19] Restitution has generally been allowed in cases in which a debtor has been coerced secretly to pay a creditor more than his agreed proportion under a composition agreement with creditors.[20] The degree of duress in such cases is doubtless no stronger than in the cases involving threatened criminal prosecutions. The different degrees of moral turpitude are, it is believed, the basis for the differing results.

 WESTLAW REFERENCES
restitution /s illegal /2 contract bargain provision
95k259 /p restitution

§ 22–8. Restitution—Locus Poenitentiae

Another exception to the general rule that the court leaves the parties to an illegal bargain where it finds them is the doctrine of locus poenitentiae. Even if the plaintiff is in pari delicto and therefore as blameworthy or more blameworthy than the defendant, he is entitled to rescind the bargain and obtain restitution if he acts in time to prevent the attainment of the illegal purpose for which the bargain was made

Peyton v. Margiotti, 398 Pa. 86, 156 A.2d 865 (1959); see 15 Williston § 1790.

16. The parties are in pari delicto where the client is the "dominant mind" in the transaction. Schermerhorn v. De Chambrun, 64 Fed. 195 (2d Cir.1894).

17. Karpinski v. Collins, 252 Cal.App.2d 711, 60 Cal.Rptr. 846 (1967) (dairyman permitted to recover kick-backs paid to president of supplier where no other supply of milk was available); 6A Corbin § 1537; Wade, supra n. 4 at 272–76.

18. Baker v. Citizens Bank of Guntersville, 282 Ala. 33, 208 So.2d 601 (1968); Union Exch. Nat. Bank v. Joseph, 231 N.Y. 250, 131 N.E. 905, 17 A.L.R. 323 (1921); Ellis v. Peoples Nat. Bank, 166 Va. 389, 186 S.E. 9 (1936); contra, Goringe v. Read,

23 Utah 120, 63 P. 902 (1901). The mere fact that an agreement is made to make restitution for a criminal act does not make the agreement illegal. The question is whether there has been a promise to stifle prosecution. Blair Milling Co. v. Fruitager, 113 Kan. 432, 215 P. 286, 32 A.L.R. 416 (1923). See also § 9–4 supra.

19. Sykes v. Thompson, 160 N.C. 348, 76 S.E. 252 (1912). Restitution may be granted if the person exercising the duress did not believe in the charge. Union Exch. Nat. Bank v. Joseph, 231 N.Y. 250, 131 N.E. 905 (1921) (dictum).

20. Batchelder & Lincoln Co. v. Whitmore, 122 Fed. 355 (1st Cir.1903); Brown v. Everett-Ridley-Ragan Co., 111 Ga. 404, 36 S.E. 813 (1900).

unless the mere making of the bargain involves serious moral turpitude.[21]

The doctrine has been justified on the grounds that it frustrates the carrying out of illegal schemes [22] and that in fairness and morality the plaintiff should have an opportunity to repent. Repentance in a moral sense is not, however, usually required and the courts will not generally inquire into what motivated the plaintiff in repudiating the bargain.[23] Indeed, in cases for restitution of money deposited with a stakeholder for wagering purposes it is often held that recovery may be had even after the event wagered upon has occurred.[24] In such cases it is usually apparent that the plaintiff does not repent having violated the law but repents only having lost the wager.

The plaintiff is generally not permitted to withdraw if any part of the illegal performance is consummated.[25] Some cases, however, permit withdrawal any time before the illegal aspects are substantially performed.[26]

Although restitution is generally not granted when the bargain involves moral turpitude, at least one jurisdiction has made a strong case to the contrary,[27] arguing that the basis of the doctrine is:

> "to protect society from the influence of contracts made in disregard of the public weal by reducing the the number of such transactions to a minimum, and by interrupting the progress of illegal undertakings before the evil purpose has been fully consummated. To hold that the hand of the court is stayed merely because of the pernicious character of the illegal promise, or solely because its performance was not sooner arrested seems like a perversion of the real purpose of the doctrine * * *. The real question at issue in any particular case is whether the ends of the law will be furthered or defeated by granting relief."

Although it is generally said that repentance comes too late if it comes only after the other party to the bargain has indicated he will

---

21. Woel v. Griffith, 253 Md. 451, 253 A.2d 353 (1969); Restatement, Second, Contracts § 199(a); 6A Corbin § 1541; 2 Palmer on Restitution § 8.7 (1978); 15 Williston § 1788.

22. Cleveland C., C. & St. L. Ry. Co. v. Hirsch, 204 Fed. 849 (6th Cir.1913); Harrington v. Bochenski, 140 Md. 24, 116 A. 836 (1922).

23. See Aikman v. Wheeling, 120 W.Va. 46, 195 S.E. 667, 669 (1938); but see Adams-Mitchell Co. v. Cambridge Distributing Co., 189 F.2d 913 (2d Cir.1951).

24. Lewy v. Crawford, 5 Tex.Civ.App. 293, 23 S.W. 1041, 1043 (1893) ("not a question of sorrow and repentance, but one of disaffirming and destroying a contract

made in violation of law and morals."); 6A Corbin §§ 1484, 1541.

25. See Stone v. Freeman, 298 N.Y. 268, 82 N.E.2d 571, 8 A.L.R.2d 304 (1948) (part of the bribe money reached its destination); but cf. Gehres v. Ater, 148 Ohio St. 89, 73 N.E.2d 513, 172 A.L.R. 693 (1947) (recovery permitted for value of bond deposited as security for payment of a gambling debt.)

26. Kearley v. Thomson, [1870] 24 Q.B.D. 742, 747 (C.A.); Ware v. Spinney, 76 Kan. 289, 91 P. 787 (1907).

27. Town of Meredith v. Fullerton, 83 N.H. 124, 139 A. 359, 365 (1927); accord, Greenberg v. Evening Post Ass'n, 91 Conn. 371, 99 A. 1037 (1917).

not perform or after attainment of the unlawful purpose is seen to be impossible,[28] this rule also finds its exceptions.[29]

 WESTLAW REFERENCES
di locus poenitentiae
"locus poenitentiae"

§ 22–9. Change of Law or Facts After the Bargain Is Made

If A and B enter into a contract which is legal at the time the contract is formed and subsequently the contract becomes illegal, the problems presented are covered under the topic of impossibility of performance.[30]

A different problem is presented if the contract is illegal when formed but subsequently contracts of that type become legal as a result of a change in fact or a change in law. The general rule is that a change of law does not validate a contract which was originally illegal and unenforceable.[31] However there are exceptions when the repealing statute expressly so states or where this is implied as for example "when the policy underlying the original statute or the extent of its prohibition is doubtful." [32]

Where the bargain is illegal and a change of facts removes the cause of the illegality the contract does not thereby become enforceable except where either party did not know or have reason to know of the illegality.[33] Where a change in fact occurs which removes the cause of the illegality the parties may subsequently ratify the agreement.[34]

 WESTLAW REFERENCES
find 107 f2d 712
95k138(6) /p illegal

---

28. Bigos v. Bousted, [1951] 1 All E.R. 92 (K.B.); 6A Corbin § 1541.

29. Liebman v. Rosenthal, 185 Misc. 837, 57 N.Y.S.2d 875 (1945) affirmed 269 App.Div. 1062, 59 N.Y.S.2d 148 (2nd Dep't 1945) (alternative ground).

30. See § 13–5 supra.

31. Fitzsimons v. Eagle Brewing Co., 107 F.2d 712, 126 A.L.R. 681 (3d Cir.1939); Reno v. D'Javid, 42 N.Y.2d 1040, 399 N.Y.S.2d 210, 369 N.E.2d 766 (1977); but see Bloch v. Frankfort Distillery, Inc., 273 N.Y. 469, 6 N.E.2d 408 (1936).

32. 6A Corbin § 1532 (e.g., Sunday law statutes and usury statutes); Goldfarb v.

Goldfarb, 86 A.D.2d 459, 450 N.Y.S.2d 212 (2d Dep't 1982); cf. Teh, the Subsequent Validation of Illegal Contracts, 9 Irish Jurist 42 (1974) (distinguishing void and unenforceable contracts). The problem here discussed is but one aspect of the general problem of the retroactive applicability of civil legislation. For a thorough survey centered on corporation laws, see McNulty, Corporations and the Intertemporal Conflict of Laws, 55 Calif.L.Rev. 12 (1967).

33. Restatement, Contracts § 609.

34. 6A Corbin § 1532.

Appendix

WESTLAW REFERENCES

The WESTLAW System

WESTLAW is a computer-assisted legal research service of West Publishing Company. WESTLAW is accessible through a number of public communications networks. The materials available from WESTLAW are contained in databases stored at West Publishing Company's central computers in St. Paul, Minnesota.

The WESTLAW user sends a query, or message, to the computer where it is processed and documents are identified that satisfy the search request. The text of the retrieved documents is then stored on magnetic disks and transmitted to the user. The data moves through a telecommunication network. The user sees the documents on a video display terminal. When the documents appear on the terminal the user can decide whether further research is desired. If another search is necessary, the query may be recalled for editing, or an entirely new query may be sent to the computer. Documents displayed on the terminal may be printed out or, on some terminals, the text may be stored on its own magnetic disks.

In addition to the federal case law databases, WESTLAW provides access to state case law databases and many specialized databases. For example, WESTLAW contains separate topical databases for areas of the law such as federal tax, patents and copyrights, bankruptcy, communications, labor, securities, antitrust and business regulation, military justice, admiralty, and government contracts. WESTLAW also contains the text of the U.S. Code and the Code of Federal Regulations, West's INSTA–CITE™, Shepard's® Citations, Black's Law Dictionary, and many other legal sources.

Improving Legal Research with WESTLAW

Traditional legal research begins with the examination of texts, treatises, case digests, encyclopedias, citators, annotated law reports, looseleaf services, and periodicals. These secondary sources of the law provide compilations and summaries of authoritative material contained in primary legal sources. The goal of legal research is to analyze and interpret these primary sources.

In their familiar printed form, such primary sources appear in the state and regional reporters, federal reporters, and in statutory codes and administrative materials. In WESTLAW, these documents are extensively represented in electronic databases.

WESTLAW permits access to the many cases that do not get indexed or digested into manual systems of secondary legal sources. With WESTLAW it is possible to index any significant term or combination of terms in an almost unlimited variety of grammatical and numerical relationships by formulating a query composed of those terms.

WESTLAW queries may be made as broad or as specific as desired, depending upon the context of the legal issue to be researched.

WESTLAW queries add a dynamic aspect to the text of this hornbook. Since new cases are continuously being added to WESTLAW databases as they are decided by the courts, the addition of queries provides a type of self-contained updating service to the publication. Since a query may be addressed to the entire range of cases contained in the database designated for a search—from the earliest decisions to the most recent—the search results obtained from WESTLAW reflect the most current law available on any given issue.

In addition, WESTLAW queries augment the customary role of footnotes to the hornbook text by directing the user to a wider range of supporting authorities. Readers may use the preformulated queries supplied in this edition "as is" or formulate their own queries in order to retrieve cases relevant to the points of law discussed in the text.

Query Formulation: (a) What is a WESTLAW Query?

The query is a message to WESTLAW. It instructs the computer to retrieve documents containing terms in the relationships specified by the query. The terms in a query are made up of words and/or numbers that pinpoint the legal issue to be researched.

An example of the kind of preformulated queries that appear in this publication is reproduced below. The queries corresponding to each section of the text are listed at the end of the section.

death deceas! die /s contract /s unilateral

This query is taken from chapter 2, section 2–20. The query, or question, that is directed to WESTLAW appears at the end of the section of the text. This query is asking WESTLAW to find documents containing the terms DEATH or DIE or DECEAS! within the same sentence as the term CONTRACT and also within the same sentence as UNILATERAL.

This query illustrates what a standard request to WESTLAW looks like—words or numbers describing an issue, tied together by connectors. These connectors tell WESTLAW in what relationships the terms must appear. WESTLAW will retrieve all documents from the database that contain the terms appearing in those relationships.

The material that follows explains the methods by which WESTLAW queries are formulated and shows how users can employ the preformulated queries in this publication in their research of the law of contracts. In addition, there are instructions that will enable readers to modify their queries to fit the particular needs of their research.

Query Formulation: (b) Proximity Connectors

Proximity connectors allow search terms to be ordered so that relevant documents will be retrieved from WESTLAW. The connectors and their meanings appear below:

Space (or). A space between search terms means "or." Leaving a space between the query terms INSANITY and INCAPACITY

Insanity incapacity

instructs the computer to retrieve documents that contain either the word INSANITY or the word INCAPACITY (or both).

& (and) or (ampersand). The & symbol means "and." Placing the & between two terms instructs the computer to retrieve documents that contain both of the terms. The terms on either side may be in reverse order. For example, if the & is inserted between the terms OFFER and ACCEPTANCE

offer & acceptance

the computer will retrieve documents containing both the word OFFER and ACCEPTANCE in the same document. In any such retrieved document, the word OFFER may either precede or follow the word ACCEPTANCE. The & may be placed between groups of alternative terms. For example, placing the & between OFFER or BID and ASSENT or ACCEPTANCE

offer bid & assent acceptance

instructs the computer to retrieve documents in which the terms OFFER or BID (or both) and ASSENT or ACCEPTANCE (or both) appear in the same document.

/p (same paragraph). The /p symbol means "within the same paragraph." It requires that terms to the left of the /p appear within the same paragraph as terms to the right of the connector. For example, placing a /p between the terms OFFER and ASSENT

offer /p assent

will instruct the computer to retrieve documents in which OFFER and ASSENT occur in the same paragraph. The terms on each side of the /p may appear in the document in any order within the paragraph. As with &, the /p connector may be placed between groups of alternative terms. Thus, the query

offer bid /p assent acceptance

will command the retrieval of all documents in which the words OFFER or BID (or both) occur in the same paragraph as the words ASSENT or ACCEPTANCE (or both).

/s (same sentence). The /s symbol requires that one or more search terms on each side of the /s appear in the same sentence. If a /s is placed between the words ACCORD and BREACH!

accord /s breach!

the computer is instructed to retrieve documents that have the word ACCORD and the word BREACH! in the same sentence, without regard to which of these words occur first in the sentence.

The /s may be placed between groups of alternative terms. Inserting a /s between the terms ACCORD or SATISFACTION and BREACH! or REPUDIAT!

accord satisfaction /s breach! repudiat!

instructs the computer to retrieve documents containing either the words ACCORD or SATISFACTION (or both) appear within the same sentence as the words BREACH! or REPUDIAT! (or both), regardless of which terms appear first.

+s (precedes within sentence). The +s symbol requires that one or more terms to the left of the +s precede one or more terms to the right of the +s within the same sentence. The query

freedom +s contract

instructs the computer to retrieve all documents in which the word FREEDOM precedes the word CONTRACT in the same sentence. The +s connector, like the other connectors, may be used between groups of alternative terms.

/n (numerical proximity-within n words). The /n symbol means "within n words," where n represents any whole number between 1 and 255, inclusive. It requires that terms to the left of the /n appear within the designated number of words as terms to the right of the connector. For example, placing a /3 between the terms PAST and CONSIDERATION

> past /3 consideration

instructs the computer to retrieve all documents in which the term PAST occurs within three words of the term CONSIDERATION. Numerical proximities may also be used between groups of alternative search terms. In addition, the +n symbol may be used to require that terms to the left of the numercial proximity symbol precede the terms to the right of the symbol. Thus, placing the +3 symbol between the words PAST or PRIOR or PREVIOUS or ANTECEDENT and CONSIDERATION

> past prior previous antecedent +3 consideration

instructs the computer to retrieve cases in which either the word PAST or PRIOR or PREVIOUS or ANTECEDENT (or all) occur within three words and preceding the word CONSIDERATION.

" " (quotation marks/phrase). The " " (quotation marks/phrase) symbol can be thought of as the most restrictive grammatical connector. Placing terms within quotation marks instructs the computer to retrieve all documents in which the terms appear in the precise proximity (i.e., contiguousness) and order that they have within the quotation marks. For example, placing the following terms within quotation marks

> "pre-existing duty"

instructs the computer to retrieve all documents in which the term PRE–EXISTING appears adjacent to, and precedes, the term DUTY. Phrases that are constructed with quotation marks may be used as alternatives by leaving a space between them. Thus, the query

> "pre-existing duty" "pre-existing promise"

instructs the computer to retrieve all documents in which the phrase PRE–EXISTING DUTY or PRE–EXISTING PROMISE (or both) occur.

This technique of query formulation is effective when used to search legal terms of art, legal concepts, or legal entities that occur together as multiple terms. Some examples are: "good faith", "requirement contract", and "firm offer".

Phrase searching should be limited to those instances in which it is certain that the terms will always appear adjacent to each other and in the same order. For example, it would not be advisable to use the following query:

> "third-party beneficiary"

Despite the entrenchment into legal jargon of the phrase "third-party beneficiary", these terms may occur in a different order and not be adjacent to each other. For example, they might appear in the language of relevant case law as ". . . a third person benefitted. . . ."

Therefore, a better query to use in searching for these terms would be:

> third /3 person party /3 beneficiary benefit***

% (exclusion). The % symbol means "but not." It instructs the computer to exclude documents that contain terms appearing after the % symbol. For example, to retrieve documents containing the term "ALTERNATIVE PROMISE", but not the term "STATUTE OF FRAUDS", the following query would be used:

    "alternative promise" % "statute of frauds"

Query Formulation: (c) A Recommended Strategy

There is no perfect methodology for query formulation. However, a systematic approach to query formulation will probably generate better search results. A step-by-step method is listed below and is suggested as a strategy for query formulation.

T Terms. After determining the legal issue to be researched, the first step in query formulation is to select the key terms from the issue that will be used as search terms in the query. Words, numbers, and various other symbols may be used as search terms.

The goal in choosing search terms is to select the most unique terms for the issue. In selecting such terms it is frequently helpful to conceptualize how the terms might appear in the language of the documents that will be searched by the query. Moreover, it is necessary to consider the grammatical and editorial structure of the document. This involves a consideration of how the writer of the document (i.e., judge or headnote and synopsis writer) has worded both the factual and legal components of the issues involved in the case.

While traditional book research generally starts with a consideration of the general legal concepts under which particular problems are subsumed, WESTLAW research starts with a consideration of specific terms that are likely to appear in documents that have addressed those problems. This is so because documents are retrieved from WESTLAW on the basis of the terms they contain. Accordingly, the more precisely terms that will single out the desired documents can be identified, the more relevant the search results will be.

A Alternative Terms. Once the initial search terms have been selected for a query, it is important to consider alternative terms and synonyms for those terms. The nature of the legal issue will determine which are desirable.

As an illustration, in formulating a query to research the effect a promise to pay a debt has on the applicable statute of limitations, the researcher might first choose the following as search terms (with appropriate root expansion):

    promis! /s pay /s "statute of limitation" /s debt

Clearly, the terms PAYING, PAID, and PAYMENT would be good alternatives for PAY. Similarly, the term INDEBTED! could be added as a synonym for DEBT. Adding these alternatives to the initial search terms produces the following terms:

    promis! pay payment paid paying /s "statute of limitation" /s debt indebted!

Note that a space, which means "or" in WESTLAW, should be left between search terms and their alternatives.

R Root Expansion (!) and Universal Character (*). When constructing queries, it is necessary to consider various forms of the search terms that are selected. Derivative forms of words should be anticipated due to the variety of ways in which the language in a document may be worded. There are two devices available on WESTLAW for automatically generating alternative forms of search terms in a query.

One device is an unlimited root expansion. Placement of the ! symbol at the end of the root term generates other forms containing the root. For example, attaching the ! symbol to the root term PROMIS! in the following query:

    promis! /s note

instructs the computer to generate the words PROMISE, PROMISED, PROMISING, and PROMISSORY as search terms for the query. This saves time and space that would otherwise be consumed in typing each of the alternative words in the query.

The other device permits the generation of all possible characters from a designated part of a term. This is done by placing one or more * symbols at the location of the term where universal character generation is desired. For example, placing two * symbols on the term SUFFICIEN in the following query:

    sufficien** /s consideration

instructs the computer to generate all forms of the root term SUFFICIEN** with up to two additional characters. Thus, the words SUFFICIENT and SUFFICIENCY would be generated by this query. The * symbol may also be embedded inside of a term as in the following query:

    withdr*w! /s bid

This will generate the alternative **withdraw** and **withdrew;** in addition withdrew, withdrawn, and withdrawing will be retrieved because of the use of the root expander.

WESTLAW automatically generates standard plural forms for search terms so it is generally unnecessary to use the root expansion devices to obtain plural forms of search terms.

Also note that WESTLAW will generate the various spellings for compound words. Whenever your search terms include a compound word, use a hyphen between the words. This way, the search will generate the compound word's other forms. For example, inserting a hyphen between the word QUASI and CONTRACT

    quasi-contract

will generate quasicontract, quasi contract, and quasi-contract.

C Connectors. The next step in query formulation is to consider the appropriate grammatical context in which the search terms will appear. Using the example provided in the preceding section

promis! /s pay payment paying paid /s "statute of limitation" /s debt indebted!

this query would instruct the computer to retrieve documents in which PROMIS! appears in the same sentence with either PAY or PAYMENT or PAID or PAYING, and also appears in the same sentence with STATUTE OF LIMITATIONS, and also appears in the same sentence with either INDEBTED! or DEBT.

Query Formulation: (d) General Principles of Query Formulation

The art of query formulation is the heart of WESTLAW research. Although the researcher can gain technical skills by using the terminal, there is no strict mechanical procedure for formulating queries. One must first comprehend the meaning of the legal issue to be researched before beginning a search on WESTLAW. Then, the user will need to supply imagination, insight, and legal comprehension with knowledge of the capabilities of WESTLAW to formulate a useful query. Effective query formulation requires an alternative way of thinking about the legal research process.

Using WESTLAW is a constant balancing between generating too many documents and missing important documents. In general, it is better to look through a reasonable number of irrelevant documents than it is to be too restrictive and miss important material. The researcher should take into consideration at the initial query formulation stage what to do if too many, or not enough documents are retrieved. Thought should be given as to how the query might be narrowed or the search broadened, and what can be done if the initial search retrieves zero documents.

Some issues by their very nature will require more lengthy queries than others; however, it is best to strive for efficiency in structuring the query Look for unique search terms that will eliminate the need for a lengthy query. Keep in mind that WESTLAW is literal. Consider all possible alternative terms. Remember that searching is done by syntactic structure and not by legal concepts.

Always keep in mind database content and the parameters of the system to date. Also, consider the inherent limitations of the computer. It does not think, create, or make analogies. The researcher must do that for the computer. The computer simply looks for the terms in the documents in the relationships specified in the query. The researcher should know what he or she is looking for, at least to the extent of knowing how the terms are likely to show up in relevant documents.

The WESTLAW Reference Manual should be consulted for more information on query formulation and WESTLAW commands. The Reference Manual is updated periodically to reflect new enhancements of WESTLAW. It provides detailed and comprehensive instructions on all aspects of the WESTLAW system and offers numerous illustrative examples on the proper format for various types of queries. Material contained in the Reference Manual enables the user to benefit from all of the system's capabilities in an effective and efficient manner.

Search Techniques: (a) Field Searching

Documents in WESTLAW are divided into separate sections called fields. The computer can be instructed to search for terms within designated fields. This technique is known as field searching. Moreover, in reviewing the documents that have been retrieved in a search, the user may instruct the computer to display specified fields. The fields available for WESTLAW case law databases are described below.

Title Field. The title field contains the title of the case (e.g., Lucy v. Zehmer).

Citation Field. The citation field contains the citation of the case (e.g., 84 Se2d 516).

Court Field. The court field contains abbreviations that allow searches for case law to be restricted to particular states, districts, or courts.

Judge Field. The judge field contains the names of judges or justices who wrote the majority opinion.

Synopsis Field. The synopsis field contains the synopsis of the case, prepared by West editors.

Topic Field. The topic field contains the West Digest Topic name and number, the Key Number, and the text of the Key line for each digest paragraph.

Digest Field. The digest field contains digest paragraphs prepared by West editors. It includes headnotes, corresponding Digest Topics and Key Numbers, the title and citation of the case, court, and year of decision.

Headnote Field. The headnote field contains the language of the headnotes, exclusive of the Digest Topic and Key Number lines and case identification information.

Opinion Field. The opinion field contains the text of the case, court and docket numbers, names of attorneys appearing in the case, and judges participating in the decision.

The format for a query that will instruct the computer to search for terms only within a specified field consists of the field name followed by a set of parentheses containing the search terms and grammatical connectors, if any. For example, to retrieve the case appearing at 84 Se2d 516, the citation field, followed by a set of parentheses containing the volume and page numbers of the citation, separated by the +3 connector may be used:

```
citation(84  +3  516)
cite(84  +3  516)
```

Correspondingly, to retrieve the case entitled *Lucy v. Zehmer,* the title field, followed by a set of parentheses containing the names of the title, separated by the & connector may be used:

```
title(lucy  &  zehmer)
```

Combination Field Searching

Fields may be combined in a query. For example, terms may be searched in the digest field and, at the same time, the query may be limited to search the court of a particular state. The following query illustrates this technique:

```
digest(promise  /s  manifest!  /s  intent!)  &  court(mn)
```

This query instructs the computer to retrieve documents containing the words PROMISE, MANIFEST! and INTENT! within the digest field that were issued from Minnesota courts, as designated with the court field restriction. Any number of different fields may be combined with this method.

Moreover, terms may be searched in clusters of fields by joining any number of field names by commas. One application of this technique is to search for terms in the synopsis and digest fields. This technique is illustrated below:

```
synopsis,digest(promise  /s  manifest!  /s  intent!)  &  court(mn)
```

In this example the terms PROMISE, MANIFEST! and INTENT! are searched in the synopsis and digest fields simultaneously.

The WESTLAW Reference Manual should be consulted for further instruction on how to perform searches using the field restrictions.

Search Techniques: (b) Date Restriction

Queries may be restricted to retrieve documents appearing before, after, or on a specified date, or within a range of dates. The date restriction format consists of the word DATE followed by the appropriate restriction(s) within parentheses. The words BEFORE and AFTER may be used to designate the desired date relationships. Alternatively, the symbols < and > may be used. Moreover, the month and day and year may be spelled out (e.g., January 1, 1984) or they may be abbreviated as follows: 1–1–84, or 1/1/84. The date restriction is joined to the rest of the query by the & symbol. For example, to retrieve documents decided or issued after December 31, 1976, that discuss unilateral contracts, any of the following formats could be used:

```
digest("unilateral contract")  &  date(after 12/31/76)
digest("unilateral contract")  &  date(>december 31, 1976)
digest("unilateral contract")  &  date(>12–31–82)
```

To retrieve documents decided after December 31, 1976, and before March 15, 1983, the following format could be used:

```
digest("unilateral contract")  &  date(after 12/31/76 and before 3/15/83)
```

Search Techniques: (c) Digest Topic and Key Number Searching

Searches may be performed using West Digest Topic and Key Numbers as search terms. When this strategy is used, the search term consists of a West Digest Topic Number followed by the letter k, followed by a Key Number classified as a subheading under the Digest Topic. The computer will retrieve all cases that contain a headnote classified with the designated Digest Topic and Key Number. For example, to retrieve cases that contain the Digest Topic classification for CONTRACTS (Digest Topic Number 95) and the Key Number for Implied Agreements (Key Number 27), the following query would be used:

95k27

A related search technique employs Digest Topic classification numbers in conjunction with other search terms. Since the Digest Topic Numbers appear in the topic and digest fields of the cases, the numbers should be searched for only in these fields by using the field restriction method. For example, to retrieve cases classified under the Digest Topic for Contracts (Digest Topic Number 95) that deal with the "Statute of Frauds", the following queries would be appropriate:

topic(95) /p "Statute of Frauds"

digest(95) /p "Statute of Frauds"

A complete list of Digest Topics and their numerical equivalents appears in the WESTLAW Reference Manual.

Using WESTLAW as a Citator

Legal Research frequently entails finding decisions that apply to specific sections of state statutes, or to other court decisions. WESTLAW can be used to retrieve documents that contain reference to such authority. Because citation styles are not always uniform, special care must be taken to identify variant forms of citations.

Retrieving Cases that Cite Codes and Statute Sections

Court decisions that cite to sections of state codes or to sections of state statutes are retrievable by including the section number in the query. For example, to retrieve cases that cite section 543.19 of the Minnesota Statutes, the following query could be used in the MN–CS database:

543.19

Since the section number is a unique term, it is unnecessary to use additional search terms in the query. The appearance of 543.19 in Minnesota case law is not likely to be anything other than a citation to that particular section. Using the number 543.19 as in the above query will retrieve all subsections of section 543.19 automatically.

Retrieving Cases that Cite Other Court Decisions

WESTLAW can be used as a citator of other court decisions if the title of the decision, its citation, or both, are known. When only the title of the case is known, use the following format:

    sherwood +5 walker

This query instructs the computer to retrieve all documents that have cited the case of *Sherwood v. Walker*. The +5 numerical connector requires that the word SHERWOOD precede and occur within 5 words of the word WALKER.

If the citation of the case is known, a query may be constructed that will retrieve documents that have cited the case. This is done by using the numbers of the citation as search terms in the query. For example, to retrieve cases that have cited to Sherwood by its citation, 66 Mich. 568, use the following format:

    66 +3 568

If both the citation and the case title are known, the following format may be used:

    sherwood +5 walker /15 66 +3 568

In the example above, the computer is instructed to retrieve all documents that contain the terms SHERWOOD, WALKER, 66 and 568 within the number of words designated by the numerical proximity connectors separating each term. This query would retrieve all documents that contain the full citation: *Sherwood v. Walker,* 66 Mich. 568.

The date restriction may be utilized to retrieve documents that cite cases within a given year, range of years, or before or after a given date. For example, to retrieve all documents that have cited *Sherwood v. Walker* after the year 1982, this query could be used:

    sherwood +5 walker & date(after 1982)

Shepard's® Citations on WESTLAW

From any point in WESTLAW, case citations may be entered to retrieve Shepard's listings for those citations. To enter a citation to be Shepardized, the following formats can be used:

    sh 84 Se2d 516
    sh 84 S.e.2d 516
    sh84Se2d516

When the citation is entered, Shepard's listings for the citation will be displayed. To Shepardize a citation it is not necessary to be in the same database as that of the citation. For example, a Supreme Court citation may be entered from the Pacific Reporter database.

West's INSTA–CITE

INSTA–CITE, West Publishing Company's case history system, allows users to quickly verify the accuracy of case citations and the validity of decisions. It contains prior and subsequent case histories in chronological listings, parallel citations, and precedential treatment.

Some examples of the kind of direct case history provided by INSTA–CITE are: "affirmed", "certiorari denied", "decision reversed and remanded", and "judgment vacated". A complete list of INSTA–CITE case history and precedential treatment notations appears in the WESTLAW Reference Manual.

An example of an INSTA–CITE reference from this hornbook appears below. The format to access the Insta-Cite display for a case citation consists of the letters IC followed by the citation, with or without spaces and periods:

ic 84 S.e.2d 516

ic 84 Se2d 516

ic84Se2d516

FIND

The FIND command allows you to retrieve a case quickly from anywhere in WESTLAW without the need to run a separate search or change databases. If you know a case's citation, FIND will take you to that case in one step.

This command is especially useful when you are reading one case on WESTLAW and find another case cited which you want to view. The FIND command allows you to retrieve the cited case quickly without losing your place in the original case.

You can also use FIND to retrieve cases listed in a Shepard's or a Insta-Cite display or cases cited in other FOUND documents. You can FIND a case even if it is not cited anywhere, as long as you know its citation.

To use FIND enter the word **find** or **fi** followed by the citation and then press **ENTER**. You may enter either the West citation or any parallel citation. For example, you may use the U.S., S.Ct., or L.Ed.2d citation. Spacing and punctuation are optional. Any of the following examples are acceptable:

find84Se2d516

fi 84 S.e.2d 516

fi 84S.e.2d516

When you are in the FIND system (e.g., if you are viewing a FOUND DOCUMENT, or have entered the word FIND), you can see a list of valid FIND publications and their acceptable abbreviations by typing **pubs** and pressing **ENTER**.

Black's Law Dictionary

WESTLAW contains an on-line version of Black's Law Dictionary. The dictionary incorporates definitions of terms and phrases of English and American law.

Included within the preformulated queries in this publication are references to Black's Law Dictionary for many important legal terms. The format of such commands is as follows:

di rescission

The command consists of letters DI followed by the term to be defined. To see the definition of a phrase, enter the letters DI followed by the phrase (without quotation marks):

di quasi contract

If the precise spelling of a term to be defined is not known, or a list of dictionary terms is desired, a truncated form of the word may be entered with the root expansion symbol (!) attached to it:

di res!

di res ipsa!

The first example will produce a list of all dictionary terms that begin with RES. The second example will produce a list of dictionary terms, the first of which is RES IPSA LOQUITUR. From the list of terms a number corresponding to the desired term can be entered to obtain the appropriate definitions.

WESTLAW Case Law Databases

This section discusses the WESTLAW case law databases, in which the preformulated queries in this publication have been designed to be used. The case law databases consist of cases from the National Reporter System.

Cases in WESTLAW are in "full text plus." That is, they include the court's decision enhanced by a synopsis of the decision and head-notes stating the legal propositions for which the decision stands. The headnotes are classified to West's Key Number classification system.

WESTLAW contains many databases not discussed here. For example, there are databases that contain the entire United States Code, Code of Federal Regulations, and topical databases covering such areas as bankruptcy, patents and copyrights, federal tax, government contracts, communications, securities, labor, antitrust, admiralty, and military justice.

The case law databases are divided into two kinds: state and federal. WESTLAW has individual state databases containing decisions from specific states. The database identifier for an individual state database consists of the state's postal abbreviation followed by a hyphen and the letters CS (e.g. MN–CS for Minnesota cases.) The available federal case law databases are: Supreme Court Reporter (SCT), U.S. Court of Appeals (CTA), and U.S. District Courts (DCT).

WESTLAW also contains individual U.S. Court of Appeals databases. The database identifier for an individual court of appeals database consists of the letters CTA followed by the number of the federal circuit (e.g. CTA8 for the Eighth Circuit Court of Appeals.)

The databases in which the queries in this publication will provide the most useful searches will vary depending upon your research needs. For example, if you are interested in the law of contracts in a particular state, these queries will yield the most useful information if used in the database that contains cases from that state. State cases can be found in individual state case law databases and in the regional reporter databases noted above.

Some issues to which the preformulated queries correspond will only appear in cases from the state databases, whereas other issues will be present only in the federal databases. However, some issues are sufficiently broad and have been so widely litigated that cases may be found with the queries in either the state or federal databases. Finally, some issues may have been litigated only in particular states and not in others, so that a given query may retrieve cases in one state but not in another.

In some instances, the query itself indicates which database it is to be used in. If a query contains a court restriction to a particular state or to a particular federal circuit, then that query can only be used in the database that contains that state or district. For example, the following query contains a court restriction for Minnesota cases:

16b.09 & court(mn)

and therefore should be used in the Northwestern Reporter (Nw) database, since that is the database in which Minnesota cases appear. Alternatively, the query could be used in the MN–CS database, without the court field restriction.

WESTLAW Hornbook Queries: (a) Query Format

The queries that appear in this publication are intended to be illustrative. They are approximately as general as the material in the hornbook text to which they correspond.

Although all of the queries in this publication reflect proper format for use with WESTLAW, there is seldom only one "correct" way to formulate a query for a particular problem. This is so even though some techniques are clearly better than others. Therefore, the queries reflect a wide range of alternative ways that queries may be structured for effective research. Such variances in query style simply reflect the great flexibility that the WESTLAW system affords its users in formulating search strategies.

For some research problems, it may be necessary to make a series of refinements to the queries, such as the addition of search terms or the substitution of different grammatical connectors, to adequately fit the particular needs of the individual researcher's problem. The responsibility remains with the researcher to "fine tune" the WESTLAW queries in accordance with his or her own research requirements. The primary usefulness of the preformulated queries in this hornbook is in providing users with a foundation upon which further query construction can be built.

Individual queries in this hornbook may retrieve from one to over a hundred cases, depending on which database is utilized. If a query does not retrieve any cases in a given database, it is because there are no decisions in that database which satisfy the grammatical proximity requirements of the query. In this situation, to search another database with the same query, enter the letter S followed by the initials DB, followed by the new database identifier. Thus, if a query was initially addressed to the NE (Northeastern Reporter) database, but retrieved no documents, the user could then search the PAC (Pacific Reporter) database with same query by entering the following command:

```
s db pac
```

This command instructs WESTLAW to search the Pacific Reporter database with the same query that was previously used in the Northeastern Reporter database.

The maximum number of cases retrieved by a query in any given database will vary, depending on a variety of factors, including the relative generality of the search terms and grammatical connectors, the frequency of litigation or discussion of the issue in the courts, and the number of documents comprising the database.

WESTLAW Hornbook Queries: (b) Textual Illustrations

This section explains how the queries provided in this hornbook may be used in researching actual problems in the law of contracts that a practitioner might encounter. Examples from the text of this edition have been selected to illustrate how the queries can be expanded, restricted, or altered to meet the specific needs of the reader's research.

A segment of the text from Chapter 2, section 2–1, of *Contracts, Third Edition,* by Calamari and Perillo appears below:

§ 2–1 Mutual Assent

Usually an essential prerequisite to the formation of a contract is an agreement: a mutual manifestation of assent to the same terms. This mutual assent ordinarily is established by a process of offer and acceptance. But it is possible to have mutual assent even though it is impossible to identify the offer and the acceptance. Thus if A and B are together and C suggests the terms of an agreement for them, there would be a contract without any process of offer and acceptance if they simultaneously agreed to these terms. Frequently, especially in transactions of considerable magnitude, the parties negotiate the terms of a proposed contract until a final draft is typed or printed. The contract may be formed when the copies of the writing are signed and exchanged. Again neither an offer nor an acceptance can be identified in this circumstance.

But, as indicated above, mutual assent usually arises through a process of offer and acceptance and, even in cases where the offer and acceptance cannot be identified, the conceptual model of offer and acceptance may be a helpful analytical tool. We shall explore the framework of offer and acceptance after establishing some important ground rules.

The text of this section discusses the circumstance when a contract will be formed absent clear signs of an offer and an acceptance. In order to retrieve cases discussing when a contract will be formed in this way, the following query

prerequisite /s formation /s contract /s agree!

is given as a suggested search strategy on WESTLAW.

A headnote of a case that was retrieved from the ALLSTATES database appears below:

```
      R 3 OF 13    P 15 OF 28    ALLSTATES  T    322 S.E.2d 474
(7)
95 27
CONTRACTS
k. Implied agreements.
S.C.App., 1984.
If one of parties has not agreed to all essential terms to alleged implied contract, then
prerequisite to formation of implied contract is lacking.
Stanley Smith & Sons v. Limestone College
322 S.E.2d 474, 283 S.C. 430
```

The relevant portion of the opinion that corresponds to this headnote appears below:

(6)(7)(8) An implied contract, like an express contract, rests on an actual agreement of the parties to be bound to a particular undertaking. The parties must manifest their mutual assent to all essential terms of the contract in order for an enforceable obligation to exist. Edens v. Laurel Hill, Inc., supra. If one of the parties has not agreed, then a prerequisite to formation of the contract is lacking. Shealy v. Fowler, supra. Therefore, Stanley Smith must prove the Board's assent by conduct to all those terms essential to create a binding contract. One such essential term is the price for which the work is to be performed. See Edens v. Laurel Hill, supra.

The query can be altered to meet the needs of individual researchers. For example, a practitioner may wish to find cases where the existence of a writing was discussed as a prerequisite to formation. In this instance, the preformulated query shown above can be modified to retrieve documents relevant to the new issue as follows:

prerequisite /s formation /s contract /s agree! /s writing wr*te written

The search terms writing, wr*te and written are added because they specifically correspond to the new issue. Below is a portion of a case retrieved by this query from the ALLSTATES database:

```
      R 4 OF 4    P 5 OF 12    ALLSTATES  T    195 Va. 603
```

It is further alleged that Broyhill Park sewerage system is governed by the ordinance of April 8, 1945; that Broyhill failed to sign a contract 'as expressly required in the aforesaid Section V.A. 5 of the ordinance', but that the said sewerage system became the property of the Board upon the completion thereof and upon approval by the said

Sanitary Engineer; that an implied contract arose by the operation of said Section V.A. 5 whereby the Board became 'irrevocably obligated', after approval of the system and its connection to the county system, to dispose of the sewage of Broyhill Park through its system in return 'for the obligation' of Broyhill to sign a written contract conveying to the Board 'title to the said sewerage works'; that the signing of the written contract by Broyhill was not a prerequisite to the formation of the said implied contract but was instead the obligation and duty of Broyhill under the implied contract; that under this obligation it was the duty of Broyhill.

Ranking Documents Retrieved on WESTLAW: Age and Term Options

Documents retrieved by a query can be ordered in either of two ways. One way is to order retrieved documents by their dates, with the most recent documents displayed first. This is ranking by AGE. Using the AGE option is suggested when the user's highest priority is to retrieve the most recent decisions from a search.

Alternatively, documents can be ranked by the frequency of the appearance of query terms. This is ranking by TERMS. When a search is performed with the TERMS option, the cases containing the greatest number of different search terms will be displayed first.

When a database is accessed by entering a database identifier, WESTLAW responds with a screen requesting that the query be entered. At this point the user may select which type of ranking, AGE or TERMS, is desired.

The queries offered in this hornbook were formulated and tested for relevancy with use of the TERMS option. Accordingly, in certain instances use of the AGE option with the preformulated queries may display less relevant, yet more recent cases, first.

Conclusion

This appendix has reviewed methods that can be used to obtain the most effective legal research concerning the law of contracts. Calamari and Perillo's, *Contracts, Third Edition,* combines the familiar hornbook publication with a powerful and easily accessed computerized law library. The WESTLAW references at the end of each section of the hornbook text provide a basic framework upon which the lawyer can structure additional research on WESTLAW. The queries may be used as provided or they may be tailored to meet the needs of researcher's specific problems. The power and flexibility of WESTLAW affords users of this publication a unique opportunity to greatly enhance their access to and understanding of the law of contracts.

Table of Cases

Mirisis v. Renda, 83 A.D.2d 572, 441 N.Y.S.2d 138 (2 Dept.1981)—§ 11–18, n. 74.

Miron v. Yonkers Raceway, Inc., 400 F.2d 112 (2nd Cir.1968)—§ 11–20, n. 28.

Mishara Const. Co. v. Transit-Mixed Concrete Corp., 365 Mass. 122, 310 N.E.2d 363 (1974)—§ 13–6, n. 80; § 13–18, n. 19; § 13–1, n. 11; § 13–6.

Misner v. Strong, 181 N.Y. 163, 73 N.E. 965 (1905)—§ 19–16, n. 83.

Mississippi & Dominion S.S. Co. v. Swift, 86 Me. 248, 29 A. 1063 (1894)—§ 2–7, n. 56.

Mississippi Bank v. Nickles & Wells Const. Co., 421 So.2d 1056 (Miss.1982)—§ 18–16, n. 34.

Mississippi State Highway Commission v. Dixie Contractors, Inc., 375 So.2d 1202 (Miss.1979)—§ 3–12, n. 44, 45.

Missouri Pac. R. Co. v. Fowler, 183 Ark. 86, 34 S.W.2d 1071 (1931)—§ 14–13, n. 23.

Mitchel v. Reynolds, 24 Eng.Rep. 347 (Ch. 1711)—§ 16–19, n. 79.

Mitchell v. Abbott, 86 Me. 338, 29 A. 1118 (1894)—§ 2–20, n. 33.

Mitchell v. Brewster, 28 Ill. 163 (1862)—§ 20–3, n. 24.

Mitchell v. C. C. Sanitation Company, 430 S.W.2d 933 (Tex.Civ.App.1968)—§ 9–3, n. 20.

Mitchell v. Ceazan Tires, Ltd., 25 Cal.2d 45, 153 P.2d 53 (1944)—§ 13–1, n. 11.

Mitchell v. Excelsior Sales & Imports, Inc., 243 Ga. 813, 256 S.E.2d 785 (1979)—§ 3–7, n. 82.

Mitchell v. Kimbrough, 491 P.2d 289 (Okl. 1971)—§ 3–7, n. 60.

Mitchell v. Lewensohn, 251 Wis. 424, 29 N.W.2d 748 (1947)—§ 14–18, n. 71.

Mitchell v. Siqueiros, 99 Idaho 396, 582 P.2d 1074 (1978)—§ 2–7, n. 51.

Mitchell Canneries, Inc. v. United States, 111 Ct.Cl. 228, 77 F.Supp. 498 (1948)—§ 13–3, n. 30.

Mitchell Properties, Inc. v. Real Estate Title Co., Inc., 62 Md.App. 473, 490 A.2d 271 (1985)—§ 21–5, n. 55.

Mitchell-Huntley Cotton Co. v. Waldrep, 377 F.Supp. 1215 (D.C.Ala.1974)—§ 16–3, n. 25.

Mitchill v. Lath, 247 N.Y. 377, 160 N.E. 646 (1928)—§ 3–2, n. 35; § 3–4, n. 32, 82; § 3–5, n. 38.

Mitsubishi Goshi Kaisha v. J. Aron & Co., 16 F.2d 185 (2nd Cir.1926)—§ 11–20, n. 96.

Mitsui & Co. v. Puerto Rico Water Resources Authority, 528 F.Supp. 768 (D.C. Puerto Rico 1981)—§ 18–14, n. 14.

Mitzel v. Hauck, 78 S.D. 543, 105 N.W.2d 378 (1960)—§ 2–4, n. 34.

Mixing Equipment Co. v. Philadelphia Gear, Inc., 436 F.2d 1308 (3rd Cir.1971)—§ 16–19, n. 93; § 16–20, n. 7.

Mobil Oil Corp. v. Prive, 137 Vt. 370, 406 A.2d 400 (1979)—§ 4–11, n. 17.

Mobil Oil Corp. v. Wolfe, 297 N.C. 36, 252 S.E.2d 809 (1979)—§ 7–3, n. 23.

Mobley v. Parker's Estate, 278 Ark. 37, 642 S.W.2d 883 (1982)—§ 11–29, n. 62.

Moch Co., H.R. v. Rensselaer Water Co., 247 N.Y. 160, 159 N.E. 896 (N.Y.1928)—§ 17–3, n. 15, 29, 50; § 17–7, n. 4, 6.

Mock v. Duke, 20 Mich.App. 453, 174 N.W.2d 161 (1969)—§ 9–23, n. 36.

Mock v. Trustees of First Baptist Church of Newport, 252 Ky. 243, 67 S.W.2d 9 (1934)—§ 11–9, n. 67.

Model Vending, Inc. v. Stanisci, 74 N.J. Super. 12, 180 A.2d 393 (1962)—§ 13–21, n. 50.

Moers v. Moers, 229 N.Y. 294, 128 N.E. 202 (1920)—§ 21–5, n. 61; § 21–6, n. 66.

Moffit v. Sederlund, 145 Mich.App. 1, 378 N.W.2d 491 (1985)—§ 22–3, n. 75.

Mohr and Sons, John v. Apex Terminal Warehouses, Inc., 422 F.2d 638 (7th Cir. 1970)—§ 4–15, n. 95.

Moline I.F.C. Finance, Inc. v. Soucinek, 91 Ill.App.2d 257, 234 N.E.2d 57 (1968)—§ 11–29, n. 58.

Monarch Marking Sys. Co. v. Reed's Photo Mart, Inc., 485 S.W.2d 905 (Tex.1972)—§ 9–27, n. 37.

Monarco v. Lo Greco, 35 Cal.2d 621, 220 P.2d 737 (1950)—§ 19–48, n. 61, 74.

Monegan v. Pacific Nat'l Bank of Washington, 16 Wash.App. 280, 556 P.2d 226 (1976)—§ 18–3, n. 27.

Monge v. Beebe Rubber Co., 114 N.H. 130, 316 A.2d 549 (1974)—§ 2–9, n. 42; § 11–38; § 11–38, n. 14.

Monroe St. Properties, Inc. v. Carpenter, 407 F.2d 379 (9th Cir.1969)—§ 11–6, n. 25.

Montana Seeds, Inc. v. Holliday, 178 Mont. 119, 582 P.2d 1223 (1978)—§ 11–20, n. 27.

Montgomery v. Futuristic Foods, Inc., 66 A.D.2d 64, 411 N.Y.S.2d 371 (2 Dept. 1978)—§ 19–23, n. 59.

Montgomery v. Stuyvesant Ins. Co., 393 F.2d 754 (4th Cir.1968)—§ 21–2, n. 18.

Montgomery Industries Intern., Inc. v. Thomas Const. Co., Inc., 620 F.2d 91 (5th Cir.1980)—§ 6–5, n. 96.

Montgomery Ward & Co. v. Johnson, 209 Mass. 89, 95 N.E. 290 (1911)—§ 2–6, n. 88.

Montgomery's Estate, In re, 272 N.Y. 323, 6 N.E.2d 40 (1936)—§ 15–6, n. 71.

Montrose Contracting Co. v. County of Westchester, 80 F.2d 841 (2nd Cir. 1936)—§ 13–3, n. 42.

Ross v. Bumstead, 65 Ariz. 61, 173 P.2d 765 (1946)—§ 13–25, n. 84.

Ross v. Harding, 64 Wash.2d 231, 391 P.2d 526 (1964)—§ 11–5, n. 13.

Ross v. Imperial Const. Co., 572 F.2d 518 (5th Cir.1978)—§ 17–9, n. 26.

Ross v. Leberman, 298 Pa. 574, 148 A. 858 (1930)—§ 2–15, n. 37.

Ross v. Warren, 196 Iowa 659, 195 N.W. 228 (1923)—§ 17–6, n. 90.

Ross Bros. Const. Co. v. State, By and Through Transp. Com'n, Highway Div., 59 Or.App. 374, 650 P.2d 1080 (1982)—§ 3–10, n. 26.

Ross Systems v. Linden Dari-Delite, Inc., 35 N.J. 329, 173 A.2d 258 (1961)—§ 9–6, n. 56.

Rossi v. Douglas, 203 Md. 190, 100 A.2d 3 (1953)—§ 9–42, n. 4.

Rotermund v. United States Steel Corp., 474 F.2d 1139 (8th Cir.1973)—§ 17–10, n. 37.

Roth v. Michelson, 449 N.Y.S.2d 159, 434 N.E.2d 228 (1982)—§ 5–7, n. 69.

Roth v. Speck, 126 A.2d 153 (D.C.Mun.App. 1956)—§ 14–19, n. 90.

Roth Steel Products v. Sharon Steel Corp., 705 F.2d 134 (6th Cir.1983)—§ 9–6, n. 63; § 19–15, n. 12; § 19–25, n. 76.

Rothkopf v. Lowry & Co., 148 F.2d 517 (2nd Cir.1945)—§ 13–5, n. 70.

Rothmiller v. Stein, 143 N.Y. 581, 38 N.E. 718 (1894)—§ 9–20, n. 18; § 9–38, n. 33.

Roto-Lith, Limited v. F.P. Bartlett & Co., 297 F.2d 497 (1st Cir.1962)—§ 2–21; § 2–21, n. 12, 19, 21, 47.

Rotondo v. Kay Jewelry Co., 84 R.I. 292, 123 A.2d 404 (1956)—§ 8–6, n. 77.

Roundup Cattle Feeders v. Horpestad, 184 Mont. 480, 603 P.2d 1044 (1979)—§ 13–15, n. 86.

Rounsaville v. Van Zandt Realtors, Inc., 247 Ark. 749, 447 S.W.2d 655 (1969)—§ 2–21, n. 3.

Rouse v. United States, 215 F.2d 872, 94 U.S.App.D.C. 386 (1954)—§ 17–12, n. 71.

Roux Laboratories, Inc. v. Beauty Franchises, Inc., 60 Wis.2d 427, 210 N.W.2d 441 (1973)—§ 22–4, n. 91.

Rowe v. Peaboy, 207 Mass. 226, 93 N.E. 604 (1911)—§ 13–3, n. 35.

Rowell v. Plymouth-Home Nat. Bank, 13 Mass.App. 1044, 434 N.E.2d 648 (1982)—§ 19–40, n. 19; § 19–41, n. 25.

Rowland v. Hudson County, 7 N.J. 63, 80 A.2d 433 (1951)—§ 13–7, n. 92.

Royal Ins. Co. v. Beatty, 119 Pa. 6, 12 A. 607 (1888)—§ 2–18, n. 62.

Royal Paper Box Co. v. E.R. Apt Shoe Co., 290 Mass. 207, 195 N.E. 96 (1935)—§ 4–13, n. 76.

Royal Typewriter Co., Division Litton Business Systems v. M/V Kulmerland, 346

F.Supp. 1019 (D.C.N.Y.1972)—§ 9–44, n. 84.

Royce Chemical Company v. Sharples Corporation, 285 F.2d 183 (2nd Cir.1960)—§ 14–9, n. 94.

RRX Industries, Inc. v. Lab-Con, Inc., 772 F.2d 543 (9th Cir.1985)—§ 14–22, n. 35, 36.

RTL Corp. v. Manufacturer's Enterprises, Inc., 429 So.2d 855 (1983)—§ 4–11, n. 37.

Rubenstein v. Rubenstein, 20 N.J. 359, 120 A.2d 11 (1956)—§ 9–2, n. 4; § 9–3, n. 16.

Ruberoid Co. v. Glassman Const. Co., 248 Md. 97, 234 A.2d 875 (1967)—§ 18–16, n. 31.

Rubin v. Dairymen's League Co-Op. Ass'n, 284 N.Y. 32, 29 N.E.2d 458 (1940)—§ 4–12; § 4–12, n. 52.

Rubin v. Fuchs, 81 Cal.Rptr. 373, 459 P.2d 925 (1969)—§ 11–6, n. 25; § 11–9, n. 71; § 11–17, n. 28.

Rubin & Sons, Inc., Harry v. Consolidated Pipe Co. of America, 396 Pa. 506, 153 A.2d 472 (Pa.1959)—§ 19–34, n. 57.

Rubinstein v. Rubinstein, 296 N.Y.S.2d 354, 244 N.E.2d 49 (1968)—§ 14–33, n. 75.

Rucker v. Sanders, 182 N.C. 607, 109 S.E. 857 (1921)—§ 2–20, n. 91.

Rudd Paint & Varnish Co. v. White, 403 F.2d 289 (10th Cir.1968)—§ 15–3, n. 17.

Rudick v. Rudick, 403 So.2d 1091 (Fla.App. 3 Dist.1981)—§ 21–6, n. 68.

Rudio v. Yellowstone Merchandising Corp., 200 Mont. 537, 652 P.2d 1163 (1982)—§ 4–9, n. 37.

Rudman v. Cowles Communications, Inc., 330 N.Y.S.2d 33, 280 N.E.2d 867 (1972)—§ 11–26, n. 23; § 14–18, n. 71.

Ruffin v. Mercury Record Productions, Inc., 513 F.2d 222 (6th Cir.1975)—§ 4–9, n. 37.

Ruggieri v. West Forum Corp., 444 Pa. 175, 282 A.2d 304 (1971)—§ 9–10, n. 97.

Ruggiero v. United States, 190 Ct.Cl. 327, 420 F.2d 709 (1970)—§ 9–27, n. 38.

Rumsey Elec. Co. v. University of Delaware, 358 A.2d 712 (1976)—§ 17–10, n. 48.

Rupert's Oil Service v. Leslie, 40 Conn. Supp. 295, 493 A.2d 926 (1985)—§ 22–1, n. 34.

Ruscito v. F. Dyne Electronics Co., 177 Conn. 149, 411 A.2d 1371 (1979)—§ 3–2, n. 55.

Russ v. Brown, 96 Idaho 369, 529 P.2d 765 (1974)—§ 9–20, n. 93.

Russell v. Stewart, 44 Vt. 170 (1872)—§ 2–12, n. 99.

Russell v. Union Oil Co., 7 Cal.App.3d 110, 86 Cal.Rptr. 424 (2 Dist.1970)—§ 2–1, n. 1.

Russo v. De Bella, 220 N.Y.S.2d 587 (1961)—§ 4–10, n. 1.

Ward v. Haren, 183 Mo.App. 569, 167 S.W. 1064 (1914)—§ **14–32, n. 71.**

Ward v. Hasbrouch, 169 N.Y. 407, 62 N.E. 434 (1902)—§ **19–21, n. 54.**

Ward v. Johnson, 13 Mass. 148 (1816)—§ **20–3, n. 24.**

Ward v. New York Cent. R.R., 47 N.Y. 29 (1871)—§ **14–5, n. 37.**

Ward v. Vance, 93 Pa. 499 (1880)—§ **13–3, n. 26.**

Warde v. Davis, 494 F.2d 655 (10th Cir. 1974)—§ **22–3, n. 73.**

Ware v. Mobley, 190 Ga. 249, 9 S.E.2d 67 (1940)—§ **8–2, n. 19.**

Ware v. Spinney, 76 Kan. 289, 91 P. 787 (1907)—§ **22–8, n. 26.**

Warner v. McLay, 92 Conn. 427, 103 A. 13 (1918)—§ **14–28, n. 96.**

Warner v. Rossignol, 513 F.2d 678 (1st Cir. 1975)—§ **21–6, n. 66.**

Warner v. Seaboard Finance Co., 75 Nev. 470, 345 P.2d 759 (1959)—§ **18–24, n. 35.**

Warner v. Texas & P.R. Co., 164 U.S. 418, 17 S.Ct. 147, 41 L.Ed. 495 (1896)—§ **19–19, n. 38.**

Warner Bros. Pictures v. Brodel, 31 Cal.2d 766, 192 P.2d 949 (1948)—§ **8–2, n. 15.**

Warner-Lambert Pharmaceutical Co. v. John J. Reynolds, Inc., 178 F.Supp. 655 (D.C.N.Y.1959)—§ **2–9, n. 30.**

Warner-Lambert Pharmaceutical Co. v. Sylk, 471 F.2d 1137 (3rd Cir.1972)—§ **19–6, n. 75.**

Warren v. Hodge, 121 Mass. 106 (1876)—§ **4–10, n. 80.**

Warrior Constructors, Inc. v. International Union of Operating Engineers, Local Union No. 926, AFL–CIO, 383 F.2d 700 (5th Cir.1967)—§ **2–7, n. 45.**

Warwick Municipal Emp. Credit Union v. McAllister, 110 R.I. 399, 293 A.2d 516 (1972)—§ **8–4, n. 46.**

Wassenaar v. Panos, 111 Wis.2d 518, 331 N.W.2d 357 (1983)—§ **14–31, n. 63.**

Wasserman Theatrical Enterprise v. Harris, 137 Conn. 371, 77 A.2d 329 (1950)—§ **13–8, n. 4.**

Wat Henry Pontiac Co. v. Bradley, 202 Okl. 82, 210 P.2d 348 (1949)—§ **9–17, n. 50.**

Watkins v. Curry, 103 Ark. 414, 147 S.W. 43 (1912)—§ **22–2, n. 41.**

Watkins v. Wells, 303 Ky. 728, 198 S.W.2d 662 (1946)—§ **19–41, n. 21.**

Watkins & Son v. Carrig, 91 N.H. 459, 21 A.2d 591 (1941)—§ **4–9, n. 47;** § **4–10, n. 85.**

Watson v. Gugino, 204 N.Y. 535, 98 N.E. 18 (1912)—§ **2–9, n. 17.**

Watson v. Kenlick Coal Co., 498 F.2d 1183 (6th Cir.1974)—§ **13–20, n. 46.**

Watson v. Loughran, 112 Ga. 837, 38 S.E. 82 (1901)—§ **14–13, n. 22.**

Watson v. McCabe, 527 F.2d 286 (6th Cir. 1975)—§ **19–30, n. 15.**

Watters v. Lincoln, 29 S.D. 98, 135 N.W. 712 (1912)—§ **2–20, n. 78.**

Watts v. Malatesta, 262 N.Y. 80, 186 N.E. 210 (1933)—§ **22–7, n. 11.**

Wavra v. Karr, 142 Minn. 248, 172 N.W. 118 (1919)—§ **14–15, n. 37.**

Wax v. Northwest Seed Co., 189 Wash. 212, 64 P.2d 513 (1937)—§ **2–20, n. 37.**

Way v. Sperry, 60 Mass. (6 Cush.) 238 (1851)—§ **5–5, n. 48.**

Weale v. Massachusetts General Housing Corp., 117 N.H. 428, 374 A.2d 925 (1977)—§ **19–15, n. 71.**

Weatherford Oil Tool Company v. Campbell, 161 Tex. 310, 340 S.W.2d 950 (1960)—§ **16–21, n. 16, 19.**

Weathers v. M.C. Lininger & Sons, Inc., 68 Or.App. 30, 682 P.2d 770 (1984)—§ **18–10, n. 92.**

Weaver v. American Oil Co., 257 Ind. 458, 276 N.E.2d 144 (1971)—§ **9–39, n. 60, 64, 69;** § **9–40, n. 87;** § **9–44, n. X;** § **9–45, n. 97, X.**

Weaver v. American Oil Company, 261 N.E.2d 99 (Ind.App.1970)—§ **9–44, n. 79.**

Weaver and Associates, Inc., R.A. v. Asphalt Const., Inc., 587 F.2d 1315, 190 U.S.App.D.C. 418 (1978)—§ **4–13, n. 79.**

Weaver Organization, Inc. v. Manette, 41 A.D.2d 138, 341 N.Y.S.2d 631 (1 Dept. 1973)—§ **9–15, n. 33.**

Webb v. Graham, 212 Kan. 364, 510 P.2d 1195 (1973)—§ **21–13, n. 59.**

Webb v. McGowin, 232 Ala. 374, 168 So. 199 (1936)—§ **5–4, n. 33.**

Webb v. Webb, 301 S.E.2d 570 (W.Va. 1983)—§ **9–28, n. 56.**

Webb v. Woods, 176 Okl. 306, 55 P. 959 (1936)—§ **19–30, n. 9.**

Webb & Co. Inc., A.M. v. Robert P. Miller Co., 157 F.2d 865 (3rd Cir.1946)—§ **2–9, n. 2.**

Webbe v. Western Union Tel. Co., 169 Ill. 610, 48 N.E. 670 (1897)—§ **2–24, n. 18.**

Weber's Estate, In re, 256 Mich. 61, 239 N.W. 260 (1931)—§ **8–13, n. 67.**

Wedner v. Fidelity Sec. Systems, Inc., 228 Pa.Super. 67, 307 A.2d 429 (1973)—§ **14–31, n. 67.**

Weeks v. Pratt, 43 F.2d 53 (5th Cir.1930)—§ **9–38, n. 26, 47;** § **16–14, n. 44.**

Wegematic Corp., United States v., 360 F.2d 674 (2nd Cir.1966)—§ **13–2, n. 16;** § **13–17, n. 12.**

Wehle v. Haviland, 69 N.Y. 448 (1877)—§ **14–14, n. 30.**

Weightman's Estate, In re, 126 Pa.Super. 221, 190 A. 552 (1937)—§ **8–13, n. 68.**

Weil v. Neary, 278 U.S. 160, 49 S.Ct. 144, 73 L.Ed. 243 (1929)—§ **22–1, n. 12.**

Table of Uniform Commercial Code Citations

U.C.C. Sec.	This Work Sec.	Note	U.C.C. Sec.	This Work Sec.	Note
1	1–7		1–205(2) (Cont'd)	3–17	98
1–102	13–26	87	1–205(3)	3–17	2
1–102(1)	1–7	54	1–205(4)	3–17	
1–102(3)	13–19	35		3–17	8
1–103	1–7	57	1–205, Comment 2	3–17	89
	3–7		1–205, Comment 4	19–30	23
	9–26	93	1–205, Comment 5	3–17	97
	13–22	62		3–17	98
	15–5	63	1–205, Comment 6	3–17	1
1–105	13–4	59	1–205, Comment 9	3–17	99
1–106	14–4	20	1–206	19–16	
	14–23	44	1–207	4–11	
	14–25			4–11	53
1–106(1)	14–3	14		4–11	56
	14–23	50		4–11	58
1–106, Comment 1	14–8	86		9–6	64
1–107	5–16			14–15	53
	11–33	16	2	1–1	9
	21–10	10		1–2	
	21–10	14		1–6	
1–201(3)	1–1	8		1–7	
	2–5	43		1–7	52
	10–1	10		1–7	54
1–201(10)	9–43	13		11–20	5
	9–44	65		18–4	
1–201(11)	1–1	8		18–4	49
	2–5	43		18–10	
1–201(19)	9–40	92		18–16	
	11–38			18–16	38
	16–16	64	2–103	5–15	
1–201(23)	12–2			11–38	
1–201(26)	2–20	67	2–103(1)(b)	9–40	92
	2–26	74		16–16	64
	18–17	52	2–103(1)(c)	13–26	99
1–201(37)	18–5	55		19–16	99
1–201(38)	2–23	84	2–104	2–21	8
1–201(39)	19–31	26	2–105	1–7	53
	19–34	54		4–12	32
1–201(42)	3–2	12	2–105(1)	19–14	53
1–201(44)	18–7	70	2–105, Comment 1	19–14	53
1–203	9–40		2–106	13–26	89
	10–1	10	2–106(1)	1–1	9
	11–38			2–6	94
	11–38	91	2–106(1)(a)	2–26	
	13–19	35	2–106(2)	2–26	75
	16–16	64	2–106(3)	21–2	23
	19–48		2–106(4)	15–3	26
1–205(1)	3–17	88		21–2	24
1–205(2)	3–17		2–106, Comment 1	1–2	12
	3–17	92	2–107	1–7	53
	3–17	93	2–107(1)	19–14	57

Index

†